RURAL CHURCH WITH PAGODA, RICHLAND PARISH, 1960s

The Louisiana Purchase Bicentennial Series
in
Louisiana History

Glenn R. Conrad, General Editor

VOLUME I
THE FRENCH EXPERIENCE IN
LOUISIANA

VOLUME II
THE SPANISH PRESENCE IN
LOUISIANA, 1763-1803

VOLUME III
THE LOUISIANA PURCHASE
AND ITS AFTERMATH,
1800-1830

VOLUME IV
ANTEBELLUM LOUISIANA,
1830-1860
PART A: LIFE AND LABOR
PART B: POLITICS

VOLUME V
THE CIVIL WAR IN LOUISIANA
PART A: MILITARY ACTIVITY
PART B: THE HOME FRONT

VOLUME VI
RECONSTRUCTING LOUISIANA

VOLUME VII
LOUISIANA POLITICS AND THE
PARADOXES OF REACTION AND
REFORM, 1877-1928

VOLUME VIII
THE AGE OF THE LONGS,
LOUISIANA, 1928-1960

VOLUME IX
LOUISIANA SINCE THE LONGS,
1960 TO CENTURY'S END

VOLUME X
A REFUGE FOR ALL AGES:
IMMIGRATION IN LOUISIANA
HISTORY

VOLUME XI
THE AFRICAN AMERICAN
EXPERIENCE IN LOUISIANA
PART A: FROM AFRICA TO THE
CIVIL WAR
PART B: FROM THE CIVIL WAR
TO JIM CROW
PART C: FROM JIM CROW TO
CIVIL RIGHTS

VOLUME XIII
AN UNCOMMON EXPERIENCE:
LAW AND JUDICIAL
INSTITUTIONS IN LOUISIANA

VOLUME XV
VISIONS AND REVISIONS:
PERSPECTIVES ON LOUISIANA
SOCIETY AND CULTURE

VOLUME XVI
AGRICULTURE AND ECONOMIC
DEVELOPMENT IN LOUISIANA

VOLUME XVII
LOUISIANA LITERATURE AND
LITERARY FIGURES

VOLUME XVIII
EDUCATION IN LOUISIANA

VOLUME XIX
RELIGION IN LOUISIANA

The Louisiana Purchase Bicentennial Series in Louisiana History

VOLUME XIX

RELIGION IN LOUISIANA

EDITED BY

CHARLES E. NOLAN

CENTER FOR LOUISIANA STUDIES
UNIVERSITY OF LOUISIANA AT LAFAYETTE
LAFAYETTE, LOUISIANA
2004

Front Endsheets:
Christ Episcopal Church, New Orleans, La., Edwin Jewell,ed., *Jewell's Crescent City Illustrated* (New Orleans, 1873).

Rural Church, Richland Parish, La., Lee Estes, *Fading Textures: Vintage Architecture, Industry, and Transportation in Northeast Louisiana* (Lafayette, La.: Center for Louisiana Studies, 2003).

Back Endsheets:
United Methodist Church, Rayville, La., Good-bye to Main Street: The Decline of Small-Town Louisiana, Photograph Collection, Center for Louisiana Studies, University of Louisiana at Lafayette, Lafayette, La.

Rear view of St. Louis Cathedral, William Coleman, ed., *Historical Sketch Book and Guide to New Orleans and Environs* (New York, 1885).

Library of Congress Catalog Number: 96-84494
ISBN Number: 1-887366-59-8

Published by the Center for Louisiana Studies
P.O. Box 40831
University of Louisiana at Lafayette
Lafayette, LA 70504-0831

CONTENTS

PART IV: THE SPANISH COLONIAL PERIOD

PART V: THE LOUISIANA PURCHASE AND ITS AFTERMATH, 1803-1830

ABOUT THE EDITOR

Charles E. Nolan is Archivist and Director of the Office of Cultural Heritage at the Archdiocese of New Orleans and Adjunct Professor of Historical and Pastoral Theology at Notre Dame Seminary (New Orleans). He chairs the Archdiocesan Henriette Delille Historical Commission. He received a doctorate in Church History from the Gregorian University in Rome and a Master's Degree in Administration from Loyola University in New Orleans. He has authored, edited or contributed to more than thirty books dealing with Southern Catholic history and records, including *St. Mary's of Natchez: The History of a Southern Catholic Congregation, 1716-1988* (1992); *Cross, Crozier, and Crucible: A Volume Celebrating the Bicentennial of a Catholic Diocese in Louisiana* (1993); *A History of the Archdiocese of New Orleans* (2000); *No Cross, No Crown: Black Nuns in Nineteenth-Century New Orleans* (2001); *The Catholic Church in Mississippi, 1865-1911* (2002); and *Religious Pioneers: Building the Faith in the Archdiocese of New Orleans* (2004). He has published numerous articles in scholarly and professional journals. He is a recipient of the Sister M. Claude Lane Memorial Award from the Society of American Archivists and was inducted into the Company of Fellows by the Association of Records Managers and Administrators.

ABOUT THE SERIES

It was in the spring of 1992 that first thought was given to the matter of how best the Center for Louisiana Studies might commemorate the bicentennial of the Louisiana Purchase in 2003. For the next few months the Center's staff and members of its Advisory Council intermittently discussed the possible project, but no consensus was forthcoming. Perhaps the reason being that the Purchase looms so monumentally in United States history there are seemingly few memorials of proper proportion to commemorate the event's bicentennial.

Nevertheless, as time passed the outlines of a project began to take shape. To properly mark the occasion the Center for Louisiana Studies should produce a lasting tribute not only to the people who crafted the Louisiana Purchase but also to the people who, during the last two hundred years, have had a role in transforming that vast wilderness into the heartland of America. But the Center's focus is not mid-America for all practical purposes, it is Louisiana, the state that took its name from the Purchase territory. Therefore, the Center's project would concentrate on a Purchase bicentennial memorial that embraced the full range of Louisiana history.

There was another reason for this decision. In March of 1999 the Gulf Coast and the Mississippi Valley would mark the tercentennial of the founding of the French colony of Louisiana and the beginning of the region's historical era. Thus, if the Center's endeavor for the Purchase bicentennial was to be a history of Louisiana, then it should tell not only about the American experience in the area but also the Native American, French, Spanish, African, British and other influences that helped to lay the foundations for the present-day state.

Questions arose: Will the Center's Purchase bicentennial memorial be yet another history of Louisiana? If so, should it be another survey or should it be a more detailed account? Who would write this account of our times and those of our forebears? What interpretation would emerge from such a monograph? Who was expert enough to incorporate a harmonious blend of the political, economic, and social ingredients of our society?

Another year slipped by while we pondered these and other questions concerning the Center's memorial to the Purchase bicentennial and the tercentennial of the founding of the colony. After more discussion, there began to emerge a collective concept that was at once imaginative, exciting, and, above all, challenging. As a fitting memorial for the

Louisiana Purchase bicentennial, the Center would organize and direct the publication of a major historical series. Marking the anniversaries, however, should not be the only reason for such an endeavor.

As discussion of the nature of the series evolved, it became obvious that there was an overriding reason for it. The series, to be known as the LOUISIANA PURCHASE BICENTENNIAL SERIES IN LOUISIANA HISTORY, would be a fine sampling of twentieth-century scholarship, particularly the scholarship of the last half of the century which embraced new methodologies leading to broader interpretations of the state's history. Here, in a multi-volume series the student of Louisiana history would be exposed to a wide range of scholarship reflecting multiple interpretations of historical events.

Thus, the decision was made; the Series would bring together in one place the very best articles, essays, and book parts that have been published about Louisiana in the twentieth century, particularly the latter half of the century. Its focus would be to inform scholars, teachers, students, and laypersons on far-ranging topics of Louisiana history drawn from a great reservoir of scholarship found in media ranging from scholarly to popular to obscure.

Most important to the development of such a series, however, was the person or persons who would select the "very best" to incorporate into the Series. The answer came quickly, only widely recognized experts, acting as volume editors, would determine from the broad spectrum of sources those essays which reflect the best in research, writing, and interpretation on topics in Louisiana history.

Initially, nineteen broad topics of Louisiana history were identified, and the Center plans to publish these nineteen volumes between 1995 and 2004. It should be noted, however, proper presentation of some topics in Louisiana history cannot be confined to a single book; hence, some volumes may incorporate several parts in order to present the full spectrum of scholarship on the subject. Finally, the volumes will not be published in sequential order, although Volume I, *The French Experience in Louisiana* was the first to appear. Each volume will be announced upon publication.

THE LOUISIANA PURCHASE BICENTENNIAL SERIES IN LOUISIANA HISTORY presents a great source of information for anyone interested in the history of the colony and the state. It stands as an appropriate memorial to the men and women who shaped the colony and state down to the dawn of the twenty-first century.

Glenn R. Conrad, General Editor

INTRODUCTION

Religion is an elusive figure to the historian. It, like comedy and tragedy, has two faces. One, the *persona* or external face, manifests itself in many ways: community and denominational development, organization, membership, and practice; shared dogma or beliefs; communal worship and prayer; individual and communal service both within and outside denominational boundaries; the relation to the body politic and society in general; interdenominational cooperation and conflict; the arts, etc. The other face, the hidden or interior face, reveals a man's or woman's inner spiritual journey. Life as a pilgrimage or spiritual journey is one of the most familiar themes in religious literature.

Religion's external face is more easily studied by the historian and in fact constitutes the complete body of literature in this volume. Louisiana has no Augustine whose personal confession reflects a dramatic conversion and spiritual journey, told against the rich background of his times. Louisiana has no Dietrich Bonhoeffer whose spiritual journey is so eloquently expressed in his prison letters. Even Henriette Delille (1812-1862), a New Orleans native, foundress of the Sisters of the Holy Family, and the first Louisianian, as well as first African American, whose Cause for Canonization has been officially initiated by the Catholic Church, has left only fragmentary written evidence of her interior journey.[1]

Even the external face of religion is open to diverse interpretations and approaches. As C. P. M. Jones observed, religion can and is viewed both as "going to church" and as something entirely private and interior.[2] Even within a single denomination a changing theology, such as Catholicism experienced after the Second Vatican Council (1962-1965), serves as a reminder of the narrow focus of past scholarship and the new challenges for the present. Avery Dulles succinctly summarizes this change and challenge for Catholic historians in *Models of the Church*, pointing out the past emphasis on Church as institution. Dulles then explores the themes of Church as community or mystical/spiritual communion; as herald or proclaimer of the Word or Message; as servant or, in Bonhoeffer's phrase, the Church "for others;" and as sacrament or the visible manifestations of the Spirit or God's presence in the communal assembly. These different theological presuppositions and approaches result in very different denominational or congregational histories. My seminary graduate students generally have little difficulty identifying the theological model or models in the parish histories they are assigned to read and analyze.[3]

Religion as an object of historical study is also elusive because it plays such an essential role in the lives of men and women who are studied from another perspective, another vantage point. One cannot write of Joseph E. Ransdell, Kate Chopin, or Bernardo de Gálvez without examining or at least recognizing the role and influence of their religious faith and practice.

Religion is finally elusive because we as historians approach it passionately—loving or hating religion or religions, trying not to let our personal faith and denominational membership, or lack thereof, shape our research, analysis, and conclusions.

More than sixty years ago, Nash Kerr Burger, in a thoughtful review of Roger Baudier's landmark *The Catholic Church in Louisiana*, succinctly summarized the challenges and pitfalls facing historians in Louisiana at mid-century:

> Professional historians of recent years, having worked through a period of history as chiefly military strategy, and having now found it an intriguing sounding board for social theories, have paid scant attention to the church. This has largely left religious history to be mulled over by denominational partisans, who frequently make up in sentiment what is lacking in sense. It is good, therefore, to find a church history as conscientiously written and as well documented as this one.[4]

The articles included in this volume respond to Burger's threefold challenge: that religion be not ignored; that research be thoroughly conducted and well documented; and that conclusions be conscientiously presented. Fortunately, many Louisiana historians have responded to this challenge over the past half-century. More than a hundred and fifty articles, book sections, presentations to historical societies, and dissertation or thesis chapters could appropriately claim a place in this volume. Only a third of these were, in the final analysis, selected.

The first criteria for limiting material was established for the series as a whole: material published since 1950 dealing principally with Louisiana. With the exception of Edwin Gaustad's introductory article on American religious regionalism (which notes Louisiana's unique status as the nation's most religiously bifurcated state), all the articles in this volume have Louisiana as their primary focus. Thus, Walter Posey's informative portrait of the frontier Baptist preacher in the South is not included.[5]

To provide a more diverse selection of articles, I, with the general editor's approval, eliminated most articles that have appeared in previous volumes of this series. These previously-included entries, many of them on an historian's list of "best books and articles on religion," are listed by published volume in the Additional Readings section.

Additional criteria for inclusion in this volume were scholarship; chronological, geographical, topical, and denominational balance; and individuality. Unlike the National Football League's annual draft, this selection process did not choose "the best available athlete regardless of position." The selection process aimed at balancing New Orleans with South Louisiana and North Louisiana, the colonial periods with the Civil War and twentieth century, the Catholic experience with the Baptist, Methodist, and Jewish experiences. Like the material published in previous volumes, these criteria still resulted in a preponderance of articles dealing with Catholicism and centered in New Orleans.

A separate volume could be published on congregational histories. Numerous studies of local congregations of all faiths have been written in the past half century. The archives of the Archdiocese of New Orleans has a collection of more than 250 such histories on Catholic parishes in the state. Few of these histories have been written by historians; most have been prepared by local members of the congregation to help commemorate an anniversary or special celebration such as the dedication of a new place of worship or to honor a pastor. Many are informative, illustrating periodic challenges and local conditions. Selections dealing with Temple Sinai in New Orleans and St. James Episcopal Church in Baton Rouge reflect some of the more scholarly or insightful studies of congregational history.

As the number of articles for this volume grew, a new, expanded format was adopted: one volume of articles arranged in chronological order and a second, in thematic order. The themes for the second volume included: Religion and the Arts; Folk Life and Folklore; Social Religion; Worship, Rituals, Devotions, and Festivals; Religion and Education; Camp Meetings, Revivals and Missions; Religion and Ethnic Identity; Religion and Gender; Religion and Political Life; Preaching and Oratory; and Historiography.

As the *Louisiana Purchase Bicentennial Series* moved forward and several multiple volumes replaced those that were originally envisioned as single volumes, the general editors realized that some limitation on the final volumes was necessary. And thus the two volumes on religion again became a single volume. Sixteen of the articles originally planned for the thematic volume found their way among the chronological chapters, in turn replacing a dozen articles originally planned there. Some, but not all, of the articles that did not make the transition are listed in the Additional Readings section.

The remaining articles are arranged chronologically. After an introductory article on regionalism and Southern religion, the nine sections follow familiar divisions of Louisiana history: Pre-colonial and Colonial: Native Americans; French Colonial Period; Spanish Colonial Period; Louisiana Purchase and Its Aftermath; Antebellum Period; Civil War and Reconstruction; Turn of Century; World War I-World War II; Post-World War II. Not all selected articles fit neatly into this framework. The articles by Priscilla Ferguson Clement, Gary Mills, and Sandra Egland span several periods.

A thematic approach to religious history is perilous at best, as multiple themes are often interwoven within a few pages. Carl Brasseaux, in his examination of Acadian folk life, cited in the Additional Readings section, succinctly treats folk theology, medicine, magic, the establishment of parishes, conflicts between clergy and laity, Freemasonry, sacramental life, family rituals, and even interfamilial and intercultural alliances in less than a dozen pages.[6] Barbara Thornhill's study in this volume, although not documented, provides a unique portrait of congregational development in a North Louisiana Civil Parish from the late colonial period through the twentieth century, intertwining information on architecture, education, camp meetings and congregational renewal, family worship, and morality.

Despite the wealth of material included and cited in this volume, major gaps in studying Louisiana's religious history remain. There is no comprehensive study, no solid overview of the state's religious traditions, history, and influence. There is no Louisiana companion volume to Randy J. Sparks' *Religion in Mississippi* (Jackson, 2001).

Louisiana religious studies generally are confined within denominational limits as reflected in most of the articles included and cited in this volume. Articles by Timothy F. Reilly, Priscilla Ferguson Clement, Caryn Cossé Bell, Dolores Egger Labbé, John Nau, William A. Poe, Sandra E. Egland, and James Dauphine are refreshing exceptions.

A half century ago, Nash Kerr Burger expressed concern that "scant attention" was being given to serious religious history, a concern that should be greatly alleviated by the growing body of scholarship reflected in this volume. But religion still finds itself occasionally ignored, either by choice or by lack of scholarly production. Tulane University's volume celebrating the 250th anniversary of the founding of New Orleans included articles on education, the arts, and "the Good Time Town," but none on religion.[7] Fortunately, the editors of this *Louisiana Purchase Bicentennial Series in Louisiana History* recognized the important role that religion has played in the state's history and included from the inception a volume on religion. The Center for Louisiana Studies itself has been a major encourager and publisher of new scholarship on Louisiana's religious history.

I wish to acknowledge and thank the staff of the Center for Louisiana Studies for their counsel and assistance in the article selection and preparation of this volume. In particular, Glenn Conrad asked me to serve as editor for this volume on religion and helped guide the initial selection process. I also thank in a special way Professor Timothy F. Reilly, not only for his significant contributions to this area of Louisiana history, but also for his assistance in identifying some of the articles that appear in this volume.

Endnotes

[1]See Virginia Meacham Gould and Charles E. Nolan, *Henriette Delille: "Servant of Slaves"* (New Orleans, 1999); Cyprian Davis, OSB, *Henriette Delille: Servant of Slaves, Witness of the Poor* (New Orleans, 2004); and the Mary Bernard Deggs article in this volume.

[2]C. P. M. Jones, "Liturgy and Personal Devotion," in Cheslyn Jones, Geoffrey Wainwright, and Edward Yarnold, SJ, eds., *The Study of Spirituality* (London, 2000), 3.

[3]Avery Dulles, *Models of the Church* (Garden City, N. Y., 1978). For a comprehensive congregational study based on Dulles' models, see Charles E. Nolan, *St. Mary's of Natchez: The History of A Southern Catholic Congregation, 1716-1988*, 2 vols. (Natchez, 1992).

[4]Nash Kerr Burger, review of *The Catholic Church in Louisiana* by Roger Baudier (New Orleans, 1939), in *Journal of Mississippi History*, 2 (1940): 111-114.

[5]Walter B. Posey, "The Frontier Preacher," in *The Baptist Church in the Lower Mississippi Valley, 1776-1845* (Lexington, 1957), 18-37.

[6]Carl Brasseaux, "Acadian Folk Life," in *Acadian to Cajun, Transformation of a People, 1803-1877* (Jackson, 1992), 31-40.

[7]Hodding Carter, ed., *The Past As Prelude: New Orleans, 1718-1968* (New Orleans, 1968).

ADDITIONAL READINGS

Selections that Appear in Other Volumes of this Series

Volume I: The French Experience in Louisiana

Baker, Vaughan, Amos Simpson and Mathé Allain. "Le Mari Est Seigneur: Martial Laws Governing Women in French Louisiana." In *Louisiana's Legal Heritage*, Edward F. Haas and Robert R. Macdonald, eds., 7-18. Pensacola, Fla.: Published for the Louisiana State Museum by the Perdido Bay Press, 1983.

Brasseaux, Carl A. "The Moral Climate of French Colonial Louisiana, 1699-1763." *Louisiana History*, 27 (1986): 27-42.

Giraud, Marcel. "The Religious Initiative." In *A History of French Louisiana, Volume One, The Reign of Louis XIV, 1698-1715*, translated by Joseph C. Lambert, 26-30. Baton Rouge: Louisiana State University Press, 1974.

Miceli, Mary Veronica. "The Christianization of French Colonial Louisiana: A General View of Church and State in the Context of Eighteenth-Century French Colonization and a Theory of Mission." *Southern Studies*, 21 (1982): 384-97l.

O'Neill, Charles Edwards. "The Lines Cross." In *Church and State in French Colonial Louisiana: Policy and Politics to 1732*, 235-255. New Haven: Yale University Press, 1966.

Volume II: The Spanish Presence in Louisiana, 1763-1803

Cummins, Light Townsend. "Church Courts, Marriage Breakdown, and Separation in Spanish Louisiana, West Florida, and Texas, 1763-1836." *Journal of Texas Catholic History and Culture*, 4 (1993): 97-114.

Greenleaf, Richard E. "The Inquisition in Spanish Louisiana, 1762-1800." *New Mexico Historical Review*, 50 (1975): 45-72.

Holmes, Jack D. L. "Do It! Don't Do It!: Spanish Laws on Sex and Marriage." In *Louisiana's Legal Heritage*, Edward F. Haas and Robert R. Macdonald, eds., 19-42. Pensacola, Fla.: Published for the Louisiana State Museum by the Perdido Bay Press, 1983.

Lemmon, Alfred E. "Music and Art in Spanish Colonial Louisiana," original article.

Lemmon, Alfred E. "Spanish Louisiana: In the Service of God and His Most Catholic Majesty." In *Cross, Crozier, and Crucible: A Volume Celebrating the Bicentennial of a Catholic Diocese in Louisiana*, Glenn Conrad, ed., 16-29. Lafayette, La.: Archdiocese of New Orleans in cooperation with the Center for Louisiana Studies, 1993.

Wilson, Samuel Jr. "Almonester: Philanthropist and Builder in New Orleans." In *The Spanish in the Mississippi Valley, 1762-1804*, John Francis McDermott, ed., 183-247. Urbana: University of Illinois Press, 1974.

Volume III: The Louisiana Purchase and Its Aftermath, 1800-1830

Labbé, Dolores Egger. "Mothers and Children in Antebellum Louisiana." *Louisiana History*, 34 (1993): 161-173.

McFillen, Nola Mae. "Methodist Beginnings in Louisiana." *Methodist History*, 5 (1967): 35-46.

O'Neill, Charles Edwards. "'A Quarter Century Marked by Sundry Peculiarities': New Orleans, Lay Trustees, and Père Antoine." *Catholic Historical Review*, 68 (1990): 235-277.

Volume IV: Antebellum Louisiana, Part A, Life and Labor

Taylor, Joe Gray. "Religion Among Louisiana Slaves." In *Negro Slavery in Louisiana*, 133-52. Baton Rouge: Louisiana Historical Association, 1963.

Volume IV: Antebellum Louisiana, Part B, Politics

Monroe, Haskell. "Bishop Palmer's Thanksgiving Day Address." *Louisiana History*, 4 (1963): 105-118.

Volume V: The Civil War in Louisiana, Part B, The Home Front

Romero, Sidney J. "Louisiana Clergy and the Confederate Army." *Louisiana History*, 2 (1961): 277-300.

Volume VI: Reconstructing Louisiana

Brady, Patricia. "Trials and Tribulations: American Missionary Association Teachers and Black Education in Occupied New Orleans, 1863-1864." *Louisiana History*, 31 (1990): 5-20.

Volume IX: Louisiana Since the Longs: 1960 to Century's End

Bradley, Jared W. "Walker Percy and the Search for Wisdom." *Louisiana Studies*, 12 (1973): 579-90.

Volume X: A Refuge for All Ages: Immigration in Louisiana History

Baiamonte, John V. Jr. "Community Life in the Italian Colonies of Tangipahoa Parish, Louisiana, 1890-1950." *Louisiana History*, 30 (1989): 365-398.

Conrad, Glenn R. "Friend or Foe? Religious Exiles at the Opelousas Post in the American Revolution." *Attakapas Gazette*, 12 (1977): 137-39.

Malone, Bobbie. "New Orleans Uptown Jewish Immigrants: The Community of Congregation Gates of Prayer, 1850-1860." *Louisiana Historical Quarterly*, 40 (1957): 110-32.

Volume XI: The African American Experience in Louisiana, Part A: From Africa to the Civil War

Reinders, Robert C. "The Churches and the Negro in New Orleans, 1850-1860." *Phylon: The Atlanta University Review of Race and Culture*, 22 (1961): 241-48.

Volume XI: The African American Experience in Louisiana, Part C: From Jim Crow to Civil Rights

Jacobs, Claude F. "Benevolent Societies of New Orleans Blacks during the Late Nineteenth and Early Twentieth Centuries." *Louisiana History*, 29 (1988): 21-33.

Volume XIV: New Orleans and Urban Louisiana, Part A: Through Reconstruction

Doorley, Michael. "Irish Catholics and French Creoles: Ethnic Struggles Within the Catholic Church in New Orleans, 1835-1920." *Catholic Historical Review*, 87 (2001): 34-54.

Reilly, Timothy F. "Parson Clapp of New Orleans: Antebellum Social Critic, Religious Radical, and Member of the Establishment." *Louisiana History*, 16 (1975): 167-191.

Volume XIV: New Orleans and Urban Louisiana, Part B: Since 1877

Blue, Ellen. "The Citizens Forum on Integration: 'Underground' Methodist Response to the Brown Decision." *Methodist History* (forthcoming).

Farley, Benjamin W. "George W. Cable: Presbyterian Romancer, Reformer, Bible Teacher." *Journal of Presbyterian History*, 58 (1980): 166-181.

Malone, Bobbie. "Southernization, Self-Righteousness, Nativism, and Social Reform: New Orleans, 1887-1891." In *Rabbi Max Heller: Reformer, Zionist, Southerner, 1860-1929*, 34-55 and 223-227. Tuscaloosa: University of Alabama Press, 1997.

Volume XV: Visions and Revisions: Perspectives on Louisiana Culture and Society

Aycock, Joan Marie. "The Ursuline School in New Orleans, 1727-1771." In *Cross, Crozier & Crucible: A Volume Celebrating the Bicentennial of a Catholic Diocese in Louisiana*, Glenn Conrad, ed., 203-218. Lafayette, La.: Archdiocese of New Orleans in cooperation with the Center for Louisiana Studies, 1993.

Baker, Vaughan, Amos Simpson and Mathé Allain, "Le Mari Est Seigneur: Martial Laws Governing Women in French Louisiana." In *Louisiana's Legal Heritage*, Edward F. Haas and Robert R. Macdonald, eds., 7-18. Pensacola, Fla.: Published for the Louisiana State Museum by the Perdido Bay Press, 1983.

Brady, Patricia. "Free Men of Color as Tomb Builders in the Nineteenth Century." *Cross, Crozier & Crucible: A Volume Celebrating the Bicentennial of a Catholic Diocese in Louisiana*, Glenn Conrad, ed., 478-88. Lafayette, La.: Archdiocese of New Orleans in cooperation with the Center for Louisiana Studies, 1993.

Brasseaux, Carl A. "The Moral Climate of French Colonial Louisiana 1699-1763." *Louisiana History*, 27 (1986): 27-42.

Volume XVII: Louisiana Literature and Literary Figures

Guillaume, Alfred J. Jr. "Love, Death, and Faith in the New Orleans Poets of Color." *Southern Quarterly*, 20 (1982): 126-144.

Volume XVIII: Education in Louisiana

Alberts, John Bernard. "Black Catholic Schools: The Josephite Parishes of New Orleans During the Jim Crow Era." *U. S. Catholic Historian*, 12 (1994): 77-98.

Fichter, Joseph H. "The First Black Students at Loyola University: A Strategy to Obtain Teacher Certification." *The Journal of Negro Education*, 56 (1987): 535-49.

Hebert, Adam Otis Jr. "History of Education in Colonial Louisiana." M.A. thesis, Louisiana State University, 1958, 61-86.

Richardson, Joe M. "The American Missionary Association and Black Education in Louisiana, 1862-1878." In *Louisiana's Black Heritage*, Robert R. MacDonald, John R. Kemp, and Edward F. Haas, eds., 147-62. New Orleans: Louisiana State Museum, 1979.

Wilson, Samuel Jr. "St. Patrick's Parochial Schools." *Louisiana History*, 35 (1994): 321-30.

For Further Reading

Amelinckx, Frans C., "Social Christianity in Short Stories and Novellas of Michel Séligny." *Louisiana History*, 39 (1998): 65-72.

Bell, Caryn Cossé. "French Religious Culture in Afro-Creole New Orleans, 1718-1877." *U. S. Catholic Historian*, 17 (1999): 1-16.

Blanton, Mackie and Gayle Nolan. "Creole Lenten Devotions: Nineteenth Century Practices and Their Implications." In *Cross, Crozier and Crucible: A Volume Celebrating the Bicentennial of a Catholic Diocese in Louisiana*, Glenn Conrad, ed., 525-38. Lafayette, La.: Archdiocese of New Orleans in cooperation with the Center for Louisiana Studies, 1993.

Bodin, Ron. *Voodoo, Past and Present*. Lafayette, La.: Center for Louisiana Studies, 1990.

Brasseaux, Carl. "Acadian Folk Life." In *Acadian to Cajun, Transformation of a People, 1803-1877*, 20-44. Jackson: University Press of Mississippi, 1992.

Brown, Mary Elizabeth, ed. *A Migrant Missionary Story: The Autobiography of Giacomo Gambera*. New York: Center for Migration Studies, 1994.

Bruns, J. Edgar. "Antoine Blanc: Louisiana's Joshua in the Land of Promise He Opened." In *Cross, Crozier and Crucible: A Volume Celebrating the Bicentennial of a Catholic Diocese in Louisiana*, Glenn Conrad, ed., 120-34. Lafayette, La.: Archdiocese of New Orleans in cooperation with the Center for Louisiana Studies, 1993.

Caravaglios, Marie Genoino. "A Roman Critique of the Pro-Slavery Views of Bishop Martin of Natchitoches, Louisiana." *Records of the American Catholic Historical Society of Philadelphia*, 83 (1972): 67-81.

Conrad, Glenn. "The Faces of French Louisiana." In *Cross, Crozier and Crucible: A Volume Celebrating the Bicentennial of a Catholic Diocese in Louisiana*, Glenn Conrad, ed., 5-15. Lafayette, La.: Archdiocese of New Orleans in cooperation with the Center for Louisiana Studies, 1993.

Dollar, Susan E. "Isle Brevelle Catholicism and Identity in Nineteenth-Century Creole Louisiana," paper presentation, Louisiana Historical Association Annual Meeting, New Iberia, La., March 2002.

Heaney, Jane Frances. "Adjustment Under the Stars and Stripes." In *A Century of Pioneering, A History of the Ursulines Nuns in New Orleans, 1727-1827*, Mary Ethel Booker Siefken, ed., 219-34. New Orleans: Ursuline Sisters, 1993.

Huber, Leonard V. *Clasped Hands, Symbolism in New Orleans Cemeteries*. Lafayette, La.: Center for Louisiana Studies, 1982.

Kasteel, Annemarie. "The Bitterness Was Intense." In *Francis Janssens, 1843-1897: A Dutch-American Prelate*, 275-300. Lafayette, La.: Center for Louisiana Studies, 1992.

Logsdon, Joseph and Caryn Cossé Bell. "The Americanization of Black New Orleans, 1850-1900." In *Creole New Orleans: Race and Americanization*, Arnold R. Hirsch and Joseph Logsdon, eds., 201-15. Baton Rouge: Louisiana State University Press, 1992.

Long, Alecia P. *The Great Southern Babylon: Sexuality, Race and Reform in New Orleans, 1865-1920*. Baton Rouge: Louisiana State University Press, 2004.

Long, Carolyn Morrow. "Voodoo Survivals and the Transition to Hoodoo: 1900-1940." In *Spiritual Merchants, Religion, Magic and Commerce*, 53-66. Knoxville: University of Tennessee Press, 2001.

Lord, Clyde W. "The Mineral Springs Holiness Camp Meetings." *Louisiana History*, 16 (1975): 257-77.

Nelson, Arnold F. "Introduction" and "Still Growing and Recognized." In *A History of Baptist French Missions in South Louisiana*, 1-2, 206-20. n.p.: 1994.

Newman, Mark. "The Louisiana Baptist Convention and Desegregation, 1954-1980." *Louisiana History*, 42 (2001): 389-418.

Nolan, Charles E. "Louisiana Catholic Historiography (1916-1992)." In *Cross, Crozier and Crucible: A Volume Celebrating the Bicentennial of a Catholic Diocese in Louisiana*, Glenn Conrad, ed., 584-634. Lafayette, La.: Archdiocese of New Orleans in cooperation with the Center for Louisiana Studies, 1993.

Orso, Ethelyn and E. Charles Plaisance. "Chitimacha Folklore." *Louisiana Folklore Miscellany*, 3 (1975 for 1973): 35-41.

Roach, Susan. "'You Gotta Go Crazy First Before You Can Be A Minister': Accessing a Speaking Role in the Primitive Baptist Church." *Louisiana Folklore Miscellany*, 8 (1993): 1-15.

Robison, R. Warren. "Small Frame Churches." In *Louisiana Church Architecture*, 46-56. Lafayette, La.: Center for Louisiana Studies, 1984.

Wynes, Charles E. "The Reverend Quincy Ewing: Southern Radical Heretic in the 'Cajun Country.'" *Louisiana History*, 7 (1966): 221-8.

PART I

Regionalism and Southern Religion

REGIONALISM IN AMERICAN RELIGION*

Edwin S. Gaustad

For so long in public expression and even longer in private assumption, the prevailing emphasis in American religion as well as in American society was on unity—mainstream, melting pot, consensus religion, the faith of our fathers. Differences were either denied or ignored; variety was either abnormal or dangerous. Unity was all.

Much has changed in this regard within the last generation, as the strength and genius of the nation have been perceived as residing in its diversity. Pluralism has been celebrated rather than denigrated. Minority viewpoints have been sought out, even as minority (and female) representation has been self-consciously encouraged on boards, councils, commissions, and presidential cabinets. This major attitudinal shift has had its clear impact on our understanding of American religion. There, the pattern in the past has been to think almost exclusively in denominational terms, which have more often concealed ethnic and gender diversity than displayed it. Hispanic Catholicism, to take a single example, has been—despite its gigantic size—virtually impotent and invisible until quite recently. "Eastern Orthodoxy" as a phrase suggested to most Americans something foreign and obscure, but the simple label scarcely hinted at the rich ethnic diversity lying underneath. Such bland official names as American Lutheran Church and Lutheran Church in America (and even these are soon to disappear) may represent a real gain in ecumenicity but they lost the nineteenth century's proud assertion of Finnish, Swedish, Danish, Norwegian, and German heritage. In denominational histories through World War II and beyond, the black churches were generally as invisible as their members were in the larger body politic.

All this invisibility in race, in gender, and in ethnic origins has greatly changed in recent times, with the clear result that we look at American religion in the 1980s through quite different eyes. Conferences are held and pastoral letters sent that highlight the place of Hispanic Catholics in America's Roman Catholic church.[1] The "black church" and "slave religion" and "black theology" have all received more scholarly attention in the last 20 years than in the previous 200.[2] And sexist language, along with sexist exclu-

*First published in Charles Reagan Wilson, *Religion in the South* (Jackson: University Press of Mississippi, 1985), 155-172. Reprinted with the kind permission of the publisher.

11

sion of women in roles of leadership in religion, are at least challenged where they have not already disappeared.[3] Never again can one generalize about American religion in ways that suppress or ignore the bountiful and bubbling, and sometimes brawling, ethnic and gender diversity in American religion. The case has been made.

It has been made with such impressiveness, however, that it is in danger of obscuring yet another long-standing source of significant diversity in American religion—its *regional* character. The South is perhaps the one region least in danger of losing its identity as a region, although, as John B. Boles has pointed out, careful and critical scholarship devoted to Southern religion is a relatively recent phenomenon.[4] He also notes, however, that this regionalism has quite particular historical roots, such as the Lost Cause cult of the Reconstruction period, and these roots have limited mobility. The "New South," for instance, can no longer be understood in terms applicable to the old Confederacy, for this region extends across west Texas, New Mexico, and Arizona to Southern California. There is great difference, to be sure, between Oxford, Mississippi, and Santa Fe, New Mexico; between Charleston, South Carolina, and Los Angeles, California. These glaring contrasts, however, must not blind one to the subtle spread of Southern culture throughout the Sunbelt, especially the spread of Southern popular religion.

Is regionalism in American religion a phenomenon peculiar to the South? Both historically and contemporaneously, the United States reveals many remarkable examples of regionalism in religion, a regionalism that has implications for community standards in morality, for economic patterns including cultivation of the soil, for public and private education, and even for presidential candidates and the issues that should be mentioned (or omitted) in certain locales.

Colonial Patterns

In considering the colonial period of American history, geography can never be ignored, whether one's attention is on religion or not. No aspect of Virginia's history, for example, can be understood apart from her great rivers. The character of soil and climate shaped New England's pattern of settlement, even as east Jersey was separated from west Jersey as much by the accidents of geography as those of politics. The best known as well as the most enduring religious regionalism of colonial America was that of Puritan New England.[5]

Puritanism made its impact not only upon the land but upon the American mind as well, so that historians speak more confidently of a "New England Way" than they do of any other colonial area. The reasons for this are well known: New Englanders in great numbers were driven by a steady purpose, and they maintained—not by accident but by design—a religious homogeneity that kept church and state connected until well into the nineteenth century. One notes in the accompanying map that New England is as thoroughly blanketed by Congregationalism in 1750 as the rest of the country is almost innocent of Puritanism. The exceptions represent migrations from New England, either overland into New York and New Jersey, or by water to Long Island and even South Carolina. These were mostly exotic plants, however; American Puritanism was rooted in New England and, when the "New England Way" moved across the continent, it drew strength, personnel, and financing largely from Connecticut and Massachusetts.

The Middle Colonies (New York, New Jersey, and Pennsylvania) reveal not one but several religious patterns in the colonial period. No single church dominated; no "Middle Colony Way" has ever been discovered. One can nonetheless find clear patterns by the middle of the eighteenth century, especially within the ranks of the Quakers, the Presbyterians, the Lutherans, and the Dutch and German Reformed. One illustration of this geographical patterning *within* a region (rather than dominating a region) will suffice— the Lutherans.[6] This migration, chiefly from Germany, followed after the earlier migration of English Quakers into west Jersey and Pennsylvania and of Dutch Reformed into New York and east Jersey. Lutherans moved, therefore, back from the coasts, or up the rivers, or even down into the backcountry valleys of Maryland and Virginia. In 1750, however, Lutheranism was almost exclusively a phenomenon of the Middle Colonies— though the reverse, one must remember, was not true. One notes in particular how hostile an environment New England is to Lutheranism. Later immigration would shift the dominance of Lutheranism markedly from its colonial locale.

In the colonial South something like a New England pattern of exclusivity prevailed, though never with the conspicuous success enjoyed in that more northern region. The Church of England, or Anglicanism, enjoyed official patronage and favor in the Southern colonies (as, of course, Congregationalism did in New England; Lutheranism did not there or anywhere else). Positively, this meant that government assistance both from England and the colonies themselves aided and abetted the planting and expansion of the Anglican church. Negatively, this meant that governments gave themselves, with varying degrees of vigor and success, to the persecution or prevention of other religious options. The Chesapeake Bay region represents by far the greatest concentration of colonial Anglicanism either in the seventeenth or the eighteenth centuries.[7] As the official church of England, however, this religion could not successfully be excluded anywhere, not even from New England. North Carolina was late to be settled, and even later to be civilized, which is another way of saying that Quakers and Baptists made major inroads there before Anglicanism managed to secure a firm foothold. In the area around Charleston, Anglican parishes were laid out in gratifying numbers and Anglican missionaries arrived in a quantity often more pleasing than the quality; interior South Carolina, however, was hardly penetrated.

Regionalism in American religion is, therefore, not a product of modern times or of sectarian exclusiveness or of secular counterattacks: it is built in from the beginning. Some of that colonial regionalism was fleeting and possibly even irrelevant, but other examples were enduring and of major cultural moment.

Nineteenth-Century Patterns

The opening of the continent in the nineteenth century also promoted religious regionalism. One might expect regionalism to be diluted on the frontier or perhaps even to disappear altogether, thinking that all of the well established groups along the Atlantic seaboard would slowly shift westward, mingling and mixing and losing any geographical identity as they went. For the most part, however, this is not what happened. Some groups were successful on the frontier, others not. Some preferred the urban centers of the East Coast or the well-cleared farmlands of their fathers and mothers. Some waited for education and civilization to go ahead; others saw themselves as the only means by which education and civilization would ever reach the West. And still other prophets and visionaries saw the frontier West as the providential opportunity to start their own church, their new movement, their colony or commune or biblical commonwealth. For these persons, the East was European and decadent; the West was American and the land of unparalleled religious opportunity.

Methodism was a denominational youngster that won its independence about the same time that the nation did. With the bloom of youth still on its cheeks, the new Methodist church set out along post roads and no roads to carry its ministry and message.[8] Across all of New York and Pennsylvania, down the Ohio River to the Mississippi; across the Carolinas and the Appalachian Mountains, down into the deep South; across the Mississippi River into the Ozarks and the piney woods of east Texas, Methodism moved in great force, eventually spreading itself rather evenly all across the United States. Even in 1850, it was not exclusively a frontier church as a glance at Maryland, New Jersey, and New England will show. Although certainly a frontier church in part in 1850, it did not rest with that regional identification, with the result that there is no peculiarly Methodist geography today. To highlight, however, the stunning success that Methodism enjoyed on the frontier a century or so ago, its advance can be compared with that of the Episcopal church in the same period.[9] Episcopalians, overly identified with England, had many problems during and after the Revolution; as a result, they were in no position to seize the opportunities presented by the new liberty and the new lands. They were, so to speak, left at the post along the eastern seaboard. While Methodism had entered virtually every county in Georgia, Alabama, and Mississippi, the Episcopal church (which had dominated the South earlier) had made no mark by 1850 in the vast majority of the counties of those three states. In Ohio, Indiana, Illinois, and Missouri, the picture was no better for Methodism's parent church.

For most denominations in nineteenth century America, the move from East to West was a move from the known to the unknown, from the churched to the wholly unchurched. For one denomination, however, this was noticeably not the case. Roman Catholicism in America was not all Irish, German, and English in 1850: it was heavily Hispanic as well.[10] Santa Fe was settled and missions planted there in 1610 and, although the Spanish were ejected by the Indians later in the seventeenth century, Spain soon returned never to depart culturally or religiously. By 1850 Father Junípero Serra's chain of missions on the Pacific Coast had long been in place. The substitution of a Mexican for a Spanish sovereignty in this region did not erase the Hispanic footsteps, nor did the Anglo conquest that followed result in the replacement of a Hispanic Catholic culture by a Protestant one.

Eastern, "old" Americans often manifested some sense of superiority toward the western, "new" Americans in California after that state was added to the Union in 1850. Such a sense of superiority was totally unjustified, argued English Catholic Herbert Vaughan when he visited California in 1864. To judge a culture, he said, one might note the way in which it treats the native American, the Indian. Here the eastern Americans who came west more for love of gold than love of God did not fare well. Even more conspicuous perhaps, said Father (later Cardinal) Vaughan, was the contrasting attitude toward the land and the names that each group gave to it. The Hispanics named it San Francisco, the Anglos Jackass Gulch; the Hispanics called it Jesus Maria, the Anglos Slap Jack Bar; Hispanics christened it Nuestra Señora de Soledad, the Anglos Skunk Gulch. Herbert Vaughan rested his case.[11] Irrespective of the question of cultural superiority, however, Roman Catholicism was rescued from a regionalism of the northeastern United States largely by a Catholic regionalism of the West, which predated the former by two or more centuries.

To return to the East Coast briefly, there was one other example of regionalism wherein a limiting parochialism (at least geographically) was evident. Unitarianism, which represented a schism within orthodox (Trinitarian) Congregationalism around the end of the eighteenth century, continued to draw its strength from the New England area.[12] Indeed, it was concentrated in, and virtually limited to, New England. Beyond that, a "saturation bombing" occurred in the Boston region giving rise to the old saw that Unitarians believed in the Fatherhood of God, the Brotherhood of Man, and the Neighborhood of Boston. Unitarianism never fully escaped this quite restricted regionalism, but it exercised an influence out of all proportion to its numbers in literature, in social reform, and even in politics. A highly literate fellowship, its power lay not in the control of geography but in the determined exercise of rationality in religion.

Dominant Patterns in the Twentieth Century

Commentators on American society often dwell on the high degree of mobility in the nation today: how few people live in the same house in which they were born, or the same town, or even the same state. Others speak of the homogenization of America by the common influences of television, mass merchandising, and inside plumbing. From coast to coast, from north to south, Americans are an undifferentiated glob. We all know better, of course, and my only point in overstating the case is to declare that the homogenization has still a very long way to go in religion. At least four "culture religions" can be identified in the 1970s and '80s—the Lutheran in the upper Midwest, the Baptist in the

Southeast, the Mormon in the far West, and the Roman Catholic in the Northeast and Southwest.[13]

Lutheranism was a Middle Colony phenomenon in 1750 and almost totally German in ethnicity. Now, a couple of centuries later, both the geography and the ethnicity have shifted. Late nineteenth-century Lutheran immigration was predominantly Scandinavian. The eastern seaboard was full; the upper Midwest was not. This latter region, moreover, represented land and latitude similar to that left behind. The region proved both hospitable and profitable, so much so that the upper Midwest contains (as has often been pointed out) more Swedes than Sweden, more Norwegians than Norway, more Danes than Denmark, and so on. But ethnicity often triumphed over theology: that is, Swedish Lutherans could find more common ground with other Swedes than with other Lutherans—just as in the eighteenth century German Lutherans and German Reformed, though from quite separate theological heritages, sometimes magnified their common Germanic origin, minimizing their separate theological ones. Permit me to quote from the grandson of Norwegian immigrants to Minnesota. The communities in that state, he writes,

> were all homogeneous and self-contained. The immigrant invasion of that part of the country was overwhelmingly Scandinavian, but the separate components of Scandinavia did not become a melting pot in the New World. A township like Aastad remained exclusively Norwegian. The Swedes and Danes and Finns kept to themselves in communities that had names like Swedish Grove and Dane Prairie and Finlandia. The different groups could have made themselves understood to one another and might have found they had much in common. But these exchanges did not occur. . . . Each [community] had its own Lutheran churches, newspapers, and social fraternities, with little or no cross-pollination. My grandfather and my grandmother lived more than sixty and eighty years, respectively, but there's no evidence they had more than glancing contact with anyone who was not Norwegian. . . . [14]

Clannishness was as American as apple pie. There was religious regionalism, but ethnic regionalism even more.

A second example of culture religion today is that of the Baptists. When speaking earlier of frontier regions, the Baptists could of course have been mentioned along with the Methodists for they too enjoyed phenomenal success in the sparsely settled wildernesses. Unlike the Methodists, however, the Baptists stayed in sufficient force to dominate a huge region south of the Ohio and Missouri rivers, and on both sides of the Mississippi. In the state of Mississippi every county but three has more Baptists than it has members of any other denominational family; in Alabama that same situation obtains in every county but one. Lutheranism's hold on the upper Midwest is not nearly so strong; that hold is weakened, moreover, by the ethnic division already noted. The major ethnic division in the Baptist South is, of course, that between black and white, but the regional dominance would be roughly the same for each group alone. Together, black Baptists and white Baptists constitute an exceptionally heavy majority, the precise figures being elusive because of the paucity of data from the black churches. Of course, Baptists in this vast region can be and are divided in many ways—theologically, ecclesiastically, politically, and socially. Fortunately, however, the concern here is only with the concept of region.

The most convincing example of religious regionalism and geographical "control" in twentieth-century America is that offered by the Church of Jesus Christ of Latter-day Saints, the Mormons. In Utah every county is a Mormon county, some to the amazing extent of 100 percent—no competing religious body at all. The region has been extended well beyond the Salt Lake Basin into adjoining states, particularly Southern Idaho and western Wyoming. Though Mormonism started in the East (Palmyra, New York) and paused briefly in the Midwest (Ohio, Illinois, Missouri), the exodus in the late 1840s to Salt Lake City represented the most striking transplanting in American history of a specific church from one region of the country to another. The Mormons encouraged further migrants from the states as well as new converts from abroad and caused the desert to bloom, as the nation's most successful utopian experiment found in the West a haven from persecution and harassment as well as a land open to religious conquest. Some observers even speak of "Mormondom," a term that points to a culture religion of recognizable influence and proved staying power.

The final dominant pattern in America today is that of Roman Catholicism, notably in the Northeast (and extending into the old Northwest) as well as the Southwest, including Southern Louisiana (and extending into the Pacific West). The dominance in the Northeast is chiefly a result of European immigration in the nineteenth century, heavily Irish before the Civil War and heavily Southern European after that war. French Catholics from Canada have also moved across the border into the United States. Ethnic strains have pulled powerfully at a church seeking to be universal, and they pull still. New York's Archbishop O'Connor and New York's Representative Ferraro no doubt have a real disagreement concerning abortion, but that difference is in no way mitigated by the long-standing tensions between Irish Catholic and Italian Catholic. The broad picture of a Roman Catholic region in the Northeast can, upon closer examination, become like the Lutheran region: a mosaic of separate, insular, homogeneous communities or parishes of Catholics who are Irish or German, Italian or Portuguese, French or Polish, Austrian or Puerto Rican, Slavic or Hungarian. In the Southwest, the Hispanic presence accounts for much of the Catholic regionalism there, but certainly not all. The French, of course, dominate the Southern half of Louisiana. Indian converts as well as Catholics from the eastern half of the United States also make their presence felt in the whole southwestern corner of the country, and on around to the Pacific Coast. A hierarchical unity gives more force to this regionalism than, say, to the Baptist, but it is a unity mitigated by differing histories, competing ethnic groups, and contending cultural perspectives.

Subtler Patterns in the Twentieth Century

A multi-colored national map may conceal almost as much about American religion as it reveals. Where, for example, are the Presbyterians, the Episcopalians, the Eastern Orthodox, the Jews, the Campbellites, and many others? It is not possible to deal with everyone left after the four macrocultures of Lutherans, Baptists, Mormons, and Catholics have been examined. A few examples of religious geography, however, will indicate that the "big picture" is far from being the total picture. There is a microcosm of religious geography, too, those little worlds sometimes surprising the cross-country highway traveler. While driving across Iowa or Kansas, for example, one may go through a county were the Mennonites are the only significant religious group. Similarly in South Dakota or Montana, one may suddenly be surrounded by nothing but Hutterite farms and Hutterite communities. And if one drives through New England, the Congregational heritage is perfectly plain, so much so that one may too readily conclude that this church still dominates the region. Such is not the case, for Roman Catholicism is the major force there.

Still, Congregationalism (now largely under the name "United Church of Christ") is stronger in New England than anywhere else in the nation.[15] In the mid-twentieth century, one observes Congregationalism moving westward, often in conjunction with Presbyterianism under what was called the Plan of Union. Congregationalism did not, however, move southward in force, with the possible exception of North Carolina. Elsewhere in the South, the Congregational presence reflects vigorous missionary and educational activity among the blacks after the Civil War. Likewise, the New Mexico-Arizona presence largely reflects Congregational missionary work among the Indians in those states — before they became states. The Southern California Congregational density represents in part just the huge population of the region but also in part the proclivity of that region to receive its immigrants from all over the nation.

The Dutch Reformed were early to arrive in America, but they arrived from Holland in two waves of immigration widely separated in time. An 1850 map of the Dutch Reformed in America,[16] would show the clear results of that first "invasion" of North America early in the seventeenth century. The New York (which was first New Amsterdam)-New Jersey axis is still clearly defined in 1850, though by this time religious dominance has long since passed to others. By 1950, evidence for that second wave in the nineteenth century is revealed.[17] The Reformed Church in America, as it is now called, is a small church (fewer than 1/4 million members), but an influential one partly because its membership is not spread thinly across the nation. Rather, it is concentrated in the upper Midwest where it does actually dominate a few counties, as well as in New York and New Jersey where it no longer controls even its own school, Rutgers University. Unhappily, many of the Dutch Reformed who arrived in the nineteenth century thought that those who had come two centuries earlier were now too much American and too little Dutch. This cultural disparity led to schism among the Dutch Calvinists in America; otherwise, their influence would be even stronger. In the study of grouping in American religion, one must pay attention to time as well as to space.

The largest of the Pentecostal churches, Assembly of God, now on its way to 2 million members, is recent in origin (1914) but is developing at a quite rapid pace.[18] It is probably still accurate to think of the Assemblies of God as a Southern church, particularly if speaking in terms of the "New South" extending from the Atlantic to the Pacific. The whole nation is exposed to this Pentecostal movement, though, and, by the end of the century, it will probably be more accurate to describe it as a national church.

Among the "subtler patterns," there is a denomination that no longer exists as a separate entity, the Evangelical United Brethren.[19] Often called the "German Methodists," this ethnic group joined with the much larger Methodist church in 1968, the latter appropriating the "United" and making it part of its official title. EUB was clearly a regional church—Pennsylvania, Ohio, and Indiana being the greatest centers of strength. By virtue of such a merger, Methodism greatly strengthened its hand in the Midwest, but hardly altered its status elsewhere in the nation. Whereas in earlier days, ethnicity was reason enough for a separate organization, that reason became less and less compelling as the twentieth century unrolled.

The Roman Catholic regionalism that was discussed before is still evident, though not quite as dramatically so. Yet the Northeast and Southwest still stand out. No state is as sharply bifurcated as Louisiana, with Catholics heavily in the South and Protestants just as heavily in the North, although Texas comes close. The Protestantism of the Midwest and the South is readily apparent; this orientation would be even more "solid" were full data from black churches available. The singular fact about another region, the West, is that church membership as a percentage of total population drops sharply—always excepting the Mormon areas. In California and Oregon less than 25 percent of the population is either Catholic or Protestant, and in both states a few instances are found were the percentage drops below 10 percent. The Gallup polls, which also divide the nation into "regions," tend to confirm the less churched status, and the less church-attending status, of the West.

The South as a Religious Region: the 1980s

As has already been noted, the dominant religion for the South is that of the Baptists. And the dominant specific institution among Southern whites is the Southern Baptist Convention, with Alabama and Mississippi enjoying the highest percentage of affiliation (about 30 percent) and Florida the lowest (less than 10 percent). The South's second strongest religious body is Methodism, with the greatest concentration to be found in North Carolina (over 10 percent) and the least in Louisiana (4 percent). Even where Baptists hold the lead on a statewide basis, as in Alabama and Mississippi, Methodists dominate many counties: eight in the former, and nine in the latter. To speak of "dominance" anywhere in the Old Confederate South is to speak almost exclusively of either Baptists or Methodists. The exceptions, to be noted below, are to be found only on the local level and not on the grander or statewide scale.[20]

The Presbyterian Church, U. S., which in 1983 merged with the larger Northern body of United Presbyterians, is the third largest denomination in the eleven states of the Confederacy. The Carolinas have the highest percentage of their population in the PCUS (about 3 percent), with Arkansas and Louisiana having the lowest (less than 1 percent). The Presbyterian Church in America, a conservative withdrawal from the PCUS in 1973, has its major base in Alabama and Mississippi; even there, however the membership expressed as a percentage of the state's total population is only about 1/2 of 1 percent. The other "mainline" Protestant body that is a visible presence throughout the South is the Episcopal church. This old colonial church fails to dominate any large region, however, serving rather as a significant cultural and religious alternative to the more popular, more broadly based Baptist, Methodist and Presbyterian denominations. The Episcopal church is strongest in Virginia (2.5 percent), weakest in Arkansas (less than 1), but in most states exercises an influence beyond that of its modest numbers.

What of the three other "cultural religions" noted above: Roman Catholics, Lutherans, and Mormons? How do they fare in the South? The Catholics do best, most conspicuously as has been noted in Southern Louisiana (over 30 percent of the state's total population is Catholic) and in Southern Texas (where Catholic strength brings the whole state's percentage to over 16 percent). But Roman Catholicism is also very strong in south Florida, this concentration being recently enhanced by heavy Cuban immigration. The Gulf Coast counties of Alabama (Mobile and Baldwin) and Mississippi (Hancock, Harrison, and Jackson) also constitute Catholic population centers. Lutheranism has penetrated the South less successfully; with the single exception of Newberry County in South Carolina, it does not dominate any Southern county and is least evident in Mississippi. The Mormons control or dominate no Southern territory at all, being nowhere more than 1/2 of 1 percent of the population in any Southern state.

If, however, such strong culture religions as Lutheranism and Mormonism have scarcely left their mark, other religious groups not prominent on the national scene find their greatest concentration to be in the South. The Churches of Christ, for example, a conservative separation around the beginning of the twentieth century from the Disciples of Christ movement, are most apparent in the border South, notably in Tennessee (about 5 percent of the population). The Cumberland Presbyterian Church, an early nineteenth century schism, also has its visibility mainly in Tennessee; even there, however, Cumberland Presbyterians are less than 1 percent of the population. The Assemblies of God, as previously observed, are strongest in Arkansas (2.3 percent); other Pentecostal and Holiness groups, on the other hand, flourish in the Carolinas, notably the Church of the Nazarene and the Pentecostal Holiness Church. Fundamentalist Baptist bodies, not affiliated with the Southern Baptist Convention, which also flourish in the South, include the American Baptist Association (over 1 million members) and the Baptist Missionary Association (about one-quarter million members). Arkansas is again the major center of these dissenting Baptists.

Some of the nation's remaining historic religious bodies, whose origins lie outside the South and perhaps even outside the United States, manage to achieve some visibility in specific locales—Judaism in Dade County, Florida; Church of the Brethren in Floyd County, Virginia; the United Church of Christ (Congregational) in much of North Carolina; and the African Methodist Episcopal Zion Church, also strongest in North Carolina but virtually nonexistent in both Arkansas and Texas. The Disciples of Christ have not surrendered all of the South to the Churches of Christ, the former being stronger than the latter in both Virginia and North Carolina. Although the South can in broad terms be described as a region in which Baptists dominate, closer inspection reveals patterns of pluralism can be found even here.[21]

Conclusion

What conclusions can be drawn about regionalism in American religion?

1. First, most obviously, religious regionalism has been common, and it is by no means limited to the South.

2. Second, there has been a great deal of tenacity, of endurance, on the part of a religion that has had at any time in its past a strong hold in a specific area: witness the Congregationalists in New England, the Dutch Reformed in New York and New Jersey, and various Germanic faiths in Pennsylvania. A notable exception to this rule, however, is the Anglican or Episcopal church in Virginia. Very strong in all of the Chesapeake region for two hundred years, the modern church is no more powerful there today than it is in most other parts of the country. (One can argue that the historical circumstances here were truly exceptional and that, therefore, the "tenacity rule" still holds.)

3. Third, that one can identify at least four powerful "culture religions" in the nation today: that is, religions that so dominate a geographical region that the line between the church and the surrounding culture grows increasingly hard to draw and the force of this unofficial alliance tends to make the religious body ever stronger and more inclusive. The four already identified on a large scale were these: Lutheran, Baptist, Mormon, and Roman Catholic. On a small scale, many more might be added to this list: hamlet by hamlet, valley by valley, county by county.

4. Fourth, one can conclude with a question. I began this paper by suggesting that the days of consensus history and melting-pot sociology appear to be behind us, and that in their respective places we have a celebration of countercultures, diverse perspectives, varied values, and "unmeltable ethnics."[22] We also have religion by region. Do we pay a price for such regionalism? Is it part of our genius and a source of our strength, or is it only an accident of history and a sketch of fault lines along which great social fissures will eventually appear? Like any proper professor, I raise the questions, leaving you full freedom to provide the answers.

Notes for "Regionalism in American Religion"

[1]In 1972 and again in 1977, National Pastoral Hispanic Conferences (Encuentros) were held to deal with the long-neglected concerns of the Hispanic Catholic minority. Then in 1983, a Pastoral Letter on the *Hispanic Presence* emanated from the nation's Roman Catholic Bishops; it was published by the U. S. Catholic Conference in 1984.

[2]See, for example, C. Eric Lincoln, ed., *The Black Experience in Religion* (Garden City, N. Y., 1974); Milton Sernett, *Black Religion and American Evangelicalism* (Metuchen, N. J., 1975); Albert J. Raboteau, *Slave Religion* (New York, 1978); and James H. Cone's and G. S. Wilmore's exceptionally valuable anthology, *Black Theology* (New York, 1979).

[3]Books dealing with the religious dimensions of feminism have multiplied rapidly, among them these solid studies: Rosemary Ruether and Eleanor McLaughlin, *Women of Spirit* (New York, 1979); Leonard and Arlene Swidler, *Women Priests* (New York, 1977); and Phyllis Trible, *God and the Rhetoric of Sexuality* (Philadelphia, 1978).

[4]John B. Boles, "Religion in the South: A Tradition Recovered," *Maryland Historical Magazine*, 77 (Winter 1982).

[5]Edwin S. Gaustad, *Historical Atlas of Religion in America*, rev. ed. (New York, 1976), Fig. 12.

[6]Ibid., Fig. 14.

[7]Ibid., Fig. 8.

[8]Ibid., Fig. 64.

[9]Ibid., Fig. 56.

[10]Ibid., Fig. 89.

[11]See Francis J. Weber, ed., *Documents of Catholic California History* (Los Angeles, 1965), 102f.

[12]*Historical Atlas*, Fig. 105.

[13]Ibid., color fold-out map in jacket.

[14]Eugene Boe, as found in Thomas C. Wheeler, ed., *The Immigrant Experience* (New York, 1971).

[15]*Historical Atlas*, Fig. 50.

[16]Ibid., Fig. 82.

[17]Ibid., Fig. 83.

[18]Ibid., Fig. 101.

[19]Ibid., Fig. 113.

[20]Ibid., color fold-out map in jacket.

[21]For all the data in this section, see Bernard Quinn et al., *Churches and Church Membership in the United States: 1980* (Atlanta, Ga., 1982). For some religious comparisons of the South with the East, West, and Midwest, see the latest Gallup Report (#222), *Religion in America* (1984).

[22]Many recent books address this large question, not all of them of course from identical stances. See, for example, Philip Slater, *The Pursuit of Loneliness*, rev. ed. (Boston, 1976); Christopher Lasch, *The Culture of Narcissism* (New York, 1978); Robert N. Bellah, *The Broken Covenant* (New York, 1975); Mary Douglas and Steven M. Tipton, eds., *Religion and America: Spirituality in a Secular Age* (Boston, 1983); and Richard John Neuhaus, *The Naked Public Square* (Grand Rapids, Mich., 1984).

PART II
Pre-colonial and Colonial Periods: Native Americans

RELIGION, IDEOLOGY, AND CEREMONY*

Jeffrey P. Brain

Religion and ideology tend to be especially resistant to change, and Tunica beliefs were no exception. Even though the Tunica were exposed to the most intensive missionary effort in the southern part of the Lower Mississippi Valley during the early French contact period, they were not easy converts to Christianity. After two decades of intermittent endeavor, Father Davion—a sincere, sometimes overly eager, if incompetent proselytizer of the Faith—acknowledged his failure, gave in to his frustration, and abandoned his mission.

Davion was old and did not live to see his efforts bear fruit. Although the Tunica resisted Christianity and largely maintained their traditional religious beliefs, they turned the other cheek when Davion defaced their temple, and they even allowed some of their children to be baptized. There is a touching (and perhaps apocryphal) story that Cahura-Joligo's dying son exhorted his father to attend services and abandon idolatry.[1] Apparently Cahura-Joligo did undergo baptism,[2] but Father Poisson considered him a Christian in name only (although even Poisson felt that the Tunica were well disposed toward Christianity).[3] Indeed, another son of Cahura-Joligo was also baptized, and given the name Jacob. During the Trudeau occupation other Tunica were identified by Christian names as well. Although all need not have been baptismal names, some definitely were, and Davion would have been immensely gratified to know that as his generation of infants became parents they sought baptism for their own children.[4] That at least one of these parents was a subchief indicates that Davion's seedlings had taken root and grown strong in a new generation.

Religious conversion at this time, however, was only superficial at best. The lack of success of the proselytizing efforts may be inferred from the fact that so few symbols of Christianity have been found at Tunica sites of the eighteenth and nineteenth centuries. From among hundreds of burials only a few crucifixes and rosary beads have been found, and not a single example of a native-made religious article showing Christian influence. Clearly, Poisson's observation was wishful thinking, and Davion's experience not simply

*First published in Jeffrey P. Brain, *Tunica Archaeology* (Cambridge: Harvard University Press, 1988), 318-9. Reprinted with the kind permission of the author and the publisher.

a matter of ineptitude. While individual Tunica may have adopted the outward forms of Christianity, and perhaps even some articles of faith, a core of traditional beliefs was retained by the society at large. Nowhere is this better illustrated than in burial 6 at Bloodhound. It contained a crucifix—indicating that the individual had been baptized—which was concealed beneath an elaborate shell necklace that was the real symbol of native values. (It is tempting to suppose that this child, obviously the scion of someone important, was that baptized son of Cahura-Joligo who died prematurely.)

The strength of aboriginal beliefs is also revealed by Tunica commitment to the mound concept. Their putative ancestors, the Quizquiz, lived among many mounds. The survivors who became the Tunica adopted the most important mound site on the lower Yazoo River and worshipped in a temple on the summit of the largest mound. They may even have enlarged that mound, the latest known example of mound construction in the Lower Mississippi Valley. At Trudeau they apparently used a mound-like bluff remnant in the same manner as a mound, the latest known "mound" usage in the valley. Even the final settlement at Marksville is not without the image: as remembered in their folklore, Tunica women were believed to have built the mounds at the nearby Marksville site,[5] although those mounds predated the Tunica by two millennia.

Other elements of the traditional Tunica belief system have persisted to very recent times as well, and some seem to be present today. In fact, there is even evidence of a reactionary return to a kind of general Indian consciousness in ceremonial behavior. This may be attributed to the success of the pan-Indian movement. An interesting example is provided by the case of the calumet pipe. A late introduction into the Mississippi Valley, these pipes were symbolic of an important ideological and ceremonial behavior. Curiously, the Tunica are mentioned only once in the historical descriptions of the calumet ceremony,[6] yet archaeologically more of the distinctive catlinite pipe bowls have been found at sites related to the Tunica than to any other ethnic group. Trudeau alone has produced at least five, the largest single assemblage from any site in the valley. If the calumet ceremony was indeed a necessary formality when two peoples met, the number of pipes among the Tunica would seem to attest to an intensive program of interaction which would fit their entrepreneurial role. No pipes are known from nineteenth-century sites, but by then calumet ceremonialism seems no longer to have been practiced in the Southeast. It persisted on the Plains, however, and the pipes—endowed with a new pan-Indian symbolism—have been reintroduced in this century. The last chief of the Tunica, Joseph A. Pierite, Sr., took one with him to his grave. The symbolic value of such pipes may thus extend to the supernatural world. Tunica cemeteries are said to be noisy places on rainy, cloudy days when "they" are talking and fussing at one another.[7] A pipe might be considered a necessity on such circumstances. The real point is that, contrary to Christian doctrine, traditional belief holds that both artifacts and spirits belong with the bones.

There has been considerable continuity, therefore, in mortuary ceremonialism. Throughout the identifiable Tunica past the dead have been interred among the living, either in or near residential areas. Furthermore, the bodies generally have been oriented with the head in an easterly direction, a fire has marked the grave, and, as noted above, burial goods have been consistently included. It is in the latter that we find some important changes. Burials early in the contact period are distinguished by a limited number of types of introduced European artifacts that because of their exotic character gained symbolic value and were quickly removed from the realm of the profane to that of the sacred. As time progressed, however, the contact became more intensive and the artifacts more common. The Tunica of the eighteenth and nineteenth centuries were increasingly well endowed with a diversity and quantity of Euro-American artifacts; and their graves were liberally furnished with commonplace items of every description. Modern mortuary practices recall earlier customs, but with important changes. When the late Chief Joseph A. Pierite, Sr., was interred, his grave may have been above ground in the local French fashion, but it was near his house, and tradition required that a light (in this case electric) be maintained over it. Chief Joe was also accompanied by artifacts that, like the calumet pipe, were of symbolic value in pan-Indian ideology and ceremonialism.

Notes for "Religion, Ideology, and Ceremony"

[1] Le Page du Pratz, *History of Louisiana*, 3 vols. (Paris, 1758), 1:123; Pierre Margry, *Découvertes et établissements des français dans l'ouest et dans le sud de l'Amérique Septentrionale 1614-[1754]*, 6 vols. (Paris, 1888), 6:247.

[2] Dumont de Montigny, *Mémoires historiques sur la Louisiane, contenant ce qui y est arrivé de plus mémorable depuis l'année 1687 jusqu'à présent*, 2 vols. (Paris: 1753), 1:166; Rueben Gold Thwaites, *The Jesuit Relations and Allied Documents: Travels and Explorations of the Jesuit Missionaries in New France, 1610-1791*, 73 vols. (Cleveland, 1900), 67:308.

[3] In 1727 there was even official recommendation for the establishment of a real parish *aux Tonicas*, but only two years later there was a call for more missionaries. Marie-Antoinette Menier, Etienne Taillemite, Gilberte de Forges Menier, *Inventaire des archives coloniales: Correspondance à l'arrivée en provenance de la Louisiane*, 2 vols. (Paris, 1976-1983), 1:163, 173; Thwaites, *Jesuit Relations and Allied Documents*, 67:312.

[4] Winston De Ville, *First Settlers of Pointe Coupée: A Study Based on Early Louisiana Church Records, 1737-1750* (New Orleans, 1974), 48-49.

[5] Here we could have a fascinating sociological insight: Could it be, at least according to the Tunica, that the women customarily built the mounds? Such a sexual division of labor might put a different perspective on the analysis of the great prehistoric public works projects. Mary Haas, *Tunica Texts* (Berkeley, 1959), 137, 141.

[6] Dunbar Rowland, A. G. Sanders, and Patricia K. Galloway, *Mississippi Provincial Archives: French Dominion*, 5 vols. (Baton Rouge, La., 1984), 4:113.

[7] Hiram F. Gregory, personal communication, 1984.

THE WORK OF MISSIONARIES[*]

Marcel Giraud

The Lower Mississippi

In reality evangelization made practically no progress in the southern part of Louisiana. The obstacles which had hindered the apostolate of the Foreign Missions from the outset became worse in subsequent years. The war weakened the resources of the Seminary of Paris: its directors attempted to make the material charge of these missions the responsibility of the Seminary of Quebec, which they reproached for having opened the missions with insufficient means; they even denied, in view of the mediocre results, having had anything to do with initiating them.[1] The directors complained unceasingly of the expenses and disappointments that such a "loose enterprise" had caused them. Tremblay considered it futile to recruit new missionaries, and in 1710 he advised simply giving up that much-too-costly experiment.[2]

Workers for the missions, consequently, became more and more rare.[3] Bouteville had left in 1703 after a useless sojourn. Davion was too worn out to serve profitably. Buisson de Saint-Cosme seemed incapable of settling down to one mission, and he did not appear to offer the moral qualities indispensable to the success of his apostolate. He was killed in 1707 by the Chitimachas: the Seminary did not seriously consider replacing him, no more than it had thought about a successor for Foucault. "That mission is reduced indeed to a mere trifle," wrote Tremblay in 1708.[4] La Vente waited in vain for the arrival of three missionaries from Quebec, among whom he expected to be the young Saint-Cosme, who was already acquainted with the peoples of the Mississippi; and when Davion took over the functions of parish priest at Mobile in 1710, there no longer remained any Seminary representative in the tribes whose evangelization the Foreign Missions had undertaken in 1699.[5] Gradually, their posts were reduced to the lone colony of Mobile.

Nevertheless the Seminarians, while acknowledging their weakness, were still not resigned to the idea of sharing with the Jesuits. The proposal of Monseigneur Laval in

*First published as Marcel Giraud, "The Work of Missionaries," in *A History of French Louisiana*, vol. 1, *The Reign of Louis XIV, 1698-1715*, trans. Joseph C. Lambert (Baton Rouge: Louisiana State University Press, 1974), 335-48. Reprinted with the kind permission of the publisher.

1704—of assigning to the Jesuits the apostolate of the tribes located above the juncture of the Arkansas and of reserving the peoples below it for the Foreign Missions—stirred up the opposition of Bergier, the grand vicar of the Tamaroas. Contradicting the argument that the Seminary of Paris had just used in order to keep the rectorship of Mobile, he asserted that if this happened the mission of Louisiana would find itself cut off from any relations with Quebec.[6] The intervention of the Jesuits among the Houmas and the Bayougoulas, which would have partially relieved the missionaries of a task they could not handle, was greeted with suspicion.[7] But by finally leaving the Seminarians in control of the mission of Louisiana, the Jesuits revealed their inadequacies all the more. None of the clergy destined for service at Mobile and at Dauphin Island was prepared to do missionary work. Davion and Huvé were excluded because of their bad health; Le Marie, who wanted to dedicate himself to the Indians when he first arrived, soon lost all sympathy for them.[8] Moreover, none of them had acquired a knowledge of the Indian languages. La Vente had lost no time in admitting his inability to learn them. Confused by the diversity and the limited radius of the dialects, he did not know how to instruct the Apalachees, and neither Huvé, nor Le Maire, nor Davion demonstrated any superior aptitude.[9]

It was impossible for the missionaries, in these circumstances, to plan any work covering great distances. All the attempts made in the interior had been successively abandoned. The priests had not reached the Choctaws and the Chickasaws, for whom the Seminary had intended Gervaise, and whose evangelization would have had the greatest importance for France.[10] Saint-Cosme died without having made any progress with the Natchez.[11] The mission of the Tunicas, finally, had not come up to Davion's expectations, even though it had been conducted with more regularity than the preceding ones. Despite his infirmities and his long sojourns at Mobile, Davion never lost contact with the tribe; he followed it even in its migrations. His presence among the Tunicas is still recorded in 1715. But the results were minimal. Davion did not hide his disappointment: "There is no longer an Indian mission," he wrote in 1711, and he never ceased requesting his recall.[12]

It was only at Fort Louis' immediate borders, among the Apalachees, that the representatives of the Seminary could act with a certain efficacy. The mission was small—it has only about one hundred persons; access to it was easy, as was the task of the missionaries, because all they had to do was maintain the faith of a group converted long before. And even though neither Huvé nor Le Maire resided there permanently nor knew the language of the Apalachees, they were able to hold these Indians to Christianity.[13]

Except for this unimportant group, evengelization remained at a virtual standstill. The director of the Seminary readily admitted this. As he saw it, the only accomplishments consisted of the baptism of some "dying infants." Duclos agreed as well that no worthwhile result had been obtained, and La Vente felt there was no reason to hope for conversion of the Indians as long as France did not apply an immigration policy conducive to reinforcing the means of the Church's work by increasing the number of French posts.[14]

The Illinois

The only remaining productive mission, then, was at the Illinois. At least there the Seminary retained its initial establishment, and when it would abandon the rectory of Mobile, after having lost the missions of the Lower Mississippi, the Tamaroas would remain its last vestige of influence in the domain that the bishop of Quebec had given it. The mission was directed by the grand vicar Louis-Marc Bergier, a man whose life was beyond reproach and whose austere dignity the Jesuits expressly recognized. He had with him two young slaves and, intermittently, a Frenchman who was his only companion at the time of his death. He worked with modest resources, his task was difficult, and the scope of his apostolate limited.[15] The rules that he claimed the right to impose on Catholics and the conception of marriage that he preached frequently aroused hostility of a society whose habits they contradicted.[16]   Because no missionary assisted him, he could not—any more than in the preceding years—exert over the Tamaroas during their hunting expeditions the permanent surveillance which was indispensable to the success of his teachings, and the Tamaroas' fear of Sioux attacks resulted in an ever-present state of uncertainty which weakened the religious life of the settlement.[17]

After 1705 the grand vicar succeeded in giving a slight impulse to his mission, and soon a nucleus of some sixty "praying people" was formed in the Tamaroas village.[18] But his death in November 1707, threatened to dismember his small community. A strong opposition, led by natives who clung to their old beliefs, immediately came out openly against his work. The village was divided and lost part of its population, while Father Marest sold what remained of the "temporality" of Bergier, thus diminishing the resources of the mission.[19]

For the Jesuits the event apparently offered an opportunity again to control the whole apostolate of the Illinois tribes. Despite the assistance that Father Marest had often given Bergier and the courtesy of their relationship, the rivalry between the missionaries of the two orders persisted. The tenacity with which Bergier defended his powers of grand vicar, and especially his pretension of applying them to all the French of the Illinois missions, aroused the sensitiveness of Father Marest, who refused to give up prerogatives that the Jesuits had held before the appearance of the Foreign Missions.[20] Bergier's death under these circumstances appeared to have freed them from the semblance of control that a grand vicar not of their order claimed over their parishioners. The long interregnum which then occurred and the indifference of the Seminary of Paris toward the fate of the mission gave the Jesuits reason to believe that it would not be long before the Illinois would be theirs.[21] But the arrival of Dominique-Marie Varlet who, having served as parish priest at Mobile, took over the direction of the Tamaroas with the powers of grand vicar in 1715, brought the situation back to what it had been at Bergier's death; and in order to prevent the "missionaries of some other corps" from "disputing the [Seminary of Quebec's] possession" of the Tamaroas, Monseigneur de Saint-Vallier officially confirmed the letters patent of 1698 in the Seminary's favor.[22]

Contrary to the desire their directors had often expressed,[23] the Foreign Missions had not, then, given up the post of the Tamaroas. Its future would be modest: the hope of making their mission the base of the evangelization of the Missouri tribes was definitely abandoned. The new vicar was wanting in personality and he was incapable of giving the mission the impetus it had had in the beginning. But the mission survived, and it had become the center of a small slow-growing French and Canadian colony.[24]

In contrast, the mission of the Kaskaskias, twenty-five leagues [about seventy miles] from that of the Tamaroas, had grown rapidly and was to become and remain something of a capital of the Illinois country for a long time. Both settlements lay in areas of rich soil, whose inexhaustible abundance the Jesuits described with admiration. Both were "compact missions," and even Father Marest agreed that the site of the village of the Tamaroas attracted "numbers of French."[25] But at the establishment of the Kaskaskias, directed then by Father Gabriel Marest and Father Jean Mermet, the presence of the Jesuits assured a dynamism and a strong direction that the center of the Tamaroas did not show.

Evangelization there was certainly not an easy task. Despite the Jesuits' tendency to contrast the superiority of their accomplishments with the modest results of the Seminary priests, they acknowledged the tenuous faith of their converts, the necessity of exerting unceasing effort in order to keep them at least superficially Christian, and the indifference that their instructions met among the men. The old pagan beliefs, defended by the shamans, created the principal difficulty.[26] But the zeal of their missionaries, their constant activity, and the remarkable instrument of conversion they had in their knowledge of the Indian languages enabled the Jesuits to fight the old beliefs effectively. The material advantages of all kinds that the Indians found in their mission, the social structure of the Illinois and the role it assigned to women also contributed, to a certain extent, to the success of their endeavors.[27] For several years, the two priests who administered the mission managed to remain in direct contact with their Indians: winter and summer, Father Marest participated in the travels of the hunters and the elderly Father Mermet remained in the village which, in contrast to that of the Tamaroas, never was entirely vacant.[28] The Jesuits thus masterfully directed the religious life of the settlement and grouped under their control a population largely won over to Christianity.[29] The mission even had a spacious church, the interior of which Pénigaut describes with its choir flanked by two side chapels.[30]

Like the mission of the Tamaroas, the Jesuit mission formed a colony of a French-speaking population composed of people from Mobile or from the Illinois Valley missions and Canadian traders, some of whom made the mission the center of their commercial operations, while others took land there and gave up moving about.[31]

It is difficult to detect the precise origins of this population. We know only that, even before the arrival of the missionaries, there existed at the Tamaroas village a small number of Canadians who frequented the Indian settlement and who perhaps already had houses there. In the neighborhood, an "establishment of French," according to the observations of Pénigaut, had been set up near the mouth of the Saline River as early as 1700. This seemed to be a group with no permanent roots that worked at the exploitation of salt and lived by hunting, thanks to the profusion of animals which the saline pastures attracted.[32] In this Tamaroas settlement early agricultural activity was probably relatively unimportant. Trading in fur and hunting were the usual occupations. The village was very much a pelt market, and Canadian merchants came there to stock themselves with articles of trade. About thirty of these merchants were found there in 1700, at the time of Pénigaut's visit.[33] The presence around the mission of a large number of *coureurs de bois*, the possibility of Sioux attacks, and the frequent moves of the population—in 1703 Bergier noted that everyone had gone "to the sea"—did not favor the growth of an agricultural economy. Some people, however, were already engaging in an elementary agriculture: the artisans who carried on their trade there—in 1703 the grand vicar indicates the presence of a blacksmith[34]—probably possessed plots of land that they cultivated. When Pénigaut ascended the Mississippi with Le Sueur, he observed that the "French of the Illinois" were accustomed to going to the cape "de Saint-Antoine" to bring back "stone to make millstones."[35] The text implies the cultivation of maize or wheat. But did this apply to the inhabitants at the Tamaroas mission?

It refers more likely to the population of the Illinois River, where we know that some small colonies were established around Fort St. Louis and the first Jesuit missions. When the latter had been supplanted by the mission of the Kaskaskias, the agricultural tradition which the Jesuits always encouraged was immediately set up there. By emigrating near the Mississippi, the missionaries did not sacrifice their post of Peoria, where a small French colony had also been formed. Abandoned in 1705, following the attempt by the Indians on Father Gravier's life, it was reoccupied in 1711 under the direction of Father Jean-Marie de Ville.[36] But from then on, it was no more than a secondary mission, definitely overshadowed by the Kaskaskias settlement. The Canadians of both French and colonial origin and the Indians who followed the Jesuits to the Mississippi had long been trained to work the land. Thus, even though there were a number of traders who did not farm—as there were the Tamaroas—from the outset, under the guidance of the Jesuits, agriculture at the Kaskaskias was practiced to a degree that it never reached at the Seminary mission. The soil at the Kaskaskias mission was extremely fertile. The Jesuits had taught the inhabitants how to plow, and agriculture there prospered under methods more advanced than those followed at Mobile. According to Pénigaut, three mills were raised near the village: one was a windmill which was the property of the Jesuits and two were horse-drawn mills which belonged to the Indians. Maize grew without difficulty and the settlement easily assured its provisioning of flour. The wheat there, whose seed had been imported from Vera Cruz because it fared better in the Louisiana climate than did the

European grain, was "as beautiful as in France."[37] Furthermore several Indians, under the direction of the French, had undertaken raising pigs and chickens, and livestock began to appear. In 1712 Father Marest noted that some cows had been brought to the settlement, and he immediately decided to use them as work animals. The pasturage was sufficiently abundant to support a large herd. Finally, the village contained some horses that the Indians, according to Pénigaut and Derbanne, obtained in trade with the tribes of the Red River.[38] Consequently the mission of the Jesuits possessed all the elements of a complete agricultural economy.

The Indians there continued their customary way of life: hunting alternated with working the fields, which was generally the lot of the women. But the two occupations solved the problem of food for the Indians as well as for the French. Only the families who practiced poultry farming dispensed with the periodic winter and summer hunts: this part of the population was never away from the village.[39]

Yet these resources did not exhaust all the advantages of the mission. The proximity of lead and tin mines (whose riches were probably still largely unknown) and of "salt springs," and the possibilities of commerce with a great number of tribes (even with the Iroquois nations) that the course of the Ohio opened where all as many assets for the future.[40] For the time being, the Kaskaskias mission owed its main superiority to its agricultural resources. The population there, sure of its food supply, escaped the uncertainties of the colonists at Mobile and, despite the high cost of all imported merchandise, it enjoyed easy living conditions.[41] In the good harvest years, such as 1711 and 1713, it even had an excess of agricultural products.

In these Illinois settlements, Indians and French maintained closer relations than at Mobile. The bond of a common religion favored the rapprochement of the two races and interracial marriages—inevitable because of the absence of French women—were not frowned upon there. The colonies were too far away and still too unimportant for their social customs to attract the attention of the French government. Consequently these unions were not contested there despite the opposition of Duclos, who warned the minister of the navy that they would invariably hasten the regression of the white man toward the primitive and would be as fatal for the French of the Illinois as they would be for the community at Mobile.[42] As far as the missionaries were concerned, there was no reason to oppose marriages performed between Christians according to the laws of the Church, and whose results did not bear out the denunciations of Duclos.[43] At the mission of the Tamaroas, the priests of the Seminary very early recorded marriages between Frenchmen and Indian women: some of these Frenchmen had Indian slaves in their service.[44] At the Kaskaskias, the Jesuits naturally continued to follow a practice that had been recorded in the registers of the mission of the Immaculate Conception as early as 1695, when it was still on the Illinois River. Among the first inhabitants, whose names we have—Michel Accault, Michel Philippe, Jacques Bourdon, Pierre Saint-Michel, Louis Philippe Delaunais, Jacques Lalande—there was hardly anyone who had not married an Indian.[45] The Indian influence was consequently more strongly felt than in the seacoast posts. Life was more primitive in the prairie region and the proximity of warlike tribes and their surprise attacks led to reprisals whose cruelty the missionaries deplored, chiefly in the village of the Tamaroas, which was more vulnerable because of its smaller size.[46]

But the daily Indian contact was offset by the increasingly frequent relations of the Illinois settlements with the French of Mobile. The economic activity of the mission of the Kaskaskias intensified, in effect, the commercial current which had been established between the Illinois country and the coast ever since the birth of these colonies. The Mississippi was more regularly used. The conditions of navigation became better known, and Dartaguiette made plans for diverting part of the river's water toward Lake Maurepas in order to shorten the distance between the coast and the interior, while Bienville, like Sauvolle at an earlier time, examined the possibility of a land route through Choctaw and Chickasaw territory which would save even more time.[47] Besides pelts and lead, the Canadian *voyageurs* brought to Mobile some bear's oil, slaves, smoked meat (which sometimes came from the Illinois and at other times was the result of their hunting on the way), wheat, and flour. And because their small boats, which reached Mobile by way of Lake Pontchartrain and the channel that ran between the mainland and the islands close to shore, could only carry modest loads, Dartaguiette advised using larger, flat-bottomed craft. These larger boats would at last make it possible to bring cargoes of food supplies ample enough to lessen the dependence of the colony on the mother country.[48]

Travelers and merchants who made the seacoast voyage played the role of liaison agents as well. They brought the missionaries' correspondence and left again with the mail from the authorities of Mobile to the Illinois colonies.[49] Sometimes it was the inhabitants at the Tamaroas or the missionaries themselves who came to Mobile to get some merchandise or letters from France.[50] Inversely, Bienville had some Canadians and soldiers carry munitions to the Indians of the interior. Frequent relations were thus established between the seacoast posts and those of the Illinois: they would have been more active still if Crozat's agents had permitted the French to establish commercial ties with the Illinois colonists as they wished to do. But the monopoly of the financier opposed other commercial possibilities and, as a rule, it was strictly enforced.[51] Having long been stocked with trading merchandise by the *coureurs de bois* and Canadian merchants, these settlements now became accustomed to more frequent connections with the lower part of the river. When the letters patent incorporated these communities into Crozat's concession in 1712, it became evident that their commercial bond with Mobile would soon be reinforced with a political bond. The visit of La Mothe to the Illinois in 1715, following that of Martin Dartaguiette some years before, is indicative of the developments which gradually linked them to the seacoast colony.

These posts of the Upper Mississippi, where no authority existed except that of the missionaries, had an essential importance for France. They made it possible to watch the progress of British encroachment. To the officers of the troops of New France detached among the Illinois and the Miamis, they offered refuge where they could receive whatever help they needed in case of sickness.[52] Thanks to these posts, it was possible to exercise a certain control over the Canadians who lived in the plains of the Illinois, independently of New France. The number of those Canadians continued to grow, for despite the official prohibition of their wandering habits (*course des bois*) more of them left Canada each year for the Ottawas, the Miamis, or the Illinois; neither threats of punishment nor promises of amnesty managed to intimidate them or make them return to their country.[53]

The missionaries of the Kaskaskias feared the presence of these Canadians. They were afraid these nomads would one day make up their minds to settle in the village, where they might very well favor a tendency to insubordination which would undermine the priests' authority over the Indians. They also dreaded the effects of the men's conduct on the Indians and their tendency to serve the interests of England.[54]

Since France had left the forts of the Great Lakes and the Illinois Valley abandoned for several years, the missionaries of the Tamaroas and the Kaskaskias became, then, the principal agents of information for the authorities of New France and Louisiana.

They denounced the disorders that the *coureurs de bois* caused in the tribes, their dealings with the British, and the efforts of the British to win over the Illinois, whose defection, if it occurred, would enable them to infiltrate the Ottawa nations.[55] Father de Ville, Father Marest, and Father Mermet thus kept the governor of Canada and the commandant of Mobile apprised of the situation in the Upper Mississippi Basin, and their warnings sometimes led to policing operations. Twice groups of soldiers were sent to the Kaskaskias and the Tamaroas to watch the *voyageurs* or the Canadian merchants there and prevent them from stirring up wars to procure slaves for the Carolina traders. At the request of Fathers Marest and de Ville, the minister ordered La Mothe to have several *coureurs de bois* arrested—Véniard de Bourgmont, Bisaillon, Bourdon—whom they accused of leading "a scandalous and criminal life" among the Indians, of opposing the rapprochement of the tribes France was striving to reconcile, and of working in the interests of Britain.[56]

Apparently the missionaries had a tendency to abuse the charge of treason, leveling it against men who were mainly guilty of loose morals. Neither Bourgmont nor Bisaillon seems to have been guilty of the treason of which the missionaries accused them. At any rate, their subsequent behavior clears them of the blame they may have incurred.[57] The missionaries' correspondence does show, however, that the situation had assumed a certain gravity, that British attempts to infiltrate the Illinois were becoming more menacing, and that France could oppose them with only limited means of action. The need for a more complete occupation of the interior became obvious if France wished to affirm her rights on the Mississippi, contain the British threat, and break the *coureurs de bois'* habits of independence. Disturbed by the warnings which came to him from Louisiana, Pontchartrain was actually planning the creation of military posts immediately after the reestablishment of peace, which would back up the colony of Mobile and the Illinois missions and would place the valley of the Mississippi under the more immediate control of France.

Notes for "The Work of Missionaries"

[1]Sém., Lettres M, no. 30, Tremblay, March 12, 1704; no. 38, ibid., June 18, 1707. Lettres O, nos. 42, 45, Tremblay, April 4, 1705, April 12, 1706; no. 52, Tremblay, 1711; ibid., no. 53, ibid., June 5, 1712. Lettres P, no. 12, Tremblay, August 11, 1707. Lettres N, no. 124, Tremblay, June 18, 1706.

[2]Sém., Lettres M, no. 38, loc. cit. Lettres O, no. 46, Tremblay to Desmaizerets, June 1706: "I confess that I am disgusted with this mission which does nothing and has no good foundation." Lettres O, nos. 49, 50 Tremblay, January 14, 1708, May 22, 1710. Lettres N, no. 122, Tremblay, April 4, 1705.

[3]Sém., Lettres R. no. 77, La Vente, September 20, 1704.

[4]Sém., Lettres M, no. 30, Tremblay, March 12, 1704; no. 38, ibid., June 18, 1707. Lettres O, no. 42, ibid., April 4, 1705, no. 49, ibid., January 14, 1708. Lettres N, no. 123, Tremblay, June 19, 1705. C 13 A, 2, f. 100-101, Bienville, February 25, 1708. C 13 C, 2, f. 134, Le Maire, January 15, 1714. B 2(M.), 167, f. 471, to Du Gué, February 28, 1703. Pénigaut, MS français, 14613, f. 101-104.

[5]C 13 A, 2, f. 553, Bienville, June 21, 1710. Sém., Lettres R, no. 86, La Vente, February 5, 1709.

[6]Sém., Lettres R, no. 69, Bergier, September 13, 1704. See also pp. 237-38, above.

[7]Sém., Lettres R, no. 70, Bergier, October 12, 1704.

[8]Sém., Lettres R, no. 84, La Vente, October 4, 1708. Lettres N, no. 123, Tremblay, June 19, 1705. Missions étrangères, Paris, 344, Davion, December 12, 1702. —C 13 C, 2, f. 123, Le Maire, January 15, 1714.

[9]Sém., Lettres R, no. 76, La Vente, September 15, 1704, no. 77, La Vente, September 20, 1704; no. 79, ibid., March 4, 1708; no. 40, Saint-Cosme, January 8, 1706. Lettres N, no. 123, Tremblay, June 19, 1705. —C 13 C, I, Bienville, February 20, 1710.

[10]Sém., Lettres R, no. 38, Saint-Cosme, October 31, 1704. Lettres O, no. 45, Tremblay, April 12, 1706. Lettres N, no. 122, Tremblay, April 4, 1705; no. 124, Tremblay, June 18, 1706.

[11]Sém., Lettres R., no. 79, La Vente, March 4, 1708; no. 38, Saint-Cosme, October 31, 1704; no. 40, ibid., January 8, 1706. Pénigaut, MS français, 14613, f. 120.

[12]D 2 C (A.C.), 51, f. 6-8, *Liste des officiers majors . . .* , August 31, 1715, notes the presence of Davion among the Tunicas. Sém., Missions, no. 46, Davion, October 20, 1711; Lettres R, no. 79, La Vente, March 4, 1708; no. 83, La Vente, July 4, 1708; no. 64, Bergier, March 30, 1704; no. 53, Tremblay, June 5, 1712.

[13]Sém., Lettres R, no. 82, La Vente, June 27, 1708; no. 83, ibid., July 4, 1708; no. 79, ibid., March 4, 1708. C 13 A, 3, f. 126027, Duclos, July 15, 1713. C 13 C, 2, f. 134, Le Maire, January 15, 1714.

[14]C 13 A, 3, f. 126-27, loc. cit. —Sém., Lettres R, no. 77, La Vente, September 20, 1704; no. 42, Bergier, February 1700; Lettres N, no. 122, Tremblay, April 4, 1705.

[15]Sém., Lettres R, no. 86, La Vente, February 5, 1709; no. 60, Bergier, March 10, 1703; no. 64, ibid., March 30, 1704. —*The Jesuit Relations*, LXVI, 256, 262.

[16]Sém., Lettres R, nos. 65, 66, 73, Bergier, June 12, 1704, April 15, 1705.

[17]Sém., Lettres R, no. 67, Bergier, July 14, 1704. However, Bisaillon (see pp. 347-48, below) appears to have usefully assisted him with the Indians. C 11 A, 35, f. 99-100.

[18]Sém., Lettres R, no. 73, Bergier, April 15, 1705, no. 86, La Vente, February 5, 1709.

[19]Sém., Missions, no. 48, Marest, April 25, 1709. Lettres R, no. 86, La Vente, February 5, 1709. *The Jesuit Relations*, LXVI, 262, Marest, November 9, 1712.

[20]Sém., Lettres R, no. 66, Bergier, 1704; nos. 67, 70, 73, Bergier, July 14, October 12, 1704, April 15, 1705. *The Jesuit Relations*, LXVI, 126, 130, Gravier, February 23, 1708; pp. 256, 262, Marest, November 9, 1712.

[21]Sém., Lettres R, no. 86, La Vente, February 5, 1709; Lettres M, no. 29, Tiberge and Brisacier, June 23, 1703; no. 30, Tremblay, March 12, 1704; Lettres O, no. 39, Tremblay, June 15, 1703, no. 46, ibid., June 1706.

[22]Sém., 15, no. 68, Confirmation des lettres patentes du July 14, 1698. D 2 C 51 (A.C.), f. 6-8.

[23]Sém., Lettres O, no. 39, Tremblay, June 15, 1703: "It would be better to shake off the dust of his feet on the Jesuits and leave them these peoples they are so anxious to take care of."

[24]Sém., Lettres R, Bergier, June 15, 1702 (no. 50). C 13 A, 2, f. 785, Marest, November 9, 1712.

[25]C 13 A, 2, loc. cit., *The Jesuit Relations*, LXVI, 226-28.

[26]*The Jesuit Relations*, LXV, 78-80; LXVI, 234-38, 240-42, 244.

[27]Ibid., LXV, 64-68; LXVI, 230-32, 264-66.

[28]Ibid., LXV, 82-84; LXVI, 252, 254.

[29]Ibid., LXVI, 230 ff. —Pénigaut, MS français, 14613, f. 201-202.

[30]Pénigaut, loc. cit.

[31]C 13 A, 3, f. 624, Crozat, April 17, 1714. *The Jesuit Relations*, LXVI, 230-32.

[32]Pénigaut, MS français, 14613, f. 53. —4 JJ (A.M.), 14, 4, f. 61, *Journal* of Le Sueur, June 19, 1700.

[33]Pénigaut, f. 53-55. —Sém., Lettres R, no. 45, Bergier, April 15, 1701.

[34]Sém., Lettres R, nos. 62, 63, Bergier, July 3, October 18, 1703.

[35]Pénigaut, MS français, 14613, f. 48.

[36]*The Jesuit Relations*, LXVI, 50-56, 121, 264-90. —C 13 A, 1, f. 594-95, Lettre du missionnaire jésuite des Cascaskias, March 2, 1706.

[37]Pénigaut, MS français, 14613, f. 199-202. —*The Jesuit Relations*, LXVI, 290-94, Marest, November 9, 1712. C 13 A, 3 f. 206, Duclos, October 25, 1713. A.D.C.M., 672, 4, Baron, *Mémoire des observations . . .*

[38]*The Jesuit Relations*, LXVI, 254, 290-94. —Pénigaut, f. 200.

[39]*The Jesuit Relations*, LXVI, 252, 254. —Pénigaut, f. 206.

[40]*The Jesuit Relations*, LXVI, 290-94.

[41]Ibid., 32-34. —Pénigaut, f. 199.

[42]C 13 A, f. 821, Duclos, 25 Dec. 1715.

[43]Pénigaut, MS français, 14613, f. 203-204.

[44]Sém., Lettres R, no. 44, Bergier, June 14, 1700; no. 29, Saint-Cosme, March 7, 1700; no. 63, Bergier, October 18, 1703.

[45]*Kaskaskia Church Records* (Transactions of the Illinois State Historical Society for year 1904, Springfield, 1904), 394 ff. Belting, *Kaskaskia under the French Regime*, 14-18.

[46]Sém., Lettres R, no. 44, Bergier, June 14, 1700.

[47]C 13 A, 2, f. 807, Dartaguiette, May 12, 1712. —B.N., MS français, 12105, f. 7, Le Maire, *Mémoire sur la Louisiane*, March 1, 1717. —Pénigaut, MS français, 14613, f. 167-68.

[48]C 13 A, 2, f. 136-37, Dartaguiette, February 26, 1708; 3, f. 206, Duclos, October 25, 1713; 4, f. 789-91, 796, *Mémoire . . . de ce qui s'est passé dans la première expédition que M. de Bienville fit aux Natchez.* —Pénigaut,

MS français, 14613, f. 104-105, 197-98. —B.N., MS français, 12105, loc. cit., f. 20. Ayer Collection (Le Valdec, 1727), *Mémoire des connoissances du Sr. Béranger* . . . , f. 100.

[49]C 13 A, 2, f. 181-82, Bienville, October 12, 1708; 4, f. 789-91, loc. cit. —Pénigaut, MS français, 14613, f. 167-68, 197-98. —Sém., Lettres R, no. 77, La Vente, September 20, 1704.

[50]Sém., Lettres R, no. 50, Bergier, June 15, 1702; no. 63, ibid., October 18, 1703.

[51]C 13 A, 2, f. 10, Bienville, February 20, 1707, f. 321, Dartaguiette, May 25, 1708. It was thus that the gentleman from Angers, Avril de La Varenne, who came over on *La Dauphine*, was able to undertake the voyage to the Illinois with trading merchandise: the difficulties that occurred unexpectedly with the Natchez interrupted his plans. Pénigaut, 14613, f. 243-53. According to La Mothe, his voyage would have been favored by Raujon for personal reasons. C 13 A, 4, f. 527-28, 533.

[52]C 11 A, 35, f. 59v-60, Dadoncour to M. de Longueuil, August 22, 1715; 36, f. 71, Vaudreuil, October 14, 1716.

[53]C 11 A, 33, f. 151, Ramezay, November 6, 1712; 34, f. 282, Vaudreuil, September 16, 1714, f. 359, Ramezay, September 18, 1714; 35, f. 87v-88, Ramezay, October 28, 1715. B 27 (Canada), f. 225, to Vaudreuil, June 9, 1706. B 33 (II), f. 71v-72, to Vaudreuil, July 7, 1711.

[54]*The Jesuit Relations*, LXVI, 290-94. C 11 A, 35, f. 224-26, Louvigny, October 26, 1715.

[55]C 11 A, 35, f. 9-11, Ramezay and Bégon, September 13, November 7, 1715; f. 73-73v, 90v, Ramezay, September 16, October 28, 1715.

[56]C 11 A, 34, f. 356v, Ramezay, September 18, 1714 —B 36 (Iles), f. 198v, to Father Le Tellier, June 10, 1714. B 37, f. 201v, to Ramezay, July 13, 1715. —Pénigaut, MS français, 14613, f. 176-77, 197-99. —On Bourmont (Veniard de Bourgmont), See also pp. 363-64, below.

[57]C 11 A (Colonies), 35, f. 91, Ramezay to the minister, October 28, 1715, f. 99-100, *Mémoire de M. de Longueil pour la justification de Bizaillon.* —See p. 352, n. 12, below.

RELIGION AND MEDICINE*

Fred B. Kniffen, Hiram F. Gregory, and George A. Stokes

The Louisiana Indians lived in a sacred world. They made no distinction between the sacred and profane, and saw none of the polarities inherent in the European world view. Their universe was a whole held together by spiritual forces that caused man to respect all things, living and nonliving.

Earth was part of a layered universe with a deep underworld and an upper world. The first humans had migrated upward through a hole, a hollow log, or a crayfish tunnel, onto earth. There the sun warmed them, and they stayed. From the chaotic, unpredictable underworld, they had ascended to a harmonic, balanced place. Everything fit somewhere; each part somehow related to the whole. The rule of existence for man as to perceive and respect this natural order. The harmony had to be maintained. Time was not a way to break apart a day but a never-ending circle of events. The repetition was an endless continuum of the seasons, days and nights, and life and death.

Animals, plants, and human beings were interchangeable parts of a single fabric. The woods were full of spirits, "little people" who could be mischievous or helpful. They often had the gift of shamanistic power. They took various forms but were known in the mythology of the majority of tribes. One had to take care not to offend them. In Indian myth, maize was once an Indian grandmother who gave her body to become food for her orphan children. Corn was analogous to a female; it had tassels like hair, and the kernels of new corn gave milk. It was the mother of life itself.

All Indians grew up feeling comfortable in the natural world. It was in the swamps, the forests, and the marshes, among the birds and animals, that man belonged. The rhythms of the land were shared by man. More than the efforts of missionaries or even the force of military control, the economy of the European finally altered the Indian religious pattern; the automobile making roads through the land, the chainsaw and the bulldozer eating away the forest, and the chemicals polluting the water and air, all played a part. The land, second only to the sun in sacredness, was torn, wasted, and broken. Even so, Indians have remained "in the woods," as isolated and as close to the natural land-

*First published as Fred B. Kniffen, Hiram F. Gregory, and George A. Stokes, "Religion and Medicine," in *The Historic Indian Tribes of Louisiana from 1542 to the Present* (Baton Rouge: Louisiana State University Press, 1987), 251-75. Reprinted with the kind permission of the authors and the publisher.

scape as possible. A modern Caddo leader, Melford Williams, once remarked, "I want to build a house in the trees where the birds and animals are, in the woods near the water. We belong there, with that."

Indians believed that animals and humans could converse freely and that certain powerful humans could change into animals and leave their bodies. Birds and animals could become humans, too. An old part-Choctaw man once remarked, when asked about the sanity of a person seen talking to a squirrel in the woods, "Your problem is simple. He speaks squirrel. *You* don't." The Indian system confused the Europeans who encountered it. Animals, plants, and even the dead were considered animate parts of life. Indians failed to understand why Europeans denied relationships with these entities.

In Louisiana, the native religions survived countless attempts by Christian missionaries to change them. Indian people were able to keep their basic view of things and to participate, to various degrees, in Christianity. Wise missionaries recognized this. Highly regarded, they had a great understanding and tolerance of traditional Indian religion. Others—perhaps less wise and certainly more zealous—punished, cajoled, and threatened Indian people. Indians politely withdrew, or, more rarely, forced the missionaries to leave. In the 1700s a few were killed. Many times the liberal priests and ministers were understood less by their European peers than by their Indian flocks. In 1719 Bénard de la Harpe described the doughty missionary Father Davion, the beloved priest of the Tunica, in somewhat ambivalent terms.

> Since he [Davion] has been with the Tunicas, he has had to "surrender" to these peoples the greatest part of their idolatry, their household gods *Dieux penates* are a toad [crapaud] and a figure of a woman that they worship. They believe both represent the sun. This nation is composed, in all, of 460 people; they have two great chiefs of the assembled nations, speaking the same language. The first is called Cahura-Joligo; he yields himself, with his family, everyday to the prayers and exhortations of M. Davion, who, although he is opposed to their feasts and plurality of wives, is strongly revered in this village.

Later, in the nineteenth century, another priest, Father Rouquette, lived with the Choctaw north of Lake Pontchartrain, near Bayou LaCombe. He wore his hair long, in Indian style, spoke Choctaw, and attended their annual ceremonial feasts. He was respectfully called Chahta Ima, "Choctaw-like," by his Indian friends.

Although the Chitimacha had killed the missionary St. Cosme in the eighteenth century, most of the priests and ministers went unmolested among the tribes. Their most common lament was simply that no one listened to them. Both the humble Spanish priests of northwest Louisiana and the politically affluent Jesuits, Dominicans, and Capuchins of the French colonies in lower Louisiana seemed equally frustrated in their efforts.

Documents from the colonial period show tribal tolerance even for excesses like the vitriolic outbursts of those missionaries who stormed temples and broke the sacred objects they found there. Even the French chroniclers seem amazed at such restraint. Had they but known that in the eyes of the Indians, such missionaries seemed mad. Surely, these sacrilegious acts must have startled the Indians into their passive attitude. Even madness was part of order, just as storms preceded great calms.

Owl hoots, the barking of foxes, and other sighs such as cracks in house walls portended death. Individuals frequently announced the day and time of day when they would die. One Tunica medicine man cut a path across a field to the site where he wished to be buried; four days later he died, just as he had predicted. Indians, then, were not taken by surprise. The omens allowed for adequate preparation. Death was to be met at home, surrounded by family and friends. To live for a long time and to live life well was part of the natural cycle. Sudden or violent events—the death of children, of young people in their prime, of warriors caught off guard—were unnatural, surprising, and usually attributed to witchcraft. A child was given a pet to grow up with; if witchcraft was directed at the child, the pet intercepted it and died.

The dead were respected and were dealt with carefully. If disturbed, they became ghosts—spirits without conscience or obligations. Ghosts were dangerous and greatly feared. Some living persons could talk with the dead and even ask them for favors, such as providing company or opening gates. Such conversations, however, were perilous and were available only to the most powerful persons.

Despite the Indian's belief that all events were part of a harmonic whole, death was traumatic, and the gaps left in family and community brought deep, genuine mourning. Although the dead were merely moving from one world to another, the path between the two might be an odyssey filled with dangers, temptations to go astray, monsters that might attack, or slippery logs that must be used to cross the streams. Consequently, the dead were prepared for such eventualities. Food and water, favorite weapons, and sacred objects were interred with the dead to help with the journey into the next life.

Some tribes, among them the Tunica, made special fires to light the paths of the deceased. Others prayed at the graves and fired guns to frighten away demons and open the road. The Alabama, Choctaw, and Koasati believed that each person had two souls, *Shillup* and *Shilombish*. One stayed at the grave with the remains for four days and nights, while the other traveled prior to the journey to the afterworld. The soul that remained at the grave might become a ghost, wandering malevolently. Cemeteries were holy places, and gifts of food were often placed there long after a person's death. The Koasati still refer to burial places as *Ilhani Snaho*, "rich man's land." Stillborn infants were buried in hollow trees with the umbilical cords of children who had lived.

The destination of the dead was conceptualized in various ways. It was a place like the home of the Indians on earth, but conditions in the upper world were better. The Choctaw described the afterworld as a place of green grass, water, and trees. The Koasati saw a land of song and dance to the west, across a rainbow. The Tunica knew of a land, like their own on earth, at the upper end of the Milky Way.

Conversion to Christianity is sometimes described by old Indian people as "being taught to pray." Prayer existed in Indian culture to express thanks and tell of need. What the European brought was prayer for salvation. Most tribal religions lacked the concepts of eternal punishment and sin. There was no hell from which to be saved. The Choctaw feared being lost in a desert of thorns, but virtually all of the others expected another life in a place much like the earth at the end of their dangerous journey. Death, then, was not confused with punishment. It was merely a part of the intricate web of natural phenomena.

To the Indian, evil simply existed, like all other things. It was a natural occurrence with which people had to contend, like cold and hunger. Although understood, evil remained locked in the context of power, a gift from the spirit world that surrounded man. Power could be used for great good or turned against one's peers and community; hence it was a danger. Antisocial behavior was evil. Punishment was immediate, not delayed to the other life, and was handled in a number of ways.

Human sacrifice, infanticide, and suicide must all be considered, at least partially, in light of the Indians' attitudes about death. Louisiana Indians observed these practices, and some of the tribes participated in all of them.

Sacrifice, noted archaeologically and ethnographically, served to release spirits to accompany the dead. Objects including weapons, pottery vessels, horses, dogs, and human beings were killed, literally or figuratively, to release the essence of their beings to accompany individuals into the next world. The Natchez chief Stung Serpent contemplated suicide so that he might enter the next world with his brother. Wives, children, and slaves were customarily strangled and interred with the deceased as retainers and friends in the other world. Close friends and family might volunteer to accompany the dead. This practice seems to have reached exaggerated peaks among the Natchez and Taensa. The roots of the once widespread custom are definable far back before the historic record began, as evidenced by multiple burials in mounds. However, it seems to have persisted into European contact times only among the Natchez and related tribes. Frightened Europeans, shocked and revolted by the behavior of the Indians, failed to understand the theological reasoning behind such actions. Only Le Page du Pratz, who lived with the Natchez, suggested that they considered sacrifice a noble deed reflecting honor and glory on surviving relatives.

Infanticide seems to have increased after white contact. Le Page du Pratz noted that women used plants to abort unwanted pregnancies, and later the Spanish authorities protested against the killing of newborn twins. The birth of twins was considered an obvious break in the natural scheme by most tribes. Charles Hudson has noted that many other phenomena were similarly regarded by Indians of the Southeast and that such drastic measures were justified as attempts to restore the natural order, the harmony of the world.

Later, infanticide was practiced by Indian women held in slavery by the French, most likely to prevent the children from becoming slaves. As late as the nineteenth century, a Tunica woman attempted suicide rather than be considered socially on the same level as a slave. Such practices were not sanctioned forms of Indian behavior but probably were responses to European impacts on traditional Indian conduct. Infanticide by women slaves is not on the same order as the killing of twins or the sacrifices described above.

The numerous accounts of human sacrifice and infanticide in the colonial period may also reflect the unprecedented stresses of new diseases and attempts to maintain the Indian world view under continuous pressure from non-Indians.

One of the oldest religious entities was a sun and temple cult. Like the corn, beans, and squash cultivated by the Indians, this religious cult had its roots in the Southwest and Mexico. The Acolapissa, Caddo, Houma, Natchez, Taensa, and Tunica all maintained sacred buildings, some of which were raised on truncated pyramidal earth mounds reminiscent of temples in Mesoamerica. Practices of the Atakapa and Chitimacha differed somewhat. They built sacred dance houses and charnel houses, but no temples. In most of the tribes, the skeletons of the upper classes; sacred objects connected with the sun, especially figurines of humans, frogs, and rattlesnakes; and quartz crystals, were kept in the temples.

A sacred fire was ritually kindled in the temple every year and kept burning by temple guardians for the ensuing twelve months. Each family fire was relit from this new fire. The temple guardians protected the building from intruders. It was an extremely holy place. Le Page du Pratz has left a detailed description of temples as he saw them in 1725.

> All the peoples of Louisiana have temples, which are more or less well cared for according to the ability of the nation, and all, as I have said, put their dead in the earth, or in tombs within the temples or very near them, or in the neighborhood. Many of these nations have only very simple temples, which one would often take for private cabins. However, when one comes to know he distinguishes them by means of two wooden posts at the door made like boundary posts with human heads, which hold the swinging door with a fragment of wood planted in the earth at each end, so that the children may not be able to open the door and go into the temple to play. In this way the door can be raised only above these posts, which are at least 3 feet high, and it requires a strong man to lift it. These are the little nations which have these temples that one would confound with cabins. The latter have in truth posts and similar doors, but the posts are smooth, and these doors open sideways, because there is no fragment of wood at the end. A woman or child is able to open these doors from the outside or inside, and at night one closes them and fastens them inside to keep the dogs from coming into the cabins. The cabins of the Natchez Suns have, in truth, posts like those of the temples, but their temple was very easy to recognize in accordance with the description I have given of it. Besides, near these little temples some distinctive marks are always to be seen, which are either small elevations of earth or some little dishes which announce that in this place there are bodies interred, or one perceives some raised tombs, if the nation has this custom.

These temples are clearly associated with the cult of the sun and the dead, sometimes termed the Southern Cult or the Buzzard Cult by anthropologists. From a city complex that developed near what is now East St. Louis, Missouri, it spread across the major river drainages of the South from about A.D. 1000 to 1400. Remnants of the Buzzard Cult were still functioning in Louisiana when the first Europeans arrived. The residual elements included temples and mounds, stratified social organizations headed by priest-chiefs, sacred fires, and special concerns with the sun, moon, wind, and cardinal directions. Life and death, the sun and moon, and rain and crops were all implicated in the temple cult.

Each day the Natchez chief climbed the temple mound and called out his father, the sun. This ritual reaffirmed his connection to the source of life, the most powerful of all the forces in the universe. The sun rose at the exact time of his call—a precise piece of astronomical knowledge. According to Archie Sam, the cross-in-palm symbol indicated the point where the power of the sun entered the worshiper's body. The crosses represented the sun and were displayed when the palms were raised toward the morning sun.

Worship of the most sacred element of the universe, the sun, seems to have been universal. The Tunica considered it a female deity. The Chitimacha had a female sky god, Kutnahin, who probably was a personification of the sun. The moon, the "night sun," was equally sacred to most of the tribes. The Alabama considered it best to wash one's body by moonlight. Myths about the sun and related human deities persist among the tribes. Dances are performed around a fire because it represents the sun. Among the Choctaw and Koasati, the discovery of red toads living under one's house is a lucky sign, as are dreams of fire.

The temples were integral not only to worship of the sun but also to the annual celebrations at the ripening of the new crops. In 1736 Father Le Petit noted that fathers of families carried their first harvests of corn and other vegetables to the temples. The priests then distributed the harvest in the villages.

Mound building had begun to lose its significance in Indian life at the time of the first white settlement in Louisiana. Both the Chitimacha and the Natchez interred their dead in mounds well into historic times. The De Soto narratives point out that both temples and chiefs' houses were raised on mounds, but by two centuries later, only the Natchez, probably the most conservative of the southeastern Indians, seem to have retained the once universal tradition. Temples, however, did survive longer, and most tribes built some such sacred edifice. Among the Alabama and Koasati, the *Ischoba*, "Big House," is still central to community patterns. Today, the word *Ischoba* is applied to Christian churches, which fulfill the sacred function.

Some tribes erected brush arbor structures at the first-fruits ceremonial. Medicine men, the ritual specialists, called the people together at the harvest of the new corn, which usually occurred in July or August, depending on the phases of the moon. The people were summoned to a ceremony called *posketa* or *bosketa*, at which many of them drank the Black Drink. The English called the ceremony the Busk. The drink, termed *asi* by the Muskogean speakers and *La Cassine* by the French, was a tea often brewed from a variety of holly (*Ilex vomitoria*). Taken in large quantities, it caused those who drank it to vomit, ritually cleansing their bodies and minds before they ate the new corn. No one could enjoy the new crop until this ceremony had been conducted. Eventually, the annual ceremonials seem to have become detached from the early temple-mound complex. The

Biloxi and Tunica preserved almost the entire new-corn ceremony, but not the temple mound, as late as 1941.

Each family harvested its own crop. The men and older boys went to a sacred water hole with the chief, usually a medicine man, in whom were combined the roles of priest and chief as observed by early Europeans. There the men and boys faced the rising sun, dove naked into the water, and bathed. The chief called them from the water and marked the forehead of each with a cross, the ancient symbol of the cardinal directions. Then each was given a kernel of corn to eat. After this ritual, they returned home, where the women had been arranging an elaborate feat in which corn was prepared in every way they knew.

Another element in the Tunica practice, called by the French the *Fête du Blé*, corn Fest, was the ritual feeding of the dead. Small boys chosen from each family were given packets of corn folded in shuck containers to place on the graves in family burial areas. This had to be done before dawn, and the dead fed before others broke the corn fast.

Except for the ancient ritual drink and vomiting, the elements described above clearly show Southern Cult roots. The sun, the cardinal directions, corn, and water all were integrated, or reintegrated, in the ceremonial. The connection between the living and the dead was reaffirmed, and the corn admitted to sacred standing.

The ritual *posketa* ceremony centered on the taking of *asi* or *ahissi*, the emetic drink. The rites were held at the square ground, an area often set apart from the community itself. Four logs pointing to the cardinal directions were laid on flat ground in the center of the dance plaza in preparation for the sacred fire. The Natchez and Cherokee departed from this custom by building the fire on a small mound raised in the plaza. According to a number of tribes, the most powerful fires were kindled from logs taken from trees that had been struck by lightning.

Then, for four days and nights at the new-corn ritual, the people of the tribe gathered. All day the medicine men in the arbors taught the men and boys, and orated. The lectures dealt with leading a virtuous life and behaving properly toward other people and nature. All night and day the people fasted; at night they danced around a fire. Koasati males drank great quantities of ritual tea, usually brewed from the roots of *toola* (bay) or *skafoto hatka* (horsemint), while women washed in it. Then all went to the edge of the sacred area, vomited, and returned. In another cleansing ritual, men and boys were scratched with a sharp implement to shed blood for the people. The scratching might be done with the teeth remaining in a garfish jaw, a sharp piece of bone, or trade needles set in a bent turkey quill by the medicine man. A dried raccoon paw was used among the Choctaw for this purpose. Scratches were inflicted on forearms, chest, calves, and the length of the spine, and the bloody marks were swabbed by the medicine man who had done the work.

Married people reaffirmed their vows, each Indian made peace with his enemies, and the harmony of the world was restored. The resolution of conflicts at every level within the community was an aspect of the green-corn feasts that Europeans generally failed to understand. Indian etiquette was complicated; one had to be careful not to give offense.

Making amends was difficult, and some Indian languages had no word for "sorry." The Bust ceremony allowed people to atone; there was ritual forgiveness, wherein each reaffirmed his ties to all the others. It is most likely that other ancient forms contained similar components that were not apparent to outsiders.

Witchcraft was universally dreaded, and it persisted long after tribal religion began shifting to Christianity. The colonial Europeans feared witches as much as the Indians did. Malevolent acts disrupted the natural order and led to unpredictable events disharmonic with normal life. Almost always, such abnormal events were discussed with the medicine people or doctors and then attributed to witchcraft.

A witch apparently had certain unnatural powers, but he or she could be overcome if the medicine person who was asked to deal with the witch was strong enough. A particularly strong Tunica witch sometimes reportedly took off her skin and traveled invisibly through the night, but when a medicine man caught her, he filled her skin with salt. The burning sensation she felt when she put it back on before dawn supposedly cured her.

The Louisiana Indian saw witchcraft and medicine as being closely related. What was great power for good could easily be turned into great power for evil. If a patient died while being treated by the medicine person, the cause of death might be considered witchcraft. In such cases, the medicine person was killed, a radical sort of compensation for malpractice.

Medicine people had various ways of diagnosing witchcraft and dealing with it. Cures were complicated and secret. In 1719 Bénard de la Harpe described a case.

> The chief of this nation had a son of 15 years, who had been baptised and instructed in the mysteries of our Saints by M. Davion. Less than a month after my departure from the Tunicas, he fell ill and died in the hands of his pastor and father, Deville, Jesuit. . . . The recovery of this young man was given over to a Tioux medicine man; after the death of this young man it is repeated that he had said had the father given him a present, he would have saved the boy's life. The Tonica chief, having received these words, ordered the immediate execution of this medicine man. Before this execution, he, the medicine man, says to Cahura-Joligo, in the presence of M. Davion, that he sees he clearly cannot avoid death, but in order to prove he is a great sorcerer; after his death the beasts and birds will respect his body without the services of the dead being performed upon him. After the Tioux was executed he was thrown on the road and truly, like he had predicted, the birds and wild beasts, though in great numbers, did not touch the body.

La Harpe attributed the incident to the use of herbs, rubbed on the body, which were repugnant to the scavengers. The role change from curer to sorcerer, nevertheless, is well demonstrated by this incident.

The term *medicine* in Indian usage connotes both power and preparations used in the treatment of disease. The medicine people who combined magic with their knowledge of plants and anatomy were the most powerful and, possibly, the most dangerous of medicine people. Each had his own territory, and like the Tioux described by La Harpe as serving the Tunica, could cross tribal and linguistic boundaries. The territories were respected, for it was believed that their violation led to vicious, magical conflicts among the medicine people.

The medicine, or power, was obtained from a visionary being, through long apprenticeship to an older practitioner, or as a gift from an animal or other spirit, such as one of the "little people" of the forest. Not everyone who sought the medicine found it, even if he heeded items essential to the search—specific herbs, thorns, water—and underwent complete isolation. Exactly what transpired during the period of isolation was never revealed. Certainly there was prayer and fasting.

The Choctaw danced around a dead tree until they saw a vision. The tree was expected to burst into life when the medicine was acquired. Some tribal medicine men knew special songs and recitations for curing, which, along with herbal medicines, are still used by Louisiana Indians.

Some forms of religious belief existed apart from the medicine involved in curing, though there was no sharp dichotomy. The medicine people existed alongside the cult leaders. It is not quite clear when, if ever, the functions of priests and medicine people fussed. As early as 1718, the anonymous author of the *Luxembourg Narrative* described the medicine people in this fashion:

> They have among them doctors, who, like the ancient Egyptians, do not separate medicine from magic. In order to attain to these sublime functions a savage shuts himself into his cabin alone for nine days without eating, with water only; everyone is forbidden to disturb him. There holding in his hand a kind of gourd filled with shells, with which he makes a continual noise, he invokes the Spirit, prays Him to speak to him and to receive him as a doctor and magician, and that with cries, howls, contortions, and terrible shakings of the body, until he gets himself out of breath and foams in a frightful manner. This training being completed at the end of nine days, he comes out of his cabin triumphant and boasts of having received from Him the gift of healing maladies, driving away storms, and changing the weather. From that time they are recognized as doctors and are very much respected; people have recourse to them in sickness and to obtain favorable weather; but it is always necessary to carry presents. It sometimes happens that having received them, if the sick person is not cured or the weather does not change, the doctor is killed as an imposter; a fact which causes the most skillful among them only to receive presents when they see an appearance of cure or of change in the weather.

The medicine people became the complicated crux of Louisiana Indian religion. Religion was the combination of philosophical concepts of how to live in the world—how to maintain the role of humans in the natural order—and the ritual and herbal magic used to maintain harmony.

Religious specialists, or priests, existed in many tribes. Among the Natchez and their neighbors in the lower Mississippi Valley, these men were Suns, descended from the sun and more like gods than men. However, in this tribe the keepers of sacred temple fires were not the Suns but old men chosen for their piety and faith. The Caddo priestly caste, the *Xenesi*, had great supernatural powers but were not necessarily medicine men. Among the more egalitarian tribes, the medicine men were sometimes religious leaders.

Some tribes, like the Choctaw, made a clear distinction between herbal and ritual medicines. The herbalists, usually older men and women, offered plant remedies and occupied a position somewhat like that of the modern pharmacist. Herbal medicine, as practiced by the Indians, was far from simple. In the 1930s, one Houma medicine man revealed to Frank Speck seventy-nine plant cures, only three of which involved plants of European origin. The French-speaking Houma called such a physician a *traiteur* or *traiteuse*. Of thirty-nine plant cures learned by Lyda Taylor from the Koasati, only four were possibly of European origin. Speck pointed out that European plants were utilized in Indian ways; dosages, for example, were computed in fours, not threes.

The application of plants in medical practice was complicated. Plant stems, blooms, bark, leaves, and roots all had their specific efficacies, and their employment varied from cure to cure. Animals, too, played a part in herbal medication. The Choctaw believed that knowledge of the mayapple medicine, used in the treatment of stomach upsets, came from the crow. The bear taught other cures, and even the dog had some medical knowledge to impart. The herbalists were careful observers of nature and especially of animals, their teachers.

Various factors were part of the Indian doctor's lore. Claude Medord has noted that the time of day was an important consideration in the gathering of medicinal plants, as were some seasonal changes. The various colors associated with the cardinal directions as well as with life and death were relevant to medicine. Red was especially powerful and almost universally viewed as a life color. Other sacred colors were black, yellow, and white. To the Koasati and Tunica, blue was sacred, signifying death to the former and winter to the latter.

Parts of plants, such as blooms, stems, and roots, were sorted by color as well as place of origin. Bags of different colors, often red flannel or a black or white fabric, were filled with medicine and carried on the sick person as amulets. The power associated with clays and natural pigments was probably derived from their association with certain sacred colors. In Louisiana and elsewhere, the Indians' emphasis on plants as agents of healing set them apart from European practitioners of medicine. Indeed, the aboriginal herbal pharmacopoeia lengthened the life of many an early American pioneer.

Among the Indians, medicines were usually administered orally, some being made into teas. Others were applied as poultices or sudorifics. The Houma and Choctaw measured medicines by "swallows" and "half-swallows." Traditionalists still find hypodermic medicine distasteful, for witches "shot" objects, including lizards and insects, into their victims.

Hypnosis, psychological suggestion, and cupping, or bleeding, were employed, along with herbal medicines. These treatments were carefully selected and skillfully administered with restraint. The feeling of balance, for example, precluded the exhaustive bleeding practiced by Europeans. Among the Indians, this treatment appears to have been cleaner and more efficiently done than by the Europeans. Choctaw curers used cups of cow or buffalo horn and lancets of flint or glass in a procedure Le Page du Pratz described as superior to the European method. Contemporary traditionalists almost always identify small lancets found at prehistoric sites as those used in bleeding, opening boils, and extracting thorns. Some of the Europeans were quick to learn that willow tea, the equivalent of aspirin, was more helpful than leeches and knives.

Smoke was also a remedy of some importance. Warm smoke blown into the ear, for example, was a widely employed cure for earache. Broken bones were skillfully set, though surgical procedures were almost unknown. Other than in the removal of bad teeth, such techniques violated the natural order.

Some aboriginal specialization developed, such as midwifery, and some curers were widely respected for their treatment of burns, fractures, and lung ailments. Some doctors were capable of handling ghostly manifestations and ghost fear. In Indian Health Service hospitals among the Mississippi Choctaw, the practices of these efficient, careful doctors, as the medicine people are still known among the Indian communities, have been integrated with modern medicine.

These medicine people were among the first practitioners of holistic medicine. They realized no only the inadequacy of a dichotomy between the mind and body but the lack of clear distinctions between the natural and supernatural as well. They used what many now consider to be advanced medical techniques. Patients, for example, were usually treated at home and were not isolated from their social unit, the family. Sweat baths, massage with a warm object such as a stone, the use of herbal incense, herbal inhalations, and the recitation of sounds that induced a sense of exaltation had all the benefits of contemporary relaxation therapy. People displaying symptoms of depression or melancholy were gathered into group sessions with family and friends. The medicine people used these support sessions to reintegrate the patient. Such meetings are clearly the forerunners of community mental health activities.

As late as the 1930s, a Koasati medicine man rejected surgery on his injured feet. He resorted to herbal medicine, and the resultant slight limp with which he walked was infinitely better to him than would have been the amputation of a foot. To be buried in two places, he explained, was unnatural. The manipulation of one part of the body, with no idea of how it fit into the larger system, was alien to the medical tradition of many American Indians, including those of Louisiana.

Le Page du Pratz, a pharmacist, was quick to note the efficacy of herbal medicines. His observations were supported by others. In the eighteenth century, French observers were amazed at the Indian doctors' abilities in curing wounds. They thought, however, that Indians had little knowledge of internal medicine. Such observers knew little of Indian herbals such as sweet-gum sap, willow-bark tea, and the various emetic plants used to treat internal problems. Le Page du Pratz not only understood the treatment of wounds to be superior but noted that the Indians' internal medicine was also excellent.

I shall not undertake to particularize all the virtues of this sweetgum or Liquid-Ambar, not having learned all of them from the natives of the country, who would be no less surprised to find that we used it only as a varnish, than they were to see our surgeons bleed their patients. This balm, according to them, is an excellent fabrifuge; they take ten or a dozen drops of it in gruel fasting, and before their meals; and if they should take a little more, they have no reason to apprehend any danger. The physicians among the natives purge their patients before they give it. It cures wounds in two days without any consequences; it is equally sovereign for all kinds of ulcers, after having applied to them for some days a plaster of bruised ground-ivy. It cures consumptions, opens obstructions, afterwards affords relief in the colic and all internal diseases; it comforts the heart.

Many of the other herbal medicines noted by Le Page du Pratz eventually were taken into modern pharmaceutical usage.

Notable, too, was that the Indian doctors were not paid. They accepted gifts, but only if they felt certain that the patient would get well. Not surprisingly, the largest gifts were given after recovery. Especially welcome rewards were tobacco and colored cloth folded in special ways. The punishment for failure might be exile, permanent ridicule, or even death.

The appearance of previously unknown diseases, particularly those brought in by Europeans, confronted the native practitioners with new problems. The fear of witchcraft increased, and the shaman became more cautious in the application of his healing arts. As early as the 1700s, the execution of medicine men may have reflected their growing inability to cope with the new diseases sweeping the tribes. Other new pressures, among them alcoholism, tribal migration and warfare, and Indian slavery, seem to have provoked more frequent accusations of witchcraft. In many cases, the medicine people suffered unjustly when their skills failed.

The medicine people, in spite of all difficulties, survived. The new strains drew the people and the practitioners closer together, and those socioeconomic stresses unique to Indian communities seemed best handled by the traditional medicine. Ancient skills had to be applied to serious new problems, worse than arrow or even gunshot wounds. The tribes were crowded onto smaller land holdings. The elders and the children, the repositories and the hope of tribal traditions, were dying. Increased involvement in the European trade brought more competitive attitudes, violating the oldest of all Indian virtues, hospitality and the sharing of resources. These problems intensified malevolent feelings, factions developed everywhere, and the medicine people had to combat witchcraft more diligently, emphasize the need for sharing, and constantly remind the people of the need to be cooperative with, and supportive of, each other.

The white men, who had transmitted their ills to the Indians, often denied them the remedies that were available. Indian leaders like Tinehouen, a Caddo chief, sought new medicine against smallpox for their people; it was never delivered. The medicine people did what they could. As the government of the United States began to treat Indians as wards, Indian doctors were driven underground, fearful of prosecution for practicing medicine without licenses.

As late as the 1930s, anthropologists could observe the old religion and collect the medicines. By the 1950s, the traditional medicine had become something understood by Indians only, and it was for the most part no longer shared with those who did not understand the depth and intensity of its spiritual components. When given to outsiders, the gift was always predicated on the admonition, "not for publication." The sacred prayers and recitations needed to make the medicines effective were once known to many people but had become carefully guarded knowledge by 1900.

By the 1920s, the medicine people had become increasingly pantribal and had extended their activities. Some, like Emma Jackson of Indian Creek and Mark Robinson, a Koasati, traveled from one tribal community to another. The late Arzalie Langley, a Choctaw from the Koasati tribal area, visited almost every Indian community in Louisiana except the Houma and the Chitimacha.

Protestant mission work among the Indians began in earnest after 1890. The first ministers were Indian medicine men, who were admirably suited to the work and were sought out for the task. Most of them knew the Mobilian jargon and so could communicate across tribal boundaries. The medicine men were sober, honest, and giving of themselves. In many ways, they surpassed the white Christians.

Their rewards, at least in this life, tended to be meager. Once conversions had been made, churches had been built, and congregations established, these early Indian leaders were often replaced by whites. One early Koasati minister, Mark Robinson, who walked fifteen miles to preach in 1922, was eventually displaced from his hard-won position, though it took two whites to do his job. Perhaps the early Indian ministers were too tolerant of the Indian medicine to relinquish that tradition; whatever the reason might have been, the Indian preachers were quickly dismissed. Non-Indian preachers drove the rituals and integrative traditions far underground. Christianity was compatible with the ministry but not with the old Indian ways.

As Indian youths began to attend schools, new assimilative pressures were felt. Not only did the native languages come under attack, but western religion was strongly advocated. Young Indian people began to acquire the notion that white values, for better or for worse, would be dominant in the world, and they began to learn the distinctions of European science and mathematics. The old ways were left for the old people. Yet the religion and medicine survived. In Indian communities, where income levels were low and children were plentiful, it fell to the lot of the older people, the grandparents, to baby-sit and to raise the children. So the earliest learning experiences were resoundingly Indian in orientation.

In colonial times, there was a tendency to exchange cultural values and behavior. Elements of European culture crept into Indian ways and vice versa. After 1900, there was a strong tendency to compartmentalize the two cultures. Recently, when a young Louisiana Indian asked his grandfather about the old ways, the reply was terse. The youth was asked if he preferred the Christian religion. When he answered that he did favor the nontraditional faith, the old man simply replied, "The medicine is for Indian people." Young Indians increasingly seem to feel that they must make a choice between the old and the new ways.

Ethnologists and others, in a well-intentioned rush to preserve the Indian culture, are equally well admonished by Chief Joseph A. Pierite, a Tunica-Biloxi traditionalist: "We have a promise from the Sun. As long as the Sun will shine we will have the medicine. As long as there is the medicine there will be Indian people. If we have, as you anthropologists say, been here 10,000 years, then we have kept medicine. We do not need it written down!" The medicine will survive in one form or another. The Sun's promise will be kept. In marshes, pine hills, and smoky streets, most Louisiana Indians continue to seek harmony, to maintain the natural balance of life. The medicine goes with them, wherever they go.

REFERENCES

While Indian religions long have quickened the imaginations of non-Indian observers and writers, anthropological literature reveals surprisingly little information on the subject. John R. Swanton discussed the Indian religions of the Southeast in most of his standard works cited herein and has provided other significant sources.

Swanton, John R. "Sun Worship in the Southeast." *American Anthropologist*, 30 (1928): 206-13.

_____. "Myths and Tales of the Southeastern Indians." *Bureau of American Ethnology Bulletin 88* (Washington, D. C., 1929).

A good summary of Swanton's works coupled with a broader southeastern Indian perspective appears in two relatively recent syntheses.

Hudson, Charles. *The Southeastern Indians.* Knoxville: University of Tennessee Press, 1976.

_____. *The Black Drink, a Native American Tea.* Athens, Ga.: University of Georgia Press, 1979.

A work tracing the connections between the archaeological evidences of religion and magic and ethnographic descriptions of those beliefs has become a classic.

Howard, James H. "The Southeastern Ceremonial Complex and Its Interpretation." *Missouri Archaeological Survey Memoir*, 6 (1968).

Antonio Waring's formulation of evidence of a widespread ceremonial complex is also seminal.

Waring, Antonio J., and Preston Holder. "A Prehistoric Ceremonial Complex in the Southeastern United States." *American Anthropologist*, 47 (1945): 1-34.

Waring, Antonio J. "The Southern Cult and Moskogean Ceremonial." In *The Waring Papers, the Collected Works of Antonio J. Waring, Jr.*, ed. Stephen Williams, 30-61. Papers of the Peabody Museum of Archaeology and Ethnology, Harvard University, (Cambridge, Mass.: Peabody Museum, Harvard University, 1968).

Another important perspective has been developed.

Witthoft, John. *Green Corn Ceremonialism in the Eastern Woodlands*. Occasional Paper from the Museum of Anthropology 13. Ann Arbor: University of Michigan Press, 1949.

Many primary sources on the religion of the Louisiana Indians and their neighbors have never been translated from the original French or Spanish. Especially important are the *Papeles Procedentes de Cuba* and the letters from the commanders at the various Spanish colonial posts of Louisiana: Lafourche (now Donaldsonville), Rapides (now Alexandria), Punta Cortada (Pointe Coupée near modern New Roads), Ouachita (now Monroe) and Natchitoches.

John R. Swanton, in 1911, used the abundant French colonial material in the *Bibliothèque Nationale* in Paris. However, he most often seems to have used translations by the nineteenth-century Louisiana historian Pierre Margry. Margry's work has unfortunate deletions, some errors in translation, and some unnecessary though interesting additions to the original sources. He has gathered a whole series of accounts in his work.

Margry, Pierre, ed. *Découvertes et établissements des français dans l'ouest et dans le sud de l'Amérique septentrionale (1614-1754)*. 6 vols. Paris: D. Jouaust, 1880-1883.

Perhaps the best observers of the religious practices of the tribes, especially in the eighteenth century, were the Jesuit priests traveling up and down the Mississippi. A look at their material is valuable.

Thwaites, Reuben, ed. *Jesuit Relations and Allied Documents: Travels and Explorations of Jesuit Missionaries in New France, 1610-1791*. Cleveland: Burrows Brothers, 1896-1901.

Another good eighteenth-century source on Louisiana Indian religion is Jean-Baptiste Bénard, Sieur de la Harpe. Most often his name is misspelled, and he is called Bernard de la Harpe. He went to Louisiana from France to found a post on Red River, and left a journal covering the period 1718 to 1720. The only manuscript copy of this journal is located at the *Bibliothèque Nationale* in Paris, as are his journals of two later trips in Louisiana and a memoir. A rather bad translation of La Harpe, by Pierre Margry, contains alterations, deletions, and additions. This version, dated 1876 to 1886, has been translated again by Ralph A. Smith.

Smith, Ralph A. "Account of the Journey of Bénard de La Harpe; Discovery Made by Him of Several Nations Situated in the West." *Southwestern Historical Quarterly*, 62, nos. 1-4 (1958-1959).

Much information from the journal of Bénard de la Harpe on the Lower Mississippi Valley and its tribes can be found in Swanton's work.

Swanton, John R. "Indian Tribes of the Lower Mississippi Valley and Adjacent Coast of the Gulf of Mexico." *Bureau of American Ethnology Bulletin*, 43 (1911): 318-26.

An important discussion of European and Indian attitudes toward witchcraft appears in Jean-Bernard Bossu's narratives.

Dickinson, Samuel Dorris, ed. and trans. *New Travels in North America by Jean-Bernard Bossu, 1770-1771*. Natchitoches, La.: Northwestern State University Press, 1982.

An interesting reference to the execution of witches by the Caddo in the nineteenth century is available.

Williams, Stephen. "The Aboriginal Location of the Kadohadacho and Related Tribes." In *Explorations in Cultural Anthropology: Essays in Honor of George Peter Murdock*, ed. Ward H. Goodenough, 545-70. New York: McGraw-Hill, 1964.

One of the best primary accounts of shamanism remains the so-called *Luxembourg Narrative*, housed in Paris. The author remains unknown, and the document apparently written in French seems to have been published at Luxembourg. The passage most pertinent to shamanistic activity is quoted in Swanton's 1911 work. Swanton believed the document was written before 1718. The full title is:

Mémoire sur la Louisiane, ou le Mississipi. Luxembourg. 1752(?).

Other early accounts appear in the Spanish descriptions of the Caddoan groups in the western area of the state. Herbert Eugene Bolton has summarized some of these in his extensive work on Texas. Further information is in the Library of Congress.

Bolton, Herbert Eugene. Letterbooks of the Caddo Agency. Manuscript on microfilm at Library of Congress, Washington, D. C. 1805-1835.

References to witchcraft among the Choctaw appear in a number of places.

Cushman, H. B. *History of the Choctaw, Chickasaw and Natchez Indians.* Edited with a foreward by Angie Debo. Norman, Ok.: University of Oklahoma Press, 1962.

Bushnell, David I., Jr. "The Choctaw of Bayou Lacombe, St. Tammany Parish, Louisiana." *Bureau of American Ethnology Bulletin,* 48 (1909): 1-37.

Some material herein came from the field notes of Hiram Gregory and the late Caroline Dormon. These references are based on work among the Koasati, Choctaw, and Chitimacha in the 1930s and 1970s. Gregory has synthesized an overview of Louisiana Indian traditional culture—religion, magic, folktales, and so on.

Gregory, Hiram F. "A Promise from the Sun: The Louisiana Indians." In *A Guide to Louisiana Folklife,* ed. Nicholas Spitzer. Baton Rouge: Louisiana Folklife Program, Office of Culture, Recreation, and Tourism, Department of Culture, Recreation, and Tourism, 1985.

Chief Pierite's statement near the end of this chapter can be found in Gregory's 1973 field notes. Donald Hunter, with several Koasati, among them Bel Abbey, Nora Abbey, and Louisa Wilson, has produced good accounts of tribal custom.

Hunter, Donald. "The Cicada in Southeastern Archaeology and in Coushatta Tradition." *Louisiana Archaeology,* 2 (1975): 219-26.

The continuity of Tunica burial customs has been documented.

Brain, Jeffrey. "From the Words of the Living: The Indian Speaks." In *Clues to America's Past.* Washington, D. C.: Special Publications Division, National Geographic Society, 1976.

Tunica practices and attitudes toward the dead have been described, along with an account of a late nineteenth-century burial.

Gregory, Hiram F. "A Historic Tunica Burial at the Coulee des Grues Site in Avoyelles Parish, Louisiana." In *Texas Archaeology: Essays Honoring R. King Harris*, ed. Kurt D. House, 146-64 . Dallas: SMU Press, 1978.

Le Page du Pratz described Indian temples.

Le Page du Pratz. *Histoire de la Louisiane.* 3 vols. Paris: Chez de Bure, 1758.

The Tunica corn feast, as described by Sesosterie Yuchigant, has been documented in a series of linguistic texts.

Haas, Mary. *Tunica Texts.* University of California Publications in Linguistics 6. Berkeley: University of California Press, 1950.

The late Louise Allen, Clyde Jackson, Mary Jones, Mr. and Mrs. Anderson Lewis, Jesse Lewis, and Dorothy Nugent, all of the Jena Choctaw, along with Clementine Broussard and the late Florence Jackson, have contributed much to our understanding of Choctaw and Tunica-Biloxi traditions. Oney Brown, a nontribal Indian, has also given of her knowledge. The late Emerick Sanson, a part-Choctaw, materially advanced our knowledge of relationships between animals and humans.

A recent work on folklore and myth among the Houma, by Bruce Duthu, a young Houma, is an impressive beginning for Indians teaching non-Indians about their tribes.

Duthu, Bruce. "Folklore of the Louisiana Houma Indians." *Louisiana Folklife*, 4 (1979): 1-32.

Faye Stouff, widow of the late Emile Stouff, a Chitimacha chief, shared some of her insights into the tribe and the medicine it used. Her publication on the tribe contains much important material.

Stouff, Faye, and W. Bradley Twitty. *Sacred Chitimacha Indian Beliefs.* Pompano Beach, Fla.: Twitty and Twitty, 1971.

Lester Sepulvado's report on curing and witchcraft along the Sabine River remains the only documentation of Hispanic and Indian syncretism in that area.

Sepulvado, Don Lester. "Folk Curing in a Spanish Community." *Louisiana Folklife*, 3 (1980): page numbers.

Many unpublished field notes are available; the notes on the Alabama, Koasati, and Tunica contain numerous references to the tribal myths and traditional religion. These are in the National Anthropological Archives. Albert Gatschet's notes are also in the National Anthropological Archives and, like Swanton's, contain many bits of information virtually impossible to find elsewhere today.

Spanish documents covering nearly forty years of Spanish administration in Louisiana are filled with detailed information on topics such as infanticide. The *Papeles Procedentes de Cuba* are now available at the Library of Congress, the Loyola University library in New Orleans, and the Archives of the University of Louisiana at Lafayette. The Bexar Archives in San Antonio, Texas, contain references to the Caddoan tribes, including some on their religion.

The Library of Congress holds English documents covering 1765 to 1790 and dealing with the tribes on the east ascending bank of the Mississippi River. More important than these sources may be the traditionalists who have shared their cherished beliefs with us: Bel Abbey and the late Mark Robinson of the Koasati; and the late Joseph Alcide Pierite, Sr., and his brother, the late Herman Pierite, of the Tunica-Biloxi.

In his work, Frank G. Speck set admirable standards—respected by Indians and anthropologists—which extended to the study of herbal medicine. His work among the Houma was seminal to the study of ethnobotany.

Speck, Frank G. "A List of Plant Curatives Obtained from Houma Indians in Louisiana." *Primitive Man*, 14 (1941): 49-73.

The regional authority on Southeastern Indian plant usage, Lyda Averill Taylor, completed her dissertation at Yale University on the Koasati. Her work, which has been published, is filled with references to herbal medicines from Louisiana.

Taylor, Lyda Averill. *Plants Used as Curatives by Certain Southeastern Tribes*. Cambridge, Mass.: Botanical Museum of Harvard University, 1940.

PART III
The French Colonial Period

"BY ALL THE CONDUCT OF THEIR LIVES": A LAYWOMEN'S CONFRATERNITY IN NEW ORLEANS, 1730-1744*

Emily Clark

On May 27, 1730, eight women called on a small community of Ursuline nuns living in temporary quarters at the west end of New Orleans and "asked to set up a congregation of women and girls, in honor of the Very Blessed Virgin Mary."[1] The nuns responded by giving meeting space and sponsorship to the confraternity that took the name Ladies Congregation of the Children of Mary. A vellum-bound folio volume was purchased, and over the years entries were made on twenty-two of its 285 pages, recording the organization's constitution, papal bulls granted to it, a fund-raising effort, election results, and membership.[2] The organization grew to include more than a third of the free women and marriageable girls living in New Orleans in the 1730s.[3] The record book they kept, which has lain almost completely ignored in the archives of the Ursuline Convent of New Orleans, offers rare insight into how French colonial women conceptualized and executed their religious and social roles in the first decades of the colony's life. It suggests strong continuity between the religious culture of France and its colony and points to the practical effects that the transference of one aspect of that culture had on the development of colonial society.[4] The picture that emerges of the confraternity limns a realm of influence and activity for these French Catholic colonial women that contrasts with that inhabited by their English Protestant counterparts; it thus provokes an inquiry into how the divergence between Protestantism and Catholicism in the age of exploration affected the evolution of colonial communities.

The question remains whether Protestantism or Catholicism offered early modern women greater scope for the expression of piety and the exercise of talents. Historians of Europe during the era of religious reform have argued that the Protestant introduction of a vernacular, participatory liturgy, promotion of literacy, and exhortation to recognize spiritual equality between the sexes benefited women in new ways. Natalie Zemon Davis remarks the empowering nature of Protestant worship for French Calvinist women, their

*First published in *William and Mary Quarterly*, 3rd ser., 54 (1997): 769-94. Reprinted with the kind permission of the author and the publisher.

voices raised in unison with their fathers and husbands in vernacular versions of the psalms. The elevation of the Word invited women not only to read but also to interpret and discuss their meditations, creating an acceptable cultural space for female intellectual activity. Wealthy women found in the promotion of Protestant causes and the patronage of ministers a rewarding avenue to power, and ordinary women profited from a new orthodoxy that glorified marriage over celibacy and exhorted husbands to love and honor their wives and to adjure the physical abuse and intimidation that marked the discipline of pre-Reformation households.[5] Other historians contend that the Reformation was the vehicle through which a patriarchy made nervous by economic and social changes reasserted control by narrowing women's options. Institutions not wholly within the compass of male authority—converts—were abolished, the Virgin Mary displaced, and women uniformly forced to make their lives within a conservatively defined domesticity.[6]

Progress in this debate, particularly in terms of how confessional differences may have affected women over time as the New World became settled and grew to maturity, is hampered by the lopsided development of the historiographical traditions on which it relies. Perry Miller's legacy shows in the prolific scholarship on Puritan women, which has attained a dense and nuanced complexity unmatched by that in colonial women associated with other forms of Protestantism.[7] As American historians embrace gender as a category of analysis, they increasingly ask questions about how religion empowered or oppressed women at different times and in different places, expanding from the base of Puritan scholarship to consider Quaker and evangelical women. The Puritan goodwife has been a point of departure; it is possible now to make comparisons among Puritan, Quaker, and evangelical women in colonial America and to place such comparisons in the broader context of their developments, such as the transition to capitalism and the Revolution.[8] By contrast, the scholarship on Catholic women in North American colonies makes even such internal comparisons difficult. It has enjoyed neither a productive focus like Puritanism nor a comparable application of gender analysis, tending instead toward biography or institutional history. There is for Catholic women very little broad historical analysis that would bring balance to a comparison with Protestant women.[9]

Evidence from the laywomen's confraternity in colonial New Orleans expands the range of scholarship on Catholic women and makes the prospect for a fruitful comparison more promising. Such confraternities, drawing on long-established tradition and attracting large numbers of women, were well within the Catholic mainstream. Their purposes and practices—and their meaning for the women who participated in their activities—may be usefully compared with the far better documented religious experience of women in the Puritan colonies of New England.

Reformed Protestant spirituality stressed the essential equality of godly souls, male and female alike. Despite this inner ideal, its expression in acceptable behavior was differentiated by gender. In a faith in which only male ministers preached and men governed and in a society where families were headed by fathers and husbands, female devotional life was marked by deference and submission. These qualities came to color women's social role as well.[10] The story of colonial Puritan women is not so much Lyle Koehler's narrative of bald masculine oppression as it is a history of a society attempting to strike equilibrium between a spiritual ideal of equality and a social order rooted in gender difference and hierarchy. The resolution lay not in stripping women of power but in defining the realm of their power in spiritual and private terms. A sophisticated ideology grew up to support the gendered division of pious labor that excluded women from roles of public authority, such as preaching and church governance.[11]

There were occasions when the ideal of spiritual equality broke through to the mundane. Cornelia Hughes Dayton writes of how, for a time, Connecticut women took advantage of Puritan legal interpretation to assert their interests through the courts. Women appear to have assumed increasing responsibility for their families' Christian education in the late seventeenth and early eighteenth centuries, perhaps as an outgrowth of the feminization of the pews that occurred in this era.[12] Even so, the essential position of women in the public, corporate institutions of the church remained unchanged. Women prayed, listened, reflected, and obeyed. They did not preach or lead religious organizations.[13] As the eighteenth century ended and the nineteenth dawned, women found themselves increasingly enclosed within the bounds of family and dependency in a male-dominated republic.[14]

By contrast, women practicing a faith that countenanced enclosure of a different kind retained a staging ground for devotional activity that stood outside the circles of family and church over which men presided. These included convents for vowed religious women and confraternities for pious laywomen that provided opportunities to express their religiosity as organized communities with elaborate internal governance structures, female-led devotional routines, and independently administered sources of wealth and programs of charity. In the very era when Protestant women gave up this separate institutional heritage in favor of a richer congregational life that joined the sexes, Catholic women not only retained their single-sex organizations but expanded them. How and why this occurred directly influenced French women's opportunities to participate in shaping Louisiana's colonial society.

Between 1535 and 1675, at least fourteen new orders and congregations of religious women were established in Europe, tripling the number in existence. The most dramatic growth took place in France, where a dozen were founded in the course of the seventeenth century. Jesuits are commonly viewed as the great soldiers of the French Counter Reformation, yet at the end of the seventeenth century their 5,000 French members were outnumbered by 10,000 Ursuline nuns living in 320 communities in every part of France and as far away as Quebec. By 1700, the Filles de Sainte-Marie founded by Francis de Sales counted 6,500 women among their ranks, the Congrégation de Notre Dame had founded sixty communities, and the Filles de Notre Dame forty. As the seventeenth century advanced, they were joined by thousands of women belonging to the Filles de la Charité, the Miramionnes, and other new religious congregations.[15]

These congregations were not only numerous and popular, they were different from their predecessors. Before the era of reform, vowed religious women lived only in cloistered communities and sought to ease human suffering and attain grace through contemplation and prayer. By contrast, the Ursulines, Filles de la Charité, and other congregations founded in the seventeenth century embraced apostolic ministries that turned their faces and their hands to the larger community.[16] Contemplative nuns had been a fixture of French Catholic life for centuries; by the opening decades of the sixteenth century, however, their numbers had stagnated along with their missions and they drew little notice from contemporaries.[17] The response their activist successors evoked suggests how jarring the innovation and sudden growth in female religious institutions must have been.

When 300 women flocked to join Vincent de Paul's charitable organization in Beauvais in the 1620s, an alarmed local official wrote that the women "meet together frequently to perform their religious exercises and other duties; which ought not to be tolerated."[18] Nonetheless, in Beauvais and throughout France they were tolerated, these women who organized themselves by the thousands into associations that took them out of their homes to pray together and to teach, to tend the sick, and to minister to the poor. Why, in France, were women able to effect such an extraordinary expansion of their institutional base? Why were the church fathers, who had firmly reasserted the role of cloister for religious women, persuaded to accept the teaching Ursulines and the peripatetic Filles de la Charité? Because, essentially, their sense of the benefits to the social fabric and the Church outweighed their fears of thousands of women stretching the boundaries of female propriety and subordination.

The new congregations provided an organized workforce to combat the threat that poverty posed to the social and moral order. As the numbers of the permanently poor expanded swelling Europe's cities and towns with men, women, and children whose desperation roused more fear than pity, medieval charitable practices proved unable to cope. Religious women in the new congregations provided the human and institutional resources needed to minister to and attempt to reform this troubling, burgeoning population.[19]

The Huguenot threat called forth a different kind of ministry but met a response in the same vein. With the Protestant heresy carried on the wings of literacy, education emerged as an obvious strategy for the Catholic counterattack. And because children learned their faith at their mother's knee, churchmen began to recognize that a Catholic mother schooled in letters and the true faith served as the best defense against the spread of Protestantism.[20] They drew on and expanded the existing base of women's religious communities to advance their campaign. Like Linda K. Kerbers' republican mothers in post-revolutionary America, in order to ensure the virtue of the larger society the mothers of Counter Reformation France found encouragement to enter the intellectual realm generally reserved to men.[21] Archbishop of Milan Charles Borromeo, the great architect of reform Catholicism after the Council of Trent (1545-1563), plucked the little teaching Company of St. Ursula from obscurity in the hills of Brescia and launched it as a formal order with papal recognition in 1682. The Huguenot-threatened clergy of southern France were quick to bring the Ursulines to France, where they spread with astonishing speed. By the end of the seventeenth century, hardly a town in France lacked an Ursuline convent school that taught girls of all social backgrounds catechism and letters along with sewing.[22]

Women advanced the goals of Trent not only by assuring the orthodoxy and effectiveness of Catholic motherhood through vowed communities but also through associations of laywomen. Tridentine Catholicism aimed to create a transnational church whose governance and practices supported loyalty to the authority of Rome. It sought to channel the devotional life of the laity in ways that supported the parish priests and churches, thus strengthening the hierarchy of pope, bishops, and secular clergy. The old array of patron saints and festivals and neighborhood confraternities created a localized piety that detracted from the progress of the Tridentine vision. The Holy Sacrament and the Blessed Virgin, on the other hand, were objects of adoration that enhanced the role of the priest and gave Catholics a patron who transcended locality.[23] The Tridentine church promoted these devotions with vigor and placed renewed emphasis on teaching Christian doctrine. Parish priests organized new confraternities around these devotions, and laypeople joined them. These organizations held particular appeal for women.[24]

The associations for pious laypeople known as confraternities had existed for centuries. During the medieval period, they drew men and women communal devotion and charity organized the rites of burial and memorial intercession. In the fifteenth and early sixteenth centuries, the organizing focus shifted, and confraternities centering on penitential flagellation came to predominate. Their communal ritual, which required flailing one's bare back, often in public procession, was thought unseemly for women, who were thus effectively shut out of the mainstream of confraternal life.[25] In the late sixteenth century, however, as clergy began promoting the new confraternities that taught Christian doctrine and centered on the Blessed Virgin and the Holy Sacrament, devotional forms changed again. Women were welcome to participate in the programs of the parochial organizations and seem to have joined them in large numbers, particularly those dedicated to the Virgin. It was not uncommon for the Marian confraternities to combine devotion to the great female saint with exclusively female membership and leadership.[26]

Although there have been no full-length studies of early modern European women's confraternities and their impact on Catholicism, a few historians have hinted at how important laywomen may have been to the French Counter Reformation church. Philip Hoffman identifies women as one of the largest constituencies supporting the Tridentine assertion of clerical control and the parochial structure.[27] Kathryn Norberg suggests that the confraternities that French women embraced during the Counter Reformation were as much their own creations as they were agencies designed by a resurgent parochial clergy intent on consolidating authority; her work implies how important these organizations were to the achievement of the clergy's aims.[28]

The new confraternities may also have served as vehicles for a campaign for moral order. Historians have linked the confraternities of the French Counter Reformation, particularly the elite male Company of the Holy Sacrament, to a desire to promote morality and exert social control amid unsettling social change.[29] Although no one has attributed similar goals to women's confraternities, the evidence of the Children of Mary of New Orleans suggests that they may have shared the ambition for moral order.[30]

In early modern France, lay and vowed religious women played a significant and visible role in advancing social and religious goals. They helped meet the challenge of the growth of poverty. They took on the fundamental task of catechesis, both as members of new religious orders established to mold Catholic mothers and as laywomen who accepted the charge to teach their children and servants the doctrines of the true faith. They joined confraternities that supported the clerical aspirations of the Tridentine church and promoted moral order. Although there were certainly wealthy individual female patrons, the majority of these women did not do these things as private persons—that is, as wives and mothers—but as members of corporate religious organizations led by women.

The French brought these organizations to America. As early as 1639, the educational missions of Ursulines in Quebec and later the Congrégationists of Montréal served as urban counterparts to the dangerous and dramatic Jesuit expeditions into the hinterland of New France to convert the Indians.[31] In 1727, less than ten years after the city was founded, a community of Ursulines traveled to New Orleans to staff the military hospital and open a school. When the laywomen of the settlement founded the Children of Mary three years later, they completed the replication of their homeland's pattern of religious institutions in the colony.

The congregation of the Children of Mary was, its constitution stated, "an assembly of persons who profess to serve the Blessed Virgin, to honor her not by their prayers alone, but also by their morals, and by all the conduct of their lives." *Confrèresses* "should have a special zeal for visiting the sick, the relief of the poor and the instruction of their children and their slaves."[32] This excerpt summarizes their essential purpose: the women were motivated primarily by piety, expressed through prayer and also through action. On its face, their mission seems unremarkable, yet it suggests a program that might have made several contributions to the community developing in the young colony. The *confrèresses'* promises to tend the sick would have had special resonance in New Orleans, where the subtropical climate brought long summer seasons of lethal fevers and dysentery. In a colony with scant economic opportunity, with many of its settlers destitute men and women deported from the poorhouses of France, their aid to the poor would not have been a superfluous nicety. Their commitment to uphold and promote a strict moral standard was almost made to order for a frontier town notorious for its rowdy populace and slack religious observance. And as settlers began families and acquired African bondsmen, the *confrèresses'* promise to take special care for the instruction of their children and their slaves implied ambitions for the colony that looked beyond stability to the creation of a community of faith and learning.

The confraternity's register thus lays out a tantalizing array of possibilities for how the Children of Mary may have acted to shape their nascent colony. Evidence of whether the *confrèresses* realized these possibilities is scant. This is largely a function of the kinds of public documents that were made and preserved in Louisiana: official dispatches between the colony and France discussing military and financial matters; minutes of the local governing body, the Louisiana Superior Council, which recorded contractual and judicial transactions; and sacramental registers noting baptisms, marriages, and deaths.[33] Although these records are voluminous, the activities of the confraternity do not fit readily into their military, legal, financial, and sacramental categories. None of them mention the Ladies Congregation of the Children of Mary. If the Ursuline nuns had not kept the confraternity's register, the organization's existence would be completely invisible in the historical record. The register provides a key that unlocks several other sources. Its membership roster enables one to identify *confrèresses* as they appear in four groups of records: colonial censuses, the city's sacramental registers, the colonial dispatches, and the proceedings of the Louisiana Superior Council. While these sources have their own limitations—censuses were in only two of the years during which the confraternity was active, 1731 and 1732, and sacramental records survive only for 1731-1733 and 1744—when combined with the confraternity register they nonetheless allow the reconstruction of a partial portrait of the *confrèresses* and their activities.

The picture that emerges leaves some things in shadow. There is no record of the charity of the Children of Mary and no testimony to their attempts to improve public morals. Nor is there anything to confirm their fidelity to their promise to educate their children. Yet the historical record delineates other features clearly. It shows the kinds of women who joined the confraternity and so reveals something of the social organization in the colony. It brings to the foreground the importance of morality for a large proportion of the women of New Orleans and illustrates what that entailed in public conduct and private piety. And it depicts the *confrèresses* making good on their promise to provide religious instruction to their slaves.

The eight women who called on the New Orleans Ursulines in 1730 formed a diverse group. Of the five who can be identified, two were very wealthy widows whose families had already established sizable land holdings worked by dozens of African slaves. Another was the wife of a carpenter. The other two were the wife and mother-in-law of a gunner in the colonial army. The membership that grew from this base was also diverse: the roster in the confraternity's record book gives the names of eighty-five women and girls, of whom forty-three can be confidently identified.[34] The circumstances of their lives that can be reconstructed from public records not only suggest a wide range of wealth and social standing within the confraternity but also give a sense of the social fabric of the young colony.

By the mid-1720s, a handful of men stand out in Louisiana's records for the property and slaves they had acquired or for their statue as members of the colonial administration.[35] Some nineteen wives and daughters of these few wealthy planters and bureaucratic officers composed a contingent of elite women among the confraternity's member-ship.[36] A sketch of several of these families gives an idea of the general circumstances of the group.

Françoise Jalot was the widow of François Carrière. François and his brothers André and Joseph were Canadians who used their friendship with the colony's intermittent governor, Jean-Baptiste Le Moyne de Bienville, to secure choice plots of land along the Mississippi and large allotments from the infrequent shipments of slaves in the 1720s.[37] By the early 1730s, the Carrière family owned seventy adult slaves, placing them among the top 13 percent of slaveholders in the colony.[38] As Françoise Jalot Carrière was one of the eight founders of the confraternity, it is not surprising that the Carrière women were well represented in its ranks. Two of Françoise's daughters belonged, as did her sisters-in-law and neighbors Marie Marguerite Arlu Carrière Tixerant and Marguerite Trépagnier Carrière.[39]

The Carrière family's financial success, if not its dynastic strength, was surpassed only by that of the Chauvin-Dubreuil family. The area on the bank of the Mississippi River just north of New Orleans known as Chapitoulas was probably the most fertile and productive section of Louisiana Plantation country, and the Chauvin-Dubreuil family dominated it. Like the Carrières, the Chauvins were colonial protégés of Bienville, a relationship that made it possible for them to become the largest private slaveholders recorded in the 1726 census. The family owned more than 250 slaves; their Dijonnais nephew, Claude Dubreuil, owned another forty-eight. The Chauvins and Dubreuils grew indigo and tobacco, crops that were readily purchased by the Company of the Indies but required such large investments in land and labor that only well-capitalized planters could grow them profitably. By 1731, the Dubreuils, father and two sons, owned seventy-six slaves. When Madame Dubreuil joined the confraternity shortly after its foundation, she was mistress of one of the wealthiest households in the colony.[40]

Wives or daughters of four families represented the bureaucratic elite of the colony in the confraternity.[41] Membership in the upper reaches of the administration assured social status, though it did not guarantee financial security. *Confrèress* Charlotte Duval, for example, enjoyed a high standard of living that threatened to evaporate at her father's death.[42] François Duval earned an annual salary of 2,000-3,000 livres as chief book-keeper for the Company of the Indies and amassed what appears to have been considerable property with his modest earnings. In 1727, he owned three slaves who served the family, and a city map drawn in 1731 identifies as belonging to his estate three large houses fronting on the quay, with outbuildings and formal gardens. Duval appears, however, to have been particularly susceptible to the temptations of speculation and credit that plagued the colony. At his death in 1729, he left a massive debt of 127,101 livres. Young Charlotte Duval's material comfort, if not her status, was saved only when her widowed mother quickly married a planter named Dauterive, who owned a large plantation and thirty-six slaves just outside of New Orleans.[43] The financial circumstances of other daughters of the bureaucracy were less precarious. Jacques de La Chaise, who came to Louisiana to straighten out the appalling finances of the Company of the Indies, appears to have been comfortably off. He took care to see that his daughters made good matches. One married a storekeeper with twenty slaves; the other, a scion of the wealthy Dubreuil family.[44]

Together with the major landowners who established profitable plantations with large slave labor forces, these officeholding families formed an elite that stood apart from the majority of Louisianians, who, having neither influence nor wealth, survived through a combination of entrepreneurship and endurance. Elite wives and daughters made up the largest constituency in the Children of Mary, but not the majority. Twenty-seven of the forty-three identifiable members were drawn from lower rungs of the social ladder.[45]

Six Children of Mary were wives or daughters of planters whose wealth hardly qualified them as elite, though their families helped lay the foundation of the full-fledged plantation economy of the late eighteenth century. Although most of the farms on the banks of the lower Mississippi by the 1730s used slave labor, the great majority (71 percent) had fewer than ten slaves.[46] Typical of these planters, the Dreux brothers, Mathurin and Pierre, mixed farming with small commercial ventures.

The Dreuxs stand out in early censuses because of the colorful nature of one of their many enterprises: they ran a brewery on their property on the river bank just downstream from the city limits. In 1726, the Dreuxs had the labor of two indentured servants and two African slaves. By 1731, the younger brother had acquired additional farmland on the opposite bank of the river and ten more slaves. Records of the Louisiana Superior Council are laced with references to the Dreuxs' entrepreneurship. In 1723, they traded boat for copper specie and free freightage and were involved in the contested brokerage of 835 pounds of bread. They were accused of trying to sell merchandise belonging to someone else in 1725; at other times, they failed to return a "borrowed" horse, advanced the concessionaire Jean-Daniel Kolly 1,700 pounds of flour, and hired out slaves to a locksmith. The Dreux brothers were resourceful, to say the least.[47] Despite—or maybe because of—their wheeling and dealing, they seem to have attained some respect within the community. In 1729, Mathurin was named arbitrator in a case before the Superior Council. And in the early 1730s both brothers took wives, one of whom joined the Children of Mary.[48]

Two other *confrèresses* married former military men who had settled down to live as planters. Marie Baron probably joined the confraternity shortly after she married François Dumont de Montigny in 1730. Her new husband was a lieutenant in the French army and is well known to historians for his memoirs illustrated with detailed, charming depictions of farms and military posts.[49] His sketch of his farm shows a plain one-story house with a central breezeway flanked by two rooms, a barn, pigeon house, chicken coop, vegetable patch, and six slave cabins. If the drawing was indeed made in 1730, as is generally supposed, De Montigny may have engaged in wishful thinking: in 1731, according to the census, he had only three slaves. De Montigny's farm was fairly typical of those that combined subsistence agriculture with cultivation of a staple crop in mid-eighteenth-century Louisiana. The material and social circumstances of Marie Baron de Montigny were probably shared by five other *confrèresses* married to modest planters along the river.[50]

In the 1730s, these planter families were acquiring property in land and slaves that augmented other sources of income and brought them a degree of prosperity. Their wealth did not approach that of the Carrières or Dubreuils, nor had family dynasties begun to form. Yet they represented a cohort of middling planters who owned enough property to invest in the colony's fledgling attempts at commercial agriculture. As Louisiana struggled to identify its most profitable staple crop, these were the kinds of families that had the resources to survive the growing pains and advance ultimately to wealth.[51]

Eight members of the confraternity were wives or daughters of professional men, artisans, and military officers who had earned enough working in the city to purchase at least one slave. Among them were a carpenter, a goldsmith, a gunner, and two attorneys with their fingers in multiple entrepreneurial pies. The carpenter, Pierre Thomelain, a hardworking, responsible tradesman who developed a solid business in Louisiana, is probably representative of this group. In 1727, he married founding *confrèress* Geneviève Caron, a widow, and with his marriage came increased wealth. In the census of 1726, the year he held the contract to weatherboard the parish church, he had no slaves; by 1732 he had acquired five, more than any other carpenter in the colony.[52] Thomelain's acquisition of slaves must have enabled him to expand his business, yet there is no indication that he lived a luxurious life. One the contrary, when he and his wife bought a house for her daughter and son-in-law in 1737, they paid 200 livres, enough for only the most basic dwelling. His own house, on Chartres Street across from the military storehouses and barracks, was a small building on a small lot. Yet Thomelain was respected enough in 1735 to be named guardian of a young orphan of means, whom he placed as a boarder at the Ursuline convent.[53]

Others of this small slaveowning group emerge less clearly from the historical record. Founding *confrèress* Servanne Edmé Banville Fabre was married to a gunner, Maximin Fabre, who had acquired a house on Royal Street and one slave by 1732. Servanne's mother, also a founder, lived with them.[54] Marie Françoise Hero married Louis Drouillon, the son of a tailor, who came to Louisiana in 1720 as a worker for an absentee planter. The couple were apparently married at the colony's remote Arkansas outpost several hundred miles north of New Orleans, later had a farm at Natchez, and in 1732 appeared in New Orleans, perhaps refugees from the Natchez Indian uprising of 1729. We do not know how this former farmer made his living and acquired a house and one slave in the early 1730s.[55]

This group of urban slaveowners managed to escape the poverty that characterized the lives of most settlers. They had come to Louisiana without benefit of Governor Bienville's favoritism or Old World wealth, but by plying their trades and making the most of opportunities that arose as the colony developed, they survived, and achieved respectability. By contrast, many members of the confraternity, like most of the struggling population of Louisiana, did not own slaves. Their lives were marked by humble origins, simple trades, and a tenuous hold on material security. Without bondpeople to ease their labor or increase their chances for material success, they experienced the full brunt of the harshness of early colonial life.

Confrèress Marie Lepron married Jacques Sautier, a carpenter, in 1730. Sautier's circumstances were marginal: in 1729, he was evicted from a house for failure to meet the terms of sale.[56] Madam Brantan was married to a gunsmith who made a salary of 400 livres and had to borrow 200 livres in 1725 for his wedding expenses. He still owed the money in 1732.[57] Marie Ann Bunel's husband was Guillaume Fauché, a nail maker. They and their child lived in a small house on the edge of town, looking out into swampy woods.[58] The family of *confrèress* La Prairie took in an orphan, perhaps because they needed the ration from the stores of the Company of the Indies that was allocated to families that sheltered such children.[59] The widow La Violette lived in a rented house on Royal Street, so desperate for money in 1735 that she attempted to collect on a promissory note of 350 livres from the estate of a colonist who had died twenty years before.[60]

One section of the confraternity roster stands apart. About two-thirds of the way through the listing, nine names appear without the deferential "Mlle." and "Mme." that precede all the others. Only three are traceable. Anne Dimanche was a widow who boarded with a family on Chartres Street. Orphans Catherine Henri and Suzanne Marchand lived at the Ursuline convent.[61] Although orphans were a common object of religious charity, Ursuline records make their disdain for their charges plain, regularly labeling them crude and ill mannered. The nuns earned a pittance for their upkeep, which did nothing to mitigate their ill-opinion to these unruly girls, who ate and took classes separately from boarding students who paid full fees.[62] Nevertheless, two orphans surmounted their obstacles to gain admittance to the confraternity.

Three of the entries grouped with the poor widow and orphans lack even a surname; these members are simply "Marie Thérèse," "Marthe," and "Magdelaine." Perhaps they were slaves or former slaves. Sacramental records and other colonial documents of the period regularly inscribed only the given name of slaves.[63] Two women of color—their fees paid by French sponsors—were boarding at the Ursuline convent during the 1730s while the confraternity was active.[64] If two orphans overcame both their reputations for crudity and failure to make a redeeming contribution to the convent purse, it seems plausible that slaves and former slaves, who were spared such derogatory epithets and paid handsome fees, may have been allowed to join the Children of Mary as well.[65]

Despite the sizable proportion of elite women and girls in the identifiable membership and the top leadership positions of the confraternity, there was clearly room for the wives and daughters of artisans and soldiers and even for poor widows, orphans, and perhaps women of color. The Children of Mary do not seem to have recognized distinctions among social groups that dictated exclusive patterns of association. The pattern of leadership likewise suggests that social boundaries were permeable. Members elected a large complement of officers annually in an elaborate ritual held on the feast of the Conception of the Virgin.[66] At the top of the organization was the prefect, who served as a moral exemplar and presided over meetings and ceremonies. The second prefect assisted the prefect and filled in for her when she was unable to attend to her duties. The treasurer received money from *confrèress* for candles and masses and rendered a written account to the governing nun and the prefect every three months.[67] The fourth officer, the instructor of probationers, played a critical role. She taught would-be members the rules and customs of the confraternity and the prayers and responses they had to recite on the day of their reception. She made sure that aspirants were of sufficiently good reputation to be considered for membership. Because the instructor of probationers had to record the names and dates as probationers entered, the office required literacy.[68] Finally, three counselors advised the officers on confraternity business, particularly the admission or rejection of members.[69]

Even though two wealthy women, the widows Carrière and Rivard, held the offices of first and second prefect more frequently than any other member, elite members did not monopolize the leadership. The gunner's wife, Servanne Banville Fabre, served as treasurer in 1730 and second prefect the next year. Madame Thomelain, the carpenter's wife, was elected second prefect in 1732 and rose to first prefect a few years later. Two women whose families owned no slaves also served regularly as officers. Marie Lepron Sautier, married to carpenter Jacques Sautier, was chosen as a counselor five times between 1732 and 1743. Madame Brantan, wife of a gunsmith, was elected treasurer twice and also served twice as a counselor.[70]

The best general history of colonial Louisiana portrays a colony in which social distinctions were clearly drawn and carefully tended.[71] A raucous dispute in 1725 over the seating of officers' wives in the unprestigious choir loft has been taken to indicate elite sensitivity to social hierarchy and protocol.[72] The women's confraternity offers evidence of a different, egalitarian setting for social relations, however.[73] There are several possible explanations. Perhaps, as some have suggested, social and racial relations during the early phase of colonization were fluid, with allowances for close association among people of very different backgrounds and means.[74] Or it may be that the early modern women's confraternities in France observed a similar inclusiveness in their membership practices, so that the practice in Louisiana may have followed form.[75] The scholarship that portrays Louisiana society as hierarchical relies on public records and the correspondence of male clergy, with an interest, probably, in presenting an image of social order. In any case, the confraternity's records show that the organization enabled a group of socially diverse women to form a nexus of common identity around religion. Its inclusiveness pointed the way for the incorporation of people of a variety of social and racial backgrounds into colonial society.

However diverse their backgrounds, the Children of Mary agreed to uphold a common high personal moral standard. Their constitution opens with a statement that members were expected to exercise piety, not simply through prayer, but, as noted above, "by their morals, and by all the conduct of their lives." The preamble goes on to say that *confrèress* should do everything possible to avoid giving scandal by passionate swearing, "Frolics," bad speech, or intemperance. They were to remove themselves from gatherings that were dangerous or incompatible with the decorum of a good Christian.[76]

The confraternity was not a refuge for the newly repentant but a haven for the habitually devout. Two of the constitution's longest articles deal with the reception of new members. The very young, newcomers to New Orleans, and women of ill-repute were to be turned away. An aspirant had to give "long evidence of certain marks of a perfect conversion." The officers and the nun in charge of the confraternity used a three-month probationary period to get to know a potential member. If her piety flagged or her behavior lapsed and she did not respond to official remonstrance, she could be rejected. On the other hand, if things went well, she might be allowed to attend the weekly assemblies during her last month of probation and finally approved for membership.[77] Once admitted, the new member became part of a selective group that was vigilant in excluding the morally unfit. Two women porters were appointed annually to stand guard at the meeting room door to make sure that no woman of ill repute entered.[78]

In keeping with this high moral tone, the constitution prescribed a demanding regimen of devotional practice. In an era when many Catholics sustained the minimal observance, only taking communion at Easter, *confrèresses* were expected to attend mass and receive the sacrament of confession and absolution more frequently. Christmas and the feasts of the Virgin and the Sacred Heart were added to their list of obligations, and the constitution directed them to attend ordinary Sunday mass regularly as well. While at public worship, their constitution exhorted, they should exhibit enthusiasm, and the women also were to provide examples of ardent observance by adhering strictly to the abstinences prescribed by the church.[79] In addition to conscientious sacramental observance and self-denial, they undertook other devotions. They were to assemble every Sunday and on feast days of the Virgin at their meeting place in the convent for a period of silent meditation, followed by litanies, other prayers, and, apparently, a homily of some kind. If a member was unable to attend, she was required to alert one of the officers. Missing more than three months without permission or a valid excuse led to probation or expulsion. Daily private devotion was also required. Each day, *confrèresses* were to recite the rosary, a *Pater Noster*, and an *Ave Maria* and to meditate on the works of various saints.[80]

Such rigorous religious observance stands in contrast to the traditional characterization of early colonial Louisiana as an especially impious place. It is true that, during this era, attendance at mass at the parish church disappointed the Capuchins serving as ordinaries in New Orleans. Few inhabitants showed up regularly for weekly services, and it sometimes required extraordinary efforts to fill the church even on major holidays. On feast days, the attorney general occasionally raided taverns where illegal gaming parties competed with divine office for the attention of the city's men. Priests continually lamented Louisianans' lack of piety.[81] Historians, taking their cue from these frustrated churchmen, have assumed that French Louisianians were indifferent Catholics at best.[82]

The register of the Children of Mary paints a different picture. The confraternity represented a thriving, if exclusively female community of the faithful that may have been key to establishing Catholicism in the colony. If early eighteenth-century confraternities continued their role as agents of the Tridentine vision, mobilizing lay piety and focusing it on the parish, their absence in the five years of the colony helps explain Louisiana's irreligious reputation. The lack of confraternities in the early years would have hampered the Capuchins' efforts to develop a viable parish community in New Orleans. The foundation of the Children of Mary thus would have been pivotal to the church's future, because the organization provided a core of observant women pledged to attend mass and prepare the young and the enslaved to become members of the church.

The Children of Mary intended their piety to be complemented by irreproachable behavior, in keeping with their constitution's charge to set an example "by all the conduct of their lives." As noted above, confraternities were important in the era's campaign for moral order. The *confrèresses'* emphasis on morality may have been both traditionally French and fortuitously adapted to the challenges of creating social order in the raw environment of Louisiana. The *confrèresses* did not have recourse to the tools of male authority—excommunication and court-ordered corporal punishment—to redress evil or to correct bad behavior. Nonetheless, they created an organization that set a clear moral standard for more than a third of the women and girls of New Orleans. In 1728, colonial officials wanted the Ursuline nuns to use one of the rooms in their convent as a reformatory, because there were so many women leading a "*mauvaise vie*" in the city. Two years after the confraternity was founded, they notified the king's minister that there was no longer any need for such an arrangement because the colony was "beginning to be purged of some dissolute women" and those who remained were now "hiding their game so that there is no scandal."[83] No direct evidence crediting the Children of Mary with the turn-around exists, although the timing suggests they may have contributed to it.[84]

The confraternity acted in another way to imprint its values on the colony. At a time when illness was frequent and mortality high, its commitment to visit the sick was more than a nod in the direction of a traditional feminine duty. As soon as a *confrèress* learned that another member was sick, she was to notify an officer of the confraternity and then pay a visit, leading the sick woman in the customary prayers of the group. Rather than a ceremonious recitation, this was to be a genuinely pious exercise with discussion and mutual reflection on the meaning of the prayers. The ladies of the congregation were further directed to extend these acts of charity to their neighbors. If death threatened, a *confrèress* was to arrange for last rites and stay at the side of the dying person as long as she could.[85] Such an organized effort to provide vigilant spiritual comfort to the sick would have been important in helping early New Orleanians survive the physical and emotional challenges of their lives, transforming sickness and death into opportunities for spiritual growth and a demonstration of community solidarity.

Moral rectitude, piety, and tending the sick and dying, each a feature of women's confraternities in France, had slightly different resonances in Louisiana and contributed in particular ways to the unfolding of colonial society. The promise that *confrèresses* made to instruct their slaves was a New World innovation that had the potential to be uniquely influential in the religious development of the colony. "Instruction" in this context almost certainly meant catechizing, not teaching reading and writing. Mothers had been recognized as the primary teachers of Christian doctrine by the fathers of the Tridentine church. The Ursulines of France trained young women to be catechizers, and confraternities marshaled and channeled their efforts.[86] The Children of Mary represented a continuation of the early modern French tradition that made women the church's primary catechizers. At the same time, they were pioneers as they extended this responsibility in the New World to include the instruction of slaves.

This inclusion may not have seemed remarkable to the *confrèresses*. In France, a woman was responsible for catechizing her household, including servants, and in 1730s Louisiana those servants were most likely to be slaves. Louisiana's slave laws, the *Code Noir*, required masters to train their slaves in the Christian faith, to have them baptized, and to bury them according to the rites of the church.[87] Ursuline nuns undertook part of the task of preparing slaves for baptism and first communion. Soon after their arrival, they began offering free classes for Indian and African slaves, presumably to prepare them for these sacraments.[88] The Children of Mary were especially instrumental in bringing Africans into the fold. Indeed, confraternity members may have been more responsible for the spread of Catholic Christianity among Africans in early Louisiana than the priests who baptized and confirmed them. Sacramental registers survive for four of the years during which the confraternity was active, 1731, 1732, 1733, and 1744. During these years, 377 individual baptisms of slave infants or children took place. Confraternity members or their close relatives acted as godparents or owned the slave in eighty-four (22 percent) of these baptisms (see Table 1).

The census of farms of 1731 and the census of New Orleans of 1732, when used together show that confraternity-linked families in the New Orleans area composed 10 percent of slave owners over this two-year period and owned 11 percent of the slaves, while they participated in 18 percent of the individual infant and child slave baptisms.[89] The French took no full censuses between 1731 and 1763; so it is impossible to determine whether the representation of such families in slave baptisms in 1733 and 1744 was also disproportionately high, but their participation in 23 percent of the individual slave baptisms in 1733 and 30 percent in 1744 suggests that they continued to be especially observant of the directives of the church and the *Code Noir* requiring the baptism of slaves.

Group baptisms of adult slaves took place twice a year, during Easter week and at Pentecost. On these occasions, between 1731 and 1744, confraternity-linked men and women owned or acted as godparents to a total of thirty-one slaves. Although they did not participate much in group baptisms in 1733 and were absent altogether from one of the two group baptisms of 1744, they represented slightly more than 22 percent of the owners and godparents in the two group baptisms of 1732, a figure more than double their representation in the general slave-owning population. In a huge baptism of May 11, 1744, they were connected to 30 percent of the baptisms (see Table 2).

The participation of confraternity members and their relatives in adult group baptisms is perhaps even more significant than their representation in infant and child baptisms. The baptismal register refers to adult slaves as "catechumens," an indication that they received some instruction in Christian doctrine before the priest conferred the sacrament.[90] Many adult slaves, participating in the group baptisms who belonged to confraternity-linked individuals or had them as godparents may well have received instruction from Children of Mary.

No other group of affiliated individuals, including the colonial officials who might be expected to have set a public example of compliance with the *Code Noir*, participated in slave baptism as frequently as confraternity members and their families.[91] As the first generation of Africans and their children became part of Louisiana's population, organized female lay catechesis appears to have played a notable part in Africans' conversions to Catholicism. Although it is not clear that sharing the faith of their masters advantaged Louisiana's bonds-people in any way, Catholicism did dictate a different cannon for the conduct of certain relations between the races. A New Orleans official was fined for failing to give his bonds-person a Catholic burial,[92] and sacramental marriage between slaves, which appears in some instances to have influenced internal slave trading, was actively promoted by Catholic religious in New Orleans through the antebellum period.[93] If, as some have suggested, colonial race relations in Louisiana were qualitatively different from those of their English counterparts, French women's role in slave conversion may well have played a part.

The record of the Children of Mary provides a rare look at a Catholic women's social institution transplanted to the Americas. The story illustrates how the divergent paths of Protestantism and Catholicism resulted not simply in different doctrines and devotional form but also in different organizational options for women. In an article that has influenced subsequent attempts at comparison between early modern Catholic and Protestant women, Davis suggests that the two confessions adopted different responses to the problem of equality between the sexes. Protestants chose an assimilationist approach, which entails making the subordinate group more like the dominant group. The spiritual equality accorded Protestant women encouraged a congregational organization that integrated the sexes in worship and joined them in matrimony. Equal souls prayed and lived in the same spaces. Single-sex religious organizations and celibacy remained workable for Catholicism, which adopted a pluralistic approach wherein "each group is allowed to keep its distinctive characteristics but within a context of society at large that is still hierarchical." Davis avoids passing judgment as to which of the two was better for women: "both forms of religious life have contributed to the transformation of sex roles and to the transformation of society."[94]

The present study looks at how those contributions differed and how the differences have affected the historical process for each. The confraternity offered colonial Catholic women an opportunity within their culture's dominant faith, to pray and otherwise act to advance religious and social goals from their own base of operations. Convening themselves in a convent, electing their own leaders, meting out their own discipline, they worked for the public good without channeling their activities, as their Protestant counterparts did, through husbands and congregations headed by men. It may well be that Puritan women of the early eighteenth century performed similar activities and drew comparable satisfaction through a variety of other avenues, but they had no single institutional arrangement that replicated the structure and range of purposes and activities of the confraternity.

As to which of these two confessions offered the better experience to women, it is impossible to say. Perhaps the *confrèresses* who met together in the segregated feminine space of the Ursuline convent to pursue a program of prayer and action felt more empowered than Puritan women, who acted from platforms of family and church that assimilated the genders spiritually while preserving external power differentials between them. The answer, if there is one, lies at the end of a good deal more work on colonial Catholic women. In the meantime, we can say that their experience was different, and that this difference gave a large group of Catholic women a distinct role in an episode in colonial development. An explanation of how the slave society of Louisiana developed must take the Children of Mary into account and in so doing press us to think more carefully about the ways in which confessional difference bear on the intertwined histories of race and gender in the Americas.

TABLE 1
PARTICIPATION IN INDIVIDUAL SLAVE BAPTISMS

Date	Non-Confraternity	Confraternity	Total	% Confraternity
1731	88	16	104	15
1732	61	18	79	23
1733	90	27	117	23
1744	54	23	77	30
Totals	293	84	377	22

Sources: "St. Louis Cathedral Baptismal Register I" and "St. Louis Cathedral Baptismal Register II."

TABLE 2
PARTICIPATION IN SLAVE GROUP BAPTISMS

Date	Non-Confraternity	Confraternity	Total	% Confraternity
May 12, 1731	7	4	11	36
April 12, 1732	9	3	12	25
May 31, 1732	11	2	13	15
March 4, 1733	24	2	26	8
May 23, 1733	24	1	25	4
April 4, 1744	7	0	7	0
May 11, 1744	48	21	69	30
Totals	130	33	163	20

Sources: "St. Louis Cathedral Baptismal Register I" and "St. Louis Cathedral Baptismal Register II."

Notes for "'By All the Conduct of Their Lives': A Laywomen's Confraternity in New Orleans, 1730-1744"

[1]"Premier Registre de la Congrégation des Dames Enfants de Marie," 3, Ursuline Convent of New Orleans Archives, New Orleans, La. (hereafter cited as "Premier Registre"). An analysis of the deaths, arrivals, and departures chronicled in "Délibérations du Conseil," Ursuline Convent of New Orleans Archives, indicates that there were only 7 nuns at the New Orleans convent in 1730. Translations from the French of manuscript documents from the Ursuline Convent of New Orleans Archives are by the author except when noted.

[2]"Premier Registre." Entries can be fairly securely dated to the period 1739-1744. See Emily J. Clark, "'Not by Their Prayers Alone': A Laywomen's Confraternity in New Orleans, 1730-1744" (M.A. thesis, Tulane University, 1995), 44.

[3]Eighty-five women and girls are named in the membership roster of the confraternity register; "Premier Registre," 13-14. The 1731 New Orleans census lists 209 free women and marriageable girls; Charles R. Maduell, Jr., *The Census Tables for the French Colony of Louisiana from 1699 through 1732* (Baltimore, 1972), 123-41.

[4]The confraternity has been noted, but not subjected to historical analysis, in scattered instances; see Roger Baudier, "The First Sodality of the Blessed Virgin, New Orleans, 1730," *United States Catholic Historical Society Historical Records and Studies*, 30 (1939): 47-53; Joan Marie Aycock, "The Ursuline School in New Orleans in 1727-1771," in Glenn R. Conrad, ed., *Cross, Crozier, and Crucible: A Volume Celebrating the Bicentennial of a Catholic Diocese in Louisiana* (New Orleans, 1993), 211; and Jane Frances Heaney, *A Century of Pioneering: A History of the Ursuline Nuns in New Orleans, 1727-1827*, ed. Mary Ethel Booker Siefken (New Orleans, 1993), 107.

[5]Natalie Zemon Davis, "City Women and Religious Change," in *Society and Culture in Early Modern France: Eight Essays* (Stanford, 1965), 88-95; Nancy L. Roelker, "The Appeal of Calvinism to French Noblewomen in the Sixteenth Century," *Journal of Interdisciplinary History*, 2 (1972): 391-418.

[6]Anne Laurence, *Women in England, 1500-1760: A Social History*, 2 (New York, 1994), 206-07. Lyndal Roper, *The Holy Household: Women and Morals in Reformation Augsburg* (Oxford, 1989), argues that the Protestant Reformation reasserted a conservative, narrow domestic role for women.

[7]Edmund S. Morgan, *The Puritan Family: Religion and Domestic Relations in Seventeenth Century New England,* rev. ed. (New York, 1966; orig. pub. 1944), is among the earliest contributions to this body of scholarship. Others include John Demos, *A Little Commonwealth: Family life in Plymouth Colony* (New York, 1970); Mary Maples Dunn, "Saints and Sisters: Congregational and Quaker Women in the Early Colonial Period," *American Quarterly,* 30 (1978): 582-601; Laurel Thatcher Ulrich, *Good Wives: Image and Reality in the Lives of Women in Northern New England, 1650-1750* (New York, 1980); Amanda Peterfield, *Female Piety in Puritan New England: The Emergence of Religious Humanism* (New York, 1992); and Gerald F. Moran and Maris A. Vinovskis, *Religion, Family and the Life Course: Explorations in the Social History of Early America* (Ann Arbor, 1992). Two very recent general works on colonial women contain updated overviews of Puritan women: Carol Berkin, *First Generations: Women in Colonial America* (New York, 1996), 21-51; and Paula A. Treckel, *To Comfort the Heart: Women in Seventeenth-Century America* (New York, 1996), 104-07, 160-72. Bibliographic essays in both books illustrate the disproportional wealth of scholarship on Puritan women.

[8]Nancy F. Cott, *The Bonds of Womanhood: "Woman's Sphere" in New England, 1780-1835* (New Haven, 1977), is an early and extremely influential study of this type. See also Dunn, "Saints and Sisters;" Mary Beth Norton, *Liberty's Daughters: The Revolutionary Experience of American Women, 1750-1800* (Boston, 1980); Linda K. Kerber, *Women of the Republic: Intellect and Ideology in Revolutionary America* (Chapel Hill, 1980); Lyle Koehler, *A Search for Power: The "Weaker Sex" in Seventeenth New England* (Urbana, 1980); Moran and Vinovskis, *Religion, Family, and the Life Course*; and Cornelia Hughes Dayton, *Women before the Bar: Gender, Law, and Society in Connecticut, 1639-1789* (Chapel Hill, 1995).

[9]For example see Charles Warren Currier, *Carmel in America: A Centennial History Discalced Carmelites in the United States* (Darie, Ill., 1989), and Louise Callan, *Philippine Duchesne Frontier Missionary of the Sacred Heart, 1769-1852* (Westminster, Md., 1957). Representative examples of scholarship on French colonial women and religion include Marie-Claire Daveluy, *Jeanne Mance* (Montreal, 1934); and Yvonne Estienne, *Undaunted* (Montreal, 1973). Although very much in the institutional-bibliographic tradition, Mary Anne Foley, "Uncloistered Apostolic Life for Women: Marguerite Bourgeroy's Experiment in Ville-Marie" (Ph.D. dissertation, Yale University, 1991), essays some larger interpretive questions, as does the essay on Marie de l'Incarnation in Natalie Zemon Davis, *Women on the Margins: Three Seventeenth Century Lives* (Cambridge, Mass., 1995). Leslie Choquette, "'Ces Amazones du Grand Dieu': Women and Mission in Seventeenth-Century Canada," *French Historical Studies,* 17 (1992): 627-55, is a narrowly focused but interesting attempt to move beyond the biographical to other themes. The introductory essay on French colonial women in Rosemary Radore Ruether and Rosemary Skinner Keller, *Women and Religion in America,* vol. 2: *The Colonial and Revolutionary Periods* (San Francisco, 1983), provides a good but extremely brief summary of the subject. Elizabeth Kolmer, "Catholic Women Religious and Women's History: A Survey of the Literature," *American Quarterly,* 30 (1978): 639-51, is almost completely silent on colonial Catholic women in North America, focusing on the 19th and 20th centuries. The survey given by Martin E. Marty, "American Religious History in the Eighties: A Decade of Achievement," *Church History,* 62 (1993): 335-37, reveals that the recent historiography of American Catholicism is richest in 19th-century subjects.

Although the elite intellectual Mexican nun Sor Juana Ines de la Cruz commands a disproportionate amount of attention, the work in Spanish colonial women and religion ranges more broadly than that on French women. Asunción Lavrin's contribution is especially notable, as is Luis Martin's. See, for example, Lavrin, "La Vida Feminina Ccomo Experiencia Religiosa: Biographia y Hagiografia en Hispanoamerica Colonial," *Colonial Latin American Review,* 2 (1993): 27-52; Lavrin, "Values and Meaning of Monastic Life for Nuns in Colonial Mexico," *Catholic Historical Review,* 58 (1972): 367-87; Lavrin, "The Role of the Nunneries in the Economy of New Spain in the Eighteenth Century," *Hispanic American Historical Review,* 46 (1966): 371-93; Lavrin, "Ecclesiastical Reform of Nunneries in New Spain in the Eighteenth Century," *Americas,* 22 (1965): 182-203; and Luis Martin, *Daughters of the Conquistadores: Women of the Viceroyalty of Peru* (Albuquerque, 1983).

[10]Laurel Thatcher Ulrich, "Virtuous Women Found: New England Ministerial Literature, 1668-1735," *American Quarterly,* 28 (1976): 20-40, provides an especially lucid development of this argument. See also, Porterfield, *Female Piety.*

[11]Porterfield provides the fullest development of this argument in *Female Piety*, suggesting that the very patriarchal authoritarianism that appears to Koehler so oppressive may instead have been the means by which New England's Puritan women exercised substantial power. Their submissiveness acted as a reminder to men of the virtues of obedience and restraint, prompting recognition of man's own subordination to an omnipotent God. Ulrich, "Virtuous Women Found," discusses a similar but slightly later resolution of the Puritan conundrum of equal souls in unequal earthly vessels.

[12]Dayton, *Women Before the Bar*; Moran and Vinovskis, *Religion, Family, and the Life Course*, 131-34.

[13]There were exceptions. K[eith] V. Thomas, "Women and the Civil War Sects," *Past and Present*, No. 13 (1958): 42-62, documents such activities for women in mid-17th century England, and the careers of Anne Hutchinson and Sarah Osborne in New England are well known. Of the English Civil War sects, however, only Quakerism survived, and it never achieved mainstream status outside pre-Revolutionary Pennsylvania. Female preachers such as Hutchinson, Osborne, and the Baptist women of the First Awakening, always rare, were punished, censured, marginalized, and ultimately suppressed.

[14]Ulrich, "Virtuous Women Found," suggests that the Puritan solution to the disharmony between an ungendered spirituality and a gendered world was not to equalize worldly opportunity for men and women but to develop an ideology that valorized the private virtue of women, laying the groundwork for the cult of domesticity. Taking up this thread and extending it through the post-Revolutionary and antebellum periods. Susan Juster and Stephanie McCurry depict mainstream evangelicalism turning its back on its potential for redistributing church power more equitable between the sexes, reasserting instead a patriarchy that returned women firmly to the enclosure of family and dependency in a male-dominated republic; Juster, *Disorderly Women: Sexual Politics and Evangelicalism in Revolutionary New England* (Ithica, 1994), 30-31, 41-44, 86, 124-44; McCurry, *Master of Small Worlds: Yeoman Households, Gender Relations, and the Political Culture of the Antebellum South Carolina Low Country* (New York, 1996), 147, 173-95.

[15]Elizabeth Rapley, *The Dévotes: Women and Church in Seventeenth-Century France* (Montreal, 1990), 40, 44, 48, 61, 93, and passim.

[16]The Ursulines began as an uncloistered order. Although they later accepted a modified form of cloister, they continued their apostolic educational activities, bringing the community into the cloister through their schools. The Filles de la Charité and several other congregations remained completely uncloistered; ibid., 48-50, 56-60, 74-112.

[17]Ibid., 4.

[18]Pierre Coste, *Le grand saint du grand siècle: Monsieur Vincent*, 3 vols. (Paris, 1931), 1:248, quoted in Rapley, *Dévotes*, 83.

[19]On the crises of demography and poverty of early modern Europe see Olwen H. Hufton, *The Poor of Eighteenth-Century France, 1750-1789* (Oxford, 1974); Emmanuel Le Roy Ladurie, *The Peasants of Languedoc*, trans. John Day (Urbana, 1974); and Robert Jütte, *Poverty and Deviance in Early Modern Europe* (Cambridge, 1994).

[20]On printing, literacy, and the Reformation see Steven Ozment, *The Age of Reform, 1250-1550: An Intellectual and Religious History of Late Medieval and Reformation Europe* (New Haven, 1980), 199-203. Rapley, *Dévotes*, is the only book that has given the phenomenal growth of women's religious communities in 17th century France the attention and analysis it deserves. She provides a sophisticated and persuasive interpretation of the goals and attainments of the 17th-century teaching congregations, 42-73, 142-66.

[21]Kerber, *Women of the Republic*, 11, 199-200.

[22]Phlippe Annaert, *Les Collèges au féminin: les Ursulines: enseignement et vie consacrée aux XVIIe et XVIIIe siècles* (Namur, Belgium, 1992), 24-25; Heaney, *Century of Pioneering*, 13-15; Teresa Ledochowska, *Angela Merici and the Company of St. Ursula, According to the Historical Documents*, vol. 2: *The Evolution of the Primitive Company* (Rome, 1968), 155-56.

[23]William A. Christian, Jr., *Local Religion in Sixteenth-Century Spain* (Princeton, 1981), provides one of the best discussions of Trent's successful campaign to suppress local religion in favor of a universalist vision.

[24]The historiography of early modern European confraternities is extensive. Ronald F. E. Weissman, *Ritual Brotherhood in Renaissance Florence* (New York, 1982); and Christopher F. Black, *Italian Confraternities in the Sixteenth Century* (Cambridge, 1989), provide especially useful discussions of how new confraternal associations facilitated the transition from localized forms of governance to more centralized models. Philip T. Hoffman, *Church and Community in the Diocese of Lyon, 1500-1789* (New Haven, 1984), 21-23, 30, speaks directly to the rise of new confraternities in France and their connection with the Counter Reformation, as do Kathryn Norbert, *Rich and Poor in Grenoble, 1600-1814* (Berkeley and Los Angeles, 1985), 41, 58, 62, and Louis Chatellier, *The Europe of the Devout: The Catholic Reformation and the Formation of a New Society*, trans. Jean Birrell (New York, 1989).

[25]On the practices of medieval confraternities see James R. Banker, *Death in the Community: Memorialization and Confraternities in an Italian Commune in the Late Middle Ages* (Athens, Ga., 1989). On the rise of flagellant confraternities and women's exclusion from them see Brian Pullan, *Rich and Poor in Renaissance Venice: The Social Institutions of a Catholic State, to 1620* (Cambridge, Mass., 971); Maureen Flynn, *Sacred Charity: Confraternities and Social Welfare in Spain, 1400-1700* (Ithaca, 1989), 23, 132-33; and Banker, *Death in the Community*, 31, 149. Robert A. Schneider, "Mortification on Parade: Penitential Procession in Sixteenth- and Seventeenth-Century France," *Renaissance and Reformation*, 10 (1986), 134, cites a rare instance of female participation in public flagellation, though it is unclear whether it took the form of lashing one's back typical of male public ritual. The autobiography of Marie de l'incarnation, a 17th-century Ursuline missionary to New France, indicates that women did engage privately in bodily mortification during the period: Irene Mahoney, ed., *Marie of the Incarnation: Selected Writings* (New York, 1989), 60, 68.

[26]Black, *Italian Confraternities*, 35-38, 103-04; Hoffman, *Church and Community*, 114; Norbert, "Women, the Family, and the Counter-Reformation in the Seventeenth Century," *Proceedings of the Annual Meeting of the Western Society for French History*, 6 (1978): 55-63.

[27]Hoffman, *Church and Community*, 124-25, 145.

[28]Norberg, "Women, the Family, and the Counter-Reformation."

[29]Hoffman, *Church and Community*, 34-38; Norberg, *Rich and Poor in Grenoble*, 41, 58, 62.

[30]See Clark, "Not by their Prayers Alone," 45, 48-49, 54-55, 60.

[31]Choquette, "'Ces Amazonnes du Grand Dieu;'" Micheline Dumont, Michele Jean, Marie Lavigne, and Jennifer Stoddart, *Quebec Women: A History*, trans. Roger Gannon and Rosalind Gill (Toronto, 1987), 32-37.

[32]"Premier Registre," 7.

[33]The dispatches are preserved in the Archives des Colonies, Archives Nationales de France. Microfilms of the series relating to Louisiana (C 13A, C 13B, B 3, and B 4) are available at several repositories in the United States, including the Library of Congress, Washington, D. C., and the Howard-Tilton Memorial Library, Tulane University, New Orleans, La. Colonial censuses are part of this material; they are published in translation in Conrad, *The First Families of Louisiana* (Baton Rouge, 1970), 2:35-75, and Maduell, *Census Tables*, 81-97, 113-41. Manuscript minutes of Louisiana Superior Council are in the Louisiana State Museum Historical Center, New Orleans, which also make these records available on microfilm. English abstracts of the Superior Council records were published in *Louisiana Historical Quarterly* between 1918 and 1939. Sacramental records are housed in the Archives of the Archdiocese of New Orleans.

[34]The membership roster contained in the "Premier Registre" in most cases provides only the member's married name. Since women are frequently identified in colonial records by their maiden names, or in some cases by their prior husbands' names, matching the names on the roster with women identified in other sources requires a process of sifting and comparison, utilizing census tables, marriage contracts, legal records, and sacramental records. A full discussion of the methodology can be found in Clark, "Not by their Prayers Alone," 16-17.

Unfortunately, the circumstances of most confrèsses can only be inferred from those of their husbands and fathers.

[35]Information on home ownership, size of land holdings, and number of slaves by owner is provided in the 1731 census of farms in Louisiana and in the 1727 and 1732 censuses of New Orleans.

[36]Clark, "Not by their Prayers Alone," 19-27.

[37]Maduell, *Census Tables*, 114; Sidney L. Villeré, "French-Canadian Carriere's [*sic*] in the Louisiana Province and Some of Their Descendents," *New Orleans Genesis*, 8 (1969): 70-75; Marcel Giraud, *A History of French Louisiana*, vol. 5: *The Company of the Indies, 1723-1731*, trans. Brian Pearce (Baton Rouge, 1992), 274, 350; Gwendolyn Midlo Hall, *Africans in Colonial Louisiana: The Development of Afro-Creole Culture in the Eighteenth Century* (Baton Rouge, 1992), 71.

[38]According to calculations based on the "1731 Census of Farms," in Maduell, *Census Tables*, 113-22, one plantation (0.4%) had more than 100 slaves in 1731; 30 (13%) had 20-100 slaves; 37 (16%) had 10-19 slaves; and 167 (71%) had 1-9 slaves.

[39]"Premier Registre," 2, 13-14; "Records of the Superior Council of Louisiana, XVIII," *Louisiana Historical Quarterly*, 6 (1923): 130; Villeré, "French-Canadian Carrière's," 72, 75; Earl C. Woods and Charles E. Nolan, eds., *Sacramental Records of the Roman Catholic Church of the Archdiocese of New Orleans*, vol. 1, *1718-1751* (New Orleans, 1987), 41-42, 97.

[40]Conrad, *First Families of Louisiana*, 2:17, 59; Giraud, *History of French Louisiana*, 5:123, 131-32, 275-76; Woods and Nolan, eds., *Sacramental Records*, 1:87.

[41]"Premier Registre," 13-14; Woods and Nolan, eds., *Sacramental Records*, 1:22, 233; "Records of the Superior Council of Louisiana, XVI," *Louisiana Historical Quarterly*, 5 (1922): 425; "Records of the Superior Council of Louisiana, XII," ibid., 4 (1921), 523; "Records of the Superior Council of Louisiana, XV," ibid., 5 (1922): 264; Alice Daly Forsyth and Ghislaine Pleasanton, eds., *Louisiana Marriage Contracts: A Compilation of Abstracts from Records of the Superior Council of Louisiana during the French Regime, 1725-1758* (New Orleans, 1980), 23.

[42]The term *confrèress* in the "Premier Registre" denotes members of the confraternity. The nearest English equivalent term for confraternity is "sorority," whose members are termed "sisters." As this is the English term for nuns, applying the same term to members of the lay confraternity invites confusion, hence the original French term is retained here.

[43] Conrad, *First Families of Louisiana*, 1:223. 230; 2:36, 58; Gonichon, "Plan de la Nouvelle Orleans tell qu'el estoit au mois de decembre 1731," Archives des Colonies, C13, C270-275, Paris, photograph of the original and accompanying notes made by Samuel Wilson, Jr., Louisiana Collection, Howard-Tilton Memorial Library, Tulane University, New Orleans, La; Woods and Nolan, eds., *Sacramental Records*, 1:95; "Records of the Superior Council of Louisiana, XIV," ibid., 5 (1922), 97; Forsyth and Pleasanton, eds., *Louisiana Marriage Contracts*, 23.

[44]Woods and Nolan, eds., *Sacramental Records*, 1:22, 87; Giraud, *History of French Louisiana*, 5:272-73; "Records of the Superior Council XII," *Louisiana Historical Quarterly*, 4 (1921): 523.

[45]Clark, "Not by Their Prayers Alone," 27-38.

[46]See note 38 above.

[47]Conrad, *First Families of Louisiana*, 2:30; "Records of the Superior Council of Louisiana," *Louisiana Historical Quarterly*, 1 (1918): 227; "Records of the Superior Council of Louisiana, VII," ibid., 2 (1919): 335; "Records of the Superior Council, VIII," ibid., 470-71; "Records of the Superior Council, XI," ibid., 4 (1921): 338; "Records of the Superior Council, XIV," ibid., 5 (1922): 340.

[48]Woods and Nolan, eds., *Sacramental Records*, 1:131.

[49]Jean François Benjamin Dumont de Montigny, *Mémoirs historiques sur La Louisiane* (Paris, 1753), also translated as "Historical Memoirs of M. Dumont" (1753), in B. F. French, ed., *Historical Collections of Louisiana*, 5
vols. (New York, 1846-1853); Giraud, *History of French Louisiana*, 212, 450; Daniel H. Usner, Jr., *Indians,
Settlers, and Slaves in a Frontier Exchange Economy: The Lower Mississippi Valley before 1783* (Chapel Hill,
1992), 36, plates 4, 5, 6; Woods and Nolan, eds., *Sacramental Records*, 1:12, 91.

[50]Usner, *Indians, Settlers, and Slaves*, 161-63, plate 5; Conrad, *First Families in Louisiana*, 2:57-64; Maduell,
Census Tables, 113-22.

[51]Giraud, *History of French Louisiana*, 5:123-24, 127-44; Usner, *Indians, Settlers, and Slaves*, 157-61.

[52]Maduell, *Census Tables*, 123-41. It was rare for artisans to have so many slaves. The 1732 census shows that
other households with 5 or more slaves were those of colonial officials or professionals. Thomelain may have
acquired his slaves through an apprenticeship program promoted by colonial officials. Perier and de La Chaise
to the Company of the Indies, Nov. 2, 1727, Archives des Colonies, Series C13A, (hereafter cited as AC, C13A,
XX: 192v-193, discusses such a program.

[53]"Records of the Superior Council of Louisiana, IX," *Louisiana Historical Quarterly*, 3 (1920): 417; Conrad,
First Families of Louisiana, 2:37, 69; "Records of the Superior Council of Louisiana, IX," *Louisiana Historical
Quarterly*, 3 (1920): 417; Woods and Nolan, eds., *Sacramental Records*, 1:41; "Records of the Superior Council of Louisiana, XXX," *Louisiana Historical Quarterly*, 9 (1926): 289; Gonichon, "Plan de la Nouvelle Orleans;" "Records of the Superior Council, XXII," *Louisiana Historical Quarterly*, 7 (1924): 339; "Records of
the Superior Council, XXV," ibid., 8 (1925): 140.

[54]Maduell, *Census Tables*, 131; Conrad, *First Families in Louisiana*, 2:71; Woods and Nolan, eds., *Sacramental
Records*, 1:101.

[55]Maduell, *Census Tables*, 131; Conrad, *First Families in Louisiana*, 2:71; Stephen and Patricia Houin, "Drouillon Family," *New Orleans Genesis*, 28 (1989): 82.

[56]Woods and Nolan, eds., *Sacramental Records*, 1:235; "Records of the Superior Council of Louisiana, XI,"
Louisiana Historical Quarterly, 4 (1921): 357; "Records of the Superior Council of Louisiana, XXIX,' ibid., 8
(1925): 683; Conrad, *First Families in Louisiana*, 2:70.

[57]Conrad, *First Families in Louisiana*, 1:229; "Records of the Superior Council of Louisiana, XXIV," *Louisiana
Historical Quarterly*, 7 (1924): 680.

[58]Maduell, *Census Tables*, 90.

[59]Conrad, *First Families in Louisiana*, 2:73: Giraud, *History of French Louisiana*, 5:272.

[60]Conrad, *First Families in Louisiana*, 2:71; "Records of the Superior Council of Louisiana, XXV," *Louisiana
Historical Quarterly*, 8 (1925): 122.

[61]Conrad, *First Families of Louisiana*, 2:69, 154.

[62]The Ursulines were paid only 150 livres for the upkeep of each orphan, half the charge for a boarding student.
AD, 13A, XIII:21, XIV: 8. Orphans were described as being harsh-natured, ill-mannered, and rude in Lettres
Circulaire, "Private Archives 4," Ursuline Convent of New Orleans Archives, 14, 18. The plan of the convent
shows separate spaces for orphans and boarders; AC, 13A, XVII, 306.

[63]See, for example, "St. Louis Cathedral Baptismal Register I, 1731, 1732 and 1733" and "St. Louis Cathedral
Baptismal Register II, 1744-1753," Archives of the Archdiocese of New Orleans (sacramental records for the
years before 1731 and for the period 1734-1743 are lost) for conventions used in the sacramental records.
Slaves are never listed with surnames, and free men and women of color only very occasionally are identified
by surname in addition to Christian name. See also "Records of the Superior Council of Louisiana, XIX," *Louisiana Historical Quarterly*, 6 (1923): 310; "Records of the Superior Council of Louisiana XXII," ibid., 7
(1924): 515, 920.

[64]A mulatto girl was placed in the Ursulines' boarding school in 1735; "Records of the Superior Council of Louisiana, XXX," *Louisiana Historical Quarterly*, 9 (1926): 310. An Osage woman whose owner's will emancipated her in 1729 and left money for her Catholic education was also at the convent; "Records of the Superior Council of Louisiana, XI," ibid., 4 (1921): 355.

[65]Lettres Circulaires, "Private Archives 4," Ursuline Convent of New Orleans Archives, 14, 18.

[66]"Premier Registre," 10.

[67]Ibid., 9-10.

[68]Ibid., 9.

[69]Ibid., 9-10.

[70]Ibid., 281-85.

[71]Giraud, *History of French Louisiana*, 5:272-85.

[72]Carl A. Brasseaux, "The Moral Climate of French Colonial Louisiana, 1699-1763," *Louisiana History*, 27 (1986): 36.

[73]Some historians of confraternities, notable Pullan, *Rich and Poor in Renaissance Venice*, 41-45, 60-62, see early modern confraternities as key vehicles for advancing social stratification and the centralization of the state. Three factors argue against grouping the New Orleans Children of Mary with such confraternities as the Scoule Grandi that are the subject of Pullan's work. First, Pullan writes about organizations in the 15th and 16th centuries, when the tasks of state building and social adjustment were arguably different from those of early 18th-century Louisiana. Pullan's confraternities differed in two other respects: they were exclusively male, and they showed a pattern of leadership and ritual that clearly buttressed notions of social rank and stratification.

[74]See, for example, Hall, *Africans in Colonial Louisiana*, 237-74; Usner, *Indians, Settlers, and Slaves*, 8-9, 106-07, 276-77; and Peter H. Wood, *Black Majority: Negroes in Colonial South Carolina from 1670 Through the Stono Rebellion* (New York, 1974), 229-30.

[75]Some 16 of the 21 members for whom nationality can be determined came from France and the confraternity's acceptance of women from all along the social spectrum may not have been remarkable from their perspective. Until more scholarship on French women's confraternities is available it will be impossible to say how innovative or unusual the membership profile of the Children of Mary was. See Clark, "Not by their Prayers Alone," 42.

[76]Ibid., 7.

[77]The constitution indicates that probationers received scrutiny from the officers and the nun in charge and that they had to be approved by the leadership and accepted by the membership, but it does not describe a voting process such as that used to select officers; ibid., 10-11.

[78]Ibid., 9-10.

[79]Ibid.

[80]Ibid., 8.

[81]For examples see AD, C13A, II: 63-64, 226, III: 48, 389-406, IV: 189, V:49v, and VIII: 418-19.

[82]Brasseaux, "Moral Climate in French Colonial Louisiana," 27-41; Henry P. Dart, "Cabarets of New Orleans in the French Colonial Period," *Louisiana Historical Quarterly*, 19 (1936): 577-83; Giraud, *History of French Louisiana*, 66, 270, 288.

[83]AC, C13A, XIV: 8, translation by Jane Frances Heaney, Ursuline Convent of New Orleans.

[84]No other likely agents for the perceived improvement present themselves in the public record. The sole priest serving as curate in the city was returned to France in 1753 because his improprieties with drink and women had made him ineffective; ibid., XVII:10v.

[85]"Premier Registre," 8.

[86]See the discussion, pp. 775, 777 above, and Foley, "Uncloistered Apostolic Life for Women," 12-13, 26.

[87]"Le Code Noir ou Edit du Roi: Servant de Réglement pur le Gouvernement & l'Administration de la Justice, Police, Discipline & le Commerce des Esclaves Nègres, dans la Province ou Colonie de la Louisiana," 1724, Article II, Special Collections, Howard-Tilton Memorial Library, Tulane University, New Orleans, La.

[88]Heaney, *Century of Pioneering*, 60-61.

[89]"Confraternity-linked" refers to individuals related to confraternity members as spouses, parents, or children.

[90]"St. Louis Cathedral Baptismal Register, I," 25.

[91]Peter Caron and Emily Clark, "Slave Baptism in French Colonial Louisiana, 1731-1744," paper presented at the Association for the Study of African American Life in History, Charleston, South Carolina, October 4, 1996.

[92]Decision of the Louisiana Superior Council, June 14, 1738, Louisiana Historical Center, Louisiana State Museum, New Orleans. The decision ordered an official named La Pommerary to transfer the body of his late slave to the Christian cemetery and to pay a fine for her improper burial in the first instance.

[93]There is no published analysis of the practice. The following examples are drawn from the author's research on the Ursuline nuns of New Orleans. The Ursulines bought a male slave in 1758 because he was married to a female slave who came to them that year through a legacy; "Déliberations du Counseil," 44. In 1798, the nuns bought a female slave because "she might marry one of our slaves who had begged us to allow him to do so;" ibid., 81. They bought a male slave named Louis Carcie, in 1845, probably because he had married their slave Helen in 1842; ibid., 118. They bought Hèlene in 1850 because she had married their slave Michel 4 years earlier; ibid., 121, 129. Baptismal records from the Ursuline Convent Chapel for 1834-1853 show that only two of the 20 children born to slaves owned by the Ursulines and baptized at their chapel were of illegitimate birth. Together with a register of Ursuline slaves kept between 1824 and 1865 that records marriages and births, these records make it possible to reconstruct the prevalence of marriage and the stability of these families for up to 3 generations; "Ursuline Convent Chapel Baptismal Register, 1835-1837;" "Livres ou sont les noms et les année de la naissance des Négres et Négresses qui sont venus au Couvent sur notre habitation le 2nd Octobre 1824," Ursuline Convent of New Orleans Archives.
    No substantial scholarship has focused on the influence of Catholicism on slavery pre-emancipation race relations since Frank Tannebaum, *Slave and Citizen: The Negro in the Americas* (New York, 1946). Other scholars have explored a variety of factors that may have distinguished French from English slavery and race relations. Hall, *Africans in Colonial Louisiana*, xv, 239-42, attributes to Louisiana a long-standing racial openness rooted in interracial sexual liaisons during the colonial period. The essays in Arnold R. Hirsch and Joseph Logsdon, eds., *Creole New Orleans: Race and Americanization* (Baton Rouge, 1992), also propose such a distinction, citing a variety of casual factors including Colbert's policy for increasing colonial population and the immigration to Louisiana of Haitian refugees with a tradition of French radicalism in the early 19th century. Mary Veronica Miceli, "The Influence of the Roman Catholic Church on Slavery in Colonial Louisiana under French Domination, 1718-1763" (Ph.D. dissertation, Tulane University, 1979), surveys the activities of Catholic missionaries and churches with respect to slaves and slavery in colonial Louisiana but offers no interpretive analysis of their influence.

[94]Davis, *Society and Culture in Early Modern France*, 93, 94.

RETROSPECT: THE FLEUR-DE-LIS
AND THE CROSS*

Charles Edwards O'Neill

These first decades of the presence of the cross and the lily on the Mississippi have shown the policy and the politics of Church-State relations in a French colony under the *ancien régime*. Where one might have expected monolithic union, one found, in reality, diversity and complexity. Along with collaboration there was conflict, or rather there was confrontation. In colonial planning, ideals and expediency were rivals; in missiology, theology stood *vis-à-vis* nationalism; on the general social scene, the design for a spiritual New France was confronted by the lawless corruption that followed forced immigration into an unstable polity.

Ancient customs appeared, like centuries-old patronage, with such concomitant problems as the hampered liberty of the apostle. More recent ones, such as the *appel comme d'abus*, also entered the colony in various forms. In public morality, as in other times and places, the shared burden of Church and State brought them together and set them apart.

Yet a review of the history of these relations would show no real doctrinal divergence in the colony: Jansenism was not mentioned. According to the legal fiction, there were no more Protestants in the realm; however, their presence in the colony, while numerically notable, was unobtrusive. French Erastianism was as yet too close to the era of the respectful Louis XIV. The resistance between Church and State in Louisiana was more a search for equilibrium within a framework of agreement. Even in the struggle between personalities and factions, there was no party of "dévots" facing the "libertins." Each civil faction was constantly claiming the side of the angels.

To the latter-day mentality it might seem unbecoming for the State to have been so clerical-minded and for the Church to have been so political-minded. The reader of history is shocked to see the State "used as a tool" by the Church, and the Church "used" by the State; yet the more he reads, the more he feels that his very phrasing of these relations is anachronistic. Seeing that things were this way, he seeks to penetrate them as they were, although it is not easy to understand the mentality of bygone epochs. In the mind

*First published in *Church and State in French Colonial Louisiana: Policy and Politics to 1732* (New Haven: Yale University Press, 1966), 283-288. Reprinted with the kind permission of the author and the publisher.

of the period under study churchmen found it quite natural to depend upon the *roi très chrétien* in patterns unthinkable today. Yet there was a separation—a separateness that involved an intricate code or system of respect, distance-keeping, and consciousness of respective limitations. While in detail Church property might have been limited, and while precise rules for the clergy's respect for civil authorities in the sanctuary might have been imposed, a humiliation of the Church or its representatives was not formally to be thought of. Conversely, civil action in sacramental affairs, including marriage, and civil trial of those vested with canonical privilege might be contested, but a repudiation of the French king as protector of the French Church was an idea that hardly any mind of that day entertained.

With that respect and that protection went a servitude, which was most particularly illustrated when the regency decided that no bishopric would be given to Louisiana. Is it not significant that a Catholic bishop was named in the Protestant-majority, English-speaking, young United States of America before Catholic-majority, French-Spanish Louisiana was made a diocese? In studies of Church-State relations in the English colonies on the Atlantic Coast, historians have observed the organized campaign, led by Non-conformists, against the transplantation of the Church of England episcopacy into America. Theirs was a "popular" or "democratic" opposition.[1] It is noteworthy that the opposite was true of French Louisiana: there the prelacy was opposed from above by centralizing absolutism, for when the French monarchy refused to set up a see in New Orleans, one of the strongest arguments was that the bishop's authority could well turn out to be disconcerting. Even though the king would name the occupant of the see, nevertheless, the prelate would be a pole in the field of authority; the civil jurisdiction wanted no rival to its own magnetism. Precisely because of the prestige and influence attributed to the bishop in the socio-juridical structure of eighteenth-century France, it was decided that the Louisiana church should have no bishop. Paradoxically, the theoretical strength of the bishop resulted in the actual weakness of the Church. For many decades after this decision of the French monarchy, the Catholic Church in Louisiana suffered crippling effects from deprivation of its customary local administration. As Robert Graham concluded in his study of papal diplomacy, the revolutionary events of the late eighteenth and early nineteenth centuries, while apparently inflicting defeats upon the Church, delivered it from many servitudes.[2]

The Church in colonial Louisiana was dependent on the monarchy or on the companies for its financial support. However, at all times it had to seek supplements from other sources in order to survive. In return for their patronage rights and power, king and company spent very little. At a time when the Church in France was regularly paying into the royal treasury millions of livres in *don gratuit* and other "substitutes for taxes," the king's *gratifications* were infinitesimal in comparison. Moreover, in the early years of the colony, the king's promissory notes were unredeemable at the royal treasury; these vouchers offered for exchange on the market would bring less than a third of their face value. Even in the late 1720s the entire operational budget for the church establishment—

including missionaries among the Indians, pastors for the French, and chaplains with the troops, together with salaries and supplies—barely equaled the emoluments which the company paid the commandant general alone. After retrocession, the monarchy was as determined as had been the company to keep the church budget down.[3]

One would err, however, in regarding the French monarch's Gallicanism as a monster in regard to the Church. It was inimical to an extent, but it must be remembered that the Church had neither the machinery nor the funds to carry on the missionary enterprise. It was the king's ships and the king's supplies that in reality kept the missions and the missionaries alive. This was less true in the eighteenth than in the sixteenth century, but the papal ministry of missions—the Congregation of the Propagation of the Faith—was far from reaching its nineteenth-century proportions. The *patronato* of the Latin monarchies was an absolutely necessary helping hand long before and fully as much as it was a stranglehold. Gallicanism was hardly different from Hispanicism or "Lusitanism," except in language and place.[4]

One can observe in the histories of Canada that the authors are often implicitly or explicitly arguing over the role of the bishop and clergy in the colonization and development of New France.[5] Whatever may be the case for the northern colony, one can conclude that in Louisiana the clergy never obtained the influence that the prelate and priest had (or were reputed to have) in Canada. On few points was there contention between the Louisiana civil government as such and the clergy as such. However, if an individual representative of the temporal authority contended with a cleric, the latter habitually lost. When La Vente excoriated Bienville, it was the churchman who was actually recalled. When Le Maire felt a coolness between himself and the leaders of the colony, he too finally abandoned the scene. If Père Raphael exercised influence, it was to the extent of his support of La Chaise. The pastor's *bête noir*, Fleuriau, remained serenely in office. Beaubois' meteoric career never brought him the solid permanence he would have needed to wield influence. And the only prelate the colony ever got was one accorded as a joke: in 1727 the farcical "Régiment de la Calotte" named the worldly Archbishop Tencin "Primate of Louisiana."[6]

Weakened by jurisdictional indecision, personality conflicts, and rivalry among religious orders, the Church ran the risk of complete subservience. There was a significant and symbolic scene in 1728: with the clergy waiting in the wings, Commandant de Périer and Commissary de la Chaise presided over the Ursuline election.[7] Weakness, however, plagued the temporal government as well; the bicephalous structure of the colony's administration kept commandant and commissary perennially at odds. Internal division, therefore, reduced the potential authority of the leaders both of State and of Church. Instead of gravitation toward lay versus ecclesiastical authority, there was rather a tendency to pair off a lay faction leader and a clerical superior of one religious group against a similar alliance of their counterparts.

In policy, as distinct from personnel, the gradual moral rise of the population in part be attributed to clerical initiative. On the other hand, it was also to the temporal advantage of the State to encourage this improvement in the conduct of the society. Increasingly often there was mention in correspondence of the role the missionary played for the good of the State; there was, of course, little question of self-effacement of the State for the sake of the missionary.

One imponderable role of the frontier missionary was that of buffer. It is striking that during the first thirty years of French contact with Indians in lower Louisiana, although there were individual robberies and murders with subsequent punitive measures against the individual or small group, warring between Frenchman and Indian was in general prevented; indeed, the natives' own inter-tribal wars decreased. Even after the Natchez massacre a missionary could cling to his idyllic hope "that Religion may ever flourish among the savages and be the bond of an eternal alliance between them and us."[8] What the relationship between settler and tribesman would have been without the missionary, the historian, of course, cannot know.

In matters purely spiritual, the Louisiana colony never attained the religious fervor of the Canadian; indeed, while there was a formal structure which paid deference to Catholicism, the society and its political organization were wanting in depth and inspiration. One might say in retrospect that religion for the Louisiana of Louis XIV and Louis XV was a pervading, tempering influence but not a dynamic, decisive force.

In these middle years of the twentieth century several dioceses and states that were part of colonial Louisiana have been brought to the attention of the national and international press because of the confrontation of polticosocial reality and the ideals of Christian doctrine. Solomon held it proverbial that "there is nothing new under the sun," and Alphonse Karr, commenting on the nineteenth-century political scene in France, wrote two volumes entitled *Plus ça change . . . Plus c'est la même chose.* While history never really repeats itself, in July 1732 Commissaire-Ordonnateur Edme Salmon complained to the Minister of Marine that, what with the lack of French wives for settlers, the missionaries had never observed the government's prohibition against interracial marriage; indeed, the official reported to Versailles, the priests said that "there was no difference between a Christian Indian and a white person."[9]

Notes for "Retrospect: The Fleur-de-Lis and the Cross"

[1]W. W. Sweet, *Religion in Colonial America* (New York, 1951), 65-72; Anson Phelps Stokes, *Church and State in the United States*, 3 vols. (New York, 1950), 1:231-40; Carle Bridenbaugh, "Church and State in America, 1689-1775," *Proceedings of the American Philosophical Society*, 105 (1961), 521-24.

[2]Robert Graham, *Vatican Diplomacy* (Princeton, 1959), 391-92; Gustave Lanctot, "Situation politique de l'Eglise canadienne sous le régime français,'" *Rapport de la Société Canadienne de l'Histoire de l'Eglise Catholique* (1940-41), 35-56.

[3]L. Bourgain, "Contribution du clergé à l'impot sous la monarchie française," *Revue des Questions Historiques*, 48 (1890), 62-132. Tremblay to Laval, March 31, 1702, Archives du Séminaire de Québec (hereafter cited as ASQ), Lettres, N 117, 16; Tremblay to Des Maizerets, June 7, 1702, Lettres, O 38, pp. 2-3; 1711, O 51, p. 10; Tremblay to Dirs. Sem. Quebec, April 7, 1710, ASQ, Lettres, M 41, p. 5. Etat des dépenses, 1728 [by way of example], Archives des Colonies, B 43, ff. 770, 775-76.

[4]Lionel Groulx writes with measure on "Le Gallicanisme au Canada sous Louis XIV," *Revue d'Histoire de l'Amérique Française*, 1 (1947): 54-90. To compare the French monarchy's activity in Louisiana with that of the Spanish to the southwest, see the theoretical, legal study of Rafael Gómez Hoyos, *La Iglesia de América en las Leyes de Indias* (Madrid, 1961), and the classic article of Herbert Eugene Bolton, "The Mission as a Frontier Institution in the Spanish-American Colonies," *American Historical Review, 23* (1917): 42-61. Also, W. Eugene Shiels, *King and Church: The Rise and Fall of the Patronato Real* (Chicago, 1961), 77.

[5]See preface of Georges Goyau in his *Une Epopée mystique: Les Origines religieuses du Canada* (Paris, 1934), x and ff.

[6]Barbier, *Journal*, 2, 23. Goyau, *Une Epopée mystique*, 263.

[7]Goyau, *Une Epopée mystique*, 210.

[8]Boullenger to [Bienville?], April 29, 1733, C 13 A 17, f. 286 and v.

[9]C 13 A 15, f. 167.

RELIGION AND THE GERMAN COAST: HISTORY OF THE PARISH OF ST. CHARLES BORROMEO CATHOLIC CHURCH*

Albert J. Robichaux, Jr.

By virtue of their 1717 charter, the Company of the West was responsible for the building of churches in Louisiana. In 1722, the province of Louisiana was divided into two spiritual jurisdictions within the Diocese of Quebec. The principal seat of the first was established at New Orleans and the second at Kaskaskia at the Illinois. The first comprised all the country from the Gulf of Mexico to the Wabash River inclusively, whereas the second included all the upper part of the colony from the Wabash. To administer each division, the bishop of Quebec established a vicar general. At New Orleans, the vicar general was the superior of the Capuchins and in the Illinois, the Jesuits. The Capuchins of the province of Champagne offered to minister to the New Orleans jurisdiction, and on May 16, 1722, an ordinance was sent for their establishment.[1]

The first Capuchins sent to Louisiana under the jurisdiction of the bishop of Quebec were three priests, Bruno de Langres, Christophe de Chaumont, and Philibert de Viauden, and one brother Eusèbe de Chaumont. In his journal, La Harpe recorded that between September 1-4, 1722, three ships, *La Loire, Les Deux Frères* and *Le Alexandre*, brought three Capuchins and a brother.[2] Appointed as the superior was Father Raphael de Luxembourg who arrived at New Orleans on April 17, 1723.

After their arrival, Father Bruno took charge of the church at New Orleans, and Father Christophe and Brother Eusèbe resided with him. By October 31, 1722, Father Philibert was serving in the capacity of missionary in an area from Chapitoulas to Pointe Coupée. From 1722 to 1723, sixteen deaths, mostly Germans, were recorded by Father Philibert.[3]

On February 1, 1723, Father Philibert entered into the registers of the parish church of St. Louis in New Orleans the marriage of Pierre Bayer and Margueritte Pellerine. In the text of the entry, Philibert referred to himself as the *Curé des Allemands*, priest of the Germans.[4] Two weeks later, on February 15, 1723, Father Philibert recorded in the same

*First published in *German Coast Families: European Origins and Settlement in Colonial Louisiana* (Rayne: Hebert Publishing, 1997), 61-76. Reprinted with the kind permission of the author.

register the marriage of Gaspart Thilly and Elizabeth Stozle, and once again wrote that he was *Curé des Allemands*.[5]

In addition to recording the religion of the earliest German Coast habitants, the census of 1724 also provides information as to the status of the church property. Among the habitations that were enumerated at the German villages, the church[6] was described, as follows:

> No. 45. The chapel at the far end of a yard surrounded by pickets and about 15 *toises* square; a house; a kitchen at the end of the yard; a garden; a cemetery containing in all an arpent and a half. . . .

Noticeably absent from the census was the mention of the name of a priest, which suggests that the parish of the Germans did not have a resident *curé*, but was served by missionaries; however, Baudier claimed that Father Philibert was the pastor at the church of *Les Allemands*, because that is how he signed the marriage register of St. Louis in New Orleans, which recorded entries between 1720 and 1730.

Further, in his definitive study of the Catholic Church in Louisiana, Roger Baudier provided a name of the parish when he wrote that "The first church which the Germans used was not under the invocation of St. Charles, as was the later church (Little Red Church on the east bank), but was dedicated to St. John. The German Coast parish was known at first as '*La Paroisse de St. Jean des Allemands*,' and is thus referred to in the registers of the St. Louis Cathedral.[7]

A thorough examination of Marriage Book 1, 1720-1730, revealed that there was only one reference to the name of the parish church of the Germans. This reference reads as follows: *Nicolas de La Cour fils d'Antoine de La Court et de Françoise Duclos habitants de la paroisse de St. Jean des Allemands je dis St. Jean des Champs Eveché de Coutance, ses père et mère paroissien des Natchez.* In translation, the document states that the parents, Antoine de La Cour and Françoise Duclos, were residents of the parish of St. Jean des Allemands "*I meant to say*" St. Jean des Champs, bishopric of Coutances.[8] This statement, when considered in conjunction with known census records, provides positive evidence that the parents were not living at St. Jean des Allemands but instead in the parish of St. Jean des Champs, in the bishopric of Coutances.

If Baudier had studied every entry in the registers of the parish church of St. Charles of the post of the Germans and St. Francis of Natchitoches, he might have arrived at a different conclusion. In the one surviving register of the old church of the Germans, on June 23, 1743, in recording the conversion to Catholicism of Jean George Schneider, the priest wrote in the text of the document, *I, undersigned Fr. Prosper, Capuchin missionary curé of the parish of St. Pierre.*[9] Additionally, on August 7, 1744, in the parish registers of St. Francis of Natchitoches, the priest recorded a baptism for Jean Maderne, whose godmother was Marguerite Thily, wife of Thomas Leger, *habitants of the parish of St. Pierre des Allemands.*[10]

Excluding the one mention of the parish of St. Pierre by Father Prosper, the surviving register does not contain any other mention of the name of the church of the German Coast; the priest signs in other entries as "*Curé* of the post of the Germans," "*Curé* of the Germans," and "*Curé* of the parish of the Germans."

On May 28, 1748, Father Prosper recorded for the first time "I, Capuchin priest apostolic missionary *curé* of the parish of St. Charles in the province of Louisiana." In view of all the documentation presented, it is the contention of this author that the parish church of the Germans was named "Parish Church of the post of the Germans" until 1748, when it was dedicated to St. Charles.

The first evidence that the church at Destrehan was named St. Charles Borromeo was found in the 1897 Annual Report by Father Leander Roth to Archbishop Francis Janssens. In that report, Father Roth wrote the name of the church as "St. Charles Baromaeo *i.e.* Red-Church." From the time of his arrival in Louisiana in 1890, Father Leander Roth had administered to the predominantly Italian parishes of Amite, Hammond, Ponchatoula, and Kenner.[11] In 1893, Father Roth was appointed as pastor of St Mary's at Kenner, and, in 1896, the parish of St. Charles, still without a resident priest since 1877 became a mission of Kenner. Because of his ministry to largely Italian congregations, Father Roth decided to add the "Borromeo" after St. Charles, and thus, a parish established by Germans since 1723 was named for an Italian Saint, St. Charles Borromeo. After 1897, the name St. Charles Borromeo was used sparingly, for the name did not appear again until 1920 followed again in 1925, 1927 and 1928. In 1930 the name, St. Charles Borromeo appeared for the first time in the Catholic directory for the Archdiocese of New Orleans, having been listed before as Red Church or St. Charles' Red Church.[12]

Having addressed the issue of the name of the church, the next question posed was the date a resident priest was assigned. In November 1724, at the time of that census, it is certain that a resident priest was not residing at the German villages. In a February 27, 1725 letter by the Superior Council of Louisiana to the General Directors of the Company of the Indies, the members wrote:

> It is not possible for the missionaries to be able to provide themselves with wine for their masses on the six hundred *livres* in the post where there are no surplice[13] fees. They ask that the food of a servant be granted to them in order that he may serve them and aid them to carry the Holy Sacrament when it is necessary. You have the Balize, the Natchez, Biloxi, and Les Allemands that are in this situation and to whom we could not refuse to give the provisions for a servant.[14]

On May 15, 1725, Father Raphael wrote to the Abbé Raguet:

> You will judge, Sir, whether in these circumstances it would not be well that there should be missionaries established elsewhere than at the posts that the gentlemen of the Company have fixed. They put three of them at New Orleans, one at the village of the Germans, one at the Natchez, one at the Natchitoches, two at Mobile, one at the Balize, one

at the Apalachees and one at the Alabamas; but you will notice, if you please, that from the Natchez to the village of the Germans there are nearly eighty leagues by water and that in this space there are several plantations that remain destitute of all spiritual assistance. From the Germans to New Orleans there are ten leagues. This community is quite populous and a single priest could not be adequate for it. . . . Those sir, are the posts at which the Company has decided that it would maintain missionaries. It has not yet been possible to fill them all both because two of our priests have died within a year and because there are several of these posts at which it is impossible for a priest to live with what the Company gives him. Such are the posts of the Natchitoches, the Germans, the Balize, and the Alabamas where there are no altar fees to be expected both because of the fewness and because of the poverty of the inhabitants.[15]

From the two documents mentioned above, the conclusion can only be that the curate at the Germans existed only on paper and had not been filled because of a shortage of priests and the poverty of the population. On January 30, 1729, Governor Perier and De La Chaise addressed a letter to the directors of the Company of the Indies in which they wrote:

As for the payment of the five *livres* per negro, we are going to issue our decree to oblige all the inhabitants to make their declaration of the number of them that they have. As *Mr.* De La Chaise will not be able to receive them all we shall commission the curate of Les Allemands to receive those of that district and of the Cannes Brulées as far as and including the Houmas; Father Maximin, the curate at the Pointe Coupée to receive those from the Houmas to the Pointe Coupée. . . .[16]

In other correspondence by *Messrs.* Perrier and De La Chaise to the directors of the Company of the Indies, dated March 25, 1729, the purpose of the Negro tax was clarified when they stated:

If we had received the decree that concerned the capitation-tax on the negroes sooner, we should not have doubted at all that it is for the Company to build the churches and parsonages. We have made a bargain with a Canadian for that of Les Allemands. We have gone to the Choupetoulas with Father Raphael and *Mr.* Baron to see the most suitable place to put a church and a parsonage there.[17]

There is a marginal note of approval from the directors who received the memorandum in September 1729.

From a letter written on June 28, 1740, by George Auguste Vanderheck, the fact that Father Philippe *was curé* of the parish at the post of the Germans in the month of July 1732 was verified.[18] After the death of Father Raphael in February 1734, Bienville and Salmon penned a status report on the church in Louisiana, dated April 20, 1734. In the document, five posts were named as vacant, including, the Chapitoulas, the Germans, the Balize, the Natchitoches and the Natchez. Further, a description was written which stated, "with regard to the Germans, the presbytery is in good condition. There is a little hut[19] in ruin which serves as a chapel, but the habitants are too poor to have a permanent one constructed. Meanwhile, they are excited to do their best."[20]

With the death of Father Raphael, the periodic detailed reports on the status of the church in Louisiana ended. From the examination of an April 14, 1785, certified copy of the April 13, 1735, baptism of Geneviève Marguerite Le Borne, it is possible to determine that Father Pierre was the *curé*, as he performed the ceremonies.[21] From a similar certified copy of the June 22, 1737, baptism of Jacque Antoine Le Borne, the conclusion was reached that by the date of that baptism, Father Philippe had returned as *curé*.[22] On February 6, 1739, the first recorded entry in the only surviving register of the church of the Germans was signed by Father Philippe, indicating that his pastorate continued. Between March 7 and April 26, 1739, three baptisms were recorded by Father Pierre. On July 29, 1739, Father Prosper signed the baptism of Marie Francoise Le Kaiser stating that he was the "undersigned priest missionary *acting* as curé of the Germans."

Although the church registers began in 1739, the chapel described in the 1724 census was still in use. According to Baudier:

> During the administration of Father Philippe after the removal of Father Matthias, work was undertaken on a new church, this time on the east bank of the river. The church was erected in 1740 and dedicated under the invocation of St. Charles Borromeo. It was constructed of logs and remained in service until 1806, when it was replaced by a frame church. Between 1739 and 1755. Father Pierre and Father Prosper served as pastors of St. Charles Church of Les Allemands.[23]

When Baudier's contentions are compared to surviving documentation, the conclusion is reached that he committed two serious errors. Although the first church probably was constructed around 1740, it was built on the west bank, not on the east bank of the Mississippi River. This fact is documented in the "General Census of the German Coast," taken in June 1766, wherein the enumeration of the inhabitants began at eleven leagues from New Orleans[24] on the right bank at the church.[25] It is also apparent from the census that the rectory was located away from the church on the location of the old chapel adjacent to the property of the commandant, Charles Frédéric Darensbourg.[26]

A review of every baptismal, marriage, burial and abjuration that was recorded in the one surviving register of the old church failed to uncover a single reference to St. Charles "Borromeo," which was Baudier's second error. Instead, as mentioned earlier, the church, with one exception, was referred to until 1748 as the church of the post of the Germans, or simply the church of the Germans. In 1748, the reference was made to the name of the church as being St. Charles; however, the name St. Charles "Borromeo" was not found between 1748 and 1755.

For the period from February 6, 1739, through March 29, 1755, Fathers Prosper and Pierre maintained a register of baptisms, marriages, burials and abjurations of the German Coast habitants. After 1755, no records for the parish of St. Charles exist until the late

1800s. The reasons for the lack of additional registers as well as the circumstances of how the one register survived have been the subject of much discussion.

In 1753, Germans arrived from Alsace and were settled on the German Coast above the original settlers; thus began the emergence of the Second German Coast, and the need for a second parish, St. John the Baptist. Within twelve years of the arrival of the Alsatians, the Acadians were established in 1765 above the Second German Coast, in an area which became the parish of St. James. From the time of the arrival of the Acadians, their spiritual needs were administered by Father Antoine Barnabé, the pastor of St. Charles of the Germans. The first evidence that Father Barnabé served as the pastor for the Acadians is found in Item 1 of St. James Catholic Church. On the first page, actually numbered 55, Father Delacasse, Curé of St. James, recopied[27] two baptisms of Acadians that were performed in 1767 and 1769 by Father Barnabé.[28]

In 1768, Louis Judice, commandant at Kabahannosse, recorded that Father Barnabé had gone to his residence on April 25, 1768 to marry several Acadian couples.[29] By 1770, the increase in population caused the relocation of the parish church of St. Charles[30] to the east bank to the present location of St. Charles Borromeo, and the creation of the parish of St. John the Baptist.[31]

As early as 1770, a chapel was located on the property of Nicolas Vicner on the second German Coast. The chapel was described in the inventory of Nicolas Vicner as "built of posts in the ground, separated from his house, situated on the habitation, in which there are two pieces of Indian furnishings, a table of cypress wood, two old benches, a cross, three communals, and a silver flambeaux holder."[32]

On February 21, 1770, Governor O'Reilly ordered the expropriation of four arpents from a tract of land owned by Mr. Dubroc, who was single without heirs, and that the land be used for the construction of a church for the Second German Coast, St. John the Baptist Church.[33]

The early history of the parishes of St. Charles and St. John the Baptist is documented in an act of deposit in the parish courthouse of St. Charles on June 17, 1795. The documents included in the act of deposit are noteworthy in themselves as they were ordered by the governor on December 4, 1782, to be transferred by Bellile to Masicot. For some unexplained reason, the documents were maintained by Masicot for a period of over twelve years before the act of deposit was made at the courthouse. Once deposited, receipt was issued by Antoine Daspit St. Amand who turned them over to François Aimé, warden in charge of St. Charles Parish.[34]

Among the documents of interest which are referenced by Conrad[35] are:

1.   Location of the church and cemetery of the parish on the German Coast, March 28, 1770.
2.   Petition presented to Governor Unzaga for permission to sell the land of the old parish, March 28, 1770.
3.   Sale of the land of the old parish by virtue of the permission granted by Governor Unzaga, May 13, 1770.

4.   Masicot named syndic of the parish, March 25, 1770.
5.   Adjudication for the project of the new church, July 1, 1770.
6.   Certificate of the experts who accepted the work of building the new church, March 8, 1772.
7.   Petition by François Castan to Governor Unzaga for what remains due him by the parish. May 29, 1770.
8.   Copy of the old notes of the colony belonging to the old parish remitted to the treasurer by Father Bernabé, January 30, 1768.
9.   Division of the bells of the old parish between the parishes of St. Charles[36] and St. John the Baptist, January 15, 1773.

The above act was a list of important documents regarding the church's history; unfortunately, these documents were not attached and, with the exception of the one for the division of the bells, have not been located either at the St. Charles Courthouse, in the Cuban or Santo Domingo Papers, or at the Notre Dame University Archives. In response to Governor Unzaga's order to divide the bells of the old parish between the parishes of St. Charles and St. John the Baptist, two subsequent documents found in the Cuban Papers provided evidence that the order was executed. In a December 30, 1772, letter written by Father Barnabé to Belille, he stated that they have "taken down one bell for the parish of St. John the Baptist according to the order of *Mr.* Belille."[37] On the following January 13, 1773, Belille informed Governor Unzaga that "conforming to the orders which you sent me, the honor of responding concerning the division of the bells between the two parishes of this coast, I have finally ended this affair."[38]

In 1973, the parish of St. Charles Borromeo celebrated its 250th Anniversary, which included the publication of a book. A history of the parish by Dr. Isabel French stated that the new church was built on the present site of St. Charles Borromeo in Destrehan, Louisiana. In evidence, French referred to a 1770 grant of land to the church, which read: "CHURCH AND PRESBYTERE, dated March 15, 1770: witnesses, LeMesle and Brazeau, inhabitants of the German Coast: 10 arpents on the left bank, about 8 leagues (24 miles) distant from the city (New Orleans); on land formerly belonging to Rousillon, bounded above by lands of De Livaudais *fils,* below by lands of Brazeau."[39]

From the above reference, the facts are undeniable that the church of the Germans, later St. Charles of the Germans, was located on the west bank of the Mississippi, and ceased to be a parish in 1770, when the church was relocated at present-day Destrehan. With this knowledge, new questions are raised concerning the fate of the registers of the parish church of St. Charles of the Germans and St. Charles Borromeo.

HISTORY AND FATE OF THE PARISH REGISTERS OF
ST. CHARLES BORROMEO

The first recordation of German Coast residents was found on a list of burials by Father Philibert, who served as the missionary for the area from Chapitoulas to Pointe

Coupée.[40] On February 1, 1723, the first marriage of German Coast residents was recorded in Marriage Book 1 of the parish church of St. Louis in New Orleans.[41]

On May 21, 1723, the Superior Council issued a decree that:

> . . . there shall be delivered at once at the suit [*sic*] of the Attorney General of the King to the curates of the posts where there are curates double registers signed and initialed with a flourish in order to insert in them at once and without leaving any blanks the baptisms, marriages, burials, names, surnames, qualities of the parties, godfathers and godmothers and witnesses, in order that one of the said registers may remain on the spot and the other be sent at the end of each year in the office of the clerk of the Council where extracts shall be given to those who need them in conformity furthermore with the title 20 of the ordinance of 1667, a copy of which shall be put at the head of said registers on the receipt of which the former one shall be delivered to the office of the clerk.[42]

Although the ordinance of 1667 was largely ignored in Louisiana, it was followed in France where today the duplicate registers are maintained in the departmental archives and the originals are found in the municipal archives.[43]

In addition to the list of deaths recorded by Father Philibert, the marriages, baptisms, and burials of German Coast residents were found in Marriage Book 1, 1720-1730 of the parish of St. Louis of New Orleans and the copies from *l'état civil* that were found in the National Archives of Paris.[44]

The first evidence that a register was maintained at the German Coast was found among documents filed with an April 11, 1785, petition of the heirs of Genobeva Borne, including several certified copies of baptisms from the registers of the parish church of the Germans between 1735 and 1760. When a certified copy of the April 13, 1735, baptism of Genevieve Marguerite Borne was requested of Father Barnabé on April 14, 1785, he used the heading "Extract from the Register of Baptisms of the Parish Church of Saint Charles,[45] Coast of the Germans, Province of Louisiana."[46] Again, on the same day, Father Barnabé wrote a certified copy of the June 22, 1737, baptism of Jacque Antoine Le Borne, and used the same statement indicating that the extract was from a register of baptisms of the parish church.

Of the registers of the church of the Germans, later St. Charles of the Germans, only one register of baptisms, marriages and deaths covering the period from February 6, 1739, to March 29, 1755, has survived. When the former parish church of St. Charles on the west bank was closed in 1770 and divided into the church parishes of St. Charles on the east bank and St. John the Baptist on the west bank, Governor Unzaga ordered Commandant Belille to divide the bells. In his response, Belille acknowledged receipt of the order and reported that he completed the division; however, there was another matter of "no less consequence." The new parish of St. John the Baptist held that the former parish of St. Charles had "six books for church affairs" that were found in duplicate, and that they were claiming three of them. In this matter, Belille reported to the governor that he responded by saying "that is of no consequence to me to make any decisions of that affair in view that the priest of St. Charles says that he accepted these last [books]."[47]

From the April 11, 1785, petition of the heirs of Genoveba Borne, it is also possible to document that on March 11, 1760, Father Barnabé baptized Jean Baptiste Verrette, son of Jean Joseph Verrette and Margueritte Le Borne. A certified copy of that baptism was issued on January 10, 1785, by Father Barnabé, whose pastorate stretched from the late 1750s until his death in 1785. Thus, the division of the "books of church affairs" were not the church registers, but probably missals, treasury books, etc. The above petition suggests that the pastor of the parish church of St. Charles on the east bank was in possession of all the church registers.

On November 18, 1785, Jacques Masicot, commandant of St. Charles, in the presence of Etienne Deslande, syndic of the said parish, Jacques Lagroue de la Tournelle and Henry Beaufin, inventoried the personal property of Father Barnabé at the parish rectory, located at one league on the right bank of the Mississippi River from the house of the commandant.[48] Unfortunately, the inventory did not mention the church registers. In the church, the appraisers found "two large books for the usage of the church." Those books, however, were probably used for the celebration of the mass. They were not the church registers, because as late as April 14, 1785, Father Barnabé was issuing certified copies of baptisms from the period 1735 to 1760, and it is certain that the registers from at least 1735 to 1785 existed and were in the rectory at the time of the inventory.

During the period after the pastorate of Father Moni, the congregation of St. Charles was thrown into controversy with the bishop over the pastorate of Father Segura. Upon his arrival from France in Louisiana, Father Segura went to the bishop and asked for a pastorate in a rural parish. As he could not provide papers from his diocese in France, the bishop stated that he must first obtain them before he could act on his request. Unknowing to the bishop, Father Segura went to the church wardens of St. Charles and assumed the pastorate, and was supported by the latter church officials. The controversy surfaced in New Orleans newspapers when the church wardens of St. Charles stated their case against the bishop.

During the controversy, the church registers were apparently removed from the rectory,[49] as Father L. Moni went to St. Charles to obtain a certified copy of the baptism of Margueritte Melanie Hardy de Boisblanc and could not find the registers. In Baptismal Book 11 (1825-1827) of the St. Louis Cathedral, Father Moni recorded that "we, the undersigned one-time Pastor of St. Charles Parish 'Des Allemands' in this State of Louisiana, and presently vicar of this parochial Church of St. Louis of New Orleans of the same State of Louisiana, after useless efforts made to recover the Register of Baptisms of the said parish St. Charles des Allemands prior to the year 1800, which Register disappeared along with others five years ago [1821]."

After the removal of Father Segura, an assistant priest from St. John the Baptist church at Edgard, Louisiana, Father François Savine, was appointed as pastor of the church of St. Charles. Unfortunately, Father Savine's ministry was short-lived, as he died during the night of May 9/10, 1832, at the rectory. Judge Labranche, in the presence of Michel Aimé and Jean François Pizeros, inventoried the personal effects. In the dining room, the appraisers found a trunk which contained "the registers of the parish."[50] From the dining room, the trunk was carried into the bedroom. Because their purpose was to conduct an inventory of the personal effects of Father Savine, no further mention was made of the church registers.[51]

In the Notarial Archives in New Orleans, an act of deposit was recorded on January 3, 1833, in the books of Felix De Armas, Notary Public, regarding Denis Christophe de Glapion. Among the documents was a certified copy of the January 18, 1790, baptism of Christobal Glapion which was performed by Father Pedro de Velet, pastor of St. Charles, "First German Coast." In certifying the baptism on July 26, 1832, Judge J. L. Labranche wrote, "I, the undersigned Judge of the parish of St. Charles in the State of Louisiana, do hereby certify that the foregoing is a true, litteral [sic] and faithful transcript of the original act, extant on the records kept by the curates of this parish of St. Charles, which Records have been deposited at my office since the death of our late Curate F. J. Savine, by the Church Wardens of the Parish of St. Charles."[52]

As Father Savine had died in May 1832, and Judge Labranche issued a certified copy of a 1790 baptism in July 1832, it is possible to document that the registers prior to 1832 were still in existence and in the care of Judge Jean Louis Labranche. After the death of Father Savine, the pastorate was vacant for a period of several years. Records of the Archdiocese of New Orleans do not indicate the appointment of a successor until 1835 when Father Auguste de Angelis assumed the pastorate at St. Charles.

Thus far, the last mention of the registers that has been found in a reference was the 1833 Act of Deposit in the Notarial Archives in New Orleans. Previously, the prevailing thought had been that all church registers, except for the one dated from February 6, 1739, to March 29, 1755, were destroyed in a fire in 1877. In 1976, this author discovered a June 1, 1877, letter by Archbishop N. Perche to the inhabitants of the archdiocese which appeared in the Sunday, June 3, 1877, issue of *The Morning Star and Catholic Messenger,* a predecessor of the present-day *Clarion Herald.*[53] That letter read as follows:

> During the night of the 30th of May, the parochial residence of the church of St. Charles, commonly known as the Red Church, was completely destroyed by a fire, which was, in all probability, the effect of design. The Rev. Father Suriray, Pastor of St. Charles, awakened by the fire, had barely time to save any of the contents of his residence. Everything became a prey to the flames—furniture, *books,* linens, provisions. He could not even save his chalice or his breviary. Father Suriray thus finding himself destitute is authorized by us to apply to charitable persons, particularly to ecclesiastics and religious communities, for at least such things as are necessary to subsistence and to exercise of the holy ministry. We exhort all persons applied to by him to assist him.

In the above letter, this author italicized the work "books" because it was the belief of the archbishop that no books survived the fire. If Archbishop Perche was correct, then how did the register with entries from 1739-1755 survive? Beginning in the 1960s, this author has heard many accounts, all unsubstantiated, but which he will relate here.

As the church of St. Charles of the Germans on the west bank serviced the early inhabitants of the parish of St. James, the priest of the latter parish had borrowed the register and it was in his possession on the date of the May 30, 1877, fire; thus it survived. From Page 55 of Item 1 of St. James Church, the fact is known that in 1783, Father Delascase, pastor of St. James, copied two baptisms from the registers of the former church into the register of the latter one.[54]

Recently, another account was related by Charles Nolan, archivist of the Archdiocese of New Orleans. According to the version that Nolan heard, the register was discovered in the basement at the St. Charles courthouse. When one of the parishioners told the pastor that one of his church books was in the courthouse, the priest went to the courthouse and took the register, claimed it as his possession, and carried it to the parish church.

As the facts are now apparent that the old church of St. Charles of the Germans became extinct in 1770, the question should be raised as to what would happen today to the registers of a parish. With the creation of an Archdiocesan archives, in such events, the register of a church parish would he deposited there. This question can be answered by the documents included in the April 11, 1785, petition of the heirs of Genobeva Borne, which included certified copies by Father Barnabé of baptisms between 1735 and 1760. These documents indicate that after the original church of St. Charles on the west bank was closed in 1770 and divided into two parishes, St. Charles on the east bank and St. John the Baptist on the west bank, the registers were placed in the care of the pastor at St. Charles, as evidenced by the fact that the registers were in the possession of Father Barnabé in the parish rectory in 1785.

Theories aside, documents provide the only definitive answers. Thus far, the letter of Archbishop Perche states that "books" were destroyed in 1877. After the death in 1832 of Father Savine, the registers were placed by the church wardens in the custody of Judge Jean Louis Labranche. Most likely, after the appointment of Father Auguste de Angelis in approximately 1834, Judge Labranche returned the registers to the new pastor.[55] If the later occurred, then the registers were in the rectory on May 30, 1877, and were burned. As to how the one register from 1739 to 1755 survived, that mystery remains unsolved. After the fire of 1877, the first mention of the surviving register appeared in an article on the first page of the magazine section of the April 17, 1921, edition of the *New Orleans Item*, which stated:

> In 1876 the parochial residence was set afire and most of the records were destroyed. Christenings, Marriages, and Funerals from 1739 to 1755 were, however, saved.[56]

STATUS OF RELIGION ON THE GERMAN COAST

On November 24 and 25, 1724, a census conducted by Perry identified the religion of the 58 heads of households, as evidenced below:

CENSUS OF 1724[57]
RELIGION OF THE HEADS OF HOUSEHOLDS

Village	Catholic	Lutheran	Calvinist	Unknown
Hoffen	16	1	1	0
1st Old Village	10	4	1	0
2nd Old Village	0	2	1	0
Karlstein	0	1	0	0
Along River	17	2	1	1
Total	43	10	4	1

Of the 58 heads of households residing in the German villages in 1724, 43, or 74 percent, were Roman Catholics; 10, or 17 percent, were Lutherans; 4, or 7 percent, were Calvinists; and 1, or 2 percent, was not indicated. Among the Lutherans was the commandant, Charles Frédéric Darensbourg, who was the subject of criticism by Father Raphael, as it was the latter's contention that, "his [Darensbourg's] religion . . . was an obstacle to the conversion of several of the inhabitants who are of the same sect."[58] Although Father Raphael spoke of a promise by Darensbourg to convert, he stated, "I fear that this is only to gain time, but in a little while I shall press him so hard that he will not be able to trifle with me long."[59]

Whether through the encouragement of Father Raphael, or the enforcement of the Black Code, which was read, recorded, and published in New Orleans on September 10, 1724, Darensbourg did convert to Catholicism in 1729.[60] In a letter written on June 28, 1740, George-Auguste Vanderheck, Darensbourg's brother-in-law, acknowledged that his wife converted to Roman Catholicism in the month of July 1732; his own conversion followed in September 1732.[61] With the exception of Darensbourg and Vanderheck, the absence of registers prior to 1739 does not provide researchers with an accurate number of conversions. In the surviving register dated from 1739 to 1755, five conversions were recorded: Jean George Schneider (June 23, 1742); Jean Adam Edelmeyer (May 10, 1743); Anne Catherine Keime, wife of Jean Adam Edelmeyer (June 8, 1743); Jean George Stally (July 7, 1743); and Jean George Seffeler (April 23, 1753).

Although Father Raphael expressed concern about the Protestant faith of the commandant, Charles Frédéric Darensbourg, he also wrote of another problem at the German Coast that would continue until the 1920s, the poverty of the inhabitants and their inability to support a parish. As early as February 27, 1725, members of the Superior Council addressed a letter to the General Directors of the Company of the Indies, in which they stated that the missionaries at several post, including *Les Allemands,* were having difficulty providing wine for the celebration of the mass.[62] On May 15, 1725, Father Raphael wrote to the Abbé Raguet that the pastorate at the Germans could not be filled because "there are no altar fees to be expected both because of the fewness and because of the poverty of the inhabitants."[63]

In a status report on the Church in Louisiana, dated April 20, 1734, Messrs. Bienville and Salmon described the condition of the church at the Germans as being "a little hut in ruin which serves as a chapel, but the habitants are too poor to have a permanent one constructed."[64]

After the death of Father Raphael, there is a cessation of the detailed status reports on the Church in Louisiana, specifically for the German Coast. Not until the establishment of the Bishopric of Louisiana and the appointment of Father Sebastian Flavian de Besançon do reports exist describing the status of the Church and religion on the German Coast. On December 29, 1795, Father Besançon wrote Bishop Penalver that, in the year 1794, of all the souls over 15 years, only 8 had fulfilled their obligations to the Church (the total population, all Catholic, was reported to be 2,232). In providing his superior with an explanation, Besançon reported that nearly two-thirds of the population of his parish resided on the west bank and that they lacked the pirogues to cross the river to fulfill their religious duties.[65]

In reporting the revenues of the church, Besançon stated that the only income was from the rental of pews and that was fixed.[66]

In a subsequent letter, Father Besançon enumerated to Bishop Penalver the "abuses" which existed in his parish, including the practice of baptizing children using the short form, not confessing before getting married, forcing slaves to work on Sundays and holy days of obligation, sending their slaves to be buried without notifying the pastor, sending their slaves for baptisms without specifying their sex, age, names of the mother, resulting in blanks in the registers, and almost never attending mass. Succinctly, Father Besançon described the status of religion in St. Charles in one word when he stated that "irreligion" is the practice in this parish.[67]

During two periods, the church wardens of the parish of St. Charles and the bishop were at odds. In 1825, during a vacancy of the pastorate, the church wardens sided with Father Segura in his dispute with the bishop. When Father Segura attempted to obtain an appointment from the bishop, he was refused until he was able to obtain the proper papers from his former bishop in France. Although Segura stated that he could, he did not. Instead, he learned that the pastorate was vacant at St. Charles and obtained the support of the church wardens, who even criticized the bishop in advertisements in newspapers in New Orleans. A committee, chaired by Father Antonio de Sedella, decided in favor of the bishop's position.

The second event was after the rectory was destroyed by fire in 1877. This dispute centered around the lack of the church wardens in obtaining a new charter. During the period from 1909 until 1918, the parish was under an interdict by the bishop, which prohibited the use of the church for the administration of the sacraments.

In 1918, the matter of the charter was resolved, and Father John Basty was appointed as pastor. In his first report to the bishop, on January 1, 1919, Father Basty described his parish as "old and delapidated."[68] As his predecessor had expressed in 1795, Father Basty also commented on the boundaries of the parish. In the latter case, the concern was not about the majority of the population residing on the west bank. Instead, Father Basty wrote that the "limits between St. Charles' Red Church and Kenner are unfair because they give to Kenner a good part of the civil parish of St. Charles settled by some 12 catholic families, renting seats in Red Church and insisting on their membership in the Red Church Congregation, to which they have a legal right of course, according the terms of land grant."[69] As a suggestion, Father Basty recommended that the boundaries of the church parishes of St. Charles and Kenner "should be the natural limits of the [civil] parishes of Jefferson and St. Charles."[70]

With the construction and dedication of a new church (the present one) and the arrival and increasing importance of the oil industry in St. Charles Parish, the Catholic church parish of St. Charles Borromeo has stabilized, grown, and prospered.

Notes for "Religion and the German Coast: History of the Parish of St. Charles Borromeo Catholic Church"

[1]*Mississippi Provincial Archives*, 2: 569-70.

[2]La Harpe, *Journal*, 213. Unfortunately, La Harpe was not specific as to which ship transported Capuchins to Louisiana.

[3]For a complete list of the burials recorded in 1721 and 1722, see Glenn R. Conrad, *The First Families of Louisiana*, 2 vols. (Baton Rouge, 1970), 2:81.

[4]*Church of the Parish of St. Louis at New Orleans, Marriage Book I*, 60, Entry No. 145.

[5]Ibid., Entry No. 147.

[6]Archives des Colonies, Series G1, Vol. 464, non-paginated.

[7]Roger Baudier, *The Catholic Church in Louisiana* (New Orleans, 1939), 71.

[8]*Parish Church of St. Louis at New Orleans, Marriage Book I, 1720-1730*, 115, No. 237.

[9]*Church of the Post of the Germans, Book I*, 23.

[10]Elizabeth Shown Mills, *Natchitoches, 1729-1803: Abstracts of the Catholic Church Registers of the French and Spanish Post of St. Jean Baptiste des Natchitoches in Louisiana* (New Orleans, 1977), 32, No. 249.

[11]Father Leander Roth was appointed pastor at St. Mary's in Kenner, Louisiana, in 1893, and the parish of St. Charles became a mission of Kenner in 1896.

[12]In 1927, Father Basty included a request in his Annual Report that his address be corrected in the Archdiocesan directory from "Red Church" in Destrehan, P. O., La., as "Red Church" was never a post office.

[13]A surplice is white garment worn by a priest, such as a tunic.

[14]*Mississippi Provincial Archives*, 2: 414.

[15]Ibid., 482-83.

[16]Ibid., 617-18.

[17]Ibid., 631.

[18]Archives des Colonies, Series C13B, Vol. 2, folio 210.

[19]As the chapel was described in 1734 as a hut in ruin, a researcher must wonder if the "chapel" was not a remnant of the Demeuves concession, as it was recorded by Le Gac that "before leaving, however, they directed the building of some huts and house with a garden for themselves. . . . " (Glenn R. Conrad, comp., *Immigration and War, Louisiana, 1718-1721, From the Memoir of Charles Le Gac* [University of Southwestern Louisiana, 1970], 7).

[20]Archives des Colonies, Series C13A, Vol. 18, folios 171-174.

[21]"Petition of heirs of Genobeva Borne, " [April 12, 1785], Records of the Cabildo, Document 2985.

[22]Ibid.

[23]Baudier, *The Catholic Church in Louisiana*, 143.

[24]The distance of eleven leagues from New Orleans is an identical reference to the lands of Taensas which was cited as early as 1722.

[25]Archivo General de Indias, Papeles Procedentes de Cuba, Legajo 187A1 (in print, see Jacqueline Voorhies, *Some Late Eighteenth-Century Louisianians: Census Records of the Colony, 1758-1796* [Lafayette, La., 1973]). The church was located above the property of Joseph Bourgeois, on land later designated Section 21, T12, S. R. 20, South Eastern District of La. West of the Mississippi River (Louisiana State Land Office, Baton Rouge, La.).

[26]Ibid.

[27]Father Delacasse presumably copied the two baptisms from the registers of St. Charles of the Germans, which are no longer in existence.

[28]Item 1, p. 55, Department of Archives, St. James Catholic Church, Diocese of Baton Rouge, St. James, La.

[29]Archivo General de Indias, Papeles Procedentes de Cuba, Legajo 187A1, folios 100-101.

[30]The location of the first church of St. Charles of the post of the Germans can be determined by a December 26, 1780, act passed before Pierre de Vaugine, commandant at Natchitoches, whereby Barbe Pommier, wife of deceased Michel Cheletre, gave power of attorney to Pierre Baillot, her son-in-law, to sell property with buildings at the Germans bounded on one side by Monsieur Darensbourg (Charles Darensbourg, *fils*) and on the other by the former church.

[31]This author is certain that the name in 1770 was St. Charles, not St. Charles Borromeo. Considering that the population was predominantly German, it is doubtful that they would have named a church for an Italian saint.

[32]"Inventory of Nicholas Vicner," [July 23, 1772], trans. by the late Earlene Zeringue, St. John the Baptist Courthouse.

[33]Archivo General de Indias, Papeles Procedentes de Cuba, Legajo 189-1. A translation of the document reads: "We the Captain General and Governor of the Province of Louisiana, on account of the representations which have been made to us by the inhabitants of the German Settlement of St. John through Mr. Michel Poché, in the name of said inhabitants the papers of which are in the files of the Government, order that there shall be taken four arpents from the land belonging to Sr. DuBroc for the purpose of building a church, the said DuBroc being alone and without family and having twelve arpents of land, will have cleared on the eight arpents remaining to him, as much land as is cleared upon the four arpents taken for the church, and also, that he be given as many new pickets as there are old ones on the four arpents. Given in our hand in New Orleans, February 21st, 1770. [Signed] O'Reilly." (Lubin F. Laurent, "History of St. John the Baptist Parish," *Louisiana Historical Quarterly*,

7 (1924): 321.

[34]Glenn Conrad, *St. Charles: Abstracts of the Civil Records of St. Charles Parish, 1700-1803* (Lafayette, La., 1974), 260-61.

[35]Ibid., 260.

[36]The reference is to St. Charles and not St. Charles Borromeo.

[37]Archivo General de Indias, Papeles de Cuba, Legajo 189-1, folio 298.

[38]Ibid., folio 273.

[39]Isabel M. French, "The First Germans and Their Church on the German Coast in Louisiana," in *St. Charles Borromeo Church, Its People, Its History, and Its Faith* (Destrehan, La., 1973), 10.

[40]Conrad, *First Families*, 2:81.

[41]*St. Louis Cathedral, Marriage Book I*, 60, No. 145.

[42]*Mississippi Provincial Archives*, 2: 291.

[43]The fact that this decree was issued by the Superior Council encouraged many researchers to write to the National Archives in Paris requesting the duplicate copies, especially for the missing records for the parish church of St. Louis in New Orleans and the church of the post of the Germans. In the 1960s, while archivist at St. Louis Cathedral, Alice Forsyth obtained some copies of baptisms and burials for the parish of St. Louis for which the originals are no longer extant. Unfortunately, no such copies were found for the church of the post of the Germans.

[44]The copies of baptisms and burials of the parish church of St. Louis in New Orleans found in the National Archives by Alice Forsyth were included in the registers of *l'état civil*. Prior to the French Revolution, all church registers were deposited in Municipal Archives in a collection which is known as *l'état civil*, or civil records. Church registers in France after the French Revolution are still in the possession of the pastors of the individual churches.

[45]In the text of the baptism, the name of the church was not mentioned. Father Barnabé stated that the register was of the parish church of St. Charles of the Germans because that was the name in 1785 when he provided the certified copy.

[46]"Petition of heirs of Genobeva Borne," [April 11, 1785], Records of the Cabildo, Document 2895.

[47]Archivo General de Indias, Papeles Procedentes de Cuba, Legajo 189-1, folio 273.

[48]Jacques Masicot, "Original Acts 1785-1786," folio 161, St. Charles Courthouse.

[49]It is possible that the registers were removed before the controversy during a period when the pastorate was vacant. Perhaps, the church wardens did not return the registers to Father Segura, or simply provided Father Moni with incorrect information due to their mistrust of the bishop.

[50]St. Charles Parish Courthouse, Destrehan, La. (Succession and Inventory of the deceased Abbé François Savine, dated May 10 and May 21, 1832, respectively).

[51]The personal possessions of Father François Savine were sold at public auction at the Presbytery of the parish of St. Charles, close by the Red Church, on the left bank of the Mississippi at 9 o'clock on Wednesday, June 6, 1832. The notice of the sale, written in both French and English, was attached to the succession, and was the earliest mention found of the church referred to as the "Red Church."

[52]Felix de Armas, Vol. 38, folio 1, Notarial Archives, New Orleans, La.

[53]Albert J. Robichaux, Jr., "The Burning of a Parochial Residence," *L'Heritage*, 1 (1978): 172.

[54]Item 1, p. 55, Department of Archives, St. James Catholic Church, Diocese of Baton Rouge.

[55]Judge Jean Louis (J. L.) Labranche died on February 7, 1869, at his residence in St. Charles Parish (*New Or-*

leans Bee, Tuesday, February 9, 1869, p. 1, col. 6). Two inventories of his personal property were conducted. On February 12, 1869, an inventory was conducted at his St. Charles residence by T. T. Baudoin, recorder of the said parish. Included in the inventory was a "library consisting of 250 volumes valued at 75 dollars"; however, no mention was made of any church registers. On February 11, 1869, an inventory was made of his property located in New Orleans. Although a section was included which was entitled "Papers of the Deceased," no books or registers were mentioned. The only papers cited were receipts.

[56]The year 1876 is an obvious error as it is certain that the fire occurred on May 30, 1877.

[57]Archives des Colonies, Series G1, Vol. 464, non-paginated.

[58]*Mississippi Provincial Archives*, 2: 489-90.

[59]Ibid., 490.

[60]Archives des Colonies, Series C13A, vol. 18, folio 105.

[61]Archives des Colonies, Series C13B, folio 210.

[62]*Mississippi Provincial Archives*, 2: 414.

[63]Ibid., 482-83.

[64]Archives des Colonies, Series C13A, Vol. 18, folios 171-174.

[65]"Father Sebastian Flavian de Besançon, O. M. C. to Bishop Luis Penalver y Cardenas," [December 29, 1795,] Microfilm Reel 4, February 1795-February 1796, Records of the Diocese of Louisiana and the Floridas, 1576-1803, Notre Dame Archives, Notre Dame, Ind.

[66]The fact that there were revenues from pew rentals in 1794 differed from the reports in the 1720s and 1730s that stated that there were no revenues; support was dependant upon assistance from the Company of the Indies.

[67]"Father Sebastian Flavian Besançon to Bishop Penalver," [December 29, 1795], Notre Dame Archives.

[68]"Father John Basty to Bishop Shaw," [January 1, 1919], Archives of the Archdiocese of New Orleans.

[69]Ibid.

[70]Ibid.

PART IV
The Spanish Colonial Period

THE FEMININE FACE OF AFRO-CATHOLICISM
IN NEW ORLEANS, 1727-1852*

Emily Clark and Virginia Meacham Gould

On the second Sunday before Easter in 1838, Henriette Delille, a free Creole woman of African descent in New Orleans, walked the eight blocks from her home to the chapel of the St. Claude Street convent and school. She regularly traversed the distance between her house and the chapel, but this morning was special. It was the beginning of the paschal season during which adults were traditionally baptized in the Catholic church, and Delille was on her way to take part in this ancient annual ritual. Waiting for her at the chapel was a free black catechumen, fourteen-year-old Marie Thérèse Dagon. Standing with Dagon at the baptismal font was the immigrant French chaplain Etienne Rousselon, who would act that day as both priest and godfather.[1]

The biracial tableau of Marie Dagon's baptism reveals the distinctive profile of Catholic tradition in New Orleans and Delille's place in it; Delille belonged to a congregation of pious women of African descent who were pledged to the corporal and spiritual care of the city's enslaved and free women of color. The spiritual aspect of that mission expressed itself in catechizing and godparenting, and by this time Delille had demonstrated her dedication to the group's aims by sponsoring more than a dozen slaves and people of African descent.[2] While each of those sacraments would have been meaningful to Delille in its own way, the baptism of Marie Dagon held particular significance.

A young adult and a free woman, Dagon came to the sacrament of her own free will. She was almost certainly led to the act by Delille herself, as it was customary for women to act as godmother to those they catechized. The ceremony took place in a religious precinct endowed with special meaning for the free black Catholic community of New Orleans. The St. Claude Street school and convent, the sacred place where free girls of color were instructed and educated, had evolved from a century-old mission to instruct females of African descent. The baptism was enacted within a space at the heart of female Afro-Catholic tradition in the city. Finally, the participation of Rousselon as both

*First published in *William and Mary Quarterly*, 3rd ser., 59 (2002): 409-48. Reprinted with the kind permission of the authors and the publisher.

celebrant and godfather signaled a distinctive and crucial partnership between women of color and the Catholic church in the city.

Dagon's baptism manifested key features of Afro-Catholicism in early nineteenth-century New Orleans: the appropriation of Catholicism by the city's free black women, the women's determination to extend the embrace of their church, and the white male clergy's recognition of their role as partners in this mission. When Delille and Rousselon shared the role and obligation of godparenting, they enacted both the spiritual equality that existed between them and their joint commitment to the propagation of the faith. The baptism of Marie Dagon—the symbolic conjoining of a French priest and a pious woman of African descent in the sanctuary of the St. Claude Street chapel—shows the dynamic that shaped the distinctive relationship between people of African descent and the church in New Orleans and illuminates Delille's extraordinary place within it.

To understand how a woman descended from enslaved Africans came to stand as a spiritual equal beside a French priest in antebellum New Orleans, we must look back to the eighteenth century and the process of religious creolization that resulted in both the feminization and the Africanization of New Orleans's Catholic Church. In colonial Louisiana, enslaved African women and their free and enslaved descendants participated in increasing numbers and with apparently growing devotion in Catholic ritual and worship. During the four decades following the Louisiana Purchase of 1803, their numerical dominance persisted and was joined to organizational innovation. By the 1830s, a large group of free women of color, led by Delille, leveraged the importance of their numbers and their piety to win acceptance and support for the first Catholic religious congregation created by and for African-American women. In 1842, Delille and a small band of companions took the first formal steps toward the formation of the canonical order the Soeurs de Sainte Famille—the Sisters of the Holy Family. The order built an educational and charitable enterprise to serve free and enslaved people of African descent that was unique in the antebellum South.[3] The establishment of the activist Sisters of the Holy Family represents an ironic culmination of a process of religious creolization that began with the crushing blow of initial enslavement.

Henriette Delille is a unique figure in the history of New Orleans and of American Catholicism, yet she and her female ancestors also exemplify a general process by which thousands of women of African descent in New Orleans became Catholic and eventually employed their religious affiliation to transform themselves from nearly powerless objects of coercion into powerful agents. This progression was highly sensitive to the particular contours of the city's colonial evolution. The development of Afro-Catholicism in New Orleans was particularly inflected by gender and the rhythm of the slave trade to Louisiana.

The evidence suggests a process of religious creolization that moved through four stages. First, West African women, perhaps predisposed by their particular religious and social traditions and responding to a unique female ministry in colonial New Orleans, were drawn into the orbit of Catholic ritual in the 1730s and 1740s. In this initial phase, enslaved females of all ages, though a minority in the general slave population, constituted the majority of slave baptisands.[4] In the next generation, a hiatus in the slave trade to Louisiana forestalled the revitalization of African religious retention, and males came to dominate most adult group baptisms. During the second half of the eighteenth century, people of African descent increasingly assumed ritual responsibility for induction into Catholicism by becoming godparents, marking a third phase in religious creolization. The final phase was characterized by the expansion and formalization of the leadership role of black women in religious instruction and benevolence. In the opening decades of the nineteenth century, women of color dominated Catholic congregations and led propagation efforts by initiating adult enslaved women from Africa and from Protestant areas of the United States into Catholicism. African women and their descendants' long tradition of participation and leadership culminated in the organization of the Sisters of the Holy Family. In each of these four stages, Henriette Delille and her matrilineal ancestors were visible actors in the process of religious creolization, forming a line of Afro-Catholic women who led the faithful and perpetuated religious practice for more than a century.

Generation after generation, Delille's matrilineal ancestors enacted these four stages. Her first female ancestor in New Orleans arrived in the 1720s amid the first immigrant wave of Africans forcibly transported to Louisiana. Known in New Orleans as Nanette, she was Delille's great-great-grandmother. One of the hundreds of adult slaves baptized in St. Louis Church in New Orleans during the 1720s, 1730s, and 1740s, Nanette is typical of the first Africans inducted into the young colony's church.[5] The record of ritual inductions indicates that the predominance of Africans in the Catholic community and the prominence of women among them originated in these early decades, but it is only when we consider the vicissitudes in the Louisiana slave trade and the specific situation of Nanette and her daughters that we are offered clues as to how and why such a pattern took shape.

French slavers brought the first shipment of captive Africans to Louisiana in 1719, and over the next dozen years roughly 6,000 bound men, women, and children entered the colony through the slave trade.[6] Male imports substantially outnumbered females, and at the end of the 1720s there were three enslaved men for every two women. This first generation of enslaved women was significantly more likely than its male counterpart to participate in the ritual of baptism. Captive females constituted nearly half the baptisms of adult African slaves performed in the 1731-1733 period, though they represented only 40 percent of the population of adult enslaved Africans in the 1730s. A similar pattern appears among the baptisms of enslaved infants. During the same three-year period, 158 enslaved infant females were baptized compared with 127 infant males. Infant female baptisands constituted a majority of 55 percent, a figure striking in view of the normative birth rate of 104 males to every 100 females.[7]

The predominance of females in these baptismal statistics confounds simple explanations for the history of slave baptism in the city. Numerous historians have argued that Catholic baptism and other forms of Christian observance were imposed on the enslaved in an effort to exert social control. The tide of slave baptism that surged through New Orleans during the French regime from 1718 until 1763 could be attributed to anxious planters' avid compliance with the *Code Noir*'s stipulation that owners have their enslaved servants baptized.[8] Yet this is an unsatisfactory explanation for several reasons. If baptism under the *Code Noir* was intended as a tool to regulate slave behavior, it was not being promptly and efficiently deployed in Louisiana. There was often a significant lag between the arrival of enslaved Africans and their baptism; the norm was two to three years.[9] Nor was baptism successfully directed toward the bound Africans who were presumably the greatest threat to white order, that is, adult males. Finally, we find that the individuals most active in the promotion of slave baptism were not colonial officials modeling compliance with the law or major planters grappling with the management of their labor force but rather colonists associated with a religious confraternity pledged to slave catechesis. The confraternity and the women's religious order that sponsored it offer a more successful starting point for unraveling the circumstances that produced the gendered slave baptism pattern of the 1730s and 1740s.

New Orleans was unique among circum-Caribbean settlements of Catholic colonial powers in that its primary missionaries were not male priests but Ursuline nuns, members of an order dedicated to advancing Catholicism through an aggressive program of female catechesis.[10] The Ursulines were the first order of teaching nuns established in the Catholic church. Before their foundation in northern Italy in 1535, all nuns were cloistered contemplatives who conducted no ministries to the public. The Ursulines remained an obscure congregation until they spread to France at the end of the sixteenth century. In France, they grew rapidly and by 1700 counted some 10,000 nuns in more than 300 convents throughout the country. Their apostolate was a radical departure from past practice in several ways. It advocated the propagation of Catholicism through the catechesis and education of women, recognizing the essential role that mothers played in inculcating faith in their children and enforcing a regimen of pious observation in their families. It also provided a rationale for female education and insisted that, for this program to succeed, it must not be limited to elites but extended to all women, regardless of their social standing. The Ursuline plan was to catechize all women, train them to become catechizers themselves, and create an army of laywomen, each shouldering responsibility for ensuring the future of Catholicism through her own pious acts.[11]

The universalism that transcended established social boundaries in France framed the Ursuline nuns' approach to emerging racial boundaries in Louisiana. Twelve Ursuline missionaries arrived in New Orleans in 1727 and quickly established a school with boarding and day divisions. In the spring of 1728, there were "seven slave boarders to instruct for baptism and first communion, and a large number of day students and Negresses and Indian girls who come two hours each day for instruction."[12] The nuns' project was advanced in May 1730, when eight laywomen visited the Ursuline convent and asked the nuns to help them organize a women's confraternity. Between 1730 and

1744, the pious association grew to include eighty-five women and girls who called themselves the Children of Mary. Although a significant number of the *confrèresses* were wealthy plantation mistresses and wives and daughters of the bureaucratic elite, many were drawn from the artisan and noncommissioned military classes, and some were impoverished widows and orphans.[13] Three members were listed without either the titles or the surnames with which white women were always recorded. "Marie Thérèse," "Marthe," and "Magdelaine" were almost certainly women of color and may have been slaves.[14]

The confraternity adopted a formal constitution, in which members pledged to honor the Virgin "not by their prayers alone, but by their morals, and by all the conduct of their lives." This promise was defined later in the constitution with some precision. "*Confrèresses*," it stipulated, "should have a special zeal for . . . the instruction of their children and their slaves."[15] An analysis of sacramental records available for the years the confraternity was active shows that these laywomen acted on their constitutional promise. In the 1730s and 1740s, *confrèresses* and their families were more involved in sponsoring slave baptism than any other group in colonial New Orleans and in numbers disproportionate to their representation in the slave-owning population as a whole.[16]

Nanette, the African captive who was Delille's ancestor, was destined to become an object of the female campaign of catechesis mounted by the Children of Mary. Nanette's service as a domestic in the household of the wealthy planter Claude Joseph Dubreuil brought her into intimate contact with two women who were among the more aggressive Children of Mary. Both Dubreuil's wife, Marie Payen Dubreuil, and his daughter-in-law Felicité de la Chaise Dubreuil were members of the confraternity.[17] The sacramental records of the 1730s and 1740s—peppered with the names of Dubreuil family bondspeople—bear witness to the Dubreuil women's zeal. Few of the Dubreuils' adult African slaves or their children were ignored—or spared. Indeed, Marie Payen and Félicité set the standard for their kin. Monsieur Dubreuil, his two sons, and his grandchildren frequently stood as godparents to adult slaves and their infants, both inside and outside their own households.[18]

Nanette's membership in the Dubreuil household explains her exposure to female Catholic catechetical efforts but does not speak to the nature of her response to it. She may simply have capitulated to the Dubreuil *confrèresses'* imprecations or demands, judging resistance to be either futile, dangerous, or disadvantageous. In such circumstances, the likelihood of choice and agency in her baptism would have been minimal and the female nature of evangelization of no significance. Some evidence related to the specific nature of the slave trade to Louisiana, however, suggests an alternate reading.

The first significant immigration of captive Africans that brought Nanette to Louisiana was distinguished by the preponderance of Senegambians. Of the approximately 6,000 Africans carried to Louisiana between 1719 and 1731, some 4,000 originally inhabited the territory in West Africa lying between the Senegal and the

Gambia Rivers and stretching from the inland headwaters of the rivers to the Atlantic littoral. There is good reason to assume that Nanette, like many of the captive women brought to Louisiana, was a member of the coastal Wolof ethnic group. Generally, slave traders acquired their male captives from inland territories, but they preferred women taken from the littoral. Coastal women, exposed through trade to European language and culture, were thought better suited for domestic service than less cosmopolitan inland women. At the same time, inland women lacked the strength that made their male compatriots attractive as field laborers.[19] Among the French, coastal Wolof women were particularly favored for domestic service and intimate companionship in both Africa and the American colonies. The eighteenth-century French missionary Jean Baptiste Labat recounts that Frenchmen living in Senegambia, to protect the interests of the slave trade, eschewed the colonial ambience of the fortress at St. Louis to live in huts with Wolof women. Le Page du Pratz, the overseer of the large plantation operated by the Company of the Indies in Louisiana, recommended that only Wolof women be selected for service in the home.[20]

Nanette's appearance in Louisiana during the first phase of African immigration makes it likely that she was Senegambian. Her position in the Dubreuil household as a *domestique* suggests Wolof origins. If she was among the many Wolof women who had mingled regularly with Europeans living along the West African littoral, she would not have been entirely unfamiliar with the French language and the Roman Catholic ritual pressed on her by the Dubreuil *confrèresses*.[21] While familiarity with Catholicism and French would not necessarily have inclined Nanette toward a fuller engagement with Catholicism, it could nonetheless have reduced two practical obstacles to conversion. Another feature of Senegambian womanhood in the era of the slave trade is more important to the story of religious creolization in Louisiana. Whether Wolof or not, Nanette came from a West African society in which women were sacred practitioners and mothers took responsibility for inducting their daughters into religious cults. Nanette came of age in a region where tradition dictated a gendered division of instruction and ritual initiation. In the cultures of Senegambian Africa, women took ritual responsibility for initiating their daughters, fathers for their sons.[22]

The gendered division of ritual responsibility in Nanette's African religious heritage is relevant not simply because it illuminates the roots of Henriette Delille's piety, but also because it was shared by a majority of the captives brought to Louisiana in the first stage of the colony's Africanization. Nanette bore four daughters who survived infancy to be baptized in Louisiana: Marianne in 1735, Fanchonette in 1737, Tonica in 1742, and Cecile in 1744.[23] Their baptisms and those of hundreds of other enslaved women and girls in the 1730s and 1740s likely reflects a confluence of complementary ritual traditions. The practice of maternally administered religious initiation in Senegambia harmonized with the mother-centered approach of the Ursulines and the Children of Mary. Mindful of their own cultural heritage, the first generation of enslaved women in Louisiana perhaps found in the daily female gatherings at the convent compound for catechism and the alien induction rice of Catholic baptism a way to sustain their accustomed religious roles. If so, their participation in these Christian rites represented something more than superficial acts of submission or meaningless mimicry. Their actions became, instead, the beginnings of a new religious tradition adapted to their new circumstances. Initially, their appropriation of Catholicism would have been largely performative, a constellation of ritual behaviors that could be read in two completely different ways. To the enslaved African women, baptism and the female sacred space and activity at the convent could represent fidelity to central, sustaining features of their traditional religion. For their part, when the nuns surveyed the African women who came to the convent with their daughters and stayed to be baptized, they saw devout women won to the true faith. This explanation of the baptismal statistics of early New Orleans, while recognizing the power differential between the European *confrèresses* and the African objects of their evangelization, uncovers crucial elements of agency and the preservation of African cultural values otherwise obscured by the tide of apparent capitulation and conversion.

The episode of European evangelization and African appropriation that marked the 1730s and 1740s represents the first phase of the relationship between enslaved women and Catholicism. While it seems unlikely that the adult women who were baptized in the 1720s, 1730s, and 1740s initially experienced conversion to Christian belief, factors operating within both the European and the African communities supported the growth of religious practice among enslaved women and paved the way for belief to follow. A hiatus in the direct slave trade to Louisiana after 1743 enhanced the influence of European forms over the African legacy and shaped the subsequent development of Catholicism among African Americans in New Orleans.

Between 1719 and 1750, much of the first generation of enslaved Africans came to Louisiana and a second, creolized generation was born. No new shipments of Africans arrived in New Orleans between 1733 and 1737, when a census was taken, and except for a single slave ship in 1743, it appears that no vessel conveying Africans directly to Louisiana arrived until after 1776, when the Spanish re-instituted the slave trade. This interval of more than three decades produced a generation of enslaved people in New Orleans who, like Nanette's four daughters, were baptized as infants and came to maturity without significant contact with adult Africans who had been untouched by Catholic evangelization. The evangelizing work of the Ursulines and the Children of Mary, with their emphasis on female participation in catechesis and religious devotion, was thus unchallenged by direct African influences during the last three decades of the French period.[24]

During this period of stasis in the slave trade and religious creolization, African mothers and their Creole daughters dominated the ranks of the city's baptisands. In the next generation, the women appear to have been influential in extending baptismal participation among enslaved males. The gender breakdown of adult slave baptism during two crucial periods in each of these two generations illustrates these trends. From

1731 to 1733, there were only two adult females for every three adult males among the city's slaves, yet women and men were baptized at roughly equal rates. The pattern was reversed during the second period, 1750-1762, when male baptismal rates outstripped male representation in the adult slave population and women's participation lagged. In eight of these thirteen years, men predominated by significant margins.

There are several possible explanations for this pattern. Men of the first generation of enslaved Africans may have resisted to greater effect than women all attempts by Europeans to evangelize them. They were physically strong and did not face the perils of childbirth, factors that lessened the appeal of the conversion as a survival strategy. And whereas the majority of enslaved women lived and worked in town as domestic servants, most men worked in the fields. This placed them beyond the surveillance of French masters and reduced their exposure to French cultural norms, especially on the larger plantations. Resistance may have played a part. The Senegambian captives who constituted most of Louisiana's laborers had a history of violent revolt both in the captivities of African coastal entrepôts and aboard ship.[25] There was also, most obviously, no male missionary program to match the effort mounted by the Ursulines and the Children of Mary. The colony's chief cleric, Abbé L'Isle Dieu, observed to the minister of the marine in 1750 that Louisiana's female slaves had grown more productive, intelligent, and well behaved under the tutelage of the nuns. In an early example of unwitting gender analysis he went on to remark that Louisiana's male slaves might be improved "if two teaching brothers were assigned to them to instruct them, cultivate their reason, and civilize their morals by the principles and maxims of religion."[26] Both Senegambians and Catholics practiced a gendered division of piety and religious induction that cut both ways for the Catholic campaign for conversion among the enslaved of New Orleans. The ministry of eighteenth-century Ursulines was restricted to women, a positive factor for the evangelization of Senegambian women who were accustomed to responding to female sacred practitioners, but an obstacle to the proselytization of men.

In the end, fewer positive incentives and an ineffective evangelizing force probably combined to retard the progress of Catholic conversion among adult male slaves. The increase in adult male baptism in the 1750s can be explained as men's voluntary submission to the wishes, injunctions, or instruction of Christian female partners. Girls born in the 1730s and 1740s were more likely than boys to have been baptized, creating a disparity in religious affiliation among young Creoles who would have become sexually active in the 1750s. The sexual unions of this generation may have been influenced by growing Christian practice as well. Sacramental marriage between enslaved people enjoyed significant growth in the 1750s: nearly a fifth of enslaved infants born in 1760 were born to married parents, compared to 12 percent in 1744.[27] Sacramental observance among the enslaved thus seems to have been advanced by both positive and negative forces. Without the arrival of fresh cohorts of enslaved Africans after 1743, the vitality of the male religious culture of the Senegambian interior would have waned, opening the way for converted women to prevail in an intimate campaign of evangelization.

Although enslaved men were baptized in increasing numbers, women of African descent continued to dominate in overall baptismal participation for the colonial population as a whole throughout the eighteenth century, usually in numbers disproportionate to their representation in the general population. In five of six sample periods (1731-1733, 1763, 1778, 1795, 1804-1805), females of African descent constituted the largest cohort of baptisands. While males of African descent consistently represent the second-largest group among the ranks of the baptized, they were often significantly outpaced by females, most notably in 1733, 1763, and 1804. Whites of both sexes never constituted more than 35 percent of the New Orleanians who joined the church.[28]

The configuration of infant baptisms suggests even more that the Ursuline female apostolate complemented the West African custom of gendered religious instruction and initiation, in each of four sample years during the colonial period, baptisms of enslaved infant females made up more than half the total, nourishing the perpetuation and growth of a feminine Afro-Catholic congregation in New Orleans.[29]

Baptism is important, but it tells us only that enslaved female Africans participated in a single rite of the Catholic church that ultimately resulted in their numerical domination of the New Orleans congregation. It speaks neither to the growth of belief nor to the ways that people of African descent employed the church as a means of advancing their own interests. Godparenting is a more reliable indication of these developments because priests required godparents to demonstrate more than a superficial commitment to the faith and because the bonds created by religious sponsorship could be turned to social purposes. Analysis of the sacramental records of New Orleans for the period under consideration reveals dramatic and sustained growth in the participation of people of African descent in this ritual function–a phenomenon that delineates phase three in our scheme.

In 1733, people of African descent, whether slave or free, served as godparents in only 2 percent of the baptisms of enslaved people that took place at St. Louis Church. By 1750, their participation had risen to 21 percent, but the most telling figure comes from 1765, which would represent the presence of the first full generation born in Louisiana, a generation whose creolization was not affected by new arrivals from Africa.[30] In that year, we see a striking jump in the frequency of people of African descent in godparenting—to 68 percent. In 1775, when the adult Creole proportion of the New Orleans slave population was probably at its eighteenth-century peak, 89 percent of the godparents of slaves were people of African descent.[31]

The most cynical reading of the growth of slave godparenting would be to see it simply as evidence of the successful exercise of coercive social control by Europeans. The cleric who remarked that the Ursulines' instruction had made the colony's female slaves "more hard-working, wiser, and better regulated in their morals" speaks volumes to the nature of the Europeans' motive to catechize their bondspeople.[32] Yet conversion was not a simple matter of imposition, nor was Christianity, once embraced, the malleable instrument of social control that slaveholders may have hoped it would be. Rather, slaves in various times and places appear to have embraced Christianity to different degrees and put it to a variety of purposes, from self-defense to armed resistance.[33]

In New Orleans, the numerical dominance of people of African descent alone exercised a form of power over the Catholic church. Clergy engaged in a demanding cycle of sacramental ceremony that offered no financial or legal reward. By the middle of the eighteenth century, the Capuchin friars who staffed St. Louis Church were called several times a week to the sanctuary to baptize slave infants. Father Eustache began the week of March 3, 1765, with the baptism of a mulatto infant, Jean Baptiste. Two days later, a Tuesday, he baptized a slave infant named François. The following Sunday, he administered the sacrament to five infant slaves and was called back to the church the next Wednesday to baptize Charlotte, another infant slave. Later in the century, the priests were called out even more frequently to baptize both free and enslaved black infants. Father Olot had little rest during the first week of May 1790. He began on Sunday, May 2, with the baptisms of Mariana, a free Afro-Creole, and Carlos, a slave. Tuesday he ministered to Honorario, a slave, and Julia Bonne, a free quadroon. The next day he presided over the baptisms of two free blacks and on Friday at the induction of a slave named Simon.[34]

Individual baptisms of infants burdened the clergy by their frequency; large group baptisms of adult slaves performed at Easter and Pentecost required lengthy and complex ceremonial effort as a succession of catechumens, sometimes numbering more than 100 stepped forward individually to receive the sacrament, each accompanied by the requisite godparents. Each baptism had to be recorded in the register, and godparents were invited to sign in witness to the promises they made. During the French period, the simple marks made by black slaves mingle with the signatures of free whites at the bottom of such entries, mute testimony to the respect accorded the slave godparents religious role, if not their civil status.[35] The Spanish clergy of the later eighteenth century ended the practice of allowing godparents to sign personally in witness of their obligation, but the demands of group baptisms remained onerous by virtue of their sheer size. At the adult baptism on Easter Eve of 1790, 112 catechumens made their way to the front in a ceremony that must have lasted hours. In some cases, the unwieldy group baptisms of the 1790s were spread out over consecutive days to ease the clergy's burden.[36]

Baptism was not the only means through which the enslaved entered and influenced the workings of the New Orleans church. Services and sacred spaces had to accommodate a large congregation of slaves. Mass would have been prolonged by the number of bound people queuing to receive communion, African voices joined in congregational responses, and black women, men, and children swelled the sections of the sanctuary reserved for their use. As the Catholic community of African descent grew to predominate, it could not have been lost on the clergy that the future and vibrancy of their mission depended on the piety of the black majority who filled the pews.[37]

Godparenting was the most formal way people of African descent laid claim to the resources and spaces of one of the city's chief institutions and made them their own. It was also almost certainly adapted to other essential functions. Enslavement resulted in a violent rupture with family and community that necessitated the refabrication of identity and social affiliation. Godparenting was an effective form of fictive kinship that helped recreate community and familial bonds, knit together the fractured polity of the enslaved, and advanced both individual and group interests.[38]

In the absence of testimony from godparents themselves, discerning the degree to which religious belief motivated them to take on the role is almost impossible. Apparently godparents at least exhibited external piety to the satisfaction of the clergy who presided over the sacrament. Catholic canon law requires that a godparent "be a Catholic who has been confirmed and has already received the sacrament of the Most Holy Eucharist and leads a life in harmony with the faith and the role to be undertaken" and take a "lasting interest in their spiritual child, and to take good care that he leads a truly Christian life."[39] As the eighteenth century advanced, those of African descent increasingly met these requirements in the eyes of the clergy of New Orleans.

The priests made their judgments on the basis of external acts, although gauging belief through behavior is difficult for any population, particularly for the enslaved. Yet, there is evidence that Catholicism and its rites did more than appease white masters and create fictive kin networks. A bondman of the Ursuline nuns, one Pierre, seems to have been anxious about the disposition of his daughter's immortal soul. Before he died in 1784, he instructed his daughter Anne to purchase her freedom from the nuns but to continue serving them and "come to die [in the convent] so that she would die like a good Christian." The piety of one woman was such that it brought the precious gift of freedom; the notarial document manumitting Julia and her three children in 1776 stated that she was being liberated because of her loyalty and love and "because she has become a good Catholic." More persuasive still of a true commitment to the faith is the testimony of the sacramental records that reveal people of African descent who acted frequently as godparents. Free blacks François and Françoise, perhaps husband and wife, sponsored four adult baptisands in 1760, 1761, and 1762. Angélique and Barthelemé, a slave couple, served as godparents in nine baptisms, sometimes together, sometimes individually.[40]

Henriette Delille's matrilineal ancestors were prominent among those who created the statistical upswing in godparenting by people of African descent in the 1750s and 1760s. During this phase of religious creolization, Delille's great-aunt Marianne and her great-grandmother Cecile sponsored numerous slaves—both infants and adults—at the baptismal font. Both women appeared regularly as godmothers throughout these decades, with a frequency that is distinctive. From an early age, Marianne exemplified a piety and devotion that history previously accorded only white women, and she did so as one of New Orleans first bound Creoles. In an extraordinary act on May 28, 1746, then eleven-year-old Marianne sponsored the adult African Victor for baptism. Victor, like Marianne, was owned by Claude Dubreuil, and Marianne may well have catechized the older man. In addition, she regularly sponsored infants born into bondage in Dubreuil's household, including Marie Anne, baptized in 1746, and Agathe, in early 1747. As she grew older, she sponsored those outside her own household, standing as sponsor later in 1747 to a male infant, Jean Baptiste, owned by colonial *ordonnateur* Jacques de la Chaise, and in 1748 to the bound infant Elizabeth. Her younger sister, Cecile, Henriette Delille's great-grandmother, also began her career as a godmother at an early age. She demonstrated her piety and devotion at age fourteen, on Pentecost Eve 1758, when she sponsored the baptism of an enslaved adult female named Therese. On two separate occasions in 1760, in May and in September, Marianne, still bound to Dubreuil, served as godmother to two separate infants. Her recently freed mother, the African Nanette, took her place as sponsor at the baptismal font in March the same year. The Creole Marianne and her African-born mother continued to demonstrate their piety among the first and second generation of the city's bondwomen, standing as godmothers in baptisms in 1765 and 1775.[41] In the actions of Nanette and her daughters we read both a homage to the West African tradition of female sacred practice passed on through the maternal line and a reflection of the female religious leadership modeled by the Ursulines and their confraternity.

Sometime after 1776, a hiatus of more than three decades, slave ships resumed their commerce with New Orleans, and in the closing years of the eighteenth century the slave population of Louisiana underwent what one historian terms a "re-Africanization." From then until the closing of the international slave trade, new Africans arrived in New Orleans in substantial numbers. Once more, Senegambians figured significantly among the forced immigrants to Louisiana.[42] The dynamics of cultural encounter and evangelization were different, however. The most effective introduction of newly enslaved Africans to Catholicism now came through a large population of Creole slaves who were second- and third-generation Catholics, as well as a substantial population of free Afro-Creoles who were active in the church.

Changes in the economy of the colony further altered the morphology of conversion by making it a largely urban phenomenon. In the last quarter of the eighteenth century, the long-struggling economy of the Lower Mississippi Valley stabilized and began to take on the familiar contours of a slave society nourished by successful staple crop agriculture. As plantation slavery matured in the region, New Orleans grew into an urban commercial center. Together, these two factors enlarged the differences between urban and rural slave communities in Louisiana. Urban blacks, whether enslaved or free, lived in close proximity to Europeans and conducted business with them as small merchants and skilled tradespeople. In New Orleans, people of European and African descent were also accustomed to sharing not only the sacred space of the church, but also the recreational spaces of ballroom, tavern, and billiard hall.[44] Like other colonial urban blacks, the Afro-Creoles of New Orleans, particularly those who were free, were economically and culturally enmeshed in a web of European behaviors and institutions, an engagement that was likely strengthened by the thirty-year suspension of the slave trade in the middle decades of the eighteenth century. The ties between European culture and the enslaved men and women inhabiting the plantations that lined the Mississippi, on the other hand, were more tenuous. The fresh infusion of religious practices that accompanied the newly arrived Africans would have found the rural slave community more fertile ground for a revitalization of traditional religion.[45] And, indeed, the majority of these newcomers was destined to join the population working on the plantations. Thus, for a variety of reasons, the re-Africanization of Louisiana brought no surge of traditional African religious repatriation for the Afro-Creoles of late colonial New Orleans. There is no evidence that the city's Afro-Creoles, bound or free, abandoned the racially integrated dances at the city ballroom for the weekly Sunday festivals of traditional music and dance mounted by native-born Africans at Congo Square.[46] Nor does it appear that Creoles of color were drawn away from the church by the reappearance of African religious alternatives. On the contrary, free and enslaved Afro-Creoles continued to bring their children to St. Louis Church for baptism, dominating the sacramental registers, and Afro-Creole women, particularly those who had gained their freedom, expanded their work of catechesis to include the African newcomers who remained in the city. The real threat to the survival of African culture that was joyfully celebrated each Sunday in Congo Square was not a local government decree that banned it, but the band of pious Afro-Creole women intent on Catholic conversion.

A close look at the adult group baptisms of 1781 reveals some interesting patterns that are typical of the late colonial period. A total of thirty-eight adult Africans were baptized that year, seventeen women and twenty-one men. Although slave women outnumbered slave men in New Orleans, among newly enslaved Africans, men substantially outnumbered women, so the male-female ratio probably corresponds to that of the population of new Africans in the city. Godparents of African descent participated in all but four of the baptisms. All four baptisands who had only white godparents were males. Nineteen baptisands were sponsored by slaves alone. Free Afro-Creoles were the next largest group of godparents, sponsoring fifteen of the baptisms. The women figured significantly, acting as godmothers in thirteen of the baptisms involving free people of color, slightly more than one-third of the total baptisms.[47]

A few speculative observations are in order. First, the association of white baptismal sponsorship with enslaved males suggests that white masters imposed the sacrament, perhaps as an aid to social control. It is also possible that some slaves chose white godparents in order to advance their status. The sponsorship of slaves by slaves can be read in two ways. Either it represents voluntary evangelization of slaves by slaves, or it suggests that white masters pressed their slaves into acting to see that new Africans accepted the sacrament. It is likely that both functions were at play. The sponsorship by free people of African descent seems less ambiguous. They of all the groups, were more likely to be acting from genuine religious motives. There were no owners pressing them to acculturate new Africans; their participation in godparenting was entirely voluntary. The numerical strength of women among these free black godparents is organic to the evolution of female participation in the church over the preceding fifty years.

Once again, Henriette Delille's maternal ancestors put flesh on the statistical bones before us. By the time re-Africanization began in the 1770s, her great-great-grandmother, great-grandmother, and great-grandmother's sister had become free women. In the years that followed, this female clan sustained a high profile as godmothers. The African Nanette and her daughters Cecile and Marianne appear time and again in the sacramental records as godmothers. In 1781, Marianne served as godmother to two enslaved infants and a free boy of color. The same year, Nanette sponsored an infant female slave.[48] Cecile's daughter Henriette Laveau sustained the tradition, appearing as a godmother in both years in the 1780s that we surveyed.[49] Whatever role fear, coercion, or expediency may have played in their initial acts of induction in the 1740s, we know from these and subsequent events that Nanette and her female descendants were ultimately led into a close and lasting association with the church. By the 1780s, these free women of color would have been familiar faces to the priests and sacristans of St. Louis Church who had seen them stand time after time beside Catholic initiates at the baptismal font.

Delille's ancestors illustrate more than the development of Catholic piety among women of African descent in New Orleans. They exemplify the growth in the city's free black population in the last quarter of the eighteenth century. Spanish rule brought an alteration in the colony's slave laws that favored the expansion of a free black community. Under the French *Code Noir*, in order to grant an enslaved person's freedom, owners had to petition the Louisiana Superior Council. Manumission could be initiated only by an owner, and it was a public act that required time, effort, and a willingness to reveal the intimate relationships between white men and women of color that sometimes lay behind such proceedings. Predictably, few masters subjected themselves to the tedious and potentially embarrassing process. Spanish slave law required only a simple, privately executed notarial act of emancipation. In the first decade of the Iberian regime, Louisiana slaveowners took advantage of the new system to free hundreds of bondspeople, most of them women and children. Although Spanish slave law also provided for *coartación*, the right of self-purchase at a reasonable price, the majority of New Orleans's free people of color gained their liberty because they were the issue of intimate interracial liaisons. Such was the case of Nanette and several of her children. Nanette, Cecile, and Cecile's daughters were freed publicly by their owner, Claude Joseph Dubreuil *fils*, in 1770. Several records relating to the emancipation of Nanette's children identify them as half-siblings of Dubreuil *fils*.[50]

Among the Afro-Creoles of New Orleans, free women of color like Nanette and her daughters were bound by both faith and blood to the Catholic church of the French colonizers. Together with the city's other free Afro-Creole women, free women of color constituted a notable segment of the population. Numbering 161 in 1777, they represented 73 percent of the free black adult population and approximately 13 percent of the total free adult inhabitants. By 1795, the number of free women of color in the city had nearly doubled to 300. The women composed 66 percent of the free colored population and 14 percent of the total free adult population.[51] In the 1780s, captives newly arrived from Africa were the primary objects of catechesis by these free black women. With the turn of the century, this situation began to change as American-born slaves from the anglophone Upper South made their way to Louisiana.

We can detect the very beginnings of this transition in the large group baptism of Easter Eve 1805, two years after the Louisiana Purchase made New Orleans part of the young American republic. African-born baptisands still predominated at this date. Ninety-two enslaved adults, nearly all Africans with their nations noted next to their names, formally entered the embrace of Catholicism on that day; many were brought to the font by free women of African descent.[52] Two-thirds of the baptisands were women, many of them adolescents. Although white men owned two-thirds of all those baptized at this ceremony, free women of African descent represented the next largest group of slaveowners. Though they owned only 21 percent of the baptisands, they were the owners of nearly a third of the women who received the sacrament. Eighteen women and two men owned by the women stood before the baptismal font that day. The women appear to have been especially conscientious in securing the sacrament for their new African slaves, but they also attended to the anglophone bondwomen beginning to appear in the city. "Una negra, Criolla Inglesa," aged thirty-two years, stood at the font, her godmother, a free Afro-Creole named Marie Mendes, at her side.[53]

With the closure of the international slave trade in 1808, "American" or "English" bondspeople sold away from the Protestant Upper South began to replace Africans as the primary object of Catholic evangelizers in New Orleans. Spanish and French priests accustomed to noting an enslaved person's nationality reserved "Creole" for those born in francophone Louisiana. Ana Maneta was sixteen years old and "de nacion Americana," according to the Capuchin friar who recorded her baptism in 1825. Most of the slaves labeled "American" by the city's priests were baptized as young adults, but there are also numerous cases of young children whose mothers are identified as "Americanas." Free Afro-Creole women are a notable constituency among the godparents of both groups. Among the seven adult female "Americanas" baptized in 1825 were Marie Françoise, aged fifteen and a native of Tennessee, and Ana Maneta, sponsored by the free Louisse Gamette and Maria Theresa Meunié. Luis Antonio, the three-year-old son of Jani, a "negra Americana" belonging to a Mr. Smith, was sponsored by the free Afro-Creole Henrieta Ducourneau. Female Catholic evangelizers paid special attention to "American" mothers with young children. The infants of Betsy, Esther, and Delsy were all baptized in 1825. Free Afro-Creole women also seem to have made certain that the older children of their "American" bondwomen were brought to the faith. Margueritte, the seventeen-year-old daughter of "Nancy de Charleston de Carolina Sud," was baptized in February 1825 under the watchful eye of her mistress, Adele Roseau, a free mulatta.[54]

The magnitude of the anglophone slave influx to Louisiana made conversion essential to the preservation of black influence in the New Orleans Catholic church. The number of bondspeople doubled in size between 1820 and 1830, rising from 7,355 to 14,440. Yet the arrival of Protestant slaves from the Upper South was not the only challenge that tested the faith and resourcefulness of New Orleans's Afro-Catholic community in the antebellum decades. White Catholic immigrants from Germany and Ireland began to trickle into the city in the 1820s and by the late 1830s had come to dominate the Catholic population.[55] Black Catholics faced the prospect of losing their hard-won place in the church if they could not retain their francophone core and expand it through the evangelization of Protestant or unconverted adults. Once again, a Delille ancestor played a prominent role in sustaining the Afro-Catholic Church. In a short interval between 1826 and 1828, Delille's mother, Maria Josefa Diaz, can be found in a spate of baptismal entries: she stood as godmother to an infant girl in November 1826 and the following May to an infant boy. Just seven months later, in December 1827, she served as godmother to an enslaved adult man. In August 1828, she stood at the baptismal font beside Josephine, an "adult negre esclave."[56]

By the 1820s when Maria Josefa Diaz appears regularly as a godmother in the sacramental records, the Delille female lineage had enacted each of the phases of religious creolization we have posited. In the first phase, the African Nanette preserved the matrifocal feature of her West African religious heritage through the vehicle of a Catholic female institution and tradition. She and her daughters represented the cadre of Christianized women who modeled Afro-Catholicism in the next generation and drew adult males into the church in the 1750s. In the third phase, when people of African descent came to dominate as godparents in slave baptism, the Delille clan was again prominent. After the turn of the nineteenth century, Delille's mother was active in the effort to sustain the Catholic Church among people of African descent. When Henriette Delille was born to Maria Josefa Diaz in 1812, she inherited the legacy of four generations of active Catholic women.[57]

When the American journalist John F. Watson traveled south to New Orleans shortly after the Louisiana Purchase, he penned an unwitting testament to that legacy. Describing Holy Week celebrations in 1805, Watson evoked a scene dominated by motherhood and female piety. "Mothers bring their infants; some cry and occasion other disturbances; some are seen counting their beads with much attention and remain long on their knees." This impressive display of femininity and maternity was especially striking, in Watson's eyes, for its racial aspect. "Visit the churches when you will," he noted, "and the chief audience is formed of mulatresses and negresses."[58] By the turn of the nineteenth century, the church had come to depend upon the support and piety of free and enslaved women of African descent like Delille's family. Without them, the churches that Watson visited would have been nearly empty.

Women of African descent advanced from powerless to powerful in the church as New Orleans Catholics entered the nineteenth century. In the 1720s and 1730s, they had been considered little more than objects of proselytization. As creolization progressed and they assumed the authority of the church, they became evangelizers themselves and were ultimately the most significant agents for Catholic propagation in the city. Following the patterns in godparenting that emerged as the colonial period gave way to the early national and antebellum eras reveals the ascendance of Afro-Creole women as agents of the church. In the 1760s, they shared godparenting with men of African descent. After 1760, however, women took the lead and retained it. Though Afro-Creoles of both sexes fully participated in the rite, significantly more women than men could be found standing as godparents at the baptismal font. White male participation as sponsors in slave baptism rose slightly between the 1770s and 1825, as new Africans and anglophone slaves from the Upper South poured into the city, though the downward trend of white female participation continued. After 1825 when Afro-Creoles, both enslaved and free, were more rigidly segregated in the city and the church, white sponsorship of blacks fell to very low levels. By 1842, nearly 90 percent of the city's slaves and free people of color were sponsored by women of African descent, while free men of color sponsored approximately 70 percent. Free women of African descent all but replaced white women in the records and, in an unprecedented move, they replaced them as ministers to their community.[59]

The loyalty of the women became even more essential to the church as a result of a structural transformation in the relationship between the secular and religious realms in early national New Orleans. The Louisiana Purchase of 1803, like the French Revolution, separated church and state. Catholic religious as well as laity in the Diocese of New Orleans, like their brothers and sisters in France, suddenly found themselves without state support. In New Orleans, the numerical dwindling of the clergy and thus their ability to respond to their parishioners as well as the rapidly growing numbers of free people and bound people who were either unconverted or actively Protestant was substantially accelerated. By 1815, only a handful of priests and a few Ursulines remained, and their decline occurred in the context of a rapidly growing population, much of it black. The deterioration of the church was only addressed in 1812, when the reluctant French missionary priest Louis William Dubourg was sent to administer a church that lay in ruins throughout the vast Louisiana territory.[60]

Dubourg's appointment to the diocese of Louisiana was pivotal, not only because he began the slow process of restoring the church, but also because he looked to France to do so. He revived the link between Louisiana and the French Catholic Church when he traveled to Europe in 1815 in order to accept his appointment as bishop of New Orleans.[61] After a brief stay in Rome, Dubourg set about his mission, first crossing the Alps to France, where he stayed for most of the next two years seeking aid for his flock. French historians who write of the revival of the missionary effort in France in the nineteenth century all point out that Dubourg's visit to France, especially to the area around Lyon, could not have occurred at a more auspicious moment. Pauline Jaricot, a dévote or secular religious woman, and her brother Philias, a Sulpicien priest, had just begun a movement in Lyon that led to the foundation of l'Association de la Propagation de la Foi (Society for the Propagation of the Faith; SPF) and eventually to Le Rosaire Vivant (Living Rosary). Both organizations were devoted, in large part, to foreign missionary work. At the same time, La Mission Étrangère (Foreign Mission) had begun to reorganize in Paris. All three organizations, and especially the SPF, responded to Dubourg's appeal by sending missionaries and financial support to Louisiana.[62]

The resurgence of missionary fervor that Dubourg found in Lyon was representative of the revival of Catholic spirit that increasingly influenced France after the revolution. To be sure, many eighteenth-century French men and women had rejected Catholicism before the revolution, and many more were to do so during the revolution, while still others remained only nominally Catholic. But by the time Dubourg reached France in 1815, significant numbers of the population were caught up in the revivalism that swept through French cities, villages, and into the countryside. As revolutionary promises remained unfulfilled, well-known Catholic thinkers and founders of religious orders renounced liberalism and rationalism. Instead, they sought to return France to a complete and coherent system that proposed a vision of a global world order responsive to all the problems of humanity and of human society. This organic universalist Catholic system was not a new one; it reflected in fundamental ways the older ideals of the seventeenth and eighteenth centuries that were so evident in the mission the Ursulines brought with them to New Orleans.[63] And as this renewal of Catholic spirit gained vigor in the nineteenth century, it took a more activist form, with its largest constituency-women-energetically seeking to remold society.[64]

The changes that swept through most nineteenth-century French convents were practical ones. Many of the older orders of women religious, having survived in clandestine havens throughout France, began to sweep off their stoops and open their windows. At the same time, new smaller groups of pious women began to emerge, gathering together in houses, doing manual labor in order to support their charitable missions. All of these women, in one way or another, began to build their communities on familiar models. Yet even as they sought to re-establish themselves in communities as if the revolutionary period had only interrupted them, they did so in a new age. For one thing, the church was no longer associated with or supported by the state; thus women living in community were forced to be financially independent, and after their experiences during the revolution, many had learned to cherish their newfound autonomy and sought to protect it. Another change was the marriage of the older missionary outlook with the activist emphasis of new female congregations. Congregation after congregation of women religious in nineteenth-century France used their autonomy in order to reform society by inculcating faith to their French sisters and their children, through instruction of the ignorant, education of the illiterate, and the provision of care for the sick, the poor, and the orphaned. The emphasis of these new communities of women was on betterment of the human condition, and as the nineteenth century unfolded, the women began to extend their ministry beyond the borders of France.[65]

At this time, significant numbers of women began to leave France in order to transmit their revived activist consciousness in other places. Nine women who left France to spread their devotion in the New World came to New Orleans in 1817 in response to an appeal—issued by the Ursulines through Bishop Dubourg—for aid. Each of these female missionaries came from a different section of France, a different background, a different walk of life. What united them was their extraordinary and personal response to the ideals of the Catholic apostolic fervor then sweeping through France. One of the women, Sister Ste. Marthe Frontière, brought the most radical form of French evangelical dedication to the poor with her to New Orleans. Before leaving France, Sister Ste. Marthe had been an Hospitalière sister in Belley, where she cared for the sick and the poor.[66] After she left Belley she became affiliated with the Ursulines, living in their convent in Bordeaux for three months while she awaited the ship that would transport her to the New World. It was there, in Bordeaux, that she received three months of novitiate training.[67] Yet even though Fontière was received by the Ursulines in New Orleans and lived in their convent for some time, she did not enter the community. Instead, she associated herself with one of their apostolates in the city, taking over the instruction of slave women and the education of free girls of color.[68] In 1824, when the Ursulines moved to a new convent several miles down the Mississippi River, Sister Ste. Marthe remained in the city, establishing a convent and a school for the girls.[69]

Sister Ste. Marthe dedicated herself to the city's women of African descent, introducing the newer French religious fervor to the city's poorest but most pious constituency. The student records for her school are no longer extant; however, the oral tradition of the Sisters of the Holy Family and the history of the community written in the nineteenth century by Sister Mary Bernard Deggs has it that Henriette Delille was educated by Sister Ste. Marthe. Her presence is documented at the school for free girls of color through 1831. During the 1830s, responsibility for the school passed through several hands. The Ursulines took it on for two interludes between 1831 and 1838 and assigned two nuns to staff it. Mademoiselle Marie Jeanne Aliquot, a French laywoman, assumed the work in 1834 and bought a new facility to house the school on St. Claude Street. When she left the city in 1836, the Ursulines resumed the commitment, until they persuaded the Sisters of Our Lady of Mount Carmel to take over in 1838.[70]

Sister Ste. Marthe, Marie Aliquot, the Ursulines, and the Sisters of Our Lady of Mount Carmel who maintained the school for free girls of color in antebellum New Orleans found themselves in more and more contentious circumstances as the city shed the flexible racial boundaries of the colonial era and fell more closely into step with the racial segregation that characterized the American plantation South.[71] The situation only began to change when the French women who had maintained control over the institutions populated by women and girls of African descent were joined by the French priest Michael Portier. Within a short time of his arrival in the Crescent City, Portier had unintentionally posed what would be a more fundamental threat to the racial order when he organized a confraternity of free women of African descent.   Founded with paternalistic enthusiasm, Portier's project quickly took on a life of its own and ultimately eluded both paternalistic and maternalistic white control.

The evidence we have of the early years of this association comes from an 1820 letter that Portier wrote to Father Cholleton, the director of the Grand Séminaire in Lyon. In that letter, Portier described what was the beginnings of the first confraternity of free Afro-Creole women: he wrote that he had a dozen young free women of color who were "fervent, like angels."   Another sixty young women, he noted, surrounded him every night, and he read the Gospel to them and then explained it.   The members of this congregation, he professed, were his consolation.   "They wear a red ribbon and a cross and they promise to fight daily like valiant soldiers of Jesus Christ."   Portier had the congregation assemble each Sunday and usually presided at their assembly.   In that way, he assured Cholleton, he regulated the manner in which the young women practiced religion.   Portier told the French priest that he had the happiness to see the young women as faithful as the seminarians in Lyon.   He pointed out, however, that the student priests in Lyon lived in a seminary while the New Orleans flock lived in "Babylon," in the midst of scandals.   These young women, he concluded, were "like angels; they teach the Blacks to pray, they catechize, they instruct, and they communicate . . . [the rest of the sentence is lost]."[72]

Sisters Ste. Marthe and Portier, both missionaries who came from the generation of activist religious in post-revolutionary France, were no doubt welcomed by New Orleans women of African descent who had themselves long been engaged in the work of the church.   Portier's letter paints a portrait of a dedicated group of followers.   The women who joined his confraternity, however, were not rapt neophytes but daughters of a long Afro-Catholic tradition poised to turn Portier's patronage into a religious foundation of their own.   In the 1830s, they took over the direction of their confraternity, and by 1836, led by Henriette Delille, they had a set of rules and regulations that named them the Sisters of the Congregation of the Presentation of the Blessed Virgin Mary.   With that move into the publicly acceptable arena of religious activism, the free women of African descent in New Orleans empowered themselves and acted on the universalist ideals brought by nineteenth-century French missionaries.[73]

The rules and regulations of this unique congregation required members to demonstrate piety and charity.   The women were to "seek to bring back the Glory of God and the salvation of their neighbor by a charitable and edifying behavior."   Each woman took a pledge to aid any of her sisters when necessary.   Finally, the women promised to serve the sick, the infirm, and the poor," who were the "first and dearest objects of the solicitude of the congregation."   These lay sisters went into homes to visit the sick and to comfort the dying.   They brought food to the hungry and warmth to the cold.   They sought out the uninstructed so they might "teach the principal mysteries of religion and the most important points of Christian morality."[74]

There can be little doubt that Henriette Delille and the women who joined her in 1836, Juliette Gaudin and Josephine Charles, were founding members of the Sisters of the Presentation. They were influenced by the Ursulines through heritage and tradition, replicating in important ways the much earlier organization and mission of the Children of Mary confraternity sponsored by the nuns in the eighteenth century. But the eighteenth-century model of female religious activism had since been revitalized and transformed by an array of more insistently activist and universalist religious orders founded in postrevolutionary France. Three of these new orders, the Sisters of Charity, Sisters of the Sacred Heart, and Sisters of Our Lady of Mount Carmel, established communities in nineteenth-century New Orleans and provided Delille and her colleagues with a contemporary French model of women ministering to the sick, the needy, and the poor and instructing the uninstructed. Marthe Frontière's personal and practical dedication to all New Orleans' women of African descent transcended in yet another way that of the Ursulines, who were willing to support the ministry but hoped it would flourish in other hands. The Sisters of the Presentation thus drew on two sources to create their new religious congregation. Delille's enterprise was grounded in the older Counter-Reformation French tradition of women evangelizing women promoted by the Ursulines and the Children of Mary and passed down to her and other Afro-Creoles in New Orleans through their matrilineal forebears. It was nourished and animated by the post-revolutionary French emphasis on women aiding other women with practical action and charity that Delille and her companions witnessed in their formative years.[75]

Delille and her companions were women who had few choices and little if any power as women of color in antebellum New Orleans. That changed when they redefined themselves as pious women and joined forces to meet the needs of others of African descent they saw around them. Yet, while the social implications of the congregation's actions are the first to strike the modern eye, the women themselves saw their project as an act of faith and piety. In 1836, Delille wrote her intentions in the form of a prayer in the front of one of her devotional books: "I believe God. I hope in God. I love. I wish to live and die for God."[76] This simple prayer exemplifies the fulfillment of the tradition of pious Catholic devotion Delille received from her ancestors. It demonstrates the culmination of the process delineated in the preceding pages. But it also previewed what was to come.

By 1842, Delille, the great-great-granddaughter of the African bondwoman Nanette, began to move toward an even more activist ministry. Not satisfied with her role as a pious laywoman, she, along with Gaudin and Charles, adopted several key features of formal religious life. They moved into a house near St. Augustine's Church in New Orleans and began to define their mission to the city's slaves and free people of color. In 1852, the three women changed their dress—from blue to black began to wear rosaries around their necks, and took private vows, committing themselves to the church and to those they called "our people." The religious order of women of color that emerged between 1836 and 1852 is recognized today as the Sisters of the Holy Family.[77]

Henriette Delille and her allies in the foundation of the Sisters of the Holy Family claimed French Catholic tradition in order to defy the social and racial conventions of antebellum New Orleans in numerous ways. Their chastity contested the sexualization of women of color and vitiated racist ideology that denied such women their claim to the feminine virtue that defined the ideal of American womanhood.[78] Their ministry to enslaved and free people of color, which came to include a school, an orphanage, nursing care for the sick and the elderly, and the provision of food and clothing for the destitute, transgressed and cast shame on the racially limited parameters of antebellum white benevolence. The institution they built conferred on them authority and power to shape the city's common welfare and denied whites a monopoly on the institutional life of New Orleans. Finally, by providing catechesis to the city's people of African descent, they ensured the continued dominance of the city's Catholic Church by African Americans and at the same time kept Protestantism at bay, effectively molding the religiosity of the city's black population.

In the 1730s, Marie Payen Dubreuil joined the confraternity of the Children of Mary that was pledged to evangelize the slaves of colonial New Orleans. One of the bondwomen of her household, an African known in Louisiana as Nanette, was subsequently baptized. A great-great-granddaughter of Nanette was Henriette Delille. In this simple narrative of catechesis and kinship, we can observe the larger movement delineated by statistics of baptism and population. The intergenerational transmission of Roman Catholicism to the people of African descent in New Orleans was a matrilineal process. It was initiated in 1727 by women who were mothers by faith alone, the Ursuline nuns, and aided by a confraternity of laywomen in the 1730s and 1740s. Enslaved African women seeking to preserve their religious traditions in an alien environment contributed the vital current of blood motherhood and brought their daughters into the ritual circle of the church. Increasingly, African American women undertook primary responsibility for the transmittal of their adopted faith, not only to their daughters, but also to all those of African descent in their city. And finally, they expressed their leadership through their own religious order. This evolution was probably nothing the first generation of European evangelizers ever imagined and contrasts markedly with the development of Catholicism elsewhere in the Caribbean and circum-Caribbean. Although the urban setting of New Orleans is an obvious point of difference from the plantation environment that characterized most other areas, the feminine nature of the initial missionary effort and the gradual assumption of leadership by laywomen of African descent during the colonial period and in the opening decades of the nineteenth century were key factors shaping the growth of an Afro-Catholic community. In a religious culture promoted by female catechesis rather than by male missionaries, leadership and responsibility for propagation of the faith was shared among a network of believers through the channel of motherhood. This method of religious diffusion was more organic to the existing West African cultural structures that enslaved women brought to Louisiana and provided more attractive opportunities for the adaptation of Catholic practices to community interests than the hierarchical model of conversion and evangelization controlled by a male priesthood.

Canon Peter L. Benoit, an English Mill Hill Father, discovered the primacy of the church in the Afro-Creole community in New Orleans when he visited there in 1875 in order to determine if there was a need for missionaries to minister to the city's freed blacks. Canon Benoit was sincere in his efforts, but his visit proved less than successful. Soon after his arrival in the Crescent City, Archbishop Napoleon Joseph Perche suggested to Benoit that there might be some need for his services in the English-speaking section of the city, where most of the blacks were Protestant. Benoit soon discovered for himself why Perche did not need Catholic missionaries to attract African Americans to their worship services in the French section of the city: "The Creoles or real French here are, I am sorry to say, as stingy here as in their own country. They support the theatres, and go to them well dressed. But they don't support their churches in the same way nor are they frequenters of the Sacraments."[79] But Benoit noted that the city's people of African descent living in the French section of the city had a different experience. While most African Americans in other cities were Baptist or Methodist, those in New Orleans were Catholic, and "the French clergy would not like to have them withdrawn from their churches because they are their chief support."[80] The missionary field of francophone Africans in postbellum New Orleans had already been successfully cultivated and had no need of Benoit's ministrations. Indeed, had it not been, the francophone church in the city would have withered from the indifference of the "stingy" white Creoles of French descent. The francophone Catholic Church that Benoit encountered in post-emancipation New Orleans quite simply owed its survival to the devout people of African descent who had come to it for generations through their women.

Notes for "The Feminine Face of Afro-Catholicism in New Orleans, 1727-1852"

[1]Ursuline Convent Chapel Baptismal Register, 1837-1845, April 1, 1838, Ursuline Convent of New Orleans Archives, New Orleans. The entry, in translation from the original French, reads: "On this first of April of eighteen hundred and thirty-eight, I baptized, in the Convent Chapel of St. Claude Marie Therese Dagon daughter of Charles Dagon and of Charlotte Diggs born the twenty-fifth of December of eighteen hundred and twenty-three. The godfather being the undersigned and the godmother being Henriette Delille. [signed] E. Rousselon, Chaplain of the Ursulines." The record does not explicitly state that Dagon was of African descent; however, it can be assumed as we have discovered no record in which a person of African descent served as a godparent to a white baptisand. Further, the St. Claude Street Chapel, no longer in existence, was a part of the St. Claude Street school for free girls of African descent. Translations of French sources are by the authors unless otherwise noted.

[2]In September 1826, Delille made her debut as a godmother in the sacramental records, sponsoring Fleurine, the 6-month-old daughter of Pélagie, the slave of Didier Livaudais; St. Louis Cathedral Baptismal Register of Slaves and Free People of Color, 1826-1827, Archives of the Archdiocese of New Orleans, New Orleans.

[3]Another order for free women of color, the Oblates of Providence, was founded in Baltimore in 1828. Several features differentiate the two orders. The Oblates, who focused on teaching, undertook a narrower ministry than the Sisters of the Holy Family. The Sisters of the Holy Family, whose members were often light-skinned

enough to "pass" for white, explicitly and continuously affirmed their identities as Afro-Creoles. By contrast, the black identity and origins of the Oblates were intentionally suppressed when one of its early leaders took its teaching ministry to the American Midwest. Finally, the impetus for the Oblates' formal foundation appears to have been external: a French priest, Jacques Joubert, organized a group of 3 women to teach and catechize free girls of color; Cyprian Davis, *The History of Black Catholics in the United States* (New York, 1990), 99. The foundation is described in Joubert, "The Original Diary of the Oblate Sisters of Providence, 1827-1842," Oblate Sisters of Providence Archives, Baltimore, 285 n. 2. See also John Thaddeus Posey, "An Unwanted Commitment: The Spirituality of the Early Oblate Sisters of Providence, 1829-1890" (Ph.D. dissertation, St. Louis University, 1993); William Leafonza Montgomery, "Mission to Cuba and Costa Rica: The Oblate Sisters of Providence in Latin America, 1900-1970" (Ph.D. dissertation, Catholic University of America, 1997); and Diane Batts Morrow, "The Oblate Sisters of Providence: Issues of Black and Female Agency in Their Antebellum Experience, 1828-1860" (Ph.D. dissertation, University of Georgia, 1996).

[4]The pattern of female catechesis that we demonstrate in this section probably began in the late 1720s shortly after the Ursulines reached New Orleans in 1717. However, the sacramental records for the 1720s were lost in a fire that destroyed much of New Orleans in 1788. Baptismal records for the years 1734-1743 met the same fate; Earl C. Woods, Charles E. Nolan, and Dorenda Dupont, eds. *Sacramental Records of the Roman Catholic Church of the Archdiocese of New Orleans*, Vol. I: *1718-1750* (New Orleans, 1987), xiv.

[5]Henriette Delille's African ancestor is called "Nanette" throughout this essay, though she appears in colonial records under both her baptismal name, "Marie Anne," and her diminutives, "Nanette" and "Manette," which were the familiar forms of the name Anne and were undoubtedly adopted to differentiate her from her daughter "Marianne." She is, for example, called "Marie Anne" in the marginal notation for her daughter Cecile's baptismal record, St. Louis Cathedral Baptism, 1744-1753, Archives of the Archdiocese of New Orleans, December 31, 1744, but is "Nanette" in the estate inventory of her owner, Claude Joseph Dubreuil; inventory of the estate of Claude Joseph Dubreuil, May 29, 1773, Louisiana State Archives, New Orleans, box 30, document 274, File 13.

[6]Gwendolyn Midlo Hall, *Africans in Colonial Louisiana: The Development of Afro-Creole Culture in the Eighteenth Century* (Baton Rouge, 1992), 60.

[7]Baptismal statistics based on St. Louis Cathedral Baptisms, 1731-1733, and St. Louis Cathedral Baptisms, 1744-1753, Archives of the Archdiocese of New Orleans. Censuses nearest in date to 1731-1733 and 1750 are those of 1737 and 1763. Our figures are drawn from Paul Lachance, "Summary of Louisiana Census of 1737," based on "Recapitulation du recensement general de la Louisiane en 1737," Archives Nationales, Archives des Colonies, série C (hereafter cited as AC), C13, C4:197, and "Summary of Louisiana Census Of 1763," based on Jacqueline K. Voorhies, trans. and comp., *Some Late Eighteenth-Century Louisianians: Census Records, 1758-1796* (Lafayette, La., 1973), 103-05. Both summaries have subsequently been published in Gwendolyn Midlo Hall, ed., *Databases for the Study of Afro-Louisiana History and Genealogy 1699-1860* CD-Rom (Baton Rouge, 2000). In these sacramental records priests usually noted whether the baptisand was an "infant" (many of whom were under age 2) or an "adult" (who was able to consent and enjoyed a different rite).

[8]"Le Code Noir ou Édit du Roi. Servant de Réglement pour le gouvernement & l'Administration de la Justice, Police, Discipline & le Commerce des Esclaves Nègres, dans la Province ou Colonie de la Louisiane. Donné à Versailles au mois de Mars 1724," in *Le Code noir ou recueil des reglements rendus jusqu'à présent concernant les gouvernment, l'administration de la justice, la police, la discipline & le commerce des nègres dans les colonies françaises* (Paris, 1742), 321. Thomas N. Ingersoll, *Mammon and Manon in Early New Orleans: The First Slave Society in the Deep South, 1718-1819* (Knoxville, 1999), 112, 135, implies that baptism could function as a means of social control, yet notes planter opposition to slave catechesis on the basis of its subversive potential and points out an annotation in a manuscript copy of the *Code Noir* that declares that the injunction to have slaves baptized was ignored in Louisiana.

[9]On the lag between slaves' arrival in the colony and their baptism, note, for example, that 151 adult Africans were baptized in 1746, 3 years after the most recent direct shipment of African captives to Louisiana; St. Louis Cathedral Baptisms and Marriages, 1744-1753.

[10]The parochial priests assigned to New Orleans were Capuchin friars. They were few in number and did not pursue a program of catechesis among the enslaved of the city and its environs. There is some evidence that the Capuchins hoped to convert Indians, but such plans were not carried to fruition. Jesuits, known for a more proactive ministry to enslaved populations, were prohibited from evangelizing in the area; AC, C 13A, 10:43-46v, 11:217-19; Charles Edwards O'Neill, *Church and State in French Colonial Louisiana: Policy and Politics to 1732* (New Haven, 1966), 55, 70-77, 130, 162-73.

[11]For full discussion of the Ursuline apostolate and descriptions of their schools see Elizabeth Rapley, *The Dévotes: Women and Church in Seventeenth-Century France* (Montreal, 1990), 3-22, 48-60, 74-75, 142-54, and Linda Lierheimer, "Female Eloquence and Maternal Ministry: The Apostolate of Ursuline Nuns in Seventeenth-Century France" (Ph.D. dissertation, Princeton University, 1994).

[12]*The Letters of Marie Madeleine Hachard*, 17211-28, trans. Myldred Masson Costa (New Orleans, 1974), 59.

[13]"Premier Registre de la Congrégation des Dames Enfants de Marie," Ursuline Convent of New Orleans Archives, 3, 7. For a full discussion of the social makeup of the Children of Mary, see Emily Clark, "'By All the Conduct of Their Lives': A Laywomen's Confraternity in New Orleans, 1730-1744," *William and Mary Quarterly*, 3d Ser., 54 (1997): 769-94; and "A New World Community: The New Orleans Ursulines and Colonial Society, 1727-1803" (Ph.D. dissertation, Tulane University, 1998), 74-79.

[14]Sacramental records and other colonial documents typically inscribed only the given name of slaves, a practice that was apparently reserved only for people of color in the colony. See, for example, St. Louis Cathedral Baptisms, 1731-1733, and St. Louis Cathedral Baptisms, 1744-1753, for conventions used in sacramental records. At least two women of color were boarding at the Ursuline convent during the 1730s when the Children of Mary were active; "Records of the Superior Council," *Louisiana Historical Quarterly*, 4 (1921): 355, and ibid., 9 (1926): 310.

[15]"Premier Registre de la Congrégation des Dames Enfants de Marie," 7.

[16]Clark, "By All the Conduct of Their Lives," 790-92.

[17]"Premier Registre de la Congrégation des Dames Enfants de Marie," 13-14.

[18]See entries for January 13, May 23, and August 15, 1733, in St. Louis Cathedral Baptisms, 1731-1733, and entries for February 6, May 12, 2(?), August 30, 31, September 22, and December 31, 1744, in St. Louis Cathedral Baptisms, 1744-1753.

[19]Liliane Crété with Patricia Crété, *La Traite des nègres sous l'ancien regime: Le nègre, le sucre, et la toile* (Paris, 1998; orig. pub. 1989), 82. The preference for taking women from the Senegambian littoral and men from further inland was first described by David P. Geggus in "Sex Ratio, Age, and Ethnicity in the Atlantic Slave Trade: Data from French Shipping and Plantation Records," *Journal of African History*, 30 (1989): 23-44. See also, Patrick Manning, *Slavery and African Life: Occidental, Oriental, and African Slave Trades* (Cambridge, 1990), 97-98; Michael Gomez, *Exchanging Our Country Marks: The Transformation of African Identities in the Colonial and Antebellum South* (Chapel Hill, 1998), 43; and Hall, *Africans in Colonial Louisiana*, 41-95, 275-315.

[20]Labat, *Nouvelle relation de l'Afrique occidentale contenant une description exacte du Sénégal et des païs situés entre le Cap Blanc et la Riviere de Serrelione, jusqu à plus de 300 lieues en avant dans les terres*, 5 vols. (Paris, 1728), 2:209, 232-33; Le Page du Pratz, *Histoire de la Louisiane*, 3 vols. (Paris, 1757), 1:342, 343n, 344-45. Hall, "African Women in French and Spanish Louisiana: Origins, Roles, Family, Work, Treatment," in Catherine Clinton and Michele Gillespie, *The Devil's Lane: Sex and Race in the Early South* (New York, 1997), 249-50, asserts the primacy of Wolof women in early Louisiana.

[21]See, for example, James Searing, *West African Slavery and Atlantic Commerce: The Senegal River Valley, 1700-1860* (Cambridge, 1993), 60, 66, 76. Searing describes the intensive interactions of the French sailors, merchants, and administrators with the coastal and river Africans who served as traders, cultural guides, and interpreters. French speakers as well as Catholics were to be found amongst these riverine and coastal

populations. Boubacar Barry, *Senegambia and the Atlantic Slave Trade* (New York, 1998), 76, describes the commercial and social power wielded by the female Afro-European *signares* of St. Louis, at the mouth of the Senegal River. See also "Lettre du Conseil Supérieur," AC, C 6:11, January 18, 1738, and La Courbe, *Premier Voyage du sieur de la Courbefait a la coste d'Afrique en 1685* (Paris, 1913), 107, 109.

[22]Assigning ethnicity and related cultural attributes to early 18th-century Senegambians is a difficult and contentious exercise, but if Nanette was from a coastal group, it is likely that she was a non-Muslim woman. From the 1670s and through the first half of the 18th century, Muslim factions waged war for political and religious control in Waalo, Futa Toro, Kajoor, Jolof, and the more inland and southern regions of Bundu and Futa Jallon. Muslims did not achieve lasting control of the northwestern areas of Waalo, Futa Toro, Kajoor, and Jolof until the second half of the 18th century. During the first phase of the Louisiana slave trade, 1719-1743, the northwestern areas of Senegambia remained in the hands of warlords who practiced traditional African religion and generally claimed succession to their positions matrilineally. A series of conflicts over succession in the early 18th century provided captives from these areas for the slave trade; Barry, *Senegambia and the Atlantic Slave Trade*, 28, 50-54, 81-105. Nanette's enslavement was likely a product of this succession of local conflicts among non-Muslim warlords. On religious behavior among non-Muslim women, see Arlette Gautier, *Les Soeurs de solitude: La Condition féminine dans l'esclavage aux Antilles du XVII au XIX siècle* (Paris, 1985), 45, and Abdoulaye-Bara Diop, *La Famille Wolof. Tradition et Changement* (Paris, 1985), 44-45, 51. Also see Peter Caron, "'Of a Nation Which Others Do Not Understand': Bambara Slaves and African Ethnicity in Colonial Louisiana, 1718-60," *Slavery and Abolition*, 18 (1997): 98-121.

[23]Nanette and her children are enumerated in the inventory of Claude Joseph Dubreuil's estate. They are identified as a family of domestics living in the household and are protected by codicil to the will; inventory of the estate of Claude Joseph Dubreuil. The fire of 1788 destroyed the baptismal records of Nanette and her children Marianne, Fanchonette, Tuyanne, and Tonica. We infer the baptisms of Nanette and Marianne from the women's appearance in sacramental records as godmothers. See, for example, May 13, 1775, in St. Louis Cathedral Baptisms, 1772-1776; March 23, May 25, and September 7, 1760, in St. Louis Cathedral Baptisms, 1759-1762; October 27, 1765, in St. Louis Cathedral Baptisms and Marriages, 1763-1766.

[24]Hall, *Africans in Colonial Louisiana*, chap. 9.

[25]Ibid., 68.

[26]Quotation in AC IIA, 96:222V.

[27]Clark, "New World Community," 136.

[28]Statistics based on St. Louis Cathedral Baptisms, 1731-1733; St. Louis Cathedral Baptisms and Marriages, 1763-1766; "Libro donde se asientan las partidas de baptismos . . . 1777 que empezó hasta el año de 1781 que es el corrente," St. Louis Cathedral Baptisms and Marriages, 1777-1786; "Libro quinto de bautizados negros y mulatos de la parroquia de San Luis de esta ciudad de la Nueva Orleans: contiene doscientos crienta y siete folios útiles, y da principio en primero de octubre de mil setecientos noventa y dos, y acaba fen 1798," St. Louis Cathedral Baptisms and Marriages, 1786-1796; St. Louis Cathedral Baptisms of Slaves and Free Persons of Color, 1801-1804; St. Louis Cathedral Baptisms of Slaves and Free Persons of Color, 1804-1805; St. Louis Cathedral Baptisms, 1802-1806; St. Louis Cathedral Baptisms of Slaves and Free People of Color, February 1824-February 1825; St. Louis Cathedral Baptisms of Slaves and Free People of Color, March 1820-December 1826; St. Louis Cathedral Baptisms, January 1822-March 1825; and St. Louis Cathedral Baptisms, April 1825-January 1827, all in Archives of the Archdiocese of New Orleans.

[29]Statistics based on St. Louis Cathedral Baptisms, 1731-1733; St. Louis Cathedral Baptisms and Marriages, 1763-1766; "Libro donde se asientan las partidas de baptismos . . . 1777 que empezó hasta el año de 1781 que es el corrente;" and "Libro quinto de bautizados negros y mulatos."

[30]For a discussion of creolization, see Edward Brathwaite, *The Development of Creole Society in Jamaica* (Oxford, 1971), 193-2, 39, who notes that creolization is a process that radiates outward from the slave community, affecting the entire culture by degrees. The process, he explains, begins when all those in a society

begin to share a common style and should be understood as prismatic with each separate group acculturating. He then adds that this concept is problematic in slaveholding societies where interculturation was channeled by the dominant class with the whip of legislation. The process, he argues, should not be understood as continual, but as one with highs and lows, ebbs and flows.

[31]Statistics based on St. Louis Cathedral Baptisms, 1731-1733; St. Louis Cathedral Baptisms, 1744-1753; St. Louis Cathedral Baptisms and Marriages, 1763-1766; "Libro donde se asientan las partidas de baptismos . . . 1777 que empezó hasta el año de 1781 que es el corrente;" "Libro quinto de bautizados negros y mulatos," St. Louis Cathedral Baptisms of Slaves and Free Persons of Color, 1804-1805; St. Louis Cathedral Baptisms, 1802-1805; St. Louis Cathedral Baptisms of Slaves and Free People of Color, March 9, 1824-February 28, 1825; St. Louis Cathedral Baptisms of Slaves and Free People of Color, March 1, 1825-December 1, 1825; St. Louis Cathedral Baptisms of Slaves and Free People of Color, December 4, 1825-December 9, 1826; and St. Louis Cathedral Baptisms of Slaves and Free People of Color, January 1840-December 1842.

[32]AC IIA, 96:222V.

[33]For these arguments, see, among others, Sylvia R. Frey and Betty Wood, *Come Shouting to Zion: African American Protestantism in the American South and British Caribbean to 1830* (Chapel Hill, 1998), which discusses both the failure of Anglican missionaries and the ways in which the enslaved took control of their religious lives; John Thornton, *Africa and Africans in the Making of the Atlantic Word, 1400-1800*, 2d ed. (Cambridge, 1998); Frey, *Water from the Rock: Black Resistance in a Revolutionary Age* (Princeton, 1991), 243-325, which places the appropriation of evangelical Christianity by slaves in the context of resistance; Gomez, *Exchanging Our Country Marks*, 263-90; and Mary Turner, *Slaves and Missionaries: The Disintegration of Jamaican Slave Society*, 1787-1834 (Urbana, 1982), 71-95, which describes slave resistance to the efforts of white evangelical missionaries to replace African religious and social beliefs and habits with Christian models. Other recent scholarship that considers the agency of slaves in relation to Christianity in more general studies of slavery includes Ira Berlin, *Many Thousands Gone: The First Two Centuries of Slavery in North America* (Cambridge, Mass., 1998), esp. 42, 51, 73, 75, 138-39, 151, 171-73, 189-90, and Philip D. Morgan, *Slave Counterpoint: Black Culture in the Eighteenth Century Chesapeake and Lowcountry* (Chapel Hill, 1998), esp. 424-25, 431-32.

[34]St. Louis Cathedral Baptisms and Marriages, 1763-1766; "Libro quinto de bautizados negros y mulatos."

[35]See, for example, the entry for the adult group baptism on Pentecost Eve, 1762, in St. Louis Cathedral Baptisms and Marriages, 1759-1762.

[36]"Libro quinto de bautizados negros y mulatos," June 3-6, 1797.

[37]Thornton, *Africa and Africans in the Making of the Atlantic World*, 2d ed., 253-71, speaks to the conversion process of Africans in Africa and in the Americas, where Christianized Africans at times acted as evangelists to other slaves. See especially p. 323, where the Kongolese of St. Jan in the Danish West Indies, "as Christians of many generations' standing, took it upon themselves to baptize all newly arrived slaves, serving as godparents of sorts to them," in the 1750s. Mechal Sobel, *The World They Made Together: Black and White Values in Eighteenth-Century Virginia* (Princeton, 1989), 180-84, 189, 204-05, speaks to the influence of slave worship styles and piety on the ministers and white congregations of the First Great Awakening, as does Morgan, *Slave Counterpoint*, 429-30. Gomez, *Exchanging Our Country Marks*, 244-90, stresses the degree to which African belief and worship forms infused the Christianity practiced by slaves.

[38]Kimberly S. Hanger, *Bounded Lives, Bounded Places: Free Black Society in Colonial New Orleans, 1769-1803* (Durham, N. C., 1997), 104-05; Clark, "New World Community," 140-45; Hall, *Africans in Colonial Louisiana*, 157-200.

[39]Canon 874, in James A. Coriden, Thomas J. Green, and Donald E. Heintschel, eds., *The Code of Canon Law: A Text and Commentary* (New York, 1985), and Stanislaus Woywod, *A Practical Commentary on the Code of Canon Law*, rev. Callistus Smith (New York, 1957), 393, 395.

[40]Acts of Juan Garic, 1776, New Orleans Notarial Archives, New Orleans; "Déliberations du Conseil," Archives of the Ursuline Convent of New Orleans, 59; Clark, "New World Community," 143.

[41]Entries for May 28, June 29, 1746, February 7, March 5, 1747, June 11, 1748, in St. Louis Cathedral Baptisms and Marriages, 1744-1753, May 13, 1775, in St. Louis Cathedral Baptisms and Marriages, 1753-1759; March 23, May 25, September 7, 1760, in St. Louis Cathedral Baptisms and Marriages, 1759-1762; October 77, 1765, in St. Louis Cathedral Baptisms and Marriages, 1763-1766; March 4, July 73, 1775, in "Libro donde se asientan las partidas de haptismos . . . 1777 que empezó hasta el año de 1781 que es cl corrente." Marianne was younger than the canonical age (16 yrs.) required for godparents, a stipulation regularly ignored according to the New Orleans records. Underage godmothers appear more often than underage godfathers.

[42]See note 24 above.

[44]Santiago Bernard Coquet and José Antonio Boniquet held the concession on a city-owned ballroom that was the scene in the 1790s of multiracial dances that became known as "tricolor balls;" Gilbert C. Din and John E. Harkins, *The New Orleans Cabildo: Colonial Louisiana's First City Government, 1769-1803* (Baton Rouge, 1996), 164, 173-75. Hanger, *Bounded Lives*, 148-49, chronicles a series of raids in the 1790s on taverns and billiard halls where whites, free blacks, and slaves were found fraternizing.

[45]Hanger, *Bounded Lives*, 136-43, portrays the free Afro-Creoles of New Orleans as thoroughly assimilated to European culture even as they embraced a revolutionary insistence on racial equality that was rejected by those of unmixed European descent in the city. The church, she notes, was a primary venue for the assertion of their European cultural identities. Hanger also provides statistical evidence of the religious observance of the city's slaves, which confounds such generalizations as "the free colored generally [adhered] to orthodox Catholicism, the slaves frequently [retained] their original religious orientation;" Thomas Marc Fiehrer, "The African Presence in Colonial Louisiana: An Essay on the Continuity of Caribbean Culture," in Robert R. Macdonald, John R. Kemp, and Edward F. Haas, eds., *Louisiana's Black Heritage* (New Orleans, 1979), 23; Michael Mullin, *Africa in America: Slave Acculturation and Resistance in the American South and the British Caribbean, 1736-1831* (Urbana, 1992), 28-29. Gomez, *Exchanging Our Country Marks*, 269-70, also comments on the cultural distance between urban and rural blacks. On the shift in the economy of colonial Louisiana, see Berlin, *Many Thousands Gone*, 325, 338-44; John G. Clark, *New Orleans, 1718-1812: An Economic History* (Baton Rouge, 1970), 189-92; Hall, *Africans in Colonial Louisiana*, 276-81, 286, 308-10; and Daniel H. Usner, Jr., *Indians, Settlers, and Slaves in a Frontier Exchange Economy: The Lower Mississippi Valley before 1783* (Chapel Hill, 1992), 118-19, 148, 177-278, 281-82.

[46]Berlin, *Many Thousands Gone*, 209, notes that the town council of Spanish colonial New Orleans, the Cabildo, promulgated a new slave law in 1777 that explicitly attempted to suppress expressions of African religion. While Berlin links this to manifestations of Creole religion still imbued with African practice, the timing suggests that it may have been triggered by the activities of newly arrived Africans.

[47]"Libro donde se asientan las partidas de baptismos . . . 1777 que empezó hasta el año de 1781 que es el corrente."

[48]There are far too many examples to cite; thus we have included a sampling: October 27, 1765, in St. Louis Cathedral Baptisms and Marriages, 1763-1766, and February 26, June 12, 1781 (one a slave, one free), in "Libro donde se asientan las partidas de baptismos . . . 1777 que empezó hasta el año de 1781 que es el corrente."

[49]August 9, 1781, in "Libro donde se asientan las partidas de baptismos . . . 1777 que empezó hasta el año de 1781 que es el corrente"; February 19, 1784, in "Libro quinto de bautizados negros y mulatos."

[50]One Marie Ann was first freed privately before the French colonial governor, Louis de Kerlerec, and was later publicly emancipated by notarial act under the Spanish regime; Emancipation of Marie Ann, Acts of Andrés Almonester y Roxas, January 10, 1770, Notarial Archives of New Orleans. Marianne and her children were freed in 1772. Cecile was freed two years later; Emancipation of Cecile, Acts of Fernando Rodriguez, 1772, Notarial Archives of New Orleans. Marianne's emancipation is recorded in Acts of Juan Garic, February 11,

September 23, 1772, Notarial Archives of New Orleans. The Spanish process would obviously have been more attractive to men wishing to free their mixed-race children and mistresses. See Hanger, *Bounded Lives*, 24-25, 31-38.

[51]See the census of New Orleans for 1795, Archivo General de Indias, papales de Cuba, legajo 216, Seville, Spain.

[52]April 13, 1805, in St. Louis Cathedral Baptisms of Slaves and Free Persons of Color, 1804-1805.

[53]Ibid. Henriette Delille owned one slave, who was probably already baptized when Delille inherited her.

[54]Ana Manetta was baptized on May 17, 1825, St. Louis Cathedral Baptisms of Slaves and Free Persons of Color, March 1, 1825-December 1, 1825; Marie Françoise on January 23, 1825, St. Louis Cathedral Baptisms of Slaves and Free Persons of Color, March 9, 1824-February 28, 1825; Luis Antonio on January 16, 1825, ibid.; Esther's son Baptiste was baptized on May 15, 1825, St. Louis Cathedral Baptisms of Slaves and Free Persons of Color, March 1, 1825-December 1, 1825; Betsy's son Louis on May 14, 1825, ibid.; and Delsy's daughter Adele on May 13, ibid.

[55]John Frederick Nau, *The German People of New Orleans, 1850-1900* (Leiden, 1958), 4-5; Earl F. Niehaus, *The Irish in New Orleans, 1800-1860* (Baton Rouge, 1965), 28-36; Lachance, "The Foreign French," in *Creole New Orleans: Race and Americanization*, ed. Arnold R. Hirsch and Joseph Logsdon (Baton Rouge, 1992), 119.

[56]St. Louis Cathedral Baptisms of Slaves and Free People of Color, March 1825-December 1826, and St. Louis Cathedral Baptisms of Slaves and Free People of Color, September 1827-June 1829, Archives of the Archdiocese of New Orleans.

[57]"Matricula," Archives, Sisters of the Holy Family.

[58]Watson, "Notia of Incidents at New Orleans in 1804 and 1805," *The American Pioneer*, 2 (1843): 230, 234.

[59]See footnote 31 for sources.

[60]Annabelle M. Melville, *Louis William Dubourg: Bishop of Louisiana and the Floridas, Bishop of Montauban, and Archbishop of Besançon, 1766-1833*, 2 vols. (Chicago, 1986). Also see Father John Marie Tessier, diary, in Archives of the Sulpiciens, Baltimore, and the letters from Dubourg to Bishop John Carroll in the Archives of the Archdiocese of Baltimore and in the Archives of the Daughters of Charity at Emmitsburg, Pa.

[61]In 1815, the Diocese of New Orleans included all of Louisiana, which in turn included the Illinois Territory.

[62]The best account of Pauline Jaricot's work is recorded in her positio, archived in the Congregation for the Causes of Saints, Vatican City. It is in Jaricot's writings that one finds the best evidence of the early activities of the Propagation de la Foi and Le Rosaire Vivant. The records of Le Rosaire Vivant are housed in La Maison Dominicaine, Lyon. Also see Edward John Hickey, "The Society for the Propagation of the Faith: Its Foundation, Organization, and Success (1822-1922)" (Ph.D. dissertation, Catholic University of America, 1922), and David LaThoud, *Marie-Pauline Jaricot*, 2 vols. (Paris, 1938).

[63]Ernest Sevrin, *Les Missions Religieuses en France sous la Restauration, 1815-1830*, vol. I (Saint Manot, 1948).

[64]Patricia Wittberg, *The Rise and Fall of Catholic Religious Orders: A Social Movement Perspective* (Albany, 1994), 58-70.

[65]Yvonne Turin, *Femmes et religieuses au XIXe siècle. Le Féminisme "en religion"* (Paris, 1989); Elisabeth Dufourcq, *Les Aventurières de Dieu: Trois siècles d'histoire missionnaire française* (Paris, 1993); Claude Langlois, *Le Catholicisme au féminin: Les Congrégations françaises à supérieure générale au XIXe siècle* (Paris, 1984).

[66]"Des Annales des Soeurs Hospitalières de Belley," Archives Départementales, Bourg-en-Bresse, France.

[67]"Des Annales des Ursulines de Bordeaux," 1816, Archives of the Ursuline Convent, Lyon; André Dallemagne, *Histoire de Belley* (Belley, France, 1979), 81, 191-99, 229, 245.

[68]Fontière does not appear in the book of professions of the New Orleans Ursulines. The annals of the New Orleans Ursulines record that Sr. Ste. Marthe "reste quelques années ici habillée comme nous, travaillant à l'institut avec beaucoup de zèle. En 1823, elle sortit pour aller établir la maison connue sous le nom de St. Claude destinée à l'instruction des jeunes filles de couleur" ("stayed here several years dressed like us, working in the school with much zeal. In 1823, she left to establish the house known under the name of St. Claude, intended for the instruction of young girls of color"); "First Book of Annals [of the New Orleans Ursulines]," 72-73, Ursuline Convent of New Orleans Archives.

[69]When the Ursulines moved to their new site, they allowed the bishop the use of their old convent compound in the city center subject to several obligations. The first of these enumerated demands was "that every Sunday and feast day an instruction or catechism will be given to the negresses of the country to replace that being given now on those days." It is possible that Sr. Ste. Marthe was the individual employed with the fulfillment of this obligation; "Délibérations du Conseil," April 1, 1826. On the Ursuline stewardship of the school for free girls of color, see entries for January 31, February 10, March [n.d.] 1836, February 26, 1837, ibid.

[70]Between 1831 and 1834, the Ursulines assigned two of their nuns to take over Sr. Ste. Marthe's school on a temporary basis. They were recalled by the convent council in 1834, but Sr. Ste. Francis de Sales chose to stay on with her sister Marie Jeanne Aliquot, who had bought the school building and property. Together they ran the school until 1836, when the Ursulines again assumed full responsibility for the institution and reimbursed Aliquot for the purchase price. Between 1836 and 1838, four Ursulines were involved as director and teachers at the school. The Ursulines spent an additional $10,000 to purchase a piece of property adjacent to the school in 1836 in order to provide living quarters for the members of their community assigned to the school; "First Book of Annals," 219-20; entries for March 7, 1834, January 31, May 2, 1836, in "Délibérations du Conseil." On the transfer to the Sisters of Mount Carmel, see the contract between Aliquot and the Ursuline Community of New Orleans, February 16, 1836, and the contract between the Ursuline Community of New Orleans and the Community of the Order of Our Lady of Mount Carmel of New Orleans, November 25, 1840, both in Acts of Theodore Seghers, Notarial Archives of New Orleans. See also Charles Nolan, *Bayou Carmel: The Sisters of Mount Carmel of Louisiana, 1833-1903* (Kenner, La., 1977), 18-21.

[71]Hall, *Africans in Colonial Louisiana*, 239-40; Usner, *Indians, Settlers, and Slaves*, 276-78; Jerah Johnson, "Colonial New Orleans: A Fragment of the Eighteenth-Century French Ethos," in Hirsch and Logsdon, eds., *Creole New Orleans*, 23. For another view, see Ingersoll, *Mammon and Manon*, which argues that a rigid racial hierarchy was established by a controlling planter regime as early as the 1730s, operating continuously throughout the colonial period.

[72]Portier to Cholleton, Sept. [n.d.] 1820, in Records of La Propagation de la Foi, Oeuvres Missionaires Pontificale, Lyon. Although Portier does not identify the gender of his confraternity members, they were undoubtedly female. Confraternities in this period were not mixed, and the overwhelming majority were for women. The activities of Portier's confraternity—catechesis and instruction—were traditionally assumed by women, as they had been by the 18th-century Children of Mary.

[73]"Rules and Regulations of the Sisters of the Congregation of the Presentation of the Blessed Virgin Mary," Archives of the Sisters of the Holy Family.

[74]Ibid.

[75]Father Joseph Rosati to Sr. Xavier Clark, April 19, 1927; Bishop Antoine Blanc to Mother Rose White, February 7, 1838, both in Records and Letters of the Daughters of Charity, Daughters of Charity Archives, St. Joseph Provincial House, Emmitsburg, Pa. Ste Madeleine-Sophie Barat and Ste Philippine Duschesne, "Correspondance: Texte des manuscrits originaux présent avec une introduction, des notes et un index analytique, Premier partie (1818-1821) et Second partie (1821-1826), Periode de l'Amérique" (Rome, 1989). Records of the Sisters of Our Lady of Mount Carmel, Convent of the Sisters of Our Lady of Mount Carmel, New Orleans.

[76]This prayer, written in French and signed by Delille, was inscribed in a French book of spirituality, J. A. Poncet de La Rivière, *Madame la Comtesse de Carcado, l'ame unie à Jésus-Christ dans le très-s. sacrement de l'autel, ou preparations et actions de grâces* . . . (Paris, 1830). The inscribed book is housed in the Archives of the Sisters of the Holy Family.

[77]The description of the changes that occurred in 1852 are found in loose notes of Sr. Mary Borgia Hart, Archives of the Sisters of the Holy Family. Sr. Mary began a history of the Sisters of the Holy Family in 1916, when Sr. Ann Fazende was still living. Sr. Ann was one of the novices who entered the community in 1852, when the women were finally allowed to take in novices.

[78]Gould, "In Full Enjoyment of Their Liberty: Free Women of Color in the Gulf Ports of New Orleans, Mobile, and Pensacola, 1769-1860" (Ph.D. dissertation, Emory University, 1991).

[79]Benoit, diary entry, April 9, 1875, in Mill Hill Fathers' Archives, copy in the Josephite Archives in Baltimore. For an excellent account of religion in the era of Reconstruction and Jim Crow in Louisiana, see Dolores Egger Labbé, *"Jim Crow Comes to Church": The Establishment of Segregated Catholic Parishes in South Louisiana*, 2d ed. (New York, 1978; orig. pub. 1971).

[80]Benoit, diary entry, April 9, 1875.

FATHER JEAN DELVAUX
AND THE NATCHITOCHES REVOLT
OF 1795*

Gilbert C. Din

In 1795 disorders rocked Natchitoches, disrupting the usually placid colonial village. Father Jean Delvaux, the parish priest, figured at the center of the disturbances. His activities represented an anomaly since the Catholic Church expected its representatives to uphold government authority, not lead the disgruntled. No other parish priest in colonial Louisiana defied government and church authority to the same extent or played as tumultuous a role as did Delvaux. Despite the priest's importance in instigating the strife that temporarily engulfed the Red River settlement, until now only two historians have examined the events that surrounded this little known cleric.[1]

The first to do so was Ernest R. Liljegren in his 1939 *Louisiana Historical Quarterly* article, "Jacobinism in Spanish Louisiana," which surveyed political and social unrest throughout Louisiana in the 1790s. Liljegren, a student of A. P. Nasatir at then San Diego State College, used his mentor's large personal collection of documents from the Spanish archives to write his essay. He devoted fifteen of the study's fifty-one pages to Natchitoches. Liljegren, nevertheless, either overlooked or lacked access to still other records that would have shed more light on Delvaux and the so-called revolt at Natchitoches.[2]

Twenty-five years later, Juan José Andreu Ocariz published "Revolt in Natchitoches" in *Louisiana Studies*, which he based on a solitary file in the Archivo Histórico Nacional in Madrid. Gov. Francisco Luís Héctor, barón de Carondelet, sent the file to Spain in 1797 to inform the government about Delvaux and the troubles at Natchitoches after they had ended. Carondelet enclosed a self-serving cover letter in which he detailed his actions in a favorable light.[3]

Andreu Ocariz, similar to Liljegren, mistakenly accepted virtually everything Carondelet wrote, and Andreu Ocariz consequently made questionable conclusions, especially

*First published in *Louisiana History*, 40 (1999): 1-33. Reprinted with the kind permission of the author and the Louisiana Historical Association.

134

about Spain's ability to impose order at the outpost. The troubles at Natchitoches eventually ended without the governor employing military force, but, guided by Liljegren's and Andreu Ocariz's articles and Carondelet's mendacity, the secondary historical literature has exaggerated the internal opposition to Spanish rule in Louisiana and Spanish impotence in quelling disturbances, especially at Natchitoches. For example, Edwin Adams Davis, in *Louisiana, A Narrative History*, wrote in 1971, "Jean Delvaux, a parish priest at Natchitoches, led an open revolutionary movement. Louisiana was practically in open rebellion against the Governor and the Spanish regime."[4]

Both sentences are wrong. This study, however, is mainly limited to an examination of the events at Natchitoches in a manner consistent with the documents exchanged between Carondelet and his subordinates in Natchitoches, and not his letters to superiors which describe the events falsely. The governor's correspondence with the captain general in Cuba and higher authorities in Spain must be used cautiously because at times he prevaricated in reporting events. Unfortunately, both Liljegren and Andreu Ocariz fail to question the accuracy of the governor's letters about Delvaux and Natchitoches.[5]

The Pointe Coupée slave conspiracy and the presence of Jacobin radicalism in New Orleans have also confused an understanding of the disturbances at Natchitoches. Although the aftermath of the black conspiracy produced hysteria in certain quarters in the province, more of it was present in New Orleans than at the outposts, and Pointe Coupée was especially quiet. Natchitoches, meanwhile, was not calm in 1795, but neither Jacobinism nor slaves were responsible for what happened there. While some of the French Creole settlers identified with the former mother country during the French Revolution, numerous others were monarchists and slaveholders and not sympathetic toward insurgent France.[6]

In 1795, the Natchitoches district held approximately seventeen hundred inhabitants, only a fraction of whom lived in the village. Tobacco and the Indian trade made up the post's two most important economic activities. But the Spanish government's reduction of tobacco purchases in the early 1790s and its entrance in the First Coalition of monarchies in the war against revolutionary France (1793-95) had adversely affected the district's economy. The war hindered the importation of goods essential for the Indian trade. These developments caused the Natchitoches economy to slump precariously, and the depressed conditions generated hostility toward the government among local settlers.[7]

Besides economic woes, Natchitoches had other problems that were purely its own. Chief among them was the division of the inhabitants into factions, largely along the line of who was post commandant. One faction consisted of the Juchereau de Saint-Denis family and friends. In the mid-1790s, this faction held power because the commandant, Louis DeBlanc, was a grandson of the post's founder, Louis Juchereau de Saint-Denis. A second faction, which was more poorly defined except for its opposition to those in power, clustered loosely around the family and supporters of Athanase de Mézières, the lieutenant governor of the post from 1769 until his death in 1779.[8] The second group probably formed after de Mézières' death, and it generally opposed the Spanish government because it was out of power.

The two factions, however, closed ranks to a point in their common hostility toward a new group that had only recently appeared in the district, the non-Gallic settlers who were mainly English, Irish, and Americans. They had entered the district despite Governor Carondelet's effort to confine English-speaking newcomers to the Natchez district on the Mississippi's east bank. The French inhabitants resented the land grants the new immigrants received and the protection the Spanish government afforded them once they settled. The dissidents exhibited no willingness to adhere to the French revolutionary concepts of "equality" and "fraternity" toward these newcomers, who, in 1795, demonstrated their loyalty to the Spanish government.[9]

The French secular priest Jean Delvaux was the central figure in the 1795 disorders. Mystery shrouds his life before he arrived in Louisiana inasmuch as he revealed virtually nothing about his past. By his own admission, Delvaux reached the colony about 1785, and the Spanish government soon employed him because of the shortage of priests in the province. He served at Natchitoches from 1786 to 1793, after which time he transferred to St. Charles Parish on the First German Coast. He, however, found his new assignment unsatisfactory since he received a salary of only twenty *pesos* per month. It amounted to only half the pay given to Irish priests who proselytized among the foreign Protestant population in West Florida. When Father Pedro de Velez, his replacement at Natchitoches, died, Delvaux returned, leaving the German Coast in December 1794. Delvaux undoubtedly hoped to supplement his meager salary with fees for church services performed for the parishioners.[10]

The background to the troubles at Natchitoches started as the priest passed through the Avoyelles post on his way to his new assignment. At that settlement, he uttered pro-French sentiments and embraced the position of Jacobin merchant Louis Badins. Avoyelles Commandant Etienne de la Morandière had placed the merchant under house arrest for making seditious remarks against the Spanish regime. The commandant labeled Badins a disturbed, insubordinate, and violent individual. De la Morandière did not appreciate the priest's interference on the merchant's behalf and reported him to New Orleans. Not long after his arrival in Natchitoches, Delvaux learned that Governor Carondelet had instructed the local post commandant, Louis DeBlanc, to investigate what the priest had done in Avoyelles. Influenced by de la Morandière, DeBlanc's report censured Delvaux.[11]

In New Orleans, the governor, in consultation with Vicar General Patricio Walsh, decided to transfer the priest to Mobile, which had fewer French inhabitants thus limiting his ability to agitate against the colonial government. Delvaux, however, had built up a following in Natchitoches among many of the parishioners during his years of service. When he learned about his recall, he refused to leave, and Delvaux helped to create an organization of rowdies among his partisans known as the *Revenants* (ghosts or spirits) to vent his anger at the government. They conspired and perpetrated hostile acts against

DeBlanc, his supporters, the governor, and the newcomers who favored the government. They especially disliked anyone who belonged to the nobility or held a government office; most of the dissidents were commoners. Although the *Revenants* have been called revolutionaries, names such as rowdies, toughs, hooligans, or "good ol' boys" more accurately describe them.[12]

At Delvaux's urging, his supporters circulated a petition at the post asking the governor to keep the priest in Natchitoches. Approximately sixty persons who were either family heads or single men signed the petition. More than half of them marked the petition with an "X" and had a scribe fill in their names. The first four to sign were among the leading dissidents at the post: Francisco Roquier the younger, Manuel [Michel] Prud'homme, Remigio [Rémy] Lambres, and a person who signed only as Prud'homme (probably Antoine Prud'homme).[13]

In June and July 1795, the *Revenants* enveloped the post in turmoil. The dissidents aimed some of their wrath at the recent immigrants. On July 5, an Irish settler in Natchitoches, Thomas O'Reilly, informed a friend about the troubles at Natchitoches:

> Some people think [Delvaux's] intention is to sow sedition among the inhabitants of [Natchitoches]. They are divided in consequence of his forming a petition to Remain heare; all who have not signed for him is marked out for punishment. Several people have been atacked by Bandities by night and day. [A] few of us English and Irish have offered our service to keepe peace by patroleing. [T]his has so provoked the Rev. Delvo that he has sent me word it was more fit for me to mind my own business than go a patroleing. My oppinion at present is you had better quit the notion of comeing here.[14]

When the disturbance in Natchitoches began, DeBlanc was in New Orleans. The militia commandant, Capt. Bernard D'Ortolant, had charge of the post, and, in June, he arrested five of the worst troublemakers, a move that stirred up more unrest.[15] Four of these dissidents had been among the first to sign the petition asking for Delvaux's retention, and the fifth was Atanasio Poisseaux. They had tried to remove the sindic Francisco Bossié (François Bossier) from his post and replace him with someone favorable to the *Revenants*. They resented anyone, such as Bossié, who refused to sign their petition. DeBlanc learned about the troubles only when he arrived at the Rapides post (near present-day Alexandria) on his way to Natchitoches. Once at the post, DeBlanc failed to act forcefully against the miscreants because his militia officers had sided with Delvaux. Although the *Revenants* donned masks and cloaks to conceal their identity, Natchitoches was such a small community that everybody knew who they were. They assaulted persons who attended social functions at DeBlanc's house; galloped recklessly through the village's main street; attempted to wreck a tavern and pool hall because they disliked the owner; guffawed about their pranks on the local parade grounds; and battered an Irishman, John O'Reilly, who participated in DeBlanc's patrols that tried to preserve the peace.[16]

DeBlanc reported the activities of the *Revenants* to New Orleans through the summer. He put Delvaux at the center of the *Revenants'* "well-liquored assemblies" and blamed him for inflaming the inhabitants' spirits. But, overall, DeBlanc minimized the disorders. He informed the governor that he had chastised the persons responsible for the unrest, and he believed that this action sufficed.[17]

Carondelet initially expected Commandant DeBlanc to handle the disorders at the post. He hoped his police regulation of June 1, 1795, could help in restoring stability. Insubordination, the governor advised DeBlanc, disrupted political society. Although he wanted everyone to render the respect that was due, Carondelet did not regard the unrest as serious at this time. Nevertheless, he believed that it was necessary "to suppress this trouble at the start and conciliate spirits, reducing them to the good harmony that is so necessary to maintain the needed order and subordination." But he refused to accept the petition that Delvaux remain as priest, preferring instead to send him to Mobile. Carondelet agreed to release the arrested persons if DeBlanc judged their mischief as trivial. Nonetheless, the commandant needed to reprimand them in the governor's name for their deplorable conduct. He emphasized that they could act only through their post commandant and not "through prohibited and tumultuous assemblies that produced disorders."[18]

The disorders, however, did not abate. In August, after learning that Carondelet had rejected their petition to let Delvaux remain as priest in Natchitoches, the *Revenants* unleashed a new wave of unruly behavior. The next month, the governor responded by sending Capt. José Vázquez Vahamonde, commandant at Baton Rouge and a regular army officer, to investigate and restore order. Carondelet also instructed DeBlanc to apprehend and dispatch Delvaux to New Orleans because of his penchant for promoting trouble. DeBlanc, however, seemed powerless to arrest the recalcitrant cleric. Furthermore, the governor's order had angered the priest and, surrounded by his stalwarts, he refused to leave. Even after his replacement, Father Pierre Pavié, arrived in early August, Delvaux remained in Natchitoches for nearly two additional months. During this time, he instigated a boycott by the parishioners against the dispirited new priest. Although Carondelet did not assign troops to accompany Vázquez, the governor permitted him to obtain militiamen from Natchez if he needed them.[19]

Vázquez, however, quickly revealed that he was the wrong man for the task. Among other things, he was related by marriage to the Natchitoches commandant, and he deferred to him. When Vázquez arrived at Rapides, DeBlanc advised him by letter that Delvaux had departed for New Orleans in late September and calm then prevailed at the post. Vázquez interrupted his journey and went no farther because, as he wrote to DeBlanc, "As you told me not to come up if it was quiet until a new order was given, I am awaiting your direction because my presence there could ignite new unrest." DeBlanc sent Vázquez that warning despite the fact that he was alone and without soldiers. The Natchitoches commandant appeared to be against the investigation. In Rapides, Vázquez learned about the *Revenants* from travelers who had come down from Natchitoches. Using their information, he reported to the governor that the name *Revenants* belonged to "six or eight drunks," who comprised "the engines of the dissension." DeBlanc coun-selled the captain to return to Baton Rouge, and he did. Vázquez then delayed nearly a month before informing Carondelet about what had happened on his journey and his in-ability to conduct the investigation.[20]

Delvaux possibly decided to abandon Natchitoches when he learned that the gover-nor had dispatched an investigator to gather information to reassign him. He descended the rivers to New Orleans, where he arrived in early October. He probably intended to defend himself in court. Carondelet, however, initially ignored him as he waited for Vázquez's report on the disorders before determining what course of action to pursue. In November, when the report failed to materialize, the governor consulted Louisiana's first bishop, Luis de Peñalver y Cárdenas, who arrived in New Orleans in August, about the errant priest. Carondelet considered it impossible to investigate him while he remained in the province. Delvaux was then showing his insubordination by writing letters to Natchi-toches and encouraging his supporters to remain vigilant against the government. He attempted to rekindle their enthusiasm by informing them that England and Spain had gone to war and that French warships would soon arrive in New Orleans to take charge of the colony. Delvaux spread other outrageous lies about himself that only his most credu-lous adherents could believe; one such story was his anticipated appointment as either the provincial vicar general or bishop. In mid-November 1795, both Peñalver and Caronde-let agreed to dispatch Delvaux to Havana for confinement at the Monastery of San Fran-cisco. Although he protested vehemently, the priest soon left by ship for Cuba, where he arrived on December 6.[21]

Immediately after entering the monastery, Delvaux resumed his letter-writing to the Louisiana governor and the bishop. In his lengthy epistles, he feigned ignorance about events and demanded to know the reason for his arrest and removal from New Orleans. He alleged that the government held documents that proved his innocence. He disputed the allegations that he had caused problems at Avoyelles; instead, he blamed Comman-dant de la Morandière for them. Contrary to the assertions of his accusers, the priest claimed that he had defended the Spanish government and that the inhabitants had been faithful and obedient vassals. Delvaux called the oldest residents, by which he meant the French Creoles, the most faithful subjects, and he declared that the newcomers "have done much harm to our customs and religion." Foreigners, the xenophobic priest as-serted, perpetrated the same injury in other districts as well. In one letter, he heatedly contradicted the charge that he was a revolutionary or a supporter of the French Revolu-tion. He, likewise, denied that his followers in Natchitoches favored revolution, claiming that in such a calamity they would gain nothing and lose everything. This last statement contains a modicum of truth because the only demand the *Revenants* made called for Delvaux's retention as parish priest. Carondelet, however, insisted on the cleric's con-finement in Havana while the investigation proceeded in Natchitoches. As a conse-quence, the priest remained secluded at the monastery during the next two and a half years.[22]

Meanwhile, Carondelet searched for another officer to conduct the inquiry that Vázquez had failed to perform. On November 26, 1795, the governor dictated detailed instructions for the commissioner, as he called the official whom he selected. Carondelet told him to choose a scribe and attending witnesses for testimony. He ordered the arrest of the culprits identified as troublemakers—Remigio Lambres, Manuel Prud'homme, Antonio Prud'homme, (Domingo) Prud'homme, Francisco Roquier, the younger, Josine de Mézières, Santiago de Mézières, and Cpl. Pedro Ramis, who was a regular army soldier stationed at Natchitoches and consorted with the *Revenants*. The governor instructed the commissioner to search the possessions of the accused in the presence of witnesses in order to collect more evidence, take the declarations of the officials, determine the reason for the unrest and identify its authors, arrest and send the accused to New Orleans, and make the remaining dissidents recognize their errors and what they would lose by disturbing a society of peaceful laborers.[23]

Two days later, Carondelet appointed Antonio de Argote, a New Orleans merchant and militia captain, as the commissioner; authorized fifteen soldiers to accompany him; and granted Argote permission to obtain militiamen from Natchez if necessary. Carondelet intended to suppress any armed resistance that might occur. In late November, Argote and the soldiers departed New Orleans.[24]

On January 6, 1796, as the commissioner proceeded upstream to Natchitoches, Carondelet reported events in Louisiana to Cuban Capt. Gen. Luis de Las Casas. For the colony's safety, the governor claimed that he needed four full battalions of soldiers, which meant adding one new battalion and bringing the three existing battalions to their respective full complements of about 600 troops each. He declared that seditious and insubordinate movements continued in Natchitoches. To impose governmental authority on that distant community, he sent Captain Argote and cautioned him to be gentle in order not to provoke an insurrection. Carondelet feared that if an uprising began, it could spread through the province like wildfire. Louisiana's governor enumerated all the invasion threats to the colony and outlined the subversive activities of dissidents within the colony. The governor claimed that thirty soldiers would have to be posted to Natchitoches for a full year to insure the post's tranquility and subservience. The remote settlement then had only three regular army soldiers, at least one of whom sided with the *Revenants*. Finally, Carondelet declared that without an increase in military forces, he could not be held responsible for failing to preserve the province for the Crown.[25]

On January 6, after delays caused by inclement weather, Commissioner Argote arrived at Rapides, where he learned that the *Revenants* had caused more disturbances the month before in Natchitoches. DeBlanc arrested three of the leaders and sent them to New Orleans in the care of retired Sublt. José Piernas and militia Sgt. Pedro Mora. The prisoners were then in Rapides, where Commandant Valentin Layssard interrogated them. Travelers who had recently descended the river from Natchitoches informed Argote that the post was up in arms. To cope with anticipated opposition, Layssard gave Argote thirty-five militiamen, most of whom were English-speakers (English, Irish, and

Anglo-Americans) who were then settling in the district in growing numbers. Before leaving Rapides, Piernas and Mora probably reported the seditious behavior of the Natchitoches surgeon Louis Monginot and the actor Dessessarts, and Argote advised the governor to order their arrest. Both had threatened government officials and their families and insulted the Spanish government in Natchitoches and Nacogdoches, Texas, the year before.[26]

To reach Natchitoches as quickly as possible, Argote left his boat at Rapides and obtained horses for his men. He departed immediately, but rain-swollen streams hampered his journey. He arrived in Natchitoches on January 13, and much to his amazement found the settlement calm and orderly. At this point, however, Argote began acting peculiarly. Rather than conduct the investigation with which the governor charged him, the captain glossed over the misbehavior of the priest's supporters. Through the next several weeks, Argote repeatedly gave the governor specious arguments that denied wrongdoing by the *Revenants*, and he attributed all the rowdiness to "two poorly advised youths," whose names he did not provide. He ignored *Revenant* mistreatment of DeBlanc's supporters and the English-speaking inhabitants. Instead, he argued both ways about the possibility of a revolt when he arrived in Natchitoches. On the one hand, he claimed that signs of unrest still lingered, but, on the other hand, he stated that the dissidents regretted their misbehavior. He believed that they were more worthy of compassion than correction. When the English-speakers handed him a petition that enumerated all the crimes perpetrated by the *Revenants*, including a threat to slit their throats before Easter, Argote merely forwarded it to the governor without comment. He appears to have adopted the position of the Frenchmen hostile to the English, Irish, and American inhabitants. Moreover, he dismissed the Rapides militiamen one week after his arrival, for which he employed different reasons in several letters: They were not needed because calm prevailed, he wanted to trim expenditures, and their presence irritated the local French inhabitants.[27]

In Natchitoches, Argote blatantly disregarded the governor's instructions. For example, Carondelet had given him copies of letters from persons who described the turmoil and named the culprits, but Argote paid no heed to them and did not investigate the individuals identified. He did not order DeBlanc to leave Natchitoches as the governor had instructed him and, instead, claimed that he needed the commandant's help. Argote wrote to Bernardo Fernández, commandant at Nacogdoches, Texas, about the disturbances the Natchitoches *Revenants* had caused there the previous October. He dismissed the utterances of the most outspoken of them, Domingo Prud'homme, claiming that swagger, not malice, had induced his imprudent talk. Argote described Prud'homme as docile, reflective, and incapable of purposely intending trouble. The commissioner passed judgment on Prud'homme only three days after arriving in Natchitoches and without knowing him to any degree. He alleged that if lawless acts had been committed they were due to ignorance, not animosity. After describing the "implacable hostility" that the French Creoles harbored for the English-speakers, he argued that the beating the *Revenants* inflicted on

John O'Reilly was due to his drunkenness, and, in doing so, Argote made the victim responsible for the thrashing he received. When O'Reilly, a cobbler by trade, soon departed Natchitoches for Rapides, Argote privately rejoiced.[28]

Soon after his arrival, Argote informed the governor that many people had recently come to see him, including twenty persons he described as "former *Revenants*." He claimed that they repented their earlier misdeeds and now supported the government. Argote promised to pardon their past conduct if they kept their pledge to behave properly.[29]

Before the commissioner left Natchitoches in mid-February after a five-week stay, he proclaimed the governor's announcement of the end of the Franco-Spanish war the previous summer. (The Treaty of Basel, which ended the war, was signed on July 22, 1795.) When the inhabitants heard the news at Sunday church services, they rejoiced. The peace helped to quiet whatever unrest still remained.[30]

In New Orleans, the commissioner's letters from Natchitoches produced results far different from what he had anticipated. The letters informed the governor that Argote had deviated from his instructions, and they caused Carondelet to explode in anger. He quickly shot off several directives to the commissioner, whom he believed was still in Natchitoches, advising him to obey orders and dispatching them by an express rider.[31]

But they arrived too late because Argote had already left the post. When the new orders reached him in early March 1796, he was in Baton Rouge, but they failed to alter his thinking. He reiterated to the governor that moderation was the wiser course to follow, and he refused to return to Natchitoches. He was then gathering depositions from witnesses about events at Natchitoches the year before. He wrote several letters to the governor about his work, among which his March 8 letter, his last, was the most important. It defined his position on what had happened in Natchitoches. He repeated his preference for what he called the "extra-judicial path" to quiet the unrest at the post because he wanted to avoid a formal legal investigation. He, nevertheless, claimed to have conducted a secret inquiry among persons he called the most important and judicious of the district. He alleged that the strife had originated from private disagreements between Delvaux and DeBlanc and then spread to engulf their friends and partisans. Argote noted the impertinence and intemperance of the inhabitants, but he denied that they exhibited a spirit of sedition or intended to separate themselves from legitimate government authority. He claimed that trustworthy informants, even persons injured by the dissidents, denied the need for a legal inquiry. He dismissed the misdeeds of the *Revenants* as unimportant, and he focused instead on tranquility, which he regarded as a greater concern. Argote alleged that had he acted forcefully, the post would have erupted in violence. Only through restraint could he calm the unrest.[32]

This excuse, however, deserves no credibility because evidence is lacking that the settlement in January 1796 verged on rebellion. Once Delvaux left the settlement in late September, his partisans began to shrink in number. The government showed three months later that it had the muscle to impose order and act forcefully. When the *Reve-*

nants engaged in what became their last outburst, DeBlanc arrested several *Revenants* and warned others about their misconduct. Delvaux, meanwhile, was secluded in Havana. The tide against the lawless behavior of the masked toughs had started to turn the month before Argote's arrival in Natchitoches. The post was not seething with dissension as the commissioner alleged.[33]

In March 1796, Carondelet felt frustrated because the two Spanish officers, whom he had sent to Natchitoches to impose government authority, had both failed to execute his instructions but for different reasons. He, however, took no punitive measures against them. Nevertheless, he had cause for wanting to punish some of the worst agitators at the post since he received indisputable new information about *Revenant* misbehavior in Nacogdoches and Natchitoches in 1795.

The information came from two eyewitnesses, retired army Sublt. José Piernas and Nacogdoches militia Sgt. Joaquín Mora. In March, both Piernas and Mora, who were then in New Orleans after having brought several prisoners from Natchitoches, gave lengthy depositions about what they had observed. They described the activities of the *Revenants* in Nacogdoches that insulted Spanish rule and officials. During religious celebrations at the Texas outpost in the previous October, the *Revenants* sang songs they composed filled with derogatory statements and threats, including their intention to kill DeBlanc, his family, D'Ortolant, and their supporters. Because Piernas showed his opposition to the *Revenants*, several of them threatened his life. The Nacogdoches commandant then ordered Mora to accompany Piernas as a bodyguard on his return to Natchitoches. At that post, Piernas and Mora witnessed more *Revenant* rowdiness in December 1795.[34]

Many of the *Revenants* met in houses to plot mischief, but drinking, eating, dancing, and card playing accompanied their intrigue, sometimes in marathon proportions inasmuch as they frequently persisted through the night and into the next day. Their revelry appeared as important to them as the plotting, so much so, in fact, that the latter can be described as "laissez les bon temps rouler" intrigue. Although some of the *Revenants* threatened Piernas, they never harmed him. Moreover, they did not use guns in their misdeeds. Much but not all of their misbehavior consisted of threats. Nevertheless, the threats, posturing, and occasional violence discomforted and intimidated persons loyal to the government.[35]

In March, after learning that Argote had not followed orders, the governor decided on changes at Natchitoches. He relieved DeBlanc as commandant and transferred him to Attakapas, but it appears that the former Natchitoches leader did not depart immediately. DeBlanc had requested the move, no doubt aware that his performance during the last eight months had been less than sterling in many respects. Carondelet then selected an outsider, Lieut. Félix Trudeau, a French Creole and a regular army officer, as the new post commandant. He assumed command on April 24.[36]

On May 15, the governor sent Trudeau instructions about the earlier turmoil. He ordered him to arrest several malefactors for their part in the unrest of the previous year and send them to New Orleans, where the governor proposed to take appropriate measures against them. He told Trudeau to implement the orders "without any fear of the results because everything is ready for the use of force if need be, in case of disobedience on the part of [the residents] who are ordered to appear [in New Orleans]."[37] Carondelet's May 15 letter reveals his commitment to using force, but it was not necessary because the *Revenants* had disbanded. On May 31, Carondelet further instructed Trudeau to send several persons involved in the unrest to New Orleans, where he intended to rebuke them. If they failed to appear, the governor warned, they would not receive pardons.[38]

In June, the governor decreed the expulsion from Natchitoches of surgeon Louis Monginot, who had threatened to kill Piernas, and Joseph Capuran, leader of the *Revenants*. Argote had recommended Monginot's arrest in January, when he passed through Rapides on his way to Natchitoches.[39]

Monginot appears not to have left Natchitoches because he underwent a political conversion and became entangled in new difficulties. In the presence of Commandant Trudeau and several witnesses in mid-June 1796, he publicly recanted his earlier behavior. He deposited two letters in the local archives, in which he expressed remorse for his misconduct and admitted his earlier disrespect toward José Piernas, whose forgiveness he now implored. Piernas, who returned to the post from New Orleans, acknowledged Monginot's change of heart and generously forgave him. At the time Monginot experienced his political metamorphosis, he languished in jail, charged with horse-stealing.[40]

Earlier, Monginot had taken offense at the government because it had not appointed him post surgeon. He expressed his displeasure loudly by mouthing revolutionary rhetoric, and he disrespectfully named his dog *Aristocrate*, to show the governor, the Barón de Carondelet, his contempt for the aristocracy. When the governor learned about Monginot's impertinence in the early summer of 1795, he became incensed. Carondelet despised revolutionary symbolism, and he shot back an order to the post commandant to kill the animal, unmindful that Monginot, not the dog, was responsible for the name. The governor directed the post commandant to acknowledge when the order had been carried out. But the dog possibly escaped execution because no other communication mentions the animal.[41]

Capuran, the recognized head of the *Revenants* who used the secret name *le Grand Rousseau*, left Natchitoches for Texas. He may have feared more punishment if he remained in Louisiana. From Nacogdoches, he wrote to Carondelet on September 27, 1796, explaining his role in the events. He seemed unrepentent for his behavior, and his attitude elicited no sympathy from the governor. When he replied on November 14, Carondelet rejected the *Revenant's* arguments. Instead, he pointed out Capuran's lack of respect for authority, his seditious behavior in forming the *Revenants*, and his mistreatment of the post's residents. The governor swore that Capuran "would never reenter" Natchitoches. Despite his hostile attitude, Carondelet later questioned Argote about Capuran. Ever the apologist for the *Revenants*, the former commissioner claimed that

Capuran had meant no disrespect and that unnamed persons had misled him. The governor, however, dismissed Argote's opinion, and Capuran remained in exile.[42]

Carondelet also ejected two other troublemakers from the province. One was Louis Armant, whose father, Joseph Marie Armant, was the Spanish commissary for East Texas. In his explanation to Spain, Carondelet tried to soften the expulsion by claiming that Armant's family wanted to teach him a lesson, and they urged the governor to send him out of the province. But that was not what happened. DeBlanc arrested Armant in Natchitoches for his part in the December 1795 disturbances and sent him to New Orleans. Carondelet then ordered Armant's deportation. He placed Armant on a vessel leaving the colony, but, as it descended the Mississippi, Armant jumped ship at Pointe-à-la-Hache and disappeared. When Carondelet later ordered Josine de Mézières' deportation, he placed the prisoner in the care of a four-soldier escort to Balize, the post at the mouth of the Mississippi, to insure that he left. As in the case of Armant, the governor claimed to Spain that de Mézières' family supported his expulsion.[43]

In June 1796, as the governor was dealing with those responsible for the unrest in Natchitoches, he adopted a new posture toward Delvaux. Carondelet gave him the choice of either going to Pensacola to serve as priest or remaining in Havana in detention while the investigation continued. When Captain General Las Casas informed Delvaux of his choices, the priest, who initially replied that he would go to Pensacola, did not, and he remained confined at the monastery in Cuba.[44]

The investigation of Delvaux continued, albeit slowly. Although Argote obtained several depositions from witnesses both for and against the priest, the inhabitants of Natchitoches, where Delvaux had committed his most serious offenses, provided few of them. Argote later claimed that had he taken more interrogatories at that post, "the said priest would have emerged whiter than snow."[45]

The commissioner's statement implied that the community supported the priest. He used that explanation as justification for not conducting the investigation, but his assessment of public opinion in Natchitoches is erroneous. Although Delvaux had many supporters at the post, numerous other people opposed the discord the priest generated. In the fall of 1796, Bishop Peñalver obtained several more depositions during a pastoral visit to the Red River settlements. In Natchitoches the inhabitants greeted him warmly and exhibited no signs of revolutionary anti-clericalism. While the priests who accompanied the bishop baptized children, Peñalver quietly questioned several people about Delvaux. One witness praised the priest, but all the others noted his involvement in the disorders and his presence at houses where the *Revenants* met. They had observed him dancing at parties and singing locally composed "revolutionary songs." These witnesses confirmed the priest's connection to the unrest.[46]

After Bishop Peñalver returned from Natchitoches with reports critical of Delvaux, Carondelet decided to eject the troublesome cleric from Louisiana permanently. On January 9, 1797, in order to obtain royal permission for his expulsion, the governor wrote a lengthy covering letter to a large batch of documents that dealt with the strife at Natchitoches. He dispatched them to Eugenio Llaguño y Amirola, secretary to the first minister (the head of government), Manuel Godoy, who now enjoyed the title Prince of the Peace for his negotiations that ended the war with France. Carondelet blamed the French Revolution for the strife, and he described Delvaux as having "the closest connections with the revolutions that were then disturbing Europe." This was not true. Moreover, the governor exaggerated the tense conditions in the colony; he described them as a powder keg, which a "revolutionary spark" could ignite. He claimed that the province's scant resources would be unable to extinguish such a calamity. He reported that had he sent a detachment of soldiers to Natchitoches to quell the disorders, the rebels would have ambushed the boats carrying them up the Red River, defeating them and spreading revolutionary turmoil throughout the province. But this was another gross exaggeration on Carondelet's part. The so-called Natchitoches "rebels" had not tried to stop the soldiers Argote took with him in early 1796. Why then should they attack a larger and better-equipped contingent of soldiers? In his letters, Carondelet overstated the strength of the *Revenants*, and he engaged in further deception when he asserted that many people in Natchitoches resisted the reestablishment of Spanish control. He told Llaguño that he did not want Delvaux investigated in Louisiana because it would arouse passions and his partisans would exonerate him.[47]

In response to the governor's request, on July 16, 1797, Godoy issued a royal order expelling Delvaux from Spain's dominions. But when the decree arrived in Louisiana, the authorities did nothing because Delvaux was in Cuba, and Cuba was either not informed about the order or failed to act. The priest, consequently, remained in detention.[48]

While these events unfolded in Spain and Louisiana, Delvaux grew increasingly restless in Havana. In July 1797, he consulted the new captain general of Cuba, the Conde de Santa Clara, demanding to know why the government had not charged him with alleged wrongdoing and why could he not defend himself in court. Santa Clara, who knew nothing about Delvaux, soon wrote to Peñalver in New Orleans to learn about the problem. The bishop forwarded the letter to the new governor of Louisiana, Manuel Gayoso de Lemos, who had replaced Carondelet in August 1797. In January 1798, Gayoso replied that a royal order had decreed the priest's expulsion from the Spanish dominions and that the captain general should obey the order to deport Delvaux. But for an unknown reason Santa Clara did not do so.[49]

On June 26, 1798, Delvaux again inquired of the captain general why had he now spent "three years" in detention without learning the charges against him. He requested copies of documents about his case that the Louisiana governor had sent to Havana. A government clerk searched the priest's file and failed to locate the letters Delvaux wanted, but he found a royal order to dispatch the cleric to Spain. Delvaux must have learned about the discovery and feared being sent there. Only two days after the clerk reported his find, Delvaux disappeared from the Monastery of San Francisco, his home for the past thirty months.[50]

What happened to the priest during the next several years remains mostly a mystery. Without difficulty, he engineered his flight from the monastery, where guards—if there were any—did not watch him closely. He escaped taking his clothing, books, and other paraphernalia, doubtlessly by cart or wagon. His pursuers soon located these belongings, but not Delvaux, at a sugar plantation called Nueva Holanda outside Havana. Perhaps the captain general launched a search for him; the priest, however, eluded capture. On October 1, 1798, Santa Clara notified New Orleans that Delvaux had disappeared, and that he, the captain general, could not provide more information about him.[51]

The cleric, however, had not vanished permanently. For several years, he either hid in Cuba or lived discreetly elsewhere unbeknown to Spanish authorities. He did not return to Louisiana while it remained in Spanish hands. After France and then the United States took charge of the province in late 1803, he resurfaced in Louisiana and resumed work as a parish priest.[52] The chastened and perhaps now contrite Delvaux no longer caused problems for the authorities, and, instead, he quietly performed his pastoral duties. During the first two decades of the nineteenth century, Delvaux served as priest at St. James Parish. From that post, he also ministered to the faithful on a part-time basis in Cloutierville (St. John the Baptist Church) and, after the priest at the Church of the Ascension accidentally drowned in 1808, Delvaux occasionally visited Donaldsonville.[53]

Without a doubt, Delvaux's role in the 1795 unrest did not endear him to the Spaniards because of the financial cost and the apprehension he caused. Although Carondelet labeled Delvaux a revolutionary, he was not, and he did not lead a revolutionary movement in the province. Despite the *Revenants'* use of radical songs and dress, the leaders of the dissension at Natchitoches espoused little revolutionary rhetoric. Their sole demand was to keep Delvaux as their priest, a demand the cleric probably instigated.[54] Had he been a genuine revolutionary, he could have caused many more problems for the Spaniards.

Moreover, the dissidents were never as powerful as Carondelet's and Argote's letters suggest. The conclusion of Spain's war against revolutionary France helped in dousing the final embers of unrest, not only in Natchitoches but throughout the province. When Trudeau assumed command at the post in the spring of 1796, he did so without trouble, and he encountered no resistance or protests when he ordered the removal of several troublemakers. The strife at Natchitoches had ebbed relatively quickly. It reached its zenith when Delvaux was at the settlement, declined significantly after he departed for New Orleans, and all but vanished when he left for Cuba.

Contrary to the assertions of Liljegren and Andreu Ocariz, the Spaniards in both Natchitoches and the province were not as weak as these historians suggest. They base their assertions on the governor's letters to higher authorities, which as noted earlier, did not report events accurately.[55] He revealed in letters to subordinates his willingness to employ force to gain submission. The governor, however, did not echo this sentiment in his letters to higher authorities, in which he presented a vastly different synopsis of events, one which magnified his weaknesses and overstated his opponents' strengths.

The threat of internal insurrection never reached the proportions Carondelet professed, nor were there as many people in opposition to Spanish rule in Louisiana as he declared. The governor frequently exaggerated. He believed that he could obtain both money and manpower from Cuba more readily if he increased the size of the forces in opposition to him. Moreover, he could minimize his responsibility if by chance a revolt occurred.

Finally, a question can be raised as to whether Carondelet overreacted in the Natchitoches "crisis." He was notorious for doing so on other occasions when crises developed.[56] This characterization of the governor, however, must be employed cautiously because the governor was a complex individual. With the exception of the punishment meted out to the dog *Aristocrate* (if it was imposed), it is this writer's belief that on this occasion he did not overreact. As governor, Carondelet bore considerable responsibilities. Above all else was his obligation to uphold Spanish authority throughout the province. He could not permit disgruntled inhabitants to engage in seditious behavior, thwart government policies not to their liking, and mistreat innocent inhabitants. To consent to such conduct could encourage similar misbehavior at other posts, thereby eroding the fabric of orderly society, and disillusioning genuine government supporters.[57]

As stated earlier, the governor's correspondence with Cuba and Spain must be read carefully, and his assertions weighed against his messages to subordinates in Louisiana so as not to be deceived by his embellishments and distortions. To reiterate, Louisiana was never "practically in open rebellion" against the governor, and Delvaux did not lead an "open revolutionary movement" in Natchitoches.[58]

Notes for "Father Jean Delvaux and the Natchitoches Revolt of 1795"

[1]Nineteenth-century historians François-Xavier Martin, Charles Gayarré, and Alcée Fortier do not mention the Natchitoches revolt in their state histories. Jack D. L. Holmes, who translated one of the two articles on the Natchitoches revolt (see Note 3), has a brief discussion based on the two articles but does not provide new information in his edited work, *Honor and Fidelity: The Louisiana Infantry Regiment and the Louisiana Militia Companies, 1766-1821* (Birmingham, Ala., 1965), 67.

[2]Ernest R. Liljegren, "Jacobinism in Spanish Louisiana, 1792-1797," *Louisiana Historical Quarterly*, 22 (1939): 47-97, with pages 65-79 devoted to Natchitoches; information given to the author by A. P. Nasatir in the summer of 1977. Despite Liljegren's use of primary documents, his article contains significant errors such as inaccurate translations of documents, omission of important points, and a flawed chronology. For example, Liljegren states that "an intense rivalry existed between the Spaniards in Texas and the *habitants* in Louisiana." Contrary to Liljegren's assertion which he bases on differing royal policies toward these two provinces, most residents on both sides of the boundary cooperated with one another, engaged in considerable clandestine trade, and attended religious and probably other celebrations in each other's communities. As Ruth Mullins McLeod wrote in 1936, "The jealousy that existed between the officials of the two governments did not affect the inhabitants of the two settlements who were far removed from their mother countries and were fighting similar battles for existence in the wilderness. These people traded together freely, and the commanding officer of Los Adaes sent assistance to Natchitoches during the siege of the Natchez." McLeod, "The History of Natchitoches" (M.A. thesis, Louisiana State University, 1936), 51. See also, Lawrence E. L'Herisson, Jr., "The Evolution of the Texas Road and the Subsequential Settlement Occupancy of the Adjacent Strip of Northwestern Louisiana: 1528-1824" (M.A. thesis, Louisiana State University, 1981).

[3]Juan José Andreu Ocariz, "The Natchitoches Revolt," trans. Jack D. L. Holmes, *Louisiana Studies*, 3 (1964):

117-32. Thomas M. Fiehrer, "The Baron de Carondelet as Agent of Bourbon Reform: A Study of Spanish Colonial Administration in the Years of the French Revolution" (Ph.D. dissertation, Tulane University, 1977), 486-93, discusses Delvaux using the same documents (which are in the Archivo Histórico Nacional, Estado, legajo 3900, expediente 2, hereafter cited as AHN, Est., leg., exped.) as Andreu Ocariz but in an extremely confused manner. A draft of the expediente is in the Archivo General de Indias, Papeles Procedentes de Cuba (hereafter cited as AGI, PC,) leg. 178B, and many but not all the documents are in the Archivo General de Simancas, Guerra Moderna (hereafter cited as AGS, GM), leg. 6920.

[4]Edwin Adams Davis, *Louisiana, A Narrative History,* 3rd ed. (Baton Rouge, 1971), 125.

[5]Carondelet wrote many letters that exaggerated the "deplorable conditions" in Louisiana because of the threats of invasions, radicals, and slaves. See, for example, Carondelet to the Duque de la Alcudia, No. 12 reserved, New Orleans, July 31, 1793, AHN, Est., leg. 3898, exped. 6; Carondelet to Alcudia, No. 14 reserved, August 27, 1793, and enclosures, and Carondelet to Luis de Las Casas, No. 444, New Orleans, October 3, 1793, all in AHN, Est., leg. 3890, exped. 13; Carondelet to Las Casas, very reserved, New Orleans, May 3, 1795, and No. 135 reserved, New Orleans, June 13, 1795, both in AHN, Est., leg. 3899. In addition to Carondelet's correspondence with officials he appointed or who served at Natchitoches, this study employs the Records of the Diocese of Louisiana and the Floridas at the University of Notre Dame, and it makes a more extensive use of the documents in AGI, PC, than either Liljegren or Andreu. See also Gilbert C. Din, "Carondelet, the Cabildo, and Slaves: Louisiana in 1795," *Louisiana History,* 38 (1997): 6-8, which briefly discusses errors some historians have made about Carondelet.

[6]For a view of the Pointe Coupée slave conspiracy and especially its aftermath based on the documentation, see Din, "Carondelet, the Cabildo, and Slaves," 5-28. Different views, and what I consider exaggerations about the conspiracy, are in Gwendolyn Midlo Hall, *Africans in Colonial Louisiana: The Development of Afro-Creole Culture in the Eighteenth Century* (Baton Rouge, 1992), 344-80; and James Thomas McGowan, "Creation of a Slave Society: Louisiana Plantations in the Eighteenth Century" (Ph.D. dissertation, University of Rochester, 1976), 349-94.

[7]Louis DeBlanc to Carondelet, Natchitoches, February 18 and April 16, 1792, both in Lawrence Kinnaird, ed., *Spain in the Mississippi Valley, 1765-1794,* 3 Parts (Washington, 1946), Part 3:9-11, 25-27 respectively; Brian E. Coutts, "Boom and Bust: The Rise and Fall of the Tobacco Industry in Spanish Louisiana, 1770-1790," *The Americas,* 42 (1985-86): 289-309; F. Todd Smith, *The Caddo Indians: Tribes at the Convergence of Empires, 1542-1854* (College Station, 1995), 81-82; Liljegren, "Jacobinism," 65-67. Liljegren, in a biased manner, claims that the post's inhabitants had "degenerated," lacked education, and wasted their lives. See also John G. Clark, *New Orleans, 1718-1812: An Economic History* (Baton Rouge, 1970), 184-85, 190.

In early 1795, Governor Carondelet was already on edge because he feared an American invasion. That year he sent an expedition to establish Fort San Fernando de las Barrancas on Spanish-claimed lands at present-day Memphis. See Jack D. L. Holmes, ed., "A 1795 Inspection of Spanish Missouri," *Missouri Historical Review,* 55 (1960): 5-17; and "The Ebb-Tide of Spanish Military Power on the Mississippi: Fort San Fernando de las Barrancas, 1795-1798," *East Tennessee Historical Society Publications,* 36 (1964): 22-44.

[8]DeBlanc to Carondelet, Natchitoches, August 4, 1795, AHN, Est., leg. 3900, exped. 2. Athanase de Mézières described opposition to him as lieutenant governor by local residents as early as 1772. It so embittered him that he claimed to prefer the company of "barbarian Indians" to that of the Natchitoches inhabitants. De Mézières to Francisco Bouligny, Natchitoches, February 12, 1772, Rosemond E. and Emile Kuntz Collection, Howard-Tilton Memorial Library, Tulane University, New Orleans, La. Herbert Eugene Bolton, ed., *Athanase de Mézières and the Louisiana-Texas Frontier, 1768-1780* (1914; New York, 1970), contains nothing about rivalry at the post. De Mézières' first wife, Marie Pétronille Féliciane Juchereau de Saint-Denis, was a daughter of the post's founder, Louis Juchereau de Saint-Denis.

[9]Carondelet to DeBlanc, New Orleans, March 7, 1792, AGI, PC, leg. 18. Overall, the de Mézières faction was more hostile toward the new settlers. On immigration policy and efforts, see Gilbert C. Din, "The Immigration Policy of Governor Esteban Miró in Spanish Louisiana," *Southwestern Historical Quarterly,* 73 (1969-70): 155-75; and "Spain's Immigration Policy in Louisiana and the American Penetration, 1792-1803," *Southwestern*

Historical Quarterly, 76 (1972-73): 255-76.

[10]Jean Delvaux to Bishop Luis Peñalver y Cárdenas, on board the *San Francisco de Borgia* at New Orleans, November 19, 1795, attached to the document dated October 1, 1798 (which contains under this date all the documentation on Delvaux and the unrest at Natchitoches) in the Records of the Diocese of Louisiana and the Floridas, University of Notre Dame, on microfilm (hereafter cited as RDLF, ND); Delvaux pay record, AGI, PC, leg. 538B; Gilbert C. Din, "The Irish Mission to West Florida," *Louisiana History*, 12 (1971): 318, 324. In the spring of 1794, Delvaux petitioned for a pay increase, and Governor Carondelet directed a memorial to the Crown on this subject, but there is no known reply. [Carondelet] to Patricio Walsh, New Orleans, May 13, 1794, AGI, PC, leg. 102. Liljegren, in "Jacobinism," 67 and note, erroneously calls the deceased priest Francisco Caldez, and he states, on page 70, that all the French inhabitants supported Delvaux, but the documentation does not substantiate his view.

[11]Patricio Walsh to Carondelet, New Orleans, January 7, 1795, AGI, PC, leg. 102; Esteban Delamorandière, Avoyelles, December 10 and 23, 1794, AHN, Est., leg. 3900, exped. 2. Delamorandière had had an unpleasant encounter with a troublemaker in his district only the year before. See Gilbert C. Din, "Domingo de Assereto: An Adventurer in Carondelet's Louisiana," *Louisiana History*, 34 (1993): 69-85. Liljegren, in "Jacobinism," 67-68, has a confused account of Delvaux in Avoyelles and his troubles with Delamorandière; he also claims that Badins was a Natchitoches merchant.

[12]Carondelet to DeBlanc, New Orleans, January 8, 1795, AGI, PC, leg. 22; DeBlanc to Carondelet, Natchitoches, February 14, 1795, AGI, PC, leg. 210; Carondelet to Delvaux, New Orleans, May 11, 1795, AGI, Audiencia de Santo Domingo (hereafter cited as SD), leg. 2566. Many of the *Revenants* seem to belong to the "de Mézières faction" because several sons of the late lieutenant governor numbered among its members. The sons of de Mézières could claim noble status through their father who belonged to the French nobility. Prior to Delvaux's return to Natchitoches in 1795, factionalism was already present at the post.

[13]Petition of the Natchitoches residents, July 10, 1795, AGI, PC, leg. 22, with a copy in the Louisiana Collection, Bancroft Library, University of California, Berkeley, Calif.

[14]Thos. O'Reilly to "Dear Friend," Natchitoches, July 5, 1795, AGI, PC, leg. 178B.

[15]Bernard D'Ortolant to Carondelet, Natchitoches, July 1, 1795, Francisco Bossié to D'Ortolant, Natchitoches, June 29, 1795, both in AHN, Est., leg. 3900, exped. 2. The effort on the part of the local inhabitants to elect their own syndic was an insult to the governor because it was his right to select them from a list of three names supplied by district commandants.

[16]DeBlanc to Carondelet, Rapides and Natchitoches, July 22 and August 4, 1795, respectively, both in AHN, Est., leg. 3900, exped. 2; DeBlanc to Carondelet, Natchitoches, October 2, 1795, AGI, PC, leg. 178B.

[17]DeBlanc to Carondelet, Natchitoches, August 4, 1795, AHN, Est., leg. 3900, exped. 2; DeBlanc to Carondelet, Natchitoches, October 2, 1795, AGI, PC, leg. 178B.

[18]Carondelet to DeBlanc, New Orleans, July 21 and 23, 1795, AGI, PC, leg. 22, with a copy of the second letter in AHN, Est., leg. 3900, exped. 2.

[19]DeBlanc to José Vázquez Vahamonde, Natchitoches, October 11, 1795, RDFL, ND. Vázquez was a forty-eight-year-old native of Galicia, Spain, and a twenty-five-year veteran of military service, all of it in Louisiana. He participated on all three of Bernardo de Gálvez's expeditions against the British in West Florida during the war. His service sheet of December 31, 1791, is in AGS, GM, leg. 7291.

[20]Carondelet to Vázquez, reserved, New Orleans, September 16, 1795, AGI, PC, leg. 178B; Vázquez to Carondelet, Rapides, October 6, 1795, RDFL, ND, which contains both quotations; DeBlanc to Vázquez, Natchitoches, October 11, 1795, RDFL, ND, and in AHN, Est., leg. 3900, exped. 2; Pierre Pavié to [Carondelet], Natchitoches, November 2, 1795, Vázquez to Carondelet, Baton Rouge, November 21, 1795, both in AHN, Est., leg. 3900, exped. 2.

[21]Carondelet to Luis Peñalver y Cárdenas, New Orleans, November 2, 1795, AGI, PC, leg. 1447; Bishop Luis to Carondelet, New Orleans, November 3, 1795, AHN, Est., leg. 3900, exped. 2; Bishop Luis to Bishop Felipe José Trespalacios, New Orleans, November 18, 1795, Bishop Luis to Luis de Las Casas, New Orleans, November 18, 1795, the Bishop of Cuba to the Bishop of Louisiana, Havana, December 14, 1795, all in AGI, PC, leg. 1458; DeBlanc to Carondelet, Natchitoches, December 22, 1795, AGI, PC, leg. 32.

[22]Delvaux to Carondelet, Havana, December 9 and 21, 1795, Delvaux to Peñalver, Havana, December 20, 1795, and January 16, 1796, all in RDLF, ND; Liljegrin, "Jacobinism," 78 and note. Although the *Revenants* used some of the symbolism of the French Revolution and sang the "Marseillaise," they issued no demands beyond insisting that Delvaux remain as their priest.

[23]"Ynstrucción para las operaciones Judiciales del Comisionado que ha de ir a Natchitoches, para averiguar el verdadero motivo de los alborotos de aquel Puesto, y quienes hayan sido sus autores y cómplices," Carondelet, New Orleans, November 26, 1795, AHN, Est., leg. 3900, exped. 2. The "attending witnesses" (*testigos de asistencia*) listened to the testimony of the witnesses or the accused and verified the accuracy of the written documents.

[24][Carondelet] to Antonio [de] Argote, New Orleans, November 28, 1795, [Carondelet] to [Vázquez] Vahamonde, [New Orleans], November 28, 1795, [Carondelet] to Carlos de Grand-Pré, New Orleans, November 28, 1795, Argote to Carondelet, on the galley *La Luisiana*, December 2, 1795, all in AGI, PC, leg. 32; Argote to Carondelet, No. 2, Rapides, January 8, 1795, AGI, PC, leg. 33. Liljegrin, in "Jacobinism," 75n, calls "Antonio Argote y Villalobos" the Spanish consul in Kentucky in 1797. Perhaps he was, but he was not the commissioner and New Orleans merchant whom Carondelet appointed in 1795. Liljegren, on page 75, inexplicably calls Argote captain of the Baton Rouge militia. For a brief description of Argote's services, see his memorial to the king, New Orleans, October 1, 1795, enclosed in Carondelet to the Las Casas, No. 766, New Orleans, October 10, 1795, AGI, PC, leg. 1443B.

[25][Carondelet] to Las Casas, No. 152, confidential, New Orleans, January 6, 1796, AGI, PC, leg. 153A. In this letter, Carondelet demonstrated his predilection for increasing the size of his enemies.

[26]Argote to Carondelet, No. 2, Rapides, January 8, 1796, AGI, PC, leg. 33; Argote to Carondelet, Natchitoches, January 16, 1796, AHN, Est., leg. 3900, exped. 2. In October 1795, many Natchitoches inhabitants went to Nacogdoches to participate in the local religious celebrations; some of them were *Revenants* who caused trouble. See two letters by Bernardo Fernández to DeBlanc, Nacogdoches, October 23, 1795, AHN, Est., leg. 3900, exped. 2, which describe the problems they caused and Fernández's offer of help to a supposedly beleaguered DeBlanc. DeBlanc, however, declined the help.

[27]Argote to Carondelet, Natchitoches, January 17, 1796, AHN, Est., leg. 3900, exped. 2; Argote to Carondelet, Nos. 5, 6, and 7, Natchitoches, January 17, 19, and 20 respectively, 1796, all in AGI, PC, leg. 33; "Statement by the English Inhabitants to Argote," Natchitoches, January 16, 1796, RDLF, ND, and in AGI, PC, leg. 208A. Possibly Argote disliked the English-speakers because of the competition he had received from their kind who were merchants in New Orleans.

[28]Argote to Carondelet, Natchitoches, January 17, 1796, AGI, PC, leg. 33; Argote to Bernardo Fernández, Natchitoches, January 15, 1796, enclosed in Argote to Carondelet, Natchitoches, January 16, 1796, AGI, PC, leg. 178B. Liljegren, in "Jacobinism," 76, states that DeBlanc left Natchitoches soon after Argote arrived, but this is incorrect. On February 7, 1797, Argote recommended to the governor to reassign DeBlanc to another post. In doing so, Argote adopted a position contrary to his earlier stance and endorsed that of some of the local inhabitants, such as the *Revenants*, who were in opposition to DeBlanc. Argote to Carondelet, Natchitoches, February 7, 1796, AGI, PC, leg. 33.

[29]Argote to Carondelet, Natchitoches, January 16, 1796, AHN, Est., leg. 3900, exped. 2.

[30]Argote to Carondelet, Nos. 10, 11, and 12, Natchitoches, February 6, 1796, Argote to Carondelet, Natchitoches, February 7, 1796, DeBlanc to Carondelet, Natchitoches, February 16, 1796, all in AGI, PC, leg. 33. The news about the end of the war had been proclaimed in New Orleans on January 1, 1796, somewhat belatedly

because the captain general of Cuba had delayed authorizing permission for its proclamation. Liljegren, "Jaco-binism," 76, states that Argote left Natchitoches "the last of February." Actually, DeBlanc was again in charge of the post by February 16, 1796.

[31][Carondelet] to Argote, New Orleans, February 16, 17, 19, and 24, 1796, [Carondelet] to Guillermo Duparc, New Orleans, February 17, 1796, all in AGI, PC, leg. 33. In his February 19 letter to Argote, Carondelet wrote: "[I]t is absolutely necessary that you do everything as directed earlier. . . . You should not listen to the fears, suspicions, or scruples that impelled you to thwart what the Instructions ordered with respect to the two peti-tions that you sent me, and which I return to serve you as a guide and provide you with all you need for your work and as I ordered you in my message of [February] 16th.

"If you are on the road returning, you shall go back immediately, take command of the Post, and inform Luis DeBlanc to leave and go to Attakapas to relieve the commandant there. Meanwhile, I shall see that an able person goes [to Natchitoches] to take command." [Carondelet] to Argote, New Orleans, February 19, 1796, AGI, PC, leg. 33.

[32]Argote to Carondelet, Baton Rouge, February 23, 1796, AGI, PC, leg. 33; Argote to Carondelet, Baton Rouge, March 4, 5, and 8, 1796, all in AGI, PC, leg. 178B.

[33]Testimony of José Piernas, New Orleans, March 16, 1796, RDLF, ND. Louis Armant, one of the three per-sons arrested by DeBlanc in Natchitoches, claimed that he was a captain of the *Revenants*. The other two per-sons arrested were Juan Archinard and Pedro Charpentier. Armant showed his rebellious behavior when he was held prisoner at Rapides.

[34]In his deposition, Joaquín Mora identified many of the *Revenants* in Natchitoches. Among them were Pablo Bonet Lafitte; Capuran; Monginot; Verdelay; Atanasio, Santiago, and Josine de Mézières who were all brothers; Francisco Bousquier; Manuel, Antonio, and Dominico or Domingo Prudhomme who were all brothers and brothers-in-law of Bousquier; Louis Armant; Bautista Andry; Poisseaux; Juan Bautista Grappe; Antonio Borde-lon; Alexo Cloutier; and Remigio Lambres (who was the brother-in-law of Bousquier the merchant and the three Prudhomme brothers). Others involved in the unrest were Juan Archinard, Francisco Charpentier, Fran-cisco Langlois Morlan, Louis Fontenau, and Antonio Sauterelle, and Corporal Ramis. Mora deposition, New Orleans, March 31, 1796, RDLF, ND. Besides the *Revenants* going to Nacogdoches for the religious celebra-tions, many other Natchitoches residents also went.

[35]José Piernas deposition, New Orleans, March 16, 1796, Joaquín Mora deposition, New Orleans, March 31, 1796, both in RDLF, ND. Both depositions provide much information on the *Revenants*. For more knowledge on José Piernas, see three articles by Jack D. L. Holmes, "Joseph Piernas and a Proposed Settlement on the Calcasieu River, 1795," *McNeese Review*, 13 (1962): 59-80; "Joseph Piernas and the Nascent Cattle Industry of Southwest Louisiana," *McNeese Review*, 17 (1966): 13-26; and "The Calcasieu Promoter: Joseph Piernas and His 1799 Proposal," *Louisiana History*, 9 (1968): 163-67. Piernas was the son of Pedro Piernas, a Spanish army officer who arrived in 1766 with the first Spanish governor Antonio de Ulloa. Piernas' father was com-mandant of the Fixed Louisiana Infantry Regiment from 1785 until his death in 1791. José was a cadet when he arrived in Louisiana in 1766, and he later became an army officer as a sublieutenant. But behavior unbefitting an officer resulted in his early forced retirement. He was in St. Louis in 1780, waiting for his discharge, when the British attempted to seize the settlement. Piernas played an important role in repelling them. For documents describing the attack, see A. P. Nasatir, ed., "St. Louis During the British Attack of 1780," in *New Spain and the Anglo-American West: Historical Contributions Presented to Herbert Eugene Bolton*, 2 vols. (1932; reprint ed., New York, 1969), 1:239-61, and A. P. Nasatir, "The Anglo-Spanish Frontier in the Illinois Country During the American Revolution, 1779-1783," *Journal of the Illinois State Historical Society*, 21 (1928): 291-358.

[36][Carondelet] to Francisco Bouligny, New Orleans, March 5, 1796, [Carondelet] to Francisco Caso y Luengo, New Orleans, March 5, 1796, both in AGI, PC, leg. 129; Carondelet to DeBlanc, New Orleans, March 5, 1796, AGI, PC, leg. 212B; DeBlanc to Carondelet, Natchitoches, April 24, 1796, AGI, PC, leg. 33. DeBlanc assumed command at Attakapas on July 10, 1796. Caso y Luengo to Carondelet, Attakapas, July 11, 1796, and DeBlanc to Carondelet, Attakapas, July 11, 1796, both in AGI, PC, leg. 34. Trudeau was the last Spanish commandant of Natchitoches. Petition of Luis Carlos DeBlanc to the king, New Orleans, May 30, 1801, AGI, PC, leg. 137A.

[37][Carondelet] to Trudeau, New Orleans, May 15, 1796, AGI, PC, leg. 33.

[38]Carondelet to Trudeau, New Orleans, May 31, 1796, AGI, PC, leg. 23.

[39]Carondelet to Trudeau, New Orleans, June 25, 1796, AGI, PC, leg. 23; Trudeau to Carondelet, No. 8, Natchitoches, July 2, 1796, AGI, PC, leg. 34. In 1792, Governor Carondelet had reprimanded DeBlanc for mistreating two subordinates, Joseph Capuran and Pablo Bonet Lafitte. Both of them figured prominently in the 1795 disorders against DeBlanc. Carondelet to DeBlanc, New Orleans, May 31, 1792, AGI, PC, leg. 18.

[40]Statement of [Louis] Monginot, Natchitoches, June 21, 1796, RDLF, ND. In some documents, such as this one, Monginot is misidentified as Francisco Monginot. He was in trouble with the governor before Delvaux began the disorders in Natchitoches. In April 1795, the governor instructed Monginot to go down to New Orleans to be reprimanded, but Monginot refused to go and remained defiantly at the post. [Carondelet] to the commandant of Natchitoches, New Orleans, April 28, 1795, AGI, PC, leg. 22.

[41][Carondelet] to the commandant of Natchitoches, New Orleans, April 28, 1795, Carondelet to DeBlanc, New Orleans, June 25, 1795, both in AGI, PC, leg. 22.

[42]Joseph Capuran to Carondelet, Nacogdoches, September 27, 1796, Argote to Carondelet, New Orleans, January 25, 1797, both in AGI, PC, leg. 33; Carondelet to Capuran, New Orleans, November 14, 1796, AGI, PC, leg. 23.

[43]Carondelet to Trudeau, New Orleans, July 5, 1796, AGI, PC, leg. 23; [Carondelet] to Joaquín Romo, New Orleans, October 29, 1796, AGI, PC, leg. 32; Carondelet to Llaguño, No. 23, New Orleans, January 29, 1797, AHN, Est., leg. 3900, exped. 2; Kinnaird, ed., *Spain in the Mississippi Valley,* Part 3:xviii. Smith, in *The Caddo Indians,* 74, 78, refers to Armant as Arman, possibly because of Spanish mispronunciation and misspelling. Liljegren, in "Jacobinism," 74, cites a DeBlanc letter of December 22, 1795, which states that the *Revenants* purposely got Armant drunk and made him appear as one of their supporters. Liljegren does not seem to know that Armant was arrested and sent to New Orleans, or that while he was in Rapides, he freely admitted his involvement with the *Revenants.* Quite possibly the Armant and de Mézières families approved the expulsions, but that was not the reason for Carondelet's action; he wanted to teach the rowdies that even if they came from "good" families, he would not tolerate their misbehavior. This is another example of Carondelet doing one thing in the colony but reporting it differently to higher authorities.

[44]Carondelet to Peñalver, New Orleans, June 2, 1796, and attachments, AGI, PC, leg. 178A; Peñalver to Bishop Trespalacios of Havana, New Orleans, June 20, 1796, RDLF, ND; Carondelet to Las Casas, No. 162 reserved, New Orleans, June 20, 1796, AGI, PC, leg. 1447; Las Casas to Peñalver, Havana, July 13, 1796, Delvaux to Peñalver, Havana, July 17, 1796, both in RDLF, ND.

[45]Argote to Carondelet, Baton Rouge, March 8, 1796, AGI, PC, leg. 33.

[46]Peñalver statement, November 19, 1996, testimony of Luis Carlos Chamard, Natchitoches, November 10, 1796, testimony of Joé Fauzin, Natchitoches, November 10, 1796, second Chamard statement, Natchitoches, November 10, 1796, testimony of Bernard D'Ortolant, Natchitoches, November 11, 1796, testimony of Pedro Mais, Natchitoches, November 11, 1796, testimony of Juan Bautista Dartigo, Natchitoches, November 12, 1796, all in RDLF, ND.

[47]Carondelet to Llaguño, No. 23, New Orleans, January 9, 1797, AHN, Est., leg. 3900, exped. 2. Carondelet included many but not all the copies of letters related to the troubles at Natchitoches in this file. Peñalver also wrote to Llaguño; see Luis, Bishop of Louisiana, to Llaguño, No. 15, New Orleans, February 1, 1797, Biblioteca Nacional (Madrid), Sección de Manuscritos, "Colección de varios documentos para la historia de la Florida y tierras adjuntas." In his letter, Peñalver did not exaggerate the unrest in the colony, and he focused on religious problems.

[48]Llaguño to the Príncipe de la Paz (Godoy), Palace, July 8, 1797, draft of royal order to the governor [of Louisiana], Madrid, July 15, 1797, AHN, Est., leg. 3900, exped. 2. The actual royal order was not issued until July 16, 1797.

[49]Delvaux to Juan Procopio Bassecourt, Conde de Santa Clara, Havana, July 1, 1797, Manuel Gayoso de Lemos to Bishop Peñalver, New Orleans, October 16, 1797, and Gayoso to Santa Clara, New Orleans, January 23, 1798, all in RDLF, ND.

[50]Delvaux to Santa Clara, Havana, June 26, 1798, and statement of Nicolás Calvo, Ingenio de la Nueva Holanda, June 28, 1798, both in RDLF, ND. Possibly the clerk who allegedly found the royal order that called for sending Delvaux to Spain misread it, and it really stated that he should be expelled from the Spanish colonies, which is what the July 16, 1797, royal order stated.

[51]Inventory of Delvaux's belongings found at the Ingenio de la Nueva Holanda, June 28, 1798, Santa Clara to Carondelet [*sic*], October 1, 1798, both in RDFL, ND. See also Santa Clara to Juan Manuel Alvarez, No. 118, Havana, May 12, 1799, AGI, SD, leg. 2567, in which the captain general reported to Spain the disappearance of Delvaux.

[52]Delvaux's expulsion from Louisiana and his return seem to have been accomplished quietly. Roger Baudier, author of *The Catholic Church in Louisiana* (New Orleans, 1939), who used New Orleans sources for his research was unaware that Delvaux had been taken to Havana, spent several years there in detention, and returned after the United States took charge. Similarly, Baudier does not mention Delvaux's role in the turmoil at Natchitoches. He presumes that Delvaux had spent these years working quietly at his parish.

[53]Ibid., 253, 285.

[54]The *Revenants* were by no means an organized cadre but an undisciplined mob that seemed as devoted to diversion as it was to opposition to the government. Perhaps having a good time took precedence with many of them. Liquor might well have been a more important catalyst for their boisterous behavior than revolutionary belief. The youth at Natchitoches no doubt welcomed the excitement as a way of relieving boredom and blowing off steam.

[55]Liljegren, in "Jacobinism," 261, alleges that the Spaniards were too weak to impose any punishment on the dissidents. Despite Delvaux's thirty-month confinement in Havana and expulsion from Louisiana, Liljegren states that he "escape[d] without having been charged with his crimes." Ibid., 262. Liljegren accepts Carondelet's claims that Spanish power was weak and the people hostile to Spain. He is unaware of the punishment imposed on some of the *Revenants*. Andreu Ocariz, meanwhile, asserts that the Natchitoches inhabitants favored French control, but this was not the reason for the unrest. Delvaux, not revolutionary fervor, accounted for the turmoil. Contrary to Andreu Ocariz's contention, the people did not support republicanism with its violence and persecution of the Catholic Church over monarchical government. Nor did slave owners endorse the French government's abolition of slavery. The Natchitoches inhabitants disliked many ideals of the Revolution. Andreu Ocariz also blames Spanish weakness for the unrest in Natchitoches and the disturbances in New Orleans. In doing so, he accepts the allegations made by Carondelet in his January 9, 1797 letter, which, in my opinion, provide a skewed version of the events.

[56]On Carondelet's tendency to overreact, see Jack D. L. Holmes, *Gayoso: The Life of a Spanish Governor in the Mississippi Valley, 1789-1799* (Baton Rouge, 1965), 81, 152, 157-60; Gilbert C. Din and A. P. Nasatir, *The Imperial Osages: Spanish-Indian Diplomacy in the Mississippi Valley* (Norman, 1983), 217, 228-29, 238-40; William S. Coker and Thomas D. Watson, *Indian Traders of the Southeastern Spanish Borderlands: Panton, Leslie & Company and John Forbes & Company, 1783-1847* (Gainesville, Fla., 1986), 157.

[57]Punishment for the offenders of the Natchitoches unrest was, in my opinion, not serious. Initially, Carondelet was not inclined to punish anyone, only reassign Delvaux. Even later, had DeBlanc, Vázquez, or Argote addressed the disorders quickly, punishment probably would have been minimal. Nevertheless, the *Revenants* participated in repeated local turmoil inasmuch as they abused non-supporters, threatened opponents, and engaged in potentially incendiary activity. Again omitting the canine *Aristocrate*, punishment amounted to the exile from Louisiana of two ringleaders, only one of whom is known to have left; expulsion of two others from the Natchitoches district, of whom only Capuran departed; and rebuking a few more. Several *Revenants* were briefly arrested. All this was in addition to Delvaux, who suffered expulsion and detention for nearly three

years before escaping. The remaining offenders got off scot-free.

[58]Many historians have made the mistake of believing that Carondelet's letters to higher officials accurately describe conditions in Louisiana. Besides Liljegren and Andreu Ocariz, they include, among others, Thomas R. Fiehrer, James T. McGowan, and Gwendolyn Midlo Hall. Historians experienced in working with the correspondence of Louisiana's Spanish governors have an advantage over novices who enter the field and accept the accuracy of all the governors' letters without question. The failure of these historians to investigate thoroughly has resulted in flawed studies. Other historians unskilled in foreign languages and paleography have compounded the problem by producing new works based on the defective studies. As a result of these mistakes which have persisted for far too long, an extensive literature has emerged based on misconceptions about colonial Louisiana under Carondelet.

THE DAWN'S EARLY LIGHT*

Glen Lee Greene

Oh, say can you see, by the dawn's early light . . . .
— Francis Scott Key

Close ties between church and state prevented the development of organized Protestantism in colonial Louisiana. Restrictive regulations did not entirely deter Protestants from entering Louisiana but did impede their organization and worship. A few Baptist voices, first crying in that strange and lonely wilderness before the close of the colonial era, eventually attracted a larger company equally intent on singing the Lord's song and hoisting the Lord's banner in the early light of dawn.

PROTESTANTS IN COLONIAL LOUISIANA

Sufficient evidence exists to refute the assertion that "no dissenters of any faith were permitted to migrate to Louisiana during the entire French period."[1] Protestants lived in and near New Orleans practically from the time that city was founded. In 1725, a French military officer at New Orleans was identified as a Lutheran, a designation "which in the vague terminology used could have applied to any Protestant whatsoever."[2] An official census, taken in 1724, disclosed the religious affiliations of the colonists along the Mississippi River above New Orleans. About 20 percent of the villagers in the German community on both sides of the river were Protestants. They were described as Lutherans, Calvinists, or Protestants.[3]

As it dealt with religious dissent, French law focused on public cult, preaching, marriage, and the education of children. There was no law excluding Protestants, but there was a policy of exclusions; yet, at least theoretically, the French Protestant who proceeded quietly could live peacefully and worship at home in Louisiana. The records show no expulsion of any Protestant, no arrest of any preacher, and no inheritance suit based on nonregistry of a Protestant marriage.[4] It appears to be a correct observation that "while no de jure freedom of worship was decreed during the entire French regime in

*First published in *House Upon A Rock: About Southern Baptists in Louisiana* (Alexandria: Executive Board of the Louisiana Baptist Convention, 1973), 35-59. Reprinted with the kind permission of the publisher.

Louisiana, nevertheless a de facto policy winked at the presence of dissenters."[5] This does not erase the fact, however, that an unjust law does not become a just one simply because it is poorly enforced.

One may reasonably surmise that few English-speaking Protestants, if any at all, settled in Louisiana during the French regime. They undoubtedly became somewhat numerous during the subsequent Spanish period, particularly toward the close of that period. Even if the Spanish generally tended to be strict constructionists in religious affairs, they desperately wanted to attract colonists and were much more successful in doing so than were the French. Restrictions against Protestant forms of public worship remained effective in spite of the fact that the Spanish authorities softened their refractory attitude as a gesture to achieve their economic and political goals. Anglo-American Protestants began to settle in West Florida, later called the Florida Parishes, as early at the 1760s. About the same time, but to a lesser extent, they entered the other settled regions of what later became the state of Louisiana. Any effort to identify Baptists who might have been among the early Protestants is complicated by the nonexistence of records by which such identifications could be made, since no known Baptist churches, associations, or conventions existed within hundreds of miles during that early period.

FIRST APPEARANCE OF BAPTISTS

Toward the close of the eighteenth century the Ouachita District attracted a rush of new inhabitants partly under the artful aegis of two pompous promoters, who styled themselves the Marquis de Maison Rouge and the Baron de Bastrop. A land speculator, Bastrop possessed an alleged Spanish land grant which entitled him to an enormous acreage in what is now northeastern Louisiana. Spurred by the demands of the Spanish authorities for colonists, Bastrop scoured the western settlements of the United States in search of recruits. He succeeded in gathering a number of families of Louisville, Kentucky, early in 1797. Divided into two companies, the colonists set out from New Madrid, now in southeastern Missouri, on their journey down the Mississippi River. They paused briefly at Natchez, where not improbably they welcomed a few additional colonists, before continuing up the Ouachita River to Fort Miro, later named Monroe.[6]

Among the colonists in the first contingent, which Bastrop personally conducted, were John Coulter and his family.[7] They landed at Fort Miro on April 19, 1797. Coulter was the first known Baptist to set foot in what is now the state of Louisiana. Probably born in Pennsylvania about the middle of the eighteenth century, he served in the American Revolution, migrated to the Newberry District of South Carolina, and from there very likely he moved to the western settlements, where he joined Bastrop's venture. While at Louisville waiting to embark, Coulter and other heads of families received from Bastrop a written contractual agreement signed by him with the following stipulations:

I will give to every family, industrious and well recommended, 400 acres of land — take where they please — six months' provisions, all kinds of seeds they want to plant out, and their children (that is to say, boys) will be enregistered; and when they come to age, 400 acres of land will be given to each of them, during this current spring.[8]

Under these conditions John Coulter selected his land soon after reaching Fort Miro. He chose four hundred acres situated in what is now Morehouse Parish, between the present towns of Mer Rouge and Oak Ridge. Morehouse Parish was a part of Ouachita Parish until 1844. After the property was surveyed in 1804, Bastrop executed a deed and delivered it to Coulter during the following year. Recorded on September 23, 1805, the deed ambiguously describes the Coulter land as "lying about half a league west of the Prairie Mer Rouge."[9] Actually it was on the west side of Bayou Gallion near the southern boundary of Prairie Mer Rouge, which the Gallion divided from Prairie Jefferson. This area was sometimes vaguely referred to as Prairie Gallion. There a number of colonists formed a settlement, perhaps the first in what is now Morehouse Parish. Coulter settled on its western perimeter.

Seeing that the so-called Bastrop grant had become the subject of controversy, of litigation, and of rumors of impending sale during the period following the Louisiana Purchase, John Coulter faced the grim truth that the legality of titles to this land was suspect and that the "headrights" of his sons were in jeopardy. Consequently, in 1805, he joined the others in a suit attempting to ensure the rights of their children. This suit, however, was later abandoned; Coulter then resolved to move elsewhere. For almost a decade he had lived in Louisiana: it had been a difficult period under three flags — flags of Spain, of France, and of the United States.

Communication and the flow of traffic had been established between the Natchez and the Ouachita districts. Coulter probably knew some of the residents in the Natchez county, many of whom had also previously lived in South Carolina. He acquired from the United States government by preemption a large tract of land in Wilkinson County, in southwestern Mississippi. From a neighbor, in 1809, he purchased a smaller tract adjoining his.[10] In all likelihood Coulter left Louisiana in 1806. Definitely, he lived in Wilkinson County in 1807, and was still living there in 1816.[11] A prominent landowner with extensive holdings, he was also a slaveholder.[12] He probably died in Wilkinson County before 1820.

Unfortunately, details of John Coulter's early Christian experience are obscure. When he settled in Wilkinson County, Mississippi, after leaving Louisiana, he united with the Bethel Church, four miles southwest of Woodville. In September 1807, the Mississippi Association convened at the Bethel Church; and Coulter attended that session as one of the two elected representatives from his church. Moreover, being a man with some education and with recognized abilities as a Christian leader, he was named treasurer of the association. The minutes tell of that event: "Brother John Coulter was nominated treasurer, and authorized to purchase a blank book for that purpose."[13] Coulter was the first treasurer of the Mississippi Association and served for several years, his last election to that office occurring at the annual session in 1812.[14]   Thus Coulter made a worthy contribution to the Baptists of Mississippi. Although his sojourn in Louisiana resulted in no spectacular impact on Baptist life, he did start there a long line of Baptists that has persisted since 1797. He founded no church, but one may validly assume that in his day, when the need for this particular kind of witnessing was imperative, he took a stand for the cherished Baptist principles of religious liberty and the separation of church and state.

OTHER TRAILBLAZERS

Shortly before John Coulter took up residence in the Ouachita country of Louisiana, a group of Baptists constituted a church in the Natchez country, some of whose members later were among the first Baptists in Louisiana. Organized in October, 1791, the Salem Church, often referred to as the Cole's Creek Church, was the first Baptist church in Mississippi. It was located in the Stampley Settlement, about twenty miles northeast of Natchez. Most of the members were from South Carolina. They suffered severe hardships on a perilous journey to a new country, endured harsh persecution after their pilgrimage, and bore up under fierce opposition in their courageous struggle to transplant a hardy branch of the Baptist denomination in the soil of Mississippi.

Afterward, in the Ouachita country of Louisiana, Abraham Morhouse acquired part of the Bastrop grant.[15] A New Yorker of unsavory character, he discovered a market for his land among the members of the Salem Church in Jefferson County, Mississippi. Morhouse struck a bargain with a surveyor, William Thomas, a charter member and the first clerk of the Salem Church.[16] Thomas surveyed much of the vast acreage which Morhouse owned in and adjacent to Prairie Jefferson, later called Oak Ridge. In 1804, he received a deed to fifteen hundred acres of choice land situated between Bayou Gallion and Bayou Little Bonne Idée, on the northern boundary of Prairie Jefferson not far from John Coulter's property.[17] After Thomas died, his land was sold for taxes in 1819; but during the following year his family redeemed it. Although a scarcity of sources precludes a particular account of his life, the known details indicate that William Thomas enjoyed the advantages of a fair education in his day, that he achieved prominence as a citizen, and that he served his church as a devoted and useful member. The official Spanish census of 1792 names Thomas among the residents of the Natchez District. Upon the creation of Pickering County, Mississippi, in 1799 (renamed Jefferson County in 1802), he took office as justice of the peace and of the court of common pleas. In 1798, the Salem Church selected him, along with several others, to assist in the organization of the Bayou Pierre Church, the second Baptist church in Mississippi.

Besides William Thomas, a number of other members of the Salem Church acquired property from Morehouse: Prosper King, 1,600 acres; John Burch, 600 acres; William Bolls, 500 acres. Likewise, in addition to Buckner Darden and James Bennett Truly, several persons linked with the prominent Curtis and Jones families, who were instrumental in organizing the Salem Church, secured land in or near the Thomas settlement. Most of them, at one time or another, were members of either the Salem Church or some other Baptist church in Mississippi.[18] In the wake of the economic problems created by the War of 1812, many landowners lost their property. Some of them returned to Mississippi. Prosper King was buried in the cemetery at the Salem Church in 1827. John Burch and William Bolls later preached in Mississippi, though it cannot be stated with certainty that they did so while at Prairie Jefferson nor that a church was organized there prior to statehood, since no known supportive documentation is extant.

In the meantime, toward the end of the Spanish regime in West Florida, where the predominantly English-speaking residents constituted a nexus joining the American community in southwestern Mississippi and its counterpart in southern Louisiana west of the Mississippi River, an extraordinary stir took place. Following the Louisiana Purchase in 1803, Spain denied that the transaction included West Florida; hence that government, aware of a threat, tightened its grip over the area. As a result, the populace became increasingly restive. Under these conditions the Feliciana planters, mounting a mini-revolution, rose against their oppressors and drove them out. They then set up a mini-republic. Declared the Republic of West Florida in the fall of 1810, this area was annexed to the United States in December of that year and was included in the state of Louisiana when statehood was granted in April 1812. The parishes carved out of West Florida have since been called the Florida Parishes. Over this region, in all, have flown six flags.

Tradition has ascribed to Bailey E. Chaney, a member of the Salem Church in Mississippi, the honor of preaching, in West Florida, the first Baptist sermon in what is now the state of Louisiana. It has further declared that, for so doing, he suffered persecution, arrest, and imprisonment. Although this legend apparently has been based solely on the recollections of Chaney's aged widow in the late 1840s, there is little reason to doubt that the episodes actually occurred; but precisely where and when it occurred is less certain.[19] Overlooking the fact that details differ in the several accounts, it seems likely that Chaney visited briefly and preached in the Feliciana section of West Florida, probably in what later became East Feliciana Parish. By the means of travel available to Chaney, East Feliciana was not "near Baton Rouge."[20] To pinpoint the exact time of that event is impossible, but it surely took place between 1798 and 1810. A date toward the end of that period is plausible, for then the Spanish authorities were most apprehensive about the loss of West Florida and the designs of the Americans against their territory.

From South Carolina, Bailey Chaney was the son of William Chaney, the first known deacon of the Salem Church. Bailey's wife Elizabeth was the daughter of William Ratliff. Both the Chaney and the Ratliff families lived in the Natchez District as early as 1792. Patriot, planter, frontier politician, and preacher, Bailey Chaney was a licensed minister, but there is no evidence that he ever sought or received ordination, that he organized a church, or that he served as pastor of a church. Perhaps he attempted too much, or he could not make up his mind whether to be a preacher or a politician; indeed, he attempted both but probably achieved distinction at neither. In 1798, when many patriots assembled at Natchez to hoist the American colors and to celebrate the passing of that territory into American hands, they called upon Chaney to deliver a sermon. It was the first sermon preached in Mississippi under the Stars and Stripes. Chaney served in the Territorial Legislature of Mississippi in 1809, in 1813, and in 1814. In 1810, living in Franklin County, adjoining the southern boundary of Jefferson County, he owned nine slaves.[21]

Oddly enough, Chaney's name scarcely appears in the minutes of the Mississippi Association: once, in 1814, during the War of 1812, when he was selected as one of a committee of three to name six days during the year as days of "fasting, humiliation, and prayer," to be observed throughout the remainder of the war; and again, in 1816, when he gave two dollars as an individual contributor to the foreign mission work of the Triennial Convention.[22] Chaney served for a time as clerk of the Salem Church. Eventually that church excluded him on charges of drunkenness and disorderly conduct, but in 1823 it restored him to fellowship and granted him a letter to unite with another Baptist church in Jefferson County. Now such an exclusion would be improbable. Then, curiously, in spite of the fact that little or no stigma was attached to social or moderate drinking, the churches usually looked sternly on drunkenness. To be sure, they meted out expeditious punishment to offenders, but they also forgave them quickly; today, by way of contrast, the churches sometimes perhaps unwittingly punish by not forgiving. In 1824 the Salem Church resolved that "Brother Chaney be required to give up the Church Book."[23] He was not the first, nor the last, church clerk to feel that, even after his tenure ended, the minute book was his personal property.

A man of action, Chaney was a Diotrephes—enamored of the preeminence—who indeed wrestled with his psyche but who often responded easily to the dark attraction of many things controversial, sensational, or spectacular. To some extent pomp and circumstance thrust a role upon him; nevertheless, as a historical figure in the burgeoning Baptist life of Mississippi and Louisiana through his furtherance of timeless Baptist teachings, he rightly won the praise of all who treasure religious liberty and the separation of church and state.

With the fact that Elizabeth Chaney, in the winter of her age and after the lapse of many years, idealized her lamented husband, few would want to find fault. But it is an exaggeration to say, whether the words are hers or those of her sincere but overeager interrogator, that Bailey Chaney "was prevented by death, and did not establish a church in Louisiana, which was a cherished object with him."[24] Chaney was still living in Franklin County in 1820.[25] There is no evidence that he ever lived in Louisiana. In a document recorded in 1828 in East Feliciana Parish, William Chaney attested an exchange of slaves between himself and Bailey on February 11, 1825.[26] Elizabeth Chaney and other members of the family acquired property in East Feliciana Parish in the late 1820s and early 1830s. Bailey Chaney probably died between 1825 and 1828, before the family moved to

East Feliciana Parish. To say that he had foibles is to say only that he was a man; to say that, despite them, in truth he tried is to say that he was a man of faith.

SOWING GOSPEL SEED

Several Baptist ministers in southwestern Mississippi undoubtedly preached in West Florida prior to statehood. A few or perhaps even all of them suffered a degree of persecution. Before the United States gained possession of West Florida, a pious old slave named Billy was not allowed to teach or to pray "vocally, even in his own hut."[27] One may conjecture that Thomas Mercer, responding to such conditions in the American settlements not far from his home in Amite County, Mississippi, ventured over the boundary into West Florida to preach to the distressed settlers. Mercer came to Mississippi from Georgia about the year 1800 or shortly thereafter. He was one of the founders of the Mississippi Association and was within its area the most popular evangelist of his time. A great lover of gospel music, he published in pamphlet form a collection of hymns for distribution among the churches.

David Cooper, who lived in Woodville, in Wilkinson County, Mississippi, was an ordained Baptist minister and was also a practicing physician. In 1817, in a letter to the corresponding secretary of the Board of the Triennial Convention, he indicated that he was probably the first minister to preach in the Feliciana area of West Florida, in the vicinity of St. Francisville. He wrote with characteristic humility: "It is a large and populous settlement, almost entirely destitute of the gospel, except the little attention they have received from your unworthy servant, and is, of course, good missionary ground."[28] Dr. Cooper came to Mississippi from South Carolina about 1802. In the Peedee section of South Carolina he owned the land on which the first meeting house of the Ebenezer Church (Jeffreys Creek) was erected. That church was among the first in the area, and Cooper was its pastor for a brief period prior to 1802. Between 1796 and 1798 he was the pastor of the Welsh Neck Church in the Peedee area. Its members agreed "to raise what they conveniently could by subscription" for his services on the second Saturday and Sunday of each month. Cooper was active in the Charleston Association; he helped to constitute the Black Creek Church in 1798 and shortly afterward helped to ordain the pastor of that church.[29] After coming to Mississippi, he engaged actively in evangelistic and pastoral work and served as missionary doctor in Mississippi and Louisiana. He helped to organize the Mississippi Association. During his latter years he was married to the widow of William C. C. Claiborne, the territorial governor and first elected governor of the state of Louisiana. Cooper died in 1830.

Dr. Cooper left a rich missionary legacy to the Baptist people of Louisiana. He made trails where none had traveled before. Arising before dawn for an early start, he crept along from Woodville to the Feliciana country, a distance of about thirty miles, at a rate of perhaps four miles an hour. Astride his horse, with saddle bags in place, sometimes singing hymns as he jogged along, sometimes dozing, sometimes coaxing his steed with a few words of encouragement, sometimes praying or exhorting in preparation for the awesome experience ahead, he completed the journey in about eight hours, alone except for his horse and the good Lord.

Somewhat less conspicuous, though by no means less significant, was the ministry of Moses Hadley, who came to Mississippi from South Carolina between 1802 and 1806. At the end of the eighteenth century he was pastor of Pipe Creek Church of Regular Baptists in the Low Country of South Carolina. At the opening of the nineteenth century he served as pastor of Black Swamp Church in South Carolina, which under his ministry experienced a remarkable revival in 1802.[30] Hadley settled in Wilkinson County, Mississippi, where he labored until his death in 1818. He participated in the constitution of the Mississippi Association. Benign and devoid of insalubrity, he inspired the worthy emulation of his colleagues. His influence upon early Baptist life in Louisiana was consequential.

About the time that Moses Hadley moved to Mississippi, or perhaps a little later, Ezra Courtney left South Carolina and settled in Amite County, Mississippi. He evidently could not have arrived in Mississippi, nor could he have begun to preach in Louisiana, as early as previous historians have declared. Members of the Courtney and Curtis families were related. Both families were in the organization of the Salem Church, the first in Mississippi. John Courtney was probably Ezra Courtney's father. John was married to the sister of Richard Curtis, Jr., the first pastor of the Salem Church. Members of both families, including John Courtney and Richard Curtis, Jr., moved to Amite County prior to 1810. This very likely accounts for Ezra Courtney's decision to migrate to Amite County. He lived in modest circumstances, as did most of the Curtises and Courtneys, all of his life. He owned one slave, probably a house servant, in 1810.

In South Carolina, Courtney was a member of the Ebenezer Church (Jeffreys Creek) in the Peedee section. This church was in the Charleston Association, which maintained a fund to render financial assistance to needy young ministers who wished to secure a ministerial education. In 1803 the church recommended Courtney as a worthy applicant for assistance, and during that year the appropriate committee of the association conferred with him, approved the recommendation, and voted to continue his assistance from the fund through the following year. He attended an academy conducted by John M. Roberts at Stateburgh.[31] His education, of course, was limited. Since David Cooper was pastor of Courtney's home church prior to Courtney's admission to the academy, the two presumably were well acquainted; and it was probably during Cooper's pastorate that Courtney was licensed to preach.

Under these conditions, Ezra Courtney did not enter Mississippi in 1802 but obviously came later, very likely late in 1805 or early in 1806. A convincing argument favoring the later date, in addition to the known fact that Courtney attended the Roberts Academy during the earlier period, is the improbability that Courtney would have remained very long in a community without either uniting with the nearest church or promoting the organization of a church in his community. According to extant records, he and his wife

Elizabeth remained in fellowship with their home church in South Carolina until they became charter members of a church organized in Amite County, Mississippi. They joined the new organization on the basis of letters of recommendation from the Ebenezer Church (Jeffreys Creek) in South Carolina. The new church was also named Ebenezer, a good Bible name for a church in the wilderness, doubtless chosen in honor of the old home church in South Carolina. Ebenezer Church, in Amite County, Mississippi—just north of the Louisiana line—was constituted with eleven members on May 9, 1806, by Richard Curtis, Thomas Mercer, James Courtney (from South Carolina), and others. John Courtney was a charter member. Still in existence, Ebenezer Church is situated perhaps twelve or fifteen miles southeast of Centreville, Mississippi, and about the same distance northeast of Clinton, Louisiana. This church ordained Ezra Courtney on July 25, 1806, and in the following November called him as pastor.[32] He was one of the organizers of the Mississippi Association in 1806 and represented Ebenezer Church at the initial session. It was during his pastorate at Ebenezer that Courtney journeyed a few miles south across the border into Louisiana and preached at American settlements in West Florida. There can be little doubt that he did this at great sacrifice or that he endured persecution in the course of such efforts.

With reference to the primal days of Baptists in the frontier areas of Mississippi and Louisiana, it is more a caricature than a portrait to draw the picture that was drawn by one not long removed from the scene: "Gospel seed was never sown upon a more ungracious and unproductive soil."[33] True, the harvest at first was not plentiful; but when planted, in time it brought forth fruit a hundredfold.

HALF MOON BLUFF: THE FIRST CHURCH

Under the otherwise favorable conditions that prevailed, such as a relatively numerous Baptist population and the comparative availability of ministers, a Baptist church could have been constituted much earlier in West Florida if that area had fallen into American hands sooner. Contrary to expectation, the first group of Baptists to organize a church in what is now the state of Louisiana appeared virtually unannounced and unnoticed in an isolated area on the Bogue Chitto River in the remote northeastern corner of the Florida Parishes, about seven or eight miles south of the Mississippi boundary and just a few miles northwest of the present Franklinton, in what is now Washington Parish. As early as 1811, at the annual session of the Mississippi Association, the Bogue Chitto group asked for fraternal assistance in the organization of a church. Accordingly, the association chose David Cooper and Thomas Mercer to help the Baptist people at Bogue Chitto and to organize a church if they deemed it "expedient."[34] In the absence of evidence to the contrary, it is a fair assumption that these two men carried out the mission assigned to them. They found, however, that it was not "expedient" to organize the church immediately; or for an unknown, though doubtless to them an acceptable, reason they did not act with dispatch but demurred. In any event the constitution of the church was delayed a full year. According to a long-standing tradition without substantial confirmation, it was organized on October 12, 1812. A few days later it affiliated with the Mississippi Association.[35]   This church adopted the name Half Moon Bluff Baptist Church. The name Half Moon Bluff was geographical rather than Biblical, its origin being the location of the church on a tiny bluff overlooking a tiny stream, the curvature of the Bogue Chitto River at that place suggesting the appearance of a half-moon. Since then, of course, the topography of the area has changed considerably.

Although the impetus that brought forth Half Moon Bluff Church was actually indigenous, for the most part the early churches of Mississippi and Louisiana stemmed fundamentally from religious influences set in motion in South Carolina. In Louisiana, practically all of the early churches were the fruit of independent local efforts by transplanted South Carolinians. Half Moon Bluff did not owe its existence to missionary efforts on the part of another church or of the association. Much like the Salem Church in Jefferson County, Mississippi, it had already been "gathered" when the association heard about it; thus, in effect, the church existed before the formal ceremonies of constitution gave it status. Because the church desired recognition, fraternal accord, and affiliation with the association, it sought through a courtesy extended by the association to authenticate what already existed. This in no way derogates from the acknowledged missionary zeal of the Mississippi Association since its inception; rather, it places in perspective and in line with known facts the authentic history of the first Baptist church on Louisiana soil.

It was not exceptional for the association to take the lead in constituting churches. In fact it also ordained ministers and otherwise appeared at times to intrude upon what would now be considered the proper concern only of the local churches. This extraordinary role of the association was gradually abandoned. Concurrence in the heretofore popular opinion that the Mississippi Association was a "mother" to the early churches in Louisiana is somewhat wide of the mark. Perhaps more to the point—to continue figuratively—it was at best a rather indifferent stepmother and at worst an improvident foster mother. This is not a great scandal if due weight is given to the predicament of the Mississippi Association during the early years of Baptist development in Louisiana: it was in its tender years, comprised only a handful of straggly churches, and was long the only association within a radius of hundreds of miles; its churches wrestled with their own problems and struggled to survive under primitive conditions; its ministers were almost exclusively men of modest means who were compelled to farm or to pursue other vocations in order to provide for themselves and their families; and it constantly labored against the hindrance of difficulties in communication and travel.

Left to their own resources, therefore, the members of the Half Moon Bluff soon erected a church building. In later years, long after its dissolution, at least two persons who had seen the building gave remarkably similar descriptions of it. A rustic log structure of modest proportions and starkly simple in its appointments, it was typical of the first meeting houses on the frontier, with a dirt floor, a mud chimney, and puncheon benches. This building was also used by the community as a school house; and, after the extinction of the church, it survived for a time as a saddlery.

Half Moon Bluff was never a large or influential church, nor did it transmit much by way of a visible heritage. From the outset it maintained a good relationship with the association. In 1814 it notified the Mississippi Association that it had unchurched Robert Smith, a minister, on charges of un-Christian conduct. Although the association concurred, by 1816 Smith had been reinstated and preached at the annual meeting of that body.

In 1812, Joseph Lewis and Joseph Erwin represented Half Moon Bluff at the association; in 1813, Nathan Morris; and in 1814, Nathan Morris, Joseph Lewis, and Lofton Fairchilds. Erwin owned the property on which the church was built and Lewis lived on the west side of the Bogue Chitto River opposite the church. The Lewis and Morris families were related through intermarriage. This union later took in members of the Erwin family. Baptist ministers in both the Lewis and Morris families were closely identified with the early growth of Baptist work in Mississippi and Louisiana, their families being scattered widely over southern Mississippi and the Florida Parishes of Louisiana.[36]

Joseph Lewis, who was surely a charter member of Half Moon Bluff Church, might have been the first pastor of that church. It is known that some years later a man having that name resided at what is now Lexie, Mississippi, south of Tylertown and perhaps fifteen miles from Half Moon Bluff; that for many years he was pastor of New Zion Church, east of Osyka, Mississippi, just above the Louisiana line; and that his son having the same name succeeded him in the pastorate.[37] Of no little interest is the fact that Miss Ruby May Lewis, a descendant of this family, was born in 1890 at Lewiston, in Tangipahoa Parish, not more than twenty miles from the site of Half Moon Bluff Church. Baptized and spiritually nurtured by the Spring Creek Church, east of Kentwood, she served from 1925 until 1954 as a missionary of the Louisiana Baptist Convention to the Italians at Independence, in her native parish.

Moreover, it is well established that Nathan Morris, who was related to Joseph Lewis by marriage, was a member of Half Moon Bluff Church for many years, apparently even after he moved to Pike County, Mississippi, where he was living at least as early as 1816. He probably lived at Half Moon Bluff prior to this. Between 1813 and 1822 he was a pastor at Half Moon Bluff and in 1818 served briefly as a missionary in the eastern portion of West Florida. If that honor is not accorded Joseph Lewis, then it seems likely that Nathan Morris was the first pastor of the Half Moon Bluff Church.[38] Of Welsh descent, the Morris family had long resided in the Peedee section of South Carolina when in 1802 Nathan attended the Charleston Association as a representative from the Beauty Spot Church.[39] Shortly afterward he and other members of the William Morris family moved to the frontier, settling in southern Mississippi and the Florida Parishes of Louisiana during the territorial period. From 1816 until 1822 Nathan Morris served as pastor of the Silver Creek Church in Pike County, Mississippi, about fifteen miles northwest of the Half Moon Bluff Church.[40] In the year following his resignation he declined another call

from the Silver Creek Church, and again in 1824 he refused to resume his pastorate because the church neglected its financial obligations. After leaving that community he
attended the Mississippi Association in 1831 as a fraternal representative for the Union
Association. Later he was accidentally killed, probably on Christmas Eve, during a celebration by some youths who were following a frontier custom of firing gunpowder on a
blacksmith's anvil. Two of Nathan's close kinsmen and contemporaries were also Baptist
ministers: one called Nathan Morris, Jr., and another named Joseph Morris, who was
among the first officers—a vice-president—of the Mississippi Convention, organized in
1836. Benjamin Morris, Nathan's brother, was an ancestor of the late James Polk Morris,
Sr. (1879-1963), a prominent merchant and civic leader who was for twenty years treasurer and for forty years a deacon of the First Baptist Church of Kentwood, in Tangipahoa
Parish. His son, James Polk Morris, Jr., now serves that church as a deacon.[41]

In 1820 Half Moon Bluff Church, along with others, left the Mississippi Association
and went into the organization of the Pearl River Association. With the rapid organization of new churches, the shifting of population, and the inevitable changes in the structure of the community, Half Moon Bluff rapidly declined after 1820 and apparently became extinct by 1830. Shortly after the Civil War a new church by the same name was
constituted and held meetings some distance east of the original site. No historical continuity between the two organizations can be demonstrated. In 1869, the new Half Moon
Bluff Church, then in Hobolochitto Association and listing Franklinton as its post office
address, reported two baptisms, a net increase of one, and a total membership of seventeen.[42] In the early 1870s other churches absorbed the second Half Moon Bluff, with the
present First Baptist Church of Franklinton likely being the principal heir to the remains
of that organization.

Marking the one hundredth anniversary of organized Baptist work in Louisiana, the
Louisiana Baptist Convention in 1912 noted the historic significance of the then long
extinct Half Moon Bluff Church. Interested Baptists erected a monument on the abandoned site. In recent years a historical marker was placed along the state highway about
a half mile from the site. When in 1962 the Convention observed the sesquicentennial of
Louisiana Baptists, a feature of the ceremonies included a pilgrimage to the spot where
once stood the first Baptist church in Louisiana.

CALVARY: THE SECOND CHURCH

Although the actual organization of a Baptist church in the Florida Parishes antedated a similar achievement west of the Mississippi River by one month, the groundwork
for such an organization was undertaken considerably earlier west of the river. There a
saga unfolded which in its particulars was at once pathetic and inspirational. In both areas the conditions that brought forth a church were much the same: Baptist frontier settlers first established their homes and then looked to the establishment of a church in the
community; a minister among them took the initiative and worked independently as a

missionary evangelist; and the Baptist community valued recognition and sought acceptance from the nearest association. When Baptists emerged in the Attakapas and Opelousas districts of Louisiana, Joseph Willis appeared as their first leader. Like a tapestry,
the threads of his life were woven into the beginnings of Baptists in central and southwestern Louisiana and formed the warp and woof of an organization that has endured
since the opening of the nineteenth century.

Unfortunately, details of the birth and early life of Joseph Willis are shrouded in
mystery. He probably did not know the exact date of his birth. Speculation by past
chroniclers, based on an imprecise record in the minutes of the Louisiana Association,
ranges from 1758 and 1762. A date closer to 1770 seems more probable.[43] Willis grew
to maturity in South Carolina; but the contention of some of his descendants that he was
born in Bladen County, North Carolina, which may be true, appears to be unverifiable.[44]
At least during his early manhood Willis lived in the mountainous northwestern area of
South Carolina, not far from the North Carolina border, in upper Greenville County between the Saluda and Enoree Rivers. There the Main Saluda River Church was organized in 1789, probably in the neighborhood of Head of Enoree, and entered Bethel Association in 1793. During the next three years Joseph Willis attended the association as
the representative of this church. He was one of "its outstanding members" but soon
united with the Head of Enoree Church. The latter church had a "large and scattered
congregation served by an unusual number of licensed preachers and candidates." Willis
was licensed to preach by the Head of Enoree Church shortly after he united with it. In
1799 he joined other "ministers" and several officers in a petition which resulted in the
incorporation of the congregation as "The Head of Enoree Baptist Society."[45]

Consequently, Joseph Willis could not have entered Mississippi prior to 1799, as
traditional accounts have inferred, but might have appeared there early enough to participate in the organization of Bethel Church in Wilkinson County in the year 1800. He tar-
ried briefly in Mississippi before making a scouting trip to Louisiana in the fall of 1804.
In November of that year, at the risk of his life, he preached at Vermilion—now
Lafayette, some forty or fifty miles southwest of Baton Rouge—the first sermon known
to have been preached by a Baptist minister in Louisiana west of the Mississippi River.
Ranging northwestward about twelve or fifteen miles northeast, he also preached at
Plaquemine Brulé, about thirteen miles northeast of the present Crowley. This preaching
tour took Willis into the heart of French-speaking Louisiana; he was the first Baptist to
undertake such a mission. Contrary to the eulogium published in the 1854 minutes of
Louisiana Association, Willis did not preach in that area "before the American flag was
hoisted" there, since the United States acquired Louisiana in 1803; yet he did suffer persecution, for even then in the rural outposts latent hostility plagued new Protestant settlers
from other parts. Concluding his tour in 1804, Willis traveled northward to Bayou Chicot, now in Evangeline Parish about thirty-five miles south of Alexandria, where he had
friends and where he decided to settle.

In 1805, accordingly, Willis brought his family to Bayou Chicot. Records at the courthouse in Opelousas reveal that he sold some slaves in 1805 and that he purchased land in 1809. His first-born, Joseph Willis, Jr., who was born in South Carolina, in later years often told of his adventures crossing the Mississippi River at Natchez when as a lad he accompanied his father to Bayou Chicot. Willis might have brought with him an infant daughter, the child of his second wife, who upon reaching maturity married William Dyer. Joseph Willis was married four times and was the father of nineteen children. At Bayou Chicot, though he was only a licensed minister, he immediately took up his work as an itinerant missionary evangelist, traveling and preaching throughout the surrounding region.

Curiously, in spite of the acknowledged effectiveness of his ministry and the fact that he repeatedly sought ordination from the nearest Baptist community—his friends and fellow ministers in Mississippi—Willis was forced to labor at Bayou Chicot for seven years without ordination. Under similar conditions, more aggressive men in other areas had organized churches without the benefit of the presence of ordained ministers. Although Willis was the first known Baptist minister to settle in Louisiana and might have organized a church in 1804 or 1805, he was not innovative; rather, conforming to his traditional orientation, he remained deferential in his attitude toward the association and its authority and possibly entertained doubts about his own competence and authority. Moreover, he was reluctant to violate what he conceived to be the "proper" procedure. His patience probably won for him ultimately what he might have lost by aggressiveness. Limited by his education, Willis nevertheless kept a diary or journal in which he recorded details of his pioneer missionary work and thus was the first historian of Louisiana Baptists.[46]

Shortly after he began his ministry at Bayou Chicot, Willis felt the need of ordination so that he might render more extensive and effective service. Consequently, he returned to Mississippi and first requested the church in which he held membership to ordain him. This church resorted to a ruse: on the pretext of not having a pastor and of lacking authority under the circumstances, it advised him to unite with another church which might be able to accommodate him. Willis then united with another church and again requested ordination. That church, more direct and to the point, refused to ordain him "lest the cause of Christ should suffer reproach from the humble social position of his servant."[47] Following the advice of a sympathetic minister friend, Willis eventually turned to the Mississippi Association. At the suggestion of his friend, he took the extraordinary step of securing recommendation from leading citizens of the community in which he lived. Thus Willis appealed to the association for ordination in 1810, the results of that appeal being published in the annual minutes of that body as follows:

> A petition was presented to the Association, from certain brethren, and from a number of citizens in Opelousas, praying that bro. J. Willis be set apart, by ordination, to the work of the ministry. Brethren D. Cooper and L. Scarborough were appointed to visit the

brethren in Opelousas, and ordain bro. Willis, if they, upon examination shall think it expedient.[48]

Willis waited a year, but there was no "examination," since nobody from the association visited him. In 1811 he attended the annual meeting of the association and was invited to participate in the proceedings. The only help he obtained was that the association
appointed Thomas Mercer and David Cooper "to visit the brethren in Opelousas."[49] During the following year this visit did not take place; however, in 1812, Moses Hadley and
Lawrence Scarborough were "appointed to ordain bro. Willis in Opelousas, and constitute
a church" in his community.[50] Soon afterward, Hadley and Scarborough traveled to
Bayou Chicot, where on November 12, 1812, they constituted a church and ordained Joseph Willis.

Organized with six members, five men and one woman, the church was named Calvary, a New Testament name that suggests the warm piety of Joseph Willis, who was a
charter member and who remained a member of Calvary Church until his death. Calvary
was the second Baptist church to be organized in the state but the first west of the Mississippi River. It has functioned continuously since its incunabula and is now the oldest
living Baptist church in Louisiana. With Willis as the sole human instrument dedicated
to its existence and survival, Calvary Church was gathered as the fruit of his individual
missionary labor and was solidly built as part of a great Baptist house upon a rock.
Throughout its history there is no record that it ever sought or received financial assistance from any source outside its own membership.

Joseph Willis was the first pastor of Calvary Church, and he remained pastor for
some eighteen or twenty years. He was apparently the first resident Baptist pastor in the
state.[51] He lived at Bayou Chicot long before the church was organized there and continued to live in the vicinity of Calvary Church until about 1830 or shortly thereafter. No
allusion to a resident pastor of that period, however, should convey the modern connota-
tion of that term: a full-time church program, a parsonage, multiple weekday administrative duties, and the like. Calvary was a quarter-time church and Willis often preached in
other areas. He was available to the people of the community, when not away on a missionary tour, to visit the sick, to solemnize marriages, and to conduct funerals, which
sometimes undoubtedly were conducted weeks or even months after the interment of the
dead. Rarely perhaps, though it did occur, funeral services for a man's late wife would be
conducted after his remarriage. Such customs arose out of frontier conditions: the im-
practicability of embalming required speedy burial of the dead; inclement weather made
roads impassable; and many communities afforded no local minister, the usually available ones frequently itinerating and being absent from home for long periods at a time.
Perhaps a carryover from earlier times, except among the Blacks, prompt burial is generally more common today in the south than in most other areas.

In the early 1830s Willis moved to Rapides Parish, where he settled briefly on Spring
Creek, east of the Calcasieu River, not far from the present Glenmora. A little later he

moved to the vicinity of Tenmile Creek, west of the Calcasieu River. In that region he founded the Occupy Church in 1833 and served as its pastor for about sixteen years. When Willis died on September 14, 1854, he was buried in the cemetery of that church (now known as Occupy No. 1). It is situated about eighteen miles west of Oakdale, not far from Pitkin in the southeastern corner of Vernon Parish. A century later, on January 18, 1954, to honor the memory of Joseph Willis, almost three hundred interested Baptists, including sixteen ministers, endured the wintry blasts of a freezing north wind to unveil a granite monument which stands seven feet tall at the head of his grave. Both the Louisiana Baptist Convention and the Louisiana Association—the first in the state, of which Willis was one of the founders, served as its moderator for several terms, and often preached at its annual meetings—have more than once acknowledged with appropriate tributes the indebtedness of Louisiana Baptists to this pioneer missionary preacher. Feeble and impoverished in his last years, Willis on occasion received generous offerings from the grateful churches at the request of a sympathetic association. Although the appraisal of an early historian that Willis spent a fortune in spreading the gospel in Louisiana is inaccurate, the Louisiana Association did not err when it published the following estimate of his work:

> Before the church began to send missionaries into destitute regions, he at his own expense, and frequently at the risk of his life, came to these parts, preaching the gospel of the Redeemer. For fifty years he was instant in season and out of season, preaching, exhorting, and instructing; regarding not his property, his health or even his life, if he might be the means of turning sinners to Christ.[52]

One of the numerous churches that Willis organized retained him as pastor almost to the end of his life, though he was virtually incapacitated by the debilities of age, and during that period, with enormous affection and profound gratitude, triumphantly announced to the association: "Joseph Willis is still living."[53] Willis requited that sentiment, for displaying the characteristic tenderness of his nature he spoke of the churches he had founded as his children and alluded to them "with all the affection of a father." One of his close friends observed:

> But when he spoke of the fact that two or three of them had already become extinct, his voice failed and he was compelled to give utterance to his feelings by his tears; and surely the heart must have been hard that could not be melted by the manifestation of so much affection, for he wept not alone.[54]

In all the history of Louisiana Baptists it would be difficult, if not impossible, to find a man who suffered more reverses, who enjoyed fewer rewards, or who single-handedly achieved more enduring results for the denomination than did Joseph Willis. He was not learned, nor was he aggressive; but he was capable, earnest, dedicated, and in his manner ideally suited to a frontier ministry.

Perhaps none of his achievements gave Willis greater joy than did the progress of his first church, Calvary Church at Bayou Chicot; yet its progress was not rapid. During the first year it received nine new members. Calvary was identified with the Mississippi Association, but its total membership then numbered only thirteen. Its representatives at that first meeting of Louisiana Association were Joseph Willis and Johnson Sweat. Not unaffected by the decline and general apathy experienced by the churches of that area during the 1830s, Calvary enjoyed revival and new growth under the ministry of John O'Quin in the early 1840s. In 1846, the church boasted the services of O'Quin once a month and of B. C. Robert twice a month and reported a net increase of nineteen members. With a membership of seventy in 1849, Calvary sent P. H. Overton and Thomas Keller as its messengers to the association. In 1880 the membership of Calvary Church totaled 62; in 1930, 111; and in 1940, 215.

Set atop a hill soaked in the abundant clean-smelling fragrance of shapely pines, Calvary has occupied the same site continuously since its organization and probably worshipped at first in a log meeting house. A more comfortable building was erected in 1845, a simple frame structure with four windows on each side and two front doors. Repaired in 1902, this building underwent extensive renovation in 1907, when the foundation was repaired and a new floor installed. Although the foundation and the floor of the earlier building were retained, this structure was completely rebuilt in 1938. The present building, which contains some of the sills from the original frame structure, was erected in 1960. It includes a modern sanctuary fronted in natural redwood trimmed in white, with a seating capacity of 250, and adequate educational facilities. Calvary Church appropriately celebrated its sesquicentennial in 1962, during which ceremonies it proudly received well-deserved plaudits from a grateful denomination. In 1971, Calvary Church reported a membership of 168, total receipts of about $11,000, and property valued at $33,000.

Thus Baptists started the founding of their churches in Louisiana at the dawn of statehood. Almost unnoticed at first by the rank and file, the War of 1812 began during the same year. As its close drew near, that conflict engaged a larger number of Baptists and, because of its adverse economic effects, momentarily cast a shadow over their otherwise bright prospects. Nevertheless, as good soldiers of Christ, they were accustomed to disappointment and had learned to wait. Though delayed, their victory was sure.

Notes for "The Dawn's Early Light"

[1] Edwin Adams Davis, *Louisiana: A Narrative History*, 2d ed. (Baton Rouge, 1965), 90.

[2] Charles Edwards O'Neill, *Church and State in French Colonial Louisiana: Policy and Politics to 1732* (New Haven and London, 1966), 273.

[3] J. Hanno Deiler, *The Settlement of the German Coast of Louisiana and the Creoles of German Descent* (Philadelphia, 1909), 82-90.

[4] O'Neill, *Church and State in French Colonial Louisiana*, 256-57.

[5]Ibid., 282.

[6]*Louisiana Historical Quarterly*, 20 (April 1937), 289-462.

[7]Glen Lee Greene, *A History of the Baptists of Oak Ridge, Louisiana: 1797-1960* (Nashville, Tenn., 1960), 37-49.

[8]*Senate Executive Documents*, 32d Congress, 2d session [1852], No. 4, 770.

[9]Ouachita Parish Conveyance Records, Clerk of Court's office, Monroe, La., Book A, 20. Civil districts that are called counties in all the other states are called parishes in Louisiana.

[10]Wilkinson County Conveyance Records, Chancery Clerk's office, Woodville, Miss., Book A, 118-9.

[11]Norman E. Gillis, *Early Inhabitants of the Natchez District* (Baton Rouge, 1963), 87.

[12]Wilkinson County Conveyance Records, Book A, 410.

[13]Mississippi Baptist Association *Minutes*, 1807, in T. M. Bond, ed., *A Republication of the Minutes of the Mississippi Baptist Association from Its Organization in 1806 to the Present Time* (New Orleans, 1849), 12.

[14]T. C. Schilling, *Abstract History of the Mississippi Baptist Association for One Hundred Years, From Its Preliminary Organization in 1806 to the Centennial Session in 1906* (New Orleans, 1908), 270.

[15]Morhouse invariably wrote his name with only a terminal *e*, in disregard of which his later admirers dubbed him "Morehouse;" incredibly enough, Morehouse Parish was named in his honor and Bastrop, the seat of government, was named in honor of the dubious Baron de Bastrop.

[16]Some authorities have confused William Thomas with William Thompson, both of whom were members of the Salem Church. The first minute book of the church is the source for the assertion that Thomas was a charter member and the first clerk; see Z. T. Leavell and T. J. Bailey, *A Complete History of Mississippi Baptists from the Earliest Times*, 2 vols. (Jackson, Miss., 1904), 1:79, 2:1521-22. Confirmation is found in the second minute book (1815-1834), 4: "our old church book kept by William Thomas." This second volume is in the archives of the Mississippi Baptist Historical Society at Clinton, Miss.

[17]Ouachita Parish Conveyance Records, Book Z^1, 135; Book E, 428.

[18]John G. Jones, *A Concise History of the Introduction of Protestantism into Mississippi and the Southwest* (St. Louis, 1866), 66-100; also see Greene, *A History of the Baptists of Oak Ridge, Louisiana*, 51-76.

[19]Bond, *A Republication of the Minutes of the Mississippi Baptist Association*, 3-6.

[20]John T. Christian, *A History of the Baptists in Louisiana* (Shreveport, 1923), 43.

[21]Gillis, *Early Inhabitants of the Natchez District*, 35.

[22]Bond, *A Republication of the Minutes of the Mississippi Baptist Association*, 42, 56.

[23]Salem Church minutes, April, 1824.

[24]Bond, *A Republication of the Minutes of the Mississippi Baptist Association*, 6.

[25]Irene S. and Norman E. Gillis, *Mississippi 1820 Census* (Baton Rouge, 1963), 23.

[26]East Feliciana Conveyance Records (Clinton, La.), Book A, 431.

[27]*Latter Day Luminary* (Philadelphia), Vol. 1, No. 2 (May 1818), 93.

[28]*Latter Day Luminary*, vol. 1, no. 1 (February 1818), 38.

[29]Joe M. King, *A History of South Carolina Baptists* (Columbia, 1964), 46, 54, 60-1.

[30]Ibid., 34-5.

[31]Ibid., 60, 67, 162.

[32]Ebenezer Baptist Church (Amite County, Miss.), Minute Book, 1806-1865.

[33]Jones, *Introduction of Protestantism into Mississippi and the Southwest*, 255-7.

[34]Bond, *A Republication of the Minutes of the Mississippi Baptist Association*, 25.

[35]Ibid., 29.

[36]Morris Collection. A collection of family and church records in the possession of Irene Reid Morris (Mrs. James Polk Morris, Jr.) of Kentwood, La.

[37]*Magnolia Gazette* (Magnolia, Miss., May 1910), article by Luke W. Conerly, author of a history of Pike Country, Miss., Morris Collection.

[38]Previously published accounts naming Ben Crawford as the first pastor appear to have no reliable basis; they probably originated from the researches of the late T. W. Gayer, whose filial interest in that area might have led him to accept a late tradition which is actually without known supportive documentation.

[39]Leah Townsend, *South Carolina Baptists, 1670-1805* (Florence, S. C., 1935), 81.

[40]Walter E. Tynes, *Centennial History of Silver Creek Baptist Church, Pike County, Mississippi, 1814-1914* (1914), 4. During this period Morris also served as pastor of Mt. Nebo Church, in Tangipahoa Parish, Louisiana, an account of which appears later; records of Mt. Nebo Church reveal that in 1815 Morris was "from Half Moon Bluff," which may indicate that he resided at the latter place but may simply mean that he was pastor of the church there.

[41]Irene Reid Morris, the wife of James Polk Morris, Jr., is librarian at First Church, Kentwood; an author and local newspaper columnist, she is also a respected local historian whose recovery of treasured local Baptist history has preserved much of a Baptist heritage in that area that otherwise might have been relegated to oblivion.

[42]Louisiana Baptist Convention *Annual*, 1870, 22-7.

[43]Willis preached at the annual session of the Louisiana Association in 1852, when he was "said to be ninety-four years old;" at the association in 1854, when his death was noted, his age at death was given as ninety-two. W. E. Paxton, *A History of the Baptists of Louisiana from the Earliest Times to the Present* (St. Louis, 1888), 214, 216. John O'Quin, a colleague and close personal friend of Joseph Willis, as was his father Ezekiel O'Quin, in a letter to John Houston Strother in 1894, wrote: "I can give you correct information, as my father was raised in the same neighborhood with Eld. Joseph Willis in South Carolina." Ivan M. Wise, *Footsteps of the Flock: or Origins of Louisiana Baptists* (Crowley, La., 1910), 115. Ezekiel O'Quin was born in 1781. Strother's correct name is given here; it was not John J., as in Wise.

[44]Greene W. Strother, "About Joseph Willis" (Th.M. thesis, Baptist Bible Institute [now New Orleans Baptist Theological Seminary], New Orleans, 1934), 16. This view also holds that Willis was born in 1750; it is based on flimsy evidence, less than convincing testimony, given about seventy-five years after the event, concerning remarks heard by youngsters attending their aged and ill grandfather. If born in 1750, Willis was pastor of a church at ninety-nine, preached before his association at one hundred two, and died at one hundred four years of age; moreover, in that event, he was not "raised in the same neighborhood with" Ezekiel O'Quin.

[45]King, *A History of South Carolina Baptists*, 109-10.

[46]Willis turned over his papers to W. P. Ford, who in 1841 arranged them in manuscript form under the title, "history of the Early Baptists of Louisiana." Paxton copied this manuscript in 1858. He acknowledged that the manuscript, together with a file of minutes of the Louisiana Association, furnished virtually all of the information he could obtain about Baptist work in that area. In 1842 the manuscript was presented to the Louisiana

Association by Ford and others as a report on the history of the association. Paxton, *A History of the Baptists of Louisiana*, 148-9, 195.

[47]Ibid., 142.

[48]Bond, *A Republication of the Minutes of the Mississippi Baptist Association*, 21.

[49]Ibid., 25-6.

[50]Ibid., 29.

[51]Christian gratuitously accorded Ezra Courtney this honor. See Christian, *A History of the Baptists in Louisiana*, 48. It is possible that the first pastor of Half Moon Bluff Church, organized a month prior to Calvary Church, might have resided in the Half Moon Bluff community. This is a matter of conjecture, since no documentation is available.

[52]Wise, *Footsteps of the Flock*, 121.

[53]Paxton, *A History of the Baptists of Louisiana*, 198.

[54]Ibid., 188.

THE FAITH OF THEIR FATHERS*

Gary B. Mills

The people of the Cane River colony had an enviable reputation. Although exceptions exist for every rule, the majority of the population earned the respect and approbation of all who came into contact with them. The most compelling forces shaping their characters were undoubtedly the Church and their father figure, Augustin Métoyer. In many respects, these forces were one and the same. The people were Roman Catholics, devout in their faith even to the smallest details. Led by Augustin, they established what may well be the oldest church built by and for free people of color in the United States.

In an era in which the whole of Natchitoches Parish suffered from a lack of formal spiritual leadership, Augustin became something of a father confessor to his community. According to tradition he was strict, yet with a piety tempered with kindness that encouraged others to seek his advice and guidance.[1] This tradition is supported by the records. No hint of scandal or indiscretion is attached to his name in any of the civil or ecclesiastical documents, and countless records portray him in the role of family counselor.

The strong presence of religion in Augustin's life can be traced to his childhood. The church registers of 1777 show the nine-year-old Augustin acting as godfather to his cousin and namesake, Nicholas Augustin, a slave of Commandant Athanase de Mézières. In 1781 he served as godfather to an Indian slave child of the Sieur LeCourt. Again in 1783 he acted in this capacity to an infant Negro slave of Mme. Gabriel Buard.[2] From this point on, the registers show him acting regularly in this role. Augustin was, without a doubt, the godfather to more children than any other free man of color in the parish.

According to legend, it was while on continental travels with his father that Augustin first conceived the idea of a church for his people. According to Father J. J. Callahan's history of the parish, "The story goes that Thomas Métoyer had taken his son Augustine [sic] to France in 1801 to visit the homeland of his people, which was the neighborhood of Lyons. It seems the latter was struck by the organization of French villages whose community life centered about the church. It recalled to his mind that there was no church at Isle Brevelle, and so, after his return, he built one in 1803."[3] However, there is

*First published in *The Forgotten People: Cane River's Creole of Color* (Baton Rouge: Louisiana State University Press, 1977), 144-63. Reprinted with the kind permission of the publisher.

no record of a church having been built on the Isle in that year, and thus is presented the crux of one of the most controversial aspects of the colony's history.

The first known chapel on Isle Brevelle was blessed by the curé from Natchitoches, Father J. B. Blanc, in 1829. Upon his return home, Father Blanc entered the record in his registers:

> The nineteenth day of July of the year 1829. I, the undersigned, pastor of the Church of St. François of Natchitoches, have proceeded to the blessing of the chapel erected on Isle Brevelle on the plantation of Sieur Augustin Métoyer through the care and generosity of the above-named Métoyer, aided by Thomas Métoyer, his brother. The above-named chapel having been constructed to propagate [*sic*] the principle of our holy religion shall always be considered as a mission of the church of St. François of Natchitoches. The said chapel erected at Isle Brevelle having been dedicated to St. Augustine, shall be considered as under the protection of this great doctor. Done and passed at Natchitoches the twenty-seventh day of July, 1829.[4]

Concerned by the discrepancy between tradition and actual records, Father Callahan questioned in his history of the parish: "If it were built earlier, why had it taken twenty-six years to have it blessed?" Answering his own question, Callahan concluded that the sanctity of priests and the social inferiority of people of color were to blame.[5]

Callahan's conclusion is not convincing. Priests were indeed scarce, but between 1803 and 1829 they made numerous trips to the Isle to perform baptisms and marriages in private homes. For example, on November 15, 1804, several baptisms were performed at the home of Sieur Pierre Jarri, white, on Isle Brevelle, including the baptisms of two children of Pierre and Dominique Métoyer.[6] Callahan felt that this was natural, since the priests of that period would go to the home of a white man before they would visit the home of a colored one.[7] Yet, the records show that it was not long before the priests did go to the Métoyer homes to administer the sacraments. As the influence of the colony increased, the priests regularly visited their homes and plantations, particularly that of Augustin, and whites from the surrounding countryside went there to be married and to have their slaves and their children baptized. But still the registers refer to such events taking place "in the home of Augustin Métoyer," with no mention of the chapel that supposedly stood next door.[8]

It is highly improbable that the priests who made annual or biennial visits during most of the period between 1803 and 1829 would have ignored a chapel for those twenty-six years while they administered the sacraments in the house next door. It was July 19, 1829, when the chapel was finally blessed. Four days later the first marriages were performed there, a quadruple wedding, representing couples of pure French, Spanish, Indian, and mixed ancestry.[9] Two days later still another marriage was performed in the chapel,[10] and from that time on the registers of the parish of Natchitoches contain frequent references to sacraments administered in the Chapel of St. Augustine.

In attempting to prove the tradition that the church was built in 1803, Father Callahan offered as evidence a letter belonging to a resident of the Isle which reputedly had been preserved by her family since the date that it was purportedly written, a letter which has been quoted frequently by subsequent writers. The letter reads:

> Cane River
> State of Louisiana
> Isle Brevelle
> 10 June 1803

Mr. Jérôme Sarpy
My dear friend and nephew,

I have just returned from New Orleans, and I suspect that you are anxious to have the news. I'll recount it all. Since you are kept to your bed, and I myself am tired after my trip, I send you my faithful servant John Baptist with this message for you. As you know we lived first under our own French government, then under that of Spain, and now we are under the authority of these new people who speak English and travel in wagons covered in white. As we all know these are unquiet times without repose. We shall all pray to our Creator for his blessings. As you know we have already spoken of building a church, and I am sure that with my brother Louis and his knowledge of building, we shall succeed. I shall give the land to the North of my house for the church and for the cemetery. That is what I have always wished to do since I visited the native land of my father in France; Paris, Marseilles, Lyons, in each one of these cities there are churches in every quarter. In one way or another I am sure that having a house of the good God in our midst, our people will live a better life, will love one another, and will live in harmony. I have heard it said that Father LaSalle admired the place I have chosen for the church. Yes, I have also heard that there have been trouble in Haiti. It seems that up to the present time, Toussaint L'Ouverture is unbeaten. I ask myself for how long. He has come up a long way, from coachman to the position he now holds. He has such love for his people and his land. To lose now would break his heart, both his and that of his beloved country.

I am sure that within a week I shall be able to visit you, when we shall have one of our long discussions. I am certain that the church will be finished by the first of August, and I am very grateful to you personally and to James Dupre for offering the main altar. With the aid of all, I know that we shall succeed. Jerome, I beg you to take good care of yourself, and bridle your impetuous temperament.

May Our Father in Heaven bless you.

> I remain

> Augustin Métoyer
> Yucca Plantation[11]

Father Callahan further asserted: "This letter contains within itself evidence of its own authenticity. It is a personal letter to a friend, whom we know otherwise to . . . have been the husband of a niece of Augustine [*sic*]. Notice also the touch of contemporary history. It was the year in which the United States had taken over the territory of the Louisiana Purchase when the settlers were already beginning to pour through Natchitoches."[12]

A comparison of the letter with the well-chronicled historical events which it mentions indicates that the letter in fact contains proof of its own spuriousness. For example, President Jefferson did not sign the treaty ratifying the purchase until October 21, 1803, and the actual announcement of the purchase was not made to the people of Louisiana until November 30, 1803.[13] Moreover, after the purchase, Louisiana was known as the Territory of Orleans until it was granted statehood in 1812. Augustin Métoyer could not possibly have written a letter from the "State of Louisiana" in June of 1803; nor would he have stated in any letter of that date that Louisiana was under American authority.

A second glaring error in the letter is the reference to the "troubles in Haiti" and the statement that Toussaint L'Ouverture was still unbeaten. In actuality, the Haitian leader surrendered in Saint-Domingue in June 1802, and in April 1803, he died in a French prison.[14] News did travel slowly in the nineteenth century, but it is inconceivable that the latest "news" which Augustin received in New Orleans in June 1803, could have contained the information that Toussaint L'Ouverture was still unbeaten.

Then, too, the date of the letter is totally contradicted by the personal family information which it sets forth. The letter is addressed to "Mr. Jérôme Sarpy, my dear friend and nephew." Yet, according to the registers of the church, Sarpy did not marry Augustin's niece until 1820, seventeen years after the date of the letter.[15] Moreover, the letter sets forth Augustin's alleged hope that having a church in their midst would enable "our people" to love one another and live in harmony. But, in 1803 the Métoyer colony consisted only of Augustin and his brothers, all of whom worked together extensively and none of whom had children over the age of ten. The family group was not yet large enough or distinct enough to term it "our people;" nor was the colony large enough to need a house of God in their midst to promote harmony between its citizens.

The letter obviously is contrived. When and why it originated can only be speculated. The location of the original letter is not known. One resident of the Isle possesses a handwritten copy; she states that she found this draft in one of the old books given to her many years ago by her mother.[16] During the period in which the letter first surfaced the numerous old and valued books owned by the colony were being borrowed, whenever they could not be purchased, by popular writers who visited a nearby plantation. According to one Louisiana historian, at least two of these writers were renowned practical jokers who had once admitted concocting a spurious "historical story" as a joke on an acquaintance. The possibility does exist that these writers, or others of a similar nature, invented this letter, and that it has been innocently perpetuated by other people.[17]

An additional documented incident strengthens the conclusion that the Chapel of St. Augustine was actually built, or completed, in July 1829. Land surveys of that area indicate that the church grounds straddled the boundary lines between two sections. The lower section was confirmed by the American government Augustin Métoyer, while the upper section was confirmed to François Lavespère. In 1829 Lavespère's widow still resided on the tract. Five months after the church was dedicated, the widow gave power of attorney to her son-in-law to "act in her stead relative to a certain difference likely to arise between her and Augustin Métoyer, f.m.c., her neighbor, respecting a certain boundary line run between their respective lands."[18] Had the church been built in 1803, with half of it standing on Lavaspère's property, it is not likely that he and his wife would have waited twenty-six years to complain about the boundary encroachment. In fact, the mistake would have been discovered and settled, undoubtedly, when the land surveys were made of these two properties in 1814 and 1815.[19]

Regardless of the date when the church was actually built, 1803 or 1829, its construction still warrants recognition as a high point in the lives of the people. It is also indicative of the value placed upon religion by this society. When the parish church at Natchitoches was burned in 1823, the parishioners there went without a house of worship for three years.[20] Finally, a special act of the legislature was passed to permit the citizens of the town to hold a lottery in order to procure the necessary sum for a new church. A ceiling of twenty thousand dollars was put on the lottery.[21] Apparently, the parishioners did not consider themselves financially able to raise the necessary funds for a church, although quite obviously many of them did not mind risking money in a lottery. By contrast, the people of Isle Brevelle set aside a tract of their own fertile land for their church and cemetery grounds and built their church themselves.

In his discussion of this church, Callahan makes an interesting observation that remains relevant whether the church was built in 1803 or 1829. Callahan cites a quotation from a study of Negro Catholicity and the Jesuit Order which asserts that the first church for the Catholics of color in the United States was established in 1860 by Bishop Michael O'Conner of Baltimore in a building purchased by the white Catholics of that diocese. Father Callahan disputes this claim: "It is no reflection on the work of Bishop O'Conner [but] the colored Catholics of Isle Brevelle had their own church . . . before that date . . . . And they did not owe their parish to money collected among white Catholics but entirely to themselves."[22]

Undoubtedly, the people of Isle Brevelle also prided themselves on the fact that their church was only the third one that had been established in northwest Louisiana.[23] There had been a church at Natchitoches, intermittently, almost since the settlement of the post. Then in 1816, a white resident of the Rivière-aux-Cannes settlement, Alexis Cloutier, erected a small chapel and grounds to the Roman Catholic "congregation" of the area. His generosity was not without an ulterior motive, however, since the church was but the first step toward the founding of a town called Cloutierville, which was to be the seat of a new parish he wanted to carve from Natchitoches.[24] The early registers of the existing Cloutierville church show that the sacraments were administered in Cloutier's chapel only between 1825 and 1829; the mission was then abandoned. Not until 1845 did the congregation reorganize and build an adequate structure.[25] The Isle Brevelle chapel, which was dedicated in 1829, probably drew much of the attendance from the mission church at Cloutierville and may account, in part, for its abandonment that year.

Although the church was built mainly by Louis Métoyer on land donated by Augustin, its furnishings were supplied by the community at large. The spurious letter by

Augustin states that James Dupré[26] donated the altar, but tradition generally holds that the altar was given by Marie Suzanne Anty, a daughter of Marie Suzanne Métoyer and the wife of Jean Baptiste Augustin Métoyer. Callahan recognizes this tradition, even though it contradicted the letter that he quoted, and states, "They say it cost five hundred dollars, quite a sum for those days, and came from Europe."[27] The altar continued to be used for over a century, even after the original chapel was twice replaced by newer and larger structures.[28]

Two of the earliest decorations installed in the original chapel were a pair of paintings, one of St. Augustine, the patron saint of the man who conceived the idea of establishing the church and donated the land for it, the other of St. Louis, the patron saint of the chapel's builder. An impressive bell was hung in the belfry above the church's vestibule; its resounding tones could be heard the length and breadth of the Isle.[29] The twelve stations of the cross beautified the interior side walls, inspiring parishioners to contemplate the burden and the sufferings of Jesus. Each station, it is recalled, was donated by a different member of the congregation.[30]

In 1836 a visiting artist painted Augustin's portrait as he stood on the verandah of his plantation home and pointed through its columns to the church of which he was so proud. In this painting we see a relatively small chapel, containing a single nave covered by a gabled roof on the front of which was erected the belfry tower. The roof extended beyond the walls to cover two galleries running along the sides of the church. According to tradition the galleries served two purposes. The slaves, who were not allowed to sit inside the sanctuary with their masters, attended mass while standing in the galleries. Also, in the event of rain, the galleries were put to use as shelter for the parishioners' carriages.[31]

Three years after the painting of his portrait with the chapel, Augustin Métoyer drafted his last will and testament, in which he explained his purpose in organizing this church:

> A portion of land of 3/4 *arpent* of frontage by 1 1/2 *arpent* of depth, situated on the portion of land above given to my children Joseph and Gassion, at its upper part, does not belong to me. The Church of St. Augustin of Natchitoches was built there by me and my family, principally for our usage, except that I desire, and such is my wish that outsiders professing our holy, catholic, apostolic, and Roman religion will have the right to assist at the divine office in the said chapel and shall enjoy, moreover, all the rights and privileges which I and my family are able to have there. After my death I wish that this portion of land continue to be destined for the preservation of the same church and of a cemetery and that it should never be able to be used otherwise, in any manner or under any pretense that may be; with the privilege to my successors of making officers of the said church the Catholic priests who will suit them and not the others.[32]

Augustin's reference to "outsiders" reflects a curious situation, since the outsiders who attended the Isle Brevelle church were, by and large, whites. Integration of Louisiana's churches (particularly the Catholic churches) was the rule rather than the exception in antebellum Louisiana. However, it was normally the whites who built the churches and permitted nonwhites to attend. On Isle Brevelle the situation was reversed. It was the Creoles of Color who organized the church, and when they extended an invitation to the wealthy white planters of the Isle who had no church of their own, the invitation was accepted.[33]

The presence of these "outsiders" was obviously important to Augustin. Upon the completion of his church, his descendants say, he set aside eight pews for the exclusive use of his white friends, located directly behind his own pew that stood in the place of honor before the statue of the Blessed Virgin.[34] For almost two generations whites regularly used these pews, obviously unperturbed by the thought of taking a back seat to a man of color, an unconventional practice even in relatively liberal Creole Louisiana. For Augustin, the establishment of his own church was undoubtedly a symbol of prestige, a measure of affluence and position that few of his white contemporaries could equal.

The presence of these outsiders, moreover, provided a legal safeguard for Augustin and his community. As racial tensions heightened in antebellum Louisiana, an increasing number of wary whites looked askance on congregations of free nonwhites gathered for religious or other purposes. Many felt that such meetings provided too convenient a cover for the planning of slave insurrections, which one element of white society believed would be instigated by free men of color. A law was ultimately passed that restricted the congregation of nonwhites, slave or free, for religious purposes. Only if whites were included in their assemblies were the *gens de couleur libres* allowed freedom of worship after that time.[35]

Such a situation could easily have resulted in white assumption of control over the affairs of the Isle Brevelle church. The people would have had no alternative but to accept that control or lose their church when the whites decamped. Descendants of the antebellum colony relate that just such an attempt was made but lacked adequate support.[36] The failure of this alleged attempt, or any other, of whites to wrest control could well be viewed as the ultimate symbol of Augustin's prestige, and a clear indication of the respect which the majority of area whites held for the integrity of the colony.

It is also related that through the years priests from many places, as they were traveling through the region, said mass in the Chapel of St. Augustine. Some came from as far away as New Orleans and even Mexico. It was Augustin, it is said, who paid the priests from his own pocket for their trouble and expense.[37] The identities of most of these priests are not known, but the parish registers at Natchitoches record two such visits made by the bishop from New Orleans. In 1836 the Most Reverend Antoine Blanc made his first pastoral visit to the parish and visited the church on Isle Brevelle which his younger brother had blessed seven years earlier. In the registers at Natchitoches he recorded the visit and noted especially "the condition of decency and cleanliness" which he found there.[38] In 1842 the bishop was again in the parish and noted in the registers his visits to three churches, the Church of St. François at Natchitoches, the Church of St.

Augustine on Isle Brevelle, and the new Church of the Nativity of the Blessed Virgin at Campti, just north of Natchitoches.[39]

On March 11, 1856, the mission of St. Augustine on Isle Brevelle was decreed by Bishop Auguste Martin of the diocese of Natchitoches to be a parish in its own right. Bishop Martin assigned his own brother, Father François Martin, to be its first resident pastor.[40] Its founder, Augustin Métoyer, died the following December 19, at the age of eighty-eight.[41] He had lived to see the fulfillment of what is said to have been the greatest wish of his old age, the establishment of a parish for his people.

Tradition relates one other story relative to Augustin and his church. After its construction or after the establishment of the parish (tradition varies), Augustin supposedly received a special letter of commendation from the pope which was read to the congregation at high mass. The letter, supposedly, was preserved by a daughter-in-law, Périne Métoyer Dupré, until it was destroyed along with many other old and valuable family heirlooms when "Tante" Périne's home burned.[42]

The spiritual activities of the people began and ended in this church. Newborn infants were taken for baptism to the holy font in the Chapel of St. Augustine as soon as a priest could be brought to the Isle to administer the sacrament to them. On rare occasions when death threatened an infant not yet baptized, the sacrament was administered privately by a family friend or relative. Should the sick one survive, however, a formal baptism still followed in the chapel when a priest next arrived. It was at his baptism that an infant was given his name, a saint's name carefully chosen; thus, at baptism was a child given the model of perfection that he was to follow. For most girls, the first name was Marie, in recognition of the most esteemed model of Christian virtue. Also at baptism each infant acquired his *parrain* and *marraine*, godparents whom he grew to love and respect as dearly as his own parents.[43]

Upon reaching puberty, the youth of the Isle received their second sacrament—confirmation. From the bishop himself, upon his periodic visits to the parish, the youth received the Holy Spirit. After his visits to the parish in 1836 and 1842, Bishop Blanc noted that he had confirmed a total of fifty-four youth of the colony.[44]

Most discussions of the religious attitudes of Louisiana's free people of color contain the usual sensational emphasis upon the illicit relations between young women of this class and their white "protectors." One modern writer, for example, discusses this aspect of their society but does note the existence of a second code of morals by observing: "Not all free persons of color entered a state of concubinage. Many of them got married and it was not uncommon for such persons to have their nuptials performed in the churches of Louisiana."[45] However, the general conclusion of this study and that of most historians in this field is that the legitimately married class of *gens de couleur libres* were an elite minority.

Among Cane River's Creoles of color, however, the situation was reversed. Perhaps due to the influence of Grandpère Augustin, who is remembered as a strict moralist, Cane River youths were expected to marry within the church and to pattern their behavior after the strict dictates of their faith.[46] Courting couples were always chaperoned. At dances the girls of good character did not permit the boys even to pay for their refreshments. A walk to the edge of the pavilion where lights were low might be countenanced, but no couple dared leave the pavilion unless accompanied by an older woman.[47]

More often than not, marriages were arranged by the parents, who met and decided upon the needs of the couple. In general, the preferences of the young people were considered, but in many cases they were not. A typical example is provided by Ambroise Sévère Dupré and his wife Sidalise Sarpy. It was Sidalise's sister for whom Sévère really cared, but she was younger than Sidalise. The fathers, Jérôme Sarpy and Emmanuel Dupré, conferred, and both agreed that no younger sister should marry until her older sisters had found husbands. Plans for the wedding were then made, with Sidalise rather than her sister as the bride. The young couple made the best of the situation, reportedly, and remained together for the rest of their lives, even though the marriage was not one of choice on their part.[48]

The marriage of Sévère and Sidalise followed the traditional pattern. The youth of the Isle were joined in matrimony at the altar of the Church of St. Augustine. Civil marriages contracted outside the church were uncommonly rare in this period. Instances of divorce or legal separation of bed and board, which did occur even among white Catholics of the parish, were nonexistent in the colony. The unions made at the chapel's altar were expected to last until death.

The church and civil records of the parish reveal that deviation from the moral code outlined by the religion was, in all respects, the exception rather than the rule. Although each family of color did begin with an illicit liaison between a white man and a woman of color, the families thereafter insisted upon contracting legitimate marriages, and for the most part the community standards were upheld by individual members. Most cases of extramarital or premarital liaisons were relationships between females of color and men of pure white blood whom they could not marry; most such liaisons also lasted until death claimed one of the partners.

It must not be assumed that the attentions of white men were indiscriminately welcomed by the people as a means of "lightening" their race. During the antebellum years when the colony was accorded respect and prestige, the maintenance of their racial composition through selective marriage was sufficient to preserve their superiority to the black race, and the maintenance of respect from the outside society by adherence to Christian precepts was necessary to their own self-respect. Although the situation was to change after the war, as all social and economic conditions underwent drastic alterations, the colony before the war generally spurned the dishonorable attentions of whites.[49]

Aside from the freed slaves, Rose Métoyer and Adélaïde Mariotte, who were the *placées* of a succession of white "protectors" (most of whom died shortly after the initiation of the relationship), the records reveal only rare incidences in which the females of the colony bore children by whites with whom they established temporary or long-term alliances. Even in such cases, the violation of family standards often had serious impact upon the consciences of the violators. Adélaïde Mariotte, for example, was apologetic for her conduct for the remainder of her life. Apparently fearing that her loved ones would not respect her life-style, she repeatedly told her children and grandchildren that she "had disgraced herself to uplift her race."[50] Assuming that personal emotions might have had a certain amount of influence upon her behavior as well, it is still indicative of the attitude of her family group that she felt such a compunction to justify her past actions.

Religious devotion among the people was a private as well as a public matter. The rosary was said at home every night before retiring, and the children were always led in their bedtime prayers by an older adult who knelt with them. The church bell rang the Angelus every morning at six, calling the faithful to daily mass if there was a priest on the Isle, and again at that hour of the evening. Men stopped and doffed their hats at the peal of the bell, and women made the sign of the cross.[51]

All homes had their little altars which were hung prominently on the living room wall. Reflecting the sentiments of the older people whom he recalled, the Louisiana storyteller Harnett Kane wrote: "In each house the altar sparkled beneath the crucifix, and the shrine must be cleaned every day. How would a saint feel if he found dust in which he could write his own name, ahn?"[52]

Although many such altars were purchased later from the people during their periods of need, one little altar owned by Sidalise Sarpy Dupré, a daughter of Jérôme Sarpy, has been proudly treasured by a granddaughter. Unlike the typical altar found in churches, this home altar resembles more a wall-hung box, shallow at the top, deep at the bottom. The sparkling glass front is a door that opens to provide access to the religious articles stored inside.

All of the holy days on the church calendar were faithfully observed by the people, but the Easter season demanded special devotion. On Holy Thursday and Good Friday all andirons and pokers were moved from fireplaces. It was believed that if on those days iron and fire met, disaster was inevitable. No chickens or any living things were killed, and meat was not eaten between Good Friday and Easter Sunday. Ground was not plowed on those days, since many held to the old belief that drops of the sacred blood of Jesus would appear in the freshly turned earth.[53]

Good Friday was a day set aside for attending to religious obligations. The most pressing necessity was the "making of the Easter duty," the annual confession and penance. After the Easter duty had been performed, the graves in the cemetery behind the church were cleaned and decorated as they had been some six months earlier on All Saints' Day.[54]

Honeysuckle, flowering quince, or other flowers that were in bloom were placed in vases on each grave, along with keepsakes of the deceased which the family had preserved through the years. A lace fan with ivory sticks, a small clock, a rakish hat, a doll, or a fluttering kite would suffice to let the dead one know that he had not been forgotten. In the earliest years, the graves were further decorated with bottles, shells, and other miscellanea of interesting shape and color, arranged in decorative patterns or outlining individual plots.[55]

Easter Sunday was a day of celebration for the entire community. After mass, coffee was brewed over small fires at the edge of the cemetery, where the people gathered to socialize and celebrate the end of Lenten fast and penance, which would be the occasion of a night of gaiety at the dance which would follow. Amid the chatter, children hid their eggs around the grave markers, while the men gathered with their own gaily decorated eggs, placed their nickle bets, and proceeded with a game of "nip and tuck." Grasping their eggs in the circle formed by the thumb and index finger, each pair of players tapped their eggs together end to end in an effort to crack the opponent's eggs while preserving their own intact. By the end of the day the churchyard and cemetery grounds were covered with white shells.[56]

The Easter gathering and resulting frolic in the cemetery indicated no lack of respect for the dead. On the contrary they were viewed as a means of sharing life once more with loved ones long departed. The Creoles of Louisiana, both white and nonwhite, exhibited a great measure of respect for the deceased. Mother Hyacinthe LeConniat, Superior of the Daughters of the Cross who established a convent in Avoyelles Parish and a second on Isle Brevelle, wrote her brother Yves-Marie in France:

> Nothing equals the care rendered to the dead here. . . . The corpse is wrapped well in white silk. The coffin is of perfect workmanship and is painted on the outside. The inside is padded and lined with velvet or satin, with gold tacks keeping the cloth in place. There is another coffin placed in the bottom of the grave; it is not as attractive as the one that holds the corpse. . . . This is naturally correct because it would be senseless to put the fine coffin in the mud. . . . This beautiful coffin which costs the rich 500 or 600 francs, is transported in a beautiful carriage or hearse. A man on horseback carries a small cross at the head of a cortege. The family and the friends accompany the body, riding in carriages or on horses. They wear on the arm beautiful bows of black lace which cost $2 or $3 apiece. At the church, which is covered with black, they sing the "Libera Me." No mass. Finally, the burial. All must throw the black crepe into the grave. They erect a fine monument. . . . This sad funeral as I described it to you is first class. If the priest goes to the house to accompany the body to the church, it is $40, and if he does not do this, it is $35. For the second class $25 or $30. For the third class $10 or $15. . . . By means of these stipends the missionary is able to live.[57]

The funerals of the colony were, apparently, first class. For example, the final account rendered by the administrator of the estate of Marie Suzanne Métoyer included a payment to the curé of sixty dollars for her burial in 1838. In 1847 the *marguilliers* of the new Church of St. Jean Baptiste at Cloutierville met to establish the tariffs on burials for that parish and set the rates at eighty dollars for a first-class funeral, thirty for a second-class, twenty for a third-class, and ten dollars for a fourth-class. When J. B. Espallier Rachal died not long afterward, his family paid the Reverend G. Guy eighty dollars for the first-class burial.[58] The hearse to which Mother Hyacinthe referred was furnished the Isle Brevelle community by the jack-of-all-trades, Oscar Dubreuil.[59]

Cane River's Creoles of Color were buried in four known locations. In the early years, those who lived nearer Natchitoches were taken into the town and buried in the cemetery of the parish church there.[60] Others who lived at the lower end of the settlement were buried in the old Shallow Lake Cemetery near the community later known as Derry. After the establishment of the church and cemetery at nearby Cloutierville, the lower Cane River people almost always used the newer cemetery.[61] Most of the family, however, was buried behind the Chapel of St. Augustine in the heart of their community. Slaves belonging to the colony were not accorded space in the family's burial grounds. Across the road, in the bend of the river, was established the cemetery for slaves. Nothing remains to mark their graves.[62]

The oldest graves in the cemetery of the Chapel of St. Augustine were marked with iron crosses. An occasional wooden cross, painted white with black lettering, marked graves of the less affluent. The most striking graves in the cemetery were the above-ground tombs, miniature white houses about five by seven feet, built to shelter the bodies of the most prominent members of the family.[63] In the place of honor nearest the church was erected one such tomb, with a marble door that identified it as the resting place of Augustin Métoyer and his wife Mary Agnès. After the death of Augustin in 1856 their tomb was twice opened, once for the burial of his favorite son, François Gassion, in the decade that followed, and then again in the early twentieth century to deposit the last remains of that son's third wife, Périne Métoyer Dupré.[64]

For the Creoles of Color on Cane River, Catholicity and its precepts were a way of life. Callahan related that the ancestors of some families in the area came to the Isle as practitioners or teachers of voodoo. Because of one side of the colony's racial heritage, these newcomers assumed the people would be eager students of this particular derivations of African religion. They were mistaken. Their culture made no inroads in the French Catholic society of Cane River, and the newcomers eventually converted to the dominant religion.[65]

Religion, to a large extent, was the cornerstone of Isle Brevelle society. The Angelus of dawn marked the beginning of each new day; the evening peal of bells from their chapel brought that day's labor to an end. The calendar of the church determined their days of work and their days of rest, their days of fast and their days of feasting. The spiritual ties of godparent to godchild were bonds that held the people together as closely as did ties of blood. The influence which their faith held upon these Creoles of color produced results that earned for the colony much of the respect which outside the society accorded it.[66]

Notes for "The Faith of Their Fathers"

[1]Confidential source to François Mignon, September 3, 1972, copy in possession of author; interview with Mrs. Lee Etta Vaccarini Coutii, March 24, 1974.

[2]Baptism of Nicholas Augustin, February 9, 1777, in Natchitoches Registers, Book 4, p. 308; Baptisms of Maria Modesta and Maria Celesia, April 17, 1781, and Baptism of small negro of Juana, June 22, 1783, in Natchitoches Registers, Book 4.

[3]Callahan et al., *History of St. Augustine's Parish*, 35. Through the years the people have consistently referred to Claude Thomas Pierre Métoyer as "Thomas," even though he always identified himself as Pierre. Perhaps they adopted the practice of referring to their ancestor by one of his less well-known names so as not to offend the white Métoyers who traced their descent from Pierre. As a result of this practice, one version of the legend insists that two Métoyer brothers settles at Natchitoches, one named Pierre and the other named Thomas. Pierre, supposedly, married a French girl at the post and was the progenitor of the white Métoyers of the Côte Joyeuse, while Thomas "married" Marie Thérèze Coincoin and was the progenitor of the Métoyers of Isle Brevelle. The tradition that "Thomas" was from Lyons cannot be supported. The Métoyer "homeland" was actually La Rochelle and Rheims.

[4]July 27, 1829, Natchitoches Registers, Book 6, 116.

[5]Callahan et al., *History of St. Augustine's Parish*, 37-38.

[6]Baptisms of Marie Susanne and Marie Perrine, November 15, 1804, in Natchitoches Registers, Book 5.

[7]Callahan et al., *History of St. Augustine's Parish*, 37.

[8]For examples, see baptisms dated October 25, 1825, and May 27, 1826, in Natchitoches Registers, Book 5, and Marriages of François Métoyer, Jr., to Marie Désirée Coton-Maïs, April 26, 1827, ibid., Book 11.

[9]Marriage of Louis Monette and Marie Louise Cottonmaïs, f.p.c., No. 10; Marriage of Étienne LaCase and Caroline LeMoine, white, No. 11; Marriage of Césaire LeCour and Marie Gertrude Maurine, French-Indian, No. 12; Marriage of Nazario Ortis and Des Nièges Aragón, Spanish-French, No. 13, July 23, 1829, all in Natchitoches Registers, Book 11.

[10]Marriage of Émile Dupart and Marie Rose Baltazar, f.p.c., July 25, 1829, ibid.

[11]Callahan et al., *History of St. Augustine's Parish*, 36.

[12]Ibid.

[13]François Barbé-Marbois, *The History of Louisiana, Particularly of the Cession of that Colony to the United States of America* (trans. from the French, Philadelphia, 1830), 324, 327-28.

[14]C. L. R. James, *The Black Jacobins: Toussaint L'Ouverture and the San Domingo Rebellion* (New York, 1963), 330-65.

[15]Marriage of Gérôme Sarpy to Marie Adélaÿde Métoyer, June 27, 1820, Natchitoches Registers, Book 11.

[16]Mrs. Coutii to confidential source, September 1973, copy in possession of author.

[17]Davis, *Louisiana*, 380.

[18]Widow François Lavaspère to Julien Rachal, in Natchitoches Parish Records, Book A, 38.

[19]Files B1806, François Lavaspère, and B1960, Augustin Métoyer, State Land Records.

[20]Beckers et al., *History of Immaculate Conception Catholic Church*.

[21]*Journal of the Senate of the State of Louisiana*, 1826, 45.

[22]Callahan et al., *History of St. Augustine's Parish*, 40.

[23]In the early nineteenth century, all of northwest Louisiana was incorporated in the limits of the parish of Natchitoches.

[24]Alexis Cloutié to the Roman Congregation, Donation, in Natchitoches Parish Records, Book 6, Misc., Doc. 142; *Biographical and Historical Memoirs of Northwest Louisiana*, 317.

[25]Baptismal Book 1 and Marriage Book 1, Cloutierville Registers; interview with Msgr. Milburn Broussard, Pastor of Church of St. John the Baptist, Cloutierville, August 22, 1970; Msgr. Broussard to author, March 15, 1974.

[26]Church and civil records of this period indicate that there was no member of the colony named James or Jacques Dupré, either in 1803 or 1829.

[27]Callahan et al., *History of St. Augustine's Parish*, 42; interview with Mrs. Coutii, April 26, 1974.

[28]This altar was finally replaced in the mid-twentieth century. The old altar was "given away;" its present whereabouts is not known. Interview with confidential source, April 26, 1974.

[29]The painting of St. Augustine and the original bell still hang in the modern church; the old painting of St. Louis has been "lost" through the decades.

[30]Nine of the twelve members of the colony who donated the Stations of the Cross are said to be Léopold Balthazar, Paul Balthazar, Vilfried Métoyer, Emmanuel Dupré, Nemour Sarpy, Nères Pierre Métoyer, Carl "Callot" Métoyer, Sévène Dupré, and Oscar Dubreuil. Mrs. Coutii to author, May 13, 1974.

[31]Interview with Mrs. Coutii, April 26, 1974; Callahan et al., *History of St. Augustine's Parish*, 42.

[32]Last Will and Testament of Nicolas Augustin Métoyer, in Natchitoches Parish Records, Book 25, Notarial Records, 77-80.

[33]Interview with Mrs. Coutii, March 24, 1974; The Rev. J. A. Baumgartner, "Isle Brevelle," quoted in Stahl, "The Free Negro in Ante-Bellum Louisiana," 362.

[34]Interview with Mrs. Coutii, March 24, 1974.

[35]H. E. Sterkx, *The Free Negro in Ante-Bellum Louisiana* (1972), 376.

[36]Interview with confidential source, April 26, 1974. It is also related that on one occasion a white "spy" was found in the loft of the church during services. The "spy," allegedly, was "removed" from the premises by several male members of the congregation and was never seen again. Apparently, the white's disappearance was never conclusively linked to the people of the colony, since no charge against them for such a crime appears in the parish records.

[37]Interview with Mrs. Coutii, March 24, 1974; confidential source to François Mignon, September 3, 1972, copy in possession of author.

[38]January 22, 1836, Natchitoches Registers, Book 12.

[39]Baudier, *The Catholic Church in Louisiana*, 346.

[40]Ibid., 46; Callahan et al., *History of St. Augustine's Parish*, 38.

[41]Tomb marker, cemetery of the Chapel of St. Augustine, Isle Brevelle.

[42]Callahan et al., *History of St. Augustine's Parish*, 43; interview with Mrs. Coutii, April 26, 1974. A search of the papal correspondence in the Vatican Archives failed to uncover a copy of the letter; Papal secretary, Archivo Segreto Vaticano, to author, April 6, 1974.

[43]Mrs. Coutii to author, October 5, 1974.

[44]Baudier, *The Catholic Church in Louisiana*, 346, 360; Louis Laraboire Morrow, *Our Catholic Faith: A Manual of Religion* (Kenosha, Wis., 1961), 274-75.

[45]Sterkx, *The Free Negro in Ante-Bellum Louisiana*, 256.

[46]According to a recent sociological study of the colony, 91 percent of the people born before 1865 contracted legal marriages, and most of the remaining 9 percent were youths who died before reaching maturity. See Sister Frances Jerome Woods, *Marginality and Identity: A Colored Creole Family Through Ten Generations* (Baton Rouge, 1972), 78.

[47]Interview with Mrs. Coutii, April 26, 1974; Mrs. Coutii to author, April 25, 1974; Saxon, *Children of Strangers*, 44-45.

[48]Interview with Mrs. Coutii, April 26, 1974.

[49]For example, refer to the discussion in Chapter VIII relative to the legal suits initiated by the colony against whites who attempted to violate the honor of females of the colony.

[50]Interview with Mrs. Coutii, April 26, 1974.

[51]Interview with confidential source, April 26, 1974; Mrs. Coutii to author, April 22, 1974.

[52]Harnett T. Kane, *Plantation Parade: The Grand Manner in Louisiana* (New York, 1945), 267.

[53]Lyle Saxon, *Children of Strangers* (New Orleans, 1948), 29-31; Hugh LaCour to author, April 22, 1974.

[54]Mrs. Coutii to author, April 22, 1974; Saxon, *Children of Strangers*, 30-32; Hugh LaCour to author, April 22, 1974.

[55]Saxon, *Children of Strangers*, 30-32; Mrs. Coutii to author, April 22, 1974. The Isle Brevelle colony, unlike many African descendants in the southern United States, retained almost no African customs or traditions. This religious practice of decorating graves with bottles, shells, and mementos of the dead appears to be one of the last vestiges. One observer of nonwhite life and customs in the antebellum South recorded: "Negro graves were always decorated with the last article used by the deceased, and broken pitchers and broken bits of colored glass." Sara A. Torian (ed.), "Ante-Bellum and War Memories of Mrs. Telfair Hodgson," *Georgia Historical Society*, 27 (1943), 350-56, quoted in Blassingame, *The Slave Community*, 37. It should be noted that the custom of decorating with bottles and shells did not long survive in the colony. The oldest descendants today have no recollection of the practice, although they do recall the days when keepsakes of the departed ones were placed on the graves during religious seasons.

[56]Hugh LaCour to author, April 6, 1974; Saxon *Children of Strangers*, 42-43.

[57]Dorothy Olga McCants, ed. and trans., *They Came to Louisiana* (Baton Rouge, 1970), 60.

[58]Succession of Marie Suzanne Métoyer, in Natchitoches Parish Records, No. 355; Memorandum of the *Marguilliers*, Cloutierville, May 9, 1847, in DeBlieux Collection; Succession of J. B. E. Rachal, in Natchitoches Parish Records, No. 927. By way of comparison, it may be noted that the son of Jean Baptiste Meuillon, a free man of color of Louisiana who is frequently recognized by modern historians for his wealth, paid only 35 piastres for the requiem mass and interment of his father in 1840; Sterkx, *The Free Negro in Ante-Bellum Louisiana*, 204.

[59]Succession of Oscar Dubreuil, in Natchitoches Parish Records, No. 1255.

[60]Natchitoches Registers.

[61]Interview with Mrs. Coutii, March 24, 1974; Cloutierville Registers, Burial Book I.

[62]Interview with Mrs. Coutti, March 24, 1974.

[63]Such tombs were not entirely unique in the parish of Natchitoches, since a handful of affluent whites erected similar monuments. These others, however, have crumbled into decay.

[64]Interview with Mrs. Coutii, April 26, 1974. It was Périne Métoyer Dupré who was responsible, more than anyone, for preservation of the legendary stories that the aging Augustin related to her during the years she and her husband cared for him.

[65]Interview with confidential source, March 24, 1974; Callahan, et al., *History of St. Augustine Parish*, 28.

[66]The religious example set by the early colony has been respected and followed for many generations since. Father Callahan quotes the following accolade to the people made by Bishop Van de Ven of the Alexandria diocese in 1917, at the dedication of the newest church on the Isle: "My dear friends . . . I must tell you that I am proud of you, my dear people, and I can without fear of contradiction, give you as a model for my whole Diocese of Alexandria. Your piety, your generosity, have just accomplished an admirable task—admirable not only because of the size and elegance of style of the building, but admirable especially because of the great sacrifices you have imposed on yourselves to realize it. Your predecessors have set a high standard for you which, if you are their true sons and daughters, you are bound to follow. As the language of your ancestors has it, 'Noblesse obligée.'" Callahan, et al., *History of St. Augustine's Parish*, 43.

A BISHOP FOR LOUISIANA*

Charles Edwards O'Neill

The Diocese of Louisiana and the Floridas, which was established in 1793, had a long history, but it is a history made up of disconnected efforts. The unifying principle is the Catholic tenet that the planting of the Church is incomplete until a resident bishop's see is established. Let us begin our history in 1520 and pursue it until 1801.

In the first two decades of the sixteenth century the Spanish were just beginning their empire in America, and no one could foresee that most of its development would come in Central and South America, in Mexico and the Caribbean islands. Already, though, dioceses were erected in Cuba, Hispaniola, and Panama. In 1513, north of Cuba, Juan Ponce de León arrived to explore a peninsula, and, since the day was Easter, in Spanish *pascua florida*, he called it "Florida." Several years later Emperor Charles V, in his role as king of Castille and León, asked Pope Leo X (Medici) to create a diocese there. In December 1520 Leo X granted Charles V's request. Like the colony itself, the town to which the pope gave the rank of see city was to be known as *Terra Florida*, that is "Floridaland."[1] (The papal document sees Florida as an *island*, which in some way is part of the *island* of Yucatán.) The cathedral church and parish were to have as patron St. James the Apostle, much revered in Spain. The pope accorded various rights and specified duties.[2] He even named a bishop—Jorge de Priego, a Spanish Augustinian. ("Floridaland" was the sixth diocese created in the Americas.) But Leo X died in 1521, and so did Ponce de León; then Charles V resigned in 1555 and died in 1558 without bringing their project to reality. In any case, the project was so premature, indeed artificial, that it was more dream than plan, for there were no Christians in Florida at that time, neither Spanish nor Indian. Nonetheless the document and procedure enable us to situate Florida and the future Louisiana—which was doubtless included in the vague extension of "Floridaland"—in the whole context of the exploration and evangelization of the Americas.

In 1565 Pedro Menéndez de Avilés founded the fort and town of Saint Augustine, but this new colonial post did not inherit the documents and the diocese of 1520. Menédez recruited members of the new religious order, the Society of Jesus, to evangel-

*First published in Glenn R. Conrad, ed., *Cross, Crozier and Crucible: A Volume Celebrating the Bicentennial of a Catholic Diocese in Louisiana* (Lafayette, La.: The Archdiocese of New Orleans in cooperation with the Center for Louisiana Studies, 1993), 96-107. Reprinted with the kind permission of the author and the Center for Louisiana Studies.

ize the native population, but the Jesuits lost so disproportionate a number of missionaries to martyrdom that the holy but pragmatic superior general, Francis Borgia, recalled the survivors from Florida and sent them to Mexico. Menédez then brought in Franciscans who served Floridians, Indian and Spanish, with such dedication and success—with martyrs too—that at the beginning of the next century their flock deserved the pastoral visit of a bishop. Arriving in mid-March of 1606 Dominican Friar Juan de las Cabezas Altamirano, bishop of Santiago in Cuba, traveled for several weeks through what is now the state of Georgia, visiting and confirming; on June 19 he got back to Saint Augustine, and returned to Havana at the beginning of October. All told, he spent a half year in this part of his diocese, where, in addition to the Spanish, the Christian Indians numbered at least 4,000 and perhaps as many as 6,000.[3]

Six decades later, Gabriel Díaz Vara Calderón, bishop of Santiago de Cuba from his appointment in 1671 until his death in 1675, traveled through the Florida missions to administer confirmation and make an episcopal visitation. He made a careful list of the mission stations as they were in 1675.[4] In 1689 the bishop of Santiago de Cuba, Diego Evelino y Hurtado, made a similar visitation and in 1701 proposed (in vain) the creation of a separate diocese because of the danger and difficulty of the sailing from Cuba to Saint Augustine in Florida.[5]

The flourishing Apalachee mission was destroyed in 1704 when Gov. James Moore of South Carolina swept down upon Florida with English troops and Indian allies. The Apalachee Catholic survivors found refuge near Mobile, where the French has newly established a colonial settlement. By some the colony was called "Mississippi;" by others, "Louisiane," the name which eventually prevailed, the name created in 1682 by Robert Cavalier de La Salle. During the 1680s one or more priest friend of La Salle hoped to become bishop of Louisiana, but no such diocese was created. Instead, after some debate, it was decided that French colonial Louisiana was to be (at least for a time) part of the Diocese of Quebec. The principle insisted on by the bishops of Quebec François de Laval, retired, and Jean-Baptiste de Saint-Vallier, his successor, was that whatever territory France acquired in New France became a part of the Diocese of Quebec.[6]

In 1702 Bishop Saint-Vallier was visiting in France while Pierre Le Moyne d'Iberville was making his voyages to and from the new colony on the Mississippi River and Gulf of Mexico. Saint-Vallier, in planning his return to Canada, considered sailing with Iberville to Louisiana.[7] But he did not carry out the idea.

King Louis XIV late in his reign thought of setting up a diocese either in Louisiana or in the French Antilles.[8] Thus Fort Louis de la Mobile might have come to have a St. Louis Cathedral before the yet to be founded city of New Orleans. Louis XIV did not act upon the matter, and thus the question of creating a new diocese in Louisiana carried over after the Sun King's death and was taken up by the regency. Just as in the colonial domains of Spain and Portugal so too in those of France the question of setting up a new diocese was a matter to be decided by the government in the name of the king.

In 1722 a French petitioner set down the obvious reasons why the king should name a bishop for the Church in Louisiana. Foreseeing the possible objection of the financially hard-pressed administrators, the proponent stated that the government should not be concerned about money, because a simple benefice would suffice for the prelate, and because the faithful both in the mother country and overseas would aid the new bishop. An anonymous rebuttal, presumably prepared in the offices of the maritime ministry, argued that the proposal was premature, for the population did not yet warrant a diocese; then, coming precisely to the financial question, the rebutter argued that, even if the first occupant of the see were content with modest means, his successor would doubtless call upon the government for more. According to the holder of the negative position, the clergy would come asking the king for cathedral, episcopal lodging, and canons' stipends—which the government simply could not afford. The result was that, even though the prime minister was Cardinal Guillaume Dubois, the regent (Duke of Orléans) and his government decided not to have a diocese in Louisiana. The southern colony was to remain a part of the northern Diocese of Quebec.[9] Since, even decades later, at the very end of the French colonial regime, Louisiana counted no more than, say, 6,000 Catholics, the argument that it was premature to create a diocese was not without foundation.

Even thought the regency was opposed to the creation of a new see, it was open to the idea of having a bishop visit Louisiana periodically. But none came. In 1723 Commissioner Jacques de La Chaise argued that Quebec was too far away for resolving disputes and granting dispensations; he recommended having in New Orleans an auxiliary bishop of the Quebec diocese. But none was named.[10] Thus the entire French colonial era passed without having a bishop set foot in Louisiana. The bishops of Quebec, too far away to make a visitation of this portion of the diocese, were in succession:

> Louis-François Duplessis de Mornay (1728-1733),
> Pierre Dosquet (1733-1739),
> François-Louis Pourroy de Lauberivière (1740),
> and Henri-Marie Dubreuil de Pontbriand (1741-1760).

For three decades, though, the individual who most attentively cared for the diocesan affairs of Louisiana was Pierre de La Rue, a priest known from his benefice as Abbé de L'Isle-Dieu; this devoted administrator, vicar-general of successive bishops of Quebec beginning in 1734, resided in Paris and served as intermediary between Versailles and Quebec and New Orleans. From afar, L'Isle-Dieu guided by correspondence and diplomacy the affairs of the Church in Louisiana, and he remained a solid pillar of support during the 1760s, a decade of uncertainty and suffering, when Quebec and New Orleans passed under different political sovereignties.[11]

Meanwhile a series of bishops had resided in Spanish Florida for short or long periods. In 1709 the elderly Dionisio Resino, titular bishop of Adramyttium, spent three weeks there, but, although he had been made auxiliary for Santiago de Cuba precisely for residence in Florida, he found the spiritual and material situation so utterly unprepared for his ministry that he returned to Cuba, where he died two years later.[12]

In 1734 Franciscan Fray Francisco de San Buenaventura—his secular name was José Francisco Martínez de Tejada—was consecrated in Mexico City as auxiliary bishop of Santiago de Cuba for residence in Florida, a role created by the king of Spain in 1732; he remained in this post until 1754, when he was transferred to the see of Yucatán.[13] Another auxiliary for Florida was soon named, Pedro Ponce y Carrasco, but, even though he was consecrated in 1746, he did not reach his territory until 1754; he remained only ten months, then returned to Cuba, and in 1762 was promoted to the see of Quito.[14]

In 1762, toward the end of the Seven Years' War, the British captured Havana, and carried off its bishop, Pedro Augustín Morel de Santa Cruz, as a prisoner to Charleston, South Carolina. At the end of 1762, with treaty negotiations already under way, Bishop Morel was released; he made his way to Saint Augustine. Remaining three months in Florida, he visited and ministered in the town and in the Indian villages.[15] By the time the bishop returned to his see in Cuba, the powers meeting in Paris had agreed upon a treaty whereby Spain was obliged to cede Florida to England, under whose rule the peninsula remained until another Treaty of Paris in 1783 reversed the treaty of 1763.

In secret negotiations a year earlier France, by the Treaty of Fontainebleau of 1762, ceded Louisiana to Spain as compensation for Spanish losses during the Seven Years War and as a buffer to protect the Spanish American empire which extended from Louisiana to the Tierra del Fuego. The Louisianians, shocked by the cession, tried to remain under France, but, when they resisted the first Spanish governor in 1768, neither their loyalty nor their philosophy obtained support in the French royal government which had given them and their land to Spain.[16] When the troubled colony settled down to being Spanish, its Church affairs passed under the royal patronage of the king of Spain, the *patronato real*. Even if Quebec, which had fallen to the English in 1759, had still been French, Louisiana could not remain under foreign, that is to say, non-Spanish ecclesiastical jurisdiction. Hence a royal order of December 20, 1771, placed the Church in Louisiana under the jurisdiction of the Diocese of Santiago de Cuba.[17]

In general the Spanish judged the French Catholics of Louisiana to be lax. In part the critics were right, but in part the judgment was based on cultural differences. In any case, when the bishop of Santiago de Cuba, Santiago Echevarría y Elgueza, proposed to go to Louisiana to examine the situation personally, the young governor, Bernardo de Gálvez, opposed the visitation because he did not wish to have ecclesiastical tensions in a colony which had but recently secured political tranquility.[18] Echevarría, bishop of Santiago from 1770 until 1789, was the only ordinary of that see to govern the Church in Louisiana.[19]

Meanwhile in Louisiana Spanish Capuchins replaced French Capuchins. After a decade had gone by with no visit by the bishop of Santiago, the king of Spain and the bishop of Santiago agreed in 1781 to ask the pope to name as auxiliary bishop of Santiago, with special responsibility for Louisiana and Florida, Francisco Antonio Sieni, in religion Fray Cirilo de Barcelona, who was superior of the Spanish Capuchins in Louisiana. Pius VI granted the bulls in June 1784, and Cirilo was consecrated bishop on March 6, 1785.[20] When Santiago in Cuba became an archdiocese, Auxiliary Bishop Cirilo and his territory were annexed to the newly created suffragan see of Havana.[21] The Diocese of Saint Christopher of Havana was erected in September 1787 and received its first bishop in March 1789 in the person of Felipe José de Trespalacios; living until 1799, he was the only Havana ordinary to govern the Church in Louisiana.[22] The situation was unsatisfactory. As auxiliary, Cirilo lacked "ordinary" jurisdiction. As a Capuchin, one would expect, he should have been on good terms with his brethren, but as a Catalan, one surmises, he clashed with the Andalusian Fray Antonio de Sedella, pastor of the parish in New Orleans. Auxiliary Bishop Cirilo did not enjoy the full support of his ordinary, nor did he win commendation from civil officials other than his good friend Gov. Esteban Miró. In 1791, after seven years in his post, Cirilo and his ordinary asked that he be reassigned.[23]

Thus in 1792 there was no longer any resident episcopal authority in Louisiana. The vacuum made it both urgent and easy for civil and ecclesiastical authorities to agree that it was time to erect a diocese there and name a bishop with ordinary jurisdiction.[24] The royal Council of the Indies was ready in late October 1792 to set up the new diocese, but agreed with the royal Contaduría on the poverty of tithes in Louisiana and hence preferred to await further reports before giving the final endorsement. The council, having heard from the bishop of Havana that Louisiana caused him more anxiety than any other part of his diocese, resolved on February 18, 1793, to go ahead; citing the example of the cases of Havana and Guiana, the councillors proposed that the ambassador in Rome seek erection of the diocese by decree rather than by a bull.[25] King Charles IV, ratifying his council's decision, writing on March 11, 1793, from the royal residence of Aranjuez, gave the order that his ambassador in Rome should ask the Holy See for the creation of the diocese.[26]

In Rome, on April 9, 1793, the ambassador of Spain to the Holy See, José Nicolás de Azara, signed the transmission of His Catholic Majesty's request and sent it to Pope Pius VI through Pietro Maria Negroni, the secretary of the Consistorial Congregation, the papal commission of cardinals whose role it was to create new dioceses. Orally Azara had already communicated the king's proposal to the pope. In writing Azara assured Negroni that Charles IV would obtain the consent of four bishops (Mexico City, Puebla, Michoacán and Caracas) to provide a subsidy for the new diocese and thereby solve the problem which had been recognized in Madrid a half year earlier.[27] On April 25, 1793, the Consistorial Congregation carved the new diocese out of the area of Saint Christopher of Havana, and designated New Orleans as the see city, with its St. Louis Parish Church to become the cathedral. The congregation took note of the subsidy to be provided by the Spanish government.[28] In the evening of that same day (April 25, 1793), Negroni brought to Pius VI the favorable action of the congregation, and the pope in that audience "deigned to adhere to the request" which had been made by the king of Spain. The very next day Negroni informed the Spanish ambassador.[29]

Azara was pleased to report to the court of Spain he had obtained not only the creation of the diocese but also the mode of procedure requested: The pope condescended most willingly, giving the order to provide the decree in virtue of which, without further bulls, one could proceed to set up the diocese and appoint a subject of the king to be its bishop.[30] Thus far the process had moved expeditiously, but over a year was to elapse before a bishop received his bull of appointment, and yet another half year before that bishop finally reached his see.

Under the *patronato* it was the king's right to choose the nominee for promotion to the episcopacy in Spanish America. The royal court was used to the procedure, and from a list of candidates the name of Luis Peñalver y Cárdenas, the forty-four-year-old Cuban-born vicar general first of Santiago and then of Havana, emerged by August 12, 1793, when he received the endorsement of the Council of the Indies. The king decided on September 6, 1793, to appoint him to the new see. Promptly on September 9, 1793, the Council of the Indies acted on the royal appointment.[31] By late December the council had completed its examination of candidacies for the canonries of the new diocese.[32]

The procedure of presentation of a bishop-to-be by the king of Spain to the pope called for a review of the candidate's aptitude by the papal nuncio in Madrid. Actually the king's presentation of Peñalver to the Holy See came only in June 1794. And only in mid-1794 did Cardinal Ippolito Antonio Vincenti Mareri, nuncio in Madrid, hold the hearings, which lasted from July 12 to 18. The nine-month delay between the royal choosing and presenting calls for explanation: Perhaps a few months were taken by correspondence between the court in Madrid and the candidate in Havana. Perhaps the French Revolution's violent events had an effect on business in the Spanish court. And perhaps the naming of Vincenti to the cardinalate in February of 1794 also added to the delay. In any case a nunciature document, notarized on July 19, 1794, assured the Holy See that its representative in Spain found Luis Peñalver y Cárdenas worthy to be made a bishop.[33]

Now all was in order. Pope Pius VI provided the bull of appointment of Peñalver under date of September 12, 1794, which confirmed the concurrence granted September 4, 1794.[34] In the appendix below one can read the Latin transcription (with abbreviations written out) and English translation of this bull, now published for the first time.

In turn the king, reminding the bishop-elect of his royal prerogative of presentation to church posts, designated as canons Don Tomás Hassett, pastor of the parish of Saint Augustine in Florida and Don Francisco Pérez Guerrero, retired navy chaplain.[35]

Peñalver received episcopal consecration in his native Havana on April 26, 1795, from the land of Bishop Francisco de la Cuerda; the newly ordained bishop arrived in New Orleans on July 17, 1795, and one week later took formal possession of his diocese (July 24).[36] His flock numbered perhaps 60,000 souls. His clergy were mainly Spanish Capuchins, with a few Irish-born English-speaking diocesan priests. Observers agreed that the level of faith and morals was low, and so the new bishop embarked upon a program of reform.

Given the history of the diocese, it was quite rightly named "of Louisiana and the Floridas." It was vast in extent, for colonial Louisiana reached to the Rocky Mountains and to Canada. Florida, East and West, while perhaps less vaguely extensive than "Floridaland" of the sixteenth century, was several hundred miles wide at the top and several hundred miles long in its north-south measurement. Nonetheless this new diocese was not nearly so vast as Quebec had once been. The Louisiana-Florida diocese's boundaries and the ministry of its first bishop, however, did not long endure.

Six years after Peñalver's installation he left New Orleans, having been promoted to be archbishop of Guatemala (July 20, 1801); subsequently, in 1805, he retired to his native Havana.[37] To succeed Peñalver, King Charles IV chose Francisco Porro y Reinado (1738-1814), Spanish-born superior general of the Clerks Regular Minor, the order of St. Francis Caracciolo. Porro, consecrated bishop in Rome, set out for Louisiana via Spain. Before leaving the mother country for Louisiana he learned that Spain was about to retrocede the colony to France. Consulting the government on whether to sail or not, Porro received word that he should stay in Spain. Eventually he received another diocese. Thus the second bishop never saw his see city of New Orleans.[38]

Napoleon obliged Spain to give Louisiana back to France, and then he sold the colony to the United States of America. So not only was the Diocese of Louisiana and the Floridas left without a bishop, but it was also divided because the political sovereignties required separate ecclesiastical jurisdictions. With unfortunate consequences and searing discord, the "widowed" see remained without a bishop for a decade and a half. In 1805 some hoped that the retired Peñalver might take up again the Louisiana miter. In 1806 some lay administrators of church property in New Orleans even proposed suppression of the diocese because they could no longer count on the subsidy provided under the *real patronato*. It seemed as though the diocese which had waited so long to come into existence might soon go out of existence, as if its creation a decade earlier had in fact been premature. Those years, however, and their difficulties lie beyond the reach of this essay.[39]

The Florida portion of the dismembered New Orleans-based diocese reverted to dependency on Cuba until the United States acquired Florida in 1819. In 1825 Florida was finally and formally separated from the territory of the Diocese of New Orleans, and joined to the Vicariate Apostolic of Alabama and the Floridas was converted into the Diocese of Mobile, but not until 1870 was the Diocese of Saint Augustine established.[40] Three and a half centuries had passed since Charles V had asked Leo X to erect a diocese in "Terra Florida."

Appendix

Pius episcopus servus servorum Dei. Charissimo in Christo Filio Carolo Hispaniarum Regi Catholico, salutem et apostolicam benedictionem. Gratiae divinae praemium et humanae laudis praeconium acquiritur et per saeculares Principes ecclesiarum Prelatis, praesertium pontificali dignitate preditis, opportuni favoris presidium et honor debitum impendatur. Hodie siquidem ecclesiae Aurelianensi Novae tunc a primaeva illius erectione et institutione per Nos Apostolica Auctoritate factis et ad praesens Pastoris solatio destitutae de persona dilecti filii Aloisii Electi Aurelianensis Novae, Nobis et Fratribus Nostris ob suorum exigentiam meritorum accepta, de consilio dicta auctoritate providimus ipsumque illi in Episcopum praefecimus et Pastorem, curam et administrationem ipsius ecclesiae Aurelianensis Novae ei in spiritualibus et temporalibus plenarie committendo, prout in Nostris inde confectis litteris plenius continetur.

Cum itaque, Fili Charissime, sit virtutis opus Dei Ministros benigno favore prosequi ac eos verbis et operibus pro Regis eterni gloria venerari, Maiestatem tuam Regiam rogamus et hortamur attente quatenus eundem Aloisium Electum et predictam ecclesiae Aurelianensem Novam suae curae commissam habens pro Nostra et Sedis Apostilicae reverentia propensius commendatos in ampliandis et conservandis iuribus suis sic eos benigni favoris auxilio prosequaris quod ipse Aloisius Electus tuae celsitudinis fultus presidio in commisso sibi curae pastoris officio possit Deo propitio prosperari ac Tibi exinde a Deo perennis vitae praemium et a Nobis condigna proveniat actio gratiarum.

Datum Romae, apud Sanctam Mariam Maiorem, anno Incarnationis dominicae millesimo septingentesimo nonagesimo quarto, pridie Idus Septembris, pontificatus Nostri anno vigesimo.

[English translation of bull of appointment:]

Pius, bishop, servant of the servants of God wishes health and gives his apostolic blessing to Charles, Catholic King of Spain.

The reward of divine grace and the acclaim of human praise are obtained when due honor and the protection of timely favor are given by secular princes to prelates of the Church, especially to those endowed with pontifical dignity. Since the Church of New Orleans, which from its erection and establishment by Our apostolic authority, has until now been deprived of the consolation of having a pastor, today, by the same authority, We intentionally provide for it and place over it as bishop and pastor our beloved son Luis, whose person is pleasing to Us and our fellow bishops because of his recognized merits; and we fully entrust to him the care and administration of the Church of New Orleans in matters spiritual and temporal, as is contained more fully in another letter of ours.[41]

Since, therefore, dear son, it is a work of virtue to foster with benign favor the ministers of God, and to venerate them in word and deed for the glory of the Eternal King, We attentively beg and exhort your Royal Majesty—who out of respect for Us and the Apostolic See recognizes as willingly recommended by Us the same Bishop-Elect Luis and the aforementioned Church of New Orleans for the extending and preserving of all their rights—we beg you then to foster them by the aid of your benign favor so that Bishop-Elect Luis, relying on the protection of Your Highness in the performance of the pastoral care committed to him, will be able to prosper by the goodness of God, and that as a result there come to you from God the reward of eternal life and from Us due expression of gratitude.

Given at Rome, at St. Mary Major, in the year of the Lord's Incarnation one thousand seven hundred and ninety-four, on the eve of the Ides of September, in the twentieth year of our pontificate.

Notes for "A Bishop for Louisiana"

[1]Bull of Leo X, December 5, 1520, Archivio Segreto Vaticano, Reg. Lat. 1400, f. 277; Félix Zubillaga, *La Florida. La Misión jesuítica (1566-1572) y la colonización española* (Rome, 1941), 42; Josef Metzler, ed., *America Pontificia. Prima Saeculi Evangelizationis 1493-1592. Documenta pontificia ex registris et minutus praesertim in Archivio Secreto Vaticano existentibus* (Vatican City, 1991), 144-53.

[2]Ibid., ff. 277v-278. The same day—*nonis decembris*—the Holy See provided a bishop for Panama: *Colección de Bulas, Breves y Otros Documentos relativos a la Iglesia de América y Filipinas*, ed. Francisco Javier Hernáez (Brussels, 1879), 2:37; Metzler, *America Pontificia*, 14, 147.

[3]Maynard Geiger, *The Franciscan Conquest of Florida (1573-1618)* (Washington, D. C., 1937), 195-210; V. F. O'Daniel, "The Right Rev. Juan de Las Cabezas de Altamirano," *The Catholic Historical Review*, 2 (1917): 400-14, hereafter cited as *CHR*.

[4]Maynard Geiger, *Biographical Dictionary of the Franciscans in Spanish Florida and Cuba (1528-1841)* (Paterson, N. J., 1940), 127-28; Lucy L. Wenhold, *A 17th Letter of Gabriel Díaz Vara Calderón Bishop of Cuba, Describing the Indians and Indian Missions of Florida* (Washington, D. C., 1935). For a recently published list of Florida missions with critical commentary that mentions the bishops' visitations, see John H. Hann, "Summary Guide to Spanish Florida Missions and *Visitas* with Churches in the Sixteenth and Seventeenth Centuries," *The Americas*, 46 (199): 417-513.

[5]J[osé] Isern, *Obispos Cubanos en Louisiana y las Floridas* (Miami, 1973), 6.

[6]Charles E. O'Neill, "Tamaroa: Mission Microcosm of Worldwide Debate" in *Ecclesiae Memoria. Miscellanea in onore del R.P Josef Metzler, O.M.I., Prefetto dell'Archivio Segreto Vaticano*, ed. Willi Henkel, O.M.I. (Rome, 1991), 393-406. Also O'Neill, *Church and State in French Colonial Louisiana: Policy and Politics to 1732* (New Haven, 1966), 52, 139.

[7]Henri-Jean Tremblay to Laval, retired bishop of Quebec, March 31, 1702, Archives du Séminaire de Québec, Lettres N, 117. Also, Tremblay to Louis Ango des Maizerets, May 1702, Lettres O, 37.

[8]O'Neill, *Church and State*, 140.

[9]Ibid., 140-45.

[10]Ibid., 151.

[11]The correspondence of L'Isle-Dieu is found in the French colonial archival series C13 and in other archives, for example, of the Congregatio de Propaganda Fide in Rome. He can be found in the index of works on Lou-

isiana and Canada. To my knowledge, no one has written a biography of this "almost bishop" of French colonial Louisiana.

[12]*Hierarchia Catholica Medii et Recentioris Aevi*, eds. Remigius Ritzler and Perminus Sefrin, (hereafter Ritzler/Sefrin), Vol. V (Padua, 1952), 68; Michael V. Gannon, *The Cross in the Sand. The Early Catholic Church in Florida, 1513-1870* (Gainesville, Fla., 1965), 78-79.

[13]Ritzler/Sefrin, vol. 4 (Padua, 1958), 415; Gannon, *Cross in the Sand*, 79-80; *Catálogo de los Fondos de las Floridas*, 14.

[14]Ritzler/Sefrin, 4:55, 351; Roger Baudier, *The Catholic Church in Louisiana* (New Orleans, 1939), 199, stated that a bishop (unnamed) from Mexico visited Los Adayes (border post between Texas and Louisiana), presumably in mid-eighteenth century.

[15]Ritzler/Sefrin, 4:240, 308; Gannon, *Cross in the Sand*, 80.

[16]Charles E. O'Neill, "The Louisiana Manifesto of 1768," *The Political Science Reviewer*, 19 (1990): 247-89.

[17]Charles Edwards O'Neill, "The United States of America," *Sacrae Congregationis de Propaganda Fide Memoria Rerum, 1700-1815* (Rome, 1974), 2:1178.

[18]Baudier, *Catholic Church*, 195.

[19]Ritzler/Sefrin, 6:240.

[20]Baudier, *Catholic Church*, 200; Ritzler/Sefrin, 6:415; Real Orden, September 14, 1781, *Catálogo de los Fondos de las Floridas* (Havana, 1944), xxxvii.

[21]O'Neill, "The United States of America," 1179.

[22]Ritzler/Sefrin, 6:164.

[23]Charles Edwards O'Neill, S.J., "'A Quarter Marked by Sundry Peculiarities:' New Orleans, Lay Trustees and Père Antoine," *CHR*, 76 (1990): 264-68.

[24]Michael J. Curley, C.SS.R., *Church and State in the Spanish Floridas (1783-1822)* (Washington, 1940), 249-51.

[25]Cámara de Indias, February 18, 1793, Seville, Archivo General de Indias (hereafter AGI), Sección Quinta, Audiencia de Santo Domingo, (hereafter SD), legajo 2674, f. 25v; Contaduría to Cámara de Indias, October 22, 1792, ibid., f. 31-33.

[26]Seville, AGI, Sección Quinta, SD, legajo 2674, f. 38v. There was no letter from king to pope. Decades later, about 1840, bishop of New Orleans Antoine Blanc, because of his secular-law problems, asked the Congregatio de Propaganda Fide whether it could furnish a copy of the relevant royal document. Officials and aides searched in the archives of the Consistorial Congregation but could find no document, and they looked in vain in other papal archives. But on July 17, 1844, Propaganda Fide was able to send Bishop Blanc a birth certificate of the diocese by citing the action of the Consistorial Congregation of 1793. Finbar Kenneally, O.F.M., *United States Documents in the Propaganda Fide Archives Calendar*, First Series, Volume I (Washington, 1966), Numbers 1844 and 2027. In preparing this essay I have not examined Cuban archives, where one might find Peñalver papers.

[27]Rome, Archivio Segreto Vaticano, Acta Congregationis Consistorialis, 1793, ff. 34r and 34v; f. 41v.

[28]Archivio Vaticano, Acta S. Congregationis Consistorialis, 1793, ff. 23 ss, cited in Ritzler/Sefrin, VI, 108.

[29]Negroni to Azara, Rome, April 26, 1793, Madrid, Archivo del Ministero de los Asuntos Exteriores, (Sección) Embajada de España cerca de la Santa Sede Número 35.

[30]Azara to Court, May 1, 1793, Seville, AGI, Sección Quinta, SD, legajo 2674, f. 39r and v. Here is the explanation why there is no papal bull for the erection of the Diocese of Louisiana and the Floridas. Donald C. Shearer, in *Pontificia Americana: A Documentary History of the Catholic Church in the United States (1784-1884)* (Washington, 1933), 91n, noted that he could not find the foundation bull in the usual printed collections of papal documents.

[31]Seville, AGI, Sección Quinta, SD, legajo 2674, ff. 42, 43, 47 and 55.

[32]Ibid., f. 56.

[33]Rome, Archivio Segreto Vaticano, Processus Consistoriales, vol. 197, 1794, ff. 21-28v. "Vincenti Mareri, Ippolito Antonio," in Gaetano Moroni, *Dizionario di Erudizione Storico-Ecclesiatica*, 103 vols. (Venice, 1860), 101: 14.

[34]In the 1960s when I came upon this bull in the Archivio de Indias, SD, legajo 2674, I brought it to the attention of the director of the AGI so that it could be given special storage and protection. The bull of appointment of Luis Peñalver has been removed from legajo 2674 and placed in *Bulas y Breves* 392. I am grateful to Rev. Paulius Rabikauskas, S.J., professor of Latin paleography in the Gregorian University, for transcribing the bull, which was indited in the highly stylized curial writing. Archivio Vaticano, Consistoria, 1794, f. 330, cited in Ritzler/Sefrin, 6:108.

[35]Archivo General de Indias, Papeles de Cuba, legajo 566.

[36]Peñalver to king, July 26, 1795, Seville, AGI, Seccion Quinta, SD, legajo 2672, ff. 102 and verso. Roger Baudier, on 224 of *Catholic Church*, complained of the delay between the creation of the diocese and the arrival of the bishop, but, when one considers the roles of the several parties in the process and also the time required for correspondence by sea between America and Spain and Rome, the interval does not appear extraordinary. Moreover, the years 1793 and 1794 were difficult. The delay between royal nomination and presentation to Rome has been treated in the text. Ten months, from September of 1794 to June of 1795, elapsed after preparation of the bull, but the times of sailing—departure of ships and duration of voyages—from Italy to Spain to Cuba to Louisiana should suffice as explanation. The Spanish ambassador in Rome received the September bull of appointment in October, and it reached Madrid in the third week of November 1794. Seville, AGI, Sección Quinta, legajo 2672, f. 95 and 99.

[37]Ritzler/Sefrin, 6:108.

[38]O'Neill, "United States of America," 1180. Letter of Father Superior General Luigi Affoni, C.R.M., to Charles Edwards O'Neill, Rome, February 8, 1991. Seville, AGI, Sección Quinta, SD, legajo 2672, ff. 141r-221.

[39]Ministre des Cultes Portalis to Cardinal Legate Caprara, Paris, March 11, 1806, Rome, Archivio degli Affari Ecclesiastici Straordinari, Francia 1805-1806, vol. 60, f. 28. Annabelle M. Melville, *Louis William DuBourg: Bishop of Louisiana and the Floridas, Bishop of Montauban, and Archbishop of Besançon, 1766-1833*, 2 vols. (Chicago, 1986), 281, 385. O'Neill, "The United States of America," 1180. O'Neill, "'A Quarter Marked by Sundry Peculiarities,'" *CHR*, 76 (1990): 235-77.

[40]Pius VIII, *Inter Multiplices*, May 15, 1829, *Colección de Bulas y Otros Documentos Relativos a la Iglesia de América y Filipinas*, May 15, 1829, ed. Francisco Javier Hernáez (Brussels, 1879), 2:789.

[41]Not found. Perhaps a formula of style.

PART V

The Louisiana Purchase and Its Aftermath, 1803-1830

THE STATE OF RELIGION IN NEW ORLEANS THIRTY-FIVE YEARS AGO*

Theodore Clapp

Multitudes suppose that genuine Christianity was not introduced into New Orleans till after its cession to the United States, the beginning of the present century. The first American missionaries, who visited the place shortly after the close of the last war with Great Britain, in their published letters and reports, expressed the opinion that the preaching of the gospel was as much needed in New Orleans as in any other spot in the whole world. They affirmed that there was pure faith of the New Testament was unknown and untaught. Yet the Catholic religion had been flourishing in that place from its commencement, one hundred years previous. Churches, schools, asylums, nunneries, and other institutions, such as are usually found in Catholic communities, had been built, with great labor and expense.

When deliberating on the expediency of making a settlement in New Orleans, I was told by divines of my own denomination, that if I went there, the most formidable enemy of the gospel would be arrayed against me—namely, the Papal church. From a child I had been taught to regard Popery as the man of sin, the great adversary of all goodness, described in the Epistles and the Apocalypse by St. John. In the chart of interpretation, pronounced orthodox at the north, numbers, dates, persons, places, and events were particularly laid down, to prove that all evils, woes and calamities mentioned in the book of Revelation were the maledictions of Heaven, denouncing the Roman Catholics. My instructors assured me that the Catholic faith was rapidly spreading in the western and southern parts of our country. It should be counteracted, they said, as far as possible, by sending out Protestant missionaries, and establishing Sunday schools throughout the great valley of the Mississippi.

One can hardly imagine how strong, blind, and hateful were the prejudices against this Christian sect which deluded my mind when I began a professional life in New Orleans. I had been there but a few weeks before I was invited to dine at the house of a

*First published as Chapter 8 in John Duffy, ed., *Parson Clapp of the Strangers' Church of New Orleans* (Baton Rouge: Louisiana State University Press, 1957), 117-28. Reprinted with the kind permission of publisher.

liberal gentleman, where I was introduced to several Catholic priests. I found them intelligent, enlarged, refined, and remarkably interesting in conversation. Not a syllable was uttered about the differences of our faith. I was charmed with their style of manners. They left their clerical robes at home, and deported themselves with all the ease, elegance, and affability characteristic of well-informed and polished laymen. Before we separated, I was assured that they would be happy to see me at their private residences any time, and in the most free and unceremonious manner. Gladly did I avail myself of an opportunity to cultivate their acquaintance. I wanted to obtain some personal knowledge of their peculiar faith, principles, and ceremonies. Heretofore, all that I had learned concerning these topics had been derived from Protestant writings and conversation. I was anxious to hear them speak for themselves.[1]

Since my acquaintance with Louisiana began, there have been, I believe, at no time, less than twenty priests stationed in New Orleans. Besides performing clerical functions in churches, chapels, convents, asylums, and hospitals, they have founded and kept in vigorous operation numerous schools and seminaries of learning for both sexes. In these respective vocations they have displayed the most unflagging zeal, and ardent, persevering industry. No Protestant ministers in the United States, of any denomination, accomplish as much hard service as they do. Morning, noon, and night, at all seasons, whether healthy or sickly, they are engaged in the prosecution of their arduous and responsible labors. Apparently, they live as if each day were their last, and as it becomes those to live who know not what a day, what an hour, may bring forth. Like the sun, which never pauses and never goes astray, so they revolve in the orbit of duty, a light, a charm, and ornament, and a blessing, to all who are embraced in their spiritual guardianship.

In addition to the duties common to churches of every name, they are required to keep their places of worship open, not on the Sabbath day only, but during each day of the week. At every altar, mass is performed at least once a day. Then, the labor involved in the duties of the confessional is inconceivable to one who has not lived among the Catholics. I have known a priest engaged from daylight till noon, uninterruptedly, in receiving penitents, and that in the most inclement weather. All this time, he sits in a small place like a sentry box, applying his ear, in a stooping posture, to an aperture in the surrounding lattice work, which separates him from those who are making their confessions to him. This toil is unintermitted and everlasting. In the intense heat of July and the cold of December, (they have no fires in their churches), it imposes a drudgery more severe than that of the poorest operative in secular life, whether he rolls a barrel and bale in the city, or digs and toils on a plantation.

In the cholera of 1832, I was the only Protestant clergyman that remained in the city except the Rev. Mr. Hull[2] of the Episcopal church, who was confined to his house by a lingering consumption, and unable even to leave his room. This gentleman never left the city in sickly seasons, but fearlessly continued at his post, however great and alarming the mortality around him. So it was that in the first cholera I had no coadjutors but the Roman Catholic priests.

One of these, Father K., was among my most intimate personal acquaintances.[3] He often dined with me, and spent hours at a time in the seclusion of my study. A better man I have not known. He was as liberal in his theological views as Dr. Channing or Bishop Fenelon,[4] and yet most ardently attached to the Roman Catholic church. He was a firm disbeliever in the doctrine of endless misery, but did not advocate this view of futurity in his public discourses. His charities, like his soul, were large and unbounded. He inherited a handsome property, which enabled him to gratify his benevolent desires. In his labors during the cholera, this gentleman gave his services to all, indiscriminately, who needed the consolations of religion, whether Protestant or Catholic sufferers. "I feel," he said, "that all men are my brethren, and heirs of the same immortality. I spend all my time among the sick, irrespective of their character or creed.

"I am not allowed, indeed, to administer the rite of extreme unction to unbelievers. I do not attempt it. But with respect to such cases, I have a peculiar service of my own devising, dictated by the condition and circumstances of the sufferers around me, and which is not in any respect incompatible with my relations to the priesthood. I propound one question only to the departing sinner. I ask him if he believes in the Almighty God, his Creator. If he answers affirmatively, (as all have hitherto done, without an exception) I then offer this short prayer: May that merciful Creator, in whom you exist, forgive and bless you, and conduct you finally to those immortal joys which Jesus has procured for all men in that 'undiscovered country from whose bourn no traveler returns.'" Could any thing be more simple, appropriate, or sublime? He added, tears starting from his eyes with the utterance, "If it were in my power to prevent it, not one of these unhappy victims would be finally and forever lost." Will not, then, infinite, everlasting, and immutable mercy ultimately achieve their deliverance?

This excellent man lost his life in carrying out an enterprise of benevolence. He undertook to establish an asylum and school for orphan boys on the Bayou St. John. He had collected quite a number of fatherless children, made suitable arrangements for their maintenance and education; and when everything, to human view, promised a rich harvest of success, the enterprise was suddenly blasted by the ravages of a tornado. It commenced about sundown, and before midnight caused the waters of Lake Pontchartrain to rise several feet, and flow towards the city like the incoming tide of an ocean. At the dead hour of night, Father K. was aroused by the rushing of the waters into his room. He made all possible haste to awaken the boys, and placed them under the direction of a tutor, who soon conducted them beyond the reach of danger. Then he took some servants with him to the stables, to save a fine stock of cows from drowning. This object was accomplished, but with great difficulty. The good man waded and swam in the water so long that it brought on a chill and typhoid fever, which in a few days terminated his invaluable life and labors. To the community in general, and to myself in particular, his death was an irreparable loss. Our views on religion, and our tastes in general, were singularly harmonious. Strong and deathless were the sympathies by which we were united.

I have not known a clergyman of my own persuasion whom I loved with a purer, intenser affection.

It is a wide-spread opinion that Roman Catholic priests practice certain immoralities, not only with impunity, but with their entire approbation of their parishioners, which, in Protestant communities, would blast completely and forever the reputation and influence of a minister. It affords me great pleasure to testify, that in New Orleans, just as much as in Boston or New York, a spotless moral life is a qualification indispensably necessary to the good standing of any clergyman, whether Protestant or Catholic. Priests are never seen in Louisiana at balls, theaters, private dancing parties, or operas even.

They do not teach that these amusements, abstractly considered, are sinful, but that, such are the weakness and prejudices of large classes in every community, they look upon it as compatible with the spirituality and refinement of the priesthood to participate in their enjoyment. In their public department, the Roman Catholic priests of New Orleans are models of clerical wisdom, decorum, and propriety. They are sufficiently grave, serious, and dignified, and at the same time free from affectations, simple, natural, condescending, agreeable, and unconstrained in their intercourse with persons of every age, character, and condition in life. I have sometimes been present when their religious peculiarities have been assailed by unjust, gross, and insulting insinuations, and beheld with profound admiration their imperturbable equanimity, meekness, and forbearance. Happy would it be if all who profess to be the ministers of Christ should faithfully follow the example of Him "who did no sin, neither was guile found in his mouth; not rendering evil for evil, or railing for railing, but contrariwise blessing, who, when he was reviled, reviled not again; when he suffered, threatened not; but committed to Him that judgeth righteously."[5]

Never, till I went to Louisiana, did I behold that living and most perfect exemplification of a Christian spirit exhibited in the conduct and benefactions of those denominated Sisters of Charity. Look at them. They were, in many instances, born and bred in the lap of worldly ease and luxury. But, in obedience to a sense of religious duty, they have relinquished the pleasures of time for the charms of a life consecrated to duty and to God. There, calm and gentle as angels, they stay at their posts amid the most frightful epidemics, till death comes to take them to a better world. What a spectacle! Their whole existence is passed in watching the sick, and performing for them the most menial offices. They, indeed, fulfill the injunction of the apostle, "Honor all men." They glorify our common humanity. They feed the hungry and clothe the naked. When I have seen them smoothing the pillow, and whispering the consolations of religion for some unfortunate fellow-being, in his last moments, dying among strangers, far from home, never again to behold the face of wife, child, relative, or friend this side of the grave, I could hardly realize that they were beings of mortality. They seemed to me like ministering angels sent down from the realms of celestial glory. O, how immeasurable the disparity between one of these noble spirits and a mere creature of the feminine gender, devoted exclusively to the follies and vanities of fashionable life, who makes a dazzling show for a few hours, and then sinks to be seen no more. These angels are seen in all our hospitals, both public and private, and in other places where their services are required, irrespective of the distinctions of name, religion, party, clime, or nation.

Indeed the Roman Catholic church is infinitely superior to any Protestant denomination in its provisions of mercy and charity for the poor. They seek to inspire the most wretched and forlorn with those hopes that point to a better world. When I was in St. Peter's Church at Rome, on a Sunday morning, I saw the poorest, most obscure and neglected persons kneeling on its splendid pavement, by the side of the most noble inhabitants of the Eternal City. In that cathedral, there is no place assigned for the exclusive use of fashionable people, any more than there is in heaven. All meet on the same level, as children of one common Father; as dependent on the same pardoning mercy; as travelers to the same grave; as partakers of the same promises, and heirs of the same immortal glory. Throughout Catholic Europe, the doors of the churches are kept open day and night, from year to year, and century to century. There, at any hour of the day, the forsaken outcast, on whom the world has ceased to smile, can repair, and falling down before the altar of his God, feel supported by the sublime faith that he has in heaven a better and everlasting inheritance. I may say that Catholic churches are the home of the poor. In countries enjoying this form of Christianity, the most fallen are incomparably less degraded than the worst of those who live in Protestant lands.

Besides, they all, without distinction, participate in the sacraments of religion. No one is permitted to die without the rite of the church. So it should be. Few Protestants know what is the nature of that last benediction, which the priest pronounces over the dying man. It runs, if I have been correctly informed, in a strain somewhat like the following: "Go forth, O thou immortal spirit, in the name of the Father who created thee, in the name of the Son who died to redeem thee, and in the name of the Holy Spirit that sanctifies thee; and when thou leavest the body, may the resplendent multitudes of angels greet thee; may the spirits of the just, clad in their white robes, embrace thee, and conduct thee to the everlasting mansions of the blessed." Could there be anything more appropriate, more beautiful, touching and grand? But with us the poor die without a clergyman, without a prayer, without a friend, without any recognition of their immortality, as if they were about to lie down with kindred brutes, in the same ditch, to exist no more forever.

No Protestant denomination, with the exception of the Methodists, have suitably remembered the poor. This remark was once made by a distinguished prelate of the church of England. In our northern cities, New York, etc., there is an actual rivalry as to which church shall be the most exclusive. And one congregation has erected a separate building for the poor to worship in. Churches are constructed on purpose to shut out the poor. The pews are sold, like the boxes of a theater, to the highest bidder. The poor can never enter there. O, what a commentary on the Christianity of our times! After spending the week in folly and dissipation, the aristocratic among us can repair to a fashionable place of worship on the Lord's day morning, to gratify a love of dress, to indulge that wicked, pitiful vanity, which one act of true religious worship would annihilate forever. I do not know where all this will end; but I do know that Protestantism will soon go down into the dust and darkness of death, unless it changes its entire ecclesiastical plans and policies. Eternal honor be to the Roman Catholic church, for practically observing the distinctive precept of our religion to remember and bless the poor. For the larger the charity of a church, the nearer it is to God.

Now, the Catholic church, as I have described it, went along with the first colonists, who settled themselves on the banks of the Mississippi. It has grown with their growth and strengthened with their strength, and the religious wants of the people of Louisiana have been as well supplied as those of Massachusetts, all things considered. I never go abroad without being compelled to listen to the utterance of the most disparaging and unjust remarks about my adopted state.

Traveling in Europe in 1847, when introduced to distinguished literary gentlemen as a resident of New Orleans, they almost invariably said, "We have always been told that your city is the most wicked, immoral place in the United States." One distinguished author, speaking of Louisiana, observed: "Its physical resources are undoubtedly very superior; but, alas! you have no literature and no history—the only things which can shed glory on a state. This is the first time I have ever met an educated gentleman from New Orleans. I am really glad to see you. Has Louisiana yet produced any scholars, poets, orators, or savan[t]s, worthy of note?" This question was asked, as I thought, in the spirit of sneering and sarcasm. It seemed intended merely to wound my feelings; for, a moment before, I had remarked that the first log cabin on the spot where New Orleans was built, then a wretched swamp, was erected within a century, and that nearly all the improvements in the state had been made within the last fifty years.

I ventured to reply thus: "Sir, you are familiar with the circle of human history. Did you ever read of an instance in which a nation only one, two, or three hundred years old had enriched itself with original works of science and literature? It took nearly one hundred and twenty years to build St. Peter's Church. What a long succession of ages was requisite to produce the cities, temples, palaces, and galleries of art, which adorn England, France, and Italy! Hitherto, the people of Louisiana have been occupied, of necessity, in reclaiming and fortifying their lowlands against the annual inundations of the Mississippi, building houses, turning cypress swamps into beautiful plantations, and providing themselves with the various physical accommodations and improvements upon which the superstructure of civilized life every where rests. At present, for the most part, they import their books, not because they want the genius, but the time and other means essential to the creations of art and philosophy. As to our history, it is very recent, but contains some items of interest. You have heard, I suppose, of the invasion of New Orleans by your countrymen in 1815, and remember the results."

"True," he said, "the victory to which you have referred must be classed with the most brilliant displays of military skill and bravery recorded in the annals of time." He was surprised to learn that the conquerors of Napoleon were subdued by a patriot band of peaceful planters and merchants, who fought for their homes with the same undaunted, invincible spirit which has inscribed the names of Leonidas, Miltiades, and Washington on the tablets of immortal glory. Charles Gayarré, late secretary of the state of Louisiana, had given to the world a noble work upon our history.[6] It is replete with narrative of wild, romantic, and thrilling interest. The author is a Creole, thoroughly acquainted with the character of Louisiana, deeply enamored of its beauties, and has painted them in elegant and polished language.

When I travel in New England, too, I am often pained by hearing Louisiana spoken of in terms of disparagement and vituperation. Last summer, a clergyman of Massachusetts observed to me that he could hardly conceive of a greater calamity than for a pious and enlightened minister to be compelled to spend his days in Louisiana, where Christianity was encumbered by the corruption of the Roman Catholic church. I have already given my opinion discerning the practical Christianity displayed by the priests, and their care for the poor, the outcast, the sick, and the dying.

There is indeed less religious display in Louisiana than in some other sections of our Union; but if what Paul asserts in the thirteenth chapter of First Corinthians be admitted, that the essence of Christianity consists in generous affections and sympathies toward our fellow-beings, I contend that the inhabitants of Louisiana have quite as much religion as those of Massachusetts, New York, or any other northern state. Charity, says the apostle, as above quoted, is the only thing absolutely needful in order to our acceptance with God, the charm and glory of the intelligent universe, the very soul, life, and breath of heaven itself. I would simply ask our traducers whether they can see our hearts, and positively pronounce them to be destitute of those noble sentiments denominated charity in the New Testament. I would invite them to remember and act in accordance with the following words of Jesus: "Judge not, that ye be not judged. For with what judgment ye judge, ye shall be judged; and with that measure ye mete, it shall be measured to you again. Who art thou that judgest another man's servant? to his own master he standeth or falleth." If gospel benevolence proves the existence of Christian principles, it is certain that true religion reigns and flourishes as vigorously in Louisiana as on the banks of the Hudson or Connecticut.[7]

A great deal has been said of late about the danger to this country in consequence of the immigration to our shores of Catholics from foreign lands. It is throughout that the poor Irish, who are constantly coming among us in such crowds, will exert a most deleterious influence, putting in jeopardy our civil liberties, and sowing broadcast over the land the seeds of moral contagion and death. The poor Irish—may Heaven bless them! I want not their aid at the ballot box. Never shall I be a candidate for their suffrages. Yet I can say with entire disinterestedness that I cherish towards them the liveliest sympathies.

I have seen much of the Irish in New Orleans, in seasons of peril and disaster. I love them, for their many generous and noble traits of character. I do not fear that their influence will be injurious to us, either in a political or religious bearing. But I am reminded that they bring to our shores degraded, dangerous characters and habits. If it were really so, is it to be wondered at, when we remember what scenes of the most atrocious despotism have been grinding them to the dust for a long series of ages? They are exiles, seeking a refuge from want and oppression. They are God's children. They are our brothers. In the extremest need and destitution, should we not open our arms to receive them with a cordial welcome, and rejoice that they can find a home in this happy land of peace, freedom, and plenty? It is not in my heart to speak of them in terms of contempt and bitterness. He who applies to them vile and opprobrious epithets virtually "reproaches their Maker."

But, some say, they are stupendously ignorant. Is it their fault, if they are so? For more than seventy years, in Ireland, a Catholic schoolmaster was liable to be transported, and if he returned, to be adjudged guilty of high treason, barbarously put to death, drawn and quartered. This most iniquitous law broke up their schools. The children of necessity grew up uneducated, and most come here ignorant, if they come at all. I rejoice on their own account; for it is an encouraging, well-established fact that, in general, Irish immigrants, as soon as they land among us, begin to improve, and rapidly to assume a more elevated character, especially when they do not forsake their national church, and prove recreant to the faith of their forefathers. Their children can hardly be discriminated from those born of English ancestors, and lose all trace of their original descent, except in those impulses of a naturally noble and generous heart, which distinguish Irishmen in all times, in all latitudes, and under every phase of outward condition and circumstances.

Some are afraid of their religion. It is perfectly safe in a free country to tolerate all forms of religion, because the principle of reverence in man, uninfluenced by coercion, can never lead to any species of immortality. If the Roman Catholics become more numerous in this republic than any other sect, the fact will prove conclusively the superiority of their teachings and mode of worship. That they should grow, till finally to outnumber all the Protestant denominations, is hardly possible. Besides, church despotism belongs to the things forever gone by. It cannot be resuscitated. We might as easily revive a belief in knight-errantry, witchcraft, the mythologies or fabulous traditions of the old Greek and Roman states. The press, the free school, the ballot box, and universal education "have already opened to every view the palpable truths that the mass of mankind was not born with saddles on their backs, nor a favored few booted and spurred, ready to ride them legitimately by the grace of God." It is a most unfounded alarm, then, that these annually increasing immigrations of foreigners into the United States can essentially interfere with our national prosperity. The majority bring with them the means of a competent support. How could we get along without them? Deprived of their aid, what would become of our canals, railways, manufactories, rising towns and cities, and public works in general, on which depends our progress in civilization, wealth, freedom, science, morals, and religion? With the help of foreigners this republic was founded; by their help it has been preserved and advanced to its present state of glory and happiness.

The first Protestant church in New Orleans was built about forty years ago, belonging to the Episcopal denomination.[8] The second was founded by my predecessor, the Rev. Sylvester Larned, and was first opened for public worship on the 4th day of June,

1819. On the lower floor there were one hundred and eighteen pews. The galleries were spacious, and capable of accommodating about four hundred persons. Both sides of the galleries contained free seats, which were always filled by strangers. On this account, our place of worship was often called the Strangers' Church. It was generally believed that its pastor was a "setter forth of strange gods," to use an expression of St. Paul. Hence those who regarded him as a false teacher not unfrequently came to the Presbyterian meetings to listen to the novelties of an heretical pulpit. Whatever may have been the cause, our church was honored by the attendance of the most respectable strangers during the winter season. The pews were always taken by the residents of the city, and there were more applicants than could be accommodated. It was a usual saying among my orthodox friends, that the merchants and planters who came to New Orleans during the healthy months to transact business never left the city without going to "the American theatre, the French Opera, and Parson Clapp's church." The insinuation is obvious. But notwithstanding the slander, perhaps the friends of truth have cause to rejoice in the greater facilities which were thus afforded for its wider dissemination. Whenever and wherever I have travelled, on this or the other side of the Atlantic, I have constantly met with strangers whose first words were, "We have seen you before; we have heard you preach in New Orleans."

I dined out in London on the second day after my arrival. When I entered the dining room, filled with a most brilliant circle, as soon as I crossed the threshold, a lady ran to greet me, saying, "Though I have never been introduced to you, I feel as if we were old acquaintances, for I visited your church several weeks in succession one winter, when sojourning in New Orleans." She then mentioned some of the subjects upon which I had preached, and the anecdotes and arguments which were employed. It affected me so deeply that I could scarcely refrain from tears. She was hardly seated before another lady claimed an acquaintance, on the same ground. One winter, it was her good fortune, she said, to be a regular attendant at our meetings in New Orleans.

In Liverpool, Edinburgh, Glasgow, Belfast, Dublin, even Paris, and Geneva, in Switzerland, I was made to feel as if I were at home, by those who recognized me at once, but had never seen me except in the pulpit, or at a funeral. Merchants, and the agents of large mercantile houses from various parts of Europe, flock to New Orleans every winter. They are, with scarcely an exception, intelligent and liberal. Among them are some of the warmest friends I have ever had. If I have spent my days in advocating sentiments essentially and fatally erroneous, perhaps no minister living has done more hurt that I have done. But if, as some believe, I have espoused the true and right, it is a pleasing reflection, that my humble efforts have perhaps contributed to the advancement of virtue and knowledge in matters of the deepest importance, both for time and eternity.

Within the last twenty years, Protestant churches have greatly multiplied in New Orleans. At the present day, I believe they number twenty-five or thirty. The Catholic churches have increased in an equal ratio, so that Christianity has the same external means of growth and prosperity in the Crescent City as in New York or Boston. The greatest hindrance to the spread of the gospel in New Orleans is the peculiar condition of its inhabitants. Nearly half of these are what may be called a floating population. They go there only for the honorable purpose of accumulating property. No one of them, hardly, looks upon New Orleans as his home. Of course, all are anxious to gain a fortune as soon as possible. What care they for New Orleans, provided their respective personal schemes of profit and independence can be achieved? Hence the number is comparatively smaller than in places where the population is stable, who feel a deep, abiding interest in building churches and other useful institutions. Those who do favor such objects are singularly devoted and self-sacrificing. The society is fluctuating and heterogeneous almost beyond a precedent. It is constantly changing. In a very short time, the settled pastor sees his pews emptied, and filled with new occupants. He has hardly time to form their acquaintance, before they vanish, to be succeeded by another set of strangers. The disadvantages necessarily attendant on such a state of things are obvious. I do not mean to intimate that the people of New Orleans are more immoral than city population in general. We do not think they are more corrupt, or depraved, or worldly, than those who live in Boston and its vicinity. It is not to be wondered at that those who go south merely to buy, and sell, and get gain, should say to the clergyman and his solicitations, "Go thy way for this time; when I have a convenient season I will call for thee." Upon the whole, New Orleans perhaps is rising as rapidly in the scale of moral and religious improvement as could be reasonably expected.

Notes for "The State of Religion in New Orleans Thirty-Five Years Ago"

[1]At this point Dr. Clapp discusses Catholic theology as it was explained to him by a Catholic priest. He concludes with a plea for toleration and understanding, supporting his plea with extensive quotations from Dr. Orville Dewey.

[2]The Reverend James T. Hull.

[3]Father Adam Kindelon, first pastor of St. Patrick's Church in New Orleans. See Roger Baudier, *The Catholic Church in Louisiana*. (New Orleans, 1939), 398.

[4]Bishop Fenélon (1651-1715), Archbishop of Cambray (François de Sélignac de la Mothe).

[5]Here Dr. Clapp gives a lengthy illustration of the virtues to be found in a good Catholic family.

[6]Charles Gayarré, *History of Louisiana*, 4 vols. (New York, 1854-66), and *Louisiana, Its Colonial History and Romance*, 2 vols. (New York, 1851-2).

[7]In the following pages which are omitted, Dr. Clapp expatiates upon the virtues of the Catholic Church.

[8]A short article in the *Louisiana Gazette*, April 30, 1805, first urged the organization of a Protestant church. Subsequently on July 16, 1805, the church came into existence. Since the majority of the members were Episcopalians, it was agreed to affiliate with that church. See Elma Leona Kolman, *The History of the Presbyterian Church in New Orleans, 1817-1860* (n.p., 1939).

CHILDREN AND CHARITY:
ORPHANAGES IN NEW ORLEANS, 1817-1914*

Priscilla Ferguson Clement

In the United States, children have constituted a large proportion of Americans living below the poverty level. In 1981, 68 percent of the recipients of the country's major public welfare program were youngsters.[1] Today such children customarily receive public assistance in their own homes, but in the last century, most enrolled in orphan asylums, whether public or private. Historians have largely ignored the thousands who were institutionalized annually in asylums due to the death, desertion, or unemployment of one or both of their parents, in favor of chronicling the experiences of the many fewer youngsters incarcerated in juvenile reformatories.[2] Although some accounts of individual orphan asylums, and several general histories of nineteenth-century methods of managing dependent youth have been published, there are few comparative studies of past methods of sheltering impoverished youngsters.[3] Many questions continue unanswered. Were orphan asylums in Southern cities like New Orleans unlike those elsewhere in the country? Were there variations between the experiences of children in orphan asylums managed by Catholics and by Protestants, in asylums administered by women and by men? Were orphanages for girls unlike those for boys?

This study addresses these questions by examining three New Orleans orphanages: the Poydras Asylum for Girls founded by Protestant women in 1817; the Asylum for Destitute Orphan Boys, opened in 1824 by Protestant men; and St. Mary's Orphan Boys' Asylum, established by Catholics in 1835 and administered alternately by male and female religious orders. The focus here is on the children admitted, their ethnic and family backgrounds, their experiences in these institutions, and what happened to them upon release. Data on the subjects was derived from a sample of admissions records of nine hundred boys and girls admitted between 1817 and 1914.[4]

This article reaches conclusions which do not wholly agree with several traditional conceptions about child-care institutions founded between 1800 and 1835. David Rothman argues that such asylums "were not part of a systematic program but the work of

*First published in *Louisiana History*, 27 (1986): 337-51. Reprinted with the kind permission of the author and the Louisiana Historical Association.

dedicated yet idiosyncratic philanthropists," and he also implies that they became more custodial in the late nineteenth century. In contrast, Peter Tyor and Jamil Zainalden state that "asylums established before 1840 typically stressed regimentation, discipline, and custody" from the beginning.[5] In actuality, the three New Orleans children's asylums herein described were founded for the same instrumental reason—to cope with orphanage caused by disease and immigration—and they were never custodial: the managers of each promptly restored children to their families. In addition, the established notions that Catholic institutions confined children longer and that Protestant asylums worked to re-press and convert Catholic youth are not applicable to the New Orleans institutions. Moreover, the history of all three asylums contradicts a recently proposed thesis that child-care institutions confined youngsters for greater periods of time at the end of the nineteenth century, presumably because of declining demand for child labor.[6]

Overall, this study establishes that the evolution of children's asylums in New Orleans was in many ways unique. Problems peculiar to this city throughout the nineteenth century, such as the high death rate from recurring epidemics, as well as Southern racial attitudes toward blacks, affected both admission and placement programs. Moreover, because in New Orleans, as elsewhere in the South, there was little or no institutional public welfare in the nineteenth century, private orphan asylums were virtually the only recourse for indigent youth. Also, the regional isolation of the South in the nineteenth century meant that children's asylums there were little affected by new methods of dealing with needy children developed elsewhere in the country. Finally, the history of these orphanages reveals differences between them based on religion and gender—distinctions that had to do with the proportion of immigrants admitted, the educational role of the asylum, and the humanitarianism of asylum programs.

In early nineteenth-century New Orleans, concerned citizens formed orphanages in response to the social problems resulting from disease and immigration. From the time the United States absorbed Louisiana in 1803 through mid-century, yellow fever reached epidemic proportions in New Orleans almost every summer. In addition, thousands perished from cholera in 1832 and 1848-9. The large numbers of children orphaned by yellow fever in 1817 so distressed Quaker Phoebe Hunter that she and several of her friends in the New Orleans Protestant community organized the Poydras Home for female orphans.[7] In 1824, some of the husbands of the managers of Poydras, troubled by the growing number of boys orphaned by yellow fever, joined with other local Protestant men to establish the Asylum for Destitute Orphan Boys.[8] Later, between 1830 and 1850 when New Orleans became an important port of entry for increasing numbers of impoverished Irish Catholic immigrants, New Orleans' powerful Catholic prelates opened several asylums for orphaned Catholic youth, including St. Mary's Orphan Boys' Asylum. From 1835 to 1871, the Brothers of the Holy Cross and the Marianist Sisters administered St. Mary's, and thereafter the Marianist Sisters assumed control of the orphanage.[9]

By 1916 the Poydras Home, the Asylum for Destitute Orphan Boys, and St. Mary's had been joined by eighteen other private children's agencies: thirteen Catholic, four Pro-

testant and one Jewish. Yet there remained little public welfare in New Orleans, no over-
seers of the poor to dispense aid to the needy in their own homes, and no public alms-
house until 1854. In 1903 there were just thirteen children in all of the public almshouses
in Louisiana. City officials in New Orleans recognized the importance of private charities and donated money to them, but such contributions were occasional and never substantial.[10] In contrast, in Philadelphia, public aid to children preceded the creation of private orphanages, and not until 1850 were there more children cared for by private than by
public agencies.[11] Because of the insignificance of public welfare in New Orleans, private aid to dependent children became the chief method by which the city sustained families in times of extreme need.

Immigrant families were the most likely to apply for and to receive assistance.[12]
None of the three New Orleans orphanages received many children who were themselves
foreign-born. But if it is assumed that all youngsters with non-English surnames were
second generation Americans, before the Civil War three-fifths, and afterwards, one-half
of the children in all three asylums were of foreign parentage. Within the orphanages
there was always a much higher proportion of children of immigrants than there were
immigrants among the city populace.[13]

Even though all three orphanages willingly accepted children of immigrants, from
1881 to 1914, St. Mary's retained the highest proportion of such children (63 percent).
As Catholic orphanages grew in size and visibility, immigrant parents, many of whom
were Catholic, seemingly preferred to send their youngsters to such asylums rather than
to Protestant institutions. This trend is confirmed by the declining number of Catholic
children in Poydras from 46 percent (1817-1839) when there were no Catholic orphanages for girls in the city, to 23 percent (1840-1861) when the first Catholic orphanages
appeared, to 13 percent (1861-1912) by which time Catholic orphanages were well established.[14] Fewer Catholics in Poydras may also have resulted from discrimination against
them within the institution, for in the nineteenth century, many Northern Protestant orphanages presumably tried to convert immigrant Catholic children. However, the Protestant managers of the Poydras Home acted differently: they released all children on Sundays to worship at churches of their own choice, for a time employed members of a
Catholic religious order to staff the orphanage, and consistently retained Catholic girls a
shorter time and returned them more frequently to their families than they did Protestant
girls.[15] Surely, had the Poydras managers been seeking to convert the Catholics, they
would have detained them in the asylum as long as possible and returned them to their
own families reluctantly.

Of course, such actions would have secured for Poydras the enmity of the city's Roman Catholics, no small matter in a principally Catholic city and might have cost the asylum its governmental financial aid. As a consequence, there was a practical as well as a
religious rationale for the tolerant attitude of Poydras managers toward Catholic youth.
Yet despite this toleration, the orphanage received dwindling numbers of Catholic children. The parents of such youngsters may have desired more than freedom of worship

for their children and the promise of a quick return home: perhaps a complete, lengthy, Catholic education, which was free to them only in Catholic orphanages.

While the three New Orleans orphanages seemingly did not practice ethnic discrimination, they did remain racially exclusive. None admitted black children. When the asylums were founded, slave children, if orphaned, were cared for by their masters; if the sons and daughters of free blacks fell on hard times, it was assumed others of their race would care for them. Even after the Civil War, the managers of these and other New Orleans orphan asylums did not alter their policies.[16] Benevolence to needy children extended only to those who were white.

Not only were the children in these three New Orleans orphan asylums racially homogenous, they were also about the same age. Between 1817 and 1914, almost three-fifths of the youngsters accepted into the Asylum for Destitute Orphan Boys, the Poydras Home, and St. Mary's were between six and eleven. The mean age at admission was 7.3.

There were several reasons why the managers of all three asylums preferred to admit children within this narrow age range. They rejected very young children, age five or below, because of their high death rate. In the two Protestant orphan asylums in New Orleans before the Civil War when yellow-fever epidemics were almost an annual occurrence, very young children were twice as likely to die as were older boys and girls. Adolescents were probably admitted infrequently because they were potential behavior problems. With the data available, the best guide to which children required disciplinary action were those who fled the asylums. Such youngsters often ran away only after they had been punished for other offenses. As an alumnus of St. Mary's reported: ". . . I always seemed to be in some trivial trouble, either directly responsible or given credit for it. . . . The environment obviously with its limitations and restrictions didn't come up to my expectations—so I ran away."[17] The child most likely to abscond was twelve or older; between 1817 and 1860, such adolescents were two times more likely than younger children to flee both from the Asylum for Destitute Orphan Boys and from the Poydras Home. If adolescents were so likely to cause problems by running off, all the more reason to admit fewer of them.

Schooling was an integral part of the regimen of these orphanages, and it also influenced their admission policies. Studies of nineteenth-century public education in New Orleans, St. Louis, and Massachusetts indicate that most youngsters attended school between the ages of six and twelve or eight and thirteen.[18] If children within this age range were ready for school, then the typical young entrant to Poydras, the Asylum for Destitute Orphan Boys, and St. Mary's, was of an age to take proper advantage of the elementary education these asylums provided.

The three orphanages also preceded the establishment of public and most parochial schools in New Orleans, and thus, for a time, offered the children of the poor their only opportunity for an education. Even after tax-supported public schools were established in New Orleans in 1841, the educational function of orphanages remained crucial to poor children, for even by the 1880s, the city's public schools could not accommodate half the children of school age. Eventually, between 1891 and 1904, after the public schools had greatly expanded, the Poydras Home and the Asylum for Destitute Orphan Boys econo-mized by closing their classrooms and enrolling their young inmates in local public schools.[19] Yet St. Mary's continued to educate orphan boys separately. Since the public schools in New Orleans had been established by Protestants, members of Catholic relig-ious orders were reluctant to enroll Catholic orphans in them. However, there were many parochial schools in the city, yet no Catholic orphan asylum in New Orleans registered its inmates in one before 1912.[20] Class prejudice, combined with a reluctance to send chil-dren from an asylum administered by one religious order to a parochial school run by another, meant that in New Orleans needy Catholic children were segregated from more affluent youngsters in the Catholic parochial schools much longer than were indigent Protestant youth kept separate from children of various class backgrounds in the public schools.

While school-age children were most likely to gain admittance to New Orleans or-phanages, only in the antebellum era were many of these youngsters full orphans. Later, all three asylums, to varying degrees, accommodated a growing number of half orphans and a few children with both parents living.

Since all three asylums were originally founded to take in youngsters whose parents had died during an epidemic, it is not surprising that before 1861 orphans accounted for 40 percent of admissions to Poydras and 65 percent of entrants to the Asylum for Desti-tute Orphan Boys. When disease abated in the city thereafter, the number of full orphans diminished. In 1915 the New Orleans Board of Prisons and Asylums reported that 15 percent of children cared for by city charities were full orphans, and that is indeed the proportion of parentless youngsters in the Asylum for Destitute Orphan Boys and in St. Mary's, for the years 1881-1914 inclusive, while in the Poydras Home just 5 percent of the girls were full orphans over this time span.[21]

With fewer full orphans in need of aid, New Orleans orphanages admitted more half orphans; their proportion of the inmate population rose less than one-half before the Civil War to two-thirds afterwards. Three-quarters of these children had no fathers. Managers assumed that all but the most sickly of men could provide for their offspring, but a single mother could usually find work only in domestic service. Since employers preferred their live-in servants to be childless, many mothers followed the example of Mary Paul, who, when she became a cook in 1885, enrolled her six-year-old son, Fred, in the Asylum for Destitute Orphan Boys.[22]

Single mothers like Mary Paul did not have large families. Before 1880, the mean size of the families of youngsters in the Poydras Home and in the Asylum for Destitute Orphan Boys was 2.7. Of course, the large number of full orphans in these institutions at this time may have kept the average family size small. Yet in later years (1881-1912), when there were few homeless boys and girls in these asylums, their median family size was just three.[23] The single mothers who sent their children to these orphanages typically had only one or two children, yet they could not afford to feed and clothe even this small number.

Such mothers often gave over all of their offspring to orphanages. The managers of all three asylums had always accepted groups of siblings, but as more parents requested admittance of several children, more were accepted. From 1881 to 1914, over half of the children in all of these orphan asylums were admitted with one or more brothers or sisters.

Parents relinquished their children to an orphanage for several reasons. Single mothers, who were often poor because in the nineteenth century the jobs open to them were few and low-paying, and because in New Orleans (unlike in most Northern cities) they could not receive public assistance in their own homes, turned to private orphanages to feed, clothe, and educate their children. Yet such reliance on orphanages did not mean the break-up of their families. Quite the contrary. Parents who sent their daughters to Poydras sometimes specified to whom they wanted the girls released, and the managers usually complied with their wishes.[24] Only at the Asylum for Destitute Orphan Boys before 1861 were the majority of sibling groups admitted separated when they left, but this was largely because the boys had no living parent to whom they could return. In later years, brothers who entered both this asylum and St. Mary's were rarely parted upon release and usually returned to one or both parents. For the children, entering an institution with a sister or brother was probably less threatening than going in alone, and once inside, siblings could look out for one another. Mothers and fathers could withdraw their children one at one time as did Mrs. Elise Plante, a widow, who in 1894 deposited her three sons in St. Mary's and returned at two-year intervals to claim each boy, beginning with the oldest. Upon release each son had secured an education and was old enough to find work. Even if the parents were dead, as in the case of Jim and Ned Lewis, aged six and eight, who entered St. Mary's in 1874, every effort was made to keep what was left of the family together. After they had spent two years in St. Mary's and had learned to read and write, the nuns placed both Jim and Ned with the same family in Avoyelles Parish.[25]

The length of time Jim and Ned spent in the orphanage was about average. Youngsters entered when they were of school age (between the ages of six and eleven) and remained two to four years, which was the typical length of time most lower class youngsters then spent in school before going out to seek work.[26] Nonetheless, there were some differences between the three New Orleans orphanages in terms of how long they retained children. Throughout its history to 1912 the Poydras Home kept girls a mean of two and one-half years, but at the Asylum for Destitute Orphan Boys and at St. Mary's, for different reasons, the average length of stay of boys declined toward the end of the nineteenth century.

After 1880 the mean length of stay at the Asylum for Destitute Orphan Boys declined from 2.5 to 1.3 years. The change occurred when the managers encountered financial difficulties after the Civil War and determined to keep the orphanage functioning, even if it meant ignoring its original purpose to serve "the destitute," by charging parents room and board fees of $1.50 per month and discharging youngsters whose families did not pay. Asylum officials, not parents, decided when youngsters should return home. In 1899 Walter and Henry Morris "were taken out by order of Mr. Blanc who considered the parents fully able to take care of them."[27] This forcible discharge policy allowed administrators to dismiss boys earlier and thus precluded costly, lengthy stays. Of course, restoring boys to parents who were too poor to pay for their maintenance in the asylum, or whom officials alone decided were ready to resume parental duties, was not always advantageous to children and was seemingly contrary to the official purpose of the asylum.

The female managers of the Poydras Home experienced similar money problems and also charged some parents for their children's upkeep, but never did they dismiss girls because their parents could not contribute for the girls' support. Herein may be a difference between an orphanage managed by men and one directed by women. Faced with comparable financial exigencies, the male managers survived by shifting the burden to poor parents, while the female directors of Poydras collected room and board fees only when they could, donated more of their own money to keep the asylum functioning, and surrendered girls to their parents at their request.[28]

The number of years youngsters spent in St. Mary's also diminished after 1880 from a mean of 4.1 to 2.5. Homer Folks was one of the first to argue that Catholic orphanages usually retained youngsters longer than did Protestant ones because extreme poverty among immigrant Catholics made it harder for them to resume support of their own children or to take in homeless orphans. Members of Catholic religious orders may also have countenanced longer stays because they assumed that a good Catholic education required some years to acquire.[29] Why then the decline in the period of time orphans spent in St. Mary's? The most likely explanation is an alteration in management, for longer stays coincided with the era when the Brothers of the Holy Cross administered St. Mary's and shorter terms with the years when the Sisters Marianne were in charge. Perhaps the Sisters Marianite felt that four years in an institution was too long for a young boy to be apart from his family, for indeed they respected family feeling more than their male predecessors, and delivered over two times more boys to their families than had the Brothers of the Holy Cross. In the late nineteenth century, Protestants at the Asylum for Destitute Orphan Boys and Catholics at St. Mary's curtailed children's asylum stays and transferred more back to their families, but for different reasons. The managers of the Protestant asylum rapidly dispatched children home at the managers' convenience, but the nuns at St. Mary's sent youngsters home only at parental request. In one case reducing length of stay in the orphanage was a harsh policy, in the other, it was not.

Actually, policies in all three asylums altered after the Civil War so that more youngsters were released directly to their parents. Earlier, just two-fifths of those in the two Protestant orphanages rejoined relatives, in part because so many were orphans and had no living relations willing and able to take them in. They resembled nine-year-old Johan Dieter, whose ailing, German-born father, himself a widower, deposited his son in the Asylum for Destitute Orphan Boys in 1835. Johan's father subsequently died and the boy, after spending four years in the orphanage, was placed out with a sea captain. At this time, indenturing provided orphans like Johan an opportunity to learn a trade and precluded retention in an asylum until adulthood. However, late in the century, the practice of indenturing became obsolete as demand for child labor decreased because of greater machine efficiency and a flood of immigrant laborers willing to work for low wages.[30] Conveniently, the number of homeless orphans then declined, and asylum entrants usually had families to whom they could and did return: after 1880, at all three orphanages, the proportion of youngsters placed out diminished to 8 percent or less, and the number restored to their families rose to over 70 percent.

Nonetheless, there were differences between the three orphan asylums in terms of how they disposed of children. Girls at the Poydras Home, even orphans, were always less likely to be indentured than were youths in the Asylum for Destitute Orphan Boys. Somehow the Poydras Managers located friends to look after fourteen-year-old Carla Bodkin after the orphaned girl had spent a year in the asylum in 1833-34, and discovered a grandparent willing to care for six-year-old Marie Danton after her parents died in 1823.[31] Poydras officials indentured fewer children before the Civil War because in a slave society, placing white girls in family homes to perform domestic chores put them on the same level with black house slaves, an unacceptable practice.[32] Even after the war, because household labor remained "black work," the directors of Poydras indentured only 11 percent of their girls and entrusted most of the rest to their families, while both the Asylum for Destitute Orphan Boys and St. Mary's Orphan Boys' Asylum indentured 24 and 15 percent respectively of their young charges.

Nonetheless, not only reluctance to indenture girls but also a strong commitment to returning children to their families dictated the placement policy of the female managers of Poydras. They maintained that, "It is not in the heart of . . . [one] mother to deny the request" of another for her child.[33] When women managed orphan asylums in New Orleans, whether they were Protestants at Poydras or nuns at St. Mary's, they restored more girls and boys to their families than did male orphan asylum managers. After 1880 when the nuns were in charge of St. Mary's, they too returned more youngsters (including orphans) to their families, even more than did the male directors of the Asylum for Destitute Orphan Boys.

By returning so many youngsters to their families, New Orleans charities for children controverted the advice and practice of the most well-known social reformers of the day. In New York, Charles Loring Brace's Children's Aid Society removed thousands of city children from their families and placed them, where they would presumably enjoy more freedom and opportunity, on farms in the Midwest. At the same time, the newest institutions for children, such as the State Public School at Owatonna, Minnesota (founded in 1885), deliberately pursued a policy of permanent separation of indigent urban youngsters from their natural families and placement of the children in healthier, more affluent farm families. From 1887 to 1908, just 27 percent of the boys and girls at Owatonna eventually rejoined their natural families.[34] Directors of New Orleans charities for children were not consciously ahead of their times in their willingness to reunite indigent parents and their children, but were simply indifferent to Northern reform ideas. The managers saw no need to change their established policy of helping impoverished immigrant parents through hard times by temporarily feeding, clothing, and educating their sons and daughters.[35]

The histories of the Poydras Home, the Asylum for Destitute Orphan Boys and St. Mary's confirms that the evolution of nineteenth-century child-care institutions was conditioned by many factors. Some of these factors were first suggested by Peter Tyor and Jamil Zainalden in their study of two Massachusetts asylums between 1847 and 1920. Even though their view that American institutions founded before 1840 were largely custodial has not proved to be the case in New Orleans, their general thesis that date and location of founding and pattern of development enormously affected the evolution of nineteenth-century institutions is confirmed by the history of these New Orleans orphanages.[36]

All three orphanages were established after serious epidemics. All were intended to serve families who faced the practical problem of how to care for children in times of extreme need. This purpose conditioned all their subsequent history, for these asylums always remained most responsive to parents who required only a temporary shelter for their children. Perhaps the regional isolation of the South in the nineteenth century also forestalled orphan-asylum managers in New Orleans from adopting the more repressive child care programs, so popular in the North and Midwest, which often involved permanent separation of needy parents from their children. Geographical locale also affected placement programs in another way: in the South, identification of household labor with blacks meant that, unlike in the North, indigent white girls could not readily be indentured as servants. Likewise, racism in the South precluded the managers of the New Orleans asylums from admitting blacks. Location in a section of the country where there was so little public welfare, also converted these private orphan asylums into a welfare source of greater importance to indigent parents than were most comparable asylums elsewhere in the country. Finally, location in New Orleans, where there was a powerful Catholic tradition, meant that managers of Protestant orphan asylums prudently avoided pursuing a policy of conversion of Catholic children in their care. This same pattern may have held true in other parts of the United States where Catholicism was strong in the nineteenth century.[37]

The date and location of their establishment greatly influenced the history of orphanages and so too did the nature of their clients. In common with the asylums studied by Tyor and Zainalden, a "pervasive gradualism" characterized the New Orleans institutions for children.[38] The directors of all three asylums consistently admitted youngsters about the age of seven and more willingly accepted children from single parent households headed by mothers than from those headed by fathers. Yet each responded to client needs as they became apparent. When fewer full orphans required care, all three asylums admitted more half orphans. When parents brought more groups of siblings to them, the managers of the asylums took more in.

Even though the Tyor-Zainalden thesis accounts for much of the development of nineteenth-century institutions for children, it does not account for all. The history of the Poydras Home, the Asylum for Destitute Orphan Boys, and St. Mary's indicates that the religion and gender of the directors of orphan asylums also influenced their policies. Religion affected both the ethnic composition and the degree of segregation of youthful inmate populations. Although asylums administered by both Protestants and Catholics in New Orleans accepted a large number of children of immigrants, by the end of the nineteenth century, the Catholic orphan asylum, St. Mary's, took more, and the Protestant asylums, fewer such youngsters. The example of New Orleans indicates that where there were many sizable Catholic orphanages, immigrant Catholic parents preferred them to Protestant orphan asylums, whether or not the latter practiced overt discrimination. Religion also affected the degree of separation of orphan asylum inmates from other children. In New Orleans, the managers of Protestant orphanages were much more willing than their Catholic counterparts to close asylum classrooms and integrate orphans into city schools. Needy Catholic orphans remained segregated from more affluent youngsters longer than did dependent Protestant youth.

The gender of the managers of orphan asylums also affected their programs in New Orleans, when asylums were directed by women, Protestant or Catholic, they were more likely than male officials of either religious persuasion to return children to their families at parental request. The period of time youngsters remained in these three orphan asylums reveals another dimension to the effect of gender on management policies. The length of stay of youngsters in each asylum remained the same or declined from early to late in the nineteenth century. This fact alone reveals that these orphanages did not become increasingly custodial, nor presumably did their managers respond to a diminishing market for child labor by incarcerating youngsters longer. Rather, the managers of all three asylums restored children to their families, but female managers were more willing to keep youngsters as long as parents desired, while male managers were more likely to release children when the managers alone saw fit.

Notes for "Children and Charity: Orphanages in New Orleans, 1817-1914"

[1]The program is Aid to Families with Dependent Children. *Statistical Abstract of the United States, 1982-83* (Washington. D. C., 1982), 340.

[2]According to Homer Folks in *The Care of Destitute, Neglected and Delinquent Children* (New York, 1902), 55, 223, before 1851 there were 77 charities for dependent children in the U. S. and 9 reformatories for delinquents. Even if we assume that each reformatory assisted 200 children annually and each orphan asylum just 50, all of the orphanages together would still have housed more than twice the number institutionalized in reform asylums. Nonetheless, the literature on juvenile delinquency in the nineteenth century is extensive. Joseph M. Hawes, *Children in Urban Society: Juvenile Delinquency in Nineteenth-Century America* (New York, 1971); Michael B. Katz, *The Irony of Early School Reform, Educational Innovation in Mid-Nineteenth Century Massachusetts* (Cambridge, Mass., 1968); Robert A Mennel, *Thorns and Thistles: Juvenile Delinquents in the*

United States, 1825-1940 (Hanover, N. H., 1973); Robert S. Pickett, *House of Refuge: Origins of Juvenile Reform in New York State, 1815-1857* (Syracuse, N. Y., 1969); Anthony M. Platt, *The Child Savers: The Invention of Delinquency* (Chicago, 1969); Steven L. Schlossman, *Love and the American Delinquent: The Theory and Practice of "Progressive" Juvenile Justice, 1825-1920* (Chicago, 1976); Barbara Brenzel, *Daughters of the State: A Social Portrait of the First Reform School for Girls in North America, 1856-1905* (Cambridge, Mass., 1983); Cecile Parris Remick. "The House of Refuge of Philadelphia" (Ph.D. dissertation, University of Pennsylvania, 1915).

[3]On individual children's charities see Priscilla Ferguson Clement, "Families and Foster Care: Philadelphia in the Late Nineteenth Century," *Social Service Review*, 53 (1979): 406-20; Arthur E. Fink, "Changing Philosophies and Practices in North Carolina Orphanages," *North Carolina History Review*, 48 (1971): 333-58; George Jacoby, *Catholic Child Care in Nineteenth Century New York* (Washington, D. C., 1941); Francis E. Lane, "American Charities and the Child of the Immigrant: A Study of Typical Child Caring Institutions in New York and Massachusetts Between the Years 1845 and 1880" (Ph.D. dissertation, Catholic University of America, 1932); Carleton Mabee, "Charity in Travail: Two Orphan Asylums for Blacks," *New York History*, 4 (1974): 55-77; Clare L. McCausland, *Children of Circumstance: A History of the First 125 Years (1849-1974) of the Chicago Child Care Society* (Chicago, 1976); A. N. Morris, "The History of the St Louis Protestant Orphan Asylum," *Missouri Historical Bulletin*, 36 (1980): Pt 1, 80-91; Peter Romanofsky, "Saving the Lives of the City's Foundlings: The Joint Committee and New York City Child Care Methods, 1860-1907," *New York Historical Society Quarterly*, 61 (1977): 49-68; Catherine J. Ross, "Society's Children: The Care of Indigent Youngsters in New York City, 1875-1903" (Ph.D. dissertation, Yale University, 1977); Jamil S. Zainalden, "The Origins of Modern Legal Adoption: Child Exchange in Boston, 1851-1893" (Ph.D. dissertation, University of Chicago, 1976); Mark Friedberger, "The Decision to Institutionalize: Families with Exceptional in 1900," *Journal of Family History*, 6 (1981): 396-409. General histories of indigent children in the nineteenth century include Robert H. Bremmer, comp., *Children and Youth in America A Documentary History*, 3 vols. (Cambridge, 1970-4); Folks, *The Care of Destitute Children*; National Conference of Charities and Correction, *History of Child Saving in the United States at the Twentieth National Conference of Charities and Correction in Chicago, June, 1893: Report of the Committee on the History of Child-Saving Work* (Boston, 1893); David J. Rothman, *The Discovery of the Asylum: Social Order and Disorder in the New Republic* (Boston, 1971); Henry W. Thurston, *The Dependent Child: A Story of Changing Aims and Methods in the Care of Dependent Children* (New York, 1930).

[4]For each institution, a sample of 300 was drawn. For Poydras, after a random start, every tenth girl admitted between 1817 and 1912 was sampled. Tulane University, Special Collections (hereafter referred to as TSC), Poydras Asylum Registers, vols. 65, 68, 71, 77, and 80. For the Asylum for Destitute Orphans Boys (since 1924 known as the Waldo Burton Home), after a random start, every seventh boy admitted, 1824-1904, was sampled. TSC, Waldo Burton Home, Admit Books, Vols. 33, 35, 36. For St. Mary's, after a random start, every twelfth boy admitted 1853-1914 was sampled. Associated Catholic Charities, New Orleans, Register of St. Mary's Catholic Orphan Boys' Asylum, 1853-1914.

[5]First quotation for Rothman, *The Discovery of the Asylum*, 207. In the same volume Rothman documents the increasingly custodial nature of late nineteenth century asylums on 237-95. Second quotation from Peter C. Tyor and Jamil S. Zainalden, "Asylum and Society: An Approach to Institutional Change," *Journal of Social History*, 13 (1979): 40.

[6]Susan Whitelaw Downs and Michael W. Sherraden, "The Orphan Asylum in the Nineteenth Century," *Social Service Review*, 57 (1983): 274-75.

[7]John Duffy, ed., *The Rudolph Matas History of Medicine in Louisiana*, 2 vols. (Baton Rouge, 1962), 2:423, 432-36. In 1817, there was only one other orphanage in New Orleans, the Ursuline Convent, which, since 1727 had taken in some female orphans. However, by the 1820s, the sisters apparently used the orphans chiefly as servants to their other pupils, who were daughters of well-to-do Catholics. Julianna Liles Boudreaux, "A History of Philanthropy in New Orleans, 1835-1862," 2 vols. (Ph.D. dissertation, Tulane University, 1961), 1:131-34. The Poydras Home derived its name from one of the asylum's most generous benefactors, Julien Poydras, a

French-born Huguenot and prominent Louisiana statesman. Shirley C. Lyons, "History of Poydras Home," 1956, TSC, Poydras Home, Box 27, Folder 4.

[8]Edna S. Gouaux, "A Study of the Waldo Burton Memorial Boys' Home" (M.A. thesis, Tulane University, 1943), 8-10, 12, 21, 33, 40.

[9]Kilian Beirne, *From Sea to Shining Sea: The Holy Cross Brothers of the United States* (Valatie, N. Y., 1966), 138, 140-3; Roger Baudier, *The Catholic Church in Louisiana* (1939, reprint ed., New Orleans, 1972), 395, 398, 400.

[10]Boudreaux, "History of Philanthropy in New Orleans," 1:157-71; New Orleans, *City Directories, 1870-1881*, microfilm edition (New Haven, Ct., Research Publications, 1974); Robert Earl Moran, Sr., "The History of Child Welfare in Louisiana, 1850-1960" (Ph.D. dissertation, Ohio State University, 1968), 31, 38; Evelyn Campbell Beven, *City Subsidies to Private Charitable Agencies in New Orleans: The History and Present Status, 1824-1933* (New Orleans, 1934), 12-18, 20, 23, 27, 43.

[11]Philadelphia's public welfare program was begun in 1700 but the city's first private orphan asylum did not open its doors until 1806. Priscilla Ferguson Clement, *Poverty and Welfare in the 19th Century City Philadelphia, 1800 to 1854* (New Brunswick, N. J., 1985), 119, 138.

[12]Unless otherwise noted, all subsequent statistics on children are based on the three samples of 300 children each admitted to the three New Orleans orphan asylums. See above, footnote 4.

[13]In 1860, 40 percent, and in 1870, just 25 percent of the city's population had been born abroad. The national origins of the children in these orphanages were also comparable to those of the New Orleans foreign-born population, with most children of Irish and a lesser number of French and German heritage. Earl F. Niehaus, *The Irish in New Orleans, 1800 to 1860* (Baton Rouge, La., 1965), 25; Charles L. Dufour, "The People of New Orleans," in Hodding Carter, ed., *The Past as Prelude New Orleans: 1718-1968,* (New Orleans, 1968), 38. To determine the ethnicity of surnames I used Elsdon C Smith, comp., *New Directory of American Family Names* (New York, 1973).

[14]The Ursuline Convent housed no orphans 1824-39 and in 1840 the Sisters of Charity opened St. Patrick's, later the New Orleans Female Orphan Asylum. There were eight other Catholic institutions that admitted girls founded in the city between 1853 and 1893. Boudreaux, "History of Philanthropy in New Orleans," 1:134, 158, 161-2; Marianites of the Holy Cross, *Marianite Centennial in Louisiana, 1848-1948* (New Orleans, 1948), 44; New Orleans, *City Directory for 1873; New Orleans Morning Star*, April, 1907.

[15]Lane, "American Charities and the Child of the Immigrant," 86-97, 117, 55-56; Boudreaux, "History of Philanthropy in New Orleans," 1:138-39, 157-58; Associated Charities of New Orleans, Minute book, New Orleans Female Orphan Asylum. The Asylum for Destitute Orphan Boys probably admitted some Catholics also, but their admissions registers contain no record of entrants' religion. Boudreaux notes that boys in this asylum were also free on Sundays to worship at the church of their choice. Boudreaux, "History of Philanthropy in New Orleans," 1:145.

[16]Robert C. Reinders, *End of an Era: New Orleans, 1850-1860* (New Orleans, 1964), 23; Andrew Billingsly and Jeanne M. Giovannoni, *Children of the Storm: Black Children and American Child Welfare* (New York, 1972), 27-8.

[17]Quotation from "Hickey's the Name" (autobiography of a boy released from St Mary's in 1917) in *Marianite Centennial,* 37. The records of the Asylum for Destitute Orphan boys also indicate that children often fled after beatings for offenses committed within the asylum. TSC, Waldo Burton Home Papers, v. 36: 69. Older dependent children were not denied admission because they had other charities to which to turn. Almost all the other asylums for adolescents in New Orleans accommodated chiefly those who broke the law. Beven, *City Subsidies,* 25; Reinders, *End of an Era,* 71; Boudreaux, "History of Philanthropy in New Orleans," 1:161.

[18]Reinders, *End of an Era,* 133; Selwyn K. Troen, *The Public and the Schools: Shaping the St. Louis School System, 1838-1920* (Columbia, Mo., 1975), 68; Ronald Cohen, "Northern Urban Schooling in Early Nineteenth Century Boston and New York," *Journal of Urban History,* 1 (1974): 119.

[19]Reinders, *End of an Era,* 131-5. New Orleans Public Schools, *Report of the Chief Superintendent, January, 1888* (New Orleans, 1888), 43; Lillian Fortier Zeringer, *The History of Poydras Home* (New Orleans, 1977), 51, Gouaux, "History of the Waldo Burton Boys' Home," 99-100.

[20]Cecile Costley, "The New Orleans Female Orphan Asylum, A Study of Foster Care in a Congregate Institution for Dependent Girls," (Ph.D. dissertation, Catholic University of America, 1941), 15. In the case of St. Mary's, the Marianist Sisters and the Brothers of the Holy Cross operated no parochial schools for young boys and so would have had to enter those in the orphanage in a school directed by another order, something which they refused to do. Beirne, *From Sea to Shining Sea,* 142.

[21]Beven, *City Subsidies,* 36.

[22]The names of all the children mentioned in this paper have been changed to protect their anonymity, although I have tried to preserve their ethnic identities with the new names given them. Fred's case history can be found in TSC, Waldo Burton Home Papers, v. 36, September 25, 1885.

[23]There is no data on household size in the records of St. Mary's.

[24]John W. Scott to Miss Daisy Hodgson, August 1, 1886, TSC, Poydras Home Papers, v. 77: 153.

[25]Associated Catholic Charities of New Orleans, Register of St. Mary's, 1853-1914, 98, 38. For Poydras it was not possible to calculate from the admission records, as it was for the boys' asylums, whether siblings were placed out together or apart.

[26]Troen, *The Public and the Schools,* 121, 126,130; Michael B. Katz, et al., *The Social Organization of Early Industrial Capitalism* (Cambridge, Mass., 1982), 277.

[27]Quotation from TSC, Waldo Burton Home Papers, v. 36: 165. The Asylum for Destitute Orphan Boys operated under monetary restraints until the 1920s when it received a sizable legacy from the father of Waldo Burton and conducted an aggressive fund-raising campaign ("Give $3,000 and endow a boy."). Gouaux, "History of the Waldo Burton Boys' Home," 69-71, 93, 102.

[28]Zeringer, *History of Poydras Home,* 43-44, 47-48.

[29]Bremmer, *Childhood and Youth in America,* 11, 247; Folks, *History of Destitute Children,* 120-21.

[30]TSC, Waldo Burton Home Papers, v. 33, April 19, 1835. The best description of the gradual decline of indenturing, 1850-70 is in Katz, et al., *Social Organization of Early Industrial Capitalism,* 249-52.

[31]TSC, Poydras Home Papers, v. 65: November 22, 1832, and November 20, 1823.

[32]In 1824, James Workman, a founder of the Asylum for Destitute Orphan Boys, explained the problems of indenturing girls faced by the managers of Poydras. Gouaux, "History of the Waldo Burton Boys' Home," 16.

[33]Zeringer, *History of the Poydras Home,* 44.

[34]On Brace see Hawes, *Children in Urban Society,* 101. On Owatonna see Priscilla Ferguson Clement, "With Wise and Benevolent Purpose: Poor Children and the State Public School at Owatonna, 1885-1915," *Minnesota History,* 49 (1984): 8-9.

[35]This tendency to stay with old established child care programs persists in the city. When institutionalization of children came increasingly under attack in the 20th Century and foster care replaced it through much of the North, orphanages in New Orleans did not close down. The Asylum for Destitute Orphan Boys is still operating as the Waldo Burton Home, St Mary's, as Madonna Manor, and not until 1959 did the Poydras Home disperse its last girls to their own or to foster homes and convert to an asylum for aged women. Beven, *City Subsidies,*

39-41; Baudier, *Catholic Church in Louisiana*, 576; Louisiana State Department of Public Welfare, *Children's Homes in Louisiana: A Directory of Licensed Child Caring Institutions in Louisiana* (Baton Rouge, La., 1971), 27; Zeringer, *History of Poydras Home*, 65-73.

[36]Tyor and Zainalden, "Asylum and Society," 39-41. Tyor and Zainalden also place considerable importance on funding source, public or private, but in the case of New Orleans, where there were virtually no public asylums, it is impossible to compare the development of the two.

[37]This point is confirmed in Timothy Walch, "Catholic Social Institutions and Urban Development: The View From 19th Century Chicago and Milwaukee," *Catholic Historical* Review, 64 (1978), 16-32.

[38]Tyor and Zainalden, "Asylum and Society," 41. The four "stages of growth" detailed by Tyor and Zainalden (40-1) are difficult to establish for the New Orleans orphanages.

HISTORY OF LOUISIANA NEGRO BAPTISTS*

William Hicks

GENERAL HISTORY

As to the general history of Negro Baptists of Louisiana, according to Dr. W. E. Paxton, author of the history of white Louisiana Baptists, we must go back to 1804 and come forward.[1] When more than half of our state was a wilderness, and there were only a few French settlements in the southern part on the Mississippi River, Bayou Teche, the prairies of the Opelousas, and the fertile bayou that threads the valleys of the Lower Red River, "there came into the state a Negro Baptist preacher, Bishop Joseph Willis, of Mississippi, but probably a native of South Carolina."[2] This was in 1804, the next year after the Louisiana Purchase. Louisiana was in her infancy and not a single Protestant or Baptist Church had been established within its bounds. The first Baptist doctrine in Louisiana was preached by this pioneer in November 1804, at Vermilion[ville], about 40 miles southwest of Baton Rouge in a day meeting.[3] At night he preached at Plaquemine Brulé. This preaching was done at the peril of his life, since he was both a Negro and a Baptist.[4] At this time, he was on a visit and had not permanently settled. His labors, however, were successful, turning many from the error of their ways. These converts were the first in Louisiana to begin marching under the flag bearing the triple declaration—"One Lord, one Faith and one Baptism."

Not being ordained, he was unable to baptize his converts and organize the First Baptist Church of Louisiana at this time. After urging them, perhaps, to be strong and steadfast in the faith, he returned to Mississippi for ordination, and for other brethren to help him organize the First Baptist Church of the state. But to his surprise, on reaching the church of his membership, he found it pastorless, and the church, therefore, felt that it could not arrange and grant his request, although they desired to do so. They advised him to take his letter and unite with a church that had a pastor. This he did, but the church refused to ordain him, claiming that the Church of Christ might suffer reproach owing to the humble social condition of this Negro preacher. This was a heavy blow to the "Apos-

*First published in *History of Negro Baptists and Early American Beginnings from 1804 to 1914*, edited by Sue Eakin (Lafayette, La.: Center for Louisiana Studies, 1998), 44-56. Reprinted with the kind permission of the Center for Louisiana Studies.

tle of the Opelousas," as he was called, but he did not give up on account of unwavering faith in God, and the large amount of iron in his blood.[5] How could he give up when he was under marching orders and had been told to go into all the world and preach the Gospel? Some prudent white friend advised Brother Willis to get a recommendation from the people among whom he had labored, and present it to the next meeting of the Mississippi Association. This he did in 1811, and the Association appointed two ministers, Bishops Thomas Mercer and David Cooper, to visit Brother Willis and his work in Louisiana. These two brethren were providentially hindered and failed to go. This Pioneer Preacher still stood undaunted, like Job, waiting for his chance to come. His petition came before the Association the next year (1812), and two other white brethren were appointed to go and examine the colored brother's work, Elders Moses Hadly and Laurence Scarborough. Meanwhile Brother Willis had returned to his field of labor only to find those who had come to Christ through his preaching deceived and led off by a Methodist preacher, who had entered the field of Brother Willis and formed the converts into a society of methods at Plaquemine. Yet this Baptist hero was not discouraged because he had preached the first New Testament doctrine and made the first disciples in the state of Louisiana. By the time Elders Hadly and Scarborough arrived, he had indoctrinated others, planted the Baptist flag, and was standing ready for ordination and organization. When they reached Bayou Chicot, in St. Landry Parish, one of the places where Brother Willis preached, there were five brothers and one sister whom they formed into a church, called Calvary, November 13, 1812, thus organizing the first church in the state.[6] These elders were also requested to ordain Brother Willis for their pastor.

The request was granted and the Lord blessed their labors by adding nine to the membership the following year. The work of these elders was approved at the next session (1813) of the Mississippi Association. Dr. W. E. Paxton, author of the Louisiana Baptist history (white), and to whom we are indebted for the above information, says concerning this pioneer: "The zeal of Father Willis, as he was called by the affectionate people among whom he labored, could not be bounded by the narrow limits of his own home, but he traveled far and wide.[7] He extended his labors to Cheneyville on Bayou Boeuf in the Parish of Rapides, some fifty or sixty miles higher up the country where many of his Mississippi acquaintances had settled, and among whom were some of the Bayou Chicot members.[8] The history of Louisiana Baptists could not be written without mention of this brother (Joseph Willis), whose name occurs so often in connection with the oldest churches in the Louisiana Association." He was born in 1762 and died at Ten Mile Creek in Rapides Parish, September 14, 1854.[9]

Another pioneer Baptist preacher of these times was Bishop D. H. Willis, grandson of Elder Joseph Willis.[10] He was born on Bayou Boeuf in Rapides Parish, December 28, 1817. At the age of 11 he was carried by his father to their new home on Calcasieu River in St. Landry Parish, a wilderness country, eight miles from the nearest white settlement. He stayed here nine years, attended school five months, and when 17 years old went to an Academy twenty miles from home, remaining only one month. Being blessed with his grandfather's push and pluck, he studied at every opportunity by the flickering light of the pine knots and in this way prepared himself for the task of continuing the pioneer work so nobly begun by his grandfather in 1804. He married March 15, 1838, and in 1840 was converted and baptized into the membership of Occupy Baptist Church, which was then a member of the Louisiana Association. In 1847, he preached his first sermon, and in 1849, on Spring Creek, Rapides Parish, at the home of Elder Willis, he was ordained to the gospel ministry by Bishops Joseph Willis, B. C. Roberts and John O'Quin.[11] This young Baptist elder continued to grow in grace, and in the knowledge of God until he became a beacon light in those dark times. Notwithstanding, he afterwards lost his sight, yet, Moses-like, he pressed forward along the rugged road of those perilous times, crying aloud, "Repent, believe and be baptized."

This period of our General History extends from 1804 to the Civil War. Elder Willis and his grandson were the only Negro Baptist preachers of prominence during the first part of this period. During the latter part, the Baptist work was carried on by white preachers who generally preached a sermon in the forenoon to white people and in the afternoon to the colored people.[12] However, a Negro Baptist minister would rise up occasionally among the slaves, and preach to them despite high water and patrols.[13] And, too, there were a few free-born Negro Baptist clergymen in some parts of the state, especially in the towns and cities, who were sometimes permitted by the slave master to preach to the slaves.[14]

Bishop Henry Adams was the most noted of this class of preachers. He labored as far back as 1837 with marked success. He was a man of education and ability. After leaving Louisiana, he continued his labors as pastor of the First Colored Baptist Church, Louisville, Ky., where after accomplishing much for the Master, during twenty-five years of pioneer life, he fell asleep in Jesus. Further mention of the early work of Negro Baptists is not necessary here, since their work before and after the war, especially in New Orleans, will be taken up in the following chapter.

PIONEER WORK IN AND AROUND NEW ORLEANS
BEFORE AND AFTER THE WAR

Because the birth of our organic denominational life is so closely connected with that of the white Baptists of the state, and especially those of New Orleans, we must know their beginnings if we would intelligently know our own. The first effort made by the white Baptists to establish a church was in 1817. In that year, the Board of the Triennial Baptist Convention sent out as missionary, Elder Jas. A. Ranaldson, who preached and taught in the "Long Room" which belonged to a Mr. C. Paulding on Dorseive Street, near Canal. In this room, Bishop Ranaldson organized the first white Baptist church in the city of New Orleans, which was admitted into the Mississippi Association. Dr. Paxton says in his history this church prospered under the pastorate of Elder Benj. Davis, of Natchez, Miss., who succeeded Bishop Ranaldson. The membership soon reached forty-eight—sixteen white and thirty-two colored. These thirty-two Negro Baptists were perhaps the first to hold membership in an association except those who were won to Christ by "Father Willis," and with all probability they were the first Negro Baptists of New Orleans. In 1820, Bishop Davis left this church, and it disbanded soon after. Following the dissolution of this church, Elder Wm. B. Johnson of South Carolina, came to New Orleans and preached in this "Long Room." From this time until 1826, Baptist preaching was only occasionally heard. Frequent preaching was resumed when Elder Wm. Bondeau arrived from England in 1826, formed a new organization, and preached about one year, first in the "Long Room," and then in a school house in Paulding's Row on St. Charles Street, and then in a brick building, corner of Poydras and Tchoupitoulas streets. Mr. W. C. Duncans says Bishop Bondeau afterwards went north and settled in Kentucky. His church at one time had about twenty members, but by the close of the year 1828, it was dissolved and scattered. Now we are nearing the organization of the first Negro Baptists in New Orleans. Dr. Paxton's history says: "There was also at this time (1827) an African church of about twenty members. They had a colored minister named Asa Goldsbery, who just before had been bound over by authority of the city, or otherwise to be silent six months under penalty of a law against colored preachers.[15] Of this body, J. L. Furman, an intelligent member of the First Baptist Church (white) and editor of the *New Orleans Baptist Messen*ger, says: "As we have been informed by the late Brother Lewis Banks, an aged colored Baptist from Virginia, who resided here many years, and who died here last January (1876) and as appears also from a book of minutes in his possession, the first colored Baptist church of this city was organized on the 31st of October, 1826, under the name of the First African Church of New Orleans." This was done in a school on Burgundy Street, by a Presbytery consisting of the already mentioned Wm. Rondeau and Elder Elisha Andrews. Asa C. Goldsbery was elected by the church and ordained pastor and Moses Jackson deacon. The church flourished for a time. Additions were made from time to time until the membership numbered forty-one males and forty-six females.

After a few years, Mr. Goldsbery died, and the church declined. About 1834, several other colored Baptists came from Virginia and elsewhere among whom were Brethren N. D. Sanders, Richard Satterfield, John Edmonds, Lewis Banks and Nathaniel Short. The church became somewhat revived, worship was maintained, and new life was apparent. Brethren Sanders and Satterfield were licensed as ministers and labored with much success. In 1837, Elder Peter W. Robert, aided by some transient preacher, reconstituted this First African Church, and ordained Brothers Sanders and Satterfield to the gospel ministry.[16] Bishop Sanders became pastor. The church purchased property and began to build on the corner of Howard and Cypress Street in 1842. Under Elder Sanders, the "Old Church" grew and became the acknowledged mother of New Orleans Negro Baptists. However, during the time Elder L. Fletcher pastored the white Baptist church (1850), the Negro members of his church were organized into a church under the care of the white brethren. This Second Colored Baptist Church numbered sixty-two members and was received into the Mississippi River Association (white), in 1859 under the fostering care of the Coliseum Baptist Church (white). This is the same church that Bishop Jackson Acox now pastors (1914), called the Fourth Baptist Church. This body owes its beginning to the new interest started by Elder R. H. Steptoe in 1857. Dr. Paxton, speaking of the work of these churches, said: "The First and Fourth African Churches had greatly prospered. They had baptized into their membership about 3,000. They had established a number of branches in the city, and extended their labors along the Mississippi above and below New Orleans. With their branches they now number 7,000."

It will also be of interest to those who scan these pages to read what Dr. John Marks, pastor Sixth Baptist Church, has to say concerning Baptist progress from 1867 to 1902. He speaks as follows: "In order that I may have a foundation to build upon, I will have to go back to 1833 when the Rev. Nelson D. Sanders, a Negro Baptist minister, was sold in Virginia and brought to New Orleans in chains by Negro slave traders. He was sold to a good master who allowed him to hire his time, and afterward bought himself. He gathered together thirty-two slaves in a little house in Gentilly Road. Under the leadership of Rev. Sanders, assisted by Revs. Satterfield, Hollands, Esau Carter, Robert Steptoe, Joseph Davenport, Henry White and others. The First Colored Baptist Church was organized in 1833. They held services on Gentilly Road until 1844. As it was against the law for colored people to hold public meetings, their meetings were often broken up, and their leaders were often arrested by the police officers and carried to jail and punished to the full extent of the law that was then on the statute books against slaves holding meetings.[17] Sometimes all in the meeting house were arrested and carried to jail—both men and women. They finally, through the kindness of some of the whites who owned slaves, obtained permission from the city authorities to allow the colored people to hold meetings two hours on Sundays from 3 to 5 p.m., under the watch of a police officer who was to be paid two dollars per hour.[18] The officer was instructed not to let the meeting continue one minute over two hours. If they should violate that order, all who were present would be arrested and punished. The city authorities and police officers were not favorably disposed to Baptist doctrine, and as the law was against colored people assembling in any meetings, they enforced the law to the letter. Under these oppressions and persecutions, the Baptists 'contended' earnestly for the faith once for all delivered to the saints." The fire of truth was kindled and could not be quenched. In 1844 they moved to Cypress Street and Howard Avenue. Here they bought the first piece of ground owned by Negro Baptists in the state, and erected a house of worship thereon. Many were the oppressions and persecutions of these humble servants of God, but their faith in Christ and his Word made their burdens light. When New Orleans surrendered and freedom removed the persecutions and oppressions, new zeal for the faith sprang up, and the once-smothered flame burst forth, and its influence spread all through the city and parish. Churches were organized in different parts of the city, and in every parish in the southern part of the state. In 1865, a large number of churches had been organized. Elder Sanders and others organized what is now known as the Louisiana Southern Baptist Association. The following year Rev. Charles Satchell and others, taking issue at the name, "Southern Baptist," withdrew from the Association, and organized the First Free Mission Association.[19] These two bodies being zealous of each other unto good works, labored earnestly and planted the Baptist banner all over the southern part of the state and as far up the Red River as Natchitoches, and in the southwestern part as far as the line of Texas.

In 1867 a very few churches owned any property. Preaching was done in the gin houses, warehouses, log cabins, under cane sheds on plantations, or rented houses in cities and towns. In 1871 Revs. Wm. Head, Whaley, and others organized the Gumspring Association in the northern part of the state; and the brethren in the northwestern part of the state withdrew from Texas and organized another Association. These two bodies extended all over the northern part of the state, organizing and building churches in every town and city, and on every plantation until the ministers were heard of from the Gulf of Mexico to the line of Arkansas, and from the line of Mississippi to the line of Texas.

The work of the Associations had grown to such magnitude in 1872, and each of them covering such large territories, that it was impossible for them to cultivate their fields properly. In order to more thoroughly organize their forces, the Louisiana Southern Baptist Association, in session at Baton Rouge, February 1872, passed a resolution inviting the other associations and churches to send delegates to meet in joint session at the First Colored Baptist Church, New Orleans, Louisiana, for the purpose of organizing a State Convention.[20] The invitation was hailed with joy all over the state, and on the appointed day, delegates from each Association and each regularly organized Baptist church met and accomplished their work.

In 1883, the Convention in annual session at Baton Rouge, passed resolutions dividing the state into fourteen Associational Districts. The districts' plans were well received by the churches throughout the state, and by July 1884, nearly every district was organized. We have our Grand State Convention with sixteen Associations. Our growth for the last thirty-five years has been as follows: In 1867 we had a few small churches organized, and about 5,000 members. The ministers had just been emancipated, and with very few exceptions, they could neither read nor write. We had no day schools nor Sunday-schools. Today (1902), we have 125,000 members; 1,200 churches at an average cost of $1,000 each, making a total of $1,200,000 worth of church property throughout the state. We have eleven well-organized and fairly equipped academies, namely: Gibsland, Alexandria, Baton Rouge, Donaldsonville, Cheneyville, Opelousas, Homer, Ruston, Shreveport, New Iberia, and Monroe. These schools value on an average of $1,200, making a total valuation of $30,000. Adding church and school property together, you have a grand total of $1,213,200. This does not include our Leland University, which is our highest institution of learning given by Mr. and Mrs. Holbrook Chamberlain.[21] We have now in the state over 800 pastors who read and write intelligently. We can count our graduates by the hundreds; also there has been wonderful improvement in divine services. All of this work has been accomplished by Negro brain and energy from the Baptist pulpits, as they have lifted up Christ to the people. We can say with thanksgiving and rejoicing: "The Lord is with His people."

The above REMARKABLE progress recorded by Dr. Marks brings us up to 1902. From that time to this, our material progress has been phenomenal. Today (1914), we thank God for our Grand Old Convention born in 1872. Further mention will be made of it elsewhere in this volume. Through this and other agencies, our pioneer and post-pioneer brethren wrought more than we knew. They set in motion snow balls of conse-crated work which gained in momentum and size as they rolled.

Notes for "History of Louisiana Negro Baptists"

[1]Rev. W. E. Paxton wrote the pioneering *History of Louisiana Baptists* and continued his research until 1881. He died two years later after the book was completed but had not been published. His co-worker, Rev. Ezra Courtney, took over the responsibility of getting the book published. Reverend Courtney added an introduction and published the book in 1888, five years after Paxton's death.

[2]Reverend Paxton was born in Little Rock, Arkansas, on June 23, 1825. When he was a twenty-year-old col-lege student at Georgetown, Kentucky, he joined the Baptist church. In 1853 he went to Bienville Parish, Lou-isiana, to teach at Mount Lebanon College. There he began "reading for the law" in the office of B. W. Egan, who later became a Supreme Court justice. A few years later, settling in the village of Sparta a few miles away, he practiced law. In his spare time, he assisted in the editing of a weekly newspaper, *The Jeffersonian.* The following year he bought a press and published his own newspaper, the *Southern Banner,* a project he continued for two years. He seems to have enjoyed his writing, and he did a great deal of it. This probably laid the foun-dation for his work in gathering the materials over a period of years. In 1857, he began his history which con-tinued through the Reconstruction period after the Civil War. Paxton was thorough, he provided priceless comment on the beginnings of the black Baptist churches in Louisiana, the centers of countless communities of blacks where uplift of the race through education was a prime consideration. By far the largest number of blacks in the state belonged to the autonomous Baptist church. Paxton's classic history contains much that is invaluable in understanding the history of black/white relations of the period. Paxton, like Hicks nearly a gen-eration later in the black church, was distressed over the lack of education of white Baptist ministers.

Joseph Willis was the son of an English planter in North Carolina named Agerton Willis, and an unknown Cherokee Indian slave girl. Since his mother was a slave, Joseph had the status of a slave. The father appar-ently had plans to free his son, but under the North Carolina law of 1741, it was not possible for Agerton Willis to do so, until the son became older. The father left a will dated September 18, 1776, by which he attempted to free his son and leave him his property. His brother, Daniel, was executor for the estate, and Daniel left a letter dated October 10, 1777 to the secretary of state of North Carolina regarding the outcome: "I have a small fav[o]r to begg if your Excellency will be pleased to grant it viz, as my Deceas'd Brother Agerton Willis gave the graitest Part of his Estate to his Molata boy Joseph and as he is a born slave & not set free Agreeable to Law my Brothers heirs are satisfied that he shall have it . . . ." The letter is signed "Dan. Willis, Sen."

Reverend Willis refers to the fact that besides the stringent rules regarding Negroes, Joseph Willis preach-ing at Vermilion [present-day Lafayette] was in traditionally Catholic territory where the Protestant church was outlawed until the 1803 Louisiana Purchase by the United States. The authority on Rev. Joseph Willis is a direct descendant, Randy Willis of Dallas, Texas, who has spent decades in exhaustive research on the life of his ancestor.

Why Reverend Hicks added "bishop" as a title to Reverend Willis (and others mentioned in the book) is difficult to understand. The singular appeal of the Baptist organizational structure was its autonomous character and lack of officials, or bishops, governing local churches. This appeal was especially strong among freedmen since bishops and higher officials in other churches were almost always white during this period, and this cur-tailed the freedom of black ministers.

[3]The City of Lafayette originated as a plantation settlement about the time of the American Revolution. In the 1820s, Jean Mouton established a village called "Vermilionville" which, in French, means "cinnamon-red." The town was renamed "Lafayette" in May 1884.

[4]There were two reasons why the Protestant, Joseph Willis, was not welcome to preach in South Louisiana. One was that this was an area almost completely occupied by French and/or Spanish migrants who were members of the Roman Catholic church. Under colonial laws of Louisiana both Protestants and Jews were banned. The other reason was the fact of Willis's dark complexion for which he was designated a mulatto. Translated in the eyes of the beholders, obviously as denoting a Negro ethnic heritage, this brought reactions from a frontier society settled in the rich lowlands along bayous and rivers with Negroes as plantation slaves. Negroes slightly outnumbered whites in Louisiana at this period, a fact which caused whites to over react with alarm to an often imagined threat from Negroes in positions of authority, such as the minister of a congregation.

[5]The term "Opelousas" refers to a far larger area than the city by that name, according to historian-genealogist Winston De Ville. The area, De Ville states, was virtually greater Southwestern Louisiana. The northern boundary was around Bayou Cocodrie and Turkey Creek. The east-west boundaries were the Atchafalaya River and the Sabine River. The exception to the Opelousas Post jurisdiction was the much smaller Attakapas Post jurisdiction.

[6]Calvary Baptist Church at Chicot, Louisiana, St. Landry Parish, is cited by Paxton as being founded November 13, 1812, by Rev. Joseph Willis. The charter membership was composed of five men and one woman. The church claims distinction not as the first Protestant church in Louisiana but as the first west of the Mississippi River. Paxton, *History of Louisiana Baptists*, 143.

[7]Reverend Willis followed "The Texas Road" hundreds of miles, from the little inland port of Washington on Courtableau Bayou through the piney woods of Central Louisiana, across the Sabine River and into East Texas. Appreciable numbers of English-speaking Protestants lived in the vicinity of this wilderness path, which took different turns through the woods depending upon the ruts or depth of the mud. Texans drove cattle over "The Texas Road" to place on steamboats headed to the New Orleans market. Tanneries, blacksmith shops, and stopping places with provisions for man and beast grew up along the way. So did the small Baptist churches of Rev. Joseph Willis, most of which exist today.

[8]Cheneyville was a plantation crossroads village that was settled around 1813 by descendants of a French Huguenot minister named Peter Robert, who had first founded Woodville, Mississippi, before migrating farther west to locate along the Bayou Boeuf. Beulah Baptist Church at Cheneyville was founded in 1816. Rev. Ezekiel O'Quin, from nearby Bayou Rouge, is credited as founder of this church with Rev. Joseph Willis of Chicot assisting.

[9]Reverend Willis is buried at his church on the Texas Road called Occupy #1. A marble tombstone gives the date of his birth as 1762, and identifies his death date as September 14, 1854.

[10]Daniel H. Willis became almost as respected for his ministry as his grandfather. Generations of Baptist ministers have been among the descendants of Rev. Joseph Willis.

[11]Rev. B. C. Roberts and Rev. John O'Quin are both credited with the founding of Beulah Baptist Church, Cheneyville, in 1816. Slaves are listed as members of the church, along with planters and shopkeepers and others.

[12]Church attendance for both blacks and whites seems to have been sporadic due to distances between houses in plantation country. Houses lined up on plantations along the bayous were estimated to average a mile and a half distance from each other, but there were many homes miles from the paths through the wilderness. When congregations were assembled, slaves were assigned segregated seating and entered the building through a rear or side door. Sometimes slaves sat in balconies. In the Campbellite church at Cheneyville, slaves were seated on the side rows with white members occupying the center pews. Various arrangements for religious participation were usually made by the planter, and in some cases, there were no provisions made at all. Preachers were often paid by slaveowners to preach to their slaves. Sarah Wright Fleming of Cheneyville wrote: "I think the Negroes were members of Beulah [Baptist] Church only; but when the Christian church was built there was no gallery and a space was reserved for the colored folks. That, together with the fact that everybody took communion at the same time instead of serving downstairs first and galleries last, impressed the Negroes favorably."

Still I do not remember that any of our Negroes left the old church. My mother paid our pastor an extra salary for visiting our Quarters & having service there for Negroes only."

[13]See above, footnote 1.

[14]Rev. John Jones was one of the most noteworthy of these free black preachers. He was a minister in Shreveport. See Hicks, *History of Louisiana Negro Baptists*, 178-79; Paxton, *History of Louisiana Baptists*, 360-61.

[15]Charles E. Gayarré, *History of Louisiana*, 4 vols. (New York, 1867), 4:644, notes that: "The situation of New Orleans cannot be considered as secure—surrounded by a numerous black population in its nature always hostile, filled up with emigrants, and free Negroes and mulattoes from all parts of the world." The cities had a "night watch" comparable to the patrols that policed plantation areas.

[16]"In 1833, Peter W. Robert, who had been ordained by Father Willis and Ezekiel O'Quinn, removed from the Opelousas country and settled in the city, where he remained eight years." See Paxton, *History of Louisiana Baptists*, 121.

[17]The fear of slave revolts and personal violence against whites increased as the numbers of slaves in the territory and state grew after the Louisiana Purchase (1803). Fear that slave gatherings would generate plans for revolt caused planters to attempt to prevent assemblies of slaves, and preachers—natural leaders—were particularly viewed with alarm for their potential for arousing their followers to revolt. In 1806, the Territory of Orleans passed a law prohibiting the assembly of slaves. The planter-merchant governing class monopolized the government, and caution had to be maintained in citing laws regarding the control exerted over slaves, punishments prescribed, and the like because the laws were enforced, or not enforced, according to the dictates of individual planters on their plantations. Slaves had some built-in protection against being murdered by masters since they were valuable property, but this did not preclude death as punishment for violations such as incitement to rebellion. The perception that such violations had, or might occur could lead to the death of a slave—with total disregard for the law. On the other hand, the 1830 Louisiana law which forbade teaching slaves to read and write was violated frequently—again without regard for the law. Since the planter code of unwritten rules dictated that the operation of a plantation was strictly a private business about which nobody, including other planters, ordinarily had the right to inquire unless there was evidence that a planter's treatment of his slaves was apt to affect attitudes or behavior of slaves on other plantations. A rigid rule of secrecy surrounded plantation affairs so what can be gleaned from court records, the diaries of scattered individuals, farm records, etc. can, at best, provide only a fragmented history of Louisiana's slavery experience. This, of course, applies to slaves' religion and church connections.

[18]In Orleans Territory Acts, 1st Legislature, 2nd Session, 1807, Sec. 3, 188; 4th Legislature, Second Session, 1820, 10, there are references to the patrols appointed by parish police juries. Patrols had the legal right to enter all plantations and check on residents of all cabins to see if a planter was violating the law that permitted assembly of slaves other than his own in his Negro quarters. Again, while this was found in the legal records, there was an unwritten rule in the plantation code that nobody stepped on a planter's plantation without his knowledge and permission. This included local law officers. Since the local planters were in control of the government, including the sheriff's office, including deputies and patrols, it is highly unlikely this law was actually invoked. Whether state, parishes, villages, towns, or cities, all had laws passed pertaining to the control of slaves. See Ethel Elizabeth Kramer, "Slavery Legislation in Ante-bellurm Louisiana, 1803-1860" (M.A. thesis, Louisiana State University, 1944), notes that the Black Code of 1806 forbade the assembly of slaves. Orleans Territory Acts, 1st Legislature, 1st Session, 1806, Sec. 12, 156. The East Feliciana Parish Police Jury included in its provisions that assembly of more than six slaves, at any time or place in the parish, was unlawful. "It was the duty of any citizen, slaveholder or patrol to dispense any assembly which violated this law and to punish offenders by whipping. Negroes who went to church with permission of their masters were not to be molested." Portions of the Black Code, which Governor Bienville promulgated in 1724 in French Louisiana, were reenacted in 1808, 1830, and 1855. Free people of color were particularly feared by the planter-merchant coalition, and the laws were likely on the books to be used to control this group. Preachers, speakers, strangers coming in from the northern United States, and assemblies of Negroes of any kind were rigidly controlled, and

violations were not apt to be repeated. Persons feared to be inciting rebellion were in almost the same position as those proven to be advocating rebellion. Violations were defined as "use of language in any public discourse from the bar, the bench, the state, the pulpit, or any place whatsoever, or whoever shall make use of language in private discourse . . . or whosoever shall knowingly be instrumental in bringing into this state, any paper, pamphlet, or book." Louisiana Acts, 9th Legislature, 2nd Session, 1830, Sec. 1, page 96; Sec. 2, page 96; 2nd Legislature, 2nd Session, 1855, Sec. 25-29, 380. In 1850, all corporations organized by free people of color for religious purposes or other secret purposes were annulled. Louisiana Acts, 3rd Session, Regular Session, 1850, 179.

[19]Associations ordinarily consisted of congenial church groups over a small geographic area about the size of a parish but sometimes overlapping parish lines. Since these organizations were originated by local churches getting together and not directed from some hierarchal position, there was no set pattern that applied to all Negro associations in the state. With regard to geographic areas, some overlapped the territory of other associations. Associations were organized whenever a number of congregations wished to do so, sometimes with two overlapping associations involving some of the same congregations. The names of the associations were those chosen by members at a period when transportation was so difficult and slow that one group could not possibly have known what another group elsewhere was doing. Consequently, the names of associations are sometimes so nearly the same as to be confusing. There were many functions of these associations, including the establishment of old folks homes. They also served as forums for political discussions, recreational pursuits, burial insurance and institution of cemeteries. One of the foremost achievements of the Baptist associations was the founding and maintenance of private boarding schools offering upper elementary and secondary education and, often, the first year, or two years, of college. In the United States Religious Census of 1910, Table 4, "Regular Baptists (Colored)," the following statistics are given regarding memberships in black Baptist associations in Louisiana:

	Organizations	Communicants
First District	31	3,194
Second District	38	2,493
Third District	9	231
Fourth District	87	5,968
Fifth District	35	2,298
Sixth District	36	2,185
Seventh District	41	2,004
Eighth District	46	4,352
Ninth District	49	4,675
West Tenth District	52	6,043
11th District	90	6,378
12th District	55	*
13th District	*	*
14th District	*	*
15th District	45	3,257
16th District	24	1,936
17th District	19	1,200
Freedmen's District	31	5,893

[20]The Louisiana State Convention of Negro Baptists paralleled that of white Baptists.

[21]Mr. and Mrs. Holbrook Chamberlain were residents of Boston, Mass., who came to New Orleans after the Civil War in an attempt to divert their attention as much as possible from the death of their only child, a daughter. In 1869, in the basement of a Baptist church on Tulane Avenue in New Orleans, the Chamberlains helped organize Leland College, or University, as it came to be known. They gave the initial funds providing for the construction of two buildings, employment of faculty, and development of the school.

METHODIST BEGINNINGS IN NEW ORLEANS, 1813-1814*

Ray Holder

The Methodist General Conference of 1812 authorized the organization of an Annual Conference embracing the territory of the "Natchez County," including New Orleans.[1] Accordingly, on November 1, 1813, the itinerant preachers in the region assembled at Newit Vick's[2] in Jefferson County, Mississippi, to set the proposed jurisdiction in motion.[3] Present were Presiding Elder Samuel Sellers, John I. Byrd, John Ford (local), Thomas Griffin, Miles Harper, Lewis Hobbs, Richmond Nolley, John Phipps, John Shrock, and William Winans.[4] Unfortunately, Bishop William McKendree was unable to be present because of "the danger of traveling through the Indian Country."[5]

Nevertheless, the business of the quasi-Conference was duly conducted. Because of his failing health, Hobbs, who had spent several months spying out the situation in New Orleans, was prevented from returning to the charmed city.[6] His replacement was William Winans who had been in the country for three years, having reached his twenty-sixth birthday during the sessions of the Conference.[7] Immediately following adjournment, he began making his arrangements to go to his new appointment. Since he would need no horse in the Crescent City, but would "greatly need money," he sold his trusty mount to Hobbs, "at a very moderate price" of some fifty dollars. Hobbs would ride back to Georgia to die within a brief time.[8]

New Orleans bound, Winans "collected together some thirty or forty Dollars' worth of Books, belonging to the Methodist Book-Concern."[9] These he hoped to sell in the city at a profit, and, together with some brief notes scribbled by his predecessor, "this was the sum of my preparation for the important enterprize [sic] to which I was assigned." He carried "no letter of recommendation, or even of introduction, to influential men," and his pocket money amounted to no more than "the price of my horse." In those days "minister[s] of the Gospel [needed] to have firm trust and confidence in the goodness and faithfulness of Divine Providence." They "went *cheerfully* to scenes of labor, where privation, neglect, persecution and sickness were their probable destiny.[10]

*First published in *Louisiana History*, 18 (1977): 171-87. Reprinted with the kind permission of the Louisiana Historical Association.

At 6 p.m. on November 17, Winans embarked at Natchez-under-the-Hill on a barge out of Louisville commanded by Captain Bradley.[11]   Other passengers included Mr. Quigles and his family from Natchez, an anonymous Frenchman, and "a yellow-woman, notoriously the mistress of . . . a U[nited] States' Officer . . . in the Custom-House Department." She "appeared to be intelligent and modest," and the others aboard, "though Spanish and French Catholics," were "pleasant and obliging fellow-travelers. The crew, too, was among the most decent of their class." Quigles and the Frenchman, however, were unhappy that Winans was put in command "during the former half of every night except the fourth and last," and "they did not scruple to interfere frequently in the management of the Boat."[12]

It was by no means a pleasant voyage. The weather was boisterous and at times "almost tempestuous," retarding their progress which was "slow enough in the most favorable circumstances."[13] They were between "five and six days" in navigating the circuitous and stump-studded course, but not even the needling of Quigles and the Frenchman, whose directions were often injudicious, was able to disturb Winans' composure at the tiller. Yet, upon asking the mulatto woman to hem a handkerchief for him, she replied: "You would not have me work on Sunday." Her response greatly unnerved, "mortified and humiliated" him. In his exhilarating role as mate he had forgotten that it was his bounden duty as a minister to keep Holy Day.[14]

Captain Bradley docked his barge in New Orleans at about noon on November 23, and his passengers disembarked. The city was much the largest that Winans had ever seen, being "rated at 30,000 inhabitants" and bounded by "the River then running where Old Levee Street now lies [1855], Canal, Rampart and Esplanade Streets." Beyond these limits human habitation was sparse. Some frame buildings and one small brick house existed above Canal Street, and a plantation, including a large orange grove, bordered on Gravier Street. For the most part, the area between the river and Saint Charles, Gravier, and Canal Streets consisted of a commons, and "back of [Saint] Charles it was an unreclaimed swamp."[15]

As Winans viewed the scene from the river, "a sense of loneliness oppressed my Spirit . . . such as I do not remember to have ever felt either before or since." He had "no reason to believe that there was . . . a single individual" in the city "I had ever known." Furthermore, with the exception of "two or three obscure white people and some twenty people of colour, there were none . . . who had evinced any partiality for Methodism, and very few with Protestant predilections [*sic*]."[16] Hobbs, however, had mentioned one man with whom Winans might "claim affinity:" Jacob Knab,[17] a "Prussian, who came to America as a private soldier in the army of Rochambeau."[18]

Knab was a tailor, a poor man, and a "deeply pious" Methodist. His wife and three of their four children lived at home with him. For five dollars per week Winans arranged for board and lodging with the family who received him with "much cordiality and affection." Mother Knab was "a notable housewife," and the couple provided liberally for their guest. Their residence was on the corner of Chartres and Bienville streets, "on the upper side of the latter and on the swamp side of the former." It was a "low one-story house, with a projecting roof" such as was common to "the early habitations in every part of Louisiana."[19]

Winans soon discovered that the hustle and bustle of the busy intersection interfered with his ability "to read or study to advantage." Particularly annoying to him, "just at the time of morning Prayer," was the cry of a Spaniard who "sold fresh Oysters from Barataria."[20] The hawker's voice "grated very unpleasantly upon my feelings, and went far towards disqualifying me for the service." Actually, the house itself was totally unsuitable for public preaching, and Winans and Knab agreed that another facility should be sought.[21]

They applied to the proper authorities for "the use of nearly all the public buildings," but their application was fruitless "except in mortification." Winans had been able to find only three white Methodists and one or two people of color on whom he could depend for support. He purchased "a suit of clothes . . . suited to [his] present position" and paid Knab for one month's lodging. Broke, and with no congregation of any consequence, Winans wondered, "what was to be done?" He could easily have yielded to the "over-whelming discouragements" and walked all the way back to Natchez, but this apparently "nevered entered [his] thoughts."[22]

Determined not to abort his mission, he resolved to find a place to preach and provide some means for pecuniary support. His predicament dovetailed with Knab's "straitened circumstances." In those "days of war and commercial depression,"[23] few new garments were being ordered, and the tailor's work consisted of "chiefly in *turning* and mending clothes." The men discussed their "gloomy condition and prospects" and decided to rent a house suitable to both their needs. It was agreed that Knab would operate a boardinghouse and Winans would open a school "to be fitted up as a preaching-place" on Sundays.[24]

Such a house was secured on the upper side of Bienville Street midway between Chartres and Royal. For fifteen dollars per month Winans occupied a bedroom on the second floor and a room on the ground floor measuring fifteen by forty-five feet. Knab paid twenty-five dollars per month for the remainder of the house. Winans opened the doors of his school to three students on December 13, 1813: Kitty Knab and James and William Ross, Junior, sons of the Irish Presbyterian flour inspector. By the end of the month William and Littleton Waters were added to the roll, and "the third month saw a considerable increase." During the final months of the term more students were matriculated than one teacher could adequately handle.[25]

This necessitated the hiring of an assistant who was "much more capable of teaching" than Winans. Together they also opened a night school enrolling some ten or twelve students, which made it possible for Winans "to bring up arrearages, pay [his] way and reserve something for future contingencies." However, his continuous confinement proved to be pernicious to his health, and at the end of six months he was compelled to retire from the classroom. He was highly respected for his "determination to establish and maintain strict discipline," which "involved the necessity of inflicting frequent and severe chastisement" upon his unruly charges.[26]

Among those whom he punished were Kitty Knab and her overgrown sixteen-year-old brother. At the same time, this chastisement was most displeasing to their mother; nevertheless, before the term had expired she "entirely approved of it." The outgoing principal strongly advised his successor to maintain the same level of discipline, but the advice was summarily ignored and the school was "broken up before the month had expired."[27] In later life, Winans "met with several young men . . . whom, in this school, I had flogged frequently and severely; and their manner toward me left no doubt that I had secured a warm and permanent place in their affections."[28]

Winans preached his first sermon in the makeshift sanctuary on Sunday, December 19. The congregation was "very small, consisting chiefly of men," and he was "much dissatisfied" with his performance. His poor showing was due in part to the "succession of discouragements" which he had experienced since arriving in the city, considerably affecting his enthusiasm. Moreover, in his "anxiety to make a favorable impression" in his initial effort he was "exquisitely sensitive to every defect or blemish" which he detected in the discourse. He was, however, "in some measure consoled and reassured by learning that Dr. Goforth professed a purpose to hear [him] again."[29]

Further reassurance was forthcoming on the following Sunday when both the morning and afternoon congregations were "much larger and of more respectable character. . . . This was encouraging." The "size and character" of the congregation on the third Sunday boosted his morale, especially when he "received more than one very flattering compliment" on his morning sermon. Soon after the turn of the year he had "succeeded in gaining a respectable standing as a preacher, among the middle as well as lower classes of Society."[30] With the advent of spring and summer he realized that his crowded facility would become uncomfortably hot. A new preaching place must be found.[31]

At that point "several Gentlemen undertook to procure a more suitable house, and resolved to bring [Winans] forth under their patronage." They were "the associated members of the Protestant Episcopal Vestry and of the Presbyterian Session," neither of whose constituents were served by "a Minister or place of worship in the City."[32] As a consequence of their combined influence with the authorities, Winans was granted permission to preach in "the Hall of the House of Representatives, in the Government House, or Capitol." The imposing structure stood on "the corner of Levee Street, and the Street running above the *Place des Armes* [*sic*]" fronting the Roman Catholic of Saint Louis.[33] The rawboned circuit rider from Mississippi mounted the rostrum of the august chamber for the first time on April 10, 1814.[34]

After having preached for several months in his rented room "independently of any patronage," Winans was now the leading Protestant preacher in the city. He occupied "a very commodious and respectable place of assembly, and under imposing and influential patronage." His congregation was "large and generally attentive," and weekly contributions pledged for his support amply covered his expenses. "The earnest attention which most of [his] audience paid to the word preached, and the *feeling* of interest often indicated were very encouraging promises of success."[35]

"But alas!" an "unpropitious circumstance occurred, which, if it did not blast the flattering prospect, detracted materially from its brightness." James F. Hull, a Presbyterian preacher, barrister, and "Political Refugee" from Ireland, arrived in the city during the spring.[36] Depending on the need for his services, he was undecided whether or not to practice at the bar or preach the Gospel. In addition to being "a boon companion at wine, and an adroit Whist-player," he was "a Scholar and an eloquent Orator." Finding the bar "abundantly and ably supplied," and the Protestant ministry represented by a young man "of no high pretensions," Hull chose the pulpit as "the scene of his exertions."[37]

On the first Sunday after Hull's arrival, Winans was requested to relinquish his pulpit to the newcomer. Having heard what he "considered obliquities in the Christian and Ministerial character" of the Irishman, Winans refused to grant the request. This "gave great offense to some," causing Winans to reconsider his position. He offered the suggestion that, since he preached a short sermon at ten in the morning, Hull could conveniently follow at eleven. The plan was agreeable to Hull's patrons, and the "arrangement continued while [Winans] remained in the City."[38]

May 22 was a warm day. Winans preached at his usual hour, scanning the congregation for the sight of Hull, but he was nowhere to be seen. He had "concealed himself in a position where he could hear me," entering the chamber only after Winans had concluded his sermon. Not wishing to "return discourtesy for discourtesy," Winans "resolved to remain and treat him with respect." Hull "occupied the pulpit with a ruffled shirt, with black gloves and with so foppish an air as would hardly have been congruous in a lawyer or a lecturer on any grave subject." Speaking of his proper theological education, he candidly confessed that he "knew of no call" to the ministry "other than that afforded by such qualification."[39]

He explained that the ministry was simply a profession which he could, with propriety, pursue or not pursue "as suited his own interest or convenience."[40] To demonstrate his professional proficiency, he delivered "a neat and sensible Discourse, in elegant language and with appropriate and graceful action." Everyone present appeared pleased with his homilectical gifts, but "the more sober-minded and pious" Presbyterians were displeased with his polished appearance and personality. Others were charmed by both. They were "the proud, the fashionable and the gay," who entertained "no higher views of Religion than as a system of decent morals and weekly ceremonials."[41]

It was clear to Winans that Hull's preaching was "not likely to disturb the quiet." Yet, it was of sufficient religious flavor to relieve "the tedium of the Sabbath" and permit his audience to "feel Christian." Supported "chiefly by Protestant Episcopalians," he was employed as pastor at an annual salary of $2,000. However, "the better portion" of the Presbyterians "refused to attend his ministry" and "drew ever closer" to Winans. One influential lawyer offered Winans a stipend of $1,500 if he would consent to continue his ministry in the city, an offer which he could not accept as a Methodist traveling preacher.

Winans wondered if it might not have been for "the Religious advantage of New Orleans" had he "been at liberty to have entered into this engagement."[42]

Hull presently went East and was ordained an Episcopal clergyman. In the meantime, "a church was built for him on the lower side of Canal Street, where he remained to the close of his life."[43] His "habits . . . changed . . . to greater and greater dereliction of Ministerial propriety" until "the scandal of his intemperance became notorious." Even in "seasons of official ministration, the effects of opium or brandy, or of both combined," frequently and utterly disqualified him for service. Winans had no hesitation in saying that "New Orleans would not have been much less injured . . . by being . . . destitute of all religious services" rather than those provided by Hull.[44]

During his final months in the city, Winans was "treated with general respect" by all who knew him well, although he was subjected to "some petty annoyances" by others. On one occasion a "supercilious young man" intercepted him on the street and accused him of impugning Hull's character. In the sharp exchange of words which followed, Winans was labeled "a tool of Edward Livingston Esqr. who was considered a Leader of the Federalists in the City."[45] The "leading Jeffersonian Republican" was A. L. Duncan, "the most prominent supporter" of Hull. Duncan, Hull, and their supporters "naturally enough" assumed that Winans was "a coadjutor of Livingston." Had they bothered to investigate, they would have discovered that "in those days" Winans was "a rather enthusiastic *Jeffersonian*."[46]

Winans was also threatened with a public horsewhipping by one Brand, a rich but "grossly ignorant" builder. Seeing Brand "coming towards me on the sidewalk, I assumed as erect an attitude and looked as brave as I could." Observing the fearless frontiersman awaiting him, Brand quickly "crossed over . . . to the opposite sidewalk . . . doubtless[ly] apprehensive that I might call him to account."[47] Returning to Knab's, Winans' dander was further aroused by a Baptist named Stackhouse, who engaged in "rude and violent attacks" upon Methodist doctrines. When Winans defended the faith in "a warm controversy," Stackhouse "became so grievously offended that he went to another boarding-house—a course which his rudeness and petulance . . . rendered very gratifying to me."[48]

Apart from these obnoxious characters, Winans formed "many pleasant acquaintances in the City," some of whom accorded him "very obliging attention." Numbered among them were Dr. Goforth, William Ross, Alfred Hennen, James Robinson, Judge Carlton, and Alvarez Fisk.[49] Former students whom he remembered pleasantly forty years afterward included the Ross boys, the Duplessis and Waters brothers, and Lucius C. Duncan. He also entertained a high regard for Mr. Paulding, a Baptist, who at the time was "deeply pious, strictly upright, and unusually liberal-minded." Paulding later became "a sordid miser," and in the end "he deteriorated, if he did not utterly apostatize . . . by his unchristian devotion to the world."[50]

Several anonymous articles by Winans appeared in the *Orleans Gazette*, published by Peter K. Wagner.[51] One was "an Eulogium on the preaching of Abbé [Louis-

Guillame-Valentin] Dubourg," whose sermons were "sensible and eloquent" and "in a high degree evangelical." The "bigotry of some Protestants, and the hatred of many Catholics" led to his bitter persecution by certain persons "who considered themselves gentlemen." They looked upon him as being a "rival of Father Antoine [Sedella], a very old and very indulgent Priest." At one point, only the intervention of the civil authorities prevented the abbé from being mobbed by the "Romanist[s] especially."[52] Winans' essay was "a severe reprehension of the indecorous behaviour" of those who vented their religious prejudices and passions upon the venerable abbé.[53]

The first of two subsequent articles was directed against the "fashionable vices" of "Sabbath-breaking, cock-fighting and *coloured* concubinage." A bill before the legislature aimed at suppressing these immoral practices was "contemptuously thrown under the table," which, to Winans, verged on an act of treason.[54] His second treatise was a "severe denunciation" of the local militia "for *refusing* obedience to the call of [the] Government" to mobilize for the defense of the city in the event of a British attack. The mutinous men twice paraded through the streets and "threw up their hats and swore they would not submit to be drafted." Both Gov. William Charles Cole Claiborne and Gen. Thomas Flournoy "backed out silently, if not meekly, from the enforcement of the Order." Winans believed they should have been summarily cashiered.[55]

Winans' slashing censures were no more warmly received by the Catholic community than the evangelical sermons of the abbé. The reason for the adverse reaction is not difficult to comprehend. One historian of the period points out the fact that evangelical religion has taken an historical stand "in opposition to excess materialism, extreme worldliness, and general secularism."[56] It was the object of that religion to save the individual soul from the evils of "the world, money, and prosperity . . . fine clothes and beautiful ornaments . . . [and] the BOTTLE."[57] As the means for achieving that salvation, evangelical preachers strongly emphasized the need for a "conversion experience" and the attainment of personal "holiness," or "sanctification." By way of contrast, the Roman Catholic's salvation was secured through the sacramental and sacerdotal system of "the church."[58]

It was therefore only natural that Catholics and Protestants often engaged in sharp encounters during the early years of the nineteenth century. No more fertile ground could be found for waging theological wars than in New Orleans.[59] Generally speaking, Methodists were less vociferous than the Presbyterians in their contest with the Catholics.[60] However, one Catholic historian maintains that Winans "attacked Roman Catholicism in no uncertain terms,"[61] being an apparent exception to the rule. Nevertheless, the fact remains that Winans vigorously defended the abbé, which indicates that the Methodist from Natchez should not be accused of indiscriminately condemning all Roman Catholics.[62]

At least two of Winans' acquaintances in the city were the objects of his uncommonly diligent pastoral ministrations. One was Richard C. Langdon, a printer and a boarder at Knab's. Although he had been religiously educated and formerly an active member of the church, he had become "a very wicked young man." His conscience caused him "frequent and painful misgivings" about the sordid life he was living. He became "warmly attached" to Winans, who, as his father confessor, "could not but feel great kindness for him." It is likely that Winans' influence induced him to alter the course of his life and, during 1820, to become editor of the *Mississippi Republican*, filling the post with "considerable ability."[63]

Winans felt an even deeper empathy for Ignatius Pigman, a fellow preacher. Pigman was "among the *first* . . . who received Ordination at the hands of Bishops [Thomas] Coke and [Francis] Asbury."[64] When Winans found him in the city, Pigman had "altogether ceased from any connection with the Church." He was living with a young widow, "reputed to be his niece, and her little child." She had recently joined the Methodist Church and appeared to be "a modest, amiable woman, disposed to melancholy." Just before leaving the city, Winans learned that she had "gone fatally astray," and that Pigman was "the partner of her guilt."[65]

Pigman was "a man of much more than ordinary intellectual power," unusually well read, and "grave and dignified in his deportment." Yet, at "near Sixty years of age" he had given up "respectability, peace of mind, [and] conviction of duty" in order to indulge in "licentiousness in a single one of its forms!" Winans could not comprehend how such a man could lose himself in "lawless love! . . . Such infatuation! . . . How often, Alas! has this current vice been found too strong for religious and virtuous tendencies associated with great mental capabilities!"[66]

One of Winans' lasting impressions of the city was its "exceedingly populous" cemetery. During high water the graves would be more than half filled with "water mixed with the obvious juices of decomposing human bodies." While conducting his first funeral in the place, a strange feeling of "mingled disgust and horror" came over him. Notwithstanding the "vigorous efforts to *bale* [sic] out the obtrusive water," it was impossible "to settle the coffin on the bottom of the grave, without perforating it and letting in the filthy fluid upon the corpse," that of a woman.[67] As he pronounced the benediction, "the ludicrous saying of a Flatboatman" flashed across Winans' mind: "I would not regard dying in New Orleans, if it were not that I must suck mud all the days of my life afterwards."[68]

Actually, Winans feared that he might be destined to be buried in that same mud. While doing double duty as preacher and teacher, his health had become "very delicate—at times, rather alarming." He suffered from frequent diarrhea and suspected that he was "going rapidly into pulmonary consumption." However, Dr. Goforth treated him "so skillfully, kindly and gratuitously" that he was able to resume his duties without undue interruption. After giving up the school, Winans "experienced a very decided improvement." Presiding Elder Samuel Sellers adjudged otherwise and ordered his junior colleague to leave the city and return to Natchez.[69]

Shortly before departing, Winans was handed a purse of more than $200 collected by non-Methodists Mr. Hennen and Mr. Robinson. This allowed him to leave the city considerably richer than when he arrived, "an event which had never before occurred in [his]

Itinerant life." His friends also "gathered round" the gangplank on the morning of July 9, 1814, to bid their pastor farewell.[70] Some, no doubt, came to see the newfangled wonder on which he had booked passage. It was the steamer *New Orleans*, "the first that was ever upon the Mississippi River," under the command of Captain DeHart.[71] The craft was expected to dock at Natchez-under-the Hill at the end of eight days of "expeditious traveling," and "the fare—very cheap!—was only $30." At half past nine the eerie sound of the steam whistle echoed across the nearby swamps, and the crew cast off.[72]

According to Winans, a seasoned mate in his own right, the hull of the steamer was formerly an "old sailing vessel." She was "too deep in her draught," heavy, and slow. Even if the engine had been "in first rate running order," it was grossly underpowered. Sleeping accommodations were primitive "bunks let into the side of the hull." Since the art of navigating the Mississippi under steam power had "yet to be invented," no pilot "dared to depend on his knowledge of the proper course for more than a few yards." Soundings were taken constantly, and because of the rapids and "adjustments of the Crazy Boat and clumsy engine," she was often obliged to tie up. Except under eminently favorable conditions "it was considered entirely too venturous to run at night."[73]

On the 13th she was tied down for the night along the western bank about a mile and a half above Baton Rouge to refit and take on wood. At daybreak Winans found the crew "strenuously endeavoring to get under way," but the craft would not budge. The river had fallen a foot or so during the night, and it was supposed that she had settled on a mud bank. Block and tackle, steam power and capstan were employed unsuccessfully, "Though she was susceptible of being moved laterally." Realizing that he had sufficient water to move out, DeHart probed the keel along with a long pole, only to discover that his steamer had settled on a high stump near midship. By 10 a.m. her old timbers began giving way, and the hull had "filled to the Boiler-deck" before the order was given to abandon ship.[74]

Less than a third of the $30,000 cargo was saved, but all passengers and crew were put safely ashore.[75] Gallant Winans accompanied two distressed damsels to a Frenchman's plantation, where they were hospitably accommodated. Leaving "the ladies kindly entertained," on the following morning Winans and five others hired a large pirogue, rowed or poled by a black man, to take them to "Bayou Sara [Saint Francisville], less than 30 miles, for which [they] paid $20." After eight miles of laborious rowing, they were forced to lay over at Mount Pleasant, where Mrs. Brogan put them up for the night.[76]

Overnight, Winans determined to abandon the boating expedition. Progress was painfully slow, the heat was unbearable, and he was "heartily tired" of the company of two "rich young roves and blackguards." Borrowing a horse from Mrs. Brogan, and accompanied by her son, Winans rode to Mr. Carters in the Plains, where he purchased a horse and proceeded five miles to Ream's place in Wilkinson County. After swapping his balking mount to J. Lott, fitting out, consulting with Samuel Sellers and Thomas Owens,

Winans rode into Natchez to labor for the remainder of the year with Thomas Griffin and Jonathan Kemp.[77] It was as if Jonah were returning home from Nineveh.[78]

Winans was not pleased with his pioneering effort in the city, but it was a beginning. Not until 1825 did "the continuous history of Methodism in N[ew] Orleans" commence under the ministry of Benjamin Michael Drake. "So difficult, and so interrupted was the introduction of Methodism into this important city!"[79] As historian John G. Jones summed it up: "Never, perhaps, in any civilized community have the Methodists had to grapple with greater and more formidable difficulties in establishing a well-ordered and respectable Church as in the city of New Orleans."[80]

Notes for "Methodist Beginnings in New Orleans, 1813-1814"

[1]This account is based on the original, unfinished manuscript "Autobiography of William Winans," (d. 1857), The Winans Papers, deposited in the Methodist Archives, Millsaps-Wilson Library, Jackson, Miss. On the decision to set apart Alabama, Mississippi, and Louisiana, see *The Journals of the General Conference, 1796-1836* (bound together) for 1812; John G. Jones, *A Complete History of Methodism as Connected with the Mississippi Conference*, 2 vols. (Nashville, 1887), 1:259, 302-18, passim. The Crescent City and Louisiana are covered in Alcée Fortier, *A History of Louisiana*, 4 vols. (New York, 1904), passim.

[2]Jones, *History of Methodism*, 1:302, spells the name "Newet."

[3]Ibid., 1:302-18. The centennial celebrating the occasion is noted in J. Allen Lindsey, *Methodism in the Mississippi Conference, 1894-1919* (Jackson, 1964), 229, 241.

[4]Autobiography, 109-10. For sketches of these men, see Jones, *History of Methodism*, 1:308, passim.

[5]Autobiography, 109. See also, Robert Paine, *Life and Times of William McKendree* (Nashville, 1899), passim; on the effects of the Creek War, Jones, *History of Methodism*, 1:288-92; Dunbar Rowland, *History of Mississippi, The Heart of the South*, 2 vols. (Chicago, 1925), 1:456-9; Eron Rowland, "The Mississippi Territory in the War of 1812," *Publications of the Mississippi Historical Society* (Centenary Series), 4 (1921): 7-233.

[6]Hobbs was so anemic that not even "voracious" ticks and mosquitoes would draw his blood. (Autobiography, 91).

[7]For sketches of Winans, see Paul Neff Garber, *Dictionary of American Biography*, 22 vols. (New York, 1928), 20:373; Jones, *History of Methodism*, 2:38-46; obituary in John Buford Cain, *Methodism in the Mississippi Conference, 1846-1870* (Jackson, 1939), 179-183.

[8]Autobiography, 109.

[9]Ibid. Origins of the enterprise are covered in H. C. Jennings, *The Methodist Book Concern: A Romance of History* (New York, Cincinnati, 1924), passim; Emory Stevens Bucke, ed., *The History of American Methodism*, 3 vols. (New York, 1964), 1:278-87, 483-4.

[10]"This was some years before the organization of the [Methodist] Missionary Society [in 1820] nor had any other reliable resource been provided for the support of Preachers engaged in Missionary labor." (Autobiography, 110). On the founding of the Society, see Bucke, *History of American Methodism*, 1:483-4.

[11]The passing of the flatboat and the advent of the steamboat is covered in Edward Quick and Herbert Quick, *Mississippi Steamboatin' . . . on the Mississippi and its Tributaries* (New York, 1926), passim.

[12]Autobiography, 110.

[13]The journey as seen through other eyes is recorded in Julia Ideson and Sanford W. Higgenbotham, eds., "A Trading Ship to Natchez and New Orleans, 1822: Diary of Thomas S. Teas," *Journal of Southern History*, 7 (August 1941): 378-99.

[14]Autobiography, 110.

[15]I.e., the inhabited area was "the old City, or that is now [1855] the First Municipality." (Ibid., 110-1).

[16]Ibid., 111. For background, see Walter Brownlow Posey, *Religious Strife on the Southern Frontier* (Baton Rouge, 1956), passim.

[17]Jones, *History of Methodism*, I: 343, spells the name "Knobb."

[18]Comte de Rochambeau commanded 5,500 French troops sent to America following Marquis de Lafayette's return home late in 1779.

[19]Autobiography, 111.

[20]Some fifteen miles south of the city on Lake Salvador.

[21]Autobiography, 111.

[22]Ibid., 112.

[23]See F. F. Bierne, *The War of 1812* (New York, 1949), passim.

[24]Autobiography, 112. See also, Jones, *History of Methodism*, 1:342-4.

[25]Autobiography, 112-3.

[26]Ibid., 113. The assistant is not named. Winans' formal education was limited to "*Thirteen and one half Days.*" (Autobiography, 1).

[27]Ibid., 113.

[28]Ibid., and adding: "It is a great mistake . . . to suppose that neglect of Discipline wins, or that the enforcement of it alienates affection—the opposite will ninety-nine times in a hundred be found to be the true one."

[29]Ibid., not mentioning Goforth's name.

[30]"And this standing I maintained, without any diminution, I believe, till I left the City." (Ibid., 114).

[31]Ibid.

[32]Ibid.; see also, Hodding Carter and Betty Carter, *So Great A Good* (New Orleans, [1956]), 18-31.

[33]Jackson Square.

[34]Autobiography, 114. Winans' patrons were Presbyterian Alfred Hennen, Vestrymen Richard Relf, J. W. Smith, et al. (Carter, *So Great a Good*, 18-93).

[35]Autobiography, 114.

[36]Ibid., and noting that Hull had acted "the part of a clergyman in Georgia, and had removed to Missouri and laying aside the ministry, had practiced at the bar for eleven years." Carter, *So Great a Good*, 18, notes that Hull had been "a licentiate of the Presbyterian Church in Ireland." On the Irish influx into the city beginning about 1810, see James J. McLoughlin in *The Catholic Encyclopedia*, 15 vols. (New York, 1909), 9:382.

[37]Autobiography, 114.

[38]Ibid., 114-5.

[39]Ibid., Carter, *So Great a Good*, 18, dates Hull's first appearance on June 11, 1814. Hull instantly recognized the fact of Winans' educational deficiency. Winans firmly believed that any man called by God to preach should be licensed whether he could "read or not!" See also, *Journal of the General Conference* (1844), 47, 59, 61, 126, 147.

[40]Autobiography, 115.

[41]Ibid., 116.

[42]Ibid., and adding "It was greatly doubted, by those acquainted with the circumstances of the case, whether [Hull] would receive more than three-fourths" of the salary.

[43]Ibid. Hull was ordained by Bishop John Henry Hobart of New York in 1816. (Carter, *So Great A Good*, 19-20.) Christ Church (Cathedral) was later moved to the 2900 block of Saint Charles Avenue.

[44]Autobiography, 117, and commenting: "The ministry of Mr. Hull was a great evil. . . . Pity that he was unfortunate as to preach a Religion he did not experimentally and practically understand to a people who emphatically needed Religious instruction, as the people of New Orleans then most unquestionably did. . . . His ministry would have been just as it was, had he substituted Socrates for Jesus Christ, and Plato for St. Paul." Hull died on June 6, 1833, never having been canonically instituted as rector. (Carter, *So Great A Good*, 31).

[45]Livingston became secretary of state during Andrew Jackson's first term, 1829-1833.

[46]Autobiography, 117, and observing that some of his warmest friends, "if not adherents of Mr. Livingston, at all events [were] not supporters of Mr. Duncan, who was too aristocratic to be popular." Winans later became a staunch Whig and ran for Congress in the Fourth District of Mississippi in 1849 against Albert Gallatin Brown.

[47]Autobiography, 117-8.

[48]Ibid., 118. For background on Baptist attitudes, see Walter Brownlow Posey, *The Baptist Church in the Lower Mississippi Valley, 1776-1845* (Lexington, Ky., 1959), passim.

[49]On Fisk's subsequent career as a Natchez churchman and businessman, see D. Clayton James, *Antebellum Natchez* (Baton Rouge, 1968), 158-9.

[50]Autobiography, 118-9. Duncan was later "an outstanding lawyer and vestryman." (Carter, *So Great A Good*, 30). "The Baptists had no formal organization in the city until 1843, though congregations met from time to time in Paulding's meeting house." (Ibid., 25).

[51]Autobiography, 119. See also, John Kendall, "Early New Orleans Newspapers," *Louisiana Historical Quarterly*, 10 (July 1927), 399-401.

[52]Autobiography, 119. Dubourg, who became Bishop of Louisiana in 1815, was "a brilliant and learned man, but was reluctant to enforce his authority against the cathedral trustees who continually opposed him." (Célestin M. Chambon in *Catholic Encyclopedia*, 5:178-9). Father Antoine had been the cathedral parish priest since ca. 1791. (Marie Louis Points in ibid., 11:10-1).

[53]Autobiography, 119. For background on "Protestants against Catholics," see W. B. Posey, *Religious Strife on the Southern Frontier* (Baton Rouge, 1965), 77-112.

[54]Autobiography, 119.

[55]Ibid., 119-20. Wagner was threatened for not identifying Winans, but he was "a powerful man, and a formidable party, it was known, would rally to his support. . . . A little more than a year after this, [Jackson] taught these recusants [sic] that there was something in lawful authority, resolutely enforced, a good deal more to be dreaded than doing Camp duty, for a few weeks, in the sight of home." (Ibid.) On the change of command from Wilkinson to Flournoy to Jackson, see James Ripley Jacobs, *Tarnished Warrior: Major-General James Wilkinson* (New York, 1939), passim; Rowland, *Mississippi*, 1:460-6; on Claiborne's terms in office, ibid., 1:401.

[56]John B. Boles, *The Great Revival, 1787-1805* (Lexington, Ky., 1972), 140.

[57]Ibid., James Smith, ed. *The Posthumous Works of the Reverend and Pious James McGready*, 2 vols. (Louisville, 1831-1833), 1:166-7.

[58]See Boles, *Great Revival*, 182.

[59]Posey, *Religious Strife*, 86-94.

[60]Ibid., 94-6.

[61]James J. Pillar in Richard Aubrey McLemore, ed., *A History of Mississippi*, 2 vols. (Hattiesburg, 1973), 1:399, citing the *Natchez Daily Courier*, October 20, 1855.

[62]Autobiography, 119.

[63]Ibid., 120, and adding that Langdon "might have done well; but being 'as unstable as water, he could never excel.'" Contrary to Winans' outspoken opinion at a later date (1849), Langdon's paper "generally favored some form of congressional control over slavery in the territories." (James, *Antebellum Natchez*, 282).

[64]Autobiography, 120, and adding: "The last notice of [Pigman] in the [Conference] Minutes is, I believe, under the year 1788; when he is reported 'partially located, on account of his family, but subject to the Conference." Pigman was ordained deacon in June following the "Christmas Conference" of 1784 at Baltimore. Abel Stevens, *History of the Methodist Episcopal Church*, 4 vols. (New York, 1868), 2:188-9. The lives of the two bishops are treated in Ezra Squier Tipple, *Francis Asbury, the Prophet of the Long Road* (New York, 1916) and Samuel Drew, *The Life of the Rev. Thomas Coke, D. D.* (New York, 1818, 1837, 1847).

[65]Autobiography, 120-1.

[66]Ibid., 121-2.

[67]Undoubtedly "Cypress Grove Cemetery, about two miles form the city." (Jones, *History of Methodism*, 2:459). Here in 1841, Winans was to bury his friend, Elijah Steele, who fell at his post during an epidemic of yellow fever. See also, Benjamin Michael Drake, *A Sketch of the Life of Rev. Elijah Steele* [and] *A Funeral Discourse by W. Winans, D.D.* (Cincinnati, 1843). Steele's "remains were deposited in a copper coffin, then enclosed in one of mahogany" and temporarily "deposited in the private vault of James Ross," awaiting the erection of "a substantial white marble tomb." (Jones, *History of Methodism*, 2:459.)

[68]Autobiography, 122, adding the later comment that he "attended burials in these shocking circumstances, till they excited no peculiarly unpleasant feelings."

[69]Ibid., 122-3, and commenting that Sellers "wanted me on the Natchez and Claiborne circuits, where I believe he thought I could be more useful than in the City, during its excessive heat and the absence of many Anglo-American Citizens."

[70]Ibid., 123.

[71]Ibid. See note on the craft in James, *Antebellum Natchez*, 193, quoting Joseph D. Shields, *Natchez: Its Early History*, ed. Elizabeth D. Murray (Louisville, 1930), 84.

[72]Autobiography, 123-4.

[73]Ibid., 124.

[74]Ibid.

[75]"Some of the passengers were interested in their loss; and they clamored against the officers of the Boat—especially the Captain. The rest of us . . . voluntarily drew up a certificate, bearing testimony to the vigilance and fidelity of the Captain, showing, by a statement of the circumstances of the loss, that no blame could be

justly imputed to any one for that loss. This silenced the clamor, and probably prevented a suit for damages."
Ibid.

[76]Ibid., 125.

[77]On Sellers, Griffin, and Kemp, see Jones, *History of Methodism*, 1:326-8, passim; Charles Betts Galloway, "Thomas Griffin: A Boanerges of the Early Southwest," *Publications of the Mississippi Historical Society*, 7 (1903): 153-70. Owens' obituary is in Cain, *Methodism in the Mississippi Conference*, 445-6.

[78]Autobiography, 125, and adding: "So long had I served these [Mississippi] people, and so kindly were our mutual feelings!"

[79]Ibid., and reflecting: "I, however, am disposed to believe that, but for the disturbance occasioned by the coming of Mr. Hull, or, if I could have remained long enough to profit by the reaction that commenced to manifest itself before I left, something effective would have been accomplished." On Drake's later ministry in the city, see Jones, *History of Methodism*, 2:31-3; Cain, *Methodism in the Mississippi Conference*, 271-5.

[80]Jones, *History of Methodism*, 1:147-8.

"HELPERS IN THE GOSPEL:"
WOMEN AND RELIGION IN LOUISIANA,
1800-1830*

Dolores Egger Labbé

In 1985 Jon Butler challenged historians of religion to direct attention to neglected areas of that history, mentioning in particular, the laity, especially women, popular religious practices, and sections of the country outside of New England.[1] In recent years there has been an explosion of interest in religion in the South with conferences, articles, and books covering many aspects of the subject.[2] However, as Sally McMillen has pointed out, antebellum Southern women in general have been slighted. Louisiana women, in particular, are often left out of Southern studies as they lived in a state that was not typical of the South, a state that did not fit the mold. In 1996 Joan E. Cashin called for more study of antebellum Southern women who were ethnic and religious minorities, noting that this is an "exciting area for more research." She mentioned in particular that more work needs to be done on Louisiana women.[3]

This article, an investigation of that "exciting area," will examine Louisiana Women and their religious experiences in the early nineteenth-century. Louisiana was not a very religious place and many women, both Catholic and Protestant, did not believe that it was the duty of women to be religious.[4] However, the Catholic and Protestant women who kept the faith were the ones most responsible for promoting Christianity in Louisiana. At times they even overcame traditional religious hostilities to join forces in their efforts.

Thomas W. Spalding has emphasized that lay people carried Christianity, and in particular Catholicism, to the American frontier. He asserts that Catholics on the frontier "knew instinctively that they were the Church, the people of God."[5] On no frontier was this attitude more evident than in Louisiana. Whether they were Catholic from Maryland, Acadian from Acadia or French from Europe or the islands, Louisiana Catholics knew that they were the people of God and knew that they had the responsibility to preserve the faith themselves. And it was the women who took this responsibility most seriously. This was not a new task for Catholics in Louisiana. Although Louisiana had had an established Catholic church under both its French and Spanish colonial governments, the

*First published in *Mid-America*, 79 (1997): 153-75. Reprinted with the kind permission of the author and publisher.

religious needs of the people had been neglected. Church parishes had been established and New Orleans made a diocese, but the official church structure was a shell and the situation did not improve for many years after the Americans came. Keeping the faith and passing it on to future generations was the task of lay people.

Protestants were in much the same situation. Although missionaries were excited with the Louisiana Purchase and its prospects of conversions, they soon became discouraged at the apathy and hostility they encountered. As with the Catholics, devout Protestants often had to preserve their faith on their own, with the assistance of the occasional visiting minister. Women, not men, were most responsible for the work of maintaining Protestant Christianity in Louisiana. Protestant women were even willing to join Catholic women, at least for a time, to work together as Christians. Neither Catholic nor Protestant women were the placid members of churches who sat docilely while men led. Women were not only the people in the pews, they were the leaders who led the rest of the people in the pews.[6]

To most nineteenth-century Americans Louisiana seemed mysterious and perhaps even a little heathen. The Louisiana Purchase introduced a new and radically different religious situation into American society. For the first time there was a sizeable area of the United States where the majority of people were Catholic. Furthermore, their Catholicism was not American Catholicism, but a French and Spanish colonial Catholicism with a tradition of dependence on government. The new territory and, after 1812, state followed a different legal system in civil matters than the rest of the country. To add to the complexities of the area, while Louisiana was a true wild frontier state, it was also home to one of the largest and most cosmopolitan cities in the country.

Louisiana Catholics included rich and poor, rural and urban, black and white, and almost all of them assumed that Catholicism was the normal religion. While a few Louisianians, such as the Ursuline nuns, were concerned about the coming of American Protestants and some, like church trustees and priests, were concerned about the end of government support, most people had a laissez-faire attitude about religion. They were nonchalant about doctrinal differences. They did not want to be converted to other denominations, but they were not particularly upset by the existence of Protestants in the world. As a whole they were rather tolerant if they were left alone.[7]

Their relaxed and apathetic attitude towards Protestants extended to their own religious beliefs. While they sometimes considered themselves devout, many were not strict practitioners of their faith. They wanted to be married, baptized and buried with the blessing of the Catholic Church, as religion was part of their heritage, but often they were anticlerical and belligerent towards anyone official in the Church.[8] This was an old problem which had been noted by the Spanish bishop, Luis Peñalver, the first bishop of the Diocese of New Orleans. In the 1790s he attributed the sad state of religious practice to contact with Americans who were moving into the colony and noted in a report to Madrid that fewer than one-quarter of the people in New Orleans attended Sunday Mass. Furthermore, he asserted that of eleven thousand estimated Catholics in the city, only three or four hundred obeyed Church laws concerning the annual reception of sacraments.[9] As late as 1820, fewer than three hundred people in the city received the sacraments during the Easter season.[10] The situation was no better in the country regions. The priest at St. John's Church at Vermilionville (Lafayette) reported in 1825 that only forty-two of the four thousand people in his parish had made Easter confessions.[11] Earlier, in 1816, Apostolic Administrator Louis William DuBourg reported in despair to Rome that everywhere in Louisiana, "morality is at an incredibly low ebb."[12]

Protestants in New England and Catholics in France had similar views of Louisiana. It was prime missionary territory, full of ignorant Catholics who needed assistance. Mission societies in France were willing to help but found difficulty in recruiting priests for Louisiana, a difficulty which continued throughout the history of the state. There were twelve priests in Louisiana in 1812 with only one man available to attend to all Catholics north of Red River from his station in Natchitoches. Between 1804 and 1824 there was no resident pastor in the Avoyelles area, and when one did arrive, he was turned away from the homes of seven Catholics before he found a family willing to shelter him.[13] The typical priest in the country like Father Blanc, was a circuit rider. Blanc, who was responsible for the frontier area north of Natchitoches, rode over about one-third of the territory and state. He held services in a few chapels and in private homes.[14] Matters did not improve for many years in the frontier area, where only two new church parishes, one at Grand Coteau in St. Landry Parish and one at Vermilionville (Lafayette) in Lafayette Parish, were founded before 1830 and the number of priests had only increased to twenty-four by 1834.[15]

Wherever Catholic services were held, whether in church, a hall, or a private home, women attended to preparations and went to the services. Often in the country there were no churches, and priests traveling along the Bayou Vermilion offered Mass in the homes of Madame Daygle on the lower bayou, at the plantation of Madame Claude Martin and in Carencro at the home of Madame Arceneaux. Seven miles above Thibodaux on Bayou Lafourche Widow Belotte opened her home for Mass. In St. Martinville an observer remarked that women went to Mass, but most men strolled in front of the church, or walked along the side to look inside and "ogle the ladies."[16] It was the same in New Orleans. Women, including free women of color, made up most of the congregation at Masses at the Cathedral. During Holy Week, when the services were numerous and long, some women had servants bring chairs for them, as only one-third of the Cathedral was furnished with pews. During Good Friday services women surged forward to kiss the crucifix, causing long lines and long delays. While they waited some women knelt and prayed, others looked around at newcomers, while others laughed and chatted. Mothers brought babies, whose crying added to the general confusion. Devout women quietly recited their rosaries, seemingly oblivious to the hubbub.[17]

Women were the ones who got babies baptized, marriages blessed, and children to First Communion and Confirmation. In a sacramental church the priests eventually had to administer the various sacraments, but until they came Catholics had to manage on their own. Judges and justices of the peace performed weddings until priests came to bless the marriages. There is some mystery about who baptized the babies. At least one researcher believes that women performed this sacramental duty until the priest made one of his infrequent visits. Women also conducted Sunday services reading various prayers from the Mass.[18] The magnitude of their efforts in religious work can be seen in the 1825 report from a missionary who noted that the sixty children who made their first communion at Natchitoches had been properly instructed. Furthermore, he baptized three hundred fifty infants and children, a feat which involved the organization of a multitude of godparents, families, and children. Credit for all the preparations was given to "the zealous women of the parish."[19] When the church burned at Natchitoches, it was the women who "got together and began collecting funds for a new church." In rural Natchitoches Parish, at Campti, Mlle. Françoise Crichet gave the land and paid for the building of a chapel for the use of local Catholics.[20]

Women were the ones who decorated and cleaned the family tombs for All Saints' Day, a very important religious day for Louisiana Catholics. Ceremonies were held in the cemeteries, and the faithful prayed for their dead friends and relatives. Although some newcomers scoffed at the tradition as being superstitious, others noted that honoring the dead was proof of parental and filial affection.[21]

There were too few Catholic church officials in Louisiana to enforce rigid rules. The Apostolic Administrator and later bishop, William Louis DuBourg, usually lived in St. Louis as he was not popular in New Orleans, where he was banned from his own Cathedral. DuBourg ordered Catholics to avoid the Cathedral under pain of sin. They were instructed to go to the Ursuline chapel for all sacraments. Most women ignored the orders and continued to attend the Cathedral. Catholics in Louisiana were independent and realized that they, not just the clergy, were the Church. When Bishop DuBourg did visit New Orleans, he depended on the Ursuline nuns for lodging and support, as the priests would not give him financial assistance. He bitterly wrote that it was the nuns who provided him with "a most precarious pittance."[22] It was indeed a novel world where the sheep provided for the shepherd.

Women were great champions of Père Antoine, a Spanish priest stationed at the Cathedral in New Orleans. The wardens of the parish decided that he should be their pastor and although women were not voting members of the group, one woman, the widow of Don Andrés Almonester y Roxas and the current spouse of the leader of the trustees, thought she had the right to help name the pastor and his assistants, as her first husband had built the church.[23] Père Antoine was kind to all women including concubines, prostitutes, and the divorced as well as the devout. He would "pass through the church" the deceased husband of any woman, whether he was a Mason, a rascal, or a good Catholic. It was said that the "beloved" Père Antoine "consents to everything." To the chagrin of the bishop and other church officials some women even displayed his picture in their homes.[24]

Priests, in both city and country, continued to wrangle over jurisdictions and provided little significant leadership. Women in religious orders were the most obvious religious leaders in the Catholic church in Louisiana. Few young men entered seminaries, but young women joined religious orders. Two elite orders, the Ursulines and the Religious of the Sacred Heart, came from France, but both orders had many American members. Two American orders from Kentucky and Maryland also sent sisters to Louisiana. The sisters were educated and served as pioneers in the professions of teaching and nursing. Each order did have to contend with a patriarchal priesthood as each group had its male spiritual director or advocate.[25] When these men were sympathetic to the work of the sisters or when they stayed out of their affairs, the orders thrived. Bishop DuBourg, who advised both the Ursulines and the Religious of the Sacred Heart, sometimes caused more distress than help. This decent man had no sense of money matters. He seemed to assume that God sent money. The nuns were much more practical, believing both in prayer and financial stability.[26] The Ursulines and Religious of the Sacred Heart owned their own property, handled their own financial affairs and were strong-minded leaders. When the Jesuits hesitated between settling at Donaldsonville or Grand Coteau in the 1830s, the Sacred Heart Sisters defeated the Donaldsonville planters by offering two hundred thousand free bricks to the Jesuits. When the bishop hesitated about building a large school on the Mississippi, the Sacred Heart Sisters were extremely polite and said they would defer to his wishes. They did add that they would have to leave and build a school in another diocese. The school was built on the River.[27]

The Ursulines were the oldest order of nuns in Louisiana, having arrived in the 1720s. Their boarding school in New Orleans dated from that period. They also assisted at the hospital, took in some orphans, had a day school, and taught religion to slaves and free children of color. In 1803 sixteen of the sisters, including the Mother Superior, left Louisiana for Havana, as they were frightened at the prospect of the change of governments. They left behind eleven apprehensive women of French descent, most of whom were Louisiana natives.[28] W. C. C. Claiborne, the American governor tried to reassure the nuns by explaining that the First Amendment protected them as well as everyone else. They were not convinced and sent a petition to Pres. Thomas Jefferson, signed by all the nuns, pleading with him to make certain that they would be guaranteed their full rights to their property.[29]

Governor Claiborne, who considered the nuns "very useful members of Society," realized their importance as community leaders. Their superior was the only woman he honored with an official, rather than a social, visit. He made frequent visits to the convent and even exchanged gifts of fans and received a portrait of Pope Pius VII. He was always alert to their concerns. When James Madison became president, he wrote to explain that Jefferson had stepped down "voluntarily." When the sisters asked him to close a play that ridiculed nuns, he explained that the same amendment that gave them freedom of religion gave others freedom of speech.[30]

The Sacred Heart sisters first went to Missouri and then established a convent in Louisiana in 1821 when Mother Eugenie Aude led a group to Grand Coteau in rural St. Landry Parish. A Maryland Catholic family had donated a large tract of land for the use of the Church and the wife in the family, Mary Sentee Smith, continued with her generous patronage after her husband's death. The Sacred Heart school flourished and had thirty-five boarding students by 1827 and the number soon increased to one hundred. A school began in St. James Parish in 1825. St. Michael's also had one hundred girls in attendance. When the superior of the order in the United States, Phillipine Duchesne, learned that the majority of students at Grand Coteau were Protestant, she consulted with Mother Sophie Barat in France and received permission for these girls to recite all prayers in English. Furthermore, they were no longer required to learn the Catholic catechism. Such accommodation helped encourage tolerance among many local planters.[31]

During this early period of the nineteenth-century most people admired the sisters. Even suspicious New Englanders were impressed by these women, who helped the sick, the orphans, the aged and educated young women. One man from the Northeast remarked that the Ursulines were females "of the most enlightened minds."[32] The people who disliked the nuns tended to be French Catholics or former Catholics such as "The Friend of Liberal Institutions" who warned that American children should not be taught by Sacred Heart sisters, because they were as dangerous as Jesuits. The *Louisiana Gazette* columnist, *Feuilleton*, who was usually sympathetic to women, had no use for convents, which he wrote, buried women alive. He also complained that the civil authorities favored nuns and did not make them fix their sidewalks which were in terrible repair.[33] Such anti-religious remarks were the exception. The selfless work of the nuns convinced many Americans that Catholics were not all bad.

Religious women had great influence on lay women. The women of elite families often kept contact with the sisters for many years after they left school, often for life.[34] Other educational institutions for young women came and went, but the convents remained and the nuns provided a source of friendship and support that was separate from family or the supervision of men. Many elite Louisiana women learned their attitudes about God, dancing, and government from nuns, not from priests, fathers, or husbands. When Claiborne was kind and respectful to the sisters, he gained respect for himself and his government not just from the sisters but from their women friends.

Protestants complained about the lack of religious fervor among Catholics. One missionary of the 1820s noted later that Methodists had more success preaching the gospel to "benighted and untutored Choctaws" than to the Catholics of southwest Louisiana.[35] However, Catholics were not alone in thwarting the efforts of the missionaries. The complainers could get little comfort from the religious enthusiasm of the typical American in Louisiana.[36] The American immigrants had not been allowed to build Protestant churches during the Spanish period, but missionaries were sadly disappointed to find that after the Louisiana Purchase there was no great rush to erect church buildings or establish congregations. Ministers found this apathy prevalent in New Orleans, the rural areas and on the frontier. The first Protestant congregation in New Orleans, an Episcopal congregation, was formed in 1805, but its members did not build a church for ten years. By 1830 the Episcopalians, Presbyterians, Methodists, and Baptists had congregations in New Orleans, but often they had few members and low attendance. Those who did attend were often women, but they did not flock to the churches in great numbers or agitate for churches to be built earlier. As late as 1827, the Baptists in the city numbered only around twenty members. Baptists tended to have biracial congregations, but there was an African Baptist church in New Orleans, established in 1826, which had about eighty-seven members in the early 1830s including forty-six women.[37]

In the country regions there was little thought of churches. A settler believed that people were too concerned about getting rich and cared too little about the next world. Other writers pointed out that on the frontier "meat, bread and shelter were the main considerations."[38]

American Protestants were as little informed about religion as the French Catholics. Many on the frontier had never heard a sermon, seen a Bible or learned the basic teachings of Christianity. Many of these people who had moved to Louisiana during the Spanish period had not worried about the religious formation of their families. One frustrated minister reported that when he preached on the Fall, people asked him what the term meant and when it was that man had fallen.[39] Another shocked minister, who founded a school for girls in the Florida Parishes spent much of his time teaching religion as he found that many of his students, all Americans, "were ignorant" of God's existence before his arrival.[40] Besides problems of religious ignorance, some Protestant churches had rigid codes which did not attract frontier people. One Baptist church, located near Clinton, in the Florida Parishes, ordered that all members renounce "Singing Carnal Songs and Carnal mirth; fiddling, dancing, etc., or vain recreation."[41] Injunctions of this sort made churches unattractive to frontier men and women.

Protestant ministers who ventured into rural Louisiana were often greeted with hostility, by both Catholics and Protestants, French and Americans. In 1808 an American woman in the Opelousas area refused lodging to a minister for the night saying that she would entertain "no such cattle." Ministers were often threatened or jeered as they spoke at courthouses. In St. Martinville, a woman with a hoe rescued a minister who had been hauled from the courthouse by ruffians. She chased the crowd and told the minister to resume his preaching.[42] Apathy was as discouraging to the ministers as hostility. A planter's wife wrote to her sister that her husband had gone into St. Francisville to hear a sermon, but she could not be bothered as it was too dusty and warm. Such attitudes were not unusual.[43]

To overcome their difficulties rural Protestants relied on the Methodist circuit rider, the Baptist preacher-farmer and the camp meeting. The camp meetings were held almost exclusively in frontier areas of northern Louisiana and in the Florida Parishes, where they were quite popular by the 1820s with Baptists and Methodists. These meetings broke the routine and boredom of everyday lives. Land was sold and other business transactions conducted, as well as souls being saved. One thoughtful woman, after considering the great excitement and pressure, wondered if many of the young converts had ever given "a thought" to religion before attending the camp meeting.[44]

Even after years of work Protestants remained discouraged about their attempts to make Louisiana a Christian state. In 1824 after twenty years of labor, the Baptists could claim one hundred fifty official members west of the Mississippi in Louisiana, while the Methodists in 1823 had one hundred fifty-six white and ninety-eight black members in the same area. The first church organized in present Calcasieu Parish, in the far southwestern part of the state, the Antioch Primitive Baptist Church, had five members, four of them women.[45] The first Protestant church, a nonsectarian one, was built in Opelousas in 1825. By 1830 several towns in the Florida Parishes had church buildings with the lovely Episcopal church in St. Francisville being the most outstanding one. A northern Presbyterian minister commented that in most American towns a church spire crowned the town with respectability, but he did not find that Louisianians worried about such matters.[46]

The few Protestants who did worry about such matters were usually women. Pious women, who had no official position in the Protestant churches, were the backbone of rural Protestant efforts, and preachers too acknowledged their importance. In remote and unfriendly areas an occasional Christian woman would open her home to itinerant preachers. Women such as Nancy Walker of Washington Parish, in the Florida Parishes, assisted relatives who were striving for visible conversions. She knelt by her brother's bed praying and "crying to God" for his conversion while his other sisters and mother also prayed. Richard Warner was finally converted.[47] Women were welcome to join men in the work of the American Tract Society and the American Bible Society. In Baton Rouge, a newspaper advertisement encouraged women to be generous in their contributions to the Tract Society. Women were often liaisons with officials of organized church societies in the East, such as the American Sunday School Union. And women taught in the few Sunday schools. In Ouachita Parish, a young teacher from New England held Sunday school for children in the courthouse before the visiting minister preached.[48] Women also gathered together in prayer groups in parts of rural St. Mary Parish and provided shelter and service space for the itinerant ministers. They were called by grateful preachers, "helpers in the gospel."[49]

The meeting of Catholics and Protestants, French and Americans in Louisiana usually occurred in New Orleans. Here religious newcomers from other parts of the United States, whether Catholic or Protestant, were shocked with what they found. These leaders did not agree on doctrine but all believed that the answer to the great religious problems in the city lay with women. The Apostolic Administrator, Louis William DuBourg, was as shocked by New Orleans as the most censorious Protestant. Bishop John Carroll of Baltimore who had heard how irreligious the city was urged DuBourg to reform the place. Carroll suggested forming groups of devout people who would live decent lives and serve as examples to other residents of New Orleans. He thought that women, in particular, might be persuaded to abandon their great attachment "to the theatre, dancing assemblies, and every species of dissipation, which now exists in N. O." He further suggested that DuBourg try to get support from government officials such as Governor Claiborne and Gen. James Wilkinson, both of whom were married to local Catholic women who could help in the reform of the city, if they had "any sparks of religion."[50]

Protestants, likewise, hoped to change New Orleans and planned to do that by converting the residents to true Christianity. Many believed that since the majority of the inhabitants were Catholic "the morals of the people [are] consequently of a dissipated cast."[51] Like the Catholic leaders Protestant missionaries placed their hopes on women. Some planned to become friendly with families, as they realized that mothers in Catholic homes were in charge of religious formation. One missionary thought that he might persuade mothers of the "necessity of a change of heart" and of "the errors of popery."[52] Missionaries were upset by French women who prayed rosaries instead of reading Bibles and by American women who had never heard of Bibles. Two New England missionaries who reported that there were no Bibles in New Orleans and very few in the entire state, easily convinced Bible societies to ship all sorts of Bibles, including French Protestant ones, to Louisiana. The missionaries bragged about causing doubts about Catholicism especially among women even including the nuns at the Ursuline convent. The Bibles might have caused some confusion, but few French Catholics were literate enough to read them or confused enough to become Protestants.[53]

All religious leaders were upset by the lack of Sunday closings. In the eastern United States some Protestants in an effort to make the United States a Christian nation were waging an active battle to force the entire population to observe Sunday as a day of prayer and rest.[54] When members of these groups migrated to Louisiana they thought they had reached a suburb of Sodom.[55] In New Orleans, not only were businesses open, but also all places of entertainment, such as billiard halls, theaters, the circus, and ballrooms. Even devout women left the Cathedral after Mass to attend the theater. To one Protestant woman, the city on Sunday had the appearance "of a fair [rather] than a Christian sabbath." Local French Catholics explained to visitors that Sunday was made for man, not man for Sunday.[56]

The Protestants, who considered the Sunday activities part of Catholicism, would have been amazed to learn that the shocked French priests viewed this relaxed attitude toward Sunday an "American" idea, the sort of thing that came to a country following a revolution. The stern refugee priests did not approve of frivolities such as dancing or the theater on any day of the week, and certainly not on Sunday. DuBourg who agreed with these views, hesitated to speak out in public, due to his unpopularity.[57] Nevertheless, John Carroll instructed him to forget his fears and to attend to the problem and to "raise shame & horror in their minds on this subject. Contrast their violations of the law of God with respectful observance of it in the U. S."[58]

Protestant women, who would not attend the theater on Sunday, persuaded the theater managers to repeat favorite performances later in the week.[59] Their ministers frowned on plays on any day of the week. Occasionally legislators tried to pass Sunday closing laws such as "an act to prevent vice and immorality on the sabbath day." Such proposals and petitions only irritated the general public and caused a flurry of letters to the editors condemning "blue laws" that would try to force everyone to follow a certain mode of behavior.[60] Louisiana was not yet ready to be Christianized in the evangelical Protestant or the official Catholic Church pattern.

Donald G. Matthews, in *Religion in the Old South* and Jean E. Friedman, in *The Enclosed Garden*, note that women formed charitable religious associations, sometimes risking disapproval for going outside the domestic sphere.[61] Such groups were formed in New Orleans apparently with the approval of men. What makes these charitable endeavors so different from the South discussed by both Matthews and Friedman was that both groups welcomed French and American women, Catholic and Protestant. The toleration for others was unique.

The first joint charitable endeavor, the Female Orphan Asylum, was a project of major proportions. It was begun several years before an asylum for boys was organized by local men. Although Protestant women from the East were the main leaders, the organization also had French members. These women wrote their own constitution, elected their own officers and ran the home entirely on their own without any male direction. This undertaking was the only instance in which women, outside of convents, organized and managed a large project.

The minutes and annual reports suggest that the officers were capable, intelligent, and practical. The women solicited aid from a variety of sources. A prominent Creole planter, Julian Poydras, gave so much money that the asylum was usually called the Poydras Asylum. The women also obtained aid from Protestant and Catholic clergy and from the state legislature. The money provided from the legislature came from gambling license fees, which might have caused concern to some of the Protestant members, but they did not refuse the assistance.

The attitude of some men was not of disapproval, but rather of amusement at the women's efforts. In the second annual report the secretary observed, "A second year has gone, that year which was to prove the limit of our exertion and the end of our society, the want of funds joined to that natural versatility so commonly associated with the female character it was predicted, would, ere this period should elapse completely exhaust the feelings that gave birth to the institution of the 'Female Orphan Society."[62] But they were still operating the orphanage and they were justifiably proud of themselves.

The Asylum was a badly needed institution in New Orleans, as the Ursuline sisters, who provided for some orphan girls, could not begin to care for the many children who were left alone after numerous epidemics. The women accepted girls from all over the state, as well as girls with one living parent. By 1828 they housed one hundred eight children ranging in age from eighteen months to sixteen years.[63]

Religion at the Asylum soon became a major problem. Protestant ministers eagerly came to the home and baptized girls into their denominations. The girls were all sent to Protestant Sunday School. The women did remember to defer to Catholics on Friday when everyone ate fish. Fish aside, the asylum had a definite Protestant flavor and some Catholics were worried about the future of small girls who were sent there. As Patrick Casey, wrote, his motherless infant, Mary, was "Baptized . . . Romancatholick" and he wanted her raised as such.[64]

The women in charge decided that Catholics had to be accommodated, so they agreed that Catholic and Protestant girls would be separated for morning and evening prayers, two nuns would be added to the staff and teachers were ordered not to dispute religious matters in front of the children or put "religious prejudices into their minds." At one point the children alternated at Sunday services between the Cathedral and the Presbyterian church. These women could not have been more ecumenical in their efforts to solve the religious problem. Their group was much more liberal than any similar women's organization would have been in Boston in the 1820s.[65] Eventually seven sisters worked at the Female Orphan Asylum. However, by the end of the 1830s as the numbers of orphans in the city continued to increase, the Presbyterians took complete charge and the sisters founded a separate Catholic orphanage.[66]

The second women's organization, the Female Charity Society, was chartered by the state legislature in 1822 for the "purpose of relieving sick and distressed persons" in New Orleans. Membership was open to free white women over twenty-one, who paid annual dues of six dollars. The names of the thirty-five charter members listed in the act are evenly divided between French and American women.[67]

The Louisiana women who were concerned about religion were the leaders of many religious endeavors, and at times they stood up to men and made their own decisions. They were not victims dragging their skirts, but women who accepted their position in society, while they also asserted a certain independence. Protestant women, as the ministers realized, were essential to the expansion of Christianity. Despite the severe lack of priests in the sacramental Catholic Church, most Catholics remained Catholic. Much of the credit belonged to the women, both mothers and nuns. Louisiana was the only place in the lower South where significant groups of professional women teachers, the religious congregations, ran schools over an extended period of time. In religious activities, women could sometimes gain the respect of men and other women for their achievements. They could enjoy the satisfaction of raising money to build churches. And they could cooperate with other women, who were not part of their family or denomination to organize charitable agencies. They realized that people of different religious groups could get along and cooperate.

By the 1830s, the population of the state increased by huge numbers. Rural areas were tamed and plowed and the frontier began to disappear. New Orleans continued to grow as immigrants poured in from Europe. Churches as institutions became important parts of the establishment. Large numbers of clergymen moved to the state and directed most religious efforts. Women would not have as much influence and power as they had had in the early years of the century.

For the early years of the century there can be no doubt, the leaders in both Catholic and Protestant churches were the laity, especially the female laity. They kept the faith and maintained and spread Christianity. Women were both the leaders and the members. They were submissive but also assertive. Church officials realized the significant leadership of women, but they preferred to speak of them, not as leaders, but as "helpers in the gospel."

Notes for "'Helpers in the Gospel:' Woman and Religion in Louisiana, 1800-1830"

[1] Jon Butler, "The Future of American Religious History: Prospectus, Agenda, Transatlantic *Problematique*," *William and Mary Quarterly*, 3d ser., 42 (1985): 167-83.

[2] Recent collections of essays include: Samuel S. Hill, ed., *Varieties of Southern Religious Experience* (Baton Rouge, 1988); and Charles Reagan Wilson, ed., *Religion in the South* (Jackson, 1985).

[3] Sally McMillen, *Black and White Women in the Old South* (New York, 1991). Jean E. Friedman, in *The Enclosed Garden: Women and Community in Evangelical South, 1830-1900* (Chapel Hill, N. C., 1985) discusses the later antebellum period and does not include Louisiana. Joan E. Cashin, ed., *Our Common Affairs: Texts from Women in the Old South* (Baltimore, 1996), 27. Even Louisiana historians neglect women of the antebellum period. For example, see Glenn R. Conrad, ed., *Cross Crozier and Crucible: A Volume Celebrating the Bicentennial of a Catholic Diocese in Louisiana* (Lafayette, La., 1993), a generally good collection of essays on various aspects of Catholic experience in Louisiana, but weak on lay women.

[4] Barbara Welter, "The Feminization of American Religion," in Barbara Welter, ed., *Dimity Convictions: The American Women in the Nineteenth Century* (Athens, Oh., 1976), 102.

[5] Thomas W. Spalding, C. F. X., "Frontier Catholicism," *Catholic Historical Review*, 77 (1991): 477.

[6] Janet Wilson James, "Women in American Religious History: An Overview," in Janet Wilson James, ed., *Women in American Religion* (Philadelphia, 1980), 2. Wilson writes that "women are the members, men lead."

[7] The women examined in this essay are, for the most part, white women of European background. Of course, many of the newcomers were not official members of any Protestant denomination.

[8] This spirit of anticlericalism is still prevalent in many parts of south Louisiana today. Protestants are often mystified by persons who are devout, but anticlerical. See Carl A. Brasseaux, *Acadian to Cajun: Transformation of a People 1803-1877* (Jackson, Miss., 1992) for a good discussion of nineteenth-century Acadian attitudes toward the official Catholic Church.

[9] John Tracy Ellis, *Catholics in Colonial America* (Baltimore, 1965), 301-2. Ellis points out that Americans were not to blame for the state of affairs in Louisiana as the practice of religion had been neglected before they began to arrive.

[10] *Notice sur l'état actuel de la mission de la Louisiane* (Paris, 1820), 24.

[11] Roger Baudier, *The Catholic Church in Louisiana* (New Orleans, 1939), 292.

[12] Bishop DuBourg to Cardinal A. Dugnani, Pro-Perfect of Propaganda, April 11, 1816, "Correspondence of Bishop DuBourg with Propaganda," *St. Louis Catholic Historical Review*, 1 (1918): 139. Bishop DuBourg was probably too pessimistic about Louisiana Catholics. Many of them did not hide the fact that they disliked him and apparently he disliked them in return and was happy when he could leave the United States and head a diocese in France.

[13] Baudier, *Catholic Church in Louisiana*, 266-7, and M. Anduze, apostolic missionary, to "M," written ca. 1825, published in *Annales de la propagation de la Foi . . .* (Lyon, 1829), 506. The reader should realize that south Louisiana is still considered as mission territory by some in the Catholic Church today.

[14]M. Blanc, missionary, Natchitoches, to "M," August 21, 1827, *Annales*, 510-1.

[15]Thomas H. Clancy, "The Antebellum Jesuits of the New Orleans Province, 1837-1861," *Louisiana History*, 34 (1993): 327-43.

[16]Baudier, *Catholic Church*, 291-2. C. C. Robin, *Voyage to Louisiana, 1803-1805*, trans. Stuart Landry, Jr. (New Orleans, 1966), 216.

[17]John F. Watson, "Notitia of Incidents at New Orleans in 1804 and 1805," *The American Pioneer*, 2 (May 1843): 230, and Benjamin Henry Latrobe, *Impressions Respecting New Orleans: Diary and Sketches 1818-1820*, ed. by Samuel Wilson, Jr. (New York, 1951), 114, 122. Barbara Welter, see note 4, writing of the feminization of religion, comments on the rather severe New England churches. Long before the nineteenth-century the rituals and ceremonies in Catholic parishes of Southern European backgrounds were full of more "flounces" than any New Englander, male or female, could have invented.

[18]Ron Bodin, "The Cajun Woman as Unofficial Deacon of the Sacraments and Priest of the Sacramentals in Rural Louisiana, 1800-1930," *Attakapas Gazette*, 25 (1990), 2-13. Bodin's evidence for this period seems rather scanty. He did interview many rural women who remembered women who baptized babies in the late nineteenth-century. Such a woman was called an "andoyée."

[19]M. Anduze, apostolic missionary, to "M," written ca. 1825, published in *Annales de la Propagation de la Foi . . .* (Lyon, 1829), 508 and Baudier, *Catholic Church*, 182.

[20]Roger Baudier, *The Catholic Church in North Louisiana: A Historical Sketch of Pioneer Days and of the Diocese of Natchitoches and Its Successor Diocese of Alexandria* (s.l., 1953), 18, and Baudier, *Catholic Church*, 318. Angela Boswell, "The Meaning of Participation: White Protestant Women in Antebellum Houston Churches," *Southwestern Historical Quarterly*, 99 (1995): 27-47, points out that raising money gave women a certain amount of control and they would assert a certain amount of independence. Furthermore, in Louisiana women controlled their separate property, so a woman like Mlle. Crichet could provide funds for a chapel without the permission of any man.

[21]*New Orleans Louisiana Courier*, November 2, 1826. The day after All Saints' Day is called All Souls' Day, a day when other American Catholics pray for their dead friends and relatives, who might still be in purgatory. In south Louisiana Catholics pray for their dead, but go to the cemeteries on All Saints' Day. Apparently, some assume that the deceased are already saints.

[22]DuBourg to Father P. Borga, February 27, 1823, *DuBourg Correspondence*, 2 (1920): 126.

[23]Letter of Father Olivier to Bishop John Carroll, February 28, 1807, cited in Annabelle M. Melville, *Louis William DuBourg: Bishop of Louisiana and the Floridas, Bishop of Montauban, and Archbishop of Besançon, 1766-1833*, 2 vols. (Chicago, 1986).

[24]Father Martial to his friend, M. Billaud, at the French embassy in Rome, *Bishop DuBourg Correspondence*, 2 (1920): 111-2, fn.5. Also see Charles Edwards O'Neill, S. J., "'A Quarter Marked by Sundry Peculiarities': New Orleans, Lay Trustees, and Père Antoine," in *Catholic Historical Review*, 76 (1990): 235-77. Martial was shocked by Antoine's lenient attitudes. O'Neill shows that the evidence against Antoine was mostly malicious gossip and that Antoine did not do anything that was in violation of his authority.

[25]For a general survey of the work of religious women in the antebellum South see Sister Frances Jerome Woods, C. D. P., "Congregations of Religious Women in the Old South," in Randall Miller, ed., *Catholics in the Old South: Essays on Church and Culture* (Macon, Georgia, 1983).

[26]Bishop DuBourg seems to have the dubious distinction of being the only bishop in America who helped to drive two superiors of religious orders to sainthood, partly by his treatment of them. The two are St. Elizabeth Seton, whose order he advised in Maryland and St. Philippine Duchesne, whom he advised in Missouri and Louisiana. Jay P. Dolan, *The American Catholic Experience* (Notre Dame, 1992), suggests that Elizabeth Seton deserved sainthood for her treatment by the French priests in Maryland, of whom DuBourg was one. The

reader of DuBourg's biography finds that he caused Phillipine Duchesne much anguish also. Most of the difficulties involved money. The nuns had more practical financial sense and DuBourg had a rather whimsical nature.

[27]Louise Callan, *Society of the Sacred Heart of North America* (New York, 1937), 188, 151-2.

[28]Baudier, *Catholic Church*, 250-1; B. Lafon, *Annuaire Louisianais* (New Orleans, 1808), 193. Lafon listed the original residences of all Ursuline nuns.

[29]"Ursuline Nuns to President Thomas Jefferson," April 23, 1804, in Clarence E. Carter, ed., *The Territory of Orleans, 1803-1812* (Washington, D. C., 1940), 231.

[30]W. C. C. Claiborne to James Madison, April 10, 1804, U. S. Department of State *Territorial Papers, Orleans Series, 1764-1813; Official Letter Books of William Charles Cole Claiborne*, Dunbar Rowland, ed., 6 vols. (Jackson, Miss., 1917), 2:203, 6:108, 4:324, 3:84-5 and 344-5. After his little admonition about First Amendment rights he did arrange with the mayor to close the play.

[31]Louise Callan, *Society*, Letter of Mother Barat to Mother Duchesne, Spring 1830, 175.

[32]Estwick Evans, "A Pedestrious Tour . . . during the Winter and Spring of 1818," in *Early Western Travels*, ed., by R. G. Thwaites, 32 vols. (Cleveland, 1904-1907), 8:341-2.

[33]*New Orleans Argus*, September 15, 1826. "Friend" wrote that he was not Catholic, but his letter, printed in both French and English sounds like it was written by a Catholic. The column, *Feuilleton: Chronique du Tems*, featured in the New Orleans *Louisiana Gazette* from 1819 to 1823, was written by Alexis Daudet. *New Orleans Louisiana Gazette*, November 19, 1819, and March 7, 1820.

[34]Within a few years other orders of sisters opened schools for daughters of small farmers and city people. A certain amount of tension existed between religious orders such as the Mt. Carmel Sisters and the Religious of the Sacred Heart. See Charles E. Nolan, *Bayou Carmel: The Sisters of Mount Carmel of Louisiana. 1833-1903* (Kenner, La., 1977), 31, citing a Mt. Carmel superior who pointed out that her order at Vermilionville was trying to educate girls to become good Catholic mothers and that those who wanted music and dancing could go to the nearby Sacred Heart convent.

[35]John G. Jones, *A Complete History of Methodism as Connected with the Mississippi Conference of the Methodist Episcopal Church South*, 2 vols. (1887 and 1908, reprint ed., Baton Rouge, 1966), 1:331.

[36]Naturally the local French and Acadians were also Americans, but the term was/is often used for those who had come from other parts of the United States.

[37]Glen Lee Greene, *House Upon a Rock: About Southern Baptists in Louisiana* (Alexandria, La., 1973), 80.

[38]Seth Lewis, Eq., Opelousas, to Rev. Robert E. Roberts, a bishop of the Methodist Episcopal Church, September 24, 1818, *The Methodist Review*, 111 (1820): 153; and D. W. Harris and B. M. Hulse, *The History of Claiborne Parish, Louisiana* (New Orleans, 1886), 48.

[39]James Pearse, *A Narrative of the Life of James Pearse* (1825, reprint ed., Chicago, 1962), 73; Mills and Smith Report, 29; Rev. Elisha Bowman, New Orleans, to Rev. William Burke, Lexington, Kentucky, January 29, 1806, quoted in John G. Jones, *History of Methodism*, 1:150-1.

[40]Rev. Randalson, St. Francisville, to the corresponding secretary of the American Baptist Mission, June 29, 1819, published in *The American Baptist Magazine and Missionary Intelligencer* (1820): 249-51. The Florida Parishes, east of the Mississippi river, were part of the Spanish West Florida until Americans took them in 1810. There was a large English-speaking population in the area from the eighteenth-century.

[41]Hephzibah Church Record Books, November 29, 1813, Louisiana and Lower Mississippi Valley Collection, Louisiana State University, Baton Rouge, La., hereafter cited as LSU Archives.

[42]Jones, *History of Methodism*, 1:445-6 and 331-2.

[43]Ann Butler, near St. Francisville, to Mrs. Margaret Duncan, Ellis's Ferry, Mississippi Territory, October, 1815, Ellis-Farar Family Papers, LSU Archives.

[44]Seth Lewis Letter, *Methodist Review*; Glen Lee Greene, *A History of the Baptists of Oak Ridge, Louisiana, 1797-1960* (Nashville, 1960), 65-6, 76; Jones, *History of Methodism*, 2:111-2 and Mary Hutchinson, Jackson, Louisiana, to her brother, John Gurley, Washington, D. C., November 1836, Gurley Family Papers, Manuscript Division, Howard-Tilton Memorial Library, Tulane University, New Orleans, La. Hereafter cited as Manuscripts Division, Tulane.

[45]W. E. Paxton, *A History of the Baptists of Louisiana* (St. Louis, 1888), 147; Jones, *History of Methodism*, 2:35 and Vivian Herbert Swent, *Antioch Primitive Baptist Church, Big Wood Louisiana* (San Francisco, 1966), 1.

[46]S. J. Mills and Daniel Smith, *Report of a Missionary Tour* (Andover, Mass., 1815), 29; Ruth Robertson Fontenot, Sue Eakin and Mary Alice Sideny, "Some History of St. Landry Parish from the 1690s," Special supplement to the *Daily World* (Opelousas), November 3, 1955, 30; and Timothy Flint, *Recollections of the Past Ten Years* (Boston, 1826), 340.

[47]Richard Warner, Washington Parish, to Rev. John P. Haney, February 5, 1826, describing his sister's aid in his conversion, in Jones, *History of Methodism*, 1:vi-viii.

[48]*Baton Rouge Gazette*, May 19, 1827 and letter from "A New Orleans Lady" in the *American School Sunday Magazine*, May 1826, 136; and James A. Padgett, ed., "A Yankee School Teacher in Lousiana, 1835-1837: The Diary of Caroline B. Poole," *Louisiana Historical Ouarterly*, 20 (July 1937): 659-60.

[49]Jones, *History of Methodism*, 1:335.

[50]Melville, *DuBourg*, 1:264. Archbishop John Carroll to Louis William DuBourg, September 1, 1812.

[51]Andrew Oehler, *The Life, Adventures, and Unparalleled Sufferings of Andrew Oehler* (Trenton, 1811), 186.

[52]Daniel DeVinne, St. Martinville, to Rev. T. Mason, Corresponding Secretary of the Missionary and Bible Society of the Methodist Episcopal Church, December 24, 1819, *The Methodist Review*, 3 (1820): 76.

[53]John F. Schermerhorn and Samuel J. Mills, *A Correct View of that Part of the United States . . . West of the Allegheny Mountains, with Regard to Religion and Morals* (Hartford, 1814), 30, 34. Bibles were always available at New Orleans booksellers and advertisements like the following were not uncommon, *Le Moniteur*, 29 January 1803, "Un assortiment de livres de piétie, tels que Bible. . . ."

[54]Jon Butler, *Awash in a Sea of Faith: Christianizing the American People* (Cambridge, Mass., 1990), 279-80.

[55]"A Stranger" asked in the *New Orleans Louisiana Advertiser*, June 12, 1826, "will it not be more tolerable for Sodom in the day of judgment than for you?"

[56][Mrs. Rebecca Burlend], *A True Picture of Emigration . . . in the Year 1831* (London, 1848), 15; and Joseph Holt Ingraham, *The South-West by a Yankee*, 2 vols. (New York, 1835) 1:219-20.

[57]Dolan, *The American Catholic Experience*, 119; and DuBourg, *Correspondence*, Letter to the Cardinal Prefect of Propaganda, April 20, 1820.

[58]Letter from John Carroll to DuBourg, September 1, 1812, Melville, *Louis William DuBourg*, 1:263-4.

[59]Niles' *Weekly Register*, April 22, 1826, 143.

[60]Louisiana, House Journal,, 3rd Leg., 1st Sess., January 21, 1817, 44 and *New Orleans Louisiana Courier*, February 13, 1824.

[61]Donald G. Matthews, *Religion in the Old South* (Chicago, 1977), 110; and Friedman, *Enclosed Garden*, 19.

[62]Poydras Home Collection, Minutes Book, 1817-1823, second annual report on January 16, 1819, Manuscripts Division, Tulane; and Louisiana, Acts, 6th Leg., 2nd Sess., April 10, 1824, 156.

⁶³Louisiana, Senate Journal, 9th Leg., 1st Sess., December 11, 1928, 27.

⁶⁴Poydras Home Collection, March 4, 1820.

⁶⁵Ibid., Minutes of the Meeting, February 17, 1825; and Flint, *Past Ten Years*, 305. Most likely the Boston women would not have allowed Catholics in their group.

⁶⁶Baudier, *Catholic Church*, 316.

⁶⁷Louisiana, Acts, 5th Leg., 2nd Sess., March 23, 1822, 102-4.

HETERODOX NEW ORLEANS AND THE
PROTESTANT SOUTH, 1800-1861[*]

Timothy F. Reilly

To the antebellum traveler, the dominant theme of New Orleanian life was its exotic contrasts to the rests of America. In the late summer of 1831, Capt. James Edward Alexander, British soldier and journalist, toured New Orleans and concluded that its social panorama was "altogether *sui generis*" in the context of American life.[1] In other words, the Southern metropolis and its institutions formed a cultural mélange which was unique and perhaps unclassifiable.

Previous visitors had emphasized the city's numerous idiosyncrasies, but few had gauged New Orleans as succinctly as young Alexander. The term *sui generis* quickly became axiomatic. Soon afterward, the traveling Irish actor Tyrone Power applied the maxim in his description of New Orleans:

> The day of my first arrival at this capital of many waters, this city *sui generis*, was one to which I had looked forward with much impatience and highly-aroused expectations. . . .[2]

Implicit in Captain Alexander's earlier pronouncement was his awareness that New Orleans contained an indecipherable mingling of different civilizations. By casual design or willful insistence, New Orleans' heterogeneous population gradually modified ethnic differences in language and temperament, formulated peculiar racial adjustments, demarcated neighborhood boundaries, and pried open new realms of social endeavor. The resultant changes deeply affected the character and tone of New Orleans society—it had no close counterpart within the radius of its Southern hinterland, which stretched from the Potomac and Ohio Valleys to the Mexican border.[3]

Cultural compromise continued as a major theme of New Orleans' life under both the French and Spanish colonial regimes in the eighteenth century, as well as in the early period of American incorporation. Even after the War of 1812, the city continued to improvise its own social patterns and arbitrate cultural differences *vis-à-vis* Southern sec-

*First published in *Louisiana Studies*, 12 (1973): 533-51. Reprinted with the kind permission of the author and publisher.

tionalism, an expanding force which was largely antithetical to New Orleans' traditional outlook.

Several antebellum visitors attempted to characterize the Crescent City's cultural distinctiveness by focusing on its peculiar religious standards and the idiosyncrasies of individual clergymen. Frequent indictments of local society hinged on the alleged profanation of the Sabbath, religious indifference, excessive liberalism among churchmen, spiritual ignorance among the laity, widespread intemperance, sexual promiscuity and racial amalgamation, and ministerial hypocrisy on the issue of slavery.

Some observers cast jaundiced eyes on the excessive fraternization between Catholics and Protestants, while others detected a distinctly un-American cultural component which was being perpetuated by a continual flood of European immigrants. Adding to the gloom was the city's role as the South's principal slave mart. Here, the most pathetic and brutalizing features of Southern thralldom were said to have taken place daily upon the public auction blocks. To an outsider, the total picture often provoked the open or implicit response that Christianity had somehow failed in New Orleans.[4]

Toward the close of the War of 1812, Samuel Mills and John Schermerhorn, Presbyterian ministers from New England, published detailed accounts of New Orleans' religious life after a tour through the Southwest. Both men noted that while life in the city possessed "many respectable families," as a whole, it was riddled with corruption and irreligion. Mills, in particular, complained of Catholic and Protestant ineffectiveness in coping with the evils of intemperance, unbridled materialism, and sloth.[5] Schermerhorn was especially critical of Catholicism's influence in the area:

> The state of society in this country [Louisiana] is very deplorable. The people are entirely ignorant of divine things, and have been taught only to attend mass, and count their beads. They are without schools, and of the French inhabitants, not one in ten can read. . . .[6]

In 1818, Estwick Evans, another New England visitor, lamented that the city's French population stubbornly resisted the "habits and modes of living" of the frontier American.[7] However, Evans managed to educe the beginnings of a cultural hybridization under the promising auspices of the city's New England immigrants:

> I am happy in being able to say that New-Orleans is much less corrupt, in many particulars, than it used to be. The American population there is rapidly increasing; and New-England customs, manners and habits, are there gaining ground. This population will, no doubt, be contaminated; but it is sincerely hoped that there will be a balance in favour of morality. . . .[8]

Between Captain Alexander's 1831 visit and the Civil War, New Orleans achieved recognition as the South's leading commercial emporium and its most cosmopolitan city. Within that time, many inquiring journalists continued to describe local religious life as being in a deplorable condition. However, some of the religious portrayals emphasized the more charming and admirable features of city church life.

Thomas Hamilton and Frederika Bremer, for example, were among those who praised religious qualities which were altogether lacking in other parts of the country. Hamilton was deeply impressed by the Catholic slave population's active participation in regular church services; Frederika Bremer once visited a local congregation of Negro Protestants and found a religious style and intensity totally new to her.[9] Indeed, Miss Bremer expressed the hope that the "children of Africa" would some day invigorate a stale Christianity with their joyful enthusiasm:

> How many there are, even in our cold North, who in their youthful years have felt an Africa of religious life, and who might have produced glorious flowers and fruits if it only could have existed—if it had not been smothered by the snow and the gray coldness of conventionality—had not been imprisoned in the stone church of custom.[10]

The more critical observers were usually traveling ministers such as the Rev. George Lewis of the Free Church of Scotland, the Rev. Benjamin Whipple, and the Rev. Ebenezer Davies of British Guiana. The accounts written by Lewis and Whipple were rather typical in their condemnation of local gambling, Sunday frolicking, drinking, hooliganism, and dandyism. Whipple termed New Orleans "the grand reservoir of the West," where everything that was bizarre and extreme converged. New Orleans was "the hottest, the dirtiest, the most sickly, and at times the most healthy, the busiest, and the most dull, the most wicked and the most orderly [of cities]."[11] Lewis' summary impression of the city was in consonance with his revulsion against the Mississippi River, which he described as "the scavenger river of the New World," a natural habitat for creatures "that love the swamp, and ooze, and slime."[12]

On the other hand, Davies' analysis of local religion was perhaps the most intimate and detailed report ever written by an antebellum outsider. As a "British abolitionist" and former missionary to British Guiana, Davies traveled to New Orleans in 1848 and spent two weeks documenting the moral efficacy of the city's Protestant clergy and laity.[13]

Davies, who was a Presbyterian, reported that in a city of 90,000 inhabitants, there were close to thirty Protestant ministers preaching the gospel in "the metropolis of a great slave country—a town in which exist many depots for the disposal of human beings."[14] Although Davies was sickened and dismayed by New Orleans' slave regime, he discovered a greater degree of flexibility within the city's religious sphere than he had anticipated.

As he conducted his investigation, Davies found opinion divided on the problems of slavery, Sabbath-observance, moral conduct, and Negro participation in local religious life. He blamed the city's social and moral ills on the growing influence of the Anglo-Saxon, and he lamented the waning impact of the older Creole civilization, whose people and institutions he characterized as more humanitarian and constructive. "The Southerners," according to Davies, "seem to have no heart—no feeling, except that of love to the almighty dollar."[15]

Ironically, the culture of the South appeared locally more dominant to Davies than the "New England customs, manners and habits" that Estwick Evans had discerned thirty years before. Actually, both men oversimplified the social chemistry of New Orleans. New England ways and Southern dictums were peripheral elements in a population which was neither northeastern nor Southern in identity and allegiance.

Out to necessity, New Orleans had become an arena of social compromise. The city's "Southern" position was more geographic than substantive, and the bases for its exotic character were more often the result of European influences than American penetration. The failure of the city to conform to any clear-cut Southern, Northern, or even western sectional pattern perplexed many a traveler as he compiled his descriptive notes.

Estwick Evans, for example, closed his mind to any possible blending of the different cultures. Either Yankee virtues would triumph or Creole licentiousness would continue to permeate the city. Later on, Ebenezer Davies offered the opposing view that the vices of the unruly Anglo-Saxon were undermining the superior Creole culture. Neither visitor could perceive that perhaps a totally new society was in the making—distinctly separate from that of any other American municipality, North and South.

Captain Alexander's *sui generis* interpretation was far more applicable to the social riddles which confronted the antebellum writer and which, to this day, continue to intrigue the social historian. It is within this vein that both the Roman Catholic and Protestant spheres of antebellum New Orleans collaborated in developing a religious prototype which was, in itself, *sui generis*. Frequent references in both the contemporary traveler's account and testimony by individual residents gave initial emphasis to the singular character of the city's early religious life. Later, the long interim of war and Reconstruction, coupled with the exigencies of a new era, terminated the old religious pattern. It was not until much later that a renewed interest was focused on the city's early religious life.

In a broad context, several twentieth century historians have purposely or casually underscored New Orleans' unique commercial role and ethnic singularity within the Old South. However, little attempt has been made to explore the specific causes which led to a religious dichotomy between the Crescent City and the adjacent Cotton Kingdom. In addition, many of the city's most important exponents of religious individualism have been slighted or ignored through lack of readily available evidence. The real impact of New Orleans' religious leadership, both in an internal and external sense, has also been misgauged or superficially examined.

However, a handful of scholars in the 1930s established some invaluable leads and perceptive observations. In an embryonic study labeled "Origins of New England Protestantism in New Orleans," Julie Koch showed how early Protestant institutions in New Orleans were tempered by an established Catholicism. Strange as it may seem, the city's Protestant inhabitants were not above emulating the older church's European formalism and parochial conceit.[16]

Shortly after the appearance of the Koch thesis, Lewis Newton contributed another article which emphasized the city's moral and religious insularity within the framework of the Old South. Newton maintained that "common economic interests tended to breed a spirit of tolerance in both Protestant and Catholic," and that the "foreign attachment" of the Roman Catholic Church slowed down the process of acculturation.[17] Somewhat later, John K. Bettersworth published a third article which focused on the rather pronounced intellectual independence of some of the city's Protestant clergymen. Like Koch, Bettersworth held that a détente between the Catholic and Protestant residents gradually produced a local ecumenism which had no parallel in the rest of the country.[18]

While the overall interpretations presented by each of these writers were laced with significant evidence and illuminating commentary, several aspects of the city's religious nonconformity were not examined. For example, the three articles provided only quick glimpses of popular clerical leaders who were instrumental in formulating New Orleans' distinctive religious setting. Other individuals, particularly those in the fundamentalist sector, were shunted aside as irrelevant or unimportant. Several religious-connected issues which prompted denominational and community-wide disturbances were also ignored.

Most importantly, the problem of slavery and its effects upon the city's religious culture were thrust into the background and only weakly projected into each of these essays. Since the inexorable spread of Southern religious orthodoxy was ultimately successful in bringing about New Orleanian acquiescence of religious liberalism in a slave society incorporate the major characters' sentiments and activities in regard to the "peculiar institution."

Aside from the specific contributions of the previously mentioned authors, other scholars have indirectly embellished the theme of religious liberalism by closely focusing on major sub-topics of New Orleanian life. Robert C. Reinders has published separate articles on different phases of Roman Catholic and Negro culture; Clarence Gohdes' classic review of Southern Unitarianism includes a brief sketch of New Orleans' contributions to the history of religious liberalism and its ranking among other Southern cities in the realms of social criticism and theological pathfinding.[19]

Other writers have concentrated on the social and economic distinctiveness of antebellum New Orleans, while commenting obliquely on the city's religious development. Joseph G. Tregle's "Early New Orleans Society: A Reappraisal," constitutes something of a landmark in this research area. Later articles by Reinders, W. W. Chenault, and John G. Clark offer additional insights into the city's singular business regimen and its ethnic accommodation.[20] In the same historiographic channel, authors Clement Eaton and Ulrich B. Phillips have briefly defined Creole Louisiana's cultural divergence from Southern civilization.[21] And standing in a class by itself, a concise study by H. W. Gilmore shows how the uniqueness of New Orleans' physical environment helped to create the city's peculiar growth pattern and ethnic hodge-podge during colonial, antebellum, and post-bellum periods.[22]

Any attempt to characterize the religious individualism of antebellum New Orleans must include the larger backdrop of Southern religious life as a whole. A prominent scholar of Southern history, Francis Butler Simkins, has observed that of all the institutions of the Old South, a peculiar religion gave the section its strongest bond of unity. Ultimately, Southern Protestantism played a crucial role in reinforcing the pro-slavery argument. By 1861, the large majority of the South's religious leaders had given their blessing to the cause of Southern nationalism and formal secession. As Simkins puts it,

> The distinctiveness of the Old South is perhaps best illustrated by its religion. Historic Protestantism was reduced to the consistencies of the Southern environment without sacrificing inherent fundamentals. Religious revivals lifted the common people out of frontier indifference to religion. The discipline of the church schools held Southerners of both races in the Christian communions. The Southern mind, which at the beginning of the nineteenth century had been under the influence of liberal deists, was captured for the orthodoxies by an aggressive group of theologians. Both church- and state-controlled colleges were dedicated to the "old-time religion." These changes prepared the way for the complete reconciliation between slavery and the Southern churches, for the breaking of ties with the antislavery churches of the North, and for their use among the Negroes of the bondage of the soul as a means of making more secure the bondage of the body. . . .[23]

The religious mind of the Old South underwent a divergent evolution from that of the Northern states between 1800 and 1860. While the religion of New England refashioned its theology by substituting rationalism in place of scriptural revelation, religious thought in the South shook off the last vestiges of deism and embraced a fundamentalist orthodoxy which disliked reason, introspection, and secularization. To the Southerner, the logical empiricism of a Ralph Waldo Emerson or a William Ellery Channing merely complicated a concept of the supernatural, which, in itself, was inexplicable to mortal man. Emotional intensity, rather than intellectual jousting, served as the connective bond between the Southerner and his God.[24]

In New Orleans, however, an opposing religious structure traditionally resisted the rising tide of religious conformity in the surrounding Southland. The city's religious heritage was Roman Catholic rather than Protestant. Its leading population component was Latin rather than Anglo-Saxon. And the city's colonial status and frontier isolation had induced a religious attitude which was decidedly liberal rather than narrowly conservative.

Finally, the religious leadership of the South sought to consecrate the institution of slavery as an integral part of the cultural landscape and Jehovah's law. Negro bondage was not the creation of Southern economics; it was said to be a social responsibility ordained by the Creator for the mutual benefit of two races, both of them bound to the Southern soil. Slavery was God's inscrutable instrument delivered into the temporal hands of the slaveholder, who was an intermediary in a Divine pattern. On the eve of the Civil War, pro-slavery arguments had finished cementing the South's religious orthodoxy, and the clergy, with few exceptions, had become the prime comforter of the Southern conscience. So deep was the pro-slavery certitude that the outspoken clergy was successful in severing formal religious ties with the Northern community.[25]

The overpowering effect of Southern religious orthodoxy, particularly in regard to slavery, was also victorious in snuffing out the last effective traces of liberalism in New Orleans. However, the city's dominant role in antebellum religious life had posed a separate identity for decades. New Orleans' established Protestantism had incorporated the formalism and decorous restraint of resident Catholicism into its philosophy and ritual. An upper-class of merchant-planters composed an urban aristocracy which was highly conscious of the proper social tone for a city which aspired to be known as a first-rate metropolis, supreme in its region and equal of all other community capitals.

Besides the city's characteristic religious style and diversity, a strong thread of tolerance created a comfortable environment for the Protestant, the Catholic, and even the Jew. New Orleans existed as a trade depot, and social antagonism in the form of religious militancy or persecution would have disrupted the routine of the countinghouse and besieged the most sacred of commercial alliances. The society was neither emotionally religious nor intellectually meditative. For the most part, religious life in New Orleans was molded to coincide with commercial priorities and the social amenities.

Those who attempted to change this superficial religious cast often proved to be unpopular. The radical evangelist, the rock-ribbed Calvinist, the Northern abolitionist, and the Southern stalwart were often forced to modify their religious attitude and style. While evangelical insurgence was never successful in converting large numbers of the city's white inhabitants, it deeply affected the black population and even adopted an intellectualism in its attempt to reach white residents. The Calvinist from New England sometimes found himself questioning iron-clad principles as a result of his experiences in the New Orleanian environment. Surprisingly, anti-slavery sentiment was not absent from the city's religious milieu, nor was it altogether a dormant feature among individual clergymen. Out of habit and practical benefit, New Orleans continually resisted a religious orthodoxy which had enveloped most of the South by 1830 and later demanded widespread submission to the South's social order.[26]

The essential incongruity of New Orleans' religious individualism *vis-à-vis* the accepted religion of the Old South demonstrated that the city was far from being a malleable adjunct to a plantation slavocracy which demanded institutional conformity and intellectual subservience. What were the peculiar social forces inside New Orleans which produced a religious separatism in style and philosophy? Why were so many of the city's religious leaders involved in disputes over church administration, theological belief, and regional differences? How did some of these divines command loyalty from their lay communicants while others reaped contempt or apathy? Most importantly, why was Southernism so late in capturing the religious mind of New Orleans?

The separate development of the city's religious institutions and the distinctive character of many of its religious leaders were the outgrowth of four basic factors, each of which exerted a decisive influence in differentiating New Orleans from a purely Southern

culture. Previous historians have emphasized one or more of these factors in their attempts to define New Orleanian singularity, but none has applied them to the city's religious sector. Throughout the antebellum era, each factor played a circuitous role in filter-
ing "alien" religious thought as it drifted into the city.

Of foremost significance was the city's Creole origin. The eighteenth century Latin
foundation molded an opposing cultural tradition in religious persuasion, as well as a
language and ethnic identification. Before the American purchase of Louisiana in 1803,
the French and Spanish colonial regimes had produced a relatively mature, albeit unpol-
ished, society at the foot of the Mississippi valley.[27] For almost a century, the Creole's
distinctive Catholicism had been relatively untouched by hierarchical discipline or Protestant competition.

However, the gradual emergence of a second factor tended to complicate Catholic
religious life. During the early half of the nineteenth century, Creole Catholicism was
inundated by large numbers of Irish, German, and French immigrants whose conservative
Catholicism frequently challenged old Creole traditions. Concomitantly, the influx of
Catholic immigrants further impeded New Orleans' swift adaptation of the Southern religious norm. While the admixture of Irish and German Catholics created a religious
enclave somewhat similar to those found in many Northeastern cities, the established
Creole religion often became overly reactionary in defending its customary prerogatives
in an Anglo-American world.

A third factor which tended to insulate New Orleans from the Southern religious
culture was the city's unusual geographic situation in relation to the Southern interior.
From its infancy as a French colonial trading post to its growth under American auspices,
New Orleans was in many ways an independent focal point of the sparsely inhabited
southwestern frontier. Before and after American annexation, the frontier expanse not
only acted as a cultural buffer, it helped to promote a diversity of social and religious
interests. It also prolonged the period of Creole and Catholic hegemony.[28]

As a somewhat exotic and ready-made metropolis shrouded by the piney woods and
cypress bogs of the Old Southwest, New Orleans could often exercise its cultural prerogatives over the Anglo-Saxon frontiersman and farmer. Incoming settlers from the
Ohio Valley region and the south Atlantic realm did not quickly revolutionize the cultural
outlook of their French-speaking hosts. Instead, the wayfaring Kentuckian and Georgia-
born merchant were often forced to re-fabricate their social and religious outlook as they
adapted to their strange new environment.[29]

Only after the War of 1812 did large-scale immigration and Americanization bring
an end to undisputed Creole hegemony. Throughout its golden age of river commerce—
roughly from 1815 to 1840—New Orleans still maintained a cultural distinctiveness and
mastery which transcended that of the nearby cotton lands. As a commercial entrepot at
the lower end of the Mississippi basin, the city owed more to the river's north-south trade
dimension than it did to Southern civilization's westward trek across the Gulf-Atlantic
coastal plain.[30] The city's easy access to the trans-Appalachian heartland, coupled with

an economic primacy, attracted the flexible westerner more often than it beckoned the Tidewater aristocrat. And in its relationship with the widely-spaced coastal and interior cities of the South, New Orleans was unrivaled in its attraction of a wide variety of entrepreneurial activities.

Likewise, the more adventurous among the frontier gospelers were apt to follow their acquisitive brethren into the city in the hope of indoctrinating a prestigious citizenry and establishing a regional base of operations. Isolated from the agrarian and sectional dictums of the Southern religious culture beyond the city, the missionary-evangelist was often compelled to change his approach and outlook after reflecting on his minority status.

The final component which effectively delineated New Orleanian religion from the mainstream of Southern orthodoxy was the city's large population of transplanted northeasterners. From the American Revolution to the War with Mexico, New Orleans' reputation as a burgeoning trading center attracted hundreds of ambitious speculators from New England, New York, and Pennsylvania. The Northern-born community casually or intentionally propagated Yankee virtues in a sultry commercial mart bereft of "true Christianity" and a coherently American identity.

Above the Creole-infested *vieux carré*, the energetic Yankee helped to build what later became known as the Second Municipality—a later version of Puritan innovation and adaptation at the continent's lower threshold. It may not have been ideally "a city upon a hill," in the context of Massachusetts Bay, but the American district prospered rapidly, and it gradually eclipsed the older part of town in directing New Orleans' growth and economic character. In terms of religious innovation, however, Northeastern Calvinism was forced to modify its original precepts in accordance with the established religious order.[31]

A Creole heritage and a permanent cultural liaison with Europe, coupled with a potent strain of northeastern business and intellectual acumen helped to form a bizarre cultural milieu in the early decades of the nineteenth century. Protected from the South's cultural center of gravity by a wide expanse of underdeveloped frontier, New Orleans' motley population maintained its socio-religious divisions or improvised its own methods of cross-fertilization and acculturation whenever expedient. Later on, while the rest of the South bolstered its agrarian credos in defense of its peculiar order, New Orleans' non-Southern components helped to deflect the incoming tides of Southern nationalism. Among the more conspicuous members of the city's tenuous resistance movement were several religious leaders.

Each of these religious leaders was directly and indirectly engaged with the four factors which bifurcated New Orleanian religion from that of the interior Southern culture. Catholic clergymen were aligned either with the liberal Creole religious tradition or with the conservative Catholicism which emanated directly from Europe. The development of the Creole clergy had long been protected by the southwestern frontier; the influence of the latter clergy was, instead, hindered by the city's isolation. And while the liberal Creole usually enjoyed a peaceful relationship with the Protestant newcomer, the conservative Catholic sometimes found himself at odds with an over-arching and dominant Protestantism. By 1850, Protestant hegemony was an established fact, and the city's Roman Catholic population was outnumbered two to one.[32]

Traditionally, Catholicism in lower Louisiana had been content to remain on its small beachhead and indulge in a policy of amiable co-existence with Protestant latecomers.[33] However, New Orleanian Catholicism finally launched defensive countermeasures during the 1850s, when its Irish and German adherents were attacked by the city's factional variant of Know-Nothingism, a political force made up of hostile Anglo-Saxon and Creole elements. At the beginning of the American aegis, social controversies and criticism among Roman Catholics centered on the issues of religious home rule and clerical discipline. The principal antagonists in the internal church battle were Friar Antonio de Sedella, who sought to maintain local autonomy, and the conservative William Louis DuBourg, bishop of Louisiana. Later, the dispute reached its climax in a confrontation between Sedella's Creole followers and their foreign-born opponents, Bishop Antoine Blanc, editor-priest Napoleon Perche, and their lay allies.

Toward the close of the antebellum era, two important side issues gradually replaced the immanent clerical struggle. Public uncertainty concerning the problems of ethnic politics and sectional loyalty was partially focused on the local Church's role in society. In defense of the Catholic immigrant, Father Napoleon Perché seized the gauntlet thrown down by the American party and led the fight against a Southern-based nativism. And on the question of secession, Father Adrien Rouquette dared to challenge both his church superiors and the sectional yoke of Southernism.[34]

Social and religious controversy constituted an equally important theme within the Protestant mainstream of New Orleans. During its early development, the city's Episcopal Church was accused of pretentiously emulating Roman Catholic dogma and ritualism. Later, the conservative Episcopalians provoked a serious inter-denominational dispute in the city when one of their outspoken divines openly challenged the clerical legitimacy of rival Protestant leaders. The Church, itself, experienced internal dissension over the matter of liturgical reform. And near the close of the antebellum period, the social activism of New Orleans' most distinguished Episcopal leader, Bishop Leonidas K. Polk, betrayed a conscience which was not in harmony with Southern dictums on slavery and religious propriety.[35]

The leaders of the Presbyterian church, however, easily overshadowed the Episcopal clergy in the realm of religious nonconformity. For almost four decades after its founding in 1818, local Presbyterianism was represented by five of the most unorthodox ministers in Southern Christendom. Only one of these clergymen was a product of the southwestern frontier; the other four were natives of far-off New England. In its infancy, New Orleans' small Presbyterian congregation welcomed two of Yale and Princeton universities' brightest scholars, only to witness their gradual abandonment of Calvinist precepts and their perplexing detour along the path of Universalism. The first pastor, Sylvester

Larned, was lost in a violent epidemic of cholera; the second, Theodore Clapp, was forcibly expelled by his more conservative parishioners in 1832.

Two years later, the Presbyterian faithful shouldered the task of defending a third minister, the New England-born Joel Parker, against community-wide charges of abolitionism and scurrilous defamation of New Orleans' good name.[36] And in the following decades, local Presbyterians played host to Tennessee's William Scott, a religious leader whose dignity was rudely buffeted by a national political wrangling, and whose conscience was frayed by the slavery dilemma.[37] Almost concurrently, another clergyman appeared on the premises and engaged in a private war against the city and its social institutions. The Rev. Robert Livingston Stanton of Connecticut proved to be an abolitionist in sheep's clothing whose obscure career as a minister-sleuth may have been unexampled in the annals of anti-slavery reconnoitering. Stanton collected enough news and personal experiences in New Orleans to launch a career as a prominent reporter and analyst of Southern affairs. His role may have been more crucial than is generally recognized. During the Civil War, Stanton published a scholarly treatise in which he blamed the Southern clergy for the secession attempt while he served as an advisor to Pres. Abraham Lincoln.[38]

Indeed, not until 1856 did New Orleanian Presbyterians come under the leadership of a genuine representative of Southern religious orthodoxy—South Carolina's Benjamin Morgan Palmer. In a brief interval before the first cannon shot grazed Fort Sumter, Palmer managed to induce the proper behavioral standard among the parishioners—in other words, their acceptance of a doctrinal rigidity blended with a sectional chauvinism.[39]

Perhaps the New England presence proved the most enduring in the Universalist philosophy which regularly emanated from New Orleans' "Church of the Messiah." It was not the oldest Unitarian congregation in the antebellum South, but in all likelihood it was the largest and strongest garrison of theological liberalism below the Potomac.[40] In fact, New Orleanian Unitarianism enjoyed a rapid growth and popularity at a time when arguments over slavery and sectional loyalty were continually battering Unitarian assemblies in Charleston, Savannah, Augusta, and Mobile, as well as the few congregations which were struggling along in the Upper South.[41]

The Church's survival in New Orleans was primarily attributable to the careful diplomacy of Dr. Theodore Clapp. Transplanted from Massachusetts, Parson Clapp enjoyed a long residence in the city, marked by a close familiarity and social integration which were often lacking among radical Protestants in other cities. Between 1833 and 1856, Clapp's special rapport with the Roman Catholic clergy, his diligent efforts in helping the sick during frequent epidemics of cholera and yellow fever, and his rationalization of slavery all helped to assure him a physical permanence and celebrity status.[42]

"Clapp's Church," along with the French Opera and the American Theatre quickly became the renowned tripod which best reflected the novel spirit of New Orleanian culture. Like the stage actor, Clapp developed a communication with his audience based on a projected intimacy and histrionic flair. His widely publicized skill as a theological lecturer and essayist was a comforting reminder to the city's upperclass that New Orleans could perhaps match the religious intellectualism and cultural arrogance of a northeastern metropolis.

The recurrent controversies afflicting these four denominations of the city's societal mainstream molded the bases for New Orleans' unique religious character. The arbitration and adjustment which followed were attempts to fashion a middle ground for the diverse opinions within the whole community. However, it was the city's leadership—its clergy, rather than its laity—which produced the social conscience of New Orleans and questioned the role of the church in the society of the Old South.

In the piney woods above the city, the uneducated preacher was often the spiritual comforter of the countryside's modest yeomanry, and the "rough and tumble" of the revival camp meeting seldom attracted the enthusiastic support of the caste-conscious planter.[43] Likewise, the Bible-toting revivalist was often rebuffed when he entered New Orleans and introduced himself to a society of planter-merchants, particularly those who were unfamiliar with frontier customs and those who sought to dissociate themselves from rural folkways.

Among the ranks of white labor, a pervasive Roman Catholicism tended to deflect the currents of frontier fundamentalism. Out of sheer necessity, the evangelist relied on the support of the city's black population and its meager supply of transplanted country folk. In time, the spiritual needs of resident Negroes necessitated segregated churches under the partial supervision of a black ministry—a development which induced a greater degree of self-sufficiency and freedom among individual members.

Within the Methodist enclave, Southwestern evangelists William Winans, Benjamin Drake, and Holland N. McTyeire were exponents of a compromising fundamentalism which attempted to alter the city's religious character, but each refrained from introducing the characteristic style and dogmatism of the piney woods. Among the Baptists, the New York-born William Cecil Duncan espoused a theological liberalism and an anti-slavery philosophy which were completely unallied with rural orthodoxy, and which were even uncomfortable to the mainstream of New Orleans' clerical life.[44] And inside a collateral religious sphere, black evangelists such as Asa Goldsbury and Nelson Sanders succeeded in carving out flourishing pastorates under the capricious patronage of a white society. In New Orleans, each of these ministers attained a level of clerical independence and tutorial skill that rarely occurred in other parts of the South.[45]

Like a motley group of castaways swept ashore by storm or resolute impulse, this odd assortment of clergymen chose New Orleans as their social laboratory. There was little unity among them; each acted out his own independent role. Some of these individuals, such as Robert Stanton and Joel Parker, silently cursed their island of partial refuge as an unworthy and unpromising realm—ill-suited to the free expression of social criticism and a proper religious decorum. To both men, New Orleans was a rather gruesome workshop where one shuddered and tip-toed about as he compiled his shocking notes.

To Antonio de Sedella, New Orleans was a comfortable retreat, whose idyllic isolation and relative obscurity helped to ensure a close, personal contact with his communicants, and a minimum of interference from an inquisitive hierarchy. To men such as William DuBourg and Napoleon Perche, New Orleans was a crucial testing ground for the inculcation of a proper orthodoxy.

Other men, such as Theodore Clapp and William Duncan, saw New Orleans as an oasis of free speech in a slough of rising intolerance—a niche within the Southern perimeter where one could express his dissenting opinions without fear of the whip, the tar, or the rail. Perhaps these men were not always warmly received by the Orleanian public, but they were given a respectful hearing. A certain charitableness was manifest in the city's culture—the result of its characteristic diversity. And it was inside the city's religious sphere that this tradition of human kindness, this mannerism *sui generis*, reached its greatest range.

The nineteenth-century mind did not easily forget the cultural distinctiveness of New Orleanian society. More than twenty years after the end of the Civil War, the visiting Charles Dudley Warner re-examined those distinctive elements of the city's heritage which had so absorbed his antebellum predecessors. In gauging his own present age, the Northern writer's conclusion echoed those of his past:

> But whatever way we regard New Orleans, it is in its aspect, social tone, and character *sui generis*; its civilization differs widely from that of any other, and it remains one of the most interesting places in the republic. Of course social life in these days is much the same in all great cities in its observances, but that of New Orleans is markedly cordial, ingenuous, warm-hearted. I do not imagine that it could tolerate, as Boston does, absolute freedom of local opinion on all subjects, and undoubtedly it is sensitive to criticism; but I believe that it is literally true, as one of its citizens said, that it is still more sensitive to kindness.[46]

Notes for "Heterodox New Orleans and the Protestant South, 1800-1861"

[1]Capt. J. E. Alexander, *Transatlantic Sketches, Comprising Visits to the Most Interesting Scenes in North and South America, and the West Indies; With Notes on Negro Slavery and Canadian Emigration*, 2 vols. (London, 1833), 2:31.

[2]Tyrone Power, Esq., *Impressions of America, During the Years 1833, 1834, and 1835*, 2 vols. (London, 1836), 2:143.

[3]See Arthur Preston Whitaker, *The Mississippi Question, 1795-1803: A Study in Trade, Politics, and Diplomacy*, 2d ed. (Gloucester, Mass., 1962), 38-47; Edna F. Campbell, "New Orleans at the Time of the Louisiana Purchase," *Geographical Review*, 11 (1921): 414-25.

[4]See Thomas P. Harwood, "The Abolitionist Image of Louisiana and Mississippi," *Louisiana History*, 7 (1966): 294-6.

[5]Samuel J. Mills, *Report of a Missionary Tour Through That Part of the United States Which Lies West of the Allegany* [sic] *Mountains; Performed under the Direction of the Massachusetts Missionary Society* (Andover, Mass., 1815), 29, 43-4.

[6]John F. Schermerhorn and Samuel J. Mills, *A Correct View of that Part of the United States Which Lies West of the Allegany* [sic] *Mountains, with Regard to Religion and Morals* (Hartford, 1814), 35.

[7]Estwick Evans, *A Pedestrious Tour, of Four Thousand Miles, Through the Western States and Territories, during the Winter and Spring of 1818; Interspersed with Brief Reflections upon a Great Variety of Topics* (Concord, N. H., 1819), 240.

[8]Ibid., 230.

[9]Thomas Hamilton, *Men and Manners in America*, 2 vols. (Edinburgh, 1834), 2:209-12; Frederika Bremer, *The Homes of the New World; Impressions of America*, 2 vols. (New York, 1853), 2:211; *America of the Fifties: Letters of Frederika Bremer*, ed. Adolph Benson (New York, 1924), 274-81.

[10]Bremer, *America of the Fifties*, 280.

[11]*Bishop Whipple's Southern Diary, 1843-1844*, ed. Lester B. Shipee (Minneapolis, 1937), 118.

[12]George Lewis, *Impressions of America and the American Churches* (Edinburgh, 1845), 201.

[13]Ebenezer Davies, *American Scenes, and Christian Slavery; A Recent Tour of Four Thousand Miles in the United States* (London, 1849), iii, 18-77.

[14]Ibid., 18.

[15]Ibid., 77.

[16]Julie Koch, "Origins of New England Protestantism in New Orleans," *South Atlantic Quarterly*, 29 (1930): 60-1, 65-7, 76.

[17]Lewis William Newton, "Creoles and Anglo-Americans in Old Louisiana—A Study in Cultural Conflicts," *Southwestern Social Science Quarterly*, 14 (1933): 36. See also pp. 35, 37-41.

[18]John K. Bettersworth, "Protestant Beginnings in New Orleans," *Louisiana Historical Quarterly*, 21 (1938): 835-7.

[19]See Robert C. Reinders, "The Louisiana American Party and the Catholic Church," *Mid-America: An Historical Review*, 40 (1958): 218-28; "The Churches and the Negro in New Orleans, 1850-1860," *Phylon*, 22 (1961): 241-8. See also, Clarence Gohdes, "Some Notes on the Unitarian Church in the Antebellum South: A Contribution to the History of Southern Liberalism," *American Studies in Honor of William Kenneth Boyd*, ed. David Kelly Jackson (Durham, N. C., 1940): 359-63.

[20]Joseph G. Tregle, "Early New Orleans Society: A Reappraisal," *Journal of Southern History*, 18 (1952): 20-36; W. W. Chenault and Robert C. Reinders, "The Northern-born Community of New Orleans in the 1850s," *Journal of American History*, 51 (1964): 232-47; John G. Clark, "New Orleans and the River: A Study in Attitudes and Responses," *Louisiana History*, 8 (1967): 117-37.

[21]See especially, Clement Eaton, "The Creole Civilization," (Chapter VI) *The Growth of Southern Civilization, 1790-1860* (New York, 1963), 125-49; Ulrich Bonnell Phillips, *Life and Labor in the Old South*, 3d ed. (Boston, 1963), 150-7.

[22]H. W. Gilmore, "The Old New Orleans and the New: A Case for Ecology," *American Sociological Review*, 9 (1944): 385-94.

[23]Francis Butler Simkins, "The South," *Regionalism in America*, ed. Merrill Jensen, 2d ed. (Madison and Milwaukee, 1965), 151.

[24]R. M. Weaver, "The Older Religiousness in the South," *Sewanee Review*, 51 (1943): 238-9; Charles S. Snyder, *The Development of Southern Sectionalism, 1819-1848*, vol. V of *A History of the South*, ed. Wendell Holmes Stephenson and E. Merton Coulter (Baton Rouge, 1948), 56, 294-5; Clement Eaton, "The Ebb of the Great Revival," *North Carolina Historical Review*, 23 (1946): 10-2; Edwin M. Poteat, Jr., "Religion in the South," in *Culture in the South*, ed. W. T. Couch (Chapel Hill, 1934), 250-3.

[25]W. J. Cash, *The Mind of the South*, 2d ed. (New York, 1967), 83-4; William E. Dodd, *The Cotton Kingdom: A Chronicle of the Old South* (New Haven, 1919): 106-10; Walter Brownlow Posey, "Influence of Slavery Upon the Methodist Church in the Early South and Southwest," *Mississippi Valley Historical Review*, 17 (1931): 541-2.

[26]For some interesting synopses attesting to the unpopularity of evangelical Protestantism in New Orleans, see Walter B. Posey, "The Advance of Methodism into the Lower Southwest," *Journal of Southern History*, 2 (1936): 442-3, 448, 450-1; "The Early Baptist Church in the Lower South," *Journal of Southern History*, 10 (1944): 164, 172-3. However, Negroes were especially numerous in the Methodist Episcopal Church, South, and the Baptist Church. See Robert C. Reinders, "The Churches and the Negro in New Orleans, 1850-1860," 243-6.

The subjects of religious intellectualism and interdenominational harmony have been briefly examined. See for example, Clement Eaton, *The Freedom-of-Thought Struggle*, 319, 321-2; John K. Bettersworth, "Protestant Beginnings in New Orleans," 823-4, 835-7, 840-2. For the best account of abolitionist and pro-slavery consternation with New Orleans society, see Thomas F. Harwood, "The Abolitionist Image of Louisiana and Mississippi," 294-6, 303-8.

[27]Whitaker, *The Mississippi Question*, 39-47.

[28]Eaton, *The Growth of Southern Civilization*, 143-4, 146; Whitaker, *The Mississippi Question*, 46-7.

[29]Phillips, *Life and Labor in the Old South*, 153.

[30]Frederick Jackson Turner, *The Frontier in American History* (New York, 1921), 187-9; Henry E. Chambers, "Early Commercial Prestige of New Orleans," *Louisiana Historical Quarterly*, 5 (1922): 451-61; Wendell H. Stephenson, "Ante-bellum New Orleans as an Agricultural Focus," *Agricultural History*, 15 (1941): 161-74.

[31]Eaton, *The Growth of Southern Civilization*, 144-4; Chenault and Reinders, "The Northern-born Community of New Orleans in the 1850s," 232-47; Reinders, "New England Influences on the Formation of Public Schools in New Orleans," *Journal of Southern History*, 30 (1964): 180-5.

[32]J. D. B. De Bow, *The Seventh Census of the United States, 1850* (Washington, 1853), 490-1.

[33]Dodd, *The Cotton Kingdom*, 13-5, 98.

[34]See, for example, "The *Catholic Propagateur* and the Know-Nothings" cited in the *Catholic Standard*, August 19, 1855, p. 1. Copies of the *Standard* are preserved in the library archives of the Notre Dame Seminary, New Orleans, La., along with copies of Perche's newspaper, *Le Propagateur*.

For information on Rouquette's unionist sympathies, see Adrien Rouquette, *Poèmes Patriotiques: Suite de L'Antoniade* ([New Orleans]: L. Marchand, 1860): 73-112. A copy of this volume is in the Archives Department, Louisiana State University, Baton Rouge, La.

[35]R. L. Stanton, *Mr. Stanton's Reply to Mr. Goodrich: Brief Notice of a "Series of Letters," Entitled "Episcopacy Maintained," "Addressed to the Rev. R. L. Stanton by Charles Goodrich rector of St. Paul's Church, New Orleans," In a Letter to Rev. Charles Goodrich* (New Orleans, 1845), passim. See especially pp. 13-15.

Evidence of Polk's disillusionment with slavery may be found in Leonidas Polk MSS, Southern Historical Collection, University of North Carolina, Chapel Hill; "Louisiana State Colonization Society," *Daily Picayune* (New Orleans), March 28, 1857, 3; and *Journal of the Proceedings of the Eighteenth Convention of the Protestant Episcopal Church in the City of New Orleans on Thursday, May 1st, 1856* (New Orleans, 1856): 56.

[36]*New Orleans Bulletin*, September 4, 1834. A clipping from the *Bulletin* is contained in the "Scrapbook: Newspaper Account of the Reverend Joel Parker Controversy, September 5, 1834-December 15, 1834," Howard-Tilton Memorial Library, Tulane University, New Orleans, La.

[37]*Proceedings of the Presbytery of Louisiana, in Special Session Convened, By Order of the Synod of Mississippi, For the Trial of Rev. William A. Scott, D. D.* (New Orleans, 1846), 10, 14; Ebenezer Davies, *American Sense, and Christian Slavery: A Recent Tour of Four Thousand Miles in the United States* (London, 1849), 27, 40, 42, 75.

[38]See R. L. Stanton, *The Church and the Rebellion: A Consideration of the Rebellion against the Government of the United States; and the Agency of the Church, North and South, in Relation Thereto* (New York, 1864), 220-1 and passim; Robert Brewster Stanton, "Abraham Lincoln: Personal Memories of the Man," *Scribner's Magazine*, 18 (1920): 32.

[39]Edwin J. Putzell, Jr., "Cui Bono: A Study of Secession in Louisiana" ([WPA] typescript, [Tulane University], New Orleans, 1935): 89-93; *New Orleans Daily Delta*, December 4, 1860, 1; Haskell Monroe, "Bishop Palmer's Thanksgiving Day Address," *Louisiana History*, 4 (1963): 105-18.

[40]Gohdes, "Some Notes on the Unitarian Church in the Ante-bellum South," 362.

[41]Ibid., 331-3, 366.

[42]Theodore Clapp, *Autobiographical Sketches and Recollections During a Thirty-Five Years' Residence in New Orleans* (Boston, 1857): 222-3, 231-3, 235-50; Clapp, *Slavery: A Sermon Delivered in the First Congregational Church in New Orleans, April 15, 1838* (New Orleans, 1838), 42.

[43]Thomas Perkins Abernathy, "Social Relations and Political Control in the Old Southwest," *Mississippi Valley Historical Review*, 16 (1930): 533-5.

[44]William Winans, "Autobiography of William Winans" MSS in Millsaps-Wilson Library, Millsaps College, 111-23; W. Winans Drake, "An Early Methodist Leader in the South: A Sketch of Rev. Benjamin M. Drake, D. D.," *Methodist Review*, 67 (1918): 76-7, 85; J. J. Tigert IV, *Bishop Holland Nimmons McTyeire: Ecclesiastical and Educational Architect* (Nashville, 1955), 100-15; "Dissolution of the Union" (editorial), *South-Western Baptist Chronicle* (New Orleans), March 23, 1850, 158; *Appelton's Cyclopedia of American Biography*, ed. James Grant Wilson and John Fiske, 6 vols. (New York, 1888), 2:256-7.

[45]William Hicks, *History of Louisiana Negro Baptists from 1804 to 1914* (Nashville [about 1915]), 26-7; "First African Baptist Church," *Chronicle* (New Orleans), May 20, 1848, 26.

[46]Charles Dudley Warner, "New Orleans," *Harper's New Monthly Magazine*, 74 (1887): 206.

THE CONSCIENCE OF A COLONIZATIONIST:
PARSON CLAPP AND THE SLAVERY DILEMMA*

Timothy F. Reilly

Of all the nation's clergymen who wrestled with the problem of American Negro slavery, surely Parson Theodore Clapp (1792-1866) of New Orleans experienced one of the more tortuous philosophical turnabouts in the intellectual history of the Old South. Initially a self-described "abolitionist," Clapp later sympathized with the colonization movement, then adopted a pro-slavery position, to be followed by his return to colonizationism, and ultimately his final commitment to the Unionist cause. As a Unitarian minister in the antebellum South, Parson Clapp actually stood alone among a handful of controversial city-based Christian "radicals" whose theology was anathema to the vast majority of Southern Christians, and whose political views often bordered on the unorthodox. Clapp's philosophical quest within the South was a veritable "Pilgrim's Progress" of calculated survival in what was perhaps the most challenging environment he could have chosen. As he grappled with the issue of slavery, he was always mindful, too, that he must achieve at all times a defensible position *vis-à-vis* his Creator and his countrymen. Complicating the task was his genuine affection for the South and most of its inhabitants, white and black.

What makes Clapp's life most notable is not so much his ultimate advocacy of colonizationism, but the reasons behind his philosophical turning points, and his assumption that whatever the course of the nation's history, the white and black races could not live together as equals. His forebodings about a multi-racial society were conditioned both by his New England upbringing and the day-to-day life he subsequently experienced in the South. His racial pessimism was not unusual for his day. Even some abolitionists would have agreed with his sentiments. He was a rare individual, however, as demonstrated by his final resolve to turn away from the pervasive force of Southern nationalism, states' rights theory, and the perpetualism of slavery.

Before his death in the post-Civil War era, Clapp's colonization cause was in ruins on both sides of the sectional border. And in Washington, Congressional leaders who had long detested colonizationism were feverishly preparing to launch the country's first

*First published in *Louisiana History*, 39 (1998): 411-41. Reprinted with the kind permission of the author and the Louisiana Historical Association.

antidotal experiment in multiracial democracy—the era of Reconstruction. In order to better understand Clapp's role in the Deep South's feeble colonization movement, one must first consider the nationwide American Colonization Society and its impact on state organizations.

A common thread uniting the varied membership of the Colonization Society involved the question of how to remove the slaves from the American continent. Judging the motives of the slaveholder in the Upper South, this did not ordinarily mean the removal of the bondsmen; it usually meant the gradual elimination of a growing free black population which was considered increasingly intractable and even dangerous. Among old-style Federalists—mostly in the North—it was thought that the removal of both enslaved and freed blacks would stabilize a republic threatened by social disorder and by the erosive force of racial inequality on its political ideals. One significant group of racial colonizationists included a large number of Protestant clergymen, North and South. They often held the opinion that the country's declining moral and ethical standards were in part the result of the pervasive influence of disorderly African Americans. It was felt that free blacks were particularly menacing. It is significant that two Protestant ministers provided the initial impetus for African colonization. In Rhode Island, Rev. Samuel Hopkins advocated returning African Americans to the British colony of Sierra Leone, founded in 1787. More than a generation later, Rev. Robert Finley of New Jersey was more successful. In 1816, Finley managed to combine an assortment of Middle Atlantic clergymen, Old School Federalists, and Chesapeake planters into the American Society for Colonizing the Free People of Colour of the United States, soon to become known as the American Colonization Society.[1]

The new colonization society initially made impressive headway throughout the country. Early members included prestigious individuals such as Bushrod Washington, John Randolph, Henry Clay, and Andrew Jackson—all Upper South slaveholders. Other supporters were Old School Federalists and philanthropists such as William Phillips and Henry Rutgers representing New England and the Middle Atlantic region. In addition to sympathetic Northern clergymen, a number of Southern church leaders lent their support; among them were William Meade and William H. Wilmer of Virginia and Stephen B. Balch from the District of Columbia. Two other churchmen were especially courageous in laying the groundwork for the future colony in Africa. Colonization missionaries Samuel J. Mills, a Congregationalist, and Samuel Bacon, an Episcopal priest, sacrificed their lives in attempts to establish a foothold on the continent in the years before Liberia's successful founding in 1822.[2]

While the American Colonization Society never succeeded in winning the long-term enthusiasm of either the United States government or large numbers of Americans, it did manage to survive against increasingly harsh attacks from suspicious, even hostile, abolitionists and Lower South slaveholders. Traveling agents often spoke in Congregational, Presbyterian, and Episcopal churches, begging contributions and emphasizing the Society's concern for Christianizing Africa, as well as repatriating the African to his original

homeland. In rebuttal, hundreds of free black leaders protested that their natural homeland was America, and they had no desire to leave the country of their birth. Nonetheless, attractive young spokesmen such as Ralph Randolph Gurley, the son of a New England Congregationalist minister, and Kentucky's James G. Birney, a former slaveholder,
traveled widely and wrote newspaper articles in praise of African colonization. Birney's
appointment as a traveling agent in 1832 was especially important, since he was scheduled to publicize the cause in the states of the Deep South. In the past decade hardly any
colonization agent had ventured south of North Carolina in as much as collections there
hardly paid expenses.[3]

In contrast to the Upper South's active movement between 1820 and 1850, the colonization crusade in the Lower South experienced stagnation and recurring uncertainty.
Mississippi, for example, sent less than one-fourth as many emigrants to Africa as the
state of Virginia. Louisiana's Colonization Society—in some ways an adjunct organization of the Mississippi movement—was perhaps the weakest state organ within the
American Colonization Society. Fewer than 180 Louisiana free blacks—less than 2 percent of the total free black emigrants—were willing to leave the state for Liberia during
the entire antebellum period.[4]

In the period from 1850 to 1860 the colonization cause in the Lower South was virtually nullified by the growing militancy of pro-slavery thought and Southern sectionalism. In Virginia or Kentucky the individual colonizationist might be judged by his
neighbors as either a farsighted visionary or an impractical idealist, depending upon the
vagaries of local racial tensions, economic possibilities or even personal popularity. To
the North, abolitionists shrilly indicted the colonizationist as a proverbial "wolf in sheep's
clothing" who sought to strengthen the institution of slavery by pretending to offer a
genuine remedy. In the Lower South, on the other hand, the "neighborhood colonizationist" was sometimes perceived as some kind of crypto-abolitionist who dangerously
threatened the stability of the South's social order and the legitimacy of its chattel property. No matter where he lived, the colonizationist often endured some degree of suspicion or scorn.[5]

Nevertheless, there were two Louisianians whose respective philosophies on colonization and slavery exhibited a number of themes shared by most colonizationists. Both
men were New Orleans residents who wrestled with the problems separately and differently, but each came to the conclusion that colonization was the only solution to the
country's racial dilemma. A well-known planter and slaveholder, John McDonogh
(1779-1850) became an active supporter of colonization rather late in his life. A calculat-
ing businessman who seldom, if ever, backtracked after a major decision, McDonogh was
a proverbial "doer" who relished the challenge of a seemingly insoluble problem. Theodore Clapp, on the other hand, underwent a thirty-year-metamorphosis—from youthful
dreamer to middle-aged conformist to aged idealogue. Clapp's most consistent belief
held that African Americans were culturally ill-suited to white America. At least in this
respect McDonogh and Clapp were alike, but the two men were probably estranged in

their religious views. When Clapp first came to New Orleans, he preached a rigid Calvinism from the pulpit of the local Presbyterian church. No doubt this was all right with McDonogh, whose religious roots were in the Presbyterian faith. There was, however, little chance that the two men would have become closer after Clapp began his theological drift in a leftward direction. In fact McDonogh had been one of the earliest members of the city's oldest Episcopal congregation, founded in 1805. Late in his life he chose to attend St. Peter's Episcopal Church, which was located closer to his plantation.[6]

During the 1840s McDonogh exchanged correspondence with fellow members and friends of the Colonization Society, including the son of the organization's founder, Robert S. Finley of St. Louis, along with John W. S. Napier of Dayton, Alabama, and Rev. Ralph Gurley of Washington, D. C. In one letter to Finley, McDonogh inquired if the St. Louis resident had obtained a published work which had recommended McDonogh's emancipation formula to the British Parliament. In another letter, Finley invited McDonogh to attend a colonization meeting in New Orleans.[7]

The practical McDonogh provided manumission and emigration on a work-merit basis for several of his slaves. He was utterly convinced that blacks and whites could not live together "as equals and brethren;" their peculiar relationship in the South as slave and master he regarded as fragile and short-lived. In the end one race or the other had to prevail in a process of relentless struggle. Until his death in 1850 McDonogh urged systematic manumission and removal of free blacks to Africa. Physical separation from white society was both natural and essential. He even advocated that Congress itself intervene with the necessary monies and organizational support to help slaveholders finance a more systematic and comprehensive repatriation of the African to his ancestral homeland.[8]

McDonogh's contemporary in New Orleans, Theodore Clapp, made no such commitment to colonization until after he had passed through at least two clearly defined states of intellectual and emotional development. As an acknowledged thinker and moral leader, Clapp was a decidedly more complex man than planter-merchant McDonogh. During his lifetime, cultural influences and personal loyalties frequently overcame Clapp's capacity for making heroic moral judgments, but in the final analysis he at least renounced the perpetualism of slavery. He had traveled a long and perplexing road. Until about the age of thirty, Clapp described himself as "an abolitionist in theory," an internalized attitude which may have influenced Clapp's initial reluctance to make his home in New Orleans. During his middle life, he dabbled for a time with local colonizationism before he assumed a pro-slavery stand which lasted for many years and seemed to betray his New England background. And finally, at the age of sixty-two, Clapp published a sermon which judged the South's institution of slavery to be "wrong;" he proposed gradual emancipation, transportation to Africa, and—like McDonogh—he pleaded for broadscale governmental assistance.

Clapp's return to an antislavery stance he had abandoned for at least thirty years makes him atypical among pro-slavery clergymen—North and South. Historian Larry Edward Tise includes Clapp in his 1979 published study of more than 250 American clergymen whose pro-slavery writings had a profound influence on the direction of events before the Civil War's outbreak. Tise divides American pro-slavery clergymen into three categories: those born before 1800; those between 1801 and 1815; and those between 1816 and 1839. As a member of the first category, the well-educated and way-faring Clapp fit the definition of a man who reached maturity before the era of a strident and damning abolitionism. And as a native New Englander and sometime Congregation-alist, he and his fellow Northerners outnumbered other like-minded clerics in the South and West. On the other hand, Parson Clapp differs from Tise's descriptive mold in that he had adopted antislavery views before he arrived in the South, had first flirted with colonizationism before converting to pro-slavery, and then finally adopted the views of a gradual emancipationist and reborn colonizationist. Even an implicit sympathy for the Union cause failed to destroy Clapp's standing as a respected member of New Orleans' Protestant establishment before and after his retirement. And though he never accumu-lated much wealth or high social standing—as so many of his colleagues did—Parson Clapp was decidedly prominent among those various pro-slavery leaders who had, to use Tise's words, "utilized their clerical careers and the prerogatives thereof to establish themselves as the preeminent antebellum arbiters of taste, morals, and style in govern-ment and society."[9]

Within his Unitarian sphere Clapp openly expressed a temporal view of his society which coincided with those of nationally prominent Unitarian clergymen such as Orville Dewey, Nathaniel T. Frothingham, and Stephen G. Bulfinch. These conservative men denounced abolitionists, women's suffrage, criminal behavior, and social revolution of any kind. Clapp and his colleagues firmly believed in the fundamental legitimacy of America's political and economic institutions; any change must be made in an evolution-ary and cautious manner. While Clapp was more restrained in his criticism of radical abolitionists, he nonetheless resembled his Northern brethren in his fear of racial disor-der, immediate emancipation, and a multiracial society. Clapp's final commitment to colonization, described by historian Douglas Strange as "the 'antislavery reform' of the conservative Unitarians," therefore partially redeemed his original antislavery views and placed him among luminaries such as Orville Dewey, Francis Parkman, Ezra Stiles Gan-nett, and Edward Everett. In his research on Unitarian membership in the American Colonization Society and the Massachusetts Colonization Society, Strange includes Clapp's name along with more than sixty other prominent leaders. According to Strange, these men were "committed social conservatives" who sought to maintain the Union at all costs. Convinced of African Americans' inferiority, they ultimately wished to separate the races by oceanic distance while at the same time disseminating a Christian legacy among black émigrés returning to Africa.[10]

Educated and licensed by the Congregationalists, Clapp became known locally as a religious radical, outspoken social critic, and a bona fide member of New Orleans' intel-lectual community whose sermons were not only published in the local press, but in other newspapers throughout the South and North. A native of Easthampton, Massachusetts,

Clapp entered New Orleans in 1822 at the age of thirty. Following his arrival, he served as the city's second Presbyterian minister, replacing Sylvester Larned who had died earlier of yellow fever. He later broke away from his conservative Presbyterian congregants in 1833 as the result of his increasing alienation from doctrinal Calvinism. By that time, Clapp had expressed doubts concerning everlasting punishment due sinners, the existence of a spiritual elect, and even belief in the Holy Trinity.[11]

On matters spiritual and temporal, Clapp could invoke a good deal of pugnacious criticism. He once attacked the local New England Society and Protestant churches for their social snobbery, while holding up local Roman Catholicism as a proper model of Christian self-sacrifice and community-wide involvement, especially during recurrent yellow fever epidemics. He condemned the rural South's revivalism as another one of those "popular delusions" detrimental to "the interests of sound morals and undefiled [C]hristianity."[12] Clapp berated the Protestant ministry in New Orleans for its ignorance of the Greek and Hebrew scriptures; he praised the local rabbis and priests for their high levels of formal education and their theological knowledge. He even denigrated New Orleans's general population, charging that nearly half the city's residents were shallow-minded fortune-hunters, transients who left without contributing anything of lasting spiritual benefit or significant material value.[13]

Yet Clapp moved cautiously on the issue of slavery despite his New England origins and his educational background at Yale and Andover Theological Seminary. While he remained in New Orleans, he came to see Southern slavery as a legitimate and durable institution given the circumstances behind its development and accommodation. He interpreted African bondage as a natural feature of Western civilization's spread across the frontier wilderness. Yes, there were moral failings and social wrongs, but these embarrassing features could be found in the so-called "free societies" of the industrial Northern states and throughout Europe's leading nations.[14]

During his early travels in the South, the young clergyman surveyed the cultural landscape with some revulsion and dismay. "I was in theory an abolitionist," said Clapp later when he wrote his memoirs. "I thought that nothing, but a blind, obstinate, unrighteous regard to 'filthy lucre,' kept the African in bondage."[15] But he slowly began to soften his views of slavery and slaveholding society. His personal experience with the hospitality of the planter class in the Upper South were very favorable. While visiting a popular Kentucky health spa near Louisville in 1821, the prim and proper Yankee was intrigued by the manners of his fellow-guests:

> At the resort I met a large number of intelligent and fashionable people from the principal cities of the west and south, and a few from New Orleans. Their time was passed in scenes of pleasure, gayety, and excess, which I had never witnessed in the staid regions of New England.[16]

The cultural seduction of Parson Clapp had begun in Kentucky, where his Puritan aloofness was introduced to Southern society's distinctive mingling of relaxed manners, graciousness, and an easy familiarity which progressed toward a privileged friendship rarely experienced before. Clapp was at first taken aback, then fascinated by these spirited upper-class folk, who eventually cajoled the shy Calvinist into coming to New Orleans for a short visit in the winter of 1821-22, then remaining there for the duration of his ministerial career. More than ever, his New Orleans friends found his cultivated personality charming and his extemporaneous sermons earnest and entertaining. Now they were determined to have this young man as the city's next Presbyterian divine despite his hesitations and fears at locating more than a thousand miles from his native region:[17]

> The first week of my sojourn in New Orleans, I assured the trustees that nothing could induce me to stay there longer than three months. At the expiration of this time I made every effort in my power to get out of the city forever. But God is stronger than man, and he was pleased to confine me there thirty-five years.[18]

During his early years in New Orleans, Clapp failed to conform quickly to the South's racial code despite all the pleasantries. In 1826, when he was president of the short-lived College of Orleans, the controversial Presbyterian pastor actually presided over a number of evening balls attended by local African Americans. There was marked uneasiness and nervous excitement in the white community, but Clapp paid only a twenty-dollar fine for defying a city ordinance prohibiting such gatherings. Clapp's involvement in the incident subsequently gained notoriety to a point where it served as one of the formally stated reasons for his ouster from the Presbyterian community.[19]

Clapp's presidency of the college was the result of his close friendship with James Workman, a liberal-minded English immigrant who became a territorial judge in Louisiana. As a trustee of the college, Workman had selected Clapp as president because of the young man's extensive formal education. Judge Workman was also convinced that a Northern-born professional man could more successfully implement "American" acculturation among the city's French-speaking youth.[20]

Workman also played a role as catalyst in altering young Clapp's strict Calvinism and in his eventual conversion to Unitarianism by good-naturedly challenging his religious dictums. Equally important was Workman's strong sympathy toward the colonization movement, since he himself was vice president of the Louisiana Colonization Society. If Clapp had openly expressed his "theoretical abolitionism" early on in New Orleans, his career there would no doubt have ended abruptly. However, an involvement with colonization—a cause which at least pleaded for slavery's eventual demise—offered the New England expatriate an opportunity to clear his antislavery conscience as he continued to preach his liberal Christianity from the pulpit.[21]

Clapp's climactic schism with the local Presbyterians in 1832-33 was based largely on theological grounds, but the break may have provided the bumptious radical with a greater freedom in secular and administrative affairs. This freedom was partly manifested when Clapp swung open the doors of his newly established "Congregational" assembly hall to regular meetings of the local Colonization Society. Those colonizationists in attendance at Clapp's church were described as polite but noncommittal. A segregated audience of white and black adherents—most of the latter free persons of color—listened intently to the likes of such visiting speakers as the Rev. Robert S. Finley of New Jersey, the peripatetic James Birney of Kentucky and Alabama, and George F. Simmons, an ardent but lesser-known slavery opponent who was grudgingly tolerated in New Orleans but run out of neighboring Mobile by an angry mob.[22]

Birney and the younger Finley differed sharply on the best colonization strategy to be used in Louisiana. Birney wrote in 1833 that the cause was languishing and he knew not what to do. He blamed the lethargy in New Orleans on the business community's obsession with immediate profits, and he complained of co-worker Finley's ill-chosen antislavery remarks to local audiences. Birney regarded Finley as a careless speaker and he was dismayed by the fact that Finley had repeatedly branded the opponents of colonization as "enemies."[23]

It was clear that Parson Clapp, in addition to his regular religious duties, played host to an anemic local colonization drive that was dying. By 1846, the African Repository pronounced Louisiana to be the American Colonization Society's least developed and least promising area. To the contrary, pro-slavery sentiment continued to harden. According to a leading twentieth-century observer of antebellum Louisiana, the slavocracy's last decade before the Civil War threatened even the local free black population with re-enslavement and offered the slave no possibility of freedom except flight.[24]

Under these harsh circumstances, how did Parson Clapp reconcile his colonizationist sympathies with his sensitive pro-slavery neighbors and the angry condemnations of contemporary Northern abolitionists? In fact, Clapp was an individual whose attitude toward slavery was largely shaped by his immediate environment, transitions in time and travel, and by people he either admired or disliked. Antislavery sentiments of his youth clearly had been shaped by his native New England culture; his inwardly suppressed abolitionism very conveniently assured some measure of privacy and safety when he first entered the Lower South as a young man. A decade later, Clapp allowed his church to be used for colonization meetings, no doubt persuaded that transportation rather than abolition was the answer to the South's "Negro problem." Later still, his religious association with Louisiana's moribund colonization movement appeared to be over by the late 1830s when he openly expressed pro-slavery views. Then, during the ensuing decades, Clapp moved from the strongest possible pro-slavery stand into a gradual transition which ultimately brought him back to the colonizationist point of view.

In the midst of all his musings, one of Clapp's more consistent beliefs was that white and black societies required some kind of permanent racial barrier. When thrust together, the two races were able to establish a measure of mutual security through the institution of Negro slavery. However, the growing number of free Negroes in the country was a threat to the stability of slavery as well as the unquestioned superiority of whites. Like many other colonizationists, Clapp believed that the removal of African Americans from the North American mainland and their re-location overseas would have provided perhaps the most effective separation of the two races. In this latter view Clapp had much more in common with abolitionists such as James Redpath and war-time Pres. Abraham Lincoln than perhaps he ever realized.[25]

Beginning with his disenchantment toward the abolitionist cause in the 1820s, it took Clapp more than thirty years to reach a permanent position with regard to the Afro-American's proper destiny in the future of the Republic. In short, he sought the black man's departure from North America. In attempting to understand the clergyman's oscillating philosophical voyage from New England abolitionism to a Southern-based colonization cause, followed by a pro-slavery stand, and ending with a re-conversion to colonization, it is necessary to consider the growing strength of the South's pro-slavery forces, Clapp's dependence upon planter-merchants in New Orleans, and his growing need to present an intellectual respectability at home and abroad.

In 1838, Clapp published a sermon in the *New Orleans Daily Picayune* which placed him among the ranks of the pro-slavery "perpetualists." "As I verily believe," he spoke and wrote, "the relation of master and servant originated in the will of God, and is sanctioned by the [C]hristian religion, it will last to the end of time."[26] The former abolitionist and colonizationist sympathizer avowed his full and unwavering support of slavery. He claimed that immediate emancipation would bring about the black man's self-destruction and imperil the public order. He pronounced slavery a civil institution; as such, the state and not the church was directly responsible for its proper management. The slave's labor he described as the price of civilization and Christianity, though he did not mention any possibility of eventual freedom in this life:

> I have no doubt but that Almighty God in his wise providence has permitted and brought about the present servile condition of the Africans in [C]hristian lands, as one of the means indispensable to the deliverance of the native country from barbarism, darkness and crime, and the final exaltation of its degraded millions to the knowledge, order, safety, refinement, pure morality and rational religion, which are enjoyed by civilized and [C]hristian nations.
>
> I would say to every slave in the United States, you should realize that a wise, kind and merciful Providence has appointed for you, your condition in life. And all things considered, you could not be more eligibly situated. The burden of your care, toils and responsibilities is much lighter than that, which God has imposed on your Master. The most enlightened philanthropists, with unlimited resources, could not place you in a situation more favorable to your present and everlasting welfare, than that which you now occupy. You have troubles. So have all. Remember how evanescent are the pleasures and joys of human life. Our fellow beings are rapidly moving off the stage, they retire behind the curtain, and are seen no more.[27]

Clapp's strong pro-slavery argument in 1838 essentially nullified any substantive commitment which may have characterized his previous experience with the colonizationists. He apparently sought to distance himself from an organization which was becoming increasingly unpopular inside the Lower South. In the very same sermon, Clapp took special pains to separate his own pro-slavery position from the controversial anti-slavery declarations of Dr. William Ellery Channing, Unitarianism's most eloquent speaker and writer. The parson's public disavowal of Channing's criticism of slaveholders may not have been easy to do, since he had long held the highest admiration for Channing. However, it became necessary for Clapp to reassure the local business community that his own brand of Unitarian theology contained no traces of abolitionist sentiment.[28]

Many of Clapp's permanent congregants were still members of the planter-merchant society. While they may have appreciated his liberal Christianity and free-wheeling style in the pulpit, they shunned abolitionism, and were becoming more and more suspicious of the national colonization leadership. In fact, Clapp's most important benefactor, Judah Touro, played a crucial role during most of his New Orleans career. Although Jewish, Touro remained sympathetic to Clapp's benign universalism. There is evidence, too, that Touro, a native of Newport, Rhode Island, had moral qualms over slavery. However, the eccentric philanthropist would likely have ended his heavy financial support of Clapp had the Unitarian minister permanently angered the South's business community by condemning slavery.[29]

Unitarian churches in New Orleans and other Southern cities harbored few aristocrats, most of whom continued to cling to the Episcopal faith. Clapp's congregation, along with those of Charleston's Samuel Gilman and Savannah's Dr. Richard Dennis Arnold, was made up of practical, "no-nonsense" merchants and slaveholding planters who, unlike members in some other church assemblies, normally tolerated the segregated seating of slaves and free colored during formal services. For more than a half-century, the planter-merchant community had helped to make Touro a millionaire; this same group had also helped to fill Clapp's successive church buildings since his arrival in the city. Without steady support from "progressive" members of the Protestant business community, both Touro and Clapp would have been forced to locate elsewhere at a very early stage in their chosen careers. In a broad sense, Clapp's transitional pro-slavery phase served as a philosophical and cultural bridge connecting Touro and his Protestant business associates.[30]   As Clapp's published sermons provided a moralistic defense of Southern civilization, his collateral religious beliefs based on deism coincided rather compatibly with Touro's personal Judaism and a common New England heritage. Even as an exponent of colonization both before and after his pro-slavery interlude, Clapp was able to question the permanence of slavery without alienating the majority of his followers.

It should be underscored that the regional colonization cause in Louisiana and Mississippi was singular not only in its lackluster state, but also in its hostility to free Negroes. The Mississippi organization, founded in 1831, was largely restricted to a group of slaveholders in a number of southwestern counties whose sole object was the removal of all local free blacks. Since local slaves greatly outnumbered the white population, it was thought that the mere presence of free persons of color—suggesting the inevitability of a free black conspiracy—might inspire a slave insurrection. In Louisiana, rumors of insurrections in Virginia and the Carolinas made life difficult for the free colored population. Virtually all of the slaveowning adherents of colonization stipulated that a slave's freedom was forthcoming only if he agreed to emigrate to Liberia. At the same time the legislatures of both Louisiana and Mississippi began to adopt adverse legislation limiting the freedoms of resident free blacks.[31]

Control of the free black population was also an important matter of consideration for Parson Clapp himself. In his 1838 sermon on slavery, he argued that Southern bondage could not be held responsible for all the nation's racial ills, particularly those in the free states:

> Were our slaves immediately to be set free, would all the sins that now infest our peace, be at once removed? . . . . In almost every newspaper published in the Northern cities, we read shocking descriptions of the vicious, idle, disorderly and atrocious conduct of the colored persons living among them. But are not these colored persons free? Neither the lash, nor the cruelties of the Southern nabob, are among the causes of the contamination.[32]

With no small degree of irony, the former abolitionist from Massachusetts later found himself in the act of consecrating his new-found faith in slavery's contribution to the social order by actually purchasing a slave in 1844. It could be said with some seriousness that Clapp was forced into becoming a slaveholder on humanitarian grounds. His mild embarrassment over the matter was revealed to a curious Northern visitor who obviously sensed the clergyman's anxiety to explain his new role as master:

> Rev. Clapp . . . owned his sexton, though with that exception he had never owned any human being. He told me that he saw this poor, broken-down old man in the [New Orleans slave] market, in great distress for fear of being sold where he would be overworked and maltreated, and so strong an appeal was made to his compassion that he paid the paltry price, and utilized the man for the light work about his church.[33]

Parson Clapp may well have believed there was at least some validity to the old man's fears of physical abuse at the hands of some "lash-wielding" ruffian or even a haughty "nabob" of the local gentry who could not have cared less about a slave's ultimate disposal. And yet Clapp's public pronouncements on the matter had previously discounted the abolitionist charge of maltreatment. "In ninety-nine cases in a hundred," said Clapp, "the conduct of the master to the slave is distinguished by the most exemplary humanity."[34] Nonetheless, he chose not to expose the old man to that one slave buyer in a hundred purported to be "unexemplary." As for his assumption of the embarrassing role of master, Clapp could have set the old man free and allowed him to work about the church at will. But perhaps Clapp retained enough Puritan business sense to realize that the carrot without the stick might prove ineffective.

A significant turning point in Clapp's pro-slavery phase came three years later while he was on a European tour. While visiting London in the summer of 1847, the Unitarian minister was indeed privileged to meet with the celebrated historian and Southern sympathizer Thomas Carlyle. It was quite a coup for Clapp since he had been warned that Carlyle regularly refused private audiences whenever he was secluded in his study. The following description of Clapp's entrance to Carlyle's home is revealing:

> A lady . . . met me at the door. I said to her, 'I have called this morning to see Mr. Carlyle: is he home?' She replied, 'Mr. Carlyle has just entered his study, and no gentleman can see him this morning. If the Queen of England should now call here and request an interview with him, it would not be granted.' I then asked her if she could oblige me by carrying a written message to his study. 'With pleasure,' said she. I sat down and wrote with a pencil the following words. 'Dear Sir: No gentleman, but a man, is at your door,—a Unitarian, a Yankee, a democrat, and a radical, all the way from the banks of the Mississippi; a careful reader and great admirer of Mr. Carlyle,—and begs the favor of a short interview, which must be granted now, or never this side of the grave.' I sent my letters [of introduction] along with this scrawl. Directly the invitation came: 'Walk up, sir; I shall be happy to see you.'[35]

The two men reportedly exchanged several ideas during a lengthy conversation in Carlyle's private study. Slavery was the major topic, and Carlyle was described as "rejoiced to hear" that the South's slaves "were well fed and clothed, not over-worked, and mercifully treated in all respects." Clapp boasted that they were "quite as well off," both materially and spiritually, "as any class of operatives, either in the field or shop, that existed in Great Britain or any part of continental Europe." This tenet, incidentally, was deeply entrenched in the clergyman's defensive rhetoric. As early as 1838 Clapp had maintained that the Southern slave was actually better off than the free blacks of the North or the peasants and urban laborers of western Europe.[36]

The words that reportedly flowed quite soothingly from the mouth of the eminent Scot presented a view of American slavery which largely absolved the Southern planter of any wrongdoing. Carlyle is said to have blamed his own imperial homeland as well as profit-obsessed New Englanders for what Clapp termed "the odious traffic" of the slave trade. According to the parson, Carlyle also declared:

> We [Great Britain] live by slave labor. . . . All those communities that use the cotton, rice, sugar, coffee, . . . produced by slave labor, are just as much implicated in the wrong as slaveholders, themselves, and just as criminal in the sight of God. In the guilt of slavery, as things are, the whole civilized world participates. How unjust, then, the reproaches and vituperation poured out upon you, for a state of things which was forced upon you by an inevitable providence, and the canceling of which is out of your power.[37]

Carlyle's statement in castigation of slavery represents something of a milestone in his listener's career. Far from disagreeing with Carlyle, the visiting Clapp appears to have acquiesced to his host's descriptive use of such phrases as "odious traffic," and the collective "criminal wrong" of not just the slaveholder, but the whole of the trans-Atlantic economic community. Verily, the "guilt of slavery" is not a phrase that Clapp would have likely shouted forth in one of his earlier sermons. By remaining silent in the presence of one of Britain's greatest historians, the Unitarian clergyman "from the banks of the Mississippi" did not allude to slavery's "positive good." Instead, Clapp's memoirs conveyed at least a momentary accord; the image of the slaveholder was akin to that of a custodial figure who was awaiting further instruction from Divine Providence.[38]

Seven years later, Clapp's published sermons in the local press as well as those in far-off New England revealed his re-conversion to the colonization ethic. But his belated timing may have seemed idiosyncratic and his acceptance of the black man's removal to Africa was certainly qualified. The year was 1854, and the colonization movement in the lower Mississippi valley was all but dead, while the national prominence of the American Colonization Society had greatly deteriorated. Both the abolitionists and the pro-slavery perpetualists were beginning to dominate events as they pressed their sectional arguments and agendas and gradually eclipsed colonizationist pleadings. Clapp's evolving philosophy, of course, was moving across the middle ground. However, his tilt toward colonization fortuitously coincided with a mild resurgence of the parent society following the independence of an improvident Liberia, and the adoption of various emigration strategies by the 1850s. Increased financial support from affiliated lawmakers, deceased members, and worried Unionists made it possible for the American Colonization Society to promote African American emigration to such distant places as Central America, Jamaica, Haiti, Trinidad, British Guiana, and even Africa's Niger River Valley. But by the outbreak of the Civil War, these schemes had ended in disillusionment for almost all of the voluntary emigrants and their supporters. In the meantime, Clapp downplayed the practicability of the Negro's instant removal and instead pressed for individual states and the federal government to establish a long-term systematic emigration policy.[39]

In a sermon which eventually found its way to the pages of the *Boston Trumpet* after its debut in the *New Orleans Daily Picayune*, Clapp beseeched the reader to attempt a better understanding and sympathy for the South's racial ills. "Suppose all the slaves in New Orleans, or Charleston, should emigrate . . . to Boston," he pondered, "would you take them to your embrace with the same alacrity and joy which you manifest when opening your arms to receive a solitary fugitive?" Clapp asked the citizens of Boston what they would do with "an army of such wanderers," and then he volunteered his own solution to what he perceived as a national, rather than a regional problem:[40]

> Prompted by Christian philanthropy only, we should keep them where they are now till ways and means can be revealed to transport them to the land of their ancestry. There is no other road by which they can reach a higher state of happiness. I see no evil in the Union that the country may not be rid of in due time.[41]

Clapp lamented that the immediate colonization of the black slave population was impossible because of the logistics and burdensome costs of such an operation under private auspices. "A vast majority of the planter South," he explained, "are too poor to provide the necessary means for sending their slaves to Liberia." The parson urged that such a transport involving hundreds of thousands of people would require "the resources of a State or nation to accomplish such a result."[42] Clapp's call for massive state and federal funding in behalf of African colonization thus echoed a similar call made by his old neighbor, slaveholder John McDonogh, who had urged Congressional support years earlier.

Clapp's strongest statement in renunciation of his old pro-slavery views came shortly afterwards in one of his last published sermons. No longer was slavery described as the South's perpetual institution, exhibiting a bonding of slave to master which "would last for eternity."[43]

> African slavery at the South is no new thing; we are all familiar with its history. Its originators, as is generally admitted, did not know that it was wrong. The present slaveholders received the peculiar institution from their fathers by inheritance.[44]

Several of the Unitarian clergyman's Southern readers must have been deeply disappointed—even angered—by his new words on an old subject. Were they now to accept his altered appraisal of institutional slavery as an accidental and immoral legacy handed down through layers of ancestral ignorance and simple-minded greed? Clapp's new interpretation was in direct contradiction to the literal Biblical reference he had invoked years before:

> Read the 44th, 45th and 46th verses of Leviticus, 25th chapter. These verses contain an exact description of slavery as it exists in Louisiana, and the Southern States generally. The children of the strangers, i.e. the Africans, are freely bought and sold among us. They become our 'possessions.' Our children receive these possessions by inheritance, and will transmit them in like manner to their descendants; and this state of things is to last forever; i.e. for that indefinite period, during which, the relations of society, now existing among us, will be continued.[45]

The contrasting features of Clapp's pro-slavery arguments in 1838 with his colonizationist rhetoric sixteen years later are striking. A full understanding of his motives in forsaking the perpetualist ranks will never be realized, but the circumstances of his thirty-year struggle are cogent. Always susceptible to friendly persuasion, especially from the wealthy and the powerful, Clapp was perhaps the last person in his very own congregation to realize that he had been firmly planted in New Orleans after arriving there in 1822. For the next decade, at least, the influential Presbyterian elders seemed confident about his retention. Then came the theological break when Clapp veered toward deism and, later on, developed his informal association with Unitarianism. Clapp's rejection of Calvinism had been partly influenced by his educational background, omnivorous reading, and quite possibly the heterodoxy of New Orleans itself. While this culminated in his abandonment by conservative members of his congregation, a liberal faction within the church asserted its staunch loyalty.

Another factor of considerable importance in Clapp's career was the continued financial assistance of Judah Touro, who remained Clapp's chief benefactor until his death in January 1854. Besides assisting Clapp, his wife, and their six children, Touro generously replaced Clapp's old church building with a brand new one after a disastrous 1851 fire. Another token of Touro's esteem was his bequest of the tidy sum of $3,000 after his death.[46]

When the parson published his 1854 sermons challenging the perpetuity and morality of slavery, he also confessed his conversion to colonization as the proper means of ridding the country of its single most important social problem. The fact that Clapp's controversial words were made public only a few months after the death of his conservative patron, Touro, is perhaps significant. And if the hard economic realities of the clergyman's personal life had indeed frustrated the public utterance of his true convictions about slavery before then, he most certainly experienced some agonized thinking late at night and in the wee morning hours.

What does the roundabout conversion of Parson Clapp signify, if anything, within the scope of Southern intellectual history? As a theologian, Clapp may well have been a lion in expressing his views on such matters as predestination and the Trinity, but he was a lamb when it came to the decipherment of slavery and its effects on American civilization. Early in his Southern career, Clapp recognized and accepted the fact that a liberal clergyman's survival required careful restraint and a good deal of judiciousness when it came to making pronouncements on the slavery topic. Like so many other Northerners who had to adapt to the regional priorities of racial caste, Clapp easily anticipated the time-honored code which defined the South as "a white man's country."[47]

It would be unfair to blame the pressures of the Southern environment alone for shaping the parson's shifting opinions on slavery and the black man's place in society. Following his entry into the South as a discreet abolitionist, he came to develop two important views which remained consistent and paramount in his mind. He sincerely regarded the presence of the African as a national, and not a regional problem; he was also tireless in his racialist maledictions upon free black societies of the North and South:

> I believe that three-fourths—perhaps nine in ten—of the Africans South, at the present time, may be lawfully subjected to the control of masters, for the simple reason that, if set free, they would pine, suffer and perish from laziness, poverty, intemperance, and mismanagement in general. Left to themselves, like most of the colored population at the North, they would be inactive, unenterprising, proverbially improvident, shiftless, dissipated, eking out a wretched existence by engaging in the meanest employments, and not infrequently by petty crimes and depredations. All things considered, immediate manumission would inflict upon them a deep and damnable wrong.[48]

Whatever his genuine feelings or his ulterior motives concerning the nation's free blacks, Clapp desired their removal from society in both his pro-slavery polemic in middle life, and his colonizationist revelation made in the ripeness of old age. From this standpoint, at least, it appears unlikely that Parson Clapp could have become an advocate of a parochial Southern nationalism, nor could he have re-embraced the notion of slavery as a perpetual institution. Neither cause was capable of solving the republic's most pressing social problem—that of impending racial conflict. Rather suddenly—and apparently for reasons of ill-health—Clapp left his Deep South home for good in 1856, and spent the remaining decade of his life with relatives far upriver in Louisville, Kentucky.

Parson Clapp made a final brief visit to New Orleans right after the close of the Civil War. The parson found his religious flock largely depleted. Having toiled during half his lifetime in his socially isolated vineyard of resident freethinkers and transient strangers, Parson Clapp must have been a bit depressed by the rather fossilized condition of his Church of the Messiah. Without a permanent minister, the elderly congregation was by now an almost ghostly relic of the antebellum South. Undoubtedly, the visiting clergyman ruminated over the time when New Orleans' cultural triumvirate included the French Opera, the American Theater, and his own "Strangers' Church." Clapp died in 1866, shortly after he returned to Louisville.[49]

Historian Douglas Strange suggests that a higher destiny for Clapp may have been thwarted by a persistent mediocrity in his character. He notes that two of Clapp's Unitarian colleagues regarded him as a shallow popularity-seeker, a local booster who avoided life's more dangerous controversies. Once considered for an honorary doctor of divinity degree at Harvard College, a mature Clapp may have missed his chance because of his earlier pro-slavery flirtation. Nevertheless, Strange cites Clapp as "a solitary exception" among Southern Unitarian clergymen in his loyalty to the Union some years before and throughout the Civil War.[50]

With regard to the future of black Americans, it is difficult to perceive Parson Clapp and most other colonizationists who were actively or theoretically engaged as representing a combined influence for good. Their advocacy of the black man's removal to Africa was apparently based on a vision of the future which saw America as some kind of white man's Elysium, at long last free of the clouds of racial discord, chronic guilt, democratic contradiction, and the threat of amalgamation. Historian David M. Streifford amplifies the colonizationist perception that the Negro's presence prevented social homogeneity and therefore equality and republican fulfillment. Successful emigration, it was thought, ensured a return to eighteenth-century political ideals.[51] On one level, Clapp's writings suggest a more immediate concern with the effects of black economic dependence and crime rates within the larger society. Like most Northern and Southern colonizationists, however, the greater fear of racial miscegenation seems to lurk in the back of Clapp's mind.[52]

Historian Lawrence Friedman has gauged the colonizationists' creed to have been one of the more contradictory and self-defeating in the American experience. While

Clapp and his fellow-colonizationists were often plagued by the guilt over slavery, many within their number still enjoyed the material comforts sustained by slave breeding, the domestic slave trade, and even the retrieval of fugitive slaves. Mere talk of African American removal followed by little or no action salved an antislavery conscience without the consequent disruption of capital depletion, unendurable labor shortages, and a system of racial hierarchy which allowed comfortable caste privileges to slaveowner and non-slaveowner, alike. It is not altogether implausible that Clapp and other colonizationists and "gradual emancipationists" deceived themselves and their followers with their high-minded rationalizations on the need for African repatriation, Christian beachheads along Africa's dark shores, and purification of American democracy. In sum, the rhetoric was profuse while the actual results proved to be underwhelming. But in the meantime, Clapp and his fellow-idealists could distance themselves from the peculiar institution and the sorrows of free blacks by enlisting the theories of colonization rather than enacting any effective practice thereof, which was for all practical purposes a seemingly impossible job.[53]

In the final reckoning of Clapp's role in Southern history, it is important to discern a common ground on which the basic attitudes of the pro-slavery advocate and the colonizationist could in some way intertwine. It is certainly clear that each asserted that American society functioned according to a strict order of racial separation, as well as caste and class divisions; the white community permanently occupied the upper strata and conjunctive sub-strata, while the blacks, both free and slave, occupied the lowest orders. Without these ironclad prescriptions, such a biracial society would not only have seemed unworkable, it would have been inconceivable to most.

It is perhaps an understatement that the proponents of slavery could not have accepted the black man's presence in America without the acknowledgement of his total subjugation. By a somewhat different philosophical route Parson Clapp and others like him had reached a consensus view that excluded any conception of black racial equality. Even in the vaunted magnanimity of their gradual emancipationism, Clapp and his fellow-colonizationists could not bring themselves to allow the black man to share a homeland, or to regard him as a brother. And yet their colonizationist alternative ultimately failed due to a lack of faith on the part of both whites and blacks.

Clapp and his fellow-colonizationists could not conceive a racially integrated society under a democratic aegis nor could they envision a workable order based on racial separateness within a "separate but equal" framework. Legal segregation, which emerged in the 1890s and expired in the 1960s, remains in the dust bin of the nation's history. Today's attempts at creating the closest approximation of racial democracy, on the other hand, represents a social experiment which nineteenth-century colonizationists, including Clapp, could have but dimly imagined.

Notes for "The Conscience of a Colonizationist: Parson Clapp
and the Slavery Dilemma"

[1]Lawrence J. Friedman, "Purifying the White Man's Country: The American Colonization Society Reconsidered 1816-40," *Societas*, 6 (1976): 2-4; Louis Filler, *The Crusade Against Slavery, 1830-1860* (New York, 1960), 20; P. J. Staudenraus, *The African Colonization Movement, 1816-1865* (New York, 1961), 13-17.

[2]Staudenraus, *The African Colonization Movement*, 27-28, 30, 37-47, 56-61, 65-67.

[3]Ibid., 79, 117-35, 146-48, 211-12.

[4]Charles S. Sydnor, *Slavery in Mississippi* (New York, 1933), 212-13, 237; Joe Gray Taylor, *Negro Slavery in Louisiana* (Baton Rouge, 1963), 166-67; Staudenraus, *The African Colonization Movement*, 140, 146-48, 236; William Sumner Jenkins, *Pro-Slavery Thought in the Old South* (Chapel Hill, 1935), 74-77, 91-95.

Like other state societies, the Mississippi and Louisiana societies managed to establish a permanent settlement in Liberia, namely the coastal enclave of Sinou. See Early Lee Fox, *The American Colonization Society, 1817-1840*, in *Johns Hopkins University Studies in Historical and Political Science*, 37 (1919), 95.

[5]As early as 1831, Mississippi colonizationist John Ker expressed his alarm that the North's "religious fanaticism" threatened voluntary emancipation in the Deep South. When the Louisiana legislature proposed an all-out ban, Ker openly defended the slaveholder's right to free his slaves with the proviso that they be removed to Liberia. Seven years later, William Winans was dismayed when fellow-colonizationist and future abolitionist Gerrit Smith of New York refused to contribute a donation for the construction of a Methodist Church in New Orleans. An indignant Smith vowed that he would give nothing to any church group which sanctioned slavery. And when Smith apparently refused to buy a number of Virginia slaves their freedom for trans-Atlantic passage, New Orleans's John McDonogh offered to pay the amount. The issue of slavery was relentlessly dividing Northern and Southern colonizationists. Writing from New Orleans in 1840, the traveling colonization speaker Elliot Cresson observed that abolitionism had made the South so paranoid that it would have taken very little in the way of public discourse to ignite serious controversy.

See Fox, *The American Colonization Society*, 158, 160, 183; "Correspondence between Gerrit Smith, Esq., of Peterborough, New York, and the Rev. William Winans of [Centerville,] Mississippi," *The African Repository and Colonial Journal*, 14 (1838): 48-51.

[6]William Allan, *Life and Work of John McDonogh* (Baltimore, 1886), 60; John McDonogh, "Self-Emancipation: A Successful Experiment on a Large Estate In Louisiana, Tract No. 10," *Colonization Journal* (1862): 4, 6-9.

[7]James T. Edwards, ed., *Some Interesting Papers of John McDonogh, Chiefly Concerning the Louisiana Purchase and the Liberian Colonization* (McDonogh, Md., 1898), 89-92, 94-96, 98-104.

[8]Carl N. Degler, *The Other South: Southern Dissenters in the Nineteenth Century* (New York, 1974), 41-46.

[9]See Larry Edward Tise, "The Interregional Appeal of Proslavery Thought: An Ideological Profile of the Antebellum American Clergy," *Plantation Society*, 1 (1979): 58-72. Tise lists two unnamed Unitarians as pro-slavery writers.

[10]Douglas C. Strange, "Abolitionism as Treason: The Unitarian Elite Defends Law, Order, and the Union," *Harvard Library Bulletin*, 28 (1980): 152-57, 166-67, 170.

[11]Theodore Clapp, *Autobiographical Sketches and Recollections, during a Thirty-Five Years' Residence in New Orleans* (Boston, 1857), 155-62, 172; *New Orleans Daily Picayune*, May 26, 1850.

[12]John C. Waldo, *Historical Sketch of the First Unitarian Church of New Orleans, La.* (New Orleans, 1907), 9-10; *Daily Picayune*, May 26, 1850.

[13]*Daily Picayune*, May 20, 22, 1850; Clapp, *Autobiographical Sketches and Recollections*, 362.

[14]Clapp's graduation from Yale in 1814 and his experiences later at Andover Seminary (1818-19) represented a broad jump from the liberal ideas of the Enlightenment to the counterweight of a conservative Calvinist theology. Founded in 1808 as the country's first divinity school, Andover sought to reaffirm a moderate Calvinism following Harvard's capture by rival Unitarian leaders. Following his 1822 ordination, young Clapp's adherence to his Calvinist faith persisted until his breach with members of his New Orleans Presbyterian flock a decade later. See Timothy F. Reilly, "'Parson' Theodore Clapp," in Glenn R. Conrad, ed., *A Dictionary of Louisiana Biography*, 2 vols. (New Orleans, 1988), 1:182-83; George M. Marsden, *The Soul of the American University: From Protestant Establishment to Established Non-belief* (New York, 1994), 74, 182.

[15]Theodore Clapp, *Slavery: A Sermon, Delivered in the First Congregational Church in New Orleans, April 15, 1838* (New Orleans, 1838), 60. Clapp's famous sermon on slavery was published and widely distributed in pamphlet-form under the same title (New Orleans, 1838). See Larry E. Tise, *Proslavery: A History of the Defense of Slavery in America, 1701-1840* (Athens and London, 1987), 327, 425. See also, Douglas C. Strange, "Abolitionism as Maleficence: Southern Unitarians versus Puritan Fanaticism, 1831-1860," *Harvard Library Bulletin*, 26 (1978): 146-71. Author Tise believes that Clapp's sermon on slavery "presented perhaps the most extended, closely argued, anti-abolitionist statement produced in the South in the 1830s." He further states that Clapp was among the foremost of Southern pro-slavery clergymen in summarizing for Southerners "the ideological message of a decade-long struggle between anti-abolitionists and abolitionists." See Tise, 327.

[16]Clapp, *Autobiographical Sketches and Recollections*, 26.

[17]Ibid., 27-29.

[18]Ibid., 29.

[19]*A Report on the Trial of the Rev. Theodore Clapp before the Mississippi Presbytery at their Sessions in May and December, 1832* (New Orleans, 1833), 98, 104. The report was somewhat vague on the precise nature of this interracial infraction of public mores.

[20]Clapp, *Autobiographical Sketches and Recollections*, 155-56.

[21]Ibid., 155-62, 172; Ralph R. Gurley to James G. Birney, February 20, 1833, as cited in Dwight L. Dumond, ed., *Letters of James Gillespie Birney, 1831-1857*, 2 vols. (New York, 1938), 1:56; *The Seventeenth Annual Report of the American Society for Colonizing the Free People of Color of the United States*, 17 (New York, 1969), xxxi.

[22]Benjamin Morgan Palmer, "An Historical Paper on the Origin and Growth of Presbyterianism in the City of New Orleans," *Presbyterianism in New Orleans and Adjacent Points; Its Semi-Centennial Held in 1873, Seventy-fifth Anniversary of the Organization of the New Orleans Presbytery, 1930*, Louis Voss, ed. ([New Orleans?], 1931), 42-46; Birney to Gurley, March 18, 1833, in *Letters of James Gillespie Birney*, 1:60-61; Staudenraus, *The African Colonization Movement*, 169-83; Clarence Gohdes, "Some Notes on the Unitarian Church in the Antebellum South: A Contribution to the History of Southern Liberalism," *American Studies in Honor of William Kenneth Boyd*, ed. by David Kelly Jackson (Durham, N. C., 1940), 358-59, 364, 366; Clement Eaton, *The Freedom-of-Thought in the Old South* (Durham, N. C., 1940), 319-20.

It should be mentioned that at least one member of Clapp's former Presbyterian assembly was a colonizationist. Alfred Hennen, a Maryland native and graduate of Yale, also became a vice-president of the Louisiana Colonization Society after settling in New Orleans in 1809 and becoming one of the city's leading barristers and businessmen. He was both sponsor and benefactor to the newly arrived Clapp and his predecessor, Sylvester Larned. But when Clapp abandoned his Calvinist precepts, Hennen held fast to his own and played a leading role in local Presbyterianism's rejuvenation. Before his death in 1870, Hennen was professor of Common and Constitutional Law in the University of Louisiana (now Tulane University), and he had accumulated the largest collection of law and literary materials in the Old Southwest. See Timothy F. Reilly, "Alfred Hennen" in Conrad, ed., *A Dictionary of Louisiana Biography*, 1:397.

[23]Birney to Gurley, March 18, April 15, 1833, in *Letters of James Gillespie Birney*, 1:60-62, 70-71. Corresponding editor Ralph Randolph Gurley characterized Finley as "excentric [*sic*] and erratic," and as a traveling

orator, he did not think Finley would "fail to stir the elements in their course." When Finley addressed a New Orleans audience in 1848, this time at the Methodist Episcopal Church on Poydras Street, he did not mince words. He said he believed that Liberia had proved to be a successful social experiment, and he maintained that when left to themselves, Africans were as capable as any other people in creating their own political and social order. See "Louisiana Colonization Society," *Southwestern Baptist Chronicle*, February 19, 1848.

[24]Taylor, *Negro Slavery in Louisiana*, 167. In addition to Clapp, there were other clergymen long associated with New Orleans who were openly supportive of colonization. Methodist clergymen William Winans and Benjamin M. Drake were both members of the Colonization Society. Other adherents included Presbyterianism's William Anderson Scott, Isaac Taylor Hinton and William Cecil Duncan in the Baptist community, and Methodism's Holland Nimmons McTyeire, whose colonizationist ideas appeared regularly in the *New Orleans Christian Advocate*, a denominational weekly which he edited. Bishop Leonidas K. Polk of the Episcopal Church was also a supporter of colonization.

[25]See Louis Filler, *The Crusade Against Slavery, 1830-1860* (New York, 1960), 225.

[26]Clapp, *Slavery: A Sermon*, 65.

[27]Ibid., 56, 66.

[28]Clapp's temporization represented a philosophical trail which was not entirely at odds with conservative Unitarian thought in the North. An antinomian theology within Unitarian doctrine militated against an evangelical-style involvement with current social problems, personal invective, and abolitionist fanaticism against slavery. While Channing himself criticized the institution of slavery, he and other conservatives supported lawful compensation for gradual emancipation and colonization as just solutions. In the end, his co-religionist Clapp reaffirmed the same measures. See John R. McKivigan, *The War against Proslavery Religion: Abolitionism and the Northern Churches, 1830-1865* (Ithaca and London, 1984), 49, 59, 173.

[29]James A. Renshaw, "Judah Touro," *Louisiana Historical Quarterly*, 11 (1928): 74-75, 84; Leon Huhner, *The Life of Judah Touro: 1775-1854* (Philadelphia, 1946), 69-71; Bertram Wallace Korn, *The Early Jews of New Orleans* (Waltham, Mass., 1969), 86-89, 218-20.

[30]Douglas C. Strange, "Abolitionism as Maleficence," 148-49; Keith S. Hambrick, "Judah Touro," in Conrad, ed., *Dictionary of Louisiana Biography*, 2:794.

[31]*Acts Passed at the Second Session of the Ninth Legislature of the State of Louisiana* (Donaldsonville, La., 1830), 90, 92, 96; Sydnor, *Slavery in Mississippi*, 203-206, 228; Taylor, *Negro Slavery in Louisiana*, 167.

[32]Clapp, *Slavery: A Sermon*, 53-54.

[33]A. P. Peabody, "Slavery as it Appeared to a Northern Man in 1844," *Andover Review: A Religious and Theological Monthly*, 16 (1891): 158. Another source suggests that Clapp, for a time at least, may have owned more than one slave. A commemorative drama written in 1933 for local consumption highlights the Clapp family's benign relationship with a high-spirited house servant known as "Mammy Lize." See Strange, "Abolition as Maleficence," 159-60.

[34]Clapp, *Slavery: A Sermon*, 52.

[35]Clapp, *Autobiographical Sketches and Recollections*, 340.

[36]Ibid., 339-43; Clapp, *Slavery: A Sermon*, 44, 54.

[37]Clapp, *Autobiographical Sketches and Recollections*, 342-43.

[38]Ibid., 343.

[39]Clapp, "Mr. Clapp on Slavery," *New Orleans Daily Picayune* [reprinted from *Boston Trumpet*], July 8, 1854; Staudenraus, *The African Colonization Movement*, 241-45.

[40]Clapp, "Mr. Clapp on Slavery."

[41]Ibid.

[42]Ibid.

[43]Clapp, *Slavery: A Sermon*, 65.

[44]Theodore Clapp, "False Impressions of Slavery," *Daily Picayune*, November 12, 1854.

[45]Clapp, *Slavery: A Sermon*, 13.

[46]John Duffy, ed., *Parson Clapp of the Strangers' Church of New Orleans* (Baton Rouge, 1957), 12-13, 45, 65-70; Huhner, *The Life of Judah Touro*, 102, 138.

[47]Ulrich Bonnell Phillips, "The Central Theme of Southern History," in E. Merton Coulter, ed., *The Course of the South to Secession* (New York, 1939), 152, 165.

[48]Clapp, "False Impressions of Slavery."

[49]Waldo, *Historical Sketches of the First Unitarian Church*, 14, 20-21; Timothy F. Reilly, "Parson Clapp of New Orleans: Antebellum Social Critic, Religious Radical, and Member of the Establishment," *Louisiana History*, 18 (1975): 186, 188.

[50]Strange, "Abolition as Maleficence," 159, 168.

[51]See David M. Streifford, "The American Colonization Society: An Application of Republic Ideology to Early Antebellum Reform," *The Journal of Southern History*, 45 (1979): 201-20.

[52]See Leonard P. Curry, *The Free Black in Urban America, 1800-1850: The Shadow of a Dream* (Chicago and London, 1981), especially 112-35.

[53]Friedman, "Purifying the white man's country," 18-19.

PART VI

The Antebellum Period, 1830-1860

CRISIS IN BATON ROUGE, 1840-1860: FORESHADOWING THE DEMISE OF LOUISIANA'S FRENCH LANGUAGE?*

Gabriel Audisio

Everyone knows that only a minority of Louisianians presently speak French, or, more precisely, Cajun French. The number of French-speakers and the size of the state's French-speaking areas were once dwindling so rapidly that Louisiana was faced with the loss of its heritage. CODOFIL, the Council for the Development of French in Louisiana, was created in 1968 in response to the urgency of this situation as a means of promoting the use of French at home and in the marketplace. At the time of CODOFIL's establishment, only the sixty-year-old-and-over generation spoke French at home. People of this generation had learned the language in their youth, but, after having subsequently to renounce the language at school, they had taught their children to speak only English. By the 1960s, the elderly had come to appreciate the cultural impact of their abandonment of French, and they began to speak French to their grandchildren.

The apparent decline of spoken French is generally believed to have occurred in Louisiana only in recent decades. Yet a strikingly similar situation existed within Baton Rouge's Catholic community in 1843. Baton Rouge is located outside Louisiana's Cajun triangle and hence it has not attracted the attention of historians interested in the Acadian migration to the Mississippi Valley, and the group's subsequent settlement and cultural evolution. Many linguists, on the other hand, have examined the region's Cajun dialect and Creole language, noting particularly how they differ from standard French. But no study has yet determined the dynamics of the French language's decline. Yet, such a transformation can be traced, and it is of crucial importance to this study. Such a transformation is accelerated by periods of stress in which the existence of the mother tongue is threatened. In such periods groups speaking the mother tongue feel that their sense of dignity is being threatened, for the reduction of the once-dominant language to minority

*First published in *Louisiana History*, 29 (1988): 343-63. Reprinted with the kind permission of the Louisiana Historical Association.

status also threatens the speakers of that language to the status of a beleaguered cultural minority.

In this context, the situation in Baton Rouge outside of the Acadian region and the strenuous objections of the French-speaking population to the anticipated demise of the French language are worthy of consideration, for they foreshadow the events which occurred much later elsewhere in Louisiana and in Quebec. The affair which precipitated the confrontation in Baton Rouge, an affair previously examined by M. L. Douglas and by Roger Baudier respectively as a linguistic and an ecclesiastical problem, occurred in the fall of 1843.[1] At that time, one Father Brogard was the curé of the local Catholic church. Almost nothing is known about him, except that he signed his first entry in the parish register on December 12, 1841.[2] Brogard soon quarreled with the parishioners of St. Joseph Church, the only Catholic church in Baton Rouge, which was managed by five wardens, elected annually in March. At their November 3, 1843, meeting, held "in the meeting room of the corporation of this town," the wardens received a protest against Fr. Brogard "signed by an important number of members of this congregation, among whom there are several citizens among the most famous and the most respectable ones in the town of Baton Rouge." The protest was directed against Brogard's decision to forego the established practice of preaching in English and French on alternate Sundays for homilies delivered exclusively in English, which only "a few people are able to understand."

Brogard responded by agreeing to preach in French on the first Sunday of every month, but the wardens objected that this concession did not adequately compensate "for the injury caused to the French population." Indeed, the wardens indicated that the said M. Brogard will be notified that the Catholic church of this town was founded and maintained until now by people for whom the usual language is French and that it is not convenient to grant them now just a minimum of ecclesiastical functions.

Continuing their complaint, the wardens indicated that they were "not requesting a favor, but we are demanding an established right." To ensure compliance with their demands, the wardens immediately suspended the priest's salary until he complied with their wishes.[3]

The local press followed the confrontation with growing interest. The *Baton Rouge Gazette*, for example, published in its November 18, 1843, issue, the minutes of the wardens' meeting without comment under the following headline: "[Pursuant] to our several friends' request, we insert this copy of the wardens' report of St. Joseph Church at Baton Rouge." But, in the following issue, dated November 24, the publisher declared his aversion toward "religious schisms" by noting that "if peace and good will does [*sic*] not exist in the sanctuary of the Most High, where on earth are we to seek it [*sic*]?" The editor also noted his support for Fr. Brogard, who had been commended by the bishop for his preference for English. The editor concluded by noting that use of English in St. Joseph Church was most appropriate because "when he [Brogard] preaches in that language he has a congregation, when he preaches in French he speaks to empty pews. . . . The majority of our citizens and of his congregation speak the English language, and thus he acts from a view of doing the greatest good to the greatest number." This contention was at odds with that of the churchwardens who maintained that "it is difficult to determine if a majority of them [the parishioners] usually speak one language or the other."

It should be noted that the warden's minutes were published exclusively in French in the *Gazette*, despite the fact that the newspaper was bilingual. The pro-Brogard editorial in the following issue, on the other hand, was printed in English. The ethnic friction underlying this linguistic dispute was a matter which *Le Propagateur Catholique*, the French-language "newspaper of the families, written by a society of literate men" and published in New Orleans, clearly sought to avoid. This Catholic publication limited itself to a detached discussion of the hostility of "some wardens" toward their parish priest and was ultimately supportive of the parishioners who did not openly side with the wardens. In fact, an editorial praised the fact that "in the wardens' election that took place on last Monday, the Catholics with a sizeable majority failed to elect those who threatened to create disunion in the parish through their attacks upon their priest."

The paper is strangely silent about the cause of the dispute, and it is not known how the quarrel evolved. But, as the foregoing quotations suggest, the tone of the conflict changed with the election of new churchwardens on March 22, 1844.[4] As early as April 3, J. J. Burke, a new warden, proposed that the priest's salary be reinstated. Discussion on Burke's suggestion was postponed until the next meeting. On April 7, the church council not only restored Brogard's salary, but also agreed to pay funds withheld earlier during the dispute. The council, while denying any intention of controlling the parish priest, gently urged Brogard to resume his original practice of alternating languages on alternating Sundays.

The minutes of this meeting as well as the reports subsequently sent to both Brogard and the bishop were written in English. These records form a point of departure in the local church archives, for they mark the first time that the English language was used to record these proceedings. Because the dispute was thus such an important watershed in the region's linguistic development, one must more closely examine the affair to determine if language was merely a pretense for a personality clash between the churchwardens and the parish priest, or whether this was a cultural clash in which the future of the French language was at stake.

I. Priests and Wardens: Let's Change Over to English

By way of introduction, it should be noted that four flags had flown at Baton Rouge since the onset of European colonization: the French flag (from 1699 to 1763), the English flag (1763-1779), the Spanish flag (1779-1810), and finally the American flag (after 1810). The impact of each governmental regime upon Baton Rouge varied in importance and permanence because of inconsistent governmental, economic and demographic factors. Many of these changes are reflected in the individuals who served Baton Rouge as parish priests.

Parish Priests

St. Joseph Church was created in 1792 and was first called Notre Dame des Douleurs (Our Lady of Sorrows). It did not become known as St. Joseph Church until 1820.[5] The first church register dates from 1793, and contains almost no trace of Latin. In fact, not until 1894 are entries made in that language. Instruments in the first register are written in Spanish and are signed by "Carlos Burke," an Irishman. Burke was one of several English-speaking Irish missionaries recruited by Governor Esteban Miro to minister to the Anglo-Saxon families of West Florida. Spanish continued to be the language of record in St. Joseph Parish until 1818, long after the Louisiana Purchase. There are scattered French instruments dating from 1805 and 1817, but these reflect personal caprice, not a change in policy.[6] The last Spanish items are three burials registered in 1832 by the sexton, Spaniard Manuel Moreno, who functioned as warden from 1843 to 1847.[7]

After 1818 most sacramental records are recorded in French. Only between 1818 and 1820, however, are the church registers maintained exclusively in French. In 1821, Antoine Blanc, a priest then ministering to West Feliciana and apparently Baton Rouge, set a precedent which was followed for many years. At Blanc's insistence, individual documents were written in either French or English, depending upon the ethnic background of the family of record. Documents relating to such Hispanic families as the Pecoras, Lopezes, Martinezes, and Linereses were consistently rendered in French, perhaps reflecting their assimilation by local Francophones.

This trend was disrupted between 1834 and 1842 by Fathers Beauprez, Evrard, and Doutreluingue, who recorded births, marriages, and burials exclusively in French, as did Fr. Brogard who arrived at Baton Rouge in late 1842. On October 8, 1842, Brogard deviated from his own practice and began to record instruments in French, Spanish, or English, depending upon the preferences of individual families. But, on January 20, 1844, Fr. Brogard began to record baptisms exclusively in English, even in documents concerning Acadian, Creole, and French-immigrant families. Between 1844 and his departure in 1846, Brogard deviated from this practice only twice, while simultaneously maintaining bilingual marriage and burial registers.

The record-keeping pattern of Fr. Martin, who succeeded Brogard in 1846, demonstrated the same progression from French to English. He began by recording exclusively in French, but, in 1848, he permitted his parishioners to select the language in which their instruments would be recorded. Martin's successors, with the exception of one Fr. de Chaignon who maintained all records in French between 1861 and 1862, also kept registers in French and English.

By mid-1862, however, it had become apparent that French had been supplanted by English as the official language of the local Catholic church. Between 1862 and 1868, French priests Larnaudie, Chassé, Delacroix, and Abbadie kept the church registers almost exclusively in English. In fact, only three documents were recorded in French during this six-year period. Between 1868 and 1894, all church instruments were recorded in English.[8]

These linguistic practices were consistently approved by the local bishop, who signed them during each of his pastoral visitations. It is thus apparent that the question of linguistics was of only minor concern to the ecclesiastical hierarchy.

The Wardens

The parish council's register perhaps reflects more accurately the sentiments of the parish regarding the question of language usage. Wardens were elected annually. Their only extant register covers the period 1837-1856, a particularly important twenty-year span in Louisiana's linguistic evolution.[9] The wardens' register is not important because of its component discussions of language usage, but because of the very language used in recording the group's minutes. In 1837, all minutes were recorded in French and would remain so until 1844. In March 1844, a new group of wardens met. Despite the fact that this group included only one new member, they abruptly began to record their minutes in English. Perhaps the defeat of A. Bessy, who had apparently championed the cause of the French-speaking parishioners, and the influence of his successor, J. J. Burke, who first proposed the restoration of Fr. Brogard's salary, interacted to create a period of English ascendancy. In any event, the council of wardens used English exclusively as its language of record for three years. Only with the election of a new council in 1846 did French regain its position as the group's official language. Before 1847, the council consisted of one French Creole, one Acadian, a person of Spanish descent, and two Anglophones. All these wardens were at least bi-lingual. Three of the five members elected in 1847, however, were monolingual Francophones and hence the switch from English to French. An English-speaking majority gained control of the council in 1848 and henceforth the group's minutes were kept exclusively in English.

The composition of the council holds the key to understanding the linguistic changes in the community. One hundred seats were available on the council during the course of its twenty-year history. Only twenty-eight individuals actually held these seats. These twenty-eight individuals included two persons of Spanish descent, six Anglos or Irishmen, and twenty persons of French descent. The French had an obvious numerical advantage in the council, and they do not appear to have been the victims of discrimination in the late 1850s.

Between 1837 and 1841, Frenchmen occupied four of the five seats on the council, the remaining seat being held by an Irishman. The French majority was eroded by the election, in 1843, of a person of Hispanic descent and, in 1844, by the election of a second Irishman to the board. The French not only no longer held a majority of the votes on the board, but one of the members, Antoine Monget who was bilingual, appears to have given the Irish the support necessary to tip the scales in favor of an English-language ascendancy in the council.

This pattern persisted throughout the 1850s. From 1847 to 1851 and from 1853 to 1855, Frenchmen held three of the five seats on the council and, in 1851, 1852, and 1854, they held four seats. In addition, Acadian A. Theriot and Creole A. Duplantier presided over the body from 1851 to 1853 and in 1854 respectively, while Acadian H. V. Babin served as secretary from 1849 to 1857. It is thus obvious that, after 1847, French-speaking members of the council accepted the English-language's ascendancy in the council without hesitation or regret.

Close scrutiny of the careers of two council members—one Irish and one French— can illustrate how this shift in attitudes occurred. Irish-native Colonel Philip Hicky served as president of the council from 1837 to 1851.[10] After a hiatus of two years, he was again elected to the presidency, but declined because of his advanced age (he was then seventy-six years old). Hicky was a notable of the town, who also served as a trustee of Baton Rouge College.[11]

Hicky's social position is also reflected in the marital alliances that his daughters concluded with prominent area families. Four Hicky marriages are recorded in the parish registers. On October 26, 1820, Elisa Hicky married James Scallan. Martha Frances Hicky married Simon William Walsh, of Natchez, Mississippi, on March 19, 1827. Caroline Hicky married Morris Morgan on December 22, 1832, and Odile Hicky married Henry Walter Fowler of Baton Rouge.

Despite the marriage of his daughters to Irishmen and despite his own marriage to an English woman, Colonel Hicky was not an anglophile.[12] While president of the parish council for at least thirteen years—the council registers for the period prior to 1837 have been lost—Hicky signed the minutes written in French for eight years without incident. This would suggest that he was bilingual and that he probably accepted as proper the use of French, despite his own personal preference for English. Nevertheless, the council's shift from French to English usage occurred during his presidency. It is difficult to believe that this shift was the work of the only new council member elected in 1844, J. J. Burke. It would seem unlikely that this individual could have exerted his influence to that extent without the council president's approval and assistance.

But perhaps the shift from French to English in the council chambers resulted less from English political ascendancy than from the gradual demise of the language in the general community. The example of Antoine Monget sheds considerable light on this process. Monget was a third generation Creole and a native of Baton Rouge. His mother was an Irishwoman, Sarah McCullough. Unlike his two sisters, who married French natives, Antoine married a Louisiana Creole.

Monget's children, on the other hand, generally married outside of their native linguistic and cultural communities. Sarah Monget married Acadian Joseph LeBlanc on September 18, 1843, but Sarah's brother, Anthony, married Letitia Parish, an English-woman, in June 1844. English immediately became the predominant language in this branch of the family, as is evidenced by the husband's signature: "Anthony" and not the original "Antoine." The two remaining Monget children, both of whom were married in

1851, followed Anthony's lead and also married into the local Anglophone community. Elisa Monget married Mayhew Bryan, and Alfred Monget married Margaret Pyburn.

The Monget family's migration across linguistic and cultural boundaries occurs at the same time that the English language is gaining ascendancy in the church council. For example, Antoine Monget, Sr., died in October 1846 and, in Fr. Brogard's absence, he was buried by E. Dupuy, pastor of the Iberville church. Monget's temporary burial certificate was written in French and glued to the parish register. The official record of the burial was written in English by Fr. Brogard upon his return to Baton Rouge.

Antoine Monget, Sr., thus serves as an excellent example of the linguistic transformation of the third generation Creoles who chose to align themselves with both the English language and the Anglo-American way of life. The families bearing French surnames were consequently not as culturally homogeneous as one would expect. Of the twenty French wardens who sat on the church council between 1837 and 1856, only three bore an Acadian surname—Babin, Daigre, and Theriot. The other "French" councilmen belonged to families that came to Louisiana directly from France. Because the Acadians constituted such a small minority of the council membership, one must look to the Creole members for an explanation of the rise of the English language, and it would appear that the Creoles were not very attached to their mother tongue. One must look at the parish community as a whole to determine if this was indeed the case.

II. St. Joseph Parish

The cultural origins of the St. Joseph Church parishioners are obscure in part because the parish registers begin only in 1793. These parish registers, moreover, must be used cautiously because the local priest resided in Baton Rouge, but served a wide rural area. One cannot be sure that the people named in the registers actually resided in Baton Rouge. The amount of demographic information contained in the records also varies in quantity and accuracy from pastor to pastor, thus complicating the problem. Finally, the lack of consistency in the types of material presented in the records prevents any type of quantitative analysis of the evidence. The background material presented below is thus based more on the author's subjective impressions than upon scientific calculations.[13]

The records dated 1793 to 1820 suggest that most St. Joseph parishioners were immigrants. There are very few "natives of Baton Rouge" mentioned in the registers. The few families bearing this designation were the Trahans, LeJeunes, Courtains, Bonvillains, Franceses, Mahiers, Henrys, and Boudreauxs. The remaining names, perhaps constituting 80 percent of the local population, were newly arrived. Most of these immigrants came from Acadia or France, and most of the Frenchmen sprang from Brittany or Normandy. If one inspects the surnames of these people, it becomes readily apparent that they are the same as those of the Acadian immigrants. These people may have been participants in the 1785 colonization project[14] that brought seven shiploads of Acadians from France to Louisiana.

Though the settlement of the 1785 immigrants throughout South Louisiana is beyond the scope of this study,[15] the establishment of these Acadians in the Baton Rouge area is indeed pertinent. Some of these immigrants arrived aboard the *Beaumont* which sailed from Nantes, France, on June 11 and arrived in New Orleans on August 19, 1785. Forty-three of the forty-six families aboard this vessel decided to live in the Baton Rouge district (roughly present-day East Baton Rouge Parish).[16] These settlers were joined by the Jean-Baptiste Guidry family from the *Bon Papa* and by one or two other people who sailed on other ships.

These settlers apparently enjoyed much greater mobility than one would expect. A 1788 list of Acadian flood victims at Baton Rouge is most revealing. Of the thirty-four families listed in Baton Rouge in 1788, only eleven had been passengers on the *Beaumont* only three years earlier. Another eleven families had arrived on other ships and had been assigned to other settlements, particularly Manchac and Nueva Gálvez. All but one of the remaining twelve families were of Acadian descent.

There can thus be little doubt that the town of Baton Rouge was also originally populated by Acadians, most of whom arrived in 1785. However, many changes occurred in the town's population between 1810 and 1830, when many Creoles migrated to the town. The Creoles were followed, between 1830 and 1840, by many Hispanic, European, and Anglo-American immigrants. The Spaniards appear to have come primarily from Mexico, the Caribbean islands, and Spain, while most of the European immigrants were Irish. Most of the Anglo-American immigrants, on the other hand, were from the northeastern United States.

The Irish migration was particularly important because of its impact upon the local Catholic community. As noted above, it is impossible to calculate the percentage of Irish immigrants in the parish, but their impact is clearly seen in a small register entitled "List of Members of Parish Societies and Catalogue of the Catholic Families of East Baton Rouge." Its component family list can help determine the distribution of the parish's linguistic groups based upon surnames. This method of establishing linguistic boundaries is admittedly imprecise, but there are presently no other means of doing so.[17]

This list ostensibly includes families admitted to the parish between 1847 and 1868, but a careful analysis of the handwriting reveals that the list was actually compiled by Jesuit J. Lavay, who served the parish between 1850 and 1858. Finally, the compiler's efforts to remove deceased parishioners' names from the list indicated that the list was actually compiled and revised between 1850 and 1853.[18]

The list contains 292 families representing 197 different surnames. These surnames have been divided into four groups, three of which drawn basically upon ethnic lines French, English, Spanish and a fourth category for the many small groups of German, Italian, and other immigrants residing in the parish.

NAMES			FAMILIES	
French	90	46%	143	49%
English	75	38%	93	32%
Spanish	20	10%	34	12%
Other	12	6%	22	7%
Total	197	100%	292	100%

On the basis of these figures, one can determine that approximately one-half of the St. Joseph parishioners were of French descent and, if one adds to their totals the number of Hispanics who usually married "French" people, one could say that they constituted a majority of all Baton Rouge Catholics. However, as noted earlier, the "French" community itself was not homogeneous, as is seen from the table below:

NAMES			FAMILIES	
Acadians	33	37%	63	44%
Creoles	57	63%	80	56%
Total	90	100%	143	100%

This sample is not sufficiently large to permit any conclusions regarding name distribution within the Acadian and Creole communities, but it does warrant two observations. First, the Acadian population was chronically underrepresented on the parish council, perhaps because of their low social status. The Creole community, on the other hand, was usually overrepresented. Out of the one hundred seats on the council available between 1836 and 1857, sixty-five were held by the "French" community, only twenty-nine for the English-speaking parishioners, and just six for the Spaniards. The rapid abandonment of French by the council was thus the result of Creole influence.

Given the dispute which took place over the linguistic question, indifference to the French language by the parish's French community would seem paradoxical. Perhaps it was simply the reaction of a minority within the Acadian or Creole population, for, from all indications, it would appear that many "French" parishioners had already definitely adopted the English language. One should not forget that many members of the "French" community were already third-generation settlers and many were either the descendants of bilingual parents or were themselves bilingual.

Thus the abandonment of the French language by the church community was not the work of the local priests or the church wardens. Indeed, only a few "French" parishioners were probably interested in the quarrel. A majority of them were English-speaking and they probably considered the defense of French as a "rear guard action" which did not concern them directly. The French community's leanings toward English were reinforced by the arrival of many Irishmen in the 1830s and 1840s. Even though the "French" were not reduced to minority status, they were quickly becoming outnumbered. At least some of the Acadians and many of the Creoles had chosen what they considered the future language of their region. This situation was not confined to the Catholic parish. It was a phenomenon underway throughout the town of Baton Rouge. It is thus necessary to look at the community as a whole.

III. "A Totally American Town"

Baton Rouge's population is difficult to determine. According to the 1830 federal census, East Baton Rouge Parish had 6,698 residents, divided almost equally between the free and slave populations. The size of the town of Baton Rouge is not indicated. In 1840, however, 8,000 people resided in the parish and 2,269 of these made their home in Baton Rouge. The parish population grew to 11,977 by 1860, while the town of Baton Rouge had nearly doubled in size, boasting 3,905 residents. If statewide trends are any indication, then approximately one-half of Baton Rouge's 1850 population was foreign-born.[19]

The 1850 census also sheds some light on the religious complexion of Baton Rouge, for it lists the number of churches, their seating capacity, and the value of the physical plants for each congregation.

	AGGREGATE CAPACITY	NUMBER OF CHURCHES	TOTAL VALUE
Episcopal	270	1	$3,500
Methodist	450	1	$7,000
Presbyterian	250	1	$2,500
Roman Catholic	400	1	$12,000

The foregoing churches boasted a total seating capacity of 1,370, which could not accommodate the existing urban population of 4,000. The foregoing table also indicates that the Protestant community was the largest and best established in the town. By 1860 there were only three Catholic churches in East Baton Rouge Parish out of a total of four-teen, while their seating capacity accounted for just one-quarter of the total. Similarly, the property value of the Catholic churches fell to one-third ($31,200 out of $92,000) of the aggregate church property values.

The decline of the Catholic church *vis-à-vis* the Anglo-Protestant community in East Baton Rouge Parish is an accurate barometer of the general decline of the local French population in terms of power and influence. This is seen perhaps most clearly in the local newspaper. Baton Rouge had two short-lived French language newspapers during the early antebellum period.[20] Far more important, however, was *the Baton Rouge Gazette-La Gazette de Baton Rouge*, a bilingual publication which operated in the parish from 1819 to 1853. Though bilingual, the paper began, in the 1830s, to reflect an editorial bias toward the English-speaking community. This bias is seen most clearly during the 1843 linguistic dispute in the Catholic church council.[21]

This bias is less reflective of the attitudes of the editors, who generally tended to remain with the paper for only short periods, than it is of the paper's readership. The *Gazette* was fully bilingual until May 13, 1843, when the paper's editor announced the abandonment of French:

> With last week, expired the existence of a French page in the Baton Rouge Gazette. While it remains in present hands, unless some remarkable changes should transpire, the only French articles we shall publish, will be advertisements and occasionally some special notices for the accomplishment of a particular object, or the accommodation of a particular friend.

The official reason for the paper's abandonment of French follows below:

> Our chief reason for so abruptly and at this time abandoning the French, will be found in the adoption of the law regulating judicial sales. Gov. Mouton, in signing that law, has given a death blow to his mother tongue in Louisiana. The stroke is heavy and its effects certainly so certain that we venture the prediction that within five years it will cease altogether as a legal language.

The pertinent legislative text is entitled "An Act Relative to the Advertisement of Judicial Sales and Monitions." It contains absolutely no reference to the use, or publication, of texts in one language or another. Thinking that he had found a defective copy of the text, this author then examined the official transcript of the state law. Once again, there was no mention of language usage in either of its bilingual versions.

> Be it enacted by the Senate and House of Representatives of the State of Louisiana in General Assembly convened, That it shall no longer be the duty of the Sheriffs, Coroners or Constables of the different Parishes of the State to cause to be inserted in any newspaper the notices or advertisements of sales to be made by them, unless the same shall be required by the plaintiffs or the defendants, or their attorneys, in which case it shall be done at the charge of the party requiring the same; and that a publication of such sale affixed at the Courthouse door and at two other public places in the Parish shall be sufficient.

What does this mean? Precisely this: Before the adoption of this act, on April 28, 1843, judicial advertisements had to be published in newspapers. With passage of that act, the obligation to publish them ceased. Why then did the *Gazette*'s editor take such drastic action? It would appear that the editor recognized that a majority of the paper's French section was published to satisfy this legal obligation and not to satisfy the wishes of his "French" readership. This is made quite clear in another paragraph in the editor's announcement.

> Since in the hands of the present proprietor, the French side of the Gazette has been a dead expense; and yet the management of the French has been at no time entirely con-

> fided to another . . . But this is a portion of his labor for which he has received no ade-
> quate compensation; on the contrary money gained on the English side has been lost on
> the French.

In other words, French readers were becoming rare, and the editor wished for linguistic assimilation of the local community into the American linguistic mainstream:

> And a sincere desire that their progress in the predominant language of the land, will en-
> able us soon to communicate with them through the medium of that impressive tongue in
> which the constitution and laws of our country are written.

The abandonment of French in the local newspaper is thus due mainly to the end of this kind of disguised subvention granted by the authorities to the newspapers through the obligatory publication of the judicial sales advertisements.

Though it would appear that French readers had become too scarce in Baton Rouge to justify continuation of the French section of the newspaper by 1843, the question of bilingual news reporting resurfaced again in 1844, when the *Gazette* was purchased by Jean R. Dufrocq and A. P. Converse. In the January 13, 1844, issue, the new editors addressed this issue:

> To the public. In conformance with the advice published in the last Saturday Gazette,
> this printing office changed its owners. It was becoming through purchase, our property
> . . . From next February [3] on, the Gazette would be published in English and in French.
> At the time when our predecessor believed he had to suppress the French side, the Sher-
> iff's numerous advice opposed the insertion of a lot of interesting articles; but then this
> obstacle does not exist anymore, we can publish, in both languages, enough pieces to an-
> swer to the most exigent subscribers' wishes of a weekly.

The new editors obviously hoped to attract new readers from the local "French" community. A February 3 editorial hailed the return of the *Gazette*'s French section.

> To the public. Establishing French again in the Gazette of which we became the owners,
> we are thinking of adopting a measure perfectly in harmony with the exigencies of the
> country; because, divided like it is, in readers understanding only French and others only
> English, we would be unwilling if we did not do what is imperiously requested by the
> most equitable and the most rigorous justice.

The editors also announced that they would use a special writer for the French section.

Did the return of the paper's French section signal a reinvigoration of the local French community? Evidently not, for the *Gazette* again suspended publication of its French section, this time without explanation, on February 7, 1846. The following week, only a few advertisements were printed in French and the reduced status of French in the publication would continue until the early 1850s. This change in editorial policy was made by Dufrocq and Converse who had restored the French section in 1844, thus confirming the decline of French in the general community.

Having presented the backdrop against which the 1843 dispute took place, one must now return to the subject of Fr. Brogard's attitude about his sermons. The priest's personal attitude is revealed in a remarkable document which confirms our findings presented above. In a letter, written in French, by Brogard to the bishop of New Orleans, and dated September 13, 1843, the curé of St. Joseph Church responds to questions about his "linguistic" behavior. The bishop was particularly sensitive about the situation in Baton Rouge because he himself had once been pastor there and had himself initiated the practice of using alternate languages on alternate Sundays.

Brogard begins his epistle by acknowledging "the very rigorous injunction that your Highness gave me to alternate my sermons every Sunday morning between French and English," but quickly proceeds to defend his decision to move away from the former language.

> [On] Sunday [September 3, 1843] I could not help announcing that, because nobody wanted to come and listen to me when I preached in French, henceforth I shall only do so on the first Sunday of every month.

It was this decision that precipitated the ensuing confrontation with the church council. Yet, according to Brogard, "the desertion was almost total." On the other hand, when he preached in English, people came. As Brogard noted

> Your Highness probably wants to know if the remarkable crowd present on the morning I preached in English was not declining when I began to preach again in French? No Monseigneur it did not decline, it quite disappeared. [Fr. Brogard's emphasis]

Brogard recognized that there were perhaps only forty Catholic families who did not speak French. Furthermore, most French people apparently understood and spoke English. The priest wrote: "There are in Baton Rouge no Creoles from 10 to 25 years of age for whom the American language is not the common language." Indeed, according to Brogard, English "is the vulgar language of 19/20ths of the town dwellers." And, the pastor continued,

> this is more proof, of the two newspapers published here, the Gazette of B.R. and the Democratic Advocate, neither one has a single line of editorial matter in French. Therefore the number of French readers must be quite small.

Brogard concluded that Baton Rouge was "a totally American town."

As a result, Baton Rouge's French community was clearly on the defensive. The priest wrote: "The hatred that the disorderly behavior of the French in this town inspires is directed toward their language, toward their church." Some Catholics became Protestants to avoid the hostility that the French community both caused and endured. "The Creoles themselves who were born of Catholic parents begin to share this American antipathy; and, if I can indicate only one, M. Larguier's second son, Isidore, who maybe did not come into our church any more after the day of his first communion, goes every Sunday to the Presbyterian church." Brogard also observed that "The French party of this town is losing its influence every day; Lanoue was just expelled as chief warden from the penitentiary and Paul Choppin as captain of the guards. The salary of the first was $1,800 and that of the latter was $1,000. Both were replaced by Americans. Here the French look at that with dark jealousy and that is the reason why some of them show displeasure when they learned that I would not preach in French anymore."

The priest's analysis of the situation appears particularly astute. According to Fr. Brogard, Baton Rouge Catholics rarely went to church "When I preach in French nobody, except some women, come to listen to me." More and more Frenchmen were speaking English, while at the same time their community was both becoming viewed as disreputable and losing its influence. With regard to linguistics, the priest's conclusion is quite definitive: "Therefore French must be considered here henceforth a dead language." Brogard therefore considered as inevitably disastrous any linkage between the French language and Catholicism. As the priest noted in his letter to the bishop, "here is the true religion threatened with total ruin in this town."

As for those individuals who complained to the bishop and in the local newspaper about Brogard, they appear to have defended the sermons in French not because of their great personal interest, but because they had come to represent the French community's last symbol of its once considerable power and prestige. As Brogard observed, "They don't care about the religion; if I only preached once a year, it would be sufficient. [But if] I did [preach] in French, the church would be considered a monument to their existence."

In the final analysis, then, the abandonment of French by St. Joseph Church was neither an Anglophile priest's obsession, nor an initiative by only a few churchwardens. It simply reflected changes in the church community as a whole: On one hand, French people rarely frequented their church; on the other hand, those who did spoke English more and more. First the priests abandoned French, and then the churchwardens followed their example. The changes began in the 1830s; the 1840s were an important transitional period; and the English language's triumph was complete by 1860. From a broader perspective, the evolution of the parish reflected the evolution of the town itself. Once a large majority, both Catholics and Frenchmen found themselves quickly sliding into the position of a conspicuous minority and, in the process, lost their social position. The abandonment of the French language constitutes the logical cultural consequence of the ethnic, economic, social, and political changes then underway in the parish.

Appendix A

Wardens' Meeting
Friday, November 3, 1843

Le secrétaire a ensuite donné lecture d'une pétition qui a été adressée au conseil des marguilliers; elle est signée par un nombre considérable de membres de cette congrégation parmi lesquels se trouvent plusieurs des citoyens les mieux famés et les plus respectables de la ville de Bâton Rouge. Elle a pour but de réclamer contre l'innovation introduite depuis plusieurs mois par Mr. le curé Brogard dans l'exercice de ses fonctions les plus augustes et qui est d'interrompre sa messe du dimanche par une lecture en anglais que peu de personnes sont capables de comprendre au lieu de suivre l'usage établi depuis de longues années de prêcher alternativement un dimanche en français et un dimanche en anglais, ce qui donnait satisfaction à tous les divers membres de la congrégation, vu qu'il est difficile d'énumérer quelle est la portion la plus considérable qui se sert habituellement et l'une ou l'autre de ces deux langues. Cette innovation a donc été intempestive et déplaisante pour un grand nombre de personnes. Plusieurs représentations one été faites à cet égard à Mr. le Curé mais il n'en a tenu compte et ce n'est qu'à grand peine et par une espèce de concession qu'il a dernièrement consenti à donner une allocution en français seulement le premier dimanche de chaque mois. Ceci n'est pas une réparation à l'insulte faite à la population française par l'innovation de Mr. Brogard : il est donc décidé en conseil et à l'unanimité qu'on notifera au dit Mr. Brogard que l'Eglise catholique de cette ville a été fondée et conservée jusqu'à ce jour par des gens dont la langue habituelle est le français et qu'il ne convient nullement de leur accorder aujourd'hui que la moindre part dans les fonctions ecclésiastiques et que si lui, Mr. Brog. [*sic*], persiste à donner ses préférences à la langue anglaise, ce qui tendrait à proscrire le français, Nous les Marguilliers représentant la congrégation de l'Eglise catholique dite de St-Joseph à Bâton Rouge, nous lui signifions que nous ne demandons point de faveur, mais que nous tenons à un droit acquis que s'il refuse, après la notification du présent, de prêcher un dimanche en français et un dimanche en anglais et de continuer de même par la suite, son traitement reste suspendu à dater de ce jour; à Bâton Rouge le 3 novembre 1843.

Appendix B

Wardens' Meeting
April 7, 1844

The following resolution offered by J. J. Burke Esq. was unanimously adopted and the secretary directed to furnish the Bishop of Louisiana and the Rev. Mr. Brogard curate of said church with copies of the same:

Resolved, that we highly approve of the ability, industry and devotion to the duties of his function of M. Brogard the parochial curate: we also hear respectful testimony to the purity of his life and manners and consider his presence and his influence among us as of inappreciable [*sic*] importance to the interests of good morals and the Catholic religion. Resolved that resolution under date 3rd September [*sic*] 1843 stopping his salary until he should conform to the requisition of preaching in the French language, be and the same is hereby repealed; and he shall be restored to his _____ and rights as they were before the adoption of the said resolution in the full sense as if this same had never passed; and further that this resolution have retroactive effect, to intitle [*sic*] him to be paid fully and for the whole period of his function, said resolution now repealed to the contrary notwithstanding.

Resolved that however from distrust of the intent of our authority and from considerations respectful and favorable to the incumbent we abstain from the exercise of any peremptory requisition with any sanction of forfeiture or other to control him as to the language to be discoursed in the pulpit nevertheless we concur in the opinion that too wide a departure from an early, long continued and uninterrupted practice to preach in the French language to a congregation composed as ours is of so large a portion of those whose maternal tongue is the French language has created a dissension but little favorable to the interests of religion and the church. We therefore recommend an immediate reoccurrence to the preaching in the English and French languages on alternate Sundays and further that copies of these resolutions be communicated to Mr. Brogard and the Bishop. The meeting then adjourned.

[Signed] J. J. Burke
Prest pro: temps

Notes for "Crisis in Baton Rouge: Foreshadowing the Demise of Louisiana's French Language?"

[1] M. L. Douglas, "Some Aspects of the Social History of Baton Rouge from 1830 to 1850" (M.A. thesis, Louisiana State University, 1952); Roger Baudier, *The Catholic Church in Louisiana* (New Orleans, 1939).

[2] Archives of the Diocese of Baton Rouge, Baton Rouge, Louisiana, no. 16, p. 71; hereafter cited as Arch. Dioc. B. R.

[3] Many of the quotations in this article are translations of the French originals.

[4] *Le Propagateur Catholique*, March 9, 1844.

[5] A new church was dedicated on December 19, 1830, as can be seen in the parish register. Arch. Dioc. B. R., no. 9; *Baton Rouge Gazette*, January 1, 1831. The present St. Joseph Cathedral dates from the 1850s.

[6] Actually in 1797, when C. Burke was absent, Gerboy signed the records and registered them in French. Gilbert C. Din, "The Irish Mission to West Florida," *Louisiana History*, 12 (1971): 316.

[7] Arch. Dioc. B. R., no. 11, p. 41.

[8] Below are the parish registers which were analyzed in the Diocese of Baton Rouge Archives: Vol. 1-Baptism (1793-1806); Vol. 3-Marriages (1793-1821); Vol. 4-Burials (1793-1815); Vol. 5-Marriages (1803-1840); Vol. 6-Baptism and Marriage (1806-1821); Vol. 7-Baptism and Marriage (1807-1822, 1835); Vol. 8-Baptism and Marriage (1816-1836); Vol. 9-Baptisms (1818-1833); Vol. 10-Marriages (1817-1861); Vol. 11-Burials (1818-1894); Vol. 12-Marriages (1822, 1840); Vol. 13-Marriages celebrated in private houses (1831); Vol. 14-

Marriages celebrated in private houses (1832-1833); Vol. 15-Marriages celebrated in private houses (1833-1836); Vol. 16-Baptisms (1833-1852); Vol. 17-Marriages celebrated in private houses (1836-1838); Vol. 18-Baptisms (1852-1868); Vol. 19-Marriages (1862-1893); Vol. 20-Baptisms (1868-1896).

[9]Arch. Dioc. B. R., no. 29, Minutes of the Warden's meetings (18337-1856).

[10]Mark T. Carleton, *River Capital: An Illustrated History of Baton Rouge* (Woodland Hills, Calif., 1981), 14.

[11]Arch. Dioc. B. R., no. 4.

[12]Ibid., nos. 3, 5, 10, 14.

[13]For the history of Baton Rouge's Catholic community, see Francis L. Gassler, *History of St. Joseph's Church, Baton Rouge, Louisiana, from 1789 to Date* (Marrero, La., 1943).

[14]Certain colonists settled in St. Gabriel in 1767; others from Maryland settled at Natchez in 1768. See Richard E. Chandler, "End of an Odyssey: Acadians Arrive in St. Gabriel, Louisiana," *Louisiana History*, 14 (1973): 69-87; Richard E. Chandler, "The St. Gabriel Acadians: The First Five Months," *Louisiana History*, 21 (1980): 287-96; Richard E. Chandler, "Odyssey Continued: Acadians Arrive in Natchez," *Louisiana History*, 19 (1978): 446-63.

[15]The bibliography concerning the Acadian *Grand Dérangement* is immense and of very unequal value. The best synthesis remains Oscar W. Winzerling, *Acadian Odyssey* (Baton Rouge, 1955). Gabriel Debien examines a lesser known aspect in "The Acadians in Santo Domingo, 1764-1789," in Glenn R. Conrad, ed., *The Cajuns: Essays on Their History and Culture*, 3d ed. (Lafayette, La., 1983), 19-78. Regarding the seven expeditions of 1785, see Milton P. Rieder, Jr., and Norma G. Rieder, comps., *The Crew and Passenger Registration Lists of the Seven Acadian Expeditions of 1785* . . . (Metairie, La., 1965). See also, Carl Boyer, III, ed., *Ship Passenger Lists: The South, 1538-1825* (Newhall, Calif., 1979).

[16]The lists of those first settlers, extracted from the Spanish archives, were published in Jacqueline K. Voorhies, comp., *Some Late Eighteenth Century Louisianians: Census Records of the Colony, 1758-1796* (Lafayette, La., 1973).

[17]Arch. Dioc. B. R., no. 30, Catalogue des familes catholiques dans la paroisse d'Est Baton Rouge par ordre alphabétique.

[18]The list of the pious societies is in the same register, arranged back to front. It was established by Fr. A. Martin before 1851. The list was maintained by Martin's successors until 1868.

[19]Demographic information extracted from the Fifth Census of the United States (1830), Sixth Census (1840), Seventh Census (1850), and Eighth Census (1860).

[20]For information regarding early Louisiana newspapers, see Edward Larocque Tinker, *Bibliography of the French Newspapers and Periodicals of Louisiana* (Worcester, Mass., 1933).

[21]The *Gazette* citations refer to the microfilm copy (microfilm no. 907) at Hill Memorial Library, Louisiana State University, Baton Rouge, La.

SPIRITUALISM'S DISSIDENT VISIONARIES*

Caryn Cossé Bell

The human soul has need of the supernatural. Reason alone cannot explain its sad condition here below.

—Alphonse de Lamartine

In the fall of 1858, a bitter rivalry between the city's Catholic leaders and the advocates of spiritualism, a radical new religious sect, culminated in a confrontation between J. B. Valmour, a black Creole medium, and police authorities. The free man of color, highly acclaimed for his success in "the laying on of hands and in the transmission of spiritual messages," enjoyed a reputation as one of the city's most renowned healing mediums. Late-night disturbances outside of Valmour's blacksmith shop near the outskirts of the city and complaints from the Catholic clergy prompted city police to take action. Accusing the Creole leader and his followers of practicing voodoo, they threatened to suppress spiritualist assemblies. The incident forced the celebrated medium to curtail his activities.[1]

For Valmour and other members of the French-speaking free black community, American spiritualism offered an enlightened alternative to the increasing conservatism of the city's Catholic Church. An anarchical religious movement based on uniquely egalitarian principles, spiritualism repudiated orthodox religion as well as other forms of institutionalized authority. Spiritualist leaders advocated a new "catholic" faith based on the Christian ideal of universal brotherhood. As the movement increased in popularity in New Orleans during the 1850s, Valmour and many other Afro-Creoles assumed leadership roles as spiritualist mediums. The social and political implications of their unorthodox new belief system represented a radical challenge to the South's entire social edifice.

Nineteenth-century American spiritualism originated in New York in the mid-1840s and swept North America and Europe during the subsequent decade. The doctrine behind the new movement represented a synthesis of the thought of three European thinkers: Franz Anton Mesmer, Emanuel Swedenborg, and Charles Fourier. The three philoso-

*First published as Chapter 6 in *Revolution, Romanticism and the Afro-Creole Protest Tradition in Louisiana, 1718-1868* (Baton Rouge, La.: Louisiana State University Press, 1997), 187-221. Reprinted with the kind permission of the author and the publisher.

321

phers had derived much of their inspiration from the scientific advances of the seventeenth century.[2]

In his theory of universal gravitation, the British scientist Sir Isaac Newton described a physical universe operating under the influence of invisible, mechanical laws. The new physics shattered previously held notions of the material world; its social and political impact was equally profound. Newton's synthesis gave new direction to human relations. The scientist's startling description of "the most subtle spirit which pervades and lies hid in all gross bodies" in the 1713 edition of his *Principia* captivated the public mind. Though the scientist himself was at a loss to explain the essence of this natural phenomenon, the existence of a transcendent and mysterious power suffusing the physical world fired the popular imagination.[3]

Less analytical but no less influential minds devised belief systems to accommodate the new scientific realities. The enthusiasm with which the discovery of a universal force in nature was received reflected an ancient and enduring quest to discover fundamental truths in nature—truths that revealed the universality of human experience and consciousness. This tendency persisted as an integral aspect of Western society.

Key social and intellectual movements within European society readily absorbed the impact of the scientific and philosophical revolution. In the eighteenth and nineteenth centuries, philosophers, artists, and other thinkers elaborated upon spirit-in-matter beliefs and universalist notions abstracted from Newtonian physics. Their efforts demonstrated a widespread craving in Western society to break free of a restrictive and archaic social order.[4]

In France in the decades leading up to the French Revolution, devotees of a new healing science called mesmerism combined the idea of a universal force in nature with discoveries involving magnetism, the flow of electricity, and the human psyche. The originator of the new medical therapy, Franz Anton Mesmer, a Viennese doctor, arrived in Paris in 1778 and announced his discovery of an etherlike substance that permeated the universe and served as a medium for gravity. Carrying light, electricity, and magnetism, the cosmic substance suffused all physical objects. In the human being, sickness resulted from an internal obstacle to the natural flow of this fluid through the body. Health, the state of man's harmony with nature. returned when the fluid's natural flow resumed.

Mesmer's treatment involved the transmission of this invisible fluid or energy by means of a technique he termed animal magnetism. In mesmerist séances, the doctor's patients sat around a large oak tub filled with a solution of water and iron filings. The fluid in the tub, Mesmer maintained, harnessed the energy of the cosmic ether. Movable iron rods extending from the tub transmitted the magnetic force to the participants when they applied the end of the rod to the body's diseased area. During the magnetic healing treatment, the mesmerizer directed the flow of concentrated fluid through the body and dispersed the internal obstacle (the disease), thereby restoring the patient's health. By manipulating magnets and engaging in an early form of hypnosis, Mesmer induced a psychological crisis in his subjects. Some patients suffered convulsions, others entered into hypnotic states of semiconsciousness, and some described sleeplike trances in which the ethereal fluid enabled them to commune with spirits of the dead. In his 1799 *Memoir* Mesmer portrayed animal magnetism as a proven scientific technique that unleashed latent powers and enabled the subject to experience clairvoyance, to comprehend universal truths, and to heal.

In eighteenth-century France, Mesmer "cured" hundreds of patients and achieved considerable popular acclaim. But his influence extended beyond the realm of medical therapy. By the eve of the French Revolution, his notion of harnessing nature's forces to alleviate human suffering had inspired a number of political philosophers and social reformers as well.[5]

Mesmerist Jean-Louis Carra based his political theory upon Mesmer's notion of a pervasive substance that acted on the political body in much the same way it affected the human body. In the invisible and superior realm of nature, the mechanism of the universe operated according to republican principles. Conveyed by the mesmeric fluid, nature's forces would, therefore, produce a revolution. Ultimately, Carra predicted, natural laws would bring the political body into harmony with the physical-moral forces of the universe. In the early 1780s, Carra, soon to be a leader in the French Revolution, prophesied that France would become a republic "because the great physical system of the universe, which governs the moral and political affairs of the human race, is itself a veritable republic." In the coming republican millennium, Carra described how the king and the shepherd would be "two men in the true state of equality, two friends in the true state of society."[6]

Mesmerism remained influential during the postrevolutionary era, when utopian socialists incorporated mesmerist concepts into their political theories. Although Charles Fourier criticized mesmerists for misunderstanding their science, he nonetheless assimilated their ideas into his own works; his view that human society could be cured of its ills by being brought into harmony with the physical universe coincided with mesmerist beliefs. And like Carra's theory, Fourier's philosophy of the physical-moral laws of nature included an apocalyptic transformation in which it would be necessary to "throw all political, moral and economic theories into the fire and to prepare for the most astonishing event . . . FOR THE SUDDEN TRANSITION FROM SOCIAL CHAOS TO UNIVERSAL HARMONY."[7]

In the first half of the nineteenth century, mesmerists exhibited their healing science at well-advertised demonstrations throughout Europe and the United States. By the time the practice crossed the Atlantic, however, French innovators had largely dispensed with the use of magnets, magnetized water, and baths. Instead, they employed more advanced techniques in hypnosis to induce sleeplike states of consciousness in their subjects. The notion of an ethereal fluid remained, however, and mesmerizers believed that this mysterious substance brought their patients into direct communication with a superior otherworldly intelligence. They described extraordinary feats of clairvoyance and telepathy in which their patients diagnosed illnesses, prescribed remedies, and communicated with distant persons and the spirits of the dead.[8]

In the United States during the mid-1840s, mesmerism underwent a unique transformation as a consequence of the experiences of a Poughkeepsie shoemaker's apprentice, Andrew Jackson Davis. Born in 1826, the uneducated Davis began to experience spontaneous trances and visions at the age of twelve. In 1843, he embarked upon a career as a medical clairvoyant after witnessing a mesmerist demonstration. In hypnotic states induced by a mesmerizer, the teenaged Davis diagnosed illnesses and prescribed cures. Although he enjoyed relative success as a seer and healer, his clairvoyant experiences took on a new character after a couple of years.

Between 1845 and 1847, under the guidance of radical Universalist ministers, he dictated a series of trance-lectures. In 1847, Davis and his associates published the spirit communications in a two-volume work entitled *The Principles of Nature, Her Divine Revelations, and A Voice to Mankind, By and Through Andrew Jackson Davis*. In the *Divine Revelations* and more than thirty other works, Davis drew upon Mesmer's healing science, Swedenborg's theology, and Fourier's socialism to lay the theoretical foundation of the spiritualist movement.

Divine Revelations met with a mixed response when it first appeared in July 1847, but Davis and his fellow reformers forged ahead regardless. They launched a paper, dispatched field missionaries, and announced their intention to bring about the "establishment of a universal system of Truth, and the Reform and Reorganization of Society." Their movement received little notice until the spring of 1848, when events in western New York attracted international attention.[9]

On a farm in Hydesville, two teenaged sisters, Margaret and Kate Fox, heard mysterious rappings on the walls of their room. The sisters and many witnesses attributed the strange noises to the spirits of the dead. The knockings and the teenagers' telepathic abilities created an immediate sensation and transformed spiritualism. Within two years, the movement had spread to most major American cities. While public attention remained fastened on the Hydesville rappings and other spirit-induced phenomena, Davis and his associates elaborated upon their vision of an earthly utopia. In the spiritualist synthesis, Emanuel Swedenborg's theology served as the basis of their new religion.[10]

During the 1740s, Swedenborg, an eminent eighteenth-century Swedish scientist, had experienced a series of visions that convinced him of the failure of orthodox religion. Guided by his mystical revelations, he described three orders of being: the natural, the spiritual, and the divine. On the basis of his doctrine of "correspondences," Swedenborg proposed to establish the transcendent unity of the three realms. Everything in the natural world, he asserted, corresponded to a higher spiritual reality. The material realm was merely an image of the superior spiritual world. The highest realm, the divine, produced and sustained the two lower orders, with God and man sharing a common spiritual essence in the life of the soul. Natural law, like the natural world, was a reflection of its superior correspondent in the upper realms. By living in harmony with divine law, the individual achieved salvation.

A highly respected physicist and astronomer, Swedenborg considered theology a science, but a literal interpretation of the Bible produced discrepancies between scientific knowledge and the sacred text. Swedenborg sought to clear away these inconsistencies by revealing the true meaning of biblical scripture. The Bible, he maintained, possessed a spiritual or inner meaning that his powers as a seer had enabled him to decipher. In his reinterpretation of the holy book, Swedenborg found the Bible to agree with science. In nineteenth-century America, the Swedish seer's unitive philosophy resonated in the thought of spiritualists, Transcendentalists, utopian socialists, and other reform-minded idealists.[11]

Inspired by Swedenborg's doctrine of correspondences, spiritualist philosopher Andrew Jackson Davis incorporated the notion of a superior spiritual realm into his "Harmonial Philosophy," a master plan for the radical transformation of existing social, economic, and religious institutions. Embodied in Davis' Divine Revelations, the Harmonial Philosophy represented the collective wisdom of the advanced societies of the upper realms.

Davis accepted Swedenborg's concept of a hierarchy of seven spheres. These concentric bands surrounded the earth and represented progressive stages of spiritual enlightenment. When a person died, the inner being of the deceased entered these invisible realms, and to the extent that the believer's spiritual life harmonized with divine law, the soul advanced through the spheres toward ultimate redemption. In the physical world, the soul of a medium during a clairvoyant trance could migrate to the spirit realm and achieve higher states of inner illumination.

Sharing Swedenborg's view of theology as a science, Davis and his followers formulated the mechanistic basis of their belief system with analogues to the physical sciences. In the spiritualist synthesis, electrical energy linked the spiritual and material worlds. Vital electricity, nature's life-giving force, permeated the universe and served as a medium of correspondence between the two realms. In mediumistic trances, the believer communed with the spirits of the dead by means of this electrical force. With the gradual loss of vital electricity, the physical body deteriorated. In death the soul migrated from the body to become the new abode of the spirit. Freed from its earthly domain, the spirit entered a new state of existence.[12]

Even though Davis, like Swedenborg, postulated a scientific basis of theology, he rejected the Swedish scientist's biblical exegesis. Whereas Swedenborg had attempted to reconcile the inconsistencies between science and biblical scripture, Davis considered such differences insurmountable. He found the doctrines of original sin, predestination, and eternal damnation completely incompatible with the true essence of human spirituality. He therefore rejected any plan of salvation based upon scriptural teachings. He described the Old Testament as "primitive history" and denied the sanctity of the Bible and the divinity of Jesus Christ. In the tradition of Confucius, Zoroaster, Muhammad, Swedenborg, and Fourier, Christ was a "great and good Reformer" who had sought the betterment of the human condition. He had died a martyr "to the cause of love, wisdom, and virtue."[13]

Davis reserved his harshest attacks for the Christian clergy. "It is a deplorable fact that all the miseries, the conflicts, the wars, the devastations and the hostile prejudices existing in the world are owing to the corrupting situation and influence of 'Clergymen.'" While science and natural religion contributed to mankind's advancement, the Bible and organized religion served as an obstacle to humanity's progressive development. Religious reform was fundamental to societal regeneration.[14]

Swedenborg's view of God's immanence in the universe also underlay Davis' concept of human spirituality. Human souls were "detached individual personifications of the Deific Nature and Essence" that would attain realization by progression through the spheres. Since all human beings possessed a share of God's divinity, all persons were equal members of a great human brotherhood. Davis admonished spiritualists to "do good and harmonious works, for the redemption and ennoblement of your fellowmen." Such works were to be undertaken "because the Human Race is but One Family—all members of one body—in which there is neither Jew nor Gentile, Nazarene nor Greek, Ethiopian nor Anglo-Saxon." In both life and death, the soul possessed the capacity for limitless growth. Davis' rejection of Hell opened the possibility of salvation to everyone. The believer's continuous advancement toward God formed the basis for all true progress, since the regeneration of the spirit would lead to the regeneration of society.[15]

While Swedenborgianism formed the basis for spiritualist theology, Fourierism served as a model for Davis' social theory. During the early nineteenth century, Fourier, who considered himself Newton's successor, proclaimed his discovery of "God's plan" for the universe. He insisted that a social analogue to Newton's principle of gravitational attraction held the key to the correct organization of society. Fourier proposed such an analogue in his theory of "passionate attraction." The principle of passionate attraction acted upon society in the same way that Newton's principle of gravitation acted upon the physical universe. Since human passions were the agents of personal happiness and social harmony, the free expression of these passions would result in a state of "unlimited philanthropy and universal fellow feeling." The repression of these benevolent instincts by civilized society had resulted in every manner of evil. Yet, salvation was at hand. Fourier boldly proclaimed his mission: "I come as the possessor of the book of Destiny to banish political and moral darkness and to erect the theory of universal harmony upon the ruins of the uncertain sciences."[16]

Like Fourier's system of Universal Harmony, the principles of Davis' Harmonial Philosophy were intended "to unfold the Kingdom of Heaven on earth, to apply the laws of planets to individuals; to establish, in a word, in human society the same harmonious relations that are found to obtain in the planetary world."[17]

Davis argued that contemporary society, instead of conforming to natural law, was divided into competing and antagonistic classes. The exploitation of the laboring poor had resulted in great inequalities. Wealth was concentrated in the hands of "Capitalists, for the wealth which the poor create is accumulated by them, and held within their grasp. Wealth that rightly belongs to those who create it, is thus given to those who earn it not, and hence have no natural title to it." The working class was uneducated and "chained in the degrading shackles of superstition, and enslaved by laws imposed by government."[18]

Davis' blueprint for the evils afflicting American society reflected the influence of Albert Brisbane, a regular attendant at Davis' lectures and the country's leading proponent of Fourierist ideas. The interests of capital and labor would be reconciled upon the basis of Associationism. Initially, agricultural laborers and artisans would implement "the law of association—which is the rudimental principle of Nature." When Fourierism's benefits were evident, all professions would join the movement toward "SOCIAL HAPPINESS AND SPIRITUAL ELEVATION."[19]

The failure to recognize nature's harmonious laws—a failure fostered by orthodox religion—led to intemperance, war, slavery, racial oppression, and other forms of human misery. When the organization of society conformed to the harmonious structure of the universe "the human race will display Light and Life, which are Love, and order and form, which are Wisdom. Thus will be established universal happiness—because the whole race will represent the harmony of all created things, and typify the express majesty of the Divine Creator."[20]

In the spiritualist journal *Univercoelum*, published between 1847 and 1849, contributors announced plans for economic reorganization along socialist lines as a first step toward establishing an ideal society. The editors of the journal published articles on socialism, trade unionism, and other cooperative organizations. They also indicated the seriousness of their reform efforts. "We are in earnest in the advocacy of general reforms and the reorganization of society, because such is the natural counterpart and outer expression of the interior and spiritual principles which we are endeavoring to set forth."[21]

Davis associated spiritualism with other reform efforts and viewed abolitionism, feminism, and the temperance and peace movements as aspects of a generalized progression toward the ideal society. At the Free Convention of 1858 in Rutland, Vermont, he explained this view: "My belief in Spiritualism is simply the door to my acceptance of the various reforms for which this convention has assembled and I trust that to you all Spiritualism is a broad and glorious triumphant archway leading in all directions into freedom, and a universal enjoyment of a heaven in the world." Similarly, Davis maintained that advances in science, the creations of artists, writers, and musicians, and the guidance received through mediums would contribute to the advancement of human society.[22]

While Davis pressed forward in the North, his followers encountered hostility and threats of violence in the South. Spiritualism's opposition to slavery, its egalitarian ideals, and its popularity among free blacks and slaves aroused southern fears. In 1859 and 1860, spiritualist lecturer Emma Harding Britten and her cohorts received threats of lynching during visits to Tennessee and South Carolina. The *Charleston Courier* unleashed a violent attack on the "incendiary practices of the abhorrent Spiritualists." At the same time, the Alabama state legislature passed a statue forbidding spiritualist demonstrations under the penalty of a five-hundred dollar fine. During the 1850s, opposition to the movement in New Orleans forced spiritualists to confine most of their séances to private residences. Nonetheless, by the eve of the Civil War, the city had acquired a reputation as a spiritualist stronghold. [23]

As in the North, the mesmerist movement paved the wary for the emergence of spiritualism in New Orleans. During the late 1820s, French mesmerists introduced animal magnetism into the United States. Mesmer's followers probably acquainted New Orleanians with the practice during the late 1830s, and in July 1843, the *Daily Picayune* reported that the "city at the present time is in a perfect state of Mesmerism." The editorialist continued: "Hard times, temperance societies, and of course we must add, the growing intelligence of the age, have made strange revolutions lately."[24]

Two years later in April 1845, Joseph Barthet, a French emigré and mesmerist propagator, organized a mesmerist society in New Orleans, the Société du Magnétisme de la Nouvelle-Orleans. Following the establishment of their formal organization, Barthet and the society's French-speaking membership corresponded with societies in Paris and elsewhere, publicized their case studies, opened a library dedicated to mesmerist works, staged public demonstrations, and preached the therapeutic value of animal magnetism in the treatment of human ailments. By 1848, the Société du Magnétisme counted seventy-one members of French extraction.[25]

While the city's conservative Catholic Church leadership opposed mesmerism, some members of the city's clergy viewed the movement favorably. One Catholic cleric, the Abbé Malavergne, belonged to the Société du Magnétisme and a number of other priests referred sick church members to the group for treatment. Barthet, who considered mesmerism "a powerful auxiliary to religion, encouraged this relationship by describing magnetic therapy as a valuable treatment for the "sickness of the soul." During the height of mesmerism's popularity in New Orleans, Barthet and his colleagues attempted to demonstrate mesmerism's compatibility with Catholicism. He and other mesmerists furnished the city newspapers with accounts of magnetism's acceptance among church leaders in France. Such testimonials notwithstanding, the city's Catholic leaders remained steadfast in their opposition.[26]

The editor of the church's official organ, Abbé Perche, conceded in the *Propagateur Catholique* that the Holy See had refrained from an outright denunciation of mesmerism and that prominent members of France's clergy tolerated the movement within their dioceses. He also noted, however, that the Congregation of the Index had condemned the works of a prominent French mesmerist, Alphonse Cahagnet, and he expressed his belief "in the imminent dangers and in the frequent a abuse of magnetism." In a subsequent editorial, he cautioned his Catholic readership to beware of the "very great moral dangers" that might accompany the practice of magnetism. [27]

In May 1852, under the cover of foreign commentary, the *Propagateur* published a particularly violent attack on mesmerists in a book review titled "Freemasonry." French author Francis Lacombe lambasted the "utopians, the *convulsionnaires*, the magnetizers, and the ecstatic somnambulists . . . the Rosicrucians, the freemasons, and the Illuminati, the avant-garde of an army of evil," which had attempted to conquer the world under the inspiration of Enlightenment thought. In the nineteenth century, these bearers of the revolutionary tradition sought the overthrow of the established order. Their esoteric confederacy carried forward the "completely subversive intentions of the French Revolution." Emboldened by their partial success in 1848, Lacombe warned, these secret societies openly pursued their aims. In relation to the avowed purposes of Barthet and other mesmerists in New Orleans and France, these accusations contained a strong element of truth.[28]

Barthet, as president of the mesmerist society, maintained direct correspondence with the Baron du Potet in Paris, who was one of mesmerism's leading proponents in France and editor of the *Journal du magnétisme*. In 1850, Du Potet offered a highly encouraging account of Barthet's progress in New Orleans. He noted that "of all the institutions founded in the last few years outside of Paris for the propagation of mesmerism, the one which has succeeded best is, without doubt, the Society of Magnetism in New Orleans." Du Potet attributed its success to Barthet, whom he considered "a zealous and capable man."[29]

For magnetists like Barthet and the Baron du Potet, mesmerism's benefits extended far beyond the boundaries of medical and spiritual healing. Mesmerism, they believed, would contribute to the transformation of society. To this end, Du Potet and his colleagues in Paris drew parallels between mesmerism and utopian socialism. They published extracts from the works of Fourierists and Saint-Simonians, and they welcomed the conversion of utopian socialists to their cause. In 1853, Du Potet published Robert Owens' mesmerist experiences in the *Journal du magnétisme* and offered an account of his changeover. Though Owen "had been until now a materialist in the strongest sense of the word," he had been "completely converted to the belief in the immortality of the soul by the conversations he has had with members of his family, who have been dead for years." Owen himself described séances in which the spirits of Benjamin Franklin and Thomas Jefferson explained "that the object of the current general manifestations is to reform the population of our planet, to convince all of us of the truth of another life and to make us all sincerely charitable."[30]

Even mesmerism's founder, Du Potet revealed, had viewed magnetism as a means for bringing about a social revolution. Between 1846 and 1848, Du Potet published installments in his journal of a manuscript Mesmer had written during the French Revolution: *Notions élémentaires sur la morale, l'éducation et la législation pour servir à l'instruction publique en France* (*Elementary Rudiments of Morality, Education, and Legislation for Use in Public Instruction in France*). In it Mesmer had outlined a radical blueprint for creating an ideal republic; he had even submitted the document to the French National Convention.

With the revolution of 1848, Du Potet's *Journal du magnétisme* railed against academic and political tyranny: "Our learned men wanted nothing to do with mesmerism, just as other men wanted nothing to do with Liberty . . . [but] the links of the despotic chain that science did not want to break have burst into splinters." The journal concluded: "Rejoice mesmerists! Here is the dawning of a great and beautiful new day . . . O Mesmer! You who loved the republic . . . you foresaw this time, but . . . you were not understood."[31]

With the rapid spread of spiritualism in the United States after 1848, Barthet became an ardent proponent of the new phenomenon. He forwarded glowing accounts of the movement to his colleagues in Paris, and in 1852, he published an instructional manual on spirit communication, the *ABC des communications spirituelles*. Before the end of the year, Barthet could report the conversion of an important new member, Charles Testut, a white French émigré and literary colleague of the Afro-Creole writer Camille Thierry.[32]

Testut, like other Romantic writers including Victor Hugo, proved especially susceptible to spiritualism's influence. The Romantic movement had fostered the belief that the artist possessed exceptional powers of moral and spiritual insight. In this view, the creative act enabled the poet or artist to commune directly with the animating spirit in nature—a spirit that permeated and unified all things. His poetic images were symbolic representations of a reality grounded in thought and moral experience that functioned as the unseen counterpart of the external, material world.

Unlike eighteenth-century classicism, which had presupposed an objective and rational reality, the Romantic movement emphasized the artist's inner impulses and passions. The urge to discover the authentic self in an act of spontaneous creativity overtook the desire to imitate accepted models of perfection. The superior value placed on the essence of things as opposed to their physical manifestation blurred the dualism of flesh and spirit. The stress on instinct, emotion, and feelings led to a fascination with the human subconscious and the ethereal.[33]

For leading European and American intellectuals, the Romantic view of human spirituality also engendered religious-political consequences. Romantic writers believed, like French socialists, that the Christian spirit was an essential element of societal progress. "La charité," Lamartine wrote in 1834, "c'est le socialisme." At a banquet in Paris in 1842, he toasted religion as one of the forces that "facilitate the divine unity, that is to say, the confraternity of all races and all men!" While French Romantics such as Lamennais and Lamartine considered themselves devoted Christians, the Catholic Church viewed their writings as heretical. In 1835, the Vatican condemned the work of Lamennais and placed the writings of Lamennais, Lamartine, and Victor Hugo on the Papal Index.[34]

In New Orleans, Testut's literary works and his social vision, like that of his Afro-Creole contemporaries, embodied many of these Romantic tendencies. In his book of poetry published in 1851, *Fleurs d'été*, Testut used the examples of Béranger, Lamartine, and other famous French writers to portray the poet as the embodiment of Christian charity—a seeker of truth and justice endowed with superhuman powers of insight and courage. In its preface, Testut introduced this image: "The true poet is the child of God; happy or suffering, he loves his neighbor; he does not envy the rich, he does not scorn the poor; his conscience is not steeped in injustice, nor his hands in blood." The poet-hero "praises the Homeland, Glory, Liberty. In the martial clamor of their poetic fanfare, they inflame hearts, bolster courage, conceal danger and pave the way to victory. In the sphere that they have chosen, they always march ahead, as if some powerful and invisible influence thrust them to the forefront of the conflict."[35]

In "The Poet," a poem dedicated to free man of color Camille Thierry, Testut indicated his belief in the poet's sacred mission:

> But still, man for his soul
> Has need of nourishment:
> God created the celestial flame
> Which must survive in the nothingness!
> In days full of frights
> Full of torments and of tears:
> Who will come to console him? . . .
>
> It is Jesus Christ! It is the poet
> Because his voice is always ready
> To console the outcast;
> Apostle of mercy
> He dies and says: "Hope
> Because our soul survives us!"[36]

In December 1852, Testut attended his first spiritualist gathering, which he later described. He and a large number of other guests crowded into a room, where over a dozen men and women sat around a large oblong table with their open hands resting on the table's surface. After a period of complete silence, each person posed a question. With each question, the side of the table opposite the questioner rose and inch or two from the floor and struck the ground once for "no" and twice for "yes." Though Testut suspected trickery, he remained fascinated and continued to experiment.

His conversion occurred in the privacy of his home. He described his experience:

> I sat down at my table, alone, at my home. I collected my thoughts, I slowly banished all images of material things—and I waited. Soon I felt myself transfused by some kind of warm and flowing liquid; a new sense of well-being came over me, and, at the same time, I experienced an urge to move the fingers of my right hand. . . . And new ideas gradually arose in my mind, all of justice, of love, and of mercy, and I finished by imagining that I poured a shower of gold over all of the wretched of the earth.[37]

Next, Testut experienced an overwhelming desire to write. He resolved to persevere, and the following night, equipped with pencil and paper, he resumed his seat at the table. After several moments of meditation, his right hand began to shake. He seized the pencil and closed his eyes while the pencil glided over the paper, then fell from his hand. He scanned the seemingly indecipherable scribblings, and when he reached the bottom of the page, he discerned the words, "Not alone."

The phrase triggered a revelatory experience. Testut explained: "These two words inundated me with light. I understood the necessity of being surrounded by brothers . . . so that our combined ardor might lead to a more complete result. Union was necessary. . . . What a lesson in these two words: Not Alone! Sacred Fraternity! you are indispensable to the pursuit of good here below."[38]

Within days of his revelation, Testut organized a spiritualist circle. From the beginning, the group met on a regular basis to receive and transcribe their spirit communications. By the time they gathered for a Christmas celebration the following year, the circle numbered over three dozen members. At their holiday banquet they sang, recited poetry, and drank to the "fraternity of all people." Near the end of the evening, they proposed to hold a spiritual séance with Testut acting as the medium. After a prayer and a reading, Testut lapsed into a mesmeric trance. His automatic writing produced a startling communication.

The message began with a blessing and then assumed a prayerful characteristic: "Let the oppressed soon feel the links of their chains fall away! Let war lead to peace, and tyranny to liberty! Look to heaven and you will see. Ask God and he will answer you: You have voices now in another sphere. You are unaware of what you have done and what you do! God, who sees and hears you, knows—and the Good Spirits surround you like a shield. . . . Eight [*sic*] centuries ago I began the mission that you continue. . . . [Signed] Jesus Christ."[39]

The communication rendered the participants speechless. Bolstered by this inspirational experience, they opened their séances to the public and transcribed their spirit messages from Christ, St. Vincent de Paul, and other spirit guides. In a further effort to propagate their beliefs, Testut published their communications in 1854 in a book titled *Manifestations spirituelles*. These "teachings" touched "on all social questions which bear on the present happiness and future felicity of humanity" and represented the "quintessence of wisdom, democracy, and love." The group remained together for five years.[40]

Testut, a productive romantic writer whose literary works often served as propaganda vehicles, later incorporated his spiritualist ideals into an anti-slavery historical novel that he wrote in 1858, shortly after his arrival in February in New York City. In the work entitled *Le Vieux Salomon; ou, une famille d'esclaves au XIXe siècle* (*Old Solomon; or, A Slave Family in the Nineteenth Century*), Testut described an underground religious society in Louisiana called the Brothers of the Universal Faith. The members of the international, interracial organization engaged in abolitionist activities and adhered to an all-embracing belief system with a religious-political mission. Testut summarized the main tenets of his fictitious religion; "The Universal Faith deals with everything: fraternity, charity, liberty, happiness, the present, the future, the greatness of man on earth and his bliss in heaven; possible equality in the social order. . . . It teaches us to love God, to honor men of good will, to scorn ill-gotten riches."[41]

Its members repudiated organized religion, and like spiritualists in New Orleans, they held the Catholic Church in particular contempt. One member offered the view that without "the adverse influence of the priests, perhaps the French colonies would soon be purged of the leprosy of slavery." His colleague responded, "What! them again! . . . They will always be, of course, on the side of injustice and tyranny, these agents of Satan who conceal themselves in the mantle of Christ!"[42]

Near the time of the publication of *Manifestations spirituelles*, Testut also embarked upon a career as a healing medium. At his *consultations spirituelle*, his patients dictated their symptoms. Alter compiling and numbering their individual ailments, Testut entered into a mesmeric trance and scribbled out prescriptions. He claimed that thirty-four of the thirty-five patients who came the day he opened his practice were healed. His only failure occurred, he alleged, when a patient expired before receiving his prescription from a messenger. Yet Testut's fame as a healing medium paled beside that of J. B. Valmour, a black Creole blacksmith.[43]

As early as 1852, Valmour enjoyed a reputation as a highly successful healing medium. The sick and the curious flocked to his blacksmith shop on Toulouse Street. At times, the eager visitors overran his small apartment and forced him to perform his spiritual healings in an outdoor courtyard. Usually, however, he and his ailing visitors sat around a large round table. After being seated, the medium lapsed into a deep state of prayerful meditation. Valmour described the nature of these trancelike states when Joseph Barthet and other mesmerists sought his advice in treating one of their patients. He advised them: "Forget that you have magnetized, because that would only mislead you; it is necessary to direct one's thinking toward God, wish for the well-being of one's neighbor, and God will do the rest."[44]

Some of Valmour's "patients" described instant cures and others returned for subsequent sessions. Upon the rare occasions when he prescribed a treatment for a sufferer's ailment, the remedy was always simple. At times the large crowds that gathered at his blacksmith shop brought his business to a complete halt. Despite these costly interruptions and his modest income, he refused to accept any form of compensation.

Valmour's admirers marveled at his powers. Barthet pleaded with the blacksmith's followers to build larger, more comfortable accommodations for the medium and his audiences. He viewed the Creole as a Christlike figure whose meager residence reminded him of the birthplace of "the great Nazarene." The white French émigré compared Valmour's lifestyle and healing feats to the life and work of a renowned magnetist in Pau, France, named Laforgue. Like the Frenchman, Barthet noted, Valmour practiced blacksmithing, possessed neither medical nor scientific training, engaged in mediumistic healing, and obtained "miracles of the same kind." Unlike Valmour, however, Laforgue suffered censorship under Napoleon III's government, when it cracked down on French magnetists. Shortly before his death in 1853, police authorities forced the French medium to suspend his activities. According to Barthet, Laforgue died "with the sorrow of having been unable, up to his last day, to do good for his fellowmen; because he was a 'true Christian,' having, like Jesus, more religion than his persecutors, though he didn't go to mass." Barthet attributed Valmour's freedom of action to the "very good Catholics" of wealth and influence among the Creole spiritualist's followers. As sectional tension mounted during the prewar years, however, even such well-placed friends could not protect the New Orleans medium from suffering a similar fate.[45]

During the early 1850s, spiritualism's rapid spread through the city and the emergence of Valmour and other powerful mediums alarmed church officials. While Catholic leaders had demonstrated a relative degree of restraint in their dealings with mesmerists, they showed no tolerance for spiritualists. In the fall of 1852, reports of a sudden flurry of spiritual manifestations involving a number of leading citizens convinced church officials to voice their opposition.

In setting forth the church's position on spiritualism, a Catholic spokesman acknowledged the intervention of spirits at séances. Indeed, Catholicism professed the existence of spirits and possessed an age-old tradition of spiritual mysticism. Such tendencies contributed to spiritualism's popularity with the city's large Catholic population, as a New Orleans observed noted: "Spiritualism has made much more rapid progress among the Creole and Catholic portions of our population that the Protestant; first, because most of them have more time for investigation than the rushing, hurrying, money-making American, and secondly, the creed of the Catholic Church does not deny the possibility of spirit communication."[46]

Although the Catholic spokesman conceded a spiritual presence at séances in the phenomenon of automatic writing, he attributed such occurrences with the work of the devil. As proof of this charge, he cited a communication in which the Islamic prophet Muhammad was compared with Jesus Christ. Certainly, the outraged writer continued, this blasphemy and other unmentionable profanations demonstrated the satanic influence of evil spirits. Biblical prophecy, he reminded his readers, warned of the coming of false prophets and an Antichrist who would perform "*great marvels and astonishing things, to lead into error . . . even the chosen.*" He cautioned his fellow Catholics that spiritualist beliefs ran counter to the teachings of the Bible, church instruction, and the example of Catholic saints. Spirit communication resembled practices that fell into the category of divination and sorcery in the Bible—practices that "the law of Moses punished by death, that the Church has always severely condemned, and that the Saints have always held in horror."[47]

In the *Propagateur*, a subsequent editorial ridiculed the movement's "spiritual investigations" into religious matters and equated spiritualists with socialists. Their efforts, the article continued, paralleled the "social investigations" of the socialists who labored "to lay the basis for society after human society has existed for six thousand years, and after

Catholic society has operated for eighteen centuries." Spiritual investigations, the piece concluded, "will only lead to foolishness and absurdities; and please to God that they do not lead to calamities and crimes!"[48]

In 1840 in Rome, Catholicism's Congregation of the Inquisition had issued a decree aimed at discouraging mesmerist practices. The church reiterated its position in a subsequent decree in 1847, and in July 1856, the Congregation prohibited spiritualist practices. Church leaders admonished Catholic bishops to suppress the "evocation of departed spirits and other superstitious practices of spiritism" in order that "the flock of the Lord may be protected against the enemy, the deposit of faith safeguarded, and the faithful preserved from moral corruption."[49]

In New Orleans, spiritualism flourished despite the condemnation of papal authorities, the dire threats of the city's Catholic leaders, and the region's hostile environment. The movement produced two national leaders, New Orleanians Thomas Gales Foster and J. Rollin M. Squire, and two local periodicals: *Le Spiritualiste de la Nouvelle-Orléans* and *Le Salut* (*Salvation*). Both Forster and Squire joined the editorial staff of Boston's nationally renowned spiritualist journal, *Banner of Light*, in 1857, then traveled widely as spiritualist lecturers.

Le Spiritualiste made its debut in January 1857; *Le Salut*, edited by G. F. Simon, a French-speaking white and close friend of the Romantic writer and black Creole medium Joanni Questy, did not appear until after the Civil War. Emboldened by the movement's success, *Le Spiritualiste* editor Joseph Barthet propagated the new religion in the pages of his monthly journal, explaining the main tenets of spiritualism, reporting on experiences of communicants, and publishing spirit communications, news, and articles from spiritualists in the North and in France. The harmonial concepts of Charles Fourier and Andrew Jackson Davis underlay the movement's religious philosophy and worldview.[50]

The spirit communications of Barthet's spiritualist circles dominated the pages of the new publication. In the articles and editorial essays accompanying these messages, Barthet and his colleagues described the nature and purpose of spiritualist beliefs. Societal regeneration, they explained, hinged on mankind's ability to live in harmony with natural laws that govern the universe. The discovery of these principles through spiritual investigation and scientific progress "is our interest, our right, and our duty." While they stressed the importance of scientific inquiry, they emphasized the greater advantages of spiritualist séances: "'Science is the apperception of the harmonies of the universe,' and we understand that human science is far from complete. There is a science superior to official science; the good *mediums* are its ministers and it can be found everywhere. Seek it; study this occult science in order to teach it; enlighten yourselves and enlighten others on the *inflexible* laws which govern the world."[51]

Spirit guides from the upper realms, acting through the agency of spiritualist mediums, would lead mankind toward a future millennium of brotherly love and harmonious human relations. These superior spirits possessed great foresight and recognized "that if we want to bring about Fraternity on Earth, we must look outside of our Capitols, where they endlessly make and unmake injurious laws; outside of our Churches, where they remain too faithful to old errors and absurd practices!" These spirit teachers were virtuous men "who preached on earth in earlier times, and who are no more *dead* than the truths that they taught." They wanted "to pursue from on high the noble task that they considered imperative. . . . Their goal is to regenerate humanity by correcting and advancing our knowledge; their language is what we call *Spiritual Manifestations*." In the tradition of the Old and New Testaments, these communications delivered at séances through spiritualist mediums, would make up a third book of the Christian Bible.[52]

Spiritualists acknowledged that the Hebrew prophet Moses, the Islamic prophet Muhammad, and the religious philosopher Gautama Buddha had possessed knowledge of the creator's transcendent laws; still, they esteemed the doctrines of Jesus Christ as the foremost expression of these precepts. Spiritualism, a synonym for Christianity, sought to restore Christ's ideals to their original purity. Down through the ages established religion had distorted his doctrines: "Spiritualism . . . is the same doctrine as Christ's, whereas the precept of Rome is nothing more than the selfish design of the Pharisees who crucified the reformer and grotesquely cloaked themselves later in the garb of Christians in order to suppress the truth and to restore the world to another kind of idolatry [the idolatry of man]."

This deception had promoted ignorance, prejudice, and most of the other evils that afflict humanity: "From infancy they deceive us; they pervert our judgement [*sic*]; they inculcate prejudices that most of us maintain all of our lives and, owing to our ignorance, that lead to most of the evils which afflict us. It will be otherwise when we take more care to enlighten our reason in order that we may he guided by it."[53]

The severity of *Le Spiritualiste*'s attacks upon the church shocked many Catholic readers. In Canada, an outraged Catholic priest seized two issues of the journal from one of his parishioners and burned them. A trans-Atlantic correspondent attributed the publication's poor circulation in France to the anti-Catholic extremism of the spirit communications. "We can do nothing about that," Barthet replied, "the spirits have often told us that they see much further than we do and they know better than us that which mortals require."[54]

In New Orleans, spiritualism's public repudiation of church authority angered Catholic leaders, and tensions mounted as the two religious factions attacked each other in the pages of their respective journals. In May 1857, when the Abbé Perche made a disparaging reference to women spiritualists, a medium who identified herself as "Marie Bar . . ." penned a stinging rebuttal in which she mimicked Perché: "A woman who thinks . . . what a monstrosity! And who writes what she thinks—what shamefulness! A woman who dares occupy herself with God, with his grandeur, with his goodness, with his essence, with his mercy, with his works, for shame! This is degrading I tell you! Go, Madame, go mend your stockings, make your preserves, beat your Negresses, tattle on your neighbors, and say your rosary. That is what is appropriate to a woman, that is what makes 'the glory of our population,' that is what will earn for you our favour in this world and paradise in the other."[55]

Spirit communications from bygone figures of French history—Catholic reformers of the French Reformation and leaders of the Enlightenment and the age of democratic revolution—dominated the pages of *Le Spiritualiste*. In an attempt to counteract spiritualism's idealization of France's dissident past, the Abbé Perche related his own version of French history in a series of articles entitled "On Liberty;" these began in the fall of 1857 and appeared in *Le Propagateur* for nearly a year. In the wake of the Protestant reformation, the abbé explained, subversive elements in France nurtured the spirit of revolt during the era of the Catholic Reformation. Conditions worsened at the time of the Enlightenment "when Voltaire appeared, surrounded by an arrogant and foul mob of philosophes." Under the influence of these free thinkers, notions of independence and revolt proliferated. Their advocacy of freedom of thought paved the way for decadence and ruin."

In the "terrible explosion" of the French Revolution, "the churches were closed, devastated, stripped of everything they possessed, and mutilated when they were not demolished" in the name of liberty. The revolutionaries' rallying cry of fraternity was as lethal as their ideal of liberty. They "had taken for a motto: fraternity or death. They should have said: fraternity is death. For, their fraternity was that of Cain." As for equality, "it was equality in servitude and misery," an equality obtained by the "equalizing level of the revolutionary guillotine."

The large numbers of "demagogues, anarchists, radicals, communists, socialists," and other present-day revolutionaries conspired to resume the agenda of the Terror: "Thus, they work ceaselessly to maintain and to increase in the masses these feelings of independence and insubordination, this hatred of all restraint, this contempt for all authority, which form the basis of the revolutionary spirit; and they succeed only too well in this work of iniquity."[56]

In a subsequent essay in April 1858, in a thinly veiled attack on *Le Spiritualiste*, Abbé Perche accused the journal of destroying the moral authority of the church and called upon government officials to suppress the publication. Surely, he maintained, local authorities "would not tolerate a journal here which would set itself up with the avowed purpose of preaching abolitionism." In a sharp rebuke, Barthet noted the irony in Perche's comparison, writing that it is certain "a Christian would have chosen another example while discoursing 'On Liberty' [the title of the article]." Barthet scoffed at Perche's allusion to abolitionism, although *Le Spiritualiste*'s enthusiastic endorsement of antislavery writers and their works appeared to confirm the abbé's accusations.[57]

In *Le Spiritualiste*, Barthet openly eulogized the life and works of Andrew Jackson Davis, an avowed opponent of slavery, and Louis Cortambert, an ardent white abolitionist, fellow French emigré, and the radical republican editor of the *Revue de l'ouest (Review of the West)* in St. Louis, Missouri. Barthet considered Cortambert a "great writer" and published extracts of his articles on spiritualism and education reform in *Le Spiritual-*

iste. The French-born author shared Barthet's view of the Catholic Church hierarchy, and he joined in the attack on Perche in the March issue of the *Revue*: "One [Perche] could not be more downrightly, more logically, and, we believe, more sincerely absurd."[58]

In its bibliography, *Le Spiritualiste* also recommended works by spiritualist radicals in France, including Baron du Potet, Alphonse Cahagnet, and Allan Kardec. In July 1857, Barthet glowingly endorsed Kardec's *Le Livres des esprits* (*Book of Spirits*) published in Paris earlier that year, in which the author condemned slavery, an institution he found inconsistent with natural law: "the human law which consecrates slavery is a law contrary to nature since it likens man to an unreasoning beast and degrades him morally and physically." Except for the question of reincarnation, Barthet found Kardec's philosophy in "perfect accord" with the beliefs of New Orleans spiritualists. Barthet considered *Le Livres des esprits* one of the best books on spiritualism and "more than worth its weight in gold," encouraging his readers to purchase a copy. [59]

If *Le Spiritualiste*'s endorsement of antislavery publications tested the limits of the 1830 state law prohibiting dissemination of seditious reading materials, the presence of an unorthodox interracial religion posed an equally provocative challenge to prevailing racial strictures. Segregationist sanctions notwithstanding, the black Creole medium Valmour assumed a leadership role within the movement as a spiritualist healer and presided over interracial séances at which he "performed many wonderful cures simply by the laying on of hands." Other members of the black Creole community, including Paul Trévigne and Constant Reynès, patronized white mediums and furnished public statements on their experiences. *Le Spiritualiste* published testimonials by Constant Reynès, Louis Courcelle, and François Carlon, black Creoles all, alongside those of their white co-religionists. While spiritualists in New Orleans did not openly attack slavery and other forms of racial oppression, their antiauthoritarian attacks on church and state, their advocacy of self-autonomy as a precondition for individual perfectionism, and their movement's interracial makeup posed a radical challenge to the attitudes, customs, and institutions of the slaveholding South.[60]

During the spring and summer, *Le Spiritualiste*, responded angrily to Perche's attacks. Labeling the *Propagateur Catholique* an ultramontane journal, the spiritualist monthly referred to the series "On Liberty" as the abbé's crusade against those "that he calls 'free thinkers,' 'liberators,' 'Voltairians,' and 'revolutionaries.'" Perche, the paper charged, "in proceeding from absurd assumptions, necessarily arrives at absurd conclusions." The abbé, it continued, "does not like the 'Free Thinkers' that he also calls 'liberators;' he requires Slave Thinkers." *Le Spiritualiste* appealed to its readers to think for themselves and to "take part in the revolution, wholly of peace and of love, that spiritualism is carrying out; make this beacon of salvation glow in the eyes of peoples still deceived, and no longer go to church, unless it be, in the example of Christ, to spread the good news and drive from the temple the merchants who prostitute it."[61]

In August, church leaders retaliated. In a public campaign launched from the pulpit, Catholic leaders labeled spiritualists "imbeciles" and complained to the police. They

described Valmour's healing feats as "monkeyshines" and accused the medium of practicing "gris-gris." In response, the authorities confronted Valmour and threatened to "quash
the movement."[62]

Barthet fulminated against the police and "a certain curé whose church is nearly deserted." He dared spiritualism's enemies to suppress the movement—"as if these little
despots had the right!" He lamented that Valmour would be forced to confine his activities to private séances, even lashing out at the medium's followers; in their refusal to pro-
claim Valmour's healing powers, they had failed the spiritualist cause.[63]

The rancorousness of the religious feud and the threat of police action forced the
movement underground. In December, *Le Spiritualiste* folded. The paper's most oft
cited spirit guide, Père   Ambroise, delivered the final spirit communication, concluding
thus: "Finally, we end in wishing the best for all men, without distinction of race or of
religion and we make the most fervent plea for the triumph of our principles because we
are deeply convinced that they alone can achieve and consolidate the work of regeneration that we have undertaken. So be it!"[64]

Even though the demise of *Le Spiritualiste* ended an acrimonious public debate,
spiritualism continued to thrive within the Creole community. Because personal revelation produced social regeneration, Barthet and his colleagues viewed spiritualist circles as
a powerful means of social reform, and the journal encouraged its readers to make "temples" of their homes. During the 1850s, such circles flourished in private residences.
Black Creole mediums Joanni Questy, Nelson Desbrosses, Adolphe Duhart, Octave Rey,
Paulin Durel, and Charles Veque participated in such a circle at the home of Henry Louis
Rey, their fellow medium.[65]

In 1835, Henry Rey at twenty-seven was a well-educated member of one of the
Faubourg Tremé's most prominent families. His father, Barthélemy Rey, had played a
leading role in the establishment of the Couvant school, the Sisters of the Holy Family
Convent, and St. Augustine's Church. At St. Augustine's the Rey family held a pew and
had financed the stained-glass windows. During the 1850s, however, as spiritualism
spread through the Creole community, Henry Rey and other members of his family converted to the new religion. Rey described the events that led to his changeover.

He recalled that during his youth his mother, Rose Agnes Rey, a devout Catholic
frequently experienced visions in which her deceased children appeared to her. At the
time, Rey dismissed these episodes as flights of imagination. He took a more sympathetic view of his mother's mystical-religious experiences, however, after his father died
in 1852. The tragedy plunged the family into a state of emotional and economic distress.
Rey's mother compounded the family's difficulties when, encouraged by a priest, J. M.
Morisot, she lavished the family's remaining finances on an elaborate Catholic funeral.

The grief over his father's death, anger at the church's role in his mother's extrava-
gance and his new responsibilities as head of the household triggered a response in Rey
similar to his mother's clairvoyance and he began to experience visions of his deceased
father. These mystical occurrences coincided with the emergence of spiritualism in the

city, prompting Rey to attend séances. He participated in a number of sessions with the black Creole spiritualist Charles Veque and other friends and relatives, including Jean François Chatry, his sister Josephine's white common-law husband. With the assistance of Chatry, a spiritualist medium and a French émigré, Rey achieved promising results. Yet his success with automatic writing and other physical manifestations frightened him. Though he found such phenomena fascinating, he remained skeptical. Finally, with spiritualism's spread through the Afro-Creole community, a dramatic experience in the spring of 1857 transformed Rey.

In April, Soeur (Sister) Louise, a popular medium and a neighbor, enticed Rey to attend a séance at her home. Under her direction, Rey took a place at the table, picked up a pencil, and laid his hand on a sheet of paper. Suddenly, he later recounted, he felt a large invisible hand seize his own. Under the power of this unseen force, his hand scribbled furiously across the paper. In the background he heard a soft, sweet voice speaking words of great wisdom. When an overwhelming sense of fatigue interrupted his concentration, his father's voice admonished him: "Write under our dictates, you are not tired." The experience confirmed Rey's belief in spiritualism and led him to become a dedicated spiritualist medium.[66]

With his conversion to the new religion, Rey opened his home in the Faubourg Tremé to a spiritualist circle that included his wife and two sisters, Alphonsine and Sylphide, and other prominent members of the Creole community. Rey's wife, a cousin of Henriette Delille and the daughter of Pierre Crocker, belonged to one of the city's most distinguished black Creole families. Nelson Desbrosses was a contributor to *Les Cenelles* and a medium whose healing feats rivaled those of Valmour, his mentor. Rey's brother Octave and his friends Charles Veque and François Estève were community activists.

In accordance with their belief in individual perfectibility, spiritualists advocated education and educational reform as an accompaniment to religious regeneration. Not coincidentally, therefore, Rey's circle of black Creole spiritualists also included prominent members of the Couvent school's teaching staff. Joanni Questy, the noted Romantic writer, was Armand Lanusse's assistant principal at the facility, and spiritualists Adolphe Duhart, Constant Reynès, and Joseph Lavigne were Questy's fellow instructors. While expressing reservations, their colleague Samuel Snaer also visited the circle.[67]

Believing that their communications constituted sacred texts, Rey carefully preserved the group's messages in hardcover books. The transcribed entries generally began with the date of the communication and included the location of the séance, name of the medium, and subject of the message. The spirit guide's name appeared at the end of the essay. Consistent with the spirit messages published in *Le Spiritualiste*, the Creole communications combined an unrelenting attack on orthodox religion with the egalitarian, liberal ideas of representative figures of France's Catholic Reformation, Enlightenment, and age of democratic revolution. Unlike the published correspondences of Barthet's journal, however, the communications of the séance registers contained messages from deceased members of the black Creole community. These spirit manifestations reflected the belief that the spirits of the dead could share their otherworldly intelligence with relatives and friends. Likewise, the registers contained a large number of correspondences from Antonio de Sedella, revealing the depth of the former church leader's influence among Creoles, even though Père Antoine's communications did not appear in *Le Spiritualiste*, Barthet, who generally considered all clergy as the "most persistent enemy of progress," described him as an "excellent man" and "a courageous and praiseworthy Capuchin."[68]

Like Davis, Barthet, and other spiritualists, Rey and his fellow mediums viewed the instructions received in the séances as guidelines to advance human society. In this regard, their communications produced a utopian formula for change based on Christian humanitarianism, universal brotherhood, and political republicanism. In November 1857, a spirit communication attributed to Bernardin de Saint-Pierre, an Enlightenment intellectual whose works influenced Charles Fourier, admonished the prosperous to share their wealth with the less fortunate and described spiritualism as the "only way to create a new world order and begin a 'New Era for humanity' in which all will be brothers and sisters and form a single family. . . . Selfishness will make way for Love of the Public Welfare; all will be Peace Harmony, Progress."[69]

The spiritualist engaged in neither the "vain and insipidly superficial practices of a Catholic nor in the bigotry of a Puritan," another spirit intoned. Rather, he exercised "a reproachless conduct full of charity towards his brothers and sisters and love for God and his fellow beings. He is truly a Christian and not a feigned one; which is to say, he follows the moral precepts of Jesus."

In other communications, the spirits of the Creole séances assured their listeners of mankind's advancement toward spiritualist ideals: "Everything in life progresses; the spirit rises, see the enormity of what we have done since Jesus." In keeping with spiritualism's view of technological advances as a key factor in humanity's social regeneration, the spirit messages glorified the discovery of the printing press, the steam engine, and the telegraph. These inventions had facilitated a freer flow of information and goods and had contributed to humanity's intellectual and material progress.

The communications pointed to events in Europe as evidence of advances in the political realm. The messages recalled the most radical phase of the French Revolution, when republican leaders proclaimed universal male suffrage and the abolition of slavery: "The Revolution of '93 contributed a great deal to human progress despite the grave mistakes of its leaders." In contemporary Europe, the correspondence continued, Italian patriots nurtured the revolutionary cause while Russia "substantiates the social pace by the emancipation of its serfs." France, "more intelligent, more advanced in its progress, has long ago abolished these unjust laws."

The spirit messages gloried in the republican ideal. One transcription showered praise on Guiseppe Garibaldi, the leader of republican forces in Italy, for his unsparing devotion to the revolutionary cause: "Garibaldi! Great hero, the new Washington, you only fight for your country and not for self-aggrandizement." And though the message ascribed divisions within the republican ranks to the egotism of the "great men of the Republican party, Lamartine, Hugo, Mazzini, and all the others," it nonetheless praised them as "ardent patriots of the Universal Republic. . . . Children, always be Republicans."[70]

Roman Catholicism, an ally of Europe's monarchical regimes and the religion "in least harmony with the laws of nature," posed the greatest impediment to social regeneration. The institutional church was the "gnawing ulcer which obstructs the progression of society." The entry warned: "Your turn is coming, like Charles X and Louis Philippe, your collapse will be heavy, the edifice will collapse and crush you under its debris."[71]

A subsequent communication inspired by Père Antoine and delivered by Rey sustained the condemnation of the church. Titled "The Ignorance of Men," the essay repudiated orthodox religion and affirmed the righteousness of spiritualist beliefs. The deity of orthodox religion, a manifestation of human egotism and ambition, was an "unjust and cruel being." Only spiritualism, the communication concluded, could reveal God's true nature. Apparently even from the grave Père Antoine fomented schism and rebellion among French-speaking Catholics.[72]

Another communication, by the medium Paulin Durel, addressed more immediate concerns. In an allusion to *plaçage*, a spirit message ascribed to Denis Affre, the radical republican archbishop of Paris who was killed during the 1848 revolution, encouraged correct behavior in sexual relations as a prerequisite to spiritual progress. The essay advised women to shun the material luxuries and fleeting pleasures of illicit relationships. A marriage based on natural law and spiritual love produced conjugal bliss, family stability, and harmonious human relations—the crucial preconditions for realizing the spiritualist ideals of "love, peace, and universal brotherhood." [73]

The spirit messages produced by Creole séances also contained a stinging critique of contemporary society. A number of Rey's communications noted the contradictions between existing realities and the Christian ideal of brotherhood. In a séance in November 1858, at the home of spiritualist J. Martino, Rey produced a communication explaining that the phrase "Our Father," which was synonymous with the concept of God, proved "that we all flow from the same source, that we are the children of the same father." Why, then, the communication continued, "these distinctions exist among us? Why this thirst for domination over your brothers? Why the selfishness with which you repulse them [your brothers] in their pain, in their afflictions, in their needs? Why still these contradictions among you?"

In a séance at Adolphe Duhart's home the following month, Rey's spirit guides resumed their attack on social injustice: "By what rights, Oh men, do you dominate your brother? By what rights do you chain him? . . . Each man in his sphere wants to dominate and yet he admits that God has created us all equal. . . . Oh! mankind when will you cease to be blind to the point of misapprehending that God created the sun for everyone and that his vast creation was made to satisfy the needs of all."

Finally, on May 1, 1860, Rey recorded his last and most prophetic communication before the outbreak of the Civil War. The spirit consoled Rey and his fellow spiritualists: "God sees with pain the calamities which you must endure, He thinks also of the injustices committed by those who dominate the unfortunate classes and who will soon know the sufferings that they [the unfortunate] are forced to endure."[74]

Denied access to traditional avenues of communication and political empowerment, Creole leaders employed nontraditional modes of expression to voice their discontent and affirm their aspirations. They seized upon spiritualism's universal and immutable principles to repudiate the established order. Having derived ideological inspiration from sustained upheaval in France and the French Caribbean and imbued with a messianic religious zeal, they stood poised to pursue their social and political objectives. In the cataclysm of the Civil War, they anticipated the realization of their ideals.

Notes for "Spiritualism's Dissident Visionaries"

[1]*Le Spiritualiste*, October 1858; Geoffrey K. Nelson, *Spiritualism and Society* (New York, 1969), 16-17; quotation from Rodolphe Lucien Desdunes, *Our People and Our History: A Tribute to the Creole People of Color in Memory of the Great Men They Have Given Us and of the God of Works They Have Accomplished* (Baton Rouge, 1973), 53.

[2]Ernest Isaacs, "A History of Nineteenth-Century American Spiritualism as a Religious and Social Movement" (Ph.D. dissertation, University of Wisconsin, 1975), 5-58; Ernest Isaacs, "The Fox Sisters and American Spiritualism," in *The Occult in American: New Historical Perspectives*, eds. Howard Kerr and Charles L. Crow (Urbana, Ill., 1983), 79-81.

[3]The impact of Newtonian physics and the scientific revolution is discussed in Margaret C. Jacob, *The Radical Enlightenment: Pantheists, Freemasons, and Republicans* (London, 1981), Chap. 1; Robert Darnton, *Mesmerism and the End of the Enlightenment in France* (Cambridge, Mass., 1968), 11.

[4]For insight into the influence of the new physics on Enlightenment culture, see Jacob, *The Radical Enlightenment*, Introduction.

[5]Darnton, *Mesmerism*, 3-14; Robert S. Ellwood, Jr., *Alternative Altars: Unconventional and Eastern Spirituality in America* (Chicago, 1979), 92. The term *animal* in animal magnetism derives from the Latin word *anima*, which refers to soul or some other life force; it is in this context that the term animal magnetism was used to describe mesmerism (Robert S. Ellwood, *Alternative Altars: Unconventional and Eastern Spirituality in America* [Chicago, 1979], 85). Mesmerists believed that magnetized subjects could see their internal organs, diagnose their illnesses, and predict the time of their cures (Nicholas P. Spanos and Jack Gottlieb, "Demonic Possessions, Mesmerism, and Hysteria: A Social Psychological Perspective on Their Historical Interrelations," *Journal of Abnormal Psychology*, 88 [1979]: 529-30). Since mesmerists often associated ill health with moral evil, they sometimes conceived of themselves as opponents of injustice and agents of moral as well as physical healing.

[6]Darnton, *Mesmerism*, 108, 110.

[7]Ibid., 143.

[8]R. Laurence Moore, *In Search of White Crows: Spiritualism, Parapsychology, and American Culture* (New York, 1977), 9; Robert C. Fuller, *Mesmerism and the American Cure of Souls* (Philadelphia, 1982), 106; Darnton, *Mesmerism*, 58.

[9]Isaacs, "A History of Nineteenth-Century American Spiritualism," 26-55, 52.

[10]Ibid., 57; Ellwood, *Alternative Altars*, 84.

[11]J. Stillson Judah, *The History and Philosophy of the Metaphysical Movements in America* (Philadelphia, 1967), 34-41; Sydney E. Ahlstrom, *A Religious History of the American People* (New Haven, 1972), 483-86; Ellwood, *Alternative Altars*, 84-89.

[12]Robert W. Delp, "Andrew Jackson Davis and Spiritualism," in *Pseudo-Science and Society in Nineteenth-Century America*, ed. Arthur Wrobel (Lexington, Ky., 1987), 100-102; Judah, *The History and Philosophy of the Metaphysical Movements*, 55-56; Isaacs, "A History of Nineteenth-Century American Spiritualism," 166-210.

[13]Isaacs, "A History of Nineteenth-Century American Spiritualism, 44-45; Frank Podmore, *Mediums of the Nineteenth Century*, 2 vols. (published in 1902 as *Modern Spiritualism: A History and a Criticism*; rpr. New York, 1963), 1:164; Robert W. Delp, "Andrew Jackson Davis's *Revelations*, Harbinger of American Spiritualism," *New York Historical Society Quarterly*, 60 (1971): 220.

[14]Slater Brown, *The Heyday of Spiritualism* (New York, 1970), 90.

[15]Judah, *The History and Philosophy of the Metaphysical Movements*, 39, 56; Isaacs, "A History of Nineteenth-Century American Spiritualism," 236, 238.

[16]Jonathan Beecher, *Charles Fourier: The Visionary and His World* (Berkeley, 1986), 65-67, 74, 226, 237-38; Isaacs, "A History of Nineteenth-Century American Spiritualism," 11.

[17]Robert W. Delp, "A Spiritualist in Connecticut: Andrew Jackson Davis, the Hartford Years, 1850-1854," *New England Quarterly*, 53 (1980): 350-51.

[18]Delp, "Andrew Jackson Davis's *Revelations*," 214-15; Isaacs, "A History of Nineteenth-Century American Spiritualism," 47.

[19]Isaacs, "A History of Nineteenth-Century American Spiritualism," 46, 48. For Brisbane's role in the American Fourierist movement, see Carl J. Guarneri, *The Utopian Alternative: Fourierism in Nineteenth-Century America* (Ithaca, N. Y., 1991), 25-32.

[20]Isaacs, "The Fox Sisters," in *The Occult in America: New Historical Perspectives*, eds. Howard Kerr and Charles L. Crow (Urbana, 1983), 81; Delp, "Andrew Jackson Davis's *Revelations*," 215-16.

[21]Podmore, *Mediums*, I, 173.

[22]Delp, "Andrew Jackson Davis," 47, 48, 52.

[23]Moore, *In Search of White Crows*, 61-62; *Boston Banner of Light*, March 13, April 3, 1858; quotation from Nelson, *Spiritualism and Society*, 17.

[24]Brown, *Heyday of Spiritualism*, 12-15; Fuller, *Mesmerism*, 17-20; Wallace K. Tomlinson and J. John Perret, "Mesmerism in New Orleans, 1845-1861," *American Journal of Psychology*, 12 (1974), 1403; *New Orleans Daily Picayune*, July 16, 1843.

[25]Tomlinson and Perret, "Mesmerism," 1403. For information on Barthet, see Manuscript Census Returns, Census of 1850, in Record Group 29, Records of the Bureau of the Census, National Archives, Washington, D. C.

[26]Tomlinson and Perret, "Mesmerism," 1403-1404; *L'Abeille*, March 15, October 22, 1847; *Propagateur Catholique*, August 9, 1851, June 26, 1852. The involvement of Catholic clerics in mesmerism may be attributed to Jansenism's continued influence in nineteenth-century New Orleans. Jansenism, often seen as a precursor to mesmerism, stressed a direct relationship between God and the believer, and the trancelike states of magnetized subjects closely resembled the visionary experiences of Jansenist mystics. Such similarities surely predisposed many of the city's Catholics to mesmerism's influence (Darnton, *Mesmerism*, 36, 61).

[27]*Propagateur Catholique*, August 9, 1851, June 26, 1852.

[28]Ibid., May 15, 1852. During the religious excitement of the eighteenth century, the phenomena of convulsive shaking and gasping accompanied spiritual revelation for a group of religious ecstatics, or *convulsionnaires*, within the French Jansenist movement (Clarke Garrett, *Spirit Possession and Popular Religion* [Baltimore, Md., 1987], 10-11, 26).

[29]Tomlinson and Perret, "Mesmerism," 1403.

[30]Darnton, *Mesmerism*, 145-46.

[31]Ibid., 146, 148.

[32]Auguste Viatte, *Victor Hugo et les illuminés de son temps* (Montreal, 1942), 29; Edward Larocque Tinker, *Les Ecrits de langue française en Louisiane su XIXe siècle: essays et bibliographies* (Paris, 1933), 30.

[33]In political exile on the English Channel island of Jersey from 1852 to 1855, Victor Hugo and his fellow French *proscrits* (proscribed republicans) engaged in spiritualist séances similar to those of their contemporaries in New Orleans, recording communications with the spirits of Molière, Dante, Racine, Marat, Charlotte Corday, Muhammad, Jesus Christ, Plato, and others. And much like Testut, Hugo in his capacity as a spiritualist medium conceived of himself as a prophet who had been chosen to lead humanity. For Hugo's exile in Jersey and mention of Pierre Soulé's visit to the island see Philip Stevens, *Victor Hugo in Jersey* (Chichester, Eng., 1985), 72. For Hugo's spiritualist activities, see André Maurois, *Olympio: The Life of Victor Hugo*, trans. Gerard Hopkins (New York, 1956), Chap. 36; Roland N. Stromberg, *An Intellectual History of Modern Europe* (New York, 1966), 213-14; J. L. Talmon, *Romanticism and Revolt: Europe, 1815-1848* (New York, 1967), 136-145.

[34]David Owen Evans, *Social Romanticism in France, 1830-1848* (Oxford, 1951), 39-40, 81.

[35]Charles Testut, *Fleurs d'été: poesies* (New Orleans, 1851), xiii-xiv.

[36]Ibid., 102-103.

[37]*L'Equité*, May 21, 1871, p. 6.

[38]Ibid., May 28, 1871, p. 6.

[39]Ibid.

[40]Ibid., May 21, 1871, p. 6.

[41]Lagarde, "Charles Testut," 26-27; Charles Testut, *Le Vieux Salomon ou une famille d'esclaves au XIX siècle* (New Orleans, 1872), 95. For a good summary of *Le Vieux Salomon*, see John Maxwell Jones, *Slavery and Race in Nineteenth-Century Louisiana-French Literature* (Camden, N. J., 1978), 81-94.

[42]Testut, *Le Vieux Salomon*, 97.

[43]*L'Equité*, June 3, 1871.

[44]*Le Spiritualiste*, May, July, 1858, pp. 136, 195-96.

[45]Ibid., July, 1858, pp. 195-196; Viatte also mentions the French government's crackdown (Viatte, Victor Hugo, 32). Laforgue gave an account of his run-in with the law in a letter to Cahagnet dated September 5, 1852; in the same letter, he also described an emotion-filled visit to his Pau residence on September 1 by four New Orleanians (Alphonse Cahagnet, *Encyclopédie magnetique spiritualiste* [Paris, 1856], 107-108).

[46]Ann Braude, *Radical Spirits: Spiritualism and Women's Rights in Nineteenth-Century America* (Boston, 1989), 29-30. For a similar contemporary view of spiritualism's popularity with the city's Catholics, see *Le Spiritualiste*, April 1857, p. 112.

[47]*Propagateur Catholique*, October 23, 30, 1852.

[48]Ibid., November 13, 1852.

[49]M. D. Griffin, "Spiritism," *New Catholic Encyclopedia* (1967), 577.

[50]Braude, *Radical Spirits*, 29-30, 211n49; newspaper clipping of Joanni Questy obituary, n. d., Charles B. Rousseve Collection, Amistad Research Center, Tulane University, New Orleans, La.

[51]*Le Spiritualiste*, October 1857, p. 261, August 1858, p. 197.

[52]Ibid., January, February, 1857, pp. 3-4, 30.

[53]Ibid., October 1857, pp. 149-50, 261-64, January 1857, p. 3.

[54]Ibid., May 1858, p. 114, September 1857, p. 234.

[55]Ibid., May 1857, p. 145. "Marie Bar" was undoubtedly Marie Barthet, wife of spiritualist leader Joseph Barthet.

[56]*Propagateur Catholique*, January 30, 1858.

[57]Ibid., April 3, 1858; *Le Spiritualiste*, May, 1858, p. 115.

[58]*Le Spiritualiste*, September 1857, p. 233, January, March, May, June, August, 1858, pp. 5-6, 59-61, 115, 167, 199-205, 207.

[59]Ibid., January 1857, p. 27, January, June, August, 1858, pp. 6-7, 166, 223; quotations from Allan Kardec, *Le Livre des esprits* (1857; rpr. Montréal, 1979), 369, and *Le Spiritualiste*, July, 1857, p. 202.

[60]*Banner of Light*, April 3, 1858; *Courier de la Louisiane*, July 1, 1857; *Le Spiritualiste*, May, October, 1858, pp. 137-38, 278.

[61] *Le Spiritualiste*, May, June, 1858, pp. 114, 117, 141.

[62]Ibid., September, October, 1858, pp. 225, 279. The term *gris-gris* is a voodoo expression meaning an evil spell; voodoo, an African-American folk religion, appeared in New Orleans in the eighteenth century (Gwendolyn Midlo Hall, "The Formation of Afro-Creole Culture," in *Creole New Orleans: Race and Americanization*, eds. Arnold R. Hirsch and Joseph Logsdon [Baton Rouge, 1992], 85-87).

[63]*Le Spiritualiste*, October, 1858, p. 279.

[64]The identity of Père Ambroise is unknown; in a historical note, Barthet wrote that Ambroise was born in Tours, France, in 1570 and died there in 1638. Given the chronology, it is possible that Barthet is referring to Dom Ambroise Tarbourier, a Benedictine monk and a Catholic reformer of the seventeenth century. See *Le Spiritualiste*, August 1858, p. 209, December 1858, p. 327.

[65]Ibid., May 1857, p. 115, March 1856, p. 73, 206; *Christian Spiritualist* (New York), May 13, 1854, p. 3; *Banner of Light*, April 3, 1858. For the spirit communications of these mediums, see the Spiritualist Registers, September 1857- May 1860, René Grandjean Collections, Earl K. Long Library, University of New Orleans, New Orleans, La.

[66]Toledano and Christovich, "The Role of Free People of Color," in *Faubourg Tremé and the Bayou Road*, eds. Mary Louise Christovich and Roulhac Toledano (Gretna, La., 1980), 94; see Rey's autobiographical sketch in his spirit communications of October 26, 1859, Spiritualist Registers, Grandjean Collection; see also ibid., November 28, 1858.

[67]Spiritualist Registers, October, 1859; Toledano and Christovich, "The Role of Free People of Color," in *Faubourg Tremé*, eds. Christovich and Toledano, 87, 99; Desdunes, *Our People*, 52-53. For *Le Spiritualiste*'s advocacy of educational reforms, see the August 1858, issue, pp. 197-206; Christian, "A Black History," Chap. 14, 13-15.

[68]*Le Spiritualiste*, August 1858, p. 209; in the registers, Sedella is affectionately referred to as "Père Antoine."

[69]For Bernardin de Saint-Pierre's influence on Fourier, see Beecher, *Charles Fourier*, 70, 342-43, 346; Spiritualist Registers, November, 1857.

[70]Spiritualist Registers, February, 1858; December 6, 1858; December 30, 1859; February 5, 1860.

[71]Ibid., November 28, December 6, 1858. The monarchy of Charles X of France (1824-30) collapsed in the July Revolution. French King Louis-Philippe (1830-48) was overthrown in the February Revolution of 1848.

[72]Ibid., November 25, 1858.

[73]Ibid., October, 1858.

[74]Ibid., November 19, December 19, 1858; May 1, 1860.

WHEN THE SAINTS CAME MARCHING IN:
THE MORMON EXPERIENCE IN
ANTEBELLUM NEW ORLEANS, 1840-1855*

David Buice

There are few if any cities in the United States that are more drastically different in spirit and outlook than New Orleans and Salt Lake City. Almost since the moment of its founding in 1718, New Orleans has been a throbbing, cosmopolitan commercial center which has benignly tolerated the foibles of its inhabitants and to this day maintains an air of convivial decadence. Salt Lake City, in contrast, was sparked by the dreams of Brigham Young and his fellow churchmen who labored to establish a haven for God's chosen ones amidst the barrenness of the American Far West.

The many disparities of these two cities and their inhabitants notwithstanding, for a brief while prior to the Civil War New Orleans played an important though now largely forgotten role in the history of the Mormon Church. Mormon missionaries scoured the city seeking converts while at the same time thousands of European Mormons passed through New Orleans en route to their New Zion in the American wilderness, and from it, they gained their first impressions of America, both good and bad.

The Mormon experience in New Orleans began during the winter of 1840-41 when two itinerant Mormon elders slipped into the city uninvited, unheralded, and unnoticed. Their names were Elam Ludington and E. G. Terrill. Exactly when they arrived and where they came from is not known but their purpose was clear: to carry their version of the Christian gospel to the multitude of lost souls in this wayward metropolis on the Mississippi. Quickly perceiving that the task which they had staked out was far beyond their limited abilities, on January 4, 1841, they sent an almost frantic letter to Joseph Smith in Nauvoo, Illinois. "For God's sake," they implored the prophet, "send help to this city before the people perish .... Send us a Peter or an apostle to preach unto us Jesus ...." With their appeal, they forwarded ten dollars to help meet the traveling expenses of the person sent to assist them.[1]

This letter struck a responsive chord in Nauvoo, and church authorities chose an elder named Harrison Sagers to proceed immediately to New Orleans to assist his two

*First published in *Louisiana History*, 23 (1982): 221-37. Reprinted with the kind permission of the author and the Louisiana Historical Association.

brethren already there. Sagers was soon on his way and reached his destination on March 28, 1841. Quickly he rented a meeting room, located over the Mechanics Exchange at the corner of Poydras and Camp streets. Advertisements appeared in the local press announcing upcoming Mormon meetings. According to Sagers' account, these early meetings were well attended, but, as frequently occurred, the uniqueness of Mormon doctrines quickly generated opposition. When people began to respond to his preaching, the alarm was quickly sounded through the city by what Sagers called the "priests of Baal and servants of the devil." He responded by issuing a challenge for some of the learned men among his critics to step forward and debate Mormon doctrines with him. None accepted, but this reticence did not indicate any newborn tolerance for the Mormons in New Orleans. On the contrary, Sagers' critics soon resorted to violence in an effort to force him to cease his activities in the city.[2]

In the spring of 1841, the Mormon elders rented a house in Lafayette, a municipality on the outskirts of New Orleans, which eventually would be incorporated into the city in 1852. Here, additional meetings were held, and one spring evening, as Sagers preached to a group assembled in the house, a mob assembled outside. After throwing eggs through the windows, the troublemakers barged through the doors intending to tar and feather Sagers, but the quick-witted elder eluded them. When the ladies present were told by the mob leaders to leave, Sagers, in the confusion, blended into the group and slipped out undetected, surrounded by a phalanx of female admirers. When his adversaries learned what had happened, they vented their anger by breaking all the windows in the house and throwing the furniture into the street to be burned.[3]

Despite the hostility which his preaching engendered, Sagers continued for a while to labor in New Orleans, but after the eruption in Lafayette he was more prudent than he had been earlier. His later meetings were apparently conducted privately and without any public notice or fanfare. Attendance was sparse, as was the number of converts. Where once he had confidently predicted that hundreds would be won over to the church in New Orleans, Sagers conceded that during his stay he converted only eight.[4]

Sagers returned to his home in Nauvoo early in June 1841, disappointed no doubt by the meager results of his labors. He planned to return to New Orleans in the fall, but it appears that he did not. What happened to Elder E. G. Terrill is not clear. Terrill's colleague, Elam Ludington, continued to preach in the city for two more years and for a while in 1842 was assisted by another elder, H. G. Sherwood.[5] But to little avail. New Orleans simply was not fertile ground for the reaping of Mormon converts, nor would it ever be in the antebellum period. In part, this lack of success in proselyting can probably be attributed to the very strong influence exerted by the Roman Catholic Church among a large element in the city's population. In addition, the dominant spirit of New Orleans worked against the Mormons; among the unchurched sons of mammon in this city of hustle and mirth, the Mormon Church, with its emphasis on the moral, abstemious life, had very little appeal.

Yet if no great number of people in New Orleans embraced the doctrines expounded by Joseph Smith, in other areas of the world Mormon missionaries were surprisingly successful, and for many of these foreign converts, New Orleans became their gateway to America. As early as 1837 the church sent its first missionaries to Great Britain and among the mechanics and tradespeople of the British Isles, thousands of converts stepped forward. Slightly later, Mormon missionaries moved into the Scandinavian countries with equal success.[6]

It is conceivable that these people once converted might have remained where they were to propagate their new faith among their fellow countrymen. Most did not, however, because of the enormous influence exerted among church members by the Mormon doctrine known as the gathering. Stated briefly, this millennial doctrine held that the Saints should remove themselves as much as possible from the sinful world and gather together in their New Zion in America where they would live together in righteousness and prepare for the return of Christ. Among those converted, this doctrine fired a fervent zeal difficult to comprehend today. Most Mormon converts were willing to leave their homes and, if need be, their loved ones, and bear any trial or hardship to gather with their fellow Saints and await their Lord's return. Indeed, as one historian of the Mormon Church has expressed it, the Mormon convert who did not feel the enormous pull of the gathering was considered a queer fish in the gospel net.[7]

But there was a serious problem which had to be confronted: how could these European converts most easily reach Nauvoo, the New Zion which Joseph Smith and his followers had established on the banks of the Mississippi? Three possibilities merited consideration. Since there was no network of railroads linking the Atlantic with the Mississippi Valley, those arriving from Europe might travel to Canada and then westward to Nauvoo by way of the St. Lawrence River and the Great Lakes. Or they could sail to some eastern seaport in the United States and by way of canals and the Ohio River make their way to Nauvoo. Finally, they might sail to New Orleans and make their way upriver to Nauvoo. All of these alternatives were used at various times by the church's early converts, but it quickly became apparent that the New Orleans route was the best of the three. It might be a little longer, but because of the large number of ships sailing between Liverpool and New Orleans and the innumerable steamboats plying the Mississippi, it was clearly superior to the others. In short, accommodations from Liverpool to Nauvoo via New Orleans were both abundant and relatively inexpensive.[8]

Once the advantages of the New Orleans route became apparent, the Quorum of the Twelve Apostles, the ruling body of the church, issued an epistle to the Saints in Europe on November 15, 1841. The missive instructed them to make New Orleans their established port as the expense was less and the convenience of water travel much greater than by either of the other routes. But there were warnings to be heeded. To avoid maladies such as cholera and yellow fever, those who were gathering should schedule their journey so as to arrive in New Orleans during the cooler months of the year. Further, while making their way to Nauvoo, they must not be surprised if their ears "were saluted by the false and filthy language of wicked and designing men who are ready to blast the character of the prophet." These and other trials, perils, and temptations were to be borne gladly, and the epistle bluntly admonished those who were not prepared to endure to the end like good soldiers to stay where they were and be destroyed.[9]

Prior to the issuance of this pronouncement, a few companies of European Mormons had passed through New Orleans en route to Nauvoo. Once church officials gave their sanctions, however, the flow of Saints through the city greatly increased. Responding to the call of the gathering, converts from England, Ireland, Wales, Scotland, and the Scandinavian countries passed through the city by the thousands. This movement was halted temporarily by the murder of Joseph Smith in June 1844, but once Smith's successor Brigham Young located the site of the new gathering place in the shadow of the Wasatch Mountains, passage of foreign Saints through the city resumed in 1848 and continued until the New Orleans route to Zion was abandoned in 1855.[10]

With the studiousness and sobriety that have always characterized their group activities, Mormon migration from Europe to Zion by way of New Orleans quickly took on a well-regulated, regimented character. In contrast to the ordinary emigrant who had to grapple with a confusing array of problems and pitfalls, the Mormon emigrant was carefully shepherded by church officials and agents who arranged, as nearly as possible, every detail of travel from Liverpool to the Great Salt Lake Valley. Because they were relieved of so many anxieties and were enormously excited by their dreams and expectations, Mormon emigrants in general soon became known for their patience, harmony, and cooperative spirit. There were, of course, some exceptions.[11]

The voyage from Liverpool to New Orleans took a minimum of four weeks and more often seven to ten, depending on the vagaries of wind and weather. Not surprisingly, simple boredom, brought on by long weeks at sea, was a frequent problem among the emigrant Saints. To combat it, the elders who led the emigrant companies put their fellow Saints to work making the tents and wagon covers needed to cross the plains. Decks were frequently scrubbed and sprinkled with vinegar to prevent the air in the sleeping quarters from becoming too foul. School was conducted for the children, if for no other reason than to keep them occupied for a few hours each day. Concerts were organized, the sacraments administered and frequent sermons delivered. Yet caution sometimes had to be used. As one diarist discreetly explained, sailors at times responded to the sermons by asking to be baptized in order to "assist in their designs upon the honour of other sisters." But not all the shipboard converts were so patently insincere. On the voyage of the *International* early in 1853, the captain and all but three of the crew members were converted and baptized, and no one questioned their motives.[12]

In addition to boredom, the monotonous diet was another source of dissatisfaction. It was largely composed of such basics as rice, oatmeal, potatoes, biscuits, salted meat and tea. Occasionally a few live pigs—called "passengers of Irish descent" by some of the English converts—might be brought on board prior to sailing to provide a little fresh meat during the voyage, but this seems to have been a rare occurrence.

The fare was not only monotonous, it was also often poorly prepared. Working on a guidebook to be used by future Mormon emigrants, artist Frederick Piercy crossed the Atlantic with a group of Saints on the *Jersey* in 1853. Noting the cooking problem, he remarked: "I do not believe that the Queen, with her Privy Council, and the Houses of Lords and Commons put together, could have legislated successfully for it." He added that two or three revolutions occurred in the galley during this voyage, and in one of these the cooks were forcibly expelled. But to no avail, as the revolutionaries not only burned their fingers but quarrelled among themselves. Piercy concluded: " . . . the [end] result was that the chuckling cooks re-took their honours, and were as impartial and as unpopular as ever."[13]

Despite the efforts to prevent it, invariably there was some complaining as one week faded into the next and nerves frayed. One Mormon diarist noted while crossing the Atlantic that there were some spirits on board who would grumble "were they in Heaven with Jesus Himself." On occasion those who complained and resisted the instructions of the elders too much were cut off from the church during the trans-Atlantic voyage, but such occurrences were rare. With their faces turned toward Zion, most endured with good cheer the hardships which the Atlantic hurled at them.[14]

Even the death of children and other loved ones was accepted stoically more often than not. The experience of English convert Jean Rio Baker was typical. Crossing the Atlantic in 1851, she watched her small son Josiah die from some unnamed malady that had afflicted him since the beginning of the voyage. After an all night vigil by the male members of Mrs. Baker's family, the child's body was sewn up in a canvas bag and buried at sea nearly a thousand miles from the land of his birth. Even in the depths of her sadness, however, this grieving mother found cause for thanksgiving—noting in her diary:

> . . . but the Lord has answered my prayers in this one thing—that if it was not His will to spare my boy to reach his destined home with us, that he would take him while we were on the sea—for I would rather leave his body in the ocean than bury him in a strange land and leave him.[15]

As the voyage neared its end and the Gulf Coast of the United States loomed in the distance, the immigrant Saints exchanged one set of problems for another. Near the coast, steam-powered tugs met the sailing vessels, dragged them across the bar at the mouth of the Mississippi and then towed them to New Orleans. The first sight that greeted the Saints were not too impressive, mostly swamps and an occasional fisherman's shack built on stilts. About sixty miles downriver from New Orleans, however, the swamps gave way to farms and plantations. To people who had seen nothing but the endless expanses of sea for weeks, the cultivated fields and citrus groves, which at that time abounded in the area, were marvelous to behold, and the spirits which had flagged during the last weary weeks of the ocean voyage began to revive. But sometimes even here there were problems. It was not uncommon for two ships to be lashed on each side of one of the tugs, and using the tug as a bridge, Gentile immigrants from another ship sometimes made their way over to a vessel carrying a company of Saints. Such an occurrence took place in 1853 when the *Forest Monarch*, carrying the first large company of Scandinavian Saints was towed upriver, and convert Christian Nielson wrote with regret in his diary that "many unclean things were perpetrated by some individuals of our people."[16]

These problems and temptations were minor compared to those to be faced once they reached New Orleans. The leaders of the immigrant companies invariably warned their brethren to be wary of the riverfront thieves who flourished in the city and to avoid quarrels in a land where deadly weapons were carried. Events soon revealed that the advice was in order, for often as soon as an immigrant ship reached the docks, thieves flocked on board to try to fleece the passengers of the money and few valuables they had. When challenged, a felon usually swore that he had a friend below deck, and when asked to name his friend, he often gave some common Irish name. Another ploy used by confidence men was to pose as riverboat employees. Cut-rate prices were offered for passage to St. Louis, and letters of recommendation, allegedly signed by Mormon church officials, were waved in the faces of the bewildered immigrants.[17] Money and baggage turned over to characters of this ilk were rarely recovered, and many Saints were first introduced in this way to Yankee ingenuity by the charlatans of New Orleans.

As much as any of its other accomplishments and attractions, New Orleans has for generations taken great pride in the rich cuisine offered by its many fine restaurants, yet to church officials this too was a temptation to be avoided. After living for weeks on the blandest of diets, newly arrived immigrants were sorely tempted to gorge themselves on the rich food and drink the city had to offer. This sudden change of diets, however, could produce unfortunate side effects, and repeatedly the Saints were warned to consume with moderation. The advice was not always heeded, especially since excellent meals in many of the city's restaurants cost as little as five cents. On one occasion a bibulous Saint who had greatly overindulged walked out into the Mississippi River, mistaking the moon's reflection on the water for a walkway. Fortunately, he was rescued by his companions before he drowned. This incident was dutifully reported in *Millennial Star*, the church's official publication in the British Isles, so that other would-be emigrants might profit from the example and conduct themselves with propriety when they eventually reached New Orleans.[18]

With typical foresight and concern for their brethren, the Mormons attempted to guide the immigrant Saints around the pitfalls of New Orleans by maintaining agents in the city from 1848 to 1855. Of the various men who served in this capacity, none was a native of New Orleans and all found the place new and strange, though not necessarily attractive. Upon arrival, the agent typically would make contact with the dozen or so Saints scattered around the city and organize among them a branch of the church. The agent invariably served as president of the branch, and through this organization, he attempted to maintain discipline and morale among those Saints who had stopped temporarily in New Orleans to earn funds to complete their trip. His primary task, however, was to meet immigrant Saints at the waterfront and move them through the city and on upriver toward Zion as quickly as possible.

The first of these agents was a Connecticut Yankee, Lucius N. Scovil, who reached New Orleans in March 1848. Upon arriving, he made his way along the riverfront trying both to locate immigrant ships and acquaint himself with the city. As he absorbed the sights, sounds, and smells of New Orleans, Scovil quickly perceived that he was in a far different climate than any he had ever known, as the customs and habits of the people were not like any he had ever encountered before. In addition to the strange environment, poverty was an ever-present affliction. Scovil wrote that he found New Orleans to be a "hard place," by which he meant that jobs were scarce and his fellow churchmen in the city were extremely poor.[19]

The financial bind that Scovil soon found himself in led to one of the most bizarre incidents that any of the church agents experienced in the city. During the winter of 1848-49, a severe cholera epidemic swept through the city. In the midst of the desolation wrought by this scourge, depressed by his lack of success in winning converts in the city, and with his funds almost exhausted, Scovil, on the morning of March 2, 1849, pondered his situation as he took a meandering walk. As he strolled through the streets suddenly, he said, he heard "an audible voice" that told him to go to a place in the city called Caliboose Square.[20] Scovil does not make it clear in his account if the voice was an earthly or a celestial one. Whatever the source, he said that the voice told him that he should go to the south side of the square where he would find a bookstore run by an old Frenchman. He should buy from the proprietor a lottery ticket bearing the number 9998, and he would win a prize.

In writing an account of this episode, Scovil said that the thought of buying a lottery ticket was alien to his natural feelings. Nevertheless, he followed the directions and in fifteen minutes found himself in the Frenchman's bookstore. When Scovil asked the man if he sold lottery tickets, he at first said no as lotteries were illegal in Louisiana. After some gentle prodding the proprietor finally admitted that for twenty years he had indeed sold tickets from the Havana lottery. When the merchant displayed his unsold wares, Scovil to his amazement found a half ticket bearing the number 9998. For $2.50 he bought it, and ten days later word arrived by steamer from Havana that he had won $250. Scovil concluded his account of this episode saying that he drew his money from a local bank and felt truly thankful to God for what had happened.[21]

A Scotsman by the name of Thomas McKenzie followed Scovil as the church agent in New Orleans and assumed his duties in the fall of 1849. During his tenure, two meeting rooms were rented by the Mormons, one at 82 Hevia Street and another on Dryades Walk, the latter described as being quite private and removed from the noise of the street. At this time also the most complete records of the New Orleans branch were kept, and these give a fascinating glimpse into some of the activities of the Saints in New Orleans. At one meeting, for example, one of the sisters complained about McKenzie visiting her on church business at the boarding house where she worked. The basis for her complaint was that she did not want her employer to know she was a Mormon, a statement which reveals that anti-Mormon sentiment still existed in the city. At another meeting, a disgruntled sister voiced the opinion that New Orleans was a "complete Hell for all manner of wickedness was carried on and practiced here."[22]

Polygamy first raised its head, at least obliquely, among the Saints in New Orleans during McKenzie's tenure and caused more than a little difficulty. One member, identified in the branch records only as Brother Russell, received permission to leave the city and move his wife and child upriver, presumably to St. Louis. Within a short time, however, he returned to New Orleans alone and began living with two female members of the church, Zelica Latete and Mary Elvin. His fellow Saints were mortified. Church officials in America had not yet publicly acknowledged polygamy, and these transplanted European Mormons knew little if anything about the doctrine at this time. At a stormy meeting held on March 6, 1850, Russell was accused of having taught "spiritual wifeism" in Scotland, and he was asked to explain his relationship to the two ladies in New Orleans. In anger Russell shouted that McKenzie was a tyrant and had once accused Sister Latete of running a house of ill fame in the city. At this point the meeting became chaotic, and a number of angry accusations were hurled across the meeting room on Dryades Walk. When tempers subsided and order was restored, Russell, on second thought, asked to be forgiven for what he had said and done. A motion to that effect carried, but whether Russell rejoined his wife and child upriver is not clear.[23]

McKenzie's successors in New Orleans were John Brown, a native of Tennessee who served from 1852 to 1854, and another Scotsman, James McGaw, who spent the winter of 1854-55 in the city. Neither liked the place. Brown reached the Crescent City on December 6, 1852. Three days later he stood on a New Orleans street and watched the passing of a funeral procession honoring John C. Calhoun, Henry Clay, and Daniel Webster. All business had stopped, church bells tolled, and as the bands, clubs and military companies passed, Brown could not help moralizing a bit:

> While viewing the procession, I could not help reflecting on the scene—think of a whole nation of professedly enlightened people mourning and making a great ado at the death of three political demagogues who lived to an old age in affluence, wealth and ease at the expense of the public; how has this same nation treated the Apostles and Prophets of God? . . . They had been seized, cast into prison and then murdered in cold blood . . . while the nation, instead of weeping, shout for joy to think they have got rid of them. O, Lord, Judge between us and our enemies and reward unto them double.[24]

A few days later, on December 19, 1852, Brown brought the few Saints residing in the city together and reorganized the New Orleans branch of the church. For the next several months, he labored diligently ministering to the members—good, honest-hearted souls he called them—and moving the immigrant Saints through the city and upriver as quickly as possible. The labor took its toll. On April 3, 1853, he wearily wrote his wife: "Sometimes I can neither eat nor sleep on account of so much care and anxiety and so many things to see and so many folks to wait on to prevent them from being imposed on . . . ."[25]

In addition to the multitude of cares which he faced daily in this strange city far removed from his home and family, Brown also endured the annual Mardi Gras madness that afflicts the city prior to the advent of the Lenten season. He wrote that during the celebration, the streets were filled with boys and men wearing masks and occasionally women's clothing. The pockets of the revelers were filled with flour which they threw on those they met in the streets. By evening, pedestrians, sidewalks, doors, and windows were all well starched, he wrote. Bewildered by this bizarre behavior, Brown ventured the guess that this form of insanity must be some strange French custom, "there being a great many of that nation here. . . ."[26]

Around mid-May, 1853, Brown left the city and returned to his home in Utah. His departure came none too soon. During the summer of 1853, a disastrous yellow-fever epidemic swept the city, and at its height, unburied bodies stacked up in the city's cemeteries and decayed in the hot summer sun while barrels of tar were burned all over the city in an effort to overpower the stench of death. Despite the pestilence, Brown returned for another round of labor during the winter of 1853-54.[27]

Elder James McGaw was the last Mormon agent in New Orleans, serving during the winter of 1854-55. By the time he arrived, the worst of the yellow-fever epidemic was over, but he still found New Orleans a most unattractive city. He reported that business activity was very dull, the streets were filled with beggars, and an epidemic of violent crime was then sweeping the city. As had been the case with his predecessors, his missionary activities were not very successful; he baptized only two converts during his stay in New Orleans, and writing to a friend in February 1855, he expressed the hope that he would soon be relieved from "this miserable place."[28]

And he was. Because of the dangers and temptations the immigrant Saints faced in all the Mississippi River towns, church officials had long contemplated abandoning the New Orleans route to Zion. No practical alternative could be found, however, until the mid-1850s when the westward expansion of the railroad network finally linked Chicago with the Atlantic seaboard. The extension of iron rails into the upper Mississippi River Valley now enabled emigrant Saints to sail to Philadelphia, New York, or Boston from which points they could travel cheaply and in relative safety about one-third of the way across the continent, avoiding the pitfalls of the Mississippi River towns. Brigham Young, in the summer of 1854, consequently instructed church officials in England to stop sending converts to Utah by way of New Orleans. The last ship carrying Mormon immigrants to the city was the *Charles Buck*, which arrived with a company of 403 Saints on March 15, 1855. Altogether in the period from 1841 to 1855, slightly over seventeen thousand Saints passed through New Orleans.[29]

Most of the European Mormons who made the trans-Atlantic crossing during those years said little about the Crescent City in their diaries, journals, and autobiographies. The omission is understandable. They usually remained in the city a day or two at most, and New Orleans was, after all, just another obstacle to be surmounted en route to the everlasting mountains of the West. Not surprisingly then, most gave the city little heed, but the brief, infrequent comments that were made give some idea of the things about the city that impressed them most. Although there were thieves in abundance, the Saints generally found the local merchants to be honest and generous. They expressed amazement that business activity seemed never to cease in this restless city with the markets remaining open even on Easter Sunday. Local folk gawked at them as they made their way through the streets dressed in heavy nailed boots, knee breeches, and smocks. The Saints, in turn, marvelled that everyone in New Orleans seemed always to be dressed in their Sunday best. Even slaves were seen moving about the city dressed in embroidered silks and satins. The reaction of the Saints to slavery was mixed; some found the spectacle of human bondage sickening and depressing while others were impressed by the cheerfulness of the slaves. Even those waiting to be sold in the city's slave markets seemed to have no cares whatever, and more than one Mormon diarist concluded that the slaves in New Orleans were better off than the poor in England.

There was also the matchless cuisine. In addition to sampling the nickel restaurant meals, those Saints fortunate enough to visit in local homes found that the tables of the middle and upper classes groaned with a plentitude of delicacies. Coffee, eggs, ham, beef, dried fish, salads, hot soda cakes, bread and butter might all be served for breakfast. For dinner, boiled fish, stewed pigs feet, rumsteaks, wild game, vegetables, pickles and salads. Similar fare was served at supper, and all was washed down with tumblers of wine and brandy. It appears certain, however, that those Saints who remained in the city temporarily to earn additional funds before continuing their journey westward rarely ate this well. Jobs were often scarce, and the wages paid immigrant Saints were usually lower than those given native workers, but not necessarily because of anti-Mormon prejudice. Many New Orleans area employers simply believed that laborers from the old countries worked more slowly than native Americans and consequently should not be paid as much.[30]

With the abandonment of the New Orleans route to Zion in 1855, the passage of the Mormon immigrants through the city ended, and today this colorful segment of Mormon and New Orleans history has been all but forgotten. For the Mormons, the New Orleans experience was in many respects a negative one. Though passage through the city provided Mormon immigrants ready access to the heartland of America, the trials and misfortunes which many encountered during their brief sojourns there left a bitter aftertaste. Brigham Young remarked that "it sickens the heart to think of the distress and deaths which have attended the Saints upon that [i.e., the New Orleans] route." Because of the hardships encountered there and because of the city's indifference to the Mormon faith, the church largely shunned the city for many years to come, and it was not until the mid-1920s that the Mormons again established a mission in New Orleans.[31] Meanwhile, most of the buildings where Mormon elders and sisters once met to preach the gospel, sing their hymns, and thrash out their differences have long since disappeared, the victims either of decay or urban renewal. But at least one place in the city which the Saints possibly used very briefly still exists, and around it there swirls a very intriguing tale.

In his 1957 work *Stories of New Orleans* the late folklorist Andrew Jackson Navard, who wrote under the pseudonym André Cajun, tells about the place known as the Brigham Young Courtyard, located at 724 Governor Nicholls Street. The gist of the tale is that after the murder of Joseph Smith in 1844, Brigham Young came to New Orleans and worked for several weeks with a local blacksmith producing the iron hubs and wheel rims the Mormons needed to make the long trek from Illinois to the distant mountains of the West. The place where the blacksmith had his shop previously had been known as the Spanish Stable Courtyard, but Navard tells us that local folk, remembering the prophet's visit to the city, began calling the place the Brigham Young Courtyard.[32]

In all probability, the story is only partially true. Zealous and dedicated as he was, it is highly unlikely that Brigham Young left his people to come to New Orleans in the dark, uncertain days following Joseph Smith's death. He says nothing about any trip to New Orleans in his published journal, and his biographers do not mention the subject either. On the other hand, Young actually did send two of his associates, Elam Ludington, who had first ventured into the city in 1840-41, and Theodore Turley to New Orleans in September 1844. Ludington wrote in his journal that he and Turley spent twenty-nine days in the city conducting "church business" and that they brought a supply of "hollow ware" back to Nauvoo from New Orleans. It appears that the hollow ware referred to was actually a shipment of two hundred muskets to be used by the Mormon militia, the Nauvoo Legion.[33] Possibly some or all of these weapons were purchased from the blacksmith whose shop was located in the Spanish Stable Courtyard. As news spread by word-of-mouth through the city about these Mormon activities, through the simple process of exaggeration some perhaps began saying that Young himself was in New Orleans, and it seems possible that in the countless retelling of the tale the Spanish Stable Courtyard became known as the Brigham Young Courtyard, the place where the prophet himself supposedly had once labored in the city.

This opinion on the origins of this tale is, of course, conjectural, but it seems a plausible explanation as to how a place in the heart of old New Orleans became associated with the name of a Mormon prophet. Whatever the truth may be, if nothing else, hopefully this gem of Louisiana folklore will now remind us that there is a highly colorful Mormon thread amidst the rich tapestry of the city's history. In brief, there was a time, many years ago, in New Orleans when, with all of their dreams, fears, and human frailties, the Saints came marching in.

Notes for "When the Saints Came Marching In: The Mormon Experience in
New Orleans, 1840-1855"

[1]*Times and Seasons,* Vol. 11, 339. Unless otherwise noted, all sources for this paper, both published and un-published, can be found in the archives and library of the Latter Day Saints Church, Salt Lake City, Utah. *Times and Seasons* was an early tabloid-type publication of the Latter-Day Saints Church which gave almost daily accounts of important church activities.

[2]*New Orleans Daily Picayune,* April 3, 1841; "Journal History," Church of Jesus Christ of Latter-Day Saints, Microfilm Reel 4, March 28, 1841. This is an unpublished historical account of the early Church compiled by the Church Historian's Office which is based largely though not entirely on newspaper articles.

[3]Journal History, Reel 4, March 28, May 15, 184 1; Kathryn C. Briede, "A History of the City of Lafayette," *Louisiana Historical Quarterly,* 20 (1937): 895-96.

[4]Journal History, Reel 4, March 28, May 15, 1841.

[5]Ibid.; Elam Ludington, "A Short History of My Life and Times," three pages, unpublished account found in the archives of the Latter-Day Saints Church, Salt Lake City, Utah; hereinafter cited as LDS.

[6]The seminal studies of Mormon missionary activities in these two areas are P. A. M. Taylor, *Expectations Westward: The Mormons and the Emigration of their British Converts in the Nineteenth Century* (Ithaca, N.Y., 1966) and William Mulder, *Homeward to Zion: The Mormon Migration from Scandinavia* (Minneapolis, 1957).

[7]Mulder, *Homeward,* 18-19.

[8]Taylor, *Expectations Westward,* 115-16.

[9]Journal History, Reel 4, November 15, 1841.

[10]Ibid., Reel 7, February 1, March 14, 1848; Andrew Jenson, *Encyclopedic History of the Church of Jesus Christ of Latter-Day Saints* (Salt Lake City, Utah, 1941), 567-77.

[11]*Latter-Day Saints Millennial Star,* 10, 40-41; Frederick H. Piercy, *Route from Liverpool to Great Salt Lake Valley,* ed. Fawn Brodie (Cambridge, Mass., 1962), xvii-xviii; Mulder, *Homeward,* 141; Taylor, *Expectations Westward,* 131.

[12]James Jack, "Journal," LDS; James Hall, "Journal," ibid.; Thomas Day, "Autobiography," ibid.; *Millennial Star,* 16, 446-8; Andrew Jenson, "Manuscript History, Louisiana," April 23, 1853, LDS; Taylor, *Expectations Westward,* 193. Jenson's "Manuscript History" is an unpublished account of Mormon activities in the individual states. Many of the diaries, journals and autobiographies used in this study are handwritten and the pages are unnumbered. Page numbers will be cited when available.

[13]George Henry Abbott Harris, "Diary," LDS; Piercy, *Route,* 66-67.

[14]Hanna Topfield King, "Diary," LDS; James Hall, "Journal," ibid.

[15]Jean Rio Baker, "Diary," 5. Typescript copy in possession of Utah State Historical Society, Salt Lake City, Utah.

[16]James Ririe, "Autobiography," LDS; Christian Nielsen, "Autobiography," ibid. Piercy, *Route,* 69-70.

[17]John Woodhouse, "Journal," 17, LDS; *Millennial Star,* 11, 72, 182-85; Piercy, *Route,* 69-70.

[18]*Millennial Star,* 10, 241-47; 11, 182-5; Piercy, *Route,* 71.

[19]Journal History, Reel 7, March 14, 15, and 17, 1848; *Millennial Star,* 10, 155-6; 11, 54-55.

[20]Scovil's account unfortunately gives no indication of the location of Caliboose Square, but there are two possibilities. As the Spanish had at one time affixed a jail to the rear of the Cabildo, Caliboose Square might have

been Jackson Square. On the other hand, by the time Scovil heard the "audible voice" a new parish prison had been constructed on the corner of Orleans and Tremé streets, across from Circus or Congo Square. This may have been the place he called Caliboose Square.

[21] Journal History, Reel 9, March 12, 1849.

[22] Jenson, "Manuscript History," October 28, December 12, 1849, LDS; Minute Books, New Orleans Branch, Latter-Day Saints Church, 1849-50, November 28, December 5, 1849; hereinafter cited as Minute Books, New Orleans Branch. The records found in the Minute Books are essentially the minutes of meetings recorded by the secretaries of the church branches and later filed with church officials in Salt Lake City. These kinds of records seem to have been kept by the New Orleans branch only in 1849-50.

[23] Minute Books, New Orleans Branch, March 6, 1850.

[24] John Brown, *Autobiography of Pioneer John Brown, 1820-1896* (Salt Lake City, 1941), 124; 128; Andrew Jenson, *Latter-Day Saint Biographical Encyclopedia*, 4 vols. (Salt Lake City, 1971), 4:694-95.

[25] Brown, *Autobiography*, 129, 135.

[26] Ibid., 130.

[27] Jenson, "Manuscript History," February 20, 1854, LDS; Donald E. Everett, "The New Orleans Yellow Fever Epidemic of 1853," *Louisiana Historical Quarterly*, 33 (1953): 381.

[28] Jenson, "Manuscript History," January 1, February 3, 1855,LDS.

[29] Ibid., August 2, 1854; March 15, 1855; April 11, 1856; *Millennial Star*, 13, 374; 14, 24.

[30] Jean Rio Baker, "Diary," 12-13, LDS; James Moyle, "Reminiscences," ibid.; John Woodhouse, "Journal," 17, ibid.; James Hall, "Journal," ibid.; "Reminiscences of William C. Staines," *The Contributor*, 11 (1890-91): 196; William Kilshaw Barton, "Diary and Missionary Journal," 2, LDS.

[31] Jenson, "Manuscript History," April 11, 1856, LDS; Mrs. Howard S. Bennion to Stephen L. Richards, June 30, 1955, Historical Reports, New Orleans Stake, 1955.

[32] André Cajun (Andrew Jackson Navard), *Stories of New Orleans* (New Orleans, 1957), 90-95. Cajun in his account erroneously gives the address as 714 Governor Nicholls Street.

[33] Ludington, "Life and Times"; Journal History, Reel 5, October 16, 1844.

ANTI-CATHOLICISM, NATIVISM, AND LOUISIANA POLITICS IN THE 1850s*

Marius M. Carriere, Jr.

During the 1850s, the American or Know-Nothing party[1] appeared on the American political scene. Although most of the party's political strength was centered in the northeastern United States, the Know-Nothings also had a following in the South. The American party in Louisiana received its greatest support in the New Orleans area, but throughout the state the Know-Nothings found enthusiastic followers.

The Louisiana Know-Nothing party's greatest success came early in its existence. The American party achieved its first significant victory in the New Orleans municipal election of 1854. Following the New Orleans election, the Americans won several local elections in the rural parishes of Louisiana. These successes in 1854 and 1855 were particularly encouraging to the Know-Nothings because the gubernatorial election of 1855 was rapidly approaching. Although the American party lost the gubernatorial election, the Democratic margin of victory was small. Democratic charges that the Know-Nothings proscribed Roman Catholics and that the American party was anti-republican failed to cause a one-sided victory for the Democrats. Americans looked forward to the 1856 presidential election.

Despite attempts by the American party to allay the fears of those who believed that the party was proscriptive, the Americans continued to suffer election defeats in 1856 and 1857. While the Democratic majority was not overwhelming in the presidential election of 1856, fewer parishes supported the American party than before. The state election of 1857 was disastrous for the Know-Nothings who lost three statewide contests and three out of four congressional races, and who watched as the Democrats increased their state legislative majority from seven to eleven in the House and from twelve to thirteen in the Senate.[2] After the 1857 defeat no American party member sought an elective state office on the American party ticket. The party retained a significant following only in New Orleans, but the party lacked unity even in New Orleans. Americans in the Crescent City even appealed to German voters. Former Know-Nothings disenchanted with the continuing violence of the American party, launched Independent movements to challenge

*First published in *Louisiana History*, 35 (1994): 455-74. Reprinted with the kind permission of the author and the Louisiana Historical Association.

American dominance. The American party consequently failed to oppose the Democrats in the gubernatorial election of 1859. In the 1860 presidential election most former Americans supported either of the two Union and conservative candidates, Stephen A. Douglas or John Bell. Know-Nothingism ended more as a Unionist movement as opposed to the nativistic movement which had originally characterized the American party.[3]

Historians have disagreed about the origin of the American party in the South. Some believe that Southerners welcomed the party, not so much because of antagonism to foreigners and Roman Catholics, but because of their hesitation to join the Democratic party which agitated the sectional question.[4] Or, more specifically, many former Whigs saw the new party as a political vehicle to oppose the Democrats.[5] The consensus is that the American party did appear to be an attractive alternative to either political stagnancy or alliance with the Democrats. However, there were some areas of the South which had a significant foreign population that, according to some contemporaries, exacerbated the existing problems of pauperism, intemperance, and demagogy.[6]

Speculation abounds about the role that nativism played in Know-Nothing success in the South and Louisiana. Ray Allen Billington notes that nativism contributed significantly to the American party's success throughout the South,[7] while W. Darrell Overdyke describes Louisiana as a "veritable hotbed" of nativism,[8] and recognizes a fanatical anti-Roman Catholic faction of Know-Nothingism in Louisiana. Overdyke, however, considers anti-Catholicism unimportant, and he considers Louisiana an exception to the anti-Roman Catholicism of the American party elsewhere.[9] Robert C. Reinders takes exception with Overdyke's thesis that Louisiana Know-Nothingism showed a "tolerance" for Roman Catholics. According to Reinders, a significant anti-Catholic sentiment existed (those Roman Catholics who belonged to the American party were mainly anti-clerical according to Reinders) in Louisiana and the Roman Catholic Church recognized this quite clearly.[10]

More recently, William J. Cooper, Jr., argues that Know-Nothing ideology mattered less for Southerners than Northerners and, in Louisiana, "political realities mitigated the influence of ideology." Thus, with the Whig party dead, former Whigs could join the Democratic party, become politically inert, or join the Know-Nothings; Cooper maintains that they chose the last option.[11] Because the Democrats were determined to press their attack against all opponents for being soft on the slavery issue, the Louisiana Know-Nothings (like their comrades across the South and the Whigs before them) spent a great deal of their time defending themselves from this charge and questioning the Democrats' ability to protect the peculiar institution.[12]

In Louisiana, the Know-Nothing party was largely a replacement party for the Whigs, and Americans continually agitated the slavery issue in Louisiana. Like the Whigs, Know-Nothing partisans argued that their party could best protect slavery, and as a result, they kept the slavery question before the voters of the state as much as the Democrats. While the slavery issue loomed large for Louisiana Know-Nothings, there was a genuine nativism that motivated many in Louisiana to participate with the Know-

Nothing party. Because many of the immigrants were Roman Catholics, a religious prejudice became part of the nativist thought in the state. New Orleans received the second greatest number of foreign-born (after New York City) during the 1850s and many remained in that city. Even though the official position of the Louisiana American party opposed the anti-Roman Catholicism of the national party, some Louisiana Know-Nothings viciously attacked the Catholic Church. Indeed, as this study will demonstrate, in North Louisiana and Baton Rouge, there were Americans who made no distinction between the liberal native-born Roman Catholics (most of whom were Creoles)[13] and the more recently arrived foreign-born Catholics. To them, Roman Catholicism, whether foreign or native, was a threat to republicanism. While the scope of this article does not go beyond this topic, it is also true that in heavily Roman Catholic South Louisiana the Know-Nothing party was weakened by its anti-Catholic stance, although there is no evidence of overwhelming rejection of the Know-Nothing party by Roman Catholics, not even in South Louisiana.[14]

II

Beginning in the 1830s and 1840s, nativistic attacks on foreigners, particularly Roman Catholic foreigners from Ireland, occurred in Louisiana. A major commercial city like New Orleans, which attracted foreign immigrants, did not escape the nativist and anti-Roman Catholic propaganda of the 1830s. American immigration eventually turned New Orleans into a Protestant city, but Protestantism was strongest in North Louisiana, where most Protestants were Baptists or Methodists. There were no Roman Catholic churches in fourteen North Louisiana parishes by 1850. In southern Louisiana, the "French" Catholics dominated that denomination, and New Orleans, the Catholic diocesan seat, remained an important Catholic center.[15]

During the 1830s, New Orleans' Catholic and anti-Catholic press were at odds, and by the fall of 1835 a nascent nativist spirit culminated in the formation of the Louisiana Native American Association. Violence marred the late 1830s and the advent of the 1840s provided no reprieve from the continuing hostility between nativists and anti-nativists. New Orleans was the site of the 1841 Native American Convention which attracted delegates from across the state, and anti-foreignism and anti-Catholicism remained important issues in Louisiana politics from 1842 to 1846.[16] By the late 1840s and early 1850s, however, the Wilmot Proviso, the Mexican War, and the Compromise of 1850 temporarily absorbed the attention of most Americans and Louisianians.

In 1853 and during 1854, nativistic and anti-Roman Catholic sentiment assumed more importance as foreign immigration increased. This continuing foreign immigration, along with the demise of the Whig party, coincided with the formation of a national nativist party which made its first appearance in Louisiana politics during an 1854 New Orleans election. The failure of the Whig party, nationally and locally,[17] left numerous Louisiana Whigs without an effective political vehicle to oppose the Democrats, and the past affinity of the Whigs for political nativism encouraged many persons to join the anti-foreign and anti-Catholic Know-Nothings.

The national Know-Nothing party was not like the Democratic or Whig parties. As one observer noted, its objectives were part religious and part political. Its end was the disfranchisement of adopted citizens and their exclusion from political office. Although Louisiana Know-Nothings denied that they were anti-Roman Catholic, opponents in Louisiana claimed that the American party intended perpetual war on Catholics.[18] Admission to national Know-Nothing ranks was restrictive, applicants having to be non-Catholic, native born citizens born of native-born parents, but Louisiana Know-Nothings waived the ban on Catholicism.

The origins of the Know-Nothing party in Louisiana are obscure, but the first trace of this secretive political party appeared during the 1854 New Orleans municipal election. The organization, however, quickly gained notoriety throughout the state. The Louisiana Know-Nothing party began innocuously with a call for a mass meeting to organize an independent reform movement.[19] The *New Orleans Daily True Delta,* however, reiterated an earlier charge that the Know-Nothings had religious objectives, for a Know-Nothing could not vote for a Catholic.[20]

The Reformers denied the anti-Catholic charges, and their ticket, Reformers noted, did include Catholic candidates. The Reform ticket listed twelve Catholics among its slate of forty-two candidates.[21] Even though the Reform candidate for mayor lost, other members of the ticket captured key municipal positions, including a majority of the alderman and assistant alderman seats.[22] Evidently disturbed by the Reform party's electoral gains, one opponent asked how could some Louisiana Catholics belong to a party with the avowed objective of waging political warfare against Catholics?[23] In addition to denying that the party proscribed Catholics, many members of the Know-Nothing society pointed out that Louisiana rejected the anti-Catholicism that characterized Know-Nothingism elsewhere.[24] But the party's critics, citing the 1854 elections in New Orleans, alleged that Roman Catholic participation in the Reform ticket was merely a ruse to attract additional voters from the city's Roman Catholic and Creole areas.[25] It would appear, however, that with the Whig party virtually defunct many Catholic Whigs, most of whom were Creoles, simply did not feel comfortable in the Democratic party.[26]

Another reason for Roman Catholic participation appeared in the Creole Catholic newspaper, the *New Orleans Semi-Weekly Creole.* This Know-Nothing paper discussed the liberal views of Louisiana's Creole Catholics who had brought from France "the opinions of the Gallican Catholic Church, which is diametrically opposed to any assumption of political or secular authority by the Pope or by any of his priesthood." The *Semi-Weekly Creole* noted that a vast difference existed between Gallican Catholics and other members of their faith.[27]

Yet a sizable segment of the population of the state belonged to the Roman Catholic Church, and Louisiana Know-Nothings had to be particularly sensitive to the anti-Roman Catholic issue. Because many members of the Louisiana American party were Roman

Catholics, the American party press made every effort to prevent the Catholic issue from dividing the party in the state.

But there were Know-Nothing supporters, who, despite party denials of a proscriptive policy against Roman Catholics, openly attacked the Roman Catholic Church and its policies. George A. Pike, publisher of the *Baton Rouge Comet,* was one of these men. Unlike his South Louisiana colleagues who displayed greater discretion in the face of large, local Catholic populations, Pike's editorials did little to convince Roman Catholics that his party did not intend to proscribe them. New York Bishop John Hughes, the Society of Jesus, and the *Southern (Catholic) Standard* newspaper were Pike's favorite targets. Pike opposed Bishop Hughes, and other Roman Catholic bishops, for holding all church property in their name.[28] To Pike and the Know-Nothings, ownership of property by a Catholic bishop resulted in the centralization of the Roman Catholic Church with the prospects of the "government . . . soon begging the church for funds to carry on its affairs."[29] Pike's fear of the Jesuits was not an isolated one. To the Know-Nothings, there was nothing more frightening than the "secretive" Jesuits, described by the American party as "a designing, scheming, and dangerous secret political order. . . ."[30] Louisiana's nativists also characterized the Jesuits as "a secret oath bound clan hourly striking death blows at the very foundation of our republic."[31] Finally, the attacks by the *Southern Standard* on the American party provoked Pike into a rage against the Roman Catholic newspaper. Calling the *Southern Standard* a "vile and slanderous sheet," Pike permitted himself to go beyond, what contemporaries considered "the bounds of propriety."[32]

If Pike was an embarrassment for the state organization, the National Council proved to be a far greater liability for Louisiana Know-Nothings. A Louisiana Know-Nothing delegation traveled to Philadelphia in June 1855 to attend the national convention. The Louisiana delegates became embroiled in a controversy over seating the delegation which included the Roman Catholic Charles Gayarré. The convention finally voted to seat only the Protestant members of the delegation, but the Protestant delegates chose not to accept admission under such terms. The convention then proceeded to write its national platform which included an anti-Roman Catholic plank.[33]

At their state convention in July, Louisiana Know-Nothings adopted a more conciliatory platform. The state platform, while essentially the same as the one adopted by the national assembly in Philadelphia, had one important exception; it rejected the anti-Catholic plank. Shortly after the state convention, over 10,000 persons assembled in New Orleans' Lafayette Square to endorse the state platform.[34]

The American party thus entered the campaign for state and congressional offices with a platform that stood at variance with the national platform on the Roman Catholic question and with Roman Catholic candidates on its ticket. Throughout the campaign Know-Nothings asserted repeatedly that they opposed religious proscription, boasted of the ticket's three Catholic candidates for high state offices, and noted that the Democrats had only two Catholic candidates for inferior offices. Therefore, the nativists asked, which ticket was most dangerous to Catholicism?"[35] Charles Derbigny, the American gubernatorial candidate, asserted that three-fourths of Louisiana's Creoles were American party members, and that he expected every Catholic parish in Louisiana to give a majority to the Know-Nothing candidates.[36]

Derbigny was optimistic because the Louisiana platform had rejected the anti-Catholic plank of the national platform. In Louisiana this would permit the Creole Catholics to sustain the American party. In addition, Louisiana's Creoles denied that the pope had any control over their temporal affairs, and they continued to insist that there was a difference between the so-called Gallican Catholics and other Catholics. American party members throughout the nation, according to Louisiana Know-Nothings, also made this distinction. Many Americans asserted that the Gallican Catholics were liberal and opposed to clerical interference while the ultra-montane Papists blindly supported the dictates of the clergy.[37]

The nativists' problems nevertheless continued during the state campaign as the anti-American press charged that Know-Nothings in predominantly Protestant North Louisiana accepted the Philadelphia platform without reservations. Democrats exploited this issue during the 1855 campaign.[38] For example, on July 23, 1855, the Bienville Parish Know-Nothing party resolved that the state "wigwam" had exceeded its authority when it repudiated the eighth article of the Philadelphia platform. This meeting, held at Sparta, Louisiana, renounced the state action and affirmed the national platform.[39] The Know-Nothing *New Orleans Daily Crescent* denied that the Sparta wigwam typified the Louisiana American party. These "hot-heads," the *Daily Crescent* charged, numbered only twenty-five or thirty members out of a total of 25,000 persons who accepted the state platform.[40]

Yet, the *Louisiana Courier* gleefully noted the abuse of Roman Catholics in Jackson Parish. The *Farmerville Enquirer* of Union Parish had an anti-Roman Catholic reputation as well. This paper suggested that Catholic institutions would be better regulated with convents opened to grand juries and *habeas corpus* extended to them.[41] The correspondent "Justice" in the *Baton Rouge Daily Advocate* reported that a Protestant minister, the Rev. Dr. R. M. Stell, who campaigned for the American party in North Louisiana, accepted the Roman Catholic test clause of the Philadelphia Platform. Reverend Stell did not stop there; he claimed that New Orleans' Charity Hospital refused admittance to Protestants. He also referred to the Sisters of Charity who administered the hospital as "women of easy virtue." In addition, Reverend Stell opposed state appropriations to various charitable causes affiliated with Roman Catholics "as pandering to Catholic influence and Romanish prejudices."[42]

Another North Louisiana clergyman joined Dr. Stell in fulminating against Roman Catholics. A minister, identified by the press as simply Rev. Dr. Harmon, campaigned in the northwestern parishes advancing the claim that Charles Derbigny, candidate for governor, "would rather see his children in their graves than Roman Catholics." This prompted the *New Orleans Daily True Delta* to ask the Americans if they were representing their gubernatorial candidate as two different people in two areas of the state.[43]

To further complicate matters in the 1855 campaign, two American tickets appeared. This turn of events demonstrated all was not well among Know-Nothings on the Roman Catholic question. Charles Derbigny headed the ticket nominated in New Orleans in July, but, in the fall, a National American ticket, headed by John Ray of Ouachita Parish, appeared in North Louisiana. The Democratic press reported that the North Louisiana Americans could not accept the Popish candidates and had presented this Protestant ticket. Democrats denounced the goals of the National American ticket, but respected their acceptance of the principles of the American party's National Council.[44] The Derbigny-slate candidates disassociated themselves from what they termed the "Bogus ticket," denounced religious proscription, and endorsed the "regular" ticket headed by Charles Derbigny. The "regulars" called the "Bogus ticket" a Democratic trick to confuse American party partisans late in the political campaign.[45]

When the election returns were published, the Democratic party had elected all of its state candidates. The Democrats also retained their legislative majority and won three of the state's four congressional seats. In the gubernatorial race, the Democrats increased their 1852 majority by over 4,200 votes. The results were much closer in the congressional races, except in the Fourth Congressional District, where the Democratic candidate won handily. It was in New Orleans where the American party did quite well. All of their candidates for the state senate won, and they won most of the representative seats from that city.[46]

III

The Democratic victory in 1855 initially left some Know-Nothings confused about the party's continued existence in Louisiana. Although the Democrats had not overwhelmed the Know-Nothings, there were those who despaired over the future of the American party in Louisiana. The editor of the *Plaquemine Southern Sentinel* emphatically announced that only one party — the Democratic party — existed in the state, and that the American party was incapable of rising from its ashes.[47] However, most American party supporters remained more optimistic, predicting that only the Know-Nothing party could avert a sectional conflict. Even the *Southern Sentinel* grudgingly predicted that a Know-Nothing would succeed Franklin Pierce as president.[48] The American party faithfully claimed that once the national organization removed its objectionable features all Louisianians would march in Know-Nothing ranks.[49] Of course, one of those objectionable features was its anti-Catholicism.

While both parties attributed the American party's defeat to the Roman Catholic Old Whigs' apprehensions regarding the Know-Nothings' proscriptive policy,[50] it is not clear if that was the major reason for the Know-Nothing loss. The *Thibodaux Minerva*, a Know-Nothing newspaper, attributed the party's loss to this, but the paper was only partially correct. Of the sixteen parishes returning majorities for the American party, nine had a significant Catholic population. Three of these had overwhelming Catholic populations, and three others had populations having large Catholic majorities. Catholic voters in these parishes would not have supported a blatantly anti-Roman Catholic party.[51] However, nine of the Know-Nothing parishes did have Protestant majorities, and even among the nine with a significant Catholic population, two (Orleans and Jefferson parishes) were strongholds of Know-Nothingism with a Protestant majority, even if that majority was small. In St. Mary Parish, the last of these parishes with a large Catholic population, Catholics constituted a minority. Four other parishes (Avoyelles, Lafourche, St. Charles, and St. Landry) had large Catholic populations, but they experienced dwindling support for the Whig-American faction; Lafourche and St. Landry parishes actually fell from the Whig-American column in 1855.[52] The 1855 election returns indicate, in part, that most Creole Roman Catholics who had supported the Whig party either moved into the American party ranks or chose not to vote at all.[53] It appears evident, therefore, that some Roman Catholics believed the American party did not represent their best interests. While the latter is difficult to prove conclusively, at least one contributor to the *Thibodaux Minerva,* published in the center of Creole Catholic Louisiana, believed this was true. This contributor wrote that "when everything religious and the secrecy is abolished from the National Organization" the party would meet with little opposition.[54]

Despite its defeat in the state election, Know-Nothingism won victories in various municipal and parish elections in the spring and summer of 1856 in Thibodaux, Washington, St. Landry Parish, Donaldsonville, Bayou Sara, Baton Rouge, and Minden.[55] The party did, however, take control of New Orleans' municipal government.[56] These victories gave the Know-Nothing party renewed hope that it could carry the national election in 1856.

Sensitive to Democratic charges in previous campaigns, the American party made every effort to allay the fears of those who still believed the Know-Nothings were proscriptive. Some Americans vowed they would leave the party if the Northern wing insisted on the religious test. This proved to be unnecessary since the American presidential nominating convention at Philadelphia in February voted to seat those Louisiana delegates who accepted Catholics in the state order. The convention also moderated the wording of its anti-Roman Catholic plank to read that "no person should be elected for political station (whether of native or foreign birth) who recognizes any allegiance or obligation OF ANY DESCRIPTION, to ANY FOREIGN PRINCE, POTENTATE, OR POWER." A nativist paper compared the revised plank with the oath of allegiance administered to new citizens and found no difference.[57] While the Americans wanted to forget the "discarded" anti-Catholic plank and pointed out that proscription was not a feature of the national party, the anti-Know-Nothing press reminded voters that proscription of Catholics remained an American party goal.

Despite claims of moderation, blatant anti-Roman Catholicism did surface in the 1856 campaign, emanating, as in 1855, from North Louisiana and East Baton Rouge Parish, particularly in the *Baton Rouge Comet.* The *Comet*'s editor continued his attack on the Catholic church's wealth and its foreign hierarchy. According to the *Comet,* the attempts to incorporate Catholic congregations foreshadowed the time when, with government sanction, the Church would "strangle the government." The *Comet*'s editorials also characterized the *Catholic Standard* as having abused "everything American."[58] Like-minded nativists rejected the "new look" of the state convention which had adopted a resolution rejecting "none, whether native or foreign," which a disgruntled Know-Nothing editor called a prostitution of American principles. This journalist did not believe it was good policy, or, that it reflected the sentiments of the party in Louisiana, and he asked, "Does the American party, now grovel in the dust, and flounder in the political cesspool as other parties have done for power and place?"[59]

This editor had expressed the sentiments of many Know-Nothings in the state. A fellow American from northwest Louisiana summarized, in one sentence, what the election was all about. To him the main issue was:

> whether this country shall be governed by the present race of Pierce office-holders, and their N. York softshell freesoiler dependents, aided by 'foreign influence," or be restored to its pristine purity and vigor, and ruled by the natives of the land, in accordance with the policy of the immortal 'Father of his Country" and the founders of the republic.[60]

Other Americans dragged out the stereotypical foreigner for this campaign, depicting the typical immigrant as living in poor houses and asylums, taking up the public domain, and abusing the franchise. Foreign immigration and foreign rule, as the nativists reminded the electorate, had caused the downfall of ancient republics.[61] Yet, even though the religious question re-emerged in this campaign, the election came down to which party would best serve the slave interests of the South and Louisiana, and would old-line Whigs continue their affiliation with the Americans.[62]

As in 1855 it is difficult to describe just how the anti-Catholic stance of the national American party affected the Louisiana election. The American party failed to win four predominantly Roman Catholic parishes which the Whigs had carried in 1852,[63] but the party still attracted numerous votes from those areas of the state containing large Catholic populations. Even in South Louisiana, Democrat James Buchanan failed to receive an overwhelming mandate from the Catholics.[64]

One thing that is certain, despite some scattered post-1856 election optimism, the defeat finished the American party, not only in the nation, but in Louisiana, except for New Orleans. The Know-Nothings would field candidates in the 1857 state and congressional elections, but defections from American ranks and pro-Democratic rhetoric appearing in former Know-Nothing newspapers contributed to yet another defeat.[65] The American party had gone the same way of its Whig predecessor.

IV

In Louisiana several factors determined why someone supported the Know-Nothing party. To a large extent, politics in the state still followed old Whig-Democratic lines.

Many voters were hesitant to join the Democratic party, as indicated above. Even as late as the 1857 state and congressional elections, former Whig cotton and sugar parishes along the Red and Mississippi Rivers, as well as the sugar parishes of St. Martin and Terrebonne, returned Know-Nothing majorities. In fact, the Democrats spent much effort in attacking the Know-Nothing movement as nothing more than Whiggery in disguise, and much of the literature on Know-Nothingism in the South and Louisiana reflects this view. Certainly some voters supported the Americans because of the nativist ideology. Native Americans found this aspect of Know-Nothingism attractive, especially in the New Orleans area, where immigrants constituted a sizable portion of the population. Other voters were influenced by the belief that the American party spoke to the issues of conservatism and preservation of the Union.

These forces help explain why there appears to be the paradox of Roman Catholics belonging to a party that subscribed to an anti-Catholic belief. Old Whigs could continue their political activity without becoming Democrats, and Creole Catholics could fulminate against the "ultra-montane" Catholics (the foreign-born Catholics who lived mainly in New Orleans). The Union, which served their interests well, could be better served with native Americans in political control. However, many Roman Catholics in Louisiana recognized that there was a serious, if only an embryonic, threat to the Catholic church and its statewide membership. Church leaders recognized this, as did many Creoles.

New Orleans, even though it had a large Catholic population, had a Protestant majority and remained a Know-Nothing stronghold up to the end of the 1850s. Two Catholic newspapers published in the Crescent City warned New Orleans Catholics of the danger posed by the American party. They knew Know-Nothingism was decidedly anti-Catholic. In addition, Know-Nothingism in the Baton Rouge area and North Louisiana was quite different from its manifestations in South Louisiana or even in New Orleans. The Know-Nothing anti-Catholic rhetoric was more extreme in Baton Rouge and North Louisiana, and it failed to distinguish between foreign-born Catholics and Creole Catholics. The emergence of a separate Know-Nothing ticket in North Louisiana—a ticket which supported the national convention's proscription of Catholics—during the 1855 state campaign did not bode well for toleration within the party. It was during the 1855 campaign that the Know-Nothings had to repeatedly defend themselves from the charges of anti-Catholicism. This was also the campaign in which Creole Catholics made a distinction between the liberal Gallican Catholics and other Catholics. The problem with this logic was that the national convention rejected the distinction by refusing to seat Creole Charles Gayarré. Many Creole Catholics probably believed that this distinction was valid, but it would have been difficult for them to ignore the so-called "Bogus" Know-Nothing ticket's acceptance of the national party's anti-Catholic plank.

In the final analysis, the growing sectional controversy began to overshadow all other issues. All Louisianians were engrossed in the more critical issues of preserving the Union and maintaining Southern rights. But the anti-Catholic bias of the Americans had received considerable attention during the 1850s, and it appears that some Louisianians willingly accepted that bias. While the Catholic issue may not have been as significant in Louisiana as the contemporary campaign literature suggests, anti-Catholicism existed, and many in the state fervently supported the national ideology. Before that ideology could be tested in Louisiana, however, the American party succumbed to the sectional crisis.

Notes for "Anti-Catholicism, Nativism, and Louisiana Politics in the 1850s"

[1]American was the official name of the party, which members organized along the lines of a secret fraternal order. Lodges, passwords, signs of recognition, a grip, and challenges were all part of the party. Members called their lodges "wigwams." Secrecy was so important that members were warned not to divulge the name of the party or any of its proceedings to non-members. When questioned about the party, members were instructed to reply "I know nothing;" therefore, the term Know-Nothing became a more commonly accepted name for the party. *The Origin, Principles and Purposes of the American Party* (n.p., n.d.).

[2]W. Darrell Overdyke, "History of the American Party in Louisiana," *Louisiana Historical Quarterly*, 16 (1933): 614; *Baton Rouge Daily Gazette and Comet*, November 3, 1857: *New Orleans Bee*, November 3, 1857; *New Orleans Daily Crescent*, November 7, 1857; hereafter New Orleans will be omitted from all future references to newspapers from that city, place names will be used, however, for all non-New Orleans papers. Leon Cyprian Soulé, *The Know Nothing Party in New Orleans: A Reappraisal* (Baton Rouge, 1961), 91.

[3]While it is beyond the scope of this study to demonstrate beyond any doubt as to the ideology of the Know-Nothing party when it ended in Louisiana, nevertheless, there is a strong, positive correlation between the American party congressional vote in 1857 and the Constitutional Union party vote in 1860. While not definitive by any means, this does point to a positive relationship between those conservative and Union men of 1860 and the Know-Nothings of the mid-to late 1850s. The coefficient of correlation between the 1860 Union presidential vote and the 1857 Know-Nothing congressional vote is +.76, while the coefficient of correlation between the 1860 Southern Democratic (Breckinridge) vote and the 1857 Know-Nothing congressional vote is -.56. The latter coefficient of correlation is not particularly strong, but its negative correlation, along with the strong, positive correlation of the 1860 Union vote and the Know-Nothings appears to confirm the qualitative evidence which also supports this conclusion. I obtained the election return data from the Inter-University Consortium for Political Research, The Institute for Social Research, Center for Political Studies, The University of Michigan, Ann Arbor, Michigan. Hereafter cited as ICPR.

[4]Avery O. Craven, *The Growth of Southern Nationalism: 1848-1861* (Baton Rouge, 1953), 238; W. Darrell Overdyke, *The Know-Nothing Party in the South* (Baton Rouge, 1950), 51.

[5]Arthur C. Cole, *The Irrepressible Conflict: 1850-1865* (New York, 1934), 146.

[6]Arthur C. Cole, *The Whig Party in the South* (reprinted Gloucester, 1962), 309-10.

[7]Ray Allen Billington, *The Protestant Crusade: 1800-1860* (New York, 1938), 393.

[8]Overdyke, *Know-Nothing Party in the South*, 13.

[9]Overdyke, "History of the American Party in Louisiana," *Louisiana Historical Quarterly*, 15 (1932): 581-88.

[10]Robert C. Reinders, "The Louisiana American Party and the Catholic Church," *Mid-America*, 40 (1958): 218-21.

[11]William J. Cooper, Jr., *The South and the Politics of Slavery, 1828-1856* (Baton Rouge, 1978), 364-65.

[12]Cooper, *The Politics of Slavery*, 365; Marius Carriere, Jr., "The Know-Nothing Movement in Louisiana" (Ph.D. dissertation, Louisiana State University, 1977), 116-22, 169-74, 195-99.

[13]I use the word Creole to refer to those descendants of colonial Louisianians.

[14]A writer in the *Thibodaux Minerva* believed that the Catholic Creoles, for example, were against the American party "owing to the implied religious test in the national platform." The coefficient of correlation, however, between the percentage of Roman Catholic church aggregate accommodations in 1850 and the American party's gubernatorial vote in 1855 is -.061. Although this is a negative correlation, it is not a high inverse relationship. *Thibodaux Minerva*, November 10, 1855; ICPR; Bureau of the Census, *Seventh Census of the United States, 1850: Compendium of the Seventh Census, Louisiana Statistics* (Washington, 1853), hereafter cited as *United States Census, 1850.*

[15]*United States Census, 1850*, 482; Roger W. Shugg, *Origins of Class Struggle in Louisiana: A Social History of White Farmers and Laborers during Slavery and After* (Baton Rouge, 1939), 62-64.

[16]Numerous examples could be cited, but a few will make it clear that anti-foreign and anti-Catholic sentiment did indeed play an important role in Louisiana politics during the mid to late 1840s. The Whig governor in 1842, running for reelection, made it clear that he stood behind the Native American Association's demand for the repeal of the "Defective" naturalization laws. On election day, the *Louisiana American* reported the issue was not between Democrat and Whigs, but "native American versus anti-Native American, and the ballot box must decide whether we are to govern ourselves or to be governed by imported patriots. . . ." In the congressional elections of 1843, the Whigs bemoaned their defeat in the First Congressional District and claimed Democrat John Slidell's election was the result of the wholesale manufacture of illegal foreign-born voters. In the 1844 election for delegates to the Louisiana Constitutional Convention, successful Whig candidate Judah P. Benjamin called for the formation of a "nativist" party. *Bee*, April 4, 6, 1842; July 6-7, 9, 1843; August 24, 1843; Overdyke, "History of the American Party in Louisiana," 584-85; Pierce Butler, *Judah P. Benjamin* (Philadelphia, 1907), 87-90.

[17]For a more detailed discussion of the failure of the Whig Party in Louisiana and the South, see Arthur Charles Cole's *The Whig Party in the South* (Gloucester, 1962), chapters 7-9. For Louisiana in particular, see William H. Adams's *The Whig Party of Louisiana* (Lafayette, 1973).

[18]*New Orleans Daily True Delta*, March 15, 1854.

[19]*Bee*, March 15, 1854.

[20]*Daily True Delta*, March 23, 1854.

[21]*Daily Crescent*, March 17, 22, 1854; *Commercial Bulletin*, March 24, 25, 1854.

[22]*Bee*, April 1, 1854.

[23]*Daily True Delta*, March 15, 1854.

[24]W. Darrell Overdyke in his "History of the American Party in Louisiana," adheres to this interpretation. See note eight above.

[25]This is the view of Leon Soulé in *The Know-Nothing Party in New Orleans*. Soulé believes that the old Creole-American animus never ceased, and during the 1850s the Creoles consciously used the immigrants to ward off American growth in New Orleans. Soulé disagrees with Overdyke's thesis that the Know-Nothing Party in Louisiana did not intend to proscribe Roman Catholics.

[26]*Daily True Delta*, March 15, 1854; Soulé, *Know-Nothing Party in New Orleans*, 48, 51-53.

[27]*Semi-Weekly Creole*, October 18, 1854. Gallican refers to a view in Louisiana that Catholicism in the state was autonomous, while the "other Catholics" refers to ultra-montane Catholics, those who upheld Papal supremacy. In general, the Creole Catholic (native-born) identified with this Gallican spirit while they considered the ethnic Catholics (Irish and Germans) who immigrated in the early to mid-1850s, to be ultra-montane. This distinction is prevalent throughout the Know-Nothing period in Louisiana.

[28]*Baton Rouge Weekly Comet*, June 21, 1855; May 3, 1856.

[29]Ibid., August 5, 1855; *Baton Rouge Morning Comet*, May 3, 1856.

[30]*West Baton Rouge Capitolian Vis-à-Vis*, September 30, 1854. Ironically, the writer for this West Baton Rouge paper (as well as other Know-Nothings) saw no contradiction in condemning the so-called oaths of the Jesuits or ridiculing their alleged secretiveness, even though the origins of the American party were steeped in rituals, oaths, and secrecy.

[31]*Baton Rouge Daily Comet*, January 23, 1856; (Clinton) *American Patriot*, June 30, 1855.

[32]Ibid., June 21, 1855; *Morning Comet*, August 14, 1856; November 2, 1856.

[33]Charles Gayarré, *History of Louisiana*, 4 vols. (New Orleans, 1903), 4:678; James K. Greer, "Louisiana Politics, 1845-1861," *Louisiana Historical Quarterly*, 13 (1930): 91; Overdyke, *Know-Nothing Party in the South*, 128; *Commercial Bulletin*, June 23, 1855.

[34]*Baton Rouge Weekly Comet*, July 11, 1855.

[35]*Daily Crescent*, August 4, 1855; *Weekly Comet*, August 12, 1855; *Opelousas Patriot*, September 29, 1855. The three Roman Catholic Know-Nothings were Charles Derbigny of Jefferson Parish, Louis Texada of Rapides Parish, and J. V. Duralde of West Baton Rouge Parish; candidates for governor, lieutenant governor, and state treasurer respectively.

[36]*Opelousas Patriot*, October 20, 1855.

[37]Henry Winter Davis, *The Origin, Principles and Purposes of the American Party* (n.p., 1855), 34-35; Anna Ella Carroll, *The Great American Battle, or, The Contest Between Christianity and Political Romanism* (New York, 1856), 178, 202. Miss Carroll noted that Louisiana Roman Catholics had stood firm against the Papacy's temporal power, and she applauded them for their resistance.

[38]The *Daily True Delta* asserted that even in New Orleans three American councils had repudiated the denunciation of the religious plank of the National Order by the State Council.

[39]*Daily Advocate*, August 1, 1855; *Louisiana Courier*, August 3, 1855. Sparta, Bienville Parish, is in North Louisiana.

[40]*Daily Crescent*, July 4, 6, 1855.

[41]*Louisiana Courier*, August 3, 10, 1855. Both Jackson and Union parishes are in North Louisiana.

[42]*Baton Rouge Daily Advocate*, August 1, 1855; September 29, 1855; *Daily True Delta*, October 5, 1855.

[43]*Daily True Delta*, October 5, 1855.

[44]*Daily Crescent*, October 2, 3, 1855.

[45]*Thibodaux Minerva*, October 6, 20, 27, 1855; November 3, 1855; *Bee*, October 8, 1855; *Plaquemine Southern Sentinel*, October 13, 1855; *Daily Crescent*, October 13, 24, 1855.

[46]Overdyke, "History of the American Party in Louisiana," 16 (1933): 276-77; *Opelousas Patriot*, March 31, 1855. In the gubernatorial race the Democrat, Robert C. Wickliffe, defeated Derbigny. Wickliffe received 53 percent of the vote (22,382 to 19,417). In the other state-wide races the Democratic candidates won with approximately the same percentage. In the four congressional contests the Democrats lost in the First District, receiving 48 percent of the vote (the American vote in New Orleans secured the First District for the Know-Nothing candidate where the American candidate won better than 52 percent of the votes cast), won the Second District race with a 53 percent majority, barely won in the Third District, and won decisively in the Fourth District. Even though the Democrats did increase their gubernatorial majority in 1855, the increase was less than 1 percent of the total vote. ICPR.

[47]*Plaquemine Southern Sentinel,* December 1, 1855.

[48]Ibid., December 15, 1855.

[49]*Thibodaux Minerva,* November 10, 1855; *Baton Rouge Daily Comet,* November 20, 1855.

[50]*Thibodaux Minerva,* November 10, 1855; *Daily True Delta,* November 14, 1855; *Opelousas Patriot,* December 1, 1855.

[51]ICPR. *United States Census, 1850.* The 1850 United States Census for Louisiana describes religion by listing a denomination's church seating capacity. While this obviously cannot reflect, with complete accuracy, the religious persuasion of parish residents, it is the only statistical evidence available and it does correspond with the qualitative sources. The three parishes which had overwhelming Catholic populations were St. Charles, St. James, and St. John the Baptist; the three parishes which had large Catholic majorities were St. Martin, Terrebonne, and West Baton Rouge.

[52]Ibid. The Whig majority in 1852 in Avoyelles Parish was thirty-nine; in 1855 the Democrats won a 158 vote majority. In Lafourche the 1852 Whig majority was 402 while in 1855, the Democratic majority was 245. In St. Landry the Whigs won with a 322 vote majority, but in 1855 the Democrats secured a victory with a majority of 294 votes.

[53]Ibid. Heavily Catholic St. James and St. Martin parishes increased their majorities for the American party in 1855 over that of the 1852 Whig gubernatorial majority. St. Charles, St. John the Baptist, St. Mary, Terrebonne, and West Baton Rouge parishes, all with sizable Catholic populations, experienced a slight to moderate decrease in their majorities in 1855 as compared to their 1852 Whig majorities. West Baton Rouge and St. John parishes are good examples of how Whigs chose not to vote. While the Democratic vote remained unchanged from 1852 to 1855 in West Baton Rouge, the American vote fell-off by twenty-two from the 1852 Whig vote. In St. John Parish the Americans increased their total vote by only one over that of the Whig total in 1852 while the Democrats received only six more votes in 1855 than they had in 1852.

[54]*Thibodaux Minerva,* November 10, 1855.

[55]*Baton Rouge Weekly Comet,* April 13, 16, 1856; *Baton Rouge Morning Comet,* April 16, 1856; July 10, 1856; *Thibodaux Minerva,* May 10, 1856; *Opelousas Patriot,* May 10, 24, 1856.

[56]Soulé, *Know-Nothing Party in New Orleans,* 64-65. At the time, the Know-Nothings controlled the legislative branch of the city, but the Democrats held the mayoralty. Violence and murder characterized election day, with both Know-Nothings and Democrats accusing each other for the mayhem, but the Americans came away with control of the city council and the mayoralty.

[57]*Semi-Weekly Creole,* March 1, 1856; *Baton Rouge Weekly Morning Comet,* October 19, 1856.

[58]*Morning Comet,* May 3, 1856; August 14, 1856.

[59]*Baton Rouge Weekly Morning Comet,* March 23, 1856; June 22, 1856; *Baton Rouge Morning Comet,* June 17, 18, 1856.

[60](Shreveport) *South-Western,* May 28, 1856.

[61]*Fillmore and Donelson Campaign Pamphlet* (n.p., 1856), Charles E. A. Gayarré Collection, Department of Archives, Louisiana State University, Baton Rouge, La.

[62]Even though James Buchanan won, and slavery had played an important role in the campaign, slave owners did not disproportionately support one or the other party. And former Whigs did, to a large extent, continue to vote the American ticket.

[63]The four parishes were Lafourche, St. Charles, St. John the Baptist, and St. Landry.

[64]South Louisiana parishes which the Know-Nothings carried in 1856 included Terrebonne, St. Martin, West Baton Rouge, and St. James, which had Catholic populations ranging from 61 percent of the population to 100 percent. As noted above, denominational preference is based on church accommodations as reported in the 1850 Census, which explains the 100 percent statistic. ICPR.

[65]*Plaquemine Southern Sentinel*, January 24, 1857; June 20, 1857; *Daily Crescent*, January 28, 1857; March 12, 1857; *Bee*, October 27, 1857.

THE FOURFOLD CHALLENGE
(THE DIOCESE, 1842-1853)*

Hodding Carter and Betty Werlein Carter

Louisiana was a fourfold challenge to the Episcopal Church.

Divine services in English must be available to a part of the country which had known none but those in Latin. Parishes must be established among those settlers who had been Episcopalians before their migration to Louisiana. Others, who were as yet unchurched, must be brought into the Church. And a ministry to the Negro population would have to be instituted.

How well would the church succeed?

At the convention of 1842 Bishop Polk gave an address which made the delegates understand better his religious emphases. The bishop considered himself as under Apostolic Orders to preserve and protect "the faith once delivered to the saints." He would, therefore, look to the Prayer Book as to a standard by which he could judge how faithful to the early teaching of the church his was.

At the convention of 1843, after a year of study of the problem of this one diocese, the bishop outlined the specific fields into which he wanted the Church in Louisiana to venture.

This convention was held at St. Francisville, which in itself was significant. It was the first time the convention had met outside of New Orleans. It was a portent of the interest the bishop would take in strengthening the Church throughout the diocese as a whole.

Another sign of his missionary interest was the meeting on behalf of missions held in Grace Church prior to the opening of the convention.

In his address the bishop, returning to his plea for a native ministry, reported that William F. Brand, a founder of St. Paul's, had gone to New York to take Holy Orders and that he had hopes of two more candidates. He enjoined the clergy to seek out potential priests. He saw that the shortage of clergy would necessarily slow extension.

---

*First published in Chapter 5 in *So Great A Good: A History of the Episcopal Church in Louisiana and of Christ Church Cathedral, 1805-1955* (Sewanee, Tenn., 1955), 58-70. Reprinted with the kind permission of the copyright holder.

He then expounded at length on the importance of a ministry to the Negro part of the population, an aspect of his ministry he was ever to emphasize. We can well listen to the words of one of the South's noblest heroes and Christian leaders:

> It is one of the chiefest charms of the Gospel of Christ, that it seeks to equalize the human condition; and to compensate, by the richness of its spiritual provisions, for the disparities existing in the worldly circumstances of our race. It is eminently therefore the property of the poor. . . . The poor are found among the laboring classes in all communities; and their claim to our attention and Christian offices here [in Louisiana] is greatly strengthened by their peculiar condition of dependence. . . . In order to ensure any great degree of success in this enterprise, we must have the countenance and hearty cooperation of our brethren of the laity. . . . I have in no instance found them [the laity] backward or indifferent to the furtherance of this object. It being distinctly understood and seen, that our purpose is to teach all orders and degrees of men, in the language of one of our formularies, "to do their duty in that state of life in which it had pleased God to call them," that we are not political crusaders, but simple and guiltless teachers of that Gospel which was preached . . . that as they [the early Apostles] did not condescend, in the execution of their high errand, to dogmatize on the civil relations or rights of individuals but rather to bind the consciences and the affections to the faithful discharge of the duties of those relations; and by the inculcation of right principles, to leave those relations themselves to be regulated by the intelligent consciences of the parties; so we, who have "part of the same ministry and apostleship," are chiefly concerned with the hearts and consciences of those to whom we go.

Bishop Polk realized how difficult it would be to reach this and other uneducated portions of the population. He visualized an order of deacons which, with less education, might better take the Word to the masses. He looked forward to the time when the Church might have:

> the services of a class of men suited to the instruction of this description of persons; and when she may, with less jealousy for her intellectual reputation, and more concern for the perishing multitudes around her, adopt measures by which she may challenge for herself, with some propriety, the character of preaching the Gospel to the poor.

Had this theory been tried, the Episcopal Church in the new West may, perhaps, have left fewer souls open to the spontaneous ministrations of self-appointed sectarian preachers of the Word. And, with more men under Orders available for missionary work in new territories and states, the Episcopal Church might earlier have approached her goal of bringing all sorts and conditions of Americans to Christ.

In conclusion the bishop requested that a diocesan missionary board be set up to receive funds for and pay out the salaries of missionaries in the diocese. This was done. Thus was constituted the diocese's first Board of Missions. Its members were the Revs. Dr. Wheaton, D. S. Lewis, Thomas Sloo, Jr., of St. Paul's, and Benjamin Lowndes of Christ Church.

But, with one, this board was to be simply a token establishment. Bishop Polk himself was to be the principal missionary resource of the diocese throughout his lifetime. He had been a missionary bishop; he knew the needs of the missionary field; he worked closely with the national Board of Missions; and his fervor and personality were such as to inspire such action by local groups as would result in organization of missions and parishes.

The Diocesan Mission Board received few contributions from the rural churches because each of these newly established parishes needed its all to get itself on firm ground. At the same time the city churches turned their energies to encouraging the formation of new Episcopal parishes in the city. The principal succor to the bishop was the missionaries sent to the diocese. These were stationed where Bishop Polk recommended and their salaries were paid in principal part by Domestic Committee could not be as large as the bishop would have liked, the period of tremendous expansion into which the young diocese now moved would have been impossible without that help which did come.

The principal fruit of the Diocesan Mission Board was the establishment of the Church of Annunciation in New Orleans.

The meeting for organization of this third parish in the city was held in Thomas Sloo's office early in 1844. The vestrymen elected were the Messrs. Sloo, Lowndes, Joseph Callender, William S. Brown, E. W. Briggs, Chauncey M. Black, and John P. McMillan. Subsequently Sloo and Lowndes, both members of the Diocesan Mission Board, were elected senior and junior wardens.

The urgent problem was then to find a priest. By the following fall the Domestic Committee had dispatched the Rev. N. O. Preston, one of its missionaries, to serve this new outpost, paying his salary of $500 a year. By September 1846, Mr. Preston was able to write the Domestic Committee:

> In presenting this, my last resort, through you to the Board of Missions, I feel constrained to speak of the goodness of God, who has blessed us in this station so much beyond our labors or deserts.
> Of our feeble beginning somewhat less than two years since you are aware: We had no organization—no place for the "Ark of God," and had it not been for the missionary stipend freely given and thankfully received, I am persuaded this field would have remained to the present unfilled. But with this aid, together with the active, united, and persevering cooperation of a few devoted and intelligent laymen, all under God, we now have a very respectable church edifice, a flourishing Sunday School and church library, and a body of vestrymen, who, at their last meeting, directed me to say to you that after the first of October, 1846, this station will assume the entire support of its rector.
> For these things I bless God, and take courage for the future.

The new parish of the Church of the Annunciation was admitted into the union with the convention in 1845. A year earlier, five others had been admitted, joining Christ Church, St. Paul's, and Trinity Natchitoches, in the Diocese of Louisiana. This convention of 1844 was held at Natchitoches in Trinity's newly erected church building, the fourth Episcopal structure in the diocese. For its construction the parishioners themselves had contributed almost a third of the cost. The rest, the diocese could say proudly, was contributed primarily by other Louisianians.

The five admitted into the union at this third convention in 1844 were St. James', Baton Rouge; St. James', Alexandria; St. John's, at Smithfield plantation in West Baton Rouge Parish; St. Mary's at Bayou Goula; and St. John's, Thibodaux.

The organization of St. James', Baton Rouge, came earlier than the Rev. Mr. Ranney had thought possible. At the second Diocesan Convention he had thought such a con-summation was not possible within the ascertainable future. But before the year was out, on February 25, 1843, he was present at a meeting at the home of F. D. Newcomb, at which St. James' came into being. Organization was completed, with Mr. Newcomb and William Markham named wardens, and Messrs. Cornelius French, Alfred Gates, Daniel Avery, William M. Fulton and A. A. Williams as vestrymen. The removal of the seat of government to Baton Rouge some two years later added to the importance of this new parish.

Of the establishment of St. James', Alexandria, Bishop Polk in his journal of 1844 records:

> In the town of Alexandria, a congregation has been organized, embracing many of the families of the parish of Rapides, which bids fair to be an inviting field of labor, and one of importance in the diocese. During my visit, there was a meeting of the vestry and friends of the church, and measures were taken for the erection, at an early date, of a suitable church edifice.

Preliminary work in the future parish had been done by the Rev. John Burke, whose territory included Alexandria as well as Natchitoches. Unfortunately, Mr. Burke's arrival in 1841 coincided with the depression. The people told him they were sorry he had come at a time when they were able to do so little to support him. He answered that he was glad he came at that time, as their hearts were the more open to the teachings of religion.

St. John's, Smithfield, and St. Mary's, Bayou Goula, were both plantation churches supported primarily by the planters on whose property they were built. Thus they were assured of support so long as the family owning the place was willing and able to main-tain a large part of the cost of the parish. St. John's was an organized congregation on Dr. Ira Smith's plantation. For it, this communicant of Grace, St. Francisville, was to be-queath the land and $200 a year for the support of the chapel. Through the plantation's many ownerships, its name would change; but the little chapel was in use into the twenti-eth century. Its Mrs. John Lobdell was one of the first regular contributors to missions in the diocese.

Bishop Polk had visited Bayou Goula in the heart of the sugar country while still missionary bishop. He had learned then that the planters were anxious to organize a con-gregation and build a church. Not, however, until 1844 was the parish formed, for lack of available priests to send if the church were built. But with the arrival of a missionary, the Rev. Charles Fay, regular services were established and the parish was accorded union with the diocese.

The parish at Thibodaux had the most personal relationship to Bishop Polk. There he had made his home and it was at his plantation, Leighton. From the time he moved to Louisiana the bishop had held services in the courthouse of the town and on the plantation, for his Negroes. On February 9, 1843, he organized the parish, and on January 1, 1844, he laid the cornerstone of "a remarkable neat" slate-covered brick church. When the Rev. David Kerr became its first rector on Easter Day, a year later, the communicants numbered 24, of whom fourteen were colored persons.

The roll call of parishes in union with the convention continued to grow. In 1845 St. Luke's, Vermilionville (now Lafayette), was admitted, and, in 1847 St. Mary's, Franklin; Zion, St. Martinsville; and Christ Church, Covington. Some to flourish, others to fade.

At St. Martinsville there lived in 1844 the Rev. Lucius M. Purdy of New York who had not, however, been transferred to the diocese. On Wednesday, April 15, 1844, Bishop Polk preached in the courthouse and the next day baptized five adults and 27 children, seven of whom were colored.

"Here there are families enough," he said, "to form quite a respectable congregation. I have appointed two gentlemen as lay readers." Mr. Purdy, however, was able to give his attention to the congregation, which requested especially that services should be in English. On December 4, 1844, a parish was organized under the name of Zion Church, and in 1847 it was admitted to union.

Zion was not admitted as soon as St. Luke's, Vermilionville. Here, in Easter week of 1845, Mr. Purdy organized the congregation which on April 14 of that year was admitted into union with the convention. This church, prematurely accepted, was not strong enough to stand alone when Mr. Purdy discontinued his ministrations and for twenty-four years this town, now called Lafayette, was to be without Episcopal services.

The Rev. Wiley Peck was the founder of the parish at Covington. Here, in a little more than a year, he organized the parish, built a trim church "with little or no assistance" beyond the local means, and saw it consecrated on April 11, 1847. A rectory, the first outside of New Orleans, was completed. He was not long to occupy it. He died of yellow fever early that fall, the first Episcopal clergyman to die in Louisiana of the dread disease. Following him came a succession of clergymen, each serving for short periods. But the parish was to persist through its many vicissitudes.

At Franklin, when Bishop Polk baptized two infants on May 19, 1844, he noted that "there are many persons who prefer the services of our Church to those of any other; and who have resolved to take measures to erect a church edifice and provide means for the support of a clergyman."

These prognostications were to come true. In that year the Rev. Edward A. Renouf of Massachusetts officiated for about six months for the Foreign and Domestic Missionary Society; and in 1846 the Rev. Samuel G. Litton settled in Franklin, organizing the parish. His salary was paid with part of the funds allotted to Louisiana and freed for other work when the Church of the Annunciation became self-supporting. By 1854 the parish had built not only its own church but also a rectory.

From 1847 to 1851 no new churches were admitted to union. But up and down the Mississippi, along the Red and the Ouachita Rivers, on Bayou La Fouche and the Teche, in the sugar lands and in the gently rolling Felicianas white men were banding themselves for worship under the Episcopal aegis and encouraging the establishment of Negro congregations.

But these people were not necessarily Episcopalians. At the Diocesan Convention of 1848, P. M. Ozanne of the French Protestant church, reorganized and affiliated with the diocese, found an amendment to the canons he had offered the year before unanimously rejected. His proposition was that none but members of the Episcopal Church and communicants be eligible for the office of lay delegates to the Diocesan or General Conventions and that every vestry of the diocese have as communicants at least one-third of it members including the wardens. Even at Christ Church, New Orleans, the Mother Church, the parish leaders were not necessarily communicants. To have passed the resolution would have meant an impossible situation. Most of the rural churches had as their parishioners all those in the area, of whatever faith, who wished to worship God in what might be the only church for miles around.

But making the services of the Church available to all was no easy matter. In the early fall of 1846 the Rev. Elijah Guion, then serving Natchitoches and Alexandria, wrote graphically to the Domestic Committee describing what the life of a missionary was like. In this report, published in December 1846, *Spirit of Missions*, he tells of his experiences:

> —the distance by land, between the two extremities of my route, will be about 135 miles, and this journey I shall be expected to perform monthly, mostly on horseback, with a horse hired oftentimes at my own expense, this being all Missionary ground, and but few seeming to think of the Missionary it at.
>
> I think, if it were possible for those at the eastward who feel interested in the success of the Church at the West, to see me on my journeyings and wanderings through the woods and swamps, now exposed to the drenching rain, and again almost fainting under the burning heat of a nearly vertical sun, that some active and efficient measures would be speedily adopted to relieve me of a portion of this burden, by sending out two or three additional Missionaries well supplied with Bibles, prayer-books, and tracts and with a support suited to the expensive nature of Missions in this part of the country.

With so little money to do with and so much to do the Domestic Committee was able to assist such missionaries as Mr. Guion only to the extent of $300 a year. The rest of his support was dependent on the generosity of those among whom he ministered.

Mr. Guion was the more discouraged at this time because he had twice been ill of "the fever," probably malaria with its debilitating chills; and prospects for erecting two churches had been "blasted by the destruction of the cotton crop by the caterpillar."

Moreover, he had other ills to contend with. Said he: "With the blighting effects of Romanism on one side, and Infidelity on the other, our little barque still keeps afloat, though contending against fearful odds."

In 1851 the missionary work of years gone by resulted in the admission of two new parishes, St. Mark's at Shreveport, and Emmanuel, below New Orleans, in Plaquemines Parish.

After the first two services held by Bishop Polk on the Red River while he was still a missionary bishop, the Episcopal Church was represented in Caddo Parish by the Rev. William Steele, an elderly missionary stationed there by the Domestic Committee which felt it was better to have the services of a devout but aging man than to abandon the district entirely.

Bishop Polk wrote:

> He is laboring as his strength will allow. But he is too feeble to fill such an arduous station, and . . . there are three stations at which highly respectable congregations could be gathered.

One congregation Bishop Polk did gather, in 1845, at Shreveport, and organized under the name of St. Paul's. But it was too far removed from the other parishes and could not last. In 1850 it had to be reorganized, as St. Mark's, when the Rev. William Scull was sent to the station. Thus strengthened, what was to be the Mother Church of the Shreveport area was admitted into union.

Mr. Scull did not limit his ministry to St. Mark's but held services on Land's End Plantation where the congregation calling itself Trinity was organized. He also held occasional services at Mansfield where there were three communicants in 1851.

The establishment of Emmanuel, in Plaquemines Parish, was accomplished by the Rev. A. B. Russell who, on June 12, 1850, laid the cornerstone for the first church in the parish.

But the foundations for the Episcopal Church in that section were actually laid by two clergymen connected with so many of the parishes in Louisiana and Mississippi, Mr. Fox and Mr. Raney. Prior to his final return to Mississippi in 1845, Mr. Fox held services at the chapel built by the Wilkinson family at Pointe Céleste, near his own place at Pointe-à-la-Hache. Farther down the river, at the Balize and Pilot Town, Mr. Ranney served as missionary from 1847 to 1850, before going to Monroe and then to Oak Ridge, Bastrop and Vernon and finally to the new Diocese of Texas.

In 1852 were admitted St. Andrews', Clinton, and the Church of the Ascension at Donaldsonville.

The work in Clinton had been started in 1842 by the Rev. William B. Lacey, D.D., president of the College of Louisiana, occasionally assisted by Mr. Ranney. Dr. Lacey continued the services while he was head of the Southern Institute of Young Ladies which he organized there in 1844. But uninterrupted services were not begun until the

Rev. Frederick Dean moved to Clinton in January 1852, from the mission station, St. Peter's, Morganza. Four months later the parish was admitted to union.

Ascension at Donaldsonville was chartered on February 5, 1852. A few months later former Gov. Henry Johnson donated a very valuable piece of property to the corporation, the deed stating that the large two-story building and school standing on it should be used as a rectory and an "Episcopal Institute." Thus, while services were still held in the courthouse, the parish had a church school. The Rev. Caleb Dowe was the rector at the time the church was admitted.

In 1854 St. Alban's, Jackson, and Christ Church, Napoleonville, in Assumption Parish, were added.

While St. Alban's had been under the tutelage of the Rev. Dr. Lacey, the labor at Napoleonville was a completely fresh effort. As Bishop Polk reported:

> Within a little more than a year . . . and that year one of great depression from a widely spread epidemic, the friends of the church in the Parish of Assumption have organized themselves into a parish; and raised, exclusively among themselves, for the support of their minister and the building of their church, above $9,500. That church is completed, and it is the most beautiful edifice of its kind I have seen in the Southern or Western country. Its style is Gothic, and very pure for its period. And its entire arrangement, within and without, exceedingly appropriate, beautiful, and in the best taste.

Other starts were made which would eventuate, finally, in parishes.

From November 1848, until 1855 the Rev. William H. Burton, who had come to New Iberia as the first settled clergyman, officiated there, living variously at New Iberia or at Bayou Sale or at Franklin. But by 1855, because of the removal of 13 communicants, only two Episcopalians remained. The Church of the Epiphany which was organized as a parish in 1852 remained a mission not in union until 1857.

The mission at Monroe was held together by the Rev. C. H. Hedges who began his labors there in September 1847, as principal in the Ouachita Female Seminary and continued until his resignation in 1849 when he was succeeded briefly by Mr. Ranney. Grace Parish was organized in 1848 but had to be reorganized in 1856.

The mission at Williamsport was undertaken in November 1848, by the Rev. Frederick Dean who came from Morganza to hold semi-monthly services. These were held on the Hopkins' land in a shell of a frame building built by the neighbors and used for a school. As the diocese's historian was later to record it, Mr. Dean usually started on the 25-mile trip from Morganza by buggy on Friday evening, fastening his melodeon to the back, and with two boys inside the buggy. They would dine and stay the night with one and then another along the way. When they got to the schoolhouse, a box would be put on the table for a desk, the melodeon brought in, the benches arranged. Mr. Dean would vest and conduct the service or play the melodeon as the service required and the boys sang—the first "boy choir" in Louisiana.

And at Opelousas, although Bishop Polk was sure enough of the people there to designate it as a mission, and the Rev. Otis Hackett was ministering for some little time, the parish was not actually organized until April 22, 1855, as St. Mark's, its name subsequently changed to the Church of the Epiphany.

Bishop Polk's diary in the convention journal of 1854 is revealing of the life of the Bishop of Louisiana, of the diocese and of the general Church.

During his spring visitations in 1853, he reported, he went to Shreveport, where thirteen years before his life had been imperiled by roistering backwoodsmen.

Here strong friends of the Church anxiously waited the arrival of a competent clergyman to minister to them. But not until after the Civil War came a rector in residence who could fulfill the requirements of leadership which the location demanded.

This Bishop Polk could not know in 1852. But he realized how important St. Mark's could be to the life of the diocese. At Shreveport that June he

> crossed the Red River with the view of visiting the Parishes of Northern Louisiana. Passing through Bossier, I stopped at Minden in the Parish of Claiborne. Here I spent two days visiting the people and preaching in the evening of each of the days that I was there, in the Methodist meeting house which was kindly placed at my disposal. During my stay I baptized four children.

Then he started for Monroe on the Ouachita which

> after a perilous journey from the swollen condition of the streams, several of which I had to swim, I reached, having traveled by boat and 50 miles by open wagon.

Here, at Monroe, he confirmed five persons, one of whom had been baptized and reared in the Church of Rome. "This flock," he recorded, "is also without a shepherd."

Truly, many were the opportunities but few the clergymen.

On his way farther down the Ouachita he heard that a child of a Churchman needed baptism. He persuaded Capt. A. W. More of the *Rockaway* to round to the boat and "the captain, the mate, all the ladies in the cabin and most of the gentlemen went ashore and were present at the administration of the sacrament."

On July 9 he stopped at the village of Trinity on the Ouachita where he "spent an hour and baptized the grandchild of an old churchman. Here too I learned there was a desire for a clergyman, and a salary of $450 has been raised toward the support of a clergyman."

On the day following he preached in Donaldsonville and the next day "I descended the La Fourche 30 miles in an open skiff to my own home [Leighton] and completed my spring visitation."

Sunday, July 17, "I read prayers in the parish church of St. John's, Thibodaux, in the morning. In the afternoon I read prayers and preached for the coloured people on Leighton plantation."

He then left on August 18 for the meeting of the Court of Bishops summoned for the trial of Bishop Doane on charges of financial irregularity. The presentment against the bishop was dismissed.

He then met members of the English delegation of the Society for Propagation of the Gospel who were visiting the Board of Missions, which held its sessions during the meeting of General Convention. The British came on an errand of fraternal sympathy and brotherly love and mainly

> to foster and cherish a feeling of sympathy and unity between the American and English branches of the Reformed Catholic Church, with a view to strengthening their hearts and hands against the common enemy, and for devising means for spreading more efficiently the doctrines and usages of the Primitive Church.

Meanwhile, inside the city of New Orleans, the Episcopal Church was also making progress. And by the convention of 1854 Bishop Polk could point with pride to what had been accomplished in the 13 years of his episcopate.

> We have after the lapse of thirteen years, thirty-two organized parishes, in which have been built and consecrated or now ready for consecration, 20 church edifices, and of the remaining twelve, several are taking active measure to build. Besides these thirty-two organized congregations, composed chiefly of white persons, we have twenty-three others, in different parts of the diocese, composed of the slaves on as many plantations; making it in the aggregate fifty-five . . . . Our list of clergy, exclusive of the three taken off by the late epidemic, has increased from six to 23. Our communicants from 238 to 1,421.

The 32 organized congregations referred to were Christ Church, New Orleans; Grace Church, St. Francisville; St. Paul's, New Orleans; Trinity, Natchitoches; Emmanuel, Plaquemines Parish; Christ Church, Covington; l'Eglise Protestante Française, New Orleans; Grace, New Orleans; the Church of the Annunciation, New Orleans; Trinity, New Orleans; Mt. Olivet, Algiers; the Church of the Ascension, Donaldsonville; St. Mary's, Bayou Goula; St. James', Baton Rouge; St. Johns', West Baton Rouge Parish; St. Andrew's, Clinton; St. Alban's, Jackson; St. James', Alexandria; St. Mark's, Shreveport; Trinity, Stonewall, DeSoto Parish; Christ Church, Napoleonville; St. John's, Thibodaux; St. Mary's, Franklin; Zion, St. Martinsville; St. Luke's, Vermilionville (Lafayette); and, not in union, St. Peter's, New Orleans; St. Luke's, New Orleans; St. Peter's, Morganza; the Church of the Epiphany, New Iberia; Grace, Monroe, and mission stations at Opelousas and Williamsport. The story of the organization of New Orleans churches will be told subsequently.

While there parishes and missions were primarily in the southern part of the state, their number and the geographical distance that separated them required some sort of districting. In 1855 at the suggestion of the bishop, the diocese was divided into seven convocations, the first such division of the diocese. But only two of the convocations ever actually met, the one centering on St. Mark's, Shreveport, the other on St. James',

Alexandria. Thus early were those two parishes keystones in the life of the Church in their areas.

Under Leonidas Polk the Diocese of Louisiana was meeting the fourfold challenge.

MOTHERS HENRIETTE DELILLE
AND JULIETTE GAUDIN*

Mary Bernard Deggs

CHRONOLOGY

1842 Founding of the Sisters of the Holy Family.

1847 Incorporation of the Association of the Holy Family.

1851 Purchase of a permanent home on Bayou Road by the community's foundress, Henriette Delille.

1861 Civil War begins on April 12.

1862 Union troops occupy New Orleans May 1. Death of Henriette Delille November 16. Juliette Gaudin assumes role of mother superior the same day.

1863 Death of Jeanne Marie Aliquot January 1. Abraham Lincoln signs Emancipation Proclamation.

1865 The South surrenders during the spring.

1866 Death of Father Founder Etienne Rousselon. Gilbert Raymond succeeds Rousselon as ecclesiastical superior. Race riots in New Orleans.

1870 The community divides on October 4; a second or split house is established on Chartres Street by Josephine Charles. Juliette Gaudin remains mother superior of the old cradle house on Bayou Road.

Sister Mary Bernard Deggs begins her historical narrative with an account of the difficulties of the early days. She tells us that the community founded in 1842 by Henriette Delille, Juliette Gaudin, and Josephine Charles, although Delille was always identified as the principal foundress, or "mother," of the community. In fact, in her history of the community written in the early twentieth century, Sister Mary Francis Borgia Hart states that Delille was chosen by Father Etienne Rousselon as the community's superior. She also explains that when the foundresses took their first official vow, on October 15, 1852, they were allowed to exchange their blue percale gowns for black ones, and that Henriette was officially named the superior and mistress of novices.[1]

*First published in *No Cross, No Crown, Black Nuns in Nineteenth Century New Orleans*, eds. Virginia Meacham Gould and Charles Nolan (Bloomington, 2001), 3-18. Reprinted with the kind permission of the editors and the publisher.

While the women changed their dress, and even their status, in 1852, their names did not change. In describing themselves and their origins, they were constant in their descriptions of their work. They said in the constitution of the Congregation of the Sisters of the Presentation of the Blessed Virgin Mary that their work was to instruct the ignorant, assist the dying, and care for the needy. Their first mission, what lay at the heart of their foundation, was evangelization, and especially the evangelization of "their people," New Orleans' slaves and free people of color. Soon after the women joined together to live in community, in 1842, they founded a school for girls. During the years that elapsed between the foundation of the community and Delille's death, many other women joined them. However, only a few remained after Delille's death in 1862.

Between the years that expired between 1842, when the women began the arduous task of founding a religious order, and 1862, when Delille died, conditions in New Orleans grew steadily more difficult for free people of color. The largest number of free people of color in New Orleans during those years were Creoles who were tied by heritage, blood, language, and Catholicism to the city's white and slave Creoles. New Orleans' Afro-Creole population emerged during the colonial period, and by 1803, when Louisiana was ceded to the United States, it had grown to occupy a significant and discrete place in the city's Creole population, numerically, culturally, and economically. During the decades that elapsed between the Louisiana Purchase of 1803 and 1830, free Creoles of color continued to strengthen their social and economic positions. While neither their demographic nor their legal position improved, the economic standing of those who remained did. By the antebellum period, they held a significant number of professional and semi-professional positions in the city; and they continued to accumulate property. Yet despite their relative stability and success, that segment of the population faced political, economic, and social decline after 1830.

Beginning in the 1830s city and state policymakers began to pass a series of laws meant to more closely regulate slavery and to restrict the positions and activities of free people of color. Notwithstanding their status, free Creoles of color were not exempt. They responded to these degrading and threatening laws in a number of ways. Some migrated to the countryside; others went to France, the Caribbean, or Mexico. Still others passed into the white community. Most, however, chose to stay in the city, and struggled to hold on to their positions. It was within that political, economic, and social climate that Delille and the women who joined her succeeded in founding a community of women religious.

As the Deggs journal makes clear, Delille and her co-foundresses faced difficult conditions during the 1840s and 1850s. Yet conditions were only to worsen after that. Shortly before Delille's death, Union forces seized the city, and her successor, Juliette Gaudin, faced dire economic circumstances. The war and postwar years economically devastated New Orleans and its population. Freed slaves poured into the city, unintentionally adding themselves to the already overwhelming mission of the sisters; some estimates put the numbers at 10,000. Those were the poorest and most uncertain years the sisters were to face. The social, economic, and political climate was constantly shifting under their feet. The population to which they ministered faced uncertainties in every area of their lives. The death of Delille complicated matters even further. Deggs tells us that several women who did remain split into two groups.

By the 1870s, economic circumstances had improved, but the sisters faced other difficulties. The years during which Juliette Gaudin led the community were tumultuous for the city's blacks. Not everyone of African descent welcomed the changes wrought by the war and Reconstruction. Color, race, and condition sometimes segmented people who otherwise had similar ideals. It was not unusual for those who had been free before the war, especially those who were mostly racially mixed, French speaking, educated, and Catholic, to segregate themselves from the newly freed people in the city. That was especially obvious in the debates of black politicians, but it did not stop there. For some, class and condition clearly outweighed race.

Is there evidence that the divisiveness in the black community in New Orleans was repeated in the convent of the Sisters of the Holy Family? Deggs writes extensively about a split that occurred in the community in 1867, but she does not even hint at its cause. It is within Borgia Hart's history of the community that the story emerges. Writing from documentation and oral tradition, Borgia Hart tells us that the sisters divided over the admission of Chloé Preval, a freed slave, into the community. It appears from the account of the split that the then mother superior, Juliette Gaudin, and her cofoundress, Josephine Charles, held differing attitudes about Preval's acceptability as a candidate.[2] For one thing, the early rule of the community stated that only women of free and elite families could be accepted.[3] The authors of the rule, Henriette Delille, Juliette Gaudin, Josephine Charles, and Etienne Rousselon, recognized that the entrance of any woman not acceptable to the increasingly racist white population would threaten the existence of the community. The formation of a community of women religious by free women of color was acceptable, if not ignored, so long as the women were from well known and prosperous families tied to the influential members of the white community. The Church fathers in New Orleans, Vicar General Etienne Rousselon and Archbishop Blanc, understood that family connection, relative wealth, and education were fundamental to the successful establishment and continuation of any such community. That had been the case in France for centuries, and it stood to reason that a community of "creole women or women born in the Americas" stood the best chance for success, especially if they were free women of color, if they were affiliated with the city's more influential citizens. Furthermore, free and elite Creoles of color in New Orleans often held slaves. It appears at first glance that Delille, Gaudin, Charles, and the other free women who joined them fully supported the race-based system of slavery that defined life in the city. Henriette Delille herself was listed as the owner of the slave Betsey for many years, although it appears that she inherited her and was then prevented from freeing her by the increasingly restrictive manumission laws passed in Louisiana. Other visible signs might suggest that the founders of the Sisters of the Holy Family were as racially rigid as were the

white slaveholders who increasingly aimed laws at them. The women educated girls
from free and elite families in an elementary school. The girls were also taught music
and sewing. Their most important subject, religion, was taught separately but was integrated as well into their other subjects. Yet while the women taught free girls of color at
least the rudiments of reading and writing, in keeping with the traditions of the Church
which reflected the legal system of Louisiana, they restricted their work among slave
girls to instruction in religion. Though, even as the women appeared to share the racist
mentality of their white neighbors, other factors hint that they were hemmed in by the
laws and mores of slavery. It was against the law to educate slaves and even illegal to
marry or evangelize them without the consent of their masters or mistresses. The women
who founded the Sisters of the Holy Family followed societal prescriptions as they defined their mission.

Yet one must ask if they did so out of necessity or if they acted discreetly against the
racial conventions that visibly defined their work. There is so little evidence left from the
early years that it is difficult to speculate that the women embraced an anti-slavery ethic
before the war. But a few clues do suggest that they followed the prescriptions of their
society overtly but rejected them in their attitudes and less public actions. In one of the
most telling actions, the sisters soon after the conclusion of the Civil War eliminated the
rule that only women from previously free and elite families were eligible to enter.

The entrance of Chloé Joachim Preval into the community is the most telling example.[4] Soon after the end of the Civil War, Father Gilbert Raymond, as the father superior
of the community as well as its spiritual director, approached Mother Superior Juliette
Gaudin about the prospect of receiving Preval, the housekeeper and a former slave, into
the community. Neither Archbishop Odin nor Raymond believed that Preval's former
status or duties as a housekeeper would compromise her identity as a Sister of the Holy
Family. Gaudin stalled. Growing impatient with her, Raymond requested that the entire
community vote on the matter. Sisters Josephine Charles, Elizabeth Wales, and Marie
Magdalene Alpaugh voted to receive Preval. The rest voted against her. In order to sub-
vert Mother Juliette's authority, Raymond rented a small house on Chartres street, between Peace and Esplanade, and sent the three sisters who had voted to receive Preval
there, appointing Charles superior. The Chartres Street community accepted Preval in
1869.[5]

One of the histories of the Holy Family Sisters suggest that Gaudin rejected Preval
because she was recently freed and had dark skin.[6] According to other evidence, her
hesitance was more practical. Preval continued to be Archbishop Odin's housekeeper.
The tradition of women serving priests as housekeepers was not unknown, especially to
the French priests in New Orleans. There are many examples. Some of the best known
are Les Apostoliques, an order of women that was founded at the beginning of the century in France in order to provide care for the domestic needs of the Oblates of Mary
Immaculate. The Marianite Sisters of the Holy Cross were founded in Le Mans, France,
in 1841 in order to serve as housekeepers to the Fathers and Brothers of the Holy Cross.[7]

While Gaudin would have been well aware of this custom, she would also have recognized that the hard-won status of her sisters would be threatened if their identities were recast as housekeepers. Why, Deggs asks, would a woman want to enter the community to do housework when she would be doing the same in the world? Indeed, during Marie Magdalene Alpaugh's tenure as superior she interrupted the service provided to the archbishops.[8] That is, except for Chloé Preval. Preval continued to work as a housekeeper until, enfeebled by age, she retired to the orphanage to care for the infants. She died of old age, sitting in a rocking chair with an orphaned infant in her arms. Chloé Preval, the former slave, served the community throughout most of her life, becoming one of its most valued and useful members.[9]

The evidence about attitudes of race, status, and condition represented in this journal and elsewhere in the archives of the Sisters of the Holy Family can be interpreted in a number of ways. Deggs clearly suggests, for instance, that lighter skin was desirable. She also stereotypes ethnicity. For instance, she writes that Sister Anne Fazende's father was Indian and her mother was Spanish, and continues, "We are all very well aware of the bad temper and malicious habits of the Spanish, French, Africans, and Indians. Just to think what it must be like to have a mixture of the four!"[10] Yet despite some evidence to the contrary the writings in this journal suggest that the sisters more closely identified with the radical black Creole leaders who emerged during the Civil War and who continued to lead the movement for equal rights through Reconstruction.[11] It was that group that insisted upon equal rights but who also used their ties to the white community to effect them.

The sisters clearly sought to bring slave women and free women together. Deggs recounts the poignant stories of slave women and their mistresses eating side by side at the same table; of slaves and free children schooled together. It was only with emancipation and the end of the war that the sisters had the opportunity to begin to break down the barriers that had been so sturdily erected as slavery found its footing in Louisiana.

J. M. J[12]
New Orleans, La., March 18, 1894

When our dear community commenced, it was very poor, but was blessed with many graces and also many crosses which are said to be the best of all other graces, as no cross, no crown. But many years of hard struggle proved their good wills. Only after thirty or more years of pain and trouble were those noble women consoled when one after another came to join them in their good and fervent work! As the gospel says, many are called but few are chosen.[13] Out of ten who came, only four remained. When the time was set to make their vows, many excused themselves saying that it would be better to go to France.

J. M. J

New Orleans, La., March 19, 1894

Sisters of the Holy Family, founded in the year 1842 and their rapid progress with its many crosses which are the key of all graces and the flowers and stones of the crown.

November 21, 1842

The founders were Miss Henriette Delille, Miss Juliette Gaudin, Miss Josephine Charles, and Very Rev. Etienne Rousselon. Rousselon was then vicar general to Archbishop Antoine Blanc. Both the archbishop and Father Rousselon did all that was in their power to assist the sisters during their lives and left them in good hands at their deaths.[14] Our dear Mother Juliette had been almost raised together with Henriette. They dearly loved each other during their whole lifetimes and had never been one week without each other.

These good sisters first came together in community in an old house on St. Bernard Street.[15] They did not remain in that house but a few months. It was intended for a home for poor, aged women, but a wounded man was one day brought to them by the parish trustees.[16] As they could not refuse to take him, both Henriette Delille and Juliette Gaudin retired to a small place on Bayou Road, and waited some twelve to eighteen months for good Father Rousselon to build them a house on Bayou Road near St. Claude Street.[17] They lived there and did much good work from 1842 until 1883. Many were the souls brought to God in that humble house and many a pain and sorrow did the women pass in their first ten years, but they never lost hope.[18] Many were the times that the foundresses had nothing to eat but cold hominy that had been left from some rich family's table. It is not necessary to say a word about their clothing, for it was more like Joseph's coat that was of many pieces and colors darned, until darn was not the word.[19] In spite of the charity of their many kind friends, they suffered much owing to the strictness of the times.

We also always had many young ladies boarding with us, but that did not prevent our needing many things to carry on the good work that we had commenced. We had the warmest feeling from all of the priests of the parish. We can truly say that our city is the true city of charity, and Almighty God could not refuse to bless it.

Our house received different donations from many friends who never felt as if they had done enough for us. One time, they even gave a fair for us and we realized over $2,500 to pay for our main building. At that time, the cost of property was very high and the smallest house could not be bought for less than $5,000 or $6,000. So it was not an easy thing to pay for a place that located just half block away from one of the city's principal churches and was surrounded by five or six different streetcars.[20]

Our linen department was among the best in New Orleans and was not better supplied than many. Many were the trousseaux made for not a hundred but a thousand of the richest and best families of this state.

We not only taught school, but also prepared children and fifty or sixty old women for their first communion, not only for one church, but two. One was St. Mary's, and the other, St. Augustine's. These girls are alive today to thank us for their being children of Christ. We are not forgotten. Since emancipation, they still show us how grateful they are.[21]

We received a monthly donation from each priest in the different churches in New Orleans. Many were ashamed they could present us only the sum of five dollars; their usual donation was from one to ten dollars a month. What a great pleasure it was for these same holy priests when they saw that our dear little community began to be blessed with so many graces.

Many a night did our dear sisters, after working all day, pray that some dear friend would send them a few spoonfuls of sugar. One time a servant came with a silver waiter with what one might call a grand dinner. Others sent us bundles of candles. Others came with a few pounds of coffee and others, if the weather was cold, with a wheelbarrow of wood and nut coal. Many ladies, knowing how poor we were, often sent us old shoes or boots to wear in the yard when it rained.

His grace, Archbishop Blanc, and our good Father Rousselon intended that we should be cloistered, but one thing or the other prevented it.[22] Both the first and second superiors were instructed by the sisters up in St. James Parish, by the Ladies of Sacred Heart.[23] Mother Juliette also received her early instruction from Madame Ste. Marthe, the first Ursuline nun who came to this city to teach the colored in New Orleans.[24] Many of our sisters, some of whom were quite brilliant, received their instruction of Madame Ste. Marthe. Many were also instructed by the Ladies of the Sacred Heart.

Our rule was well kept even in the beginning. Our first members were strikingly edifying and also very charitable; their love drew many graces. Would to God that many of our first sisters had lived some years longer to enjoy the fruit of their work, they who had toiled so had in the beginning for the love of God. When we think how many times they worked and were obliged to wait until some rich or charitable lady sent them the cold food from her table for their meals. Would it not seem strange if our dear Lord were to refuse to grant them so many striking graces after so many sacrifices for His holy love.

Our dear sister, Jeanne Marie Aliquot, was from a wealthy family in France and had four sisters.[25] She refused to take money from her family, and instead came to New Orleans. When she saw that there were six or eight young quadroon or octoroon ladies who wished to found an order, she was delighted and offered herself as mistress of novices. We were only too happy to accept her for she was just as holy as she could be.

When the bell was rung, Miss Aliquot would not wait to put on her shoes but would take them in her hand and come down.[26] She was a good mistress of novices and left a good example. Even when she was just as sick as she could be, she would say, "Get up Aliquot. Laziness, you shall not be my mistress," even when she was burning up with fever. A sister her age, she was forty-five or fifty, who was always ready to teach the Word to everybody she met! Many laughed at her, but she never noticed because she was so holy. She often told such beautiful stories that one would think that she had read them in a book or paper, but it just came from an inspiration and holy feeling. Humility was her most striking virtue. She was rich, but was poor for the love of others.

She not only loaned us $17,000 or $18,000, but she also went out to all of the richest planters to beg sugar and syrup for the sisters and she brought two or three slaves to work for us. When the soldiers during the late Civil War were posted in the city, one of them went off with a girl about the age of ten who followed him to camp. When our poor Sister Aliquot was told that the girl was in the camp, she went to get her. That was her last act of charity. She took cold and was brought to our convent almost speechless. She asked if that was the convent of the Holy Family and they said, "yes." When the sisters went to take her, she fainted from joy and died a very short time after that.[27]

Many times Miss Aliquot left her own dinner to give it to some old black man whom she had paid to come and learn his prayers. Many times she took off her own clothing to give it to some old colored woman whom she saw in the streets. We regretted her death very much for we have not found a friend a dear as she was nor as holy a religious.[28]

Once Henriette Delille, our Rev. Mother Foundress, became disgusted with the house on account of the malice of our precursors. So we decided to move and rent out our home and take a place near St. Mary's Church where we might live in peace. But even though good Father Rousselon would not give his consent our Mother Foundress, Henriette, did it of her own accord. But she regretted it much afterwards, for that very night, she was taken quite sick and one of the young sisters lost her mind and came near killing herself. After that, she would have been glad to return, but the parties who had leased our house were unwilling to break the lease. So we were obliged to remain until the lease expired which was over twelve months. During that time, we passed many pains. But we bore them patiently to show how pleasing our obedience was to our dear Lord who was obedient even to death, and death on the cross.

After that, we were able to move home again and we were not sorry to get back and were ever contented there with our many crosses which we were not wanting, for they came right and left.

At one time, the sisters were made to close up all of their windows on the north side of their house. They had just completed a payment on one of the back buildings to screen themselves from a vulgar set of men who had much annoyed them when they moved there. The sisters had spent many dollars to pay for the improvements on the two back buildings. That was during the Civil War. It had just broken out a few months previous to that.[29]

At another time, the girls in our boarding school became sick with measles and scarlet fever and left. Afterwards we came near starving and could not get anyone to go and see about a donation. At that time our good Father Rousselon had gone to France. We had no bread nor anything to make bread. So we prayed to St. Leven.[30] Just as soon as we had prayed the last word, someone rapped at the door, and there was a barrel of the best flour and rice. So we did not need anything for a long time. At another time, we were out of oil and when the prayers had been said, someone sent us a basket of olive oil and another sent two bottles. We were so thankful to God for so many graces that we say every day a prayer for them.

Another trouble was with the parish priest. We wanted to have a chaplain to have the privilege to say mass in our house and to keep the blessed sacrament in our chapel. But we were obliged to go out to church to make our visit.[31]

One more obstacle was to pay a tax for our home until we could incorporate our property, which was no easy thing. That required prayers.[32]

Our next cross was that some complained our school children in their recess made too much noise. That was another trouble for us, for everybody knows that children in playing most always make noise at recess, even the very best of children.

Our next trouble was with the family who complained of those with whom their children were playing. The ones who complained were of a better class and said that they did not want their children to mix with those whose mothers had been slaves. That gave our sisters much pain. But what could we do but all in our power to avoid offending them as we needed bread. That had been one our best means of getting by. If we could have lived without their tuition, it would have been more agreeable to us. Unfortunately, we were too poor and thus obliged to depend on the charity of our friends who had been more than kind to us. They are still willing to do any favor that is in their power.

Others wished us to have their children instructed in one place, and others in another. All of those things were unpleasant to us. But what must we do, for "no cross, no crown."

One of the greatest pains for us after emancipation was that those owners who had previously sent their slaves to us to be instructed wished us to refuse to give them any more lessons. But that as asking too much of our sisters, for our dear Lord said, "Go and teach all nations."[33] We, as sisters, are more obliged than others to teach all to know their God. And the day that we would refuse would be the day of sin for us, for our dear Lord said in another place that He had not come for the just, but to save sinners.[34] This would have been preaching one thing and practicing another, for the rich have many friends when they have money. We would work in vain if we were to seek to please them and to neglect the poor, for he that is in health has no need of a doctor.

After the death of Rev. Mother Foundress, our dear little community came very near failing, for there were four or five of the most accomplished young ladies whose families objected to them remaining with us after Rev. Mother's death. Some of the most useful members who left were Misses Allean, M. Shannaue, J. Valks, M. Marrianne, and D. Vaenuneas. Others who left and went to France were Misses J. La Rue, D. Doulard, and F. Lourta. They were not successful. But even after they left, we had many dear friends and also, like the Church of Christ, many enemies. But the slave is not better than his master.[35]

The first band of sisters who made their vows were Misses Juliette Gaudin of Cuba, Suzanne Navarre of Boston, Josephine Charles, Orphise François, Henriette Delille, and

Harriette Fazende, the last three of this city. There were many who, with the consent of their families, would have entered, but they did not want to displease their relatives and friends, not knowing whether they would remain and then have to return back into the world.

Another heavy cross was the death of our good Father Founder Rousselon, which happened a few years after that of Rev. Mother Henriette.[36] At New York City, he fell in the hatchway of the steamer on which he returned from his dear old home in the middle of France where he had made the voyage in search of better health which he much needed. It had seemed with his death that all was lost, for dear Father Rousselon had proved himself a true and faithful friend until his departure from this world of pain and toil.

But God, the Father and Consolation of his loved ones, sent us a dear friend in Father Gilbert Raymond, Father Rousselon's old schoolmate and his lifelong and dear friend. Our good Father Rousselon had left Father Raymond to replace him while he was away. It pleased God for Father Raymond to remain for fifteen years with us after our good Father Founder's death. In many things, Father Raymond was more attentive than our good Father Rousselon was himself. When Father Raymond resigned, he went to Opelousas and died in his own home with his only brother, Rev. François Raymond. Very Rev. Gilbert Raymond had left the care of a very fine and flourishing academy to his brother; it is one of the most successful of St. Landry Parish although the boys might have gone to Grand Coteau, a college of the Jesuit Fathers where so many famous and brilliant young and capable businessmen have completed their instruction for the last fifty or sixty years and they are still as bright as then.

Our holy habit that our good Father Rousselon had intended to give us was lost and someone else was obliged to give us another in its place. That was the habit Very Rev. Gilbert Raymond gave us with much pleasure some years later, and that habit was very pleasing to us all. That is the one that we have at present. Our habit was completed on March 19, 1881, when we came under the direction of the Jesuit Fathers.[37] We have been under the direction of the Jesuit Fathers up to the present time.

There was much trouble after the death of our Mother Foundress. The differences between Sisters Juliette Gaudin and Josephine Charles were so striking that it caused the establishment of a new branch or rather split house. That happened eight years after our dear Mother Foundress' death. Sisters Josephine and Juliette were both very holy, the former so bright, and the latter so docile. The split made such a change in the community that only prayer calmed their differences.[38] As both were well disposed to work for Almighty God, a word from our good Father Gilbert Raymond was enough to calm their displeasure and put them on their right path again, for they were like the lambs who were guided by the voice of their pastor. No doubt the split had its effect, but all was for the love of God. Henriette Delille's death as of course a great trial for those beautiful souls who would rather have died themselves than to have lost her so soon.[39]

The first split or branch house on Chartres Street was made the motherhouse instead of the old house at Bayou Road and Rampart Street which had been the first motherhouse of the community. The old house at Bayou Road and Rampart Street had been established for the instruction of novices when our dear Father and Mother Foundresses opened our dear little community in the beginning. But many years later it became too small and our dear old Mother Juliette became too feeble to conduct it as a house for the new members who desired to give themselves to God to work for His poor.

Because of respect for Mother Juliette's age as one of our principal members and because she had a superior intellectual capacity and had kept all the books of the community since her entrance, she was made assistant to the first mother superior who was very holy but not a very brilliant instructor and had not enough knowledge of finances to direct a community that was in its cradle and was not half paid for yet.[40] So our dear old Mother Juliette worked harder than any of the first members who had opened our community.

With the grace of God, our religious order is at present one of the most flourishing in this city, even after the little trouble between Mother Juliette Gaudin and Sister Mary Elizabeth Wales in the summer of 1870 when the first branch house was opened on Chartres Street.[41] After the split in the community, six sisters remained at Bayou Road under Mother Juliette's direction for three years.

On October 16, 1874, Sister Marie Philomene was named superior at Bayou Road, but that gave poor Mother Juliette much pain.[42] She felt that Mother Juliette was too old to be ruled by her; [thus] on March 8, 1876, Marie Philomene asked Father Raymond if she might resign as mother superior in favor of Mother Juliette.[43] He consented. Sister Marie Philomene went to the house on Chartres Street and Mother Juliette resumed her former duties as superior of the old cradle house on Bayou Road.

The poor soul, Mother Juliette, was again persecuted a second time for about eighteen months by another old sister, Sister Anne. Sister Anne took charge on December 27, 1876, but she was taken from the superiorship on April 3, 1878.[44] After that, the fathers of the parish were obliged to justify Mother Juliette's actions. Only to think what Mother Juliette suffered from the two girls whom she herself had received and had given their vows. That made her feel worse. She was so badly treated that she left every day for the first mass and stayed in the churchyard until the sunset, without coming home to take a bite of bread.

The subjects who were under Sister Anne saw that she was very unkind to our dear Old Mother Juliette. After one of them reported her to our mother superior, Sister Anne was soon taken out of the position and sent away for a time to collect for the orphans and the old people who needed to repair their old building that had much need of roofing.

At the same time that Sister Anne was removed, another of the oldest sisters went over to the other house on Chartres Street. That left old Mother Juliette almost alone on Bayou Road with a sister who was so old and sick that she was not able to do her duties. Dear old Mother Juliette then hired a teacher who had very kind feelings for her and God blessed them both by sending them a great many scholars. Her classes were again full of children.

The intentions of those at the split house on Chartres Street were to crush Mother Juliette so as to get her to come to them. But God loves the true soul who is willing to suffer for His glory. Mother Juliette and the other sisters on Bayou Road were independent of the help of those at the split house on Chartres St. The sisters at the old motherhouse had many friends who loved them much and were always ready to do everything that they could to aid them. They were never more cheerful and received many applicants from women who wanted to join the community from other cities. They received two young ladies of the first rank who made their classes flourish. It was only then that Mother Juliette regained the good will of those at the split house. The growth of her school was the only means of reuniting those who had not been on good terms for over twelve years.

Dear old Mother Juliette, the oldest member of the order, accepted the will of His Grace, Archbishop Napoleon J. Perché, who advised her to take the holy habit of our dear community which she had never consented to take. She received the habit on July 2, 1882, for the love of the Holy Family for which she had labored and suffered for so many years.[45] She did not receive the habit where we usually took it. Instead, she obtained permission to go up to St. John the Baptist Church in this city to receive the habit from the hands of Rev. Father Kenny who was visiting his mother for the last time. He died a few months later that of lung trouble.[46]

Mother Juliette afterwards said that she never felt a happier day in her whole life than she did that day she took the habit. Her only regret was that she had not taken one of our dear sisters instead of a child with her on that beautiful day. Instead, she was assisted by a nun of St. Dominic whose convent adjoined the Church of St. John the Baptist.[47] From that time, dear old Mother Juliette was as happy as she could be. She had often expressed to us that her greatest wish was to pardon and be united with those who had been against her and to die in union with them. God, who loves union, granted these graces to her before her death. She had been installed as mother superior at the house on Bayou Road on November 17, 1862, and remained in that position until December 17, 1883, when she moved to the house on Orleans Street where she lived in perfect love and holy joy with her dear sisters.

She was ever holy and edifying until her death which occurred on January 1, 1888.[48] She had made her jubilee for the Holy Father, the Pope.[49] On the day of her death, she made her communion in the chapel and was in bed only a few hours. She had been joking all that day, getting up and sitting on the side of the bed. Two or three times she told the sisters to pray and what prayers to say. One never dreamt that she could or would have died so soon. We had gone for the doctor two or three times that day. But as it was New Year's Day, it was hard to find one. That day is the only day that the gentlemen take for their amusement, and it is just that they should keep it once a year after working the year indoors. The doctor himself said that he never traced any symptoms of death on her.

So we all said that she had received the indulgences of the jubilee and was too holy to live. One of our sisters went across the street to call one of the parish fathers to come and give her the last sacraments. But he was baptizing a child and could not stop, so she started to come back and let Rev. Mother know and to see what she was to do. Just as she placed her hand on the doorknob, she heard the step of someone behind her. When she looked to see who it was, it was our chaplain who was coming to wish us a Happy New Year and to give us a benediction of the blessed sacrament. Just as he got up to the last step and reached the room, the priest who had been our previous director entered the door. One gave her the last sacraments and the other acted as an assistant. While one read the prayers, the other responded. It seemed so striking that although both the doctor and our good father director had been called away, one priest remained and another whom we had never hoped to see soon came. God must have been pleased to send them both to console her. God will reward them for their charity to her. Even though she was old and had been taken from her post as superior or second foundress, she had done much for our dear community. She had been the most brilliant of the four young ladies who founded our dear order, having kept the books for the acts of business for more than twenty-one years or until five years before her death.[50] Her death was so very calm and unexpected that one would never call it death, for she never seemed more gay than that day.

Mother Juliette's love for the poor had no limits. Many was the time that she was seen in rags because she had given her clothing to some poor child who had none. Many were the nights that she went to bed after having taken a glass of sweetened water, for she had saved her supper to give to some widow and her little children.

She was never so angry as when the sisters refused anything to the poor. Many a tear I have seen her shed when going to bed in bad weather for fear that someone was too poor to have the comforts that they ought to have. When she had her likeness taken, many said that her face was too sad, but her compassion for the poor was stamped on her face. All who knew her said the same of her. They said that when she was at the school, she was quite a child. The children always loved her for it. She was charitable to the poor and sick who knew and loved her. Many of them imposed on her kindness when they did not need it at all. The calmness of her death very plainly showed her many virtuous qualities that made her esteemed by all who knew her. More than one of the children of that time received their instruction from her and a great many grand persons were converted to the faith by their children's edifying conduct. Not so many of those are alive today, but those few have not forgotten the true oath to God. They are the first ones at the holy table and never miss mass on Sundays. We can also refer to some members of our dear community who were taught by her to make the sign of the cross. They are the most valuable sisters that we have and belong to some of the best and first families of this city.[51]

Dear Mother Juliette Gaudin was also a hero at the bedside of the dying of all colors and conditions. If at that time she came in contact with people of different colors living in a state of mortal sin, she would give them no rest until they had their union blessed by the holy Church of Christ, so as to draw God's blessing.

Our dear old mother's modesty and prudence surpassed all her other virtuous qualities. She shunned appearances so that many would have sooner taken her for the subject rather than the superior or the head of the house. One of her most striking qualities was her spirit of forgiveness, even to the smallest child in the house.

When we first fell into the hands of our good old Father Raymond, who was so very different in ideas from our good old Father Founder Rousselon, it seemed to Mother Juliette that she was being harshly treated. With the good advice of her confessor, however, she became one of his most compassionate friends.[52] She often expressed her deepest regret at having treated him so indifferently. But she received him with the greatest respect the last time that they met. That was a very short time previous to their deaths, which took place, one on January 1, 1888, and the other, Father Raymond, on April 5, 1889.

Her love for children had no bounds. She used to spoil them so that it was a very hard thing to manage them afterwards. I can remember that after she and I came to this house from the old cradle house, once or twice, the sister in charge of the boarders had two children who had been quite sick.[53] Mother Juliette had given them something that made them very sick. After that, this sister forbade them to eat anything from Mother Juliette. But one day Mother Juliette gave them a piece of cake and it gave them a relapse. Another time, the same sister noted something quite strange but did not say anything to anyone. She later said that the child was drunk from wine and said that Mother Juliette had given the child the wine that made her sick and drunk.

Mother Juliette did many things that made the children worse, but she did not mind. It was the strangest thing to see someone like Mother Juliette who could not speak but a very few words of English together with many of the children who could not speak a word of French. But they managed to understand each other in some way. At first sight in the yard every day just as they came to school, the smallest child would run after her for cake. They knew that she would save something for them, even if she starved herself to give to them. How often did some sisters conceal themselves to see her give the children nuts and cake that some of her friends had brought or sent her, thinking they would please her as she was so old and careworn. Many of the young ones were the children or grandchildren of some of her dear old schoolmates. Others were her father's scholars, for he had been a professor at one of the principal young men's high schools in the French part of New Orleans.

Notes for "Mothers Henriette Delille and Juliette Gaudin"

[1]Sister Mary Francis Borgia Hart began writing her history of the community, officially published under the title *Violets in the King's Garden*, in 1916. She explains, however, that other duties drew her away from her task and that it took her several decades to finish. The timing is important. In 1916, Henriette Fazende, who had

taken the religious name Anne, was still alive. She had come into the community in the 1850s and thus knew the foundresses as well as their struggles and triumphs.

[2]Sister Mary Francis Borgia Hart, SSF, "A History of the Congregation of the Sisters of the Holy Family of New Orleans" (M.A. thesis, Xavier College, 1931), 21.

[3]See below, Part I.

[4]Chloé Preval was born in St. Bernard Parish, January 21, 1839, at 11:30 P.M. She was the legitimate daughter of Jean Baptiste, negro slave of M. François Chaler, and of Marie Louis [sic] negress slave of Mlle. Aimée Rousseau. She was baptized June 18, 1839.

[5]Borgia Hart, "History of the Congregation," 22-23.

[6]Ibid., 23.

[7]Archives of the Oblates of Mary Immaculate, Rome, Italy; Archives of the Marianites of the Holy Cross, New Orleans.

[8]For a discussion of the problems housekeeping evoked, see *No Cross, No Crown, Black Nuns in Nineteenth Century New Orleans*, eds. Virginia Meacham Gould and Charles Nolan (Bloomington, 2001), Part III.

[9]Random notes Borgia Hart gathered from interviews with her religious sisters, Borgia Hart collection, Archives, Sisters of the Holy Family (hereafter cited as ASHF).

[10]See *No Cross, No Crown*, Part III.

[11]Caryn Cossé Bell and Joseph Logsdon, "The Americanization of Black New Orleans, 1850-1900," in *Creole New Orleans*, eds. Arnold R. Hirsch and Joseph Logsdon (Baton Rouge, 1992), 218.

[12]Jesus, Mary, and Joseph.

[13]Matthew 20:16; 22:14.

[14]New Orleans became an archdiocese in 1850. Father Antoine Blanc was its first archbishop. He died in 1860.

[15]This description is confusing but appears to be reasonably factual. Apparently the community's foundresses first moved into a rental house on St. Bernard Street. It proved to be too small, so the women moved into a rental home and then a few months later into a more permanent house on Bayou Road at Rampart. In 1851, Delille purchased a permanent house on Bayou Road. After the disagreement between Sisters Juliette and Josephine, Josephine and two sisters moved to 350 Chartres Street. Juliette stayed on Bayou Road with six other sisters. In 1881 the women united at 717 Orleans. Another document suggests that the foundresses of the community had some control over other property besides the houses on Bayou Road and Chartres Street. For instance, L'Association de Sainte Famille was incorporated on July 11, 1847, with Henriette Delille as its president and Juliette Gaudin as its secretary. The foundresses, along with several other officers, incorporated as a religious association in order to be legally recognized in Louisiana, raise funds, own property, and avoid taxes. On September 18, 1848, the association, represented by president Madame Cecilia Denouy LaCroix, spouse of François LaCroix, purchased property on St. Bernard Street between Marais and LaHarpe streets for 540 piastres from Widow J. J. Collard. Printed act of incorporation and purchase agreement, ASHF.

[16]Catholics parishes had lay trustees who managed the finances, property, and in this case, the needs of the poor.

[17]Throughout the manuscript Deggs refers to Bayou Road as either Bayou Road or Hospital Street. The editors have regularized the name to Bayou Road. Henriette Delille purchased the Bayou Road property, which included buildings and improvements, for $1,400, form Aristide Polenne on December 12, 1850. Of that, $1,091.25 was cash. She signed a one-year note for the outstanding $308.75. Jeanne Marie Aliquot loaned Delille $700.00 at no interest for the down payment and also guaranteed the $308.75 note. The contract of sale states that Delille was determined to establish "in perpetuity an establishment or asylum of charity for the religious education according to Catholic doctrine of colored people." Felix de Armas, notary, December 12, 1850, and June 13, 1853. Originals in the New Orleans Notarial Archives, hereafter cited as NONA.

[18]It was important for Deggs to be able to follow the movement of the foundresses from house to house, or motherhouse to mother house. Deggs does not identify any of them as a convent; they were always simply houses to her. Yet from the very beginning one house after the other served the women as a convent and a sanctuary. The possession of a house/convent demonstrated the women's commitment to religious life and their rejection of worldliness.

[19]Genesis 37:3, 23, and 32-33.

[20]A fair to benefit the sisters was advertised in *Le Propagateur Catholique*, December 20, 1851; May 7, 1860, fair brochure in ASHF.

[21]The first work of the foundresses was to evangelize slave women and free women of color. For the organization that served as a precursor to the religious community, see: Règles et règlements pour la congregation des Soeurs de la presentation de la B.V. Marie . . . fondé à la Nouvelle Orleans le 21 November 1836, ASHF. The association was founded by Henriette Delille and Juliette Gaudin. This pious group of free women of color, known as la Congregation de la Presentation or the Congregation of the Presentation, appears to have been a transitional group, bridging the gap between an early group of pious lay women and the later group that took their identities as women religious. The pious congregation of the Sisters of the Presentation was affiliated with one of the ancient Catholic sodalities in Rome in 1841 at the request of Bishop Antoine Blanc.

[22]By 1836, there were four communities of women religious in Louisiana: the Ursuline Nuns, the Sisters of Charity, the Religious of the Sacred Heart, and the Sisters of Mount Carmel. The New Orleans Ursulines were originally cloistered, although the cloister was modified to meet local needs. Concerning the evolution of women religious communities in France, see Elizabeth Rapley, *The Dévotés: Women and Church in Seventeenth-Century France* (Montreal, 1990).

[23]The first and second superiors were Henriette Delille and Juliette Gaudin. According to oral tradition, both were educated by the Sisters of the Sacred Heart in Convent, St. James Parish, Louisiana. Borgia Hart writes in her account that Delille had become aware by 1850 that it would be impossible to give prospective members the proper training if she had not received it herself, so she turned the direction of the house over to Gaudin and traveled to the Sisters of the Sacred Heart in St. James Parish, or Convent, to be instructed "in the principles and duties of the religious life and subjected to the trails of a novice." She would have returned to New Orleans near the beginning of 1851, at which time, Borgia Hart writes, she spent a year instructing her two companions on what she had learned. There is no record in the Sacred Heart archives that Delille was instructed either there or at the Sisters of the Sacred Heart, St. Michael's Convent, in St. Michael's, Louisiana. American Archives of the Religious of the Sacred Heart, Saint Louis, Mo. Borgia Hart, *Violets in the King's Garden*, 10. Yet, Archbishop Blanc was very close to the sisters of the Sacred Heart and it would have been the logical place to send Delille for a more formal religious formation. The annual reports and chronicle of St. Michael's convent and school reveal that the sisters of the Sacred Heart regularly taught and even provided retreats for slaves and persons of color; Borgia Hart writes that Delille spent nearly a year with the sisters at St. Michael's.

[24]Sister Ste. Marthe Fontière was a member of the French religious community Les Dames Hospitalière when she arrived in New Orleans in 1817. Les Dames Hospitalière signified many different communities of religious women in France in the nineteenth century. Sister Ste. Marthe left France for New Orleans in response to a request made by the Ursulines to Bishop Dubourg. Upon arriving, she took charge of the classes for free girls of color that the Ursulines had conducted. When the Ursulines arrived in New Orleans in 1727, they established a school that included African girls among their first catechism and boarding students. By 1823, Sister Ste. Marthe had established a separate school for free girls of color on St. Claude Street. Records demonstrate that by 1829, the school had about eighty girls in attendance; monthly tuition was $1.50 to $5.00. The Ursuline nuns, the pious woman Jeanne Marie Aliquot, and the Sisters of Mount Carmel successively took over Sister Ste. Marthe's school in the early 1830s. 1829 report on the Status of the Diocese of New Orleans by Bishop Joseph Rosati. Historical Manuscript Collection, 1.8. Archives, Archdiocese of Boston. Archives of the Ursulines, New Orleans.

[25]Jeanne Marie Aliquot came to Louisiana from France in 1832, according to the oral tradition of the community, in order to join the Ursulines. She was following the lead of one of her biological sisters, Félicité Aliquot,

or Sister Francis de Sales Aliquot, who was an Ursuline. Another sister, Adele Aliquot, also traveled to New Orleans but died of yellow fever in 1833. However, Jeanne Marie Aliquot did not join the Ursulines, but rather devoted herself to the salvation and care of blacks in the city. As the story is told by Borgia Hart, Jeanne Marie slipped and fell into the Mississippi River while disembarking from the ship upon her arrival in New Orleans. A black man dived into the river and rescued her. In response to that experience, she vowed to devote her life to the city's blacks, a mission that was not possible as a member of the Ursulines. Consequently, Jeanne Marie began teaching at the St. Claude Street School. However, in 1836 she sold the school to the Ursulines, who in turn sold it to the Sisters of Mount Carmel. Ursuline Archives, New Orleans, Archives of the Sisters of Mount Carmel, New Orleans. Nolan, *Bayou Carmel*, 19; Borgia Hart, *Violets in the King's Garden*, 7.

[26]The bell was rung to notify each person in a religious community that they were to report to a particular activity or place. The idea of promptly responding to the bell reflected an immediate response to duty.

[27]Deggs confuses the 1881 debt on Orleans Street with Aliquot's $700.00 loan to Delille in 1851. Jeanne Marie Aliquot was buried in St. Louis Cemetery #3 on April 12, 1863, not in the Holy Family tomb in St. Louis Cemetery #2. And while she was closely associated with them, she was never included in any official list of early sisters. St. Louis Cathedral Funeral Expenses, 1860-1871, p. 285, act 840. Archives, Archdiocese of New Orleans, hereafter cited as AANO.

[28]According to Borgia Hart, the sisters were perturbed when Aliquot's body was claimed by white friends after her death and laid out on the second floor of a house a short distance from the convent; a fire broke out, and the fire department was called. Just as it appeared that it would be impossible to retrieve the body because the stairs had burned, the fire died down. The bucket brigade was able to bring it out by way of a ladder. It was then taken to the convent, where it lay in repose until interment, "when all classes of persons in New Orleans gathered to pay their respects to the mortal remains of one who had sacrificed her life for its down-trodden people." Borgia Hart, *Violets in the King's Garden*, 17.

[29]The house to which Deggs refers was the old motherhouse on Bayou Road, where the sisters lived from 1851 until 1881.

[30]St. Leven has not been identified.

[31]Because the women could not have mass said in their chapel they were obliged to go out to one of the local churches and to visit the blessed sacrament.

[32]The Sisters of the Holy Family were incorporated in 1847, under the name La Société de la Sainte Famille. The incorporation was created to "aid indigent sick people" and to eventually purchase a hospice for them.

[33]Matthew 18:19-20.

[34]Matthew 9:13; Mark 2:17; Luke 5:32.

[35]Matthew 10:24; Luke 6:40. The biblical text refers to disciple and master; Deggs substituted slave for disciple. The women Deggs lists here were not included in the community's Matricula or official book listing the professed sisters. We do not recognize these names from other sources; most are probably phonetic. These were apparently "not successful" in joining another religious community, and kept in contact with the women who remained in the community.

[36]Rousselon died on June 15, 1866, while returning from a trip to France, from injuries sustained when he fell through the hatch of his ship. Burials of Clergy, in AANO.

[37]In her book, Borgia Hart recounts what she learned about the evolution of historical significance of the habit. The omen wore a blue percale dress and a black bonnet during the early years of common life together, or between 1842 and 1852. It appears that Father Rousselon recognized that they needed to be as discreet as possible and thus advised them to dress simply and without pretension. On October 15, 1852, when the women too their first vows, Rousselon allowed them to change their blue dresses for black ones. So as not to threaten the white nuns in the city or to alarm their fellow New Orleanians, who would have seen them as having pretensions, they wore dresses instead of habits. However, in 1866, when the war was over and the sisters were attempting to

break down the prewar racial barriers, Rousselon obtained permission for the sisters to wear a habit, and was bringing a pattern for one from France when he died en route. In the confusion that followed his death, the pattern disappeared. For a time, the sisters wondered if someone who disapproved of black women wearing habits had disposed of it. There is some evidence that the sisters began wearing a habit designed by Josephine Charles in 1876. Yet, as Deggs states in this passage, it was not until 1881 that formal permission for the habit was obtained by Gilbert Raymond.

[38]The word "differences" is the editors'. Deggs wrote "eareations," most likely meaning "variations." We substituted "differences" in order to make the text more accessible.

[39]The community split in 1870 when Josephine Charles left the old motherhouse located on Hospital at Rampart Street, near St. Claude Street. It is not clear how many women Charles took with her, but she established the split house, or second house, at 350 Chartres Street. The split lasted until 1881. Deggs in several passages addresses the issue and personalities involved in the rift between Sisters Juliette Gaudin and Josephine Charles, including the influence of Sister Elizabeth Wales and Sister Juliette's refusal to accept the religious habit. Yet even though Deggs never describes exactly what led to the split, oral tradition has it that it was over whether the women should accept a freed slave into their community. Supposedly Charles was willing to accept the freed woman into the community, while Gaudin was not.

[40]The original text confusingly reads: "She had disrespected her age as one of principal and having had a more superior intellectual capacity and having kept the all off the books for the whole community since the entrance and long before it was opened. So by those means she as assistant for the first general superior had worked more as she."

[41]Bayou Road is now called Governor Nichols. Deggs identifies the house on Chartres Street as "the split house."

[42]Sister Marie Philomene left the community before the Matricula was composed; she is not included in that list of sisters.

[43]The original text reads March 8. Other information she gives indicates the year as 1876.

[44]Deggs wrote 1877 in the original text, but other records prove that to be incorrect. There were two women named Sister Anne in the community during the nineteenth century. In this passage, Deggs refers to Sister Anne (Harriette) Fazende, one of the oldest members of the community. Deggs describes her as both gifted and abrasive. Harriette Fazende, daughter of Martin Fazende and Marcellite Lange, was born on August 11, 1826, in New Orleans, and baptized January 25, 1828, at St. Louis Cathedral. Her parents had been married at St. Joseph Church in Baton Rouge on April 9, 1821; Diego Pintado was one of the marriage witnesses. St. Louis Cathedral Baptisms of Slaves and Free Persons of Color, 1827-1829, p. 59, act 266. AANO. Diocese of Baton Rouge Catholic Church Records, 1820-1829, Volume 4 (Baton Rouge, 1983), 338. She entered the community in May 1858. She died February 5, 1919; thus, she was still alive at the time Deggs wrote this historical account.

[45]The date, 1882, given for Juliette Gaudin's taking the habit, was only a few months after the houses were reunited. And since Gaudin went alone, out of the parish, to St. John the Baptist Church, to accept the habit, it appears that there was still a considerable amount of discord in the community.

[46]Fr. Thomas Kenny was the pastor of St. John the Baptist Parish at this time. He died on August 19, 1881. Roger Baudier, *St. John the Baptist Church, New Orleans: A Century of Pastoral Service, 1852-1952* (New Orleans, 1952), 31-32.

[47]The Dominican Sisters staffed a school for white girls in St. John the Baptist Parish in the American sector of New Orleans.

[48]The obituary of Mother Juliette Gaudin appeared in the *New Orleans Daily Picayune*, January 2, 1888.

[49]Leo XIII, who was pope in 1888, had declared that year a papal jubilee year with special prayers and indulgences. Pastoral Letter of Archbishop Francis Janssens, New Orleans, December 3, 1888, AANO.

[50]Both the Deggs journal and other community records suggest that Juliette Gaudin and Josephine Charles received a more formal education than did Henriette Delille.

[51]Deggs does not say if she herself is among this group.

[52]The community confessor by church law was someone other than the community's clerical superior.

[53]Deggs was evidently in the house on Bayou Road with Juliette Gaudin.

THE NEW ORLEANS GERMAN AND
HIS CHURCH, SCHOOL, LODGE, AND
ELEEMOSYNARY INSTITUTION*

John Fredrick Nau

In March 1721, two hundred Germans arrived in Biloxi to continue their journey to the land concession of John Law, a notorious Scotch financier, located in the lower Arkansas River Valley. After a little more than a year, these immigrants were joined by two hundred and fifty more of their countrymen.[1] While their lot in this region was hard and trying, their coming and settlement proved to be the beginning of German immigration to Louisiana and New Orleans, which by the mid-1830s had culminated in the establishment of a German colony within the city, numbering about 7,000.[2]

As far as religious persuasion was concerned, there were Catholics, Protestants, and free thinkers among these German immigrants. Within the Protestant element, Reformed, Evangelical, and Lutherans predominated, however, all were without any clear conception as to the distinctions among the three. This was the result of the spiritual condition in their homeland, largely the outcome of the Prussian Union of 1817.[3]

The establishment of the Prussian Union was an event of the first importance in the history of Protestantism in Germany. Two years earlier, the Congress of Vienna had deprived the German states of the right to determine the religion of their subjects. The adherents of all Christian creeds were placed on a footing of legal equality in all states. In some of them, which had been partly Lutheran and partly Reformed, this led to great confusion; and to end the confusion the government attempted to force a union of the two churches. In 1817, Fredrich William III decreed such a union for his kingdom of Prussia and issued, at the same time, a new liturgy for the use of all the congregations in the kingdom. The example of Prussia was followed by other states. Only a few of the smaller states attempted to unite the Protestant churches, but practically all of them adopted the new method of church control. The state churches were placed under the direction of consistories, appointed by the rulers, and the rulers themselves became "ex officio" heads of the churches.[4]

*First published as Chapter 5 in *The German People of New Orleans, 1850-1900* (Leiden: E. J. Brill, 1958), 69-95. Reprinted with the kind permission of the copyright holder.

Circumstances favored this move. Both in the Lutheran and in the Reformed churches comparatively little stress was laid upon distinctive confessional doctrines; and the philosophies of Pietism and Rationalism, which preceded the era of the Prussian Union, had for different reasons taught the relative unimportance of dogma. Consequently, in Prussia and in many other German states an Evangelical national church with a common government and liturgy existed. This ecclesiastical body embraced three variant doctrinal viewpoints, a Lutheran, a Reformed which held to its distinctive doctrines though not regarding them as a cause of separation from this body, and an Evangelical which completely abandoned the points of difference seeking a real union church between the Lutherans and the Reformed. Squeezing these divergent viewpoints into one church organization, the Prussian Union became more and more identified with doctrinal indifference and the slighting of all church symbols.[5]

The greater number of Protestant German immigrants coming to New Orleans were by religious persuasion children of this merger in which doctrinal distinctiveness had been superseded by the effort at unity. While this feeling of outward unity among them led to the founding of the first German Protestant congregation in 1825, it also became the direct cause of strife, bitterness, and division in their early church life when it was seen that no true spirit of ecumenity existed among them.[6] Diversity of religious thought and conviction was the dominant factor in the origin of German congregations of many different denominations.[7] Those of Catholic faith also experienced strife and division in their churches mainly because of the language question, yet not as intensely as among the Protestant element. They were a part of the dominant religious faction in the city and state under the jurisdiction of much higher and more united church officials.[8]

Prior to 1825, the Germans of the city had no church of their own which offered them spiritual solace in the language with which they were familiar. Catholic Germans worshiped either in Saint Patrick's Cathedral on Camp Street or in Saint Louis Cathedral at the *La Place d'Armes*. Protestants attended services either in Christ Church, the first Protestant congregation in Louisiana, on the corner of Canal and Bourbon Streets, or in the First Presbyterian Church and in the First Methodist Episcopal Church.[9] Eager to have the Word preached in their own language and being unable to understand too readily the preaching in a "foreign language," some Germans gathered for worship in a school house on Burgundy Street near Canal. By 1839, a church building was erected on Rampart Street which, however, was abandoned the very next year when this group moved into a new church structure on Clio Street between Saint Charles and Carondelet. The congregation gave itself the name of the Clio Street Church.[10]

The ensuing decades were propitious for the founding of German Protestant congregations, as well as those of the Catholic persuasion. In 1840, two Protestant churches were organized, one a Methodist, and one giving itself the name of the Deutsche Evangelische Orthodoxe Kirche in New Orleans. The former found a leader in Peter Schmucker, who in the winter of that year gathered a number of members placing Matthaeus Tautau in charge. The group rented a plot of ground on Erato Street between

Camp and Magazine and built a small church. The latter was of a German-evangelical character but was not Lutheran.[11] Holding services in the fire engine house on Chartres Street, between Clouet and Louisa, and later in a private dwelling on the same street near Port, this congregation built a modest building on the corner of Port and Burgundy streets, dedicating it on October 1, 1843.[12] Six years later, in 1849, the church records revealed that one hundred and eighty-five baptisms were performed, ninety-seven weddings solemnized, and thirty-nine confirmants received into membership.[13] In March 1872, the congregation adopted a more doctrinally conservative constitution and gave itself the name of the German Evangelical Lutheran Saint Paul's Congregation of New Orleans, Louisiana.[14]

Many Germans lived in the vicinity of Jackson Avenue and the river, known as the City of Lafayette, and among them were many of the Catholic faith. Warehouses, slaughter-houses, and other kinds of business had sprung up in that area which led to an increased population. The Germans living in that location had no church. The closest one to the neighborhood was the Church of Saint Thérèse. The attention of Bishop Blanc was directed to the situation, but being sorely in need of priests, especially German-speaking priests who could work among the many Catholic immigrants settling in and around the city, he was unable to begin work.

In 1836, the opportunity to start work in this area appeared. The Superior of the first Redemptorist order in the United States sent Father Czackert, then thirty-five years old, on a tour of the large cities of the country to collect funds for the Redemptorist Fathers' mission of Pennsylvania. Father Czackert came to New Orleans and was welcomed by Bishop Blanc, who gave him lodging at the episcopal residence, the old Ursuline convent on Chartres Street. The bishop was so impressed with the young Redemptorist that he asked him to remain for a time, at least, and do some work of gathering the Germans of Catholic faith at the Kaiser Hall, a popular dance hall located on Josephine Street and Chippewa. By paying a monthly rental Father Czackert was able to obtain permanent use of the hall from its Protestant owner. He fitted up the former dance hall as a church, and it became the center of religious activity for the City of Lafayette. He organized several catechism classes for children and adults, giving daily instructions, particularly to those of German birth, thus gradually building a German Catholic congregation about the makeshift dance-hall chapel. Bishop Blanc, noting the good work of Father Czackert and realizing the continued shortage of priests, was inspired to offer the work in the City of Lafayette to the Redemptorist Fathers. Accordingly, he wrote Father Passerat, the Superior-General of the Redemptorists, who, moved by the bishop's plea, accepted the offer. In 1843, Bishop Blanc purchased two lots of ground on Josephine Street with the expressed intention "for a church to be built for the special use of the German Catholics living in Lafayette."[15]

Consequently, a church edifice was constructed which was blessed by the bishop on Sunday, April 14, 1844, and was called Saint Mary's Assumption Church. This was the first German Catholic Church not only in New Orleans but also in the state of Louisiana.[16] A frame structure, ninety by forty-five feet in dimensions, resting upon high pillars of brick, with a wide stairway leading into the interior, housed the first worshipers.[17]

The first Saint Mary's edifice served the congregation until 1858, when Father Anwander was successful in having the congregation venture upon building a second and more pretentious house of worship. The site chosen was right next to the original church. Parishioners worked hand in hand with the Fathers to erect the building. Even the women lent their aid carrying the bricks in their aprons from Jackson Avenue, since the deep mud permitted no traffic on Constance Street, then called Live Oak.

Of modified Gothic style, its beautiful majestic lines attracted attention and aroused enthusiasm from natives and visitors alike. As the years passed by, all that could enhance the beauty and the reverential atmosphere of the church was added. The gorgeous stained glass windows, the melodious bells, named "Mary-Joseph," weighing 4,000 pounds, and her companions, "Pius" and "Gabriel," and the great organ—all were installed as time went on. Finally, on Christmas Day 1874, the high altar, made in Munich, Germany, which was one of the finest examples of the wood-carvers' art to be seen in this country, was solemnly dedicated. All which the church symbolized was a tribute to the pioneering Catholic Germans of the City of Lafayette.[18]

Expansion of the church among the German Catholics of the city was very orderly, directed to take care of the Germans living in various sections of the city and its outlying areas. Just as the City of Lafayette attracted a goodly number of German immigrants, so also were the City of Carrollton and the Faubourg Marigny popular sections for the concentration of these people. In Carrollton preaching began in 1847 in a private home on Cambronne Street near Maple. A German priest from Saint Louis came at regular intervals to read the mass and give instructions, assisted by the priest of Saint Charles Borromeo, the little Red Church of Destrehan. Bishop Blanc realized that the Catholics of Carrollton consisting principally of German and French people, but including also Irish and American, should have a church with a resident pastor. In 1848, in compliance with the request of these Catholic people, he commissioned Father F. Zeller, a Lorrainian, to form a parish in Carrollton and to build a church. On May 2 of that year, Father Zeller bought three lots of ground upon which a church and a rectory were built. The dedication took place on September 8.

Preaching was carried on in German only. This angered the French- and English-speaking people of the congregation who plotted to burn down the church building. The threat brought out guards to protect the building but also the wise decision to preach in German, French, and English. This practice of preaching in three tongues was continued until 1861, when Father Franz Ceuppens, a Belgian priest, took charge of the congregation and discontinued German preaching since he could not speak the language. Discontent among the Germans resulted. In answer to their dissatisfaction, Father Anton Bicklmayer was sent as assistant to Father Ceuppens with instructions to work especially with the German-speaking people of the parish. All was well until the days of the Franco-Prussian War in 1870, at which time Father Ceuppens was in Europe.

Bicklmayer was preaching in German only at that time, and the Germans, filled with patriotic fervor, were clamoring for their own church. With the return of Ceuppens, Father Bicklmayer was forced to leave to assume work in another parish and was ordered by his superiors "not to visit Carrollton under any circumstances."[19] Immediately the Germans of Carrollton went into action. They organized themselves into a congregation, bought a piece of ground measuring a hundred feet from the old church on the other side of Cambronne Street and built their own building. Meant to serve the German Catholics of the area, it received its own pastor in Father Bicklmayer and its own name, German Mater Dolorosa Church.[20]

One section of the Faubourg Marigny was popularly known as "Little Saxony" because of the large number of Germans living in that area. Here the Catholic church concentrated its efforts to establish a congregation among them. Success was realized in 1847, when Father J. M. Masquelet founded Holy Trinity Catholic Church, erecting a small frame building at a cost of $3,000.00 on the corner of Saint Ferdinand and Dauphine Streets. The first church was blessed on July 18, 1848. Three years later, however, while Father Scheffer was pastor, the first church burnt. The members, all German Catholics, at once proceeded to rebuild and on the feast of the Holy Trinity 1853, the new church was dedicated.

Misunderstanding on the part of the priest and the trustees and members of the congregation in regard to incorporation and proper assignment of the property as required by Bishop Blanc caused considerable confusion. For a time it seemed as if serious trouble would destroy the young parish entirely, but Father Scheffer carried on his ministrations and soon affairs were straightened out and settled. Holy Trinity rapidly forged ahead to become one of the outstanding parishes of the church in the city.[21] Its era of greatest achievement came during the pastorate of Father P. Leonhard Thevis, who served the parish from 1870 to 1893.[22] He was followed by J. B. Bogaerts from 1893 to 1898, and Anthony Bicklmayer from 1898 to 1900.[23]

Wherever German Catholics settled in any number, they always insisted upon a church of their own, where instruction, the Gospels, announcements, sermons, and catechism were given in the German language. Such feeling led directly to the founding of Saint Henry's Catholic Church on Berlin Street between Constance and Magazine Streets in the year 1856; to the organization of Saint Boniface Catholic Church on Lapeyrouse and North Galvez Streets; and the chartering of Saint Joseph Catholic Church on the west bank of the river in Gretna, Louisiana.

Saint Henry's served the Germans living in the area known as Jefferson City, which was located between the City of Layette and the City of Carrollton. From 1870, when the parish received its first resident pastor, until 1900, the members received their spiritual guidance from four priests: Father M. Radamaerger from 1870 to 1871; Father J. Bogaerts from 1871 to 1872 and from 1874 to 1891; Father M. Radamaergerts from 1873 to 1874; and Father Louis Rich from 1891 to 1900.[24]

Saint Boniface was organized by Father Joseph Koergerl in 1869. He had been ordered by Archbishop Odin to establish a congregation among the Catholic Germans living in the area below Canal Street and in the rear of Holy Trinity German parish. These
people had repeatedly petitioned the archbishop for a church of their own stating that the
distance between their homes and Holy Trinity parish was too far and too difficult to
traverse. In a rather short time Father Koergerl gathered about him a large flock, which
grew in membership and included many French and Creoles who lived in the rear of the
city.[25]

Saint Joseph had its beginning in 1859, after many German Catholics living on the
west bank of the river in the vicinity of Gretna had been served for a number of years by
priests coming from New Orleans parishes. In that year a church was built and dedicated.
By 1870, the Germans of the city and its vicinity were able to worship in and work for
five prosperous and growing churches of the Catholic faith.[26]

Among the Protestant Germans church building and church organization were likewise going forward, with more individual congregations established than among the
Catholic element. After the founding of the Clio Street Church, the First Methodist
Church, and the Deutsche Evangelische Orthodoxe Kirche, Protestant groups mushroomed in all parts of the city. While a growing German population was one of the
dominant reasons for the appearance of so many different church groups, the German as a
religious individualist, the inability to obtain capable pastors, and the presence of dissentient elements within existing congregations were strong contributing factors.[27]

Germans who could not forget that they were children of the "Evangelical" movement in the fatherland were busy, soon after establishing their homes in the city and its
outlying sections, in organizing their congregations. One of the earliest church groups
assembled on September 21, 1845, in the home of Caspar Auch at Rousseau and Fourth
Streets. There was great rejoicing when on August 16, 1846, the members, who had
given much of their time and labor in the construction program, were privileged to dedicate a church building on the corner of Philip and Chippewa Streets. Since the location
of the church was in the City of Lafayette, it was known as Lafayette Evangelical
Church.

Strife and dissension plagued the congregation in its early history. The first pastor of
the flock, C. A. Schramm, was dismissed for writing jocose sayings into the church records.[28] From 1849, the year of his dismissal, to 1864, the congregation was served by
seven pastors, four of whom ministered only one year. The height of strife occurred in
the year 1858, when Hermann Pressler, the pastor, was literally chased out of office by
the women of the church wielding whips and umbrellas, and scattering salt, pepper, and
sand. Pressler had made himself unbearable to a large number of his members by his
belligerent attitude, first toward the teacher of the church school and then toward any and
all who questioned his right as a clergyman.[29] Lasting peace came to the congregation,
however, in 1864, when the Reverend Ludwig P. Heintz assumed the pastorate and
served until 1900.[30] Under his guidance and inspired leadership a new house of worship

was erected in 1875 on the corner of Jackson Avenue and Chippewa Street, which received the name of Jackson Avenue Evangelical Church.[31]

Another German Evangelical congregation was organized in the City of Carrollton on Zimple Street between Monroe and Leonidas Streets on April 22, 1849. Five years after the founding, at the time of the arrival of L. P. Heintz as pastor, a split occurred in the membership since some refused to stay with Heintz but followed the newly-arrived Basel preacher, Martin Otto. The result of this action was that from 1855 to 1884 there were two evangelical groups in the City of Carrollton, one known as the "Rooster Church" because of a cock adorning the tower, the other, the "Otto Church." They were within a few blocks of each other, the "Rooster Church" on Zimple Street and the "Otto Church" on Dante Street.

It was not a matter of faith or conscience but simple human selfishness and jealousy which kept the two apart. As early as 1878, an attempt at reunion was unsuccessful because the two groups could not decide which building to use. Finally, in 1884 when the two united, the "Otto Church" building housed the newly-merged group, named the German Evangelical Church of Carrollton 7th District of New Orleans; while the property of the "Rooster Church" was sold to the Evangelical Lutheran Church-Missouri Synod for $600 and was used for the organization of a Negro mission. The old "Otto Church" structure did not, however, serve as the house of worship of the united group for any length of time, for during the year of the merger a new church building was erected on Dante Street near Elm Street. In 1890, the name of the congregation was changed to the German Evangelical Saint Matthew Church.[32]

An evangelical splinter was organized into a congregation by John H. Kleinhagen in 1854. After serving Clio Street Church and Zion Lutheran Church, he started his own congregation by rallying around a small splinter group of evangelical Germans and, locating on Felicity Street, called it the German Evangelical Bethlehem Church. The organization remained in existence until the 1890s, when the group disbanded, selling its church building to a Negro mission which moved it to Felicity Street and Claiborne Avenue.[33]

Two more evangelical congregations were organized among the Germans of the city before the close of the century. In Jefferson City a group of them led by Preacher J. J. Ungerer organized in 1862. For a while it seemed as if they would join the Lutheran church, being served for a time by ministers of that body. In 1864, however, a Reformed pastor, G. Dietz, was called, who immediately launched a building program by erecting a structure on Milan and Camp Streets, and who by 1877 was successful in placing the congregation in line with the Evangelical Synod of North America. This affiliation was made final in 1891 under the pastorate of Julius P. Quinius.[34] The other evangelical flock was gathered by Hermann Perpeet, who in 1879 left the Clio Street Church to form an independent congregation on North Derbigny Street. In this particular neighborhood Saint John's church, a Protestant group with definite Lutheran leanings, was already active; and, after 1881, another church group, Emmanuel Lutheran, began activity in the same area. These conditions undermined the efforts of the independent church of Perpeet, which consequently disappeared in 1887.[35]

The Lutheran faith was a dominant one in the religious life of the German-speaking people. This was clearly reflected in the days when New Orleans Germans were laying the foundations of their church life in their adopted home. On September 12, 1847, J. H. Kleinhagen preached to a number of Germans in the Saint Marie Church on Gainie Street.[36] The effort led to the organization of Zion Evangelical Lutheran Church on July 2, 1848. While not possessing all the marks of a confessional Lutheran church body, the congregation was conscious of its heritage by incorporating the word "Lutheran" into its official name. During October and November, negotiations for the purchase of a piece of property on Euterpe Street were completed, and on March 18, 1849, the erection of the first church building was completed by contractor Friedrich Koch.[37] This group of Germans, together with Saint John's Church and the German Evangelical Lutheran Saint Paul's Congregation, was influential in bringing confessional Lutheranism to New Orleans during the early years of the 1850s.[38]

On January 18, 1852, a group of Germans organized a congregation on the corner of Customhouse and North Prieur Streets and gave it the name of Saint John Evangelical Lutheran Church. Brother J. H. Hollander was appointed the lay preacher in October of that year. Immediately after his appointment the members cast about for a trained spiritual leader, and it was soon evident that they would not be satisfied with any kind of pastor. On January 3, 1853, Pastor Press was recommended to them. Since he held to doctrines and practices not in accord with those of the congregation, he was not received.[39] About that time, C. F. W. Walther, president of a confessional Lutheran body with headquarters in Saint Louis known as the Evangelical Lutheran Synod of Missouri, Ohio, and Other States, heard of this congregation and its needs through the medium of a New Orleans daily newspaper.[40] He came to New Orleans accompanied by George Volk, a young candidate for the Lutheran ministry. Three days after, Volk was ordained and installed as Saint John Lutheran Church's first pastor. The rite was performed by Walther in the presence of a large gathering.[41] By this act the congregation came into official membership of the Missouri Synod, which in time established more firmly the teachings and practices of this confessional body in the city of New Orleans.[42]

Germans of Zion Lutheran Church and of Saint John Lutheran Church, together with their pastors, participated in many joint efforts which created in both church groups the hope and desire to form a closer association with the Missouri Synod. As this spirit grew, Kleinhagen, the pastor of Zion, became dissatisfied and consequently resigned. The leaderless congregation sent an urgent request for a pastor to the officials of the Synod and on December 3, 1854, received W. A. Fick in response to their call. The coming of Fick as pastor of Zion strengthened the tie between Saint John and Zion since both were served by ministers trained in the teachings and practices of the Missouri Synod of the Lutheran Church. By the beginning of 1855, through the combined work of the members of Saint John and Zion, Lutheranism was firmly established in the city of New Orleans.[43]

A consciousness of confessional Lutheranism gradually worked its way into the life of the members of the Deutsche Orthodoxe Kirche of New Orleans. In 1858, a new constitution was adopted in which it was stated that the congregation adheres "to all the symbolic books of the Evangelical Lutheran church, as the form and norm drawn from God's Word, according to which, since they have been taken from the Word of God, not only the doctrines taught in our church shall be proven or taught, but all eventual doctrinal and religious differences shall be judged and regulated."[44] Finally, in the early years of the 1870s, the congregation, then known as the First Evangelical Lutheran Church of New Orleans, Louisiana, united in fellowship with Zion and Saint John.[45] At about the same time, Lutheran churches among the Germans living in Algiers and Gretna were established.[46]

Germans of the city also affiliated themselves with congregations of the Presbyterian faith. Churches of this denomination among the Germans were usually the result of splits occurring in existing ecclesiastical organizations. In 1853, a number of members of the Lafayette Evangelical Church, because of the liberalism of its pastor who was in like mind with the Turners of the Forty-Eighters, left and founded a German Presbyterian church on First Street between Laurel and Annunciation Streets. From 1865 to 1878, it was affiliated with the Northern Presbyterium, because the pastors serving the congregation were in general closely associated with this conference of churches. In March 1878, however, under the leadership of Professor Lesko Triest, the group returned to the Southern Presbyterium. Shortly thereafter, Candidate Louis Voss became the pastor, who served the church throughout the remainder of the century. He was a leading clergyman of the city who was not only interested in building the Kingdom but also in furthering German culture. During his ministry, the name, First German Presbyterian Church of New Orleans, was given the congregation.[47]

The Second German Presbyterian Church grew out of the Deutsche Orthodoxe Kirche on Port and Burgundy, where in 1861, strife broke out over the problem of changing from an Evangelical to an Evangelical Lutheran church. Dissatisfied members moved over to Saint Roch Street between Rampart and Saint Claude Streets to erect a modest building in 1863. Work was carried on at that location on Allen Street near North Claiborne Avenue, very close to the present location. At the time of the move, the group numbered one hundred and six members and was affiliated with the Northern Presbyterium. Two years later, however, under the strong leadership of the Reverend F. O. Koelle, which projected the congregation into an influential position in the city's religious life, the congregation returned to the Southern Presbyterium.[48]

In 1877, a number of the Milan Evangelical Church withdrew and organized a separate unit under the leadership of Owen Riedy. At the same time, the group joined the Northern Presbyterium. By 1880, the congregation took the name of Immanuel Presbyterian Church and purchased a suitable building for worship on Camp and Sonnet Streets. It continued to serve a number of German people throughout the remaining years of the century.[49]

After the founding of the First German Methodist Church in 1840, Germans in the City of Carrollton organized a Methodist congregation during February 1845, being ably led by N. Brickwaedel. The very next year the members received two building lots from Isaac T. Preston "to be held in trust for the benefit of the Germans in Carrollton."[50] In spite of this generous gift, the church was not incorporated until 1853 and did not erect a building in the area of Jefferson, Fourth, Leonidas, and Plum streets until 1859. Such a struggle seemed to foretell the eventual fate of this Methodist group for in 1883 it closed the door of the church structure and sold all the property to a Negro congregation.[51]

There were several other ventures to organize Methodist German churches. One of the older and more successful ones was the Soraparu German Methodist Church, located in the City of Lafayette and organized in 1853. The congregation weathered several serious splits which were caused by the break that came in the Methodist church between the North and the South. In 1893, however, the group discontinued its services and disbanded. Another effort which achieved success was the founding of Felicity Street German Methodist Church in 1868. By 1871, the group had erected a building on Loyola and Saint Andrew Streets, shifted its activities to that location, and continued its work well into the years of the twentieth century. In the populous Third District of the city several Methodist German churches were organized. Perhaps, one of the more successful was the dissentient faction of the Burgundy Street group which in 1874 established the Third German Methodist Church on North Rampart Street between Press and Saint Ferdinand Streets. This congregation prospered at that location until 1900.[52]

There were never many Baptists among New Orleans Germans. An attempt was made to have a branch of the Coliseum Place Baptist Church in the Third District. A piece of property was bought on Spain Street, but late in 1872, the venture was discontinued.[53]

With the heavy immigration from Germany in the 1840s, Jews settled in the city in considerable numbers and in family groups. Their coming was a boon to the congregation Shaarei Chesed, or Gates of Mercy, which had been organized in 1828 on North Rampart Street. By 1849, two hundred German members were affiliated with the Jewish church. Since it was found impracticable to unite all Israelites of New Orleans in one congregation, another group with the Portuguese ritual organized on August 21, 1846, under the name of Nefutsoth Jehudah, or Dispersed of Judah. Both of these congregations were fortunate to enter synagogues in 1850, the latter receiving the building located on Canal and Bourbon Streets as an outright gift from Judah Touro.[54] Pursuing separate ways for thirty-two more years, Shaarei Chesed and Nefutsoth Jehudah finally merged in the year 1882 under the name of Touro Synagogue, which at the time had its house of worship on Carondelet Street. Under the dynamic leadership of Rabbi J. L. Leicht, who became the spiritual leader of this congregation, a most beautiful house of worship was erected on the corner of Saint Charles Avenue and Berlin Street in 1892.[55]

In the town of Lafayette, lying along the river between Felicity and Toledano Streets and extending back to the "woods," a number of Jews, mostly Alsatian Germans, settled.

From the very first, these newcomers had to depend largely on their own resources for the satisfaction of their religious needs because of the difficulty of getting into New Orleans. By 1848, about forty families considered the purchase of ground for a synagogue. In the same year officers were elected and the German ritual adopted. After a series of vicissitudes the work of organization was completed with the founding of the Congregation Shaarei Tefiloh, or Gates of Prayer, of the City of Lafayette. A house believed to have been on Washington Avenue was rented for a synagogue. When repeated attempts to unite with the congregation Shaarei Chesed failed, Shaarei Tefiloh worked toward obtaining its own church building, which was accomplished in 1855, when a two-room frame house was purchased. Four years later, a building site on Jackson Avenue and Chippewa Street was obtained. While the civil conflict interfered with the plans, the desire to erect a new edifice did not die but culminated in the dedication of an attractive synagogue on April 5, 1867.[56]

Toward the end of the 1860s, the reform movement was beginning to make itself felt in both of the German-Jewish congregations, Touro and Shaarei Tefiloh. In the latter congregation, reform was by evolution instead of revolution; while in the former some thirty members became impatient with conservatism and seceded to form Temple Sinai as a reform congregation. Rabbi James K. Gutheim, who had served Shaarei Chesed on two different occasion, assumed the ministerial responsibility of this newly-organized reform group.[57] Temple Sinai was the only representative of Reform Judaism in the city.[58]

Around 1875, when the second generation of former German immigrants had been greatly influenced by the predominant power of the English language and consequently saw no necessity in continuing to preserve the German tongue, all German-preaching congregations of the city felt the first impacts of the use of the English language. Every church introduced services in which the English language was used exclusively, although the German language remained the official one of the pulpit, the classroom, and the meeting room. Wherever a congregation was too stubborn to introduce services in English, it soon noticed a drop in membership or a wave of dissatisfaction, which in several instances led to splits and the organization of churches in which the English language was used exclusively.[59] Prophetical were the words of Louis Voss:

> In the absence of German immigration the time cannot be far distant when German preaching will no longer be necessary and our German churches will cease to be German speaking churches. This does not imply that in that event they will have outlived their usefulness and must cease altogether, but the only means to prevent their extinction is their transformation into English speaking churches.[60]

The German language, however, survived in a measure in the church and school until 1939.[61]

Practically every German church, regardless of its membership and wealth, supported its own school for a longer or shorter period of time.[62] Christian Sans, organizer of Saint Paul's school, was the first to launch an educational program for the children of his congregation. Taking note of this event, one of the newspapers commented:

> Our particular attention has lately been called to the efforts of the Reverend C. Sans, pastor of the German Church of this city, to promote the cause of religion and education among his countrymen around him. It is estimated that there are upwards of 14,000 Germans, forming a large class of our most industrious and intelligent citizens. Among these, Mr. Sans, by great labor and perseverance, has formed a church and a large congregation. He has established two large schools containing in all nearly three hundred scholars. One of these schools is in the second municipality, corner of Race and Constance Streets, the other in the third municipality in Moreau Street. In each of these schools several assistants are employed, and sixteen branches taught after the Pestalozzian and Prussian Systems.[63]

The purpose of their existence was manifold. The Germans' cherished theory of education in the nineteenth century was to give attention both to the intellectual and to the spiritual training of children. This principle, therefore, became the desired objective of all instruction in their schools. A thorough knowledge of the tenets of Christianity and of the subject matter fields, such as reading, writing, arithmetic, spelling, grammar, geography, and United States history or natural history for each child was the burden of every teacher of these schools. In this manner, it was believed, a child would be an upright member of the church and a "useful citizen of the United States."[64] It was erroneous to suppose that the prime purpose of these schools was to teach and thus preserve the mother tongue of their native land. Although this was in a great measure accomplished, the schools continued to exist even after English became the medium of instruction.[65]

Unpopularity of the public school system in the state throughout the days of Reconstruction was undoubtedly a contributing factor to the appearance of so many church schools. In 1870, almost no white children were attending the public school system, while the church schools were generally filled to overflowing.[66] But the church schools continued to exist even after the number of public schools in the state increased to 2,276 in the year 1889. About that time, nineteen private schools sponsored by churches and related agencies had an enrollment of 2,835 pupils.[67]

These prosperous days were short-lived for in the 1890s one church school after another closed its doors because of the scarcity of funds and the inability to match the progress of the public school system. Two of the German church groups, however, held on tenaciously with their school system, that of the Catholic and Lutheran churches, whose schools continued in operation throughout the remaining years of the old century and into the days of the new.[68]

Private schools were also conducted by individuals and secular organizations. One of the most successful private schools which had even more than a city-wide reputation was founded by John and Jacob Ueber. In 1850, after having taught for ten years in the city, these two brothers started their private school on North Rampart Street between Port and Saint Ferdinand Streets and for fifty-one years served as teachers for thousands of

New Orleans children. The famous school differed from most in having no summer vacation. Except for the customary holidays, it continued the year round and at times had more students in the summer than in the winter. This was particularly true during the Civil War, when Federal authorities sought to intimidate the two brothers and demanded the teaching of Union songs in the school. The brothers replied that the only songs they would teach were Sunday School songs, and that they were rebels to the core. No effort was made to molest the school. At the time of Butler's authority in New Orleans, the Ueber school was crowded beyond its capacity, the attendance on one day, by actual count, reaching two hundred and seventy-nine. The average daily attendance during the winter was one hundred and fifty and during the summer seventy-five. Unlike other schools, the charges were not graded according to the classes but in consideration of the circumstances of the family. When the Ueber brothers celebrated their fiftieth anniversary of teaching in the year 1890, they had taught more than 3,000 pupils, of whom the greater number were of Teutonic origin. Among these were some who became prominent citizens of New Orleans, as, Capt. Gustave Gersdorff, who became a well known bar pilot, L. A. Wiltz, one time governor of Louisiana, Prof. Henry E. Chambers, Albert Winterhalder, manager of the *Times Democrat,* Ferdinand Dudenhefer, R. J. Whann, the Blum brothers, and many others.[69]

Another well known private school was conducted by the Turn-Verein of the city.[70] This school, known as the *Turn Schule,* was opened to some of the members and during the summer only gymnastics were taught. During the winter, however, the course included foreign languages, history, mathematics, and singing.[71]

Textbooks used in the German schools were similar to those used in all public schools; and, although most of the German boys and girls in those days did not go any further than grammar school, those who wished to do so were prepared to enter the high schools and academies maintained by public tax funds or by the Catholic Diocese of Louisiana.[72] Public high schools were few and far between in the days of the nineteenth century. Only McDonogh High School and two high schools for girls under the direction of a Mrs. Lusher and Miss Marion Brown were included in the public school system.[73] The Catholic Church, however, maintained a very strong system of girls' academies and boys' high schools. Students of all denominations were welcomed, and many non-Catholics attended.[74]

Discipline was quite severe in the schools of that day. It was said of John Ueber that "he wielded the rod over unruly boys, taught sweet little girls their alphabet, coerced or persuaded boys to study and learn."[75] Nevertheless, the schools were looked upon with great pride not only by the Germans themselves but by all the citizens of New Orleans.

The non-Catholic Germans of the city responded enthusiastically to the American craze for lodges and secret societies. Among the more successful German secret orders was the "Order of the Druids." It was founded in England in 1781 and introduced into the United States in 1832 but did not get well underway until 1839. The Order was a moral, social, and beneficial society. Its objects were to unite men together, irrespective of nationality, tongue or creed, for mutual protection and improvement; to assist socially and materially by timely counsel and instructive lessons; by encouragement in business and assistance to obtain employment for those in need; and to foster among its members the spirit of fraternity and good fellowship.[76] In 1856, the Magnolia *Hain* received its charter from the National *Hain* of the United States, bringing the first German Druid grove to the city.[77]

In quick succession came the formation of three more German groves, the Oak *Hain* Two and the Goethe *Hain* Four, both established in 1857, and the Mispel *Hain* Six, in 1859. Not until 1872 came the founding of the fifth Druid grove, the Louisiana *Hain* Thirteen. These five groves of Druids existed until 1880, during which time they enjoyed prosperous days. After this time, however, because of the decline in German immigration to the South, the membership of these organizations dwindled and consolidations became the order of the day. The Magnolia, Oak, and Goethe merged to form the Concordia *Hain* One, which continued until 1901, when it was forced to consolidate with the Louisiana *Hain* Thirteen. Through the remainder of the century, the Louisiana *Hain* Thirteen and the Louisiana Mispel *Hain* Six served those Germans of the City who desired to be affiliated with a Druid order. The motto of this society was appealing to the German mind for it called for "Unity, Peace, and Good Will."[78]

The work of the Masons was likewise attractive to the German immigrant of the city. As early as 1853, two German lodges of this secret organization were in existence, the Germania Lodge Twenty-Nine and the Germania Lodge Forty-Six. These two functioned separately until March 12, 1882, when a merger took place forming the Germania Free Mason Society. The first officers were J. H. Koehn, president; John Runte, vice-president; Philip Pfeffer, secretary; and J. G. Abry, treasurer. The purpose of the society was to help those in need and to offer a social opportunity for its members. Every German-speaking Free Mason could become a member. The hall on Saint Louis Street, which had been the property of Germania Lodge Forty-Six, was used by the new order. In spite of the group's ups and downs, its headquarters was a regular rendezvous for Germans throughout the last decades of the century.[79]

Many other lodges existed among the Germans, particularly during the years before the 1880s.[80] Their purpose was to give aid to those in need, especially those who were members. To accomplish this end, most of these orders bought burial plots where their deceased members were placed at rest, paid funeral expenses, and gave a small insurance to the deceased member's closest kin.[81] This service, which was highly beneficial to many Germans because of their meager incomes, proved the very feature which not only insured the life of these societies but caused them to multiply even after the decrease of German immigration to New Orleans had set in. By 1897, more than twenty-five of such benevolent associations were in existence and most of them were in very good condition as to membership and finances.[82]

Deeds of mercy were common among the New Orleans' Germans.[83] These were done for friend and foe alike, but especially for the unfortunate, the orphans, and the aged. The first German orphanage was founded in 1854. On the Feast of the Most Holy Redeemer, the cornerstone of Saint Joseph German Orphan Asylum was laid, and on December 28, its doors were opened. Ever since its beginning, the orphanage has annually taken care of two hundred to three hundred children who, under the fostering care of the good Sisters, have been very happy and content.[84]

During the hectic days of Reconstruction, the Germans of the city organized two more orphanages which rendered great service throughout the remainder of the century. These were the German Protestant Orphan Home and the Bethlehem Lutheran Orphan Asylum. The spirit behind the founding of the former was Pastor Ludwig P. Heintz, minister of Jackson Avenue Evangelical Church. In the year 1866, Heintz had thirty-one orphans in a confirmation class of one hundred and fifteen. On Good Friday of that year, he closed his sermon with the words: "Next year we must have an orphan home."[85] Consequently, a meeting was held on November 4, at which time those present elected the first directory of the home.[86]

This venture of mercy made rapid progress. After a sum of $4,000.00 was raised, it was decided to purchase a plot of ground on State Street at the cost of $18,000.00. The additional sum needed to purchase the lot was soon gathered and a building program was undertaken. While the building was in progress, additional ground was purchased for the sum of $5,000.00. There was great rejoicing on June 2, 1867, when the dedication rites of the ground and buildings were solemnized. At that time the organization had about four hundred active contributing members. Another wing was added to the building in 1869, and already in 1870, president Del Bondio was able to announce to the general assembly that the organization was debt free.

On January 16, 1871, the ladies auxiliary of the home was founded. The first officers were Wilhelmina Jackson, president; Dora Clerc, assistant chairman; Fannie Strohmeier, secretary; and Christine Kuhlmann, treasurer. With the help of the ladies, the first general benefit for the home was scheduled and successfully carried out in the summer of 1847 at the New Orleans Fair Grounds. This event was the forerunner of annual benefit Volksfests which brought profit to the home and a good time to all who attended. After 1899, these affairs were held on the grounds of the home. Over the many years the home cared annually for seventy to one hundred children aged from one to sixteen years.[87]

Organizing an orphan home among the German Lutherans was the dream of the Reverend C. G. Moedinger, pastor of the Deutsche Orthodoxe Kirche. In 1866, a society for the support of needy orphans was organized. This association interested itself in the care of orphans, finding homes for them and supplying the needs for their physical well-being. The effort to secure a site for the building of its own home, however, was not successful. Seventeen years were to pass and two other German Lutheran churches were to join hands with the members of the Deutsche Orthodoxe Kirche, then known as Saint Paul Lutheran, before an old time, but well-preserved plantation house, a one story frame structure resting on brick pillars, located on the river front of the Mississippi River, became the Bethlehem Lutheran Orphan Asylum.[88] On November 15, 1881, Saint John and Zion congregations joined the Bethlehem Orphan Asylum Association, which had been incorporated by Saint Paul in June of that year; and with united action, the Association purchased the property for a home in 1883.[89] Since that time eight hundred orphans have been harbored in the safe retreat of "Bethlehem."[90]

While Germans of Catholic and Protestant faiths were erecting institutions of mercy through joint efforts of their churches, the German Jews were just as active and just as successful. November 25, 1854, was an epochal date for the Hebrew Benevolent Society. Under the leadership of J. K. Gutheim, rabbi, and Joseph Simon, president, a decision was reached at a mass meeting held in the Masonic Hall to create a home for widows and orphans. The following year the cornerstone was laid, and on January 8, 1856, the dedication took place.[91] The home was a blessing to many widows and orphans, and by 1886, it was found necessary to build a larger and more serviceable home. This new Jewish Orphan Home was built on Saint Charles Avenue and Peters Street.[92]

Two German Protestant Homes for the old and crippled were founded during the 1880s. Both of them were the results of the dynamic leadership of the Reverend F. Otto Koelle, pastor of the Second German Presbyterian Church. The first of these was organized in 1885, with Koelle assuming the presidency of the institution located on Magazine Street between State and Eleanore Streets. The work was supported by voluntary offerings and gifts, together with annual festivals which always netted good financial returns.[93]

The second institution for the care of the old and crippled resulted after Koelle withdrew his active interest in the home on Magazine Street. Seeing the need for administering to the poor and sick of his congregation in the downtown area of the city, he inspired the women of the church to do something about it. Consequently, on February 28, 1889, the women of the Second German Presbyterian Church conceived the idea of organizing a deaconess society to help with the poor and sick and to assist in spiritual work as well. As this work progressed, it was discovered that the greatest need was for a place to shelter the homeless and aged Protestants. It was decided to expand the work and establish an institution dedicated to this purpose. On November 1, of the same year, the deaconess society developed into the German Bethany Home Society, and a piece of property on North Claiborne and Allen Streets was acquired for the sum of $4,500.00. The next year, 1890, the "home" was opened with five inmates. Under the loving solicitude of the members of the deaconess society, especially of the wife of the pastor of the congregation, the "home" prospered so that need for expansion was felt at the turn of the century.[94]

The Germans of New Orleans manifested their love for charity not only through the agency of their churches. During the turbulent days of the Civil War the Germans contributed through their various societies, such as the theater and the German Society, thousands of dollars for the relief and support of New Orleanian Confederate families.[95] This kind of activity continued throughout the decades as the many German benevolent and singing societies participated in innumerable benefits for charities and other worthy causes.[96]

A living monument to the Germans' sympathy for mankind's suffering was the work and labor which have gone into the building of one of the great hospitals of the city, Touro Infirmary. This institution began operating as a charitable agency in May 1854, in accordance with the will of Judah Touro, in the building located at the corner of Gaiennie and Celeste Streets.[97] By 1880, Julius Weiss, then president of the Infirmary, saw the need for e₂pansion; and with the ardent support of Dr. Frederick Loeber, who had been the house surgeon since 1869, had erected a new building on Prytania Street, the present site of the hospital.[98] This institution offered many Germans, particularly those of the Jewish faith, an opportunity to care for the sick. It was here that both Doctor Loeber and Dr. William Kohlman made outstanding records as surgeons and administrators which have lived in the memory of many New Orleanians.[99]

It was through church, school, lodge, and eleemosynary institution that the Germans of the city not only preserved their religious and cultural heritage but also contributed to the development of the ideals of the metropolis of the Deep South. These ideals continued to live in the lives of many to come.

Notes for "The New Orleans German and His Church, School, Lodge, and Eleemosynary Institution"

[1]J. Hanno Deiler, *Geschichte der New Orleanser deutschen Presse* (New Orleans, 1901), 1; François-Xavier Martin, *The History of Louisiana* (New Orleans, 1882), 140. Deiler stated that of the 1,200 Germans who left the Palatinate in 1721 only two hundred arrived in March of that year. One thousand of them died on board ship.

[2]Deiler, *Geschichte der deutschen Presse*, 2; J. Hanno Deiler, *Geschichte der deutschen Gesellschaft* (New Orleans, 1897), 41. The 1850 census of Louisiana showed that from 1820 to 1849, 50,597 German immigrants landed in New Orleans. This compared with 68,854 from France and 50,656 from Great Britain.

[3]John Henry Kurtz, *Church History*, 3 vols. (New York, 1890), 3:178; Charles M. Jacobs, *The Story of the Church* (Philadelphia, 1925), 369-70; Lars P. Qualben, *A History of the Christian Church* (New York, 1936), 385.

[4]Kurtz, *Church History*, 3:178-79; Jacobs, *Story of the Church*, 369-70.

[5]Kurtz, *Church History*, 3:178.

[6]*Hundred Years with St. Paul's 1840-1940* (New Orleans, 1940), 4; W. Robinson Konrad, "The Diminishing Influences of German Culture in New Orleans Life Since 1865" (M.A. thesis, Tulane University, 1940), 16-17; G. J. Wegener, *Kurzgefasste Geschichte der Deutschen Evangelisch-Lutherischen Kirche St. Paulus Gemeinde U. A. C. zu New Orleans, Louisiana* (St. Louis, 1890), 6.

[7]Konrad, "The Diminishing Influences of German Culture," 12; J. Hanno Deiler, *Zur Geschichte der deutschen Kirchengemeinden im Staate Louisiana* (New Orleans, 1894), 63-7.

[8]Ibid.

[9]Letter of Bishop Blanc to the Trustees of the Saint Louis Cathedral, September 4, 1837; Deiler, *Zur Geschichte der deutschen Kirchengemeinden*, 20; Konrad, "The Diminishing Influences of German Culture," 28.

[10]Henry Rightor, ed., *Standard History of New Orleans, Louisiana* (Chicago, 1900), 507.

[11]Deiler, *Zur Geschichte der deutschen Kirchengemeinden*, 29, 37. This congregation played a vital part in the history of the Lutheran church in Louisiana.

[12]Ibid., 29; *Hundred Years with St. Paul's 1840-1940*, 8-10.

[13]G. J. Wegener, *Geschichte der St. Paulus Gemeinde* (St. Louis, 1890), 8-10.

[14]Ibid., 19; G. J. Wegener, "Continued Progress of the Missouri Synod in the South—St. Paul's in New Orleans," *Southern District Bulletin*, 8 (1932-33): 1:1-2.

[15]Roger Baudier, *The Catholic Church in Louisiana* (New Orleans, 1939), 368-69.

[16]Ibid.; Deiler, *Zur Geschichte der deutschen Kirchengemeinden*, 39-41; *One Hundred Years in New Orleans, Louisiana*, 7-8. The first members of the Redemptorist Fathers, a German religious order, came to the United States in 1832 and worked among the Indians in Ohio and Michigan. In 1839, the Fathers took charge of a German congregation in Pittsburgh, and this event marked the beginning of their long apostolate among the Germans in various parts of the country. Matthew A. Pekari, "The German Catholics in the United States of America," *Records of the American Historical Society*, 36 (1925): 4:352.

[17]*One Hundred Years in New Orleans, Louisiana*, 9.

[18]B. J. Krieger, *Seventy-Five Years of Service* (New Orleans, 1923), 53-56; *One Hundred Years in New Orleans, Louisiana*, 11-12.

[19]Deiler, *Zur Geschichte der deutschen Kirchengemeinden*, 70, 72-73.

[20]Baudier, *Catholic Church in Louisiana*, 368; Deiler, *Zur Geschichte der deutschen Kirchengemeinden*, 70, 72-73; *New Orleanser Deutsche Zeitung*, May 1, 1898.

[21]Deiler, *Zur Geschichte der deutschen Kirchengemeinden*, 63; Baudier, *Catholic Church in Louisiana*, 367.

[22]Baudier, *Catholic Church in Louisiana*, 367; Rightor, ed., *Standard History of New Orleans*, 492; Deiler, *Zur Geschichte der deutschen Kirchengemeinden*, 63. During the year 1867, Archbishop Odin was in Europe and there he met Father Thevis, inviting him to take up his work in his diocese in Louisiana. Father Thevis was a native of the Diocese of Cologne. The young priest accepted and came to New Orleans arriving during the yellow fever epidemic of 1867. He was assigned as assistant at Holy Trinity and at once plunged into the work of the parish. Seeing with dismay the toll of dead in the city, Father Thevis prayed to Saint Roch to intercede for the congregation among whom he labored. He promised Saint Roch that if the congregation were spared he would construct a shrine in honor of the saint with his own hands. Though many in Holy Trinity were stricken, there was not one death, according to Thevis. Keeping his promise, he visited mortuary chapels in Bavaria and Hungary to plan the one he had promised. He bought land in the rear of the parish and set to work alone to build the shrine. He directed all the work, laid the marble flooring and installed an altar and stained-glass windows. In the shrine he placed a statue of Saint Roch. The good priest himself led the congregation in procession to the shrine for its dedication. The building is regarded as a masterpiece of Gothic architecture. It has become a favorite shrine in New Orleans and thousands visit it annually.

[23]Rightor, ed., *Standard History of New Orleans*, 492.

[24]Deiler, *Zur Geschichte der deutschen Kirchengemeinden*, 90; Rightor, ed., *Standard History of New Orleans*, 490, 493. Berlin Street was changed to General Pershing after World War I.

[25]Deiler, *Zur Geschichte der deutschen Kirchengemeinden*, 107-9; Baudier, *Catholic Church in Louisiana*, 415-16.

[26]Deiler, *Zur Geschichte der deutschen Kirchengemeinden*, 94.

[27]Konrad, "The Diminishing Influences of German Culture," 13.

[28]In the wedding register he wrote: *Similis simili gaudet* (like and like loves each other's company); and in the death register he wrote: *Finis coronat opus* (All's well that ends well). Deiler, *Zur Geschichte der deutschen Kirchengemeinden,* 50.

[29]Deiler, *Zur Geschichte der deutschen Kirchengemeinden,* 51-53.

[30]Ludwig P. Heintz lived in New Orleans for fifty-one years. In 1864, he took charge of the German Evangelical Church in Lafayette, coming from the Carrollton Evangelical Church where he had served since 1854. Besides being influential in the construction of a large new edifice on the corner of Jackson Avenue and Chippewa Street in 1875, he was instrumental in organizing the German Protestant Orphan Home in 1866. He was also active in masonry, founding the Humboldt Lodge in 1858 and later identified himself with the Kosmos Lodge, both of which conducted their meetings in the medium of the German language. *Souvenir of the Eightieth Anniversary of the German Society* (New Orleans, 1927), 35.

[31]Deiler, *Zur Geschichte der deutschen Kirchengemeinden,* 49-52; Rightor, ed., *Standard History of New Orleans,* 503.

[32]Deiler, *Zur Geschichte der deutschen Kirchengemeinden,* 57-60; Konrad, "The Diminishing Influences of German Culture," 18-19; Rightor, ed., *Standard History of New Orleans,* 503.

[33]Konrad, "The Diminishing Influences of German Culture," 22; Deiler, *Zur Geschichte der deutschen Kirchengemeinden,* 89.

[34]Deiler, *Zur Geschichte der deutschen Kirchengemeinden,* 100-2; Konrad, "The Diminishing Influences of German Culture," 22.

[35]Deiler, *Zur Geschichte der deutschen Kirchengemeinden,* 120; Konrad, "The Diminishing Influences of German Culture," 18.

[36]Minutes of Zion Lutheran Church, August 26, 1849. Gainie Street has been changed to Saint Peters Street. John H. Kleinhagen had been pastor of the Clio Street Church.

[37]Ibid., November 26, 1848; January 15, 21, 1848; April 15, 1849.

[38]Confessional Lutheranism subscribes to the symbolical books of the Evangelical Lutheran Church. These are: the three Ecumenical Creeds (the Apostles' Creed, the Nicene Creed, and the Athanasian Creed), the Unaltered Augsburg Confession, the Apology of the Augsburg Confession, the Smalcald Articles, the Large and Small Catechisms of Luther, and the Formula of Concord, 1580.

[39]Minutes of St. John Lutheran Church, May 21, 1853; January 3, 1853.

[40]J. W. Behnken, *The Missouri Synod in the South and Southwest* (St. Louis, 1922), 365-66. The Evangelical Lutheran Synod of Missouri, Ohio, and Other States was organized in the city of Chicago on April 26, 1847. Walther was its first president. H. Kowert, *The Organization of the Missouri Synod in 1847* (St. Louis, 1922), 95, 99. Carl Ferdinand Walther was born October 23, 1811, at Langenchursdorf, Saxony, Germany. He migrated with the Saxon Lutherans to America in 1839, and served as pastor of Trinity Lutheran Church in St. Louis from 1841 to 1850. He became professor at Concordia Seminary in St. Louis, where he remained until his death on May 7, 1887. Walter A. Baepler, *A Century of Grace* (St. Louis, 1947), 47-48.

[41]Minutes of St. John Lutheran Church, May 21, 1853.

[42]The term "Missouri Synod" was the abbreviated form of the Evangelical Lutheran Synod of Missouri, Ohio, and Other States. In this thesis the abbreviated form has been used for this church body was known by this name throughout the world.

[43]Minutes of Zion Lutheran church, May 21, June 1, 7, 9, 1854; Minutes of St. John Church, June 12, December 4, 1854.

[44]The Constitution of the First Evangelical Lutheran Congregation of New Orleans, Louisiana, adopted December 19, 1858.

[45]G. J. Wegener, "Continued Progress of the Missouri Synod in the South—St. Paul's in New Orleans," *Southern District Bulletin*, 1 (year):2.

[46]Minutes of Salem Presbyterian Church, November 6, 1871; *New Orleans States*, May 25, 1913; undated clipping, *Algiers Herald*, in possession of Trinity Lutheran Church, Algiers, Louisiana.

[47]Louis Voss, *History of the First Street Presbyterian Church* (New Orleans, 1929), 1; Deiler, *Zur Geschichte der deutschen Kirchengemeinden*, 50, 85-88; *New Orleans Daily Picayune*, October 10, 1890; Rightor, ed., *Standard History of New Orleans*, 502. Voss was born in Schleswig-Holstein, Germany, on March 7, 1856. In 1879, he graduated from the German Theological Seminary of Newark, New Jersey. He became pastor of the First German Presbyterian Church of New Orleans in October, 1880. He is the author of *The Beginnings of Presbyterianism in the Southwest, Louisiana's Invitation to German Settlers,* and *History of the German Society. Souvenir of the Eightieth Anniversary of the German Society*, 13.

[48]Deiler, *Zur Geschichte der deutschen Kirchengemeinden*, 97-98; *Celebrating the Seventy-fifth Anniversary, 1863-1938—Claiborne Avenue Presbyterian Church, New Orleans, Louisiana* (New Orleans, 1938), n.p.; Louis Voss, *Presbyterianism in New Orleans and Adjacent Points* (New Orleans, 1931), 354; Konrad, "The Diminishing Influences of German Culture," 25; Rightor, ed., *Standard History of New Orleans*, 503. Koelle was born in Elberfeld, Germany, April 19, 1839. He came to New Orleans in 1868. In April 1869, he was called to the pastorate of the Second German Presbyterian Church (now Claiborne Avenue Presbyterian Church) at the corner of Claiborne and Allen. He was organizer and first president of the Protestant Home for the Aged on Magazine and Eleanore Streets. He founded the Protestant Bethany Home on Claiborne and Allen. *Souvenir of the Eightieth Anniversary of the German Society*, 33.

[49]Konrad, "The Diminishing Influences of German Culture," 25-26.

[50]Deiler, *Zur Geschichte der deutschen Kirchengemeinden*, 48.

[51]Ibid.

[52]Deiler, *Zur Geschichte der deutschen Kirchengemeinden*, 84-85, 112; Konrad, "The Diminishing Influences of German Culture," 27-28.

[53]Deiler, *Zur Geschichte der deutschen Kirchengemeinden*, 92.

[54]Nathaniel S. Share, *One Hundredth Anniversary of Congregation of Gates of Prayer* (New Orleans, 1950), n.p.; Maximillian Heller, *Jubilee Souvenir of Temple Sinai 1872-1922* (New Orleans, 1922), 5; interview with Nathaniel S. Share, rabbi of New Orleans Temple Gates of Prayer Congregation, New Orleans, Louisiana, on May 28, 1954. Judah Touro was a successful merchant of New Orleans who was remembered for his many deeds of charity.

[55]W. E. Myers, *The Israelites of Louisiana—Their Religious, Civic, Charitable and Patriotic Life* (New Orleans, 1904), 42; Share, *One Hundredth Anniversary of Gates of Prayer*, n.p. Leucht was born in Darmstadt, Hesse, Germany, on January 25, 1844. He came to the United States in 1864 and to New Orleans in 1868 as assistant to Gutheim. He was a member of the state school board for two terms, president of the prisons and asylum commission, president of Kingsley House, first vice-president of Touro Infirmary and the Jewish Orphan's Home. Myers, *The Israelites of Louisiana*, 43, 69.

[56]Share, *One Hundredth Anniversary of Gates of Power*, n.p.

[57]Ibid.; Heller, *Jubilee Souvenir of Temple Sinai*, 49-52. Gutheim was born in 1817 at Menne, District of Wartburg, Westphalia, Germany. He was trained at the Teachers' Seminary in Muenster but never followed this profession. He came to the United States and New Orleans in 1849 to serve Shaarei Chesed.

[58]Myers, *The Israelites of Louisiana*, 43, 69.

[59]Minutes of Zion Lutheran Church, July 5, October 4, 1875; Minutes of St. John Lutheran Church, January 2, 1882; Minutes of Salem Lutheran Church, Gretna, Louisiana, 1880; a letter addressed to First English Lutheran Church by St. Paul Lutheran Church, 1890, in which it was stated that "services in the English language have been conducted at St. Paul for the last seven years." This letter is in the possession of Wegener's family in New Orleans; Rightor, ed., *Standard History of New Orleans*, 503; Share, *One Hundredth Anniversary of Gates of Prayer*, n.p.

[60]Konrad, "The Diminishing Influences of German Culture," 28.

[61]Interview with G. M. Kramer, Lutheran pastor of New Orleans and superintendent of the Lutheran Mission among the Colored, on December 10, 1947, who preached the last German sermon at Zion Lutheran Church in New Orleans on April 7, 1939. Preaching in the German language is occasionally heard in a New Orleans church today.

[62]Deiler, *Zur Geschichte der deutschen Kirchengemeinden.* Histories of various Catholic, Protestant, and Jewish churches of New Orleans.

[63](Lafayette) *City Advertiser*, January 29, 1842.

[64]L. Schwickhardt, *History of Saint Matthew Evangelical Church* (New Orleans, 1924), 29.

[65]Philip Vollmer, "What Germans Have Contributed to Our National Life," *Souvenir of the Eightieth Anniversary of the German Society of New Orleans*, (1927), 42,44.

[66]Richard Lineberger, *Zion Lutheran Church Centennial, 1847-1947* (New Orleans, 1947), n.p.; *Souvenir of the Diamond Jubilee of the St. John's Evangelical Lutheran Congregation, New Orleans, Louisiana* (New Orleans, 1927), 7-8.

[67]"The History of Education in Louisiana," *United States Bureau of Education* (Washington, 1898), 107-9.

[68]Konrad, "The Diminishing Influences of German Culture," 36; Beryl M. Hoffman, "German Education in Louisiana" (M.A. thesis, Tulane University, 1939), 29-30. Catholic and Lutheran parochial schools are in operation in New Orleans.

[69]*New Orleans Daily Picayune*, March 22, 1906; Hoffman, "German Education in Louisiana," 47-48.

[70]The first Turngemeinde in the United States was organized in Cincinnati in October, 1848. In theory, the Turner endeavored to educate men physically, ethically, intellectually, and culturally. Their goal was more a "refined humanity" and their leaders regarded their organization as a vital education force for progress in culture and freedom and good citizenship. Much money went into libraries, singing societies, debating clubs, lectures, and dramatic performances. Carl Wittke, *Refugees of Revolution—The German Forty-Eighters in America* (Philadelphia, 1952), 148, 152.

[71]Jeanette K. Laguaites, "The German Element in New Orleans, 1820-1860" (M.A. thesis, Tulane University, 1940), 33.

[72]Hoffman, "German Education in Louisiana," 32.

[73]Rightor, ed., *Standard History of New Orleans*, 242.

[74]Roger Baudier, *Catholic History Collection,* files on Catholic Education in Louisiana. Replies to questionnaires by Religious Teaching Congregations, notes from Annals of Religious Congregations. Mr. Baudier stated that there were eleven girls' academies in New Orleans during the nineteenth century. The better known boys' schools were: College of the Immaculate Conception by the Jesuit Fathers, St. Aloysius College by the Brothers of the Sacred Heart, St. Mary's College of the Christian Brothers, 1851-1875, and Holy Cross College by the congregation of the Holy Cross in 1878. "1954 Annual Catholic Directory," *Catholic Action of the South*, 32; *A Century of Service for the Sacred Heart in the United States, 1847-1947* (Brothers of Sacred Heart, 1946), n.p.; Angelus Gabriel, *The Christian Brothers in the United States* (New York, 1948), 472-73.

[75]*New Orleans Daily Picayune*, September 22, 1901; March 22, 1906. A. L. Rau, speaking of S. Speicher, teacher of the Evangelical church on Milan Street, says: "As a disciplinarian he was almost unequaled. The writer remembers distinctly the first Monday he made his appearance at school, and the fact that when he returned after his noon lunch, he had availed himself of the opportunity to purchase a good strong cowhide of which he made abundant use, as a number of scholars who read this can no doubt testify." A. L. Rau, *Some Interesting Facts Gathered from the Early Records of Our Church, The Echo* (n.p., 1904), 1.

[76]*The Encyclopedia Americana* (New York, 1953), 9:351.

[77]The English translation of the word *Hain* is Grove. This was the official name given each Druid group.

[78]*Program of the Third German Day Festival—October 6* (New Orleans, 1912), n.p.

[79]New Orleans *Deutsche Zeitung*, May 26, 1853; *Program of the Third German Day*, n.p.

[80]New Orleans *Deutsche Zeitung*, May 26, 27, 1853; January 8, 1854.

[81]Minutes of the *Deutscher Verin Zweiter Distrikt*, August 3, 1884; *Program of the Third German Day*, n.p.

[82]*Program of the Franz Schubert Festival* (New Orleans, 1897), n.p.

[83]Deiler, *Geschichte der deutschen Gesellschaft*, 72-73.

[84]Krieger, *Seventy-Five Years of Service*, 47.

[85]*Program of the Third German Day*, n.p.

[86]Members of the first directory were: Jacob Nussloch, Jacob Hassinger, Fredrich Del Bondio, H. F. Stuerken, G. L. L. Mayer, F. Rickert, H. Zuberbier, George Strohmeier, H. F. Klump, J. G. Haas, G. Hufft, H. R. Gogreve, G. Spitzfaden, F. W. Haussler, T. Schorr, A. Bohne, Leon von Zinken, T. Pelle, N. Mueller, G. Gemming, A. Winkelmann, A. Goldmann, and C. Bornwasser. The first officers were: F. Del Bondio, president; F. Rickert, first vice-president; H. Zuberbier, second vice-president; G. Strohmeier, first secretary; H. F. Klumpp, second secretary; and J. G. Haas, treasurer.

[87]*Program of the Third German Day*, n.p.

[88]*Golden Anniversary—A Memorial of Fifty Years of Labor of Love—Bethlehem Orphan Asylum, New Orleans, Louisiana* (New Orleans, 1931), 11.

[89]Ibid. The "Home" was bounded by North Peters, Flood, Andry, and Douglas streets.

[90]Records of Admission, Bethlehem Orphan Asylum, New Orleans, Louisiana, 1883-1952.

[91]Heller, *Jubilee Souvenir of Temple Sinai*, 8.

[92]Myers, *The Israelites of Louisiana*, 50.

[93]Deiler, *Zur Geschichte der deutschen Kirchengemeinden*, 99; *New Orleanser Deutsche Zeitung*, May 24, 1898; *New Orleans Daily Picayune*, October 26, 1890.

[94]Voss, *Presbyterianism in New Orleans and Adjacent Points*, 358; *Celebrating the Golden Anniversary of the Protestant Bethany Home* (n.p., n.d.), n.p.

[95]Robert T. Clark, Jr., "The New Orleans German Colony in the Civil War," *Louisiana Historical Quarterly*, 20 (1937): 100. The German Society contributed $7,469.30 at one time, the proceeds of a huge Volksfest, while the city government voted only $2,000.00 to the support of families of Orleanians in the Confederate service.

[96]Minutes of the German *Liedertafel*, April 3, 1882; Minutes of the German *Quartette Club*, February 3, May 2, 1889, March 9, 1900.

[97]John Nash, "Brief History of Touro Infirmary" (New Orleans, February 5, 1954), in possession of Dr. John MacKenzie, director of the hospital. Judah Touro was the individual who in 1840 donated $10,000.00 to complete the building of the Bunker Hill Monument and in his will left a sum of money to start the work of the Touro Infirmary. A typed copy of an article on the life of Judah Touro taken from Number 13 of the American Jewish Historical Society, in the private files of Dr. MacKenzie.

[98]M. J. Magruder, "Some Incidents in Connection with the Early History of Touro Infirmary" (New Orleans, November 30, 1936), in private file of Dr. MacKenzie, director of Touro Infirmary.

[99]Letter of A. J. Hockett to Mr. Thomas Ewing Dabney, November 30, 1936. In the private file of Dr. MacKenzie. Dr. William Kohlmann was born in Germany, June 6, 1863. In 1897, he became a resident surgeon at Touro and then surgeon-in-chief until 1906. Alceé Fortier, *A History of Louisiana*, 4 vols. (New York, 1904), 3:236.

THE IRISH AND THEIR CHURCH, 1830-1862*

Earl F. Niehaus

The most important institution for the immigrants in New Orleans, as for the Irish in most American cities, was their church. The Catholic church and the priest, usually Irish-born himself, were visible links with their past. An active Irish parish meant that not everything was new and puzzling to the immigrants. The public worship of the sacrifice of the Mass, the administration of the sacraments, and the preaching were no different from similar services in the homeland.

Since many other group activities, not exclusively religious, centered on the parish, this institution became the major social discipline for the newly arrived from Ireland. Not only did the national church promote spectacular temperance crusades, but many of the more permanent benevolent societies and social charity agencies were parish-centered. In addition, much of the social life of the immigrants depended on parochial organizations; and most important of all the clergy guided the educational endeavors of the immigrants. Nuns, religious brothers, and priests came to New Orleans to found and staff schools. As the headquarters of these various functions of the Irish community, the Irish parish was clearly an ethnic institution.

The Irish Catholics in the city insisted on a complete parochial plant, emphasized in the practice of their religion the reception of the sacraments, and were notably loyal to the bishop—practices and attitudes regarded as peculiarly characteristic of the American Catholic church.[1] Thus the Irish parishes which became the principal vehicle of the Americanization of the Irish in turn made the New Orleans Catholic church American.

Before the first Irish church was established the immigrants dreamed, talked, and perhaps threatened to have their own parish where "God spoke English." Naturally their church would be dedicated under the invocation of St. Patrick and would be the finest edifice in the city. In the interim the Irish Catholics attended Mass either at St. Louis Cathedral or at one of the three chapels—the Ursuline Convent in the heart of the Latin Creole section, St. Antoine's Mortuary Chapel on North Rampart, or Pierre Foucher's private chapel on Delord (now Howard) near Tchoupitoulas. The immigrants preferred the cathedral but were not happy there because the priests usually preached in French.

*First published as Chapter 7 in *The Irish in New Orleans* (Baton Rouge: Louisiana State University Press, 1966), 98-111, 181-3. Reprinted with the kind permission of the publisher.

The Irish appreciated visits to the city by distinguished Irish prelates such as Bishop John England of Charleston, South Carolina, in 1830, and flocked to St. Louis to hear their English sermons at the High Mass on Sunday.[2] These visitors were rare, however, and did not furnish what the immigrants wanted—an English sermon every Sunday.

During the early months of 1833 the Irish hope was fulfilled. With Thomas Fitzwilliams and Charles Byrne as leaders, a small group of Irish businessmen purchased four Camp Street lots from W. W. Caldwell, built a small frame church, and obtained an act of incorporation as the Roman Catholic church of St. Patrick from the state legislature. The charter authorized the trustees to establish also a school, an orphan asylum, and a cemetery; it further specified that the trustees would be in complete control of the finances of the new corporation. The anticipated source of revenue was the annual auction of pews; but the income never quite equaled costs, and St. Patrick's was burdened with a heavy debt during the entire antebellum period.[3]

In April 1833, the newly appointed Bishop of New Orleans, Leo de Neckere, "with impressive ceremonies" dedicated the new church and appointed as pastor Father Adam Kindelon, a native of Ireland.[4] The career of the first pastor illustrated the role of the Irish parish as a social welfare center. St. Patrick's was established within a year of the devastating cholera epidemic of 1832. Father Kindelon soon founded the first Catholic orphanage in New Orleans—St. Mary's Orphan Boys Asylum, located on Bayou St. John—to house the numerous Irish orphans.[5] Its administration proved to be a full-time task, and in 1835 Father Kindelon resigned the pastorate of St. Patrick's. The Bishop appointed Father James Ignatius Mullon as the new pastor, a position he fulfilled so remarkably for thirty-two years that the antebellum history of the parish and his life are inseparable.

Father Mullon came with his parents from Londonderry to Emmitsburg, Maryland, where his father founded a school. After fighting with the American navy during the War of 1812, young James Ignatius began his studies for the priesthood. Ordained in Cincinnati, he served there as a teacher and on the Catholic newspaper before coming to New Orleans in 1834.[6] Physically and temperamentally Father Mullon was the priest the Irish in New Orleans wanted. Big, forcible, outspoken, rough, a born and trained orator, more than a match for impudent trustees, bully Know-Nothings, and even Gen. Benjamin Butler, he became a mythical figure for his flock. The Irish in New Orleans had a hero.[7]

Father Mullon also exercised influence beyond his congregation, frequently addressing civic groups and making friends throughout the city. Thoroughly American, "he tendered the use of St. Patrick's to the citizens for the celebration of our great national festivals." As a consequence the press praised him for his liberality of sentiment, and non-Catholic friends contributed generously to a drive to pay the debt on his church. Not quite as invincible as his admirers depicted him, he made concessions to the climate by occasional trips to the North or to Europe for reasons of health. And his paper, the *Catholic Sentinel*, failed.[8]

As soon as the mortgage was paid on the small church, the authorities decided that the ever increasing Irish immigration made a larger edifice imperative. This time a Gothic structure, modeled on the cathedral in York, England, was planned, and the prominent architectural firm of Dakin and Dakin received the $115,000 contract. Before the second St. Patrick's was finished the Irish in New Orleans must have suspected that their national saint had withdrawn his blessing. The 185-foot tower began to lean precariously; the architect was dismissed; the trustees muddled the finances so hopelessly that St. Patrick's was sold at a sheriff's sale in 1845; a huge bell imported from Europe was cracked; and for over a decade the Irish had to suffer the embarrassment of reading in a friendly paper stories similar to the following: "We do hope to see this stately and noble structure made in the course of the coming spring an ornament to the First District instead of an eye-sore as it has too long remained in its state of reproachful incompleteness."[9]

In time the obstacles were overcome. The new architect, the elder Gallier, shored up the tower and finished the structure. As a result of the financial muddle Bishop Blanc acquired complete control of the church.[10] The ladies of the parish purchased a 2-ton bell and an organ described in the papers as probably the largest in America; and the three enormous oil paintings in the sanctuary, executed by the Frenchman Leon Pomarede, were the pride of the city.[11] The completed St. Patrick's received recognition from varied sources. When Bishop Blanc was elevated to the rank of archbishop he chose to receive the symbol of his office, the pallium, at the Irish church called by the press the "St. Patrick's Cathedral." Tourists agreed that the best view of New Orleans was from its tower, and the city even placed a fire watcher there.[12]

Once his church was finished in 1851, the pastor concentrated on another important parochial function, education. Two schools were opened, both for boys and both staffed by faculties composed of Christian Brothers and lay teachers; St. Mary's charged tuition, but St. Patrick's was a free parochial school. Although the annalists of the decade recorded little about these institutions, apparently both were well attended until they were closed at the beginning of the Civil War.[13]

Father Mullon took an active interest in the many Catholic orphans. At the request of the New Orleans Catholic Association, which had assumed the task of financing St. Mary's Orphan Boys Asylum, he made frequent appeals from his pulpit for its support. He also asked his parishioners to support St. Patrick's Orphan Asylum, established by the Sisters of Charity on Camp Street in the late 1830s.[14] (After 1840 St. Patrick's Orphan Asylum was called the New Orleans Female Orphan Asylum.) It had as its most prominent benefactor Margaret Haughery (née Gaffney), an Irish widow with simple tastes and keen business sense. Margaret, because of her devotion to the orphans, became a legend in the Irish Channel. After her death a marble statue with the simple inscription "Margaret" was erected in a little park in front of the asylum, the first public monument erected to a woman in the United States.[15]

Faithful to their national heritage, the Irish immigrants considered care of the dead almost as important as care of the living. This was reflected in the daily press, diaries, and travel accounts, which recorded little information about Irish schools and orphan asylums but an abundance of data about Irish wakes and St. Patrick's Cemetery. Wakes were the occasion of humor and criticism. When a Recorder reprimanded a Patlander for getting drunk at one, the immigrant replied, "Not take anything at a wake? Well that 'ud be a purty way, indeed, to show respect for a decent corpse. Faith, it's come to a purty time of day wid us if we are to be put in the calaboose for takin' a dhrop at a wake."[16]

The funerals were often extravagant pageants, as the length of the mourning cortège to St. Patrick's Cemetery was a prestige factor of the greatest importance. Irish families sacrificed home comforts and "often involved themselves in debt . . . to encompass the one great and final end—large funerals."[17] The final resting place was St. Patrick's Cemetery, located on the Metairie ridge. It was a spacious cemetery and a source of pride to the Irish community; but when the rains came the primitive roads became quagmires, and complaints multiplied that the trustees should have anticipated these emergencies.[18] A most unfortunate public argument occurred during the terrible 1853 epidemic when the chairman of the cemetery committee of the Board of Health appointed an Enniskillen Orangeman to supervise burials at St. Patrick's Cemetery. (Enniskillen or Inniskilling was the site of the 1689 battle in which the forces of William III defeated those of James II; the famous regiment of Enniskillen Dragoons was formed at that time.) Father Mullon considered this appointment a studied insult and published a protest. Although the chairman threatened to close the cemetery, the tragedies of the epidemic quickly distracted men from their petty differences.[19]

For no other activity did the Irish parish and its pastor receive such widespread and sincere praise as for its temperance association. In its comment on Father Matthew's temperance crusade in Ireland, the *Picayune* early in 1841 urged a similar movement in New Orleans: "If a temperance society were to be established in New Orleans among this class of our population . . . what a benefactor to their best interest would its originator prove! . . . Who will come forward? What says our friend, the pastor of St. Patrick's Church?" For seven months the paper continued its suggestions; finally Father Mullon announced that on the Feast of the Assumption, the 15th of August, he would administer the temperance pledge after the last Mass. The pastor then inaugurated the practice of enrolling members of his congregation after the Sunday High Mass. His public reward came on the following St. Patrick's Day when the "St. Patrick's Total Abstinence Society" was the pride of the parade. The press reported the temperance association and its effect on the Irish community in glowing terms and concluded that the merit of the moral reformation was Father Mullon's. In a way the effusive praise gave a distorted picture of the association's work. The movement was effective because the priest avoided wholesale and spectacular pledging; his aim was true and permanent reform.[20]

Father Theobald Matthew, the Irish temperance crusader, arrived in New Orleans ten years after Father Mullon's pioneering work. No other Irish visitor received as much publicity as he. In fact, the newspaper coverage was comparable to that for a stage celebrity, and the pre-visit announcements were similar to the ballyhoo which his benefactor, P. T. Barnum, used to attract attention to his shows. For example, in February 1850, the papers announced that "Ireland's savior—the good Father Matthew—may now be daily looked for in the city."[21] A wit even thought of a new title for the good padre, "the great Mississippi of humanity, the venerable Father of the Waters."[22]

Upon his arrival the missionary was greeted by a delegation from the Common Council and escorted to St. Patrick's Church where he preached his first temperance sermon, appropriately, on St. Patrick's Day 1850.[23] The crusade lasted for two months, pledges being taken and temperance medals being distributed in all the Irish Catholic churches. At the midway point the *Picayune* enthusiastically reported "the cry 'still they come' may well be applied in recording the progress of this devoted missionary of temperance. . . . The hardy sons of the 'Emerald Isle' are foremost in the ranks."[24] According to the final count 13,000 had taken the pledge, and a deputation of citizens in a public testimonial acknowledged that

> the happy results which have followed your benevolent labors are abundant. . . . Directing your especial attention to that valuable class of our population who contribute by their labor to the augmentation of the commercial wealth and importance of our city, the change already produced is truly gratifying. Improved health, increased mental and intellectual energy, and an attention to the sacred duties of religion and morality, are among the blessings that have flowed into many a hitherto disconsolate household.[25]

Evidently one crusade was not sufficient for the moral reformation of the Irish in New Orleans, for at the end of the year the "Apostle of Temperance" was once more in the city's pulpits. He remained until after St. Patrick's Day 1851, rebuking the pledge-breakers and aiding the Irish pastors in fund-raising drives to pay for the churches built during the previous year.[26] Before he departed for Florida, Father Matthew spent a few weeks at the plantation of Col. Maunsel White, also a native of Tipperary and the priest's outstanding local benefactor. But the visiting priest was a pledge-taker not an organizer. As a result of his crusade a few teetotal societies were founded which survived until the Civil War, but the overwhelming majority of the 13,000 pledges were not observed.[27]

St. Patrick's received almost as much praise for providing outstanding musical programs as for encouraging the virtue of sobriety. A "Grand Oratorio" or concert was held yearly to secure funds for the organ, a painting, or a new school building. Visiting Irish stars of the stage also received invitations to sing in the church. In 1852, Miss Catherine Hayes, "The Irish Skylark," gave a sacred concert; and in the same year on St. Patrick's Day the Heron family sang Mozart's High Mass.[28] No one objected to this means of collecting money for the church, and as contributions to the cultural life of the community the programs were sincerely appreciated.

By mid-century, the increased Irish population made establishment of more Catholic parishes imperative. The diocesan authorities dedicated two churches for Irish Catholics in 1850 and another in 1851. The parish of St. Alphonsus was located in the City of Lafayette on the edge of the Garden District, the parish of St. Peter and St. Paul in the Third Municipality below Esplanade, and the parish of St. John the Baptist in the rear of the so-called American section (the Second Municipality). Evidently the Irish in New Orleans were widely scattered. The activities of these new parishes were similar to those of St. Patrick's; even the construction pattern was imitated, each of the congregations first building a small wooden church and then within a decade constructing a large brick edifice.

The early Irish in Lafayette long had plans for a parish in their suburb. A year before St. Patrick's on Camp Street was incorporated, five Irishmen published the following notice in the *Louisiana Advertiser*: "Architects are requested by the undersigned to send in their plans for the erection of St. Patrick's Church in the fauxbourg [*sic*] Lafayette. The dimensions to be 60 by 100 feet."[29] These Irishmen waited twenty years for their plans to materialize, and since the Hibernian immigrants on Camp Street had preempted the name of Ireland's national saint, the new church was named in honor of St. Alphonsus, the founder of the religious society staffing the parish. These religious priests, popularly called Redemptorists, ministered in reality to an ecclesiastical complex—a German church, an Irish church, and a French church in the same section. These three large national churches were concrete evidence of the cosmopolitan nature of the suburb's population.

Father John B. Duffy was in charge of the Irish church. Although the large Renaissance structure was built during the early years of his pastorate, this priest's principal interest was education. Soon after he arrived in New Orleans, Father Duffy instituted classes for boys desiring to study for the priesthood; among the young men he influenced was James Gibbons, the future cardinal of Baltimore. In 1853 St. Alphonsus's parochial school began, with the pastor as superintendent and six lay teachers as instructors. The conviction that the public school was a danger to the faith of the Irish children was a strong motivation.[30]

The Know-Nothing hysteria had an effect on the social behavior of the Irish in the fourth district, as the City of Lafayette was called after its incorporation into New Orleans in 1852. St. Alphonsus Church organized a great festival for the Fourth of July 1855. The Irish military companies paraded to the church and attended a Solemn High Mass. Later in the day there were lectures and entertainment—all in all, a grand and ostentatious display of patriotism to silence the criticism of the Americans.[31]

St. Peter and St. Paul, established for "the English-speaking Catholics of the Third Municipality," was the second church for Irish Catholics dedicated in 1850. Most members of this parish were newly arrived famine refugees. They resided below Esplanade Avenue where rent was cheap and where they were within easy walking distance of their work at the wharves and at factories located on the riverfront. Obviously this congregation was much poorer than those of St. Patrick's or St. Alphonsus's. Odious comparisons were made such as "Why is it that . . . the Irish Catholic ladies of the Third Municipality do not originate temperance societies similar to those of the second?"[32] The *Orleanian* stressed class differences between the Irish sections, its editor hinting that the wealth of St. Patrick's was because of its cemetery monopoly. He also criticized the pastor of St. Patrick's for being indifferent toward the immigrants crowding into the lower regions of the city.[33]

The distinctive feature of the third new Irish parish was the dedication of the pastor, Father Jeremiah Moynihan, to education. St. John the Baptist parochial school was probably the largest Catholic school in the archdiocese during the antebellum period. On the eve of the war, Father Moynihan invited a group of Dominican Sisters from Dublin to establish a girl's academy in his parish, thereby bringing to New Orleans a new group of educators.[34]

In the farthest *faubourg* of the third district, called La Course after a race track within its boundaries, the archbishop decided to build the church of St. Maurice contiguous to the United States barracks because of the large number of Irish Catholic soldiers stationed there. Prendergast, ever willing to submit an opinion, thought that the United States government should contribute to the construction insofar as the edifice was principally for the convenience of the soldiers.[35] When the War Department transferred the artillery unit to Baton Rouge, the ecclesiastical authorities canceled this plan for expansion.

The larger community approved or at least did not seriously object to the parochial expansion of the Irish Catholics and had effusive praise for the temperance crusade. Yet conflict between Irish Catholics and Protestants, and between the Irish as self-appraised good Catholics and the indifferent Latin Creoles, was not unusual. The Irish reacted most vehemently against various forms of Protestant proselytizing. The persevering efforts of colporteurs to deliver tracts to Irish householders was a frequent occasion of friction. Irish pastors had instructed their congregations to have nothing to do with the heretical tracts. Thus the zealous spreaders of the saving word who would not take "No" for an answer were occasionally thrown bodily from Irish homes.[36] Irish leaders also protested against Protestant Americans inducing Irish servant girls to attend non-Catholic services. Allegedly the hired girls were either made to feel ashamed of their faith as a public mark of inferior status, were teased into a denial, or were too young to realize what they were doing.[37]

As in other American cities the principal dispute between Catholics and Protestants arose over Bible reading in the public schools. Their parents and pastor instructed the Catholic children in New Orleans to leave the classroom during the reading of the selection from the Scriptures. This strategy was not effective, for when the children returned they were punished by the instructors. Catholics began to ask, "Are Roman Catholics not to send their children to Public Schools, without having them abandon their religion, and have other creeds, either directly or indirectly, forced upon them?"[38] The non-Catholics considered the Irish more devoted to the instruction of their pastor than to the revealed word of God.

The judgment of the immigrants on this non-Catholic activity was formed quickly and decisively: the effort of the Protestants to convert the Irish was terribly wrong, but, after all, they did not know any better. In their conflict with their coreligionists, the Latin Creoles, the Irish did not regard ignorance as an excuse. How could these men claim to be Catholics and at the same time openly profess to be Masons? Even some of the trustees of the cathedral were important Masonic officials. The immigrants were suspicious of this Latin Creole Catholicism and puzzled by Catholics whose moral criteria did not cut as sharply as their own. Men who were more faithful to the lodge meeting than to Sunday Mass simply were not true Catholics, at least not according to the Hibernian tradition.[39]

The Irish had an excellent opportunity during the early 1840s to demonstrate officially their dislike of "those who call themselves Catholics." In the diocese of New Orleans, as in many American Catholic dioceses, the temporalities of parishes were managed by a group of laymen called trustees. When this group endeavored to exercise the right to review episcopal appointments of pastors, a struggle inevitably resulted. American historians of the Church call the struggle for control of parishes between the bishop and the trustees, "the Crisis of Trusteeism." Trustees of St. Louis Cathedral were known as *marguilliers*, and the local crisis is referred to as the "war of the marguilliers."[40]

When the struggle began, the Temperance Society of St. Patrick's—1,570 strong—immediately notified Bishop Blanc that he could rely on the support of the American Irish. They deplored his persecution by the marguilliers "and other evil minded persons styling themselves Catholics,"[41] and thereby won the undying gratitude of the Bishop. Not only was the St. Patrick's group thanked in the Catholic paper, but praise of their action echoed throughout the United States. Bishop Blanc himself wrote to a brother bishop, "It is important especially to lead and encourage the American and Irish population because they are and will be the chief support for authority."[42] A visiting bishop in another letter added, "The Irish have conducted themselves nobly, as thank God, they always do, when their religion is concerned."[43] Not only had the Irish publicly censured the Latin Creoles, they experienced the satisfaction of having their action officially commended.

In the 1850s the Irish Catholics publicly criticized the Latin Creoles for joining and supporting the Know-Nothing party. Creole membership in the nativist party was no secret, for both Archbishop Blanc and Father Mullon reported it to Northern friends.[44] The articulate Irish were indignant at the betrayal, granting, however, that a few sincere Catholic Creoles were victims of illusions. Irish writers asserted again and again that "it is not against the birthplace but against the religious creed of adopted citizens that Know-Nothingism hurls its envenomed shafts" and that "the war against the foreigners is little more than a pretext. War to Catholicism is the true aim."[45] They cited as proof the rejection of the Catholic Charles Gayarré as a delegate from Louisiana to the American National Council meeting in Philadelphia in June 1855. Irish editors urged the Latin Creoles not to whine about the religious test included in the platform of the American party, but "to cut the connection, to sever the tie that binds them to an order whose intolerance they admit."[46] In this conflict the Irish knew that once again in the eyes of their religious superiors they were on the side of the angels.

Although the lay leaders among the Irish in New Orleans were bold in denouncing the latitudinarian posture of the Latin Creoles, they were by no means "clerical" in their own attitude. Boasting that they were completely free and "not vassals to priestly authority," the laymen rebuked the Irish members of the American Catholic hierarchy and vehemently criticized the Roman Catholic press.[47] Strong Irish nationalists remained bitter toward the Catholic hierarchy of Ireland for not supporting the revolution of 1848. When leaders of the American Church refused to give their blessing to John Mitchell, the exiled hero of 1848 and publisher of the radical *Citizen*, they transferred their hatred to the American Irish bishops. Archbishop John Hughes of New York was their sworn enemy. Local Irish editors took advantage of every opportunity to praise Mitchell and condemn the obsequious clergy who aided the monstrous British.[48]

The rumor that the papal nuncio, Archbishop Bretano Bedini, might visit New Orleans gave the Irish editors another occasion to declare their freedom from clerical control. "We trust no silly parade," one wrote, "fulsome laudation, or debasing and disgusting demonstrations will be consequent."[49] The nuncio wisely terminated his trip without visiting New Orleans.

The Catholic Institute, an organization much less spectacular and less publicized than the mass temperance campaign of Father Matthew, satisfied the need of a segment of the Irish community. The association offered cultural and intellectual lectures on the controversial questions of the day and publicized what it considered the Catholic intellectual heritage. During the 1850s societies with these aims were established in many American cities, undoubtedly with an unannounced purpose of answering the calumnies of the nativists. In 1854 Irish and American Catholic lay leaders, considering the times critical, organized the Catholic Institute of New Orleans. Its program called for an annual series of lectures, a library, and a newspaper.[50]

The institute did not purport to be an ethnic society; in fact, the officers deliberately recruited support from the non-Irish Catholics in the city. The list of the officers of 1855, however, shows an Irish dominance: J. C. Dinnies, president; R. M. Kearney, vice-president; G. W. Byrne, treasurer; M. B. Brady, D. P. Scanlon and C. Noonan, directors.[51] Unofficially the institute considered the Catholicism of the Latin Creole men a shallow sentiment. In a letter to Orestes Brownson, a prospective lecturer, the secretary wrote: "The men among the native population are generally infidels, tho' the women are pious."[52]

Brownson was not only the best known of the speakers whom the lecture committee secured but also the most controversial. Local Irish editors had been as disturbed by his sharp observations on Irish immigrants, as had those in Boston, New York, and Baltimore. Journalists have short memories, however, and the same editor who labeled him a man of paltry ideas in September praised him as a distinguished publicist on the eve of his lectures the following April.[53] Among the other speakers were Christian Roselius, a local law professor and politician, and a number of members of the Catholic hierarchy, including Bishop Spalding of Louisville, the most learned of the Catholic bishops in the country. The subject matter of such a diverse group of orators cannot be briefly categorized. The lectures did reflect a common concern with the nature of liberty, its history, and contemporary threats, supposed and real, to its integrity.[54] The lecture program of the Catholic Institute was evidence both of a willingness to initiate discussions with non-Catholics and of local Irish thinking on the big questions of the day.

The *Southern Standard* was the institute's newspaper. Published in English only, it explicitly appealed to the Irish Catholics. The library seems to have been very limited. Its leading promoter was Thomas O'Donnell, proprietor of the Catholic bookstore on Camp Street, and all the acknowledged donors of books were Irish.[55]

A comparison of the Catholic Irish in New Orleans with those in Boston, New York, Philadelphia, and Baltimore reveals that the experiences of extensive parochial expansion, publicized temperance crusades, and bitter conflicts with nativists were common. The influence of the Irish on their urban communities and on local Catholicism appears to have been more far reaching in the northeastern Atlantic ports. Their influence made Catholics in those cities a numerically important group, whereas New Orleans had already been to some extent a Catholic city. As the first, largest, and most articulate Catholic ethnic group in the eastern cities, the Northern Irish assumed local leadership in the Church and eventually set the tone of Catholicism in America.

Not being the first Catholic group in New Orleans, the Irish were not the early leaders, and their influence on the character of Catholicism in the city was not immediately evident. Indeed, having assumed the continual local dominance of French culture, many have completely ignored the influence of the immigrants on the antebellum Catholic church in New Orleans.[56] The population of the city changed radically, however, as a result of immigration from abroad and from the southern states between 1820 and 1850, and the dominance of French culture and Catholicism was inevitably challenged.

The Latin Creoles, even when allied with the "foreign French," had so slipped in the important battle of numbers by 1850 that they were outnumbered at least three to one.[57] A study of census returns for that year leads to a further conclusion that only a bare majority of the city's residents were Catholics, and about half of these were Irish Catholics. These estimates are based on the generally accepted assumptions that the Americans were overwhelmingly Protestant, that the "new" Irish were as overwhelmingly Catholic, and that the other large immigrant body, the Germans, were equally divided between the two religious groups. Roughly speaking there were 50,000 Catholics in New Orleans, of whom a little more than 25,000 were Irish. By sheer weight of numbers the Catholic Irish in New Orleans, to use Will Herberg's apt phrase, "plebeianized" the Catholic Church in New Orleans.[58] For them the orphan asylum, the benevolent societies, and free parochial schools were more important than the very proper academy of the Ursulines or a social event at the cathedral. The priest serving them was more than a chaplain enlisted to solemnize weddings, preside at funerals, and grace banquets. At least two antebellum observers explicitly described the Irish priest as "a staff in adversity and trouble" for the poor immigrants.[59]

The Irish in New Orleans believed in going to church. The typically American label, "practical Catholics," accurately describes them. On Sunday mornings they crowded their churches, the congregation even overflowing onto the sidewalks. This faithfulness to religious services was in marked contrast to the advertised indifference of the Latin Creoles. Because of their numbers, their professed loyalty to authority, and their regularity in attending Mass and receiving the sacraments, the Irish exercised a profound influence on the tone of New Orleans Catholicism.

Notes for "The Irish and Their Church, 1830-1862"

[1]Thomas T. McAvoy, "The Catholic Minority in the United States, 1781-1821," *Historical Records and Studies*, 39-40 (1952): 33-50.

[2]Roger Baudier, "St. Patrick's of New Orleans, 1833-1958," in *St. Patrick's of New Orleans, 1833-1958: Commemorative Essays for the 125th Anniversary*, eds. Charles L. Dufour and Roger Baudier (New Orleans, 1958), 55-56; *Louisiana Advertiser*, May 14, 1830; November 12, 1831.

[3]Baudier, "St. Patrick's of New Orleans," 56; *Acts of the Louisiana Legislature, 1833*, 86; *Bee*, April 24, 1833; *Argus*, April 26, 1833.

[4]*Argus*, April 20, 1833; *Bee*, November 19, 1834.

[5]*Bee*, November 19, 1834; *Daily Picayune*, October 14, 1837.

[6]Baudier, "St. Patrick's of New Orleans," 60-61.

[7]John S. Whitaker, *Sketches of Life and Character in Louisiana* (New Orleans, 1847), 54.

[8]*Daily Picayune*, April 8, December 15, 1838; March 5, 1839; June 7, December 15, 1840; January 13, October 6, 1844.

[9]Antoine Blanc to John Baptist Purcell, December 29, 1843, in John B. Purcell Papers, University of Notre Dame Archives, Notre Dame, Ind.; *Daily Picayune*, December 18, 1846; *Daily True Delta*, September 19, 1852.

[10]Blanc to Purcell, April 15, 1845, in Purcell Papers.

[11]*Daily Picayune*, March 28, April 1, 1843; September 24, 1847; *Daily True Delta*, September 19, 1852.

[12]*Daily True Delta*, March 16, 1852; *Daily Orleanian*, February 16, 1851; February 8, 1855; *Daily Delta*, April 25, 1852. At the time Archbishop Blanc received the pallium, St. Louis Cathedral was undergoing extensive repairs.

[13]Aloysius B. Goodspeed, "The Schools in St. Patrick's Parish," in *St. Patrick's of New Orleans, 1833-1958: Commemorative Essays for the 125th Anniversary*, eds. Charles L. Dufour and Roger Baudier (New Orleans, 1958), 113. Abbé Perché, the French-born priest-editor, consistently supported St. Patrick's free school and urged an expansion of these facilities. See *Le Propagateur Catholique*, January 11, December 20, 1851; January 15, 1853; May 20, 1854.

[14]*Mercantile Advertiser*, February 24, 1834; *Daily Picayune*, October 20, 1837; November 22, 1839; October 21, 1838; *Daily True Delta*, October 21, 1855.

[15]Edward F. Murphy, "Margaret: The Story of a Parishioner," in *St. Patrick's of New Orleans, 1833-1958: Commemorative Essays for the 125th Anniversary*, eds. Charles L. Dufour and Roger Baudier (New Orleans, 1958), 96-102.

[16]*Daily Picayune*, August 2, 1840.

[17]Robinson, *The Diary of A Samaritan*, 83; *Daily Orleanian*, December 12, 1856.

[18]*Daily Orleanian*, July 28, 1853; September 30, 1854.

[19]*Daily True Delta*, August 24, 25, 26, 1853.

[20]*Daily Picayune*, January 29, August 15, 1841; March 18, May 7, October 19, 1842; January 8, 1843.

[21]Charles G. Rosenberg, *Jenny Lind in America* (New York, 1851), 156; *Daily Orleanian*, February 21, 1850.

[22]Charles Olliffe, *Scènes américaines: dix-huit mois dans le Nouveau Monde* (Paris, 1853), 48.

[23]*Daily Orleanian*, March 12, 15, 1850.

[24]*Daily Picayune*, April 13, 1850.

[25]*Daily Orleanian*, May 10, 1850; *Daily Picayune*, May 19, 1850.

[26]*Daily Orleanian*, November 12, 20, 28, 1850; February 7, 1851; *Daily True Delta*, March 13, 1851.

[27]Aaron I. Abell, "The Catholic Factor in Urban Welfare: The Early Period, 1850-1880," *Review of Politics*, 14 (1952): 299; Blanc to Purcell, April 6, 1853, in Purcell Papers. See Reinders, "A Social History of New Orleans," 496-97, for information on the temperance efforts.

[28]*Daily Picayune*, May 16, 1841; February 21, 1852; *Daily Orleanian*, March 17, 1852; April 25, 1857.

[29]*Louisiana Advertiser*, April 5, 1832.

[30]Byron J. Krieger, *The Corner Stone: Centenary Souvenir of St. Alphonsus Church, 1855-1955* (New Orleans, 1955), 10-22.

[31]*Southern Standard*, July 8, 1855.

[32]*Daily Orleanian*, September 28, 1850.

[33]Ibid., September 6, 1850; November 1, 1854.

[34]*Daily True Delta*, September 3, 1856; James A. Burns, *The Growth and Development of the Catholic School System in the United States* (New York, 1912), 81.

[35]*Daily Orleanian*, January 29, February 25, 1854; Reinders, "A Social History of New Orleans," 275. See Baudier, *The Catholic Church in Louisiana*, for detailed histories of the parishes. The collections of jubilee and centennial histories in Howard-Tilton Library, Tulane University, and Notre Dame Seminary Library, New Orleans, are also useful. The annual *Metropolitan Catholic Almanac and Laity's Directory* (Baltimore, 1840-61) includes statistical data for the archdiocese of New Orleans.

[36]*Daily Orleanian*, September 1, 1857; *Semi-Weekly Creole*, June 30, 1855.

[37]*Daily Orleanian*, May 1, 1853.

[38]Ibid., October 5, 1850. See the *Semi-Weekly Creole*, February 21, 1855, for the nativist position on Bible reading in the schools.

[39]Thomas J. Semmes to Orestes Brownson, March 5, 1855, in Brownson, *Orestes A. Brownson*, 2:609; Reinders, "A Social History of New Orleans," 370; *Daily Orleanian*, February 21, 1855.

[40]See Alfonso Comeau, "A Study of the Trustee Problem in the St. Louis Cathedral Church of New Orleans, Louisiana, 1842-1844" (M.A. thesis, Notre Dame University, 1947).

[41]*Le Propagateur Catholique*, November 18, 1843.

[42]Blanc to Purcell, January 10, 1844, in Purcell Papers. See also John Gilmary Shea, *History of the Catholic in the United States from the Fifth Provincial Council of Baltimore, 1843, to the Second Plenary Council of Baltimore, 1860* (New York, 1892), 270.

[43]John Timon to Purcell, December 5, 1843, in Purcell Papers. Timon was bishop of Buffalo, 1847-67.

[44]Blanc to Purcell, March 31, 1854, in Purcell Papers.

[45]*Southern Standard*, July 1, August 19, December 25, 1855.

[46]*Daily Orleanian*, September 4, 1855.

[47]Ibid., April 8, 1852.

[48]Ibid., September 10, 1849; June 24, 1854; April 12, 1855; John Maginnis to John McKowen, July 18, 1849, in McKowen Papers, Department of Archives, Louisiana State University, Baton Rouge, La.

[49]*Daily Orleanian*, December 22, 24, 1853. See Billington, *The Protestant Crusade*, 300-3, for a brief account of Bedini's visit.

[50]Reinders, "Orestes A. Brownson's Visit to New Orleans, 1855," 2n.

[51]*Southern Standard*, July 1, 1855.

[52]Semmes to Brownson, March 5, 1855, in Brownson, *Orestes A. Brownson*, 2:609.

[53]*Daily Orleanian*, September 5, 1854; March 16, 1855.

[54]Abbé Perche lectured on "The Harmony between Catholicity and Liberty;" Mr. T. S. Semmes, on "The Harmony between the Spiritual Relations of Catholics to the Church and their Allegiance to the State;" and Bishop Van de Velde, on "Genuine Liberty."

[55]*Southern Standard*, July 15, 1855.

[56]Charles F. Marden, *Minorities in American Society* (New York, 1952), 71.

[57]See Earl Niehaus, *The Irish in New Orleans* (Baton Rouge, 1966), Chapter 2.

[58]Herberg, *Protestant-Catholic-Jew*, 152.

[59]Power, *Impressions of America*, 2:153; Robinson, *The Diary of A Samaritan*.

RELIGION AND EDUCATION IN
NORTH LOUISIANA, 1800-1865*

William A. Poe

North Louisiana settlers not only brought established religious denominations to the area but even adopted familiar names for their new churches. This transfer of traditional religion to the North Louisiana region is a familiar pattern in American history.

In the following essay, William A. Poe, of Northwestern State University, describes the religion of North Louisiana as conservative and comprising a two-fold theological heritage—that brought to America's shores by colonists from England and Europe and the "indigenous theological controversies and divisions" which emerged in the original and early states. A basic characteristic of North Louisiana frontier religion was its Protestant and Anglo-Saxon antipathy toward Roman Catholicism.

Baptists and Methodists were most numerous in Louisiana, and they dominated the rural area. However, the Baptists had the largest overall membership in North Louisiana. Revivalism, emotionalism, hymn singing and a lack of emphasis on education for ministers characterized both Baptists and Methodists. Presbyterians and Episcopalians, who centered their activities in the river towns and plantation areas, were less numerous. The latter were better educated, disciplined, and less inclined to revivalism.

The schools established by the denominations in North Louisiana depended on local support, and schools within a denomination often competed with one another for church support. Although none of the denominations' schools survived to the twentieth century they fostered a legacy of denominational higher education in the area.

Perhaps there was a certain drama in the history of South Louisiana that was lacking in that of the North. Rather than possessing a distinctive and peculiar history, the latter may be viewed against the background of the westward movement. The hill parishes were less an extension of Europe than those of South Louisiana. Specifically, they represented the outreach of the older Southern states. As late as the Civil War, frontier condi-

*First published in *North Louisiana, Volume 1: To 1865, Essays on the Region and Its History*, ed. B. H. Gilley (Ruston: McGinty Trust Fund Publications, 1984), 113-30. Reprinted with the kind permission of the publisher.

tions prevailed in almost all of the Protestant churches of North Louisiana. Indeed, aspects of pioneer religious culture lingered long afterwards.[1]

Pioneer religious leaders sought to reproduce churches and organizations that were similar to those they had left behind. Innovation and purposeful adaptation to conditions on the frontier were not in vogue.[2] In their search for continuity, church members in new settlements created those organizations which they had known in the old communities.[3] The meticulous and even legalistic interpretation of church letters and other forms of membership transfer practiced in North Louisiana portrays this vividly. An historian of Methodism noted that the journals of its pioneer ministers abounded with "illustrations of people in new places yearning for the old faith."[4]

This yearning embraced theological dogma as well as ecclesiastical organization. Western settlers adopted familiar names for new churches. In 1852 when some wealthy and cultured planters migrated from the black belt of Alabama and found land in DeSoto Parish, they organized a Presbyterian church at Frierson and named it Good Hope after one in Lowdnes County, Alabama.[5] Scores of North Louisiana churches received their names in a similar way. Blacks were allowed membership in churches. Good Hope had four times as many black members as white. At about the same time and in the same parish, Evergreen Baptist Church was founded by people from the Alabama black belt. Its records show that in the 1850s there were 130 black female members, but only one third that number of white women. The number of black males was about forty. Evergreen made use of "suitable colored brethren to watch over and advise the rest."[6] They reported breaches of moral and spiritual conduct that necessitated discipline. In May 1854 the church appointed a white member "to inquire among the servants whether they be at peace among themselves or not." He reported that all were at "piece" [*sic*].[7] Such procedures for supervising blacks in religious organizations had been standard in the South from the time that whites first manifested spiritual concern for them in Virginia and along the Charleston-Savannah coast. The procedure was practiced in North Louisiana down to Reconstruction.

The deep conservatism and perpetuation of established ways meant that the theological heritage which American colonists had transplanted from Europe was very much alive in nineteenth century North Louisiana. This was also true of indigenous theological controversies and divisions which had emerged in the older American states. They experienced new life in North Louisiana. One such controversy was the anti-missionary movement among Baptists. However, the most comprehensive and overriding legacy from Europe, shared by all Protestant groups, was Anglo-Saxon fear and distrust of Roman Catholicism. Anglo-Saxons in the northern parishes clung to this legacy with a tenacity not unlike its sixteenth century form.

Religious changes in England during the sixteenth century had culminated in a lingering distaste of that island's people for the Roman Church. Two events of the century exacerbated this sentiment. One was Mary Tudor's (1553-58) attempt to reestablish Catholicism after its overthrow by her father. The tale of persecutions, exaggerated or not, which Protestants underwent at the hands of this queen were for centuries retold through the reading of John Foxe's *Book of Martyrs,* This lore was a legacy of the culture which was planted in North Louisiana. A generation after Mary, Englishmen under the Protestant Queen Elizabeth I (1558-1603) successfully defended their island from Philip II (1556-98) of Spain. The defeat of the Spanish Armada fostered national pride and identification with Protestantism that lasted until modern times. After Elizabeth's excommunication in 1570 the work by John Foxe became enormously popular among the English people.

These historical shadows from the sixteenth century may have had more influence on Anglo-Saxon hatred of Roman Catholicism than did more recent movements such as English resentment of the Irish and fear of Catholic migration to the United States. It should be remembered that the people who came into North Louisiana had long been conditioned by reading the King James version of the Bible. They had imbibed the spirit of John Foxe through cultural transmission. As late as 1884 the graduating class of one North Louisiana college heard an address praising Queen Elizabeth I for "her invincible courage . . . in repelling the persistent attempts to destroy the Protestant religion by the able and gloomy fanatic [Philip II]." For the younger generation the speaker contrasted the vitality of contemporary Protestant civilization to the "shallow and sluggish" life of Catholic Spain.[8]

So overwhelming was the rejection of Catholicism that in North Louisiana numerous parishes did not have a Catholic church during the nineteenth century. There were a few Catholics at Monroe, Lake Providence, and a scattering elsewhere. Catholic worship had been organized in Shreveport in 1856 around Holy Trinity parish, and church records at Natchitoches date back more than a century before this. However, the North as a whole was solidly Protestant.[9] In the early fall of 1865 a thirty-two year old Protestant minister rode horseback from his home in Bienville to DeSoto Parish to hold protracted meetings. He passed only one Catholic church and recorded his impression: "Passed a large persimmon grove, some French settlements and catholic church. The cross was erected on the house and on the graves."[10]

Along with the rejection of Protestantism there was an absence of ecumenical spirit within Protestantism. Walter B. Posey noted that on the Southern frontier there was little to suggest the wide and tolerant attitude which emerged in the last half of the twentieth century.[11] The background for this was the proliferation of European sectarianism in the sixteenth and seventeenth centuries which came in the wake of the Magisterial Reformation of Luther and Calvin. Lutheran theology had far less influence in North Louisiana than did Calvinism. The latter was the rockbed of theological understanding among both Baptists and Presbyterians, and to a lesser degree among Episcopalians.[12] While the two major Calvinist denominations actually had a great deal of common heritage, it was not stressed. Instead, theological and ecclesiastical differences, such as baptism and church government, were emphasized.[13]

The northern portion of the state developed an ecclesiastical structure much later than did the Southern part. An ecclesiastical structure did not emerge in North Louisiana until long after statehood. Individual Protestants settled in North Louisiana in the colonial era but organized churches did not emerge. For example, the first Baptist to live in the North was John Coulter who arrived in 1797. Although Coulter lived for a number of years in the territory that would become Morehouse Parish, no church was founded there.[14] The purchase of Louisiana by the United States in 1803 made it attractive to Anglo-Saxon Protestants, and within a few years their interest in the region began to increase. In 1808 Methodists made a foray into the territory. Learner Blackman, who visited the Ouachita country was the first itinerant of that denomination in the region.[15] Other pioneer contacts were made from Mississippi, but these were unpretentious beginnings, and a year after Louisiana entered the union (1812) there were only about ninety-nine Methodists in the entire new state; ten of these were black.[16] In the next half century and down to the Reconstruction era the percentage of black Methodists who constituted the denomination in the state dramatically increased.

In 1826 Methodists held their first camp meeting at Allen's Settlement in northwest Louisiana. A participant left this observation:

> We went prepared to camp out at night, as the weather "as warm and there were too many of us to crowd into the little cabins of the new settlers. It was the most primitive camp meeting we ever attended. We tethered our horses out to graze in the daytime and tied them up to the trees at night. The tents, pulpits, and seats were of the cheapest. . . . Each preacher both local and traveling had to preach at least once.[17]

While Methodists appear to have made greater use of camp meeting evangelism than did other denominations, it was not limited to them. Of the camp meeting one paper affirmed that, "Viewed in a denominational light simply, there is scarcely any other means of grace that has been more potent for the extension and establishment of Methodism."[18] In a typical meeting ministers of several denominations might preach. This highly informal religious institution remained part of the North Louisiana scene throughout the period in spite of claims that it was no longer useful.

A camp meeting site in Jackson Parish was beautifully situated with an abundance of fresh water. Families erected their own dwellings which usually had two large sleeping rooms, one for men and one for women. Pallets made of straw and quilts filled these rooms. An adjoining shed provided shelter for tables laden with "chicken, pork, ham, beef, mutton, vegetables, pies, cakes, and jams." Campers were free to wander around and eat at any of the tables. Four times a day they retired to an arbor for preaching which took place at sunrise, morning, afternoon, and at night.[19] An apologist for such a schedule wrote, "It gives the stony heart of the sinner four regular hammerings each day for several days together. . . . On any other occasion the sinner finds respite."[20]

Camp meetings were never a substitute for the local church. Local churches multiplied steadily throughout the region in the nineteenth century. The first Baptist church in

North Louisiana was founded in 1821 by the Rev. James Brinson who, with several related families, came from Tennessee.[21] This church, Pine Hills, was located approximately five miles north of present-day Ruston. Progress, however, was slow. In 1832-33
there were still only sixteen Baptist churches in North Louisiana with a membership of
728.[22]

At about the time that Baptists were pioneering in the hill country of North Louisiana, Presbyterians were turning their attention to the area. In May 1822, Mississippi Presbyterians moved to employ a missionary in the Red River country. For reasons unknown, however, the project did not materialize and it was not until around 1836 that the
Rev. Alexander Robinson Banks made the first missionary journey into North Louisiana
in behalf of the denomination. By 1838, at Overton (not far from Minden) he had conducted the first Presbyterian meeting in Old Claiborne Parish.[23] By that time, Baptists
had inaugurated a work which proved to be far more significant than Pine Hills Church.
This was Mt. Lebanon in what is now Bienville Parish. Its settlers, from the Edgefield
District of South Carolina, not only established Rehobeth Church, which was for years
the leading congregation of the denomination in the state, but in the middle decade of the
century inaugurated an antebellum college.[24]

Not long after the Baptists established a thriving work at Mt. Lebanon, an infant village destined to move in the opposite direction received its first Protestant witness. This
was Shreveport, and the preacher was Episcopal Bishop Leonidas Polk. Bishop Polk,
whose name is plowed deep in Louisiana history, visited Shreveport in March 1839.[25]
The little town had been organized only three years earlier as Shreve Town Company; it
was eight streets wide and the same number long[26] but Polk is reputed to have foreseen
that it would become the second metropolis of Louisiana.[27] Two years later, in February
1841, he arrived in Shreveport a second time and once more conducted religious services.
The spiritual destitution of the town is reflected in Polk's comment that in his absence of
two years no sermon had been preached by any clergyman.[28] He baptized a few people
while in the area.

By 1850 Episcopalians had placed their work in Shreveport on a firm basis. Episcopal ministries also had been commenced in Monroe under the Rev. C. H. Hedges.[29] In
1841 the denomination was planted in Natchitoches with the establishment of Trinity
Church. Mansfield had Episcopal work shortly before the Civil War. This can be attributed to the fact that many of its citizens were from the Alabama black belt where the
Episcopal Church had strength. Episcopalians did not occupy many towns in North Louisiana until later. The Diocese of Louisiana held only one session in North Louisiana
before 1922. This meeting was at Natchitoches in 1844.[30] In fact, the Episcopal Church
as a whole rarely addressed itself to the spiritual problems of the American frontier and,
as one historian maintains was quite willing to leave frontiersmen to be ministered to by
Baptist, Methodist, and Presbyterian groups.[31]

Episcopal occupancy of the river towns was in marked contrast to Baptist activity
which flourished in the rural hill regions. As late as 1884, one who knew Baptists well

alerted the denomination to expect little financial support from struggling city and town churches. "Our strength numerically, and financially, is in the rural districts among small farmers, members of country, churches. To these we must look in the main."[32] Presbyterian churches were located in the towns and on plantations; Methodist congregations appeared in the countryside as well as in almost all the towns. The strong predilection of Baptists for the hill people is illustrated by their slow development in towns. They were forty years later than Episcopalians in founding a work at Natchitoches. Even then it remained weak. In Monroe, the denomination struggled to survive.[33]

In the 1840s strong sectional rivalry in the United States began to create divisions in the Protestant churches of the land. At the General Conference of the Methodist Church in New York in 1844, ominous questions relating to slavery loomed large and a Plan of Separation was drafted. The Plan recognized that a peaceable division of the Church, North and South, might be necessary.[34] The following year representatives from the Southern Conferences gathered in Louisville, Kentucky and established the Methodist Episcopal Church South. Two years later the Louisiana Conference was formed, and it affiliated with the Southern Church.[35]

About the same time a similar break occurred in Baptist ranks. In May 1845 more than three hundred messengers from eleven Southern states met in Augusta, Georgia, and formed the Southern Baptist Convention.[36] Although slavery was the root cause of tension between Baptists of the North and South, there were other grievances. One Southern objection was that too few of the denomination's resources, both money and missionaries, were being expended in religiously destitute areas of the region. Louisiana was cited as one of the most destitute areas in the country yet few missionaries had been sent there.[37] The formation of the Southern Baptist Convention did much to strengthen the denomination in North Louisiana, and it influenced the founding of a Baptist convention at Mt. Lebanon in December 1848.[38]

The previous year Methodists had gathered in Opelousas to organize the Louisiana Conference of the Methodist Church South.[39] A principal difference between the Baptist and Methodist organizations, which between them had almost a monopoly on church membership in North Louisiana, was that Baptists were more regionalized as indicated in the name of their convention, "Baptist State Convention of North Louisiana.[40] Leaders of this convention did not foresee a day when churches in South Louisiana would affiliate with it, and it was not until 1889, at Lake Charles, that one of its sessions was held in the south.[41]

Illustrative of how regionalized Baptists were, parishes with major representation at the annual convention of 1853 were Claiborne, Jackson, DeSoto, Ouachita, Winn, Caldwell, and Bienville, with only a sprinkling of delegates from the northeastern parishes.[42] Baptists were also bothered by regionalism in another way. Several local associations had been formed in the North prior to the formation of the convention. Among these were Concord (1832), Ouachita (1844), Sabine (1847), and Red River (1848). For a time the associations were acutely jealous of the new convention and only reluctantly affiliated with it.[43] Regionalism with its concomitant local jealousies manifested itself strongly among Baptists in Louisiana until well after the Reconstruction era. Geography was the chief cause of regionalism. As late as 1875 the expression "persons coming from abroad" more often than not meant someone from a section of the state remote from the scene of the convention.[44] In contrast to Baptist regionalism, the Louisiana Conference of the Methodist Episcopal Church South was statewide with well-balanced districts such as Attakapas, Alexandria, Monroe, and New Orleans.

Presbyterian organization followed that of Baptists and Methodists a few years later. In February 1854 representatives gathered at Minden to organize the Presbytery of Red River. Its territory comprised all of North Louisiana above Alexandria, except the extreme northeast which was added later. Nine churches constituted this new presbytery which had been authorized on December 17, 1853, by the Synod of Mississippi. The Presbytery voted that every member of the presbytery "pay a tax of 50 cents at each semi-annual meeting."[45] Unlike Methodists and Baptists, Presbyterians in the United States had not yet split over slavery. However, in 1861 they separated into Northern and Southern Churches. An earlier schism in the Church, the Old School-New School controversy, took place in 1837-38. Louisianians sympathized with the Old School which dominated Presbyterian thought in the state before the Civil War. One important feature of the Old School was its pro-slavery sentiment. Before the war Presbyterians in the state moved from an antislavery position to a strong defense of the institution. This church is an example of ecclesiastical adjustment to Southern culture.[46] The early Presbyterians in Louisiana, who became exponents of Southern civilization, were in the lower portion of the state. Presbyterian expansion in North Louisiana was not dramatic. A decade after the organization of the Presbytery of Red River the number of' churches had reached seventeen but most were very small.[47]

Another feature of Old School Presbyterianism was anti-revivalism. For the most part Presbyterians did not share in the great revivals of North Louisiana which swept so many members into Baptist and Methodist churches. They relied primarily on finding those who were already Presbyterians before coming to the frontier and organizing them into churches. Baptists and Methodists sought people who had no religious affiliation, a large part of the population, as potential converts and members. This is not to say that Presbyterians ignored evangelism altogether. Through the efforts of the Presbytery of Red River, Vernon Church in Jackson Parish was organized in 1856, as was the church in Monroe.[48] Vernon functioned well for a few years. Settlers poured into the frontier parish and later the church supplied some of the members who constituted the Ruston Presbyterian Church.[49] During various sessions of the presbytery, ministers were urged to plant new churches. One who did so was the Rev. J. T. Davidson who commenced the work at Horner and at several other locations in North Louisiana. In 1860 he directed a two-week meeting at Rocky Mount in Bossier Parish out of which more than forty persons joined the Presbyterians.[50] This is striking, for throughout the period under review there were few years in which any Presbyterian church of the region could report such an accretion.

Though few in numbers, Presbyterian ministers were well educated and came from exceptionally good backgrounds. Most were graduates of Princeton Theological Seminary, and a very close bond developed between Louisiana Presbyterians and the New Jersey school.[51] Some of the ministers had taught in prestigious schools before coming to Louisiana. For example, the Rev. Philo Calhoun taught at Washington and Lee University. One of his pupils at a private school in Prince Edward, Virginia was Henry Watkins Allen, who later served as governor of Confederate Louisiana.[52]

Baptists and Methodists dominated the religious pattern. The Rev. J. Q. Prescott, who traveled four thousand miles in North Louisiana in 1852-53, stated that "a very large portion of professing Christians belong to the Baptist denomination."[53] Most of these were missionary. Anti-missionary Baptists, or Primitive Baptists, were popularly called "Hardshells" and were rigid Calvinists. They showed some strength in North Louisiana and all along the Southern frontier. However, the anti-mission movement in the United States peaked between 1820 and 1840. The fact that it was already in decline accounts for its relatively light impact in North Louisiana. In Ouachita Parish, the movement was vocal and divisive in the middle decades of the century. The Rev. Thomas Meredith led some churches from Ouachita Association and in 1851 formed a Primitive Baptist Association. These churches practiced foot washing and were opposed to ecclesiastical boards, agencies, and Sunday Schools. It appears that their objections to missions and organized work were the same as those which had plagued the denomination on earlier frontiers.[54] This opposition included a strong prejudice against Bible and tract societies as well as opposition to state and national conventions. Whatever strength the anti-mission movement in Louisiana enjoyed was in serious decline by the century's end, at which time it was but a shadow of Missionary Baptists and of Methodists.

Methodists were stronger than Baptists in the northeastern parishes and in Rapides. However, Baptists most likely had the larger membership in North Louisiana. White Methodists at the time numbered approximately fifty-seven hundred and black members, fifteen hundred. With the latter included, 54 percent of these were in Monroe, Farmerville, Sparta, Minden, Homer, and Mt. Lebanon. Other areas of Methodist concentration were Alexandria and Shreveport, and far behind them was Lake Providence. Fifty-six white and twenty black ministers in North Louisiana.[55] At this time William E. Paxton had begun to compile statistical data on Baptists. His figures for associations that covered roughly the same area numbered white Baptists at about nine thousand. The number of white Baptist ministers in North Louisiana was not less than eighty: no more than four were economically able to give all of their time to the ministry. The number of black Baptist ministers at the time is undetermined.[56]

In spite of a Baptist numerical advantage, there was a remarkable balance of strength between them and Methodists throughout much of the nineteenth century. For example, Methodists led in the number of Sunday School teachers and also in the value of church property. In Lincoln Parish a school girl, rather than ask a new acquaintance "What is your religion?," asked instead "Are you a Methodist or Baptist?" It was assumed that she was one or the other.[57] A prominent educator, who spent his youth in Jackson Parish, recalled that in the village of Vernon there were three frame church buildings. Methodist, Baptist, and Presbyterian, with numerical strength in that order.[58]

On the frontier the two major denominations shared certain advantages and disadvantages. In the years before the Civil War both had shed their Northern ties and this placed them in the vanguard of Southern nationalism. Methodists were episcopal in administration and, therefore, less democratic than the congregationally organized Baptists. But the democratic theology of Methodism offset its authoritative hierarchy. Methodists, who were Arminian in theology, stressed free will as opposed to the predestination of John Calvin.[59]

> The Methodist alone stand pledged as a sect, to the doctrine of universal redemption, to proclaiming the soul-cheering news that every man may be saved—if lost his own fault. People go to Methodist churches to hear such tidings; no where else are they sure of hearing them in candor and fullness avowed. . . .[60]

As Calvinists, Baptists and Presbyterians stressed that Christ died for the elect only. In the nineteenth century Presbyterians carried this further than did the Baptists, but the Baptists were far closer to this doctrine than their modern lineal descendents. By the close of the Civil War, Baptists had discarded much hyper-Calvinism, but some still adhered to it. Among these were the Primitive Baptists. All in all, the Baptist denomination in Louisiana was well equipped to win a strong following. Revivalism, emotionalism, hymn singing and lack of emphasis on education as a ministerial requirement characterized the denomination, as was also true of Methodism. By way of contrast, Presbyterians were definitely regarded as a more orderly, formal, educated, and disciplined denomination.

The subject of baptism was always explosive. Nineteenth century religious journals regularly devoted long columns to its discussion. Readers avidly digested the popular theology which was doubtless used in many debates at the local level. It was welcome news when a member of one denomination won adherents from another. James Scarborough reported baptizing five Methodists in Winn Parish in 1853 and three in Natchitoches Parish into Baptist churches.[61] Cyrus Harrington, a leading Presbyterian minister, started out as a Baptist. While in college he argued with a roommate over baptism and became convinced that the Presbyterian practice of affusion was right. In 1852 he joined this body and prepared for their ministry.[62] Following the Civil War, Harrington was for a number of years pastor in Mansfield at the same time Green W. Hartsfield was at the Baptist Church. Few men of that era were more convinced Baptists than Hartsfield, and since he was influenced by Graves, the town of Mansfield must have witnessed some lively polemics.

The desire to win members from other denominations in the competition for souls prompted colporteurs to enter the area with religious literature. A Baptist expressed this succinctly.

> We believe a great deal of good might be done by procuring certain denominational books . . . and put into the hands of our pastors, and others who would distribute them as colporteurs. . . . If we do not supply the people with books, other denominations will, and their cause will be built up at our loss.[63]

In spite of strong denominational consciousness, evidences of cooperation between religious groups could be seen.[64] Occasionally editors chided the people for their sectarianism and called for a turning away from "perpetual disputations on baptism, and church policy, and the thousand theological questions of the day. Is this the way to provoke one another to love and good works?"[65] The good works between denominations were frequently manifested by their lending the use of buildings to one another. Such instances were common and require little elaboration. The Presbytery of Red River met in the Methodist Church in Minden in 1854 for its organizational session. The following year the Baptist Church in Homer opened its doors to this body. The Louisiana Baptist Convention gathered for the first time in Shreveport in 1854 and both the Presbyterian and Methodist Churches opened their doors for its use, whereupon the convention adopted a resolution of thanks to the ministers and their congregations "for their high-minded and Christian courtesy. . . . "[66]

During the Civil War the Baptist Church in Mansfield, like several others in North Louisiana, was destroyed by fire. Following the war an interesting case of interdenominational cooperation developed there when the Baptist congregation for several years made use of the Christian Church building. This is appealing in that relations between Baptists and Christians were severely strained on the western frontier. Baptists referred to this group as Campbellites after their founder, Alexander Campbell, who for a few years was a Baptist. Prior to this, he had been a Scotch-Irish Presbyterian. About 1832 Campbell broke with the Baptists and founded the Disciples of Christ. On the frontier as far west as Texas hundreds of Baptist churches joined his movement. However, the "Campbellite" threat, as it was popularly called, was not serious in North Louisiana. Throughout the century the Disciples of Christ was a minor denomination in the region.[67]

Frequently denominations conducted union Sunday Schools for children, but this seems to have been most prevalent among Presbyterians and Methodists, and even they did not regard it as ideal.[68] Denominational sentiment did not curtail occasional courtesy visits of ministers to other churches. Green W. Hartsfield was perhaps a little surprised to have five Methodist preachers in his Baptist congregation at Sparta on November 26, 1865. They were en route to the annual conference, meeting that year at Mansfield. The pastor stated that one of them publicly endorsed his sermon.[69] Later, while he lived at Mansfield, Hartsfield sometimes attended the services of the Episcopal Church where the Reverend John Sandels was minister, but these more liturgical services held little appeal for him.[70] When the Baptist Convention, the Methodist Conference, and the Presbyterian Presbytery assembled, ministers from other denominations were sometimes present. Minutes of the proceedings of these bodies, however, reveal that this was not a common practice. There was little cooperation between the denominations in the realm of Christian education.

By the 1850s the ecclesiastical structure of the major Protestant denominations in North Louisiana was complete so far as state organizations were concerned. In that decade Baptists and Methodists turned vigorously to the founding of academic institutions. The fifties was a time when the Southern Methodist Church manifested unusual zeal for higher education. Methodist colleges were formed in every Southern state where they had not been previously established.[71] Methodists of Louisiana and their Mississippi cohorts supported Centenary College at Jackson, Louisiana. This institution did not become part of the North Louisiana scene until early in the next century. Important for North Louisiana was the establishment in 1854 of Mansfield Female College under the presidency of the Rev. H. C. Thweatt, a Methodist minister educated in Virginia. In 1855 the college had 104 students, a solid enrollment for that day, and within two years a substantial building was erected at a cost of $25,000.[72] Homer College in Claiborne Parish was established and in 1856 a large building was begun. The college was jointly controlled by a local board of trustees and the Methodist Church. By 1858 a group of prosperous citizens at Pleasant Hill in DeSoto Parish had subscribed $50,000 to establish a third college, Pierce and Payne, which they wanted to place under the auspices of the Methodist Church. This institution reported purchasing 570 acres of land at $2.63 1/2 per acre.[73]

Baptists inaugurated Mt. Lebanon University in 1853 in Bienville Parish, the first institution of higher learning in Louisiana. In 1857 they established Keachi Female College in DeSoto Parish. Presbyterians discussed the possibility of commencing a school but did not do so until after the Civil War.[74]

Auxiliary to Mt. Lebanon University was its female college which had an enrollment of 101 at the end of the antebellum era. Mt. Lebanon's trustees failed to attract the administration and faculty they desired, but they did secure the services of a few outstanding men. The trustees especially wanted the chair of theology to be filled by a prominent clergyman, since upgrading ministerial education was a basic goal of the Baptist Convention. Dr. Jesse Hartwell and Dr. William Carey Crane successively occupied this chair. The former died after a brief tenure, and Crane, having become involved in a dispute at the University and with the local church, moved to Texas where he sustained a long relationship with Baylor University and served as its president. One obstacle to attracting more suitable men was the decision to limit the search to Southern men, or at least to those with sectional sympathies.

> In view of the very exciting political manifestation of northern ministers of every denomination, they would best subserve the interest of education in Louisiana by limiting their selection to Southern men . . . or to men who have formed just and proper views of the peculiar institutions of the South.[75]

Some generalizations may be made concerning church schools. For one thing, they tended to be local and had only limited support. Keachi College was largely supported by only one Baptist association, Grand Cane. Concord Baptist Association gave its patronage to Concord Institute, a high school located at Shiloh in Union Parish.

Isolated settlements, coupled with the difficulties of travel, discouraged attendance at distant centers of learning and fanned the desire for local schools. Mrs. E. A. Rembert, a North Louisiana widow, was billed four dollars trunk fare for her daughter who travelled to Keachi. Since boarding students paid eight to twelve dollars per month, this was equivalent to half a month's board.[76]

Community pride was another factor in founding academies and colleges in the growing communities of North Louisiana. Shortly before the Civil War the Methodist Conference asserted that there was more interest in education in the state than in any other Southern Conference.[77] The presence of an academic institution greatly increased property values in an area where there was still much evidence of the frontier. Methodists appealed to community pride by calling upon towns to found schools and to align them with the denomination. They offered to bestow patronage on any institution which raised $100,000.[78]

Few institutions which called themselves colleges would have measured up to modern standards. The range of the standards in the academies, institutes, colleges, and universities—whatever the title—was wide. Many were ephemeral. Although institutions might be only indirectly related to their denomination, most had religious foundations because their presidents usually were ordained ministers. Most Presbyterian pastors, such as J. Franklin Ford and J. E. Bright, taught school. Both served as president of Minden Female College. In 1864 Ford left to found an academy at Shreveport. Prior to this the Rev. S. P. Helme had conducted his Collegiate Institute in that city.[79] When a minister opened a private school it usually received endorsement, but not financial support, from his denomination.

It was inevitable that not all institutions would survive the ravages of war, population shifts, and social changes. The effects of the war devastated Mt. Lebanon which had shown promise before the conflagration. The University never quite recovered and when the Vicksburg-Shreveport railway failed to pass through the town the institution was further weakened. Mansfield College had been financially weakened in 1862 and was closed for a time but came out of the war strengthened because the Methodist Conference acquired it. It claimed, as did most of the schools, a healthy location and boasted that in thirty years no boarding student had died. Meanwhile, Methodists had disclaimed any ties with Homer College. Pierce and Payne, which had shown financial promise before the war, failed during Reconstruction.

The religious patterns which developed on the North Louisiana frontier were not dissimilar to those which had emerged elsewhere on the American frontier. The Christian form of expression in this region was solidly Protestant. Within Protestantism only a small number of denominations gained strength in the area. Baptists and Methodists were successful in winning the allegiance of large numbers of people, a success which stemmed from adapting to the needs of the area. Presbyterians offered stability and high ecclesiastical ideals to a minority who preferred more conservative approaches to evangelism and church growth. Small denominations like Episcopalians, Primitive Baptists, and Disciples of Christ, appeared in scattered areas. Protestant Christianity in North Louisiana touched the lives of thousands, both black and white. This was achieved despite a shortage of ministers, particularly of those who were economically able to devote full time to the ministry.

Competition between denominations was pronounced. In some areas cooperation among religious groups occurred. Baptists and Methodists promoted higher education. Both founded colleges in North Louisiana, a few of which survived the Civil War and Reconstruction and were still functioning in 1880. None of the North Louisiana antebellum schools survives today. Methodists and Baptists fostered a legacy of higher education which both denominations sustained in the twentieth century. Methodists did this by moving Centenary to Shreveport while Baptists commenced a new school at Pineville which overshadowed their pioneer colleges.

Notes for "Religion and Education in North Louisiana, 1800-1865"

[1]Emphasis on the frontier in this paper is not to overlook the work of recent scholarship which has tended to modify frontier influence on American religion which William Warren Sweet stressed so strongly a generation ago. Sweet was highly influenced by Frederick Jackson Turner. For a work which plays down the importance of the frontier on religion see Winthrop S. Hudson, *Religion in America* (New York, 1965).

[2]Of course organized religion was in time molded by the new environment but there was little conscious effort to do so.

[3]Donald G. Mathews, *Religion in the Old South* (Chicago, 1977), 54.

[4]Emory Stevens Buckem, ed., *The History of American Methodism* (Nashville, 1964), I:365.

[5]B. Charles Bell, *Presbyterianism in North Louisiana to 1929* (Presbytery of Red River, 1930), 16. Later durng Reconstruction Good Hope became an all black Presbyterian Church, a rare thing in North Louisiana.

[6]"Minutes of Evergreen Baptist Church," June 1853, Kingston, Louisiana, Archives, Northwestern State University Library (hereinafter cited as NSU). This once influential church is no longer in existence.

[7]Ibid., May 1854.

[8]General John Young, "Address Before Keachi College, June 11, 1884," Harris Collection Box 12, Folder 12, NSU.

[9]Roger Baudier, *The Catholic Church in Louisiana* (New Orleans, 1939), 147, 406, 437.

[10]"Diary of Green W. Hartsfield," September 38, 1865, author's collection.

[11]Walter Brownlow Posey, *Religious Strife on the Southern Frontier* (Baton Rouge, 1965), xiii-xiv.

[12]Both of these denominations had modified to some extent their Calvinistic heritage. This was less true at the time of Presbyterians than of Baptists. However, some Baptists in North Louisiana were hyper-Calvinists. This was particularly true of Primitive Baptists.

[13]Presbyterian and Baptist similarities and parallels are briefly but ably treated in Winthrop S. Hudson, *American Protestantism* (Chicago, 1961), 99. 21-24.

[14]Glen Lee Greene, *House Upon A Rock: About Southern Baptists in Louisiana* (Alexandria, La., 1973), 37-39.

[15]Robert Henry Harper, *Louisiana Methodism* (Washington, D. C., 1949), 3.

[16]Holland N. McTyeire, *A History of Methodism* (Nashville, 1904), 556.

[17]Quoted in Wade Crawford Barclay, *History of Methodist Missions*, 5 vols. (New York, 1949), 1:238.

[18]*Southern Christian Advocate*, August 19, 1858.

[19]C. A. Ives, *As I Remember* (Baton Rouge, 1964), 11-12.

[20]*Southern Christian Advocate*, August 19, 1858.

[21]Greene, *House Upon A Rock*, 113.

[22]*Ford's Christian Repository*, 38 (October 1884), 318. This data, which was gathered half a century later, may not be precise; it does seem to be appropriate.

[23]Penrose St. Amant, *A History of the Presbyterian Church in Louisiana* (Synod of Louisiana, 1961), 99, 101-02.

[24]Shortly before the Civil War the church changed its name from Rehobeth to Mt. Lebanon. Its building burned while under construction in December 1856. Apparently workmen who worked late had left live coals. The fine spirit of its members is reflected in their comment. "Our plan is to remedy our calamity, not to grieve over it." *Louisiana Baptist*, December 18, 1856.

[25]Hodding Carter and Betty Werlein Carter, *So Great A Good . . .* (Sewanee Tennesse, 1955), 53.

[26](Shreveport) *The Times*, July 31, 1980.

[27]Carter and Carter, *So Great A Good*, 54.

[28]Robert Campbell Witcher, "The Episcopal Church in Louisiana, 1805-1861" (Ph.D. dissertation, Louisiana State University, 1969), 175.

[29]Carter and Carter, *So Great A Good*, 65-67.

[30] Ibid., p. 407.

[31]Posey, *Religious Strife on the Southern Frontier*, 33-34.

[32]S. C. Lee of Arcadia in *Baptist Record* (Mississippi), June 9, 1884.

[33]Walter G. Mangham, *The Church That Would Not Die . . .* (Monroe, 1979), 6-7.

[34]William Warren Sweet, *The Story of Religion in America* (New York, 1930), 436-37.

[35]Harper, *Louisiana Methodism*, 1.

[36]William Wright Barnes, *The Southern Baptist Convention: 1845-1953* (Nashville, 1954), 29.

[37]Ibid., 15-16. Baptists and Catholics were at the time widely regarded as the two polarities in American Christianity. The large number of Roman Catholics in the state led Baptists to look upon it as a major mission field. Methodists and Presbyterians shared this view to an extent.

[38]Greene, *House Upon A Rock*, 146.

[39]Methodist Episcopal Church South, *Minutes of the Annual Conference* (1847), 2 (hereinafter cited as Methodist Annual Conference, *Minutes*).

[40]Greene, *House Upon A Rock*, 150.

[41]Ibid., 331.

[42]Louisiana Baptist Convention, *Minutes* (1853), 2.

[43]Greene, *House Upon A Rock*, 118, 125, 130, 133, 152.

[44]*The Baptist* (Memphis), June 19, 1875.

[45]Bell, *Presbyterianism in North Louisiana*, 22-23.

[46]St. Amant, *Presbyterian Church in Louisiana*, 71-72, 74-75; Walter Brownlow Posey, *The Presbyterian Church in the Old Southwest: 1778-1838* (Richmond, 1952), 117-23.

[47]Presbytery of Red River, "Minutes" (1865, 1870, 1890).

[48]Bell, *Presbyterianism in North Louisiana*, 33.

[49]Ibid., 93.

[50]Ibid.

[51]St. Amant, *Presbyterian Church in Louisiana*, 72.

[52]Presbytery of Red River, "Minutes" (1873); Vincent H. Cassidy and Amos E. Simpson, *Henry Watkins Allen of Louisiana* (Baton Rouge, 1965), 60. Allen remembered Calhoun as one "who used to flog me unmercifully."

[53]Louisiana Baptist Convention, *Minutes* (1853), 13.

[54]Edward Lynn Bouriaque, "A History of the Ouachita Baptist Association During the Nineteenth Century" (M.A. thesis, Northwestern State University, 1971), 21-24; T. Scott Miyikawa, *Protestants and Pioneers: Individualism and Conformity on the American Frontier* (Chicago, 1964), 145.

[55]Methodist Annual Conference, *Minutes* (1870), 6-7.

[56]Louisiana Baptist Convention, Minutes (1870), 22-27. Paxton calculated that the number of black Baptists might equal whites. However, this writer is inclined to think that they did not come close to approximating white strength at the time.

[57]Kathleen Graham, *Notes on a History of Lincoln Parish Louisiana: Louisiana Polytechnic Bulletin*, 33 (November, 1934), 34.

[58]Ives, *As I Remember*, 10.

[59]Jacobus Arminius (1560-1609) was a Dutch theologian who argued that divine sovereignty was not in conflict with the free will in a man. Christ died for all men and not merely the elect. Arminian doctrines came to represent a strong theological reaction to Calvinism.

[60]*New Orleans Christian Advocate*, July 10, 1850.

[61]Louisiana Baptist Convention, *Minutes* (1854), 28-29. Scarborough claimed that many other Methodists were experiencing dissatisfaction with their baptism.

[62]Bell, *Presbyterianism in North Louisiana*, 104.

[63]W. J. Larkin in Louisiana Baptist Convention, *Minutes* (1850), 6.

[64]Methodist Annual Conference, *Minutes* (1855), 23.

[65]*Southern Christian Advocate*, June 2, 1854. *The New Orleans Christian Advocate* very early in its career stated its policy in this way. "Brethren of all orthodox denominations will be greeted by us." Ibid., February 21, 1851.

[66]Louisiana Baptist Convention, *Minutes* (1854), 9.

[67]Baker, *The Southern Baptist Convention*, 148-50.

[68]The minutes of the presbytery clearly indicate that they preferred the churches to have Presbyterian Sunday Schools rather than union. However, when this was not feasible, union schools were encouraged.

[69]"Diary of Green W. Hartsfield," November 26, 1865.

[70]Ibid., April 16, 1866.

[71]Hunter Dickinson Farish, *The Circuit Rider Dismounts: A Social History of Southern Methodism: 1865-1900* (New York, 1969), 237.

[72]Methodist Annual Conference, *Minutes* (1855), 25.

[73] Ibid., (1858), 38.

[74]Presbytery of Red River, "Minutes" (1890-93).

[75]Louisiana Baptist Convention, *Minutes* (1854), 20.

[76]Harris Collection, Box 4, Folder 18, NSU.

[77]Methodist Annual Conference, *Minutes* (1858), 26.

[78]Ibid., (1855), 26. The $100,000 would be placed with the state treasury and was expected to produce an annual return of 8 percent.

[79]Bell, *Presbyterianism in North Louisiana*, 40, 90, 96.

PART VII

Civil War and
Reconstruction, 1861-1877

MOTHER ANNA JOSEPHINE SHANNON (1810-1896):
CROSSING THE LINES IN THE CIVIL WAR*

Mary Blish, RSCJ

Anna Shannon, born in 1810, entered the newly founded boarding Academy of the Sacred Heart in Florissant, Missouri, when she was fourteen. For the next seventeen years, as student, novice, and professed religious, she was under the austere and prayerful influence of St. Philippine Duchesne, who had brought the first group of Religious of the Sacred Heart to Missouri in 1818. In the early years of her religious life, Shannon taught in the Academy and the Indian school and also looked after the business affairs of the house while serving as interpreter for Mother Duchesne. Then Shannon was sent to Louisiana. After a decade spent at Grand Coteau and three years as founding superior of the house in St. Joseph, Missouri, in 1856 Mother Shannon was appointed superior of the Academy of the Sacred Heart in Convent, Louisiana, familiarly known as St. Michael's. A thriving boarding school located on a large property, St. Michael's also had a free school for children of the parish.

In 1864, Mother Shannon was called to New York, where she was told that at the just-completed General Chapter in Paris[1] she had been named Vicar of the houses in Louisiana—St. Michael's, Grand Coteau, and Natchitoches. Since late summer of 1862, New Orleans and the river parishes, including Convent where St. Michael's was located, had been under the authority of Federal troops, while Grand Coteau and Natchitoches were in Confederate territory. Consequently, although Shannon at St. Michael's was able to communicate with the motherhouse in Paris as well as with houses in New York and other parts of the north, she was separated from the two other Louisiana houses which were now her responsibility.

Shannon was known for her business acumen, and her manuscript notebook includes this entry: "I spent several thousand dollars, of Confederate notes, in buying goods, that would last several years, such as clothing for the community, wine for Mass, sugar, pa-

---

*First published in *Religious Pioneers: Building the Faith in the Archdiocese of New Orleans*, eds. Dorothy Dawes and Charles Nolan (New Orleans: Archdiocese of New Orleans, 2004), 39-51. Reprinted with the kind permission of the publisher.

per, flour, etc. etc. We had plenty for Saint Michael's, and our other houses, during several years."[2] Between late 1863 and early 1865, she twice took supplies across the Federal and Confederate lines. These journeys are detailed in the following account, edited
from her biography,[3] which was based on extensive conversations both with Mother
Shannon during the months before her death in 1896, and with others familiar with the
events of her life.

In late 1863 an active smuggling trade was going on between New Orleans and the
interior, thanks to the connivance of some Federal officers who did not scruple to share in
the profits of this clandestine traffic. A great many letters crossed the lines in this way,
for the disasters of the time made everyone feel the need of helping his neighbor. Shannon saw that by availing herself of this means of communication, she would be laying
herself open to suspicion on the part of the Federal authorities should any of her letters be
captured, and she therefore prudently refrained from it. But as time went on she grew
increasingly uneasy, and, towards the end of 1863, she formed a plan of going herself to
Grand Coteau to deliver supplies and certain letters just received from the motherhouse in
Paris.

Before taking any decisive step, she went to New Orleans to consult Archbishop
Jean-Marie Odin. He not only gave his entire approbation to the project, but also supplied her with a letter in which he strongly recommended her to General Lalor[4] who, besides being a Catholic, was in command of the Artillery Corps of the Army of Louisiana.
She had a good deal to ask, for she wished to obtain passports, not only for herself and a
companion, but also for quite a number of persons, some of them priests, who wished to
cross the lines under her protection. Moreover, she desired to purchase supplies, a part of
which she intended to take with her to Grand Coteau, with the rest for Natchitoches. Nor
was this all; to carry out this latter item of her program, she had to secure the cooperation
of the Federals themselves. The fortunes of war were in her favor. Gen. Nathaniel P.
Banks was organizing an expedition against the northeastern part of Texas. The fleet was
to ascend the Red River, and the general impression was that it would reach Natchitoches
before any adequate resistance could be made to the advance of the army. While deplor-
ing the ruin and desolation the expedition would leave in its track, Shannon considered
that the religious there would stand in greater need of assistance than ever and resolved to
make use of the Federals themselves to send it to them.

Her plans were laid with her usual sagacity. In New Orleans she lodged with the Sisters of Mount Carmel, who resided near St. Augustine Church, but she spent the greater
part of the day at the Poeyfarre Street residence of Mr. George Byrnes, agent of St. Michael's in New Orleans. After a visit to General Lalor to present her letter of introduction, her next step was to ask her host to invite that officer and his wife to dinner. This
was a heavy demand to make upon his friendship, considering the aversion with which
the people of New Orleans viewed all those who had any dealings with the invaders.
These feelings were fully shared by Mr. Byrnes himself. He yielded, however, and General Lalor accepted his invitation. Needless to say, the general was completely won, and

Shannon as able to specify her wishes, which she had expressed in only a general way in her first interview. The general promised to do his best for the success of her enterprise. "Madame," he said on taking leave, "you may count upon me. You should reach your destination if I have to take you there myself on one of my caissons." He was as good as his word. When Shannon called upon General Banks himself, she was most graciously received. His daughters were in school at Manhattanville, the Sacred Heart Academy in New York where Mothers Aloysia Hardey and Susannah Boudreau, both from Louisiana, were superior and mistress general respectively. He addressed Shannon as "Mother" and refused her nothing. General Lalor visited her again several times and promised that whatever supplies she wished to send to Natchitoches should be delivered there. And, though the Red River expedition was a complete failure, he found means to fulfill his promise.

The enterprises of this energetic nun were always accompanied by many prayers and placed under the protection of St. Joseph. In this instance, the first token of his care was finding a very competent guide; Mr. J. B. Noel Jourdan, a planter of the vicinity and father of four Religious of the Sacred Heart, gladly offered his experience and services to Mother Shannon and her party. When they reached Grand Coteau, nothing could equal the joy of the community after so long a period of isolation, while the visitor, hearing of their privations, rejoiced in having brought them assistance.

In January 1863, the Federals had occupied the Attakapas region, establishing their headquarters for a time at Opelousas. The invaders had stripped the inhabitants of all they could find, cotton, sugar, corn, forage, and livestock of every sort, leaving them on the verge of starvation and, for the time, without the means of cultivating the ground, to say nothing of the wanton destruction indulged in by the soldiers.

Though the convent had not been disturbed, the community soon endured the same scarcity as elsewhere, but the Heart of Jesus did not forget them. Blackberries were in extraordinary abundance that year, and the religious with their few remaining pupils gathered great quantities in the woods belonging to the convent and preserved them. They had secured in time a considerable quantity of sugar that, before the invasion, had been very cheap because of the blockade, which prevented exportation. These preserves, with corn bread, coffee made of roasted acorns, together with vegetables from their gardens, supplied them with food. There had also been an abundance of wild grapes in the woods, from which they made wine for Mass. Many of the nuns were wearing carpet shoes and well-patched habits.

Shannon had remembered the Jesuits of St. Charles College, to whose devotion the community of Grand Coteau owed the spiritual assistance they received. They had always been the best of neighbors, and she was doubly glad to have rendered them a service when she learned that the men had insisted on giving the nuns a share of their own none too abundant stores. She had added to her list whatever she thought they would need, and in noting down her items she had to use no little ingenuity. She had been greatly amused at the scruples of her companion, on seeing the item "six dozen straw hats suitable for Negroes" and knowing for whom they were intended.[5]

After two weeks' stay at Grand Coteau, she and her companions departed. They made the journey in December, partly in a cart by almost impassable roads, and partly in a flatboat through lake and bayou without any shelter from the weather, even at night. Shannon's second trip took place the following year under similar circumstances, and the record provides a detailed account of her experiences.

The following December (1864), Shannon set out to take to Grand Coteau and Natchitoches supplies which were needed more than ever. From the trip to New York that November, where she learned of her appointment as vicar, she had returned to Louisiana by sea, bringing with her a very considerable quantity of goods and provisions for the three houses. General Banks had been recalled after the failure of the Red River expedition, but General Lalor was ready to obtain the necessary passports and permissions. Her party comprised herself with two companions, her ever faithful guide Mr. Jourdan, and several others, including one or two priests. In her company, they knew they could cross the lines in security and without hearing anything of the oath of allegiance.

Shannon had still another concern. Among the planters whose cotton, sugar, and other crops had been confiscated and carried away by the Federals, there were some who, as foreign subjects, had a right to an indemnity. These had put in their claims, and a certain number of them, apparently cotton planters on the Red River, had written asking her to use her influence to bring the matter to a speedy issue. The petitioners were required to produce documents to prove their foreign nationality, and to obtain these was one of the secondary purposes of her journey. There is no documentation to show how this affair ended, but tradition holds that she at least obtained official recognition of their claims. She was never known to refuse a service if it was in her power to render it. "Where charity and obedience are concerned," Mother Amélie Jouve [whom Shannon replaced as vicar] used to say, "Mother Shannon never sees any difficulty in the way." Indeed, there were few difficulties her tact, perseverance, and personal influence could not overcome.

A considerable part of the December 1864 trip lay across the territory occupied by the outposts of both armies, and the travelers had to be alert to avoid any encounters with either.[6] They had to be particularly careful about the places where the Confederates had placed artillery batteries. She ran no personal risk, nor did anyone with her. She was well known and her religious habit was a title to respect and deference. What she feared were delays and perhaps the seizure of the supplies she had with her should she come across some over-zealous subaltern. She and her party went to Berwick's Bay by railway. From there, they traveled through the network of lakes and bayous close to the route usually followed by smugglers to reach Butte La Rose, not far from the town of St. Martinville. These smugglers were for the most part traders and small planters of foreign nationality, settled in the country and entirely favorable to the Confederate cause.

The party landed in safety near the home of a planter named De la Peyrouse who, because of his dealings with the Federals during their occupation of the area, had become so obnoxious that he dared not show himself at St. Martinville. Being now within the Confederate lines, Shannon's fellow-travelers could easily find their way to their respective destinations while, after nightfall, Mr. De la Peyrouse conducted her and her two companions to the outskirts of St. Martinville, leaving them at the house of a butcher. Early the next morning she found some sort of a conveyance and on December 12[7] she was with the community at Grand Coteau.

The supplies having been safely landed within the Confederate lines, there was every reason to believe that the venture had been a complete success. But this was not the case; Mr. Jourdan had arranged for the transportation of the numerous boxes, trunks and barrels from St. Martinville, but just as the goods were nearing the convent in wagons, they were seized by the Confederate authorities. The motive for this action is unknown, but the loss of this merchandise, which amounted to four thousand dollars, was a cause of real affliction for the community. Shannon did not lose courage; she committed her cause to St. Joseph. Novenas, holy hours, and acts of mortification were multiplied while she herself went to Opelousas and to Washington, not far from Grand Coteau, to negotiate in person with the military authorities. Her friends also seconded her with all their powers, and she secured all that the officers at these two posts could grant: namely, that the goods should be sent to the convent to be kept there under seal, until she could obtain from the higher authorities a revocation of the order under which it had been seized.

The merchandise was deposited in the old part of the building. "It was like the torments of Tantalus," wrote on the nuns, "to know that there within our reach were so many things of which we had so urgent a need and not be at liberty to touch them." The prayers of the community continued unremittingly and Shannon placed in the hands of St. Joseph the keys of the room, which had been left in her keeping. Then, joining action to prayer, she set out to plead her cause with Mr. Henry Watkins Allen, Governor of Louisiana, and Gen. Richard Taylor, commander of the Confederate Army, both then at Marshall, a small town in northeast Texas where Taylor had for the time established his headquarters.

She left for Grand Coteau in the little open carriage belonging to the convent, with Mother Mary Jane Miller and Mr. Jourdan. It took nearly four days to reach Natchitoches. She could only remain a few days, however, as she was anxious to settle the affair of the sequestered merchandise as soon as possible; but there was time enough to satisfy the eager desire of her daughters to hear about the Society, and especially about the other two Louisiana houses, and to listen to the story of their own experiences. Since the capture of New Orleans and the Mississippi River had forced the state government to remove to Shreveport nearly two years previously, the Natchitoches community had been completely isolated from the rest of the Society. She probably heard also how the supplies forwarded by General Lalor a year earlier reached the community.[8]

When the little party arrived at Natchitoches and were making their way to the convent, Mr. Jourdan caught sight of his son, a lieutenant in the famous 18th Louisiana Infantry. The young officer offered his services and by the time they resumed the journey he
had obtained an extension of his leave to accompany Shannon in place of his father.
Their conveyance was the same small open carriage in which they had left Grand Coteau,
and closed curtains with a few blankets were their only protection against the frosty air
and cold wind of December. They had to travel at a moderate pace so as not to overtire
the stout mule on whose services they had to rely for the whole journey.[9] At midday,
they halted at some convenient place to take their dinner. Whenever they passed by a
church, they stopped to visit the Blessed Sacrament and recommend to Him the success
of their undertaking.

On one of these occasions, while passing through a small town near Shreveport, the
two religious were descending the steps of the church when a merry throng of little
schoolgirls poured out from a neighboring house and caught sight of the travelers. They
stopped to gaze at the sisters in wonder. "Oh! Just look at them! Where did they come
from? What kind of thing is that on their heads?" were some of the exclamations that
reached the ears of Shannon and her companion. At least one of them, of a cautious turn
of mind, said to her companions in a startled tone, "Maybe they're crazy! We'd better
run."

"Poor little things!" exclaimed Shannon, "they can hardly be Catholics. But," she
added with smiling earnestness, "they have only given expression to the judgment of the
world. And would, indeed, that we were possessed by the folly of the Cross."

Prayer and religious exercises had their place in the travelers' order of day, but during the rest of the time Shannon conversed pleasantly with her companions, breaking the
tediousness of the journey. Towards nightfall they would stop at the nearest plantation
house, where they were sure of being entertained with the liberal Southern hospitality.
During a halt at a little town in Texas, she was noticed by a lady who ran up to her eagerly and asked if she was not Madame Shannon. Then naming herself, she insisted upon
taking her and companions to her home, showing them every possible attention. In 1844
at Grand Coteau, Shannon had had in her class of religious instruction a pupil who had
grown up in exclusively Protestant surroundings and felt nothing but horror and contempt
for Catholicism. Shannon had prayed a great deal for her and induced her other pupils to
do the same, but at the same time to refrain from all discussion upon religious topics.
Her prejudices being dispelled by all she saw and heard, she began to study the catechism
and listen to the instructions given to the class. Still, she left at the end of the year without
giving any further sign of conversion. This pupil was the lady who had just recognized
Shannon. After leaving school, she had begun to work for the conversion of her family,
and with such success that eleven of them had entered the Church. She herself had married a good Catholic and was bringing up her young family very piously. Feeling that,
under God, she owed to Shannon the gift of faith, she had longed to meet her again and
express her gratitude. This providential encounter seemed an answer to her prayers, and

she counted it as one of the greatest joys of her life. Shannon had cast her bread upon the waters and it had come back after many ears.

When Shannon reached Marshall, she immediately called upon Governor Allen and General Taylor. It was probably on her way to the headquarters of the latter that the following characteristic incident occurred. As she neared the house, two sentinels barred the way with crossed bayonets and a peremptory, "You can't pass!" "Oh! I pass everywhere," answered Shannon with her humorous smile and that air of confidence and simplicity with which she was accustomed to set aside opposition. At the same time, she coolly parted the bayonets with both hands and passed through with her companion. When the soldiers recovered, they laughed and made no effort to detain her. She was very courteously received by both officials. They lent a favorable ear to her petition, but delays were inevitable. And, besides, there were no means of communicating with Opelousas except by bearers of dispatches on horseback. During the progress of this affair, Shannon was begged to try to obtain the release of a priest who was incarcerated in some town further inland. She proceeded to negotiate the matter directly and in a day or two the captive was able to thank her for his recovered liberty.

The business being concluded, and that of the sequestered goods being advanced as far as possible, she left to one of the friends that she had made at Marshall the task of forwarding to her the documents necessary for the recovery of the impounded goods, and hastened back to Natchitoches where she had determined to await them.

Shannon set out again in the beginning of January 1865, taking with her Mother Adine Guinand. Her other companions were Father N., Mary McGloin, a young lady going to New Orleans under her care, and Mr. Jourdan, her helpful and devoted guardian. They directed their way towards Alexandria, following the highway along the river. The two religious, the priest, and the young companion occupied the carriage, Mr. Jourdan rode beside it with his son the lieutenant and Frank McGloin, a volunteer of the 2nd Louisiana Cavalry, who had obtained a furlough to accompany his sister a part of the way.[10] When Mr. Jourdan thought the priest might be tired, he changed places with him and took the reins to drive.

They had to travel at a leisurely pace, for the sake of the mule. The party must have reached Alexandria towards the evening of the second day. Many former pupils of the Sacred Heart lived in this region and, wherever Shannon halted, the news of her arrival spread to families within a radius of several miles. The announcement soon brought to the house a troop of girls and young women. She listened with earnest sympathy, comforting and strengthening them with motherly tenderness and practical wisdom. Shannon had a gift for shedding around her the sunshine of her own joyous nature, and her wit and humor made it hardly possibly for her to speak without exciting laughter. These touching scenes were renewed at every halt. "The journey," wrote Shannon's young companion, "was a continual ovation."

At Alexandria, Shannon remained several days with the Ransdell family, awaiting the cessation of the rain which had been falling since their arrival, and also, probably, to attend to the business of the cotton planters already mentioned. When the weather cleared up and she was about to depart for Grand Coteau, the two young volunteers took leave of the party and returned to Natchitoches, where the lieutenant was to await the documents from Marshall and forward them.

Mary McGloin's notes of this journey include these incidents:

> On our first day from Natchitoches, we had something of a scare. As we advanced down the road, we saw signs of increasing excitement. People were hurrying in every direction. Some women called out to us that the Yankees were coming. A man took our mule's head and turned him out of the road. "You'd better take care," he said, "the Yankees will confiscate your mule and carriage. They are down the road." A man on horseback came hurrying up and exclaimed, "They're at ____," I forget the name of the place. After a while the excitement quieted down and we continued our way. Of course, it was only a false alarm. The Federals had their hands full elsewhere; but these simple country folks had too lively a remembrance of the ills they had suffered through the invasion of the preceding spring not to be easily thrown into a panic by any rumor announcing a renewal of that calamity.
>
> When we left Alexandria, we found the roads heavy from the recent rains, and we made very little headway. The next day conditions were better, but the distance to our intended stopping place seemed interminable. We kept asking everyone we met how many miles it was to ____, I forget the name of that place also. It was thirty years ago. The miles kept growing fewer, but not fast enough for our wishes. They had fallen well below ten when a queer-looking man came along on a mule. We stopped, of course, and asked the usual question. 'Forty-five miles' sang out the man in a high rasping voice. The priest turned towards us in blank amazement—towards Mother Shannon and me, for Mother Guinand was absorbed in prayer and seemed unconscious of what was going on around us. Mother Shannon was the first to recover from the shock, and then such a gale of laughter! The priest was put in possession of the key to the riddle and "four to five" gave gaiety to the few remaining miles of the road.

During the journey Shannon had to practice some degree of forbearance. Mother Guinand was a very holy soul, compared more than once to the saintly Philippine Duchesne. She kept silently in the background and gave herself up to recollection and prayer, leaving Shannon to keep up the conversation. The latter was not less humble or less united to God, but her humility was of a different type. Under different circumstances, Mother Guinand had demonstrated that she knew how to forget herself in favor of her companions. Her heroic devotion to the community of St. Michael's during the yellow fever epidemic of 1855 caused her to be greatly appreciated by those who knew her, and their priest companion on this trip looked upon her at the model of a true religious, while he did not accord the same approval to Mother Shannon.

He had a second grievance against her. He was convinced that her young companion, Miss McGloin, had a religious vocation, and he repeatedly urged her to come to an immediate decision. The young girl parried his attacks with ready wit and smiling good humor; but the priest was persistent. Now and then Mother Shannon would come to her rescue by bringing in some new subject of conversation. His obvious disapproval was the price she paid for her charitable intervention, but his actions did not disturb her equanimity or diminish the respect with which she treated him;

The travelers reached Grand Coteau towards January 10, 1865, and a few days later Lieutenant Jourdan himself arrived with the expected documents. He had traveled the whole distance from Natchitoches to Grand Coteau in two days and three nights without stopping to rest, except for a few hours at Alexandria. The only mount he had been able to secure for the journey was an old mule. When it reached the convent gate, it stopped short and refused to advance another step until its rider dismounted, when it trotted off to the stable.

The business of the sequestered goods, however, was still not finally settled. New difficulties arose and Shannon was compelled to depart from Grand Coteau, leaving the matter still in abeyance. The community continued their prayers, for their needs were pressing. It seemed at one time that the goods were to be sold for the benefit of the Confederate government. But such persevering prayers were answered at last. An order from the local authorities handed them over to the house, converting the supplications of the community into fervent thanksgiving. Unfortunately, some of the supplies had become spoiled and unserviceable.

When Shannon resumed her journey her party had increased to ten. Besides a young sister from Grand Coteau, it was joined by Mrs. Hardey, the lately widowed step-mother of Mother Aloysia Hardey, together with her daughter Pauline, aged thirteen, and two of her cousins, all three to be placed at school in New York. The trip to St. Martinville offered no trouble except for the bad roads, but it was quite a different thing when they entered upon the country between the Mississippi River and Bayou Teche, consisting alternately of virgin forests, stretches of prairie, and extensive swamps, the branches of their cypress trees hung with Spanish moss. The travelers spent the first night at St. Martinville and the next day they traversed the Grand Bois, an immense forest surrounding Grand Lake, to reach Butte La Rose, the point from which they were to embark. Here, Shannon with the other ladies rested upon seats of moss and dry leaves that had been piled up for them. As she arose to depart, however, she noticed that she had lost her profession cross which had hung from a cord around her neck. After a careful search made in vain, they were compelled to leave without it.

The cross was restored to her about a year later. Madame Richard, a former pupil of Grand Coteau residing in St. Martinville, happened one day to be visiting a friend, whose young son noticed her Child of Mary medal. "You have such a pretty medal, Madame," said he; "the heart on it is just like the one on a silver cross Mr. Breaux wears about his neck." The description he gave of the cross answered so exactly to that of the professed Religious of the Sacred Heart that, a few days later, she called upon Mr. Breaux and asked to see the cross he wore about his neck. He showed it to her at once, mentioning that he had found it at the foot of a tree when he was deer-hunting in the forest near Butte la Rose. On hearing that it was a profession cross of the Sacred Heart, he handed it over to her at once. "If that is the case," said he, "pray oblige me by returning it to the nuns;

only tell them that the finder claims a Hail Mary for its ransom." Madame Richard kept it as if it were a relic. At the same time, she sought a safe opportunity to send it to Grand Coteau.[11]

At Butte La Rose, the party embarked upon a large flatboat, such as smugglers were accustomed to use. The baggage trunks filled up the space in the middle, and upon those were piled the mattresses and covering that served as seats during the day and beds for the night. Mr. Jourdan had secured the services of several trusty young men of the country who knew every inch of the way. The sons of small planters and tradesmen of foreign birth, they were not liable to conscription; but they were willing to lend a hand to the guerillas in a quiet way or even to the smugglers. By means of a long pole, the boat was propelled along the almost imperceptible current of the bayous at the upper end of Grand Lake. The stream could scarcely be distinguished from the dark, stagnant waters around except by "blazes" made at intervals by fire and axe upon the trunks of the trees that lined its borders.

A little before sunset, if they could find a suitable spot, they landed for the night. Moss and dry leaves were heaped together and upon these the mattresses were placed. Then stakes were driven into the ground and a curtain extended them to break the force of the wind. At the same time a large fire was kindled, nor only for the purpose of preparing hot coffee and dispelling the dampness and chill of the night, but also to keep at a respectful distance the wild animals, of which only the wildcats were at all ferocious. As soon as they had taken their suppers and said their night prayers, the ladies wrapped themselves up in their blankets, their heads towards the curtain and their feet towards the fire. Mr. Jourdan and the priest watched alternately during the night to keep up the fire and care for the safety of the little camp. One morning, Miss McGloin noticed a hole burnt in the fabric of her dress. A bit of live coal had leaped out of the fire during the night and the little flame had been promptly extinguished by Mr. Jourdan without disturbing her slumbers.

One evening they came upon an abandoned hut, roofless and in ruins, and in it they took their quarters for the night. Shortly afterwards they learned that it had been the scene of a murder of a woman by her husband. On another evening, they continued after sunset through a tract of forest flooded by the Atchafalaya, when they suddenly emerged into a broad lake. Upon its shining surface the full moon poured its silvery light. It was a scene that filled the travelers with a sort of religious awe. After a momentary hush the priest, interpreting the thought of all, intoned the *Ave Maris Stella*, which was continued in chorus by eight or ten voices.

At last they found themselves in the vicinity of the Mississippi River, after as favorable a journey as could have been desired. As they drew near the river, they encountered a Federal outpost, but the officer in command recognized Mother Shannon and gave her a most friendly reception. They continued their way up Bayou Plaquemine, and a little later they saw a man in a skiff heading for the same place. On perceiving them he began to row away hurriedly, but Mother Shannon called after him herself and he turned and rowed towards them. He proved to be a man who had formerly worked at Grand Coteau, and for a bonus of one hundred dollars he agreed to take the party to the town of Plaquemine.

Mother Shannon was very well known there and she was received with the same rejoicing as all along the route. The place, being situated on the Mississippi at its junction with the bayou, was held by the Federals. She and Mr. Jourdan were the only ones who had passports, but she had no difficulty in getting the others through. The priest, whose knowledge of English was very slight, was quite in the dark as to what was being said. Seeing Mother Shannon and Mr. Jourdan present their passports, he thought he would be required to do the same, and determined to venture upon a bold stroke. Taking out of his pocket-book a printed Latin document, he handed it to the Provost Marshal. The latter, who was speaking to Mother Shannon, merely glanced at it and handed it back. "It's lucky these Yankees do not understand Latin," said the priest replacing it in his pocket-book, greatly amused at the supposed success of his little ruse.

Next, the Marshal inquired if the travelers had any letters. Mother Shannon never refused to be the bearer of letters from the Confederates to their families or vice versa. Her companions also had letters to deliver in New Orleans, but feeling that she would be sure to get these through more safely than they could, they had handed them over to her. To the officer's question, she answered, "Yes, I have them all. They're in my trunks. That little white one is full of them. I refuse nothing from rebels or Yankees." She said this with her usual air of amiable frankness and the officer, who was not suspiciously inclined, said with a laugh, "The little white trunk may pass with the others. It would not be in such good company if there were any treason in it."

The party left Plaquemine for New Orleans by the first steamer. Mother Shannon was detained there by business for about a week and did not reach St. Michael's until the last days of January. Her long journey, with all the business she had to transact, had lasted less than two months.

Following the Second Council of Baltimore in 1867, Archbishop Jean-Marie Odin asked Shannon to open a school for black children. This was done at both St. Michael's, which had an enrollment that grew from twenty to sixty in the first two years, and Grand Coteau, with both becoming long-lived parish schools. In the same year, she founded a day academy on Dumaine Street in the French Quarter of New Orleans.

In 1872, Anna Shannon was asked to return to the house in St. Joseph, Missouri; she had founded it twenty years earlier and now it needed her business acumen. She never returned to Louisiana where she had spent some thirty years of her life. After five years in St. Joseph and another five years in St. Charles, Missouri, where her charity as well as her business sense was widely known, she retired to Maryville, a boarding school in St. Louis. There she gave formal testimony to the sanctity of Philippine Duchesne before the Ecclesiastical Tribunal meeting in June 1895 to study the historicity of Mother Duchesne's virtues. She rode to her meeting with the Ecclesiastical Tribunal in an electric car.[12] A few months later her strength began to fail and she died on August 4, 1896.[13]

Notes for "Mother Anna Josephine Shannon (1810-1896):
Crossing the Lines in the Civil War"

[1]The last chapter presided over by the founder, St. Madeleine Sophie Barat.

[2]English typescript translation of *Vie de la Reverende Mère [Anna] Josephine Shannon* (Roehampton, 1920): 79-97. Both the original and the translation are by Ellen McGloin, RSCJ, National Archives of the Society of the Sacred Heart, St. Louis, Mo. (hereafter NASSH).

[3]Ms. 18-19, St. Louis, NASSH.

[4]Probably Gen. Michael Kelly Lawlor; see also, John D. Winters, *The Civil War in Louisiana* (Baton Rouge, 1963).

[5]Shannon apparently surmised that the Jesuits would need replacements for the hats they customarily wore as protection from the sun.

[6]The author noted, "Since this journey, over forty years have gone by. Already when the notes for this sketch were collected, many of those who had taken part in it or were familiar with its details had passed away, and the reminiscences of those who remained had in course of time lost something of their clarity, while at the same time the archives of the Louisiana houses furnish very scanty material for its history. It is impossible therefore to retrace the itinerary with perfect accuracy."

[7]The House Journal of Grand Coteau has November 26th, NASSH.

[8]There follow three single-spaced pages describing the situation in Natchitoches during those years.

[9]The distance from Grand Coteau to Marshall by today's roads is approximately 225 miles.

[10]The two McGloins were sister and brother of the author of this account (see note 13). Frank McGloin was later a judge on the Louisiana Court of Appeals, writer, and prominent Catholic layman in New Orleans; for a time he edited a weekly, *The Holy Family Journal.*

[11]Later she had the consolation of learning from Mother Shannon herself how happy she had been to recover the cross which had been her faithful companion for thirty-six eventful years.

[12]Ruth Cunningham, RSCJ, *Anna Shannon, R.S.C.J.* (Society of the Sacred Heart, U. S. Province, 1991), 31-36.

[13]The author of Mother Shannon's biography, Ellen McGloin, was received into the Society of the Sacred Heart by Anna Shannon in 1870. In 1874, she was sent to Chile and in 1880 was among the founders in Buenos Aires, Argentina. In 1891 she moved to Lima, Peru. She returned to the United States in 1894 and went to Maryville in St. Louis where she was responsible for preparing the documents of the Ecclesiastical Tribunal considering the cause of Philippine Duchesne. Thus she was with Mother Shannon in the last months of her life. Later McGloin was moved to Eden Hall in Philadelphia where she died March 5, 1918. Her manuscript life of Anna Shannon ends with the notation, "Eden Hall, August 4, 1905."

AN HISTORICAL OVERVIEW OF
AFRO-AMERICANS IN NEW IBERIA, 1865-1960*

Sandra E. Egland

THE OVERVIEW

History is the record of people, it is the story of humankind. Theoretically it is complete, it cannot be flawed by omission or distortion. But, as we all know, that occurs and when it does it is usually the fault of the recorder of history, the historian, who consciously or unconsciously chooses between what will be remembered or recorded and what will become the chaff of history. Too often, however, hidden in the chaff are grains of a people's heritage which, if one takes the time to discover, reveal the potential for a rich harvest. Such a potential should never be mistakenly underrated; nevertheless, that has been true among American historians who, until recently, have overlooked, disregarded, or generally ignored the Afro-American experience since emancipation.

To suggest that people of African descent have not had a significant history in America is to admit an ignorance of the story of the race and of our country. From the beginning, blacks have been integral to the American cavalcade; they are not incidental to American history; they are not intruders; they are Americans. Nevertheless, throughout most of the Afro-American experience, blacks have sometimes been pushed and shoved by people who chose not to see the African descendant as a partner in the evolution of the American dream. History, however, provides a means for anyone who has it in his heart to see and to understand the black experience. History gives everyone a chance to judge wisely the past, to properly focus on the present, and to correctly plan for the future.

The historical tapestry of the United States is woven of many threads of different fibers. Louisianians have long contributed to the natural skein, and the Louisiana contribution is itself a multiplicity of human endeavor. Part of that endeavor is found in the historical tapestry of New Iberia, a fabric of many colored threads. Unfortunately for the history of the town, some threads have long been overlooked, thus detracting from the

---

*First published in *New Iberia: Essays on the Town and Its People*, comp. Glenn R. Conrad, 2d ed. (Lafayette, La.: Center for Louisiana Studies, 1986), 432-42. Reprinted with the kind permission of the author and the Center for Louisiana Studies.

fullness and richness of our past. What follows is an account of one overlooked thread—an attempt to weave it into the story of New Iberia.

Religion

Because religion has always been important to most African Americans and because the black church is and has been a significant institution, this overview of black life in New Iberia will begin with a look at a few of the older African American churches.[1]

Most of the African American churches in the major cities north and south were organized in the 1770s. Blacks frequently took the initiative in bringing about separation, especially when it became obvious that they were not welcome in the white churches. Most of the African American churches in New Iberia were organized shortly after the Civil War, with the exception of St. Edward's.

The role of the non-Catholic African American church was not limited to Sunday services. The black's church was a highly socialized institution with many functions and responsibilities, a community center where one could find recreation and release. It was a welfare agency, dispensing help to sick and poor members. It was a training school in self-government, in handling money, in doing business, and it was a newspaper. It was the black man's very own, allowing him to make decisions for himself which was seldom possible elsewhere.

St. James United Methodist Church, formerly called St. James Methodist Episcopal Church and St. James Methodist Church, is the oldest black congregation in New Iberia. As the Civil War was drawing to a close, a few black New Iberians gathered together out of concern for a place to worship God and serve mankind through fellowship, service, and mission. On April 9, 1865, they organized St. James Methodist Church. Their first pastor was the Rev. William Davis who toiled and struggled with the congregation to provide a place of worship. Beginning as a mission church, the congregation grew to the point where a new church was constructed in 1893 under the pastorate of the Rev. A. H. Banks. The Rev. S. E. H. Morant, presiding elder, and Bishop J. M. Fitzgerald were of great help in making this dream a reality. Pastors who have subsequently served the congregation are the Rev. W. Davis, Rev. C. D. Bryant, Rev. C. Shallonhorm, Rev. M. J. Dyer, Rev. H. J. Wright, Rev. Valco Chatman, and Rev. J. F. Johnson.

St. James congregation is proud to record in the pages of its history the fact that it has supported and inspired several persons to further their education and become Christian ministers. They were J. D. Richard, Q. W. Obee, Ed Richard, Travic Larkins, J. J. Obee, Eugene Johnson, Robert Wilkins, William and Russell Jones. These men have served the Louisiana conference with pride and dignity. The Joneses continue to serve the conference.

A great highlight in the history of St. James occurred in 1918 when the annual state-wide conference was held at the church. The Rev. Henry Taylor served as the Host Pastor, and the late Bishop Thirkield presided.

For 121 years, and with twenty-nine ministers serving as spiritual leaders, the St. James congregation has stood as a beacon in the community.

This establishment of the separate houses of worship for blacks, as inconsistent as it may seem with the teachings of their religion, gave to blacks an unusual opportunity to develop leadership. In New Iberia, one such leader was the Rev. Jessie Giles, who, in 1869, with only a small group of dedicated Christians, among whom were Joe Morris, Ann Levy, Sylvian Thornton, Ben Ramey, Sally Butler, and Louis Randolph, pulled together to form the Old Ironside Church. Ten years later the church's name became Star Pilgrim Baptist Church. Rev. Giles served this community until his death twenty-eight years later.

Thereafter, the Rev. A. J. Horton continued the mission of service and leadership. He was followed to the pastorate of Star Pilgrim by the Rev. Prince Albert (1916-1931), the Rev. William Bowers (1931-1932), the Rev. John Parker (1932-1956), and the Rev. Cyrus V. Jackson (1956-). Assistant pastors have been the Rev. James Simmons and the Rev. McKinley Smith. The Reverend Jackson and many members of his congregation have long been associated with civic and community activities, and the church is used for numerous civic programs.

Another church established in New Iberia shortly after the Civil War was St. Paul's United Church of Christ. St. Paul's began as a Congregational Church sometime between 1866 and 1868, several years after the freed slaves had held religious services in houses on the Gall Plantation. The church was organized by William Butler, a missionary of the American Missionary Association of the Congregational Church. The first church built by the congregation was on Washington Street near the railroad depot. After the edifice burned, the American Missionary Association assisted in the building of a new church on the corner of French and West Pershing streets. In 1891 the church was renovated and enlarged.

Although St. Paul's began as a Congregationalist church, it became St. Paul's Congregational Christian Church in 1931, when the Congregational and Christian churches were united. In 1957 there occurred the merger of the Congregational-Christian churches and the evangelical and reformed churches. The merger gave birth to the United Church of Christ and the name of St. Paul's became St. Paul United Church of Christ.

A never-to-be-forgotten pastor of St. Paul's was the Rev. R. V. Sims who served as shepherd to his congregation from 1897 to 1940. The Rev. B. J. Robertson, the current pastor, came to his flock in 1956.

Mt. Calvary Baptist Church was organized in 1875, with a membership of eighteen, under the leadership of Rev. J. B. Livingston who served as pastor until 1922. Other pastors to serve the congregation were the Rev. F. M. Boley, 1922-1949; Rev. H. M. Jones, 1949-1972, under whose leadership the present edifice was built. The Rev. L. M. Norbert, the fourth pastor of Mt. Calvary, has served since January 1973. He was baptized and grew up as a youth in Mt. Calvary.

Property acquired with God's help include four houses: two 2-story houses and one single-story house located on Julia Street to the rear of the church and another one adjacent to the church. Next to this property was another single-story house on Weeks Street. The site of this house is now the church's parking lot.

Through the Bus Ministry, needed transportation is provided by bus and van for persons who are able to get out to enjoy and participate in worship service and Christian fellowship.

For the sick and shut-in, there is available the Radio Ministry which includes a broadcast of the regular Sunday morning services. In addition to the church site and property adjoining it, the Mt. Calvary congregation owns an eight-and-one-half-acre tract of land in rural New Iberia which is the site of Mt. Calvary Memorial Park, a cemetery under development.

Classrooms for Sunday School, the Summer Tutorial Program and the annual Winter and Summer Institutes are located at 419 Julia Street. At 423 Julia Street is housed Operation Sharing Center which provides food and clothing on regular bases and financial assistance (when feasible). Mt. Calvary's general membership exceeds 575.

The churches were places of real release for a people who worked long hours, usually in the full sunshine of an open field, and who had few material pleasures. More than that, however, the church was a place where black people could get recognition for achievement, sympathy for sorrow, and the strength and love of brotherhood. The church was a place for maintaining community and family values—it was a place for hope.

During the 1920s, and '30s and '40s, these and other black Protestant churches served as centers of social life as well as places of worship. Fairs and other social fund raisers were held to promote the work of the churches. Many of the great cooks of the town showed off their culinary skills, producing sweet-potato pies, peach pies, coconut delights, blackberry cobbler, ice cream, pralines, fudge, and a host of other good foods to delight the palate. To raise money there were Friday night fish fries, Saturday fairs, and Sunday services with lemonade and fried chicken dinners interspersed between religious teachings.

Churchgoing was an extended family affair. Women and girls wore dresses starched stiff as cardboard and carried lace handkerchiefs and fans with funeral home advertisements. Every Sister (as all women were called and all men were addressed as Brother), wore a hat, but if they were deaconesses and/or missionaries they wore a specially made headdress. The men and boys, of course, always donned their Sunday best for church services.

In those days of no-air-conditioning, fainting was as commonplace in Baptist and Holiness churches as Hollywood's conception of swooning among antebellum white women. Shouting was also common. Baptisms by Baptists were done in Bayou Teche until the 1940s and 1950s. Ladies who were to be baptized wore long white dresses that tied at their feet in order that their dress would not float when they were emerged. Beginning in the 1940s and 1950s, pools were constructed in the church for the purpose of baptism.

A social function performed by the black churches was to provide a place for courtship. Young men would go to church to meet their sweethearts, or they would walk with them to church. If those who were courting walked to church, they did so always a few feet ahead of the accompanying chaperons. In church and on the church grounds the young couple was permitted to hold hands only.

The development of separate black Catholic churches across South Louisiana, including the one in New Iberia, was the result of complex political, sociological, and religious factors.[2] From colonial days to the time of the Civil War, black and white Catholics had worshipped together, even though they did so from segregated seating. Such an arrangement held sway even after the Civil War and emancipation. But change was in the wind. With emancipation, black Protestants established black churches, conducted worship services, and participated in the social activities of their community. Many black Catholics yearned for a similar religious life. In politics, when Reconstruction ended and whites regained political domination, tensions developed between the races at all levels, even the religious; hence, black Catholics came to understand that their presence in the mixed congregations was embarrassing for many whites. Numerous black Catholics therefore began to drift away from their lifetime religious experience. Also, between 1890 and 1900, the Louisiana legislature passed a series of laws designed to separate the races at certain points of contact and to deprive the blacks of the franchise. Official segregation therefore fueled racial tensions that finally burst into violence. Between 1882 and 1903, for example, there were 285 confirmed lynchings in the state. A combination of these political, sociological and religious factors, therefore began to impact upon the black population of Louisiana and especially black Catholics.

The Catholic hierarchy was aware of deteriorating race relationships and was deeply concerned about the consequences. The official response to this multifaceted problem came when, in 1888, Francis Janssens was appointed archbishop of New Orleans. After consultation with clergy and laity, the archbishop found a possible solution to the many problems facing black Catholics in the concept of a national church. National churches for various ethnic groups, Irish, Italian, German, for example, were common in most American urban centers. The national churches were designed to accommodate the immigrant family until it sought integration into the American social system. No member of any ethnic group was compelled to belong to a national church, he could belong to his territorial church. The national church thus provided the model from which Janssens drew his plan for Louisiana's black Catholics. The archbishop "was certain that blacks were leaving the church and he was just as certain that the attraction of an active parish life would serve as strong reason for remaining in the church and perhaps persuade some who had left to return."[3]

Janssens' plan was gradually put into practice during the archbishop's tenure, and continued at a slow pace during the episcopacy of Archbishop Louis Placide Chapelle.

When, however, James Herbert Blenk became archbishop of New Orleans in 1909, the program of separate parishes accelerated as a result of the archbishop's appreciation of two facts: the rapid decline in the black Catholic population of the archdiocese and the mounting racial tensions.

Thus, when Monsignor J. M. Langlois, pastor of St. Peter's Church in New Iberia, petitioned the archbishop in 1916 (the Diocese of Lafayette had not yet been created) to establish a black parish in New Iberia, Blank moved swiftly to act upon the request. In February 1917 the archbishop received agreement from the Holy Ghost Fathers to staff the new parish. In the meantime Mother Katherine Drexel, founder of the Sisters of the Blessed Sacrament and heiress to a large fortune which she had used to fund the purchase of land and the construction of buildings for the next black parish in New Iberia. The actual donation came from Mother Drexel's sister, Mrs. Louise D. Morrell, who asked that the new parish be named St. Edward's as a memorial to her husband Edward Morrell.

Fr. F. Xavier Lichtenberger, the first pastor, arrived in New Iberia on October 1, 1917. He moved into his new house on January 1, 1918, and celebrated the first Mass in St. Edward's Church on November 10, 1918. In May 1919, St. Edward's was the first church to be blessed by the bishop of the new Diocese of Lafayette, the Most Reverend Jules B. Jeanmard. St. Edward's is therefore considered by many people to be the mother church of all churches in the diocese that were founded as national parishes for black Catholics.

Fr. Lichtenberger faced an enormous task. His congregation was scattered over a large geographical area; more importantly, many members of the flock strayed from the Catholic church. He therefore spent his pastorate in the work of gathering the flock. His two successors continued this work with success thereby making it possible for Fr. John McGlade, after he became pastor in 1924, to begin the work of conversion.

The Holy Ghost Fathers continued to minister to this congregation until 1977 when personnel problems necessitated the order's withdrawal from the parish. After a brief transition period, priests of the Society of the Divine Word have taken up the work of shepherding the flock.[4]

In 1933 St. Edward's School was accredited by the state board of education. The school had seven grammar grades and four grades of high school. Thousands of children have graduated from this school to continue their education and assume responsible positions in society. The school is now part of a unitary system serving all Catholic children of New Iberia from kindergarten through third grade.

Today's St. Edward's is a thriving complete parish unit with church, school, and rectory built largely through the generosity of the parishioners. The convent is the only remaining original structure. This parish and its mission, St. Jude's in Olivier, stand as monuments to the dedicated black men and women who kept their faith.

Notes for "An Historical Overview of Afro-Americans
in New Iberia, 1865-1960"

[1]These histories of the churches were obtained from the Rev. C. V. Jackson, Rev. Larry Norbert, Rev. Burnell Robinson, Rev. Alvin Dixon, the *Daily Iberian*, church programs, commemorative brochures, and other reference materials. Also supplying information were Mr. Edran Auguster, Mrs. Ruth Sophus, Mrs. Ruby Egland, Mrs. Ruth Bolden, Mr. and Mrs. Borie Stinson, and Mr. Leander Viltz.

[2]An excellent account of the establishment of black Catholic parishes can be found in Dolores Egger Labbé's *Jim Crow Comes to Church: The Establishment of Segregated Catholic Parishes in South Louisiana* (Lafayette, La., 1971).

[3]Labbé, *Jim Crow Comes to Church*, 38-9.

[4]Pastors of St. Edward's: F. X. Lichtenberger, 1917-19; T. A. Wrenn, 1919-21; J. A. Pobleschek, 1921-24; John C. McGlade, 1924-35; Anthony Walsh, 1935-36; J. P. Lonergan, 1936-45; J. E. Stegman, 1945; James McCaffrey, 1945; Herbert Frederick, 1945-49; Clement Roach, 1949-58; Eugene Monroney, 1958-66; Martin Kirschbaum, 1966-68; John Schlicht, 1968-71; John Burns, 1971-76; William Havenar, 1976-83; J. Gus Johnson, 1983-84; Alvin Dixon, 1984- .

THE "SOUTHERN WORK" OF THE REVEREND JOSEPH C. HARTZELL, PASTOR OF AMES CHURCH IN NEW ORLEANS, 1870-1873[*]

Anne C. Loveland

During the years of presidential and congressional reconstruction, various Protestant denominations were implementing programs aimed at the religious and moral reconstruction of the former Confederacy. Northern Methodists in particular looked upon the post-Civil War period as an opportunity to continue the efforts for national regeneration that had claimed their energies and those of other Protestants before 1860. The defeat of the South, a region previously closed to their efforts, opened up a vast field for missionary and educational efforts, particularly, though not exclusively, among the freedmen.

In New Orleans, the "Southern work" of the Methodist Episcopal Church was prosecuted by the Rev. Joseph C. Hartzell, pastor of Ames Church from 1870 to 1873. Born in Illinois in June 1842, and educated at Illinois Wesleyan University and Garrett Biblical Institute, Hartzell was serving in his first pastorate in Pekin, Illinois, when the Rev. John P. Newman invited him to become his successor at Ames Church on St. Charles Avenue.[1] "The Church," Newman wrote, "is one of the largest & most elegant in the South, & the congregation a power in the city." The position would also offer Hartzell an opportunity to become involved in the educational work of the Church—he would be principal of "the State Normal School" which was under the supervision of the Methodist Church. Newman spoke optimistically of Ames' financial situation. A debt of $5,000 had just been paid and the trustees were prepared to offer Hartzell a salary of $150 per month "and more proportionately if you are married."[2]

Hartzell was unable to accept Newman's invitation until almost a year later. Only then did Bishop Edmund Janes agree to release him from Pekin for work in the South.[3] He arrived in New Orleans in February 1870 and discovered that Newman had painted a somewhat exaggerated picture of Ames and its congregation. Hartzell's salary was not as munificent as Newman had promised, with local debts of $5,500 coming due and the Church Extension Society threatening legal procedures to obtain repayment of a mortgage of $5,000. Hartzell's most pressing task at Ames would be to shore up the finances

*First published in *Louisiana History*, 16 (1975): 391-407. Reprinted with the kind permission of the author and the Louisiana Historical Association.

of his new church, first by securing an adjustment of the debt owed the Extension Society and then by waging yearly financial campaigns for donations from the congregation and other friends of Ames.[4]

During his pastorate, Hartzell quite naturally looked to Newman for advice and inspiration. "I hope occasionally to hear from you," Hartzell wrote in June 1870. "There is so much of soul warmth and encouragement in your letters that they are received with great pleasure."[5] For his part, Newman continued to take an interest in the Methodist work in New Orleans. In one letter he advised Hartzell to "Make your pulpit a power, by hard study, much prayer, & by preaching on *live* subjects. The people of the South appreciate oratory as no other people in the world. . . . Make your church a *spiritual* power. Have a revival, Save souls." Newman also counseled his successor to "Call upon the Governor at his house, & interest the State offices, [*sic*] whom you may benefit & who will afford financial support to your Church," and he advised making friends with T. G. Tracy, editor of the *New Orleans Republican*. Hartzell should take care to be "dignified," yet "cordial;" this, Newman declared, was the way to win friends and benefactors. "Quietly but surely gain the confidence of your brethren & they will honor you when honors are to be conferred," he wrote. Finally, Newman urged the new pastor to "Be kind to our colored preachers, and manifest a lively interest in all their welfare." He admitted that "It will take *time* to gain their confidence, but it sticks when once secured." In particular, he advised Hartzell to "Pay special attention" to three of the black "fathers" affiliated with the Methodist Church in New Orleans: Anthony Ross, Scott Chinn, and H. Green.[6]

Hartzell's initial impression of New Orleans was what might be expected of a pious Northern missionary venturing for the first time into the cosmopolitan port city. Writing to a friend in Evanston, he described it as "without a doubt the wickedest city in the Continent. Catholicism has almost complete sway. Jews, Mexicans, Chillians [*sic*], Spaniards, Germans, French, Negroes—people of every clime & shade of color, and shade of religious belief—are here. Among the lowest classes of Negroes there are actually some forms of worship and many shades of superstitions—of *Voudouism*." He and his wife had encountered some hostility. "The educated & wealthy," he noted, "are very largely *bitter rebels* politically. So bitter are they that they knowingly will not associate with a Northern family." But such things did not discourage Hartzell. Indeed, he declared, "Since coming each day has only confirmed our faith that we are where the Father wants us to work. . . . this city is in God's territory and must be conquered for him." Moreover, he continued, "From among the heap there are many true warm & noble souls, who are well known at *head quarters*, and are doing manfully for God. Our church is not large and yet is composed of those who have been loyal enough to their country and God, to 'come up through' the 'great tribulations' of the rebellion and reconstruction." Thirty new members had been added to the church since his coming to New Orleans and Hartzell was able to report, exaggerating slightly, that "Financially the church with its friends is strong—The Governor and most of the leading state and city officers support us financially. Several attend and some are members."[7]

Like their pastor, many of the congregation of Ames Church were carpetbaggers. Hartzell's parishioners included Gov. Henry Clay Warmoth, Judge Henry C. Dibble, and Cyrus Bussey, along with other prominent politicians and businessmen of the Reconstruction period.[8] Hartzell once characterized them as "men who have risked *everything* for our cause here and to whom we are largely indebted for our standing among the whites, *and especially among the colored people*;" and he emphasized "the sacrifices and actual cost in dollars & cents it cost them . . . to sus[tain] Methodism in this rebel and wicked city."[9] Bussey was the most generous contributor to the support of the church. Hartzell reported that the wealthy cotton factor had donated $1,000 during a recent financial campaign. The list of other subscribers included some of the leading members of the Ames congregation: "Page, Heath, Warmoth & McMillan 500$ each. Dibble, Noyes, Beldon, Spranley, Lowell 250$ each."[10] Another friend of the Church was H. S. McComb, president of the New Orleans, Jackson, and Great Northern Railroad Company, who donated somewhere between $1,000 and $1,500 over a two-year period.[11]

Many of Hartzell's parishioners were Republicans. He himself was a strong Unionist and Republican and often officiated at political ceremonies. One time he offered the opening prayer at American Union Club observances of Decoration Day at Chalmette Cemetery, and on another occasion he performed a similar service at a meeting in Lafayette Square following a procession celebrating the passage of the Fifteenth Amendment.[12] Like most other Northern Methodist missionaries to the South, Hartzell saw no conflict in linking religious endeavors and Republican politics.[13] Ames was in his view to be the "one loyal church" in New Orleans; and from the very beginning of his pastorate Hartzell sought to make the Church a "power for good" in the "great and wicked city."[14]

As a result, Ames Church was almost inevitably drawn into the maelstrom of Reconstruction politics. In February of 1871 Hartzell reported to Newman that the church had suffered "another terrible blow. Bro. S. C. Emley has been compelled to resign his place on the city government on account of defalcation." Hartzell refused to believe that Emley had been "dishonest intentionally," though Warmoth and Bussey had told him that Emley "had ample warning given him to straighten his accounts." Another parishioner, Brother Cambias, "has been dismissed from the police force for *swindling*." Hartzell declared him "a persecuted man," but reflected that "nevertheless the effect on the church is the same."[15]

Although Hartzell was concerned to make Ames serve as a kind of religious haven for Northern politicians and businessmen who came to New Orleans during Reconstruction, he was chiefly interested in extending its regenerating influence among the natives of the city and its environs. White Louisianians were not very receptive to his missionary efforts, though he did receive occasional appeals like the one from W. D. Beaumont, who wrote from White Hall Landing in Plaquemine Parish to request books for a Sunday School:

> We wish to open a Sunday School in this settlement there is about forty children what
> would attend it but we have no books to teach them they are all colored children and very
> anxious to have a Sunday School and what they want is books if you could send them
> books they would pay for them in course of a few months by taking up a Sunday School
> Collection they are all able and willing to pay for them if you Can send us such books as
> are necessary for the school I will see that they are paid for[.][16]

On another occasion Hartzell received an invitation to preach at West Pearl River.
Mrs. L. S. Sadler, in making the request, noted that "The people here as in other places in
the South, are considerably prejudiced towards the Northern Methodists. The principle
objection is because they think they wish to force Negro equality on them. They have no
objection to your preaching to the colored [sic] people but they must not wish them to
meet together." But, she added, "I presume that you are perfectly aware of all these little
peculiar ideas of the southern people." Apparently the desire for more frequent preaching
had overcome the suspicions of some of the West Pearl community. Mrs. Sadler explained that there was circuit preaching once a month by a preacher belonging to the
Methodist Church, South, and that "He said he would be glad to have you come over and
Preach here." Moreover, "My Husband says he will donate the Methodists a lot for a
church if they will build one." Appealing to Hartzell's benevolent instincts, Mrs. Sadler
told him, "You might probably see an opening here to do much good."[17]

Hartzell's missionary endeavors among black Louisianians also met with difficulties,
though of a different nature from those attending his efforts among whites. He attempted
to cement good relations with the black Methodist churches in the city. On one occasion,
he reported to Newman, he and his wife, "Invited the Colored brethren to take tea with
us. Or rather I should say we invited the members of the Preachers meeting and none
came but the colored brethren. Such a time! I'll never forget the pleasure they seemed to
take in conversation, and how appreciatively they gave their hearty 'God bless you' to
us."[18] But his efforts among the blacks were no doubt undercut by Ames' policy of segregation, which had been established before his coming to New Orleans. In 1869 the
church had twenty Negro members who, according to John Blassingame, "apparently sat
where they wished in the church." One of the trustees objected, and the church adopted a
policy requiring Negroes to sit in the balcony.[19] When Hartzell assumed the pastorate, he
avoided confronting "the direct issue" by maintaining that "our only work now is to let
points of difference go and labor for Jesus." After he left Ames, the issue was raised
anew in 1874, when a few blacks requested admission to the church. Hartzell's successor
and the lay officials decided against admitting them and a bitter conflict ensued. Hartzell,
having become presiding elder and editor of the *Southwestern Christian Advocate*, found
himself in the middle. "I am appealed to on both sides, in my official capacity, as the
representative of the church," he wrote to Bishop Simpson. There was, he reported, "a
most intense excitement among the colored people—and in fact through the entire city."
But he noted that this time, in arguing their case, "the colored people are more advanced

and make the issue on the [Methodist] *discipline*."[20] After months of debate and controversy, in 1875 the Church adopted a policy of nondiscrimination.[21]

Hartzell's "Southern work" included educational as well as missionary efforts. Indeed, the opportunity to become engaged in what Newman had termed "the educational department of the church-a life work" was what had attracted the young minister to New Orleans.[22] Hartzell became principal of the Union Normal School, founded in 1869 by the Freedmen's Aid Society. When he took charge in 1870 the school had 68 pupils and 3 teachers, and was housed in two "Wooden buildings . . . two stories high 44 x 36 x 42 x 30."[23] In addition he supervised the Thomson Bible Institute which had been established on Bayou Teche in St. Mary Parish to prepare young black men for the ministry.

Thomson Institute was part of a larger benevolent scheme undertaken by a wealthy Methodist layman, John Baldwin, of Berea, Ohio. In 1867 he had purchased the 1,700-acre Darby Plantation in St. Mary Parish for the sum of $20,000. He offered to donate to the Methodists some thirty or forty acres on Bayou Teche, along with about twenty buildings, to be used in establishing a school which, according to the conditions of the grant, would be for both blacks and whites and open to women as well. Baldwin Seminary, as the new institution was called, was established in 1868, but when its nondiscriminatory policies appeared to be hindering operations, the founder decided to continue it for whites and endow another school for blacks. In 1868 he offered a portion of the plantation to the trustees of Thomson University, a school for Negroes studying the ministry which had been established in New Orleans under the auspices of the Freedmen's Aid Society.[24] The board of trustees, which included J. P. Newman, Cyrus Bussey, John Page, R. K. Diossy, and N. L. Brakeman, accepted the offer, and Thomson was moved to the Darby Plantation that same year.[25] Apparently relations between officials of the two institutions, Baldwin Seminary and Thomson Institute, were never entirely happy; among other things there was a prolonged controversy over the building of a fence between the schools.[26] In addition, relations between John Baldwin and his Methodist brethren were strained by various disagreements. In 1870, for example, there were reports that Baldwin had "sold a lot right in front of [Thomson] University to a rumseller who is making drunkards at a fearful rate." This was a direct challenge to the temperance principles of the Methodists. R. S. Rust, of the Freedmen's Aid Society, wrote Baldwin a strong letter admonishing him to "Banish rumselling from your vicinity if possible, or our interests are fearfully jeopardized."[27] Despite these and other problems, Thomson continued in operation and in 1873 merged with Union Normal School to form New Orleans University, the precursor, along with Straight University (founded by the American Missionary Association) of present-day Dillard University.[28]

The education provided by Union Normal, Thomson, and other Methodist institutions in the South was highly sectarian and moralistic. Indeed, the schools were as much engaged in missionary as in educational work. Churches and schools were often one and the same building; teachers were frequently preachers as well, and served in both Sunday and day schools.[29] At Union Normal School the schedule included daily chapel sessions and prayer meetings, three church services on Sunday, and "special convocations 'for the promotion of holiness.'"[30] The report of the Freedmen's Aid Society for 1868 suggests the general purpose of Methodist educational efforts:

> Our schools have rendered essential aid in the work of restoring social order; in bringing about friendly relations between the employers and laborers; in promoting habits of cleanliness, industry, economy, purity, and morality; rendering more emphatic the grand distinctions between right and wrong, falsehood and truth; enforcing fidelity to contracts; portraying the terrible consequences of intemperance, licentiousness, profanity, lying, and stealing; teaching them to respect the rights of others while they are prompt to claim protection for themselves. The teachers have furnished for the freedmen a vast amount of valuable information in regard to the practical matters of life which could be obtained nowhere else. The schools have met a great want which no military or political organization could supply, and without which it will be impossible for peace and harmony to be restored. Our teachers have been pioneers in the work of reconciliation, and are laying a foundation upon which the most enduring superstructure can be reared.[31]

Hartzell's co-workers at Union Normal School and Thomson Institute were young men and women, most of them, like him, from the Midwest or the northeastern part of the United States, and all dedicated to the cause of "the Master."[32] Like their counterparts throughout the South, they worked long hours for pitifully small salaries, lived with their students in crowded dormitories and shared their often meager diet, and frequently met with social ostracism, economic sanctions, even violence, from the surrounding white community.[33] Rosetta Coit, a teacher at the Union Normal School, even spent her vacation in Hasting's Center, New York, trying "to interest the people I have met from time to time, in the cause of Education among the Freedmen, & especially the subject of Normal schools—ours in particular." She reported to Hartzell that one business firm had donated fifty dollars, "by far the largest sum," but noted that "Our church has so many Interests & so many *regular collections*, that it is impossible to secure a large one, for any one object." Yet she consoled herself with "the consciousness, that I have tried very hard to accomplish something for the cause."[34]

Besides Union Normal School and Thomson Institute, Hartzell also supervised the Freedmen's Orphan Home located on a plantation next to the one owned by John Baldwin. Like the Union Normal School, the "Home," as it came to be called, was partly subsidized by the Freedmen's Bureau until 1868; after that it was self-supporting from the proceeds of the sugar industry.[35] The orphanage combined educational and missionary efforts, sharing some of the same characteristics and encountering some of the same difficulties as Hartzell's other ventures. Thus one of the teachers at the Home, Emerson Bentley, attempted to link Republican politics and religious activities, much as Hartzell did. He reported that "The Republicans of this parish have nominated me as their candidate for the State Legislature. I will take part in this contest not as a professional politician, but with a Christian spirit, and a desire to do something for the general good. I thought best to accept the position when offered me, because of the many advantages it afforded me to do practical good." The Home met with some hostility from the surrounding white community, but Bentley declared that nevertheless the institution "is doing a great work and its influence is extending." Noting that the orphanage had "a representative now in every important point in this parish," he observed that "when the children leave the institution one by one, either by marriage, or the aid of friends, or to enter business pursuits, and settle in its immediate vicinity, the Home will become the mother of a wholesome Christian influence which cannot help affecting the future control of politics and morals." No doubt Hartzell shared Bentley's view that "It is a pleasure to think of this."[36]

Hartzell was also able, perhaps remembering his initial reaction to New Orleans, to sympathize with another teacher's lament over "the irreligious influences" at work in the Home. S. L. Beiler, a young Ohio Wesleyan student who divided his time between Thomson Institute and the orphanage, explained that "when my scholars come to me with old infidel theories that have been exploded long since, and want to know what they mean; and others advance the detestable doctrines of Roman Catholicism, as that of a purgatory, and the interposition of saints, in Sabbath School; I am made to feel that if this is to be a Methodist institution, Methodists ought to be in it, and not infidels and Roman Catholics." The problem was compounded by the fact that, as Beiler believed, "They do not work openly, and in a manner they can always be met, but secretly, silently, and many times unknown to us, until the mischief is done."[37]

In supervising the Home, Hartzell not only heard complaints from the white teachers, but was also forced to respond to criticism from the black community. What the precise issue was remains obscure. In part it seems to have been a personality conflict between the matron of the Home, Mrs. J. S. Roberts, and some of the blacks. Newman wrote to Hartzell that he had received several letters on the issue indicating that "The colored people are excited on this matter." He advised Hartzell to talk with the Negroes, particularly Brother Boinir, who "reflects the mind of the colored people;" and, he wrote, "as the 'Home' is for their children, their wishes should be complied with." He urged Hartzell to "Go to work *quietly* & get another matron." Newman admitted that "it is not right to turn a person out for any little prejudice, yet when the 'Blacks' get a prejudice it is hard to uproot it." Besides, he noted, hinting at the political implications of the controversy, "We must have them with us for the 'Home.'" If Mrs. Roberts remained, the blacks would turn against the orphanage, "& through them the *State*, & the 'Home' will suffer."[38]

The dispute at the Home also involved a sort of power struggle, if the report of W. H. Gray is accepted. Gray, a doctor who had contracted with the board of managers of the Orphans Home Society to see to the medical needs of the children, reported in 1871 to John Baldwin on the outcome of the controversy surrounding Mrs. Roberts:

> The star of the house of Diossy has culminated and now tends rapidly to the Western horizon. The Board of Managers of the Home seem to have their eyes fully open to the duplicity and scheming of that house. . . .

Madam Roberts found that many votes had been passed at the Board meetings which *many of the Board knew nothing of* and measures were engineered through by the manipulations of the House of D. which were not in accordance with the wishes of the majority of the Board. In this way were passed, a vote cutting down Madam's salary— and afterward another *dismissing her from the Home.* . . . It is all over now and the further interferance [*sic*] of the D's in the affairs of the Home. . . [39]

What position Hartzell took regarding the controversy at the Home is not known. Probably he confronted that issue in much the same way that he did all the others, confident that such trials and tribulations were only temporary obstacles in the way of remaking the South into "God's territory." Notwithstanding financial and other troubles, Hartzell was generally optimistic as pastor of Ames, sustained in his efforts by the feeling that he was succeeding, however slowly, in his enterprise. "Ames Church," he wrote in February 1871, "is gradually but surely rising to be a *power* for good in this city."[40] Yet, in just a few years, Northern Methodists would lose interest in the church's work in the South.[41] In addition, two other factors, which were largely outside Hartzell's control, had a significant bearing on his efforts. One was the generally unsympathetic response of Southern whites toward the missionary and educational efforts of Northern Methodists among the freedmen. The other was the ultimate abandonment of the cause of the Negro by the Republican party. Hartzell's work, which drew much of its inspiration from the antebellum abolitionist movement, was, for just that reason, suspect to Southern whites. At the same time, the fact of his alliance with the Republican party meant that when Republicans—and Northerners in general—abandoned the social and political goals of Reconstruction, the Southern undertaking of the Methodist Church lost a good deal of the moral, financial, and political support on which it depended. Hartzell would continue his "Southern work" in the late 1870s and 1880s, but he would labor against increasing odds.[42]

Notes for "The 'Southern Work' of the Reverend Joseph C. Hartzell,
Pastor of Ames Church in New Orleans, 1870-1873"

[1]Biographical information from Inventory Folder, Joseph C. Hartzell Papers, Louisiana State University Archives, Baton Rouge, La. (hereafter cited as Hartzell Papers). Terry L. Seip, assistant professor, University of Southern California, and Frank J. Wetta, assistant professor of history, Galveston College, also provided information on Hartzell. Ames Church was within the Louisiana Conference of the Methodist Episcopal Church, established in December 1865 by Bishop Edward Thomson and embracing the states of Louisiana and Mississippi. At that time the organization had twelve traveling preachers and approximately 1,000 lay communicants. By 1881 the Northern Methodist Church had in Louisiana a membership of almost one hundred whites (not including numerous German Methodists in New Orleans) and over 10,000 blacks, many of whom had originally been affiliated with the Methodist Episcopal Church, South. Ralph E. Morrow, *Northern Methodism and Reconstruction* (East Lansing, Mich., 1956), 45-6, 99, 128-30. For the later history of Ames Church see Rev. O. E. Kriege, D. D., *A Century of Service by the Napoleon Avenue Methodist Church and Its Forerunners* (New Orleans, 1942), 40-5 and passim.

[2]J. P. Newman to J. C. Hartzell, New Orleans, February 8 and February 19, 1869, Hartzell Papers. See also, Newman to Hartzell, Washington, D. C., April 8 and December 21, 1869, ibid. John P. Newman was perhaps

the best known of the Northern Methodist missionaries to the South. He arrived in New Orleans in 1864 to take charge of Methodist work in that city and helped found Ames Church; a year later he began publication of a weekly newspaper, the *New Orleans Advocate*. In 1869 he became pastor of the Metropolitan Church in Washington, D. C., ministering to a congregation that included the president, vice president, and chief justice of the United States, numerous senators and representatives, as well as other prominent political and financial figures. William Warren Sweet, *Methodism in American History* (New York, 1953), 295; Morrow, *Northern Methodism and Reconstruction*, 55, 216-7, 221.

[3]M. Simpson to Hartzell, Philadelphia, March 23 and December 5, 1869, Hartzell Papers.

[4]See the correspondence between Hartzell and the Reverend A. J. Kynett, corresponding secretary to the Church Extension Society, March 1870 through May 1871, especially Hartzell to Kynett, New Orleans, March 21, 1870, ibid. The Church Extension Society had been established by the General Conference of 1864. Along with the Missionary Society it offered loans and donations for the support of new churches and their ministers in the South. Morrow, *Northern Methodism and Reconstruction*, 32.

[5]Hartzell to Newman, New Orleans, June 6, 1870, Hartzell Papers.

[6]Newman to Hartzell, Washington, D. C., February 25, 1870, ibid. Anthony Ross, pastor of the Wesley Chapel, a black Methodist Episcopal church, was ordained a deacon and elder of the Methodist Episcopal Church by Bishop Thomson in 1865. He had been born into slavery in Maryland in 1805 and taken to Louisiana in 1831. Reverend Scott Chinn was pastor of the La Harpe Street Church, a black Methodist Episcopal church. H. Green was a black preacher. Matthew Simpson, ed., *Cyclopaedia of Methodism. Embracing Sketches of its Rise, Progress, and Present Condition, with Biographical Notices and Numerous Illustrations*, rev. ed. (Philadelphia, 1880), 767; *Edwards' Annual Directory to the Inhabitants, Institutions, Incorporated Companies, Manufacturing Establishments, Business, Business Firms, Etc., Etc., in the City of New Orleans and Suburbs. for 1870* (New Orleans, 1869). Besides Wesley Chapel and the La Harpe Street Church, *Edwards' Directory* lists eight other black Methodist Episcopal churches: Port Street Church, Green's Chapel, First Street Church, Winans Chapel, German Church, Marais Street Church, Sixth Street Church, and St. Mary's Street Church.

[7]Hartzell to Sister Pearson, New Orleans, June 30, 1870, Hartzell Papers. Writing to A. J. Kynett almost a year later, Hartzell reported "a membership of 84" and "a congregation of *less than 200*," Hartzell to Kynett, New Orleans, March 21, 1870, ibid.

[8]Dibble was appointed judge of the Eighth District Court by Governor Warmoth in March 1870. Francis Byers Harris, "Henry Clay Warmoth, Reconstruction Governor of Louisiana," *Louisiana Historical Quarterly*, 30 (1947): 602. Cyrus Bussey, a prominent Methodist layman, was born in Indiana and entered the Union Army on August 23, 1861, as colonel of the 23rd Iowa Volunteers. After the war he moved south, and during Reconstruction was a cotton factor in New Orleans, serving for a time as president of the Cotton Exchange. Simpson, ed., *Cyclopaedia of Methodism*, 150. Professor C. Howard Nichols of Southeastern Louisiana University also provided information on Bussey. Since Hartzell referred to many of his parishioners only by last name, it is difficult to be certain as to the membership of Ames Church. The following state officials have been tentatively identified as members of the congregation: Edward Heath, former mayor of New Orleans; W. L. McMillan, elected to the United States Senate in 1873; J. O. Noyes, chief of the Bureau of Immigration; Dr. James G. Belden, former state treasurer; C. W. Lowell, elected speaker of the Louisiana house of representatives in 1872, and later postmaster; W. B. Armstrong, former acting quartermaster of the Freedman's Bureau in Louisiana, M. C. Cole, secretary to the state superintendent of education.

[9]Hartzell to Kynett, New Orleans, May 23, 1870, Hartzell Papers.

[10]Hartzell to Newman, New Orleans, February 13, 1871, ibid. I have not been able to identify Page; F. Spranley was listed as a salesman for Emley & Co. in *Edward's' Directory, 1870*.

[11]Hartzell to McComb, New Orleans, January 3, May 13, May 25, 1871; McComb to Hartzell, January 9, May 22, 1871, Hartzell Papers.

[12]Invitation dated May 13, 1870, from Headquarters, American Union Club, New Orleans, to attend the ceremony at Chalmette Cemetery; Programme for Decoration Day, May 30, 1872, sponsored by American Union Club; invitation to participate in procession, signed William H. Pemberton, chairman, Committee of Arrangements, ibid.

[13]Ralph Morrow points out that a number of Northern clergymen held positions in various state governments during the Reconstruction period. One of those who corresponded with Hartzell was George W. Honey, who administered the Texas Treasury Department and also served as secretary for the Texas Conference of the Methodist Episcopal Church. Morrow, *Northern Methodism and Reconstruction*, 220. See, for example, Honey to Hartzell, Austin, November 9, 1871, Hartzell Papers.

[14]Hartzell to McComb, New Orleans, January 3, 1871; Hartzell to Newman, New Orleans, February 13, 1871, Hartzell Papers.

[15]Hartzell to Newman, New Orleans, February 13, 1871, ibid. *Edwards' Directory, 1870* lists Emley as a partner in the firm of Emley & Co., flour merchants; and George A. Cambias as police sergeant.

[16]W. D. Beaumont to Hartzell, White hall landing Parish placiemine [sic], May 8, 1870, Hartzell Papers. See also, T. W. Hawkin to Hartzell, Bayou Lafourch [sic], April 6, 1872, ibid.

[17]Mrs. L. S. Sadler to Hartzell, West Pearl River, May 31, 1871, ibid. Mrs. Sadler was the sister of Benjamin F. Crary, editor of the *Central Christian Advocate*, a Methodist periodical published in St. Louis, Missouri. Morrow, *Northern Methodism and Reconstruction*, 109.

[18]Hartzell to Newman, New Orleans, June 6, 1870, Hartzell Papers.

[19]Blassingame, *Black New Orleans, 1860-1880* (Chicago, 1973) 199.

[20]Hartzell to Bishop Matthew Simpson, New Orleans, April 2, 1874, Simpson Papers, Division of Manuscripts, Library of Congress, Washington, D. C.; Morrow, *Northern Methodism and Reconstruction*, 188. During Hartzell's pastorate at Ames, the issue of racial segregation in the church as a whole arose in connection with the anti-segregationist "Louisiana Platform" advanced at the 1872 General Conference by Lucius C. Matlack, former abolitionist and presiding elder of the New Orleans District. See Morrow, *Northern Methodism and Reconstruction*, 192.

[21]Blassingame, *Black New Orleans*, 199.

[22]Newman to Hartzell, New Orleans, February 8, 1869, Hartzell Papers.

[23]Notation by Hartzell on a letter from E. W. Mason, Superintendent of Education, Bureau Refugees, Freedmen and Abandoned Lands, State of Louisiana, dated New Orleans, June 9, 1870, requesting information on the Union Normal School. The Freedmen's Aid Society, formed in 1866, was the educational agency of the Methodist Church. During Reconstruction it established schools of various grades throughout the Southern states, often with assistance from the Freedmen's Bureau. Union Normal School, for example, received an initial grant of $12,500 from the Bureau. Howard A. White, *The Freedmen's Bureau in Louisiana* (Baton Rouge, 1970), 191. As Ralph Morrow points out, though the Methodist schools were "variously designated as universities, colleges, institutes, normal schools, and seminaries" in fact "the label . . . bore no correspondence to the caliber of its academic offerings." He suggests that in the 1870s New Orleans University which grew out of Union Normal School) was probably equal in academic standing to an academy or high school. The institutions were advertised as open to all students, regardless of race, but after 1866 few whites attended. By the spring of 1870 the society was sponsoring 60 schools throughout the South and employing 110 teachers. The following year, when Bureau funds were cut off, the number decreased to 35 schools and 75 teachers. Morrow, *Northern Methodism and Reconstruction*, 163-6, 197. See also William Edward Highsmith, "Louisiana During Reconstruction" (Ph.D. dissertation, Louisiana State University, 1953), 385.

[24]Judge A. R. Webber, *Life of John Baldwin, Sr., of Berea, Ohio* ([Cincinnati?], 1925), 139-41. Baldwin's enterprise involved more than education. He ultimately laid out a town (which was named Baldwin), hired Meth-

odist freedmen to farm the land on shares, and operated a sugar mill. That the community was part of a larger venture contemplated by Northern Methodists is suggested in a letter of R. K. Diossy to Baldwin regarding plans to hire men to work on the plantation. Diossy wrote that

> Several good men are already on the list, and will meet you here or on the place, when you arrive. . . . There will be no difficulty in finding good reliable men of family to take all the land you wish to hire out, and I think it will be an excellent plan. Your enterprise will greatly benefit our colored people, fostering self-respect, and encouraging them to show themselves worthy of freedom, franchise, and every privilege they enjoy. All these renters should plant some cane; 10 to 20 acres each. This could be hauled to the mill and thus give the miller plenty of business. Then we shall have the renters on the Orphans Home place, and send the cane to *John's* mill. . . . I hope others will come. It is important that the adjoining places, above and below (Fusiliers and Hardins) get into the right hands. They are beautiful plantations, and will now sell cheap. . . . They are very large places and several persons might unite in the purchase. This would give us and our friends the whole strip of Bayou between the Indian and Irish Bends, with land on *both sides*, altogether making a splendid town site.

R. K. Diossy to John Baldwin, Franklin, St. Mary's Louisiana, September 3, 1867, John Baldwin Papers, Western Reserve Historical Society Library, Cleveland, Ohio (hereafter cited as Baldwin Papers). Compare the letter of W. H. Gray to Baldwin inquiring on behalf of some people in Bethel, Maine, the terms on which Baldwin was renting land. Gray was convinced that the Maine farmers "are the right material to make a prosperous and virtuous community. If they can only be induced to settle in that heretofore rebel ridden country the results for good would be almost incalculable." W. H. Gray to Baldwin, Bethel, Maine, June 16, 1869, ibid. According to Morrow, Baldwin's enterprise went bankrupt in 1877. *Northern Methodism and Reconstruction*, 175.

[25]Resolutions of meeting and board of trustees of Thomson University, New Orleans, January 29, 1868, Baldwin Papers. See also the following other items in the Baldwin Papers: N. L. Brakeman to Baldwin, July 17 and 22, 1867; Newman to Baldwin, New Orleans, July 28, 1867; R. S. Rust to Baldwin, Cincinnati, November 2, 1867; J. S. Leavitt to Baldwin, New Orleans, March 12 and November 7, 1873; Minutes of meeting of Board of Trustees of Thomson University, New Orleans, January 11, 1871.

[26]S. L. Beiler to Baldwin, Thomson University, Baldwin, Louisiana, May 16, 1871, ibid.; Beiler to Hartzell, Baldwin, April 27 and May 28, 1871, Hartzell Papers.

[27]R. S. Rust to Baldwin, Cincinnati, November 9, 1870, Baldwin Papers.

[28]Jay S. Stowell, *Methodist Adventures in Negro Education* (New York, 1922), 111; White, *Freedmen's Bureau in Louisiana*, 191; Dwight Oliver Wendell Holmes, *The Evolution of the Negro College* (New York, 1934), 192-4.

[29]Morrow, *Northern Methodism and Reconstruction*, 161; A. D. Mayo, "The Work of Certain Northern Churches in the Education of the Freedmen, 1861-1900," in *Report of the Commissioner of Education for the Year 1902*, 2 vols. (Washington, D. C., 1903), 1:296.

[30]Morrow, *Northern Methodism and Reconstruction*, 171.

[31]Quoted in Mayo, "Work of Northern Churches," 296.

[32]Rosetta Coit to Hartzell, Hasting's Center, New York, July 23, 1870, Hartzell Papers.

[33]Mayo, "Work of Northern Churches," 290.

[34]Rosetta Coit to Hartzell, Hasting's Center, New York, September 14, 1870, Hartzell Papers.

[35]Stowell, *Methodist Adventures in Negro Education*, 112-3; White, *Freedmen's Bureau in Louisiana*, 79, 81-2. Like John Baldwin, the managers of the Orphans Home Society, which sponsored the orphanage, rented out land to farmers, furnishings, cabins and sugarcane for planting in return for a portion of the crop. See W. H. Gray to Baldwin, Bethel, Maine, August 16, 1869, Baldwin Papers.

[36]Emerson Bentley to Hartzell, Baldwin, September 30, 1870, Hartzell Papers. See also Bentley to Hartzell, Baldwin, June 27 and July 17, 1870, ibid. According to C. Howard Nichols, Bentley became a prominent Republican and newspaper editor in Louisiana during Reconstruction.

[37]S. L. Beiler to Hartzell, Baldwin, May 28, 1871, and see also Beiler to Hartzell, Baldwin, April 27, 1871, Hartzell Papers.

[38]Newman to Hartzell, Washington, D. C., November 15 and 16, 1871, ibid. *Edwards' Directory, 1870* lists a George Boiner as colored porter.

[39]W. H. Gray to Baldwin, Baldwin, Louisiana, May 17, 1871, Baldwin Papers.

[40]Hartzell to Newman, February 13, 1871, Hartzell Papers.

[41]See, for example, Morrow, *Northern Methodism and Reconstruction*, 228, 246.

[42]During the late 1870s and early 1880s Hartzell served as presiding elder of districts in the Louisiana Conference, editor of *Southwestern Christian Advocate*, and assistant secretary of the Freedmen's Aid Society. The Methodist General Conference of 1888 elected him corresponding secretary of the Freedmen's Aid and Southern Education Society. In 1896 he became Missionary Bishop for Africa, an office which he held until retirement in 1916. Inventory Folder, Hartzell Papers. For information on Hartzell's activities as Missionary Bishop, see Mary Searles, "Letters of a Missionary Bishop in Africa," *World Outlook*, 29 (1939); on his religious and educational activities in Louisiana during the late 1870s and 1880s, see Barbara Myers Swartz, "The Lord's Carpetbagger: A Biography of Joseph Crane Hartzell" (Ph.D. dissertation, State University of New York at Stony Brook, 1972).

A PATRIOT, A PRIEST, AND A PRELATE: BLACK CATHOLIC ACTIVISM IN CIVIL WAR NEW ORLEANS*

Stephen J. Ochs

The lives of three very different men converged on Wednesday afternoon, July 29, 1863, a hot, humid, oppressive day so typical of New Orleans in the summertime. That of Capt. André Cailloux, a thirty-eight-year-old black Catholic, had ended two months earlier, on May 27, 1863, as he gallantly led Company E of the First Regiment Louisiana Native Guards in an assault on the Confederate fortress at Port Hudson, Louisiana. He would be buried that day in the Federal-occupied city, the first black war hero of the Civil War and an officer in the overwhelmingly Catholic First Regiment of Louisiana Native Guards, the first black regiment to be mustered into the United States Army and the first to engage in a major battle.

The priest who would officiate at the funeral was French-born Claude Paschal Maistre, the lone champion of racial egalitarianism among the local Catholic clergy and one of the relatively few Catholic abolitionists in the nation. He would perform the funeral rites of his church in defiance of New Orleans' formidable archbishop, Jean-Marie Odin, who, like Maistre, was also a native of France, but who, unlike the priest, and like most white New Orleanians, was a Confederate sympathizer. Two months earlier, Odin had suspended Maistre and had placed his parish church, St. Rose of Lima, under interdict in reprisal for Maistre's refusal to desist from advocating emancipation and equal rights for blacks, in Odin's view, "inciting Negroes." The huge crowds of people of color who gathered for the service and who lined the route of the funeral procession to pay their respects did so in defiance of Odin's interdict. They knew that by their participation they also could incur an ecclesiastical penalty that, according to the archbishop's edict, could be removed only by him personally.

A patriot, a priest, a prelate: the intersection of their lives highlights the unique historical experience of Catholics of color in New Orleans, one of the largest and most dynamic of the diverse black Catholic communities in the United States. Throughout the second half of the nineteenth century, these black Creoles, as they were known, played a

*First published in *U. S. Catholic Historian*, 12 (1994): 49-75. Reprinted with the kind permission of the author and the publisher.

leading role in the struggle for racial justice in church and state. Cailloux's funeral dramatized their resilient, sometimes defiant, Catholic identity, an identity rooted in a French Catholic tradition, personified by Maistre, that supported their aspirations for freedom and equality. The interplay of the stories of Cailloux, Maistre, and Odin underscores what historian Randall Miller has called the "failed mission"[1] of the nineteenth-century church in the United States to people of color, a failure characterized not only by institutional opposition to racial equality, but also by repression of those few white clerics who challenged racial orthodoxy by allying themselves with black aspirations for freedom.

II

Cailloux's death had a profound impact on people of color in New Orleans. *The Daily Picayune* reported an "unprecedentedly large" turnout of blacks for the funeral, by far the largest public event since the burial of the first rebel Louisiana officer killed in the war. To blacks, this funeral for one of their own attested to their capacity for patriotism, courage, and martial valor. They also intended the public tribute to atone for the desecration that had been visited upon Cailloux's corpse, which had lain rotting on the battlefield for forty-one days until the surrender of the fortress on July 8. Meanwhile, as word of his death filtered back to New Orleans, women of color donned crepe rosettes in mourning. Immediately after the Confederate capitulation, Cailloux's body, identifiable only because he wore the ring of the Friends of the Order (probably a Masonic lodge), was recovered and was sent to New Orleans via the steamer *Old Essex*.

Arriving on July 25, the body lay in state for four days in the hall of the Friends of the Order where Cailloux had been a leading member. The coffin was draped with the American flag, on which rested Cailloux's sword and belt, uniform coat and cap. Flowers were strewn in profusion around the coffin and candles were kept burning in strict observance of Catholic rule as a guard solemnly paced to and fro.

At the appointed time on July 29, the band of the 42nd Massachusetts Regiment made its appearance, and "played the customary solemn airs." According to a witness reporting for the *New York Times*, Father Maistre, the officiating priest, performed the Catholic service for the dead. The clergyman then delivered a glowing and eloquent eulogy on the virtues of the deceased. He called upon all present to offer themselves, like Cailloux, as martyrs to the cause of justice, freedom, and good government, and he characterized Cailloux's death as one that the proudest might envy.

Immense crowds of people of color had, by this time, gathered around the building, rendering impassable the surrounding streets. Two companies of the Sixth Louisiana (colored) regiment acted as an escort while representatives of over thirty black male and female mutual aid, fraternal, and religious societies lined Esplanade Avenue for more than a mile, waiting for the hearse to pass through. The vast majority of the organizations bore the names of saints (viz. St. Alphonsus Society), were clearly Catholic, and witnessed to the rich communal life of the Creoles of Color.

The procession to the cemetery included a large number of black officers and also the carriage bearing Cailloux's widow, Félicie Cailloux, and their children. Thousands of people, born in slavery and disenthralled enough by the events of the war to appear in the city's streets, waved miniature flags in their hands, or wore them tastefully on their persons.

After moving through the principal downtown streets, the body was taken to the "Bienville Street" cemetery (probably St. Louis #2) and was interred there with military honors. Since ecclesiastical censure prevented Maistre from securing the aid of any other priests or assistants, he turned to Col. Spencer H. Stafford, commander of the First Louisiana Native Guards, who had bragged that his regiment represented so many trades and professions that he could build a town on the prairie in sixty days. Two privates immediately volunteered and helped at the graveyard services. A private of the regiment also left the ranks to perform the duties of bricklayer in constructing the tomb, which was built above ground.[2]

Northern newspapers such as the *New York Times*, the *Herald*, and *Harper's Weekly*, which had urged the use of black combat troops in the war, gave extensive coverage to Cailloux's funeral. The *Times* correspondent noted that the scene called forth a single sentiment in those who witnessed it: "the struggle must go on until there is not legally a slave under the folds of the American flag."[3] *L'Union, a* newspaper published in New Orleans by free people of color, observed that "In Captain Cailloux the cause of the Union and freedom has lost a valuable friend" [who] had defended the cause of liberty and whose demonstrated valor, patriotism and courage had "vindicated his race from the opprobrium with which it was charged." In New Orleans, the American flag remained at half mast in Cailloux's honor for thirty days and people of color formed Cailloux Societies to support the cause of the Union, of emancipation. and of equal rights. Cailloux was memorialized in an ode by popular poet George H. Boker, and thirty years later, Rodolphe L. Desdunes, in a history of New Orleans Creoles of Color, recalled him as "this American Sparticus" who had proved that "the black man is able to fight and die for his country."[4]

III

This man, whose life and death came to symbolize so much to so many, was, like most of his 11,000 fellow free people of color in New Orleans in 1860, Afro-French in ancestry, French in culture, and Catholic in religion. Unlike the majority of free people of color, however, he was born a slave. His mother was Josephine, a slave of Joseph Duvernay, a planter in Plaquemines Parish, south of New Orleans. His father, André Cailloux, about whom little is known, was probably a black man, judging from his son's ebony complexion. According to tradition, young André's forebears came from St. Domingue (Haiti) as part of the mass emigration that brought thousands of whites, free blacks, and slaves to Louisiana to escape revolutionary turmoil between 1791 and 1810. André was born on August 25, 1825 and baptized at St. Louis Cathedral on July 15, 1827. His godparents, Bernard and Antoinette, were also slaves.[5]

Joseph Duvernay, André's first master, was a member of a large clan with many branches (white and mixed-race) spread throughout Orleans, Plaquemines and St. Charles civil parishes. Joseph fathered at least one other natural son by Josephine: André's half-brother Antoine, whom he freed at baptism in 1827. It was probably as a result of Joseph Duvernay's premature death at the age of 32 in 1828 that André passed into the possession of Duvernay's sister, Aimée, and her husband, Mathieu Larthet (also spelled Lartet), who resided in the second municipality in New Orleans at the corner of Girod and Carondolet streets. Whether at this time André and his mother were separated is unclear, but at some point, the two were parted and she became the property of Charles P. Daunoy. As André grew to maturity, he learned the cigar-making trade, quite possibly from members of the colored branch of the Duvernay family, such as Molière Duvernay, Aimée's nephew, many of whom were cigar-makers. As an artisan, young André would probably have been "hired out" by his master to cigar-making establishments for a fee.[6]

André so pleased his master and his mistress that they decided to manumit both him and a fellow slave named John. Aimée declared in a petition that "both slaves form part of a family of slaves who have always given much satisfaction by their good behavior" and that she desired to emancipate them in return for their good services and those of their family. She assured the court that both bondsmen were fully capable of earning their livelihood as cigar-makers. C. S. Léonard, a commissioner of the second ward of the second municipality who had lived in the same square as the two slaves for several years, testified to their industry, sobriety, and perseverance and expressed confidence that they possessed the skills by which they could maintain themselves and achieve affluence in a few years. After meeting all of the requirements of law, Aimée and Matthew freed André on July 8, 1846. Since André declared that he could not write, he made his mark on the notarial document and moved into the ranks of New Orleans' large population of free people of color.[7]

Free people of color, or colored Creoles, in antebellum Louisiana occupied an anomalous position legally and socially between whites and slaves in a tri-partite caste system. Though they lacked political rights, they could own property, make contracts, and testify in court against whites. They were easily the most prosperous free black population in the United States. On the eve of the Civil War, a majority were artisans, professionals, and proprietors; many even were slave owners. In 1850, Cailloux was one of 156 colored Creole cigar-makers in New Orleans, the third largest group of artisans after carpenters and masons. He, like many of his fellow Creoles, had secured a dominant position in occupations that were closed to people of color in Anglo-America. Most but by no means all Creoles of Color were mixed-blood; but they ran the spectrum of skin color. Cailloux, for example, took great pride in his ebony hue and liked to boast that he was the blackest man in the Crescent City.[8]

The overwhelming majority of free people of color were Catholic. Culturally and religiously they were part of the French world. Their Gallic Catholicism, with its tinge of anti-clericalism, tended to emphasize communal activity and celebration organized around holy days and patron saints rather than a rigorous adherence to rules of conduct or to dogma. They sought the church, especially at critical transitions such as birth, marriage, death (as is evident from the sacramental registers of Catholic parishes in New Orleans, such as St. Louis Cathedral, St. Augustine's, and St. Mary's Chapel adjoining the former Ursulines Convent), and at times of communal festivals.

Their religion helped to shape their individual and group identity and to give meaning and dignity to their lives. It also produced vocations. From their ranks in 1842 rose a congregation of women religious: the Sisters of the Holy Family. Free people of color also established and supported Catholic schools in which catechism was regularly taught. The most famous of these was *L'Institution Catholique des Orphelins Indigènes* (Catholic Institute for Indigent Orphans or *Institut Catholique*) whose faculty included Creole intellectuals, poets, novelists and dramatists and whose students included children of the Creole elite. (The first principal of the Institute in 1848 was Félicie Cailloux: "an exceedingly intelligent, highly respected, and devout Catholic" woman, whose relationship to André Cailloux is unclear.[9] Those Creoles who could afford to do so often sent their sons to study in France. The French cultural connection introduced colored Creole leaders to the radical currents associated with the 1848 Revolution, which had led to the abolition of slavery and to the grant of universal suffrage to former slaves throughout the French empire in 1850. Some French bishops also embraced emancipation. The provincial council of Bordeaux, in 1853, for example, had condemned slavery. The most prominent French Catholic clerical opponent of human bondage was the bishop of Orleans, Félix Antoine-Philibert Dupanloup (1802-1878).[10]

Catholic Creoles of Color formed numerous religious, fraternal, social, occupational, and mutual aid societies, many of which turned out *en masse* for Cailloux's funeral. They also contributed to building funds for parish churches such as St. Augustine (which opened in 1842), but they were required to sit in separate pews from whites (to whom they were often related); slaves sat in galleries or on the side on benches. Diocesan regulations required separate sacramental registers for whites, slaves, and free persons of color.[11]

The relationship between free people of color and slaves was complex and never as simple as a division between light and dark complexion. Some free people of color owned slaves for economic reasons and emphasized the social distance between themselves and their slaves by zealously guarding their separate church seating. But many free persons of color, such as Cailloux, were only recently removed from slavery. Free people of color fraternized, cohabited, and intermarried with Francophone slaves and also formed benevolent organizations, such as the *Société des Artisans de Bienfaisance et d'Assistance Mutuelle* (1834) and *Dieu Nous Protège* (1844), to help blacks purchase their own or their families' freedom. One of the most devout of the religious confraternities, the all-male Christian Doctrine Society of New Orleans, made the evangelization and spiritual care of blacks its major practical work.[12]

Cailloux's life reflected the above complexities. A Catholic former slave, who spoke both French and English, he married a French-speaking ex-slave, Félicie (sometimes referred to in legal and ecclesiastical records as Félicité or Louise Félicité) Coulon on June 22, 1847, in the church of St. Mary's Assumption in the town of Lafayette, an up-river suburb of New Orleans that was annexed by the city in 1852.[13] Félicie had been born about 1818 at Grande Isle, a barrier island in the Barataria region near the mouth of the Mississippi River, to Féliciana, a slave of Valentin Encalada. Féliciana had cohabitated for a time with her master and had borne him a son. Félicie's father, Antoine Coulon, was probably a slave of the Coulon family of Grand Isle. She owed her freedom to her mother, a remarkable woman who, receiving her freedom in New Orleans from Encalada in 1835, had acquired cash and real estate in Lafayette. She had purchased her daughter, along with the daughter's natural son Louis and another male slave from Encalada in 1841 for $1,200. Five years later, in December 1846, the same year that André Cailloux secured his freedom, Féliciana Encalada (as she was now known) obtained permission from the police jury to free her daughter and her grandson, now identified as Jean Louis. Féliciana attested to Félicie's ability to earn her own livelihood and further stated her intention to provide for the support of Jean Louis until he was able to maintain himself. André Cailloux's former owner, Mathieu Larthet, with whom Féliciana had business dealings, testified to Félicie's good character and conduct.[14]

Larthet and Féliciana were probably cooperating in these manumissions because they knew that André and Félicie wished to marry. On April 18, 1847, André and Félicie signed a marriage contract. In it, they expressed their intention to legitimize "their" six-year-old natural son, Jean Louis, thus ensuring to him the advantages that the law extended to legitimate children. Jean Louis's baptismal certificate from St. Louis Cathedral, dated April 3, 1839, identifies another man, Antoine Philippe, as his father. This suggests that either André begot Jean Louis at the tender age of fourteen and Félicie named the wrong man as father, or, as seems more likely, André recognized another's child as his own, in essence adopting Jean Louis and making him legitimate. By the time of his marriage, André (though not Félicie) could sign his name, in a somewhat large, unsteady hand, and apparently had entered the ranks of the estimated 80 percent of free people of color who could do so.[15]

In 1848, Cailloux also became a property-holder, purchasing a small $200 lot on New Orleans Street in the American-dominated Second Municipality from Mathieu Larthet. In doing so, he reflected the tendency among Creoles of Color to invest their surplus cash in real estate. The 1852 New Orleans directory listed André as a cigar-maker on Perdido Street between Adeline and St. Jane Streets. He was hard-working and ambitious — a self-made man determined to better his lot in life.[16]

The young artisan also became a slaveholder. On January 22, 1849, he paid Charles F. Daunoy, a state senator from New Orleans, $100 cash for a female slave. Slaveholding by people of color was not uncommon: in 1860 over 700 in Louisiana owned slaves, most fewer than five. The motives of colored Creole slaveholders were mixed. Some purchased family members with an eye to freeing them: others bought, sold, and held slaves for economic gain or as domestic servants. Cailloux fell into the first category. For the forty-five-year-old woman whom he purchased from Daunoy was his mother, Josephine. Cailloux acquired her for cash and with the understanding "that said purchaser shall emancipate and set free the said slave 'Josephine,' as soon as practicable. . . ." On August 20, 1850, the Caillouxs added another member to the family, a baby daughter named Athalie Clémence.[17]

By the mid-1850s, Cailloux had sold his first lot and with an assist from his mother-in-law had purchased another, slightly larger, one that had once belonged to Féliciana. It was on Coffee Street (subsequently renamed Bacchus and then Baronne) in the former faubourg (suburb) Lafayette. The Cailloux family lived in a modest house in a racially and economically diverse square bounded by Dryades, Philip, and Jackson streets. The property owners in the square included seven whites (one whose real estate was assessed at $8,000) and at least two other free men of color, including André's brother-in-law, Bastien Encalada. On May 6, 1857, in the Coffee Street house, a second daughter, Odile, was born. The following month, her parents had her baptized at St. Theresa of Avila church.[18]

Cailloux was a respected but struggling artisan who, by 1858, was producing cigars in a shop at Union (Touro) and Casacalvo (Royal) streets, two blocks downriver from the *Vieux Carré*, or French Quarter. He was not a man of wealth and property. He bought tobacco on credit and did not have access to much ready cash. Owning real estate that was assessed for tax purposes at $500 in 1860, he fell far short of the $2,000 benchmark that signified "relatively prosperous." His property was also heavily mortgaged, and in 1856, in 1859, and again in 1860, he was forced to borrow money against it, usually at six-percent interest, to cover notes that fell due. His sterling reputation for integrity undoubtedly enabled him to obtain the loans. But in 1856 and in 1857, the city of New Orleans attached small liens to Cailloux's property for past due taxes. In addition, he found himself enmeshed in a lawsuit which, although he eventually won, dragged on for two years.[19]

Cailloux also faced increased competition from other Creole and foreign-born artisans and from businessmen such as Lucien Mansion and George Alcée, who operated sizable cigar factories. Indeed, the relatively privileged position of free people of color in Louisiana society became more tenuous after 1852 as sectional tensions grew. An expanding number of whites demanded the expulsion or re-enslavement of the free black population and the state legislature considered repressive measures aimed at them.[20]

Six months after the attack on Fort Sumter plunged the nation into civil war, Cailloux sold his property on Baronne Street. The buyer was James P. Fréret, a noted architect, who paid $1,070, or over three times what Cailloux had paid. Fréret gave Cailloux $200 in cash and agreed to assume Cailloux's outstanding $400 note. Fréret also signed a promissory note to Cailloux for the remaining balance of $470, which he finally paid off on August 19, 1864. Cailloux probably rented lodging for his family after the sale, perhaps above his shop at Union and Casacalvo streets.[21]

Meanwhile, Cailloux and numerous other free people of color had responded to the governor's call to organize a militia regiment for the defense of the state. The result was an organization designated the First Native Guards, Louisiana Militia, Confederate States of America. Though a few of the colored Creoles may have been Confederate sympathizers, most probably joined in the hope of improving their increasingly threatened civil and political status by demonstrating their loyalty to the state as their forbears had earlier done, first under the French and Spanish, and then later under Andrew Jackson at the Battle of New Orleans. They may also have been reacting to veiled threats of property confiscation and bodily harm if they failed to "volunteer." Cailloux's rank of first lieutenant of Order Company indicated the respect and esteem that he enjoyed among his peers.[22] The name of Cailloux's unit also suggested a link between its members and one of the Masonic lodges in the city known as *Los Amigos del Orden* (The Friends of the Order). Despite ecclesiastical opposition, membership in Masonic lodges was common among Catholic free people of color who were influenced by radical French movements associated with the Revolution of 1848 and who saw no incompatibility between their Catholicism and the professed humanism and brotherhood of the masonic lodges.[23]

The thirteen companies of Louisiana Native Guards, about 900 strong, busied themselves with drills and parades and participated in large Confederate troop reviews in November, 1861, and in January, 1862. They inspired pride in the Creole community and fired the imaginations of students at the *Institut Catholique*, who recorded their impressions in weekly English compositions that were transcribed in copybooks. In February, 1862, officers (presumably including Cailloux) and members of his Order company assisted at a "grand mass" at Annunciation Church that celebrated, according to the student chronicler, the anniversary of the "True Friends" (probably the Friends of the Order), from whose membership the Order company had apparently been formed. Morning reports of the regiment, however, indicated that "The number of absentees is large owing to the fact that many have not their uniforms." Many also lacked muskets.[24]

The Confederacy placed little confidence or trust in the Native Guards, limiting their military service to training and ceremonial duties. Their suspicions may have been confirmed when Federal troops under Gen. Benjamin F. Butler occupied the city on May 1, 1861 and the Native Guards did not withdraw along with other Confederate forces. Rather, through a committee, they offered their services to the Federal cause. Butler, though impressed by the intelligence and sincerity of the Creole officers, initially demurred. But Confederate Gen. John C. Breckenridge's attack on Baton Rouge in August 1863, which seemed to presage an attack on New Orleans, convinced Butler of the necessity of raising additional troops to defend the city. He therefore decided to "call on Africa" by issuing General Order No. 63 on August 22, 1862, which authorized the recruitment of three regiments of free people of color. According to J. B. Roudanez, a mechanical engineer, within forty-eight hours, more than one hundred shops and businesses of free people of color were closed as men rushed to enlist, encouraged no doubt, by promises of bounties, rations for families and equal pay with white soldiers.[25]

As they had done under the Confederates, leading and respected free people of color, such as Cailloux, raised companies and served as officers (one captain and two lieutenants per company). On September 27, 1862, ten companies were mustered into the service as the First Louisiana Native Guard Infantry (approximately 1,000 strong). Two other regiments of Native Guards (the Second and Third regiments, composed largely of freedmen) were also organized shortly thereafter. Capt. André Cailloux of E company was one of the First Regiment's nineteen company officers: the field officers, such as Spencer H. Stafford, colonel commanding, were white. The muster roll for Cailloux's company, dated September 27, 1862, lists 82 privates, two musicians, eight corporals, five sergeants, and three officers, for a total of one hundred men.[26] Colored Creoles viewed the First Regiment as uniquely their own and flocked to Camp Strong Station on Gentilly Road, where the regiment trained, to view the daily drill and the dress parades. The charismatic, thirty-eight-year-old Cailloux was one of the regiment's toughest, most effective, and most striking officers. (He was also one of its oldest, since the average age of the black company officers was thirty.) Polished in manners, athletic, and daring, he was, according to contemporaries, a born leader and "a fine looking man who presented an imposing appearance" and commanded attention.[27] Attributes of character rather than economic or social position accounted for his prominence.

Most of the men of the First Regiment shared Cailloux's Catholicism. Colonel Stafford recognized this in December 1862, when he recommended that the appointed regimental chaplain, a Methodist preacher named Asa Barnes, be promoted to major. Stafford explained that "As most of my men are French Catholics, we have no use for a protestant chaplain . . . ." Certainly the men saw little of Barnes. One of them recalled years later that Barnes came around only "once every other month." Later in the war, even after desertions, casualties, transfers, enlistments and inductees had diluted the Catholicity of the regiment, Barnes' successor, the Rev. Samuel S. Gardner, a Presbyterian minister, noted that, unlike some other black regiments with which he was acquainted, "Night exhortations in the open air are not held. . . ."[28]

The First Regiment was composed, for the most part, of free people of color, many of whom were mulattos. Twenty percent had been bricklayers, 15 percent carpenters, 12 percent cigar-makers, 6 percent shoemakers and 45 percent laborers. Some members of the regiment, however, were also escaped slaves, who had flocked to the city after its surrender to the Federals and who swore on enlistment, often using aliases, that they were free. Hilaire Zénon, for example, a member of E Company, recalled that "I was a slave before the war and until I enlisted. Many men in our regiment were slaves but all were put down as free men." Cailloux apparently cooperated in this subterfuge, since he personally enrolled the members of his company and counted many of them as friends and acquaintances drawn from the tightly-knit colored Creole community.[29] He almost certainly recognized any who were not legally free, but did not balk at enlisting them. Indeed, in his person, he appeared to reconcile both slave and free, black and mulatto. His life suggests that the boundary between slaves and free people of color was more permeable than some historians have maintained. The absence of conflict within the First Regiment based on ethnicity or color further confirms this. A common agenda of liberation bound their ranks and held out the promise of cooperation between free people of color and freedmen in the postwar struggle for equality.[30]

A student at the *Institut Catholique* captured that spirit in a letter to a friend in November 1862. Implicitly recognizing an inner logic and inevitability to the war, L. Lamanière wrote that he was "very glad since the Federals are here, [*sic*] they are telling that General Butler is going to make the colored men of this city who were born free vote, [*sic*] if he does that the colored men will be very glad to see equality reign here and if he is ever to be elected President of the United States, [*sic*] I am sure that he will be President because the colored man will vote for him. And I must tell you another thing. The [white] Creoles of this city will die when they see the Negroes vote as well as them, [*sic*] those Negroes whom they were always whipping in the plantations take their tickets and put it in the [ballot] box. . . ."[31] The student had conflated the rights of free people of color and of freedmen and now interpreted the war, at least implicitly, as a struggle for emancipation and equality. Colored Creole activists, such as Paul Trévigne, who began to publish *L'Union* in the same month that the First Regiment was mustered into service, viewed black participation in the war as a vehicle for obtaining equal rights. An editorial declared that "From the day that bayonets were placed in the hands of the blacks . . . the Negro became a citizen of the United States."[32]

While the First Regiment trained at Camp Strong, which lay north of St. Rose of Lima church, his church on Bayou Road, the forty-one-year-old priest Claude Paschal Maistre visited the troops, ministering especially to the sick. (Camp fevers were a great menace throughout the war). Maistre's priestly career had been tainted by the scent of scandal since his arrival in 1851 in the United States from the diocese of Troyes in France where he had run afoul of the law. Expelled from the dioceses of Detroit and Chicago on charges of immorality, indifferentism, and simony, he had come to the New Orleans archdiocese in 1855. After several assignments and after alienating several fellow priests (one of whom complained in 1856 that he spouted abolitionist doctrine), Maistre had received an appointment in 1857 as the first pastor of St. Rose of Lima parish from Archbishop Antoine Blanc. In that capacity, he erected a small frame church that held fewer than forty pews.[33]

As pastor of the racially mixed congregation of St. Rose, Maistre showed great interest in the free people of color, especially encouraging the formation among them of quasi-religious benevolent societies, the first being *La Société des Soeurs de la Providence*. These sponsored special high masses and usually took up collections for worthy causes. They afforded, in the words of one historian, "opportunities for common action, solidarity and communication." Emboldened by the Federal occupation of New Orleans, and perhaps influenced by Bishop Dupanloup's well publicized pastoral letter of April 6, 1862, which condemned slavery as a violation of both the unity of the human family and the law of love. Maistre became increasingly outspoken in his support of emancipation and racial equality. In December 1862, in defiance of diocesan regulations, he wrote in the parish registers "Nota Bena—From the date of January 1, 1863, acts (baptisms and marriages) for persons of color will be found inscribed in the principal register without discrimination, together with whites." He also assisted desperate black refugees, some of whom were still legally slaves. Maistre later charged that the local clergy refused absolution and the last sacraments to them unless they consented to return to their former masters.[34]

Maistre's opinions and actions angered his fellow priests. The clergy of the city, from archbishop down, were overwhelmingly pro-Confederate. Odin, the former bishop of Galveston, had been installed as archbishop in May 1861, shortly after the war had begun. A prelate of unyielding attitude and determination, he ruled by the letter of the law and set out to establish discipline and regularity in what had been an unruly diocese; he also publicly supported the Confederate cause, asserting in an 1862 pastoral letter that justice lay on the side of the South. Odin appealed for chaplains for Louisiana forces and at least ten priests answered his call. Absent from the city when it fell to Union forces, he maintained a cool and civil relationship with the occupation authorities after his return. They in turn, treated him respectfully while keeping him under surveillance. Napoleon L. Perche, editor of the diocesan newspaper *Le Propagateur Catholique*, however, was so outspokenly pro-Confederate in the pages of the paper that Federal officials suspended it and placed him under house arrest for a time.[35]

The sight of colored Creoles sporting Federal uniforms particularly outraged some Catholic clergy. When the Native Guards had born arms for the Confederacy, priests had blessed their regimental and company flags and the archbishop had urged them to fight valiantly. All that changed when they donned Federal blue. Vicar General Etienne Rousselon expressed fear that "A new San Domingo" [a reference to the bloody slave uprising in Haiti at the turn of the century] was in the offing. According to *L'Union*, some priests voiced their opposition to racial equality in front of Creole children during catechism classes. Soldiers were spat upon and church doors were closed to them. Several families allegedly encountered difficulty in securing church burials for troops who had died in camp and only fear of scandal resolved the matter. One soldier, who had confessed the previous day, was refused communion at Mass because he wore a Federal uniform. Women, with parents and husbands in the Native Guards, banded together and requested that a mass be sung for the protection of their loved ones. Their parish priest responded that he would gladly sing a mass for those same soldiers if it were a funeral service. Knowing the rebel sympathies and the hostile sentiments of neighboring priests, they turned to Maistre at St. Rose. Their presence in the church frightened the white parishioners and led many to abandon the chapel. Maistre, however, sang the Mass and preached a consoling sermon on the love of God, the love of neighbor, and the benefits of unity and peace. Not surprisingly, no priests of the archdiocese accompanied any of the three units of Native Guards when they left the city in late October.[36]

The hostility of the Catholic clergy was simply a manifestation of the animosity felt by the majority of white New Orleanians toward the Native Guards. According to one lieutenant in the regiment, "When we enlisted we were hooted at in the streets of New Orleans as rabble. . . ." The men were, according to their commanding colonel, grossly insulted and provoked in the streets. Their families were harassed by white landlords and those men married to slave women were often denied access to their families by masters. The government failed to deliver on Butler's pledge of a land or cash bounty. Thirty-eight dollars in advance, and thirteen dollars per month for enlisted men. Indeed, they received no pay until February 1863. Rations, which had been promised for the soldiers' families and that were to be distributed by relief committees, proved sub-standard.[37]

Soldiers of the First Regiment also had to endure suspicion, hostility, and harassment from Union officers and enlisted men. Staff officers threw impediments in the way of procuring supplies and equipment. Ordered into the Bayou Lafourche to reopen rail communications, the regiment spent most of its time on backbreaking fatigue and guard duty to the detriment of its combat training. The assignment of black troops to fatigue duty placed a stigma of inferiority on black regiments and reinforced doubts about their martial abilities. The *New York Tribune* on May 1, 1863, observed that loyal Northerners "have generally become willing that [blacks] should fight but the great majority have no faith that they will really do so. Many hope that they will prove cowards and sneaks—others greatly fear it."[38]

Further complicating matters was the implacable opposition shown to black officers by Gen. Nathaniel P. Banks, who replaced Butler in December 1862, as commander of the Department of the Gulf. In February 1863, he signaled his intention to remove the black officers from the Native Guard regiments and began forcing them out of service. Within eighteen months his purge was complete. He moved first, however, against the officers of the Third and Second regiments respectively. Cailloux and the officers of the First Regiment escaped the initial assault and in the late spring of 1863 still remained at their posts, yearning for an opportunity to prove their mettle.[39]

That opportunity came in May 1863. The First Louisiana advanced its part of General Banks' force against the Confederate bastion of Port Hudson, one of the last two Confederate strongholds on the Mississippi River (the other was Vicksburg), which was besieged in the last week of May. Early on the morning of May 27, the First and Third Native Guards, who were stationed on the far right of the Union line, were ordered to assault a virtually impregnable position of bluffs and rifle pits protected by swamp and a Rebel-engineered backwater from the Mississippi. Cailloux's Company E, the color company, would man the center of the regiment and lead its charge.

At roll call prior to the attack, Sgt. Anselmo Planciancios,[40] the color sergeant of Company E, accepted the regimental banners from his colonel, who ordered Planciancios to "protect, defend, die for, but do not surrender these flags." The men cheered his response: "Colonel, I will bring these colors in honor or report to God the reason why." Planciancios, who had been baptized forty-one years earlier that month at St. Louis Cathedral, would, later that day, make his report to God.

As the regiment advanced, Cailloux moved along the line encouraging his men both in English and in French. With the First Regiment leading the way, the entire force advanced in skirmish formation through the tangled woods. At 10 a.m. the bugle sounded and the regiment charged, emerging from the woods in good order, advancing first at quick and then double-quick time toward the bluff about 600 yards away. The First Native Guards led off, followed closely by the Third. Each regiment formed a long line, two ranks deep. The Confederates directed a withering fire of musketry and artillery at the advancing troops from a distance of about two hundred yards. The first volley threw them into confusion, but their officers rallied them for another charge. Confederate fire again broke the ranks and sent the men rushing for cover, but again their officers rallied them. This scene was repeated numerous times with the denouement played out as the regiment managed to approach the backflow, within two hundred yards of the main position.

At that point every available Confederate weapon that could be brought to bear opened up on the black phalanx. Only the availability of trees, stumps, and other obstacles prevented a complete slaughter. As it was, Cailloux and Planciancios were hit. Cailloux, his face ashen from the sulfurous smoke, his left arm dangling by his side, broken above the elbow by a ball, brandished his sword (one witness said a flag) in his right hand and hoarsely cheered on his men. His color company presented an inviting target for Rebel sharpshooters. As Cailloux moved in advance of his troops urging them to follow him across the flooded ditch, he was killed by a shell that struck him in the head. Planciancios, flourishing the flag, was also felled by a missile that cut the flag in two and carried away part of his skull. Two color corporals nearby struggled to raise the blood stained standard; one of them was wounded; the other shouldered it and bore it throughout the remainder of the battle. Second Lt. John Crowder was also killed.

The regiment fell back in disarray under a hail of Confederate artillery. While some officers vainly attempted to rally the troops among the willow trees, others evidently fled headlong into nearby swamps for cover and were subsequently dismissed from the service for cowardice. In the midst of a hail of shell and solid shot and lethal splinters from fragmenting trees, the regiment attempted to provide covering fire for some thirty to forty volunteers of the Third Regiment who attempted to ford the backwater and continue the attack. Only six of the volunteers returned alive. The attack was called off that evening.

The men of the First Regiment had demonstrated courage in desperate circumstances. They suffered only from the incompetence of their commanding general and the cowardice of their commanding colonel. In addition, they lacked preliminary intelligence of the dangerous terrain and failed to receive artillery and infantry support that had been promised. A *New York Times* correspondent noted that "In the midst of the carnage, when men in every form of horrible mutilation were being sent to the rear . . . —after fighting as few white men could have fought—not a single ambulance or stretcher was there to gather their torn and incarcerated bodies." Nor, parenthetically, was a priest present to tend to their spiritual needs.

During the truce of May 28, the remains of all the white soldiers were retrieved and buried. But the Louisiana Native Guards, including Cailloux, lay where they had fallen. The *New York Times* correspondent wrote that although "by a flag of truce our forces in other directions were permitted to reclaim their dead, the benefit, through some neglect was not extended to the black regiments." The unbearable stench led the Confederates to offer a truce for burial. General Banks, however, rebuffed the proposal, reportedly replying "that he had not dead there." So Cailloux and the rest lay where they fell until the surrender of the fortress.[41]

IV

Félicie Cailloux's choice of Father Maistre to conduct her husband's funeral represented both a religious and a political statement and reflected the extent to which the priest had become associated in the public mind with the cause of black liberation. To people of color he was a hero: a visible sign of that French Catholic tradition that embraced abolition and suffrage. To most white New Orleanians he was a pariah. A little more than a month before the First Regiment's assault on Port Hudson, Maistre celebrated a well-publicized high Mass at St. Rose that was attended by hundreds of people. The Mass was one of thanksgiving for the Emancipation Proclamation (which did not apply to large portions of Louisiana) and of petition for an end to slavery in Louisiana and in the nation. In his sermon, Maistre emphasized liberty as a gift from God, a theme that he would repeat countless times in succeeding years. Most white parishioners, repulsed by Maistre's abolitionism, had, by this time, left the parish. More dangerously, some hinted darkly at lynching, including one fellow priest, who declared that a cord would be too good for him—that his stole would suffice.[42]

Shortly thereafter, on Good Friday, April 1863, Archbishop Odin returned to New Orleans from Europe (where he had been since before the Union capture of the city) and heard accusations from clergy that Maistre had "incited the Negroes against the whites." In a later report to the Congregation of the Propaganda in Rome, under whose jurisdiction the American Church fell, Odin would charge that Maistre had offended white Catholics from St. Rose and had attracted a large number of slaves and persons of color "to whom he preached the love of liberty and independence" and whom he excited "to insurrection against their masters."

Seizing on the pretext of Maistre's earlier legal difficulties in France, which a priest of the diocese had made public at a gathering of clergy, and professing concern about possible public scandal, Odin demanded that Maistre leave his parish and repair to a monastery to do penance. When Maistre used his friendship with the chief Union military chaplain, a Protestant, to secure an "order" from the provost marshall to continue his ministry, Odin suspended him and placed the parish under interdict. Maistre, however, held the keys to St. Rose and continued to occupy the church until January 1864, when Odin finally prevailed upon the military authorities to compel the recalcitrant priest to vacate the premises.[43]

Meanwhile, Maistre, with the aid of lay trustees who included Charles Honoré, a prominent Creole figure in the Equal Rights League, constructed a new edifice on Ursulines and Claiborne streets called Holy Name of Jesus church. That the freedmen and colored Creoles alike regarded the schismatic priest as a hero was evident from the archbishop's contemptuous description of Maistre's congregation as "a great number of irreligious and ignorant Negroes who consider him as a virtuous persecuted victim for the love that he carried for their race." Yet baptisms at Holy Name of Jesus, almost all of them of blacks, jumped to 150 in 1864, up from 59 the previous year at St. Rose.

As the war ended, Maistre attempted to negotiate an end to the impasse with Odin that would allow him to remain in the archdiocese. In the spring of 1865, he appealed to Cardinal Alessandro Barnabò, prefect of the Congregation of the Propaganda, who advised him to submit "with complete docility of spirit," implying that Odin would show him mercy. Maistre then wrote to Odin begging his pardon for the pain that he had caused the archbishop and promising obedience and docility in the future. Odin, however, refused any compromise, insisting on Maistre's complete submission and on his departure from the archdiocese. A last meeting between the two men on February 19, 1866, ended in a shouting match, during which Maistre accused Odin of despotism.[44]

The standoff between the archbishop and the priest dragged on until 1870. Maistre's schismatic parish, based as it was on his standing among blacks, remained his sole bargaining chip with ecclesiastical authorities. He claimed that his ministry preserved the Catholicism of many blacks who had been scandalized by the behavior of Odin and his clergy and who threatened to leave the church. Thus, Maistre continued his highly visible alliance with the anticlerical Creole activists associated with *L'Union* and its successor, the *New Orleans Tribune*, who spearheaded the drive for equal rights and who bitterly attacked the archbishop and the local clergy for their racism. He chanted a *Te Deum* at Holy Name of Jesus in May 1864, on the occasion of the ratification of the state constitution that abolished slavery; offered the opening prayer at the founding convention of the Equal Rights League in Louisiana; marched at the head of his congregation at a mass meeting assembled in Congo Square to mourn President Lincoln's assassination; celebrated masses commemorating John Brown's death; and lent his presence to numerous other public gatherings of blacks.

Maistre's backing increased the other activists' credibility among Creole Catholics. By emphasizing his influential role among blacks, the radical press in turn strengthened his hand in future dealings with the archbishop. Maistre's appointment in 1870 as profes-

sor of modern languages in the collegiate department of newly founded and predominantly black Straight University underscored the esteem that he enjoyed among blacks,
especially among the Francophone Catholics who comprised a considerable segment of
the university's student population. His presence on the faculty of Straight, an institution
that was sponsored by the Congregationalist American Missionary Association, moreover, illustrated yet again his willingness to collaborate across racial and denominational
lines to promote black empowerment, this time through education. In June of that year,
in a rather remarkable gesture, the University chose Maistre to deliver one of the principal addresses at its first commencement exercises.[45]

That address however, was Maistre's valedictory. During the following month he
submitted finally to ecclesiastical authority in the person of a new archbishop, Napoleon
J. Perche. Odin's death and Perche's accession made possible a resolution of the schism
that Odin's intense personal animus toward Maistre had partly fueled. (Sacramental records also suggest that membership in Holy Name of Jesus parish had begun to decline
after 1867). Maistre worked out an arrangement with his old friend Perche that allowed
him to remain in the archdiocese. In a letter that appeared in the July 17, 1870 issue of
Le Propagateur Catholique, Maistre publicly disavowed his actions and submitted to
Perche. After some months of retreat and penance he was reinstated and was assigned to
a remote pastorate in Chacahoula, Louisiana, where he served until illness forced his return to New Orleans. He died there at the archbishop's residence on January 29, 1875, at
the age of 53.[46]

V

The patriot had perished; the priest had submitted; and the archbishop (or at least his
successor) had ostensibly won. Yet Cailloux's valor and Maistre's defiance had helped to
fuel a drive by Catholic people of color for equal rights, a drive that in December 1864,
saw nearly 1,000 of them sign a petition to President Lincoln and to Congress asking for
the right to vote. For a few brief years during Reconstruction, they won that political
equality but failed to convert their own church. In the post-Reconstruction South, as the
forces of disenfranchisement, violence, and segregation gained momentum, Catholic
people of color in New Orleans would once again stand against the gathering storm and
mount another campaign against discrimination in church and state. Men like Homer
Plessy, married at St. Augustine's Church in 1888, whose name would be immortalized in
the *Plessy v. Ferguson* case, could draw on the inspiration of Cailloux and the witness of
Maistre to insist to pastor and politician alike that caste, founded on prejudice against
color, violated a central concept of Christianity: its recognition of the common paternity
of the human race: that one could not be a true Christian, in the words of an editorial
from *L'Union*, "without adhering to that doctrine of love and charity which forms the
distinctive traits of the Christian philosophy."[47] In espousing those ideals, they per-

formed a prophetic role in church and society, a role that would be little recognized or appreciated until much later in the twentieth century.

Notes for "A Patriot, A Priest, and A Prelate: Black Catholic
Activism in Civil War New Orleans"

[1]Randall Miller, "The Failed Mission: The Catholic Church and Black Catholics in the Old South," in Randall M. Miller and Jon Wakelyn, (eds.), *Catholics in the Old South: Essays on Church and Culture* (Macon, 1983), 149-170.

[2]*New Orleans Daily Picayune*, July 30, 1863; David C. Edmonds, *The Guns of Port Hudson: The Investment, Siege and Reduction*, 2 vols. (Lafayette, La., 1984), 2:131, 377; deposition of Mary Lewis, June 26, 1894, in Pension File of John Louis, RG 15, National Archives (hereafter NA), Washington, D. C.; *Harper's Weekly*, August 29, 1863; *New York Times*, August 8 and August 9, 1863. The following societies participated in Cailloux's funeral: Friends of the Order, Society of Economy and Mutual Advance, United Brethren, Arts and Mechanics Association, Free Friends, Good Shepherd Conclave No. 2, Artisans Brotherhood, Good Shepherd Concalve No. 1, Union Sons' Relief, Perserverance Society, Ladies of Bon Secours, La Fleur de Marie, Saint Rose of Lima, Children of Mary Society, Saint Angela Society, the Sacred Union Society, the Children of Jesus, Saint Veronica Society, Saint Alphonsus Society, Saint Joachim Society, Star of the Cross, Saint Theresa Society, Saint Eulalia Society, Saint Magdalene Society, God Project Us Society, United Sisterhood, Angel Gabriel Society, Saint Louis Roi Society, Saint Benoit Society, Benevolence Society, Well Beloved Sisters' Society, Saint Peter Society, Saint Michael Archangel Society, Saint Louis de Gonzague Society, Saint Ann Society, the Children of Moses. See *Harper's Weekly*, August 29, 1863; and *New York Times*, August 8, 1863.

[3]*New York Times*, August 8, 1863. Opponents of the use of black troops also reported on Cailloux's funeral. The *New York World* mocked it in an article captioned: "A Defunct Darkey [illegible]." See *New York Times*, August 9, 1863, which reprinted the piece from the *World* as an example of Copperhead journalism.

[4]*L'Union* is quoted in *Harper's Weekly*, August 29, 1863; Ronald C. McConnell, "Louisiana's Black Military History, 1729-1865," in *Louisiana's Black Heritage*, eds. Robert R. Macdonald, John R. Kemp, Edward F. Haas (New Orleans, 1972), 60. Boker's poem appears in Joseph T. Wilson, *The Black Phalanx* (1890: repr. New York, 1968), 217; Rodolphe Lucien Desdunes, *Our People and Our History*, ed. and trans., Sister Dorothea Olga McCants (Baton Rouge, 1973), 125.

[5]H. E. Sterkx, *The Free Negro in Ante-bellum Louisiana* (Rutherford, 1972), 154. At the end of the French period in 1763, there were 165 free people of color in the colony of Louisiana. Manumissions and refugees from Saint-Domingue, and, to a lesser extent, natural increase helped to swell that number to 1,500 by 1803, of whom 1,200 lived in New Orleans. See, Jerah Johnson, "Colonial New Orleans," in *Creole New Orleans: Race and Americanization*, eds. Arnold R. Hirsch and Joseph Logsdon (Baton Rouge, 1992), 52-53. The last and largest wave of St. Domingue refugees reached New Orleans in 1809 and early 1810. Of the more than ten thousand emigres, 3,102 were free people of color and 3,226 were slaves. See Paul F. Lachance, "The Foreign French," in Hirsch and Logsdon, *Creole New Orleans*, 104-105. Baptismal Register of Mulattos and Negroes, St. Louis Cathedral Parish, vol. 20, 197, act 618, in Archives of the Archdiocese of New Orleans (hereafter AANO), New Orleans, Louisiana; Duvernay family history in the possession of Jack Belsom, New Orleans, Louisiana; Alice P. Dunbar, "People of Color in Louisiana," *Journal of Negro History*, 2 (1917): 69; Extract from the Register of the Acts of Marriage of the Church of the Assumption, June 22, 1847, in Pension Record of André Cailloux (misspelled Caillaux), RG 15, NA; Marriage Contract between André Cailloux and Louise Félicie Coulon, in Octave de Armas, vol. 40, #88, April 18, 1847, New Orleans Notarial Archives (hereafter NONA), New Orleans, Louisiana; Baptismal Register of Mulattos and Negroes, St. Louis Cathedral Parish, vol. 20, 197, act 618, AANO.

[6]See Manuscript Census of the United States, 1850; Duvernay family history; Vendee Book 1, 35-36, in Conveyance Office, Orleans Parish, New Orleans, Louisiana; Sale of slave to André Cailloux, in H. B. Cenas, Vol. 41, 505-507, January 22, 1849, NONA; *New Orleans City Directory*, 1849; Testament of Joseph Duvernay,

April 14, 1834, in L. T. Caire, Vol. 37, 376, NONA; Duvernay family history; Extract from the Register of Marriages of the Church of the Assumption, June 22, 1847, and sworn affadavit of Recorder of Births, Marriages and Deaths, Parish of Orleans, October 10, 1871, in Pension file of André Cailloux (misspelled Caillaux), RG 15, NA; Moliere Duvernay witnessed André Cailloux's marriage to Félicie Coulon; Richard C. Wade, *Slavery in the Cities* (New York, 1964), 38-54.

[7]Orleans Parish Police Jury, Petitions for the Emancipation of a Slave, Book C (vol. 3), October 10, 1845, and March 8, 1846, both in the Louisiana Collection (LC) of the New Orleans Parish Public Library, New Orleans, La.: *New Orleans Annual Directory and Commercial Register, 1846* (New Orleans, 1846); Act of Emancipation Aimée Duvernay to André, in Achille Chiapella, Volume 2, #233, July 8, 1846, NONA. Louisiana law required the approval of a police jury for the manumission of slaves born in Louisiana who were younger than thirty years-of-age. On March 8, 1846, the jury gave its unanimous approval and stipulated that André and John would not be required to leave the state. A printed notice in both French and English was then posted by the sheriff for forty days, during which time no one raised any legal objections and several residents and free holders of New Orleans testified to the good character of both slaves. André Cailloux's manumission reflected the increasing stagnation and subsequent decline of urban slavery in New Orleans in the fifteen years between 1845 and 1860. The number of slaves in the city dropped from 23,448 in 1840 to 17, 011 in 1850, and to 13,385 in 1860. Between 1840 and 1860, the number of free people of color living in New Orleans also dropped significantly from 23,448 to 13,385. See Richard C. Wade, *Slavery in the Cities* (New York, 1964), 18-19, 26-27, 326, and David Rankin, "The Impact of the Civil War on the Free Colored Community of New Orleans," *Perspectives in American History* (1977-1978), 380-381. Beginning with William Wells Brown's *The Negro in the American War of the Rebellion: His Heroism and his Fidelity,* which was published in 1867, historians have consistently described Cailloux as "finely educated." None indicated that he had been a slave. If Cailloux received any formal schooling, it most likely was not in France, as many have suggested. See, for example, William Wells Brown, *The Negro in the American Rebellion: His Heroism and his Fidelity* (Boston, 1867), 169, and Joseph T. Glatthaar, *Forged in Battle: The Civil War Alliance of Black Soldiers and White Officers* (New York, 1990), 124.

[8]Ira Berlin, "The Structure of the Free Negro Caste," *Journal of Social History,* 9 (1976): 312-13; Manoj K. Joshi and Joseph P. Reidy, "To Come Forward and Aid in Putting Down this Unholy Rebellion': The Officers of Louisiana's Free Black Native Guard During the Civil War Era," *Southern Studies,* 21 (1982): 326; H. E. Sterkx, *The Free Negro,* 223 and passim: Joseph Logsdon and Caryn Cossé Bell, "The Americanization of Black New Orleans," in Hirsch and Logsdon, *Creole New Orleans,* 204; David C. Rankin, "The Impact of the Civil War on the Free Colored Community of New Orleans," *Perspectives in American History,* 9 (1977-1978), 379-86; William Wells Brown, *The Negro in the American Rebellion,* 169.

[9]For the French connection see, LaChance, "The Foreign French," and Logsdon and Bell, "The Americanization of Black New Orleans," in Hirsch and Logsdon, eds. *Creole New Orleans,* 91-130 and 189-261; Ralph Gibson, *Social History of French Catholicism, 1789-1914* (New York, 1989), 159-63, 165; James W. Blassingame, *Black New Orleans, 1860-1880* (Chicago, 1973), 108; Desdunes, *Our People and Our History,* 29; Roger Baudier, "The Story of St. Louis School of Holy Redeemer Parish, Formerly l'Institution Catholique pour l'Institution des Orphelins dans l'Indigence (Widow Convent's School), AANO; Cyprian Davis, *The History of Black Catholics in the United States* (New York, 1990), 73, 104-5; Sister Mary Francis Borgia Hart, S.S.F., *Violets in the King's Garden: A History of the Sisters of the Holy Family of New Orleans* (New Orleans, 1976), 3-4.

[10]Logsdon and Bell, "The Americanization of Black New Orleans, in Hirsch and Logsdon, eds., *Creole New Orleans,* 195, 208-209; Benjamin J. Blied, *Catholics and the Civil War* (Milwaukee, 1945), 26-7.

[11]Roger Baudier, *The Catholic Church in Louisiana* (New Orleans, 1939), 365; Randall M. Miller, "A Church in Cultural Captivity: Some Speculations on Catholic Identity in the Old South," in Miller and Wakelyn, eds., *Catholics in the Old South,* 42.

[12]Logsdon and Bell, "The Americanization of Black New Orleans, in Hirsch and Logsdon, eds., *Creole New Orleans,* 204; Randall M. Miller, "Slaves and Southern Catholicism," in John B. Boles, ed., *Masters and Slaves*

in the House of the Lord: Race and Religion in the American South, 1740-1870 (Lexington, 1988), 146-7; John T. Gillard, S.S.J., *The Catholic Church and the American Negro* (Baltimore, 1929), 18-19.

[13]Extract from the Register of the Acts of Marriage of the Church and the Assumption, June 22, 1847, in Pension Record of André Cailloux (misspelled Caillaux), RG 15, National Archives, Washington, D. C.

[14]Marriage Ccontract between André Cailloux and Louise Felicie Coulon in Octave de Armas, vol. 40, #88, April 18, 1847, NONA; Extract from the Register of the Acts of Marriage of the Church of the Assumption, June 22, 1847, in Pension Record of André Cailloux (misspelled Caillaux), RG 15, NA; Testament of Valentin Encalada in L. T. Claire, vol. 19, #319, March 27, 1832, all in NONA; Sally Kittredge Evans, Frederick Stielow and Betsy Swanson, *Grand Isle on the Gulf—An Early History* (Metairie, La., 1979), 26; Sale of Property, James Armour to Feliciana and Bastien, in William Chrsity, vol. 44, p. 715, February 17, 1842, Emancipation of Feliciana and Bastien, in L. T. Claire, vol. 47, p. 715, September 21, 1835, Purchase of Slaves by Feliciana, in C. V. Foulon, vol. 7, #187, October 11, 1841, Manumission, Feliciana Encalada to Slave Felicie and Son, in Achille Chiapella, vol. 11, #419, p. 841, December 23, 1846, all in NONA; Sale of a Slave, Feliciana to M. Lartet, Conveyance Book 36, p. 460, August 10, 1844, in Conveyance Office, Orleans Parish.

[15]Marriage Contract between André Cailloux and Louise Felicie, in Octave de Armas, vol. 40, #88, April 18, 1847, NONA; Baptismal Register of Negroes and Mulattoes, St. Louis Cathedral, vol. 27, Act 140, April 13, 1839, in AANO; Sterkx, *Free Negro*, 223.

[16]Sale, Lartet to Cailloux, in Achille Chiapella, vol. 14, April 3, 1848, NONA; Robert C. Reinders, "The Free Negro in the New Orleans Economy, 1850-1860," *Louisiana History*, 6 (1965): 280; *Cohen's New Orleans and Lafayette Directory* (New Orleans, 1852).

[17]Purchase of a Slave by André Cailloux, in H. B. Cenas, vol. 41, pp. 505-507, January 2, 1849, NONA: Birth record of Athalie Clemence Cailloux, Vital Records Section, Louisiana State Archives, Baton Rouge, La.

[18]Sale of the naked property of land by Jean Pocte to André Cailloux and renunciation by Féliciana Encalada of the usufruct in favor of Jean Pocte and André Cailloux, in Paul Emile Laresche, vol. 17, #197, June 30, 1855, Sale of property by André Cailloux to Pane Blair, f.m.c., in Paul Emile Laresche, vol. 17, October 15, 1855, both in NONA; Tax Registers, City of New Orleans, 1857-1960, in LC; affidavit of Henriette Lamott, October 4, 1871, and affidavit signed by Molière Duvernay, Office of Recorder of Births, Marriages, and Deaths, State of Louisiana, Parish of New Orleans, August 19, 1871, in pension file of André Cailloux (misspelled Caillaux), RG 15, NA; St. Theresa of Avila Baptismal Book #2, 1857-1868, p. 10, Act #162, in AANO.

[19]See, *A. Mygatt and Company, New Orleans Directory* for 1858 and 1859, in 873:2, City Directories, Microform Reading Room, Library of Congress, Washington, D. C.; Joseph T. Glatthaar is the latest to describe Cailloux as a man of great property. See, *Forged In Battle: The Civil War Alliance of Black Soldiers and White Officers* (New York, 1990), 124; Testimony of Martin Lamothe, Docket #6358. *Cailloux, f.m.c., v. Nuba, f.m.c.* (June 1860). Unreported: 15 La, Ann. xiii. Accession 106, p. 8, in Supreme Court of Louisiana Collection of Legal Archives, University of New Orleans Archives and Manuscripts/Special Collections Department, New Orleans, La. (hereafter cited as SCLC); Loren Schweninger, "Prosperous Blacks in the South, 1790-1880," *American Historical Review*, 95 (1990): 33; Mortgage by André Cailloux in favor of Thomy Lafon, in Paul Emile Laresche, vol. 19, #240, October 16, 1856, Mortgage by André Cailloux to Joseph M. Zardais, in Octave de Armas, vol. 74, #321, October 19, 1859, Mortgage from André Cailloux to L. F. Parent, in Octave de Armas, Vol. 77, #332, October 22, 1860, all in NONA; Docket #6358. *Cailloux, f.m.c., v. Nuba, f.m.c.* (June 1860). Unreported: 15 La, Ann. xiii. Accession 106, in SCLC.

[20]See Robert C. Reinders, "The Free Negro in the New Orleans Economy, 1850-1860," *Louisiana History*, 6 (1965): 278; Schweninger, "Prosperous Blacks in the South, 1790-1880," 38; Logsdon and Bell, "The Americanization of Black New Orleans," in Hirsch and Logsdon, eds., *Creole New Orleans*, 208-209; Sterkx, *The Free Negro*, 286-315.

[21]Sale of Property by André Cailloux to James P. Freret, in Felix Grima, Vol. 27, #756, September 13, 1860, NONA; Tax Assessment Records, Board of Assessors, Names of taxable persons in Square 270, 1864, in LC, *Gardner's New Orleans Directory* (New Orleans, 1861).

[22]Roland C. McConnell, "Louisiana's Black Military History, 1729-1865," in Robert R. Macdonald, John R. Kemp, and Edward F. Haas, eds., *Louisiana's Black Heritage* (New Orleans, 1977), 47; Ted Tunnell, *Crucible of Reconstruction: War, Radicalism and Race in Louisiana, 1862-1877* (Baton Rouge, 1984), 69-70; Mary F. Berry, "Negro Troops in Blue and Gray: The Louisiana Native Guards. 1861-1863," *Louisiana History*, 8 (1967): 166-67; Howard C. Westwood, *Black Troops, White Commanders, and Freedmen During the Civil War* (Carbondale, 1992), 43; Compiled Service Records, Confederate Soldiers who served in units from Louisiana, in National Archives microfilm, A-G, M320-94.

[23]Masonic Temple Archives of New Orleans, New Orleans, La.; *Gardner's Directory for 1861* (New Orleans, 1861); Baudier, *The Catholic Church in Louisiana*, 218, 275-76, 278, 339; Logsdon and Bell, "The Americanization of the Black New Orleans," in Hirsch and Logsdon, eds., *Creole New Orleans*, 211, 234-35.

[24]F. Richard to H. Relf, November 27, 1861, S. Toussaint to E. Lafargue, December 18, 1861, L. L. to F. Richard, December 19, 1861, E. Perault to J. Enagerrot, January 29, 1862, S. Toussaint to M. Perault, January 29, 1862, F. Bordenave to H. Isidore, January 30, 1862, E. Perault to F. Drahcir, February 19, 1862, and S. Toussaint to S. B. Peaucrup, February 5, 1862, all in Catholic Institution, English Composition Copy-book, First class begun on 13th March, 1861, Wm. Vigers, Teacher, in AANO; Morning Report, 1st Regt. Native Guards La. Militia, January 10, 1862, in Compiled Service Records, Confederate soldiers who served in units from Louisiana, in National Archives microfilm, A-G, M320-94; S. Toussaint to M. Perault, January 29, 1862, in Catholic Institution, English Composition Copy-book, in AANO.

[25]McConnell, "Louisiana's Black Military History," in Macdonald, Kemp, and Haas, eds., *Louisiana's Black Heritage*, 47; Howard C. Westwood, *Black Troops, White Commanders, and Freedmen During the Civil War*, 43-44; Supplemental Report (b) of the American Freedman's Inquiry Commission of James McKaye, 1863, in Letters Received by the Adjutant General's Office, box 1054, folder 3, in RG 94, NA.

[26]Berry, "Negro Troops in Blue and Gray," 176; Muster Roll, Company E, September 27, 1862, in Regimental Muster Rolls, 73rd USCI, RG 94, NA.

[27]*L'Union*, January 13, 1863; Joshi and Reidy, "To Come Forward," 328-29; Berry, "Negro Troops in Blue and Gray," 175; Glatthaar, *Forged in Battle*, 124; Brown, *The Negro in the American Rebellion*, 168-69.

[28]Col. Spencer H. Stafford to Maj. George C. Strong, December 2, 1862, in Compiled Military Service Record of Asa Barnes, 73rd USCI, RG 94, NA; Deposition of Joseph Fille, May 6, 1905, in Pension File of Joseph Fille, RG 15, NA; Samuel S. Gardner to Gen. Lorenzo Thomas, November 2, 1862, in Letters Received by the Adjutant General, RG 94, NA. Pension records of the 1st Regiment (designated the 73rd United States Colored Infantry in 1863) contain additional evidence of the Catholicism of the men of the regiment, usually in the form of extracts from parish marriage registers.

[29]The descriptive book of Company C (the only extant company descriptive book) indicates that of the ninety-five men enrolled between August 28 and September 8, twenty-six were "fair," "bright," "yellow," or "light;" thirty-four were "brown," and thirty-five were "black." Of the thirty-seven whose occupation was listed as laborer, only seven were light, bright or yellow. Unfortunately, the descriptive book for Company E appears to have been lost or destroyed. See, Descriptive Book, Company C, 73rd USCT, in Regimental Papers, 73rd US-CInf., RG 94, NA; Mary Berry, "Negro Troops in Blue and Gray," 175: deposition B, Hillaire Zenon, June 9, 1911, deposition A, Basil Ulgere, June 3, 1911, and Copy of Records of Baptisms from Register #4 of Baptisms for the parish church of St. Louis Cathedral, March 13, 1841, all in Pension File of Basil Ulgere, RG #15, NA.

[30]*L'Union*, October 18, 1862; Logsdon and Bell, "The Americanization of Black New Orleans," in Hirsch and Logsdon, eds., *Creole New Orleans*, 220-221.

[31]L. Lamaniere to J. Burel, November 19, 1862, in Catholic Institution, English Composition Copy-book, in AANO.

[32]*L'Union*, January 13, 1863.

[33]Roger Baudier, *Centennial, St. Rose of Lima Parish* (New Orleans, 1957), 22; Jean-Marie Odin to Cardinal Alessandro Barnabo, August 14, 1863, in vol. 20, fols. 358rv-361rv, and Odin to Barnabo, November 8, 1865, vol. 20, fols, 1658rv-1659rv, both in *Scritture Riferite nei Congressi: American Centrale*, Congregation of the Propaganda Archives (PA) (microfilm), University of Notre Dame Archives, Notre Dame, Indiana; Bishop John Mary Matthew, September 21, 1844, certificate of ordination of Claude Paschal Maistre, V-5-b, Passport issued by the French Consul to Father Claude Pascal Maitre-Simonnot, London, June 26, 1849, V-5-k, Belgian passport issued for Father Claude Pascal Maitre Simonnot, June 29, 1849, V-5-k, Bishop Pierre-Louis Coeur, June 1, 1849, V-5-k, all in New Orleans Papers in UNDA: Notre Dame Indiana; Passenger lists of vessels arriving at Atlantic and Gulf Ports, 1820-1874, Supplemental Index Roll 107, in RG 36, NA; Portfolio of Father Claude Paschal Maistre, January 10, 1855, V- 1-i, in AANOND; *Metropolitan Catholic Almanac and Laity Directory* (Baltimore, 1852), 137; *Metropolitan Catholic Almanac and Laity Directory* (Baltimore 1853), 109; *Metropolitan Catholic Almanac and Laity Directory* (Baltimore, 1854), 152-53; *Metropolitan Catholic Almanac and Laity Directory* (Baltimore, 1855), 167; *Diamond Jubilee of the Archdiocese of Chicago: Antecedents and Developments* (Chicago, 1920), 255 (copy in the Archives of the Archdiocese of Chicago); Bishop Anthony O'Regan to Archbishop Antoine Blanc, June 6, 1855, Bishop James Oliver Vandevelde to Archbishop Antoine Blanc, October 23, 1855, November 6, 1855, November 26, 1855, all in VI-1-i, (AANOND); Rev. Ennemond Dupuy to Archbishop Antoine Blanc, January 3, 1856, Claude Paschal Maistre to Antoine Blanc, January 14, 1856, Maistre to Blanc, April 9, 1856, November 6, 1856, all in VI- 1-j, AANOND; Baudier, *St. Rose of Lima*, 16-18.

[34]Baudier, *St. Rose of Lima*, 20-21; *L' Union*, April 14, 1863; Benjamin Blied, Catholics and the Civil War, 26-27 (a copy of Bishop Dupanloup's pastoral is included in "Speech of Hon. T. [Thaddeus] Stevens in Reply to the Attack of General Hunter's Letter," in the Library of Congress; Baudier, *St. Rose of Lima*, 22; *L'Union*, January 13, 1863; Claude Paschal Maistre to Cardinal Alessandro Barnabo, May 15, 1865, vol. 20, fols. 1461-1462rv, in *Scritture Riferite nei Congressi: American Centrale*, (PA).

[35]Baudier, *The Catholic Church in Louisiana*, 411, 425; Pastoral letter of Jean Marie Odin, February 16, 1862, in Vol. I (1844-1887), Pastoral Letters, AANO; Baudier, *St. Rose of Lima*, 19-23. As late as March 1865, Odin passed information about Union troop movements to the Confederate secret service. See, Gen. E. Kirby Smith to Maj. Gen. J. G. Walker, March 7, 1865, in *War of the Rebellion: A Compilation of the Official Records of the Union and Confederate Armies*, 128 vols. (Washington, D. C., 1880-1901), series I, vol. 48, pt. 1, p. 1,412.

[36]F. Richard to Janus, February 5, 1862, Catholic Institution, English Composition Copy-book, in AANO; *L'Union*, December 25, 1862; Etienne Rousselon to Jean Marie Odin, October 15, 1862, in VI-2-f, AANOND.

[37]"The Negro in the Military Service of the United States, 1607-1889," 973-75, in United States Colored Troops, RG 94, NA; Ira Berlin, Joseph Reidy, and Leslie Rowland, eds., *Freedom: A Documentary History of Emancipation, 1861-1867. Series II: The Black Military Experience* (New York, 1982), 684-86; S. H. Stafford to Maj. George L. Strong, October 23, 1862, in Letters Received, 1862, ser. 1756, Department of the Gulf, RG 393, pt. 1; Gen. Benjamin J. Butler to Edwin M. Stanton, December 3, 1862, in Letters Received, 1863, ser. 1756, Department of the Gulf, RG 393, pt. 1; According to the muster role for June-August 1863, the Regiment was paid on February 28, 1863, for a period extending to June 30, 1863. See, muster rolls, 73rd USCInf., RG 94; Westwood, *Black Troops, White Commanders, and Freedmen During the Civil War*, 49.

[38]Spencer H. Stafford to Capt. Wickham Hoffman, Asst. Adj. General, February 23, 1863, in Letters Received, 1863, ser. 1756, Department of the Gulf, RG 393, pt. 1, NA; Berry, "Negro Troops in Blue and Gray, 178-79; deposition of Edgar Davis, May 28, 1884, in Pension File of Louis B. Boute, RG 15, NA; quoted in James M. McPherson, *Ordeal by Fire: The Civil War and Reconstruction* (New York, 1982), 353-54.

[39]Joshi and Reidy, "To Come Forward," 331-32; early in 1864 the officers of the 1st Regiment began to resign. Banks' actions, if not his words, undermined the authority of Cailloux and his fellow black officers and encour-

aged disrespect by white soldiers toward them. Capt. Joseph Follin of Company C attributed his resignation in 1864 to "daily events [that] demonstrate that prejudices are so strong against Colored Officers, that no matter what would be their patriotism and their anxiety to fight for the flag of their native Land, they cannot do it with honor to themselves." See, Joseph Follin to George B. Drake, February 18, 1864, Compiled Service Record of Joseph Follin, 73rd USCInf., RG 94, NA.

[40]The spelling of the name varies depending on the source. It appears, for example, as "Anselme Placencio" in the St. Louis Cathedral parish baptismal register. See, St. Louis Cathedral Baptismal Register 17, p. 132, Act #1014. I have used the spelling found in the first company muster role, which is dated September 1862. See, Muster Role of Company E, September 1862, in Regimental Papers, 73rd USCInf., RG 94.

[41]Affidavit of Rosa Ulgere, October 26, 1904, and deposition of L. A. Snaer, August 25, 1864, in Pension File of Athanase Ulger, RG 15, NA; Edmonds, *The Guns of Port Hudson*, 2:49-58, 128-29, 377; McConnell, "Louisiana's Black Military History," in Macdonald, Kemp, Haas. eds., *Louisiana's Black Heritage*, 51-53; Benjamin Quarles, *The Negro in the Civil War* (1953; repr. New York, 1968), 217; Joseph T. Wilson, *Black Phalanx* (1890; repr. New York, 1968), 214; George Washington Williams, *A History of the Negro Troops in the War of the Rebellion, 1861-1865* (1888; repr. New York, 1969), 218-19; Laurence Lee Hewitt, *Port Hudson: Confederate Bastion on the Mississippi* (Baton Rouge, 1987), 147- 50; *New York Times*, June 13, 1863, Edmonds, *The Guns of Port Hudson*, 2:57; *New York Times*, June 13, 1863.

[42]St. Rose of Lima and Holy Name of Jesus Baptismal and Marriage Records (microfilm), reel 222, in AANO; Baudier, St. Rose of Lima, 21-23. According to *L'Union*, Maistre, in his sermon, marvelled at the changes wrought by the war over the course of the year and referred to the Emancipation Proclamation as the most difficult "first step." He insisted on the nobility and the necessity of free labor, noting: "That which ennobles work is liberty." Declaring that slaves were "men like us," who needed guidance, Maistre expressed confidence that God's justice would prevail and spoke so powerfully that many in his large audience were moved to tears. See, *L' Union*, April 14, 1863, and December 6, 1862.

[43]Jean-Marie Odin to Cardinal Alessandro Barnabö, August 14, 1863, in vol. 20, fols. 358rv-361rv, March 1, 1864, vol. 20, fols. 703rv-704rv, and November 8, 1865, vol. 20, fols. 1658rv- 1659rv, all in *Scritture Riferite nei Congressi: American Centrale*, PA; James Bowen to Monsignor Jean-Marie Odin, May 25, 1863, in Letters sent by the Provost Marshall (press copies), ser. 1843, vol. 1, RG 393, pt. 1, NA; Capt. W. Killborn to Odin, July 30, 1863, in VI-2-g, AANOND; Odin to Killborn, August 1, 1863, Letters Received, Provost Marshall General Records, Department of the Gulf, ser. 1845, in RG 393, pt. 1, NA; Baudier, *St. Rose of Lima*, 23. The dispute between Maistre and Odin will be treated more thoroughly in a forthcoming article.

[44]Baudier, *The Catholic Church in Louisiana*, 413; Jean-Marie Odin to Cardinal Alessandro Barnabò, August 14, 1863, in vol. 20, fols. 358rv-361rv, in *Scritture Riferite nei Congressi: American Centrale*, PA; St. Rose of Lima and Holy Name of Jesus Baptismal and Marriage Records (microfilm) reel 222, in AANO; Claude Paschal Maistre to Bamabò, May 15, 1865 (Fr. Josaphat note appended), vol. 20, fols. 1461rv-l462rv, and Odin to Barnabò, November 8, 1865, vol. 20, fols. l658rv-1659rv, both in *Scritture Riferite nei Congressi: American Centrale*, PA; Barnabò to Maistre, January 5, 1866, vol. 357, fols. 7v, 7r, 7rv, in *Lettere Di S. Congregazione*, PA; Maistre to Odin, February 13, 1866, in V1-2-k, AANOND; Maistre to Barnabò, February 20, 1866, vol. 21, fol. 15lrv, and Odin to Barnabò, April 12, 1866, vol. 21, fol. 216rv, both in *Scritture Riferite nei Congressi: American Centrale*, PA.

[45]Claude Paschal Maistre to Cardinal Alessandro Barnabò, May 15, 1865, (Fr. Josaphat note appended), vol. 20, fols. 1461rv- 1462rv, *Scritture Riferite nei Congressi: American Centrale*, PA; *L'Union*. May 14 and 31, 1864; *New Orleans Tribune*, January 13, 14, and 22, 1865, October 1, 1865, December 1, 1867, January 9, 1869; "Straight University, Charter. Board of Trustees, and Faculty," #45869, in American Missionary Association Archives, Amistad Center, New Orleans, La.; Joe M. Richardson, "The American Missionary Association and Black Education in Louisiana. 1862-1878," in Macdonald, Kemp and Haas, eds., *Louisiana's Black Heritage*, 148, 155-61; *New Orleans Republican*. June 30, 1870.

[46]Baudier, *St. Rose of Lima*, 24.

[47]"Memorial of a large number of citizens of Louisiana asking that citizens of African descent residing in this state who were free at the breaking out of the rebellion may be registered as voters," in Select Committee on the Rebellious States, January 20, 1864 to January 23, 1865, HR 38A -G25.6 #1418, Records of the House of Representatives, RG 233, NA; Marriage of Homer Plessy and Louise Bordenave, St. Augustine Marriage Book 6 (1882-1894), pg. 281, in AANO; *L'Union*, January 13, 1863, and June 21 and 28, 1864.

SLAVERY AND THE SOUTHWESTERN EVANGELIST IN NEW ORLEANS (1800-1861)*

Timothy F. Reilly

Within the Protestant community of antebellum New Orleans, the Methodists and Baptists represented an alien force in religious style and social adaptation. Evidence also indicates that several of the city's early Methodists and Baptists evinced a racialist philosophy which was at variance with the clerical mainstream. From 1805 to 1858, almost all of the fundamentalist preachers who entered New Orleans sought to proselytize among white and black alike, either through mixed assemblies or in separate meeting houses. Operating on the periphery of New Orleans' older religious society, the first wave of evangelical interlopers carved out independent bailiwicks where they circulated the word of Scripture among the city's motley population.

Only the Methodist and Baptist organizations allowed the city's Negroes the freedom of expression and the luxury of a semi-autonomous black clergy, however limited these features of religious participation may have been. Available evidence indicates that all of the other churches in the city were reluctant to permit any degree of black leadership among their parishioners; to do so would have compromised a paternalistic premise that was central to Southern thought.

Methodist and Baptist recruitment of blacks began as a necessity. Evangelical idealism, too, played a significant role, but late beginnings had forced the itinerant to concentrate his ardor among the uncommitted fringes of society. Both black and white were called upon to abandon Satan by freely extolling the joys of heavenly contact. By the 1840s, large black memberships and informal religious style were characteristics which set the Methodist and Baptist circles apart from the city's religious mainstream.

Evangelical forces in New Orleans also utilized the press in an effort to enlarge memberships and increase their public appeal. In its traditional advocacy of Negro proselytism, colonization, and unionism, the fundamentalist press in the city was directly at odds with the pro-slavery elements which were mounting their attacks with increasing frequency during the 1850s. The independent course of the editor-evangelist was not unlike that of the earlier missionaries who entered the city for the purpose of establishing

*First published in *Journal of Mississippi History*, 41 (1979): 301-17. Reprinted with the kind permission of the author and the publisher.

a foothold in the South's commercial metropolis. In their own minds, the odds against success were formidable; but the possible rewards far outweighed the dangers of personal sacrifice.

In the late winter of 1805, the migrating Elisha Bowman introduced Methodism to the Crescent City, only to be snubbed by the general public and harassed by the newly formed Episcopal Church.[1] Nearly eight years later, Lewis Hobbs had managed to attract a small congregation of six whites and twenty blacks.[2] When the city government strongly objected, young Hobbs answered that the blacks came of their own free will and could not be denied the preaching of the Gospel. Following his early departure in 1814, Hobbs sent a plaintive letter to his successor, William Winans, in which he expressed greetings to his "poor black people" and their white brethren.[3]

There were only three white Methodists inside New Orleans when Winans arrived in 1813. Almost all of the twenty-odd black Methodists he had expected to meet had mysteriously vanished. The Pennsylvania-born minister at first met resistance from the city government, but after he built "a respectable standing," he was allowed to preach in the Cabildo.[4]

Winans did not look upon the black man as an inferior being, nor did he resent the Catholic Church's domination of Orleanian religion and social life. Earlier experiences with converted Negroes in the North had convinced him that there were no intellectual or spiritual barriers between the races.[5] Winans' positive attitude toward local Catholicism was enhanced by his spirited defense of Bishop Louis DuBourg when the latter was threatened by the radical preachings and personal attacks of Father Antonio de Sedella and his aggressive followers:

> . . . I published several articles, anonymously, in the New Orleans paper [*Orleans Gazette*]. . . . One was a Eulogism on the preaching of Abbe Dubourg, and a severe reprehension of the indecorous behaviour of certain men, who considered themselves Gentlemen, while he was preaching. I have heard few better or more faithful preachers than was the Abbe. He was, when I heard him, sensible and eloquent, and his Discourse was, in a high degree [,] evangelical. The bigotry of some Protestants, and the hatred of many Catholics, for whom his preaching was too faithful, and who considered him the rival of Father Antoine [Sedella], a very old and very indulgent Priest in the City, led to his being bitterly hated and persecuted. Only the authority of Government prevented his being mobbed, and by Romanists especially. . . .[6]

Nominal Christianity and immorality in New Orleans had somehow prompted a strong bond of empathy between a Methodist frontier preacher and a French-born Catholic missionary. At the same time, Winans openly criticized his Protestant archrival, the Reverend James Hull, for his flamboyant dress and alleged intemperance. Hull's increasing prestige and popularity among "the fashionable and the gay" strengthened the Episcopal church as it weakened the appeal of Methodism.[7] As a backwoods evangelist, Winans was no match for the urbane Episcopal leader. After his transfer to the Natchez area in 1814, Winans himself described the New Orleans pastorate as the dread of the [Missis-sippi] Conference."[8]

The status of Methodism within the community improved slightly between 1824 and 1826, when another traveling evangelist, Benjamin M. Drake, attempted to popularize his faith by engaging in humanitarian endeavors. During his two-year sojourn, Drake went out of his way to visit prison inmates, hospital patients, and wayfaring sailors. He risked his life by caring for the seasonal victims of yellow fever and cholera. Before his depar-ture, he was successful in constructing New Orleans first Methodist church in 1826.[9] Membership in Drake's Church reportedly increased by "twenty and thirty whites and about sixty colored people."[10]

In addition to the open-mindedness Drake often displayed toward the city's Presbyte-rians and Episcopalians, the Methodist minister paid his respects to the majority Catholic population by frequently visiting the St. Louis Cathedral and quietly meditating in the midst of somber frescoes and ghostly statuary. The Protestant frontiersman was certainly an individualist, since he found such exotic surroundings conducive to prayerful inspira-tion.[11]

During his ministry in New Orleans Drake initiated the strong alliance between Southwestern Methodism and the American Colonization Society. This partnership brought considerable hardships in future years. At a regional meeting of the Mississippi Conference in Tuscaloosa, Alabama, in 1826, Drake submitted the first proposal of recip-rocal aid ever made before that body. His trial balloon met with enthusiastic acceptance. The Conference formally recommended that "members and patrons" give their support, and Methodist preachers were asked "to take up collections . . . and remit the same to the Treasurer of the [Colonization] Society. . . ."[12] At the time, the Colonization Society had been in existence only ten years.

Near the close of the regional conference of Southwestern Methodism, Drake deliv-ered an address on the status of Methodism in New Orleans. He reported that even though membership was slowly increasing and the new church property would soon be out of debt, "Methodism in New Orleans was like a partridge in the wilderness."[13] It was still apparent that the Church's missionary outposts in the Catholic city represented one of the most precarious undertakings of frontier Methodism.

It was not until 1841 that the Orleanian Baptists adopted a formal organization. Prior to this time they had been forced to rely on visiting missionaries. Baptist evangelists had never experienced undue persecution; in fact, a high degree of cordiality existed among the competing groups. For example, in 1817 Father Antonio de Sedella invited a visiting Baptist, the Reverend William B. Johnson of South Carolina, to deliver a sermon to a Catholic audience in the St. Louis Cathedral.[14] Another early missionary was the Rever-end James A. Raynoldson, who preached in the city for one year.

Reminiscing about his brief stay in New Orleans Raynoldson later emphasized the importance of converting "the poor Africans in our country who bear the heat and burden of the day." He also felt that his successor, the Reverend Benjamin Davis, had a special talent for instructing the Negroes, and he hoped that city officials would not impede Davis' efforts.[15] Davis' tenure in New Orleans was brief and the results of his labor were rather meager. When he left the city in 1820, his congregation numbered only forty-eight persons, two-thirds of them black.[16]

Between 1820 and 1845, the city's white Baptists drifted aimlessly, as itinerant preachers made abortive attempts to establish a permanent church. Toward the close of this unproductive interim, James Huckins, a Baptist missionary on his way to Texas, complained that a "dictatorial spirit" within New Orleans had subdued "nearly every Baptist preacher who has ever visited this city."[17] It was not unusual that the black and white amalgam was given a hard time in view of the local evangelists' recurring interest in Negro proselytism.

As early as 1826, an English missionary by the name of William Rondeau helped to establish the "First African Church of New Orleans." The black congregation was led by a free Negro, the Reverend Asa C. Goldsbury, and his assistant, Deacon Moses Jackson. Goldsbury was eventually forced into a six-month period of silence under penalty of a local law barring the activities of blacks. In the meantime, Rondeau's white congregation dwindled to seven persons, and the disheartened missionary finally left the city in 1828. But the fortunes of the black Baptists rose as those of their white brethren declined. Before Goldsbury's death a few years later, the First African Church boasted a respectable membership of eighty-seven persons.[18]

Like the local Baptist Church, Orleanian Methodism eventually produced a black ministry before the Civil War. The activities of the Negro Methodists, however, were more circumscribed. In its paternal restrictions against its slave and free colored adherents, the Methodist Episcopal Church, South, gradually excluded blacks from Sunday services by setting up three all-black congregations. Both races had previously occupied separate sections of the same church; but after 1850 segregation was intensified. Blacks attended the Wesley, Soulé, and Winans Chapels where the Reverend Holland N. McTyeire, a white man, provided the necessary instruction and supervision.[19]

In spite of its strong segregation policies and closer supervision after 1850, Orleanian Methodism was still troubled by a public suspicion which held that too many church leaders were not conforming to Southern dogmas on race and slavery. The recent history of Southwestern Methodism provided substantial evidence of philosophical aberration and individual floutings. As late as 1851 the official *Discipline*, a booklet setting forth the creed of Southern Methodism, still contained the controversial "Section IX," which condemned slavery. The institution was termed a "great evil," slaveholders were barred from the ministry, and lay members were compelled to encourage their slaves to read the Bible.[20]

Accompanying the factious *Discipline* were abolitionist church leaders who persistently created havoc in different parts of the Southwest. The aggressive James Axley, traveling through Mississippi and Louisiana, included the institution of slavery, along with Freemasonry, whiskey, tobacco, and fashionable dress, in his "Sermon on the

Abominations."[21] In 1826 the so-called "Hale Storm" disrupted Methodist communities in Southern Arkansas when the Reverend Jesse Hale, presiding elder and an "ultra-abolitionist," attempted to enforce literally "Section IX."[22]

During the 1830s and 1840s debates over slavery were still raging in some Methodist conference meetings within the Deep South.[23] By 1860 there were more than 3,300 Methodists in the Crescent City, and almost sixty percent were black. Rural Louisiana's Methodism claimed more than 14,000 members, of whom almost forty percent were black. New Orleans' still higher proportion of black communicants signified urban Methodism's potent appeal among slaves and free colored persons, as well as its more limited appeal to the city's white population.[24]

Although William Winans had adopted Mississippi as his permanent home, his strong identification with the city of New Orleans lasted throughout his career. As late as 1845 the venerable Methodist joined the Reverend Isaac Hinton, an English-born Baptist, in furthering the city's sporadic colonization movement. Both ministers presided at an inter-denominational gathering at the Methodist Church on Poydras Street.[25] Continued support of colonization and black proselytism was later given by the local Methodist and Baptist newspapers, which were under the editorship of the Reverend Holland McTyeire and the Reverend William Cecil Duncan, respectively.

Both Winans and Mississippi's Benjamin Drake, who had also remained in frequent contact with New Orleans, were sometimes called upon to defend their church from local and outside enemies. When colored missions in the South were threatened with closure in 1835, Winans wrote a defensive tract, which aimed at placating jittery authorities. Both Mississippians collaborated five years later in the authorship of a catechism for "colored people under Methodist pastoral charge."[26]

Winans frequently pleaded on behalf of the struggling Orleanian Methodists. After requesting a sizable donation for the construction of a permanent meeting house inside the city, Winans was curtly rebuffed by his former friend and fellow colonizationist, Gerritt Smith of Peterborough, New York. Smith issued an indignant reply that he would contribute nothing toward the upkeep of a religion which sanctioned slavery.[27] In his published rebuttal Winans attempted to portray Southern Methodism's dilemma, as well as his own reservations concerning the institution:

> . . . It is true, that *professors* of religion in the south may, as *professors* in the north do, sometimes sanction those things which are incongruous to the pure Gospel of Christ, but this no more convicts the religion of the south than it does the religion of the north of either heathenism or imperfection. . . . [The religion of the South]. . . condemns slavery as clearly and as strongly as . . . [the Saviour and his apostles] . . . ever did; and it goes no farther toward sanctioning the abuses of slavery than they did. It is this sort of religion for which a sanctuary in New Orleans is contemplated. . . . Would you, sir, have met a requisition of St. Paul, to aid in propagating the religion which he taught in Rome, at Ephesus, or at Colosse, by such an excuse as that by which you would vindicate your refusal to contribute to the erection of a Methodist Church in the city of New Orleans? . . . Come over, then, to our Macedonia, and help us. . . . [28]

Winans' declining health forced him to retire permanently to his Mississippi pastorate in Centreville after 1850. Despite his somewhat cloistered existence, the feeble church leader still managed to carry on a regular correspondence with his Methodist successors in New Orleans. In 1851 the *New Orleans Christian Advocate* published a controversial letter from Winans in which the elderly minister urged Southern Methodists to retain "Section IX" of the *Methodist Discipline*. Winans pleaded that any whole-hearted sanctioning of slavery by the Southern Church would alienate the border states and furnish the North with additional propaganda grist. The *Advocate* introduced Winans' plea by beseeching the reader's moderation and understanding, since the distinguished churchman had "long enjoyed the highest respect and affection of the country."[29] Winans died in 1857 at the age of 68 following a "protracted and painful illness."[30]

The following year the General Conference of the Methodist Episcopal Church, South, formally renounced the antislavery clause of the famous *Discipline*. At a meeting in Nashville, Southern church leaders eliminated "Section IX" of the Methodist code by the overwhelming vote of 140 to 8. It was charged that the ill-adapted rule was "ambiguous in its phraseology, and liable to be construed as antagonistic to the institution of slavery."[31]

When Union forces occupied New Orleans in 1862, the Methodist flock was scattered and church property was temporarily seized in order to meet wartime needs. The New Orleans church did not fully recover until the post-war Reconstruction period.[32] In fully characterizing the effects of southwestern evangelism in New Orleans, Methodists Winans and Drake must be given primary recognition as Southerners who were unwilling to accept the dictums of the status quo. Whether they lived in the Crescent City or in the piney woods of Mississippi, Winans and Drake consistently attempted to moderate sectional bitterness among their fellow-Methodists and to alleviate the human suffering connected with slavery.

Despite the numerous difficulties, local and outside observers of the late antebellum period placed considerable importance on the direction of New Orleans' Methodist and Baptist organizations. The city symbolized a potential source of religious prestige and influence, particularly among the Baptist evangelists of the Lower South. One Baptist leader writing in 1853 saw New Orleans as a crucial battlefield between "true Christianity and the anti-Christian Popery."[33] A decade earlier, visiting journalist from Louisville proposed that the church employ a much more dynamic approach toward converting the mind of New Orleans:

> . . . People in cities who are borne along with the influence of the world, and unaccustomed to regular attendance on the worship of God, will not attend ordinary preaching, unless they are drawn out by some attractive influence. Hence popular lectures of a literary, scientific historical or prophetic character, interspersed with religious considerations, and appeals to the conscience have proved eminently successful in some instances. . . .[34]

The dormancy of New Orleans' white Baptists was broken in 1845, when the English-born Isaac Hinton entered the city and launched a serious effort to improve the Church's social position. Within two years Hinton increased the white membership at the newly constituted First Baptist Church from 29 to 122.[35] The young Englishman was a supporter of the Colonization Society. He apparently held liberal theological views as well. In February 1845, one member of his audience recorded that the earnest clergyman delivered a Sunday sermon on the compatibility of science and religion, adding somewhat critically that Hinton "had not properly digested his subject."[36]

Following Hinton's untimely death in the yellow fever epidemic of 1847, the Baptist missionary cause was led by William Cecil Duncan. In his small newspaper office on Poydras Street, this young preacher-journalist regularly published his denominational weekly, the *Southwestern Baptist Chronicle*.[37] He began his liberal publication in 1847 at the youthful age of twenty-three, one year before his ordination into the Baptist ministry. The son of a Scottish immigrant, Duncan had spent most of his early life in Mississippi's northeast hill country. The young idealist hoped that his New Orleans newspaper would strengthen the local Church, unify Baptist opinion in the sparsely settled Gulf states, and further promote the Crescent City's reputation as a commercial and educational center.[38]

During the *Chronicle*'s three-year existence, Duncan's espousal of gradual emancipation for slaves developed along slow and circuitous lines. There were favorable accounts of the activities of the state colonization society and its parent organ.[39] Occasionally there were reportings of an ingeniously devised slave escape, or a sensational piece on some alleged white victim being accidentally sold into slavery.[40]

In another instance, Duncan reviewed a recent talk given by the Reverend Robert S. Finley, a peripatetic colonizationist who had recently given a speech on Liberia before a mixed audience at the Methodist Episcopal Church on Poydras Street. Elaboration on the contents of Finley's address paraphrased an equalitarian premise that many Southerners would have considered inflammatory:

> . . . The question, whether the negro is capable of governing himself, he [Finley] considered as forever settled by the result of the present experiment. The history of Liberia, and its prosperity, prove beyond a doubt that the sable sons of Africa, when left to themselves and subjected to no civil restraint save those imposed by their own consent, are as capable of making their own laws, and managing their own affairs, internal and external, as other nations. . . .[41]

The best measurement of Duncan's growing antipathy against slavery existed in his numerous editorials. In the fall of 1847 the *Chronicle* maintained that Northern critics were incorrect in their assertion that the institution of slavery was crumbling in the city of New Orleans. The newspaper noted, however, that within the city "there always has been, and there still is, a great diversity of opinion on this subject [slavery]."[42]

Following the close of the Mexican War, Duncan broadened his editorial focus to include the sectional disputes over the newly acquired Western territories. In the spring of

1850 Duncan finally advocated a policy of popular sovereignty in the Western states. And appearing in the same issue of the *Chronicle* was the twenty-six-year-old evangelist's unexpected declaration against slavery. In the context of antebellum Southern liberalism, the young Mississippian's public stand had few parallels:

> . . . That the time will come when the institution [of slavery] will exist among us no longer, we no more question than we doubt, that, but for the interference of Northern abolitionists, its area would at this time be more circumscribed than it is, and the prospects for its disappearance be more hopeful than they are today. Nay, we go farther. We shall rejoice to see that period arrive when slavery shall no longer be recognized in any part of the United States. Its existence in the South at the present day we honestly believe to be a check upon the prosperity, and an incubus upon the energies of the Southern people. As a civil institution, then, it is, we admit, an evil. We will go yet farther. We believe its prevalence in the South to be deleterious both in a moral and social point of view, and a barrier to the free progress of many useful institutions and to the free dissemination of general intelligence. . . .[43]

Duncan proposed that the individual slave states enact their own policies of gradual emancipation, followed by a program of systematic colonization.[44] His plan for the black man's removal from the South may have been impractical and morally questionable, but he nevertheless gauged slavery as the greatest of all evils. Duncan was explicit in his belief that slavery brutalized white and black alike, that it retarded Southern material development, and that it constricted the flow of new ideas and insights.

Two months later, Duncan was forced to close down his newspaper office through lack of funds. His paper's circulation had always been limited. It is likely that the *Chronicle*'s subscribers numbered less than two thousand farm folk and small townspeople in the Florida Parishes of Louisiana and in the Piney Woods and Coastal Meadows of Mississippi.[45]

Between 1853 and 1855 William Duncan coedited another denominational weekly, the *New Orleans Baptist Chronicle*, but religious conservatives were disturbed by the editor's doctrinal commentaries.[46] Across the cotton provinces in Nashville, the Reverend J. R. Graves, editor of the *Tennessee Baptist*, continually attacked his New Orleans competitor as a dangerous revisionist and interpolator of fundamentalist doctrine.[47] Just before the demise of his second journalistic venture, Duncan observed that his Tennessee rival had finally succeeded in damaging the new *Chronicle*'s reputation among Southwestern Baptists:

> . . . [Editor Graves' misrepresentation] . . . has done our paper a serious injury among the discussion loving brethren of the South-West. Their denominational feelings are strong (perhaps too strong); and they are not willing to support a paper, however ably conducted, that is not a decided advocate of Baptist principles and practices.[48]

In 1861 Duncan decided to leave New Orleans for the North. Shortly after Union forces occupied the city the following year, Duncan returned and became an active participant in the city's Unionist activities. But the frail minister's renewed engagement with social reform was abruptly cut short in 1864, when he died of tuberculosis.[49] The local Baptist community almost died with him. Toward the close of the Civil War there were perhaps no more than twenty white Baptists attending services in the city of New Orleans.[50]

William Duncan's capacity for dissent was best shown by his opposition to slavery and secession. In the 1840s and 1850s, leading clergymen in New Orleans dutifully supported the South's peculiar institution by basing their arguments on selected Biblical references. Liberal Unitarianism's Theodore Clapp employed this tactic. Some Christian leaders, including Presbyterianism's Benjamin Morgan Palmer, did not hesitate to rank the principle of sectional honor ahead of all other defenses. Duncan's opposite assumptions were based, instead, upon a non-Biblical premise that asserted slavery's ill-effects on the moral and social values of Southern life, as well as the tragic division the institution was creating in the country as a whole.

In one sense, the elements of time and location combined to make Duncan's gradualist position more venturesome than the immediate abolitionism espoused by Northern assailants who were protected by distance and public moderation. At mid-point in the slavery agitation, Duncan cranked his press "in the heart of the beast," protected only by the thin buffer of Orleanian forbearance. The editorial commentary of Mississippi evangelists William Winans and William Duncan could have easily provoked more violent reactions in the border realms of the South.[51]

The liberal proclivities of the southwestern evangelist in New Orleans have been heretofore ignored. It is doubtful that such activity could have been initiated and sustained in the rural sector of Southern life. But New Orleans' peculiar seedbed had been cultivated in advance of the evangelical design. Catholicism and the old Protestant mainstream of society had accepted the reality of religious pluralism. The very character of the city itself induced improvisation while it beckoned the explorer and the idealist. The Southwestern evangelist sometimes recognized his opportunities and attempted to create a religious culture responsive to urban needs. In a broader context, some of these city evangelists even hoped to influence the mind of the entire South.

Notes for "Slavery and the Southwestern Evangelist in New Orleans (1800-1861)"

[1]Elisha Bowman to William Burke, January 29, 1806, as cited in "New Orleans Territory," *New Orleans Christian Advocate*, April 12, 1851, 2.

[2]John G. Jones, *A Complete History of Methodism as Connected with the Mississippi Conference of the Methodist Episcopal Church South*, 2 vols. (Nashville, 1887), 1:288; Robert Alan Cross, *The History of Southern Methodism in New Orleans* ([New Orleans], 1931), 11.

[3]Robert Henry Harper, *Louisiana Methodism* (Washington, D. C., 1949), 38.

[4]William Winans, "Autobiography of William Winans" (unpublished MSS in Millsaps-Wilson Library, Millsaps College, Jackson, Mississippi), 111-14.

[5]Ibid., 11.

[6]Ibid., 119; John S. Kendall, "Early New Orleans Newspapers," *Louisiana Historical Quarterly*, 10 (1927): 399-401.

[7]Winans, "Autobiography of William Winans," 116-17.

[8]Quoted in Cross, *The History of Southern Methodism in New Orleans*, 1-14; Winans, "Autobiography of William Winans," 112-14, 123.

[9]W. Winans Drake, "An Early Methodist Leader in the South" A Sketch of Rev. Benjamin M. Drake, D. D.," *Methodist Review*, 67 (1918): 76-77.

[10]Quoted in Harper, *Louisiana Methodism*, 60.

[11]Drake, "An Early Methodist Leader in the South . . . ," 85.

[12]Jones, *A Complete History of Methodism . . .* , 2:117.

[13]Ibid., 120.

[14]John T. Christian, *A History of the Baptists of Louisiana* (Shreveport, 1923), 61-62; W. E. Paxton, *A History of the Baptists of Louisiana from the Earliest Times to the Present* (St. Louis, 1888), 119.

[15]J[ames] A. Ra[y]noldson, St. Francisville, La., to Dr. [William] Staughton, [Philadelphia, Pa.], March 20, 1818, as cited in "Louisiana in 1818," *Ford's Christian Repository*, n.s., (1884), 38, 26.

[16]Paxton, *A History of the Baptists of Louisiana . . .* , 119.

[17]Quoted in Christian, *A History of the Baptists of Louisiana*, 64.

[18]"Louisiana Baptist History," *New Orleans Baptist Messenger*, July 29, 1876, p. 2; Paxton, *A History of the Baptists of Louisiana . . .* , 120-21.

[19]*Minutes of the Annual Conference of the Methodist Episcopal Church, South* [1855-57] (Nashville, 1878), 610-11, 729-30.

[20]See *The Doctrine and Discipline of the Methodist Episcopal Church, South* (Louisville, 1851), 197-98. Since its organization in 1784, the Methodist Church was known for its strong attacks on the institution of slavery. In 1796, the Church passed legislation which expelled slave traders and demanded that all other members emancipate their slaves. Literal enforcement of the antislavery code, which had been incorporated into a national "Discipline," eventually led to the formal separation of the Northern and Southern churches in 1845. See William Warren Sweet, *The Story of Religions in America* (New York and London, 1930), 421, 435-39; and *Religion in the Development of American Culture, 1765-1849* (2nd ed.; Gloucester, Massachusetts, 1963), 143.

[21]Harper, *Louisiana Methodism*, 51-52.

[22]Jones, *A Complete History of Methodism . . .* , 2:109-110, 489.

[23]Ibid., 109-110, 489.

[24]Holland N. McTyeire, *A History of Methodism: Comprising a View of the Rise of this Revival of Spiritual Religion in the First Half of the Eighteenth Century, and the Principal Agents by Whom it was Promoted in Europe and America; With Some Account of the Doctrine and Polity of Episcopal Methodism in the United States, and the Means and Manner of its Extension Down to A. D. 1884* (Nashville, 1884), 562.

[25]Entry of April 16, 1848, Luther F. Tower MSS Diary, Vol. I, Louisiana State University Library.

[26]Cross, *The History of Southern Methodism in New Orleans*, 13-14, 18; Jones, *A Complete History of Methodism . . .* , 2:347, 443.

[27]"Correspondence between Gerritt Smith, Esq., of Petersborough, New York, and the Rev. William Winans of [Centreville,] Mississippi," *African Repository and Colonial Journal*, 14 (1838): 48-49.

[28]Ibid., 50-51.

[29]"Dr. Winans and the Ninth Section," *Advocate*, February 15, 1851, p. 2. Microfilm copies of the *New Orleans Christian Advocate* from July 10, 1850 to December 26, 1860, are located at the Millsaps-Wilson Library, Millsaps College.

[30]"Death of the Rev. William Winans," *New Orleans Daily Picayune*, September 5, 1857, p. 2.

[31]"The Methodist Church and Southern Slavery," *Daily Picayune*, May 28, 1858, p. 4.

[32]Cross, *The History of Southern Methodism in New Orleans*, 34-35.

[33]Christian, *A History of the Baptists of Louisiana*, 134.

[34]"Editorial Wanderings," *Baptist Banner and Western Pioneer*, March 24, 1842, p. 1.

[35]E. R. Witter, "Baptist Cause in New Orleans" [from the *Mississippi Baptist*], cited in the *Louisiana Baptist* (Mount Lebanon), February 11, 1858, p. 1; Christian, *A History of the Baptists of Louisiana*, 65-67.

[36]Entry of February 16, 1845, Luther F. Tower MSS Diary, Vol. I.

[37]Perhaps one of the reasons why Southern historians have traditionally overlooked Duncan' liberal career in New Orleans is the limited amount of primary source material. Since all his private papers are presumed to be lost, the only direct links to Duncan's slavery views are microfilm copies of his newspapers located at the James P. Boyce Centennial Library, Southern Baptist Theological Seminary, Louisville, Kentucky. Although Duncan's presence in New Orleans was briefly noted by post-Civil War church historians W. E. Paxton and John T. Christian, both writers ignored the controversial aspects of Duncan's life.

[38]*Appleton's Cylcopedia of American Biography*, ed. by James Grant Wilson and John Fiske, 6 vols. (New York, 1888), 2:256-57; Paxton, *A History of the Baptists of Louisiana . . .* , 530-33; "South-Western Baptist Chronicle," (editorial), *Chronicle* (New Orleans), April 8, 1848, p. 2; "South-Western Baptist College" (editorial), *Chronicle*, January 6, 1849, p. 157.

[39]See, for example, "Louisiana Colonization Society," *Chronicle*, February 19, 1848, p. 182; "From Liberia," September 2, 1848, p. 86; "College in Liberia," September 16, 1848, p. 95; and "Moses Allen, Treasurer of the Colonization Society," September 30, 1848, p. 104, in *Chronicle*.

[40]"The Running of Slaves," June 16, 1849, p. 207; "A White Slave," August 4, 1849, p. 28, in *Chronicle*.

[41]"Louisiana Colonization Society," *Chronicle*, February 19, 1848, p. 182.

[42]"Slavery in New Orleans," *Chronicle*, October 2, 1847, p. 102.

[43]"Dissolution of the Union," *Chronicle*, March 23, 1850, p. 158.

[44]Ibid.

[45]"South-Western Baptist Chronicle," *Chronicle*, April 8, 1848, p. 2.

[46]Four copies of the *New Orleans Baptist Chronicle* are located at the James P. Boyce Centennial Library, Southern Baptist Theological Seminary, Louisville, Ky. William C. Duncan's name, along with his title of "Senior Editor," appears in the "Lengthy and Controversial Articles," (editorial) *Baptist Chronicle* (New Orleans), February 1, 1853, p. 2; see also Paxton, *History of the Baptists of Louisiana . . .* , 529.

[47]See "Much Ado About Nothing!" (editorial), *Tennessee Baptist* (Nashville), December 24, 1853, p. 2.

[48]"Defense Against False Charges and Misrepresentations of Rev. J. R. Graves," *Baptist Chronicle*, November [?], 1854, p. 3.

[49]*Appleton's Cyclopedia* . . . , 2: 256-57; Paxton, *History of the Baptists of Louisiana* . . . , 530-33.

[50]C. V. Edwards, *Manual and Directory of the First Baptist Church, New Orleans, Louisiana*, 37.

[51]Although newspaper editor Cassius M. Clay of Lexington, Kentucky, styled himself as a gradual emancipationist, and not an abolitionist, his *True American* was violently suppressed in 1845, and the press of the Upper and Lower South gave its resounding approval of mob action against any newspaper which expressed a critical view of slavery. See Clement Eaton, *The Freedom-of-Thought Struggle in the Old South*, 2nd ed. (New York, 1964), 185-89.

LOUISIANA PRESBYTERIANS AND TUMULTUOUS TIMES*

Penrose St. Amant

WAR

On July 9, 1861, a special meeting of the New Orleans Presbytery was called by several ministers, led by Dr. B. M. Palmer, pastor of the First Presbyterian Church in New Orleans, "to consider the course pursued" by the General Assembly and "to take whatever action may be judged necessary."[1] Why were these Presbyterians concerned about "the course pursued" by the General Assembly? It was because the Spring Resolutions, adopted by that body in Philadelphia on May 1861, declared that it was the "duty" of the churches under the care of the General Assembly "to promote and perpetuate the integrity" of the United States and "to strengthen and encourage the Federal government."[2] This was an ultimatum to the Southern churches, which faced the alternative of staying in the General Assembly at the price of surrendering slavery or of disrupting the General Assembly by supporting it. Actually, the course of the church in the slaveholding states was clearly determined by the adoption of the Spring Resolutions. Fort Sumter had already been fired upon and President Lincoln's call for volunteers made. No battle had been fought but battle lines were being drawn and war was imminent. The disruption of the Presbyterian Church was inevitable.

The response of the New Orleans Presbytery was a studied statement of historic importance in the emerging controversy. On July 10, 1861, the Presbytery stated, "[In view of] the unconstitutional, Erastian, tyrannical, and virtually excinding act of the . . . General Assembly sitting at Philadelphia in May last, we do hereby, with a solemn protest against this act, declare in the fear of God our connection with the General Assembly of the [Old School] Presbyterian church . . . be dissolved."[3] The Presbytery did not stop with a declaration concerning itself but called upon "each presbytery" in the slaveholding states "for itself and by its own sovereign power also" to dissolve its relationship with "the General Assembly" and "appoint commissioners to the General

*First published as Chapter 5 in *A History of the Presbyterian Church in Louisiana* (Richmond, Va.: Synod of Louisiana, 1961), 111-33. Reprinted with the kind permission of the publisher.

Assembly of the Presbyterian Church in the Confederate States of America to sit in the City of Augusta, Georgia, on the fourth day of December 1861."[4] The New Orleans Presbytery was one of the first presbyteries in the slaveholding states to dissolve its connection with the General Assembly of the Presbyterian Church and was active in promoting a separate Southern church. The action of this Presbytery was widely publicized and furnished a pattern to the presbyteries generally.

In October 1861, the Mississippi Synod, of which Dr. B. M. Palmer was moderator, declared that "existing circumstances" made it necessary to "dissolve" relations with the General Assembly of the Presbyterian Church in the U.S.[5] Nothing was said concerning the Spring Resolutions but it is clear they were in the background as a precipitating factor. Palmer was the dominating figure in this historic meeting of the Synod, at which the break with the General Assembly was declared, as he had been in the Presbytery of New Orleans.

Ten synods and forty-five presbyteries, including three from Louisiana, were represented by a little less than one hundred people at the organization of the Presbyterian Church in the Confederate States of America at Augusta, Georgia, on December 4, 1861. The central role which Dr. B. M. Palmer played in these proceedings is suggested by the fact that he was unanimously chosen to preach the opening sermon and elected moderator. The new church numbered 840 ministers and 72,000 communicants. Its existence was justified by the celebrated J. H. Thornwell, who, though ill, gave a penetrating address which brought together the grievances of Southern Presbyterians. The involvement of the church in a "political" issue by the Philadelphia Assembly in May 1861, was cited first. This action, he said, was unconstitutional and created a situation in which delegates from the North and South could not meet in harmony. Furthermore, it was better to have a separate Southern Church free from controversy on the subject of slavery. As long as the church was "even partially under the control of those . . . hostile to slavery" it would be impossible to have "free and unimpeded access to the slave population." Reaching the crux of his argument, Thornwell declared: "This is too dear a price to be paid for nominal union." He then concluded with a defense of slavery.[6] This address succinctly summarized the position of the entire Southern Presbyterian Church. Dr. B. M. Palmer's remarks on the subject were, of course, in complete conformity with Thornwell's sentiments. Both men believed in "the purely spiritual character of the Church,"[7] which with reference to the issue that precipitated the division among Presbyterians meant a church which preserved its neutrality on the issue of slavery. The effect of this view was to put the Presbyterian Church in the South solidly on the side of the status quo and thus of slavery and the slavocracy.

Toward the end of April 1862, Commodore David G. Farragut's fleet fought its way past the Confederate batteries and captured the Crescent City. On May 1, Gen. B. F. Butler led his Federal forces into New Orleans. The divisive effect which this had upon the Presbytery of New Orleans is reflected in the *Minutes* of that body for December 19, 1862, which speak of "the present troubled state of the country which prevents communication with brethren who live outside of the city." "Very few" ministers were left in New Orleans.[8] That part of the Presbytery outside of the city met several times during the Civil War. Meetings were held at Amite City in the Helena Church, April 15, 1863, and at Summit, Mississippi, a year later. On March 9, 1864, that part of the New Orleans Presbytery which was confined to the city dissolved its connection with the General Assembly of the Presbyterian Church of the Confederate States of America and became an independent Presbytery.[9] In April, the Presbytery spoke of the "hopeful prospects" which had obtained two years before when there were "twenty-four or more" ministers and the churches were in a "flourishing" condition and lamented that of these only five ministers remained—one had died—and the churches were weak and discouraged.

Dr. Palmer was not in New Orleans when it was occupied by the Union Army. Early in April 1862, he left the city to visit the army of Gen. Albert Sidney Johnston and to attend the meeting of the General Assembly, scheduled to meet in Memphis, Tennessee. Just before the Battle of Shiloh, according to a tradition, he delivered a moving address, astride a horse, to a portion of Johnston's army. A Confederate officer stated that Palmer's "services were worth more to the Rebel cause than a soldiery of ten thousand men."[10]

Palmer found it impossible to get to Montgomery, Alabama, to which the meeting of the General Assembly was moved from Memphis due to fighting near that city, and spent several weeks in Tennessee speaking in behalf of the Confederacy. By this time, General Butler had occupied New Orleans. It was evident that Palmer, regarded rightly as an archenemy by Union men, should not return home. His family was sent to him and in August he established his home in Columbia, South Carolina, with Mrs. George Howe, his wife's mother. From this time until July 17, 1865, when he resumed his pulpit in New Orleans, he labored unstintedly in behalf of the Church and the Confederacy. He continued to preach at every opportunity and did some teaching at Columbia Seminary. On September 17, 1862, Palmer delivered a eulogy upon Dr. Thornwell, remarks which formed the nucleus of a biography of this fallen leader of the Southern Church, entitled *The Life and Letters of John Henley Thornwell, D.D., LL.D.*, which was published in 1875. To the General Assembly convened in Charlotte, North Carolina, in 1864, he reported that he had preached in all the brigades of one corps of the Army of Tennessee and observed "the greatness of the work God was carrying on" among the troops. He still harbored live hopes that victory would come to the Confederacy. But soon these hopes were shattered and he was forced to flee from Columbia, which, with his "private papers, books, and household effects," was burned by the Union forces. Returning to the devastated city, he labored to bind up the wounds of war and resumed his spiritual ministrations in the Church until the close of the conflict.[11]

On October 13, 1865, following the end of the war the previous April, the New Orleans Presbytery resumed meetings of the entire body which had not been held since April 1862. The two sets of minutes from the two parts of the Presbytery, which met separately during the war, were both accepted "without raising any question of precedence between the two."[12] The three and one-half years during which the Presbytery was divided by the fortunes of war were described as years of "separation and peculiar trials." Gratitude was expressed that "with few exceptions" houses of worship were retained by their respective congregations, permitting the immediate resumption of worship when hostilities ceased. Notice was taken of the fact that ministers of the Presbytery had served as chaplains in the Confederate Army. A "hopeful condition" prevailed in the "united, earnest, and spiritual" congregations, and attendance at church services showed "an encouraging increase."[13]

The Louisiana Presbytery, made up of eleven ministers and seventeen churches, dissolved its connection with the Presbyterian Church in the United States at Jackson, Louisiana, on October 16, 1861. The *Minutes* for that meeting record at random several matters which cast light upon conditions in the Presbytery: "Congregations have generally diminished in consequence of enlistments in the war." "The instructions of servants is regularly attended to, and with special success upon some plantations." "Contributions to benevolent operations of the church have fallen off in amount in consequence of the claims of our troops for outfits, which have been met with great liberality, and in consequence of the arrest of cotton sales."[14]

In March 1862, "the desolating and widespread influence of the war" was noted in the *Minutes* of the Presbytery,[15] and a year later the situation in the church was dark— "very little" was reported. This meeting, held at Comite Church on March 18, 1863, was the last until after the war, when the Presbytery met at Baton Rouge on November 8, 1865. Divine worship was observed in "most" of the churches in 1864-1865. The spirit of the people was set forth in a sentence of the records of the meeting at the Comite Church: "We have much over which to mourn," as indeed they did, but this was a temporary mood soon overpassed with concern for the gigantic task of rebuilding the Church.[16]

The Red River Presbytery ended its relationship with the Presbyterian Church in the United States at Minden on July 18, 1861.[17] It is clear that this Presbytery and the Louisiana Presbytery followed the leadership of the New Orleans Presbytery and Dr. B. M. Palmer in severing ecclesiastical ties with the General Assembly. What happened in North Louisiana in the war years is another version of the same dreary story which occurred elsewhere in the state. An interesting sidelight on this story is the minute book of the Red River Presbytery for this period, purchased in 1863, when, due to the scarcity of paper because of the war, a curious looking tablet of poor quality paper—with sheets joined at the top rather than the side—was all that was available. Readers were assured in a sentence written in pencil that it was "the most suitable record book obtainable."[18]

On March 21, 1863, the Presbytery "heartily" approved the proclamation of Jefferson Davis to observe Friday the 27th "as a day of humiliation, fasting, and prayer to Almighty God" for His "gracious interposition" in behalf of the Confederate forces. But the tide of war was turning against the South.[19] An anticipated meeting of the Presbytery at the Mt.

Zion Church on September 20, 1863, was not held "on account of the invasion of this section . . . by the Yankee Army."[20] It was not until September 25, 1865, that the Presbytery met again, after a lapse of more than two years. At this meeting, the Presbytery acknowledged "the hand of God . . . in the overthrow of the Confederate government and in the establishment of the authority of the United States" and recommended that the General Assembly should rename the Southern Church "in strict conformity with the facts of history."[21] This view was shared by Presbyterians generally in the South and the Presbyterian Church of the Confederate States of America was named the Presbyterian Church in the United States at the 1866 General Assembly.

The consequences of the defeat of the Confederate States were more devastating to the Red River Presbytery than the two sister presbyteries in Louisiana. The economy of North Louisiana was based primarily on the plantation system and the churches relied largely upon the plantation owners for support. The *Minutes* for September 20, 1866, speak of the "diminished fortunes and even poverty of those who were once wealthy" and lament the "absence or death of many . . . ministers."[22]

POST-WAR PROBLEMS

A declaration of the Presbytery of New Orleans in 1866 is typical of the condition and outlook of the Presbyterian Church in Louisiana shortly after the war. The churches were "for the most part self-sustaining" but hampered by debts on houses of worship only partly paid for at the outbreak of hostilities. When the war ended "everything was dark and discouraging [and] . . . the hearts of many had yielded to despondency, so fatal to Christian effort." In the "general overthrow of private fortunes [some] were in danger of being swept away by a spirit of worldliness in the superhuman efforts made to escape insolvency and utter ruin." Deep concern was expressed for the "young and gay" who, in the view of the framers of the presbyterial statement, "threatened to take reprisals upon the sorrows of the past and to flee from the gloom of the present by plunging recklessly into every form of earthly pleasure." But conditions were improving and there was a growing inclination on the part of the people in the churches "to accept their lot from the hand of God"[23]—a recurring belief reflected in the *Minutes* of the three presbyteries. Gratitude was expressed that the congregations were as large as before the war.[24]

The secular spirit of the post-war period is reflected equally in the *Minutes* of the Louisiana and Red River Presbyteries. In 1866, four problems were taken up by the Louisiana Presbytery. Dancing by members of the church was frowned upon and those who persisted in "this amusement" faced the possibility of dismissal. "Persistent neglect of worship and the ordinances" of the church might result in "eventual suspension." People who moved from one community to another were admonished to affiliate with the church at their new residence. Failure to do this within two years could result in dismissal. "Open disregard for vows" could have the consequence of a public trial and possible exclusion.[25]

At the same meeting, the Presbytery deplored the "general eagerness to recuperate lost fortunes," which bordered on "avarice" but recognized that there was a legitimate anxiety for "the supply of daily recurring wants . . . by many." The plight of the ministers was particularly severe. "Our ministers," the report continued, "are not supported in a single congregation within our bounds." Many clergymen were forced to secure "secular labor."[26]

In September 1868, the Louisiana Presbytery reported "dead and dying churches, scattered people, and wasted fortunes. . . . " Churches in the Louisiana Presbytery at this time were Oak Grove, Unity, Liberty, Bethany, Comite, Clinton, Jackson, Plaquemine, Baton Rouge, and Woodville. The following year, the Presbytery declared that not a single minister received "a competent income." [27] A little later, the records of the Presbytery reveal that "not more than one, if one," minister of this Presbytery received "adequate support in his labor."[28] The situation was so desperate financially that not a single minister received such "support as would enable him to lay aside sufficient money for his own burial."[29] At this same time, the Presbytery of New Orleans asked the General Assembly to reconsider its action of listing salaries of ministers. Such "public exposition of the estate of individual churches" was deemed unwise and embarrassing to many.[30]

In 1870, it was stated at the meeting of the Louisiana Presbytery that there was "not a solitary" Presbyterian minister in the territory of the Presbytery west of the Mississippi River.[31] Three years later, the situation had not improved, for Evangelist R. E. Patterson reported in 1873 that he found the "field . . . on the west side of the river very destitute." Only one sermon had been preached in two years in the Atchafalaya area, which had been "almost abandoned by all denominations."[32] The Red River Presbytery recorded its "sad need of young ministers."[33]

These conditions were the result of the war and were thus temporary. The 1870s were years of discouragement but also years of reassessment and new beginnings. For example, the Napoleon Avenue Presbyterian Church in New Orleans completed a new edifice in 1872, except for "plaster on its walls and pews on its floor." The ladies then took the problem in hand and through "a series of entertainments" in the church—"music, vocal and instrumental, recitations, and tableaux, with refreshments"—helped to complete the church and provide needed facilities. People were invited to visit the church, which could be reached on "a pleasant ride [which afforded] the enjoyment of fresh suburban air."[34] That was when Napoleon Avenue was in the suburbs!

The Rev. Benjamin B. Wayne served as "stated supply" of this church from the beginning, a position he retained until his tragic death in 1879, which was the consequence of an accident sustained while swimming in Lake Pontchartrain at Mandeville. In order to supplement his modest income Wayne taught in the public schools of the city and was principal of McDonogh No. 10 when he died. He counted Paul Tulane, the generous philanthropist, among his close friends.

Wayne's successor was the Rev. R. Q. Mallard, who also served as editor of *The Southwestern Presbyterian* for twelve years. He was elected moderator of the General Assembly in 1896. But his main concern was the church, which, under his leadership, moved into "the front ranks of the Presbyterian Churches of the city," according to Georgia Mallard Seago, who wrote a history of the church for the celebration of its Diamond Jubilee in 1936.

During the pastorate of Dr. Mallard, a young man of nineteen years of age, Dunbar H. Ogden, who in 1930 was to become pastor of the Napoleon Avenue Church, spoke at prayer meeting in the church in the interest of Chamberlain Hunt Academy. He talked on the subject, "How to bring up a child." After the service, the young preacher went over to the manse with Dr. Mallard, who commended him for his excellent discourse and then, with a twinkle in his eyes, remarked, "But you were preaching to old maids and widows."[35]

A picture of the situation in South Louisiana in 1871 has been preserved by the Rev. J. A. McConnell, an evangelist, who lived at Thibodaux. He listed and described briefly the following "preaching points:" Brashear City, now Morgan City, with "thirteen members waiting to be organized" into a Presbyterian Church; Centerville on Bayou Teche, where a church of thirty-five members (four elders) without a building had been organized; Franklin, "no organization;" Jeanerette, "four members, no organization"; New Iberia, the "largest and most flourishing town on the Teche" River, where there were six Presbyterians and only a Roman Catholic and a Methodist Church; Abbeville, "five or six members [and] no Protestant Church."[36] He also preached at Vermilionville, now Lafayette, and Opelousas, where there was a small Presbyterian Church.[37] The Presbyterians in Brashear City who were "waiting to be organized" into a church effected an organization in 1872, under the leadership of the Rev. Charles S. Dodd. On March 14, 1876, it became the First Presbyterian Church of Morgan City.[38] The church at Opelousas, which belonged to the Louisiana Presbytery, requested that it be made a part of the New Orleans Presbytery in 1871 but the request was denied.[39]

POST-WAR GROWTH

There were many problems but there were also many heroic souls, ministers and laymen, for whom the problems were occasions which elicited courage and labor, not despair and inertia. The unnamed pastor-elect at Plaquemine was such a person. Excerpts from a letter he wrote in 1872 give a glimpse of his first trip to Grosse Tete, near Plaquemine, where he was also pastor. Multiply what he recorded many times and some impression is gained of the labors of obscure leaders in this period who were determined that the Presbyterian witness should be maintained and extended in outlying areas of difficult access.

He left Plaquemine at dawn on a Saturday morning for Grosse Tete to officiate at a communion service. Down Bayou Plaquemine in a skiff propelled by two men with oars, he and two others proceeded on a journey which required twelve hours to cover twenty-six miles. Reaching a point on Bayou Grosse Tete four miles from the church, he disembarked and spent the night with a friend. On Sunday morning, he and his host traveled to the church by horse and buggy. They found "a goodly number" gathered for worship and two young ladies were received into full communion. They were the first fruits of his new charge and he was much encouraged as he faced the missionary challenge of the Plaquemine-Grosse Tete field. The two churches persisted until 1911, when the Grosse Tete Church was dissolved and its members joined the church at Plaquemine. [40]

The history of the Presbyterian Church in South Louisiana in this period must give a large place to the Rev. Charles M. Atkinson, who in 1878 accepted the position of Evangelist in the Teche Country under the direction of the New Orleans Presbytery. He lived first at Morgan City and was remembered particularly by the people there for his devotion to them during the yellow fever epidemic of 1879-1880. He lost two of his children during this terrible scourge but strove valiantly through it all to give comfort and courage to the suffering and stricken people. [41]

In 1880, he moved to Thibodaux, where for eight years he served as pastor of the church there. Eight years later he transferred to Centerville and remained there until his death in 1906. During the twenty-eight years of his ministry in South Louisiana he preached at Morgan City, Thibodaux, Houma, Berwick and Centerville. He and the Rev. G. E. Chandler were instrumental in organizing Presbyterian churches in Jeanerette,[42] called Calvary, in 1880, and New Iberia on July 14, 1895.[43] Until June 15, 1901, when the Rev. J. N. Blackburn arrived at Houma, Atkinson was the only Presbyterian minister between Lafayette and New Orleans. In spite of advancing age and poor eyesight, which grew steadily worse, he continued to supply the churches at Centerville, Berwick and Morgan City until 1906, when at the age of eighty-seven he concluded his earthly pilgrimage. In his honor, the church at Morgan City was named the Atkinson Memorial Presbyterian Church in 1913.

Illustrative of another type of endeavor in this period of rebuilding is a report given in 1878 by the Committee of Colportage to the Presbytery of Red River. [44] The Committee was granted the authority to "select and purchase" books and tracts to sell and give away, provided they were publications approved by the General Assembly. The Committee was given the power to employ colporteurs to visit the homes of the people and dispose of literature by gift or sale. It was also the function of these itinerant propagandists to advertise such church papers as the *Earnest Worker, Children's Friend,* and *The Southwestern Presbyterian.* Each colporteur was furnished a horse, a "suitable wagon," and other "things necessary" for his work at a cost not to exceed $250.00. His salary was set at $30.00 per month and essential expenses, subject to increase "if the business should justify." He was expected to devote at least six months of the year traveling in the territory of the Red River Presbytery. The rest of the time could be spent anywhere in Louisiana.

It is difficult today to recapture the important role which colporteurs played in strengthening and extending the Gospel at this time. These men, poorly paid, making their way with wagons filled with books, magazines, and tracts, were an important feature of the missionary strategy of the Church after the Civil War. Innumerable materials published in the nineteenth century, especially in the last three decades of it, now buried in archives and accumulating dust, are reminders of a significant segment of the missionary task.

The most significant factor in the growth of the Presbyterian Church in Louisiana after the Civil War was the rapid expansion of the railroads. The first region affected was served by the New Orleans Presbytery. In 1875, for example, the Evangelistic Committee of that Presbytery indicated that missionary efforts were being expended along three recently completed railroad lines operating from the Crescent City.[45] This "outlying territory" so difficult to "overtake with the Gospel" was open in a new way to Presbyterian extension due to its easier accessibility. The three directions were southwest, northeast, and roughly north.[46] A year later the "city missionary" reported that he worked with the seamen in the Bethel Society and along "three lines radiating from the city," presumably in the directions mentioned above. Each line stretched "one hundred or more miles" and was "dotted with feeble churches unable to maintain the Gospel." He was concerned because many communities were entirely devoid of Presbyterian churches.

But the situation was improving. This is reflected in a report made to the New Orleans Presbytery in 1878: "Outside the city [of New Orleans], our field embraces the territory along the Jackson and Great Northern Railroad, which has six churches supplied by an evangelist; the country along the Mobile and New Orleans Railroad has three churches, two mission stations, and the services of two ministers; and the country along the Morgan Railroad and Bayou Teche, which has the services of an evangelist; there are also stations on, or near, Lake Pontchartrain, which have occasional services from pastors in the city."[47]

The six churches to the northeast of New Orleans on the Jackson and Northern Railroad were: Amite City (Helena Church), twenty-four members; Tangipahoa, Louisiana, seven members; Summit, Mississippi (Pisgah), twenty-five members; Magnolia, Mississippi, fifteen members; McComb City, Mississippi, ten members; Osyka, Mississippi, twenty-two members. The total membership of these churches, all except one in the state of Mississippi, was one hundred and three. All belonged to the New Orleans Presbytery. The six churches were served by an evangelist, the Rev. J. C. Graham.[48]

The three churches on the Mobile and New Orleans Railroad were at Pass Christian, Mississippi, fifty-one members, of which the Rev. W. C. Clark was pastor; Hansboro, Mississippi, nineteen members, and Moss Point, Mississippi, forty-two members, both of which were served by the Rev. I. J. Bingham as stated supply. There were also two mission stations at Biloxi and Bay St. Louis. The total membership of these churches was one hundred and twelve. All were in Mississippi and all belonged to the New Orleans Presbytery.

Southwest of New Orleans on the Morgan Railroad and along Bayou Teche were four churches: Thibodaux, thirty-two members; Houma, six members; Centerville, forty-two members; and Morgan City—known also as Brashear—sixty-six members. Three "stations" on or near Lake Pontchartrain were Madisonville, Mandeville, and Covington, for which the Rev. C. M. Atkinson served as evangelist.[49] The churches at Madisonville and Covington which had been founded in the late 1840s were disorganized by the Civil War and ceased to function except for occasional preaching until the 1890s.

In 1878, the total membership of the churches in the New Orleans Presbytery outside the city was three hundred and sixty-one. There were 2,245 members in the remaining nine churches in New Orleans. The total membership of all the churches in the Presbytery was just above twenty-six hundred. There were two evangelists in the city— the Rev. A. J. Witherspoon and the Rev. J. G. Gruber.[50]

In the 1880s and early 1890s, the records of the presbyteries reflect a growing awareness of the impact of expanding railroad transportation upon the church. The growth of railroads would "change the centers of population" and should, therefore, elicit "special efforts to commence work" in the new settlements thus created. For example, when Vienna, the Lincoln Parish seat, was left four miles from the Vicksburg, Shreveport, and Pacific Railroad, the town of Ruston was founded at the point where the railroad intersected the old dirt road linking Vienna and Vernon. In October of 1884, the Presbyterian Church at Ruston was organized through the efforts of the Rev. James A. McLees, an evangelist for the Red River Presbytery.[51]

The missionary opportunity which confronted the church as a result of the shifting population must have prompted some to consider the use of ministers without professional education because the Louisiana Presbytery declared its "disapproval of any steps to lower the educational standards of the ministry" and insisted that the times demanded not less but "more thorough mental discipline than any former time. . . . "[52] The New Orleans Presbytery also opposed "any change" which would lower "the qualifications for entrance into the Gospel ministry" and made its position known to the General Assembly.[53]

The railroads were not an unmixed blessing. The Presbytery of Louisiana declared that Sunday excursions were "a great evil" not only because they lured people away from public worship but also because of the bad effect which the "excursionists" had upon the communities in which they spent the day.[54] Riding on trains on Sunday by ministers going to and from preaching appointments could not be justified, the Presbytery stated, "on the grounds of necessity or mercy."[55]

The same warnings against the failure to observe the "Sabbath" properly came from the other presbyteries. "Flagrant desecration" of the day by excursions on the railroads, "by parades, picnics, and parties of pleasure, [and by] traversing the city streets and filling the parks" was frowned upon by the New Orleans Presbytery in 1877.[56] Serious consequences from such behavior were sure for God would not permit such desecration indefinitely, the Presbytery declared, and the people were reminded of Israel's punishment for profanation of the sacred day. [57] The Red River Presbytery in 1878 registered its disapproval of using Sunday as a time for "visiting." Concern was manifested by the New Orleans Presbytery six years later about the laxity with which the "Sabbath" would be treated during the World's Industrial and Cotton Centennial Exposition in New Orleans.[58]

It is not surprising that the Synod of Mississippi made an extensive report on the Sabbath, which was published in the December 8, 1881, issue of *The Southwestern Presbyterian.* [59] Dr. B. M. Palmer was chairman of the committee which framed the statement: "The increasing evil of Sabbath desecration" could be arrested by recognizing that the church had "no power to abate in the least degree the rigor of the Divine law," by recognizing that the only limitation of "the law of the Sabbath" permitted by Jesus is found "in works of necessity and mercy," and by "the exercise of church discipline." The intent of this statement was to bring the growing influence of the Presbyterian Church to bear on "secular authorities" through "her members as citizens of the Commonwealth" in order to secure "by wise legislation . . . a national Sabbath."[60]

Exactly ten years later, in 1891, Dr. Palmer was waging a sustained campaign against the Louisiana Lottery Company. On June 25, he spoke in the Grand Opera House in New Orleans following an introduction by Col. William P. Johnston, Chancellor of Tulane University, who described Palmer as "the first citizen of New Orleans." His opening words were: "I lay the indictment against the Lottery Company of Louisiana that it is essentially an immoral institution whose business and avowed aim is to propagate gambling throughout the state and throughout the country."[61] He regarded lottery as not merely a nuisance but a crime and because he believed it was a crime he held that it was incompatible not merely with the safety but with the very being of the state. This thesis he advanced with eloquence and logic. Its effect was literally tremendous. The lottery was doomed and Palmer played a major role in its collapse.

The continuing intellectual vitality of this remarkable man is evidenced by an invitation extended to him to join the faculty of the Theological Seminary at Columbia, South Carolina, in 1892, when he was seventy-four years of age. He was offered the chair of Pastoral Theology, which he declined. This was the last of many efforts to persuade Palmer to leave his beloved church and city. [62]

In 1898, the city fathers, responding to a widespread sentiment of New Orleanians of every creed, named that part of Henry Clay Avenue which lies east of St. Charles Avenue for the veteran minister and citizen, "Palmer Avenue."

THE SOUTHWESTERN PRESBYTERIAN—
HENRY MARTYN SMITH

It required great courage to begin *The Southwestern Presbyterian*, a weekly synodical newspaper, whose first issue appeared in New Orleans on February 25, 1869.[63] *The True Witness*, a paper published under the editorship of the Reverend R. McInnis, was suspended during the Civil War and not reissued at its close. This prompted the Board of Trustees of Presbyterian Publications of the Synod of Mississippi, organized January 22, 1852, to establish *The Southwestern Presbyterian*. The editor, Dr. Henry Martyn Smith, pastor of the Third Presbyterian Church in New Orleans since March 22, 1857, was well aware of the problems confronting the project. "We are not ignorant of the difficulty and perils connected with a new newspaper enterprise," Smith said. His trepidations about the venture are easy to understand. The war was only four years past and "the tragic era" had just begun. But Smith's faith was more formidable than his fears. "The end in view," as he put it, was worth "all the risks."[64] The success of the enterprise was assured by the distinguished character of the Board of Trustees, which was made up of nine of the leading Presbyterians in Louisiana: Editor H. M. Smith, B. M. Palmer, T. R. Markham, E. S. Keep, Moses Greenwood, David Hadden, W. C. Black, H. T. Bartlett, and Frederick Stringer.

The first editorial in *The Southwestern Presbyterian* bore the unlikely caption of "Lazy Elders." The editor admitted it was a strange beginning to speak critically of the lay leadership of the Church but made it quite clear that a discussion of "lazy elders," of whom he felt there were too many, was "nothing at all compared with some things" he expected to say when he and his readers got better acquainted![65] It would be hardly accurate to say that this brief editorial was typical of the man, either in terms of outlook or interest, but it does suggest a certain bluntness and also a touch of gentleness and wit which marked his work.

Smith was a Pennsylvanian who, after finishing college in his home state and starting to study at the Allegheny Theological Seminary, went south to Columbia, South Carolina, where he completed his divinity studies at the seminary there. One of his instructors was Dr. B. M. Palmer, who taught at Columbia Seminary from 1853 to 1856. In the autumn of the latter year, Dr. Palmer accepted the invitation to become pastor of the First Presbyterian Church in New Orleans and prevailed upon Smith to go to New Orleans to occupy the pulpit of the First Church until he should arrive in December. At the expiration of this period, Smith became pastor of the Third Presbyterian Church in the Crescent City, his only pastorate, which he served for thirty years and ten months. Ill health forced him to retire from the church, then on Royal Street facing Washington Square, in 1888. Until that time he bore with grace and distinction the double responsibility of the pastorate and editorship of *The Southwestern Presbyterian*, which he finally relinquished in 1891. His resignation was reluctantly accepted by the Synod of Mississippi on November 11, 1891, and his name appeared for the last time as editor of the paper the next day. He died less than three years later. He was a leading figure in Louisiana Presbyterianism in the tumultuous times that followed the Civil War. His facile pen and rugged courage were known not only in the community in which he lived and labored but also throughout the territory of the General Assembly, of which he was elected moderator in 1873.[66]

Notes for "Louisiana Presbyterians and Tumultuous Times"

[1]*Minutes of the Presbytery of New Orleans* (July 9, 1861): 240.

[2]*Minutes of the General Assembly, Presbyterian Church in the U. S.*, 16 (1861): 303.

[3]*Minutes of the Presbytery of New Orleans* (July 9, 1861): 240. The mood of the members of this historic presbytery has been vividly captured by T. C. Johnson, who wrote that the passage of the Spring resolutions "involved a subordination of Church to State, a violation of the Church's Constitution as well as a usurpation of the crown rights of the Redeemer; and a cruel trampling upon the God-given rights of their [sic] brethren throughout the whole Southland." See T. C. Johnson, *The Life and Letters of Benjamin Morgan Palmer* (Nashville, 1906), 240. According to Fred H. Ford in his *Historic Continuity of the Presbytery of Louisiana of the Presbyterian Church, U. S. A.*, "a small group of churches and ministers struggled courageously to maintain the original New Orleans Presbytery." The Second German Presbyterian Church, organized May 24, 1863, reported to the General Assembly of the Presbyterian Church U. S. A. in 1872 and later returned to the Southern Church. This church became the Claiborne Avenue Church in 1915. See *Presbyterian Journal*, 1:8 (June 7, 1916): 15-16, for a historical sketch of this church.

[4]Ibid., (July 10, 1861): 250.

[5]*Minutes of the Synod of Mississipi*, October 1861.

[6]See R. E. Thompson, *History of the Presbyterian Church in the U. S.* (New York, 1895), Appendix 19, 388-406.

[7]B. M. Palmer, *The Life and Letters of James Henley Thornwell, D.D., LL.D.* (Richmond, 1875), 501.

[8]*Minutes of the Presbytery of New Orleans* (December 19, 1862): 286.

[9]Ibid. (March 9, 1864), First Presbyterian Church, New Orleans. At the end of the war, the relationship between this part of the Presbytery and the General Assembly of the Southern Church was reestablished. See ibid., 2 (October 12, 1865): 311 ff. and ibid., 2 (Summitt, Mississippi, 1868): 118.

[10]Quoted in Henry Wilson, *Rise and Fall of the Slave Power in America* (New York, 1877), 700.

[11]Johnson, *B. M. Palmer*, 287.

[12]*Minutes of the Presbytery of New Orleans*, Special Committee on Minutes of the Presbytery, 2 (October 13, 1865): 311 ff.

[13]Ibid., (October 13, 1865): 319 ff.

[14]*Minutes of the Presbytery of Louisiana* (October 16, 1861).

[15]Ibid. (March 19, 1862).

[16]Ibid., Comite Church, Louisiana (March 18, 1863): 395-6.

[17]*Minutes of the Presbytery of Red River*, Minden, Louisiana (July 18, 1861): 103-8.

[18]Ibid., 2.

[19]Ibid., (March 21, 1863): 20.

[20]Ibid., 21

[21]Ibid., (September 29, 1865).

[22]Ibid., (September 20, 1866): 24.

[23]*Minutes of the Presbytery of New Orleans*, Thibodaux, Louisiana (October 13, 1866): 60-1.

[24]Ibid.

[25]*Minutes of the Presbytery of Louisiana*, Liberty, Mississippi (October 13, 1866): 421-23.

[26]Ibid., 8: 5-6.

[27]Ibid., Plaquemine, Louisiana (March 20, 1869): 61.

[28]Ibid., Bethany Church, Louisiana (March 18, 1871): 163.

[29]*Minutes of the Presbytery of New Orleans*, Centerville, Louisiana (1871): 230. See *Minutes of the General Assembly* (1871): 505.

[30]*Minutes of the Presbytery of Louisiana*, Liberty, Mississippi (October 1, 1870): 150.

[31]Ibid., 10, Clinton, Louisiana (October 12, 1873): 42.

[32]*Southwestern Presbyterian*, 4:12 (May 9, 1872): 2.

[33]Ibid., 4:15 (May 30, 1872): 2.

[34]Georgia Mallard Seago, *Historical Sketch of Napoleon Avenue Presbyterian Church* (n.p., 1936), 6-13.

[35]Ibid.

[36]*Minutes of the Presbytery of New Orleans*, 2 (October 11, 1871): 245.

[37][George Summey], "Home Mission Work of New Orleans Presbytery," in *Presbyterianism in New Orleans and Adjacent Points, 1818-1930*, comp. Rev. Louis Voss (Presbyterian Board of Publication, Synod of Louisiana, 1931), 67, 69.

[38]*Minutes of the Presbytery of Louisiana*, Comite Church, Louisiana (September 28 and 30, 1871).

[39]Letter of the "Pastor-elect" at Plaquemine to Brother Smith in *Southwestern Presbyterian*, 4:4 (March 14, 1872): 2.

[40]*Minutes of the Presbytery of Louisiana*, Opelousas, Louisiana (October 5, 1911): 76.

[41][Summey], "Rev. C. M. Atkinson," in *Presbyterianism in New Orleans*, 71. In 1892, Calvary Church was named Jeanerette.

[42]Minutes of the Session, New Iberia Presbyterian Church, 1.

[43]*Minutes of the Synod of Louisiana*, Baton Rouge, Louisiana (November 15-18, 1906): 223-6.

[44]*Minutes of the Presbytery of Red River*, Alabama Church, Louisiana, 2 (April 11, 1878): 149.

[45]*Minutes of the Presbytery of New Orleans*, Amite City, Louisiana, 2 (April 1875): 354.

[46]Ibid., (April 1876).

[47]Ibid., New Orleans (October 9, 1878): 3:6-7.

[48]Ibid., Moss Point, Mississippi (April 16, 1879): 32-3.

[49]Ibid.

[50][George Summey], "After the War," in *Presbyterianism in New Orleans and Adjacent Points, 1818-1930*, comp. Rev. Louis Voss (Presbyterian Board of Publication, Synod of Louisiana, 1931), 71.

[51]*Abbeville Progress*, May 21, 1938.

[52]John P. Graham, *An Historical Sketch of the Presbyterian Church of Ruston, Louisiana* (n.p., 1934), 5.

[53]*Minutes of the Presbytery of Louisiana*, Liberty, Mississippi, 10 (April 21, 1883): 22.

[54]*Minutes of the Presbytery of New Orleans*, Hansboro, Mississippi (April 14, 1892).

[55]*Minutes of the Presbytery of Louisiana*, Plaquemine, Louisiana, 10 (October 3, 1884): 111.

[56]Ibid., Wilson (October 28, 1887).

[57]*Minutes of the Presbytery of New Orleans*, New Orleans (October 1877): 456.

[58]*Minutes of the Presbytery of Red River*, Alabama Church, Louisiana (April 12, 1878): 152.

[59]B. M. Palmer, "Report upon the Sabbath," in *Southwestern Presbyterian*, 13:44 (December 8, 1881), 1.

[60]*Minutes of the Presbytery of New Orleans*, New Orleans (October 10, 1884).

[61]*Southwestern Presbyterian*, July 2, 1891. See Johnson, *B. M. Palmer*, 553-63.

[62]B. M. Palmer, quoted in Johnson, *B. M. Palmer*, 554.

[63]The *New Orleans Observer* has served as a paper read by Presbyterians in the 1830s. In 1843, the Louisiana Presbytery proposed to establish the *New Orleans Presbyterian*. See *Minutes of the Presbytery of New Orleans*, Jackson, Louisiana, 1 (September 29, 1843): 350.

[64]Henry Martyn Smith, "Prospectus," in *Southwestern Presbyterian*, February 25, 1869, 1:1.

[65]Ibid.

[66]See B. M. Palmer, "Rev. Henry Martyn Smith, D.D.," in *Presbyterianism in New Orleans and Adjacent Points, 1818-1930*, comp. Rev. Louis Voss (Presbyterian Board of Publication, Synod of Louisiana, 1931), 273-8.

PART VIII

The Turn of the Century, 1878-1916

THE WOMEN OF THE TEMPLE: JEWISH WOMEN IN LAKE CHARLES AND SHREVEPORT*

Janet Allured

The story of women in Protestantism has been told and retold many times, but little has been written about Jewish women, particularly in Louisiana. One reason is that their numbers were fairly small. Jews made up 3 to 4 percent of the population of the United States throughout most of this century, but they were only about 1 percent of the population in the South. The percentage of Jews in Louisiana has ranged from nearly 2 percent in the 1890s to under 1 percent in more recent years.[1]

Jews have traditionally been more influential than their small numbers would suggest. In the towns across the South in which Jews settled, they were among the most active community leaders. They were prominent businessmen and businesswomen, civic leaders, and philanthropists. Southern Jews were far more urban than the general population, more likely to be middle class, and usually better educated. Their outlook was cosmopolitan rather than parochial, liberal rather than conservative, and tolerant rather than narrow-minded.[2] Most were also Reform Jews.[3] Reform Judaism, a product of the Enlightenment, encouraged a rational, scholarly study of the Bible. Eschewing most of the traditional laws and rituals, Reformers modernized Judaism. American Reformed congregations began the practice of holding their services in English, introduced congregational singing (rather than using the traditional cantor), and used an English-Hebrew prayer book. They adopted many of the trappings of the Protestant churches, building their temples with pulpits, choir lofts and altars.

Reform Judaism also elevated the position of women in the Jewish faith. Traditionally, women were not obligated to perform religious tasks or to attend regular synagogue services. Because there was no obligation for them, they were not considered full participants in the religion. They could not participate in communal prayer or study sacred texts. Needless to say, they were also excluded from any decision-making roles in relig-

*First presented at the thirty-seventh meeting of the Louisiana Historical Association, Houma, Louisiana, March 1995. Printed with the kind permission of the author.

ious life.[4] Reformers, however, changed all of that. They allowed girls to be educated alongside boys and, for the first time, to be eligible for confirmation. The old practice of segregated seating was abandoned; women sat beside men in family groups, and were counted in the *minyan* (the legal quorum of ten required for a religious service). And finally, Reformers abolished the man's traditional morning benediction thanking God for "not having made me a woman."[5] Rabbi Isaac Wise, who popularized an Americanized Reform Judaism in the 1840s and 1850s, believed participation in worship was as much an obligation for women as for men.[6] This meant that Jewish education, philanthropy and social services were now their responsibility as well. Thus, while men were busying themselves in the secular world of business, their increasingly leisured wives were able to take over these religious roles for them. Women, in other words, became more active in Jewish life as men became less so.

In the nineteenth century, Jewish congregations in this country, like Protestant churches, were seeing their churches "feminized." That is, the women sitting in the pews began to outnumber the men.[7] Jewish men, like Protestant and Catholic men, were increasingly diverted from religious duties by the demands of a capitalist economy, leaving the women to serve as the bastions of religion in this country. But Jewish men suffered a dilemma not faced by other religions—the exigencies of American life forced them to work on their holy day, the Sabbath. Increasingly, then, rabbis looked to women to be the keepers of religion. That the rabbis were preaching to congregations which were predominantly female is reflected in the new respect accorded women in Reform Judaism.

A central concept in Judaism is *rachmonus*. The literal translation of this term is "compassion," but it implies responsibility as well. As a Jew, one had a responsibility to be charitable towards those in need. This had always been true for women as well as men. Thus, some of the first organizations of Jewish women, all of which were associated with a synagogue, were devoted to charity.[8] For example, the women of Shreveport formed a Hebrew Ladies Benevolent Association as far back as 1861, which provided charity, not just to other Jews, but "in times of distress, epidemics, overflows [flooding]," the *Shreveport Times* commented on the occasion of the association's twenty-fifth anniversary, "has nobly taken its place in the front ranks of those ever ready to alleviate want and suffering."[9]

These first organizations of women in Reform congregations, often called "Ladies Aid Societies," or "Women's Leagues," were forerunners of the Temple Sisterhoods. The women of a prominent temple in New Orleans formed themselves into "The Women's League of Touro Synagogue" in 1895. The purpose of the organization was to care for the synagogue and the grounds, to oversee the Sabbath school, and to visit the sick of the Congregation. In addition, the women obligated themselves not to miss any of the "divine services."[10] The organization, like the Sisterhood into which it evolved, basically replicated women's role in the home, but gave them a sense of obligation to the temple community as well. That is, it extended their role outside of the home into the religious community.

The organization of these Sisterhoods became more formal in 1913, when the National Federation of Temple Sisterhoods (hereafter referred to as NFTS) was founded at the instigation of J. Walter Freiberg, president of the Union of American Hebrew Congregations (the Reform organization). At the time, Reform was losing ground to Conservatism, the choice of many newly arrived immigrants. According to the rabbi who gave the opening address at the Cincinnati convention, the role of the NFTS was not to initiate change but to "maintain an organization."[11] Its goal was to strengthen Reform Judaism by fostering religious commitment in the home and in the synagogue. The members of the Sisterhoods pledged themselves "to urge all our members to realize that it is one of our solemn duties as Jewish women to abstain from shopping, diversions and secular preoccupations that interfere with our religious duties; to attend divine worship and to advance in every way possible the holy cause of Judaism."[12]

The women of Temple Sinai in Lake Charles followed this model. Temple Sinai was built in 1904, serving about nineteen or twenty Jewish families, many of whom were engaged in business and commerce. In fact, most of the first retail and jewelry stores in Lake Charles were owned by Jewish families, such as Gordon's Jewelers; Love's and Muller's department stores; The Fair, Riff's, and The Fashion clothing stores. Two families, the Reinauers and the Abelmans, ran real estate businesses. Some men in the Temple were lawyers; others were doctors. In fact, a substantial percentage of Lake Charles's first doctors were Jewish.[13] These occupations produced enough income that their wives did not need to work outside the home, and were thus free to do the volunteer work necessary to the Temple's survival.

The temple women formed a Ladies Aid Society which, in 1916, changed its name to Temple Sinai Sisterhood and affiliated with NFTS. In addition to seeing to the upkeep of the Temple and its grounds, the purpose of the Sisterhood was "to promote a feeling of common interest between Rabbi and Sisterhood," to aid the Sabbath School in every way, and "to aid and assist our poor."[14] The women raised money through dues, cake sales and sale of cookbooks, Uniongrams, and religious items and teaching aids in the Temple gift shop. These fundraising activities were important to the service of the Temple, but NFTS leaders found it necessary to remind the members that "It is not the primal business of the sisterhood to raise money, but TO RAISE JEWS."[15] The purpose of the sisterhood was to draw women into synagogue affairs so that they could in turn "revive Jewish religious home observance."[16]

Among the most important vehicles for achieving this goal was the Sunday School. The concept of a Jewish Sunday School was the brainchild of Rebecca Gratz of Philadelphia, who founded the first one in the United States in 1838, and modeled it upon the Sunday schools that Protestant women were founding. Gratz shattered Jewish tradition by having women teach both male and female students.[17] Since middle class women had more leisure time than women had ever had before, and since their husbands were occupied with work, it made sense to solicit female teachers for those Sunday schools. Thus, despite some controversy, women became teachers of the Jewish faith. Sunday schools were an important way to prevent apostasy, and Gratz had founded hers partly to counter the evangelism of Protestant women in Jewish neighborhoods. Thus, by seeing to the successful functioning of a Sunday school, Jewish women were carrying out the mission envisioned by Rabbi Wise: nurturing a sense of cultural identity while preserving the faith. The women of Temple Sinai in Lake Charles fulfilled this role as well. They provided the funds to keep the Sunday school going, secured the services of the teachers, and volunteered their time to teach the children themselves. They also sponsored social events for young adults.[18] Undoubtedly, this was a way to try to keep their children from marrying non-Jews.

Assimilationism was a chronic problem for Southern Jews. In Louisiana, with the exception of New Orleans, most Jews lived in small towns where there were few other Jewish families.[19] Their children, attending the local schools, had as many Catholic and Protestant friends as Jewish ones. Parents tried to combat this by cultivating and maintaining strong connections with the other Jewish communities throughout Louisiana and even in neighboring states. Adolescent children were frequently sent to stay with friends or relatives in other towns. Mothers took their new babies to see relatives; men on business trips stayed in the homes of Jewish friends.[20] These trips helped to introduce children to potential spouses throughout the state. Still, the influence of Protestant society was powerful and, fearful of anti-Semitism, many Jews were also careful to cultivate links with their non-Jewish neighbors by joining country clubs and other organizations which were predominantly Protestant. The results, predictably, were that their children often married non-Jews. Thus, within two or three generations of their settlement in this country, they had become completely assimilated.[21]

By supervising the Sunday schools, then, the Sisterhoods were seeking to counteract the powerful pull of the surrounding secular world upon their children. But the Sisterhoods did not confine themselves to this role. The money raised by the Lake Charles women supported a variety of causes. Most of the funds were devoted to the upkeep of their own Temple, but other monies went to support Jewish causes elsewhere. The Sisterhood sent money every year to the Jewish Children's Home in New Orleans (an orphans' home), to the Hebrew Union College (the Reform seminary) in Cincinnati, and the National Jewish Hospital in Denver. In keeping with their mission to care for other Jews in need, the Sisterhood devoted funds to care for the two refugee families who settled in Lake Charles in 1939.[22]

The Sisterhood also made donations to local branches of well-established charities such as the Calcasieu Parish Association of the Blind, the Red Cross and the Infantile Paralysis Fund, and to the local hospital.[23] During World War II, the women devoted themselves to war work, making bandages, knitting, hosting USO functions, and donating to the local chapter of Bundles for Britain.[24]

In all of these activities, they were implementing their traditional responsibility to help those in need, but by assisting such projects, the women were also making links to the larger non-Jewish community. These ties, in turn, undoubtedly helped to discourage nascent anti-Semitism. Since anti-Semitism could harm their husbands' business or profession, the women were in effect protecting their homes and families, as well.

But Sisterhood women also worked in more formal ways to build bridges between Christians and Jews. This was an activity encouraged by the national organization: when the director of the NFTS spoke to the state convention in 1957, she noted that, nationally, the sisterhoods held institutes for 10,000 Christian church women per year to help them understand Judaism.[25] The women of Lake Charles did their part by hosting an interfaith tea or dinner every year, attended by anywhere from 100 to 250 people. At these dinners, one of the women, or perhaps the rabbi, would give a lecture about Jewish traditions and then answer questions.[26] Such events served the Jewish community by helping to counter anti-Semitism while simultaneously defending the faith.

Besides encouraging work in the community, Sisterhood served as a vehicle for self-improvement. At the meetings, the members themselves gave talks (topics ranged from world peace to the role of women in Judaism), or they invited speakers. In addition, the women stressed the importance of reading, not only about historic Judaism, but about any topic of current interest. Such activity encouraged independent thinking and a broad-minded outlook, which often translated itself into a more liberal vision of the world than that held by their Protestant neighbors. Traditionally, Jews have been encouraged to fight oppression and discrimination. For example, the annual celebration of *Purim* celebrates the defeat of tyranny, and in the service, the congregants recite this prayer: "Strengthen us to combat prejudice and oppression. Let not divisions of blood and faith create distrust and strife." Thus, the women of the Temple supported the Civil Rights legislation, and the organization urged its members to write their Congressmen indicating their support.[27]

The women of the sisterhood, then, helped to modernize Reform Judaism by teaching ritual to women, creating women's studies circles in Judaism, and improving synagogue religious schools.[28] The Lake Charles Sisterhood, like sisterhoods elsewhere, provided much-needed support to the Temple congregation. Not until the 1960s, however, did the sisterhood demand greater participation in the running of the Temple. Though the president of the sisterhood had long advised the Temple's governing board, in 1964, the president of the Temple Sinai Sisterhood asked the board to give the president active (voting) status.[29] This was done, and the Sisterhood soon began to encourage the board to consider including women for other positions on the board as well.[30] The number of women on the board increased, and in 1980, the board elected its first female president, Shirley Reinauer.[31]

If the Temple Sisterhoods were one vehicle for Jewish women's activity, the National Council of Jewish Women (NCJW) was another. The NCJW was founded in Chicago in 1893.[32] Similar to and modeled on Protestant Social Gospel organizations, the NCJW was dedicated to "religion, philanthropy and education." Believing that women were badly undereducated about their own faiths, the founders wanted NCJW to "encourage the study of the underlying principles of Judaism; the history, literature and customs of the Jews, and their bearing on their own and world's history." This knowledge was not for the benefit of the women themselves, but for the greater good: "the improvement of the Sabbath Schools, and in the work of social reform."[33] This was a major step forward in the evolution of Jewish women's organizations.

The women of New Orleans organized a local branch of NCJW in 1987.[34] Another section formed in Shreveport in 1919. As council women had done in other cities in America, the Shreveport chapter began the city's first school lunch program. In November 1920, several council members appeared before the Caddo Parish School board and requested that the council be allowed to operate a cafeteria at a local school. The women would serve the children themselves and absorb all expenses other than building alterations. The board concurred, and the city's first hot lunch program soon began operation. The NCJW continued to run it until the school board agreed to take over the program in 1925. The city had thus accepted its responsibility to provide a decent meal to hungry school children, a responsibility made clear to them by the women of the NCJW.[35]

Another popular program begun in the 1930s and operated for fifteen years by the Shreveport NCJW was the Toy Loan library. The women accepted donations for the program and offered, in addition to a lending library, story-telling, free swimming lessons, movies, and supervised outdoor play. The Toy Loan operation eventually expanded to include nine branch lending facilities, most located at schools.[36]

In the 1930s, the Shreveport chapter of the NCJW became involved with the Association for the Blind. The council purchased two Braille transcription machines and committee members transcribed books into Braille. In 1947, the council created a Sick Loan Closet which provided small and large medical supplies to needy citizens. This closet served everyone, white and black, based only upon the family's need.[37]

The Shreveport Council remained active in the 1950s and 1960s and initiated a number of community programs which continue to this day, such as Meals on Wheels, educational programs about child abuse, and a program to tutor learning disabled children. But it disbanded in 1981, at least partly because Jewish women were now admitted to the Junior League, which often supported similar programs.[38]

It was not until 1948 that a section of the NCJW was founded in Lake Charles.[39] In addition to creating a recreation program for the elderly, called "the Sixty-Plus Club,"[40] the Lake Charles women, as in Shreveport, started a Sick Loan Closet to make available to doctors and others of the area scarce and expensive medical supplies such as splints, wheelchairs and crutches.[41] As this project illustrates, providing medical aid to those who needed it was among the top priorities for Jewish women, a priority not normally found among Protestant women. This may have been because no one else was filling the need, or perhaps it was because many Jewish men, often their husbands, were medical professionals. The Lake Charles women in the NCJW worked with the Red Cross Mobile Blood Bank, volunteering as registrars and canteen workers, and in 1950 they started the St. Patrick's Hospital Ladies' Auxillary.[42] The volunteers devoted their time to reading to patients who were unable to read to themselves, provided clerical help, and even assisted "emergency cases to the operating room."[43] Finally, like the Shreveport women, the Lake Charles NCJW assisted the "sight conservation program" in the Lake Charles schools.[44]

Like the Sisterhoods, the NCJW women used their meetings to educate themselves, particularly about the achievements of women. For example, one of the few female doctors practicing in Lake Charles, Dr. Janie Topp, was invited to give a talk about "Women in Medicine." Another speaker lectured on female composers, another about female playwrights, and still another about women in journalism.[45]

The two organizations, the Temple Sisterhood and the local section of the NCJW, were composed of the same women. Dividing their time between the two organizations got to be too much, and as the congregation saw its membership dwindle, fewer women were able to shoulder the burden, and the NCJW section closed down in 1966. Temple Sinai's Rabbi, John Rosenblatt, lamented that "an important service to the Jewish Community has been lost."[46]

Jewish women were active in their communities in secular organizations such as the Community Chest and the Junior League as well.[47] So active, in fact, that at the 1963 state NFTS convention, two Lake Charles sisterhood women were honored for "outstanding service to the community."[48] These same women were also prominent in the artistic life of Lake Charles: in the Lake Charles Symphony, Community Concerts, and the Lake Charles Little Theatre, which was founded by Rosa Hart, a member of Temple Sinai Sisterhood.[49] In more recent years they have worked to found and support the Calcasieu Women's Shelter for battered women; the Southwest Louisiana AIDS Council; the Samaritan Counseling Center, which provides counseling for free or at a reduced rate to those who need it; Family and Youth Counseling Agency, the ETC program (Education, Training, Counseling), which provides counseling for teenagers; to support a *kibbutz* in Israel; and to raise money for scholarships for McNeese State University. Abraham's Tent, which feeds homeless people a hot meal once a day and is now supported by many different churches in the area, was actually founded by the Temple's Rabbi Sherman Stein, and the women have devoted countless hours to its success. To raise money for these activities the women hold an annual art auction which showcases artists from all over the country.

Some women of the Temple have been willing to brave hostility and criticism for their cause. In the early 1980s, Shirley Goldsmith, concerned about industrial pollution streaming from the area's chemical plants, became one of the area's first environmental activists. Like many Jewish women, she had a religious motivation for her actions: "God loaned us this earth to be stewards and take care of it," she said, "not to destroy it for the sake of money." Though she initially got little support from the Temple community, she nonetheless went on to found the Calcasieu League for Environmental Action Now (CLEAN) in 1982, which is still the foremost grassroots environmental organization in the area.[50]

Jewish women in Louisiana, then, have been active in their community in a variety of ways. Though Judaism is not an evangelistic religion, members of the Jewish community seek to influence their neighbors individually, rather than trying to impose their brand of morality upon the entire society. An important concept in Judaism is *tikkun olam*, meaning "to repair the world," or to make the world a better place. This is also considered a Jew's responsibility, a reciprocal obligation of the covenant with God. Jewish women, like Jewish men, have more than upheld this concept in their activities in the community.

Notes for "The Women of the Temple: Jewish Women in Lake Charles and Shreveport"

[1]Benjamin Kaplan, *The Eternal Stranger: A Study of Jewish Life in the Small Community* (New Haven, 1957), 42. See also Leo Shpall, *The Jews in Louisiana* (New Orleans, 1936).

[2]Alfred O. Hero, Jr., "Southern Jews," in *Jews in the South*, Leonard Dinnerstein and Mary Dale Palsson, eds. (Baton Rouge, 1973), 217-250; Elliott Ashkenazi, *The Business of Jews in Louisiana, 1840-1875* (Tuscaloosa, 1988), especially Chapter Three, "Country Stores and Cotton." See also "The Children of Israel," *Times of Acadiana*, April 3, 1996, which mentions that Main Street in New Iberia was "dotted with Jewish-owned businesses, a pattern repeated in many small towns across the state."

[3]The Jewish population of Louisiana is mainly of German extraction, and most of the congregations, therefore, are Reformed congregations. Leonard Reissman, "The New Orleans Jewish Community," in *Jews in the South*, 189.

[4]Linda Gordon Kuzmack, *Woman's Cause: The Jewish Woman's Movement in England and the United States, 1881-1933* (Columbus, 1990), 4-5.

[5]Ibid., 24.

[6]Ibid., 25.

[7]Ann Douglas, *The Feminization of American Culture* (New York, 1977); Barbara Welter, "The Feminization of American Religion, 1800-1860," in Mary Hartman and Lois Banner, eds., *Clio's Consciousness Raised* (New York, 1973), 137-155; Kuzmack, *Woman's Cause*, 25.

[8]Jenna Weisman Joselit, "The Special Sphere of the Middle-Class American Jewish Woman: The Synagogue Sisterhood, 1890-1940," in Jack Wertheimer, ed., *The American Synagogue: A Sanctuary Transformed* (New York, 1987), 206-230. See also, Beth Wenger, "Jewish Women of the Club: The Changing Public Role of Atlanta's Jewish Women (1870-1930)," *American Jewish History*, 76 (1982), 312. The first organization of Jewish women in the country was the Immanuel Lodge of the United Order of True Sisters, founded in New York City in 1846. Its purpose was to help its members "become familiar with current arts and affairs and to foster solidarity among the women of the Temple." Kuzmack, *Woman's Cause*, 25, 31.

[9]*Jewish Ledger*, August 2, 1895. This was a reprint of an article which first appeared in the *Shreveport Times*.

[10]*Jewish Ledger*, November 22, 1895.

[11]Kuzmack, *Woman's Cause*, 173-74. Conservative and Orthodox women formed similar organizations within a few years. Joselit, "Middle-Class American Jewish Women," 213. For a general history of both the NFTS and the National Council of Jewish Women, see June Sochen, *Consecrate Every Day; The Public Lives of Jewish American Women, 1880-1980* (Albany, 1981), especially chapters four and five.

[12]*Proceedings of the Fourth Biennial Meeting*, NFTS, 1921, 72, quoted in Joselit, "Middle-Class American Jewish Women," 211.

[13]David Reinauer, "The Jewish Influence in Southwest Louisiana," paper delivered in a local program called "The Many Faces of Southwest Louisiana," June 12, 1973, in Temple Sinai Archives, Lake Charles, La. (hereafter cited as TSA); author's interview with Corinne Davidson and Fay Barnhart, June 1999.

[14]Typewritten Constitution, 1935 Scrapbook, TSA.

[15]Mrs. Abraham Simon, "Woman's Influence in the Development of American Judaism," *41ˢᵗ Annual Report, Union of American Hebrew Congregations*, 1915, 76-90.

[16]Quoted in Joselit, "Middle-Class American Jewish Women," 213.

[17]Kuzmack, *Woman's Cause*, 19.

[18]Every issue of the *Jewish Ledger* published information written by correspondents in cities around the state, about various social events being held for Jewish youth.

[19]Kaplan, *Eternal Struggle*, passim.

[20]Each issue of the *Jewish Ledger* contains a full page or more reporting on the comings and goings of Jews in various communities. The reporters say who is visiting whom, how long the stay is, and what the purpose of the trip was (visit, honeymoon, business, etc.).

[21]Kaplan, *Eternal Stranger*, passim. See also the film by Brian Coehn, *From Pushcarts to Plantations* (New York, 1997), which notes that the Museum of Southern Jewish Experience in Utica, Mississippi, is, sadly, made up of the objects from defunct temples from small towns across the South.

[22]Sisterhood Minutes, April 26, 1939, TSA.

[23]Sisterhood Minutes, March 20 , 1950, January 19, 1942, November 20 , 1939.

[24]April 17, 1944, Annual Report of the Chairman, Mrs. E. R. Kaufman, War Service Activities Committee, TSA; March 24 , 1941, Sisterhood Minutes, TSA.

[25]Newspaper clipping (newspaper unknown), 1957 Scrapbook, TSA.

[26]There is a report of such a dinner in each year's minutes, beginning in the 1940s. See, for example, February 20, 1950, and March 1954 newsletter.

[27]See, for example, May 22 , 1957, Sisterhood Minutes.

[28]Kuzmack, *Woman's Cause*, 174; Sochen, *Consecrate Every Day*, 68.

[29]April 1, 1964, Temple Sinai Minutes, TSA.

[30]April 20 , 1966, Temple Sinai Minutes, TSA.

[31]Author's interview with Fay Barnhart, February 1995. At the time of the interview, Barnhart was president of Temple Sinai.

[32]For a history of the NCJW, see Faith Rogow, *Gone to Another Meeting: The National Council of Jewish Women, 1893-1993* (Tuscaloosa, 1993).

[33]Rogow, *Gone to Another Meeting*, 23-24.

[34]*Jewish Ledger*, January 13, 1897.

[35]Kay Goldman, "Southern Jewish Women's Response to Progressivism," paper delivered at the Women's Leadership Program First Annual Conference, LSU-Shreveport, 1998, 17-18.

[36]Ibid., 21-22.

[37]Ibid., 19.

[38]Ibid., 22-24.

[39]1948 Scrapbook, TSA; Goldman, Southern Jewish Women," 17.

[40]Clipping from the *Southwest Citizen*, March 6 , 1951, Scrapbook, TSA.

[41]Clippings, 1948 Scrapbook, TSA.

[42]Clippings, November 1951, 1951 Scrapbook, TSA.

[43]Clippings, 1950 Scrapbook, TSA.

[44]Clippings, April 1954, Scrapbook, TSA.

[45]Clippings, Scrapbooks, 1950-1951, TSA.

[46]"Temple Newsletter," 1966, Scrapbook, TSA.

[47]Clippings, Scrapbooks, TSA; interview with Corene Davidson, Temple Sinai member and past-president of Temple Sisterhood, February 1995.

[48]March 1963, Sisterhood minutes.

[49]See, for example, the *Lake Charles Sisterhood News*, September-March, 1947, which lists the various activities of the members.

[50]Author's interview with Shirley Goldsmith, March 1999.

RELIGIOUS RITUALS AND FESTIVALS*

Barry Jean Ancelet, Jay D. Edwards, and Glen Pitre

Religion has played a powerful role in shaping institutions such as the family. But what *is* religion in a folk society? Is it even legitimate to ask which kind of religion exerts more influence on the lives of the average Cajun—the formal church with its clergy and teachers, or the complex system of extra-ecclesiastical and informally transmitted religious beliefs that have remained a basic ingredient of the life of rural people such as the Cajuns?

Folklore is knowledge passed along from one person to another, or from one generation to another, through traditional, nonofficial channels. In this respect, folk religion includes beliefs and practices that are not sanctioned by a church but have become an integral part of the religious lives of a people by custom. This includes such practices as giving gifts on Christmas and New Year's Day, as well as events like the immensely popular Mardi Gras, which occurs on the day before Lent begins. However, less well-known practices are also popular in Acadiana: the making and giving of king's cakes between the beginning of Epiphany and Mardi Gras, the special commemoration celebration of certain saints' feast days, like the making of bread altars for St. Joseph's Day (influenced by the Italian community of New Orleans), or the whitening and decorating of tombs for *La Toussaint*, or All Saints' Day.

Often there is considerable overlap between nature beliefs and folk religion. Even within the Catholic Church, Christmas day was originally determined by the time of the winter solstice, and Easter is still defined as the first Sunday after the first full moon after the spring equinox. It is perhaps a consequence of the ritual importance of spring as a period of rebirth that a number of traditional activities take place during this time of year. The huge bonfires that are lighted on the levees of the Mississippi River between New Orleans and Baton Rouge on Christmas Eve are descendants of the bonfires lit by ancient European civilizations, particularly along the Rhine and Seine rivers, to encourage and reinforce the sun at the winter solstice, its "weakest" moment.

Epiphany is announced by the making of king's cakes in which a bean, a symbol of growth and fertility, is hidden. The one who gets the piece with the bean is chosen king

*First published as Chapter 5 in *Cajun Country*, Folklife in the South Series (Jackson, Miss.: University Press of Mississippi, 1991), 77-94. Reprinted with the kind permission of the authors and the publisher.

for the day. The fertility symbolism is even more overt as a tiny plastic baby is now substituted for the bean in the thousands of commercially baked king cakes consumed before Mardi Gras in the cities of southern Louisiana. Getting the baby in your piece of king cake is now said to obligate you to buy the next king cake from the bakery.

The relative lack of traditional religious activity during the late spring, summer and fall may reflect the effort needed to plant, maintain and harvest crops. There are, however, a few folk religious practices directly associated with farming and fishing. Each year, priests go out into the fields in places like New Iberia and Jeanerette to bless the sugar cane. In many coastal towns, such as Lafitte, Delcambre, and Morgan City, priests formally bless the shrimping fleets by saying prayers over them and sprinkling them with holy water. Participants devote considerable effort to decorating the shrimp boats for these occasions.

Also included in folk religion are personal or family rituals, such as the building and maintenance of home altars in Cajun and Creole households. Home altars serve not only as places for prayer but also as shrines to commemorate deceased family members. They are illustrated with holy cards and death announcements, and contain tokens like watches, rings, scapulars, rosaries, and prayer books. These home shrines are often lovingly kept with fresh flowers and other decorations.

Another popular kind of folk religious observance among Cajuns and Creoles alike is lawn statuary. Many Cajun families pay their respects to their patron saint, usually Our Lady of the Assumption, with homemade grottoes or shrines that house statues of the Virgin. Other popular statues include the Sacred Heart of Jesus and Saint Theresa (who is often confused with the Blessed Virgin). Some of these shrines simply present the statue all alone. In others the statues nestle in havens such as porches, carports, or under trees. Still other shrines can be quite remarkable, consisting of complex brick or cement grottoes and elaborate landscaping, with small ponds and flowering bushes. Makeshift grottoes are also fashioned from such things as used bathtubs or oil drums.

Because of the predominance of the Roman Catholic faith among Cajuns and Creoles, religious rituals surround the major steps in a person's life, including birth, courtship and marriage, and death. Children are almost invariably baptized as Catholics within the first few months of their lives. The business of godfathering and godmothering is still very important in Cajun country. Almost always referred to by their French names, even by non-French-speaking youth, *parrains* and *marraines* are not just spiritual guides and insurance in case of the loss of both parents. They become family. They enlarge the circle of people who like you "just because." They give gifts at Christmas and on birthdays. They are also among the ones children can run to in case of trouble at home. A typical statement concerning godparents can go something like this: "Well, my dad can't go fishing this weekend, so my *parrain* is taking me." Consequently, there has long been a great deal of importance given to choosing these representatives. One commonly held tradition is that one cannot ask to be made a child's godparent. There may, however, be a great deal of lobbying and jockeying for position behind the scenes as soon as a woman becomes pregnant—and sometimes even before.

Death involves another set of religious rituals. Long ago, most families held wakes for their dead in the home. Nowadays, most use funeral homes. Yet there are a few durable traditions no matter where the body is exposed. Traditionally, wakes can last nonstop through the night for several days, which requires special arrangements so that the body is never alone, even in the middle of the night. Recently, funeral homes have begun closing at 10 p.m. or midnight, easing the strain on survivors, but upsetting many who are disturbed that their loved ones are left alone. At intervals during the wake, the rosary may be recited for the departed. Certain members of the community, in addition to the priests and members of the lay clergy, become known as leaders of rosary, primarily for their ability to recite unwritten prayers that occur between decades and at the beginning and end of the rosary. Those who are able to perform this ritual in French are in especially high demand today.

Another aspect of folk religion includes the relationship between religion and everyday life. This ranges from the belief that the Virgin will slap children who whistle at the dinner table to doubts concerning the celibacy of the clergy. It includes the belief that it is forbidden to break ground on Good Friday, and that if one does, one will see the blood of Jesus Christ. Paradoxically it is also holds that Good Friday is the best day for planting parsley. This combination of beliefs has caused many a gardener to come up with a clever plan for the preparing and planting of a parsley patch. Many Cajun families still go to church on Palm Sunday to receive blessed palm leaves and holy water, which they keep in their houses to sprinkle during storms.

Praying is considered an important part of life, and prayer is thought of as a means of intercession with which one can change the course of fate. Some persons, not necessarily appointed by the church, are thought to have a particularly good relationship with the Deity and/or the saints and are frequently asked by others to help in obtaining favors. These individuals thus become mediators between the Deity and people, in much the same way as the prophets and high priests of their ancestors.

Traditional observances like the eating of seafood on Fridays and during Lent provide another example of the relationship between religion and everyday life. Fish markets gear up for a heavier demand on days historically set aside for fasting, despite the fact that the Catholic Church has officially eased its rules in this matter. In south Louisiana even public school cafeterias continue to provide alternatives to meat for the predominantly Catholic student body on Ash Wednesday and Fridays during Lent. Waitresses in restaurants will often gently remind regular patrons what day it is if they choose a meat entree on days like Ash Wednesday and Good Friday—just in case they may have forgotten.

While Mardi Gras signals the beginning of Lent, Good Friday signals its approaching end. It is celebrated with a ceremonial Way of the Cross procession on the road between Catahoula and St. Martinville. The stations of a Way of the Cross are usually mounted on the walls of a church, but the stations of this one are hung on the largest oak trees between the two towns. Members of the faithful gather in St. Martinville and walk or drive the length of the road to Catahoula (about eight miles), stopping at each station to pray.

Easter has traditionally been a time of family gatherings. Many Cajun families have now adopted most of the features of the general American celebration from the media and from personal contacts outside of Acadiana. Rituals now incorporated into the Cajun repertoire include the giving of baskets of dyed eggs and chocolate bunnies, and Easter egg hunts. Historically, however, eggs were not given but prepared for a contest called *pâcquer*, after the French name for Easter, *Pâques*. Participants still boil and dye their eggs and bring them along on visits to friends and relatives where they will strike them against other eggs to see which is the strongest. Formerly, the winner was allowed to take the loser's broken egg as a prize. This meant that the winners had more to eat than the losers, and there was much competition in these quests for the strongest eggs. This, along with a natural love of practical joking, still leads some to dye smallish goose eggs or largish guinea hen eggs (both renowned for their tough shells) or even rocks in an attempt to stack the odds. Others distribute dyed *uncooked* eggs to grateful but unsuspecting friends just for the fun of watching their faces when the inevitable occurs.

Perhaps the most important element of this tradition is the visiting and socializing it makes possible, which explains why the tradition is still very popular among many Cajun families today. Extended families and friends take advantage of the spring holiday to get together, not only for a little egg *pâcquing*, but also for a crawfish boil or a barbecue as well. Many of the usual rites of spring are also observed: baseball, volleyball, kite flying, fishing, and napping outside. Easter is, in many ways, a day on which to stake a claim on summer.

Christmas is the other major religious holiday celebrated by the Cajuns. These days, Cajuns buy Christmas trees and exchange battery-operated playthings just as in most of the western world. Cajun children now eagerly await the arrival of Santa Claus, whereas traditionally they once awaited the arrival of *le Père Noël*, or Father Christmas, and received small, often handmade presents. In fact, in the nineteenth century Christmas was more important as a time for family gatherings, family meals, and going together to church for mass (often at midnight) than for exchanging gifts. Although some gifts were given on Christmas Day, the major gift holiday for most Cajun families was New Year's Day, when families and friends gathered and exchanged gifts called *étrennes*.

Mardi Gras

Almost synonymous with Cajun Louisiana itself, Mardi Gras (also called Carnival) occurs on the day before Ash Wednesday, which marks the beginning of the Lenten season. This popular traditional festival has roots in ancient springtime fertility rituals and rites of passage. These often involve such obvious sexual symbols as mock abduction and seduction, real or symbolic nudity, and whips—these last being part fertility symbols, part instruments of intimidation. Mardi Gras is based on medieval European adaptations of even older rituals, particularly those that included reversals of the social order with the lower classes parodying the elite. Men dress as women, women as men; the poor dress as rich, the rich as poor; the old as young, the young as old; black as white, white as black. Survivals of these earlier versions are still evident in contemporary Cajun celebrations of Mardi Gras. Yet even ritualized chaos still has its own system of rules to act as a framework for the ritualistic play. Mardi Gras is usually a processional celebration. Groups of revelers move through towns and countryside alike, taking the celebration to the places they visit and invading public spaces such as roads, making them impassable, and commercial districts, rendering them inoperable. Masks provide anonymity and an opportunity to shed inhibitions and to act out roles for the day. The ritual altering of consciousness, in this case through the consumption of alcohol, enhances the ability of participants to play beyond themselves.

The country Mardi Gras celebration of south Louisiana is also a processional festivity, but unlike its urban counterpart, it stems from the medieval *fête de la quémande*, a ceremonial begging ritual, modified by frontier influences. The *fête de la quémande* was celebrated by a procession of revelers who traveled through the countryside offering some sort of performance in exchange for gifts. Costumed children on Halloween, Christmas carolers, and Irish mummers are all modern vestiges of this ancient rite. In the *course de Mardi Gras*, masked riders visit farmhouses, singing and dancing to the traditional Mardi Gras song. The goal of these performances is to obtain a contribution to the communal gumbo, to be shared later that day. The ideal gift is a live chicken, which is released by the homeowner and must be captured by the celebrants who are hampered by masks, costumes, and their various states of inebriation. This entails considerable buffoonery and generates great merriment and entertainment for the members of the visited household.

The traditional costumes for *la course* have roots in medieval dress. In addition to the inevitable modern clowns, monsters, movie heroes, and villains, one sees conical hats (in parody of noblewomen and also long associated with dunces or fools), miters (to ridicule the clergy), and more rarely, mortarboards (mocking scholars and clerics). The medieval atmosphere is enhanced by the processional nature of the celebration, which moves through the countryside. Like medieval jesters who remained marginal to the festivities for which they provided entertainment, the Mardi Gras musicians accompany the ride in a closed wagon or truck and never participate in the activities of the riders.

In some towns such as Kinder, Basile, and Iota, participants are flogged with whips of burlap sacking rolled or braided, reminiscent of the medieval processions of flagellants who whipped themselves and each other to purge their past sins and escape the horrors of Hell. This practice also has roots in the ancient Roman *lupercalia* when masked and costumed men ritually beat women with animal pelts to insure fertility. Brief spontaneous skits are also sometimes performed, including *The Dead Man Revived*, a modern version of the pre-Arthurian fisher-king legend. One participant feigns death and his companions "revive" him by dripping wine or beer into his mouth. In *The Animal Burial,* revelers bury a chicken that has succumbed to the rigors of the day in a ceremony that parodies the Catholic funeral liturgy, replacing Latin sounds with obscene or irreverent Cajun French.

Ancient and medieval elements of the *course de Mardi Gras* have been modified by the Louisiana frontier experience. In many communities there is a mystique of toughness reminiscent of the American Wild West. The anonymity of the masks once provided an ideal way to settle scores with some impunity. At times the riders mildly terrorized the visited households, forcing women to dance, vandalizing property, or stealing from the kitchen. With Americanization and the civilizing effect of schools and churches, the of-ten rowdy *course* was banned from many communities. The World War II draft further weakened the celebration's social support, and it eventually disappeared from the annual cycle in most communities. In the early 1950s, a group of cultural activists in the Mamou area, under the leadership of Paul Tate and Revon Reed, undertook to revive the tradi-tional Mardi Gras *course,* with guidance from older members of the community.

In reviving the tradition, Tate and Reed took pains to render the celebration respect-able and relatively safe for both riders and hosts, while maintaining its traditional aspect. This effort, anchored in the absolute control of the *capitaine,* encouraged the continuation of the *course* by virtually eliminating fights and the element of real danger. The whip now became an element of the *capitaine*'s control. The ritual tension between supplica-tion and chaos persists even today. Riders await permission to approach a house, then charge it as though taking it by storm. They sing and dance for an offering, then chase the chicken through the barnyard as though stealing it. Riders play at changing roles from beggar to outlaw to clown, singing and dancing while intimidating and fooling non-participants.

Other towns have since revived the *course* as well, and sexuality continues to be an important element in these revivals. Most towns, including Mamou, Church Point, L'Anse Meg, and Kinder, limit participation to men only. Petit Mamou (where the cele-bration never lapsed) and Basile have separate versions for men and women, while Eunice and Scott allow both sexes to run together, as was the custom there long ago. The "males only" restriction is said to have originated among the women of Mamou to ham-per anonymous carousing among their men. Among the riders, there exists the same sort of freedoms that one encounters in other sexually exclusive groups. For example, male riders dance together, walk arm in arm, and embrace each other. In fact, a popular cos-tume on male rides involves the reversal of sexual identity as men wear wigs, dresses, and even false bosoms. The principle is that only the toughest men can afford to play at being feminine without arousing any suspicions concerning their sexuality.

A certain aura of outlawry has not entirely vanished from the modem versions of the Prairie Cajun Mardi Gras, which effectively resists reduction to a simple tourist attraction by virtue of its sheer toughness. In fact, the celebration continues to function as a rite of passage for the young men and women in many communities. Reminiscent of similar rites in primitive societies, the social initiation on the morning of the ride is accentuated by the anonymity and the removal of inhibitions through alcohol. But the essential part of the initiation lies in the ritual play of the day: being all that one dares to be. Except for the list of rules designed to contain the game, there is virtually no limit to the personal freedom of expression available to each participant.

Participation in the Mardi Gras *course* can begin several weeks in advance with a series of informal meetings to discuss administrative and support roles, such as beer truck personnel, tractor drivers, and musicians. The *capitaine,* named for life by his predecessor in most cases, chooses his *co-capitaines,* often the toughest riders and the hardest to control, thereby channeling their energies in a positive direction. Business is settled quickly, and these meetings become rallies building excitement for the coming ride. In the days before the celebration, riders make final preparations for the *course,* completing their costumes, preparing tack, and locating horses, often in great secrecy. To avoid being recognized by their mounts, many riders exchange horses several times before Mardi Gras day. In fact, under these circumstances, it is said that one can effectively avoid recognition by riding one's own horse. At dawn on Mardi Gras next morning, riders don their costumes and masks, saddle their horses, and start down country roads and back streets to join their fellows at an appointed gathering place, usually near the center of town. When enough have gathered, the *capitaine* brings the riders to order and takes charge of them for the day. In some cases, there is a formal reading of the rules. The *capitaine* and his *co-capitaines* are unmasked so that they may represent the band of revelers to each household they visit. In most communities they are further identified by their cowboy hats and long multi-colored caps, usually a two-color combination of the traditional Mardi Gras colors: purple, red, yellow and green.

From the time he takes command of the celebration at the initial gathering to the reentry into town later in the day, the *capitaine*'s reign is absolute. This is the result of a tacit, and necessary, agreement among all riders who play the game. For an entire day, a considerable number of adults willingly suspend reality for the sake of the celebration, the very nature of which demands unquestioning submission to the authority of a chosen leader who acts as intermediary between the ritual madness of the procession and the people they will visit.

The rules of most celebrations are also designed to provide a framework for the festivities. Some are preventative: no Mardi Gras rider shall advance beyond the *capitaine* on the route. No rider shall enter private property without the explicit permission of the *capitaine.* No rider shall consume any liquor except that which is distributed by the *capitaine* or his assistants. No rider shall bear arms or weapons of any kind, including knives, guns, or sticks. Other rules are meant to keep the tradition intact: no rider shall throw beads, doubloons, or trinkets of any sort anywhere along the route. All riders are expected to dismount from horses and wagons to sing and dance at the homes that agree to give an offering for the gumbo. The rules are more than symbolic; riders are actually frisked to enforce the "no weapons" rule. And *capitaines* of male-only rides diligently supervise their bands to prevent women from infiltrating the ranks.

After the rules are read, riders mount their steeds, unmounted participants enter the wagons, and the procession leaves town to the incessant strains of the Mardi Gras song. As the procession approaches the first house, the *capitaine* halts the band of riders on the road and rides ahead alone with raised white flag to ask the residents' permission to enter. According to custom, if permission is refused, he simply turns and leads his troupe to the next house. Many homeowners avoid an outright refusal by arranging to be absent during the visit. If permission is granted, the *capitaine* drops his flag to signal the invitation to approach the house. Mounted participants usually take advantage of this opportunity to charge the homestead as if taking it by assault.

Surrounding the front yard, the riders dismount and begin singing and dancing, often in ritual supplication poses, to the Mardi Gras song, played by the musicians who accompany the ride in their own wagon or truck. Some riders openly express a certain machismo, along with excellent horsemanship, by dancing on their mounts. Some of the more daring riders might playfully snatch up the lady of the house and her daughters and dance with them in the crowd. Children are often the object of a little mock terrorism, being whisked away from their parents for a brief moment. (This teaches them a short and relatively harmless lesson in the risks of being away from the safety of home and family.) Gardens and kitchens are sometimes raided. Riders sometimes play at stealing livestock, such as pigs and calves, but this behavior is carefully controlled by the *capitaine* who is ultimately responsible for any real damage. This ritual play functions best when the home owners know the masked visitors but cannot recognize them. Participants speak in falsetto and wear gloves to avoid being recognized despite their masks. All this is intended to produce a few uneasy but playful moments for the families that are visited.

After an appropriate amount of revelry, the man of the house brings out an offering for the Mardi Gras, a contribution to the communal gumbo to be shared later that day. This may be flour, rice, onions, oil, or even money. The favorite gift, however, is a live chicken which is thrown high in the air. Those closest to it chase it down, and the captor jubilantly holds up his prize for all to see before surrendering it to one of the *co-capitaines* who will place it in a cage until it can be transported back to town to find its way into the gumbo. After a bit more dancing and socializing, the *capitaine* blows his cow horn to call the riders back to order, and the procession moves on to the next house.

At regular (and frequent) intervals between houses, the *capitaine* calls a halt to the procession for a beer stop. A loaded pickup truck parks in the middle of the road and the riders file by to receive their ration of beer under the scrutiny of the *co-capitaines*. On especially cold days, wine and whiskey are also available. Consumption is controlled but liberal, and many riders easily work themselves into a state of ritual inebriation.

The entire scene is repeated as many as twenty or thirty times during the day. Ironically, the smaller rides usually succeed in collecting more chickens than the larger ones. The processions in Mamou, Church Point, and Eunice have a certain amount of inertia due to sheer numbers. The countless photographers, journalists, ethnographers, and other "foreign" observers who accompany huge processions further impede their progress through the countryside. Today the larger rides are often forced to augment their catch with chickens from the market, while smaller bands, usually more mobile and less affected by outside visitors and the media, can visit more houses. Some rides have adapted custom to physical realities. In communities such as Iota, the large distances between farmsteads have made visiting them on horseback impractical, so riders now hitch a wagon to a truck or tractor to cover a larger area during the day.

By mid-afternoon the riders, now weary and ragged from a day on the road, approach the edge of town. The *capitaine* often orders a stop to regroup and repair tack and costumes, and to regain a certain composure for the re-entry parade. Riders present themselves as "survivors" to those who did not participate in the ordeal. With a strong sense of brotherhood based on shared experiences, they parade down the length of the crowded main street, waving to spectators along the way. In towns where organizers have street dances (to keep as many visitors as possible in town) the band yields the stage to the Mardi Gras musicians for a final performance of the Mardi Gras song and other Cajun music. This can last up to half an hour, while riders dance in the crowd. Most riders then retire to a quiet spot to await their hard-earned supper, the ceremonial gumbo. Riders eat first. Some go home to rest or take their horses back to the barn before returning later for the masked ball, which marks the final hours of this revelry before the beginning of Lent the next day. All festivities stop abruptly at midnight, and many of Tuesday's rowdiest riders can be found on their knees receiving the penitential ashes on their foreheads on Wednesday.

METHODISTS, OTHER DENOMINATONS, PUBLIC EDUCATIONAL DEVELOPMENT, AND THE CULTURAL BOUNDARY*

James G. Dauphine

While Catholics and Baptists built the majority of denominational schools in Louisiana before World War II, Methodists, Presbyterians, Episcopalians, Lutherans, and Jews all became involved, at one time or another, in educational ventures. Most schools built by religious groups other than Methodists did not survive the Reconstruction period. In general, these minority religious groups had their greatest impact on education through the activities of individuals who were members of their faiths.

Following the state's 1845 legislation creating a public educational system, little progress ensued toward the construction of public schools. As a result, antebellum education was largely handled through the agency of private schools, although a public system did emerge in the city of New Orleans before the war. Most of the private schools in the state were small non-denominational schools opened by individuals who ran them for profit. Since many of the state's educated Protestant ministers had small financial support from their congregations, ministers often taught in the small private schools as a means of supplementing their income.[1]

Many antebellum planters in the sugar parishes of Louisiana were Catholic and made use of Catholic private schools for their children. Even in the Southern parishes, planters were well-represented in the ranks of the state's Episcopalian, Presbyterian, and Methodist populations, although the first two denominations were always concentrated most heavily in New Orleans before World War II. An influential political group, both Catholic and Protestant planters usually did not support the public educational system. They reasoned "with some justification," as noted by Joe Gray Taylor, "that they would have to pay for them," if the public schools were allowed to proliferate into a truly extensive state system. As a result, planter opposition to public schools retarded the growth of the state system into the twentieth century and allowed private denominational and nondenominational schools to flourish.[2]

*First published as Chapter 7 in *A Question of Inheritance: Religion, Education, and Louisiana's Cultural Boundary, 1880-1940* (Lafayette, La.: Center for Louisiana Studies, 1993), 99-111 and 144-8. Reprinted with the kind permission of the author and the Center for Louisiana Studies.

For a brief time between 1868 and 1877, the state did try to expand the public system. In demonstrating concern for the educational disparity among freedmen following the war, the state's Reconstruction government attempted to racially integrate the public schools. Encountering massive resistance in the rural parishes, the state government made no attempt to enforce integration, except in Orleans Parish.[3]

Although Lousiana's black population outnumbered the white in 1860 and would continue to do so until the 1900 census, blacks made up only 8 percent of the population of New Orleans in 1860 and were still outnumbered nearly three to one by whites in 1890. As the capital of the state during Reconstruction, the only metropolitan center, and the home of the majority of the state's former "gens de couleur libre," New Orleans became the testing ground for the experiment in school integration. Despite assurances that a majority white population would mean no cases in which blacks outnumbered whites in the public schools, white flight from public schools occurred after 1868.[4]

There were ten private schools in New Orleans in 1868. One year later, there were thirty. In 1870, the number increased to seventy-three. By 1875, there were over one hundred. About half of these were Catholic schools, which had increased in number from eight to forty-nine between 1868 and 1875. Much of this Catholic school construction represented a Catholic attempt to assume dominance of education in New Orleans. Unfortunately, the attempt proved costly in later years, as indebtedness caused by the rapid school construction of the 1870s precluded further Catholic educational expansion until 1906.[5]

With seventy-six public schools in 1874, New Orleans had 67,272 educable children, youths of both races aged six to twenty-one. Highest public school enrollment during Reconstruction was 17,194 in 1874. This figure represented enrollment of 25 percent of the educable youth—a low figure even for the pre-1920s period of generally low enrollments. Public school enrollment in 1874 should have been higher (over 30 percent), but were low because of protest against the integration of approximately five hundred Negro children in the schools. The accompanying increased attendance in private schools was a consequence of those protestations.[6]

Besides the Catholics, German immigrant denominations in the city opened parochial schools after 1870. Between them, German Evangelical Lutherans, German Evangelical Protestants, and German Presbyterians opened seven schools by 1877. Southern Methodists opened a high school in the city, four Episcopalian parochial schools appeared, and Presbyterians built six grammar schools, plus a boys' and a girls' high school. Presbyterians even organized their own school board and hired the former superintendent of city schools, William O. Rogers, to head it. The majority of these schools were discontinued when Democrats assumed control of the state government in 1877 and ended the experiment with school integration. Some of the Protestant schools that survived Reconstruction, such as the Presbyterian girls' high school, were forced to close during the 1880s.[7]

With the return to power of Bourbon Democrats in 1877, the school system was reorganized. Throughout the state, however, public schools continued to be too few, poorly equipped, and lacking in adequate monetary support from local governments. State Superintendent of Education William G. Brown recognized in 1874 that, "unless local authorities tax themselves, present schools only can be maintained." Because of restrictions on the power of local authorities to tax themselves for educational purposes—written into the 1879 Constitution—public schools continued, for the rest of the century, to rely on state appropriations that were too small to effectively augment the funds provided by local property taxes.[8]

Indications were that local authorities in many parishes were not interested in educational expansion. Prior to 1877, the State Board of Education received little cooperation from local governments. An extreme example of educational indifference occurred in St. Bernard Parish, where the state school appropriation, small as it was, was partly "appropriated" by school officials. One public "school" was operated in a mule stable with children having to endure the smell from a stall just six feet from them. White Leaguers in Red River Parish murdered the parish school board treasurer after forcing him to open the safe containing the parish school funds. The parish treasurer in Plaquemines Parish got caught embezzling $8,000 from the state school appropriation in 1874 and was subsequently acquitted by a sympathetic jury. After the "Radical Republican" regime disappeared in 1877, interest in public educational expansion continued to flag.[9]

In the meantime, until the 1898 state constitution allowed parishes to collect special taxes for school construction and maintenance, small, private, and non-denominational—albeit Protestant—schools continued to handle much local educational need. In the years before Catholic expansion of parochial schools after 1906, small non-denominational schools flourished even in the Southern Catholic parishes. Varying in quality, even bad schools still required tuition and were consequently beyond the reach of poorer citizens. As the net result of educational neglect in the state—by government officials, by religious denominations, and by the public in its apathetic acceptance of the absence of educational opportunities—illiteracy soared. William Ivy Hair aptly concluded that, among Southern states, Louisiana "climbed from fifth to first place in ignorance between 1880 and 1890," with a rate of illiteracy of over 70 percent for blacks and over 20 percent for native whites.[10]

Negro denominations did what they could to alleviate the disadvantaged educational condition of blacks in the state, but could provide educational opportunities—of the kind not geared toward agricultural or vocational pursuits—only to a miniscule fraction of the black population. The seventeen Negro Baptist associations in Louisiana, affiliated with the National Baptist Convention, were most involved with construction of black denominational schools. In 1916, they owned sixteen of the eighteen black denominational secondary schools not affiliated with Northern white missionary agencies. Negro Methodists maintained the other two—Homer College, in Claiborne Parish, and the Lampton Literary Institute, in Rapides Parish.[11]

Negro Methodist denominations, as offshoots of the white dominated Methodist Episcopal Church, or of the Methodist Episcopal Church, South, continued into the 1870s to be dominated by the episcopal structures of the white denominations. Lacking the autonomy of the Negro Baptists, the Negro Methodist denominations attracted fewer converts than the Baptists prior to the 1870s and never attained the large memberships of the Negro Baptists in Louisiana. Despite declaring education an avowed priority of Negro Methodist church activities, Negro Methodist denominations could never develop the educational organizations and financial support for schools that Negro Baptists, through sheer numbers, could muster. Where Negro Methodists were numerous, as in Alabama, Georgia, and the Carolinas, they built more schools and pursued a stronger educational mission than in Louisiana.[12]

Although never as strong an educational force as other Northern missionary agencies, the Lutheran Board of Colored Missions established nine schools for Negroes in the South in 1879. Eight of those schools, all primary parochial schools, were in New Orleans. Still operating in 1916, these Lutheran schools had a collective monetary value of $25,500, employed twenty teachers, and enrolled 1,037 black elementary students. All were one-room schools in mission chapels or in rented buildings. The evangelistic impact of these schools on the black population of New Orleans appears to have been at least as strong as that of the Northern Methodist schools—Gilbert Academy and New Orleans University. It is probable that the majority of Lutherans in New Orleans were blacks and Lutherans did outnumber Negro Methodists in the city by 1936. Elsewhere in the state, the numerical strength of Negro denominations was also strongest where schools maintained by those denominations were located.[13]

In 1890, St. Mary Parish ranked second only to Orleans in the size of its Negro Methodist population, among twenty-seven southern Catholic parishes. The black Methodist Gilbert Academy located in St. Mary moved to Now Orleans in 1919. Afterwards, St. Mary's Negro Methodist population declined ranking only seventh among the Triangle parishes by 1936. Claiborne Parish, the site of Homer College, maintained by the Colored Methodist Episcopal Church, contained the second largest Negro Methodist population of the thirty-five northern parishes in 1890. By 1936, Claiborne had the largest Negro Methodist population in the state, followed by Orleans, with its two black Methodist institutions.[14]

Rapides Parish, site of the only other black Methodist academy, was a slight exception to the rule. Seventh among the northern parishes in 1890 in numbers of Negro Methodists, Rapides ranked only ninth in 1936. Still, in both 1890 and 1936, Rapides contained the largest number of Negro Methodists of any parish in the central part of the state.[15]

With white denominations, the pattern of numerical strength correlated less obviously to the existence of denominational schools, partly because only Catholics erected white denominational schools in any great numbers. Also, white Protestants favored either non-denominational private schools—most numerous during the nineteenth century—or public schools, as the Protestant-dominated public school system expanded in the twentieth century.

One white Protestant denomination that never fully accommodated its position on education to reliance on public schools was the Protestant Episcopal Church. Every year from 1865 to 1886 resolutions were introduced at the Episcopalian General Convention calling for the establishment of parochial schools. Many Episcopalians disliked public schools, both for their secular nature and for their generally poor quality, as common schools for the masses. Although Episcopalians did build parochial schools in the North, they did not do so in Louisiana until after World War II.[16]

A good explanation for the failure of Episcopalians to establish schools in Louisiana is found in the religious statistics of Louisiana before World War II. There were only 5,162 Episcopalians in the entire state in 1890, nearly three thousand in New Orleans alone, where they constituted all of 3 percent of the religious population. By 1936, the number of Episcopalians had grown to over 17,000, nearly half still in New Orleans. Over the years since 1936, Episcopalian growth in the state has made Episcopalian schools feasible.[17]

Presbyterians were even less numerous in Louisiana than Episcopalians. The Presbyterian population grew from just under 4,000 in 1890 to just under 14,000 in 1936. Over half resided in the urban areas of New Orleans, Baton Rouge, and Shreveport. The remainder were scattered throughout the state in much smaller groups. Few parishes had more than one Presbyterian church before World War II and the congregation in Lafayette, first organized in 1875, was probably typical of Presbyterian congregations in most of the state. In 1920, the pastor in Lafayette complained that only about half of the church members attended service regularly. Those who did attend did no evangelistic work outside the church. He concluded that "worldly conformity is too prevalent for the Church's good." Four years later, the same pastor commented: "Our People here generally are like the people in most places and try out almost every fad."[18]

Concluding, probably correctly, that such behavior among Church members was the result of a lack of proper religious indoctrination, the Louisiana Synod created a Department of Religious Education in 1924 that began operating in 1927. As with other Protestant groups in Louisiana, the Presbyterian Educational Department placed a great deal of emphasis on the improvement of Sunday Schools. These had been deficient in teacher quality, in lesson materials, and in enrollments. With the onset of the Depression, Presbyterian Sunday Schools continued to struggle, until increased affluence and population growth after the war brought improvements in all phases of Church activity—especially in the area of physical plants.[19]

Neither Northern nor Southern Presbyterians operated denominational schools other than colleges after the 1870s. Since then, Presbyterian absence in the private school field has been characteristic of the denomination. In formal recognition of long-established practice, the Northern Presbyterian General Assembly adopted a strong statement in 1957 declaring its "support of public education and its role in the United States." That statement might also have applied to the educational stance of the Southern Presbyterians as well.[20]

White Southern Methodists, with larger numbers of religious communicants, showed greater educational ambitions than either Presbyterians or Episcopalians before World War II. With an educational outlook similar to that of Southern Baptists and equal organizational capabilities, Southern Methodists evolved a program of educational activity nearly identical to that of Southern Baptists.

With the founding of Centenary College at Jackson, East Feliciana Parish, in 1825, Methodist interest in higher education manifested earlier than that of Baptists in Louisiana.[21] Three more colleges were built during the 1850s. Homer College, in Claiborne Parish, came under the control of the Colored Methodists, who splintered from the white Southern Methodist Church in 1870. Pierce and Payne College, in DeSoto Parish, did not survive the Civil War and Reconstruction. However, Centenary and the Mansfield Female College, in DeSoto Parish, did survive into the twentieth century, as counterparts to the Baptist Mt. Lebanon University for men, and Keatchie College for women.[22]

Like the Baptist colleges, Centenary and Mansfield entered the new century with old and inadequate physical plants. Two years after Baptists established Louisiana College, near Alexandria, to replace Mt. Lebanon, the Methodists moved Centenary to a new urban location in Shreveport, where the school has since remained. Both female colleges, Keatchie and Mansfield, were eventually abandoned by their denominations—Keatchie by the Baptists in 1912, and Mansfield by the Methodists in 1930.[23]

As did Baptists, Methodists established academies in various parts of the state that were abandoned when public high schools came into existence about the turn of the century. Evergreen Institute, established in Avoyelles Parish in 1856, was one of the largest Methodist denominational schools of the nineteenth century. Also like Baptists, the Methodist college and Sunday Schools became the educational priorities of the Annual Conference by 1919.[24]

In 1919, as the Southern Baptist Convention was launching its $75,000,000 Campaign ($20,000,000 for education), the Southern Methodist General Conference launched a similar drive to raise $23,000,000 for denominational education. Like the Baptist campaign, the Methodist funding drive fell far below its goal, collecting only about $8,000,000 by 1928. As a result, improvements made on Centenary College created serious indebtedness on the school, a problem similar to that of the Baptist Louisiana College during the Depression years. In further similarity to Baptist education, a Sunday School teacher training program brought better quality and higher enrollments to Methodist Sunday Schools after 1920.[25]

One difference between Methodist and Baptist education in Louisiana was that Methodists supported their denominational college with better funding than Baptists gave Louisiana College. Instead of retiring debts on Centenary College during the 1930s as Baptists did with Louisiana College, Methodists increased their debts in order to upgrade their school. In 1939, the conference Board of Education reported that Centenary had qualified for accreditation by the Southern Association of colleges and Secondary Schools—an important measure of commitment to meeting educational standards that Baptists failed to display with Louisiana College.[26]

In addition, Louisiana's Southern Methodists began requiring a minimum of two years of college work by its ministers in 1926. In 1945, a Southern Baptist minister could still lament the lack of education on the part of Southern Baptist ministers: "Ignorance is one of the greatest sins of the church. . . . Many of our ministers are 100 years behind the times." With improvements at Centenary and better educational standards, Methodist ministers in Louisiana did not have to bear such criticism. While Louisiana College, in 1951, had one Ph.D. on its faculty, 40 percent of Centenary's faculty held doctorates by 1953. Further, Centenary was in sound standing with the Southern Association, both academically and financially, as Louisiana College was not.[27]

One other important religious group existed in Louisiana before World War II. This was the small minority of Louisianians who were Jewish, of both the Reformed and Orthodox faiths. According to Leo Shpall, the first Jewish congregation in Louisiana was founded in 1828, in New Orleans. By 1842, there were about 2,000 Jews living in New Orleans. From this point, little growth occurred in the Jewish population for the remainder of the century, as the 1890 census reported 2,750 Jews in Orleans Parish and 3,374 in the entire state. By 1936, Jews numbered over 13,000 (8,700 in New Orleans) and were about as numerous in the state as Presbyterians.[28]

Partly because of the effects of the Civil War, in drawing whites closer together, Jews experienced little discrimination in Louisiana of the kind Jews endured in other parts of the country. Small numbers, business acumen, and social philanthropy on the part of Louisiana's Jews are other reasons, as well as the fact that, in Louisiana, Reform Jews predominated, creating less divergence from Christian religious practices than would have been true if the majority were Orthodox.[29]

The Jews of New Orleans organized the Hebrew Educational Society in 1866, which opened a school available to Jews and non-Jews alike. This institution gave way in 1910 to the New Orleans Hebrew School. Already in existence, since 1896, was the library, gymnasium, and lecture facilities built by the Young Men's Hebrew Association and the Young Women's Hebrew Association. However, the private philanthropy of Jewish individuals had broader significance to education in Louisiana than the activities of Jewish organizations.[30]

One such individual was the New Orleans businessman, Isidore Newman. The Isidore Newman Manual Training School, which Newman founded in New Orleans in 1903, reflected its benefactor's interest in promoting the training of skilled workers. By the 1930s, however, the Isidore Newman School had become the state's model secondary school. Educational innovations, proven successful there, were sometimes copied by the state's public schools. To the present day, the Newman School is still considered by many to be the finest academic secondary school in Louisiana.[31]

Jews in Louisiana had little problem with the cultural boundaries existing in the state. As a distinctive and highly successful minority, Jews were as culturally alien to North Louisiana Protestants as they were to South Louisiana Catholics. They posed no danger to the dominant cultures of either section and avoided clashes with the politically dominant Protestants through a shared outlook on church-state separation as best for the health of both religion and government.

A Jewish lawyer from Shreveport, Sidney L. Herold, built a reputation after 1912 for involvement in legal cases concerning the separation of church and state. He brought suit against the Caddo Parish School Board in 1913 for the Board's approval of Bible-reading in public schools, winning his case against Bible-reading in 1915 on the grounds that this practice violated the separation of church and state. Jews subsequently became members of the Caddo Parish School Board in the 1920s and two Shreveport high school principals in the 1920s were Jewish. In 1928, following Protestant protest against Louisiana's new Free Textbook Program, which distributed free books to church schools and became the first such program in the country to be justified by the child-benefit theory in state aid to education, Herold brought suit against the state on the grounds of violation of separation of church and state. Herold took the case to the Supreme Court, where his suit was denied in 1930, a decision hailed as a victory for the cause of Catholic education in the United States. Herold's action in both suits demonstrated a consistent position by the Jewish minority in cases concerning separation of church and state—a position necessary for a religious minority seeking guarantees against religious discrimination.[32]

Episcopalians and Presbyterians also had little trouble with the cultural boundary, for they too were minorities in both sections of Louisiana. Although these Protestant religious groups should have felt at home in Protestant North Louisiana, few lived there. The 1890 religious census revealed that all but 7,110 of 115,808 Protestants in North Louisiana belonged to the major Baptist and Methodist denominations. About half of those who were not members of the major religious groups belonged to sectarian offshoots of those groups, such as the Primitive Baptists; or the Methodist Protestant Church. Out of the remaining 3,570, 2,969 were either Presbyterians or Episcopalians. There were 1,257 Presbyterians and Episcopalians out of a Protestant population of 40,320 in twenty-four South Louisiana parishes (excluding Orleans), almost exactly the same percentage of Presbyterians and Episcopalians, among Protestants, as in the Northern parishes (3.11 percent to 3.06 percent).[33]

Perhaps the rural nature of Louisiana throughout the nineteenth century best explains the establishment of the boundary by 1890 between Catholic populations on one side and Baptists and Methodists on the other. Walter Brownlow Posey made the observation that Episcopalians had been content during the first half of the nineteenth century to leave the field of evangelism on the frontier to Methodists, Baptists, and Presbyterians. In Louisiana, with large areas of sparsely settled territory little removed from frontier conditions, Presbyterians as well as Episcopalians abandoned the field of evangelism during the nineteenth century. It made little difference to Presbyterians and Episcopalians in the towns and cities, or on the plantations, whether the country people were Baptists, Methodists, or Catholics.[34]

Minority religious groups were most represented in urban areas and in the black-belt parishes, where their adherents were often among the most prominent and influential leaders in economic and political affairs. From positions of power in local and state government, individual Presbyterians and Episcopalians exerted great influence over public educational development. Such influence reflected upper-class interests that conflicted with the best educational interests of the majority of rural Baptists, Methodists, and Catholics on both sides of the cultural boundary. After 1898, upper-class influence in government became evident in that educational reforms tended to benefit black-belt and urban parishes to the exclusion of areas where rural Baptist or Catholic religious influence was greatest.

In 1888, the Louisiana legislature passed a General Public School Act that required parishes to collect at least a one and one-half mill tax, based on property assessments, for public schools. This provision was nearly identical to one in the 1898 Constitution that allowed parishes to tax beyond a one and one-quarter mill requirement, if they wished. Collection of such taxes was hailed as a new beginning for the public school system after 1898. Few parishes, for some years beyond 1898, collected more than the required one and one-quarter mill. However, collection of the minimum requirement represented improved funding for schools since the 1888 Act had been ignored by most parishes. In commenting on the change in support of public education from 1888 to 1898, Rodney Cline referred to the "time-honored principle that laws enacted upon an unwilling or an unready populace are likely to be ineffective." However, Cline did not explain what made Louisiana's population seem more receptive to public educational expansion in 1898.[35]

Perhaps the most important provision of the 1898 Constitution was the disfranchisement of Negroes. For the public educational system the important provision was that state funds for public schools were to be apportioned to parishes on the basis of the total number of educable children in the parishes of the state, aged six to eighteen. What this meant to the Bourbon Democrats in charge of school boards and police juries was that, since Negroes were disfranchised, there could be no opposition to counting the children of both races, receiving the state appropriations, and then spending a disproportionate share of the school funds on schools for white children. Unfortunately for the predominantly white, hill-country parishes, they had few blacks to count as educables and the system worked to increase their educational disparity with the urban and black-belt parishes.[36]

Such disparity contributed to a situation in which there were two large groups of whites in the state who were educationally disadvantaged: rural Baptists and Methodists in the North Louisiana pine woods and uplands parishes, and rural South Louisiana French Catholics. Other religious denominations with largely urban memberships had better access to both public and private educational facilities. As the most educationally disadvantaged group, Negroes used their religious organizations to found schools in an attempt to overcome educational disadvantages. Rural white Protestants and Catholics, with traditions of low educational attainment, suffered from the lack of public educational development in their parishes at a time when their religious denominations were either abandoning denominational schools or facing financial barriers to educational expansion.

As a truly silent majority, Louisiana's rural white population got left out when the urban and plantation whites finally decided to support an expanded public system. With the educational reforms of the 1898 constitution, it was not the religious minorities of the state who were disadvantaged. Quite to the contrary, it was the religious majority of Negro Baptists and Methodists, rural white Southern Baptists and Methodists, and rural white and Negro Catholics.

The cultural, religious, and economic practices of these rural people were rooted in their eighteenth and nineteenth century origins. Social and cultural change was much less evident among them than among others in the cities and towns. They were the people most responsible for the presence and persistence of the cultural boundary, for they also constituted the majority of people in the state.

For the state's religious minorities, found mainly in urban places or on plantations, the cultural boundary was less meaningful. Represented in the state's economic, political, and intellectual elite out of proportion to their small numbers, Presbyterians, Episcopalians, and Jews were, in the main, a more prosperous group of people than the majority of Baptists, Methodists, and Catholics. They conducted their activities without regard for the religious prejudices and cultural heritages of the major religious groups. Insulated by economic status, along with the Baptist and Catholic elite, they represented the vanguard of progressivism in Louisiana. By World War II, changes in society introduced by progressives indicated a greater interest in protection of economic status than in sponsoring widespread social reform. Despite Huey P. Long's introduction of social reform on an unprecedented scale after 1928, the cultural boundary remained intact by World War II as Louisiana's religious majority remained largely unrepresented in the state's political and economic power structure.[37]

Up to World War II, the political and economic processes that produce social and cultural change had not greatly affected the older process of religious continuity and cultural persistence in large areas of the state. An emerging "civil religion," characterized by materialism and nationalism, was not yet strong enough in Louisiana to challenge or to share the loyalty that Louisianians gave to their conventional religions. As rural values reinforced by conventional religious tradition persisted, educational expansion failed to subsume provincialism. Common class interests of rural white and black Baptists and Catholics remained buried beneath disunity caused by racial and cultural antagonisms between themselves. Unbound by these cultural antagonisms and having economic interests to protect, planter and industrial elites, in league with the growing middle-class of the towns and cities, exploited the political and cultural disunity of the rural population to retain political and economic hegemony in Louisiana.[38]

Leaders of the major denominations, less bound than most members of religious groups to nineteenth century rural values and traditions, recognized a need for social uplifting on the part of their denominational activities. Although in different ways, all the major denominations turned to education as key to the process of social uplift. The years between about 1910 and 1940 witnessed a transformation in the educational values of the religious majority, as the educational influence of the minority of religious leaders slowly bore fruit. While urban/rural, black-belt/pine woods, and black/white educational disparities were partially a result of the class differences that religions reflected, these disparities were not caused exclusively by political and economic exploitation. To a great extent, educational disparities were the result of educational disinterest on the part of adherents of the major religious groups, although this was less true of black religion.

To the extent that religious antipathy and cultural boundary maintenance between Baptists and Catholics politically divided rural whites between the two sections of the state, class exploitation emerged as a plausible cause of educational disparities. However, that explanation implies that Huey Long, who managed to politically unite North and South Louisiana after 1928 and to institute educational reforms and expansion, somehow accomplished the feat through educating rural whites to sudden awareness of their exploitation and became the cause for increased public interest in educational expansion and reform during the 1930s.

A better explanation is one that accounts for change in the educational attitude of the religious majority by 1928 so that an astute politician like Long could take advantage of an existing social reality. While Louisiana religions were socially conservative and promoted the persistence of traditional values and cultural expressions, they also came to embrace an educational ideal calling for the social advancement of their adherents within the two sections of the state. The expansion of their educational programs after 1910 attest to the existence of that ideal—as did Long's political interest in educational reforms after 1934.

After 1898, as rural Baptists and Catholics of both races experienced fewer benefits from public educational reform than other groups, religious education programs began to expand, reflecting spread of the progressive, organizational reform spirit to these groups. Catholic parochial schools in South Louisiana copied administrative and curricular trends in the public school system, serving to supplement that system and to increase its benefits for greater numbers of poor blacks and whites. Black Baptists in North Louisiana attempted to maintain denominational schools until public school expansion began to reach poor rural blacks in the 1930s. White Baptists abandoned denominational schools, except for colleges, after 1898 but significantly expanded their system of Sunday Schools. Centralized organization, standardization, and direction of that system after 1910 transcended the otherwise independent, isolated character of locally autonomous Baptist congregations. Over time, Sunday School expansion and operation resulted in development of stronger educational desires and ideals by Louisiana Baptists.

When Long introduced a plan to equalize funding for public schools in all areas of the state in 1934, rural Baptists and Catholics in both sections of the state enthusiastically supported this reform. By the 1930s, both Catholics and Baptists had become committed to strong educational programs adapted to coexistence with the public educational system. The result was less political tension across the cultural boundary, greater educational opportunities for adherents of the major religious denominations, and no threat to the continuing religious dominance of Baptists and Catholics on either side of the cultural boundary.

Notes for "Methodists, Other Denominations, Public Educational Development, and the Cultural Boundary"

[1]Louisiana historian Joe Gray Taylor commented that many of the non-denominational private schools "could almost be termed Protestant parochial schools, because they were taught by Protestant clergymen to supplement their meager incomes." Joe Gray Taylor, *Louisiana: A Bicentennial History* (New York, 1976), 81-82; Roger A. Fischer, *The Segregation Struggle in Louisiana, 1862-77* (Urbana, Ill., 1974), 90.

[2]Taylor, *Louisiana*, 81; J. Carlyle Sitterson, *Sugar Country: The Cane Sugar Industry in the South, 1753-1950* (Lexington, 1953), 84-86; in referring to Bourbon neglect of education, William Ivy Hair has suggested "that there was probably truth to the charge, made by Populist reformers in the 1890s, that the Bourbon Democracy deliberately sabotaged Louisiana's school system; and sabotaged it not so much for the sake of economy, but in order to hold public intelligence down to the lowest common denominator and so keep rural people of both races docile." William Ivy Hair, *Bourbonism and Agrarian Protest: Louisiana Politics, 1877-1900* (Baton Rouge, La., 1969), 124.

[3]Fischer, *The Segregation Struggle*, 90-99.

[4]Presently New Orleans is about 55 percent black. Fred B. Kniffen and Sam Bowers Hilliard, *Louisiana: Its Land and People*, revised edition (Baton Rouge, La., 1988), 193; U. S. Bureau of the Census, *Historical Statistics of the United States, Colonial Times to 1970* (Washington, D. C., 1975), Part 1, 28; U. S. Bureau of the Census, *Compendium of the Eleventh Census: 1890; Population* (Washington, D. C., 1892), Part 1, 489-490.

[5]Fischer, *The Segregation Struggle*, 115-116; Roger Baudier, *The Catholic Church in Louisiana* (New Orleans, 1939), 461, 501, 507-508.

[6]Louisiana Department of Education, *Annual Report of the State Superintendent of Public Education*, 1874 (Baton Rouge, La., 1875), xv, xix-xx; Fischer, *The Segregation Struggle*, 131.

[7]Fischer, *The Segregation Struggle*, 16-18.

[8]Louisiana Department of Education, *Annual Report, 1874*, xxi; the Orleans Parish School Board reported in 1893: "It is a matter of great pride to our Board that the Public schools of New Orleans have arrived at a degree of intrinsic excellence and general popularity never before attained, and they compare most favorably with any system of schools to be found elsewhere." Quoted in Louisiana State Board of Education, *Official Proceedings, 1869-1909*, State Board minutes of May 24, 1893, Louisiana State University Library, Baton Rouge, La.; Taylor, *Louisiana*, 120, 134; C. Vann Woodward, *Origins of the New South, 1877-1913* (Baton Rouge, La., 1951), 61-63, 66.

[9]Louisiana Department of Education, *Annual Report, 1874*, 80-81, 89, 96, 98-99, 129-133; Taylor, *Louisiana*, 120.

[10]T. H. Harris Papers, 3:30, Southwestern Archives, University of Southwestern Louisiana, Lafayette, La.; Fischer, *The Segregation Struggle*, 101-102; Roger Baudier, *One Hundred Years of the Upper Teche* (Arnaudville, La., 1953), 43-44; Hair, *Bourbonism*, 122-123; as late as 1898, when, now, parishes were constitutionally mandated to collect local taxes of at least one and one-quarter mill of property assessments for education, private schools still flourished in even non-Catholic areas of the state. For example, Jackson Parish, with no Catholics in its population, had thirty white private schools. Red River Parish, also with no Catholics, had fifteen white private schools. Union and Winn Parishes, with no Catholics, had forty-four and thirty white private schools, respectively. Louisiana Department of Education, *Biennial Report of the State Superintendent of Public Education, 1898-99* (Baton Rouge, La., 1900), 32-35.

[11]National Baptist Convention, *Annual*, 1899, 96; ibid., 1900,181; ibid., 1901, 98, 165; Thomas Jesse Jones, *Negro Education: A Study of the Private and Higher Schools for Colored People in the United States*, 2 vols. (Washington, D. C., 1917), 1:345, 374-375.

[12]Negro Methodists had eighteen academies in Alabama, Georgia, and the Carolinas. Ibid., 1:155-158. L. M. Hagood, *The Colored Man in the Methodist Episcopal Church* (Westport, Conn., 1970), 88, 142-147, 299, 306. In 1890, three Negro denominations (African Methodist Episcopal, African Methodist Episcopal Zion, and Colored Methodist Episcopal), plus the predominantly black Methodist Episcopal Church (Northern Methodists), represented 30 percent of Louisiana's black religious communicants, as compared to 64 percent for Negro Baptists. By 1936, Negro Methodists declined to 15 percent of the black religious, compared to 66 percent for Negro Baptists. In 1936, over 40 percent of all members of the Negro Methodist denominations, nationally, resided in Alabama, Georgia, and the Carolinas. U. S. Bureau of the Census, *Report on Statistics of Churches in the United States at the Eleventh Census: 1890* (Washington, D. C., 1894) (hereafter cited as *Religious Census*, 1890); U. S. Bureau of the Census, *Religious Bodies: 1936; Denominations A to J: Statistics, History, Doctrine, Organization, and Work* (Washington, D. C., 1941), II, Part I, 1179, 1183, 1190, 1213; U. S. Bureau of the Census, *Religious Bodies: 1936; Summary and Detailed Tables* (Washington, D. C., 1941), Vol. L (hereafter cited as *Religious Census*, 1936).

[13]Jones, *Negro Education*, 1:138; ibid., 2:313; *Religious Census*, 1936.

[14]*Religious Census*, 1890; *Religious Census*, 1936; Jones, *Negro Education*, 1:345; Sue L. Eakin, "The Black Struggle for Education in Louisiana, 1877-1930s" (Ph.D. dissertation, University of Southwestern Louisiana, 1980), 192.

[15]Jones, *Negro Education*, 2:304-305; Religious Census, 1890; Religious Census, 1936.

[16]Richard Ognibene, "Catholic and Protestant Education in the Late Nineteenth Century," *Religious Education*, 77 (1982): 14-16; There were twenty-six Episcopalian schools in the North and Northeast, in 1930. Of nineteen Episcopalian schools outside of the North and Northeast in 1930, there were in three in the West, eight in Maryland and Virginia, three in the District of Columbia, two in Tennessee, and one each in Georgia, North Carolina, and Texas. Porter Sargent, A *Handbook of Private Schools for American Boys and Girls: An Annual Survey*, 14th ed. (Boston, 1930), 791, 805-806, 823.

[17]*Religious Census*, 1890; *Religious Census*, 1936. Beginning with a high school in Metairie in 1947, the Episcopal Church has since sponsored several more denominational schools in both North and South Louisiana. Rebecca A. Shepherd, ed., *Peterson's Annual Guide to Independent Secondary Schools* (Princeton, N. J., 1982), 119, 297; Episcopal School of Acadiana "School Profile," informational sheets on mission of the school, in personal possession of author; John T. Russell maintains that the Episcopal school movement, resulting in the establishment of schools across the country, was a reaction to the Supreme Court decision of 1947, in *McCollum v. Illinois*, which banned prayer in public schools—and not a reaction to the Brown decision of 1954. John T. Russell, "The Parish School Movement: An Appraisal," in Kendig Brubaker Cully, ed., *The Episcopal Church and Education* (New York, 1966), 73-86.

[18]Religious Census, 1890; Religious Census, 1936; *Synod of Louisiana of the Presbyterian Church in the United States, Presbyterian Activities in Louisiana: A Synopsis for Use as a Study Book by Auxiliaries, Sunday Schools, Young People's Societies, and Others* (New Orleans, 1927), 14-17; Records of First Presbyterian

Church, Lafayette, Louisiana, August 1875-May 1975, Southwestern Archives, University of Southwestern Louisiana, Lafayette, La. (hereafter cited as Presbyterian Records), April 25, 1920, April 13, 1924.

[19]Synod of Louisiana, *Presbyterian Activities*, 49-50; The Presbyterian Church in Lafayette collected contributions of $4,739.50 in 1924. All but $430 of this went to paying the salary of the pastor and expenses on the church building. $42.50 went to conducting the Sunday School, which had an enrollment of 87. During the Depression, contributions were lower but topped $6,400 in 1946. A new church was built in 1947 and contributions rose to $24,735 in 1954, $64,667 in 1958, and ever higher after that time. Presbyterian *Records*; William B. Kennedy, "New Orthodoxy Goes to Sunday School: The Christian Faith and Life Curriculum," *Journal of Presbyterian History*, 58 (1980): 326-328, 365-367.

[20]Paul W. Koper, "The United Presbyterian Church and Christian Education—An Historical Overview," *Journal of Presbyterian History*, 59 (1981): 304.

[21]Taylor, *Louisiana*, 82; William A. Poe, "Religion and Education in North Louisiana, 1800-1865," in B. H. Gilley, ed., *North Louisiana; Essays on the Region and Its History, Vol. One: To 1865* (Ruston, La., 1984), 121.

[22]Poe, "Religion and Education in North Louisiana," 128; Hagood, *The Colored Man in the Methodist Church*, 306.

[23]Taylor, *Louisiana*, 82; *Baptist Message*, October 25, 1962, 14; *Annual* of the Louisiana Conference of the Methodist Episcopal Church, South (hereafter cited as MECS, *Annual*), 1930, 43.

[24]Sue L. Eakin, *Avoyelles Parish . . . Crossroads of Louisiana Where All Cultures Meet* (Baton Rouge, La., 1981), 87; Centenary's importance was in its mission to train more and better ministers, as well as to conduct a new correspondence course to improve the training of Sunday School teachers. MECS, *Annual*, 1919, 23.

[25]MECS, *Annual*, 1919, 22-23; ibid., 1929, 77; Sunday School enrollments climbed from about 33,000 in 1920 to over 42,000 in 1977. Only slight decline in enrollments were experienced during the early years of the Depression, as enrollment hit its low of 37,000 in 1937, climbing thereafter to an all-time high of over 45,000 in 1940. By 1955, enrollment had increased to over 73,000, a figure representing nearly 70 percent of the entire church membership in the state. Ibid., 1920, 44; ibid., 1927 ,71; ibid., 1937, 92-93; ibid., 1940, 20-21; ibid., 1955, 105.

[26]Ibid., 1938, 57; ibid., 1939, 67.

[27]Ibid., 1926, 51; *Time*, April 16, 1945, quoted in Porter Sargent *The Continuing Battle for the Control of the Mind of Youth* (Boston, 1945), 95; Centenary enjoyed some good fortune that Louisiana College did not. Having been selected by the U. S. Army as a site for training schools for aviators and nurses during World War II, Centenary enjoyed the benefits of government military spending. In addition the college's endowment fund was tripled in 1951 by a two million dollar bequest, left in the will of William Arch Haynes of Shreveport. Haynes had earlier donated over $105,000, in 1942, for the purchase of Dodd College, a Baptist women's junior college in Shreveport, which became the Haynes Campus of Centenary College in 1944. MECS, *Annual*, 1943, 35; ibid., 1944, 36; ibid., 1951, 58. Louisiana College, having to struggle to raise endowment funds to meet the standards of the Southern Association, could not qualify academically for membership. In 1953, the Southern Association required that at least 25 percent of college faculties hold a Ph.D. Ibid., 1953, 73; Greene, *House Upon a Rock*. 267.

[28]One reason for the small growth of the Jewish population was the Civil War, which split the Jewish population. Those Jews in New Orleans in 1890 were apparently the ones who chose to cast their fortunes with the Confederacy in 1861, such as Judah P. Benjamin, Attorney General, Secretary of War, and Secretary of State of the Confederate government during the war. Leo Shpall, *The Jews in Louisiana* (New Orleans, 1936), 9-12, 17; Religious Census, 1890; Religious Census, 1936.

[29]Shpall, *The Jews in Louisiana*, 13, 43-44, Beverly S. Williams, "Anti-Semitism and Shreveport, Louisiana: The Situation in the 1920s," *Louisiana History*, 21 (1980): 389-392; Elliott Ashkenazi, *The Business of Jews in Louisiana, 1840-1875* (Tuscaloosa, Ala., 1988), 14, 77.

[30]Shpall, *The Jews in Louisiana*, 13, 24, 27-28, 43-44. Isaac Delgado, the philanthropist who endowed the Delgado Trade School in New Orleans in 1912, is presented as Jewish in Shpall's book. The Delgado Trade School became very influential as a model for other such schools, which came into vogue in the wake of the Smith-Hughes Act of 1917. Although possibly of Jewish descent, Delgado was also of Spanish-Portuguese descent, and was a member, in New Orleans, of the Episcopal Church. Glenn R. Conrad, ed., A *Dictionary of Louisiana Biography*, 2 vols. (New Orleans, La., 1988), 1:230-231.

[31]*Dictionary of Louisiana Biography*, 1:600; Robert Nielson, Headmaster at the Episcopal School of Acadiana (an academically rigorous college-prep school) wrote in 1987 that he has "always considered Newman to be the finest high school in Louisiana, public or private." However, the preceding was written in a context of introducing a new faculty member from the Newman School, who claimed that the Episcopal School was better academically, because of the more rounded nature of the curriculum at a religious school, which can attempt to impart moral values. Episcopal School of Acadiana, Informational sheets on the school in personal possession of author.

[32]Interestingly, an Alexandria lawyer, H. H. White, defended the state's interest in the free textbook case. White was prominent in the Southern Methodist Church, becoming involved with the unification of several Southern Methodist denominations in 1939. White was also a longtime president of the Louisiana State Board of Education. Beverly S. Williams, "Anti-Semitism and Shreveport, Louisiana: The Situation in the 1920s," *Louisiana History*, 21 (1980): 392-394; *Herold v. Parish Board of School Directors* 136 La. 1034, 68 So. 116 (1913); *Bossier Parish School Board, et al., Caddo Parish School Board, et al. v. Louisiana State Board of Education, et al.* 123 So. 665 (1929); *Cochran v. Louisiana State Board of Education* 281 U. S. 370 (1930).

[33]Religious Census, 1890.

[34]Walter Brownlow Posey, *Religious Strife on the Southern Frontier* (Baton Rouge, La., 1965), 33-34.

[35]Rodney Cline, *Education in Louisiana—History and Development* (Baton Rouge, La., 1974), 29; Minns Sledge Robertson, *Public Education in Louisiana After 1898* (Baton Rouge, La., 1952), 3-4; for a breakdown, in 1901, of parishes collecting special school taxes, and the amounts, see minutes of State Board of Education meeting of April 29, 1902, in Louisiana State Board of Education, *Official Proceedings, 1869-1909*, Louisiana State University Library, Baton Rouge, La.

[36]Ibid., 3-4, 188, Woodward, *Origins*, 321, 326-328, 340, 342.

[37]Dewey W. Grantham explained that Southern Progressives faced the challenge of reconciling urban, industrial progress with Southern tradition. They were "in no sense involved in the promotion of fundamental social change. Nor were they, as a rule, democrats with an implicit faith in the masses or a concrete program for assisting the poor and disadvantaged. . . ." As representatives of "the emerging professional and bourgeois elements of the South's social structure, . . ." they accepted or accommodated themselves to a system whose major institutions were dominated by powerful economic and political interests." Dewey W. Grantham, *Southern Progressivism: The Reconciliation of Progress and Tradition* (Knoxville, Tenn., 1983), 417-418, 422.

[38]In support of J. Morgan Kousser, in *The Shaping of Southern Politics: Suffrage Restrictions and the Establishment of the One-Party South, 1880-1910* (New Haven, 1974), Matthew J. Schott pointed out that in Louisiana, as in the rest of the South, electoral reform and progressivism were tied in with each other. Use of the Australian (Secret) ballot was an effective disfranchiser of both whites and blacks in such states as Louisiana, with large rural and uneducated populations, unable to use secret ballots that required English literacy. Both Kousser and Schott submit that Louisiana's elites instituted the Secret ballot with full knowledge of the high rates of illiteracy in the state, and that the success of the Australian ballot, as a tool for disfranchisement of the rural people, provided motivation to prolong illiteracy in the non black-belt, rural parishes. Progressive educational reform after 1898 tended to benefit mostly the urban population, as well as the white population of the black-belt parishes. As Schott aptly wrote, "progressivism in Louisiana . . . was motivated and influenced by upper-class, elite reformers with undemocratic attitudes and goals: That is to say, by Progressives against democracy." Matthew J. Schott, "Progressives Against Democracy: Electoral Reform in Louisiana, 1894-1921," *Louisiana History*, 20 (1979): 249-251.

MINUTE BY MINUTE:
CASE STUDIES FROM THE LEADERS' AND STEWARDS' MINUTES OF AN AFRICAN AMERICAN METHODIST CHURCH, NEW ORLEANS, LOUISIANA, 1896-1906*

Rosalind F. Hinton

Wesley Methodist Episcopal Church was founded in 1838 as a multi-racial congregation in New Orleans, Louisiana. In 1844, the church was reorganized into an all-Negro congregation and members, many of whom were slaves, built a showcase church that seated 1,200 people at the corner of South Liberty and Perdido streets.[1] By the early 1900s this neighborhood was a red light district known as the Battlefield. It was a few blocks west of Storyville, a prostitution district created in 1897. Louis Armstrong described this area, where his mother lived, in his autobiography *Satchmo*: "My mother went to a place at Liberty and Perdido Streets in a neighborhood filled with cheap prostitutes who do not make as much money for their time as the whores in Storyville, the famous red-light district."[2]

The historiography surrounding the Battlefield focused on the sensational life in the area and erased the church and family life that existed alongside the notorious street life. Case studies from the Leaders' and Stewards' Meeting Minutes, 1892-1906, of Wesley Methodist Episcopal Church, North reveal a disciplined communal ethic that sharply contrasts with the romantic portrayals of licentious street life that white audiences demanded from early historical accounts. The minutes also show how church disciplines created a politics of respectability for a working-class community of laundresses, laborers, and upwardly mobile black professionals during the Jim Crow Era.

Jim Crow was the turn of the century system of segregation that confined African Americans to the bottom of the Southern racial and economic order. In the late 1890s, three successive national depressions placed their signatures on the urban landscape of New Orleans. The bottom fell out of cotton prices and black and white farmers swelled the city's population. The influx of people created a large labor pool and fierce job com-

*This previously unpublished selection is printed here for the first time with the kind permission of the author.

the city's population. The influx of people created a large labor pool and fierce job competition for very low wages. White claims of black laziness and immorality justified a host of Jim Crow customs, ordinances and laws that restricted African America advancement.

And advance was exactly what the Wesley community did between 1865 and the early 1900s, especially in the field of education. Wesley members helped charter New Orleans University in 1873. The university had a medical school, theological school, nursing and normal departments as well as a grade school, preparatory, and traditional college program. The Women's Home Missionary Society at Wesley started a school for freed women that became the Peck Industrial School for Women and shared the prestigious St. Charles Avenue address with New Orleans University.[3] Wesley also started Faith Kindergarten which had an enrollment of two hundred children.

Musical performances at Wesley embodied the educational accomplishments of African Americans. For instance, in 1877 Wesley sponsored, "A Grand Concert, Dialogue and Tableaux Exhibition . . . under the auspices of the New Orleans Jubilee Singers."[4] The New Orleans Jubilee singers sang in the European classical style of the Fisk Jubilee singers who originated the concertized spiritual in 1871. These spirituals blended the European song form with the lyric elegance of the field spiritual. This new song form was created on a fundraising tour that kept the doors of Fisk University open. It bore witness to the desire for education shared by African American communities after the Civil War.[5] But, as the congregation engaged new musical styles, it also remained faithful to traditional forms developed in slavery. A case in point was the traditional Methodist love feast held at the quarterly Louisiana Methodist Episcopal Conference hosted by Wesley in 1880 where "one thousand people joined in stirring exhortations and the singing of our hymns and the weird songs so familiar in the olden times."[6] This account implies that the community kept alive not only the emotionally stirring love feast rituals of early Methodism, but also the black meter tradition that arose at religious camp meetings and revivals during and after slavery.[7]

These performances of Wesley provided counterpoint, not discord to life in the Battlefield. In fact, the women of Wesley were busily recruiting young members from the ranks of the neighborhood. In 1905, calling themselves the Crusaders, the women of the church broke into squadrons and took a block by block census of children in the area. They tabulated the number of children attending and not attending church in the neighborhood and offered to subsidize fifteen children without financial means at Sunday school.[8]

The early Methodist Church organized its members into intergenerational classes. Wesley maintained this tradition. The six hundred members of congregation were divided into intimate classes that averaged thirty members. Each class had a class leader. Classes met faithfully on Tuesday nights at 8 p.m. Class members became lifelong religious, educational and artistic colleagues who planned programs, raised money, prayed together and shared in the problems and the celebrations of the larger community. No one simply disappeared from the class roster. They were expelled for immoral behavior, formally withdrew or died.

Wesley's congregation was made up of a number of upwardly mobile black professionals, but its primary base was "a community of laundresses and servants for white people."[9] The weekly class collections confirm that there was little in the way of economic resources at Wesley. On February 7, 1896, the funding total from the seventeen classes was $14.60. Some classes gave as little as 25 cents that week with the highest amount at $1.35. And, 1896 was a good year. By 1898, the members felt the shut down of capital into the black community as Jim Crow customs became law.[10] The October 4 class records totaled $7.25 with individual class donations at 15, 30, and 35 cents. By the time the minutes concluded in 1906, the community had not yet matched their 1896 financial figures.[11]

The disciplines of Methodism—thrift, temperance, hard work, moral purity, and responsibility—were reinforced and monitored at the class level. As we have seen, members were responsible for weekly dues. The member also had to be physically present and contribute to the social uplift of the larger community. The disciplines were not simply about personal advancement in the new Southern industrial economy. Indeed, communal rituals such as love feasts, class meetings, and church trials were abandoned by upwardly mobile white Methodist communities as early as 1866.[12] African Americans at Wesley, on the other hand, maintained these early Methodist traditions and disciplines because they helped express a collective ethos that was deeply rooted in West African religious traditions, persisted in the ring shouts and collective rituals of slavery, and continued nurturing the church community during the difficult period of Jim Crow. The rituals of Methodism provided a means for spiritual exhortation and communal expressiveness and nurtured a rigorous discipline that maintained a purposeful interdependence. Events as basic as class attendance reveal a three-way dialectic between individuals, their community, and their God. Frequent absences were not simply a personal offense, but a breach of relationship with God that also threatened the survival of the church community.

The song, "There Ain't No Hiding Place Down Here," comes to mind in reading through the minutes. Trials were held when class leaders accused church members of an offense. For instance, if a member missed three consecutive classes, he or she was brought before the stewards on the serious charge of "having neglected the means of grace."[13] When Sisters Lilly Bell and Edwina Reed were charged with "willful neglect of the means of grace. They were not reinstated until they "showed the proper humiliation, promised to be more dutiful to God and the Church and, were reprimanded in a very impressive and fatherly manner by the Pastor."[14]

Members were sometimes expelled in front of their class and then reintroduced to the class the following week and placed on probation. All members in the Methodist church served a probationary period before they were recommended for full membership, so this sentence was a form of starting over. For instance, one trial began with a hymn "A

Charge To Keep I Have" and a prayer from the pastor. Sister Lucina Crayon was charged with fraud and immoral conduct. She allegedly spent ten dollars during an illness that she had collected from the class for another purpose. Sister Crayon pled guilty, but said that she only raised $7.50. She was expelled one week and then put on probation the following week. She was also granted a fixed time in which to settle the full account of ten dollars.[15]

The Leaders and Stewards' Meeting minutes show that men dominated the list of church officials and women dominated the unofficial positions. Men were the class leaders, deacons, stewards, and trustees. They were generally the people who brought charges against class members and they also acted as judge and jury at the trials. Women were prayer leaders, exhorters, teachers, musical soloists, and fundraisers. Women dominated the entertainment roster. They organized concerts, teas, socials and entertainments that rallied support and money around trustees and stewards' planning. These events helped the various organizations within the church fund new initiatives and retire old debt.

In 1900, the sisters of the church instituted Silver Dollar Day. The minutes read, "The sisters will on the second Sunday in July have this day known as Silver Dollar Day and they [will] all pay one dollar each." Benevolent associations also collected money during anniversary celebrations and gave the money to the Church. For instance, the New Ladies Providence Benevolent Association collected $12.05 at one Sunday service.[16]

Classes and choirs also held rallies and concerts for the church. The concert announcements were always celebratory, "There will be a grand concert on Monday night, Sept. 26, by the New Ladies Providence Benevolent Association." A concert by church soloist Nellie Williams raised $4.75 for the Trustees. On May 28, 1905, a "grand green and black tea" was held and tickets were sold for five cents. Class number two held a concert with the senior choir and raised $25.00. Class number fourteen brought in $4.00 with a rally. The women of the church sponsored a trolley ride excursion that was so successful the trustees had their own trolley ride a few months later.[17]

Women held candy pulls, fish fries, and house parties as church fund-raisers. One announcement stated, "There will be a grand entertainment at the residence of Sister Ophelia Talbert under the auspices of the Stewards Sisters." There are no accounts of the fish fries in the Wesley minutes, but musician Pops Foster described the house parties and the fish fries in his autobiography,

> All over New Orleans on Saturday night there'd be fish fries. The lawn parties were usually Monday or Wednesday night. . . . The wife usually did the cooking in the morning. She'd fry catfish, cook gumbo, make ham sandwiches, potato salad and ice cream to sell. . . . When it got toward dark, you'd hand a red lantern out on the front door to let anybody going by know there was a fish fry inside and anybody could go in. A plate of catfish and potato salad or a plate of gumbo was fifteen cents. It usually cost twenty-five cents to get in and it was a good way to make a little change.[18]

These entertainments were more than mere fundraisers for the Wesley community. Musical performance was the method and the means by which Wesley passed on the traditions and aesthetic values of slave ancestors. Memory and morals, in a sense, rode the musical aesthetic styles into a new generation. In performance new forms were developed that held the social and musical memory of past traditions in new aesthetic configurations. New aesthetic forms such as the Jubilee Spiritual and Traditional Jazz both liberated African Americans from their slave past and protected the memory of that past in musical counter-narratives.

A child's earliest musical experiences revolved around the weekly concerts, rallies, and friendly competitions staged by the classes, benevolent associations, choirs, and church musical soloists. The events enculturated young members into the aesthetic and moral life of the church community. A letter from an older to a younger woman member of the church reveals the intergenerational mentoring process that took place, "I remember how in your childhood you had been so near and dear to me. How I used to take delight in learning you to recite and together we won many applause . . ."[19]

Wesley's children were not given casual lessons, but ancient survival techniques. Speaking, singing and acting helped children develop poise under pressure and other life skills necessary for survival in a hostile world. The pageants, class rallies, and concerts also instilled within children a communal ethic of responsibility. Children learned the purpose of developing their own gifts and talents. Talents were gifts from God that became gifts to the larger community. Children at Wesley also learned the ethic of social uplift and the value of a dollar.

Wesley could make a dollar cover a multitude of needs. The week's financial coffers often began with not much over a dollar on the books. The total weekly receipts often amounted to no more than $45.00. Out of this sum, the pastor, the recording steward, sexton, and the organist had to be paid. The number of groups and individuals "in need of temporal relief" also grew weekly. Wesley made monthly contributions to New Orleans University, The Freedman's Aid Society of the Methodist Church and the local home for the aged. They met requests for contributions from other religious denominations and paid Sunday school fees for children without means. There were also the utility bills and notes that came due on church property.

The class structure, church trials, and musical performances were closely tied to community survival. The rolls were purged and negligent members were brought to trial because each person's singing, speaking, organizing and fundraising contribution was vital to the success of the whole. Many of the activities scholars attribute to denominational jealousies were actually sincere efforts to keep the membership rosters current and effective. It was an "All that can do, will do" approach and only the old and infirm were allowed to sit on the sidelines. Performances reveal what most institutional histories ignore: women were involved at every turn. Women were not only active in more traditional roles as teachers, but were integral to the financial life of the church and offered

musical training that was the basis for the vibrant New Orleans culture most often identified with jazz men.

The minutes of Wesley Church offer additional insights into the importance of African American church life during Jim Crow. The church was a piece of property whose
ownership was shared by the members. The benefits of property ownership came to most
Wesley members, not through the purchase of private property, but through the collective
ownership of the church. Most of the Wesley members would never own their own property, house or business. Contributing even dimes and nickels to the church, gave the
members a very real stake in its ownership. These contributions offered the church
community the same type of independence that home ownership gave to African Americans with financial means. Home ownership was more than a middle class status symbol
for African Americans during Jim Crow. For instance, at home, family members had a
certain amount of control over their own destiny. As a black presence on the white landscape of Jim Crow, home ownership was a form of resistance against erasure. It also
enabled family security for future generations.[20] All three of these benefits existed for the
members of Wesley. An important event in 1903 illustrates this point.

In February of 1903, the leaders and stewards of Wesley, with the unanimous support of the congregation, rejected a ministerial appointment by the presiding head of the
black Mississippi, Louisiana and Texas Conference. The Wesley community, a congregation made up of many illiterate servants and day laborers, rejected the minister "on the
grounds that he was not an educated minister." The leaders and stewards publicly refused
to let the minister, Reverend Walker, take the pulpit. Walker filed for a restraining order
against the leaders and stewards in criminal court. In an amazing moment of cooperation
between white public authorities and African Americans, the chief of police of the City of
New Orleans advised the trustees and stewards to close the church and hold services in
another building that they owned. The judge ruled in favor of the congregation. Their
success in this case was so important that the recording steward wrote the entire ruling
into the minutes. The judge said that the Bishop could not "arbitrarily ignore the almost
unanimous wishes of the congregation." The judge urged the Bishop to assign another
minister so that Wesley, "may prosper for another seventy years as in the past seventy
years, without the city police and criminal courts aiding their minister in preaching the
Gospel."[21]

The fact that they owned their own property helped the Wesley congregation lever-
age support from local and municipal leaders against the conference bishop. In the ruling, the judge made note of Wesley's good reputation, "It [Wesley] owns its own church
property and pays by voluntary contribution the largest salary to its minister of any of the
Methodist churches, colored, in the state. Its pulpit has been filled with educated intelligent ministers since its organization (and) until this suit it has never had any trouble in
the church or in the court."[22] Property ownership and the practice of Methodist disciplines provided a type of social capital that facilitated relations with the white world
when issues could not be contained within the black community.[23]

The church minutes at Wesley also reveal a scrupulousness surrounding black women's moral behavior. Adultery charges were most often filed by class leaders who were men, but women also brought charges against fellow members. Church women protected their own reputations by vigilantly policing sexual misconduct. For instance, Sister Francis West of class number two was accused of "living in adultery (and) giving birth to a child with no lawful husband." At her trial, Ms. West stated that she was living with the father of the child and that they were not married. She also said, "the child was born in April and is now dead." The committee found her guilty as charged and she was expelled. In another case, Sister Georgiania Pines pleaded guilty to adultery and asked for the prayers of the committee but was pronounced expelled by the pastor.[24]

The apparent harshness of the proceedings must be seen against the backdrop of the neighborhood. The Battlefield occupied a section of Storyville that was not policed. It is estimated that half of the prostitutes in Storyville were women of color. Official blue books that advertised this red light district reinforced white mythology that characterized black women as desirable and exotic. The poorest of the black prostitutes lived and worked in close proximity of the church. Louis Armstrong explained, "In that one block between Gravier and Perdido Streets more people were crowded than you ever saw in your life. There were church people, gamblers, hustlers, cheap pimps, thieves, prosti-tutes, and lots of children. There were bars, honky-tonks and saloons, and lots of women walking the streets for tricks to take to their "pads," as they called their rooms."[25]

The manipulation of the image of African American women as symbols of the erotic placed black women in danger.[26] This fact was doubly true in the Battlefield, where all women who walked down the street were automatically considered sexually available. Strategies that countered assaults on females were developed around a woman's ability to get protection from within her community.

Women who lived outside of formal church communities developed their own meth-ods of protection and self-determination. "Mary Jack the Bear" was a female prostitute who was known for using a switchblade when trouble started. Madame Paploos gained strength for herself and for her clients through the practice of voodoo.[27] One female jazz musician in New Orleans said that she sold her body in back alleys for a quarter to avoid having it taken for nothing. This woman developed a strategy that was similar to one mentioned by Linda Brent in her slave narrative, "It seems less degrading to give oneself than to submit to compulsion."[28]

Church women had some knowledge of these alternative coping mechanisms and rejected these methods of self-protection. Instead, they asserted their own strategy of respectability. Moral righteousness became their weapon. Wesley woman were living witnesses of moral purity and discipline whose very personhood countered racist my-thologies that degraded the entire black community. They policed this strategy them-selves. As Evelyn Higgenbotham has noted, the strategy of respectability "demanded that every individual in the black community assume responsibility for behavioral self-regulation and self-improvement along moral, education and economic lines."[29]

There had to be an enormous amount of anxiety and a certain amount of fear and empathy around the economic situations that led women into occasional prostitution. People in the neighborhood most likely knew women who turned intermittently to prostitution in order to make ends meet. This strategy was not tolerated in the church environment where women defined their own virtue on a daily basis against the backdrop of explicit prostitution. In one Wesley trial, Sister Hill was accused of "walking disorderly." Walking disorderly was a term for prostitution. Sister Hill did not show up to refute the charges, but sent a message through another woman of the church. She said, "She is not forced to attend these balls but the church gives her nothing and she will go to them if they were given every night."[30] Sister Hill claimed that she got no help from the church and, therefore, found other ways to provide for herself.

The details of another trial demonstrate how women could occasionally guide the proceedings to their own advantage. One woman brought forward a charge of adultery against a fellow member because battery and assault charges against women were not taken seriously, especially when the perpetrator was a church insider. The case was against Brother Brooks, a class leader and deacon in the church.

Sister Henry accused Brother Charles Brooks of adultery after she was accused by Brother Brooks of "neglecting the means of grace." Sister Henry was exonerated from her charge in a July hearing. Brother Brooks' trial was held in November of 1902.[31] It came out in the trial that Brother Brooks approached Sister Henry on the street and threatened to kill her if she spoke to a woman named Miss Lena. He then repeated "vile oaths" and accused Sister Henry of being a "low down dirty rat."[32] The trial revealed that Brooks lived with Miss Lena and had thrown her out of his apartment on a number of occasions. Two other witnesses, both women, took care of Miss Lena after these incidents and were also threatened by Brooks. The all-male jury did not condemn Brooks for physically threatening at least four women. Brooks was not convicted of perjury for lying when he swore that he did not live with Miss Lena. Instead, the women of the community forced a charge of immorality because Brooks was living with a woman without being married to her. Unlike the women accused of adultery, Brother Brooks was not expelled immediately, but had his case deferred to the district conference for trial.

This case demonstrates the vulnerability of women even to men within their own church community. It also shows that they could influence, but not alter a system that defined morality in male terms. It reveals the triple jeopardy of black women who had to contend with the economic, sexual, and racial politics of Jim Crow as it was played out within their sanctuary as well as on the streets of New Orleans. The moral trials at Wesley support Evelyn Higgenbotham's observations that black moral conduct of women was overpoliced. Yet, this last trial explains one reason why women participated in this intense moral surveillance. Within the church, women could sometimes manipulate a patriarchal system of justice to their own satisfaction and protection.

The minutes of Wesley Church show how African Americans, betrayed by white America, and forced to live under the tyranny of Jim Crow, poured their considerable energies into influencing the only territory they often collectively owned, the black church. Church culture became an economic, social and spiritual outlet. At church African Americans had something they could fashion in their own interests. Their opinions mattered and their contributions were noticed.

The rituals and disciplines of Methodism were maintained at Wesley long after they were abandoned in many white church communities because they supported deeply rooted communal values and aesthetic traditions. In other words, Methodist values were also African American values. Methodist disciplines nurtured a collective identity and facilitated self-determination and economic self-sufficiency. Early Methodist rituals and class structures were easily tailored to African American performance and worship aesthetics that also nurtured communal interdependency. Traditional values such as thrift, self-help and moral purity helped create a very modern politics of respectability. As seen in the court case that blocked an uneducated minister, this politics of respectability could function as a bridge to the white world during Jim Crow. Church women also used respectability as a form of protection from both black and white assault. They defined their own images by setting themselves apart from the racial, gender and economic politics of Storyville and by manipulating the politics of respectability to their own advantage.

Before I conclude, I would like to return to the musical life of the community. One myth that arose from jazz autobiographies was that jazz was born in the brothels of Storyville. This myth negates the strong influence of the African American church on the creation of jazz. It plays into the myth that the communal improvisation of traditional jazz was somehow less rigorous and required less training and musical discipline than Western classical music. It also erases the role women played as unpaid mentors and educators who made significant contributions to the musical life of the city of New Orleans. Women as well as men passed on the African American communal values and disciplined training that became part of the jazz aesthetic.[33] The numerous performances on Wesley's calendar give us a hint as to how black performers acquired what whites called a "natural ease" in performance.[34] The sheer number of concerts and opportunities for performance helped create the virtuosity and genius for which many black musicians were noted.

Louis Armstrong remarked that his early musical training was at Sunday school. We should take Louis Armstrong seriously when he discussed the importance of Sunday school. He said, "In church and Sunday school I did a whole lot of singing. That, I guess, is how I acquired my singing tactics. . . . At church my heart went into every hymn I sang." Armstrong was born in 1900 and lived in the Battlefield. He could have been one of the "children without means" caught in the Sunday school safety net woven by the women of Wesley.[35]

Musical aesthetics reveals facts that are not always documented in historical accounts that rely on texts. Wesley members moved easily between the classical style of the Jubilee Singers, the traditional style of the Methodist love feast with its "weird songs so familiar in olden times," and the hot jazz arrangements of fish fries and house parties.

Each voice was more juxtaposed than blended as one, but each contributed to the vitality of the whole. The aesthetic styles, kept in tension, communicate the cultural diversity and survival techniques of the Wesley community.

Notes for "Minute by Minute: Case Studies from the Leaders' and Stewards' of an African American Methodist Church, New Orleans, Louisiana, 1896-1906"

[1]Wesley was Northern Methodist Episcopal (M.E., North), not African Methodist Episcopal (A.M.E.) After the 1844 general conference, the Methodist Church split over the question of slavery into a Northern and Southern conference. Wesley remained with the Northern Methodist Episcopal Conference (M.E., North). In 1867, the congregation helped form an African American Conference that included Mississippi, Louisiana and part of Texas. http://www.umc.org/churchlibrary/discipline/history/the_slavery_question.htm

[2]Louis Armstrong, *Satchmo: My Life in New Orleans* (New York, 1984), 8.

[3]New Orleans University (NOU) was located on the site of present-day De La Salle High School. New Orleans University and the Straight University merged and became Dillard University in 1932.

[4]Lynn Abbott, "'Do Thyself a' No Harm'": The Jubilee Singing Phenomenon and the 'Only Original New Orleans University Singers,'" *American Music Research Center Journal*, 6 (1996): 13.

[5]*Wade in the Water: African America Sacred Music Traditions*, Bernice Johnson Reagon, Curator, Smithsonian Institution Traveling Exhibition Service with the National Museum of Natural History; Bernice Johnson Reagon, interview by the author, Birmingham Ala., October 1998.

[6]Abbott, "'Do Thyself a' No Harm,'" 29.

[7]Love Feasts and class meetings (discussed later in the article) were "intimate gatherings of spiritual renewal." They often were very emotional as participants discussed trials, tribulations and hopes that included hymns and exhorters who called forth the spirit. Randy Sparks, *Religion in Mississippi* (Jackson, 2001), 48-49. Black meter music history begins with lined hymns of the 1500s. Presbyterians in Scotland used lined hymns as a way to enable their illiterate congregations to participate in the singing during the church services. Two lines of a hymn were quickly intoned by a leader and then sung in unison by the congregation then more lines were repeated until the song was finished. The tradition was brought to the New World and spread throughout Christian Congregations during the Great Awakening Revivals of the 1750s. African Americans took Watts and Wesley hymns and "blackened them" which meant they incorporated an African American musical aesthetic into the singing of the hymns which endured into the 20th century. The leader intoned text in call and response manner. Leadership changes and communal improvisation required disciplined interdependency between members of the congregation to move the song forward. It also meant that no version was the same way twice. The traditional meter was thrown out and a surging swinging beat was reinforced with handclaps and the sound of feet keeping time. The songs were sung in unison, but created a heterogeneous sound ideal common in African American musical aesthetics. The next lines "raised" or intoned by the leader set off a new level of intensity building to a musical, emotional and spiritual catharsis. Wyatt Tee Walker, *Somebody's Calling My Name: Black Sacred Music and Social Change* (Valley Forge, 1992), 73-96.

[8]Leaders and Stewards' Meeting Minutes, Wesley M. E. Church, March 5, 1905, 401. The Amistad Research Center, New Orleans, La.

[9]Matilde Smith, interview by the author, telephone transcript, October 28, 1998, New Orleans, La.

[10]Laws were passed that directly and indirectly affected social, educational, and political advancement. Vagrancy laws, enforced only against Negroes, made travel dangerous. *Plessy v. Ferguson* made separate public facilities legal. By the early 1900s the dismantling of Reconstruction school systems was written into Southern state constitutions, as was disenfranchisement. By the mid-1920s, nets would be thrown to catch those who were still sliding through the cracks of white supremacy. Residential segregation ordinances were instigated in

the North and the South.

[11]Leaders and Stewards' Meeting Minutes, October 4, 1898, 102-3. Class records read: Class 1-95¢, 2-50¢, 3-65¢, 4-50¢, 5-$1.00, 6-40¢, 7-60¢, 8-5¢, 9-40¢,10-35¢, 11-30¢, 12-30¢, 13-30¢, 14-30¢, 15-15¢, 16-25¢, 17-25¢, Total $7.25. On Feb. 7, 1896, Class 1-$1.35, 2-90¢, 3-$1.35, 4-90¢ 5-$1.10, 5-25¢, 7-$1.80, etc., total of $14.60.

[12]Randy Sparks, *Religion in Mississippi*, 117-118.

[13]Leaders and Stewards' Meeting Minutes March 24, 1899, stated: "Each member of this church be present at class and any one missing three successful meetings will be notified of the same and if they then do not attend or show just cause they shall be charged with neglect of the means of grace and must answer according to the nature of the charge," 162.

[14]Leaders and Stewards' Meeting Minutes, October 15, 1897, 96-97.

[15]Ibid., February 24, 1900, 11.

[16]The Ladies' Prayer Meeting Minutes capture the creative lives of the women of Wesley, Ladies Prayer Meeting Minutes, August 17, 1900, Special Collections, Amistad Research Center, New Orleans, La.

[17]Ibid., September 26, 1904, June 26, 1904, July 27, 1904; November 13, 1904.

[18]Pops Foster, *The Autobiography of Pops Foster New Orleans Jazzman as told to Tom Stoddard* (Berkeley, 1971), 17-18.

[19]Correspondence from Nannan to Alma Lillie Hubbard, November 20, 1930, Special Collections, Schomburg Center For Research in Black Culture, New York, N. Y.

[20]In a significant number of my oral interviews, people would tell about the hardship of Jim Crow and then add, "But we always owned our own house." Home ownership, for those who could afford it, was an important factor in resistance in rural and urban communities.

[21]Leaders and Stewards' Meeting Minutes, February 8, February 12, June 22, August 24, 1903, p. 65-71, 104-107, 130-131.

[22]Ibid.

[23]Evelyn Brooks Higginbotham makes note of this bridge: "The WC's (Woman's Convention of the Baptist Church) advocacy of "respectable" behavior attempted to bridge the emotional distance between blacks and potential white allies." *Righteous Discontent: The Women's Movement in the Black Baptist Church, 1880-1920* (Cambridge, 1983), 197.

[24]Leaders and Stewards Minutes, April 28, 1905, October 29, 1902, 395, 19.

[25]Armstrong, *Satchmo*, 8.

[26]Images of African American women are discussed in the following texts: Darlene Clark Hine, *Black Women and the Re-Construction of American History* (Brooklyn, 1994), 37-47; Evelyn Brooks Higginbotham, *Righteous Discontent: The Women's Movement in the Black Baptist Church, 1880-1920* (Cambridge, 1983), 204-211; Patricia Hill Collins, *Black Feminist Thought: Knowledge, Consciousness, and the Politics of Empowerment* (New York, 1990), 67-90.

[27]Jelly Roll Morton said "She would get lamb and beef tongues from the markets and stick pins and needles all through them in order to tie the tongues of the prosecuting attorney and the witness and the juries so they couldn't talk against whoever the victim's supposed to be—not the victim, but the one that arrested." Alan Lomax, *Mister Jelly Roll* (New York, 1993), 68.

[28]John D'Emilio and Estelle B. Freedman, *Intimate Matters: A History of Sexuality in America* (New York, 1988), 103.

[29]Higginbotham, *Righteous Discontent,* 196. Hazel Carby comments that church women sublimated desire into duty. Hazel Carby, "It Just Be's Dat Way Sometime: The Sexual Politics of Women's Blues," *Radical America,* 20 (1986): 9-22.

[30]Leaders and Stewards' Meeting Minutes, August 25, 1905, 453.

[31]Ibid., November 5, November 7, 1902, 26-40.

[32]Ibid.

[33]Traditional New Orleans Jazz, often called "Trad. Jazz," favors group improvisation which is kept in tension with individual virtuosity. These aesthetic values stylize the patterns of living within black communities in New Orleans at the turn of the century.

[34]I use the word natural with irony. What whites called "natural" was often a virtuoso's continued refinement of technique.

[35]Armstrong, *Satchmo,* 11.

U. S. SENATOR JOSEPH E. RANSDELL,
CATHOLIC STATESMAN: A REAPPRAISAL*

Vincent J. Marsala

Historians have almost completely overlooked the life and contributions of Joseph E. Ransdell (1858-1954), a citizen of East Carroll Parish in Northeast Louisiana.[1] There is no authoritative account of his thirty-two-year tenure in the United States Congress, his national accomplishments, and his role as a Catholic lay leader. This lack of recognition may result from Ransdell's association with the Bourbon oligarchy, who controlled Louisiana politics from 1876 to 1928.

Bourbon politicians have often been dismissed by historians as being selfish and greedy, with little concern for the public good. Noted historian T. Harry Williams characterized Ransdell as "one of the most ineffective members of Congress, practically a cipher in Washington's political community."[2] No professional historian or political scientist has challenged Williams's seemingly authoritative assessment; yet Ransdell's record of public service clearly shows that T. Harry Williams' cavalier evaluation, grounded upon a simplistic, stereotypic view of the Bourbon oligarchy, is misplaced. Indeed, the historical record clearly shows that Joseph E. Ransdell was actually a progressive, innovative policymaker and a precursor of the New Deal.

Joseph E. Ransdell was born October 7, 1858, on Elmwood Plantation, nine miles south of Alexandria, La. His father, John Ransdell, had migrated to Alexandria from Kentucky. John Ransdell, former editorial staff writer for the *Louisville Courier*, assumed control of the *Red River Whig*, but he soon turned to farming. His wife, Amanda Louise Terrell, had inherited Elmwood Plantation. Joseph's Catholic mother was educated by the Ladies of the Sacred Heart at Grand Coteau.

Joseph Ransdell's early schooling consisted of both public schools and private Catholic schools. At an early age, he was influenced by the Catholic priests of Alexandria, particularly Father Menard, then assistant pastor of St. Francis Xavier Church. At the age of eighteen, Ransdell found employment as a teacher at Spring Creek, twenty-five

*First published in *Louisiana History*, 35 (1994): 35-49. Reprinted with the kind permission of the author and the Louisiana Historical Association.

miles from his home. While teaching, he also studied law in the Alexandria office of Judge Michael Ryan. Robert Bringhurst of Alexandria recognized Joseph's academic potential and secured a scholarship for him to Union College, Bringhurst's alma mater in Schenectady, New York.[3]

Unable to afford the cost of transportation home, Joseph Ransdell spent four long years in New York. While at Union College, Ransdell demonstrated an affinity for politics. Appointed by one of his professors as a student senator to participate in the "mini-government" or "congress" at Union College, he assumed the role of a policymaker. Having witnessed destructive flooding along the Red and Mississippi rivers during his youth, Ransdell introduced a mock flood-control bill and then convinced his fellow student "congressmen" to approve it. Joseph Ransdell's oratorical abilities again gained campus-wide attention when, during his senior year, he won the coveted Blatchford Oratorical Medal for his address on "The New South."

Ransdell received an A.B. degree (Scientific) from Union College in 1882.[4] His graduation coincided with a search by Field F. Montgomery of Lake Providence in East Carroll Parish for a young man to assist in running his law office. Joe accepted the position, and after "reading the law" for one year, passed the Louisiana bar examination in 1883.

Shortly afterward, Ransdell met and fell in love with Olive Irene Powell of Lake Providence. Though Olive's family was Methodist she had never become an active member of that church. During their engagement, she studied the Catholic religion with Father Celestine Mahe, the pastor of St. Patrick's Church in Lake Providence, and was baptized a Catholic. Two days later, on November 15, 1885, she and Ransdell were married. Although Joe had purchased a home for his bride, it was still occupied by the former owners. Father Mahe came to the newlyweds' rescue and invited the couple to spend their honeymoon in the rectory of St. Patrick's Church while he traveled to Tallulah in Madison Parish. It was a comfortable arrangement, at least for Joseph, since previously he had roomed at the rectory for two years due to the lack of accommodations for single men in Lake Providence.

As his life assumed a new direction, Joseph Ransdell embarked upon a career of public service to the citizens of Northeast Louisiana, the state, the nation, and the Catholic Church. In 1883, he was appointed parish surveyor. One year later, Ransdell was elected district attorney for East Carroll and Madison parishes. In 1897, he was elected as a delegate to the Louisiana Constitutional Convention; and in 1899, he entered the Fifth District Congressional race after the death of incumbent Congressman Sam T. Baird. In the primary race, Ransdell won a clear majority over four opponents. After fourteen years in the United States House of Representatives, Joseph Ransdell won a seat in the U. S. Senate and served in that body from 1914 until 1932.

It is historically significant that a North Louisiana Catholic could win election and re-election in a section of the state that did not hide its anti-Catholicism. Ransdell himself candidly recalled that, in the Congressional elections of 1903 and 1907, opponents attempted to stir up anti-Catholic feelings against him because Louisiana's Fifth Congressional District was only 1 percent Catholic. Ransdell's effectiveness in Congress and his issue-oriented campaigns largely neutralized such underhanded tactics.[5]

Congressman Ransdell's first order of business in the 56th Congress was "to learn the ropes." In the 57th Congress, he secured a seat on the Rivers and Harbors Committee and quickly developed a national reputation for his advocacy for water and harbor projects throughout the United States. He poured all of his energies into studying America's waterways. As a pragmatic politician, Ransdell realized in 1900 that by helping to develop the economic potential of the Great Lakes, inland rivers, lakes, and canals, he would win support from his Congressional colleagues for flood control on the lower Mississippi, Ouachita, and Red rivers.[6] In 1904, he secured passage of a bill to appropriate $30 million to restore and maintain channels and improve harbors. In 1906, his growing national reputation as an expert in navigation and flood control led to his election as chairman of the board of directors of the National Rivers and Harbors Congress, a national conference promoting federal appropriations for waterways improvements. This position provided Ransdell a national forum for his flood-control proposals. In one year alone, he travelled over 20,000 miles addressing conventions, commercial groups, and waterway associations from Florida to California to Canada and throughout the Missouri River Valley and Mississippi River Valley systems. This exposure enhanced Ransdell's national reputation, and his name became synonymous with the national development of waterways and flood control.[7]

In 1911, Ransdell sought election to the United States Senate against incumbent Murphy J. Foster. Ransdell received a majority of the votes, carrying forty-one of sixty-four parishes—including his own Fifth District. During his eighteen-year tenure in the Senate, Ransdell served on the Commerce Committee, which was responsible for waterways, and the Agriculture Committee. Both committee assignments were extremely important to the economic development of Louisiana, as well as his service as chairman of the Senate Committee on Public Health.[8]

As a member of the Senate Commerce Committee, Ransdell continued his fight for flood-control appropriations. In 1917, the first substantial federal aid for levees resulted from the passage of the Ransdell-Humphreys Bill, which appropriated $45 million for flood control. In 1923, Ransdell was successful in getting an additional flood-control appropriation for $60 million. A few years later, he sponsored legislation that established the National Hydraulic Laboratory.[9]

The great Mississippi River flood of 1927 underscored the necessity for more federal flood-control projects to protect villages, towns, cities, and agricultural lands along the Mississippi. Affecting areas far beyond Louisiana, this natural disaster developed widespread support for Senator Ransdell's efforts to place the burden for control of the Mississippi River on the federal government rather than on local governments and communities. As a result, in two minutes the Senate approved by a 69-0 vote a bill appropriating $325 million for flood control on the Mississippi. The House passed the bill in essentially the same form, and President Coolidge signed the Flood Control Act on May 15, 1928. As a direct result of Ransdell's Congressional leadership in securing waterway legislation from, 1899 to 1928, as well as his fourteen year tenure as president of the National Rivers and Harbors Congress, he was recognized as the "father of waterways appropriations."[10]

A second major area of Congressional legislation initiated by Joseph E. Ransdell concerned his humanitarian efforts to improve the public health of the American people. His interest in public health was triggered by memories as a young boy in Alexandria when yellow fever ravaged his hometown. In fact, his departure for Union College was delayed three months while his family sought refuge in White Sulphur Springs from a yellow fever epidemic. Later, he learned that these outbreaks were common in many areas of the United States, as well as abroad. Ransdell was particularly moved to act when he read the words of Benjamin Disraeli who wrote, "Public health is the foundation on which reposes the happiness of a people and the power of a country. The care of the public health is the first duty of a statesman."[11]

As a young Congressman, he was also greatly influenced by a visit to Panama to view the construction of the Panama Canal. Gen. William Gorgas, the chief sanitary officer of the Panama Canal Commission, gave him a tour of the hospital in Colon and explained the process of eradicating malaria and yellow fever by cleaning up the mosquito breeding areas. This collective effort to improve public health poignantly demonstrated to Ransdell what could be done with concerted governmental action in the United States. His concern for the physical well-being of citizens was certainly not characteristic of a self-centered Bourbon oligarch. Rather it reflected a progressive humanitarian who realized the responsibility of government to improve the quality of life for all citizens.

Ransdell's first effort in the field of public health concerned the dreaded disease leprosy. In 1916, as chairman of the Senate Committee on Public Health, he was approached by W. M. Danner, secretary of the American Mission to Lepers, for assistance. Danner explained the pitiful condition of lepers in the United States and expressed the need for a national leprosarium. Ransdell had some knowledge of leprosy, for Louisiana in 1894 had established a Control Board to create and maintain what would be the first home for lepers in the United States. This board had leased property at Carville, sixty miles north of New Orleans, where cabins were constructed, and the Sisters of Charity of St. Vincent de Paul were asked to take charge of the facility.

Ransdell, in typical fashion, promised Mr. Danner that he would take action on the matter. As with the problems of America's waterways, Ransdell thoroughly researched the disease by reading everything he could find on the subject. Also, he consulted personally with those who dealt with the disease first hand such as, the Samaritans of Molokai, Father Damien, and Brother Dutton, Dr. L. R. Luskie of Molokai, the Carville staff, and Dr. Victor G. Heiser of the Rockefeller Foundation, the world's foremost specialist in leprosy. He accompanied Dr. William C. Fowler, the medical inspector of the District of Columbia Health Department, on a visit to John Early, a leper who was confined to a hut within sight of Washington, D. C. Ransdell quickly foresaw the need for federal assistance and drafted a bill establishing a national leprosarium. The bill passed Congress, and President Wilson signed it on February 3, 1917, as Public Law 299 of the 64th Congress.[12]

Senator Ransdell then suggested that the federal government take over the state leprosarium at Carville. With Gov. John M. Parker's assistance, the Louisiana legislature passed an act authorizing the sale of the Carville leprosarium to the federal government for $53,000. The property was transferred on January 3, 1921, and Senator Ransdell secured an appropriation of $2,500,000 to build a new institution. The modern hospital, which was essentially a self-contained community, was completed in 1941.[13]

Senator Ransdell's most important achievement was his successful effort to establish a federal research and scientific agency to improve the daily life of all human beings. As in his other legislative achievements, he prepared himself intellectually by researching and collecting as much data as possible on illness, disease, and death in the United States. He again actively sought out those in powerful positions who could help achieve his goal. In this case, he turned to fellow Sen. Royal S. Copeland of New York, a medical doctor; F. L. Hoffman, the consulting statistician of the Prudential Insurance Company of America; Dr. Charles H. Herty, president of the Synthetic Organic Chemical Manufacturers' Association; Francis P. Garvan, president of the Chemical Foundation of New York. These individuals were instrumental in his efforts, and in 1926, he introduced a bill to establish a "National Institute of Health." The purpose of the NIH was "to conduct and promote scientific research relating to the cause, prevention and cure of disease affecting human beings."[14]

Ransdell launched an intense four-year lobbying and public relations campaign to see his dream for the NIH come true. He actively sought physicians, researchers, business and industry leaders to support his humanitarian legislation. His personal success is reflected by the organizations which supported his efforts: the Rockefeller Foundation, Chemical Foundation, National Research Council, Metropolitan Life Insurance Company, American Chemical Society, American Medical Association, American Public Health Association, American Pharmaceutical Association and the International Society for Crippled Children. On May 26, 1930, President Hoover signed the NIH bill into law. This significant legislative achievement won him the title, "Father of the National Institute of Health." The *Washington Star* noted that this was his third great legislative achievement dealing with humanitarian relief. The others included the bill establishing the National Leprosarium at Carville, and the measure to eradicate Texas tick fever.[15]

Ransdell's long service in the United States House and Senate was further distinguished by his sponsorship of a variety of bills that revealed the inner self of a man who was truly concerned with the national well-being of his country, as well as the growth and development of his beloved South. In 1905, for example, he led the fight to eradicate Texas tick fever which caused annual losses of $75 million to the Southern cattle industry. Prof. Hartwell Morgan of Louisiana State University, later president of the University of Tennessee, persuaded the Congressman of the need for legislation providing aid to cattle growers. In 1906, Ransdell sponsored the initial Texas tick fever bill which was passed and led to the eradication of tick fever from the South.[16]

Ransdell also appealed to Southerners to reverse the waste of deforestation of virgin timberlands by reforestation; he supported the Jones Act to give the U. S. Merchant Marine protection from foreign competition; he supported Woodrow Wilson's League of Nations to limit arms, reduce the size of armies, and limit destructive weapons such as poison gases; he encouraged migration of citizens from the north and east to the South, and he supported woman's suffrage. Throughout the United States, he spoke eloquently on all of these topics and was recognized in the press as a national leader.[17]

Joseph E. Ransdell's strong commitment to Catholicism was fundamental to his public service. He was proud of his faith, and church, and took every opportunity to express his personal beliefs. His active role in sponsoring significant national legislation led directly to numerous speaking engagements throughout the United States. He was far from being a "cipher in the Washington community," as described by Professor Williams. Quite the contrary, Ransdell was a statesman with a national reputation, reflected in his numerous public appearances and landmark legislation.

In Ruston, in 1907, Ransdell made what was probably his first public speech regarding his personal religious beliefs. In a presentation entitled, "The Spirit of Progress in Our Time — Where Is It Leading?" he reviewed the excesses of the Roman empire, and then warned, "We are the greatest and most progressive people on the globe. . . . Do not let us swell with a false pride . . . but remember, that by sin fell the angels. Let us gird on the armor of humility, of trust in heaven, of hope, and of that spirit of wide progress which leads not only to temporal, but to eternal welfare."[18]

During that same year, Ransdell was invited to his alma mater, Union College, to deliver the Chancellor's Address, and to receive an honorary LL. D. degree. The topic of his speech "The Responsibility of Wealth," would have made any self-respecting Louisiana Bourbon oligarch in Louisiana shudder. He began by reminding his audience that wealth is held merely as a trust of heaven and that it should be used in ways to benefit mankind. He maintained that the rich should use their money to do the greatest good; to relieve the sufferings of the needy, to help orphans, the decrepit and aged poor, to aid in church and civic works, to assist in the general education of the masses in the manner of philanthropist George Peabody. Ransdell then reminded the rich that they earned their wealth with the help of thousands of workers and that the wealth should, in turn, help their workers "to become the owner of a little home and property valued at $5,000 or more."[19]

Ransdell practiced what he preached. He believed that small farm ownership was necessary for the general welfare and that the small landowner, black or white, was a better citizen than the transient laborers, tenant farmers, or sharecroppers who did not own the land they worked. In 1885, as a young attorney in Lake Providence, he subdivided tracts of land into twenty to 100-acre farms and sold them at reasonable rates to Negroes who built small homes on them. East Carroll Parish at that time had no small white farmers, only white-owned plantations worked by black field laborers. His purpose was to help poor men acquire land and a home. Ransdell's innovative program to increase the number of family farms was in the progressive tradition and based on his Catholic philosophy. His effort was a forerunner of the Resettlement Administration (CRA) and the Farm Security Administration (FSA) programs of the New Deal.[20]

Notre Dame University, America's premier Catholic institution of higher learning, invited Senator Ransdell to the June 1914 commencement to receive an honorary doctor of laws degree in recognition of his service as a role model for the nation's youth. In his acceptance speech, entitled simply "Divorce," Ransdell expressed his personal fear that divorce would increase and eventually weaken the home, and America as a whole. For this reason, and the fact that divorce was a violation of the sacrament of marriage, he refused, as an attorney, to represent any parties to a divorce in Louisiana. He warned those attorneys in attendance, "Marriage is not only a civil contract, but a sacrament, and as such you have no moral right to assist in breaking it, to become an agent in its sacrilege."[21]

To Ransdell, belief in God and patriotism were inseparable. In Richmond, Virginia, he gave a stirring speech on "The Patriotism of Catholics" at a Knights of Columbus celebration of George Washington's Birthday. He said, "He loves his country best, who loves his God best. . . . No man can be a good Catholic without being a good member of the state or nation . . . in other words, a good citizen. . . . The better the Catholic, the better the citizen, is as true as proof of holy writ."[22]

In a speech entitled, "What the Nation has a Right to Expect From the Catholic College Graduate," delivered at Villanova College in 1918, Ransdell assured the new graduates that as educated Catholics they could show by their daily lives that the Church has instilled in them patriotism and religion. He reminded them that they could show that they recognized the rights of everyone to life, liberty, and the pursuit of happiness, and that they should be ready to assist not only the people of the United States, but the oppressed of all nations.[23]

Throughout his life Joseph Ransdell equated the practice of religious faith with good citizenship and patriotism. Of particular importance to him was receiving Holy Eucharist at Mass. At the convention of the Federation of Catholic Societies in New Orleans in 1926, he spoke on the Eucharist and described it as "incomparably the greatest of the seven sacraments." He also noted that "among Catholics, no one can be a frequent communicant without being a good man, a patriot who obeys the laws of God and country and whose daily life sets good example for his fellowmen." Likewise, devotion to God, as shown by loving Jesus and participation in the Eucharist, "is very helpful not only in spiritual, but also in worldly affairs." However, the essence of Ransdell's personal philosophy was summed up in a simple, eloquent admission before a Knights of Columbus meeting in Monroe, Louisiana, when he said, "I am convinced there is no genuine, real happiness in this life except for those who love their Creator and their fellowmen."[24]

Ransdell demonstrated his devotion to his church and his fellow man through efforts to provide a chapel for Lake Providence's black Catholics. Upon learning that Bishop Desmond of Alexandria planned to build a church for African Americans in Lake Providence and one in Tallulah, Ransdell immediately informed the bishop that the first church should be in his hometown of Lake Providence. The senator indicated that he would donate the necessary land and make the first monetary contribution toward its construction. Desmond accepted the offer and the chapel for the "colored" in Lake Providence became a reality. Needless to say such an undertaking was not well received by all residents of this small town.[25]

Senator Ransdell's long political career came to an end in 1930 with his defeat by Gov. Huey P. Long. Long was elected in 1928 on a populist platform of reform in education, road and bridge construction, and the philosophy that government should initiate social programs for the majority of its citizens. However, Long was not content with being the "Kingfish" in Louisiana and actively sought to spread his "share the wealth" program to the entire nation by election to the U. S. Senate and eventually the presidency of the United States.

After thirty-two years in Washington, Ransdell was an easy target, in spite of his significant accomplishments. He had never developed a personal political organization in Louisiana. Instead he devoted all of his attention to his work in Congress and relied on his reputation as a productive national legislator and his impeccable public service to the citizens of Louisiana to win re-election. Long, on the other hand, had a well-organized political machine that covered every village, town, city and country store, and he was immensely popular with the mass of voters. Long won 57 percent of the vote in the September 9, 1930, election.[26]

After his defeat, Ransdell remained in Washington for three years as executive director of the conference board of the National Institute of Health. The former senator was to spread the news of the NIH through public speeches, writing, and personal contacts. This he did with great effectiveness. Finally, in 1933, he returned to Lake Providence at age seventy-five to concentrate on his farming business, to work for his beloved Catholic Church, and to attend his weekly Rotary meetings. He also turned his attention to another of his favorite projects—that of subdividing land into small farms of 20-80 acres which he leased to poor whites and blacks with the option to purchase at a fixed price. He also helped them build homes, and advanced them money for living expenses while they improved the land. Ransdell was especially proud that he had not had to take back one acre.[27]

Even though historians have ignored Senator Ransdell's achievements, he did receive recognition from his contemporaries. On July 12, 1930, scientists, physicians, and business leaders from throughout the United States hosted a dinner at the Jung Hotel in New Orleans in honor of Senator Ransdell's successful efforts in creating the National Institute of Health. Speech after speech toasted Ransdell for his contribution to his country. Dr.

Hugh S. Cumming, the surgeon general of the United States Public Health Service added his praise by stating

> The passage of the Ransdell bill will mean much to the future happiness and increased health of the American people. I am proud to praise him; to praise that gentle, quiet, persistent and persuasive way in which he carried on this work. Whatever Senator Ransdell's many other achievements for the benefit of his state and country, the National Institute of Health will be the monument which will perpetuate his memory.[28]

Ransdell was most deeply moved by a ceremony that occurred on February 26, 1950, at Lake Providence. Over 200 friends, Catholic priests, nuns, and political figures gathered at St. Patrick's Church and school auditorium to honor his service to his church and country. Bishop Charles Paschal Greco of the Alexandria diocese conferred on Joseph E. Ransdell the papal distinction of "Knight Commander" of the Order of Saint Gregory the Great.[29]

Ransdell died four years later on July 27, 1954, at the age of ninety-five. Ransdell's exemplary life of service to his state, country, and church should be used as a yardstick by which other public servants in Louisiana history should be measured.[30]

Notes for "U. S. Senator Joseph E. Ransdell, Catholic Statesman: A Reappraisal"

[1] The author reviewed all major historical and political monographs, journals, and books relative to Louisiana history and politics from 1900-1992. The primary documents used in this research are found in the Joseph E. Ransdell Papers, 1898-1948, Louisiana and Lower Mississippi Valley Collection, LSU Libraries, Louisiana State University, Baton Rouge, La. Hereafter cited as, Ransdell Papers. The author particularly thanks Anne Edwards and Luana Henderson, Archivists, of the LSU Library for their professional assistance.

Special thanks also to Betty Allen, Assistant Archivist, Union College, Schaffer Library, Schenectady, New York, who provided valuable primary information relative to Joseph E. Ransdell's attendance and graduation from Union College in 1882.

For Ransdell correspondence to the Broussard brothers, Robert and Edwin, who both served in the U. S. Senate from South Louisiana see, Broussard Papers. University of Southwestern Louisiana, Lafayette, Louisiana. See, Ann Wakefield, "The Broussard Papers of the University of Southwestern Louisiana: New Light on Louisiana Progressivism," *Louisiana History*, 31 (1990): 293-300.

Matthew Schott clearly recognized the lack of historical research relative to the pre-Long period of Louisiana political history. See Matthew J. Schott, "Huey Long: Progressive Backlash?," *Louisiana History* 27 (1986): 33-145. See Schott's revisionist view that explores the failure of Louisiana historians to provide a synthesis of Louisiana history because of their reliance on the class-conflict model in, Matthew J. Schott, "Death of Class Struggle: End of Louisiana History?," *Louisiana History*, 31 (1990): 349-71.

[2] T. Harry Williams, *Huey Long* (New York, 1969), 462. The *American Heritage Dictionary* defines "cipher" as the mathematical symbol (0) denoting absence of quantity; zero. Also, a person or thing without influence or value; a nonentity.

[3] This early sketch of Ransdell's life is taken from Adras La Borde, *A National Southerner: Ransdell of Louisiana* (New York, 1951), 1-10. La Borde was a newspaper friend of Ransdell and interviewed him for this biography. However, it lacks citations and bibliography and is poorly organized.

[4] Union College Papers, Trustees Minutes, June 23, 1874-June 26, 1895, and Graduate Council Personnel Information Sheet, November 15, 1949.

[5]Ransdell Papers. Information given in interview of Senator Ransdell by Roger Baudier, December, 1946.

[6]Ransdell Papers. Random Notes About Joseph E. Ransdell Made by Him at Odd Times—More or Less Disconnected, p. 11. Also, see La Borde, *Ransdell of Louisiana,* 14-16.

[7]Ransdell Papers. Extracts from Speech of Hon. J. E. Ransdell, M.C. of Louisiana, delivered March 6, 1906, Annual Banquet of the North Side Board of Trade of the Bronx, New York City. Also, Brief Report of Joseph E. Ransdell, Chairman of Rivers and Harbors Congress, December 6, 1906, Arlington Hotel, Washington, D. C.

[8]For the 1912 U. S. Senatorial race see, Sidney J. Romero, Jr., "The Political Career of Murphy James Foster, Governor of Louisiana, 1892-1900," *Louisiana Historical Quarterly,* 28 (1945): 1129-1243. Ransdell and Broussard recommended to President Wilson that Murphy Foster be appointed Collector of Customs at New Orleans, which he did.

[9]Ransdell Papers; Ransdell interview with Roger Baudier, December 1946; *Shreveport Journal,* March 3, 1931.

[10]"One Life Was Not Enough," *Times-Picayune, Dixie Roto Magazine,* December 9, 1951, 25; La Borde, *Ransdell of Louisiana,* 131-46.

[11]La Borde, *Ransdell of Louisiana,* 17, 68; Ransdell Papers; Baudier Interview. p. 1.

[12]Ransdell Papers; Address of Hon. Joseph E. Ransdell, Executive Director of the Conference Board, National Institute of Health, Before the American Mission to Lepers, October 28, 1932, New York. This speech explains in detail events leading to the founding of the National Leprosarium at Carville. See also, Philip A. Kalisch, "Lepers, Anachronisms, and the Progressives: A Study in Stigma, 1889-1920," *Louisiana Studies,* 12 (1973): 489-531. This is an excellent study of the leprosarium movement which began in the 1880s and culminated with the opening of the U. S. Hospital in Carville, Louisiana.

[13]La Borde, *Ransdell of Louisiana,* 61-66.

[14]Charles Holmes Herty Papers, Emory University, Special Collections Department, Robert W. Woodruff Library, Atlanta, Ga. This collection contains correspondence between Dr. Herty and Senator Joseph E. Ransdell. La Borde, *Ransdell of Louisiana,* 122-23.

[15]Ransdell Papers; Senator Joseph E. Ransdell, Radio Broadcast, "Half Hour with the Senate," NBC, May 3, 1930. In this nationwide broadcast Ransdell explained to the American people that the NIH bill "seeks to prevent sickness and suffering among all human beings, regardless of station, the rich and poor alike, being subject to the same illness and pain." Francis P. Garvan, president of the Chemical Foundation, upon hearing the NIH bill was signed gave the first gift, $100,000, to establish fellowships in chemistry.

[16]Ransdell Papers; Baudier interview.

[17]Ransdell Papers, "Reforestation or Deforestation?" Senator Ransdell, Southern Forestry Congress, New Orleans, La., April 5, 1929; Senator Ransdell, President, National Merchant Marine Association, "What's Wrong with Our Merchant Marine," Advertising Club, New York, November 2, 1921. (Ransdell resigned as head of the National Rivers and Harbors Congress and, in 1915, organized and became president of the National Merchant Marine Association.) See Ransdell's Speech on League of Nations, Congressional Record, 66th Congress, First Session, Washington, D. C., July 31, 1919, pp. 3617-3623. "Remarks of U. S. Senator J. E. Ransdell on the Suffrage Amendment to the Constitution," U. S. Senate, June 27, 1918. Senator Joseph E. Ransdell, "The Lure of the Southland," U. S. Senate, July 7, 1916.

[18]Ransdell Papers; Address by Hon. Joseph E. Ransdell, M.C., Louisiana, "The Spirit of Progress in our Time—Where is it Leading," Ruston, La., April 19, 1907.

[19]Ransdell Papers; Chancellor's Address by Hon. Joseph E. Ransdell, LL. D., of Lake Providence, Louisiana, Delivered at Union College, Schenectady, New York, on June 12, 1907, on "The Responsibility of Wealth."

[20]See *Dixie Roto Magazine*, 25; Ransdell Papers, Undated statement entitled, "Developing Small Farms." This statement details Ransdell's efforts to increase small farm ownership in East Carroll Parish from 1883-1935. See in particular, Donald Holley," Old and New Worlds in the New Deal Resettlement Program: Two Louisiana Projects," *Louisiana History*, 11 (1970): 137-65. Also, Donald Holley, *Uncle Sam's Farmers: The New Deal Communities in the Lower Mississippi Valley* (Urbana, Ill., 1975).

[21]Ransdell Papers, Commencement Address of Hon. Joseph E. Ransdell, "Divorce," Notre Dame University, Indiana, June 16, 1914.

[22]Ransdell Papers, Address of Senator Joseph E. Ransdell, "The Patriotism of Catholics," at a Celebration of Washington's Birthday, Knights of Columbus, Richmond, Virginia, February 22, 1917.

[23]Ransdell Papers, Graduation Speech of Senator Joseph E. Ransdell, "What the Nation Has a Right to Expect from the Catholic College Graduate," Villanova College, Pennsylvania, June 11, 1918.

[24]Ransdell Papers, Senator Joseph E. Ransdell before the Convention of the Federation of Catholic Societies, New Orleans, October 10, 1926; Speech of Senator Joseph E. Ransdell to Knights of Columbus at Monroe, Louisiana, March 30, 1941.

[25]Ransdell Papers; Letter of Msgr. John C. Vandegaer to Roger Baudier, editor, *Catholic Action of the South*, January 5, 1947.

[26]Ransdell Papers; Interview with Baudier, p. 9; Allan P. Sindler, *Huey Long's Louisiana; State Politics, 1920-1952* (Baltimore, 1956), 70-71.

[27]Ransdell Papers; Interview with Baudier, p. 9. See also, *Dixie Roto Magazine*, 25; La Borde, *Ransdell of Louisiana*, 195-97. Ransdell was appointed by Gov. Sam H. Jones to the LSU Board of Supervisors and served from 1940-44. One of his projects was to push for the establishment of a Department of Religion which was approved during his term on the Board but was not formally established.

[28]Ransdell Papers, Article from *Times-Picayune*, July 13, 1930.

[29]"Hundreds Honor Northeast Louisiana's Top Citizen, Senator Joseph Ransdell," Vicksburg, Miss., *Sunday Post Herald*, March 1950.

[30]*New York Journal-America*, July 28, 1954; *Washington Star*, July 28, 1954.

SABINE PARISH BAPTISTS*

Joanne Hudson Pickett

Although Baptists began the founding of churches in Louisiana in the year of statehood, 1812, it was thirteen years before the first Baptist church was established in the remote wilderness of what later became Sabine Parish. Several factors contributed to the long delay.

The area remained sparsely populated for many years. Geographically, it did not provide the same attraction to settlers as some other areas of Louisiana with rich bottom lands. The Sabine River did not deposit rich loam as did the Red and Mississippi Rivers. Much of the region was sand hills and ridges. The Los Ormegas (1795) and La Nana (1798) grants from Spain covered much of the area, but they were never developed into large agricultural holdings. The population lived as small, isolated farmers along the Sabine River and adjoining bayous, few of whom were Anglo-Saxons. Not until 1819 would the American migrations of small farmers from Tennessee, Mississippi, Alabama, and the Carolinas begin to trickle into the area along the Sabine River and Bayou Negrete (Negreet).[1]

Upon withdrawal of the Spanish from the Mission at Los Adais in 1773, the territory lying between the Sabine River and Arroyo (Rio) Hondo was left a virtual wilderness. The sparse settlers were of Spanish and Indian descent whose religion was Roman Catholic. In the sale of Louisiana in April 1803, the exact boundary of west Louisiana was not established. For the next seventeen years this area between the Sabine River and Natchitoches would be disputed territory. By agreement between General Wilkinson and the Spanish General Herrera, the United States withdrew to Natchitoches and the Spanish withdrew to the west of Sabine River. This mutual withdrawal left a vast area, later to comprise Sabine, Vernon, Beauregard, and Calcasieu parishes, under no country's jurisdiction. By 1810, the "Neutral Strip" had developed into a major problem for both Spanish and American authorities, and an attempt was made to evict "squatters" violating the regulation against additional settlers entering the territory. The requirement of passports was virtually ignored. It had become a haven for outlaws and riff-raff. Several filibuster groups were organized in this area.[2]

*First published in *Journal of Louisiana Baptist History*, 2 (1989): 30-45. Reprinted with the kind permission of the publisher.

By treaty with Spain in 1819, the western boundary of Louisiana was fixed at the Sabine River, thus ending the era of lawlessness, but not settling the boundary question technically. Boundary litigations continued as late as the 1960s. The activity of the Spanish in Texas, the filibusters, and continuing crimes committed by robber bands on travelers, drew the attention of the United States Government to the need of a military outpost. In 1823, the clearing for Fort Jesup was begun. During this period, a military road was opened from Pendleton Ferry, on Sabine River, to Fort Jesup, located about five miles east of the present town of Many. The road went by the Blockhouse near Pendleton Ferry. It had been built by the military in 1812 for the storage of goods coming up the Sabine River into the territory, and for the purpose of housing a few scouts and rangers to keep some semblance of peace on the border. Their presence also served to keep a watchful eye on Mexico.[3]

While evidence exists for the movement of people through the area during this period, land and census records fail to substantiate the statements of some writers that settlers "flocked" into the region.[4] Census records for 1810 give a total of only 2,970 people for the whole of Natchitoches Parish, including 1,476 slaves. The 1820 census for District I, west of Rio Hondo, gives a total for that district of 3,263 inhabitants, including 547 foreigners and 250 slaves. A better measure of the number of households of settlers is the occupational totals: 866 farmers, three commerce, thirty-nine manufacturing. These are relatively small figures when the size, length of time Louisiana had been part of the United States, and other factors are considered.

The building of Fort Jesup attracted people into the territory. Social activities flourished around the fort, giving the general impression of a healthy population during the period 1825-1835. Several hotels operated on the military road at various times and places, which accommodated travelers and transients. Few of these people remained in the territory as permanent settlers. Some few men discharged from the military post took land grants or bought acreage, but the majority moved on to Texas or returned to their native states.

Property transactions were very light, averaging only two to five filings a year until 1838. There was a marked increase in filings in 1838-1840, which continued to increase each year through 1950. This is the period when the Anglo-Saxon immigrants really began to move into the parish as permanent settlers.[5] Prior to the late 1830s political unrest and boundary disputes as well as the geography of the area slowed immigration of Anglo-Saxon Protestants. The established Roman Catholic Church also discouraged them. Problems within the Baptist denomination itself probably delayed the movement as much as any other factor. Early Baptist mission efforts were not aimed at the frontier region of the South. Before 1832, when the American Baptist Home Mission Society was formed, there were fourteen states with active missions, but emphasis was on missions to the Indians and Blacks, not on the Southern frontier to their own people. Such mission efforts as were made on the frontier centered in the Illinois-Missouri area of the frontier and in the upper Mississippi Valley.

These factors contributed to the late establishment of the Baptist churches in Sabine Parish. They were not established as the result of missionary endeavors. Transplanted Carolinians and Virginians, by the way of Alabama and Mississippi, who were zealous in the faith founded the first churches in isolated areas of Sabine Parish.

Some time after 1805, Green Cook received by assignment of grant some 841 acres of land on Bayou Negrete (Negreet).[6] Still known locally as "Green Cook Ridge," it is the first ridge of land on Bayou Negrete that one encounters after leaving the Sabine River bottom, a choice spot near the water but out of the mosquito area of the river. Green Cook's preacher brother, Elder William Cook, moved into the same vicinity about three and one-half miles to the east of Green Cook's farm. Elder Cook was, in 1810, a member of the Yadkin Association, North Carolina. He was in Mississippi in 1818, as his name appears as a messenger from Baley Chitto Church to the Mississippi associational meeting at New Providence, Amite County, of that year. He is last mentioned in the Mississippi minutes in October 1821, so he likely came to Sabine Parish shortly thereafter. Elder Cook preached the first Baptist sermons in this part of the country, traveling back and forth across the Sabine River into East Texas.[7]

Zion Hill Baptist Church, at Negreet, Louisiana, was organized December 27, 1826, with William Cook and James Martin constituting the presbytery. Charter members were John Thompson, Nancy Thompson, J. T. Montgomery, Lavina Montgomery, William Iles, John Dove, Nancy Morris and Easter, a colored sister.[8] This was the first Baptist church organized in what became Sabine Parish in 1843 and has existed without interruption to the present.

Elder William Cook was called as first pastor of Zion Hill and continued until his death on September 19, 1829. His obituary in the Louisiana Association minutes read:

> Brother William Cook, of Zion Hill Church, Parish of Natchitoches, has been called home . . . He has left behind him to mourn their loss, a little church in the planting of which he was instrumental, in the hands of the Lord . . .[9]

After the formation of this first Baptist church, it was twenty-one years before another such church was organized in Sabine Parish. The slow influx of settlers was a contributing factor. Between the years 1832-1845, only seventy-five settlers registered land claims on government land. There were some private land sales and evidence of "squatters" (those who occupied the land with no attempt to claim title), but they were few and insignificant to the overall settler population.

Evidence of the impact of the anti-mission element on Baptist work is found in the minutes for the Louisiana Association of which Zion Hill was a member until 1848, and in the writings of Ivan W. Wise and William Paxton.

Wise commented on those conditions:

> For fourteen years, Louisiana Baptists depended on Louisiana Association for fostering care, but in 1832, Concord, and in 1844, Ouachita [*sic*] and Sabine in 1847, were orga-

nized from Louisiana Association. This swarming time seemingly came at an unfortunate time for the Mother Body. . . . Yes, Louisiana Association from 1832-1847 had hardshellism and Campbellism at the same time. . . . These were hard financial time [*sic*] and preachers went to manuel [*sic*] work; of course, as always in such situations, the spiritual interests of the Kingdom went to ruin.[10]

Louisiana Association met with Zion Hill Church again in 1846, and the divisive controversies were still evident. The committee on the Abstract of Faith presented its report entirely in biblical language. Paxton stated that this was done to hush the clamors of the brethren of Campbellite tendencies, of brethren whose watch-word was: "No creed but the Bible."[11] Wise made the following comments: "At this session B. C. Robert presented an Abstract of Faith in Bible language; it is a singular and able document, but it did not close the mouths of Campbellites and Hardshells."[12]

There was, however, a general optimism manifest in the reports of the churches, marking the beginning of a period of growth and solidarity among Baptists all over the state. Of the Zion Hill Church (still the only one in Sabine) it reported: "Zion Hill is at peace, and brotherly love abounds; enjoys the labors of brother E. A. Campbell, one of her own members and a licentiate, but complains of coldness; has increased three."[13] In the next few years Sabine Parish would see an increase in population, and the mushrooming of Baptist churches through the parish.

By 1847, settlers were steadily moving into the territory via the Sabine River route. They traveled up the Sabine River, settling on Toro Bayou in South Sabine, and on Bayou Negrete farther up the river. Rattan, Columbus, Negrete (Negreet), Sabine Town, and Gaines Ferry (later known as Pendleton and East Pendleton) were some of the early settlements along the Sabine River and the bayous of Sabine Parish. This was the beginning of a period of great progress for Baptists in Sabine Parish. Most of the churches naturally located in the settlements near the waterways. Many Church, an exception, was in the town of Many, located on Gaines' Military Road to Fort Jesup. Many was chosen for the parish seat that year.

Two permanent churches in the parish and three outside it were organized in 1847, and they, with the Zion Hill Church, constituted the Sabine Baptist Association. The order of business of the organizational meeting stated that the sermon was delivered by Elder Alison Phillips and letters were read from the six churches. Although the six churches were not named, the statistical table of 1848 gives the following information: Zion Hill (1824) (six); Liberty (1847); Pleasant Hill (1847); Mt. Zion (1847); Mt. Pleasant (1847); and Many (1847). These were the six constituting churches of the Sabine Association.[14]

The associational minutes, 1847, read:

> Agreeable to previous arrangements a convention met with the Many church in the Parish of Sabine, on the 22nd and 23rd days of October, 1847, and after examining the Articles of Faith of the Churches and finding them orthodox adopted a constitution resolved

themselves into an Association and adjourned to meet with the Zion Hill Church, October 6th, 1848, said Association to be called the Sabine Baptist Association.[15]

Pleasant Hill was the second Baptist church in the parish, located in the Southwest corner near Sabine River on Toro Bayou. The original minute book of Pleasant Hill was burned in a house fire, but the charter and organizing information was previously copied from one book to another so that the record is extant. The presbytery was Alison Phillips and J. C. McCaully with fourteen charter members: William Curtis, Ezra Byrd, I. McCollister, W. C. Southwell, I. Nettles, N. C. Hanley, J. Skinner, Wm. Ellzey, Nancy McCollister, Lucretia Broadway, Eviline Southwell, Martha Nettles, Rhoda Byrd, and Winiford Ellzey.[16] Descendants of these families are still prominent in the community. The church congregation was rather large with charter groups usually consisting of no more than six to ten members. It indicates that the community was rapidly being settled, and there was a larger population than usual for a rural Sabine Parish community.

In July 1848, Little Flock Church was organized near Sabine River north of Pleasant Hill Church but South of Zion Hill.[17] It petitioned the Sabine Association for membership in October of 1848. At that time, its location was given as Newton County, Texas. In 1850, Little Flock Church was dismissed to unite with the East Texas Association. The next reference to it was in 1855, and in 1856 it was listed as a Sabine Parish church.[18] The Texas-Louisiana border was finally established in this area and Little Flock Church was situated in Louisiana by one mile.

In its letter to the Association in 1848, Little Flock "humbly prays God would send more laborers into the destitute region; begs ministers of the gospel to come over and help them."[19] A resolution by the association that the churches observe a day of prayer and fasting to God, "that he would send laborers into this part of his vineyard . . . and revive pure and undefiled religion throughout the churches."[20] This indicates that the population had increased and the problem was now not one of sparse population but lack of leadership for the people.

In 1848, a group of people migrated from Washington Parish into Sabine Parish, settling on Walker Creek about three miles east of the present village of Florien, and probably twenty to twenty-five miles from the nearest Baptist settlement of Pleasant Hill. This was the first Protestant group to settle inland from the Sabine River, in South Sabine Parish, marking the beginning of a definite pattern of settlement for the parish away from the river. The settlers had been residents of Washington Parish for several years and had filtered into that area from Mississippi. The terrain of the Walker Creek vicinity was very much like that of Washington Parish with sandy hills and clear creeks. These were strong, dedicated Baptists and their church, Toro, was to be the mother church for three other congregations that are still functioning, namely Middle Creek (1857), Mt. Carmel (1863), and Beulah (1867?).[21]

On September 21, 1848, the following statement was drawn up by the group:

State of Louisiana Parish of Sabine 21st day September_____ the undersigned members of the Beulah Baptist Church of Christ of Washington Parish State for holding letters from said Church have this day met on Walker Creek for the purpose of constituting a church under the state of Regular Baptist Church of Christ and known by the name of Toro.

Being assembled with the Presbatery [*sic*] composed of Elders D. D. McCalley and W. L. Sibley being aded [*sic*] by G. W. Edwards this 21st day of September year of our Lord one thousand eight hundred and forty-eight. Letters presented and members found to be in order and in fellowship one with another also orthodox in faith do agree to give ourselves to the Lord and to one another by the will of God in gospel bonds agreeing to be governed by the Law of Christ and do adopt the following articles of faith. . . .

Charter members of Toro Church were Robert F. Sibley, W. L. Sibley, A. K. Addison, Averilla Sibley, Mary A. Addison, Ann Self, (blacks, Glass and Ellen). A petitionary letter to join the Sabine Association was the first motion voted on after the Rules of Decorum and Articles of Faith. Two members were accepted by letter from Pleasant Hill Church the first Sunday of regular services, Robert Sibley, Jr., and his wife, Mary L. Sibley.[22] In the first statement on Toro appearing in the associational minutes it was reported as being in a flourishing condition. The people had been active church members in Washington and the Feliciana parishes. Their names appear many times in the minutes of the Mississippi Association as messengers, clerks and ministers.[23] The majority were not new converts, but rather faithful, strong, orthodox, churched people. This explains why Toro became the mother church for three congregations that are still active. This may also explain the ultimate survival of these churches against Landmarkism, antimission movements, and the chaos and problems of the Civil War and Reconstruction. Another measure of this growth and emigration of Baptists into the area was the rapid increase of ministers.

In 1846, E. A. Campbell, licentiate, was the only minister in Sabine. Within two years the number of ordained ministers had increased to five: William L. Sibley, D. C. McColley [*sic*], J. L. Ritter, E. A. Campbell, and Alison Phillips, with two licentiates: W. C. Southwell and N. H. Bray.[24] A strong ministry in numbers and quality was indicative of active, strong churches. Several of these men would become influential pastors in Sabine, Vernon and Natchitoches parishes, especially Nathan Bray, Sibley, and Southwell.

Nathan H. Bray was born in Petersborough, England, in 1809. He emigrated to New Orleans and came into Sabine in the 1860s as a rough and boisterous character. Bray was converted to the Baptist faith and immediately assumed an active and prominent role in the Baptist work, being referred to in later years by Paxton as the "Apostle of the Sabine."[25] Elder Bray was elected moderator of the Sabine Association at its formation in 1847 and served in that capacity until 1871. He became moderator of the Vernon Association in 1871 and served until his death in 1875.

Perhaps Bray's greatest contribution to the Baptist cause was his tremendous work promoting the Sabbath schools. In 1853, he was appointed General Sunday School Agent for the association and was advanced $27.64 for his expenses.[26] His report in 1854 declared:

> I am happy to say the Union System to [sic] work well as all sectarianism has been avoided. . . .[27] Within your bounds are now to be seen hundreds of children gathered on every Sabbath morning at the house of prayer, receiving that pious instruction . . . and the field is still white unto harvest. . . .[28]

Sunday schools were only for children at that time. It was much later that adults were included in Bible study.

Elder Bray promoted the state convention work, sometimes being the only representative from Sabine Parish at the annual meetings. He helped organize numerous churches, traveling from DeSoto to Calcasieu Parish.

An active co-laborer with Bray in Baptist work in Sabine was W. L. Sibley. He was ordained while still a member of Beulah Church, Mississippi Association. In 1842, while Sibley was its moderator, that association was actively promoting Sabbath school work, Bible study, libraries and the Foreign Mission Society. Sibley, therefore, was not unfamiliar with the work when he came to Sabine Parish. Unlike Bray, Sibley's work was restricted to the parish and association. He was a member of the organizing presbytery and served as pastor of numerous churches in Sabine Parish.

Another Elder who contributed substantially to Baptist work in Sabine was W. C. Southwell. His work differed from Sibley's and Bray's in that it seemed to be more of a pastoral nature. In the margin of the minute book of Zion Hill Church is a note written in 1899 by the church clerk, E. P. Curtis, concerning Elder Southwell:

> Elder Southwell preached his first sermon at this church August 18, 1849, and on this date, September 17, 1899, he preached his last sermon also at this church, and he has preached continually for this period of fifty years and one month in West Louisiana and East Texas and it can truthfully be said that there was much good done as he was well educated and an able preacher.[29]

This note and many other references to his labors in the churches and association attest to his reputation as a pastor and preacher.

Other evidence of the flourishing Baptist work was reflected in the committee reports. The original committees of the association were arrangements, preaching, finance, state of the churches, correspondence and delegates. By 1855, the committee work had expanded to include Sabbath schools, domestic missions, temperance, and a special committee on the condition of Blacks.

Sectionalism was having a great impact politically in the United States in the 1840s. This was also true in religion where the Baptists were concerned. Baptists of the Southern states charged that they were not getting a fair share of the missionaries, that the Northern states controlled the agencies, were sending them into the Northwest to their own people, and that the bulk of the missionaries were northern and did not want to work in the South.[30]

Apparently the charge had some merit for missionaries in the Sabine area were non-existent until the late 1840s, and then they were supported only by the state convention and the local association. The populations of Sabine Parish had increased by 1850 to 4,515.[31] The number of Baptist churches had increased from one in 1846 to nine by 1850 with a total of 172 members.[32]

By 1854, the Sabine Association had a committee on domestic missions. The report of that committee stated:

> . . . We take this means of acknowledging our gratitude to said convention [Louisiana State Convention] for sending Bros. I. N. McCollister and J. Scarborough to labor in our destitute field; also to the Southern Domestic Board for sending Bro. Bray whose labors have been blessed even beyond our expectations . . .[33]

A mission offering was collected at the 1855 associational meeting.[34] With the mission activity the organizing of new churches was a natural result.

At the May conference of Toro Church, 1857, Henry A. Coburn, Albert (Abner) Coburn, Elizabeth Coburn, Elias Weldon, Sister Sara Ann Cassady, Jane Lemmons, John Dixon and Lucy Dixon all made application to the church for letters of dismission.[35] Although no explanation was entered in the Toro minutes for the request, these people met the same month to organize the Middle Creek Church under the guidance of Nathan Bray.

The minutes of the Middle Creek Baptist Church for May 30, 1857, reflect the following entry:

> May 30th, 1857, at a meeting held this day at Mt. Enterprise, we the undersigned members of regular Baptist Churches and holding letters of dismission from the same being sided by Elders N. H. Bray and Bro. W. L. Sibley who formed the Presbytery to ade [*sic*] us in organizing a Regular Baptist Church by the name of Middle Creek Church.[36]

Members in the constitution were John Bolton, John Putnam, Elias Weldon, H. A. Coburn, Abner S. Coburn, Mary Ann Bolton, Nancy Ann Putnam, Sarah Ann Weldon (Cassady?), Jane Lemmons, Elizabeth Coburn, Loretta Putnam.[37] After preaching by Elder N. H. Bray, the church met in conference by appointing N. H. Bray as moderator and S. T. Sibley the church clerk, pro tem, when it was resolved that the Rules of Decorum for the church be adopted. The record of the first business session reads:

Business Conference Number One:

Resolved that this church be known by the name of Middle Creek Church. Resolved that this church make a choice of a clerk which resulted in the choice of Bro. John Putnam who agrees to serve.

Resolved that John Bolton serve this church as Deacon he being already ordained to that office who also agrees to serve.

Resolved that our next meeting be on Saturday before the first Sabbath in June at Kirkham School House.[38]

Resolved that N. H. Bray be requested to purchase a church book and record the proceedings of this meeting and draw on the treasure for the same seventy-five cents.

The extant minutes of Toro Church, Middle Creek Church, associational records, and associational minutes give a graphic picture of the typical church community in Sabine Parish from 1847-1869. The first houses of worship were usually the log cabins of the settlers because of the small number of six to ten members. The first meeting house was usually of round logs to be followed in a few years with one of hewn logs or rough lumber. If a church was prosperous it might also have a fireplace.

Middle Creek was typical of the early churches in its physical facilities. The church worshipped in two different buildings in its first fifty years. The original was built of logs in February 1859, two years after the church was organized. The material and the land was furnished by Henry A. Coburn, one of its charter members.[39]

The second building was of rough lumber with wooden shutters over the windows and was constructed in the early 1880s. At night the congregation worshipped by candlelight.[40]

The rules and customs of the early churches of Sabine were standardized from their inception. They were closely patterned after the earlier Baptist churches in the South. Business meetings, or conferences, were held once a month on Saturday. Sunday was a day of rest and worship. The church did not take care of business on that day. The minister served as moderator at business meetings.

A large part of the monthly conference was concerned with the discipline of members. Church discipline served a multi-purpose in both the community and the church during these formative years. It primarily enforced the rules of the church. The basis for these rules was the belief that the work of the church could only accomplished within an atmosphere of peace and harmony between its individual members. It was the church's responsibility to set the moral standards for Christian living. The minutes of almost every conference included a statement on the peace and harmony of the church.

Members could not plead ignorance of the rules for they were read regularly at conference. It was expected that when one joined the fellowship of the church he understood its rules and agreed to abide by them.

Discipline in the church served a useful purpose in helping to maintain law and order in isolated communities. Disturbing the peace and being drunk and disorderly was not easily taken care of by the sheriff because of the great distance of communities from the parish seat, the mode of travel, and the lack of adequate roads. These types of disturbances were considered more of a moral matter than criminal.

Exclusion from the church was a very serious matter. An individual's position in the church was a status symbol in the community. But if a church was quick to mete out discipline, it was willing to grant forgiveness. It was common for a member to be "voted out" at one conference and be reinstated at the next monthly business meeting. After reinstatement a member was permitted to participate in the observance of the church ordinance of communion.

The Civil War wrought havoc with churches throughout the South, as it did in other areas of life. Sabine Parish was the scene of only one battle, Battle of Pleasant Hill. Physical destruction was at a minimum, but it took its toll in capable men and finances needed for promotion of the programs of the church such as Sabbath schools, ministers' salaries and missions.[41]

Paxton's statistics show an increase in church membership during the war years and Reconstruction.[42] There were two new churches established in the Southern portion of Sabine: Mt. Carmel (1663), Beulah Church (1867?); and the Baptists brought about a general upswing in the churches by 1870, but it was short lived.[43] The economic and political impact of Reconstruction was too severe. By the 1870s they were again in bad condition financially and spiritually.

The effects of Reconstruction were only seen in subtle ways through the church minute entries. The contributions to defray the expenses of the association dropped drastically that year with six of the churches giving nothing, and the largest single amount contributed by any church in the association was $8.00.

In 1874 there were only three ordained ministers and one licentiate in the association and the committee on missions exhorted the churches to "support their ministers in a way that permits them to leave the plow handles, schoolrooms, to devote full time to preaching so missionaries are unnecessary." The reason for so few preachers in the association was given as poor pay and poor support. The committee suggested prayer meetings and Sabbath schools to strengthen the churches, showing much concern for their weakened condition both financially and spiritually.[44]

In summary, the impact of the Baptist work in Sabine Parish and its contribution of stable Christian citizens to the development of the economic, social, and political life was considerable. The strength of the first seven churches, Zion Hill, Pleasant Hill, Little Flock, Toro, Middle Creek, Mt. Carmel and Beulah was due to: 1) the charter members were generally not new converts, but rather, strong Baptists who came as a group into this frontier area; 2) their ministers, as a whole, were a particularly orthodox, faithful few who worked unceasingly promoting the churches; 3) the churches guarded their theology with diligence against the schism of Campbellism and other schismatic groups. The result was that, although historically Sabine Parish had been Spanish Catholic for over a hundred years, its Catholicism would be overshadowed by 1900 and the parish would have become a part of the Anglo-Saxon "Baptist Belt" of north Louisiana.

Notes for "Sabine Parish Baptists"

[1] U. S. Department of the Interior, General Land Office, Washington, D. C., *Louisiana Tract Book*, Vols. 19-23, 1880. Exemplified copy, dated April 21, 1931, on file in Pickett Abstract and Title Company, Many, La.

[2] J. Fair Hardin, *Northwestern Louisiana: A History of the Watershed of the Red River, 1714-1937* (Shreveport, La., 1993), 92-98. Some of these groups were the Miguel Menchaca Expedition, 1811, Gutienrez-Magee, and many unorganized bands. See also Dan L. Flores, "The John Maley Journal: Travels and Adventures in the American Southwest, 1810-1813" (M.A. thesis, Northwestern State University, 1972), 40.

[3] Ibid., 92-98.

[4] Louis Raphael Nardini, Sr., *My Historic Natchitoches, Louisiana, and its Environment* (Colfax, La., 1963), 104.

[5] Legal Records on file in Office of the Clerk of Court, Sabine Parish, Many, La.

[6] U. S. Department of the Interior, *Louisiana Tract Book*, Vol. 23, insofar as it relates to T5 R13W Louisiana Mer. Louisiana. No. 126 (Rio Hondo).

[7] Ivan M. Wise, *Footsteps of the Flock, or Origins of Louisiana Baptists* (Crowley, La., 1910), 90-91. Also from the private papers of Miss Myra Addison (a descendant of Elder Cook), Many, La. William and Temperance Cook were in the Horeb Baptist Church, Mayfield, Georgia, in 1814, coming from Powellton Church, Georgia. William Cook was licensed to preach September 18, 1814, at Horeb and dismissed from that church in November 1817. Verified by church records from Sparta Baptist Church, Sparta, Georgia.

[8] February 19, 1848, members of the church met to certify the date, charter members and organizing presbytery, because the original minute book had recently burned in the house of Isah Flanakin, Church Clerk. The following members singed the statement: I. N. McCollister, Joseph White, Isah Flanakin, John Brown, William Eaves, Lavina Montgomery (charter member), (illegible) White, Nancy Cook, Elizabeth Arthur, Mary Garlington, Patsy Cain, Nancy Brown, Sarah Arthur, Mary Turner, (illegible) Whitley. W. E. Paxton, *History of the Baptists of Louisiana, From the Earliest Times to the Present* (St. Louis, 1888), 385-86, quotes from the Rev. N. H. Bray, giving a different date, presbytery and charter members. The statement adopted by the members is probably correct. Paxton's work is a very valuable one for Baptist history, but there are many instances of incorrect names and dates.

[9] Paxton, *History of the Baptists of Louisiana*, 182.

[10] Wise, *Footsteps of the Flock*, 21-24.

[11] Ibid., 200.

[12] Wise, *Footsteps in the Flock*, 29.

[13] Paxton, *History of the Baptists of Louisiana*, 206.

[14] Although reference will be made occasionally to other churches for statistical purposes, concentration is on those churches organized 1826-1880, who have continued to function composing the Sabine Association. Their physical locations are in the South half of Sabine Parish, the exception being the Baptist Church of Many, which was active in the Sabine Association until the 1880s when it apparently merged with Jerusalem Church, selling its property to the Methodists in 1897; another Baptist Church was organized in the town of Many, which is the present First Baptist Church.

[15] Sabine Association minutes of organizational meeting, October 22-23, 1847 (New Orleans) *Southwestern Baptist Chronicle*, 1848, 29.

[16]This name is spelled in the church minutes and the published works of Paxton and Wise as McCaulley, McCalley, McCauley, McColley, but it is obviously the same minister.

[17]I. N. McCollister to Wade Barr, July 20, 1950. Original in the possession of the Clerk of Little Flock Church, Route 5, Many, La.

[18]Sabine Association minutes, 1848, 1855, 1856.

[19]Ibid., 1848.

[20]Ibid.

[21]This date was arrived at by comparing the earliest listings in Beulah's earliest extant minute book with the date of removal of letters from Toro and the dates Beulah joined the Sabine Association.

[22]Toro Baptist Church minutes.

[23]Mississippi Association Minutes.

[24]Paxton, *History of the Baptists of Louisiana*, 389.

[25]Ibid., 494.

[26]Ibid.

[27]Ibid., 393.

[28]Ibid., 397.

[29]Zion Hill Church minutes, in possession of the church clerk, Negreet, La.

[30]Robert A. Baker, *The Southern Baptist Convention and Its People, 1607-1972* (Nashville, 1974), 153-55.

[31]U. S. Census, Sabine Parish, 1850.

[32]Paxton, *History of the Baptists of Louisiana*, 387-92.

[33]Sabine Baptist Association minutes, 1854.

[34]Ibid., 1855.

[35]Toro Baptist Church minutes, 1857.

[36]Middle Creek Baptist Church minutes. All material on Middle Creek Church, unless otherwise stated, comes directly from the original minute books with all spelling and names exactly as recorded. The books are in possession of the church clerk.

[37]Leah Townsend, *South Carolina Baptists, 1670-1805* (Florence, S. C., 1935), 248, 250, 182. The Putnams and Boltons were prominent Baptists in the early churches of South Carolina.

[38]The congregation continued to hold its meetings at the school until 1859.

[39]Middle Creek Baptist Church minutes, February 1859, "Building Committee composed of Brethren H. A. Coburn, John Bolton, A. J. Norsworthy, A. Weldon, and Josiah Canaday to select a place of ground on which to build a church house and also to superintend the building of the same, in which act the church is bound to sustain the committee."

[40]Annie Durrett Norsworthy, pamphlet written on the occasion of the 100th anniversary of the Middle Creek Church, 1957, privately owned by Joanne H. Pickett, Many, La.

[41]Abner Coburn is a good example of the loss. He was the very capable church clerk for Middle Creek and wrote excellent minutes. He died in a prison camp in Illinois. Letters dated 1864 from a fellow prisoner to Abner's father, private collection Coburn family, Katy Coburn Hyatt, Florien, La.

[42]Paxton, *History of the Baptists of Louisiana*, 404-11.

[43]Mt. Carmel and Beulah's charter members came from the Toro congregation. Beulah is later known as the "Old Blockhouse Church," because of its location, but nowhere in any of the associational or church records is it referred to by any name except Beulah.

[44]Paxton, *History of the Baptists of Louisiana*.

PART IX

World War I-World War II, 1915-1945

THE FIFTH JOURNEY OF *ST. PAUL* IN LOUISIANA (1917-1918)*

Roger Baudier, Sr.
Edited by Charles E. Nolan

The Chapel Car Manuscript

On January 6, 1956, Archbishop Joseph Rummel of New Orleans forwarded an urgent request for information on the activities of the Catholic Church Extension Society's railroad chapel cars in Louisiana to Roger Baudier. The original request came from Bishop Francis Leipzig of Baker, Oregon, who was in the final stages of preparing a short book on these "chapels on wheels."[1]

Roger Baudier-journalist, editor, apologist, advisor to the archbishop, official archdiocesan chronicler, and the South's most prolific Catholic historian—put aside his other pressing projects and delved immediately into his vast, personal historical collection, a few published sources, local Catholic newspapers, and archdiocesan administrative records.

Within a month, the completed manuscript, "The Chapel Cars of The Catholic Church Extension Society in the Louisiana Dioceses," was on the archbishop's desk. Despite some lacunae, Baudier reported, "I have been able to piece all the fragments together and give a creditable survey of the work done." Unfortunately, the manuscript sat on the archbishop's desk for a month before it was forwarded to Oregon. By that time, Bishop Leipzig's book was already at the printer. The Louisiana chapel car story remained unpublished and the manuscript became another folder in Baudier's extensive historical collection.[2]

The original Baudier article was divided into four sections: 1) the Chapel Car *St. Anthony* in Louisiana in 1909; 2) the building and blessing of the Chapel Car *St. Paul*; 3) the five journeys of *St. Paul* in Louisiana; and 4) the chapel car's later use by St. Leo the

*First published in Glenn R. Conrad, ed., *Cross, Crozier and Crucible: A Volume Celebrating the Bicentennial of a Catholic Diocese in Louisiana* (Lafayette, La.: Archdiocese of New Orleans in cooperation with the Center for Louisiana Studies, 1993), 233-48. Reprinted with the kind permission of the editor and the Center for Louisiana Studies.

Great Parish in New Orleans. The present essay is an abridgement of the third section and recounts only the car's final Louisiana journey; material from other sections is briefly summarized.

While retaining Baudier's unique style and content, some narrative rearrangement and grammatical editing was necessary. The most significant difference between this article and the original manuscript is the addition of footnotes.[3]

The Chapel Cars of the Catholic Church Extension Society

The Catholic Church Extension Society was founded in 1905 by Father Francis C. Kelley to assist American dioceses in building up the Church in rural, mission areas. By 1912, the society was operating two railroad chapel cars, "churches on wheels," the *St. Anthony* and the *St. Peter*. In 1909, the former had operated briefly in Louisiana and Mississippi, where large areas had neither chapels nor resident priests.[4]

In late summer 1912, Peter Kuntz of Dayton, Ohio, offered to provide funds to build a third car for exclusive use in the South, "convinced that money invested in it is productive of more good than anything else."[5]

The Extension Society contacted Archbishop James H. Blenk (1905-1917) of New Orleans who appreciated the venture's possibilities for immense good. His archdiocese embraced all of southern Louisiana and included the South's largest Catholic population. The number of priests needed to minister to the scattered faithful fell far short. The northern half of Louisiana constituted the vast Diocese of Alexandria. In late October 1912, with support from the region's bishops, Archbishop Blenk accepted the Extension Society's offer. Construction began immediately at the Barney and Smith Company shops in Dayton, Ohio.

The copper-roofed steel car measured eighty-six feet in length; the interior was finished throughout in Cuban mahogany. The car could be heated by steam or its own oil-burning heating plant, and lighted by electricity or gas. The car's main section consisted of a furnished chapel, with pews, an altar, and seventy-five seats. There were also living compartments for the chaplain, manager, and porter, as well as a compact kitchenette. At each end was an observation platform.[6] In honor of the great Apostle of the Gentiles who had journeyed to so many lands to preach the Gospel, the new car was named for St. Paul, since it too was intended to go far afield to bring the Gospel to many.

On March 14, 1915, James Cardinal Gibbons, archbishop of Baltimore, presided at the colorful cavalcade down New Orleans' Canal Street and the blessing of the new car at a nearby railroad siding. Bishop John Gunn of Natchez delivered a masterful address, touching upon the great work of the Extension Society, the necessity of disseminating knowledge as an antidote for the calumnies from which the Church in America was suffering, and the good work that would be achieved by the car.[7]

The new car's operating expenses were supplied by local donations and a subsidy from the participating dioceses. The Apostolic Mission House in Washington, D. C., generally provided the chaplain's monthly $100 salary. The railroads granted free transportation. Father E. B. Ledvina of the Extension Society observed in 1916, "The railroads have recognized the help that such cars give in the way of assisting to pacify old, and to induce new settlers to locate along the line. From a mere business standpoint, it is good policy to grant such a concession."[8]

The First Journeys (1915-1917)

The *St. Paul* left New Orleans on March 18, 1915, for North Louisiana.[9] The following day, the car, with Father Alvah W. Doran, C.P., [*sic*] as chaplain, made its first stop at Bunkie, a growing town on the Texas and Pacific Railroad in Central Louisiana.

The initial accomplishments of the Chapel Car *St. Paul* are told in the Bunkie parish annals:

> On Passion Sunday, 1915, Fr. Doran opened a mission in Bunkie for Catholics and non-Catholics. Interest in the mission grew so much that it was soon impossible to accommodate in the car all who came. The sermons had to be delivered in the [local] chapel. By means of the question box, the missionary imparted some very useful information to his hearers, and did much to dissipate ignorance about things Catholic. Many sincere Protestants assisted and asked questions, and all expressed themselves as much pleased with the way services were conducted.
>
> The immediate fruits of the mission were about 200 holy communions. . . ; twenty-four children were further instructed and made their first communion, and two converts were received into the Church; many Italians received the sacraments, being able to make their confessions in their own tongue, as the missionary knew the language. The amount of good done for the cause of religion, however, cannot be estimated.[10]

A year after the chapel car had made its historic visit to Bunkie, the first pastor was appointed.

The experiences at Bunkie were typical of events all along the *St. Paul*'s route. The car continued to operate in North Louisiana until May 1915, when it moved to the Dallas diocese.[11] In fall 1915, the chapel car returned to North Louisiana where missions were conducted at Monroe, Shreveport, and "the various small interior, sawmill towns, where there are very few Catholics and no churches."[12] For the next two years, the car crisscrossed the state with summer layovers in New Orleans because of the heat. In 1916, the Redemptorist Fathers from New Orleans took charge of the missionary endeavor. They were assisted by Mike J. Cousins, the car manager, who rendered great service to the chaplains, not only serving the car and looking after its physical upkeep, but also teaching catechism, distributing literature, and acting as factotum and secretary.

The schedule of Reverend John Diederich, C.SS.R., car chaplain in late 1916 and early 1917, was typical. His missions at Egan, Lacassine, and other towns in Jeff Davis, Acadia, and surrounding parishes included 7 a.m. Mass in the chapel car, catechism for children at 4 p.m., and a lecture at night. In between, he spoke with people and heard confessions. A question box, installed in the car, was used considerably, and the questions usually revealed the tenor and views of the local population. On the first day, attendance was usually not very large, but when word-of-mouth comments got around, interest was aroused and attendance jumped.

The Extension Society and the Louisiana chapel car mission lost a great friend and loyal supporter when Archbishop James H. Blenk died on April 20, 1917. The capable and determined Father Jules Jeanmard, acting administrator, *sede vacante,* assumed direction of the chapel car movements. Father Jeanmard's burden was increased by America's entry into World War I; war conditions would eventually halt the chapel car's journeys.

The Fifth Journey (1917-1918)

Father Jeanmard and Father Francis Leon Gassler, archdiocesan vicar general, planned the chapel car's 1917-1918 winter itinerary in the small towns along the Gulf Coast Lines from Palmetto in St. Landry Parish, through Pointe Coupée Parish, and down to Port Allen in West Baton Rouge Parish. This was certainly an area that needed attention.[13]

The *St. Paul* left New Orleans on October 6, 1917, on the Gulf Coast Lines, with Reverend Bernard Kalvelage, C.SS.R., in charge. The first stop was Krotz; Springs, a sawmill town east of Opelousas. There were ten Catholic families out of a total population of seventy-five persons. The car was "entrenched" on a siding about a mile from town and close to the sawmill. A small delegation came to extend a welcome. During the eight-day mission, forty-five persons, including ten non-Catholics, attended each night. A mission for children was also held and fourteen children were prepared for first communion. "There was a little prejudice," the missionary reported, "among those who had been baptized Catholic. Of these, two returned to the Church and had their marriages revalidated. The Methodist minister is in the habit of visiting Krotz Springs once a month and most of the people flock to hear him. Hence the loss of Faith among the Catholics." Father Kalvelage recommended that the local pastor, who resided fourteen miles away, visit the place occasionally.[14]

On October 14, the chapel car was moved to Lottie. About two miles from the town were two sawmills, employing some 300 men, most Negroes and non-Catholics. Introduction to the town was very cold and the departure still colder. At the depot, the missionary was met by the community's only Catholic family—husband, wife and four children. Despite the "wise remarks" of the curious and the spirit of religious indifference, eighty persons showed up for the opening of the mission. Father Kalvelage realized that this was mostly from curiosity, because next night only forty-five attended, and that was the number for the rest of the visit. But he also learned that local Baptists had sent an S.O.S. to their minister to come at once. He opened a revival immediately, although a general revival had been held a few weeks previously. "He was a very respectable man,"

Father Kalvelage reported, "and indirectly conveyed to us his deep sorrow that his mission should be simultaneous with ours and that he would not have held his nightly meetings, if he had known that the chapel car was here although everybody in town had known two weeks in advance that the car was to come. However, he did no damage."

A number of non-Catholic men were members of the Masonic Lodge at nearby Fordoche, which the car was to visit later, so the question box was a chance for them to find out what the missionary had to say about Masonry. When he explained the oaths of the first three degrees, the only Catholic Mason renounced the fraternity. Sixteen children, between the ages of eight and seventeen, were instructed, went to confession, and made their first communion; sixty-eight communions were received; and twenty-two adult confessions were heard at Lottie; one marriage was revalidated.[15]

Several persons had come from nearby Blanks for the mission, and they assured Father Kalvelage a better reception when he went there. On October 23, the car was moved to this thrifty little lumber town, where most of the white workers were Catholics. The mill supervisor, an Episcopalian, gave the missionary and the car a warm welcome. A good location was given to the chapel car close to the mill. Most of the men regularly attended the nightly services. Some had lost the faith, had married out of the Church, and had joined secret societies. Some careless Catholics returned to their duties, and Father Kalvelage stated that "our stay at Blanks was indeed blessed." Average attendance at the mission was about seventy. Nearly all the non-Catholics of the town attended in the evening and many, through the question box, had false impressions about the Church removed. There were forty-two confessions; ninety-eight communions; fourteen children's first communions; two marriages revalidated; and one baptism.[16]

On October 31, 1917, the *St. Paul* moved to Livonia. Father Kalvelage had many misgivings, as some of the women from there had warned him not to expect any men to go to confession. Furthermore, the pastor of the nearest church (Father J. Murgue) had obtained a Passionist Father to give a mission at Livonia just two months previously. After four days, the priest had given up in disgust. Only two men had gone to confession. Many had contracted civil marriage.

The mission opened in the Livonia school on All Soul's Day, November 2. The cane-grinding season was in full swing, so only from seventy-five to 100 people attended. The missionary thereupon resumed services in the chapel car. Only about five men of the residents received the sacraments. Even some of the women remained away. To make matters worse, whooping cough was prevalent, so that the missionary experienced much difficulty. Despite all this, Father Kalvelage kept the car at Livonia for twelve days. On Sunday, he offered two Masses, which some 200 people attended, but not more than seventeen men approached the Holy Table. Finally, with Father Murgue's approval, the missionary suggested formation of a committee to prepare the way for erection of a church. Enthusiasm ran high, and soon $400 was promised. Already $352 had been collected. A lot was donated, and the non-Catholic manager of the lumber mill promised a supply of lumber. Only last year [1955], the chapel at Livonia became a parish church.[17]

From Livonia, the Chapel Car *St. Paul*, now under the direction of Reverend Joseph A. Girven, C.SS.R., was taken to Baton Rouge to take on a supply of water. This was made possible through the courtesy of the vice-president of the Gulf Coast Lines, all of whose officials, Father Girven stated, were always ready to come to the aid of the car and its personnel.[18]

On November 19, the car moved to Erwinville, a little town twenty miles west of Baton Rouge. The population was then composed of eighty white and fifteen Negro families, nearly all Catholics. This area was formerly a vast forest, but a sawmill had operated in the vicinity, so the cleared land was turned to truck farming and sugarcane. The nearest church was at Chenal, ten miles away, but the road was a hard one to travel.

As Father Girven was leaving to invite the neighbors to the services, a woman and her husband appeared. She wanted to know if services were held in the car, then if any other than Catholic services would be offered, and, finally, "How much do you charge?" When told there were no charges, she sighed with relief and assured the chaplain that she and her husband would be there that night. Dodgers had been distributed a few days in advance. Only fifty-five appeared the first night. The second evening saw the car jammed with 120 inside, twenty in the library room, and nearly 100 outside. The rest of the evenings saw 260 people at the car. The Catholics were certainly delighted over the opportunity to attend services—they came to morning Mass and evening services too.

The children's mission was a great success. Each morning early, sixty children came to the mission before they left for the school some distance away; forty-one made their first communion. Father Girven was surprised to find nearly every child well instructed in prayers, a job the mothers had done well. The parents deplored the fact that they were unable to have regular services, since they just could not make the twenty-mile round-trip to Chenal every Sunday.

Practically all of the fallen away or indifferent Catholics came back to their duties. Just a few months before, a Methodist minister had spent some weeks at Erwinville, but in vain, because the Catholics remained firm. However, he had promised to return.

The good will of the people at Erwinville was shown by their calls with food for the priest and his helpers, something they regarded as a privilege. Even some of the non-Catholics brought food. Before the close of the mission, a delegation called on Father Girven, as was usually done, to solicit his help in building a chapel, disclosing they already had $500 promised. Confessions at Erwinville numbered 160; holy communions, 232; first communions, forty-one, revalidations, two.[19]

On November 27, the chapel car went on to Oscar Crossing, where only a brief, five-day stop was made because most of the people were Italians and did not speak English. Average attendance at night was ninety and in the morning, fifty. The Italians called on Father Girven and asked that the mission be conducted in Italian; the chaplain suggested that they ask Father Louis Savouré, their pastor at nearby Chenal, to send an Italian priest to help them. Several non-Catholics attended the evening services. Eleven children were prepared for first communion. A class for young adults, aged nineteen to twenty-six, was held and seven made their first communion. A married Methodist woman came for instruction and was baptized at the close of the mission.[20]

On December 2, 1917, the car moved along the Texas and Pacific Railroad tracks to Morrow, where it stayed nine days. Father Girven and the crew were amazed upon arriving in Morrow to behold a great array of autos, buggies, and saddlehorses. They were soon informed by locals that the large gathering was not for the chapel car. Three saloons, two for whites and one for Negroes, were pointed out. The large number of people was explained by the fact that surrounding towns were "dry," so folks made the trek to this town to satisfy their thirst.

Morrow was in the care of Lebeau, twelve miles distant. Twice a month the priest came to offer Mass on Sunday at the town chapel, which had been built by Mr. Morrow on his own land, and he looked after it as well as the priests on Sundays. The congregation was made up of thirty-five to forty families. Many spoke only French. When they learned that the mission would be in English, they decided not to attend.

The first night's service, at the pastor's advice, was held at the local chapel, but the attendance was small. The chapel car was used thereafter. On the first night in the car, fifty-five people came, including twenty non-Catholics. The second night the number increased to ninety, of whom fifty were non-Catholics, and so it continued for the rest of the week. A number of anxious non-Catholic inquirers came during the day for private chats with the missionary. The children had been cared for by the nearby pastor, so there was no mission for them. One little fellow came for instruction and made his first communion. Adult confessions totaled only nineteen at Morrows; holy communions, fifty-two; and revalidations, one.[21]

The little town of Rosa, population about ninety, was next to be visited by the chapel car. The mission opened on December 10 in wet, cold weather. In fact, the rain and cold continued for the ensuing six days. This played havoc with already bad country roads, so attendance was restricted. Most of the area's twenty-five Catholics made the mission. Some three miles out there was a French settlement, but those people could not reach Rosa because of the bad roads. Attendance the first night was a discouraging fifteen, but the second night saw thirty-five present, ten of whom were non-Catholics. One long-time resident said no Catholic services had been held in Rosa for forty years. The Catholics were well posted. The Methodist ministers were frequent visitors around the area as in other little towns, but their efforts were in vain.[22]

On December 15, the car was moved to Palmetto, a nice little town, as Father Girven styled it, but with a very poor Catholic chapel compared to the Methodist church. The chapel was an abandoned schoolhouse with a seating capacity of seventy-five. On opening night, the chapel car was comfortably filled. The second night eighty-five were present. The average stood at 110 for subsequent evening services, including twenty-five non-Catholics. Many of those attending came four or five miles, but many others could not brave the inclement weather and the mud roads. Some of the town leaders asked Father Girven to have the car make a return visit in more favorable weather.

A little mission was held for the children and ten were prepared for first communion. The indifference of the young people in the town was the result of the Methodist Sunday school with its many inducements for attendance. Catholics had Mass only on Sunday every month or two. A delegation that called on the missionary informed him that their pastor, a Josephite, worked principally among the Negroes. They pledged $1,000 and a lot of ground to build a church. At Palmetto, there were forty-five confessions; sixty communions; two first communions; and three baptisms.[23]

On December 23, 1917, Father James H. Dreis, C.SS.R., replaced Father Girven as chaplain and the car was moved to Melville. The town boasted of a population of 1,000, including twelve Catholic families. A chapel had been built there several years previously and the priest from Lebeau offered Mass once each month. A two-weeks' mission was scheduled. However, because of the Christmas spirit and family gatherings, Father Dreis decided to postpone opening the mission until after Christmas. The day after the car's arrival, a circus set up quarters near the chapel car, and remained for the holidays.

The first night of the mission proved a disappointment-four people came. The second night was better—seven attended. On the third night, the car was filled and for the rest of the mission there were not less than seventy, of whom ten were non-Catholics. On the first day, a woman, a Methodist from birth, came for instructions, told Father Dreis that she was convinced of the Catholic Church as the true Church, and asked for admission to the Church. Wednesday at 3 p.m. was set as the time for conditional baptism. At 2 p.m. word was sent to the chaplain that the convert's mother, a bigoted Methodist, had swallowed poison when she heard of her daughter's action. The convert did not come to the car.

Because of the large number of children at Melville, instructions were given for them twice daily and four children made their private first communion. There were fifty-eight confessions; including children; sixty-two communions; and one baptism.[24]

On January 5, 1918, the car moved to the farming town of Fordoche where about ten Catholic families lived. The mission started with the baptism of three Italians. People attended well, despite the cold weather, said to be the coldest in twenty years. A children's mission proved a blessing, because the children knew little of their religion, and many could not even make the sign of the cross. Twenty-four children and two adults made their first communion. Holy communions numbered fifty-nine. On the last day of the mission it snowed—something very unusual—and the thermometer dropped to four degrees above zero. Very few attended the closing exercises.[25]

The car's next point of activity was Morley. From the chaplain's very entrance into the hamlet on January 13, he felt that the car was among friends, as attendance proved. After three sermons, four converts presented themselves for instruction.

The chapel car congregation was given an unusual treat—a resident served as organist and a friend came from Edgard to sing. Men came every morning to Mass at 5:30. Although there were only fifty-seven confessions heard, communions totalled 110— many being daily communicants. Two men forsook secret society membership; one marriage was revalidated; the nuptial blessing was imparted to two convert couples; and seven adults and eight children made their first communion.[26]

On January 20, the *St. Paul* continued along the Texas and Pacific Line to Addis, a railroad center where many members of train crews resided. There was no church there, but thanks to Father Eugene Royer, the pastor at Brusly, the people were well acquainted with their religion. From the first day of the mission to the last, the car was crowded; on closing night, the car was jammed and seventy people stood outside.

The town counted 200 Catholics, all of whom were looking forward to the day when they could have a chapel. In fact, a delegation of men led by the mayor called on Father Dreis for some action in this regard. They were directed to the pastor who approved a subscription. A lot was donated and $400 was quickly raised. Thirteen children received their first holy communion, and there were, all told, 117 confessions and 165 communions. Two converts were received into the Church.[27]

Torras, a plantation site near the junction of the Red and Mississippi rivers, was reached on January 30. Unfortunately, the postmaster had not received the advance dodgers, so arrival of the *St. Paul* was somewhat of a surprise. The parish church at Morganza was twenty miles away and the pastor, Father Dominic Perino, came to Torras once a month on a weekday to offer Mass and give instructions. A little chapel had been built several years before by the late Mr. Torras, the town's namesake.

Only four adults appeared the first night; sixteen adults and children attended the second service. The area had practically no Catholics, judging from the attendance at the mission. Only eighteen people, including four non-residents, approached the sacraments. Some Catholics living only one-and-one-half miles from the depot failed to attend, but the few who did come were edifying. At the time of the mission, roads were bad from recent heavy rains and levee repairs. There were eighteen confessions; eight first communions; thirty communions; and one revalidation. The five-day mission closed on February 5.[28]

Attendance was also very small at Lettsworth (February 5-10). Although the mission had been well advertised, the first night saw only thirteen whites and thirty non-Catholic Negroes present. Lettsworth was predominantly Presbyterian and not one of them came near the car, even to inspect it. Only three French families made the mission. One Italian family lived a short distance from the car, but only their children attended and they received their first communion. Father Dreis reported twenty-one confessions; three first communions; thirty communions; and one baptism.[29]

On February 10, the car arrived in Batchelor, which, like Lettsworth, was a parish station of Morganza, fourteen miles away. Batchelor had a population of about 100, most of whom were Catholics, but it had no church—the nearest being eight miles away at New Texas. Sixty people came to the mission on the first night, but the number increased until there were 180 following the services, including fifty non-Catholics. Father Dreis learned that many of the Catholics were careless or indifferent, but they all returned to their duties and made their peace with God. Ten non-Catholics asked for literature on the

Church. One aged man received his first communion, after revalidation of his marriage. One woman and her three children came for instruction and asked to be received into the Church. A children's mission was conducted and nine made their private communion. Confessions at Batchelor totalled 120; and communions, 140.[30]

The last stop along the Texas and Pacific railroad line was at a sidetrack at Chamberlin, fifteen miles from Baton Rouge (February 16-18). There was no chapel at the town, and Catholics there had to go about five miles to Lobdell, where services were held once a month.

When the chapel car arrived, Father Dreis was welcomed by a group of people who wanted to know the hours of services. Next morning there were about forty in the car; at evening instructions, there were sixty-five. At the end of the week, it was an overflow crowd. Average attendance was 110, including twenty-five non-Catholics. Many non-Catholics came for private chats with Father Dreis. One of them was a Methodist judge; he was baptized and received his first communion. A few days later, on his fifty-eighth birthday, he invited the crew of the *St. Paul* to his house for dinner. A non-Catholic plantation owner sent to the car a young dressed pig; many other donations were made. At the close of the children's mission, ten children received the sacraments. At Chamberlin, Father Dreis reported seventy-nine confessions; 145 communions; and one convert.[31]

The missions on the west side of the Mississippi River closed at Chamberlin on February 28, 1918. Father Gassler and Father Arthur Drossaerts then arranged for a trip by the chapel car to the stations along the Baton Rouge, Hammond, and Eastern Railroad, from east of the state capital, to Hammond, a stretch of some thirty-five miles without a single parish church. The nearest church south of the railroad was at French Settlement, some ten miles away, and northward there was none at all to the Mississippi state line, another thirty miles.

The Reverend Byron J. Krieger, C.SS.R., was in charge of the car. Missions were given at Sharp (March 10-16) and at Denham Springs (March 17-23). One of the dodgers widely distributed by Father Krieger was headed: "Notice to Travelers Going to Heaven" and included a list of "Important Rules for Passengers:"

> PRICE OF TICKETS - 1st Class on Limited Express: Poverty, Charity, Obedience. 2nd Class on Fast Express: Piety, Devotion, Sacraments. 3rd Class on Local Accommodation: Commandments, Penance.
>
> NO RETURN TICKETS are issued. NO EXCURSION TRAINS are run. Don't miss the train. Trains leave on time at all hours—day and night—when DEATH strikes the clock. Arrival: When God wills. Travelers can take passage on any part of the road. Travelers are advised to bring no other baggage but good works. Children who have not attained the age of reason are carried free, provided they are held on the lap of their mother-the CHURCH. For further particulars apply to YOUR PASTOR, General Passenger Agent, or to THE CHAPLAIN of The CAR, Joint Agent.[32]

The tour of the Florida Parishes ended the mission work of the Chapel Car *St. Paul* in Louisiana. Newly appointed Archbishop John W. Shaw, formerly of San Antonio, arrived in New Orleans in June 1918. He soon decided to discontinue use of the car until after the war. New wartime restrictions on civilian railroad travel limited even the possibility of moving the car at private expense, since the *St. Paul* was classified as a private car.[33] The archbishop's interest was further diverted by the tragic influenza epidemic that broke out in the winter of 1918-1919.

Father Ledvina of the Extension Society wrote to Archbishop Shaw that the Society felt "in honor bound to keep the Chapel Cars operating" and reminded the New Orleans prelate of his predecessor's commitment to use and maintain the car. Archbishop Shaw responded with a non-committal "let's-wait-and-see."[34] However, there were no developments.

St. Leo the Great Chapel (1920)

The Chapel Car *St. Paul* slept in its wraps, tucked away on a siding in the outskirts of New Orleans for almost two years. In early February 1920, Father Vincent Prats, newly appointed to establish St. Leo the Great Parish in midtown New Orleans, was searching for a place to celebrate the parish's first Mass. From a streetcar, he noticed an abandoned railroad spur next to the Mylam-Morgan Grain and Feed Mill and suddenly remembered the *St. Paul*, "now peacefully sleeping, but suddenly to be awakened by a Macedonian call."

The pastor went immediately to the archiepiscopal house and burst excitedly into the usual placid life of Archbishop Shaw. "Your Grace, I have a church next Sunday—that is, if you say so. All I have to do is to roll it into place." The archbishop, the Extension Society, and the mill owners soon gave permission. On Sunday, February 13, 1920, Father Prats offered St. Leo the Great's first parish Mass in the Chapel Car *St. Paul,* on a sidetrack next to the Mylam-Morgan Grain and Feed Mill, a short distance off Gentilly Road. The car continued in use as a chapel until November when a temporary church was ready and the car was moved out of the archdiocese.[35]

Conclusion

Father Byron Krieger, the chapel car's last chaplain, later summed up the work of the *St. Paul* and its Redemptorist chaplains.

> They visited places that had no resident priest and no church; and in a great many instances, found people who had not had the services of a minister of God in a score or even two scores of years.
> It goes without saying that in this pioneer work, there were many to be baptized, adults as well as infants, likewise numerous marriages to be validated. Naturally in most of these places, the unfortunate Catholics were in woeful ignorance of the most elementary doctrines of the Church. While in most localities, the chapel car and the missionary Father were received joyously and enthusiastically, and shown every mark of esteem and

courtesy by the townspeople, non-Catholics as well as Catholics, in some instances the priest had to contend against the aggressive bigotry. The car and the missionary were cursed outright; the services were disturbed, and food had to be ordered from places as distant as thirty miles, because the fanatics refused to sell to the hated priest and his car. Often therefore, there was nothing on hand, but canned goods, unless some generous family would go to the next town to purchase fresh provisions. Sometimes, bigotry was so rife and so wild that the protection of 'parish' officials had to be sought. Examples of this kind make interesting reading, but they proved rather uncomfortable for those who had to submit to them.

This condition was by no means general; it was rather the exception. In most places, the non-Catholics who came to hear the discourses, at first perhaps through curiosity, became attentive listeners; and in the end, even if they were not converted to the truth, they went away less prejudiced against their Catholic fellow-citizens; and thus the spirit of bigotry and intolerance was greatly allayed.[36]

Notes for "The Fifth Journey of *St. Paul* in Louisiana (1917-1918)"

[1]J. F. Rummel to Roger Baudier, New Orleans, January 6, 1966, Baudier Collection [BP, 1:19], Archives, Archdiocese of New Orleans; hereafter [BP, 1:19], AANO.

[2]Roger Baudier to Richard O. Gerow, New Orleans, January 28, 1956; Roger Baudier to Joseph F Rummel, New Orleans, [n.d.-cir. January 30, 1956]; J. F. Rummel to F. P. Leipzig, March 2 and 12, 1956; F. P. Leipzig to Roger Baudier, March 8, 1956, [BP, 1:19], AANO.

[3]The manuscript, research notes, and correspondence are now housed in Baudier Collection [BP, 1:19]. AANO. Baudier's detailed research notes allowed the editor to reconstruct and review all of the author's original source material with one exception as noted below.

[4]Concerning the 1909 visit, see *New Orleans Morning Star* (hereafter *MS*), January 16, 23; February 6, 20, 27; March 20; April 3, 10; June 19, 1909.

[5]Francis C. Kelley to James H. Blenk, Chicago, September 20, 1912. The Catholic Church Extension Society File, Records Center of the Archdiocese of New Orleans. Unless otherwise noted, all reports, brochures, and correspondence cited below are located in this file.

[6]"Souvenir of Your Visit to the Chapel Car 'St. Paul' . . ."

[7]*MS*, March 13, 20, 1916; and Catholic Church Extension Society File.

[8]E. B. Ledvina to F. L Gassler, [Chicago], January 24, 1916. Also, E. B. Ledvina to James H. Blenk, Chicago, July 7 [*sic*], 1917; E. B. Ledvina to J. B. Jeanmard, Chicago, August 15, 1917; Jules B. Jeanmard to E. B. Ledvina, [New Orleans], August 24 and September 26, 1917.

[9]*MS*, March 20, 1915.

[10]Baudier's source for this quotation has not been identified. On the Bunkie mission, see also, *MS*, April 3, 10, May 29, 1915. Father Alvah W. Doran was a priest of the Archdiocese of Philadelphia, not a Paulist. Paulist priests took charge of the car after the May 14 mission in Mansfield.

[11]After Bunkie, the car visited Sacred Heart Church in Alexandria, then went on to Cheneyville, Lecompte, Boyce, Colfax, Aloha, Montgomery, Robeline, and Mansfield where the mission closed on May 14, and Father Doran left the car. *MS*, May 29, 1915.

[12]*MS*, March 20,1915.

[13]E. B. Ledvina to James H. Blenk, Chicago, July 7 [*sic*], 1917; E. B. Ledvina to J. B. Jeanmard, Chicago, August 15, 1917; Jules B. Jeanmard to E. B. Ledvina, [New Orleans], August 24 and September 26, 1917. Jules B. Jeanmard to E. B. Ledvina, [New Orleans], September 26, 1917; includes a copy of the proposed itinerary.

[14]Report of Father A. B. Kalvelage, C.SS.R., Krotz Springs, October 14, 1917. "I left out entirely all references to difficulties that arose between pastors in the archdiocese and the Redemptorists who were in charge of the Car St. Paul. This arose from criticism contained in reports of the chaplains about conditions in some parishes . . . Bishop Jeanmard was Administrator at the time, and he cautioned the chaplains to be more discreet and judicious." (Baudier was generally hesitant to publicly criticize the local clergy.) Baudier to Rummel, New Orleans, [n.d. circa February, 1966], [BP, 1:19], AANO.

[15]Report of Father A. B. Kalvelage, C.SS.R., Lottie, La., October 23, 1917.

[16]Ibid., Blanks, La., October 31, 1917.

[17]Ibid., Livonia, La., November 13, 1917.

[18]Report of Father Joseph A. Girven, C.SS.R., Erwinville, La., November 27, 1917.

[19]Ibid.

[20]Ibid., Oscar, La., December 2, 1917.

[21]Ibid., Morrow, La., December 10, 1917.

[22]Ibid., Rosa, La., December 15, 1917.

[23]Ibid., Palmetto, La., December 23, 1917.

[24]Report of Father James H. Dreis, CSS.R., Melville, La., January 5, 1918.

[25]Ibid., Fordoche, La., January 13, 1918.

[26]Ibid., Morley, La., January 20,1918.

[27]Ibid., Addis, La., January 20, 1918.

[28]Ibid., Torras, La., February 5, 1918.

[29]Ibid., Lettsworth, La., February 10, 1918.

[30]Ibid., Batchelor, La., February 16, 1918.

[31]Ibid., Chamberlin, La., February 28, 1918.

[32]"Notice to Travelers Going to Heaven."

[33]E. B. Ledvina to John W. Shaw, Chicago, September 4, 1918; Jules B. Jeanmard to E. B. Ledvina, [New Orleans] September 10, 1918; E. B. Ledvina to Jules B. Jeanmard, Chicago, September 19, 1918.

[34]E. B. Ledvina to J. W. Shaw, Chicago, March 17, 1919; J. W. Shaw to E. B. Ledvina, New Orleans, March 21, 1919.

[35]"The material about use of the car *St. Paul* as a parish church for St. Leo the Great, I got from Father Prats years ago in long interviews that I had with him while he was at Hotel Dieu, when I was preparing to write the history of that parish." Roger Baudier to Joseph Rummel, New Orleans, undated [circa February 1, 1953]. [BP, 1:19]. The Chapel Car *St. Paul* later served in North Carolina and Oklahoma and was exhibited at the 1933 Chicago World's Fair. *The Grail* (August, 1933): 127. Copy in [BHC, 28:83]. AANO.

[36]B. J. Krieger, *Seventy-Five Years of Service* (New Orleans, 1923), 145-46.

DEFYING THE HAPLESS TWENTIES
(THE DIOCESE, 1919-1930)*

Hodding Carter and Betty Werlein Carter

The post-war decade of the 1920s was to be one of perilous disillusionment and decay throughout the United States of America. The ideals for which the nation had so well and willingly fought were dissipated at Versailles and, afterward, in American inertia and Europe's ancient hatreds and scheming. We turned away, disillusioned; yet how could the millennium for which the world had already waited nearly 2,000 years be ushered in by a few months of American participation in world affairs?

Few stopped to reason thus, and Church and State suffered. For the reaction was the Jazz Age.

The moral shock of world war contributed greatly to the increased number of divorces plaguing the American family. Chancellor J. Zach Spearing found the number of cases referred to him for canonical interpretation by parish priests increasing constantly. Did the canon permit or forbid the remarriage of certain individuals? The Prohibition amendment to the Constitution had brought, perversely, an increase in drunkenness. Woman's new status was evident in the national female suffrage amendment.

And many old standards of conduct became, for a time, derided antiquities.

Seemingly, the only verity was the dollar. The first post-war depression of 1922 was followed by the pseudo-prosperity which ended with the stock market crash of 1929. Speculation was as hard on the rural areas, where land values skyrocketed and then fell, as in the city markets. The great flood of 1927 brought more trouble to Louisiana. Most of the missionary area of the diocese was submerged. Churches were damaged and Churchmen saw their homes partly submerged in the Mississippi's grasping waters. The *Living Church* and the Presiding Bishop collected funds for the relief of the Church in Louisiana, and contributions were sent direct to Bishop Sessums.

Many individuals held true to their faith and their God. Because of them the Church in Louisiana continued to grow. But the pervasive atmosphere of the period was one of

*First published as Chapter 20 in *So Great A Good: A History of the Episcopal Church in Louisiana and of Christ Church Cathedral, 1805-1955* (Sewanee, Tenn.: University Press, 1955), 265-88. Reprinted with the kind permission of the copyright holder.

unbelief, cynicism, or lighthearted neglect of the soul. The courage of true Christians can be tested in such a time as well as in eras of physical persecution.

Within Louisiana, the Ku Klux Klan, cruel and cowardly distortion of the Reconstruction bands, brought strife and murder to the rural parts of the state, as it did in many and widely separated regions. Against this organized, powerful embodiment of mob rule the Reverend Alvin W. Skardon, missionary priest-in-charge of St. Andrew's in the Klan's stronghold of Mer Rouge, bore strong witness for the faith which teaches the brotherhood of man. Tendered a check for $100 by the Klan, the Reverend Mr. Skardon tore it up contemptuously; and, coming into the church for an early celebration of the Holy Communion, he faced his small congregation and said:

> There will be no service of the Holy Communion this morning. There is no Christian charity in your hearts and no peace in mine.

Turning, he left the church, its small band of worshippers brought to shame-faced realization of what Christianity had to mean.

The Church needed strong leadership at this period. The bishop was not able now to give it. By 1920 Bishop Sessums was 61 years old. The first period of his episcopacy had been brought to a close with his illness which caused a 19-month interruption of his work. The World War had caused another interruption of equal length. In the fall of 1920, the bishop's youngest son, Davis, a boy in his early 'teens, for whom the family had already had great concern because of a lung condition, was run over and fatally injured by an automobile. The death of the boy was a great shock to the aging man. Thereafter he took less interest in the boards, committees, campaigns and drives with which the diocese abounded. All were necessary, each had its place, but he could not regain the energy to direct and channel them.

Then, into what might have been a vacuum, moved a man whose whole life had been largely dedicated to the service of God and man. Able, intent, and autocratic, Warren Kearny gladly assumed most of the executive details of diocesan operation.

Mr. Kearny had been brought up in Trinity Parish, New Orleans, the son of a father who had also been a vestryman there. Watts Kearny, his father, took his two sons into partnership with him in his building materials firm. Early the other brother was placed in charge of the day-by-day operation of the family business, freeing Warren for the civic and church activities he loved.

In 1910 he was elected to the Standing Committee on which he then served continuously until his death in 1947, being named its secretary every year from 1916 on. As chairman of the Church Pension Fund Drive he had learned to work with clergy and laymen throughout the diocese. Preferably, Mr. Kearny served on committees as secretary; and in the 1920s he was secretary or chairman of almost every important committee in the diocese with the exception of the Board of Religious Education.

Much of Mr. Kearny's detailed knowledge of diocesan affairs came from his chairmanship of the Nation-wide Campaign. The Nation-wide Campaign broadened the concept of the Every Member Canvass. Instead of putting the emphasis on reaching every member in the parish alone, its very name emphasized that throughout the nation all Episcopalians were together facing their responsibilities for the total Church program. It was devised at about the same time that radical changes in the structure of the general Church were authorized.

These changes were passed at General Convention in 1919. Under new canons, the presiding bishop, on the death of Bishop Tuttle who was then serving, would be elected, rather than take office through seniority. A National Council was organized, putting under one roof various commissions and boards, making each a department of the Council. Thus the old Board of Missions came to an end like the other boards, taking on the new name of the Department of Missions. A new Department of Christian Social Relations was established. Some twenty years later the Louisiana diocese would pattern itself after this new structure and the "Bishop and Council" would then become the administrative cabinet of the diocese. In the meantime the sessions of the Diocesan Convention continued to be called the council.

Under the Nationwide Campaign plan devised by the old Board of Missions and then sponsored by the National Council, a Nation-wide Campaign Committee was named by each diocese in the Church. This committee was then charged with collecting all money for what the Church hoped to accomplish in the diocese as well as in the nation and abroad. The Church's Program, as it came to be called, was seen as one unit, whether administered by the diocese or the national Church.

For years the expenses of running the diocese had been apportioned to the parishes on the basis of a percentage of what each gave for its own expenses. A usual assessment was 11 percent of the parish budget. In the Nation-wide Campaign solicitation, the local budget, the diocesan budget, and the overriding Church's Program would all be explained.

An efficient person who ran the Nation-wide Campaign for the diocese would know in time what each parish and mission was spending, what the bishop and each agency of the diocese required, what each mission needed, what the Church hoped to accomplish. If less were collected than anticipated, the committee would have to decide which part of the program should not be slighted.

The bishop named the Reverend Alfred R. Berkeley of St. Paul's chairman of the diocesan committee, and Warren Kearny secretary.

The first Nation-wide Campaign in the Diocese of Louisiana was a tremendous success, though in that fall of 1919 only about half the churches actually participated.

The chairman, reporting to the 1920 convention that $35,000 had been pledged, said

> When we recall that total contributions for missionary endeavors at home and abroad have never exceeded $12,000 per annum, it will be seen that we have secured

pledges for three times that amount from only about one-half of the churches in the Diocese.

The *Living Church* rejoiced editorially that in the first year of the Nation-wide Campaign "the miracle of leveling mountains was wrought before our eyes."

There were resultant procedural changes in the diocese. The old days for special collections, with the exception of that for the Children's Home, were abolished in 1924. The Church Pension Fund and Nation-wide Campaign had superseded most of them. The Committee on Apportionment which functioned from 1908 to 1920, allocating the national missionary budget requirements to the Louisiana parishes, were discontinued. The time set aside annually at convention for pledging to diocesan mission needs was no longer scheduled. The diocesan Board of Missions told the Nation-wide Campaign what it would need, and its requirements were met from the campaign funds, as far as possible.

The first year of the Nation-wide Campaign, the diocese sent three-fourths of what it had collected for the Church's Program to the general Church. With one-fourth kept in the diocese, Louisiana not only gave its missionaries nearer to a living wage but also added a city missionary in New Orleans, built a new church for St. Nathaniel's mission at Melville, replacing one destroyed by storm, and expanded its educational program. The publicity and inspiration of the drive brought larger pledges for parochial needs. Christ Memorial at Mansfield, for instance, was able for the first time to call a rector of its own.

The diocesan mission funds also went to buy automobiles, where imperative, for the missionaries. The coming of passable roads had put the missionaries behind the steering wheel rather than riding a train or sitting on or behind a horse. In one case it meant closing a mission, St. Andrew's, Lindsey, for lack of roads leading to it.

Few new stations were opened but some long untended were reopened and many were given more regular and more frequent ministrations. Two were finally closed, St. Mary's, Bayou Goula, and St. John's, Laurel Hill. Their parishioners had died or moved away.

The bishop loved the missions and spent ever more time visiting them and the rural parishes. The regular meetings of the convocations, now for the first time held regularly, required more of his time.

In the mission activities of the diocese Mr. Kearny was to be his right-hand man. The entire clerical half of the diocesan Board of Missions changed in 1921, because of death or removals from the Diocese. The four new archdeacons were the Venerable E. N. Bullock, the Venerable J. D. Cummins, the Venerable J. M. Owens, and the Venerable W. S. Slack. Three of the five lay members served over an extended period: Warren Kearny from 1901 to 1942; George W. Law from 1908 to 1940; and R. P. Mead from 1914 to 1933.

In the diocese, the placing of the Reverend Caleb B. K. Weed as city missionary in New Orleans to minister in the hospitals and prisons and to transients re-opened a field of service dormant since the Reverend Mr. Bakewell had become incapacitated by age. In the automobile given him by the Woman's Auxiliary Mr. Weed was soon traveling 10,000 miles a year, almost entirely within the city limits.

The Auxiliary grasped the idea of Christian social relations faster than the diocese as a whole. Mrs. William Lamb, its first secretary of Christian Social Relations, saw to it that the Auxiliary gave Mr. Weed all the assistance he needed. Churchmen gradually came to realize that their service for the Red Cross and Community Chest, on the boards of welfare institutions and in civic and community agencies could be sacramental in nature. Mr. Weed and Mrs. Lamb were both to become active in the province's Department of Christian Social Relations.

Another fruit of the Nation-wide Campaign was that it gave the diocese enough funds to supplement what was contributed by individuals in Sewanee's Million Dollar Endowment Fund Drive so that the diocese met its quota in full and on time.

The Nation-wide Campaign provided the Board of Religious Education, as all other diocesan boards, with the funds it needed. And Louisiana was alone consistently to meet its full obligation to the provincial board.

While the Reverend Mr. Tucker headed the province's Department of Religious Education, the supervision of diocesan religious education became more and more the responsibility of the field secretary, Mrs. Fry. She held teacher training courses throughout the diocese, and in 1927 Louisiana was second only to Tennessee in the national Church in the number of teachers holding approved teachers' certificates. At St. Mark's, Shreveport, Mrs. Cooper Nelson, the first parochial director of religious education in the diocese, conducted a weekday school of religious education.

Mrs. E. A. Fowler, Mrs. Fry and Miss Alma Hammond started an Episcopal Teachers' Association in New Orleans in 1923 to train teachers for the Sunday Schools. Once a month during the eight months of the school year, the teachers met at different parishes for instruction by clergy and lay leaders. Soon other adults began coming.

In 1938 the schedule of classes would be changed to once a week for eight consecutive weeks in the fall and the instructional series would be designated as the School of Religion. This continues to the present.

A program of Christian service for the Sunday School scholars was co-ordinated by the Woman's Auxiliary. The Church School Service League was organized in the diocese in 1920, taking the place of the old Junior Auxiliary of the Woman's Auxiliary and including boys as well as girls in its program. This League had supervision of the Lenten Offering, the Birthday Thank Offering, the Little Helpers' Offering, and the Christmas box. Shortly, the Young People's Service League would take its place.

After its first impact, the Nation-wide Campaign was gradually to lose its appeal. The National Council asked for smaller parts of the total collected in the dioceses as the dioceses failed to meet the percentage expected. Within the diocese, with difficult times, the money contributed for the Church's Program had to be juggled. Decisions as to which diocesan missionaries should be placed where, which stations should be manned, had to be made. Mr. Kearny, the Nation-wide secretary, saw to it that the bishop's decisions were carried out. Annually, he made the report for the committee. He knew the facts, and had the time to study them.

During the decade and a little earlier some changes in canon and procedure were voted.

Part of the work formerly done by the treasurer of the diocese was turned over in 1918 to a new officer, the custodian of the trust funds of the diocese. H. E. Grice was to serve in this capacity from then until the reorganization of the administration of the diocese into Bishop and Council. An analysis of the funds which he received then showed the diocese had capital of $25,000 invested for the endowment of the episcopate: $14,000 in the Aged and Infirm Clergy Fund; $1,000 in the totally inadequate Widows and Orphans of Clergy Fund; $4,050 in the Goodrich Fund; and the two funds given by the Reverend E. Wallace Hunter.

In 1919 the date of the annual meeting was changed so that from 1920 on the council was held in January. Also, on motion of Mr. Kearny, the bishop was urged to consider having some sessions of the council elsewhere than New Orleans, in order to stimulate the parishes outside that city. By canonical revision it was ordered that henceforth each alternate session should be held outside the city. The place of meeting in New Orleans was at first left as Christ Church Cathedral. But later revisions removed this provision. The first council meeting anywhere but at Christ Church Cathedral in thirty-five years was held in 1922 at St. Mark's, Shreveport. The council would have met there a year earlier except that fire all but destroyed the church and it was not rebuilt in time for the council of 1921. The cost of transportation for the clergy to the Diocesan Council meetings was also assumed by the council for the first time at this council meeting. A year later canonical provision was also made for the travel of delegates to the General Convention, Provincial Synod, and meetings of the Board of Trustees of Sewanee, though funds were not always to be found for these purposes.

The Reverend Dr. Herman Cope Duncan was not to live to attend the out-of-city sessions which his committee on Canons put into canonical form. In 1917 he had retired from St. James', Alexandria, after thirty-seven years as its rector, the longest rectorate to date in the history of the diocese. At the council of 1920 he retired as secretary of the diocese, an office he had filled for forty-five of the past fifty years. At this, his last council meeting, wearied by the multiplicity of reports through which the council had to sit, he proposed that the old council committee on dispatch of business be re-instituted. This change was his last action as chairman of the Committee on Constitution and Canons. Bishop Sessums held the service and gave the address at his funeral in December. His death brought to a close the service of a second generation of a family connected with the diocese since its earliest days.

The Finance Committee became a more workable unit by reducing its size, a suggestion of T. J. Bartlette, its chairman. And a council committee on publicity, proposed by the Reverend Menard Doswell, Jr., was named in 1921. A motion for such a committee some 20 years earlier had then been defeated. The diocese had come, in the meantime, to realize the need of spreading the Word by every possible medium.

Charles W. Arny, prominent in the Brotherhood of St. Andrew and the Church Club, served for several years as business manager and editor of the *Diocese of Louisiana*, continuing for a short period as business manager only when the pressure of personal business made it impossible for him to continue as editor. The Reverend Sidney L. Vail, secretary of the diocese, took over its editorship and became managing editor shortly thereafter.

The Woman's Auxiliary had broadened in concept; it was no longer an auxiliary to the Board of Missions, but to the National Council, and so was interested in the work of the Church, and of the diocese as a whole. In many parishes it was to become the single parochial organization through which all work by women was channeled. However, in many, the Parish Aid and other local societies continued. In 1917, the Daughters of the King had been organized in the diocese with Miss Mary Levy as its first president. This remained, save for the Woman's Auxiliary, the only diocese-wide organization for women.

The primary missionary expansion of the diocese during these years was through two institutions, one of which, the Gaudet School, the diocese accepted as a gift; the other of which, the Student Center at Louisiana State University, was achieved through the vision of the Reverend Malcolm Lockhart of St. James', Baton Rouge.

The Gaudet Normal and Industrial School for Negro Boys and Girls was formally turned over to the diocese on March 14, 1921.

This school had been founded by Mrs. Frances A. Joseph-Gaudet, daughter of a lowly Protestant, Negro minister and an Indian mother. Mrs. Gaudet was born November 25, 1861, in Holmesville, near Summit, Mississippi. She lived with her first husband ten years. Because he drank heavily, they were legally separated and the then Mrs. Joseph, while supporting herself as a seamstress in New Orleans, began her work in the Women's Christian Temperance Union, becoming president of the Louisiana Negro chapter. Through this interest, she began to visit the prisons of New Orleans and found in them many adolescent boys awaiting trial. If guilty, these boys were sent to the boys' House of Refuge, and if innocent they were, of course, released. But in prison they heard and saw many things the young should not be exposed to. To protect colored boys and girls from these influences, she would have the judge put them in her custody. It was then that she dedicated her life to protecting outcast young Negro children.

In 1902 she founded the school which bears her name and that of her second husband. Already she was world-famous for her mission work in prisons. She had visited twenty-two prisons in the United States and had gone to Europe, bearing letters of introduction from the mayor of New Orleans to prison directors of England and the continent.

Early she won the backing of Mrs. T. G. Richardson. Some few questioned the propriety of Mrs. Richardson calling a meeting at which a Negro woman would be present. But so correctly did Mrs. Gaudet present her case that soon afterward an advisory board was formed of the most prominent people in New Orleans, including such Churchmen and women as Albert Baldwin, Mrs. Mary Henderson, Miss Sarah Henderson, Alfred LeBlanc, Mrs. Richardson and others.

There was talk in 1907 of the diocese assisting in the development of the school, but no concrete steps were then taken. The principal support of the school above the sacrifices and efforts of Mr. and Mrs. Gaudet came through the publicity given it by the *Times-Democrat.*

In 1911 the girls' dormitory was built and named in honor of the school's first patroness, Richardson Hall. In 1913 the three main buildings were added. By 1921, the school plant, four buildings on 105 acres of fertile soil at 4118 Gentilly Road, was estimated to be worth $100,000, and could accommodate 100 boarding students. In its last year of independent operation the school received $3,306 in revenues, of which $1,200 was given by the City of New Orleans for the support of children sent to the home by the judge of the juvenile court. On its advisory board then were such Churchmen as Robert H. Marr, George G. Westfeldt, and Alfred LeBlanc, its president for many years.

Mrs. Gaudet, a Methodist herself, decided to turn the school over to the Diocese of Louisiana because she wanted to be sure that there would be continuity in the management of the school.

Under the terms of the agreement, Mrs. Gaudet would have a room in the main cottage as long as she lived. The property could only be sold to further the purposes for which the institution was founded.

In this manner the Diocese of Louisiana undertook a new service for Negroes. It was to receive the assistance of the national Church, as it had through the years for St. Luke's, New Orleans. In the present instance, the help was to come from the American Church Institute for Negroes.

After the resignation of Mrs. Gaudet as principal because of her almost complete loss of sight, a succession of principals was placed in charge, several of them clergymen. A blacksmith taught his trade, a carpenter his. The boys at the school assisted the resident farmer in the truck gardening which produced vegetables for the dining hall and for sale. The girls were taught cooking, washing and sewing. Regular classroom subjects were taught.

The first board of trustees for the diocese consisted of the bishop, *ex officio,* and the Reverends A. R. Berkeley, Matthew Brewster, A. R. Edbrooke and, of the laity, Warren Kearny, Alfred LeBlanc, Walter Guion, William A. Bell, and G. G. Westfeldt.

In 1926 the Gaudet School was accepted as a member of the Community Chest. While some of the children were placed there by the city, others came as paying students. The religious character of the institution was emphasized after a fire had burned down the boys' dormitory in 1925, by the erection of a new building on whose first floor was an assembly room used for chapel and other purposes.

To look ahead, the history of the school, as such, was to end in 1954. Gaudet was not able to compete with the modern equipment and expanded curriculum available in the public schools. Despite determined efforts by the parents' organization which undertook to raise a large sum to meet the deficit in the costs of operation, it became obvious that the school would have to be closed.

But Mrs. Gaudet's work did not die. The cause to which she had dedicated herself for so many years was the welfare of Negro Children. After long hours of conference and study, the board decided that her prayers could best be fulfilled by developing the buildings as a group home for normal but neglected Negro children for whom there is no other provision in the city of New Orleans. From this home the children can be placed in foster homes. The protection and loving kindness with which Mrs. Gaudet wanted the boys and girls surrounded will be theirs, in fuller measure, through this change. The New Orleans Council of Social Agencies, which had long seen the need for a place to send such normal, non-delinquent children, endorsed heartily the new function of the Gaudet institution.

The 1920s were marked by an increase in emphasis on youth work. The importance of maintaining contact with the young people of the Church throughout their school years was thoroughly recognized. Thus the Board of Religious Education gave $300 a year to the Y.M.C.A. and Y.W.C.A. to keep in touch with Episcopal young people there and on youth work in the parish church.

In 1921, the Reverend J. S. Ditchburn came to St. Paul's, New Orleans, as curate. With enthusiasm and fresh energy, he founded a branch of the Young People's Service League which, in the fall of 1923 was organized as a diocesan body under the sponsorship of the Board of Religious Education. First officers of the Louisiana Y.P.S.L. were Edmund Thrash, president, Dorothy Foulkes, vice-president, and Richard Morse, secretary-treasurer. The strong New Orleans assembly was headed by John Gooch, with Dorothy Davis as vice-president, and Ruth Palfrey secretary-treasurer. In June, 1924, the organization held its first camp at Bay St. Louis with a total enrollment of 85.

Each successive camp was named for a Louisiana clergyman. By 1930 the Y.P.S.L. numbered 15 parish leagues with a membership of 300. Thus, the high school age group was organized for participation in Church activities.

Work with college students had long been carried on by St. James', Baton Rouge. With the removal of the university to its new location three miles from the old campus, the rector, Dr. Malcolm Lockhart, suggested to the vestry the need for an Episcopal center on the new campus. Such vestrymen as Dean Charles E. Coates, Col. A. T. Prescott and Pres. T. D. Boyd, members of the staff at the university, and such other Churchmen as J. Hereford Percy and C. Vernon Porter were in enthusiastic accord with the idea.

At the prompting of St. James', the diocese put $1,000 into its budget in 1925 to help St. James' expand its work with students. The Reverend Richard Baker, later Bishop Coadjutor of North Carolina, was chosen by the vestry as curate for this work. However, the diocese was unable to give this money, and though the council of 1926 endorsed building a student center on the campus, the work among the students continued entirely at the expense of the local parish.

St. James' went ahead, however, and by 1927 it had secured pledges of $10,000. Then, a committee appointed in 1923 by the bishop and headed by Dr. Coupland proceeded to raise and borrow the rest of the required $50,000. The Woman's Auxiliary made the first pledge, $1,000, to the diocesan fund. The state legislature passed, in July 1928, the necessary legislation, leasing the diocese a 200 by 200 foot plot on the campus. That November was begun the construction of the first Episcopal student center in the province and the first owned by any communion in Louisiana. Of the same type Spanish provincial architecture as the rest of the university buildings, it consists primarily of an auditorium, a chapel, and, on the second floor, an apartment for the student pastor.

The Reverend Mr. Ditchburn became in 1930 the first student pastor, serving until 1949. St. James' had made the center possible. The building was named in honor of the bishop in whose episcopate it was constructed, the Davis Sessums Memorial.

The center in the years that were to follow would more than prove itself as a point of continuing contact with the youth of the Church. From among the young men who took part in its campus life were to come twelve priests in its first twenty-six years: Ivenson B. Noland, to be Suffragan Bishop of Louisiana; Skardon D'Aubert, Julius Pratt, John Womack, Harry Tisdale, Frank Wall Robert, J. Philson Williamson, Edwin C. Coleman, James Douglass, James M. Barnett, John Stone Jenkins and Balfour Patterson; and Carey Womble, a medical missionary in Puerto Rico.

It is interesting that part of the costs of building the center were met through sale of one of the oldest diocesan missions, Trinity Chapel, New Orleans.

Although other priests had served the chapel after the death of the Reverend A. G. Bakewell on February 22, 1920, its days were really numbered with his passing. By then few could look back to the time when the tall soldier-priest had been a layman, in business and wealthy enough to provide the first warehouse in which the Children's Home was housed. When, in 1930, the chapel was condemned as unsafe because of termite infestation, the council voted to sell the property rather than rebuild. This was done, and part of the proceeds were turned over to the center committee.

Thus, through the Davis Sessums Student Center, Trinity Chapel lives on.

At the end of the 1920s, the Children's Home, which had long been looked on as diocesan property, was officially turned over to the Diocese of Louisiana. Children's Home Chapters spread in the 1920s throughout the diocese, thereby augmenting donations by the New Orleans churches, individuals, and the Community Chest. But not until November 30, 1929, was the Home actually turned over to the official ownership of the diocese.

Henry M. Allen, who had been serving as treasurer and to whom had been entrusted the many details of the improvement of the building during the past decade, was selected by the bishop to continue as treasurer of the diocesan Board of Managers. With the bishop as *ex officio* chairman, the Reverend R. S. Coupland, D.D., was named vice-chairman and the Reverend Nicholas Rightor, chaplain. On the board were the Reverend Edward F. Hayward, the Reverend James M. Owens, D.D., the Reverend W. E. Vann,

Jeff D. Hardin, Rollo C. Jarreau, Archie M. Smith, Chris Stander, Mrs. George A. Wiegand, president of the Children's Home Guild, Mrs. Alonzo Church, president of the United Chapter (which supervised the actual manual details of improving things at the home), and Miss Alice Parkerson, then social service secretary of the Woman's Auxiliary.

Just as the multiplicity of activities and committees in the parishes caused the earlier need for parish houses, a business headquarters for the diocese was now obviously required. The bishop had his office in the See House next to the cathedral, to which came his secretary to attend to his correspondence. Each board kept its papers wherever its secretary and treasurer wished. The Board of Religious Education was the first to need formal offices, which were procured in 1925. But it was apparent that all needed headquarters. The old Diocesan House on Carondelet Street had been rented as a family home since the closing of the school for deaconesses, and its location then seemed too far removed from the downtown offices of the businessmen who made up the committees; so diocesan headquarters were established in the Louisiana Building in the business section in 1926.

In earlier days, rectories and parish houses had been the principal new building requirements of the parish churches. In the 1920s church edifices, outgrown and antiquated, were replaced. Fire forced the rebuilding of St. Mark's, Shreveport, and the Church of the Good Shepherd, Lake Charles. The Reverend Mr. Slack designed and supervised construction of a new St. James', Alexandria. And the Episcopal Church came back at last to Canal Street in 1920, after an absence of 36 years. Grace Church, New Orleans, quitted its quarters on Rampart Street and under the Reverend Mr. Edbrooke built on Canal and Marais. The Church of the Annunciation under the Reverend Mr. Vail moved closer to its parishioners and built on South Claiborne and Jena.

Smaller churches were also raised, among them St. Timothy's, Eunice; St. Matthew's, Bogalusa; and Christ Church, Slidell. St. George's mission, St. Philip's, finally built its church, at Henry Clay and Chestnut. And at Bayou du Large, members of the congregation built their chapel in 1922 with their own hands.

Two events were to have a profound effect on the spiritual life of the diocese. One was the meeting of the General Convention in New Orleans in 1925. The other was the Bishops' Crusade of 1927.

Many good Louisiana Episcopalians began their spring flower planting earlier in 1925 than did their neighbors. Moreover, they showed preference for two colors, the purple of ageratum, wild heliotrope, tiny Michaelmas daisies and asters, and the gold of cosmos and zinnias. These were the glorious colors to be used at the General Convention which in October was to meet in New Orleans, the only Triennial ever held south of Richmond, Virginia. Six years before the actual gathering in New Orleans, preparation for the 48th General Convention began when, at the annual meeting of the diocesan Church Club, its president, F. H. G. Fry, suggested that the men give serious thought to inviting the 1925 Triennial to Louisiana.

The council of 1922 passed overwhelmingly a supporting resolution presented by the Church Club. Then, prior to the General Convention in Portland, Oregon, a committee headed by the Reverend Dr. Coupland wrote every Southern diocese asking cooperation. Bishop Sessums wrote an invitation in rhyme. The official invitation was formally presented by the bishop and Archdeacon Slack on the respective floors. The General Convention voted to come to New Orleans.

Immediately thereafter Bishop Sessums appointed an executive committee with Warren Kearny as general chairman, and Mrs. James McBride, president of the Woman's Auxiliary, as head of the Women's Advisory Committee. General Convention Headquarters were set up in the Commercial Building on Canal Street, with the Woman's Auxiliary offices in the same suite. Mrs. McBride moved temporarily to New Orleans from Houma, and enlisted the aid of 400 women. The Finance Committee, led by L. M. Pool, quickly raised the $32,000 needed to meet expenses of the convention. Mr. Fry as chairman of the Committee on Halls was to oversee all details connected with the convention halls, from procuring the meeting places themselves to providing the thumb tacks for the bishops' desks and the sanitary drinking cups by the water coolers.

The General Convention met on October 7, 1925, at the Athenaeum on St. Charles Avenue; the Woman's Auxiliary at the nearby Jerusalem Temple.

The Bienville Hotel at Lee Circle was headquarters for the National Council, administrative heads of the Church and its departments. But lodging for 2,200 delegates and 2,500 interested visitors also had to be provided. The Very Reverend J. D. Cummins headed the Committee on Hotels, T. J. Bartlette the Committee on Registration and J. D. Hardin and Edgar Mouton the Committee on Transportation. Mrs. A. R. Pierson and her diocesan Woman's Auxiliary's Hospitality Committee worked for practically eight months checking the suitability and price of accommodations offered in private homes.

Mrs. George Williams organized the Motor Corps which met the trains, took the guests to their lodgings, to the services, to the meetings, to the diocesan reception at the New Orleans Country Club, to the regatta and tea at the Southern Yacht Club. So well was the corps organized that in less than an hour it transported 1,200 visitors from the Jerusalem Temple to the steamboat landing at Canal Street for a boat ride.

The Committee on Publicity headed by Clem G. Hearsey worked so closely with the Publicity Department of the National Council that the newspapers of New Orleans and of the United States printed nearly 50 percent more news of this convention than had ever been provided for any previous one. Mrs. George F. Wharton headed the committee of the Woman's Auxiliary which prepared the Convention Issue of the *Diocese of Louisiana* with brief histories of every parish in the diocese.

Mrs. F. J. Foxley, vice-president of the diocesan Auxiliary, arranged the entertainment of the Negro delegates. At the General Convention and at the meetings of the national Auxiliary these delegates sat with the delegations from their dioceses as always. At the close of each day's sessions sightseeing busses waited to take them to the Gaudet School for tea. Mrs. Foxley's handling of the problems involved in their entertainment and housing in a deep Southern city was described by Mrs. McBride as having been done "with a tact and understanding that virtually made history and paved the way for future conventions here and elsewhere."

Mrs. F. H. G. Fry was chairman of the committee on places of meetings and services for the Woman's Auxiliary; Mrs. Matthew Brewster planned for the afternoon teas; Mrs. William Lamb was charged with registration and checking; Mrs. Gustaf Westfeldt had encouraged the planting of the flower gardens and her committee assembled the flowers with which the arrangements in the two convention halls were made.

Mrs. McBride was elected by the Woman's Auxiliary of the host Province of Sewannee to preside at all sessions of the national Auxiliary.

The business sessions of the General Convention began at 3 p.m. on October 7, exactly 140 years after the end of the first General Convention in Old Christ Church, Philadelphia. For three weeks the entire Episcopal establishment was centered in New Orleans. From the Arctic Circle, the jungles of Africa, and tropical South America, from China, Japan and the Philippines, the bishops and other servants of the Church throughout the world gathered here to make decisions by which the next three years could bring closer the Kingdom of God.

Louisiana's deputies for this General Convention were the Reverend R. S. Coupland, the Reverend A. R. Berkeley, the Reverend W. S. Slack, the Reverend J. M. Owens, Warren Kearny, J. Zach Spearing, R. P. Mead and F. H. G. Fry. The alternates were the Reverend S. L. Vail, the Reverend C. B. K. Weed, the Reverend G. L. Tucker, the Reverend Matthew Brewster, D.D., and J. L. Caillouet, E. G. Palmer, Dr. J. N. Thomas and George W. Law.

The convention would decide that a bride would no longer have to promise to obey; that Bishop Brent of Western New York was right in asking that the Protestant Episcopal Church have fuller membership in the Federal Council of Churches in several of whose commissions it was already participating; that a budget of $4,500,000 for the triennium should be trimmed to proportions more acceptable to some of the delegates. The Right Reverend Ethelbert Talbot, the presiding bishop, would utter the formal decree deposing the aged Bishop of Arkansas, the Right Reverend William Montgomery Brown, from the ministry for heresies. The convention would for the first time elect its presiding bishop, choosing for this highest office the Right Reverend John Gardner Murray, Bishop of Maryland, in a vote which was a triumph for the High Church wing of the Church. The United Thank Offering of the Women of the Church would be $909,813.50, of which the Louisiana Auxiliary would give $14,048.

But on the morning of October 7, the principal question was: Would it rain? The reason for such anxiety was that under the great live oak trees in Audubon Park which came together to form a vast natural cathedral the General Convention was to meet in its first open air service.

The morning broke clear and warm, so warm that the 10,000 people who gathered in the park were glad of the programs which could serve them as fans. So warm that the women of the diocese who had carefully placed 2,000 stuffed eggs in the lunch boxes for delegates who might want to picnic after the service removed them just as carefully, and more hurriedly.

But that was behind the scenes.

What the mighty assemblage saw and heard and experienced was a profoundly moving service of praise and thanksgiving to Almighty God. Here, under the oaks which had led to the De Boré plantation where sugar was first successfully made in Louisiana, history of another kind was being made.

From a distance could be heard the sound of a trumpet. Soon it was joined by a second. And then the waiting multitude standing under the moss draped trees heard the first words of the hymn, *Onward Christian Soldiers*. Down the central aisle came first the crucifer and cross, and then the combined choirs of all the parishes in the diocese, led by the Reverend Dr. Coupland, who was chairman of arrangements for the service, and W. S. Cudlipp, choir director of St. George's. As the first of the 300 choir members reached the raised platforms on either side of the wading pool, they turned and stopped to form a lane through which the bishops marched to their appointed places on the tiered seats. The hymn changed. Now the choristers sang *The Son of God Goes Forth to War*. Slowly the secretaries of the two houses, the Reverend Charles L. Pardee, D.D., of the House of Bishops and the Reverend Carroll M. Davis, D.D., of the House of Deputies marched between the singers, the American flag carried behind them. And then came the bishops of the Church in stately array, 130 strong, in black, purple and white. They, like the deputies and the thousands who had come from the farthest places of the world, from the smallest parishes of the diocese, from the proudest and poorest homes of the city, would all kneel together in general confession.

The first words of the first service of the General Convention were read aloud:

> From the rising of the sun even unto the going down of the same my Name shall be great among the Gentiles; and in every place incense shall be offered unto my Name, and a pure offering: for my Name shall be great among the heathen, saith the Lord of hosts.

The Convention sermon was to have been delivered by Bishop Bratton of Mississippi. But the night before he had been taken to the hospital and his address was read by Bishop Gailor of Tennessee, president of the National Council, whose clear tones were carried far with the help of amplifiers, a modern innovation.

The service came to a close with the second recessional hymn, *Stand up, Stand up, for Jesus*.

That morning the two Houses had held Corporate Communion at Christ Church Cathedral. The next day the Woman's Auxiliary would present the United Thank Offering at Trinity Church. It was to be used for a chapel and gymnasium at the mission school in Hankow, China, to help St. Agnes's School in Kyoto, Japan, and to keep the Auxiliary's many women missionaries at work in the field.

That afternoon the deliberations of the bodies began.

During the period of the convention the great preachers of the Church spoke in the parish churches of the diocese, bringing new zeal to those who could not attend the convention as deputies.

Not only did the convention quicken the interest of the Church in the Diocese of Louisiana but it was an especial inspiration also to all the Southern dioceses, which thereby felt closer to the general work of the Church.

The funds raised for the convention were so skillfully handled by the chairman, Mr. Kearny, the finance chairman, Mr. Pool, and the treasurer, C. S. Williams, that $7,000 was left after expenses of the convention were paid. Five thousand dollars of this were used to meet the full quota of Louisiana to the Nation-wide Campaign, thereby putting the diocese on the Roll of Honor. The rest was allocated by the bishop to help build the churches at Ponchatoula and Bogalusa, to restore the church at Ruston, to repair several rectories, and for use as needed by the Diocesan Board of Missions.

The Triennial was held at the same time that in Locarno, Switzerland, the Western powers were hammering out a pact which, it was hoped, would mean peace for many years to come. Surveying the world in which the Church of God prayed that the spirit of love might hold sway, the bishops prepared their pastoral letter which was read on the final day of the convention by Bishop Manning. It spoke of storm warnings in the East and forecast "racial conflicts greater and more disastrous than any this earth has yet known" unless there be found a "power strong enough to bind men together in world brotherhood."

The Bishops' Crusade was an evangelistic campaign throughout the Church.

All diocesan clergy save five were present at the Crusade planning meeting held the last week in November 1926. Then came special services in the diocese on St. Andrew's Day with continuous prayers throughout the day. In some parishes, neighborhood group meetings for prayer and study were held. The week from January 9 to 16 was set aside as Intensive Week, with daily celebrations of the Holy Communion culminating on Friday with continuous intercessions.

The Crusade itself was inaugurated in the Louisiana diocese on Sunday afternoon, January 23, with a meeting for young people at Christ Church Cathedral. After that, for six successive evenings the cathedral was crowded to capacity, several hundred people having to be turned away because not even standing space was available. The crusaders who came into the diocese to preach and teach the usefulness of life in the service of God were the Right Reverend Frederick B. Howden, D.D., Bishop of New Mexico, the Reverend Robert N. Spencer, rector of Grace and Holy Trinity Church, Kansas City, and Thomas Q. Dix, of St. Louis. Bishop Howden held the night services, Mr. Spencer the afternoon conferences, and Mr. Dix the supper conferences. The combined choirs of the city, 200 strong, sang at the Sunday mass meetings, and on the intervening nights these choirs alternated in groups of two. The great singing of the Crusaders' Hymn "in procession" as sung in English cathedral pilgrimages was acclaimed one of the most inspiring features of the Crusade.

At the closing service on Friday night, just before Bishop Howden's final sermon, the chairman of the diocesan committee, the Reverend Dr. Coupland, summoned to the chancel all those who had volunteered to take the evangelistic message throughout the parishes as diocesan crusaders. Here Bishop Sessums gave them a ringing charge, and then the crusaders, kneeling, received his blessing. At the conclusion of Bishop Howden's sermon, the crusader struck the keynote of the Crusade by calling upon the congregation to stand up with him and renew their baptismal vows.

The diocesan crusaders, as a great regiment in the army of the Lord, went forth on the following Sunday and for several weeks thereafter, carrying the Crusade throughout the diocese.

In only one parish and mission in the diocese was the Crusade not held. Just as the crusaders were about to board the train to go to Bogalusa a message was received that the church had been so badly damaged by wind storm that it could not be used.

The Crusade was to have its effect not only in the private lives of those who participated. From then on, the diocese was to have a committee on evangelism, to see that its spirit did not die.

Without the publicity which accompanied the Bishop's Crusade and the meeting of General Convention in New Orleans, and both as a stimulant to spiritual life and because of it, the period just before the opening of the 1920s marked the beginning of a weekly prayer group which for over 37 years would offer prayers for the healing of the sick on every Friday afternoon in the year except Good Friday. This oldest continuous prayer group in the nation continues still.

In November 1918, two friends, Mrs. Frederick Foxley and Mrs. Charles O. Elmer, met daily for a week in St. George's Church, New Orleans, to pray for the healing of a mutual friend, a young woman who had developed epilepsy so that her mind was as that of a little child. At the end of this week of prayer a priest of the English Church who was in New Orleans, Father Gain Duffy, suggested that the sick woman be taken to church and have the "Laying on of Hands." When Father Duffy placed his hands on her head and demanded the evil spirits depart, in the name of Christ, she fell to the floor in the worst convulsion she had ever had. The women feared she was dying. But from that moment she began to improve and, her mind returning, she resumed her active life in the world, cured.

Other women joined the first two and with Bishop Sessums's permission weekly meetings were begun in Christ Church Cathedral. The women got in touch with the Reverend Henry B. Wilson, founder of the Society of the Nazarene, in Mountain Lakes, New Jersey. As a branch of this society, the intercessory prayers were continued. Later, when the Society of the Nazarene's national headquarters were dissolved, the new name of the Cathedral Intercessory Prayer Group was adopted.

In addition to the weekly prayers at the cathedral, the group was later to organize its membership so as to have women available at a moment's notice to accept requests for immediate prayers for those in critical condition. The names of those for whom prayers are desired are sent in from all over the United States.

The leaders of the intercessory group—only three in its 37 years—have been Mrs. Foxley, Mrs. William Nes, whose husband, the dean of the cathedral, had been active in Maryland in the healing mission of the Church, and Mrs. Donald Everett MacDonald.

Mrs. Foxley, president of the diocesan Woman's Auxiliary when the prayer group was organized, later attributed the fact that the Auxiliary went through the war years without loss of membership of diminution of funds as a sign of the power of prayer.

The diocese, through the grace of God and with the help of His servants, weathered one of the most worldly decades in the history of the nation.

But the diocese too had had its unsavory moments.

The erratic Mr. Hunter, rector of St. Anna's, had become more and more original in his interpretation of the rubrics and dogma of the Church. Finally, he left the ministry of the Church, asked for and was given the money in two funds he had established in 1905, and precipitately announced that the parish church owed him some $18,000 for which he held a mortgage. To save the historic church, in which Bishop Sessums had been elected bishop, and the only Episcopal Church below Canal Street, from going on the public auction block, the bishop and Mr. Kearny borrowed the money in the name of the diocese to pay the court judgment, and the parish became a mission.

In 1929 the diocese was forced to hold its first ecclesiastical court. Charges of immorality were brought against the Reverend Francis Van R. Moore, former assistant rector of Trinity, New Orleans. After a trial of several weeks he was found guilty of only one of the five charges and sentenced to a year's suspension. The court consisted of the Reverend R. R. Diggs, New Iberia, president; the Reverend Walter Lennie-Smith, retired diocesan missionary; the Reverend A. R. Price, the Reverend E. F. Hayward, and the Reverend C. E. Shaw, Covington. Mr. Spearing, the chancellor, was the prosecutor.

At Christ Church, Bastrop, on December 22, 1929, Bishop Sessums celebrated the Holy Communion in the morning, and at 7:30 that Sunday evening confirmed five candidates and preached. These were the last episcopal acts of the man who had been Bishop of Louisiana for thirty-eight years.

Two days later, on Christmas Eve at 4:30 in the afternoon, there came from the See House the unbelievable news that he had died of a stroke. The bishop who had confirmed most of the Episcopalians in the diocese had been gathered to the Church Expectant. The diocese he had guided for two-fifths of its life would have to seek another shepherd.

The Standing Committee on that sad Christmas Eve called into session by its president, the Reverend Dr. Coupland, asked Bishop Gailor of Tennessee, who had presented the episcopal ring to his friend Bishop Sessums in 1892, to take charge of all arrangements for the funeral. Bishop Gailor was assisted by Bishop Bratton of Mississippi. Bishop H. J. Mikell of Atlanta and Bishop Coadjutor William Mercer Green of Mississippi were to participate in the service. The date of the funeral was set for Friday, December 27, at 11 A.M. The place was to be the church Bishop Sessums had made his cathedral.

The clergy of the diocese, the lay members of the Standing Committee, the chancellor and the wardens of the parishes and missions were honorary pallbearers. The active pallbearers were the clerical members of the Standing Committee and the archdeacons of the diocese. Following the funeral service in Christ Church Cathedral some 150 automobiles drove in the funeral cortege to Metairie cemetery.

Not for many years had the diocese held an election for a bishop. No member of the Louisiana clericus in the diocese in 1930 had been present for the election of Bishop Sessums in 1891. No delegate to the sessions that year had been a delegate when the coadjutor was sought. The procedure of election was explained in the constitution of 1898. What did it say?

During the years since its adoption, the laity had become ever more prominent in the government of the Church. To the surprise of clergy and laity alike the articles of incorporation very clearly provided, as had the constitution of 1838, that clergy and laity should meet in separate bodies, the clergy to elect the bishop, and the laity only to confirm or not confirm the clerics' choice. Other surprises came to light. Certain parishes — the Church of the Nativity at Rosedale, Trinity at Natchitoches, and Christ Church, St. Joseph, missions as far back as man could remember — were permitted by the canons the same number of delegates they had had in 1895 — as many as the large self-supporting parishes were entitled to. It was too late to change the provisions before the election; but a commission was named by the Ecclesiastical Authority to study and make revisions of the charter, constitution and canons, article by article.

The regular meeting met in Baton Rouge on March 12, 1930. The opening session was held at the Student Center, and then the clergy organized separately at St. James'. After eleven ballots the clergy had elected as bishop, the laity concurring, the Reverend Charles Clingman, D.D., rector of the Church of the Advent, Birmingham, Alabama. Many Louisianians had heard and met him at General Convention in New Orleans.

But the Reverend Mr. Clingman did not then accept the election to the episcopate. In 1936 he became Bishop of Kentucky.

A special session was called at St. James', Alexandria, for May 14, 1930. The Reverend Matthew Brewster, who was elected president of the Standing Committee on the resignation of Dr. Coupland, presided. On the first ballot of the Right Reverend James Craik Morris, D.D., Missionary Bishop of the Panama Canal Zone, was elected Bishop of Louisiana.

Bishop Morris accepted the invitation, but asked to be permitted to attend the Lambeth Conference as he had earlier planned. The Service of Institution was therefore postponed until the Feast of St. Simon and St. Jude, October 28, 1930, when it took place at Christ Church Cathedral, at eleven in the morning followed by Holy Communion at which he was celebrant. Bishop Gailor of Tennessee, chancellor of the University of the South, preached.

LOUISIANA BAPTISTS AND THE SCOPES TRIAL*

Wallace Hebert

An event of great importance to Louisiana Baptists occurred during the period between July 10 and July 21, 1925, in Dayton, Tennessee. John T. Scopes was tried under the Tennessee anti-evolution law of March 13, 1925. His trial attracted nationally known personalities such as Clarence Darrow, Dudley Field Malone, and Arthur Garfield Hays for the defense and William Jennings Bryan for the prosecution. Also present were countless experts, acknowledged and self-appointed. Dayton became a showcase for the extremists, and circus tactics prevailed even in the courtroom.[1] The Dayton trial was to involve Louisiana Baptists more intensely in the issues surrounding the evolution question and spur them into public action. In particular, it would direct the interest of Louisiana's Baptist congregations to the specific problem of evolutionary theories in textbooks, and would ultimately lead to a declaration by the Louisiana Baptist Convention to the State Board of Education and to a campaign for state legislation.

The issues of the trial were carried to the public mainly through newspapers, with 2,310 daily and 13,627 weekly papers providing details of the proceedings.[2] The *New Orleans Times Picayune* carried a series of articles on historical evolution reconciling the scriptural account with the theories of science.[3] Some pastors of that city took a different view. The Reverend W. A. Jordan of the Central Baptist Church announced two consecutive sermons, "The Alive, Active, and Age-Abiding Bible," and "The Final Issue," centered on the Scopes trial for the Sundays of July 12 and July 19, 1925.[4] The *Times Picayune* of July 18, 1925, stated that the Reverend L. T. Hastings of the Coliseum Place Baptist Church would preach a sermon in which certain phases of the evolution trial would be touched upon. Hastings' sermon was entitled "Jesus' Theology Versus Jungle Theology," and in it he stated that the "Book of Natural Science" and the Bible were both inspired of God. Although much was being written in an effort to sunder them, no conflict could arise, "else God would be at variance with himself." Hastings further asserted that not everything that postured as science was worthy of the name, and that "not a single established fact of science" contradicted the Bible.[5] Hastings was far from conciliatory as he dealt with the issues of the trial. "Darrow, Malone, and Hays, Inc.," together with all other agnostics, skeptics, freethinkers, and Darwinites, he asserted, should be

*First published in *Louisiana Studies*, 7 (1968): 329-46. Reprinted with the kind permission of the publisher.

reminded of a passage in the writings of Paul referring to false teachers who, "thinking themselves wise, became as fools," and who altered the glory of an "incorruptible God into an image like to a corruptible man, to birds, and four-footed beasts and creeping things."[6] The conclusion was that the evolutionists' theology was the theology of the "jungle, plunging the race into hopelessness, despair, doubt, darkness, without God and without hope in the world to come."[7]

In the editorial sections of Louisiana newspapers, meanwhile, the trial and Baptists' attitudes toward it were not being ignored. In an editorial entitled "Baptists Deny Evolution," the *Bogalusa Enterprise and American* stated "its best exponents admit that the causes of the origin of species have not been traced."[8] The *Farmerville Gazette* in an article covering a speech by Shreveport Mayor L. E. Thomas, a prominent Baptist layman, reported that Thomas argued that all men accept the idea of beginning in time and the corollary idea that the universe must have had creation. Thus, if God could make the universe, who could deny Him the right to create man in His own image?[9] The *Gazette* also stated that the Bible was too deeply rooted in America "for the tree to disease and die because a small gnat of an agnostic lights on its branches."[10]

The *Baptist Message*, like other state religious periodicals, generally depended on news articles and regular newspaper coverage of the trial for detailed accounts of the proceedings.[11] Editorially, the *Message* took note of the trial even before it began. In a guest editorial of June 18, 1925, the Scopes trial was regarded as a battle to answer the question, "Is the Bible correct, or did man evolve from the monkey?" At Dayton, "paganism and materialism are being weighed in the balance and found wanting."[12] This view that the trial was to be conclusive, a vindication of the wrath and judgment of God, shortly gave way to the realization among Louisiana observers that little was going to be accomplished in Dayton. Even so, the Scopes trial bathed the issues in enough publicity to force expression of all shadings of opinion.

In a guest article in the *Baptist Message* of July 9, 1925, Dr. M. E. Dodd, a prominent Shreveport minister, penned one of the most complete expressions of articulate fundamentalism by a Louisiana Baptist. Entitled "Evolution or Creation, Which?" Dr. Dodd's article divided evolutionary theory into two aspects. The first, a God-directed evolution which placed God as a sort of prime mover, had a certain number of adherents in the Baptist faith. The second, based on the Newtonian framework and its laws of the conservation of matter and energy, postulated that matter was self-perpetuating and changed within itself. Viewed as a basically atheistic or at best agnostic system, this second alternative was the target of Dr. Dodd's arguments. Scientists who accepted this theory would "deny the hand of God a place anywhere along the line and revel in . . . Materialism."[13]

Evolutionary theory, Dodd charged, did not "harmonize itself with the observable facts of nature," failed to answer the thousands of questions that arose, and resulted in a "brutal, beastly, and devilish view of life and of living." Dodd's insistent theme was that Darwinian evolution simply created more problems that it could ever hope to solve. Life, when left to itself, "descends rather than ascends." Observing that hybrids failed to re-produce and that evolutionists had failed to produce a missing link, Dodd asked why does not man continue to evolve? Why are there no evidences of animals having become men? Why have certain species never improved? Finally, evolution established the most "inordinately selfish" principles of life and living.[14]

Dodd then commented on the conflict between the Darwinian principle of the strug-gle for existence and Christian altruism. "If it can be shown," he said, "that any living species does something simply for the sake of another, evolution will be discredited." Quoting Herbert Spencer's statement, "If God is admitted in one place, we had as well admit Him in all," Dodd turned to his affirmative case. In Genesis, the word "created" meant made out of nothing, he said, and it was used in the very places scientists agreed there was a huge gap; therefore, the only missing link man needed were the words "and God created."[15]

The first issue of the *Baptist Message* after the beginning of the trial featured an edi-torial entitled "The Dayton Trial and the Daily Press." It charged that the daily papers and the "evolution crowd" were treating the trial as if the entire fate of evolutionary the-ory and of the Bible were to be determined. Although the *Message* had taken much the same stand in its editorial of June 18, it now stated: "Whether the case goes on the Su-preme Court or is settled in the district court, conditions will be the same as before." The trial could only decide if the Tennessee law should be obeyed.[16] Further, only an "evolu-tionist crank" would deny to the citizens of Tennessee the right to protect their children, and it was predicted that the trial would be watched with interest by the people of the United States and would be followed by the enactment of similar laws in other states. Special invective was reserved for the daily press, which was accused by an editorial en-titled "The Evolution Case Is Closed" of an attempt to "ridicule the evolution law out of countenance before the public." In this campaign, radical evolutionists had the "full backing and cooperation of the Hearst news agencies." The editorial contended, how-ever, that most observers would recognize the journalistic fraud and be "aware of the wiles of the enemy and not be moved by cheap propaganda."[17]

The July 30 *Baptist Message* also printed a guest sermon by Mayor L. E. Thomas of Shreveport. After calling the Dayton events "unparalleled in the history of our country," he declared that the enemies of the Bible were "filling the daily press with their damnable declarations relating to God's Word and its infallible teachings." Baptist leaders were thus very much aware of the role the newspapers had in portraying the trial and in shap-ing public opinion. There seems to have been considerable fear on the part of Baptist spokesmen that H. L. Mencken and other persuasive Hearst writers would penetrate the fundamentalist phalanx.

The personalities of the trial received, usually, more attention than their causes. Pro-evolutionists might claim that William Jennings Bryan was a "broken old man, champion of lost causes and pathetic again in his mischoice of an issue,"[18] but Louisiana Baptists saw him as "one who met the enemies of God with unanswerable truth."[19] As for Darrow, no vilification was too stringent, and Baptist writers reached new heights in invective while attempting to find suitable adjectives for him. He was a "blatant atheist and ridiculer of the scriptures, and his compatriot in evil," Malone, had a personal grudge against Bryan.[20] Richard Edmunds, a Louisiana Baptist, in August of 1925 stated that the "whole trial was a travesty, purely a publicity-seeking scheme of publicity seekers."[21] Louisiana Baptists seem to have confused the personalities and the issues of the trial, making a complete identification of Darrow and Bryan with their respective positions.

In a proclamation which appeared in the *Baptist Message* of August 13, 1925, the members of the New Hope Baptist Church in Independence, Louisiana, claimed to be reliably informed that "textbooks teaching evolution are being taught at Louisiana College," a Baptist institution, and at the state-supported institutions of learning. The doctrine of evolution, claimed the church, was a dangerous teaching among "civilized people." The teaching of evolution in any of the public schools of Louisiana was condemned "for the reason that the evolutionary theory is in direct contradiction to the teachings of the Bible." Other churches, associations, and religious assemblies in the state were urged to pass resolutions memorializing the state legislature at its 1926 session to enact laws proscribing the teaching of evolution. Evolutionary theories were held to cause "unbelief and infidelity in generations yet unborn." Two parish associations, the Vernon Missionary Baptist Association and the Acadia Baptist Association, in their summer sessions passed resolutions against the teaching of evolution in colleges and secondary schools.[22]

The drive was to culminate at the state convention to be held in Winnfield, Louisiana, November 17-19, 1925. Some three years before, a committee had been appointed to investigate for the convention the treatment of evolution in textbooks used in the state. Since 1923 no reports had been recorded,[23] but the committee in 1925 "felt compelled" to make a statement. The committee claimed to have given considerable time to the investigation of evolution and was convinced that it was being taught "in many of the textbooks being used." The committee believed that the number of teachers endorsing the evolutionary hypothesis was small, and urged that only anti-evolution teachers be employed. Especially commended were the policies of Texas and Mississippi, where school officials refused textbooks teaching evolution, and the Louisiana Baptist Convention was urged to memorialize the Louisiana State Board of Education to adopt the same policies.[24] The committee's report was accepted as read, and it was moved that a commission be appointed to prepare a memorial.[25] Isaiah Watson, who had been instrumental in the passage of the Vernon Missionary Association's resolution, also proposed the adoption of a statement. It declared that Louisiana College, despite the fact that it was one of the Christian schools in the state, admittedly had in use textbooks that presented the doctrine of evolution. Watson urged the convention to express its joy in the assurance that the teachers there did not favor evolution, and to urge them to act immediately to obtain textbooks not favoring the theory.[26] Mention at the state convention was made of particular texts guilty of teaching evolution as a fact, but no acceptable non-evolution texts were listed.[27]

The special concern of Baptists for Louisiana College, their denominational institution, was a matter frequently mentioned. The *Baptist Message*, in September of 1925 had printed an article entitled "Louisiana College—the Pride of Louisiana Baptists." After affirming its wholehearted support of Louisiana College, the article stated that "every effort possible was being expended" to furnish textbooks on science free of "all error which is calculated to wreck the faith of our boys and girls in the Bible." Louisiana College had escaped criticism because "we have a faculty who believe in the Bible as God's infallible and revealed Word to men."[28]

The schools, not the courts, were to be the battlefield for fundamentalists and evolutionists. One of the earliest Louisiana Baptist writers to advocate the field of education as the ultimate area of decision was Dr. C. C. Carroll of the Baptist Bible Institute in New Orleans. Carroll, in an article facing the issues as he saw them in 1924, had characterized evolutionist authors as "pedagogical opportunists." These false teachers, he said, described "speculative philosophy" as matured conclusions and established tenets of science. Carroll had advocated the training of teachers by responsible instructors who would insure their receiving responsible information. The great fundamentalist intellectual leaders, he added, should write textbooks which would properly draw the lines between established fact and theory.[29]

Edward Lassiter Clark, writing on the history of Baptists and Darwin's theory, has affirmed that biology as a discipline had a late start in Baptist schools and that classes were carelessly scrutinized with regard to doctrine unless an intense amount of publicity prompted concern.[30] The great and overpowering significance of the Tennessee trial lay in its direct focus on evolution in the schools. The almost universal Baptist conviction that the church must support education caused the expression of conservative opinion. Men like Dr. M. E. Dodd and the members of the state convention's textbook committee came far closer to approximating Baptist desires than extremist views of any kind. The trial, by effecting the transformation of fundamentalism into the most living of issues, prepared Louisiana Baptists for their most significant statement against evolution, the "Memorial" to the State Board of Education. Louisiana Baptists, by deciding to prepare the "Memorial" had committed themselves to working within their state's administrative and legislative system in a determined and constructive manner.

Once a course of action had been decided upon, the members of the "Memorial commission" began their work. Leon W. Sloan, state convention president and head of the commission appointed at the 1925 convention in Winnfield, personally composed most of the "Memorial."[31] When the document was completed, Sloan sent copies to all members of the commission. The final draft was signed by all but one of the commissioners.[32] Sloan then began correspondence with E. L. Kidd of Ruston, Louisiana, who was president of the State Board of Education, and with T. H. Harris of Baton Rouge, the state superintendent of education, to arrange for presentation of the "Memorial." On May 19, 1926, Sloan and a delegation from the Louisiana Baptist Convention traveled to New Orleans, and the "Memorial" was presented the following day.[33]

The "Memorial" began by declaring that the consideration at hand was the use of texts teaching the evolutionary hypothesis in tax-supported schools of the state. Mention was made of the constituency that Louisiana Baptists represented, with Negro Baptist membership included.[34] The report of the committee on textbooks at the 1925 convention in Winnfield was read in its entirety, including its emphasis on the examples of Texas and Mississippi where state authorities refused contracts for textbooks unless evolution was deleted. The "Memorial" contended that the explanation of man's origin as either "descending or ascending" from other life forms was inimical to the Bible. Since Louisiana courts had held that teaching the Bible in tax-supported schools was unconstitutional, the teaching of an explanation so opposed to the Bible should be equally unconstitutional.[35] The "suppression of theories of evolution would not be a violation of academic freedom of either teacher or pupil," nor a contravention of free speech. It would be a "just protest" against the teaching of evolution as a fact when at best evolution was an "unproven hypothesis or guess."[36] Evolutionists had the right to their own schools and textbooks, and could hire their own teachers, but not at the expense of all of Louisiana's taxpayers. Despite isolated and individual exceptions, the "Memorial" continued, all Christian fellowships in the state believed in the integrity of the Bible and were steadfastly against the teaching of evolution to young people. Such teaching made the minds of the pupils "prejudiced against the truthfulness of the Bible," prevented young people from enjoying any "laudable pride of ancestry," and failed to furnish an ideal of the future. Nothing in the "Memorial" should be interpreted as condemning the teaching of "true science." Scientific facts were in complete accord with the Bible, but evolution was not fact, only guess. The State Board of Education, reminded that the "Memorial" represented the views of more than 700,000 people, was urged to decline contracts for books which taught evolutionary theories. All references to evolution in textbooks then in use should be deleted. Teachers should be prevented from teaching evolution in tax-supported schools or on the property of the state's schools.[37] According to the minutes of the meeting, the Baptist delegation left after "Dr. Pritcher"[38] addressed those present in behalf of the "Memorial." Upon his return home, Sloan received a letter from E. L. Kidd in which he stated that the "Memorial" had made a "profound impression" on the members of the board, and he pledged their "future earnest consideration."[39]

With the "Memorial" completed and formally presented, Southern Baptists in Louisiana next centered their attention on a specific campaign in the Louisiana legislature. On May 2, 1926, the *Baton Rouge Morning Advocate* weighed the possibilities of an anti-evolution law. The newspaper commented that "someone may be stirred into introducing an anti-evolution bill" but the agitation in other states "seems to have reduced the opportunity for great excitement." Anticipating the possibility of a law similar to Tennessee's famous Butler Act under which Scopes had been tried, Louisiana State University's Episcopalian St. James Club published a declaration stating that anti-evolution legislation was contrary to democratic principles and that anti-evolutionism was based on a "false antithesis" between science and religion. In an interesting reversal of an argument used frequently by Baptist spokesman, the Episcopalian students held that restrictions on the teaching of evolution were unconstitutional just as the teaching of any religion in a tax-supported school was unconstitutional.[40]

When the 1926 session of the legislature opened on May 11, 1926, Representative C. H. Hudson of Farmerville introduced a bill "to prohibit the teaching of evolution in all the universities, normal, and other public schools and state institutions in the state of Louisiana." Opposition to the bill began to develop almost immediately.[41] After the defeat of a motion to indefinitely postpone the bill, it was sent on May 13 to the Committee on Public Education where it began a long rest.[42]

Meanwhile, Baptist clergy and laymen supported efforts to secure legislative action. In an article entitled "Should the Legislature Now In Session Pass An Evolution Bill?" the *Baptist Message* of May 23, 1926, advocated state action to squelch the teaching of evolutionary theories. In the *Baptist Message* of May 27, Dr. W. H. Knight, the leading Baptist spokesman and pastor of the First Baptist Church in Baton Rouge, attempted to prove the desperateness of the problem. Against the contention that legislation would abridge the freedom of the teacher, Knight replied that a teacher had the right to teach whatever he wanted, but not wherever he wanted. Such a law would not compromise a teacher's right to seek other employment. Knight also linked evolutionary theories with bolshevism and asserted that "since the Bible must not be taught, it must not be abused."

Another anti-evolution bill was introduced into the legislature on May 25 by Representative T. Sambola Jones of East Baton Rouge Parish. House Bill 208 prescribed the qualifications of local school superintendents, principals, teachers, and lecturers at institutions supported in whole or in part by state funds. Echoing Jones's phrases in presenting his bill, it came to be referred to as the "atheist and infidel" measure.[43] A few days before, the "Memorial" had been presented to the State Board of Education, and the *Baptist Message* of May 27, 1926, published the entire "Memorial" and accompanied it with an editorial urging Baptist awareness of legislative developments.

On May 28, Representative S. O. Shattuck, a Southern Baptist lay preacher,[44] introduced still another anti-evolution bill. House Bill 279, containing a key passage identical to the phrasing of the "Memorial," would prohibit teaching that mankind either "descended or ascended" from another animal form. Textbooks teaching evolution as fact rather than theory were to be forbidden at schools, colleges, normals, and other institutions supported by public funds.[45] Like its two predecessors, this bill also was sent to the Committee on Public Education.[46]

Baptist support of the Shattuck bill came from Dr. Knight who passed out copies of it at the First Baptist Church in Baton Rouge.[47] The text of the bill was also printed in the *Baptist Message* of June 3, 1926, along with an editorial stressing the need for its passage. Louisiana Baptists were urged to communicate with their senators and representatives to ask for their support of the bill.[48] Mail response favoring anti-evolution legislation was reported to be high,[49] and the *Baptist Message* continued urging passage in its editorials on June 10 and 17.

On June 16, 1926, the Committee on Public Education brought its report. The Hudson bill was reported without action. The Jones bill was reported unfavorably by a 10-2 vote. Shattuck's bill was reported favorably 11-1.[50] Jones and Hudson withdrew their bills the following day.[51]

The *Baton Rouge Morning Advocate*, on June 19, 1926, printed an article which noted the rising opposition to the bill, and predicted that the bill would not be passed. On June 22, that newspaper predicted a close ballot. On the same day, the Shattuck bill was passed in the house of representatives by a 52-43 roll-call vote, with only four representatives absent.[52] The *Morning Advocate*'s headline read, "Churchmen Offer Prayer as Evolution Bill Wins House Approval." The *New Orleans Times Picayune* of June 23 called the bill a "futile undertaking."

The state senate began its deliberations with a roll call after which it was moved that House Bill 279 be sent to the Committee on Public Education. Senator P. H. Gilbert of Napoleonville made a substitute motion that the bill be postponed indefinitely. A few excited whispers greeted his motion as senators began to recognize that it was the Shattuck bill in question. The senate voted 17-15, with seven absences, to postpone the bill.[53] Four senators who had been absent later proclaimed that they were in favor of the postponement, but most observers were surprised at the bill's early demise. Opposing senators, concluded the *Times-Picayune*, were convinced that the bill was a "thinly disguised religious measure" and contended that the legislature was no place for religious legislation.[54] The *Baptist Message* expressed no surprise at the bill's defeat.[55]

At the Louisiana Baptist Convention at Natchitoches, November 23-25, 1926, Pres. L.W. Sloan was able to assure the convention that "your 'Memorial' had, along with other agencies, much to do with the passage through the House of the Shattuck bill."[56] He also reported receipt of a letter from T. H. Harris,[57] the state superintendent of education, who declared that he was corresponding with the publishers of textbooks which taught evolution in an attempt to eliminate all references to the evolutionary theory of man. Harris had, Sloan reported, also issued instructions to all parish school superintendents directing them to request that their teachers of science delete all reference to evolution in their instruction. Sloan stated, "This accomplishment alone is well worth the efforts put out."[58]

First reactions to the developments of 1926 indicated that Louisiana's Southern Baptists were not satisfied, and it was predicted that anti-evolution lobbyists would try again to pass laws forbidding the teaching of evolution in tax-supported schools.[59] L. W. Sloan, at the 1926 Baptist Convention, had proposed that a new textbook committee be appointed to consider further action.[60] These plans never materialized, however. The minutes of the Louisiana Baptist Convention after 1926 show no record of the formation of another textbook committee, and the anti-evolution legislation efforts of 1926 were never to be duplicated in Louisiana. This apparent loss of interest can be partially credited to State Superintendent of Education T. H. Harris' assurance to the 1926 convention that the teaching of evolution would be suppressed at the local level and that he would examine the matter of textbook revision.[61] Harris' action was significant enough to lead at least one observer to classify Louisiana among those states passing anti-evolution legislation.[62]

The year 1926 was the peak period of Louisiana Baptists' involvement in the evolution controversy, and the Scopes trial was the single most important catalyst in that involvement, causing Baptist interest to be centered on the question of the teaching of evolution in the schools. The leadership of the Louisiana Baptist Convention had prepared the "Memorial," the most significant formulation of Louisiana Baptist fundamentalism, and had presented it to the State Board of Education. Although defeated in the legislature, Louisiana Baptists had established that the Baptist constituency when applied to a problem could be a powerful force in state affairs. Baptists in key positions, whatever their motives, were willing to acknowledge that their convention's stand on evolution had influenced their decisions. And, even with the defeat of the Shattuck measure, Baptists could point to the action of the state superintendent of education as a partial victory.

A striking point about Louisiana Baptists in the evolution controversy was the extent to which they depended on their leadership to express their conscience for them. It required the stimulation of the leadership of the state convention for Louisiana's Baptist laymen and ministers to become deeply involved. Any list of these leaders would include M. E. Dodd,[63] Leon W. Sloan, W. H. Knight, and Finley W. Tinnin, editor of the *Baptist Message*. These leaders made frequent use of two arguments, which, with a few corollaries, can be traced throughout Louisiana Baptist literature between 1923 and 1926. One of these was the argument that evolution was only a hypothesis or guess rather than fact. The second was the constitutional argument: if it was unlawful to teach the Bible in public schools, it was also wrong to teach evolution because evolution was anti-religion.

Another important fact about Louisiana's Baptists in the evolution controversy is that they committed themselves to the support of their state's legislative and bureaucratic processes. In deciding to prepare a "Memorial" to the State Board of Education, Louisiana's Baptists were not merely agreeing in convention that an undesirable situation existed; they were embarking upon a program to convince other groups that their remedy was correct. It is difficult to establish the importance of a Baptist congregation acting within its local area with relation to a dispute such as the fundamentalist-evolutionist controversy. Edward Lassiter Clark has stated that public school teachers had little hope of retaining their positions if they chose to teach evolution in communities with strong Baptist concentrations.[64] This would seem to have been particularly true in Louisiana, considering the stand taken by T. H. Harris.

However, Louisiana Baptists only partially fit within the generalizations of the historians of fundamentalism. Although individual differences of opinion were obvious, Louisiana's Baptists were able to unite behind their great "educational and missionary" goals to the exclusion of internal discord.[65] Various observers of fundamentalism declare that the southern fundamentalist never understood that evolution could refer to anything except Darwinism, but this was not completely true of Louisiana Baptists. Although they could speak of transmutation of species as meaning specifically "man from the anthropoid ape,"[66] for the most part, from 1923 until 1929, they referred frequently to various types of evolution.

Historians of fundamentalism place the decline of the evolution controversy at about 1930. Gasper, along with John T. Scopes, contending that the Dayton trial was the turning point, places the decline of fundamentalist expression in 1925.[67] The actions of Louisiana's Baptists seem to support the latter view. They had shifted the emphasis of their anti-evolution campaign by 1927, and by 1930 had turned to other issues such as prohibition.[68] After 1926, evolution was allowed to become, if not forgotten, at least unmolested as a public issue.

Notes for "Louisiana Baptists and the Scopes Trial"

[1]Jerry R. Tompkins, ed., *D-Days at Dayton* (Baton Rouge, 1965), 37.

[2]H. W. Odum, "Duel to the Death," *Social Forces*, 4 (1925): 190.

[3]*New Orleans Times-Picayune*, various issues, July 1925.

[4]Ibid., July 11, 18, 1925.

[5]Ibid., July 18, 20, 1925.

[6]Rom. 1:20-30.

[7]*New Orleans Times-Picayune*, July 20, 1925.

[8]*Bogalusa Enterprise and American*, July 10, 1925.

[9]*Farmerville Gazette*, July 22, 1925.

[10]Ibid., August 5, 1925.

[11]Personal interview with Dr. James E. Carter, Pastor, First Baptist Church, Natchitoches, La., May 6, 1968.

[12]*Baptist Message*, July 16, 1925. The *Message*, printed in Shreveport, was the news organ of the Louisiana Baptist Convention and the sounding board for Louisiana Baptists. From 1920 to 1957 it was published under the rigorous, theologically conservative editorship of Finley W. Tinnin.

[13]Ibid., July 9, 1925. Dr. Dodd was a pastor of the First Baptist Church in Shreveport from 1912 to 1950. With regard to evolutionary theory, he was "solidly with Southern Baptist theological orthodoxy" and often voiced his opposition to evolution. John P. Durham and John S. Ramond, eds., *Baptist Builders in Louisiana* (Shreveport, 1934), 163; Clyde W. Averett, "Monroe Elmon Dodd: His Life and Work among Southern Baptists" (Ph.D. dissertation, New Orleans Baptist Theological Seminary, 1966), 126.

[14]*Baptist Message*, July 9, 1925.

[15]Ibid. See also the issues for January 1 and February 1, 1925.

[16]Ibid., July 16, 1925.

[17]Ibid., July 30, 1925.

[18]Odum, "Duel to the Death," 4:190.

[19]*Baptist Message*, July 30, 1925.

[20]Ibid.

[21]Ibid., August 27, 1925.

[22]*Associational Minutes of the Vernon Missionary Baptist Association* (Shreveport, 1925), 13; *Associated Minutes of the Acadia Baptist Association* (Shreveport, 1925), 7.

[23]In 1922 a committee on textbooks had been appointed which presented a report to the Louisiana Baptist Convention in November, 1923. The report held it to be a matter of "common knowledge" that textbooks teaching evolution were in use in colleges and universities, condemned scientists for exceeding the limits of their disciplines, and asserted that the theory was being repudiated by scientists themselves. One anti-evolution argument advanced by the committee was to appear in Louisiana Baptist polemics for some time: since religion could not be taught in the schools, it should be equally true that no "irreligious or anti-christian" teachings were allowed. The committee asked for time to make a more complete investigation of textbooks and to prepare a further report. *Annual of the Louisiana Baptist Convention* (Shreveport, 1923), 20-23.

[24]*Annual of the Louisiana Baptist Convention* (Shreveport, 1925), 37.

[25]Ibid., 34.

[26]Ibid., 37.

[27]*Baptist Message*, May 27, 1926.

[28]Ibid., September 4, 1925.

[29]C. C. Carroll, "Baptist Schools and the New Theology," *The Review and Expositor*, 21 (1924): 212. For other articles indicating the concern of Louisiana Baptists over the teaching of evolution in the schools in the period immediately preceding the Scopes trial, see *Baptist Message*, February 5, April 2, 9, 16, 1925.

[30]Edward Lassiter Clark, "The Southern Baptist Reaction to the Darwinian Theory of Evolution" (Ph.D. dissertation, Southwestern Baptist Theological Seminary, 1952), 8.

[31]*Annual of the Louisiana Baptist Convention* (Shreveport, 1926), 17. Numerous attempts to arrange for a meeting of the commission proved futile, usually because most of the members were bound by other duties. The Winnfield convention had made no provision for expenses. Because the members felt that their group was too large to arrange a general meeting at their own expense, it was decided that Sloan would collect expressions of opinion from the various members, act as commission chairman, and draft the "Memorial."

[32]Examination of the listings of officers reveals that J. P. Durham, corresponding secretary, had failed to sign. While the "Memorial" was being prepared, the *Baptist Message* editorialized about the growing nervousness among some Baptists about evolution. A product of "modernism and the Devil," evolution should be feared, and Baptists should be "thoroughly aroused to the danger of this insidious enemy of truth" which appealed largely to a "superficial class of people parading under the name of scholarship." By the individual effort of Southern Baptists, however, the theory could be "dashed to pieces on the rock of faith." *Baptist Message*, April 29, 1926.

[33]The delegation included two executive officers of the convention, E. D. Solomon and J. J. Wise; two members of the faculty of the Baptist Bible Institute, G. H. Crutcher and R. P. Mahon; J. J. Bristow, New Orleans Baptist Hospital superintendent; and three New Orleans ministers, W. W. Hamilton, B. E. Massey, and W. A. Jordan, *Annual of the Louisiana Baptist Convention* (1926), 3, 17.

[34]Louisiana, State Board of Education, *Official Proceedings*, May 24, 1926, 4. Cited hereafter as *Official Proceedings*. Technically, the commission could speak only for Louisiana's white Southern Baptists.

[35]Ibid., 5.

[36]This became one of the most popular arguments used by Baptists in opposing evolutionary theories after Dr. M. E. Dodd, postulated it in articles for the *Baptist Message*, January 1, February 5, 1925.

[37]*Official Proceedings*, 5, 6.

[38]Dr. Crutcher, not Dr. Pritcher. *Annual of the Louisiana Baptist Convention* (1926), 18.

[39]Ibid.

[40]*Reveille* (Louisiana State University), May 5, 1926.

[41]Louisiana, House of Representatives, *Official Journal* (1926), 11. Cited hereafter as *Official Journal*. *New Orleans Times-Picayune*, May 12, 1926. Louisiana State University students were the source of much of the lobbying against the Hudson bill. They were joined by members of the faculty and President Thomas D. Boyd. *Baton Rouge Morning Advocate*, May 16, 1926; Norman F. Furniss, *The Fundamentalist Controversy, 1918-1931* (New Haven, 1954), 93.

[42]*Official Journal* (1926), 24. The motion to postpone made by Rep. Allen J. Ellender of Houma effectively killed debate on House Bill 41. *Times-Picayune*, May 13, 1926.

[43]*Official Journal* (1926), Calendar of Bills, 84.

[44]Personal interview with Mrs. Billy Willy, granddaughter of Rep. Shattuck, May 28, 1968.

[45]Violation of the act was to be a misdemeanor punishable by a fine of not less than $50.00 nor more than $100.00. *Baptist Message*, June 3, 1926.

[46]*Official Journal* (1926), 110.

[47]*Morning Advocate*, May 30, 1926. See also the issue for June 6, 1926.

[48]Opposition to the bill came from Louisiana State University biology students who presented a series of resolutions to the Committee on Public Education. A major concern of the students was the cancellation of a course on evolution for which some twenty-five students had registered. *Reveille* (Louisiana State University), June 6, 1926.

[49]*Gazette* (Farmerville), June 9, 1926.

[50]*Official Journal* (1926), 574, 575.

[51]Ibid., Calendar of Bills, 3, 4.

[52]Ibid., 762.

[53]Louisiana, Senate. *Official Journal* (1926), 597.

[54]*Times-Picayune*, June 24, 1926.

[55]*Baptist Message*, July 1, 1926.

[56]*Annual of the Louisiana Baptist Convention* (1926), 18.

[57]Harris was a Baptist and the son of a Baptist minister. Henry E. Chambers, *A History of Louisiana: Wilderness, Colony, Province, Territory, State, People*, 3 vols. (New York, 1925), 2:3.

[58]*Annual of the Louisiana Baptist Convention* (1926), 18.

[59]*Baton Rouge Morning Advocate*, June 24, 1926.

[60]*Annual of the Louisiana Baptist Convention* (1926), 18.

[61]Ibid.

[62]Furniss, *The Fundamentalist Controversy*, 93. At the same time Louisiana Baptists were deciding not to press their campaign with regard to textbooks, either in future legislatures or in their own convention, more attention was being given to the prevention of the teaching of evolution in denominational institutions as opposed to state-supported schools. The formation of Dodd College for girls was one result. For information on Dodd

College, see *Baptist Message*, various issues throughout 1927; *Encyclopedia of Southern Baptists* (Nashville, Tenn., 1958), 378; Averett, "Monroe Elmon Dodd," 126; C. Penrose St. Amant, *A Short History of Louisiana Baptists* (Nashville, Tenn., 1927), 40; *Annual of the Louisiana Baptist Convention* (Shreveport, 1927).

[63]Dodd, perhaps the first to provide leadership in the controversy in Louisiana, wrote numerous articles on the subject. At least one source credits him with the authorship of the McDaniel statement at the Southern Baptist Convention in 1926, and none contest that he was probably privy to the plan to sidestep the issue of a doctrinal statement on evolution. He was the only Louisiana Baptist included in the "Memorial" commission who was not an officer of the convention or the head of a state Baptist institution or agency. *Baptist Message*, April 15, 1920; February 17, 1927; *Morning Advocate* (Baton Rouge), May 13, 1926; *Annual of the Louisiana Baptist Convention* (1925), 34.

[64]Clark, "Southern Baptist Reaction to the Darwinian Theory," 72.

[65]*Baptist Message*, July 30, 1925. Louis Gasper, one of the most recent writers of fundamentalist developments, states that Southern Baptists, because of the congregational character of their church polity, suffered less dissension over the question of evolution than did some other religious groups. Louisiana Baptists are a case in point. Louis Gasper, *The Fundamentalist Movement* (Paris, 1963), 21.

[66]*Annual of the Louisiana Baptist Convention* (1923), 20.

[67]Gasper, *The Fundamentalist Movement*, 18. Mr. Scopes, a resident of Shreveport, declared his trial to have been the turning point in a recent interview. See also Tompkins, *D-Days at Dayton*, 31.

[68]Examination of the district association minutes between 1924 and 1926, the climactic period of the evolution controversy in Louisiana, reveals that only two Baptist district associations drafted statements on evolution, while more than half of the state's thirty-five district associations had standing committees on "Prohibition" or "Temperance." Prohibition articles and editorials increased during the years after 1926 in the *Baptist Message*. See also Furniss, *The Fundamentalist Controversy*, 178.

PARTISON PARSON: AN ORAL HISTORY ACCOUNT OF THE LOUISIANA YEARS OF GERALD L. K. SMITH*

Glen Jeansonne

Gerald L. K. Smith, notorious in the years after 1935 as an anti-Semitic speaker, author, and publisher, never forgot the happier years he spent in Louisiana from 1929 to 1933 as pastor of the Kings Highway Christian Church in Shreveport and from 1933 to 1935 as organizer of the Share Our Wealth Society for Huey Long.

During the early years of the Great Depression, Smith was a popular Shreveport minister, a dynamic, fund-raising, spellbinding ministerial speaker, and an organizer of athletic, social, and charitable events. After the onset of the Depression, he asked Senator Long to intercede in saving the homes of his congregants from mortgage foreclosure. Long did so, and Smith never forgot it. Smith's association with Huey Long provided him with a taste for politics, and after joining Long's organization he never returned to preaching. Indeed, under Long's tutelage he became advocate of a secular salvation, the Share Our Wealth Society. A highly effective speaker, Smith became the "front man" for Long: the crowd pleaser, the public organizer, and the gregarious extrovert.

Smith was impressed by strong personalities; he later would be a lieutenant of both Father Coughlin and Henry Ford. But it was Huey Long who gave him his start in politics, and he never quite recovered from Long's death. Smith once told me that, aside from his father, Huey Long had been the most important influence in his life.[1]

I first became aware of Smith while doing research on Leander Perez, who, like Smith, was a Long lieutenant. I began corresponding with Smith. I told him that I planned to write his biography, and that his cooperation was essential. At first he temporized, explaining that he had no time for interviews in his busy schedule. However, his vanity was aroused, and he was interested in my Louisiana connection and my work on Perez and Long. It was my Louisiana origin and upbringing which finally convinced Smith to cooperate.

Smith had voluminous papers, but they were not available to the public. Therefore, I concluded that oral interviewing was the only method to employ in learning about certain

*First published in *Louisiana History*, 23 (1982): 149-58. Reprinted with the kind permission of the author and the Louisiana Historical Association.

aspects of Smith's career, particularly his early life, before he attracted journalists and historians. I corresponded with Smith for two years before he finally agreed to a personal meeting. But the meeting produced a breakthrough. Smith wanted to speak for history because he thought that time would vindicate him.

Eventually, I interviewed Smith on four occasions,[2] corresponded with him, visited his headquarters at Eureka Springs, Arkansas, and Los Angeles, admired his art, lunched with him, saw his Passion Play, and stayed in his guest house. In addition to my own interviews, I had access to interviews with Smith taped by my friend Leo Ribuffo, associate professor of History at George Washington University. I also interviewed people who knew Smith: his staff at Los Angeles, his three leading aides at Eureka Springs, and his wife. I interviewed members of the Kings Highway Christian Church in Shreveport, where he preached for five years before giving up the pulpit to become a political organizer for Huey Long.

This essay concerns the relationship between Smith and Long and the years Smith spent in Louisiana—pivotal years in his career. I will also discuss my efforts to document these aspects of Smith's career, the molding of his opinions, and the insights into his personality obtained through oral interviews.

The story told by the subjects of my interviews begins in 1929. Smith came to Louisiana just four months before the stock market crash to pastor the large, staidly affluent Kings Highway Christian Church in Shreveport. The church had never seen the likes of Smith. He talked before the Kiwanis and Rotary clubs, organized lumber workers into a union, managed the community chest drive, spoke over a network of radio stations— criticizing sweatshops and debt peonage—and helped host the Chinese delegation at the Los Angeles Olympics.[3] I interviewed most of the surviving members of Smith's church, some of whom remembered Smith vividly. On the whole, they were cooperative, although a few insisted on anonymity, and some refused to permit me to tape the interviews. Two of the interviews were conducted over the telephone.

Most of the church members interviewed recalled Smith's energy and abilities. A woman who had baby-sat for Smith's adopted son termed the minister "lovable," "dynamic," and added, "You couldn't help but like him."[4] They all remember him as a spellbinding speaker who could preach a rousing sermon on a moment's notice. One confidential source told me of an experience he and his father had with Smith. The minister appeared at church one Sunday morning with a hangover, after carousing the night before. As he entered, he asked my source's father: "Mr. A., what shall I preach on today?" Mr. A. replied: "John 3:16." Smith proceeded to preach a brilliant sermon precisely on that Scripture.[5] His ability to preach without preparation was confirmed by Mrs. K. A. Miller, who had baby-sat for the Smiths. She said:

> I think, I've heard it said, that he did a lot of preaching from the cuff. He didn't have to really [prepare]. That may have been part of what got him in trouble. He was spending time with other things. But he was smart enough to get up there and preach that sermon on Sunday mornings without a lot of preparation.[6]

Others speak of a less appealing side to Smith—things which did not seem appropriate for a minister. One member remembers him using profanity.[7] In fact, in my interviews with him, his language was what one would expect from a working man, not a minister. He repeatedly told me that in the exuberance of youth, he had been "filled with piss and vinegar."[8] One of Smith's congregants remembers him as an arrogant, unprincipled individual, "a junior edition of Senator Joseph McCarthy," who was so ambitious that "Kings Highway Church was too small to hold him." Another recalled that Smith had asked to borrow his red sportscar to tool about town ostentatiously; the man found the request presumptuous and declined. But Smith could also be considerate. In the depths of the depression, when teachers were going unpaid, he lodged and fed several at his home, without payment, so that they could continue teaching.[9]

It is in his relationship with Huey Long that the pieces of Smith's personality began to fit together. In their initial encounter, Long befriended Smith and interceded to save the homes of some of Smith's congregants from mortgage foreclosure. After that, Smith worshipped Long. He exaggerated the Kingfish's virtues and dismissed cursorily his vices. He claimed: "His family, you know, were indeed aristocrats. They go back to Maryland and they are among the most sophisticated people that ever moved to Louisiana."[10] Actually, Long's forebears were neither as distinguished as Smith insisted nor as impoverished as Long himself claimed in his campaigns.

To Smith, Long was a giant—intellectually, morally, and politically. In a *New Republic* article he characterized Long as a "superman."[11] Of course, Long's flaws were so obvious that it was impossible even for one as uncritical as Smith to deny all of them. Consequently, he attributed Long's vices to his advisers, particularly the rising Jewish hotel magnate, Seymour Weiss. Smith explained to me how Weiss gained influence in the Kingfish's councils: "Back when Huey Long was wild and woolly and full of fleas, Weiss was his pimp."[12] According to Smith, most of Long's errors of judgment were due to the sinister influence of this Jewish manipulator. Smith said: "And against my judgment—Huey Long was over-influenced by Seymour Weiss." Smith told interviewer Leo Ribuffo that he personally had collected over half a million dollars for Long's 1936 presidential campaign. It was kept in the safe of the Roosevelt Hotel where Weiss was an employee. After Long died, according to Smith, Weiss "just opened the safe, took the money, and bought the Roosevelt Hotel."[13]

Smith's own moment of glory in the aftermath of the assassination of his mentor was his delivery of Long's funeral oration. Smith said that it was "the will of his [Long's] aged father" that he deliver Long's eulogy. He bristled at charges that he had plagiarized the address. According to Smith, the eulogy was entirely his own except for the fact that it was inspired by God. He claimed to have arisen many times during the night to change words and phrases. Charges of plagiarism were inspired by jealousy, he argued. Smith asserted that his opponents within Long's organization had underestimated his oratorical ability. "It was just too good for them to believe."[14]

In this he was not, in fact exaggerating; those who heard Smith, Franklin Roosevelt, Father Coughlin, and Huey Long believe that Smith was the best speaker among them. H. L. Mencken said that Smith was the greatest orator he had ever heard, and he had heard every presidential candidate since the turn of the century, including William Jennings Bryan.[15]

Unfortunately for Smith, his undeniable oratorical prowess was insufficient to win him control of the Long organization. After Long's death, he was outmaneuvered by Seymour Weiss and Robert Maestri in the internal power struggle which ensued, and was forced to leave Louisiana and apply his oratorical and organizing talents elsewhere.

When I asked Smith about the leadership struggle in the wake of Long's demise, he stated heatedly: "There was no leadership except the gangster role of Seymour Weiss who engineered the selling of Huey Long's blood to the Roosevelt machine."[16] Smith denied, however, that what he termed his "alleged" anti-Semitism in later life was due to his experience with Seymour Weiss:

> My so-called anti-Semitism is not related to my contempt for Seymour Weiss or even the Jew that shot Huey Long. Those did not trigger what some call anti-Semitism in my mind. The thing that gives me the attitude I have toward organized Jewry is a careful study of their history and behavior.[17]

After Long's death, the remaining Longite leaders, with the exception of Smith, made peace with Roosevelt and supported the Democratic President's re-election in 1936. Smith termed this "sellout" the "Second Louisiana Purchase" and glamorized his own refusal to join the cabal. In a typical exaggeration, he reported to Leo Ribuffo that a Roosevelt emissary had told him: "You're the only bright one in the bunch, and if you come along with us there isn't anything in Washington that you want which you cannot have." According to Smith, he told Roosevelt's man: "Well I only want one thing, and that is for your man to be impeached, and I'm going to fight him as long as he's alive."[18]

Smith's hatred for Roosevelt only increased after Long's death. He explained to Leo Ribuffo his reasons for opposing FDR: "In the first place, Roosevelt was completely captured by the Marxist, Socialist elements, even down to the brazen, self-confessed Communists. Then of course he was the super hypocrite of all times."[19] Smith told me angrily that the press had ignored Roosevelt's vices:

> They [the press] never even raised an eyebrow when even Elliot Roosevelt revealed that his father was sleeping with his secretary in the front room, and by an understanding with his lesbian wife, she slept in the back room . . . [20]

Smith rationalized his exclusion from the leadership—sour grapes on his part. "I wasn't interested in anything in Louisiana because it all represented a deal, trading off the blood of my assassinated friend." He claimed that as part of the arrangement the mailing lists of the Share Our Wealth Society were destroyed. Long's widow was helpless to prevent the "sellout" because she was blackmailed by the Internal Revenue Service. "They led her erroneously, dishonestly, to believe that there were manipulations in Huey Long's income that would embarrass the whole family, but the fact is that Huey Long died virtually impoverished." He added that incumbent governor O. K. Allen, after helping to destroy the mailing lists, "dropped dead of fright from the Internal Revenue Department."[21]

While condemning Long's survivors for opportunistically reconciling with Roosevelt, Smith admitted that he himself became an opportunist after Long's death. This opportunism led him first to Dr. Francis E. Townsend, then to Father Charles E. Coughlin, and to both in 1936. He said: "So I had to devise opportunistically ways to get in touch with the public." The result of this tripartite alliance of convenience was the Union Party, which ran North Dakota Congressman Gerald Lemke for president and suffered a crushing defeat. Smith insisted that Lemke was no Huey Long, maintaining that the North Dakotan had "about as much charisma as a deserted telephone." He dismissed the two major party candidates: "Landon was nothing and Roosevelt was a package of brilliant political satanism." But Smith insisted to his death that "If Huey Long had been alive in 1936 he would have been nominated by the Democratic party and would have been elected."[22]

Smith never lost his admiration for Long. In his declining years he erected a bronze statue of Long at the St. Maurice Mansion near Natchitoches, Louisiana, and converted the antebellum plantation home into a Long museum. He also wrote a fawning biography of Long which was distributed at the site of the statue. Natchitoches was chosen instead of Long's hometown because Winnfield already had a statue of Huey's younger brother, three-term governor Earl Long. Although he had returned to Louisiana to campaign for Earl in 1940, Smith disliked Earl and the rest of the Long family. He explained, "God had just a certain quota for the Longs and he gave it all to Huey." He called Earl "a sort of erratic wild man."[23]

The personality profile of Smith which emerges from my interviews with him and with persons who knew him is that of a highly emotional individual, engaged in frenzied activity all of his life, who loved and hated with intensity, was blind to the faults of friends and virtues of enemies, a man who uncritically accepted a conspiratorial theory of the nature of politics. But all of those I interviewed, whether they liked or disliked Smith, insisted that he was a man of great personal magnetism and charisma. In my personal interviews with Smith himself, I was also impressed by his charisma. Even his appearance—stocky, upright, and vibrant—was that of a man who dominated everything around him.

In my earlier projects utilizing oral history—a biography of Leander Perez and an account of Louisiana's 1959-60 gubernatorial campaigns—my sources were conveniently limited to Louisiana. Such was not the case with Smith. After leaving Louisiana in 1935, he never returned except to visit. He traveled extensively and cultivated alliances, open and covert, from coast to coast, living first in New York, then moving successively to Detroit, St. Louis, Tulsa, Los Angeles, and finally, Eureka Springs. The logistical problems of conducting interviews over such a large geographic area, over a span of more than forty years, and of locating and interviewing even a tiny fraction of those who knew Smith, are formidable. Nonetheless, as one who wished to study Smith's entire life, there was no alternative to utilizing the technique of oral history.

When interviewing Smith himself, I had to weigh carefully his testimony, tempering it with common sense when he was obviously altering the record. In my four interviews with him, he was a willing discussant, but not entirely reliable. He exaggerated—about himself, about his enemies, and about almost every aspect of the curiously conspiratorial intellectual world in which he lived. Those who knew Smith were sometimes equally biased. He was a man who evoked strong responses. By interviewing most of his former congregants still living, however, it was possible to reconstruct a composite profile.

The chief problem in interviewing members of the Kings Highway Christian Church was not so much deliberate falsification as the unreliability of the memories of events which occurred more than forty years earlier. In these interviews, it was important to establish the relationship of the interview subjects to their former minister and their feelings toward him. Most subjects were quite candid, although some preferred to remain anonymous. At this point it was necessary to determine what was more important: protecting a confidential source or footnoting every fact. There was no single encompassing rule. Compromises between fidelity to footnoting and the importance of critical information were inevitable.

In contrast to the problem of reluctant witnesses is the problem with "overly cooperative" subjects. I found some who tried to tell me what they thought I wanted to hear. Other recollections were mixed with material from books about the period which the interviewees had read long after the events in question. Careful probing was required to establish the extent of the subjects' information which came from their own experience.

My interviews with Smith himself, members of the Kings Highway Christian Church, and others who knew Smith in Louisiana constitutes the first phase of my research. These people knew him at the earliest stages of his ministerial and political career. There were no other sources: no articles, diaries or memoirs, monographs or essays. These recollections, the oldest, might have altered over the years by knowledge of what Smith became after leaving Louisiana. Tapping them proved an exercise in the most delicate aspects of oral history, asking individuals to recall episodes from their youth which interest the historian but were incidental to their own lives. Some of the things I asked them about were controversial, some, unpleasant. It required coaxing, gentle prodding, establishment of rapport and, occasionally, promises of anonymity.

The fact that I had completed research in written sources about the Louisiana phase of Smith's career before conducting interviews proved propitious. I knew which questions to pursue because I had established previously the gaps in my knowledge. Thus the interviews could be focused or directed toward obtaining material which could not have been derived from written sources. I was able to test the veracity and accuracy of my subjects by asking the same questions to several subjects and, sometimes, by asking questions to which I already knew the answers. Information could be clarified and expanded upon within the interview process. Much could be learned from expression and intonation. And each interview could lead to other sources.

The interviews taken altogether produced the image of a vigorous young man seeking a cause into which to channel his extraordinary energies and substantial talents. Most of my subjects had liked Smith, but a few had seen the seeds of his later extremism and egocentricity. My fears about fading memories, although not entirely unfounded, proved only a minor problem. Smith had touched their lives; he was unforgettable.

However, Smith's impact on Louisiana was not as important as the state's impact on him. It was the launching pad for a man who for the next forty years was one of the leading spokesmen of extremism on the right, the author of thousands of tracts and articles, the mentor and associate of hundreds of personalities involved in practically every reactionary movement. The Louisiana years comprised a period in his life which he recalled nostalgically. It converted him from a local to a national figure, heightened his ambitions, and developed his vanity. He loved to reminisce about those days and speculate about what might have been.

One indeed may speculate on the direction Smith's career would have taken had Huey Long lived. He then would have had a strong power base and an effective tutor. He may not have careened off into rabid anti-Semitism. (Long himself was no anti-Semite and Smith was not overtly so while a member of the Long organization.) Perhaps his energies would have been channeled more productively. Certainly as his opportunities for real political power faded, his became a shriller and shriller voice, finally appealing only to fanatical extremists.

Notes for "Partisan Parson: An Oral History Account of the Louisiana Years of Gerald L. K. Smith"

[1]Gerald L. K. Smith, taped interview with the author, August 10, 1974, Eureka Springs, Ark.

[2]I taped interviews with Smith on August 10 and August 11, 1974 at Eureka Springs, Ark., and on December 28, 1974 and January 21, 1975 in Los Angeles. His wife submitted a written response to my questions on August 11, 1974.

[3]Smith was invited to Los Angeles by Olympic officials as a reward for his fundraising efforts for American athletics. Ibid., August 11; David H. Bennett, *Demagogues in the Depression: American Radicals and the Union Party, 1932-1936* (New Brunswick, N. J., 1969), 116; "Gerald L. K. Smith," *Current Biography*, 1943, 707-08. For a detailed discussion of Smith's early career see my "Preacher, Populist, Propagandist: The Early Career of Gerald L. K. Smith," *Biography*, 2 vols. (1979), 2:303-27.

[4]Mr. and Mrs. Marion Jouett and Mrs. K. A. Miller, taped interview with the author, Shreveport, La., June 12, 1979. The praise was that of Mrs. Miller. The Jouetts and Miller were members of the Kings Highway Christian Church. Mrs. Jouett was too young to remember Smith and her husband had been in college during Smith's pastorate and had only attended church when he was home for weekends. Mrs. Miller baby-sat for the Smiths' adopted son, Jerry, and had distinct impressions of Smith.

[5]Confidential Communication. This source was confirmed by Mrs. Miller. John 3:16: "For God so loved the world that he gave his only son, that whoever believes in him should not perish but have eternal life."

[6]Jouett and Miller, taped interview with the author, June 12, 1979.

[7]Mrs. Ralph King, interview with the author, Shreveport, La., June 12, 1979.

[8]Smith, taped interview with the author, August 28, 1974.

[9]Confidential Communication.

[10]Smith, taped interview with the author, December 28, 1974.

[11]Gerald L. K. Smith, "How Come Huey Long? . . . 2. Or Superman?," *New Republic*, 82 (1935), 14-15.

[12]Smith, taped interview with the author, December 28, 1974.

[13]Smith, taped interview with Leo Ribuffo, Eureka Springs, Ark., August 25, 1969. Ribuffo furnished me with partial transcripts of his two interviews with Smith.

[14]Smith, taped interview with Ribuffo, Eureka Springs, Ark., January 8, 1973.

[15]"Smith," *Current Biography*, 707. Mencken said: "Gerald is the greatest of them all, not the greatest by an inch or a foot or a yard or a mile, but the greatest by at least two light years. He begins where the next best leaves off. He is the master of masters, the champion boob-bumper of all epochs, the Aristotle and Johann Sebastian Bach of all known earsplitters, dead or alive."

[16]Smith, taped interview with the author, January 21, 1975

[17]Smith, taped interview with Ribuffo, August 25, 1969.

[18]Ibid.

[19]Ibid..

[20]Smith, taped interview with the author, August 10, 1974

[21]Smith, taped interview with Ribuffo, August 25, 1969.

[22]Smith, taped interview with the author, January 21, 1975.

[23]Smith, taped interview with Ribuffo, August 25, 1969.

THE ZENITH OF MY CAREER*

Bobbie Malone

As the Balkan powder keg exploded and its flames ignited the rest of the European continent, Max Heller's professional energies peaked, sparked by enough "trouble to keep one's edges clean." World War I inspired both the Wilsonian vision of a world made safe for democracy and the Balfour Declaration, which promised the fulfillment of the Zionist dream. Together, these wartime impulses allowed Heller's idealism to soar to new heights. Although sometimes exhausted by his physical limitations, he nevertheless fiercely battled for his Progressive and Zionist principles. Heller well understood that the war years constituted a key era in his life. In fact, he admitted to his sons in 1916, "I am probably at the zenith of my career."[1]

Characteristically, Heller responded to the outbreak of the European conflict by becoming enthusiastically engaged in the promotion of peace. In October 1914, the *New Orleans Item* published his "Prayer for Peace," the first indication that he had enlisted in the ranks of the peace movement. He offered his prayer on behalf of the "misguided brothers . . . divided by bitter animosities" in hopes that God might speedily terminate "their efforts at mutual destruction." Heller hoped that, out of the anguish, some "incalculable good" might arise and that "hatred and prejudice . . . between races, nations and faiths" might vanish. In the earthly paradise he envisioned, the stronger would generously help the weaker in an effort to establish the "reign of genuine brotherhood. "[2]

In June of the following year, the major headline of the *New Orleans American* carried news of the sinking of the *Lusitania*, and on the same page, a large photograph of Heller appeared with the caption "Jewish Leader of New Orleans Who, with His People, Stand for Peace." The long accompanying article quoted Heller extensively. "No nation ever existed for which the word peace had greater attraction than it always had for the Jew." In the years that preceded America's entrance into the Great War, Heller's activity in the American Peace Society yielded him leadership in the organization. He was twice elected as president of the local chapter. A Wilsonian in spirit, even before he openly campaigned for the president's reelection in 1916, Heller also worked with the Louisiana

*First published in *Rabbi Max Heller, Reformer, Zionist, Southerner, 1860-1929*, Judaic Studies Series, Leon J. Winberger, general editor (Tuscaloosa: University of Alabama Press, 1997), 164-88 and 242-7. Reprinted with the kind permission of the author and the publisher.

Society for International Concord. The promotional circular sent over his signature and that of three other leaders bore the imprint of his style. In advocating international law, the authors argued that they were not "commending a policy of peace in preference to justice" nor "peace at any price." While denouncing the spirit of militarism that might lead to "martial castes," the organization encouraged "military preparedness" for self-defense. Their sole purpose was to rouse public awareness, to insist that neutrality had not "lost all value."[3]

Before vigorously working for Woodrow Wilson's reelection, Heller had never taken an active role in a presidential campaign. Isaac, while a law student at Harvard, was also campaigning in the Boston area for Wilson. Calling Wilson "the greatest progressive President this or any other country has ever had," the father listed some arguments for his son to use in trying to persuade prospective voters. As the election approached, Heller worried about the prospects of the "schoolmaster turned practical reformer." He wrote to his sons that he wished he "were sure of W. W.'s election," adding that it would be "a real relief which would make me deeply thankful both for the sake of the country and of humanity in general." In an elated letter to Stephen Wise written shortly after the president's reelection, Heller pronounced the "Wilson triumph . . . a vindication of a great man of progressive policies" and of the "justice and good sense of the American people." The good news made the rabbi "feel like newborn."[4]

In the spring of 1916, Heller also campaigned enthusiastically for the Progressive Louisiana gubernatorial candidate, John M. Parker. Unlike other contemporary Southern governors, Parker distinguished himself as an arch-enemy of the Ku Klux Klan and a fighter against bigotry. Attending a large campaign meeting for Parker, Heller bragged to his sons that he had seated himself "conspicuously" on the platform, "to emphasize my friendship for him." In the service of progressivism, Heller overcame some past grudges, even praising a speech of Charles Rosen's "which seemed to me very excellent." The hall where the Progressives met was jammed with a "splendid class of people." Parker's bid was successful, and the following November, Heller sang Parker's praises again because the governor had actively campaigned for Wilson's reelection. Telling a local friend, chairman of a banquet to be given in Parker's honor, that he would be "most eager" to be included on the guest list, Heller added that he wanted to pay tribute to Parker at the affair. When Parker saw Heller's letter, the future governor called it "the finest compliment paid me" and asked Heller's permission to publish it. Heller gladly consented and confided to Stephen S. Wise that Parker was a man "after your and my heart, with moral courage and staunch backbone, a sincere friend of the Jews and a real lover of progress."[5]

But work on behalf of war sufferers abroad demanded much more of Heller's energies than did politics. In the fall of 1914, even as he solicited funds to help the civilians displaced by war, he worried that Jewish agencies like the B'nai B'rith and the American Jewish Committee might duplicate efforts and waste precious money raised. Heller told Isaac that although "*schnorring* [begging] for the Jewish war-sufferers" proved to be "a nasty and difficult job," the older Heller derived a great deal of satisfaction from using the skills he had developed in "fighting hard for justice." Now he considered himself "in prime time for attacking tight purses and flinty hearts."[6]

Encouraged by the Federation of American Zionists (FAZ) to make an appeal to the Reform rabbinate on behalf of Zionism, Heller had sent out a circular to most of his Reform colleagues, encouraging them to rethink their attitudes toward Palestine in the light of the war. He admitted that he was writing as a "radical Zionist" but asked his colleagues, "Are not many of us, despite their opposition to political Zionism, disposed to favor the setting aside of Palestine as a neutral zone of Jewish shelter? It is a queer coincidence," Heller noted, "that orthodox Jews and Julius Rosenwald should understand that monthly contributions are called for, not skimpy donations." He told them that, as rabbis, their positive influence could go far in remedying "prevailing indifference toward Palestine."[7]

Good Progressive and amateur sociologist that he was, Heller decided to poll the Reform rabbinate and included a list of four questions that he wanted answered briefly and returned. This circular and questionnaire marked his first systematic efforts to create a dialogue on Zionism within the rank and file of the Central Conference of American Rabbis (CCAR) membership. The effort to relieve suffering among Jews abroad had opened a door for Heller's larger mission of reconciliation between the two movements that might otherwise have remained locked. Heller was very much aware of his role. In January 1915, he told his sons that he now realized that the circular constituted "a highly important step, together with my appeal for funds, in the rapprochement between Zionism and Reform Judaism." The effort enabled him "to prove that at least 1/3 of the CCAR membership" sympathized with Zionism "(41 replies, so far out of 209)." By February, fifty-five had notified him that they would help raise funds to support the colonies in Palestine.[8]

By early February 1915, Louis Brandeis, recently converted to Zionism and already its leading American spokesperson, had sent Heller a telegram, urging him to collect funds for Palestine, where suffering was particularly intense. Heller expressed his frustration to his sons, "Find myself utterly unable to do more than to send of my own. From the people I cannot collect again." Less than two weeks later Cyrus Sulzberger, secretary of the American Jewish Relief Committee (AJRC), told Heller that, thus far, no funds "commensurate with the well-known generosity of the South" had been raised in Louisiana. Sulzberger felt compelled by the "crisis in the affairs of our coreligionists abroad" to call upon Heller to take the chairmanship for the AJRC for the state. Heller may have wished to refuse but could not do so. He worked hard to raise whatever additional funds he could.[9]

Heller's additional responsibilities placed new items on an already crowded agenda. After resigning from his position as weekly columnist for the *American Israelite* in the fall of 1914, he had begun publishing more regularly in the *Maccabaean*. In January 1915, Louis Lipsky, the journal's editor, wrote that he was "heartily glad" that Heller had turned all his "literary abilities to Zionist service" and affirmed his interest in Heller's monthly contributions to the *Maccabaean*. But even as Heller responded to Lipsky's call, he found himself deeply enmeshed in a policy crisis at Hebrew Union College (HUC) that involved James, his son, who had enrolled there as a rabbinical student.[10]

The previous December, when James and three other students who formed the board of the college's Literary Society learned that Horace Kallen would be coming to Cincinnati, they invited him to speak on a subject of his choice at the Literary Society meeting the evening before his address to the Menorah Society. Kallen accepted and told the student board that his topic would be "The Meaning of Hebraism." Two days before Kallen's scheduled arrival, the president of the Literary Society telegraphed him that the HUC authorities "commanded" the board to rescind the invitation because of some of the positions Kallen had taken publicly. Kallen was deeply disturbed by the affair not so much for the criticism of his Zionism or atheism as because he worried about the apparent lack of academic freedom at an institution responsible for training American rabbis. He told Stephen S. Wise that restrictions on academic freedom would only weaken the *morale* of the rabbinate and would undermine "the freedom of Judaism." Furious, Wise demanded of Heller, "Is nothing to be said or done about this? Are you satisfied with that spirit at the college and are you going to sit silent under it?" Personally, professionally, and philosophically, Heller could hardly avoid being swept into the vortex of the dilemma.[11] More fireworks lay ahead. The members of the Literary Society's board apologized to Kallen, stating that the invitation had been canceled "over our heads" and that they were writing "at the risk of appearing disloyal" to the college. They made the mistake of sharing the letter with Kohler, who, in turn, initiated disciplinary actions against them for insubordination. Wise and Heller protested to the HUC Board of Governors, and the board president issued an all-expenses-paid invitation to both of them to attend a special executive conference in Cincinnati at which they could express their grievances. Before leaving to meet the board, Heller circulated a letter to its members outlining the situation. Heller contended that HUC's current rage of censorship discredited I. M. Wise's spirit of "broad toleration." Heller cleverly argued that Kohler's policy only resulted in "rendering Zionism the more alluring to youths of independent spirit" while fostering "habits of servility and toadyism in those who are disposed to cater to superior power." He entreated the board members, as "spiritual heirs of Dr. Wise" to "exercise their influence on behalf of a reasonable measure of academic liberty" when they met in Cincinnati in mid-February.[12]

Even before the mid-February meeting, Heller anticipated success. He persuaded the HUC board members to pass a resolution stating that the topic of political Zionism was not too dangerous for discussion, provided that the lecturer were "competent" and free of "insulting hostility to the institution [HUC] or its officials" and could "speak in a spirit consonant with genuine religiousness." Moreover, a student could advocate Zionism from the chapel's pulpit if the "temper and manner of his Zionist support" were "sincerely religious." Heller felt gratified by the "openminded earnestness" that the board had displayed in considering the proposals he had presented.[13]

Involvement with the demands of congregation and community and commitment to Zionism and with the problems at HUC did not detract from his concern as a parent for his younger son, Isaac. Although a deeply spiritual man, once he became a rabbi, Heller rarely talked about God, preferring such terms as "divine Providence" when he infrequently approached the subject in a sermon. Thirty years of serving in the rabbinate heightened his sense of spiritual maturation. While Isaac was attending Harvard Law School, Max received a letter not unlike the postcard he had mailed from Prague to his own father nearly forty years earlier. Isaac had entertained the idea of becoming a rabbi, but he wrote to say that he had definitely decided not to do so.[14]

Unlike Simon, his father, Max was able to identify with the feelings Isaac expressed. Telling Isaac that his letter "touched me deeply," Max recalled his own rebellion. "A father tries his best to guide his boys right; when he himself was crowded [?] away by such circumstances from the dream of his childhood he cannot, especially as a believer in selfguidance, force a vocation on his boy," Max replied. "Because a boy goes through the feverish measles of scepticism [*sic*] and agnosticism therefore he thinks the ministry is not for him, or else his brother is already studying, or his father has a stormy road to travel. But all the time that boy does not know the deep fountains of his yearning at the bottom of his nature . . . , the hunger for the . . . eternal values of the soul-life, the unspeakable satisfaction of pouring out one's being in the communication of one's innermost to souls that long for their food. Religion which is my blockhead's joke to-day, has been the intoxicating wine and the nourishing meat of all the deepest and most luminary souls in history." But Max did not push the rabbinate. Instead, he reassured Isaac that, as an attorney, he could "do a great deal of good in Judaism . . . , broadening and deepening your moral life, owing to the contact you may have had with these strange sides of human nature." To show Isaac that he accepted his decision, Max warmly told him that he was sending him a tallis (prayer shawl). "It belonged to your great-grand father on my father's side," Max wrote, and then he shared instructions about the proper way to wear it. Prayer shawls were not used in Reform worship, but Heller was now anxious to initiate his son into more traditional Jewish forms, even if Isaac had chosen to pursue a career different from that of his father and older brother. He trusted that Isaac would also carry on the fight for Zionism.[15]

At the CCAR conference at Charlevoix, Michigan, in 1915, Heller practically single-handedly championed the Zionist point of view. While Stephen S. Wise was beginning to feel overwhelmed by the obstinate leadership within the CCAR and did not attend the conference, he relayed to Heller that younger Zionist rabbis present had spoken of his superb fight "against the powers of darkness." Heller and Wise differed radically in their approach to the CCAR. When frustrated by intransigence, Wise was ready to pull out of the organization, but Heller's loyalties to his HUC education and to the memory of I. M. Wise made him persist in attempts at reconciliation. Perhaps the unpleasant isolation at the conference inspired Heller's powerful attack, waged in October 1915, in the *Jewish Comment*. Calling his pulpit enemies "Philistines," Heller excoriated them for the "colorless liberalism" that seldom ventured beyond safe platitudes rooted in middle-class comfort. He deplored such rabbis' effusive discourses on social maladjustments, with their tendency to represent social justice "as the core of Judaism," and simultaneous criticism of Brandeis's leadership in the American Zionist movement. Brandeis, the model of social justice, had no formal Jewish training, but, Heller wondered, "Must a man know Hebrew grammar in order to be entitled to an opinion on Jewish psychology?" Wise again communicated his frustrations. He agreed with Heller that the future battles in Judaism would be waged not between the Orthodox and the Reform "but over a real and fundamental Jewishness expressed racially or, if you please, nationally, and with milk-and-water emasculate Judaism which is the sad survival of the German-Jewish Reformation." Moving far from the position he had taken in opposition to Heller's bid for CCAR president some years earlier, Wise now claimed to feel closer to Orthodox Jews not ashamed of their Judaism than to "our reform colleagues many of whom have fundamentally ceased to be Jews, who prate about the religion of the Jew when religion is furthest from their own souls."[16]

Just as Heller had opened 1915 by giving a memorable address at the University of Michigan, so he closed the year with another major sermon on Jewish identity delivered in mid-December at Temple Israel in St. Louis, at the Jewish Chautauqua Service. In "The Jewish Consciousness," he traced the historic evolution of Jewish consciousness, dwelling particularly on the dilemmas posed by emancipation. He saw the Jew unhappily caught "between the Scylla of truculent self-assertion and the Charybdis of shame-faced self-obliteration." In his confusion, the modern Jew lacked the appropriate language for self-definition, unsure whether to call the bonds between him and his brethren racial, religious, or national. Heller eloquently pleaded for a synthesis, for a Jewish manhood yearning to be its "unhampered self." He believed that all humanity needed "the soil-rootings of nationality" in order to flourish, a condition clearly impossible in the "assimilative environments" of the West. In a similar vein, earlier that month, Heller had published an unsigned article, "Uprooted," in which he argued that while a "man without a country" was a pathetic creature, even sadder was the man "whose heart has cut itself loose from all rootage in its natural soil." Even as Heller realized that nationalism run amok had plunged Europe in the throes of war, he embraced nationalism as an "indispensable" ingredient in the evolution of consciousness, "a prime factor in the cultural diversification and, thereby, the progressive unfoldment, of the human race."[17]

Heller's continued allegiance to Zionism only renewed and deepened his commitment to the larger themes of brotherhood. Strengthened by his own insights and his determination to spread the gospel of his own convictions, in December Heller also returned to preach at the Central Congregational Church in New Orleans, in the same pulpit from which he had first addressed an African American audience several years earlier. This time he gave a memorial sermon, "Booker T. Washington, a Modern Prophet." Heller compared Washington to Moses; both men had found their mission in building the foundations for their people. Washington deserved praise, Heller argued, because he had taught and uplifted his race without renouncing his dignity, his self-worth, and his race pride. Like a Jew concerned with fulfilling God's laws, Washington had spent his entire life in "one consistent preachment of duties, rather than a demand for rights." Heller prophesied that the time would come when the South would "count it among her glories" that one "dark-skinned man, in the space of one generation," had fought his way "out of the night of slavery into the full daylight of wide esteem and incalculable service."[18]

But Heller well understood the limits of the gains that Washington had made. Just a few months after the sermon, Heller wrote his sons that he and Ida had gone to see *The Birth of a Nation*, D. W. Griffith's neoconfederate racist epic. Heller was appalled. He found it "replete with prejudice of the worst kind and historic misrepresentations." Although he considered sending a letter to the *Times-Picayune*, "warning parents against sending their children to see it and denouncing this way of stirring up feeling against the negro," or preaching a sermon against both the film and the book on which it was based, he eventually did nothing. Temporarily exhausted from his exertions or unwilling to face a fresh barrage of criticism, he admitted that he was "not in the mood . . . to take up another fight." He added that, unfortunately, no one else seemed ready to "trouble himself about it."[19]

In 1916, however, Heller did take up another fight. Even though he was not a central protagonist in the battle to establish an American Jewish Congress, his presence made a difference in the conference skirmishes where he debated the mainstream leaders of the CCAR and in the editorial bouts where his pen became his weapon of choice. The war in Europe coincided with and helped change the structure of the American Jewish community. The increase in the needs of Jews abroad placed additional pressure on communal resources already stretched to meet the demands of the large numbers of immigrants who had arrived steadily before war broke out in Europe.

When the thoroughly assimilated Louis D. Brandeis mediated a garment workers' strike in 1910, he encountered Russian immigrant Jews for the first time and as a pragmatic idealist found himself deeply moved by the workers' intellectual acumen and Jewish pride. The journey from sympathy to activism proved short, as it had for Heller a decade earlier. Tutored by his friend Horace Kallen, Brandeis converted to Zionism. When he took over the leadership of the Zionist Provisional Executive Committee, which sought to alleviate the emergencies of Jews overseas, he used his immense energies to transform American Zionism into a movement that could more efficiently meet the needs abroad. "Men! Money! Discipline!" he demanded. In addition to the prestige and organizational abilities that Brandeis brought to American Zionism, he offered his own synthesis of Kallen's cultural pluralism, which proved to be the perfect formula for recruiting. He smoothly blended American patriotism with Zionism, a fusion that harmonized the tensions inherent in the specter of "dual loyalties" feared by assimilated German-American Jews. "To be good Americans," he announced, "we must be better Jews, and to be better Jews, we must become Zionists."[20]

The movement mushroomed under his leadership, and the ideals of his skillfully engineered progressivism seeped not only into Zionism but also into a movement to organize democratically for Jewish defense, to establish an American Jewish Congress that truly represented the American Jewish community. Brandeis became the titular head of the pro-Congress group. Before the fight for and establishment of an American Jewish Congress, the exclusive and oligarchic American Jewish Committee (AJC) had represented the Jewish community with prestigious patriarchal leaders like Jacob Schiff and Louis Marshall. At the opposite end of the spectrum, the working-class Zionist organizations spearheaded the Congress movement, which by 1916 was being actively debated at the CCAR convention. Heller asked the organization to support the Congress movement, "endorsed by the masses of our people," instead of the AJC, which had resisted the idea of a democratically elected organization. Although democratization in the American Jewish community reflected larger trends in American political culture like the Seventeenth Amendment that provided for the direct election of senators, Heller's close friend, Joseph Stolz, disagreed with his support of an American Jewish Congress, fearing that the Congress would destroy the AJC.[21]

Although Stolz and Henry Cohen had been Heller's closest friends in the rabbinate, neither sympathized with his Zionism, and now Stolz argued against the Congress movement. When, in the fall of 1916, Isaac dejectedly wrote that the young woman he loved no longer returned his affections, his father responded by revealing his own disappointment in friends. Isaac worried that his limp from his bout with polio had made him unattractive. Heller reassured him that some day he would meet an "aspiring, noble-hearted woman, the sympathetic echo of your innermost yearnings." Although Rabbi Heller had often boasted that he had "the two most admirable friends of any one in the rabbinate, your Uncles Joe and Henry" and many others, he rhetorically asked Isaac, "Do you imagine I have one perfect friend, one solitary friend whom I could trust to the very end?" He added defensively, "Don't you know how often my friends have failed to stand by me, not because they didn't love me, but because they lacked the moral courage?" The father's own moral courage did not diminish the loneliness he experienced because he advocated unpopular positions.[22]

As the United States moved away from its policy of isolation, Heller continued to support Wilson. Heller told his congregants that the country could remain neutral no longer, since modern civilization had already "entangled us into alliances without number which bind up our commerce, our intellectual progress, our sympathies, our daily life with the welfare and the peace of Europe." When the United States entered the war in the spring of 1917, Heller professed boundless optimism and was fully invested in Wilson's democratic mission. In his sermon "Boons from the World War," Heller asked his congregants, "Is there not such a thing as a democracy of nations as well as of individuals?" The metaphors he had been using for the past decade when addressing the needs of African Americans and Eastern European Jews he found serviceable once more. He foresaw a day when even the "least gifted and most backward nations" would be able to live and develop freely, having been given "its right of unhampered unfoldment" in living "according to the inner law of its own individuality," rather than subsumed under the "selfish interests of some powerful elder-brother nation." Heller believed that from the current travails there might "emerge as victor the dove of peace bringing the olive-leaf of perfect reconciliation, of universal disarmament" and "free fellowship."[23]

That same spring, Heller accepted an invitation to give the commencement address at Tuskegee Institute. With the international situation very much on his mind, he found striking parallels between the international struggle for minority rights and the fight against racial barriers confronting African Americans at home. He told the graduates that he had always been "deeply touched by the problem of the Negro." His sympathies were aroused on behalf of the downtrodden race, "partly because, as a Jew, the perplexity of national problems and race problems comes home to me as it would not to other men." Heller confessed that he had been too often "depressed" by the "bigoted prejudice" that had hindered the efforts of "even otherwise well-meaning people" in attacking the "delicate problems of race." He cleverly merged the Wilsonian concern in the international arena for smaller nations and the national rights of minorities with the racial situation in America. Now his paternalistic devotion to African Americans, expressed in "The Elder Brother" title of his sermon, had broader overtones than a simple echo of Atticus Haygood. Heller took for his biblical passage Genesis 25:23, "One people shall be mightier than the other, but the elder shall serve the younger." He moved from questioning how the stronger might protect the weaker individual or race to wondering how the small nations and "backward races" might be protected "against the aggressions and exploitations, against the violences and rapacities of their brother-nations and races." While he did not offer any innovative solutions to the aggressive segregation of the day, Heller did admit that, especially in the South, there could be no prosperity "while our colored brother is languishing." The South could foster no "enduring culture" while shutting out the black citizen "from the best which our generation has to offer." The only real solution was to "take our colored brother with us on our march of progress" or else "lag with him in the rear, as we shall, then, deserve to lag." He also compared the difficult road ahead for the aspiring, educated black student with the plight of the Jewish people, some of whom had "climbed to the heights of culture," while the other half had "only left Russian bondage" two months earlier.[24]

The next month in the *Jewish Ledger*, Heller once again advocated an American Jewish Congress. He believed that the projected meeting of a Congress presented a significant departure from the historic methods of self-defense Jews had used for centuries to fight bigotry. Typically, prominent Jews had pleaded "against injustice as individuals." Although later external circumstances departed radically from those of medieval Poland, essential features of the initial pattern of self-defense endured. Structurally, the most intriguing feature was the emergence of the *shtadlan*, the "intercessor" who presented himself to the gentile community as the representative of the Jews, as one acting in their behalf. Inevitably, the *shtadlanim* were also *maskilim*, or enlightened Jews. The enlightened, assimilated, secular Jewish leader acted at the expense of the traditional *ke-hilla* authority—the rabbi—but the self-appointed leadership function of the *shtadlanim* did not go unchallenged by working-class Jews. The latter refused to identify with either the assimilationist means or the bourgeois ends of the community elites. Now, for the first time, in America, "under the shadow of the greatest of democracies, under a President who seems to be the world's outstanding champion of democracy," Heller saw Jews who were ready to model themselves in the image of the country of their allegiance. They were choosing a democratic method of organization to unite in offering assistance to those abroad. "To impress upon the nations the rights of our brothers to freedom and self-unfoldment we must stand together," he counseled. In June, when elections for delegates were held throughout the United States, Heller was selected from New Orleans. But the meeting of the Congress was postponed for a year and a half. With the country now at war, American Jews decided to put their energies into the war effort and put aside their own agenda until after peace had been reestablished.[25]

The "zenith" of Heller's career as a journalist began at the end of 1916, when he told Stephen Wise that he was looking for a forum that would allow him to try his hand at "joining Zionism with Liberal Judaism." A new format in the *Maccabaean* provided the perfect venue for Heller's forceful essays. Beginning in the spring of 1917, Heller produced a frequent column in a section entitled "With Malice Toward None." The timing proved to be particularly fortuitous, because 1917 was a turning point both for progressivism and Zionism, and Heller had positioned himself to comment on both to a national audience.[26]

"Dollarland Spirituality" was the first column to appear in which Heller blasted those who preached "blessing and prosperity" as salvation. "What a fine gospel from unctuous pulpit-lackey to beatific millionaire!" he sneered, as if "our millions" could "bring back the faded Jewish life" or prosperity could "cure our snobbish attitude towards Jewish history." He deemed anti-Zionism a certain brand of "commercialized soul life" fit only for the philistines who still championed the obsolete notion of a Jewish mission in dispersion. "The Mission in Dispersion" followed. Here he used suggestive natural images of weakening, like the "subsidence of Jewish consciousness" or spiritual "barrenness" that occurred when Jews were planted in soil too rich in diversions, a condition "notoriously unsuited to the blossoming forth of religious genius."[27]

Just before the CCAR met in Buffalo the following July, Heller published in the *Maccabaean* a column, "Nationalism and Religion," that went beyond Brandeis's formula equating being a good American with being a better Jew, or a Zionist. Heller succeeded in his resolution of the central tensions in liberal Judaism by claiming that Jewish nationalism and religious Judaism were completely interdependent. Responding to the Zionists who discounted religiosity as well as to Reform Jews who discounted nationalism, Heller achieved his own synthesis. He maintained that Jewish nationalism needed the "consecration of Judaism" just as Judaism, "in the long run," needed nationalism to "maintain life."[28]

But the majority of the rabbis present in Buffalo, including Joe Stolz, reaffirmed the Jewish mission idea, declaring that "that essence of Israel as a priest-people" lay in its "religious consciousness . . . , not in any political or racial national consciousness." Heller submitted his own minority report, arguing that the tenets of Reform Judaism did not "insist on the dispersion of the Jews as an indispensable condition for the welfare and progress of Judaism." Attempting to secure a "publicly and legally safe-guarded home for Jews in Palestine," he declared, violated none of the principles of the Reform movement. He and Stolz parted ways again when the subject of the American Jewish Congress was debated, and this time Heller's other dear friend, Henry Cohen, also opposed the Congress. Heller tried to point out that because the American Jewish Congress already had a slate of delegates, the new body stood "before the world" in representing American Jewry, and the CCAR needed to be counted among its participants and supporters. Like the majority of his colleagues, Cohen disagreed, feeling that because a Zionist majority had been elected as delegates to the Congress, that body did not truly represent "American Israel." Three other Southern rabbis present, Edward Calisch of Richmond, Morris Newfield of Birmingham, and David Marx of Atlanta, sided with Cohen. Heller's New Orleans colleague Rabbi Emil Leipziger, Leucht's successor at Touro Synagogue, editorialized on the CCAR conference in the *Jewish Spectator*. He mentioned that the majority had achieved "a significant diplomatic victory." Even though a resolution opposing Zionism would have caused the "secession of a number of valuable men from the Conference," one favoring Zionism would have been "unthinkable in the rabbinical body" As with his positions on Zionism and race, the Congress movement found Heller isolated again both in the CCAR and in his region.[29]

Despite defeat at Buffalo, Heller remained optimistic, discerning in the movement "a strong, influential and growing minority . . . openly espousing Zionism," while the majority had refused to condemn Zionism completely. Only a small group of "rabid irreconcilables" remained, and their numbers, he believed, were "dwindling." Heller believed that the younger men, those with "triumphant enthusiasm," might yet revitalize American Reform Judaism. Stephen Wise agreed, telling Heller, "As you rightly put it, the best thing about the debate on Zionism was the fact that we now see that the younger men are with us,—and that is everything."[30]

In "Our Spiritual Golus [diaspora]," however, Heller expressed the darker side of his feelings and fears about America, even as he proudly championed the president, the war effort, and Jewish patriotism. This essay in the *Maccabacan* conveyed the depths of discomfort in the Americanized immigrant's soul. Convinced that the Jew could not be "welcomed, as Jew, into the innermost life of American culture" and therefore faced outsider or pariah status in the United States, Heller discussed social anti-Semitism as "the silent unarticulated, but invincible power of a sense of uncongeniality" increasingly prevalent in America, from boardrooms and hotels to fraternities and schools that sought to exclude Jews from their midst. Although Heller was a liberal intellectually, his life experiences in the South and his observation of recent Western European Jewish history had forced him to qualify his trust in liberalism. "We ought to be abundantly aware," he cautioned, how much more "administrative policy, public feeling, social atmosphere matter" above the "mere formal letter of the law." He cited countries like Austria, in which "even the socialist and radical have not been above entering into bargains at the expense of the Jew." In his adopted country, Heller was wary because Americanization tended to equal "de-Judaization," a process that set up an "insoluble antagonism" for the Jewish citizen. Zionism, with its "restoration to our historic soil," provided the only cure for "spiritual homelessness."[31]

In the fall of 1917, the British issuance of the Balfour Declaration, recognizing Jewish rights to a homeland in Palestine, cast such light onto the Zionist world that Heller's diaspora depression lifted. He busily set to work to rally support among American Jews and gentiles alike. Earlier that spring, when the Russian Revolution seemed to offer relief for all the oppressed minorities there, including the Jews, David Philipson had predicted that it would lead to "Zionism's End." When the Balfour Declaration and the Bolshevik Revolution occurred almost simultaneously, Heller and the Zionists were vindicated. "In these days of the Russian chaos," he crowed, "as little as the Jewish problem is susceptible of a lightning solution, just so little is the Zionist movement in danger of a sudden and complete collapse." As Russia retreated from liberation and reverted to "pogrom conditions," Heller hailed Great Britain, "the greatest empire in the world," declaring itself "in full accord with the aims and aspirations of the Zionist movement." To Jacob de Haas, Heller cabled, "England, politically the ripest of commonwealths, boldly hews the path towards this triumph of international justice. America is certain to follow." While Heller believed that the world had been moving in the direction England now spearheaded, he understood that "the last to be convinced" would be "the snobs and autocrats in our ranks," although they, too, would ultimately "fall into line."[32]

David Philipson, one of the principal unnamed "autocrats," wrote an editorial for the *American Israelite* in which he proudly defended his allegiance to America, and he claimed that the Balfour Declaration in no way changed the terms of debate on Judaism's mission. "Are the Jews an international religious people unique and distinct in their status," he queried, "or are they merely a small nation in the political sense like other small nations of the earth?" For Philipson, the ideologue, no doubt existed as to the answer. He pledged his allegiance to the United States, considering Palestine "dear only as a memory," having been the home of my very remote ancestry." Besides, he considered Judaism "much larger than Zionism," an essential element in his argument that Jews formed a religious and not a national group.[33]

Heller's close friend, Henry Cohen, was also among those who fell in line with the anti-Zionist activists after the Balfour Declaration, and the correspondence between the two leading Southern rabbis never quite recovered its prior warmth and rapport. In late December, challenging his Galveston colleague, Heller wondered if the "historic changes" of the past few weeks had softened Cohen's attitude toward Zionism. Heller wanted to know the outer limits of Cohen's anti-Zionism, how far Cohen aligned himself with "rabid, purblind, selfish Anti-Zionists in fearing a nationalist experiment as prejudicial to the safety and comfort of Western Judaism." Henrietta Szold, a passionate Zionist and the founder of Hadassah, planned a trip to Galveston. If Cohen were to "chime in with that chorus" of anti-Zionists, Heller feared, it would seem "your holy duty to proscribe or, at least, cold-shoulder Henrietta." Heller assured Cohen that he was not trying to "beg a favor," but respecting and loving both Szold and Cohen, he would feel "greatly pained" if a conflict ensued. "What's the use, Max?" Cohen had responded to a similar request. "We've threshed the matter out thoroughly, for lo! these many moons & that's the result. Why you should call it intolerance I don't know!" Cohen tried to patch over their differences. "Seemingly your experiences are different," he told Heller, "but I know mine. You are a Zionist & your people know it. I am not & my people know it."[34]

The Moravian-born historian Gotthard Deutsch, Heller's close friend at HUC, was an anti-Zionist intellectually but emotionally kept his distance from those like Kohler and Philipson. Deutsch enjoyed playing the devil's advocate. Complimenting Heller on one of his journalistic pieces on anti-Zionism, Deutsch could not resist asking if Heller actually believed that a Jewish commonwealth in Palestine would help retain the "Judah P Benjamins . . . , the Joseph Pulitzers . . . , and even the Mary Antins and their descendants within the fold of Judaism." Deutsch believed that the assimilationists would always find an "easier way of slipping out of Judaism," just as, with the intense anti-German sentiment of wartime America, prominent Americans of German descent were now proclaiming that their ancestry was "a matter of strictly historic interest."[35]

A real maverick, Deutsch intensely admired German culture and had never become an American citizen. In April 1917, he was completely disheartened, upset with the injustice of what he considered an unjust war. Factional problems between Zionists and anti-Zionists seemed beside the point. Deutsch still had family in Germany. James Heller and Deutsch's sons were all in the army. To Deutsch, the "great need of the moment" was to make the American nation "appreciate the monstrosity of a patriotism that demands of my boys to consider it the highest virtue to kill the only son of a widow who happens to be their father's only sister." Deutsch's sympathies during the war were becoming problematic. He sarcastically commented to Heller, "You go on preaching the making of the world safe for democracy, when 100 innocent niggers are cruelly done to death in broad daylight." Deutsch's vulnerability wounded him. While Heller preached democracy, the Board of Governors warned Deutsch to abandon his activity with the "council for peace and democracy," an organization evidently critical of the war. Deutsch closed with the line, "Give me humanity or Cherokkeee canibalism [*sic*]."[36]

In a city with so large a German population, when wartime anti-German feeling crested, Deutsch came under suspicion for his German affections and his German citizenship. He was accused of disloyalty. Many in Cincinnati's German Jewish community, fearful lest Deutsch's idiosyncrasies cast aspersions on their own patriotism, tried to pressure the HUC Board of Governors to dismiss him. Deutsch's loyal out-of-town friends on the board of HUC alumni, including Stolz and Heller, came to his aid, and the college retained him. In a statement submitted to the board by the Alumni Association, the organization decided that Deutsch should make a "public declaration of loyalty" to clear the college of suspicion. After Deutsch was exonerated, Heller congratulated him but warned him that he needed to be "watchfully discreet," "to abstain" from giving the "slenderest provocation."[37]

Following Deutsch's death in 1921, Heller wrote a biographical sketch of him for the *Hebrew Union College Monthly* in which he tried to explain Deutsch's wartime problems. Heller maintained that Deutsch's "heart clung to the German people" and that "his affections . . . ruled his judgment." But, Heller continued, Deutsch had also been stung by the "general discredit under which everything associated with Germany had fallen in the exaggerated wave of chauvinistic bigotry which had come with the war." Heller himself had sent a letter to the editor of the *Times-Picayune* to protest when the local school board threatened to remove German from the public high school curriculum. Heller argued that teaching the German language perpetuated "that glorious German spirit" that far antedated and would long survive "the menacing spectre of Prussian Kulture."[38]

Heller's overwhelming concern, after the issuance of the Balfour Declaration, however, lay in publicizing the renewed possibility that Zion would be restored, a subject he entertained both in the pulpit and in the local press as well as in the Jewish press. Unlike Deutsch, Heller was now caught up in the vision of a Jewish Palestine, the most "glowing romance of the world war." But while the younger men in the CCAR well may have sympathized with Zionism and, like many American Jews formerly indecisive over the issue, were more likely to embrace the movement since the appearance of the Balfour Declaration, the anti-Zionists were motivated to organize as never before. In the spring of 1918, Heller's venom reached a literary peak in a letter to the editor of the *American Israelite* in which he compared the anti-Zionist to the Bolshevik, arguing that the two exhibited "many points of congeniality and resemblance." He called the Anti-Zionist the "Bolshevik of Jewishness." Both Bolsheviks and anti-Zionists were prisoners of their own dogma; both would discover, "too late, that by their blindness, they have struck their adored cause of actualized social justice a stunning blow from which it will take a long time to recover." The anti-Zionist belatedly might awaken to learn that he had "injured the prestige of his own faith and race by stubbornly seeking to retard" what was already "beyond his power to prevent."[39]

The following June, Heller was jockeying behind the scenes to shape the CCAR summer convention in Chicago, even though he had decided not to attend. He stayed away, he sarcastically remarked, because the unpleasant decisions at the Buffalo convention had "satisfied" him "for some time to come." Although he refused to resign from the CCAR and was "keeping Wise and [Martin] Meyer from doing so," he complained to Stolz that he felt "worn out with the pettiness, weakness and folly of the rank and file" and "nauseated by the spirit of leaders like Philipson and Schulman." The "blinkered" positions spouted by Heller's antagonists on issues from Zionism to "social maladjustments" and "industrial evils" dampened both his "pride of vocation and glow of idealism." A "divorce" may have been out of the question, but he needed a period of "separation" from the Conference. The leadership's response to the Balfour Declaration particularly displeased him, and in referring to the subject, Heller revealed his peevishness even to Stolz. "If the rest of you cannot recognize an epoch when it has come," he wrote, "I want to be absent when you record yourselves" standing in the way of historical development. Although he still felt the tug of old loyalties and apologized for the bitterness in his heart, he concluded that it was best to stay away even while he continued his work for the CCAR in other areas.[40]

Heller's premonitions were sound. He was far from being paranoid on the growing intransigency of the anti-Zionists, even if he remained unaware of the extent of their underground activities. In late April 1918, a group of rabbis and laymen, including Schulman and Herman Enelow, met in New York at the request of Ephraim Frisch, a young anti-Zionist rabbi there. Frisch wanted to initiate a League of American Jews, an official anti-Zionist organization similar to the League of British Jews. In July, as Heller was lobbying for a more positive statement from the CCAR on the subject of the Balfour Declaration, Frisch, Philipson, and other anti-Zionists were busily planning a counterattack. Philipson noted that since the CCAR had reaffirmed its position at Buffalo, the Conference had to deal with Zionism again at the 1918 convention only because the Balfour Declaration had been issued, bringing "Zionistic propaganda into the field of practical world politics." The CCAR very much favored facilitating the immigration of Jews to Palestine when "economic necessity or political and religious persecution" made Palestine the obvious haven, he argued, but the Conference refused to subscribe to the phrase in the Declaration stating that Palestine was to be designated as "a national home-land for the Jewish people." The CCAR opposed the idea of Palestine as "THE homeland of the Jews" and maintained that the Jewish people had a right to be at home wherever they chose to live."[41]

Heller waged his attack on the outcome of the CCAR convention in an essay, "Zionism and Our Reform Rabbinate," in an unusually long *Maccabaean* column that presented a concise historical overview of the encounter between America's Zionists and anti-Zionists during the preceding two decades. Now that more of the seminary's students were of Eastern European parentage, Heller believed that perhaps a majority were sympathetic toward the movement, but he sadly noted that, when faced with the hostility of their congregants, many of these young men would "abandon their Zionist ideals" in order to maintain their pulpits. As if predicting that more favorable conditions might exist in the future, he mentioned that Zionist rabbis now headed five of the largest congregations in the country-New York, Philadelphia, Cleveland, San Francisco, and New Orleans-and that the most influential rabbi in the movement [unnamed, but undoubtedly Stephen S. Wise] was also a Zionist. Again equating anti-Zionism with philistinism, Heller concluded, "Whenever, if ever, the multitudes of the prosperous will adopt Zionism into fashion, they will be followed, reluctantly by their spiritual leaders."[42]

Anti-Zionists wasted no time in pushing their agenda past a limited audience of Reform Jews-rabbinical and lay. Just a few days after the Chicago meeting, Henry Cohen sent a letter to Robert Lansing, Wilson's secretary of state. No friend of the Jews, Lansing was a logical and well-chosen target of anti-Zionist propaganda. In December 1917, he had already cautioned Wilson to "avoid endorsing the British position." Cohen's letter got to the point very quickly. He told Lansing that "an overwhelming majority of native born Americans and numbers of Jews who have made the United States the country of their adoption" appreciated Balfour's good intentions, but felt the Declaration to be an "act of mistaken kindness." He argued that Reform Jews, having "outgrown the conception of Jewish nationality," were much "too deeply attached" to the United States to seek another political affiliation. Truly, these anti-Zionists reacted "with repugnance and alarm" to the very idea of a newly established Jewish state. Obviously, Cohen wished to pressure the State Department, and ultimately the president, to withhold support for the British Declaration.[43]

Now when he advocated the Zionist position, Heller used Wilsonian-Brandeisian terminology, seeing the new Jerusalem "in the shape of a realized pattern of social justice." The Jews would establish in their regained homeland a "perfectly ethical social order," which would lead to "higher spirituality." In another article, he spoke of the harmony that would exist in the homeland, where "every class-interest and party-complexion" would be assuaged.[44]

The dream of Jewish harmony in the promised land vividly contrasted with the intra-ethnic fighting that the idea of a revived Palestine provoked. In August 1918, both the Reform Zionists and the anti-Zionists were aggressively promoting their viewpoints. Heller, Stephen Wise, and Martin Meyer circulated a counterstatement (endorsed by several other Zionists within the CCAR) to the recent CCAR resolution. When Cohen received his, he scribbled a response at the bottom, castigating Zionists for propagandizing to members of Congress. Evidently he interpreted his "private" letter to Lansing in a different light. At the end of August, Frisch, Philipson, and Cohen, among others, were ready to put forward their League of American Jews and proposed that a conference be held in New York at the end of October. While the anti-Zionist organizers exchanged letters containing a variety of agendas for the meeting and their future campaign against the Declaration, on the last day of August, President Wilson's Jewish New Year's greeting to Stephen S. Wise undermined all of their plans. Wilson warmly endorsed the progress American Zionists had made since the Balfour Declaration and generally looked forward to the British government's fulfillment of its promise to facilitate the establishment in Palestine of a national homeland for the Jewish people.[45]

Zionist leaders capitalized on the statement by sending copies to rabbis throughout the country, suggesting that they read it aloud to their congregants during high holiday services. In light of Wilson's pro-Zionist sentiment, anti-Zionists like Kaufman Kohler decided that the time was not propitious for launching a new anti-Zionist organization. He worried that such an action would not only expose the "weakness and smallness of numbers" in the anti-Zionist camp but might even seem un-American. "I consider it detrimental to our cause to start an opposition during war time," he told his cohort David Philipson, since the League could be "looked upon as unpatriotic." Kohler decided not to allow his name to be used in the call for the anti-Zionist conference. "I trust . . . that you yourself have by this time come to the same conclusion," he added. Louis Marshall's letter was even stronger. "I not only am unwilling to permit the use of my name" in calling for a League conference, "but I sincerely hope that you and your associates may abandon the project," Marshall began. He warned that only negative consequences would result from the effort, creating "a bitter feeling among the Jews of this country and of misapprehensions which can only bode evil."[46]

Frisch, however, followed his own counsel and, after Wilson's letter to Wise had been published, telegraphed the president himself. Embarrassed by Frisch's ill-timed, impetuous, and bold reaction, Zionists and anti-Zionists alike castigated him. In his statements to the press the unseasoned young rabbi had, perhaps inadvertently, revealed the plans for the League of American Jews. Henry Berkowitz, an influential Philadelphia rabbi originally sympathetic to the League, now reversed himself. "Circumstances have placed us in a position in which we are robbed . . . of doing anything that would prove effectual," he told Philipson. Berkowitz regretted that Frisch had destroyed any possibilities "to make known our position in a dignified and effective way to the President and the country." But the die-hards like Philipson, Cohen, Frisch and some committed laymen did not give up so easily.[47]

Frisch's action motivated Heller to vent his anger in a scalding letter to the editor of the *American Israelite*, which remained one of the most ideologically anti-Zionist publications in the country. He acknowledged that Zionists had been portrayed as "impractical dreamers . . . irreligious or even anti-religious in tendency." But now that the national association of Orthodox Rabbis had endorsed Zionism, the argument that the movement was anti-religious could be seen as fallacious. While Heller acknowledged that the president's letter was not an official sanction, he nevertheless believed that Wilson, in "speaking on behalf of 'all Americans'" and in alluding to Palestine's "promise of spiritual re-birth," favored the cause. Heller's conclusion was particularly strong. "If Zionism succeeds, the glory will certainly be that of the Jew and Judaism," he predicted. But should the movement fail, "the discredit can not be escaped by Jew and Judaism," especially if the failure resulted, "not from outward impediments," but from "inner divisions and factious antagonisms." Elsewhere Heller called antinationalism a "prejudice" that Jews still needed to outgrow. He continued to blame an assimilated, comfortable American Jewish community who refused "to measure a world-wide question otherwise than with the yardstick of domestic interests."[48]

Although now badly crippled, the anti-Zionists continued to work more discreetly. After armistice was declared in November 1918, the core of League-supporting anti-Zionists now hoped to limit the Zionist influence on the peace process. When the American Jewish Congress finally convened in Philadelphia the following month, and Judge

Julian Mack, Brandeis's disciple and president of the Zionist Organization of America, was elected to chair the delegation going to Paris,[49] anti-Zionists felt duty bound to re-double their organizational efforts.

President Wilson's reassurance to Stephen S. Wise that he would stand by his prom-ise to help secure a "Jewish commonwealth," only spurred the anti-Zionists to find a leader to deliver their message to the president. In March 1919, the same month that Wilson personally met with the American Jewish Congress delegation, California Con-gressman Julius Kahn presented the president with an anti-Zionist manifesto that had been signed by nearly 300 prominent American Jews, including rabbis from nearly every major Reform congregation in the South except Temple Sinai.[50] These leaders identified completely with the Classical Reform mission of dispersion, an attitude reinforced by the anxieties aroused by wartime antihyphenated campaigners like Theodore Roosevelt, who stridently insisted that America was for Americans. David Philipson quoted the Califor-nia congressman whose concluding remarks praised the recent elimination of "hyphen-ism" in the United States. "Thank God for it! . . . And what is Zionism endeavoring to do? Create a new form of hyphenism? . . . We want no such thing. . . . For me the United States is my Zion and San Francisco is my Jerusalem." But these sentiments proved to be practically the anti-Zionists' last hurrah of the World War I era.[51]

In response to the renewed anti-Zionist thrust, Heller continued to promote the mes-sage of the essential reciprocity between Reform and Zionism as lie patiently and pas-sionately explained that the two movements needed each other. In his neatly balanced argument, he ably described the inner reconciliation that allowed him to fight actively for the two movements that, at the moment, appeared to be poised in opposition. Signifi-cantly, he now perceived both as processes that, in time, were bound to "fructify and in-terpenetrate one another." While Zionism needed the "liberal temper . . . to save for Ju-daism its vigor and freshness of ever renewed readaptation to historic environments," Reform Judaism required "the inspiring wing-beat of the Zionist hope" with its "hot, red blood of Jewish loyalty and . . . brotherhood, its thirst for the sincerity and the fulfillment of being ourselves." Now when he waged his war of words, Heller called those who still opposed a Jewish homeland not anti-Zionists but anti-Semites. Paraphrasing Brandeis's famous call for men, money, and discipline, he implored American Jews to "observe dis-cipline ourselves." Then he presented his own plea. "Let us fall into line," he urged, "uphold our leaders and build the one permanent refuge for our downtrodden brothers." Rabbi Leon Harris, a non-Zionist from St. Louis and a friend of Heller's, provided a posi-tive long-term perspective on the Zionist question within the Reform movement. He agreed that to oppose the rehabilitation of Palestine was not anti-Zionistic but anti-Semitic, and he believed that there was "room in Jewry . . . for those who are sympathetic with Zionistic aspirations, without actually sharing them."[52]

At the two major CCAR events of 1919, the celebration in Cincinnati in April in honor of the centenary of I. M. Wise and the annual summer convention to which Heller was now ready to return, the New Orleans rabbi underscored his major arguments with new variations on his well-worn theme of rapprochement. Although anti-Zionism remained the official position of the Reform movement, Heller detected in the turn of events since the Balfour Declaration the beginning of the sea change he had anticipated in the Reform rabbinate. In spite of much waving of the "bloody Anti-Zionist shirt" at the Wisc celebration, he discerned the "Zionist skeleton at the Reform feast" apparent in the momentous topics assiduously avoided in the CCAR president's address. Missing was all reference to Palestine, Wilson's communiqués to Wise, the meeting of the American Jewish Congress and the Zionist presence at the peace conference-clearly the most noteworthy recent events in American Jewish life. Heller could see that the "best men" in Reform Judaism had become "painfully aware" that the movement had lost its vitality. Any rabbi sensitive to his own Jewishness would be troubled to see that the officially sanctioned Jewishness among CCAR leaders consisted merely of "trite quotations and cant phrases" uttered by men whose minds were as "inelastic as their hearts" were cold. The topic of Zionism, however, served as fair game for constant dissection and denouncement in other venues at the centenary. In an intriguing metaphor, Heller noted that although Jewish nationalism had played the role of "St. Sylvester to a shower of passing arrows, " he still believed that "conversion to Zionism" had to precede the "revitalization, in America, of Reform Judaism."[53]

In his critique of the president's paper at the CCAR summer convention, Heller parted ways with the dominant Brandeisian Zionism that had won over so many American Jews. The souring of the Progressivist vision in the ashes of World War I, coupled with the xenophobia and racial hysteria that ran rampant throughout the country in 1919, served as elements to diminish, once again, his belief in American exceptionalism. He echoed sentiments that he had expressed earlier that year when he noted that those Jews who worried about Zionism and dual loyalty and who readily denounced "Ghetto ways" were actually those most clearly bearing the "deepest Ghetto marks." They were undoubtedly the Jews who were unsure of their acceptance in American society, and their anxiety expressed itself as "Ghetto Americanism" with its frantic appeals to Zionists not to "substitute Jerusalem for Washington." While Heller exalted America as "the ideal of perfection . . . above all other national loyalties," he considered excessive patriotism to be in bad taste, indicative of insecure Jews' desperate need to feel equal to other Americans. The ills of assimilation had lessened his expectations that Judaism could thrive on American soil. "We have lost our Sabbath and our Jewish feeling towards the Sabbath," he complained. Having known the Sabbath as a "child of the ghetto" in Prague, Heller understood the great value of that loss, and he for the first time openly said that he wished to live in Palestine, where he could celebrate the Sabbath as the essence of a Jewish way of life. Although he acknowledged that, in his "advanced years," he had "nothing to offer Palestine at this time," his sentiment was not as a result "any less sincere."[54]

If Heller had been younger or stronger that year, he would have been able to participate in a couple of events that he would have found stimulating. Stephen Wise invited him to join Justice Brandeis on a fact-finding mission to Palestine, an experience that could later be used in pro-Zionist fund-raising. Heller declined because he did not think he had the physical stamina to "repay that wonderful experience by an adequate propaganda tour;" his energies would have to be devoted to the efforts of his own congregation in building a new temple. He told Wise that he planned to ask his congregation for a winter vacation in recognition of his thirty-five years in Sinai's pulpit, and he hoped to make the pilgrimage to Palestine at that time. He also declined another propaganda tour, this time under the auspices of the National Association for the Advancement of Colored People (NAACP). Among the several rabbis who had written to James Weldon Johnson, executive director of the NAACP, offering to speak on race relations on behalf of the organization, Heller was the only Southerner. Now he felt that his poor health precluded his participation in promoting "the cause of an Association . . . very dear to me." He hoped that the following year he would be sufficiently rested to do so.[55]

Unfortunately, while Heller was never able to speak on behalf of the NAACP, he did muster the vigor, psychological as well as physical, to face the CCAR convention the following summer. Between the two meetings, the British mandate for Palestine had been confirmed at the San Remo Conference. Heller undoubtedly realized that the CCAR leadership might still not bow before the reality of this momentous decision. He was right. The committee on the president's message found that it could not "rejoice" when the mandate for Palestine was heralded as the "Redemption of Israel." The Reform movement remained "convinced" that the mission of the Jew was to trumpet ethical monotheism throughout the world, rejecting any assertion of Jewish nationality as "long ago outgrown." Israel's Redemption would be realized only "when the Jew will have the right to live in any part of the world" with "all racial and religious prejudice and persecution ended."[56]

Heller, along with Horace J. Wolf, a younger Zionist rabbi, dissented. The CCAR, they argued, must realize that "conditions annihilate theories." The treaty of San Remo had "stamped the sanction of the civilized world upon the program of political Zionism," and the CCAR should go along with the majority of Jews throughout the world in lifting "our hearts in fervent gratitude to the mysterious Providence . . . guiding the Jewish people . . . into the Promised Land." Although the majority report received the lion's share of the vote, Heller felt that a strongly "spiritual aspect" was already surfacing at the convention. The majority had trounced the Zionists' report, but Heller believed that "in Judaism, minorities have a trick of changing to majorities." He and Stephen Wise had already recognized that Zionism held an attraction for younger rabbis. Now Heller felt that more rabbis could flock to the "standards of Zionism, despite . . . pressure . . . exercised in the opposite direction."[57]

Anti-Semitism, moreover, was once again on the rise, even in the United States, in the resurgence of the Ku Klux Klan and in the pages of Henry Ford's *Dearborn Independent*. Heller felt that Jews could not continue to deceive themselves that no danger existed here. In "Dangers of the Hour," Heller mentioned the reappearance of "deep-rooted antagonisms" that would "take generations to overcome." He also identified signs of a brighter future to come. First, the "guiding principle of minority rights" had been recognized in the postwar peace negotiations, and Jews had succeeded in sending representative delegations to the peace conference at Paris. Most important, even though Jewish persecution was on the rise, the prospect of a national homeland "endorsed by the great powers of civilization" offered some hope of rescue. Heller prophetically perceived that the next few decades would prove to be "a critical period in Jewish history" that would "largely determine the nature and scope of our contribution to the reborn world." A Jewish world divided between assimilationists and nationalists could not respond adequately to the dual tasks of rebuilding a Jewish homeland and rehabilitating "our impoverished brothers" in Europe "where they would never be able to live at peace." During the early 1920s, in addition to occasional articles and essays in the local press and in Jewish publications where he had earlier published, Heller served as a special correspondent to the *B'nai B'rith News*. In article after article, he analyzed the rise of anti-Semitism abroad and at home. In January 1925, Heller's article "The Quandary of the Apostate Jew" appeared in the *B'nai B'rith Magazine*. Now the rabbi's analysis gained a new sense of urgency, eerie in its insights of the changing nature of anti-Semitism. "The anti-Semite becomes impatient with science," he warned. "Refractory archaeologists have disappointed him by failing to discover any mysterious Arian meaning in the history of his cherished Swastika; another science must come to the rescue; anti-Semitic microscopes promise to detect Jewish blood, nay, even the half-blood the quarter-blood."[58] Although Heller could not imagine the dimensions of the dangers he envisioned, he truly believed that moral courage and the spiritual vision of a reunited Jewish people would ultimately triumph.

Notes for "The Zenith of My Career"

[1]Max Heller, New Orleans, to "Boys" (Isaac and James), Cincinnati and Boston, February 3, 1916, Box 17, Folder 11, Max Heller Papers, American Jewish Archives, Hebrew Union College-Jewish Institute of Religion, Cincinnati, Ohio (hereafter cite as MHP).

[2]Max Heller, "Prayer for Peace," *Item*, October 3, 1914.

[3]Max Heller, New Orleans, to "Boys" (Isaac and James), Cincinnati and Boston, March 29, 1916, Box 17, Folder 11, MHP; Arthur D. Call, Executive Director, American Peace Society, Washington, D. C., to Max Heller, New Orleans, July 8, 1915, Box 1, Folder 14, MHP; "Orleans Jews Are in Sympathy with Peace Movement," *American*, June 3, 1915, clipping, Box 14, Folder 5, MHP; untitled promotional circular on stationery from the Louisiana Society for International Concord, New Orleans, January 20, 1916, Box 6, Folder 15, MHP.

[4]Max Heller, New Orleans, to "Boys" (Isaac and James), Cincinnati and Boston, October 29, 1916, Box 17, Folder 11, MHP; Max Heller, New Orleans, to "Boys" (Isaac and James), Cincinnati and Boston, November 9, 1916, Box 17, Folder 11, MHP; Max Heller, New Orleans, to Stephen S. Wise, New York, November 14, 1916, Box 45, Folder 16, Stephen S.Wise Papers, American Jewish Archives, Hebrew Union College-Jewish Institute of Religion, Cincinnati, Ohio (hereafter cited as SSWP).

[5]Matthew James Schott, "John M. Parker of Louisiana and the Varieties of American Progressivism" (Ph.D. dissertation, Vanderbilt University, 1969), 409-65; Max Heller, New Orleans, to "Boys" (Isaac and James), Cincinnati and Boston, April 5, 1916, Box 17, Folder 11, MHP; Max Heller, New Orleans, to Harold A. Mosie,

New Orleans, November 15, 1916, Box 4, Folder 1, MHP; Moise told Heller that Parker "requested that this letter be saved for him to hand down to his children and grand children [*sic*]," Harold A. Moise, New Orleans, to Max Heller, New Orleans, November 17, 1916, Box 4, Folder 1, MHP; Max Heller, New Orleans, to "Boys" (Isaac and James), Cincinnati and Boston, November 18, 1916, Box 17, Folder 1, MHP; Max Heller, New Orleans, to Stephen S. Wise, New York, November 14, 1916, Box 45, Folder 16, SSWP.

[6]Adolf Kraus, president, B'nai B'rith, Chicago, to Max Heller, New Orleans, November 27 and December 2, 1914, Box 3, Folder 14, MHP.

[7]Max Heller, New Orleans, to Isaac Heller, Boston, November 20, 1914, Box 17, Folder 8, MHP; Max Heller, New Orleans, to Samuel Rosinger, Beaumont, Texas, October 8, 1914, Box 4, Folder 21, MHP; Bernard A. Rosenblatt, honorary secretary, FAZ, New York, to Max Heller, New Orleans, August 18, 1914, Box 4, Folder 21, MHP; David Philipson, Cincinnati, to Max Heller, New Orleans, September 3, 1914, Box 1, Folder 7, David Philipson Papers, American Jewish Archives, Hebrew Union College-Jewish Institute of Religion, Cincinnati, Ohio.

[8]Max Heller, New Orleans, to Stephen S. Wise, New York, December 31, 1914 (circular), SSWP, Box 111, Folder 8; Max Heller, New Orleans, to "Boys" (Isaac and James), Cincinnati and Boston, January 1, 1915, Box 17, Folder 10, MHP; Max Heller, New Orleans, to "Boys" (Isaac and James), Cincinnati and Boston, January 11, 1915, Box 17, Folder 10, MHP; Martin A. Meyer, San Francisco, to Max Heller, New Orleans, March 29, 1915, Box 4, Folder 10, MHP.

[9]Louis D. Brandeis, *Zionism and Patriotism* (New York, 1918); Cyrus Sulzberger (?), American Jewish Relief Committee (hereafter cited as AJRC), Philadelphia, to Max Heller, New Orleans, January 14, 1915, Box 1, Folder 1, MHP; Max Heller, New Orleans, to "Boys" (Isaac and James), Cincinnati and Boston, February 2, 1915, Box 17, Folder 10, MHP; AJRC, unsigned circular, Philadelphia (?), to Max Heller, New Orleans, February 2, 1915, New York, Box 1, Folder 1, MHP; Cyrus Sulzberger, Philadelphia, to Max Heller, New Orleans, February 11, 1915, Box 5, Folder 22, MHP; Cyrus Sulzberger, Philadelphia, to Max Heller, New Orleans, May 24, 1915, February 25, 1916, Box 1, Folder 1, MHP.

[10]Louis Lipsky, New York, to Max Heller, New Orleans, January 15, 1915, Box 3, Folder 29, MHP.

[11]Summaries of the Kallen-HUC affair can be found in Melvin I. Urofsky, *A Voice That Spoke for Justice: The Life and Times of Stephen S. Wise* (Albany, 1982), 89-90; Zola, "Maximilian Heller," 391; Horace Kallen, letter to the editor, *Jewish Comment,* December 25, 1914. When James told his father what had happened, Heller replied, "Too bad about Kallen.... He is one of the most glorious human beings I have ever met, though very eccentric," Max Heller, New Orleans, to "Boys" (Isaac and James), Cincinnati and Boston, December 27, 1914, Box 17, Folder 10, MHP; Horace Kallen, Madison, Wisconsin, to Stephen S. Wise, New York, Box 3, Folder 15, SSWP; Stephen S. Wise, New York, to Max Heller, New Orleans, December 28, 1914, Box 6, Folder 8, MHP; editorial, *Jewish Comment,* January 1, 1915.

[12]Sam S. Mayerberg, Simon Cohen, I. J. Sarasohn, James G. Heller, Cincinnati, to Horace Kallen, Madison, Wisconsin, Box 13, Folder 1, Horace Kallen Papers, AJA; Isaac Bloom, secretary, HUC Board of Governors, Cincinnati, to Max Heller, New Orleans, January 27, 1915, Series D, Box 8, Folder 15, HUC Papers, AJA; Stephen S. Wise, New York, to Isaac Bloom, Cincinnati, to Stephen S. Wise, New York, undated, Box 3, Folder 17, SSWP; Max Heller, New Orleans, to "Boys" (Isaac and James), Cincinnati and Boston, January 28, 1915, Box 17, Folder 10, MHP; Max Heller, New Orleans, to Edward Heinsheimer, president, HUC Board of Governors, Cincinnati, January 29, 1915, Series D, Box 8, Folder 15, HUC Papers; unsigned (secretary of the HUC Board of Governors?), Cincinnati, to Max Heller, New Orleans, February 1, 1915, Series D, Box 8, Folder 1, HUC Papers; Max Heller, New Orleans, to Henry Cohen, Galveston, February 1, 1915, Series 3, Box M233, HCP; Max Heller, New Orleans, to Stephen S. Wise, New York, February 3, 1915, Box 3, Folder 17, SSWP; J. Leonard Levy, Pittsburgh, to Max Heller, New Orleans, February 3, 1915, Box 3, Folder 26, MHP; Max Heller, New Orleans, to Joseph Stolz, Chicago, February 5, 1915, Box 8, Folder 7, MHP.

[13]Max Heller, Chicago, to Joe Stolz, Chicago, February 18, 1915, Box 8, Folder 7, MHP; Max Heller, New Orleans, to Isaac Blum, Cincinnati, March 1, 1914, Series D, Box 8, Folder 15, HUC Papers; Blum replied that

Heller's "expressions of pleasure and satisfaction at the happy finale of our conference sound[ed] a note of pleasure in the hearts of all those who attended the meeting," Isaac Blum, Cincinnati, to Max Heller, New Orleans, Series D, Box 8, Folder 15, HUC Papers; Zola, "Maximilian Heller," 391-92.

[14]Max Heller, New Orleans, to Isaac Heller, Boston, October 16, 1912 (?), Box 17, Folder 8, MHP.

[15]Max Heller, New Orleans, to Isaac Heller, Boston, October 16, 1912 (?), Box 17, Folder 8, MHP. Isaac's sons, Theo and Edward Heller, both assert that their father had a personality and temperament far better suited for the rabbinate than that of his older brother, James; informal conversations, New Orleans, 1989-1994.

[16]*CCAR Yearbook*, 25 (1915): 497-99; Urofsky, *A Voice That Spoke for Justice*, 9-10; Max Heller, "The Philistines Are Upon Thee, Samson," *Jewish Comment*, October 2, 1915; Stephen S. Wise, New York, to Max Heller, New Orleans, November 15, 1915, Box 6, Folder 8, MHP.

[17]Max Heller, "The Jewish Consciousness," *Temple Israel Pulpit*, December 31, 1915; "By a Prominent Rabbi" [Max Heller], "Uprooted," *American Jewish World*, December 10, 1915.

[18]"I speak to the negroes to-night on Booker Washington," Heller mentioned to his sons, Max Heller, New Orleans, to "Boys" (Isaac and James), Cincinnati and Boston, December 12, 1915, Box 17, Folder 10, MHP; Historical Events Notebook, Central Congregational Church Records, Amistad Research Center, Tulane University, New Orleans, La.; Max Heller, "Booker T Washington," *Olio*, 30 (January 1916): 2-6, Box 15, Folder 2, MHP.

[19]Max Heller, New Orleans, to "Boys" (Isaac and James), Cincinnati and Boston, April 3, 1916, Box 17, Folder 1, MHP.

[20]Melvin I. Urofsky, *American Zionism from Herzl to the Holocaust* (Garden City, N. Y., 1975), 127-29.

[21]Gerald Sorin, *A Time for Building: The Third Migration, 1880-1920* (Baltimore, 1992), 211-23; Urofsky, *American Zionism*, 127-29. The Jews already settled in Palestine also impressed Brandeis, and he again drew a thoroughly American analogy to their struggle. He regarded them as "Jewish Puritans" and saw Zionism as the "Pilgrim inspiration and impulse over again"; Howard Morley Sachar, *A History of the Jews in America* (New York, 1992), 252, 228-29. Brandeis also added a neat summation about the work of the "Jewish Pilgrim Fathers;" Brandeis, *Zionism and Patriotism*, 2; *CCAR Yearbook*, 26 (1916): 88-89; Sachar, *A History of the Jews in America*, 262-64; Stephen S. Wise, New York, to Max Heller, Kennebunk Port [sic], Maine, August 10, 1916, Box 6, Folder 8, MHP; Joseph Stolz, Chicago, to Max Heller, New Orleans, April 27, 1916, Box 8, Folder 7, MHP.

[22]Max Heller, New Orleans, to Isaac Heller, Boston, October 16, 1916, Box 17, Folder 8, MHP.

[23]Max Heller, "Rabbi Indorses [sic] Peace Proposal of President," *Times-Picayune*, January 27, 1927; Max Heller, "War Will Result in Great Benefit, Says Rabbi Heller," *Times-Picayune*, April 28, 1917.

[24]Heller, "The Elder Brother."

[25]Max Heller, "The Need of a Jewish Congress," *Jewish Ledger*, June 29, 1917; Stephen S. Wise, New York, to Max Heller, Kennebunkport, Maine, July 15, 1917, Box 6, Folder 8, MHP; Lederhendler, *The Road to Modern Jewish Politics*, 84-110, clearly and perceptively analyzes the emergence and role of the *shtadlanim;* Sachar, *The Course of Modern Jewish History*, 265-66.

[26]Max Heller, New Orleans, to Stephen Wise, New York, November 14, 1916, Box 45, Folder 16, SSWP; Zola, "Maximilian Heller," 394.

[27]Max Heller, "Dollarland Spirituality," *Maccabaean*, April 1917, 198-99; Max Heller, "The Mission in Dispersion," *Maccabaean*, May 1917, 224-25.

[28]Max Heller, "Nationalism and Religion," *Maccabaean*, June-July 1917, 247-48.

[29]*CCAR Yearbook*, 27 (1917): 132-45; *Jewish Spectator*, July 20, 1917.

[30]Max Heller, "Zionism at the Buffalo Convention," 1917, *American Jewish Chronicle*, Stephen S. Wise, New York, to Max Heller, Kennebunkport, Maine, July 15, 1917, Box 6, Folder 8, MHP; Zola, "Maximilian Heller," 393.

[31]Max Heller, "Our Spiritual Golus," *Maccabaean*, August 1917, 314-15.

[32]Henry Hurwitz, New York, to Max Heller, New Orleans, April 5, 1917, Box 3, Folder 8, MHP; Max Heller, New Orleans, to Editor of *New York Times*, New York, April 9, 1917, Box 6, Folder 15, MHP; Max Heller, "Nationalism in English Diplomacy," *Maccabaean*, December 1917, 415; Max Heller, Chicago, to Jacob de Haas, New York, undated, Box 3, Folder 2, MHP.

[33]David Philipson, "The British Declaration," *American Israelite*, November 29, 1917; Douglas Kohn, "David Philipson: American Anti-Zionist," manuscript, HUC-JIR, 1986, AJA, presents an excellent discussion of Philipson's consistent ideology, forged when he was a student of I. M. Wise and maintained until his death sixty-six years later.

[34]Max Heller, New Orleans, to Henry Cohen, Galveston, December 31, 1917, Box 3M, Folder 236, HCP; Henry Cohen, Galveston, to Max Heller, New Orleans, January 27, (year?), Box 1, Folder 18, MHP.

[35]Gotthard Deutsch, Cincinnati, to Max Heller, New Orleans, February 6, 1918, Box 2, Folder 2, MHP.

[36]Gotthard Deutsch, Cincinnati, to Max Heller, New Orleans, April 14, 1917, Box 2, Folder 2, MHP; Gotthard Deutsch, Cincinnati, to Max Heller, New Orleans, July 30, 1917, Box 2, Folder 2, MHP; Kerry M. Olitzky, Lance Johnson Sussman, and Malcolm H. Stern, *Reform Judaism in America: A Biographical Dictionary and Sourcebook* (Westport, Cpnn. 1993), s.v. "Gotthard Deutsch."

[37]Olitzky et al., *Reform Judaism in America*, 38-39; circular to Executive Members of the HUC Board of Alumni Association, from Julian Morgenstern, President, Board of Alumni, Cincinnati, HUCP, Box G1, Folder 9, AJA; Max Heller, Kennebunkport, Maine, to Gotthard Deutsch, Cincinnati, June 28, 1918, Box 2, Folder 9, Gotthard Deutsch Papers, AJA.

[38]Heller, "The Personality of Gotthard Deutsch," 149-52; *Times-Picayune*, September 5, 1917.

[39]"Rebirth of Holy Land Glowing Romance of War; Rabbi Max Heller Speaks on Restoration of Palestine at Temple Sinai," unidentified newspaper clipping, February 17, 1918, Box 14, Folder 7, MHP; "Rabbi Heller Tells of Plan for the New Jerusalem," *New Orleans Item*, undated clipping, Box 14, Folder 5, MHP; Max Heller, "An Intellectual Affinity," *American Israelite*, March 14, 1918.

[40]Max Heller, Kennebunkport, Maine, to Joseph Stolz, Chicago, June 13, 1918, Box 8, Folder 7, MHP.

[41]Stuart E. Knee, *The Concept of Zionist Dissent in the American Mind, 1917-1941* (New York, 1979), 49-50; Untitled, April 29, (1918), Box 1, Folder 1, Ephraim Frisch Papers, AJA, contains a list of those present; unsigned circular, initialed "DP/PF," undated, Box 1, Folder 15, David Philipson Papers; David Philipson, "The Rabbinical Conference on the Balfour Declaration and Zionism," editorial, *American Israelite*, July 11, 1918.

[42]Max Heller, "Zionism and Our Reform Rabbinate," *Maccabaean*, July 1918, 180-81, 190-91.

[43]Urofsky, *American Zionism*, 196, 206, 210, 216; Henry Cohen, Galveston, to Honorable Robert Lansing, Washington, D. C., July 15, 1918, Box 3M, Folder 236, HCP; David Philipson, Cincinnati, to Henry Cohen, Galveston, July 19, 1918, Box 3M, Folder 236, HCP.

[44]Max Heller, "A Realized Pattern of Social Justice," *Menorah Journal*, August 1918, 236; Max Heller, "A National Resurrection," *Times-Picayune*, September 8, 1918.

[45]Edward N. Calisch, Richmond, Virginia, to David Philipson, Cincinnati, August 3, 1918, Box 1, Folder 2, David Philipson Papers; circular suggesting the formation of an organization "somewhat along the lines of the League of British Jews," signed David Philipson, Chairman, and Ephraim Frisch, Secretary, August 8, 1918, Box 3M, Folder 236, HCP; circular from Max Heller, Martin A. Meyer, Stephen S. Wise, New York, August 8,

1918, Box 3M, Folder 236, HCP; Ephraim Frisch, New York, to Leo Franklin, Detroit, August 24, 1918, Box 1, Folder 2, Leo Franklin Papers, AJA; Leo Franklin, Detroit, to Ephraim Frisch, New York, August 26, 1918, Box 1, Folder 2, Leo M. Franklin Papers; Ephraim Frisch, New York, to Henry Cohen, Galveston, August 26, 1918, Box 3M, Folder 236, HCP; A. H. Fromenson, New York, to Henry Cohen, Galveston, September 5, 1918, night lettergram, Box 3M, Folder 287, HCP.

[46]Circular from Julian W. Mack and Jacob de Haas, New York, September 5, 1918, Box 3M, Folder 287, HCP; Kaufman Kohler, Cincinnati, to David Philipson, Cincinnati, September 4 and 5, 1918, Box 1, Folder 10, David Philipson Papers; Louis Marshall, New York, to David Philipson, Cincinnati, September 5, 1918, Box 1, Folder 13, David Philipson Papers.

[47]Ephraim Frisch, New York, to President Woodrow Wilson, Washington, D. C., undated, Box 1, Folder 15, David Philipson Papers; Ephraim Frisch, New York, to David Philipson, Cincinnati, undated, Box 1, Folder 5, David Philipson Papers; Ephraim Frisch, New York, to Max Raisin, Brooklyn, undated, Box 11, Folder 16, CCAR Papers; Max Raisin, Brooklyn, to Ephraim Frisch, New York, September 19, 1918, Box 11, Folder 16, CCAR Papers; "Messages Favoring and Opposing Zionism Sent President Wilson by American Jews," *Independent*, September 13, 1918; David Philipson, Cincinnati, to Henry Cohen, Galveston, September 11, 1918, Box 3M, Folder 326, HCP; Henry Berkowitz, Philadelphia, to David Philipson, Cincinnati, September 11 and 13, 1918, Box 1, Folder 1, David Philipson Papers; Louis Wolsey, Cleveland, Ohio, to David Philipson, Cincinnati, September 12 and 13, 1918, Box 2, Folder 4, David Philipson Papers; Ephraim Frisch, New York, to David Philipson, Cincinnati, September 20, 1918, Box 1, Folder 5, David Philipson Papers; Thomas K. Kolsky, *Jews Against Zionism: The American Council for Judaism, 1942-1948* (Phildelphia, 1990), 34-35, 44, notes that, after the 1937 Columbus Platform of the CCAR (for which James Heller fought strongly) affirmed Palestine as a "center of Jewish culture and spiritual life" as well as a "haven for the oppressed." Those dissenting from the Columbus Platform founded the anti-Zionist American Council for Judaism, and the leaders included veterans of the League of American Jews.

[48]Max Heller, "The Status of Zionism," *American Israelite*, October 3, 1918; Max Heller, "Outlived Viewpoints," *B'nai B'rith News*, September-October 1918.

[49]Max Heller, "Impressions of the American Jewish Congress," *Chicago Israelite*, December 26, 1918.

[50]Included among those signatories to the anti-Zionist manifesto were rabbis of the following Southern pulpits: William Rosenau of Baltimore, Morris Newfield of Birmingham, William Greenburg of Dallas, Henry Cohen of Galveston, Harry Merfeld of Greenville, Mississippi, Henry Barnstein of Houston, Louis Witt of Little Rock, James Rauch of Louisville, William Fineshriber of Memphis, Isidore Lewinthal of Nashville, Emil Leipziger of Touro Synagogue, New Orleans, Moses Jacobson of Shreveport. Notably absent was also David Marx of Atlanta, even though he was an anti-Zionist, "Citizens of the U. S. of America: Signers of the Manifesto to the Peace Conference at Paris delivered to President Wilson by Congressman Julius Kahn, March 1919," small collections, documents file, AJA.

[51]"The Hon. Julius Kahn Sounds a Warning Note," *American Israelite*, February 6, 1919, Sachar, *A History of Jews in America*, 264-67; Knee, *The Concept of Zionist Dissent*, 55; Higham, *Strangers in the Land*, 198; Kolsky, *Jews Against Zionism*, 31. A representative sampling of the rich vein of anti-Zionist materials of this brief period scattered in the collections of the AJA includes the papers of Max Senior, David Philipson, Samuel Schulman, and Henry Berkowitz; secondary accounts of personalities and issues in the anti-Zionist camp include Micah D. Greenstein, "Classicity in the American Reform Rabbinate: A Study Based on the Unpublished and Published Papers, Sermons, and Works, of Moses J. Gries and William Rosenau, Two Presidents of the Central Conference of American Rabbis" (rabbinical thesis, HUC-JIR, 1991); Goldblatt, "The Impact of the Balfour Declaration in America," 455-515; Cohen, "The Reaction of Reform Judaism," 361-94.

[52]"Synopsis of Rabbi Max Heller's Address at Carnegie Hall, Jan. 15," *Jewish Criterion*, January 17, 1919; Max Heller, "The Congress Question," *Jewish Ledger*, March 7, 1919; Leon Harris, St. Louis, to Max Heller, New Orleans, February 21, 1919, Box 3, Folder 4, MHP.

[53]Max Heller, "A Zionist's Appraisement of the Isaac M. Wise Centenary," *Jewish Exponent*, April 18, 1919; Max Heller, "When Zionism and Reform Meet," *Maccabaean*, May 1919, 112-14. After the centenary, Stephen Wise promised Heller that, should the CCAR pass a "really anti-Zionist resolution" at its summer convention, "I for one will have to withdraw, and I think my congregation would go with me," Stephen S. Wise, New York, to Max Heller, New Orleans, April 16, 1919, Box 6, Folder 8, MHP.

[54]Max Heller, "Americanism and Zionism," *Maccabaean*, March 1919, 69; *CCAR Yearbook*, 29 (1919): 229, also cited by Michael A. Meyer in "American Reform Judaism and Zionism," 63-64.

[55]Stephen S. Wise, New York, to Max Heller, New Orleans, May 9, 1919, Box 6, Folder 8, MHP; Max Heller, New Orleans, to Stephen S. Wise, New York, May 15, 1919, Box 45, Folder 16, SSWP; Max Heller, New Orleans, to James Weldon Johnson, Washington, D. C., March 18, 1919, NAACP Administration Files, C-172, Manuscript Division, Library of Congress, Washington, D. C. "List of Speakers for NAACP Meetings," NAACP Administration Files, C-172, Manuscript Division, Library of Congress; a footnote in Hasia R. Diner, *In the Almost Promised Land: American Jews and Blacks, 1915-1935* (Westport, Conn., 1975), 159, alerted me to Heller's communications with the NAACP.

[56]Knee, *The Concept of Zionist Dissent*, 58, notes that the CCAR accepted the San Remo decision because the majority of the members believed that the decision would serve as a "death blow to Zionism;" *CCAR Yearbook*, 30 (1920): 138-43.

[57]Max Heller, "San Remo and the Reform Rabbis," *Maccabaean*, August 1920, 39-41; Michael A. Meyer, "American Reform Judaism and Zionism," 64; Max Heller, "The Rochester Convention from a Zionist Viewpoint," *Scribe*, July 23, 1920, also cited by Zola, "Maximilian Heller," 345.

[58]Max Heller, "Dangers of the Hour," *Maccabaean*, September 1919, 270-71; Louis Marshall, New York, to Henry Ford, Dearborn, Michigan, June 3, 1929, copy of telegram, Box 4, Folder 5, MHP; Dearborn Publishing Company, Dearborn, Michigan, to Louis Marshall, New York, June 5, 1920, copy of telegram, Box 4, Folder 5, MHP; Max Heller, "The Quandry of the Apostate Jew," *B'nai B'rith Magazine*, January 1925, 138-39, 149; Heller, "The Anti-Semitic Twins," 165-66, 183.

ANTI-SEMITISM AND SHREVEPORT, LOUISIANA: THE SITUATION IN THE 1920s*

Beverly S. Williams

Anti-Semitic prejudice in the United States has never reached the proportions evidenced at times in other nations of the world. Yet, in the 1920s, this nation witnessed an enormous increase in prejudice with anti-Semitism reaching a previously unknown degree.

The growing mood of prejudice began during World War I when some American Gentiles came to doubt the patriotism of this country's Jews. Their suspicions were founded upon the fact that many prominent American Jews were known to be opposed to the policies of Tsarist Russia and were thought to be favorable toward the new Bolshevik regime.[1]

Perhaps the most influential reason for the increase in anti-Semitism in the 1920s was the influx of Jewish immigrants into the United States before and during the early years of that decade. Before the 1880s Jews comprised a relatively insignificant numerical segment of the nation's population, but, between 1877 and 1917, Jewish numbers increased from about .52 percent to 3.28 percent of the total population. The rise in anti-Semitism obvious in the 1920s was owing, in large measure, to this numerical increase and to the desire of Jewish immigrants for a better social standing than that which most earlier immigrants had attained.[2]

The ideological catalyst for the postwar campaign against American Jewry was provided by Henry Ford. In May 1920, Ford began publishing in his newspaper; the *Dearborn Independent*, a series of articles concerning "The International Jew." The *Independent*'s attacks on Jews, lasting until 1927, were founded upon the assertion that Judaism and Bolshevism went hand in hand, and more particularly, upon belief in the existence of a Jewish conspiracy to establish a world dictatorship.

The idea of a secret Jewish plot for world dominance was first presented in France by Abbé Barreul in 1807. His exposé was written in response to Napoleon's "French Sanhedrin" which had been called to ease tensions between French Jews and Gentiles. Nearly one hundred years later, in 1905, Barreul's book served as the basis for a Jewish

*First published in *Louisiana History*, 21 (1980): 387-98. Reprinted with the kind permission of the Louisiana Historical Association.

conspiracy myth which was disclosed in "The Protocols of the Elders of Zion." This pamphlet, first published in Russia, linked the supposed conspiracy to Bolshevism. When the "Protocols" appeared in the United States in 1920, during the era of heated reaction to the 1917 Bolshevik Revolution, Ford and his associates were quick to offer it as a justification of their anti-Semitic campaign.[3] The pamphlet, of course, was a hoax; but American reaction to its assertions combined with a concern over the growing number and influence of Jews to produce a national climate of fear and intolerance.

Prejudice spread quickly across the land; and, throughout the decade, it was expressed in many forms. Jews were denied employment, especially in the teaching profession. Admission quotas for Jews were established in colleges and universities, particularly in the Northeast where Jews came to be excluded from medical schools. Property owners refused to sell to Jews; and subdivision restrictions from New York to Florida discriminated against them. Across the nation they were frequently denied hotel accommodations and were systematically excluded from country clubs and other social organizations. Finally, exclusion of Jews from sororities and fraternities, which had begun earlier, became universal in the 1920s.[4] Even Congress became involved in the temperament of the times when it passed the Immigration Act of 1924. Although the quotas set by this act appear to be directed toward people of various nationalities, "proponents of measure said that it was aimed at the Jews . . . "[5] On occasion, the anti-Jewish mood of the nation took on a violent character; for example, in Milwaukee in 1928 and 1929 when Jewish-owned lakeside cottages were burned.[6]

Here, then, a sampling of conditions under which Jews lived in many areas of the country during the 1920s. This was not the case, insofar as Jews were concerned, in the South, for "the South has traditionally been one of the least anti-Semitic regions in the nation, and a considerable body of data suggests that it remained so until the 1940s."[7] Moreover, in Shreveport the nationwide outbreak of anti-Semitism did little to affect the long-standing cordial relations existing between Jews and Gentiles. A Jewish resident of Shreveport, who has lived in other Southern cities, confirms the fact that there was never a great degree of discrimination in the South generally, and that there was, even in the 1920s, less discrimination in Shreveport than anywhere else she had ever lived.[8] Certain events in Shreveport's history together with long-established attitudes of its residents combined to make the community more tolerant of Jews than was normally the case in the 1920s.

Primarily responsible for this was the fact that Shreveport's Jewish community was not a newly arrived immigrant group. Rather, Jews were among the area's first settlers, some having been in the region "as long or longer than a lot of the non-Jewish people."[9] As a result, the wave of immigration which fueled anti-Semitism elsewhere in the twenties was not a factor in Shreveport. The town's Jews were not considered aliens; instead, they were seen as established and respected members of the community.

The first known Jew to come to the Shreveport region was Jacob Bodenheimer. At age fourteen he left his native Germany and crossed the Atlantic as a stowaway on a ship destined for New Orleans. He lived there until1827 when he undertook a trading venture to North Louisiana. During the trip north the keelboat on which he was traveling sank, and, rather than return to New Orleans for more trade supplies, Bodenheimer simply settled at Moscow Landing, a community on Lake Bistineau in what is now Bossier Parish. In the early 1840s he moved to Bellevue, also in Bossier Parish, and there lived out his life. Bodenheimer's wife, Eliza, and their four children eventually moved to Shreveport, where Jacob was buried in Oakland Cemetery in 1865.[10]

As the population of Northwest Louisiana increased, the Jewish community grew in size until over one hundred families were resident in Shreveport in 1900.[11] Some of these early residents—Jewish and non-Jewish—had known each other in Europe. Upon their arrival in Shreveport there was a considerable amount of intermarriage between Jews and Gentiles, a situation which obviously lessened tensions between the groups.[12] Moreover, intermarriage has continued throughout the years. In some cases these marriages have been accepted by both families; in others, one partner has reportedly felt alienated from the spouse's family.[13]

Shreveport's first formal Jewish congregation, Har-El-Mountain, was established in 1861. On April 2, 1866, the group was reorganized as the Hebrew Zion Congregation. Until that time the group had worshipped in the home of Abraham Winter. From 1866 until 1870 they met in Bogel's Hall, an old hotel. The immediate goal of the congregation, however, was the establishment of a permanent house of worship, and this dream was realized in 1870 with the construction of a temple on Fannin Street. In 1875 the congregation was reorganized, took the name Emmanu-El, but continued to hold services in the old Hebrew Zion temple until 1915 when a new temple was built on the corner of Cotton and Common streets. That year the congregation changed its name to the current B'Nai Zion.[14]

B'Nai Zion, the original Jewish congregation in Shreveport, had been joined, by the 1920s, by a second active congregation. In 1902 the Congregation Agudath Achim was formed, and in 1905 its synagogue was consecrated. This young congregation differed from B'Nai Zion in that it was Orthodox, whereas the older group practiced the Reform ritual.[15] The fact that the earliest Jewish congregation in Shreveport was affiliated with the Reform movement may be seen as still another reason for the good relations existing between Jews and Gentiles.[16] Differences between the Reform and Orthodox congregations allow the former to be more early assimilated into a predominantly Gentile community.

Orthodox Jews still look for the coming of a messiah who will lead in the political restoration of Palestine. As a result, they adhere to all Jewish laws which, according to their beliefs, set them apart as the chosen people of God. They are concerned with maintaining both their moral and national integrity. Reform Judaism, on the other hand, views the Jewish people as destined to lead the world into an era of peace and brotherhood. The Messianic Age is, for them, that era of peace rather than a time of Palestinian restoration. The Reform movement, however, does generally support the establishment and maintenance of a Jewish state, but sees it simply as a safe homeland for Jews who are being persecuted elsewhere.

Together with these differing views of Israel's destiny, the groups also differ on the degree of adherence to ceremonial laws. These include rules governing diet, seating and the use of vernacular in worship services, separate confirmations for boys and girls, and the use of an organ and a mixed choir to provide music in their services. Although there is much variation among Reform congregations regarding ceremonial matters, all resemble Christian practices far more closely than do those of the Orthodox Jews. The resulting ability to be more easily assimilated into the larger community is looked upon by Reform Jews as an essential adjunct to their Messianic mission, whereas the Orthodox regard maintenance of a separate identity essential to the Messianic restoration of Palestine.[17] The earliest Jewish settlers in the Shreveport region were to be blatantly different from their Christian neighbors and were accepted, from the first, as equals.[18]

The relationship between Jews and Christians in Shreveport continued friendly during the twenties largely because of the longstanding respect for property owners. Gentiles elsewhere in the nation might resent the upward social mobility of Jews, but the majority of Shreveporters have traditionally held large property owners in esteem regardless of their ethnic origin. Members of the Jewish community, long before the 1920s, had become some of the larger property owners of the city.[19] Mr. Levi Cooper, for example, owned and operated Cooper Brothers' Livery Stable. He also owned a large tract of land on the outskirts of town known as Cooper's Pasture. For years he used this land to retire horses, but in 1920 Cooper sold the land to W. H. Werner who developed it into Werner Park Subdivision .[20] Cooper, together with Alfred Leonard, was responsible for developing Cooper Road Subdivision, an area which has only recently been incorporated into the city.[21] Indeed, instead of an outbreak of anti-Semitism in Shreveport, there was a continuation of the warm relationship between Jew and non-Jew which had long characterized the community. The unimpeded participation of Jews in all facets of public and commercial life is further testimony to the low level of anti-Semitic prejudice in the Shreveport area.

At a time when anti-Semitic prejudice restrained many Jews from contributing fully to American society, the Shreveport Jewish community was actively engaged in a broad spectrum of professional endeavors. Throughout the era of the 1920s, Jews continued to serve on the Caddo Parish School Board. Elias Goldstein, the son of a former school board member, served with distinction. Rachel Goldenberg and Josephine Wolff taught for years in Shreveport's schools before serving the community as school principals.[22]

Members of the Jewish community distinguished themselves in the field of medicine. In 1920 Dr. Jacob Bodenheimer, grandson of a Shreveport pioneer, served as president of the Shreveport Medical Society, and in 1927, Dr. A. A. Herold, Sr., was elected president of the Louisiana State Medical Society.[23] When the Woman's Auxiliary of the local Medical Society was founded in 1928, Mrs. Herold and Mrs. Bodenheimer served as officers of the organization.[24]

Jews assumed an active role in the legal profession in the 1920s. In 1921, the Shreveport Bar Association was headed by A. B. Freyer, and, that same year, Sidney L. Herold was elected as a delegate to the Louisiana Constitutional Convention.[25]

Herold had built a reputation as a leading attorney through his participation in legal suits pertaining to the principle of separation of church and state. As early as 1912, he was involved in a suit to prevent Bible reading in Pennsylvania schools,[26] and a year later he began a two-year-long crusade against mandatory Bible reading and recitation of the Lord's Prayer in Caddo Parish public schools. The case, *Herold v. Parish Board of School Directors*, 136 La. 1034, 68 So. 116, was cited many years later in the U. S. Supreme Court case of *School District of Abington Township, Pennsylvania, et al. v. Schempp et al.*, 374 U.S. 275, 292. The decision rendered in this case declared such devotionals and Bible reading to be unconstitutional.[27]

Herold had initiated the action against the school board after bringing the matter to the attention of the state superintendent of education, T. H. Harris, in 1913. The case went into the state courts and in March 1915, a decision was handed down favoring Herold's position.[28]

In 1928 and 1929, Sidney Herold was again involved in a legal battle with school officials. The contest this time was over Gov. Huey P. Long's free school textbook legislation, and, in this instance, Herold represented the Caddo Parish School Board in a suit against the State Board of Education. The case, a joint action with the Bossier Parish School Board, was one of a series of actions designed to test the constitutionality of Long's plan to provide textbooks to both public and private schools. Opponents of the plan argued, among other things, that it threatened the separation of church and state. In June 1929, however, the parish school boards lost their case.[29]

Sidney Herold was not the only member of Shreveport's Jewish community to take an active role in the legal-political arena. Several city officials during the twenties were Jews. Among these were Leon Kahn, a member of the park commission in 1928, and David B. Samuel, Shreveport City Court Judge from 1916 to 1937. Emmanuel M. Bodenheimer served as the first and only mayor of South Highlands before the village was incorporated into Shreveport in 1927.[30]

These men were part of a long-standing tradition of Jewish political leadership in Shreveport. Prior to the twenties the city had had three Jewish mayors, Samuel Levy, Ben Holzman, and Earnest R. Bernstein.[31] Moreover, Paul Lowenthal, a city councilman around the turn of the century, conducted a campaign in the first quarter of the century which resulted, in 1926, in the development of Cross Lake as a source of the city's water supply.[32]

Jewish involvement in the commercial activities of Shreveport dates from the antebellum era. Abraham Winter founded Winter and Weinstock in 1849, and M. Levy & Son, clothiers, was founded in 1857. Following the Civil War, these firms were joined by J. Kahn & Bro., a dry goods business, and E. & B. Jacobs, drygoods and hardware. In

1869 Emanuel Phelps opened Phelps Shoe Co., Ltd. All of these firms were located on Texas Street.[33]

By the 1920s Jewish involvement in the commercial community of Shreveport was widespread. In 1903 Winter & Weinstock had become The Winter Company and was being operated by Abraham's son, Henry. Another son, William, went into business for himself, representing the New York Life Insurance Company. A. Kahn, Herman Loeb, Henry and Abry Cahn established themselves as Shreveport businessmen.[34]

The continuing success of Shreveport's Jewish businessmen in the 1920s was demonstrated by the expansion of their businesses. During the decade the Selber brothers, with the aid of Andrew Querbes, president of the First National Bank, built the Ricou Brewster Building which included expanded facilities for their clothing business. M. L. Bath Company moved to expanded facilities in 1921, and Brenner's Furniture Company relocated in a new building in 1924. Finally, Rubenstein's Department Store, a business established before the turn of the century, relocated in a new building in 1926.[35]

Some of these Jewish businesses expanded regionally or nationally during the 1920s, as, for example, in the cases of Big Chain Grocery, Feibleman's-Sears, and Saenger Enterprises. In 1922 I. E. Weil and Louie Levy, in association with Earl Sandifer opened the Big Chain Grocery. In time the business grew and a chain of these food stores dotted Shreveport. In addition, the owners of Big Chain Groceries opened several cafeterias. In 1956 Big Chain was purchased by The Kroger Company, and while the grocery business name was changed, the cafeterias, also owned by Kroger, still carry the name of Big Chain.[36]

Another Jewish firm to merge with a nationally known operation was Feibleman's. Feibleman's was a retail store dealing in high quality clothing, diamonds and furs. For some time after Sears, Roebuck and Company opened their Shreveport store, much of their merchandise was purchased through Feibleman's. In 1930 Sears bought out the Feibleman interest but continued to operate the store at the same location until September, 1961.[37]

A Shreveport firm that became nationally known in the 1920s through its own expansion was Saenger Enterprises. In 1895 the Saenger brothers, A. D. and Julian, opened a pharmacy which incorporated a popular soda fountain. Using the profits from the Saenger Drug Company, the owners began investing in the entertainment business. The Saengers were initially interested in vaudeville, but they knew very little about the entertainment business. To fill this gap came E. V. Richards, a former carnival barker, who went into partnership with the Saengers.[38]

The Saenger Company grew from inauspicious beginnings into one of the country's largest motion picture theatre chains. In 1925 Saenger-Ehrlich Enterprises built the Strand Theater in Shreveport, and within a short time thereafter put together a theatre empire which stretched from this country into Central and South America.[39] In 1929 they sold their theatre interests to Paramount for millions of dollars.[40]

Jews were also prominent in Shreveport's financial institutions. Arthur T. Kahn, who began working for Commercial National Bank in 1898, was vice-president of that firm and manager of its affiliate, Commercial Securities Company of Shreveport, Inc., at the time of his death in 1927. Early in the 1920s Philip Leiber became president of the Shreveport Mutual Building Association, now known as First Federal Savings and Loan Association.[41]

One of the most active organizations in Shreveport during the 1920s was the American Legion. The local post sponsored a Boy Scout troop, worked for the Community Chest and the Salvation Army, and provided continuing support for Veterans' Hospital No. 27 in Alexandria.[42] Lowe-McFarland Post No. 14 of the American Legion was chartered in Shreveport on September 22, 1919. Jews were among its earliest members and included such individuals as Malcolm Kaffie, Aaron Selber, Sr., Isadore Leiber, Seymour Van Os, Earl Weiner, Abry Cahn, Dr. J. M. Bodenheimer and Sam Weiner.[43]

Although the Jewish community was involved in much of the social activity of Shreveport, they were among the staunchest supporters of the city's most important social activity, the Louisiana State Fair. The Fair began its annual operation in 1906 and its success was in large measure owing to men such as Earnest Bernstein, Samuel Dreyfus, Julian Saenger and L. Wolff.[44]

One man, more than all others, was responsible for the continued success of the State Fair. William Hirsch, a Jewish businessman, was president of the State Fair Association in 1914 and 1915. In 1916 he became the Association's secretary and in 1921 was named secretary-manager. He served in the latter capacity for over three decades, and today the coliseum, built during his years as secretary-manager, honors him by carrying his name.[45]

While conditions in Shreveport did not closely resemble national conditions, and anti-Semitism was low key, there were instances of prejudice and discrimination. Jews were admitted to the local country club, but it has been suggested that the club may have set a quota.[46] Jewish girls, while invited to all their social functions, were not admitted as members of sororities at Centenary College.[47] Fraternities at Centenary, on the other hand, appear to have been somewhat more liberal, as it is reported that at least one Jewish boy was a member of a fraternity there in the 1920s.[48]

Additional evidence that conditions in Shreveport were less than perfect has to do with the Ku Klux Klan. The only reported confrontation between the Klan and the Jewish community involved Sidney Herold. While there are many versions of this story, and no one seems to know all the details, one highly credible source reports that Herold conducted an ongoing battle with the Klan in the twenties in an attempt to stop the lynching of blacks. Herold even went so far as to plant a spy in the Klan. According to this source, the Klan, to put an end to Herold's interference, engaged the services of a hired killer. Herold in turn, reportedly hired people to protect him.[49] Outside of this incident, however, there does not seem to have been a major confrontation between the Klan and the Shreveport Jewish community during the 1920s.

One can conclude then with the thought that the relationship of Jews and Gentiles in Shreveport during the Roaring Twenties did not reflect the typical relationship between these groups found then in many areas of the United States.

Notes for "Anti-Semitism and Shreveport, Louisiana:
The Situation in the 1920s"

[1]Oscar Handlin, *Adventure in Freedom: Three Hundred Years of Jewish Life in America* (New York, 1954), 202-03; Marshall Sklare, *America's Jews* (New York, 1971), 6-7.

[2]Handlin, *Adventure in Freedom*, 84; John Higham, *Strangers in the Land: Patterns of American Nativism, 1860-1925* (New Brunswick, N. J., 1955), 266-67.

[3]Higham, *Strangers*, 265, 279-80, 284; Carey McWilliams, *A Mask for Privilege: Anti-Semitism in America* (Boston, 1948), 34; Vamberto Morais, *A Short History of Anti-Semitism* (New York, 1976), 193-94, 197-98, 202-03.

[4]Higham, *Strangers*, 278; McWilliams, *Mask for Privilege*, 37-39, 128, 132-33.

[5]McWilliams, *Mask for Privilege*, 36.

[6]Ibid., 125.

[7]Charles Hebert Stembert, et al., *Jews in the Mind of America* (New York, 1966), 390.

[8]Interview with Mrs. Armand W. Roos, Shreveport, La., April 11, 1977.

[9]Interview with Mrs. Albert Elmer, Shreveport, La., April 8, 1977.

[10]Louise Matthews Hewitt, *Days of Building: History of a Jewish Community* (Shreveport, La., 1965), 4, 7-10.

[11]Ibid., 16.

[12]Elmer interview.

[13]Interview with Mrs. James W. Stone, Shreveport, La., July 28, 1979.

[14]Hewitt, *Days of Building*, 33-39.

[15]Ibid., 43-44.

[16]Elmer interview.

[17]Joseph L. Blau, *Modern Varieties of Judaism* (New York, 1966), 38-39, 57-58, 125-26, 147-49; Handlin, *Adventure in Freedom*, 76-79; Frank S. Mead, *Handbook of Denominations in the United States*, 6th ed. (Nashville, Tenn., 1975), 162.

[18]Elmer interview.

[19]Interview with Thomas Ruffin, Shreveport, La., March 3, 1977.

[20]Caddo Parish, Louisiana, Conveyance Records, Book 144, 647, filed and recorded April 28, 1920; interview with Henry Cahn, Shreveport, La., August 16, 1979.

[21]Cahn interview; City of Shreveport La., Department of Public Works, Annexations and Areas (1977).

[22]Cahn interview; interview with Mrs. George S. Franklin, Shreveport, La., April 8, 1977; Hewitt, *Days of Building*, 116-117; Caddo Parish, Louisiana, Board of School Directors, "Minutes," vol. 2, June 20, 1913.

[23]Hewitt *Days of Building*, 93-94.

[24]Mary Lilla McLure and J. Ed Howe *History of Shreveport and Shreveport Builders* (Shreveport, La., 1937), 191.

[25]Hewitt, *Days of Building*, 96-97.

[26]Interview with Sidney H. Lazard, New Orleans, La., August 20, 1979.

[27]*Herold v. Parish Board of School Directors*, 136 La. 1034, 68 So. 116 (1915); *School District* of *Abington Township, Pennsylvania, et al. v. Schempp, et al.*, 374 U.S. 275, 292 (1963); letter from Mr. Simon Herold to author, September 12, 1979; William K. Muir, Jr., *Prayer in the Public Schools: Law and Attitude Change* (Chicago, 1967), 12-14.

[28]Caddo Parish, Louisiana, Board of School Directors, "Minutes," vol. 2, April 9, 1913*; Shreveport Journal,* March 13, 1913, March 22, 1915; *Shreveport Times*, March 13, 15, 27, 1913, March 23, 1915.

[29]*Bossier Parish School Board, et al v. Louisiana State Board of Education, et al., Caddo Parish School Board, et al v. Louisiana State Board of Education, et al.*, 12 3 So. 665 (1929); Caddo Parish, Louisiana, School Board Minutes, vol. 6, August 22, September 5, 1928; *Shreveport Times*, August 25, September 1, 6, 1928; T. Harry Williams, *Huey Long* (New York, 1969), 340-341.

[30]Hewitt, *Days of Building*, 57-59.

[31]Ibid., 52.

[32]Cahn interview; *Shreveport Times*, October 28, 1926.

[33]Cahn interview; McLure and Howe, *History of Shreveport*, 134-35; Maude Hearn O'Pry, *Chronicles of Shreveport and Caddo Parish* (Shreveport, La., 1928), 393; *Shreveport Times*, May 2, 1925.

[34]Calm interview; O' Pry, *Chronicles of Shreveport*, 393.

[35]Zeak M. Buckner, *The Selber Story* (Shreveport, La., 1964), 14-16, 30-34; Hewitt, *Days of Building*, 71-77.

[36]Cahn interview; interview with Mrs. Aaron R. Selber, Sr., Shreveport La., August 27, 1979; *Shreveport Times*, April 23, June 2, 1922; letter from J. L. Sneyd, Personnel Manager, Dallas Division, The Kroger Co., to author, August 29, 1979.

[37]Interview with Gene Clark, Operating Superintendent, Sears, Roebuck and Co., Shreveport, La., August 16, 1979; letter from Belinda Jagers, Public Relations Dept., Sears, Roebuck and Co., Southwestern Territory, Dallas, to author, August 27, 1979; *Shreveport Journal*, May 5, 1928; September 2, 3, 1930; September 13, 1949.

[38]Cahn interview; *Shreveport Times*, September 6, 1928.

[39]Cahn interview; Hewitt, *Days of Building*, 82-83.

[40]Hewitt, *Days of Building*, 83; *Shreveport Times*, September 6, 1928.

[41]Hewitt, *Days of Building*, 77-78; O'Pry, *Chronicles of Shreveport*, 308.

[42]Cahn interview; Lowe-McFarland Post No. 14 of the American Legion, Shreveport, La., "Minutes of Meetings," (1921-1932).

[43]Cahn interview; Lowe-McFarland Post, Minutes (1921-1932); Lowe-McFarland post No. 14 of the American Legion, Shreveport, La., Pictorial Record of Post Commanders and Ladies Auxiliary President; Selber interview; *Shreveport Times*, August 25, 1928; March 24, 1968.

[44]Viola Carruth, *Caddo: 1,000. A History of the Shreveport Area from the Time of the Caddo Indians to the 1970s* (Shreveport, La., 1970), 123; Hewitt , *Days of Building*, 133; McLure and Howe, *History of Shreveport*, 144-46; O'Pry, *Chronicles of Shreveport*, 159.

[45]Hewitt, *Days of Building*, 133; McLure and Howe, *History of Shreveport*, 147; O'Pry, *Chronicles of Shreveport*, 160.

[46]Cahn interview; Roos interview.

[47]Elmer interview.

[48]Stone interview.

[49]Lazard interview.

PART X
Post World War II, 1946-2004

MEETING THE CHALLENGES OF THE LATE
TWENTIETH CENTURY*

Edward L. Bond

Although St. James had seemed to prosper during the 1950s, with a new education building, a flourishing school, and nearly 2,600 baptized members, there were also signs of discontent. Downtown Baton Rouge was changing. Formerly a residential area, it was in the process of becoming a business district, and some members of St. James believed the parish could not survive in this new environment. In the late fifties an insurgent group of parishioners held an alternative parish meeting and proposed that St. James move out to the suburbs. They thought the church building downtown could best be preserved as a chapel. At the parish's annual meeting in 1960, [Reverend Philip P.] Werlein expressed his belief that attendance at divine worship was the "heart of the church." The recent Epiphany service had particularly disappointed him-only two communicants attended-and he exhorted the congregation to come to church more regularly.[1]

Early in 1960, federal judge F. Skelly Wright of the Eastern District of Louisiana ordered the Orleans Parish School Board to comply with *Brown v. Board of Education of Topeka, Kansas* (the 1954 United States Supreme Court decision that declared segregation in the public schools unconstitutional) and to submit a school desegregation plan by mid-May. When the school board refused to act, Judge Wright formulated a plan calling for the integration of Orleans Parish first grades when the school year began in the fall. When the school board half-heartedly attempted to integrate the first grades at two New Orleans schools, a crisis ensued. Mass demonstrations, threats of violence against board members, attacks on blacks, and harassment of white parents who sent their children to integrated schools marked the local scene.[2]

Some leaders of the Episcopal Church in Louisiana worked to keep the public schools open and were roundly criticized by segregationists within the Church. Clergy should "stick to the gospel," these critics declared. Louisiana's Bishop Girault Jones, who

*First published in *St. James Episcopal Church, Baton Rouge: A History, 1844-1994* (Baton Rouge: St. James Church, 1994), 153-76 and 193-4. Reprinted with the kind permission of St. James Episcopal Church.

became a leader of Save Our Schools, a New Orleans group dedicated to preserving the public schools, responded to this charge in his 1961 address to the annual diocesan convention. Those who insisted that the Church should stick to the gospel, Jones pointed out, were "actually preaching the Communist line" in their attempt to "confine Christianity to the four walls of the church." What about the Ten Commandments? the bishop asked; were Christians to stick to the gospel and "say they [the Commandments] have no bearing on life?"[3]

Early in 1961 the Church Responsibility Committee tried to address some of the parish's spiritual concerns. They emphasized church attendance and asked if Werlein could arrange to have a preaching mission held at St. James. They also proposed to present a lecture series by laymen that would focus on significant Protestant thinkers of the twentieth century. Having gained the rector's permission, once a week for ten weeks in the spring of 1961 local laymen presented lectures on different Protestant thinkers. Those who attended this series heard lectures on topics ranging from German theologian Paul Tillich to former archbishop of Canterbury William Temple to Albert Schweitzer, missionary and author of *Quest for the Historical Jesus*. Although the lectures were of an academic nature, they also had a spiritual focus in that they addressed the future of Protestantism in the modem world. The underlying theme of the lecture series centered on whether Protestantism could measure up to the alluring challenge of political ideologies in the battle for men's minds.[4]

Werlein fell ill during April 1961, and the vestry granted him indefinite leave until he recovered his health. A month later, on May 8, the Ministerial Association of Baton Rouge published an "Affirmation of Basic Religious Principles" in the local newspapers. Racial tensions then confronted Baton Rouge—as they did much of the South—and the ministers' "Affirmation" spoke in favor of keeping the city's public schools open. The group further stated that "discrimination on account of race or religion is a violation of the divine law of Love." The Reverend A. Stratton Lawrence, president of the Ministerial Association and the rector of Trinity Episcopal Church, signed the document, as did the rector and the assistant rector of St. James, Phillip Werlein and Nelson Longnecker.[5]

At the vestry meeting that evening, Werlein asked to retire from the active ministry during the summer of 1962. Fielding Phillips, the parish's junior warden, expressed his and the congregation's thanks for Werlein's twenty-six years of service to the parish. The time, he added, "has passed too quickly." Phillips then moved and the vestry passed a resolution asking Werlein to appoint a committee to begin searching for a new minister. The Parson then explained to the vestry that signing the Ministerial Association's resolution did not affect his belief in segregation or his acceptance of the doctrine of separate but equal facilities. He told the vestrymen that he thought an individual could be a Christian and still believe in segregation.[6]

While citizens throughout the South confronted issues of integration and civil rights, many parishioners at St. James faced change in other areas as well. Expansion of the city's industrial base brought new families and new wealth to Baton Rouge, and many of the old families who attended St. James found that their influence and their world were shrinking, or at least bad to be shared with others.

On the evening of June 12, 1961, the St. James vestry met at the church. A report was introduced from St. Mark's Episcopal Church in Shreveport critical of the National Council of Churches of Christ in America and its political activities. Some speakers at the meeting alleged that although the NCC was not a Communist or a Communist-front organization, many of its policies had Communist leanings (the NCC had advocated both abolishing the House Committee on Un-American Activities and admitting Red China to the United Nations). In addition, according to a letter distributed by vestryman Fred Drew, the NCC claimed to speak for Protestants—and thus for Episcopalians—when it did not actually have this authority. Werlein, however, spoke in support of the NCC, explaining that it was "the one Church movement toward one Christian Church." After an intense discussion, filled with resolutions and counterresolutions, the vestry tabled action on the NCC until its July meeting.

After taking care of some routine business regarding the welcoming of newcomers and the scheduling of vacations for Werlein and Longnecker, the vestry next tackled the issue of segregation. Following publication of the Ministerial Association's "Affirmation of Basic Religious Principles," some parishioners at St. James had raised questions about the church's stand on segregation. They wanted to know whether the parish had changed its "longstanding policy regarding segregation of the races in its religious services and activities and in the conduct of its Day School." The vestry then debated a resolution emphasizing the church's commitment to the "continuation of segregation" in all its various social, educational, and religious activities. After a lengthy discussion, the vestrymen took a voice vote on the resolution. There was one "no:" the parish's assistant rector, the Reverend Nelson Longnecker, opposed the resolution.

At the end of the meeting, Longnecker told the vestry that he believed passing the resolution was wrong. Since the rector had not opposed the resolution, Longnecker later recalled, he could no longer support Werlein as his assistant and believed he was obligated to resign his position at St. James. He then submitted his resignation to the vestry, effective September 1, 1961. Several vestrymen asked him to reconsider. They were particularly impressed with the job he had done in fostering the growth and development of the day school and hoped he would stay at St. James. Despite their support for his work with the school, however, the vestry reiterated that passing the resolution was a reaffirmation of their belief.[7]

Longnecker remained at St. James until the school started up again in the fall and then left for his new position as director of religious education at Trinity Church in New Orleans.

At the end of June 1962, the Reverend Werlein retired. During his long tenure at St. James, the number of communicants had nearly doubled and the parish had acquired additional property that would facilitate its work into the future. Bishop Jones later praised Werlein, stating that his "pastoral zeal . . . kept [St. James] from suffering the fate of so many downtown parishes." In a resolution published shortly before Werlein retired, the vestry particularly complimented his career as their pastor. None of his accomplishments, they wrote, had "been as great or will be remembered as long, as his untiring, unselfish and devoted dedication to his flock. The nights have never been too dark, the distance too long, the time too inconvenient, the sacrifice too great, for the Parson when one of us needed him." Werlein's accomplishments had indeed extended beyond the parochial borders of St. James. Under his direction, St. James had founded or assisted in starting four different Episcopal missions in Baton Rouge: St. Michael's, Trinity, St. Augustine's, and St. Luke's. When Werlein retired in 1962, approximately 2,600 baptized Episcopalians were members of these four churches.[8]

In July 1962, the vestry called the Reverend Robert Witcher (1926-), a former curate at St. James, to become the parish's new rector. Then the canon pastor at Christ Church Cathedral in New Orleans, he accepted and soon took charge of the parish in which he had been ordained to the priesthood nearly ten years earlier. Shortly after accepting the position, Witcher received a letter from the Parson. Werlein explained that he held great respect for Witcher and his abilities but thought he was too young and too high-church to be rector of St. James. Since Witcher was in fact the new rector, however, Werlein wished him well and asked him to take into consideration the low-church ambience of the parish. The vestry, in fact, expressed concern over just how they should address their new priest—did he prefer to be called "Nuster" or "Father"? Witcher told them to address him in whatever manner they felt comfortable and explained that he would make no liturgical changes for at least a year.[9]

Although Witcher intended no immediate liturgical changes, he soon made proposals that would help bolster the parish's financial base. At one of the first vestry meetings he attended as rector, Witcher—apparently unaware of the meager fund already in existence—recommended to the vestrymen that they look into establishing an endowment fund to finance long-range capital projects, that they encourage parishioners to remember the church in their wills, and that they urge members of the congregation to make St. James the beneficiary in their insurance policies. Werlein had earlier told Witcher that he believed the only way St. James could survive downtown was by developing a viable endowment. Werleien's previous work with parishioner Mrs. King Harding Knox had, in fact, resulted in the first significant bequest to St. James. When she died in 1965, Mrs. Knox left $100,000 to the church to be used for work among the needy, the infirm, and the aged.[10]

Witcher also moved forward with plans to begin an Episcopal high school in Baton Rouge. Aware that he was unable to run both a church and a school, he told the vestry in October that he planned to interview the Reverend Ralph K. Webster to be the parish's assistant rector, with the intention that Webster would eventually become headmaster of the proposed high school. St. James extended a call to Webster, who was then the chaplain of Christ School, in Arden, North Carolina. He accepted and came to Baton Rouge in the summer of 1963. Later in the year, a charter was drawn up, and by mid-February, 1964, Episcopal High School was incorporated.[11]

There was plenty of other activity at St. James during the early years of Witcher's tenure. In October 1963, the parish's Long Range Planning Committee made plans to begin construction on a new parish house and office complex in the spring of 1965. Intruding on these local matters during the fall of 1964, concerns over the National Council of Churches had again riled some vestrymen at St. James, and the vestry spent a significant portion of its September meeting discussing the NCC's programs, organization, motives, and purposes. Many vestrymen held strong feelings about the NCC, but others did not know enough about the organization to judge its merits. In the hope of holding a more informed discussion in the future, the vestry asked L. L. Feickhert to reproduce copies of an outside report, "The Episcopal Church and the National Council of Churches," and distribute them to each vestryman. After everyone had a chance to read the report, Witcher could then call a meeting of vestry members interested in discussing the problem further.[12]

Ten days later a group of vestrymen drafted a letter to be sent to Louisiana's delegates to the coming general convention of the national Church. They had read the report on the National Council of Churches. "Frankly," they wrote, "we do not like what we see." Their letter conceded that the NCC did a good job in some areas but claimed that in others the council's work was detrimental to the Episcopal Church. Although the council's stated policy was that its Washington office was not to attempt to influence legislation or to participate in any lobbying activity, the vestry complained that the NCC had in fact done just that. Furthermore, some of the NCC's other activities had created resentment against the Episcopal Church and brought "shame and disillusionment to many thousand [sic] of its members." Some Episcopal clergy, encouraged by the NCC, had participated in civil rights demonstrations, broken laws, and even served time in jail in what the critics, letter called a "misdirected effort to help a minority group achieve certain goals." The letter also criticized the NCC's support for the previous summer's voter-registration drive among blacks in Mississippi. It denounced the "invasion of the State of Mississippi by large groups of misguided youths, whose action, in our opinion, was partly responsible for the disturbance, lawlessness and crimes, committed in the State in connection with this invasion." National church leaders who had supported these demonstrations, the letter added, also had to share the blame. Apparently unfamiliar with or unpersuaded by the centuries-old Augustinian and Thomistic assertions that an unjust law is not a law, the vestrymen deplored the NCC's theory that encouraged people to break established statutes.[13]

The furor over the National Council of Churches soon died down at St. James. As a matter of fact, when St. Mark's in Shreveport stopped paying their diocesan assessment because the diocese contributed to the NCC, St. James's vestry voted to raise their assessment in order to help make up the shortfall. Recalling this situation, Father Witcher later remembered two conservative vestrymen pointing out that St. James "was either part of the diocese or it was not a part of the diocese," and that withdrawal from the organization would leave the parish with no voice to help bring about the changes the vestry desired. The two men convinced the whole vestry to vote in favor of helping the diocese make up St. Mark's former contribution.[14]

At the diocese's annual convention in 1965, held at St. James, Bishop Jones responded to those parishes still complaining about the Church's speaking out against social injustice. "The National Council of Churches is only a symbol," he asserted. "What many people really protest is the involvement of our own Church in civil rights issues." Many serious churchmen, the bishop said, had told him that local civil laws were supreme forms of law and should not be violated. Neither advocating reckless lawbreaking nor trying to trivialize civil disobedience, Jones confronted these critics with a parable. A man was standing on the bank of a lake, he told them, watching some children playing in a canoe. Suddenly the boat capsized, throwing the youngsters into the deep water. The man dove in to try to help them. There were others there, however, who criticized his action. They pointed to a No Swimming sign and told the man they protested his "deliberate violation of the law." Bishop Jones then exhorted the gathering to identify themselves with the eternal truths revealed by Christ, truths "which down deep in our hearts-we know to be right." (Not everyone in the parish agreed with the bishop's views on civil rights. Jones later recalled that during these difficult years a "prominent layman" from St. James attended one of Jones's Lenten services in New Orleans. The bishop's sermon that day addressed the unwillingness of many "to apply the catechism's Duty Towards My Neighbor to Negroes." The St. James parishioner got up while Jones was preaching and left the church. Concerned that the man had fallen ill, the bishop asked the usher after finishing the service if that were the case. It was not. The parishioner from St. James had told the usher exactly why he was leaving: "I did not come to Church to hear communist propaganda."[15]

Whatever its entanglements in diocesan and civil rights affairs, St. James continued to address local problems and projects. Under the direction of former senior warden George Vordenbaumen, the parish initiated a fundraising campaign in the early months of 1966 to raise money to replace the "old and dilapidated" parish house. The campaign resulted in pledges totaling over $330,000, to be paid during the next three years. Architects A. Hays Town and William Hughes drafted final blueprints for the proposed addition, and that summer construction began on the new two-story parish house and office complex (complete with air conditioning).[16]

Building the new parish house caused some problems for St. James's growing day school, since both the old parish house and the Maxwell house, which had long since served their purposes, had to be demolished, leaving the school without adequate facilities in which to conduct classes. Fortunately, the parish was able to lease the old Baton Rouge Junior High School buildings on Florida Street; with the exception of the kindergarten, all the day-school classes met there for the next two years.

The year 1966 was an important one for the Episcopal high school then evolving out of St. James's day school. Having realized that no single parish could adequately maintain the high school and that for one parish to try to do so would ultimately lead to friction among Baton Rouge's several Episcopal parishes, the board of trustees of Episcopal High asked the Diocese of Louisiana to accept the school as a diocesan institution. The diocese agreed to this request, and Episcopal High became one of only two Episcopal parochial high schools in the Louisiana diocese (the other being St. Martin's in Metairie). In the fall of 1966 the day school added an eighth and a ninth grade. In the spring of 1970 students from that ninth grade became Episcopal High's first graduating class; meanwhile, however, in December 1966, the parish learned that for legal reasons the high school would have to separate from the day school by the time classes began in the fall of 1968. During the intervening period, the high school's board of trustees acquired fifty acres of land in the Woodland Ridge area of east Baton Rouge: the board purchased thirty acres and accepted donations of five acres apiece from four individuals (including St. James parishioner Dr. Henry Miller) who wanted to see the school become a reality. By the time the 1968-1969 school year began, a three-story school building, a mechanical building, and a dining hall had been constructed on this property.[17]

Much of St. James's work in the late 1960s demonstrated that a downtown church could succeed as a viable and active parish despite demographic factors working against it. Four decades earlier, in the 1920s, the Reverend Malcolm Lockhart had warned the vestry that unless a parish had work to do, congregations tended to grow indifferent both to church attendance and to service in the name of the church.

St. James's initiative then had resulted in an Episcopal student center at Louisiana State University. Baton Rouge had changed considerably in the years that followed, but the parish's leading role in establishing Episcopal High and in constructing a modern physical plant with the capability of serving the parish into the next century served notice that despite its location, St. James could survive.

Challenges more serious than a downtown location, however, confronted orthodox Christians during the 1960s, and Witcher responded to these challenges as well. The New Theology and the Death of God movement gained a measure of respectability in some quarters, and many parishioners at St. James became confused by what they were hearing from adherents of these ideas. Witcher believed that part of his job as a priest was to defend the faith, and he reacted vigorously against these heterodox theologies. To him, they represented an "erosion of revealed truth." He admonished his congregation to remember Heb. 13:8-9, "Jesus Christ is the same yesterday and today and forever. Do not be led away by diverse and strange teachings." Witcher also emphasized the changeless character of faith in Jesus Christ. "Our faith is true and forever," he proclaimed, "and it gives us a stable center in these changing times."[18]

The civil rights movement, the war in Vietnam, and the sexual revolution all caused and embodied change during the sixties. The decade also brought significant changes in the Episcopal Church's liturgy and in its liturgical practice. The Second Vatican Council

(1962-1965), called by Pope John XXIII to help modernize some aspects of Roman Catholicism, plus the liturgical movement of the early sixties, led many Episcopal churches to move their altars out from the walls. This was not a simple matter of taste in church interior design; moving the altar away from the wall—in effect turning it into a table—implied a different emphasis in the Eucharist. Before, the priest had celebrated the Eucharist facing the altar with his back to the congregation. This practice emphasized the sacrificial nature of the rite. When the altars stood free, the priest celebrated facing the congregation, and the new practice placed a larger emphasis on the Eucharist as a communal meal. By 1967 the altar at St. James had been pulled out from the wall of the sanctuary, and the parishioners easily adjusted to this alteration. Witcher accepted the change as well; however, he later confessed that during a penitential season like Lent he often felt an urge to push the altar back into its former place.[19]

There were other liturgical changes during the decade. At the parish's annual meeting in 1968, Witcher announced that later in the year St. James would begin using the experimental *Liturgy of the Lord's Supper*. The Diocese of Louisiana had directed its parishes to use this new liturgy at all public services between Ash Wednesday and September 1, 1968. Trial use of the new liturgy was part of the procedure for revising the *Book of Common Prayer*. Witcher explained to the congregation that this was the first time in the church's history that the laity had been invited to participate in the process of liturgical change. He asked them to take this opportunity seriously. Three years later, in September 1971, St. James began using *Services for Trial Use*, the second of the three trial liturgies authorized by the Standing Liturgical Commission of the national Church. Some Episcopalians may remember this version as the "green book" and the third trial liturgy, *Authorized Services*, as the "zebra book."[20]

Witcher helped ease St. James's transition to the new liturgy by explaining the reasons for the proposed changes. Before the diocese introduced *Services for Trial Use* and a modified liturgical year in 1971, he told the members of St. James that "there is no change just for change's sake in these particular proposals." Many of the proposed changes in the *Book of Common Prayer*, in fact, brought the Episcopal liturgy back in harmony with the rest of Christendom. The trial eucharistic liturgy rearranged parts of the service and modernized some of the rite's language, while the proposed church year intended to restore "Sunday to its prime place as 'The Lord's Day'" by not allowing saints' days to replace it. Witcher also pointed out that the changes were designed to assist Episcopalians in their spiritual pilgrimages.[21]

The Episcopal Church's renewed emphasis on Sunday as the Lord's Day helped Witcher move St. James toward becoming a more sacrament-centered parish. When Parson Werlein retired in 1962, the Sunday services at St. James had been morning prayer at 7:30, 9:00, and 11:00 A.M., and evening prayer at night. The Eucharist was celebrated one Sunday a month at the eleven o'clock service. Although Witcher and Werlein shared similar theological views of the sacrament per se, Father Witcher was much more Anglo-

Catholic than the parson, and he believed the Eucharist "should be the center of the parish life."

At the parish's annual meeting in 1971, Witcher told his congregation that each parishioner should set a goal of receiving the Holy Sacrament at least once a week, preferably on Sunday. "There are duties and obligations expected of Christians," he reminded his charges, "and they are for the sake of your own soul's health." By the fall of 1971 St. James's Sunday schedule had been changed to encourage weekly attendance of the Eucharist, which was now celebrated each Sunday at 7:30 A.M. and 5:30 P.M., and every other week at 9:00 A.M. and 11:00 A.M. This schedule reflected a distinct change from the Werlein years and the former rector's belief that church members should "worship God every Sunday in his church" but not necessarily receive the Sacrament. [22]

In the fall of 1971 St. James began the process of emending certain archaic portions of the parish's charter. At the annual meeting in January 1972, the parish voted by a greater than two-thirds majority to lower the age requirement for church membership from twenty-one to seventeen and to remove racial and sexual restrictions regarding membership in the church and on the vestry. The charter no longer restricted church membership to white communicants at least twenty-one years of age, nor did it exclude women from membership on the vestry. These changes brought St. James in line with the canons of the national Church and the Diocese of Louisiana. A year later, in January 1973, Mrs. Mildred McVea became the first woman elected to the vestry of St. James. [23]

As St. James moved forward into the 1970s, it would look back on the decade of the 1960s as a period of crisis and redefinition. For nearly fifteen years the parish's mission had been directed within. Its parishioners had struggled with social change, liturgical change, and the question of whether the church should continue to exist on the same downtown corner where the original building had been constructed 130 years earlier. The members of St. James had learned that their parish could survive downtown, and they had taken steps to help ensure its existence. The day school continued to prosper, and the parish was developing a growing endowment fund. And although membership in mainline churches declined nationwide during the sixties and early seventies, St. James actually gained members.

By the mid-1970s St. James's mission was beginning to look out toward the world once again. In April 1974, the vestry started discussing the feasibility of establishing a retirement home for elderly persons. This idea had been raised as far back as the 1950s, when the Women's Auxiliary had strongly supported it, but little had come of the proposal. Now some vestry members began reexamining the concept, and in June they announced that there might be considerable support in the parish for moving forward with the project. [24]

The retirement-home project was still in the proposal stage when, in November 1974, Witcher announced that he had recently been elected bishop coadjutor of the Diocese of Long Island. He accepted the call in January 1975, and told the vestry his resignation would be effective sometime around the end of March. At the parish's annual meeting in 1975, Witcher spoke in favor of establishing the projected retirement home: it would help combat the isolation and the loneliness with which many older people had to contend. As St. James went about the process of calling a new rector to replace Father Witcher, the vestry continued to develop plans for the retirement community. In February, they decided it would be an exclusive project of St. James.[25]

When Witcher left St. James in March, the parish was much stronger than it had been when he was called to be its rector nearly thirteen years earlier. His years at the parish had been years of reflection—did St. James want to remain downtown or move to the suburbs?—and of decision: the church would remain on the corner of Fourth and Convention. Witcher had guided the parish through a difficult period, and he had helped St. James develop an endowment that would buoy it in the years ahead. By the time he left, St. James's endowment totaled approximately $200,000. Moreover, as a result of Witcher's ministry, when parishioner Mrs. Helen Barnes died a few years later, she left a bequest of over $1.25 million to St. James.[26]

Witcher had also found time to earn a Ph.D. in history from Louisiana State University during his years at St. James. His dissertation, "The Episcopal Church in Louisiana, 1805-1861," contributed to the historiography of the diocese.[27]

In May 1975, the vestry called the rector of Christ Church in Martinsville, Virginia, the Reverend Dr. James Coleman (1929-), to St. James. He accepted and late in the summer became the parish's new spiritual leader. During his first five months, Coleman conducted public worship, administered the sacraments, visited parishioners, attempted to reorganize the administrative apparatus of the church to conform with its increasing size, and generally became acquainted with his new parish. He also attended two special conventions called to elect a new bishop for the Diocese of Louisiana. The Right Reverend Iveson Noland (bishop of Louisiana, 1969-1975), a former curate at St. James, had died in a plane crash in New York on June 25, 1975.[28]

By the time St. James held its annual parish meeting in January 1976, Coleman had identified three ministries that the parish needed to develop or expand: a more active ministry to its elderly parishioners; a more diversified program of Christian education for the adults, emphasizing spiritual growth; and a program encouraging parishioners to get to know and support each other.[29]

St. James began implementing these programs that year. To help parishioners living in the same area get better acquainted, the parish instituted the Neighborhood Group Ministry program in February. Two months later, in April, Coleman talked to the Reverend Herbert Bolton, a former chaplain at Bellevue Hospital in New York, about assisting with St. James's ministry to shut-ins and elderly members of the congregation. Bolton, then retired and living in New Orleans, accepted and began his work at St. James in June.

In the activity surrounding these new ministries, the vestry had not forgotten the plan to establish a retirement community in Baton Rouge. Members of the Retirement Home Committee met with Bob Murtha of Medical Management Systems of Westerville, Ohio, in June. Murtha recommended that before making any plans, St. James conduct a market analysis and survey to ascertain the Baton Rouge area's need for a retirement home. The vestry accepted this counsel and authorized the survey, paying for it out of the Knox-Dunbar endowment for work with the needy, infirm, and elderly. During 1977 the feasibility study was completed. The results indicated that the Baton Rouge area indeed needed a retirement community, and St. James decided to proceed with the project.[30]

The parish also introduced a new Sunday school curriculum that year. The Christian Education Committee, led by chairman Jesse Coates, Jr., suggested that St. James make a complete change from the traditional Sunday school program, which they believed failed to make a lasting impression on children. For example, it rarely outweighed the influence of science classes the children attended during the week. The committee recommended that the parish begin using the New Media Bible, a program based on films and filmstrips that emphasized the theological concepts in the Bible. The committee believed the visual nature of this program would have a greater effect on "today's children [who] are visually oriented." The vestry agreed, and the parish implemented the New Media Bible curriculum later in the year, showing the first film, *The Creation*, in September. Early in 1978 St. James instituted a Bible-study program, the Bethel Bible Series, for the adult members of the congregation.[31]

A new vitality was evident at St. James during the late 1970s. Confident now that the church could survive in its downtown location, the parish had begun expanding its ministries. The parish had a new Christian education program and an expanded ministry to the elderly and shut-ins, and was moving forward with plans for the retirement community. At the annual parish meeting in January 1978, Coleman told the members of St. James that he did not know "of a congregation anywhere that has accomplished so much over the years and yet has so much potential for the years ahead." He then shared with the congregation part of a letter he had received from a former communicant who had moved out of town. The letter accompanied the former parishioner's final payment on his family's 1977 pledge. "This brings us up to date . . . financially speaking," he wrote, "but what of the gifts of the Spirit given us . . . by this generous congregation?" "'I was a stranger,'" he continued, quoting Scripture, "'and ye took me in' as I am sure many other newcomers feel that they have been welcomed and, well, helped, through the years by St. James, Baton Rouge."[32]

St. James continued its mission of service both to members of the parish and to those in the larger Episcopal community during the years that followed. In addition to the church's internal ministries, at the urging of Warren Green, chairman of the Long Range Planning Committee, the parish in 1979 made one-time grants of $5,000 to the Presiding Bishop's Fund for World Relief, Episcopal High School, All Saints' School (in Mississippi), the bishop of Louisiana's mission fund, and the University of the South. The parish also gave gifts of $5,000 to both the student center at LSU and an Episcopal school in Honduras, and established matching grant funds for these two institutions. By February 1980, matching funds of nearly $7,500 had been raised for the student center and over

$33,000 for the school in Honduras. St. James added $10,000 and $35,000, respectively, to these monies.[33]

In 1980 the parish again expanded its facilities. The Capital Savings and Loan Association had moved to another location in the downtown area, and in November 1980, St. James purchased the company's former building on the southeast corner of Florida and Fourth streets adjacent to the church. After some minor (yet costly) alterations, the parish began using the new building as an activity center, complete with a gymnasium for the day school and several general-purpose meeting rooms. The Episcopal Young Churchmen held their meetings here, and the building later became the focus of St. James's outreach ministries. St. James also permitted several local businessmen to play basketball in the building after work.[34]

Work on the retirement community, to be known as St. James Place, continued as well. The board of trustees acquired nearly forty acres of land in the vicinity of Highland Road and Lee Drive on which to build the facility. As the retirement-community plan developed, it became clear that St. James Place was to be a "total living" facility and not a nursing home. Part of the center's mission, as Witcher had pointed out years before, was to help overcome, by bringing people together, the loneliness and isolation that plagued many elderly people in the late twentieth century. Baton Rouge responded enthusiastically to the proposed retirement community. By the time the groundbreaking ceremony for the facility was held in August, 1981, over 75 percent of the nearly two hundred units had been reserved. In January 1983, the first residents moved into St. James Place.[35]

Two other significant events in the life of St. James occurred in 1983. First, the vestry decided to make an addition to the parish house to alleviate crowded conditions in the building. Second, under the leadership of Warren Green, the parish established the St. James Episcopal Church Outreach Endowment. At its 1982 national convention in New Orleans, the Episcopal Church had adopted the tithe (10 percent of one's income) as the minimum standard of financial giving. The vestry proposed that this standard apply not only to parishioners, but also to the total amount pledged to the church each year. In other words, St. James would tithe 10 percent of its operating budget. "Those funds considered to be tithed by the church," the vestry continued, "should be used for the Lord's work outside our own parish, and particularly (but not exclusively) for the relief and succor of those who are homeless, ill, starving, alone, without access to the Lord's word, or otherwise in great physical or spiritual need in our country and throughout the world."[36]

The vestry established an increasing scale of outside giving intended to reach the tithe level within three years. St. James failed to reach this standard within that period, and the resulting failure led to some tension at the parish. During the mid-1980s the parish had difficulty meeting its annual pledge to the Diocese of Louisiana (20.5 percent of the parish's operating budget at that time), and in order to fulfill its commitment to the diocese, the parish spent amounts of less than 10 percent of its operating budget on outreach. As a result, the parish later reorganized its outreach plan. St. James resolved to pledge 10 percent of its operating budget less its pledge to the diocese (which the vestry considered a form of outreach) to furthering the Lord's work outside the parish. By 1989, the parish had reached this goal.[37]

During Coleman's years at St. James, assistant rector Edward Robertson organized a food ministry for needy people in the downtown area. The parish had also donated considerable sums to help the St. Michael's mission build a day care center, and to St. Margaret's, an Episcopal mission in southeast Baton Rouge. Under Coleman's direction, the parish not only ministered to its own members, but also extended its outreach programs to the larger community.

In December 1988, Father Coleman announced to the vestry that he had accepted a call to St. John's, Memphis, in his native Tennessee. By the time he left the parish at the end of February, St. James had more than 1,400 communicants and approximately 300 students in the day school.[38]

While the vestry searched for a new rector, they also began preparing for the parish's 150th anniversary in 1994 by establishing the Sesquicentennial Restoration Fund. St. James needed $150,000 to pay for repairs to the interior of the ninety-three-year-old church building. The campaign was a great success, and the parish was soon able to renovate the pews, restore much of the woodwork, and lay new carpeting in the church.[39]

After Coleman's departure, St. James's rectorate lay vacant for nearly nine months. In October 1989, the vestry extended a call to the Reverend Francis Daunt (1945-), a native of Ireland then serving as rector of the Church of the Holy Trinity in Decatur, Georgia. Daunt accepted, and on the First Sunday of Advent, 1989, he was installed as St. James's twenty-first rector. Shortly after he took charge of the parish, Daunt asked the vestry to begin a scholarship fund to help children of parishioners to attend St. James Day School and Episcopal High. The vestry established the fund a few months later.[40]

A survey conducted before Daunt came to St. James indicated that most parishioners were committed to keeping the church at its downtown site. Having chosen to remain downtown, the parish had to decide how it could best further the Christian mission from this location. One obvious need was to expand St. James's outreach to the poor in the downtown community. Daunt later recalled that during his first few months at St. James, a constant flow of people came to the church office to ask for financial assistance. Most lived near the downtown area and needed money to help pay for food, utilities, or medical care. The vestry allocated a certain amount each month to a discretionary fund that the rector could use to assist people as he saw fit, but Daunt soon discovered that the funds for an entire month could be used in a day or two.

Daunt asked the priests and ministers at Baton Rouge's other downtown churches how they addressed the problem of helping the poor in the area. Most, he learned, let their secretaries handle the matter, and for the most part, the secretaries were turning people away. Those parishes that did offer assistance did so in much the same way as St. James—scattered donations to individuals of ten to twenty dollars with no follow-up. In some respects, the assistance was as much a way of getting the poor to go away as it was an attempt to help people in need. Many people who received funds from St. James also approached the other downtown parishes; some managed to learn when the priests and ministers at the various parishes received additional discretionary monies and were able to ask for assistance when they knew funds were available. This practice led to abuses of the system as some individuals, through craft or luck, often received proportionately greater assistance than others who were just as needy.[41]

With the help of John Pine, chairman of the Outreach Committee, Daunt furthered the parish's recent mission of Christian outreach. His former parish in Decatur had taken part in an interracial, interdenominational cooperative ministry designed to help many segments of the city's population. This ministry had developed programs to assist people without adequate food, clothing, or money to pay for rent or medical care. A night shelter for women with children, many of whom had been abused, was housed in the Episcopal church. Daunt believed that a similar program could work in downtown Baton Rouge, and he discussed the idea with clergy at the other downtown churches. They supported it, and the group began developing a plan for a Christian Outreach Center. The chief obstacle to implementing this combined ministry of St. James Episcopal Church, St. Joseph's (Roman Catholic) Cathedral, First Presbyterian Church, First Methodist Church, and First Baptist Church was lack of a building in which to house it. In early 1991, however, Father Frank Uter of St. Joseph's closed the cathedral's bookstore and gave the downtown churches permission to use it as a site for the outreach center.[42]

The downtown churches worked with Volunteers of America, a national organization that helps coordinate volunteers working on community problems, and on April 15, 1991, the Downtown Christian Outreach Center opened. The downtown churches were, in effect, reclaiming part of the church's mission to the poor that had been taken over by federal, state, and local governments. Volunteers of America supplied a staff person to administer the center and provided training to volunteers from the five downtown churches involved.

By pooling their limited resources, the churches were able both to assist more people and to prevent potential abuses of the system. John Pine encouraged lay members of St. James to donate their time to this ministry, and the parish soon developed a small but active core of volunteers, ranging from housewives and retired persons to an economics professor at LSU. In addition to addressing immediate concerns, the center also attempted to investigate the underlying causes of a problem and to help the individual work toward a solution.[43]

For much of his first year and a half at St. James, Daunt went through the process of assembling a ministerial staff to help implement the parish's programs. He called two priests to help with pastoral and sacramental duties; both were former rectors themselves and brought many years of experience to St. James. The Reverend Reginald Gunn, a Georgia native, became St. James's associate rector in July 1990. In the summer of 1991, the Reverend Robert Burton accepted a call to be the parish's assistant rector. Before coming to St. James, Burton had been rector of St. John's in Fort Smith, Arkansas. His primary area of ministry was to elderly members of St. James; he also served as chaplain of St. James Place.

The parish also hired a full-time director of religious education, a full-time director of youth ministries, and a new principal for the day school (Mrs. Mona Terry, the principal for twenty years, had retired in June 1991). Ironically, the parish's downtown location, once a potential threat to the church's existence, had become a strength for the day school. As long as people who worked downtown had school-aged children, St. James Day School had a ready market.[44] One theory of parish management in the 1990s asserted that many young families no longer cared what denomination they belonged to as long as the church served their needs and the needs of their children by providing good schools during the week and good Christian education programs on Sunday. In effect, what they wanted was a "full service" church. More by accident than by design, St. James was well on the way to becoming just that by the end of 1991.[45]

St. James had strengthened its ministry to the elderly and to the youth of the parish, and it had developed a strong Christian education program for adults and children alike. Furthermore, the parish's clergy—especially Father Gunn, whose responsibility it was to direct, organize, and schedule the parish's worship activities—were committed to doing a first-class job at public worship. As the parish had done so many times before, St. James was responding to new challenges in the early nineties. Through various forms of service directed within as well as outside the parish, St. James was implementing the Christian's mandate to "seek and serve Christ in all persons." Nearly seventy years earlier, during Inspiration Week in 1925, Bishop James Freeman had proclaimed that the days of merely walking down the aisle and receiving the Sacrament were over. "We must exert the faith by which we live," he said. As St. James parish of Baton Rouge approached its 150th year of service, it was confidently putting the bishop's words into action.

Notes for "Meeting the Challenges of the Late Twentieth Century"

[1]Diocesan Convention, 1960, 266; Right Reverend Robert Witcher interview, December 16, 1991, Baton Rouge, La.; Annual Meeting, January 12, 1960, Archives of St. James Episcopal Church, Baton Rouge, La.

[2]Bennett H. Wall, ed., *Louisiana: A History* (Arlington Heights, Ill., 1984), 335-41.

[3]Girault M. Jones, *Some Personal Recollections of the Episcopal Church in Louisiana* (New Orleans, 1980), 83-84; Diocesan Convention, 1961, 52-54.

[4]Vestry Minutes, March 13, 1961.

[5]*Baton Rouge State Times*, May 8, 1961; Vestry Minutes, May 8, 1961.

[6]Vestry Minutes, May 8, 1961.

[7]Ibid., June 12, 1961.

[8]Reverend Nelson Longnecker interview, June 18, 1991, Baton Rouge, La.; Vestry Minutes, June 11, 1961 (the vestry resolution is filed with this date as well); Diocesan Convention, 1965, 38. The total of 2,600 baptized members is an average of the numbers recorded at Diocesan Convention, 1962, 186, and Diocesan Convention, 1963, 183.

[9]Witcher interview; *Episcopal Clerical Directory, 1991*, 866.

[10]Witcher interview; Vestry Minutes, October 8, 1962, March 8, 1965.

[11]Witcher interview; Vestry Minutes, October 8, 1962, February 10, 1964; Ralph K. Webster, "St. James Day School, the Forerunner of Episcopal High School," August 10, 1991 (photocopy of typescript), 1-3, in Archives of St. James Episcopal Church, Baton Rouge, La.

[12]Vestry Minutes, October 21, 1963, September 14, 1964.

[13]St. James Episcopal Church in Baton Rouge to Louisiana Deputies to the Sixty-first General Convention of the Protestant Episcopal Church in the United States of America, September 24, 1964, filed with Vestry Minutes, September 14, 1964.

[14]Witcher interview.

[15]Rt. Rev. Girault Jones to the author, January 13, 1992; Diocesan Convention, 1965, 46-47.

[16]Annual Meeting, January 10, 1967.

[17]Witcher interview; Webster, "St. James Day School," 4-7; Day School Committee Report to Vestry filed with Vestry Minutes, December 12, 1966.

[18]Witcher interview; Annual Meeting, January 11, 1966; Annual Meeting, January 9, 1968.

[19]Witcher interview.

[20]Annual Meeting, January 9, 1968; Messenger, September 9, 1971; Witcher interview; Robert W. Pritchard, *History of the Episcopal Church* (Harrisburg, Pa., 1991), 251.

[21]Witcher interview; Annual Meeting, January 24, 1971.

[22]Witcher interview; various issues of *Messenger* for Fall, 1971; Annual Meeting, January 24, 1971.

[23]Vestry Minutes, October 11, 1971; Annual Meeting, January 16,1972; Amendment of Charter of the Rector, Churchwardens, and Vestrymen of the Church of St. James in the Parish of East Baton Rouge, in Communion with the Protestant Episcopal Church in the United States of America, January 19, 1972, in Archives of St. James Episcopal Church; Annual Meeting, January 21, 1973.

[24]Vestry Minutes, April 8, June 10, 1974; Witcher interview.

[25]Vestry Minutes, November 18, 1974, January 13, February 10, 1975. Witcher's remarks at the Annual Meeting, January 19, 1975, are appended to Vestry Minutes, February 10, 1975.

[26]Annual Meeting, January 19, 1975; Financial Records of St. James Episcopal Church.

[27]Witcher, "Episcopal Church in Louisiana," title page.

[28]Vestry Minutes, May 5, September 8, 1975; Annual Meeting, January 18, 1976.

[29]Annual Meeting, January 18, 1976.

[30]Vestry Minutes, February 9, April 12, September 13, 1976; Annual Meeting, January 16, 1977; Annual Meeting, January 15, 1978.

[31]Vestry Minutes, April 11, September 12, 1977; Annual Meeting, January 15, 1978.

[32]Annual Meeting, January 15, 1978.

[33]Vestry Minutes, May 14, December 23, 1979, February 11, 1980. Although one certainly should not discount the efficacy and legitimacy of such financial donations, they do seem to represent a form of piety that is more

institutional than some past expressions. In a sense, the parish's community has in some instances become both larger and more impersonal.

[34]Vestry Minutes, October 13, November 10, 1980; Annual Meeting, January 18, 1981; Reverend James Coleman, telephone interview by the author, March 25, 1992.

[35]Vestry Minutes, March 10, May 12, December 8, 1980; Annual Meeting, January 27, 1980; Vestry Minutes, August 18, 1981, January 10, 1983.

[36]Vestry Minutes, October 10, 1983; Annual Meeting, January 22, 1984; Coleman interview.

[37]Vestry resolution in Vestry Minutes, December 8, 1986; Rev. Francis Daunt, interview by the author, January 10, 1992, Baton Rouge; Annual Meeting, January 8, 1989; Financial Records of St. James Episcopal Church.

[38]Vestry Minutes, December 13, 1988; Diocesan Convention, 1988, 165.

[39]Vestry Minutes, March 12, April 16, 1990; Annual Meeting, January 21, 1990; Annual Meeting, January 20, 1991.

[40]Vestry Minutes, October 9, 1990, April 16, November 12, 1990. Daunt's biographical material is from *Episcopal Clerical Directory, 1991*, 185.

[41]Daunt interview; *Faith and Works* (a monthly publication of St. James), August, 1991, in Archives of St. James Episcopal Church.

[42]Daunt interview; *Faith and Works*, August, 1991.

[43]Daunt interview; *Faith and Works*, August, 1991.

[44]Daunt interview; Letter of agreement between St. James Episcopal Church and the Reverend Reginald Gunn, in personal papers of Francis Daunt.

[45]Daunt interview.

A HISTORY OF THE LOUISIANA BAPTIST HISTORICAL ASSOCIATION*

Perry Lassiter

In Memoriam

Gratefully dedicated to Truman Kerr, who died the week before writing began. As the reader will see, Truman was invaluable to the establishment and development of this Association, as he was to so many other Louisiana Baptist projects. I also called him my friend, as did so many others. His impact as a servant of God and a man of prayer will last into eternity.

Introduction

Historiographers debate whether history is—or should be—objective or subjective. This account intends some of both. As I participated in this development from before the beginning, and since I was one of the "prime movers," the account must be subjective. Nevertheless, I write with the primary documents at my right hand (and sometimes at my left and beneath my feet). Hopefully, the reader can easily distinguish between the "facts" of the written record and my memory. One caution: in several places my memory differs from the written record, and I believe with good reason that my memory is correct. I will try to point these places out. Of course, the opposite will prove true in other places.

If another person had collected this record from me with the aid of a tape recorder, the material would be labeled "oral history." I intend to capture some of the personal flavor of that type reportage. I will give my impressions, which are highly subjective by definition. Again, I hope to moderate these by recounting events more or less factually. This is the story of the emergence of the Louisiana Baptist Historical Association. Should anyone read it in the future, the story may also reflect a common pattern of committee and organizational structure in the last quarter of the twentieth-century. He or she may also find an introduction to some of the personalities and issues of the day.

*First published in *Journal of Louisiana Baptist History*, 7 (1994): 17-41. Reprinted with the kind permission of the author and the publisher.

The History Committee

I attended my first Louisiana Baptist History Committee meeting sometime in 1983. That committee is nominated by the convention committee on committees and usually "rubber-stamped" by the convention in annual session. The job assignment given in the LBC by-laws reads "The committee shall advise the Convention regarding historical material and encourage activities concerning the development of historical data about Louisiana Baptists and giving appropriate recognition of places figuring importantly in denominational history."[1] The committee consisted then of only six members, plus some ex officio members.

I don't remember the matters discussed at the first couple of meetings I attended. I do recall a strong impression that a group of intelligent people loved history and loved talking about history. But I had the feeling that this conversation kept them from focusing on the issues for which the committee met. The meeting turned mostly into a historical "bull session." A great bull session, true enough, but still not germane to whatever the stated purpose of the day was.

The next year, by some alchemy I was appointed vice-chair by the committee on committees. Then Chairman Carl Conrad either spoke to me in person at the convention or phoned me (or both). He absolutely refused to serve as chairman and laid that task on me. (Carl and I had known each other for some time. He had been director of language missions for many years and done a superb job. In retirement he has continued to work in missions in South Louisiana.)

I checked with Bob Lee, then the executive secretary for Louisiana Baptists. He said Conrad's "passing the buck" was kosher, so I went ahead. On February 1, 1984, I mailed a letter to the committee calling a meeting for March 8, 1984, at the Baptist Building in Alexandria. "Chief purpose of the meeting will be to plan the work of the committee for the remainder of the year. We will also give attention to the media conference which includes a history section for the first time."[2]

Further, I suggested the need for a job description. I had reviewed the assignment in the by-laws and felt it rather vague. So I included an extra sheet entitled "Thoughts about the LBC History Committee."[3] The list began by outlining several basic actions in the field of history: Awareness, Collecting, Preserving, Writing, Publishing. I commented that the committee should probably be involved with the first three ("four" was written in error), but foresaw a role only of encouraging writing and publishing. As events turned out, several committee members did, in fact, write, and the committee (plus its offspring, the Association) jumped up to its neck in publishing.

I also mentioned encouraging the writing of histories of all our LBC agencies, including the Executive Board and its subcommittees. The sheet mentions biographies and the encouragement of church and associational histories. The shortest line reads, "Support, encourage, and promote the Historical Society."

The committee meeting convened March 8, 1984, in a committee room just off the executive offices on the second floor of the Baptist Building. (A copy of these minutes and all minutes are filed in an appendix section in the archives at the Baptist Building.) During this meeting the committee outlined an ambitious series of goals to seek in the coming months and years. Most of these goals are not relevant to the history of the Association. One specific recommendation does relate directly to that history, however, and a trend among other actions should also be noted. The last item in the "job description" reads: "7. Obtain information on the Louisiana Baptist Historical Society (secure copy of constitution)."[4] Notice a developing trend to encourage an increased outreach and involvement of Baptists outside the committee. We invited associational and church historians to the media conference. We encouraged both groups to write histories and send them to Kathy Sylvest in the Baptist Building. We kept a list of names and addresses of those attending to begin a mailing list.

Attending that meeting were several people who have been of great help both to the committee and the Association over the years. Dr. Robert L. Lee was very much interested in Louisiana Baptist History. He has himself written in the field and joined the Association, attending meetings after his retirement. As executive director of the LBC, he helped us in numerous ways to steer through rules, protocol, and practicabilities. Truman Kerr bridged two administrations, and gave inestimable service. We shall see his hand at several points throughout this history. Kathy Sylvest holds several responsibilities in the state convention. Chief among them is media specialist. But she also finds time for her assignment to history and archives. She has a genuine interest in history and gets excited whenever someone turns up a real find for her collection. She has been of help in many, many ways—both small and large. (1994 Update: She is now treasurer of the Association.) Carolyn Sterne is executive secretary to the director of the convention. I've always suspected that secretly she runs the building and probably most of the convention. She was most faithful in attending after hours (Saturdays) and recording the minutes until the Association elected its own recording secretary. She also helped in numerous other ways.

The history committee met again on September 18, 1984, following a 12:15 p.m. lunch. Present were Lassiter, Dixie Moss, and A. W. Robbins. Ex officio attenders were Christine Hunt (from the Historical Society), Glen Lee Greene (convention historian), Kerr, and Sterne.[5] Near the beginning of the meeting I suggested that Dixie Moss condense her history of Half Moon Bluff Baptist Church and submit it to the national journal of the SBC Historical Society. Dr. Robbins agreed, and added that we should direct it to Lynn May.[6] At the time I had no thought this article would be the first in our first journal!

Dixie Moss impressed me the first time I met her. She was about seventy years old and had driven to Alexandria from Baton Rouge. She commented in general conversation before the meeting that she had ten years of projects laid out to do. Writing this nine years later, I suspect she has completed most of them and started on others. Among them, she has endowed a chair at Louisiana College. I appreciate the fact that she made a significant contribution to the work of the committee and beginning the association.

Christine Hunt outlined the background of the Historical Society. The group was formed the first Saturday of December 1978, at First Baptist Church of Minden with Eugene Spruell taking the major responsibility for promoting the meeting. Spruell was elected president, and Hunt was elected secretary. The Society had a second meeting in 1979 in Franklinton with 25-30 people attending. Most were from the Franklinton area. The Society charged a $5 membership fee and currently had $120 in the treasury.[7] There may have been discussion of the Society not mentioned in the minutes. I have the impression the general feeling was that the Society was not likely to be revived at that time. We had been talking about getting associational history chairpersons together and challenging them to help attain some of the goals we had been discussing. The possibility of including Historical Society members was discussed, which led to Christine Hunt's summary.

An idea was forming in my mind. The group conversation and certainly Dr. Hunt's summary helped shape it. I asked whether the committee might want to set up a conference on Baptist History. At that conference we might ask Dixie Moss to present the paper on Half Moon Bluff and follow up with a discussion on collecting and writing church histories. Note the focus was still on getting associational leaders together to achieve our goals. Robbins spelled that out in asking that they be invited. I suggested we promote the meeting in an attractive way that would make it "sound interesting and informative to those attending."[8]

Dr. Robbins summed up the discussion with a motion, seconded by Dixie Moss, which carried unanimously: "to postpone reviving the Historical Society, but invite associational history representatives to a meeting (date to be set later). If the association does not elect a history representative, the moderator could be asked to attend." Truman Kerr added that the convention could cover expenses of such a meeting.[9]

Somewhere along the way, the meeting grew from one paper to three. In a memorandum dated March 4, 1985, I announced to the committee a "three-fold meeting in the Church-Minister Relations Building . . . on Saturday, March 30." The agenda listed in the memo was:

9:30 a. m.	Orientation and Training Session for Associational History Committees
10:30 a.m.	Historical Society Meeting
12:00 Noon	Lunch Break
1:30 p.m.	History Committee Meeting

Note that the memo still used the term "Historical Society," even though the conference was actually sponsored by the committee. I think we all hoped at that point to revive the Society. The memo also stated that I was sending a news release to the *Baptist Message*, promoting the meeting.

I can find no documentation on what happened between the fall committee meeting and the spring conference. The committee report to the Convention in November 1985, listed three papers presented.[10] This accords with my memory and with the three papers published in the first issue of the journal. I also have a cassette tape of the three papers as delivered. Those three first papers were

> "Half Moon Bluff Baptist Church" by Dixie Moss
> "Origins of Louisiana Baptist Journalism" by William Poe
> "Four Past Presidents of Louisiana College" by Landrum Salley

Traditionally, many committees in Baptist life work informally. I remember discussing the papers with each of the presenters. Likely, over the phone and perhaps at the state convention, we made suggestions to each other about the latter two papers. I would then have called Poe and Salley and asked whether they could present something, and they agreed.

I also took it on myself in that first conference to set some standards that have been repeated to each participant. In the papers presented to the conference and published in the journal, we wish excellent and thorough scholarship. However, we ask that the material be presented in a popular and interesting style without sacrificing that excellence. We also ask the presenters to confine their presentation to 15 or 20 minutes if possible to allow the additional part of a half hour for questions and comments.

Incidentally, I plan for this present paper to have three incarnations: one to be read before the group at the May 1993, meeting, another more complete paper to submit for journal publication, and a still fuller work to be deposited in the archives along with the originals of the materials in my possession, such as minutes.

In the History Committee meeting after lunch, I brought up the question of "revitalizing the Historical Society." Christine Hunt, member of the committee and treasurer of the Society, stated there was not enough strength to reorganize at that time. Several of the committee members who had belonged to the Society agreed with her.[11]

At that meeting we were still trying to develop an organization built around history committees—or at least chairpersons—for each association. A. W. Robbins suggested that the state might be divided among the History Committee members, and each member could be responsible for associations in his or her area. Truman Kerr said he had asked the directors of missions to find contact people who have an interest in history. The chairman suggested developing a mailing list of contacts. Then, over a period of time, a good group of interested people would emerge. Kathy Sylvest reported ten associational history chairmen.

The group agreed to continue the History Committee organization as it was, but strive to locate a contact person in each association.[12] Thus, following the first seminar program, the Committee deliberately rejected trying to begin or revive a separate Historical Society. Rather they focused on similar associational structure used by other programs, such as Sunday School

Before adjourning, several members expressed approval of the days' program and expressed a desire to repeat the same type meeting. About twenty people had attended. Lassiter stated that he would like future programs to continue to interest all people, not just history scholars.[13]

1987-1988

I believe I rotated off the History Committee for a year after that meeting. I don't have the records for 1986, and there was no seminar that year. I was present and presiding as vice-chairman on October 8, 1987, however. Chairman William Poe was absent for some reason.[14]

At that meeting I raised the question about hosting a spring meeting similar to the one in 1985. (The minutes say "1984" in error, possibly my error. Carolyn Sterne's minutes are almost always accurate.) Christine Hunt agreed and added she would like to publish the reports if possible. This statement by Dr. Hunt is the first recorded mention of publishing.

(Christine Hunt is the former chairperson of the old Historical Society. She is principal of a school in Minden. The press of her duties made attending some later meetings difficult for her, but she made considerable contributions to our thought in the early days.)

A. W. Robbins and Joanne Pickett agreed the idea of another program was good. Following discussion Robbins moved and Pickett seconded that the "History Committee have a spring meeting at 10:00 a. m. at the Baptist Building or Louisiana College, April 23, 1988." The motion carried unanimously.[15]

Further discussion resulted in the group's deciding again on three papers. Each was projected for twenty minutes, with ten minutes for discussion. Chairman Lassiter asked Joanne Pickett to present her thesis on Sabine Parish as one of the reports given at this meeting.

The committee considered combining the seminar with other anniversary celebrations elsewhere in the state. As I recall, the purpose was to build interest and increase attendance. Following discussion, however, the group decided against this because others were planning their own programs which might not blend well with ours.[16]

A number of other suggestions were given for speakers. The committee also talked about setting a permanent, recurring date in the spring. (This was later done.) Lassiter would contact some of the proposed writers and speakers to set up the spring seminar.[17]

I talked by phone with Dr. Thomas Howell, history professor at Louisiana College, and Dr. Claude Howe, his counterpart at New Orleans Baptist Theological Seminary. Each school offered a student to give a paper. Kevin Fontenot was a senior at LC and very highly recommended. His paper was entitled "The Legacy of W. C. Beall." A doctoral student from NOBTS, who worked with the deaf, presented a paper on "Baptist Deaf Ministry in Louisiana." As the WMU was promoting history as part of an anniversary celebration, we talked with Kathryn Carpenter, former state executive director of the WMU. We found she was writing a history of WMU in the state, and she agreed to present a paper on "Early WMU in Louisiana."[18]

Artie Varnado is the sister of Dixie Moss, who is described earlier in this paper. Artie was in her seventies at this time and more energetic than most of us. Her historical fixations were her family genealogy and an early Baptist preacher named Ezra Courtney. She called me one night as excited as a teenager with her first date. The first words I heard over the phone were "I've found Ezra's grave!" And indeed she had. She and her pastor, Joe Nesom, have done considerable work in finding old minutes and records of Ezra Courtney. She agreed to share a report on the grave finding and restoration at the April meeting.[19]

The second seminar was held in a room of the Student Center on the Louisiana College Campus on April 23, 1988. Everyone considered the program a success, although the attendance remained small. William Poe, who belongs to other historical societies has told us that small attendance is the norm at meetings of this sort. The spirit of the group was undiminished, however. Probably twenty or so were again attending.[20]

The history committee convened at 1:00 p.m., following the seminar. The minutes state that Chairman Perry Lassiter was presiding. This meeting was significant in that the Committee followed through in launching the *Journal of Louisiana Baptist History*. The previous meeting saw the conception of the idea. On this day the committee actually laid plans to publish.[21]

Someone suggested we get copies of each paper for Kathy Sylvest to keep in the archives. (Lassiter had received, or would receive, copies he had requested from each participant.) The chairman then asked whether the committee would want to offer copies of the papers for distribution at the Louisiana Baptist Convention in November. Another additional possibility would be to publish them.

According to the minutes, Dr. William Poe was the first one to suggest that the papers could be "compiled in a 'Journal' and be published annually."[22] Lassiter concurred and suggested a journal the size of a Sunday school quarterly. Dr. Herbert Gregory agreed with Poe that the morning's papers were good. He added that by printing the papers, more interest would be created in LBC history.

Truman Kerr then began to discuss how to market the papers. He thought they were excellent and should be published, but he wondered how best to achieve the committee's purpose. He further suggested a booth at the Louisiana Baptist Convention that November in Baton Rouge. Copies could be produced within the Baptist Building at minimal cost on "Pagemaker" software. From there we went on to other business.

During the summer I got the papers together for publication. Mrs. Carole Hays of Hodge Baptist Church did much necessary typing to get them in order for printing. As I recall we made some phone calls back and forth to gather information to bring us to the point of the meeting next described.

The committee again convened at the Baptist Building on October 6, 1988, at 10:00 a.m. Our first order of business was the details of printing the historical papers presented in 1985, 1986, and 1988. The group decided to arrange them in alphabetical order by author. The book was to be about six inches by nine inches in size.[23]

Chairman Lassiter stated the committee had about $800 which had been transferred from the now defunct Historical Society. Christine Hunt, who had formerly chaired that group, and others had agreed to the shift. The minutes show that I also reported that 1,000 copies would be printed for distribution at the convention and elsewhere and that a sketch of the Half Moon Bluff Church would be on the cover. I believe I recall discussing the number with either Truman Kerr or Mark Short. (Dr. Short replaced Robert Lee as Executive Director of the LBC. He has been equally helpful to the work of both the committee and the Association. Since the Association has been up and rolling, however, Dr. Lee has been much more active although Mark Short is certainly very supportive.) We must have made that decision on the phone as necessary to get the printing done in time for the convention. I don't recall who secured the picture of Half Moon Bluff, although we do know it was drawn for the 175th anniversary of the founding of that church.[24]

We discussed possible titles and agreed on one that the minutes give credit to me for proposing. As I recall, however, we sort of hammered out the title by bouncing around several possibilities, some rather jocular. We settled on *The Journal of Louisiana Baptist History.*

A New Society Proposed

Dr. Herbert Gregory then commented that the title implied an organization to support the journal. He hoped the Historical Society would be re-established in the future and the Journal would relate to that organization. Note that we had toyed with this idea a number of times. In addition to those times reflected in the minutes, the thought had been discussed in private conversations. Up until Dr. Gregory's remark in the committee, however, our official position was the "NO" vote taken a couple of years before and chronicled above. Herbert Gregory started the ball rolling again, and this time the ball kept rolling until it scored a strike![25]

The time was ripe and approval came quickly. Mark Short suggested that Kathy Sylvest might serve as liaison between the society and the History Committee. Later he suggested the president of the society could serve ex officio on the committee. In fact this suggestion was later written into the LBHA constitution, and a reciprocal arrangement allows the chair of the committee to sit on the board of the Association.[26]

Although the committee then returned to discussion of the Journal and plans for the convention, I would personally date this meeting—October 6, 1988—as the launching point of the Louisiana Baptist Historical Association. From that point on, everyone had a different attitude. We did not question whether we were going to begin an association.

Rather we focused on the ways and means. Credit Herbert Gregory and Mark Short with giving us the launching impetus.

Following that discussion on reviving a society, William Poe moved "That the title of the history paper be 'Journal of Louisiana Baptist History, Volume 1, 1988.'" Richard Lisk seconded the motion and the group voted unanimously.

The rest of the discussion on the journal involved which papers to be printed and the number of copies. The committee decided on 1,200 copies with about 200 to be given out at the convention. Since this was the first issue, we decided to mail copies to each of the 521 church libraries in the state and 64 parish libraries. We would also mail to the state universities and our seminary.

The committee then discussed arrangements for a booth at the convention. Kathy Sylvest would request an eight-foot table in the display area. Herbert Gregory would assist Kathy in setting up the booth and contact Dixie Moss and Artie Varnado who live in the Baton Rouge area.[27]

Some time was also spent in arranging the program for next spring's seminar (1989). Lassiter asked Joanne Picket to present her paper about the history of Sabine Baptists, and she agreed to do so. A number of other suggestions were given, and the chairman was given the responsibility of calling or writing people until the necessary papers were secured.[28]

I remember arriving at the convention to find the table set up and a nice display of artifacts on the table. The two sisters (Dixie and Artie) had brought them. We gave away a number of the booklets and also copies of Glen Lee Greene's book *House upon a Rock*. We felt the day a reasonable success, although we would have liked to give away more. I don't remember, and I'm not sure anyone has a record of how many we gave away.

The Birth of the Association

Yet another seminar was held in the Baptist Building with four speakers on April 3, 1989. Following the program and lunch, the History Committee met and gave birth to a new organization.

The meeting began with a discussion of the Journal and its financing. I reported that it had been well received. We had received letters from all over thanking us for sending copies to the libraries. I reported that we produced the Journal for a total cost of $800 or $1.00 each ($0.66 for printing and $0.34 for mailing). Apparently we were not able to produce the full 1,200 we had voted previously for lack of funds. The book was printed within the Baptist Building, using convention equipment.[29]

The next question was how to pay for the next issue since we were out of funds. Truman Kerr said the convention had no provision for the committee beyond its meeting expenses. We would have to generate our own funds.

Kathy Sylvest reported that at a recent meeting of the Southern Baptist Convention's Historical Commission, she learned that other states have historical societies mainly to fund a historical journal. At that point someone raised again the idea of the Historical Association. Only three members of the committee were present on that day: myself, Kathryn Carpenter, and Richard Lisk. Lisk was pastor of FBC, Vidalia, and later became chairman. JoAnne Pickett was also present, perhaps by mistake, having rotated off the committee. Her input was valuable, however. Kathy Sylvest and Truman Kerr were present ex officio, and Carolyn Sterne was present to take minutes.[30] This, then was the group that officially gave birth to the new LBHA.

Minutes of virtually all meetings fail to record much discussion. The History Committee minutes are outstanding in their compass. Nevertheless, one must assume that considerable discussion went on around the table before some of the statements recorded in the minutes.

Actually, we had several purposes from the very beginning. Chief among them was the ability to involve more people in Baptist history. The committee had worked toward that goal since 1984. The History Committee was selected by the convention and rotated through three-year terms. That involved about nine people at a time in historical work for Louisiana Baptists. A society or association would be open to all who were interested. They could continue projects over a long term with the same people involved. (Even with a rotating board, members not on the board can chair committees and projects.) They have a freedom in fund raising that might not be appropriate for a convention agency.[31]

The committee then decided by common consent to finance the Journal by membership fees from the new organization. The committee passed the following resolution. I do not recall who wrote it. Usually, those type things are sort of hammered out by the group. One of us might dictate a line or two with others modifying. Eventually, we usually ask the secretary to read back to us the final product on which we vote.

RESOLUTION

BE IT RESOLVED, That the Louisiana Baptist Historical Association be established,
That charter memberships be offered from June 1, 1989, through April 28, 1990,
The annual membership fee will be $10.00,
Membership in the Historical Associadon will entitle one to:
  A. Certificate of membership
  B. Copy of Joumal
  C. Voting Rights
The official organization meeting will be Saturday, April 28, 1990, at which time officers will be elected and a constitution adopted.[32]

Kathryn Carpenter moved the adoption of the resolution. Richard Lisk seconded the motion, and the vote was unanimous.

The committee then acted vigorously to follow up the motion. Truman Kerr offered to talk with executive board attorney Jean Pharis about incorporation papers for a non-profit organization. Kathy Sylvest offered to prepare the membership certificates and promotional brochures. She intended to collect similar materials from other states to use as resources. She also volunteered to mail a letter and brochure to pastors, WMU directors, librarians, and clerks. Kerr commented that $400 remained in the history reserve account which might be used to print and mail these materials.[33]

Kathryn Carpenter then moved that the committee publish Volume 2 of the *Journal of Louisiana Baptist History* this fall with the state convention as the publication date (November 13, 1989). Lisk again seconded the motion, which also carried unanimously. Someone suggested we might include something about the author of each journal piece, and the committee agreed.[34]

By the fall meeting on October 5, 1989, Kathy Sylvest was able to report that the membership of the newborn LBHA was 113.

The journal had been printed at a cost of $658.16 for 500 copies. Postage came to $193.93. We were now distributing the journal primarily to members of the association and not to the wide assortment that had received Volume 1. I did request that we send complimentary copies to NOBTS, Louisiana College, and the Historical Commission in Nashville. We set a price on remaining copies (for those not in the Association or members wanting extras) of $2.00 apiece. An extra fifty cents was added if the booklet needed to be mailed.[35]

Sometime between when the resolution passed at the last meeting in April and this meeting, the date of the organizational meeting of the association was changed. Notices had gone out to members that the LBHA would be formed at 1:30 p.m. on October 5, 1989 'in the Baptist Building. I sent out a memorandum on September 15, calling the committee meeting and announcing the other meeting as well. In each of my letters to committee members (and later to association board members) I included a proposed agenda in notifying them of the meeting. I felt this gave them time to consider what input they may want to give as well as other matters I might have omitted. I likewise began most meetings with a review of the agenda and requests for additions. Then I called for prayer after we had some idea of what we were about that day. In that particular memo I included on the agenda the "Status of the Historical Association" and "Review agenda of Association."[36]

We discussed what should take place that afternoon. We agreed that we needed to come out of the meeting with a Nominating Committee to report back in April 1990, and we needed a Constitution and Bylaws Committee, which would present a draft to the April meeting. And, of course, we needed a temporary slate of officers to carry on until the committees could report.[37]

We then turned to Articles of Incorporation. Truman Kerr stated that Jean Pharis had drawn up a set for our committee and the association to use as a guide in organizing.[38]

Kerr also reported that he had some ideas for bylaws and suggested some responsibilities for the board of directors:

1. Planning and continuing the History Seminar and Conferences
2. Publishing materials in consultation with the History Committee
3. Enlist members, maintain membership roll, receive dues, and give report at annual meeting
4. Board members elected at annual meeting and should be Baptist.

Kerr continued that he felt we needed the two committees already mentioned, but had not developed other committees in his thinking as yet. He did suggest two meetings a year—October and April—with the October meeting being the official annual meeting of the group.[39]

Herbert Gregory then suggested that the members of the board be selected geographically as a statewide recruiting device. The committee agreed by common consent to ask executive director Mark Short to serve on the board ex officio. I requested that Kathy Sylvest also serve both because of her job assignment as archivist and because she had handled the charter membership so well. I suggested her for treasurer. I also asked whether Carolyn Sterne would be willing to serve as secretary for the first two meetings until we could elect a recording secretary. I also felt that Carolyn produced the best minutes I had ever seen, and I coveted that quality reporting for our first meetings.

The committee asked Kathy Sylvest to do another membership mailing after the first of the year. We wanted at that time to establish a fiscal year of April to April. That is, all memberships would be renewed each April. The problem of when memberships come due was to plague us for several years before we solved it (if indeed we have).

The committee also discussed the April Seminar with suggestions for possible speakers. They felt that the program should be limited to three papers, each taking no more than thirty minutes, divided between the reading of the paper and group discussion. William Poe suggested a panel discussion on missions with several persons involved. Each could give a formal presentation, after which the discussion could ensue.

The committee also worked out a proposed agenda for next April's meeting including the program, business session for the LBHA, and the History Committee meeting.[40]

The Organizational Meeting of LBHA

At the request of the sponsoring committee on Louisiana Baptist History, I called to order the first meeting of the Louisiana Baptist Historical Association at 1:30 p.m. on October 5, 1989. We met in the large auditorium of the Baptist Building with 37 present. I announced that we had 113 members who had joined so far. Richard Lisk led in our opening prayer.[41]

I then made an opening statement explaining the purpose of forming a new Association. I gave a very brief summary of the background and the desire to involve more people in the study of Louisiana Baptist history. I explained the committee's plans regarding the seminar and the Journal. The April meeting would be the time for adopting a constitution and bylaws. At that point the new organization could take over both the Journal and the seminar program. I concluded by outlining an agenda which we followed as no one objected or amended.[42]

Dr. Arnold Nelson then made the motion that brought the organization into official existence: "That the Louisiana Baptist Historical Association be organized as of October 5, 1989." William Poe gave the second, and the vote was unanimous.[43]

Richard Lisk then moved that Perry Lassiter be elected temporary president of the LBHA. The minutes do not record a second, nor who made the following motion to cease nominations and elect Lassiter by acclamation. The motion carried.

Lynn Clayton then moved, seconded by Herbert Gregory, that Richard Lisk be elected temporary vice president. Again came the motion and vote for acclamation.

Austin Tucker moved, seconded by Richard Lisk, that President Lassiter be given the authority to appoint the secretary and treasurer of the historical association. This vote was also unanimous. I then appointed Carolyn Sterne as temporary secretary and Kathy Sylvest as temporary treasurer.[44]

I then laid before the group other discussions of the committee. We proposed the April meeting as the "Organizational Meeting." (So the minutes. And so our previous resolution. But what was this assemblage I was chairing at present?) I told of the need for a committee to draft a constitution and bylaws and work with a lawyer on articles of incorporation. We also need a nominating committee.

Emile Rousseau then moved, seconded by Tucker, that the president in conjunction with the temporary officers appoint both committees. Again, unanimous.[45]

Next, we had a "brainstorming" session with the group tossing out suggestions of things they might like to see the LBHA accomplish. Sixteen items are recorded in the minutes that people suggested. After this several announcements were made. One was the completed remodeling of the archives in the Baptist Building. The group was invited to visit following adjournment. Dr. Poe commented that the association had begun well, since the old society stayed around 45 members, and we already had 120.

Austin Tucker raised a question that had been previously discussed, but merits another mention. He wondered whether the president of the association should be ex officio a member of the History Committee. Kerr explained that convention bylaws already allowed the officers of the society to be members. (The bylaws were later amended to change the wording to the name of the new organization.) Lassiter added that earlier discussion had suggested only the president, rather than all the officers belong to the committee.

William Poe led the adjourning prayer, and the first meeting of the Louisiana Baptist Historical Association adjourned at 2:45 p.m.[46]

The Second Meeting

The second meeting convened again at the Baptist Building about six months later on April 29, 1990, at 10:00 a.m. with forty-three people present. This group was to be our largest attendance through the time of writing this paper (1994). Appropriately enough for a Louisiana Baptist group, the theme of the program was missions. Three men who devoted their lives to missions gave us varied histories. J. D. Scott, who had served as consultant to rural churches in Louisiana for years, spoke on that work. Carl Conrad spoke from his autobiography, which itself is a history of missions in a large area of South Louisiana. And Arnold Nelson delivered a paper on the "History of Missions in Southwest Louisiana."[47]

Immediately after the October meeting, the temporary officers set to work carrying out the responsibilities given them. We communicated largely by telephone and established both a bylaws committee and a nominating committee. Correspondence relating to the details is filed with this paper in the archives. James Carter chaired the Constitution and Bylaws Committee. Dr. Carter had a distinguished career as a pastor, broken by a period as assistant to the executive director of the LBC. At this time (and now) he was director of Church-Minister Relations for the LBC. Carter is a writer of curriculum materials and books and holds a seminary doctorate in church history. Copies of the proposed document were distributed to those present for review. Carter pointed out the major provisions and then moved the adoption of the constitution as printed. Arnold Nelson gave a second, and the motion passed without dissent.

Next Dr. Carter reviewed the proposed bylaws and indicated two typographical changes. He then moved the adoption, Scott seconded, and the vote was unanimous.

As a result of grappling with the question of board terms in writing the bylaws, the committee had discovered a problem. James Carter thus asked the association whether they would prefer to begin the rotation of board members after their first six months of service, or wait eighteen months. As the annual meeting was October, but we were to elect the first board today, that first board could not serve an even twelve-month period.

Leon Hyatt therefore moved that the board begin rotation in eighteen months, that is, October 1991. Grace Beall seconded the motion, and it carried unanimously.[48]

Joe Baugh had been appointed nominating committee chairman and had served in that capacity. However, he was unable to attend this meeting, so Richard Lisk reported for the committee. He then moved its adoption, and Robert Lee seconded the motion, which then carried.[49]

Kathy Sylvest then brought encouraging news, both of membership and finances. Membership had grown to 182 members. Finances in the past eleven months since June 1, 1989, had been excellent. We had received over $2,100, spent about $1,500, and had an exact balance of $608.49. The journal had cost $730.91 for printing and mailing. We had spent an even larger amount ($765.25) for a heavy promotion emphasis to launch the organization. That amount paid for printing, postage, and supplies. The fact that we brought in 182 members indicates the promotion was successful.[50]

The First Board Meeting

Our first board meeting convened at 10:00 a.m., May 19, 1990, in the Rare Books Room of the Louisiana College Library. Librarian Landrum Salley had invited us to use that space, and most board meetings took place there except when combined with a program meeting. Then we have used a conference room in the Church-Minister Relations Building.

That first meeting was poorly attended, but a great deal of work was done. Vice President Christine Hunt also took minutes for the absent secretary at my request. Treasurer Oscar Hoffmeyer was there, along with board members Virginia Joyner and William Poe. Hoffmeyer was the retired public relations worker from the LBC. He put our finances on computer and gave us detailed print-outs. We hated to lose his conscientious work when he moved out of state about 1993. Virginia Joyner is a long-time member of FBC Shreveport and a granddaughter of M. E. Dodd, the subject of one of our historical papers (by Austin Tucker). She and her husband run a travel-tour service. Tucker is a long-term pastor from Shreveport, who did his graduate work on Dodd. He has been strongly supportive of the association from the beginning. Regretfully, as this is written, Austin is recovering from a severe fall while pruning a tree. He has been paralyzed from the chest down, and it is not yet apparent whether he will regain feeling and use below that area.

A good deal of this meeting was spent discussing the journal. After some discussion of editorial policy, Hoffmeyer moved and Poe seconded this motion: "The Board will consider publication of papers presented at Seminars of the Association and other suitable manuscripts on Louisiana Baptist history. Decision to publish will be based upon quality of scholarship, space available, and guidelines of the Association." The motion carried unanimously.[51]

Poe then moved that we maintain a directory of research through which current projects on Louisiana Baptist history would be publicized in the journal and *Baptist Message.* Joyner gave the second, and this passed.

I recall considerable discussion about how to finance the work of the association. We felt that people should be given the opportunity to give more than the standard $10 membership fee. Various possibilities were discussed, although they are not recorded in the minutes. Finally, Hoffmeyer moved that the president appoint a committee to formulate guidelines for financing the work of the association and report to the next board meeting. Virginia Joyner seconded the motion, and it carried.[52] After the meeting I appointed Mrs. Joyner to chair that committee. She sent out a letter dated May 25 for the committee to meet June 9, at FBC in Shreveport.[53] We discussed also in this meeting that committees could include association members who were not on the board. We felt this a good way to involve as many people as possible in the work of the association. We did prefer in most cases a board member as chair in each committee, so that we could keep up with what was going on. We have been able, in fact, to accomplish this to some degree.

We moved back to a discussion of the Journal. We thought we needed an editorial board of some sort. Further reflection led us to a simple organization that divided the responsibilities between editing and publishing. One group would focus on editing the writing, pretty much as any editors will do. The other group would be responsible for securing materials, deciding on the cover, making decisions on print and the like, and generally getting the product out. Eventually Oscar Hoffmeyer moved that I appoint a seven member committee to publish the journal. Joyner seconded, and the motion passed. I appointed William Poe to chair the committee and delegated to him the authority to appoint six additional members, three to focus on style and three on general publishing procedure. Grace Beall and Oscar Hoffmeyer were named to the committee that day.[54]

We now turned our attention to the seminar program. We looked over the membership list and Hoffmeyer recommended Jim Cooper to chair the Program Committee for the 1991 seminar. He was to appoint two more members. (As it turned out, Jim had to decline. Saturdays were a bad day for him.)

We then set the date for the fall meeting as October 6, 1990. The remainder of the meeting covered routine "housekeeping" chores, and we adjourned at 12:20 p.m.[55]

The Third Association Meeting

The results of a brief September board meeting and two committee meetings were brought to the whole association on October 6, 1990, at the Baptist Building for approval. Nineteen were present.

The financial report continued to look good. The funds were now in an interest-bearing account and the balance was $1,047.29 plus $30 collected that morning in dues.[56]

The major actions of this meeting were the adoption of a plan of membership categories and discussion of the journal. Virginia Joyner was not present, so Austin Tucker reported for her committee. Each category was voted on separately and a change or two was made in the committee report. The following categories emerged from the votes:

1. Regular memberships remained $10 as in the past.
2. Institutional memberships would be $15. Such institutions as churches and schools would receive two Journals, but no votes.
3. Lifetime memberships cost $100. These would be placed in an endowment fund. Tucker suggested the Baptist Foundation, and the funds were indeed placed there. The original report called these Charter/Lifetime Memberships. In discussion the charter concept was amended and dropped.

4. Sustaining Membership is $20 or more a year. This category fits anyone who may wish to contribute more, but is not able to reach the $100 for a Lifetime gift. Names of these will be published.

5. Honorary Membership may be granted to persons who have made outstanding contributions to Louisiana Baptist history. As of this writing, only Glen Lee Greene has been so honored. It turned out the award was made posthumously, although we voted to do so while he was still alive.[57]

We then turned to a discussion of the journal. Oscar Hoffmeyer began by reporting costs. As a result, we raised the price from $2.00 to $3.00. Poe reported that the next issue would contain four articles and two book reviews. A memorial section would list deceased members from the past year. He intended to put out a style and format sheet for articles which he hoped to be ready by the Spring 1991 meeting.

At that time Sally Beall (daughter-in-law of Grace Beall) was typing the journal. (I believe she was keying it into a computer.) Bill Poe did the final editing, and LBC printer Ken Nichols was to complete the printing by November 1.[58] (I believe this is still pretty much the situation as I submit this paper. James Carter also edits, and Grace and Kathy are heavily involved in the process.)

A discussion of publicity and a suggestion by Mrs. Joyner that each member of a Baptist church somehow receive a membership application led to the formation of a Public Relations Committee. I appointed Frances Griffith chairman. They held a brief meeting after the big meeting to get a direction. Frances comes across with boundless energy and worked hard initially. However, she had a baby within the next year, left her job, and has been unable to continue. Another member, Judy Camp, picked up the leadership for awhile, but recently the committee has gone dormant.[59]

We then adopted our first budget—$1,200! Of that, $800 was for the journal, $200 for postage, and $200 for stationery, supplies, and miscellaneous. Somehow, we have always had enough funds to accomplish our purposes, most notably to publish the journal. (The seminar costs us very little, although in the last year we have offered a small stipend as a token of appreciation or expense defrayment.)

Conclusion

At this point the Louisiana Baptist Historical Association was really up and running. As Glen Lee Greene might have said, the foundation was laid, the framework was up, the roof kept out the rain, and now we were putting up the walls.[60] In other words, the committee on Louisiana Baptist History had dreamed a dream of involving more people in preserving and sharing our heritage. They had created a new organization as a vehicle for so doing. That group, the Louisiana Baptist Historical Association, had now been formed with a strong number of charter members and a reasonably sound financial base. The group had elected officers, set up a constitution and bylaws and begun its work. They had successfully taken over the annual seminars and the publication of the *Journal of Louisiana Baptist History.* Many other details had been taken care of. The LBHA was up and running!

Afterword

From the vantage point of one who has been involved from the beginning, I'd like to make a few observations. We gave birth to a good, healthy organization. The key to that health was involvement, the involvement of many people. The key to our future health will be the continued involvement of many people. I feel that the ability to keep producing fine seminars and good quality journals is also the key to attracting people to meetings and other involvement in the association.

We must also avoid inbreeding. We must constantly search out new members who can be included on committees and on the board. Former board members must be willing to remain active supporters, serve on committees, and attend meetings, while deliberately pushing others to the front.

We must be open to change. I have no idea what I mean. Change, by definition is unpredictable. If we are able to embrace new forms, new ways of doing things, then we shall not merely study and record history, we shall become history . . . dead history!

I do have some miscellaneous suggestions, remembered as I wrote the history. Most of these have been rejected or passed by. They are not all mine. I would still like to try some regional seminars. I still believe some folks would turn out in the Lafayette area, for example, if we did a seminar at the Southwestern BSU on Baptist missions in the area. Likewise for any other area of the state. Someone has suggested a panel discussion for a program, an excellent idea. What about one day selecting the best of the journal and publishing a book?

The last word is . . . don't forget the imperative of administration! Whatever contribution I have made to this group, it lies in that area. We can love history and talk about it, but only as we plan and act do things begin to happen!

Appendix
Louisiana Baptist Historical Association
First Fifty Charter Members

Kathy Sylvest	Marguerite Hebert
Oscar Hoffmeyer	Robert L. Lee
Wanda Berry	Don F. Mabry
James E. Carter	Mrs. Woodrow May
Kenneth Everett	G. O. McGuffee
Karen Garner	Arnold F. Nelson
Myrtlene Grant	Clara Parker
R. C. Hammock, Jr.	J. L. Pollard

G. Robert Richardson
Ethma Roberts Rush
Kevin W. Sandifer
Southside B.C., Baton Rouge
Austin B. Tucker
R. Chip Turner
Gaddis L. White
L. C. Williams
Richard A. Lisk
Mark Short
Joe Baugh
Kathryn Carpenter
Kathleen G. Clements
Roger P. Freeman
Thomas Goodman
Nancy Greenwood
Kim Hall

Ruth T. Keener
Birdie B. Lewis
W. A. Massey
Bruce McGee
John H. Monk
Arnold F. Northsworthy
Malcolm G. Parker
Joe M. Rice
A. W. Robbins
Landrum Salley
Eddie Savoie
T. W. Terral
Artie S. Varnado
Erma Villers
Jacqueline B. Wild
Xavier University Library, New Orleans

Notes for "A History of the Louisiana Baptist Historical Association"

[1] 1992 Annual, Louisiana Baptist Convention, 12.

[2] Letter from Perry Lassiter to Committee, February 1, 1984.

[3] Perry Lassiter, "Thoughts about the LBC History Committee," appended to committee letter of February 1, 1984. See appendix.

[4] Minutes: Convention Committee on Louisiana Baptist History, March 8, 1984.

[5] Minutes: Convention Committee on Louisiana Baptist History, September 1984, 1.

[6] Ibid.

[7] Ibid.

[8] Ibid.

[9] Ibid., 3.

[10] Ibid.

[11] Minutes: Convention Committee on Louisiana Baptist History, March 30, 1985.

[12] Ibid.

[13] Ibid.

[14] Minutes: Convention Committee on Louisiana Baptist History, October 8, 1987.

[15] Ibid.

[16] Ibid., and personal recollection of the author.

[17] Ibid.

[18]Personal recollection of the author.

[19]Personal recollection.

[20]Personal recollection, supplemented by minutes (vd. #[21]).

[21]Minutes: Convention Committee on Louisiana Baptist History, April 23, 1988.

[22]Ibid.

[23]Minutes: Convention Committee on Louisiana Baptist History, October 6, 1988.

[24]Ibid.

[25]Ibid.

[26]Ibid.

[27]Ibid.

[28]Ibid. and personal recollection.

[29]Minutes: Convention Committee on Louisiana Baptist History, April 29, 1989.

[30]Ibid.

[31]Personal recollections of purposes discussed numerous times in the Committee and later in the Association.

[32]Minutes: Convention Committee on Louisiana Baptist History, April 29, 1989.

[33]Ibid.

[34]Ibid.

[35]Minutes: Convention Committee on Louisiana Baptist History, October 5, 1989.

[36]Memorandum to History Committee dated September 15, 1989.

[37]Ibid.

[38]Ibid.

[39]Ibid. and personal recollections and personal practice.

[40]Ibid.

[41]Minutes: Louisiana Baptist Historical Association, October 5, 1989.

[42]Ibid.

[43]Ibid.

[44]Ibid.

[45]Ibid.

[46]Ibid.

[47]Ibid.

[48]Ibid.

[49]Ibid.

[50]Treasurers report attached to minutes.

[51]Minutes: LBHA Board Meeting, May 19, 1990.

[52]Ibid.

[53]Copy of letter dated May 25, 1990, from Virginia Joyner.

[54]Minutes: LBHA Board Meeting, May 19, 1990.

[55]Ibid.

[56]Minutes: LBHA Meeting, October 6, 1990 and Board Meeting, September 8, 1990.

[57]Ibid.

[58]Ibid.

[59]Ibid. and personal knowledge.

[60]Compare Glen Lee Greene's analogies in *House upon a Rock: About Southern Baptists in Louisiana* (Alexandria, La., 1973).

VIETNAMESE CATHOLICS IN LOUISIANA*

Jesse W. Nash

Coming to America

The Vietnamese are perhaps the most recent Catholic immigrants to make their home in Louisiana, particularly in the Archdiocese of New Orleans. Relatively speaking, their numbers are small compared to those of other ethnic populations in the area. Approximately seven thousand Vietnamese live in the metropolitan New Orleans area, and a total of around twelve thousand Vietnamese live in Louisiana.[1] The Vietnamese, however, have become highly visible, significant, and influential, especially in the New Orleans metropolitan region, largely because of their Asian-Catholic heritage and their practice of the faith. The Vietnamese parish has become the largest in the archdiocese. Accordingly, the Vietnamese community has become a political force to be reckoned with in local elections. Their increasingly activist positions on such issues as the environment, education, and abortion make them not simply a Vietnamese or Asian voice but also a Catholic one. It is no surprise then that bishops and other Catholic leaders frequently point to this ethnic group as symbolizing what it can mean to be Roman Catholic *and* American.

It is ironic then that this peculiarly rejuvenating Asian presence in Louisiana has come about only because of the tragic consequences of America's involvement in Vietnam. Even before that "war," however, Vietnamese Catholics already had a venerable tradition of almost four centuries of the faith and a long and illustrious line of martyrs to prove the sincerity of their faith. European missionaries brought the faith and helped introduce an alphabet distinct from the traditional Chinese characters. The present Vietnamese alphabet, in a very real way, helped create Vietnam and spurred on the development of a specifically native Vietnamese literary tradition. Not surprisingly then, literacy

*First published in Glenn R. Conrad, ed., *Cross, Crozier and Crucible: A Volume Celebrating the Bicentennial of a Catholic Diocese in Louisiana* (Lafayette, La.: Archdiocese of New Orleans in cooperation with the Center for Louisiana Studies, 1993), 70-6. Reprinted with the kind permission of the Center for Louisiana Studies.

has been a characteristic feature of the Catholicism practiced in Vietnamese communities and spiritual reading remains an encouraged pious practice.

The faith brought to the Vietnamese reflected the Counter-Reformation piety of the European missionaries descending on Southeast Asia in the sixteenth and seventeenth centuries as well as those who followed and continued to evangelize Vietnam well into the twentieth century.[2] Special emphasis has always been placed on the family, various spiritual exercises, convent and seminary education, the cult of the Blessed Virgin Mary, and the call to priestly and religious life. Many of the early missionaries were themselves heavily influenced by Jansenism and Quietism. This in turn influenced what many Vietnamese call their rather unhealthy attitude toward sin, a fear that God will not forgive sins, and the conviction that tragedies and accidents in everyday life are the result of God's judgment and vengeance.[3] Having noted this tendency, however, it would be a mistake to label the Vietnamese Catholic community Jansenistic. There are other factors which have helped to shape Vietnamese Catholicism.[4]

They include Confucian and European humanism and eventually those movements that led to the Second Vatican Council. A stroll through a Vietnamese bookstore will dispel any suspicions that Vietnamese Catholicism was ever isolated from developments in the world or the Church. In that bookstore, one will find not only the traditional religious literature of the fathers and saints but also works by Japanese writers, Sartre, Camus, the great Russians, and others. In short, the Vietnamese Catholic community has been an international community for a long time and remains so today. The Church in Vietnam had been regularly sending students to schools in Europe, the United States, and Japan for years before the war broke out between the north and the south.

The Church in Louisiana's contact with Vietnamese Catholicism began in 1975 with the fall of Saigon and the South Vietnamese government. Refugees, fearing reprisals from the new Communist government, fled with the last of the departing American soldiers and diplomats or fled as soon as they could. Many did not escape—they died or were imprisoned before they could leave Vietnam. The Vietnamese Catholic community in the New Orleans area boasts of priests and laity alike who were imprisoned because of their faith and only released to be deported to this country.

It began with only sixteen refugee families.[5] They fled here to escape a government that would not allow them to practice their faith. They did not flee here to escape their homes or Vietnam. As any visitor soon learns from adults and the elderly, the Vietnamese love their country and continue to miss it. They became Americans so they could practice their faith safely.

Adapting to New Orleans and America

After the fall of Saigon, New Orleans became a major resettlement center. Archbishop Philip M. Hannan and the Archdiocese of New Orleans invited Vietnamese refugees to resettle in the metropolitan region. The archdiocese historically has been concerned about a Catholic refugee population, and in the case of the Vietnamese, its various agencies and Associated Catholic Charities sponsored the first families and helped them adjust and find employment. The archbishop, himself a World War II veteran, took an active and personal interest in the fate of America's displaced allies. Moreover, the Vietnamese themselves expressed a preference for "the subtropical climate" similar to those in New Orleans and Louisiana, a climate comparable to that of their homeland. Both New Orleans and Louisiana attracted and still attract fishermen.

Under the leadership of now-Monsignor Dominic Luong and with the help of the archdiocese, the fledgling Vietnamese community took root and began to grow in New Orleans. Pockets of Vietnamese congregated throughout the area, especially in New Orleans East and on the Westbank. At first, jobs were available and many Vietnamese worked on the docks and at the shipyards, but the shipping industry soon entered a recession and the Vietnamese community faced its first crisis, an economic one. In a chronically depressed economy, the Vietnamese were forced to return to trades they had practiced earlier in Vietnam. Many of the unemployed men took jobs as fishermen. Vietnamese became common sights as they opened restaurants and stores all over the New Orleans area and took employment wherever they could. As a community, they soon prospered and were talked of as models of achievement and American know-how. The community recovered, earning for itself the admiration of many people, but, as so often has happened in American history, the community suffered from a subsequent outbreak of racism and nativism. Refusing to be intimidated, the Vietnamese community nevertheless prospered in New Orleans and in other parts of the state, especially in Baton Rouge.

Always of some assistance in these formative years was the local Vietnamese parish, Mary Queen of Vietnam, in New Orleans East, and later the mission communities founded on both sides of the river, especially Assumption of Mary in Avondale in 1987 and Immaculate Heart of Mary in Marrero in 1990. A Vietnamese church is never simply a place one routinely goes to on Sundays. It is very much a part of all aspects of Vietnamese life, economic as well as spiritual, social as well as liturgical.

No area has been more influenced by the Vietnamese Church's presence than that of education. The Church encouraged and sponsored programs to assist in teaching English. At the same time the church has sponsored programs to assist in teaching Vietnamese to the children born and raised here. Scholarships and assistance was provided to students to help them in high school and college. Seminary students too were sponsored. The results were a little less than amazing. By the early 1980s, Notre Dame Seminary could boast of a disproportionate number of Vietnamese vocations. Vietnamese high school graduates were also over-represented as valedictorians and salutatorians in area schools.

Such initial success brought with it ethnic conflicts and misunderstandings, some of which continue today, but despite this, the community has been able to develop and adapt to American culture. In New Orleans East, the Vietnamese community quickly spread out, people moving out of apartments and project housing into their own homes. As the community prospered and grew, the small church building was no longer adequate. The old church building's official name was the Vietnamese Martyrs Chapel on the corner of Alcée Fortier and Peltier Drive. It had been blessed and dedicated in 1978 by Archbishop Hannan. In some ways, that chapel had itself been something of a breakthrough for the community. When the Vietnamese community had first moved out to New Orleans East, a mobile home had served as its chapel.

It is sometimes difficult for other Americans to understand the importance of a parish church for the Vietnamese. The Vietnamese community is made up of neighborhoods, neighbors often being related by virtue of their practice of the faith and membership in one or more sodalities or parish organizations. The Vietnamese believe that ideally one should be within walking distance of the church building. That building should be at the center of all Vietnamese communal functions and exercises. The problem with the old church building was that it was simply not big enough to accommodate the number of worshippers or the types of liturgies the Vietnamese are justly famous for. Vietnamese liturgies, such as Tet, the celebration of the Chinese lunar New Year, involve great processions, bands, and parades. Similarly, Vietnamese Holy Week ceremonies demand great space. Moreover, since the community's population had shifted, the church needed to shift with it.

A new church building was planned, and a campaign to raise the necessary funds was successful. In 1983, Archbishop Hannan published the decree permitting the foundation of a new parish, the Mary Queen of Vietnam Parish. The new church building was built off MacArthur and completed by 1986. Since then a school and meeting building have also been added, and plans are under way to build a new school and eventually open a grammar school for the area. In addition, the Westbank area boasts of two Vietnamese churches now, Assumption and Immaculate Heart of Mary.

These building activities are testimony to the vitality and commitment of the Vietnamese. They are also testimony to the vision of the community. The Vietnamese community understands its future to be tied to its practice of the faith. It is no surprise then that the Vietnamese Church is creating numerous smaller faith communities on both sides of the river and is focusing on the future in terms of the education of young Vietnamese Catholics. The Vietnamese Catholic community understands itself to be responsible for both the religious and secular education of its young people. Mary Queen of Vietnam Church in New Orleans East has inaugurated a summer school program offering courses in English, Science, Social Studies, and Math. The same parish also opened a kindergarten and pre-kindergarten school for the youngsters of the parish. A tutoring program for elementary and high school students was established as well as an ACT preparation program. A Vietnamese language program is conducted every summer and is part of a regular tutoring program. Music lessons and a church band are provided under the auspices of the parish.

But it is in the religious education domain that the community has so far excelled. During the school year about one thousand students participate in the weekly CCD program. Young people are always present at the packed liturgies on holy days and Sundays. Many of these young people's religious education is continued and complemented by their participation in Catholic scouting, young people's modalities, choir, etc. It is not unusual for the young people to go camping, and as part of that camping their faith is celebrated and recalled. Retreats are a common feature of the young person's spiritual diet, and almost any gathering will be marked by the presence of a religious leader of some kind.

Adults too participate in numerous retreats, cursillos, and sodalities. The education of the adults is seen to with the same care as that of the young people. In fact, so many adults belong to so many parish organizations that one can spend Sundays simply going to and from organizational luncheons and dinners. One will note that these festive Vietnamese are hardly Jansenistic. Their faith is celebrated and their hard work is rewarded with a meal and conviviality.

Values of the Vietnamese Community[6]

If the Vietnamese Catholic community of Louisiana was born in tragedy, it continues to receive its inspiration from the martyrs of old Vietnam. A crowning achievement for the community was the canonization of the Vietnamese martyrs by Pope John Paul II in Rome in the summer of 1988. This faith and this pride in their ancestors in the faith is a traditional value of the community. The Vietnamese Catholics are unabashed pietists. They celebrate feast days; they read the lives of the saints; and they place themselves within the line of the saints. In a very real way, the Vietnamese Catholic community celebrates its dependence on the past in such activities. As more than one Vietnamese has explained to me, the community has been given a trust, a faith which must be handed on to the succeeding generations. The community roots itself in history so that it can determine its own future and not to be a victim of the future.[7]

This veneration of the saints is of course very Roman Catholic but it is also Confucian. The values of the community derive from at least two founts of wisdom, the Judeo-Christian and the Chinese-East Asian. The community, because of its history, is also Confucian. One can see this immediately in the celebration of Tet, the Chinese New Year. The symbols used in the celebration are Chinese, Taoist, and Confucian, traditions which avoid extremes and espouse a moderate path, the middle way, and traditions which promote a humanism of sorts, a respect for and love of fellow human beings, if not all of nature.[8]

The Chinese symbols utilized in the Tet celebration locate the human between heaven and earth in a mediation role. Like Christian symbolism, the human is in the image of the divine but is of this earth. The things of the earth, the plants and the animals, are to be cared for and respected. The Vietnamese Catholic community is amenable to environmental and ecological concerns in this country precisely because of this Chinese influence in this regard.

One can deduce from this liturgical symbolism that for the individual Vietnamese then, his or her happiness is pursued in sympathy with the rest of creation, divine, human, and non-human. To the Vietnamese way of thinking, one cannot be happy if everybody else is miserable; there is something fundamentally wrong with someone being happy in isolation. One's first responsibility then may not be to himself or herself but to the group; and this is perhaps where the values of the Vietnamese Catholic community differ from other ethnic groups in the area. Vietnamese Catholics are group-oriented and find their identity in the group and not in opposition to the group.[9]

This latter point is the object of considerable confusion and misunderstanding among others in the New Orleans area. Vietnamese Catholics are not robots who simply do what they are told; they are not simply authoritarian; they are group-oriented. There is a difference. A Vietnamese is responsible for the feelings of other people besides himself or herself. Unlike many other Americans, for a Vietnamese a choice is always rather complicated because others are involved in that choice. Being group-oriented, the Vietnamese sometimes make decisions others would call less than individualistic, but the community names such actions by the value of the self-sacrifice, of being Christ-like and Christian.

These values are crystallized in the Vietnamese family, which has received much comment from other Catholics in this country. A Vietnamese family is always a thing of history, a memory, a child who is also a great grandparent's heritage, the future. The family is at the heart of what it means to be a Vietnamese Catholic, and to be a member of a Vietnamese family is to be at the intersection of many strands of the past and the future. This is not to say that there are not conflicts in the Vietnamese family; it has its share of conflicts; the difference is that the conflicts do not invalidate the family; the family persists and is valued in spite of the fact that it is composed of individuals; there is, in a word, a value to being a member of a family and not simply alone. One can see how this value has helped in the formation of a tightly knit community, a parish, archdiocesan participation, and an amazing sense of the universal Church on the part of the Vietnamese. The Vietnamese Catholic is a series of concentric circles of relationships beginning and ending with Christ, an elderly Vietnamese mystic once explained; "but then," he added, "all the circles are Christ."

It is only fitting to end this description of the Vietnamese Catholics of Louisiana with this reminder. It is precisely their great valuation of the family and self-sacrifice that has led so many of their young men and women to enter the priestly and religious life. In the New Orleans metropolitan area especially, Vietnamese vocations may in the future help rejuvenate a general interest in vocations and in the meantime alleviate an increasingly chronic shortage of priests. We are a Church increasingly dependent on our Vietnamese brothers and sisters who define themselves primarily as children of God.

Notes for "Vietnamese Catholics in Louisiana"

[1]See Jesse Nash, *Vietnamese Catholicism* (New Orleans, 1991), appendix 1; Paul Rutledge, *The Role of Religion in Ethnic Self-Identity* (New York, 1985), 4-5. See also Professor Rutledge's recent *The Vietnamese Experience in America* (Bloomington, Ind., 1992), 39.

[2]Dieter Brotel, *Franzosischer Imperialismus im Vietnam* (Zurich and Freiburg, 1971).

[3]For an ethnographic discussion of Vietnamese theological attitudes toward tragedies, misfortunes, suffering and divine predestination, see the title essay in Jesse W. Nash, *Tales of God and Beautiful Women: Gender, Romance, and Religion* (New Orleans, 1993), 1-10.

[4]See Nash, *Vietnamese Catholicism.*

[5]I am grateful to Msgr. Dominic Luong, pastor of Mary Queen of Vietnam Parish in New Orleans, for his assistance in re-creating the early history of the community.

[6]For a fuller exposition of this topic, see Nash, *Vietnamese Catholicism.*

[7]Nash, "Confucius and the VCR," *Natural History*, 97 (May, 1988): 28-31.

[8]See the essays "Disciples and Masters" and "Ghosts" in Nash, *Tales of God and Beautiful Women.*

[9]Nash, *Vietnamese Catholicism*, Chapter 3; Nash, "Form Preferences of Seminarians: Cultural and Institutional Conflicts," *Human Mosaic*, 22 (New Orleans, 1978): 71-93.

Index

UNITED METHODIST CHURCH, RAYVILLE, LA.